HANGAR DESIGN GROUP

H

as I told you before
IDEAS
NOT AIRSHIPS

SKIRA

THANKS TO

Thanks to the possibility we have had, in the past thirty years, of succeeding in everything we have wanted to achieve. And thanks also to the fact that we have never strayed from our dream of seeing projects become real.
Thanks to us and you, all of you.

CONTENTS

Thirty years of passion for design are nothing compared to the potential for cross-contamination by future opportunities. This is to say that what the Hangar Design Group has achieved reflects a part of the people who achieved it.

In fact, the production is the fruit of an astonishing intersection of abilities and suggestions. The abilities are the result of intelligences, occasionally including artificial ones, which have always driven projects linked to design. Everything in Hangar Design Group is filtered through a momentous aspiration: to produce design.

When a logo is being designed or when architectural dimensions are the focus of attention, there is a constant emphasis on proceeding in accordance with a unique design imperative. It is never "a consequence of." Rather it is "the unique thing in itself."

As indeed are suggestions. Suggestions which permeate all corners of each group branch. Those who work or have worked at Hangar have always *lived* by suggestions. Generating them oneself or getting caught up in them when you least expect it. When some partners tackle a project with their collaborators, they never think that they must produce something "useful" for someone, rather they think of how they can develop a mental attitude in themselves and in each of their collaborators which allows the design imperative to be developed and nurtured within themselves and the others. This very design imperative occasionally borders on a more spiritual sensibility.

Like when the primary emphasis is on defining, organiz-

IN HANGAR THERE WILL ALWAYS BE ROOM FOR RAPTURE AND FANTASY AND IMAGINATION, BECAUSE IT IS THROUGH IMAGINATIVE RAPTURE THAT THE FUTURE IS CREATED. AND A DESIGNER WITHOUT IMAGINATIVE RAPTURE HAS NO FUTURE.

ing and monitoring the potential focus on ego, in order to guide it into a relationship with the client.

We can say that, whatever is produced at Hangar is designed completely with its own end in view – design – and then, that complete whole is offered only afterwards to a third party, usually a client.

This has had a powerful impact on the internal organization of Hangar Design Group, since it has broken all the traditional models of collaboration within a professional studio context. It should be said that this did not generate monsters.

Instead, it has produced a *modus operandi* which has transformed into a veritable *school*, and probably a unique one at that.

The rotation of individual professional skills and the strongly pragmatic approach, capable of transforming Hangar Design Group into a big design machine, are not based on schemes of production organization or policies tied strictly to times and methods, but they are based on variable intuitions and approaches, reflecting in recent years the market and customer base itself.

When Japanese designer's design meets Chinese fantasy within a clearly European production logic, it becomes clear that one is dealing with a recognized brand that aims to leave its design trace, through its signs and through ideas.

These very signs and ideas emerge from the almost "anguished" activity of all the designers working in the hangars, who set traps and generate intrigues and snares, reflecting the very nature of design itself.

The designer is a shrewd operator who seeks to present his or her own reality by his own hand, sign, brain.

The designer is capable of everything but inhibiting his or her idea and in order to achieve this, he or she transforms, changes and orients himself (or herself) in accordance with the guiding light of his or her design. And it is this imaginative rapture that makes his or her design unique. In Hangar there will always be room for rapture and fantasy and imagination, because it is through imaginative rapture that the future is created. And a designer without imaginative rapture has no future.

This is valid above all if one thinks of a future capable of meeting the long-time challenge launched by the architects at Hangar, who have always resisted attempts to tie down their field of endeavor.

The history of Hangar Design Group began in the 1980s in the Treviso countryside, and it is the story of an organizational model rather than an actual design style.

It is a story that began inside two old hangars for dirigibles and testifies to an unshakable faith in work, in pragmatism and in the principle that "things happen only if you organize your affairs in such a way that they can happen."

This, together with the great

ability of the duo – Alberto Bovo and Sandro Manente, two Venetian architects who are in many ways definite opposites – and of their creatives to transform anything into a communication project, has made possible the development of the organization as well as its expansion beyond national borders.

The creative process is infiltrated by the suggestions of the group, which help generate a creative work environment and lend a momentum to new projects and experiences with clients, designs and productions, ranging from a glass bottle for mineral water to a mobile home, from a lamp in a technical style to a fashion advertising campaign.

A design activity without pause, expressing the nature of design today as a response to the demand for a design and lifestyle that are contemporary, involving a small element of functionality and a large element of seductiveness. This book is an inexhaustible mine of images and memories, all reflecting ideas which were born within the crucible of the Hangar Design Group.

We believe that passion lies irremediably at the foundation of things: passion for our work, passion for challenges, passion for change.

And also the awareness that, through what we do, we commit to the mission – beyond pure pleasure – of making some contribution to building the landscape of signs that surrounds us. A honorable responsibility for someone who, once upon a time, picked up a pencil and started to sketch with the light enthusiasm of the young creative. Because if communication is never uni-vocal, it follows that the signs which we trace in their dozens, if not hundreds, each day in our professional practice rebound on our daily experience and go towards composing the visual symphony that accompanies our lives.

Over the horizon of Hangar Design Group has hovered – from the very beginning – the figure of the dirigible, the huge flying machine which marked the dawn of the conquest of the skies and which, while technically obsolete, has over time maintained the aristocratic superiority of a machine consecrated to utopia itself, in which the most emblematically aesthetic characteristics have become increasingly prominent: lightness, silence, ethereal energy, the calculated lightness of materials, the nautical tradition of group control, power, plasticity, scientific knowledge of structures that are strong but feather-light.

These characteristics have created irresistible reverberations over time on the work of the group.

The lightness of the sign, the power of the communication, the attention devoted to messages from throughout the world, the sense of space understood as a window to the universe, technical rigor and the serene abandonment to the winds of creativity – which distinguish this group in contemporary design and communications culture – are all signs of a stylistic tendency that legitimately invokes the archetypal image of the dirigible as its own heraldic emblem.

What the world seeks from the design culture is – today more than ever – a *world design*.

The Hangar style – if we wish to use the word "style" – has been shaped from different ingredients, both material and immaterial, from places, from persons, but primarily from the factor of equilibrium.

Experimentation – whether in the headquarters of Treviso or in the Milan branch, in the American branches first and then in the Chinese ones, is promoted while always ensuring that the imperatives of functionality are respected and that excesses are limited within the group identity. The approach taken has not been concerned to explain the products or designs in an explicit way, but rather to take the more lofty road of suggesting, evocating and of the philosophy of the group, more than, or beyond, the mission itself.

Hangar Design Group has become a kind of think tank in the Italian thought, a point of reference often resorted to by universities, by creatives and by companies.

And for this reason, instead of reciting successful case histories, it was thought preferable to discuss and reveal the development of the group, as well as the philosophy and the vision that animate and energize it from within.

The chapters of the book have evocative titles and demonstrate the essence of the group's design culture. More than that, they reveal its soul.

H.D.G.

*A HANGAR IS A CLOSED STRUCTURE TO HOLD AIRCRAFT
AND/OR SPACECRAFT IN PROTECTIVE STORAGE. MOST
HANGARS ARE BUILT OF METAL, BUT OTHER MATERIALS
LIKE WOOD AND CONCRETE ARE USED AS WELL. THE
WORD HANGAR COMES FROM A NORTHERN FRENCH
DIALECT, AND MEANS "CATTLE PEN."
HANGARS PROTECT AIRCRAFT FROM WEATHER
AND ULTRAVIOLET LIGHT. HANGARS MAY BE USED
AS AN ENCLOSED REPAIR SHOP OR, IN SOME CASES,
AN ASSEMBLY AREA. ADDITIONALLY, HANGARS KEEP
SECRET AIRCRAFT HIDDEN FROM SATELLITES
OR SPYPLANES.*
[FROM ENCYCLOPAEDIA BRITANNICA]

*A HANGAR, IN A MORE APPROPRIATE WAY, IS
A PLACE WHERE AIR MACHINES ARE GOING TO LEAVE
AFTER AN INDULGENT STAY. HANGAR APPEALS TO ALL
DESIGN MINDED PEOPLE WHO APPRECIATE WORK WITH
THE ENGINE OF IDEAS IN ORDER TO MAKE THEM FLY.
BASICALLY, PEOPLE WHO FEEL A LITTLE BIT
AS MECHANICS OF THE APPEARANCE.
HANGAR IS EVIDENTLY ARCHITECTURE, ART, DESIGN,
ADVERTISING, PHOTOGRAPHY, FASHION, LIFESTYLE.
BUT DEEPLY, IT IS OIL FUEL, MONKEY WRENCH, SCREW
BOLT. BEHIND THE GOOD-LOOKING SHAPES.
HANGAR IS NICE TO SEE BECAUSE IT'S INNER
THOUGHT.
FINALLY, IT'S ONLY A JOB. BUT A GOOD JOB.*

danilo, 84

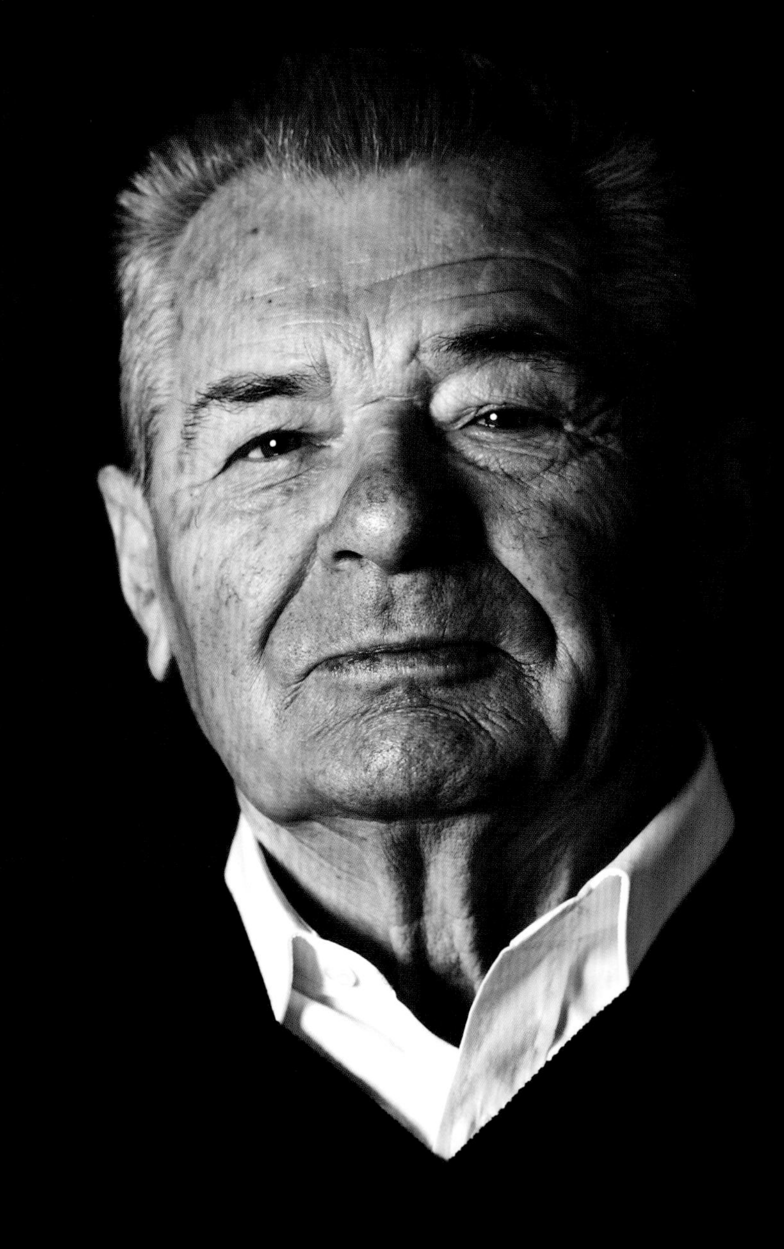

A graphic design project starts out as a relationship, transforms into a process of loose analysis and more-or-less insightful speculation, then enters into a practically autistic phase of visual generation, followed by a synthesis of speculation and experimentation that morphs into a purely computational and mechanical production – accomplished with or without the involvement of any number of outside trades – and finally emerges in the world through a complex of socialization and acculturation that includes publicity, public relations, distribution, retailing, advertising, focus testing, and criticism. Some version of this process is applied to everything: from high art to low commerce, from the intellectual to the banal, from the edifying to the disingenuous. And the process may be interrupted at any point – in ways both positive and negative – by collaborators, authors, editors, clients, vendors, users, lawyers, censors, and politicians, all demanding modifications that range from the minor to the catastrophic.

Add into the mix that the studio is comprised of headstrong individuals engaged in multiple, overlapping projects – all utterly out of sync – concerning wildly different subjects, players, timelines, technologies, audiences, budgets and geographic locations.

On top of that, designers have their own private agendas, ambitions, anxieties, compulsions, and references that they attempt to implement. Those agendas may mesh with the

EVERYTHING I WILL SAY COULD BE WRONG.

content at hand – and with the overarching, collective vision of the studio – or may be grafted onto content and live on parasitically. Personal vision is the designer's added value; it's an indexical presence assumed so resilient it can survive in any context, from the base to the effete. The compelling aspect of design is that each part of this messy process produces things. There is a constant stream of material pumping out of the studio at all times. This superabundance defies any simple definition of the "object" (and any simple declaration of completion). Design can never be reduced to a direct process of transmission because the design object carries multiple messages: some overt, others sublimated, some literal, some haptic.

And besides, the actual receptor of the communiqué is also opaque. It could be an imagined audience, an ideal audience, a peer, a studio mate, a passerby, whomever. Design is always about creating a physical effect: it is both read and felt. Designers make things – deliverables – but these are not always the discrete things for which one gets paid. The simplest study can yield an idea, effect or emotion.

Printing, binding, programming and building don't necessarily have anything to do with it. A designer's "things" happen at every stage of a design process; they are always finished and never finished. But the bigger project, the one that is never complete, is the one that is carried over many projects and many years. It's the project that demands persistent, diligent, never-quite-satisfying attempts.

That's the work, and the life, of the studio. So this book superimposes diverse projects, scales, eras and voices onto a typical trajectory, starting from first contact and concluding with delivery into the world.

It makes no attempt to segregate the polished from the in-process. Each thing is complete. Through rude juxtaposition it attempts to find an intuitive master narrative in a day-to-day process where clients come and go, the population of the studio is in constant flux, and projects fall into our lap or slip away without rhyme or reason. This is not a book about what our work is about, but about the way it is about it. From the ephemeral to the concrete, each page is drawn from a pastiche of projects: some finished, some dead in the water, some successful, some not.

It includes sketches, models, prototypes, collages, animations, drawings and site photographs – the things we make every day. Here ends the attempt to explain it, the rest is left to the things themselves. They are what they are.

HANGAR
DESIGN
GROUP

(Ideas,
not Airships)

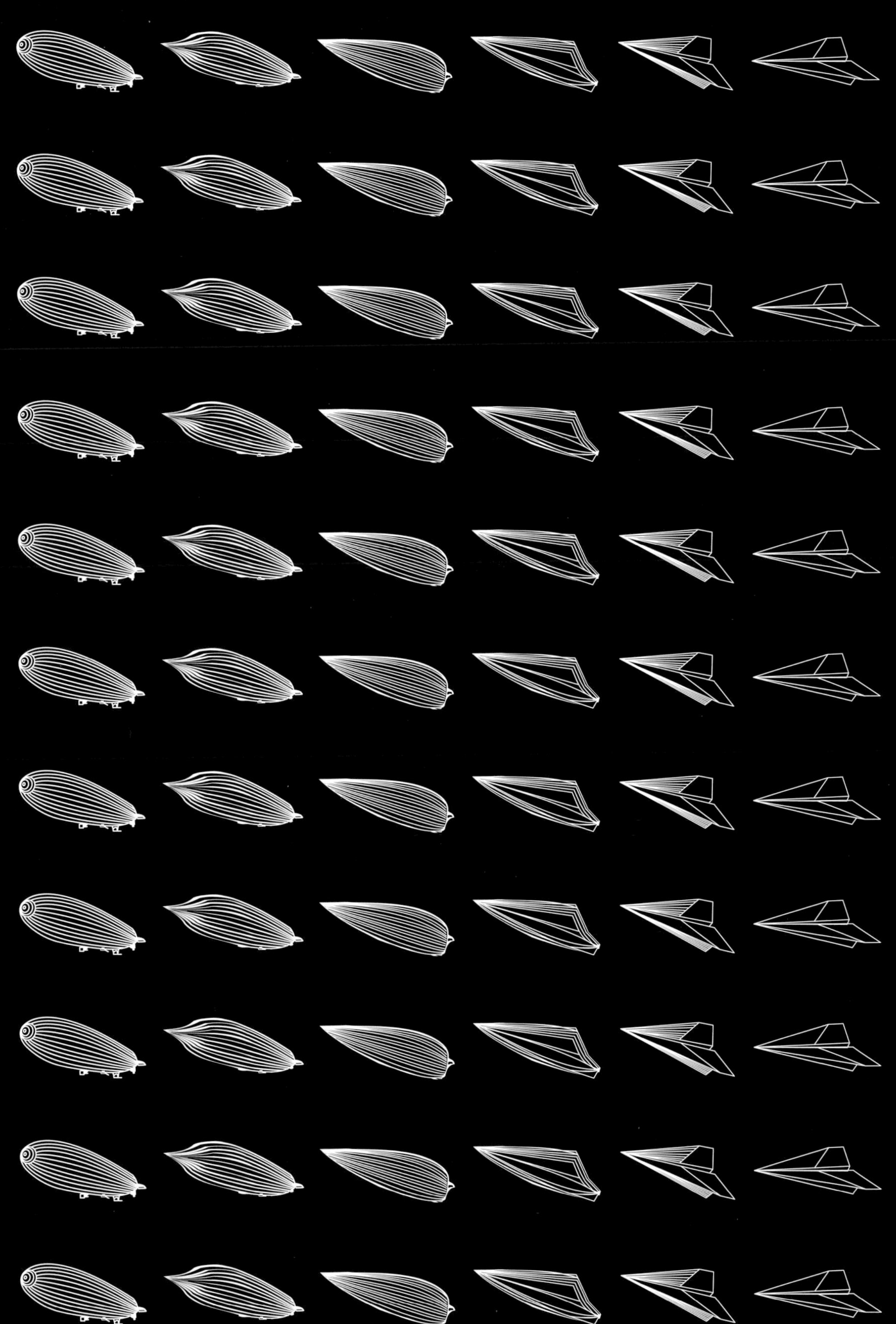

toBE HDG

What I do is

~~what I have to do.~~
~~what someone tells me to do.~~
~~what is right.~~
~~the easy way.~~

what I like.

Back in 1980.
With quick step along the streets of Treviso,
in the government offices to understand how
to fill a form in order to set up a company.
The bureaucracy didn't frighten us at all.
<u>Spending one's day on paperwork
made us feel entrepreneurs.</u>
They were years of social rebellion in Italy.
Who wanted to a be a creative had to
be necessarily "counterculture."
We wanted to apply a business approach
in the creative field, giving us rules.
Quite frankly, we were the heretical.
<u>And we liked it.</u>

Corporate *culture*

or AUTHOR ?

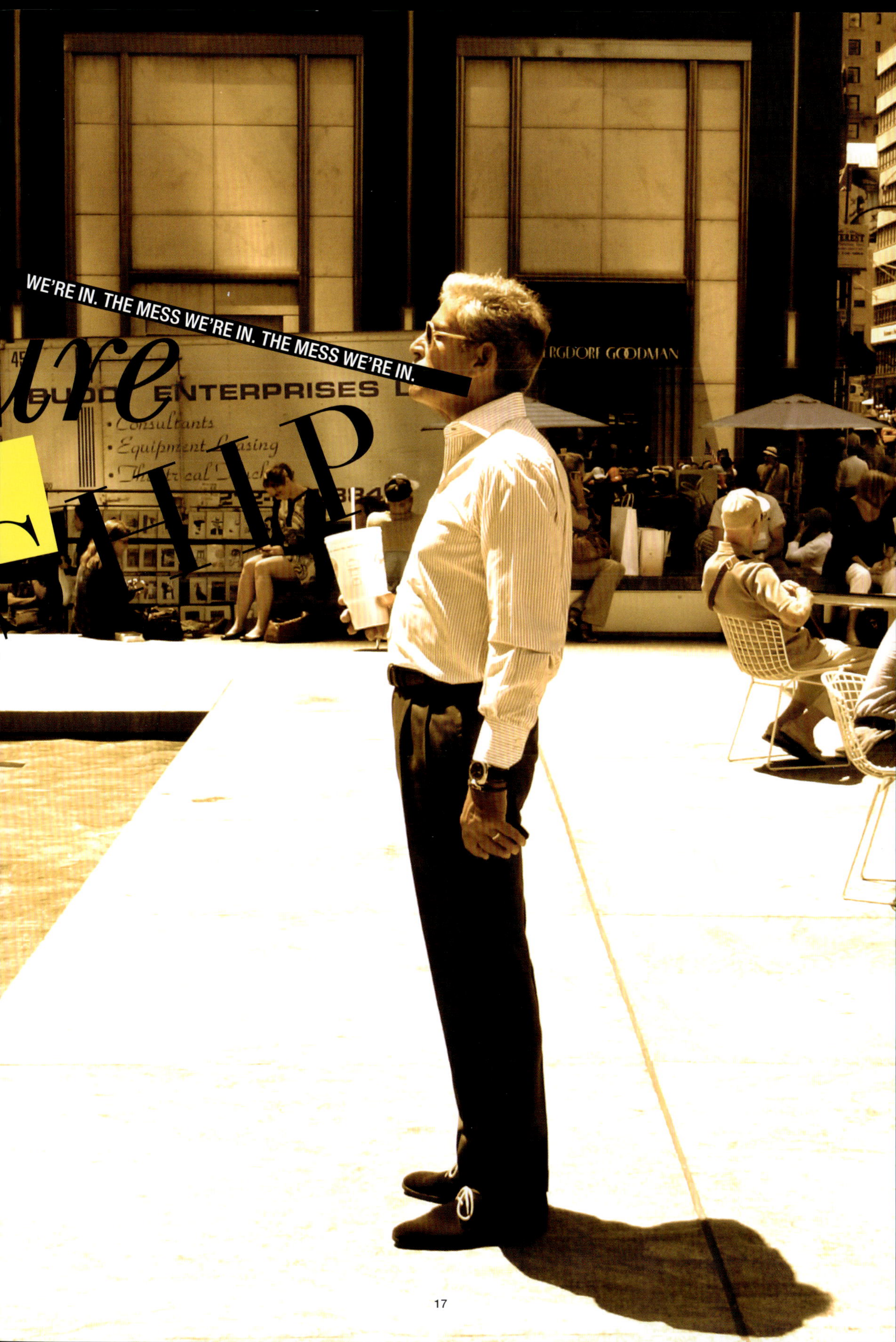
WE'RE IN. THE MESS WE'RE IN. THE MESS WE'RE IN.

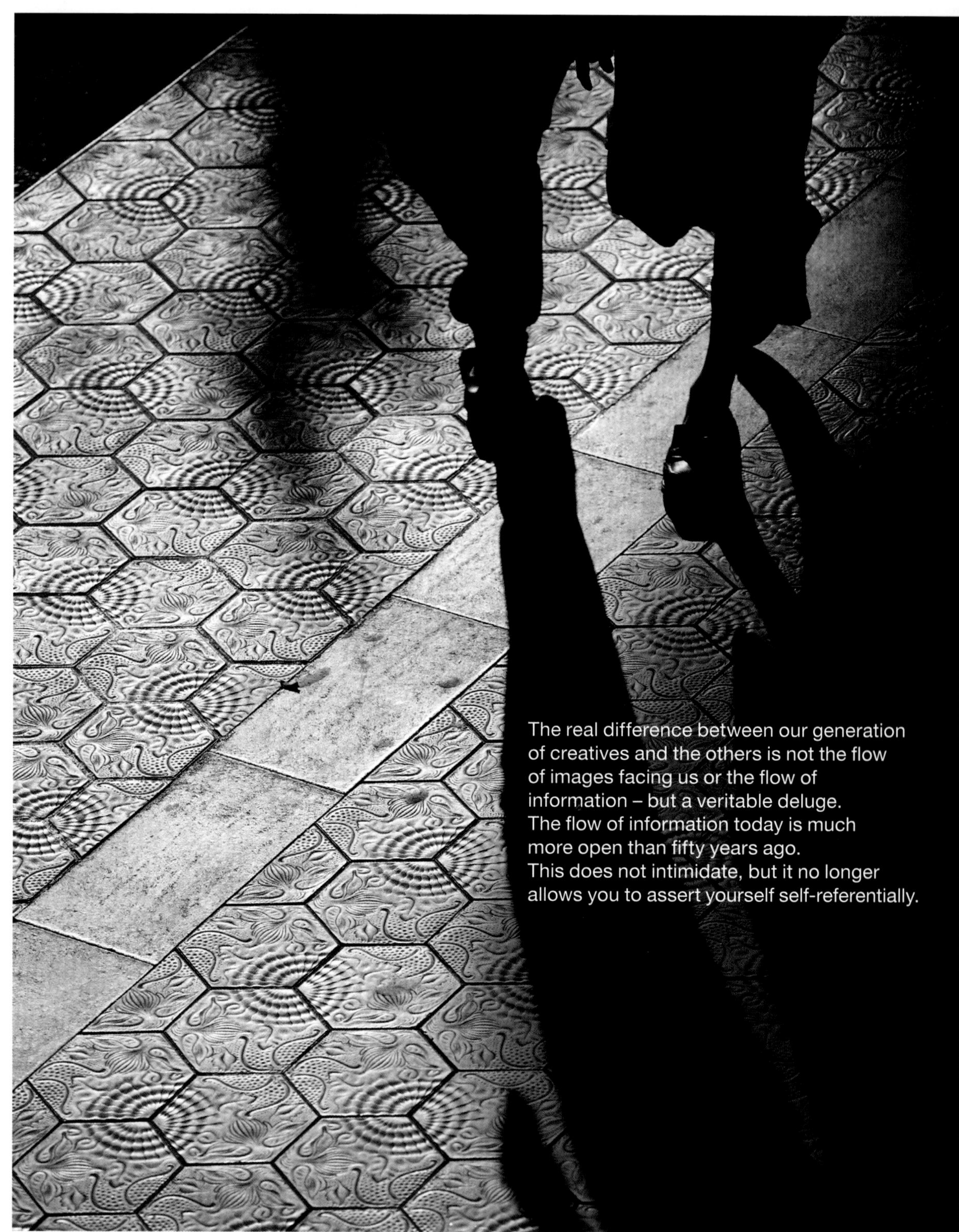
The real difference between our generation
of creatives and the others is not the flow
of images facing us or the flow of
information – but a veritable deluge.
The flow of information today is much
more open than fifty years ago.
This does not intimidate, but it no longer
allows you to assert yourself self-referentially.

Move,

How stable one's own principles are depends
on the level of passion for one's own work.
The more the passion, the fewer the creative
compromises. In design, for example,
we start off with a design project and often
arrive at a simplified solution, a compromise.
We are more interested in processes than
solutions. The images, for instance, must be
the result of a primordial process of creative
elaboration. It must be a pre-creative action.

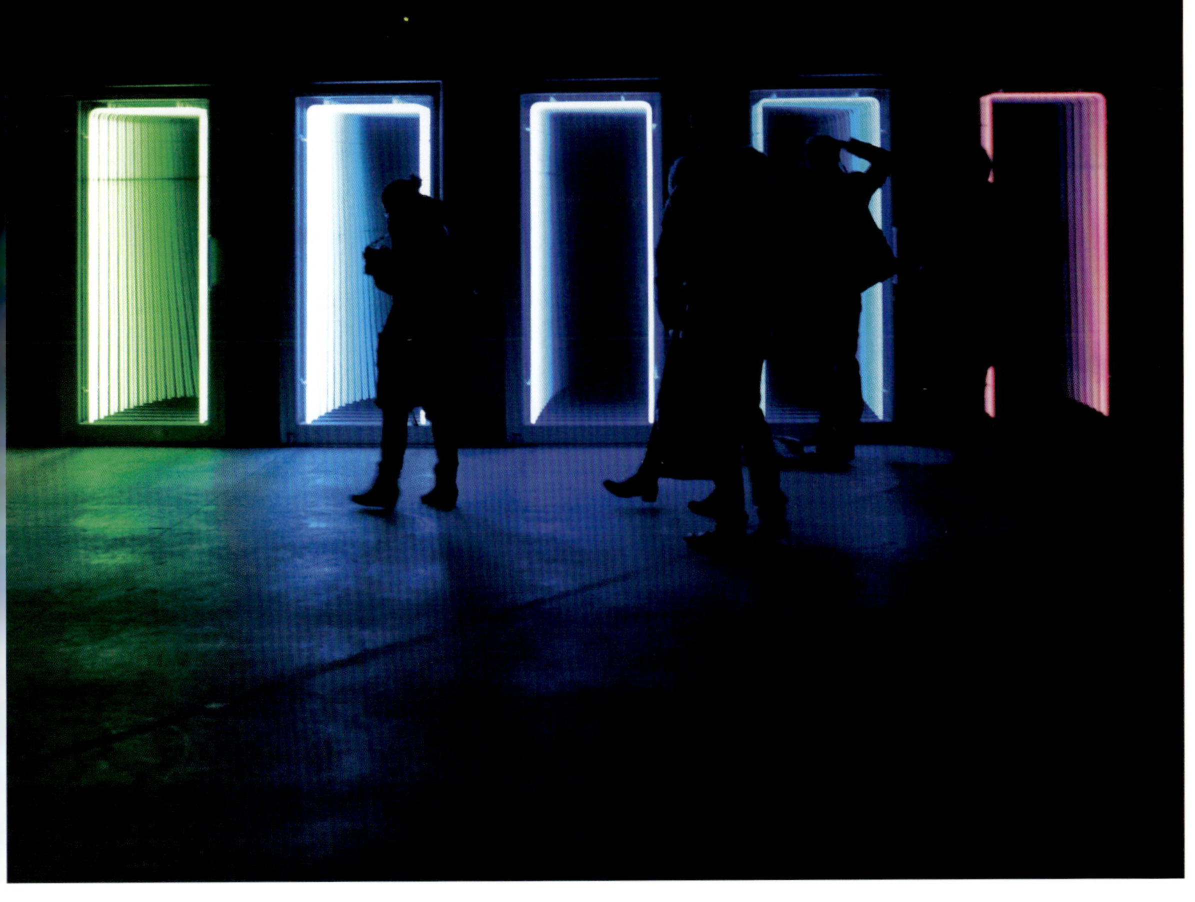

watch,

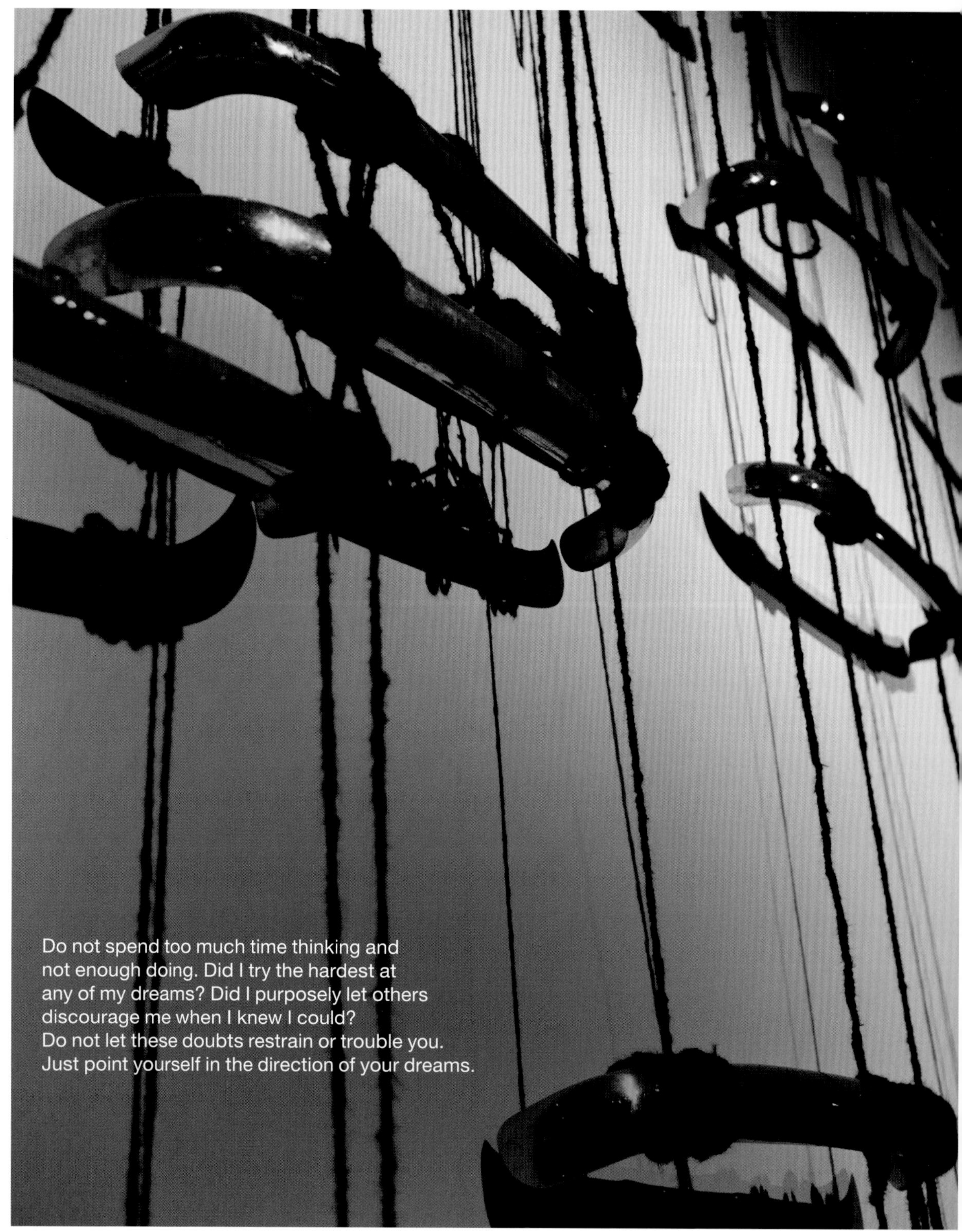
Do not spend too much time thinking and
not enough doing. Did I try the hardest at
any of my dreams? Did I purposely let others
discourage me when I knew I could?
Do not let these doubts restrain or trouble you.
Just point yourself in the direction of your dreams.

share,

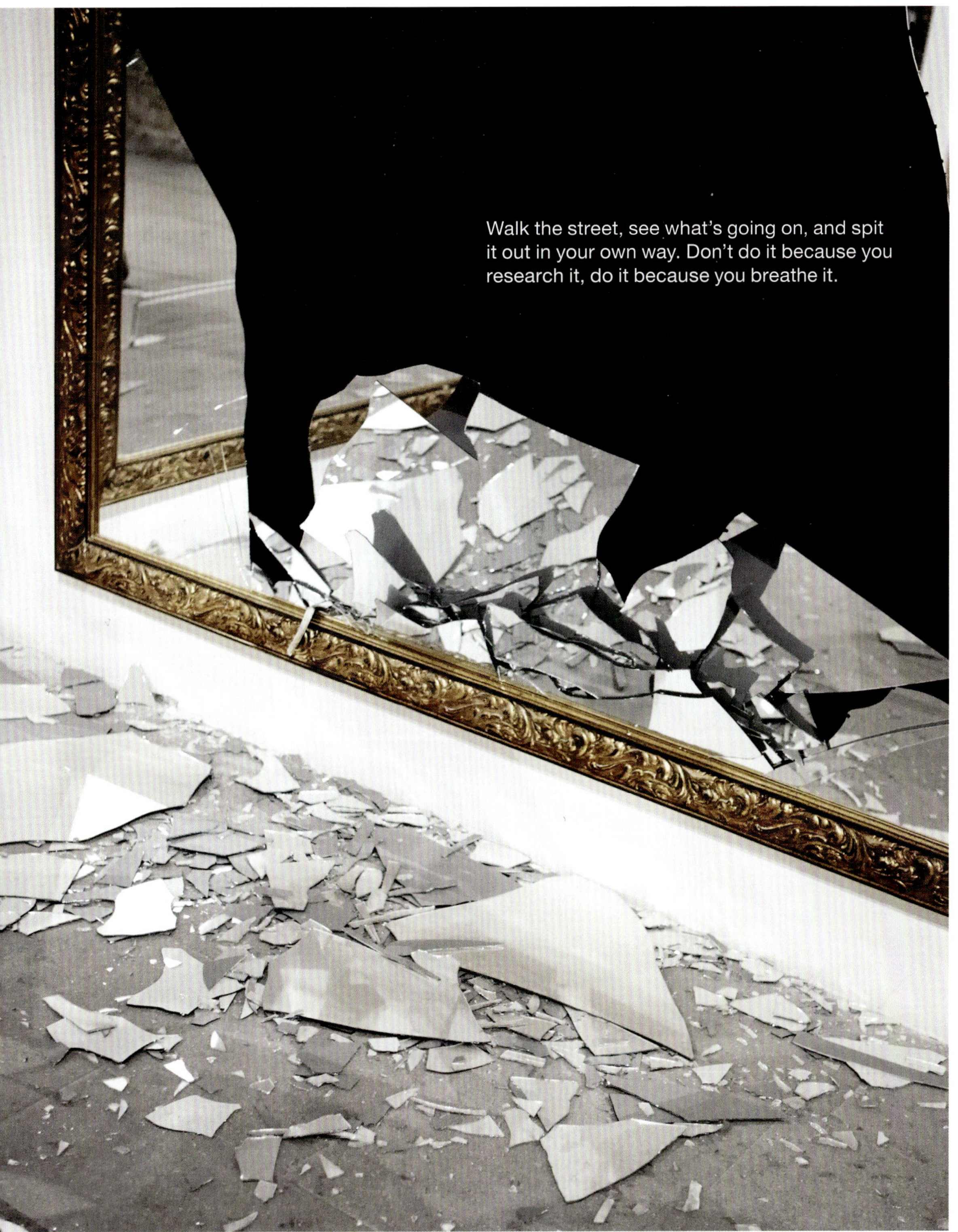

Walk the street, see what's going on, and spit it out in your own way. Don't do it because you research it, do it because you breathe it.

do!

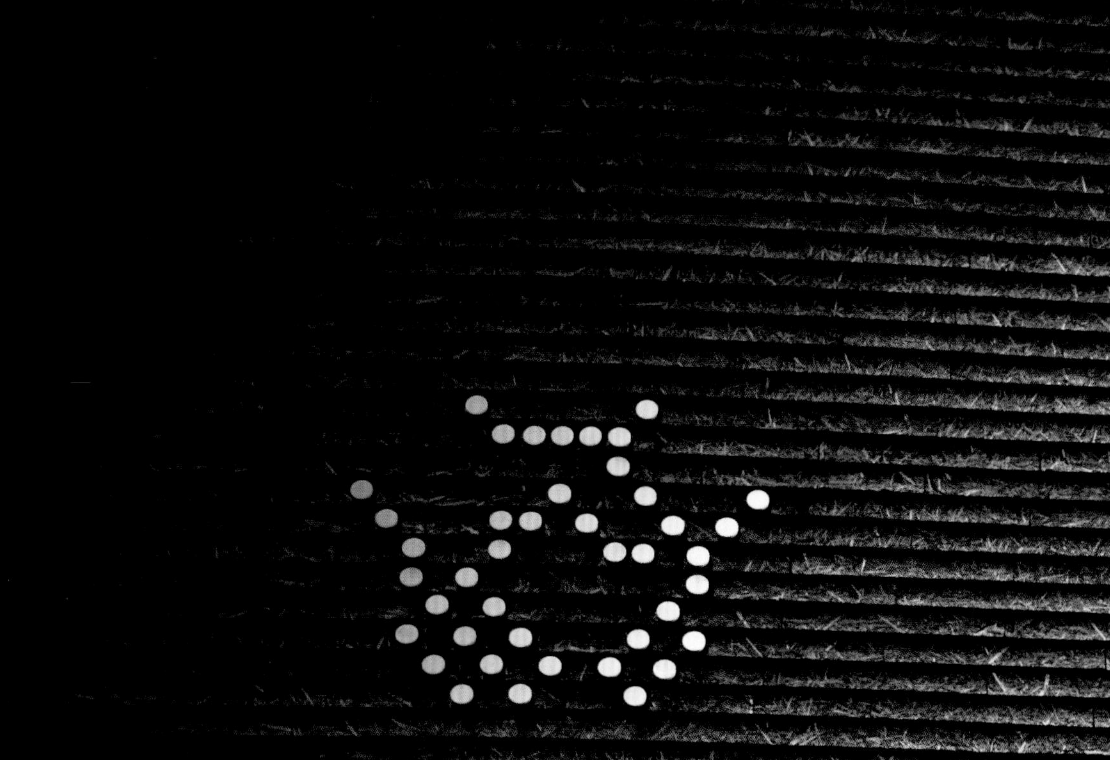
THE POSSIBI

the survival of an idea

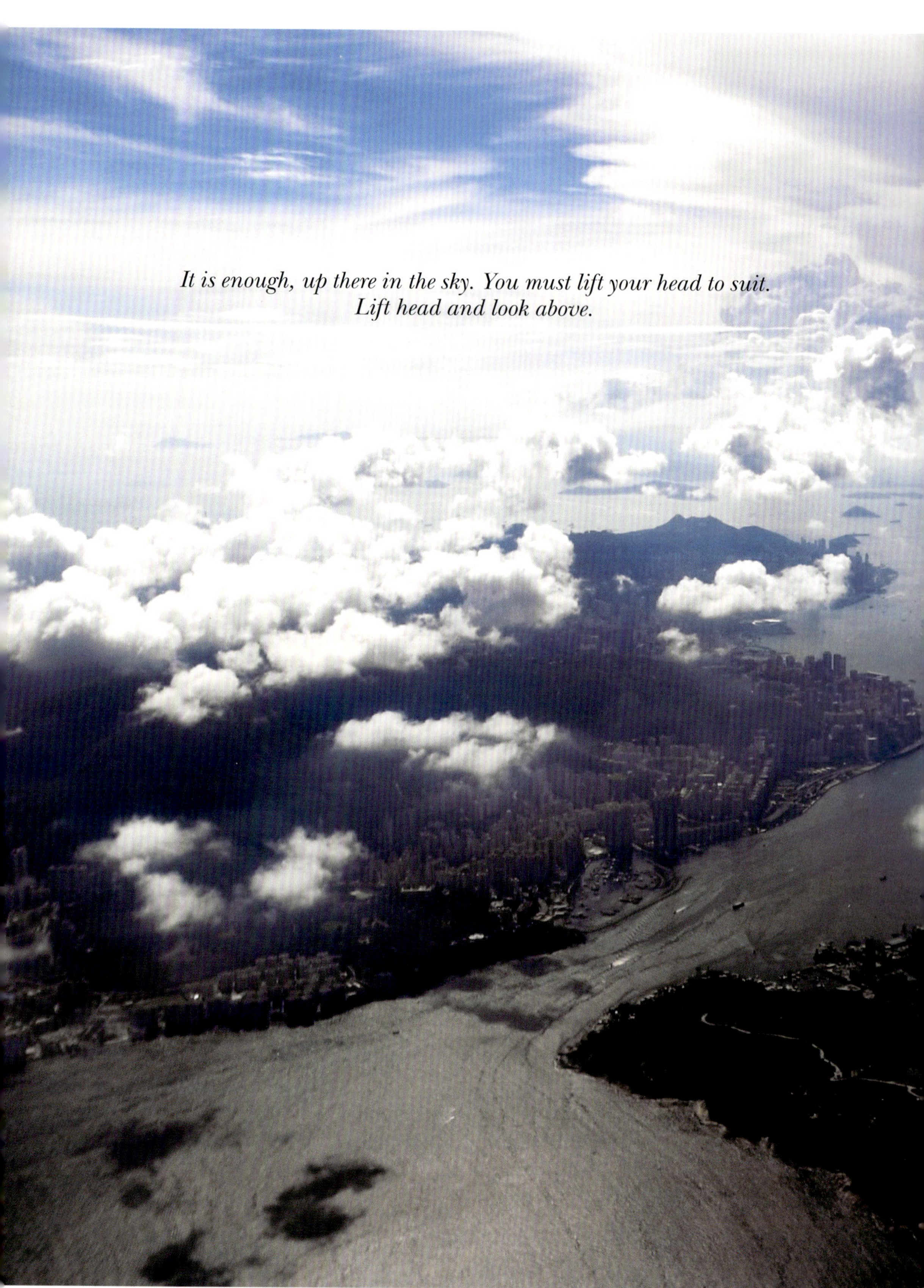

It is enough, up there in the sky. You must lift your head to suit.
Lift head and look above.

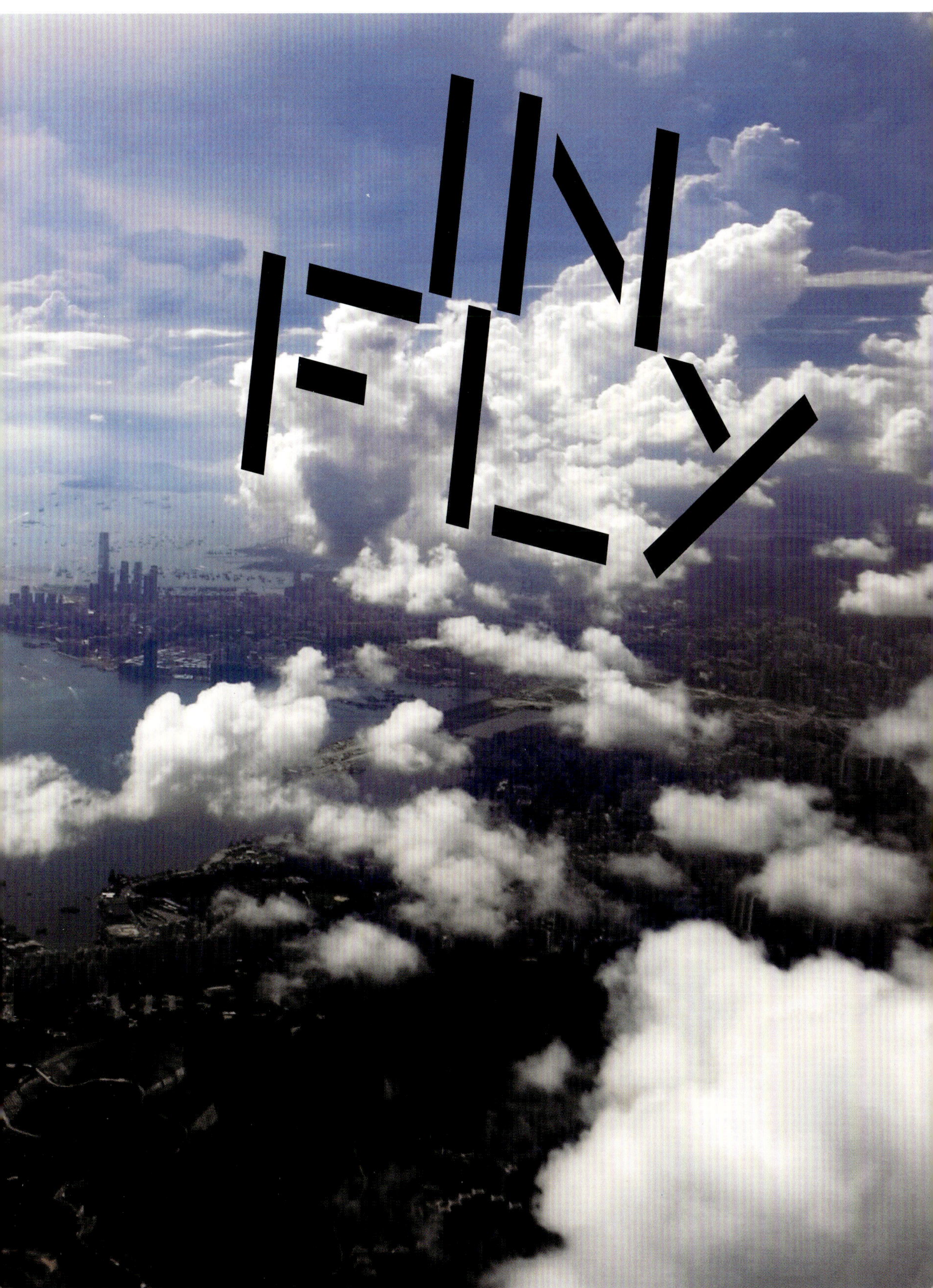
IN
FLY

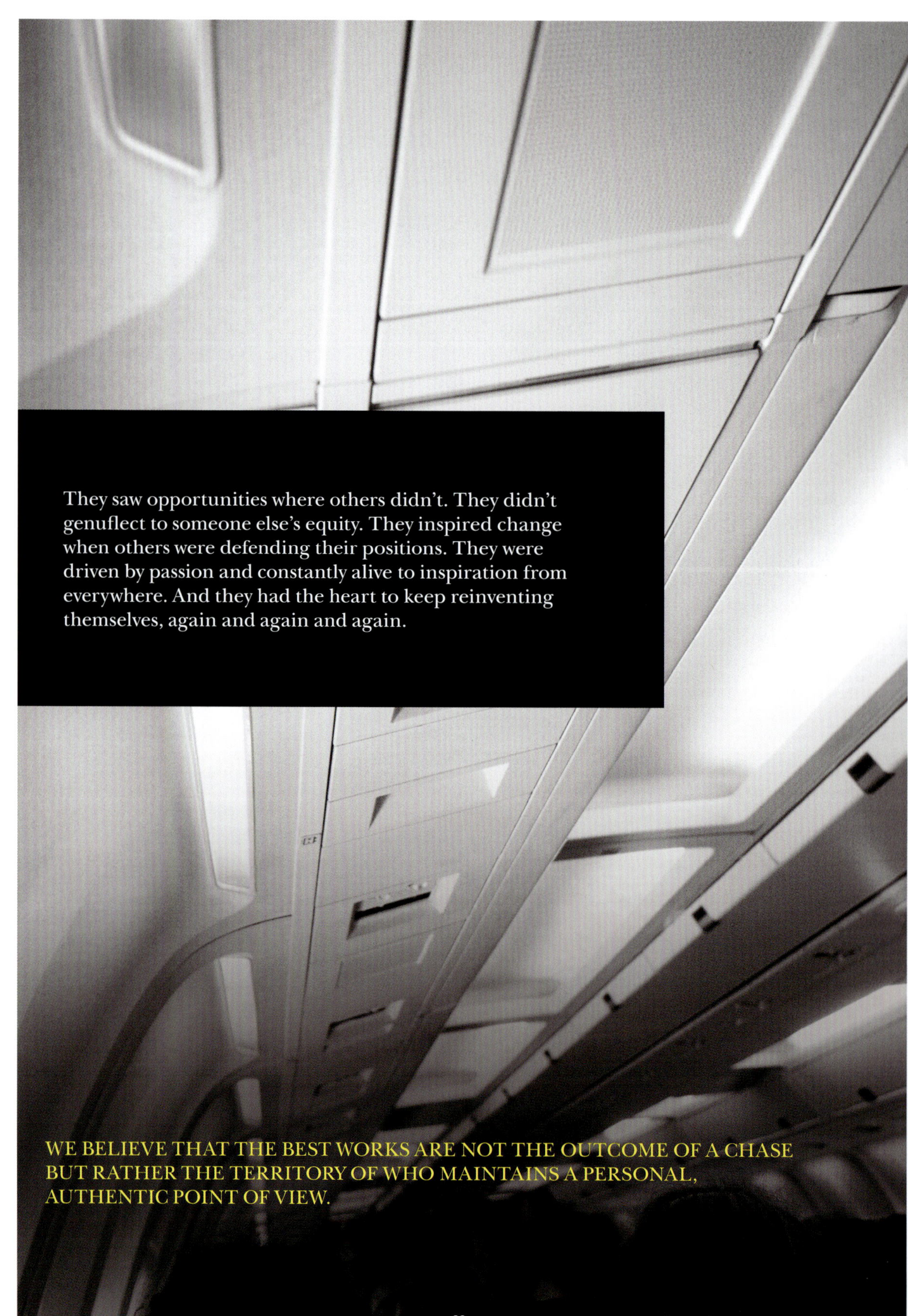

They saw opportunities where others didn't. They didn't genuflect to someone else's equity. They inspired change when others were defending their positions. They were driven by passion and constantly alive to inspiration from everywhere. And they had the heart to keep reinventing themselves, again and again and again.

b&w　　　　but also

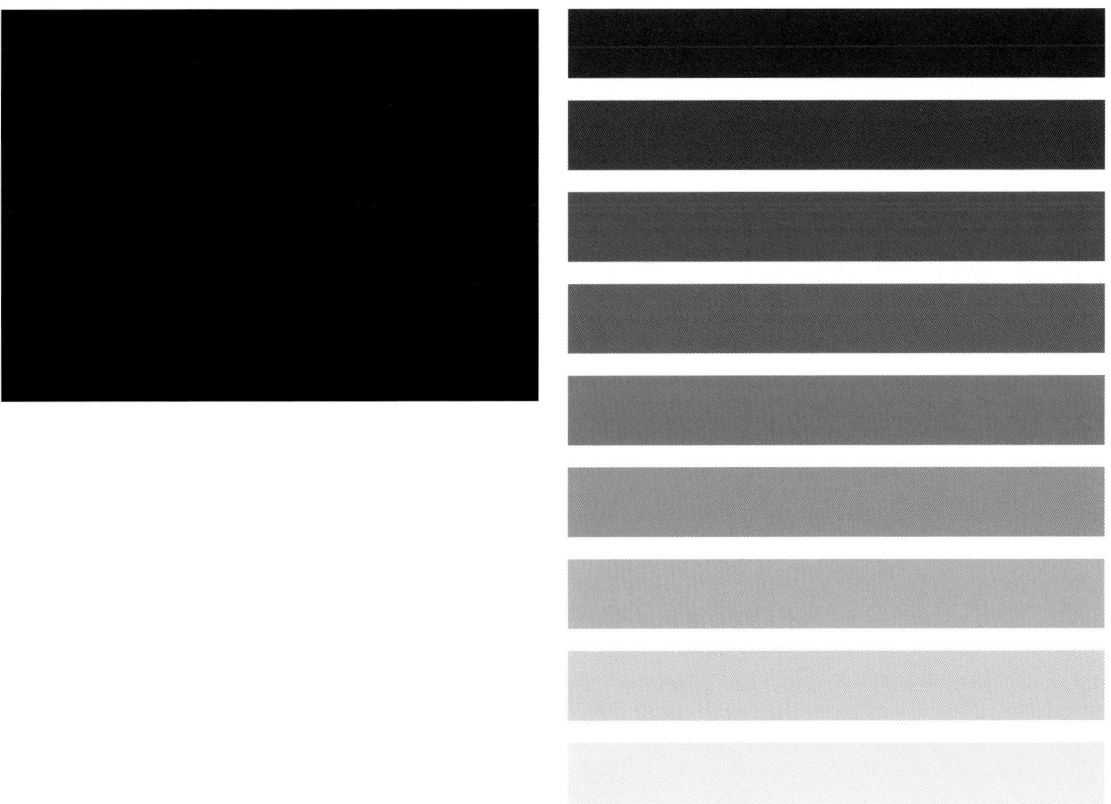

All the companies or agencies or people we admire
were driven by this type of personal vision.

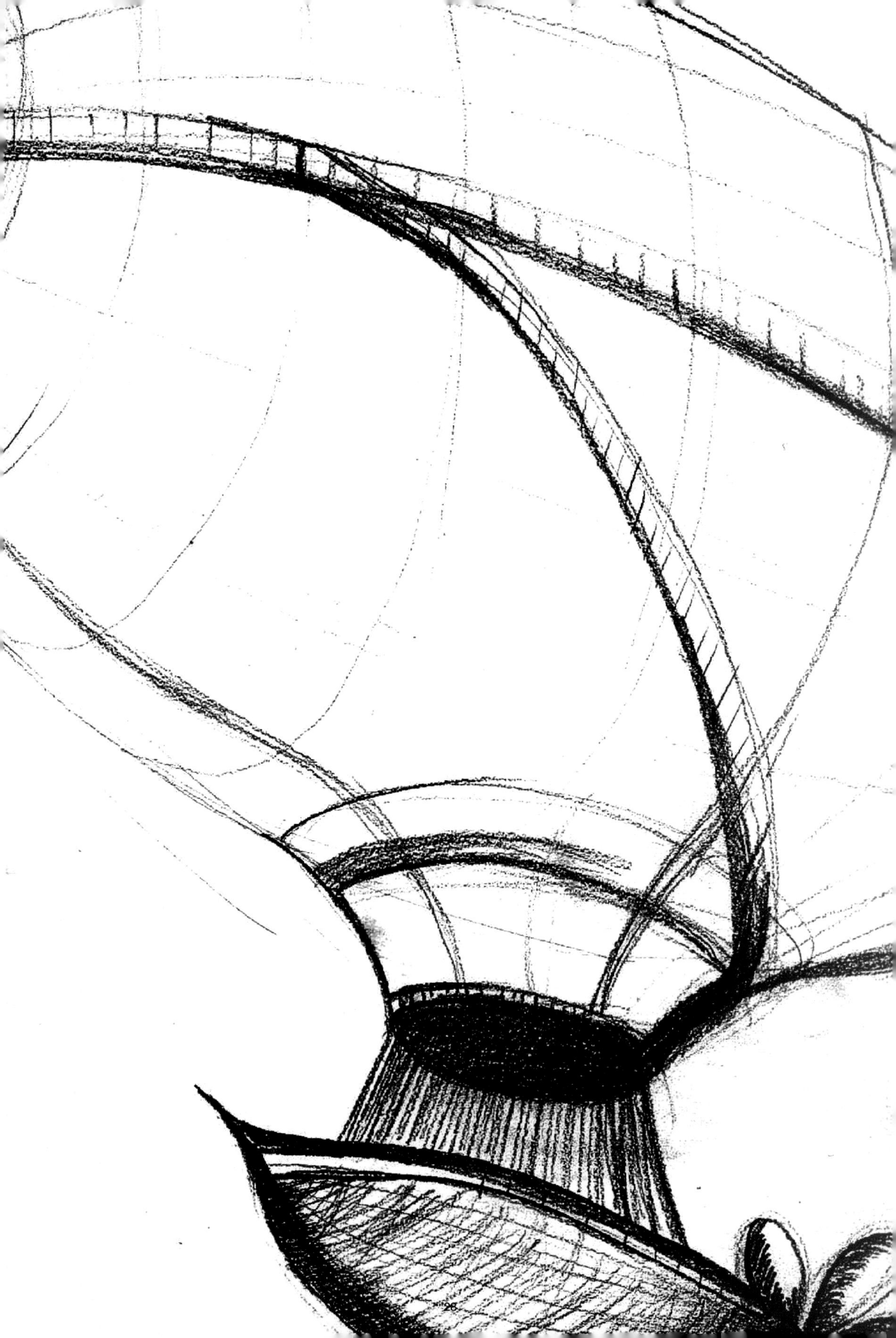

WE WORK

The spaces of Hangar Design Group arose from the desire to represent a kind of logbook of travel through time and through the architectures of the world, without a particular will to achieve a single formal and representative dimension, but simply selecting the chords, playing the notes of the mix.

IN THE MOST BEAUTIFUL

The site bequeathed two twin buildings, built as workshops for the maintenance and repair of zeppelins during the Great War, which an initial restructuring in the 1990s remedied along analogous design lines, but using different structures and materials.

PLACE

The two buildings, which are absolutely identical on the outside, represent an experiment with the trilithic system, in one building in steel and cement, and in the other in reinforced concrete and in masonry and cement.

IN THE WORLD

Vegetation is an integral part of this design process. It defines space in a precise way, it maintains the stony pathway, it juxtaposes a filter, with maples and willows towards the farmed countryside, it delimits and protects from the surrounding environment.

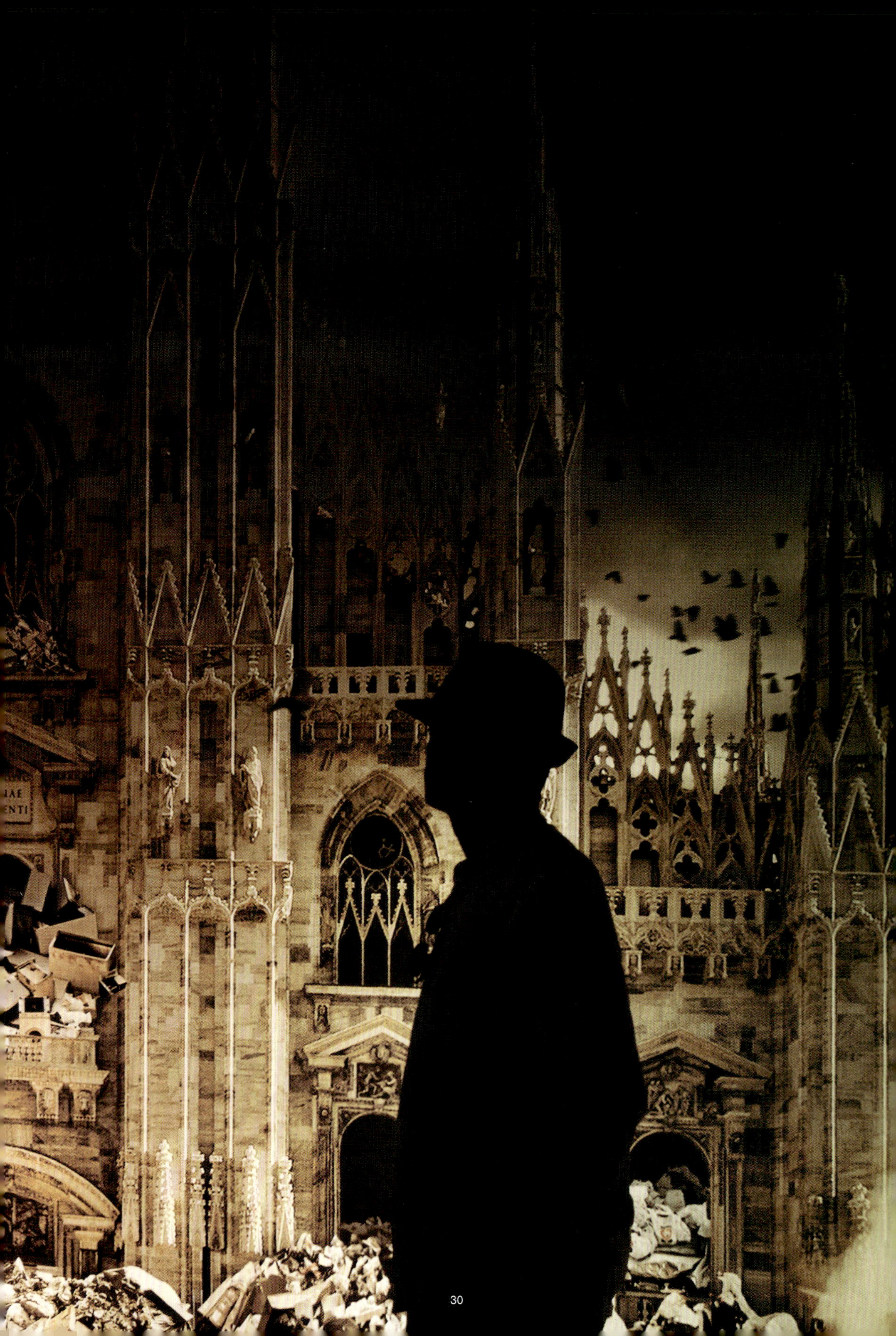

THE ONLY WAY IS THROUGH

The Special Extra Mysterious, Magical, Immeasurable. Beauty.
In this troubled context and historical crisis, fraught
with sensible anxiety we wish to make the case for beauty
as the only thing. Beauty is all we have.
Let the subject of beauty – form, image, color, coherence measure up
to the quantitative crisis we now collectively confront.
Our only hope is the Special Extra Mysterious, Magical, Immeasurable.
Beauty Now. Only beauty holds the key.

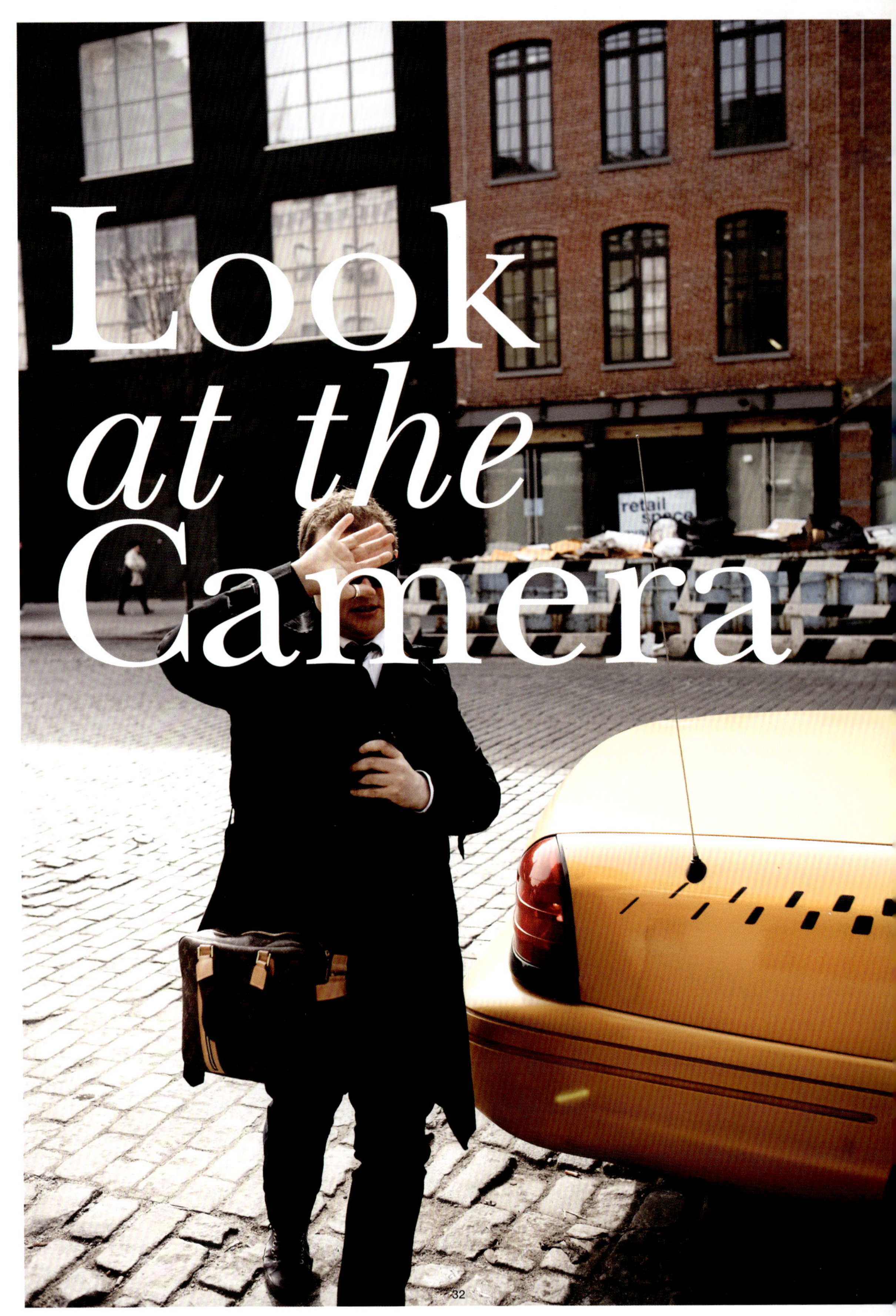
Look
at the
Camera

TIM
WE N
TO T

Hello./ It's time for a new conversation./ Come on in and let's talk./ Letting your light shine doesn't count if the effort won't be spread to the crew./ The worry is just for the self-referential attitude./ Rather keep believing in autarchism. Cultivating the quality of being self-sufficient as the statement of a strenuous opposition to conformity./ Act according to self rules undoubtedly, but the pleasure is to share them.

WE NEED TO TALK

"In our mind, Hangar Design Group belonged securely to ourselves – its founders – but also to whoever worked there and to all those who came into contact with it. Like the blues, which generated new music through its intersecting influences and alternative trajectories, it's the same with us: everyone can and must provide ideas, resources, means. Each person must bring his or her own experience."

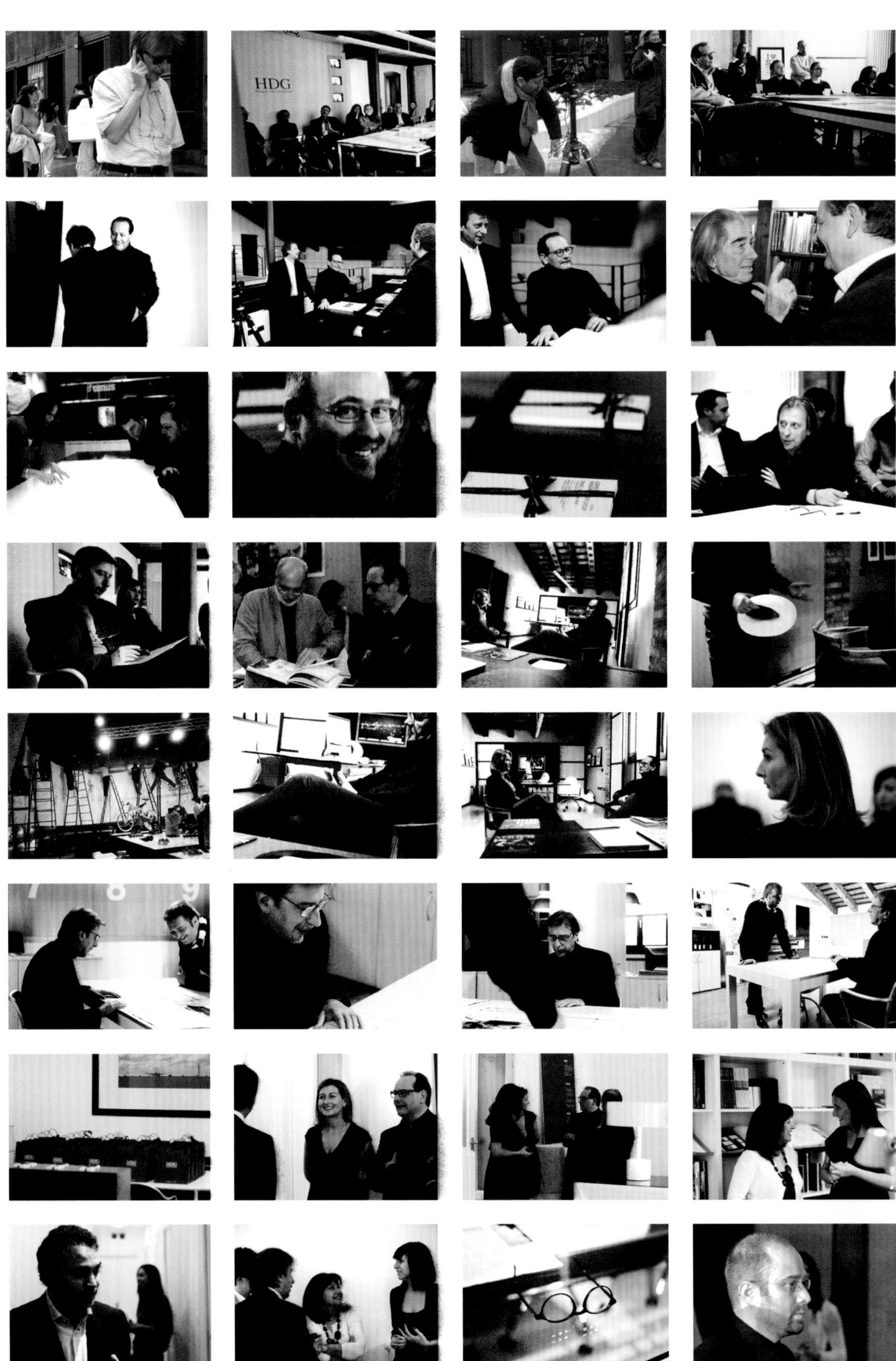

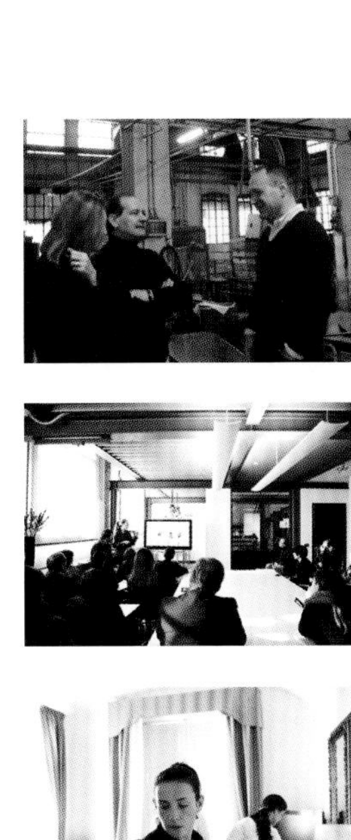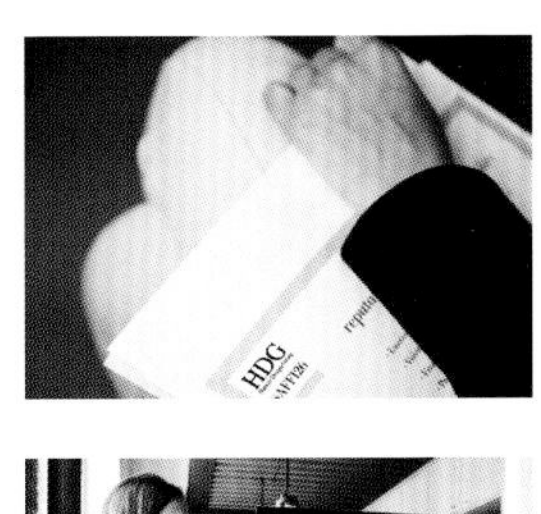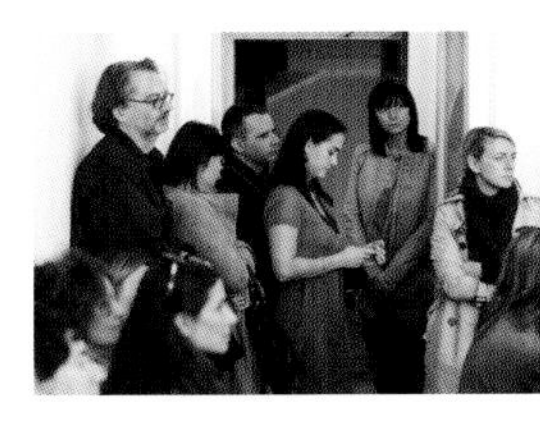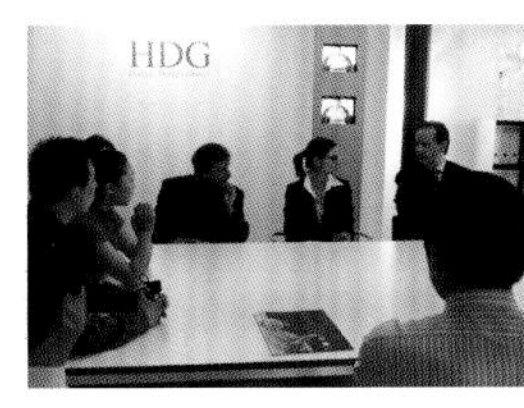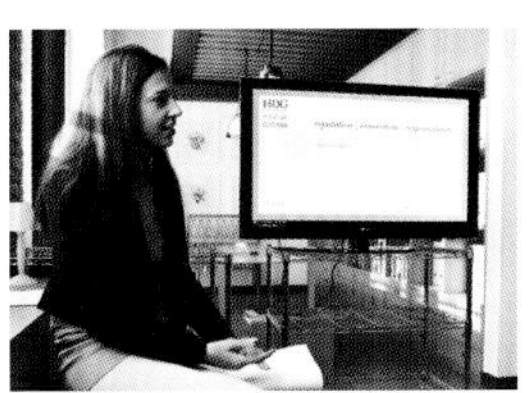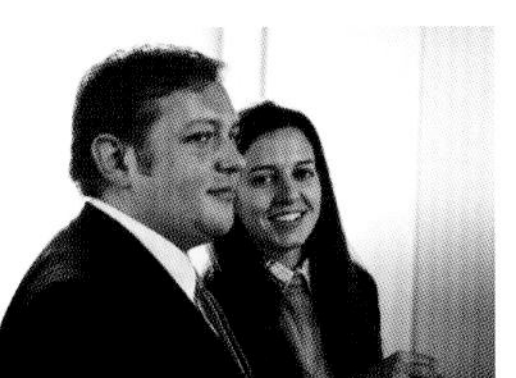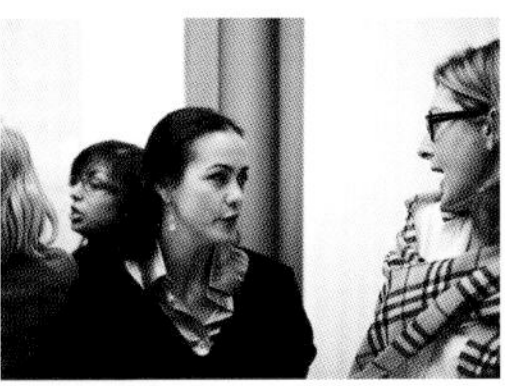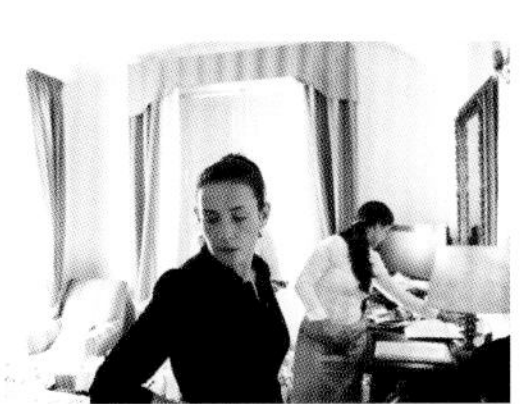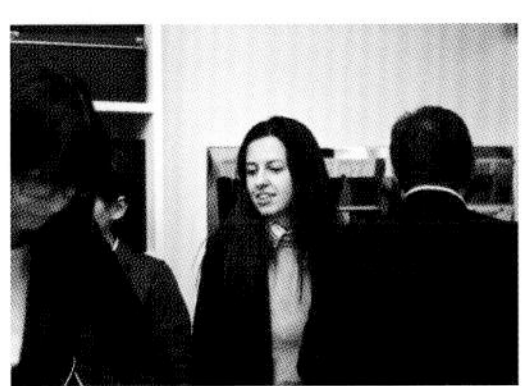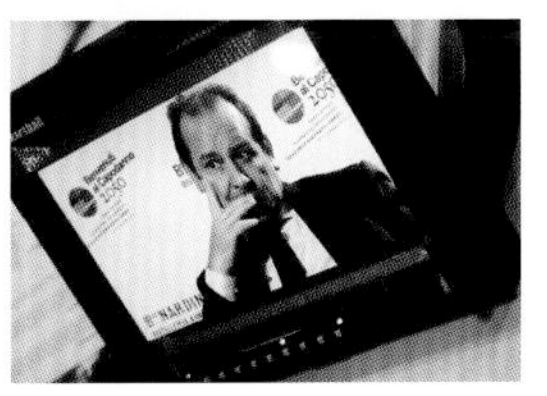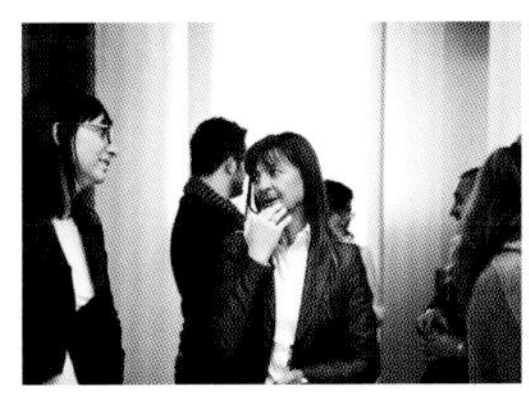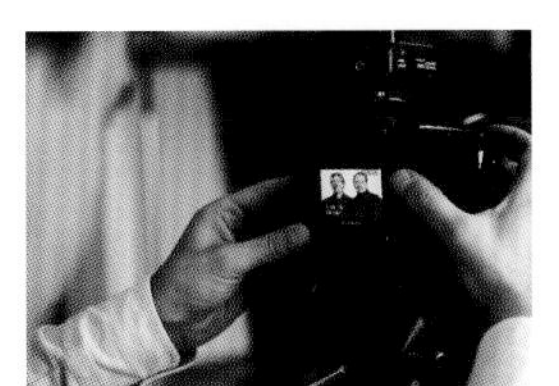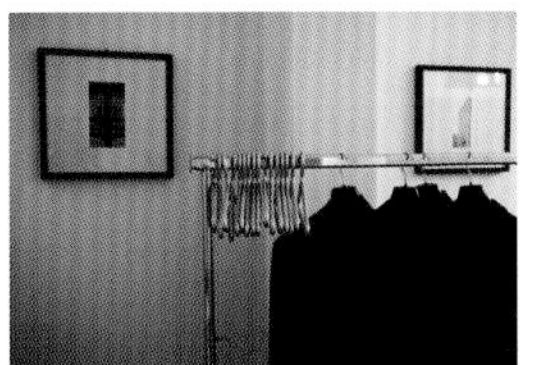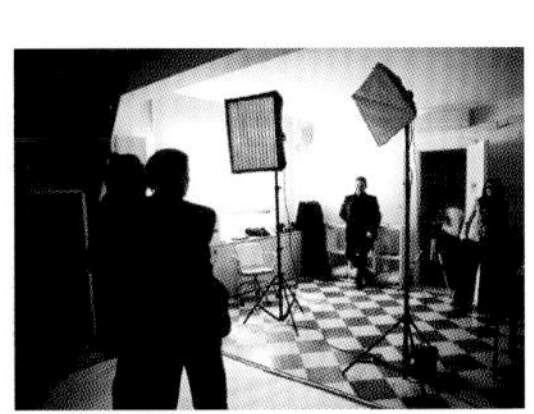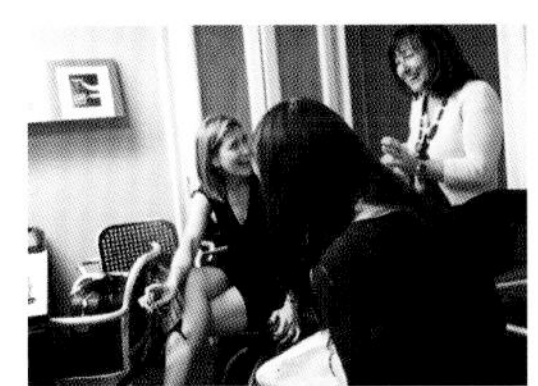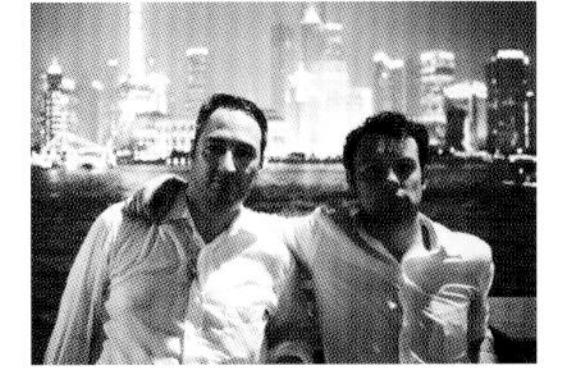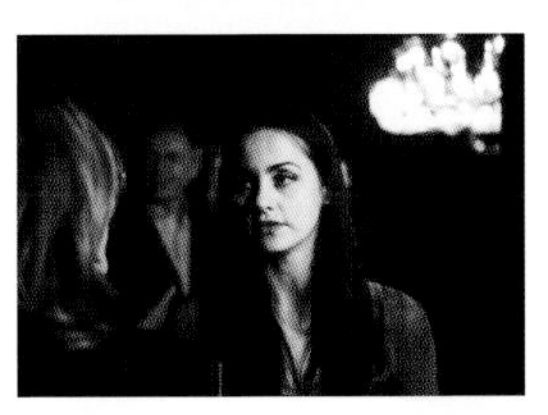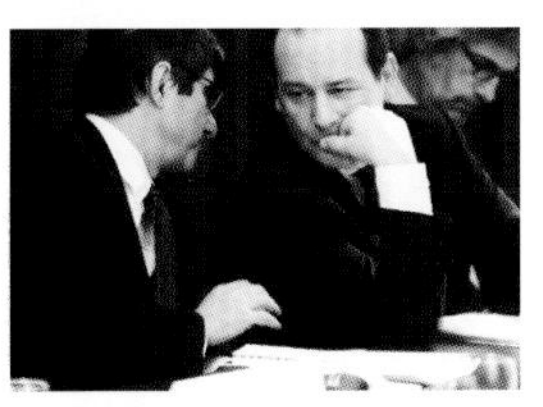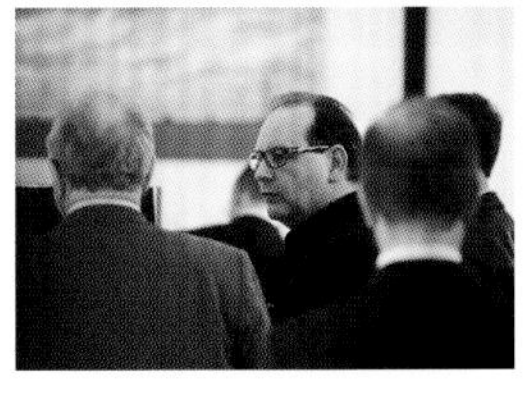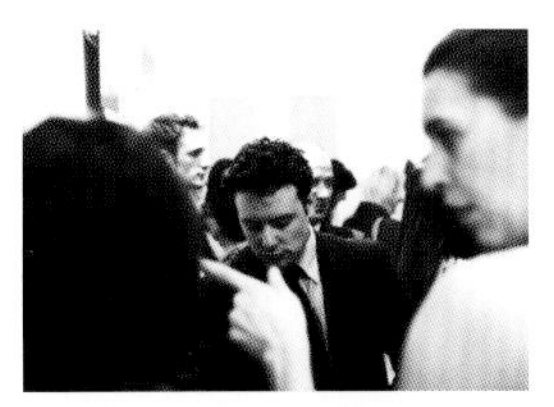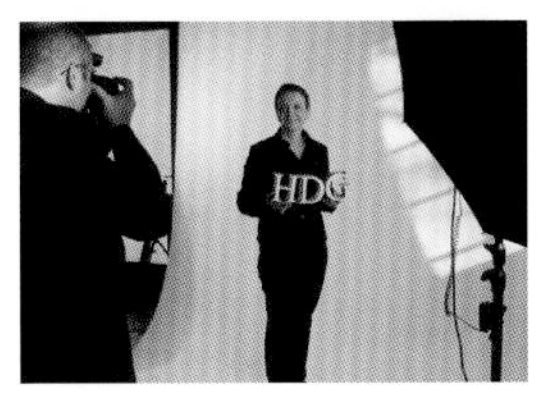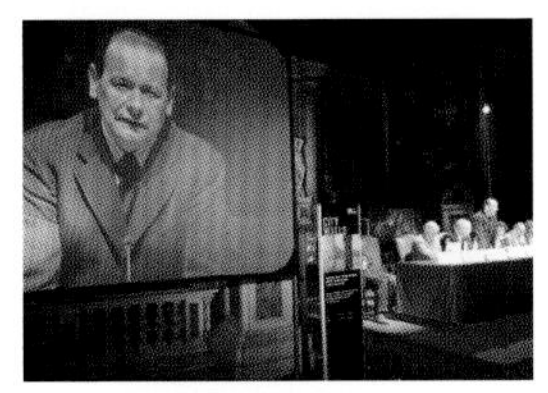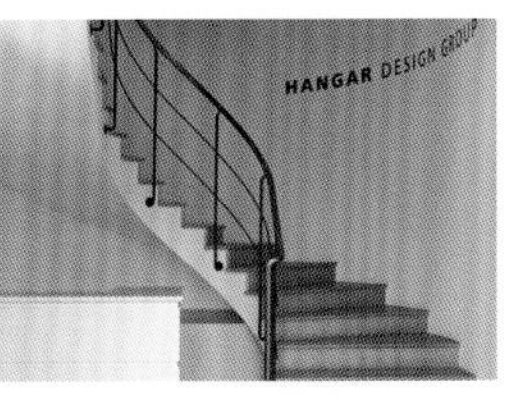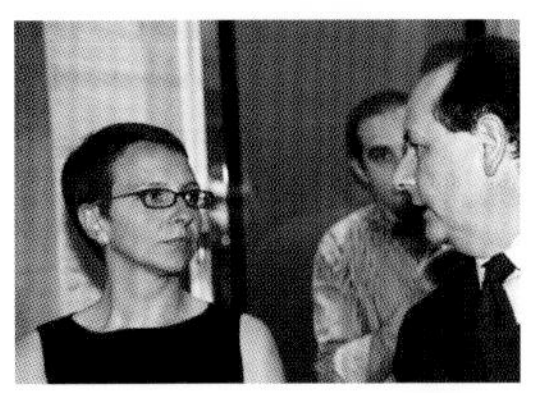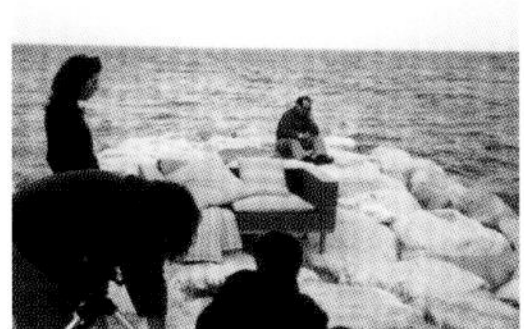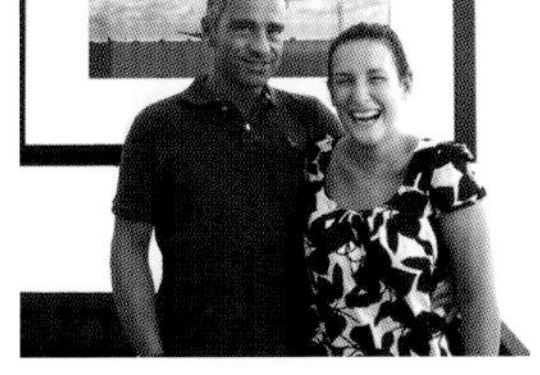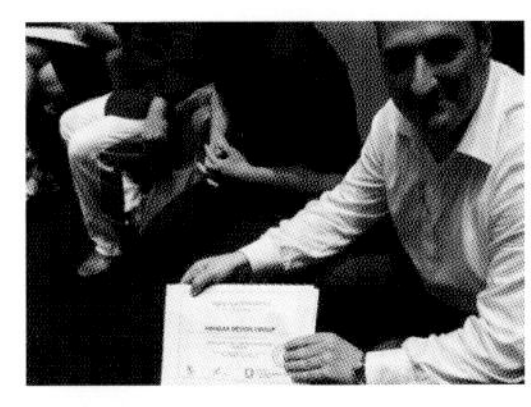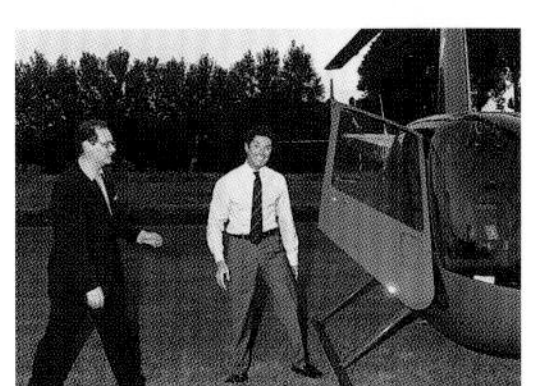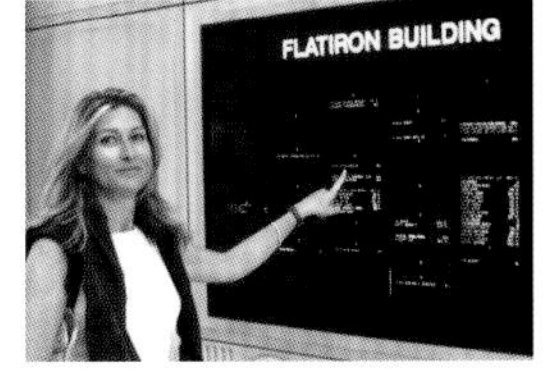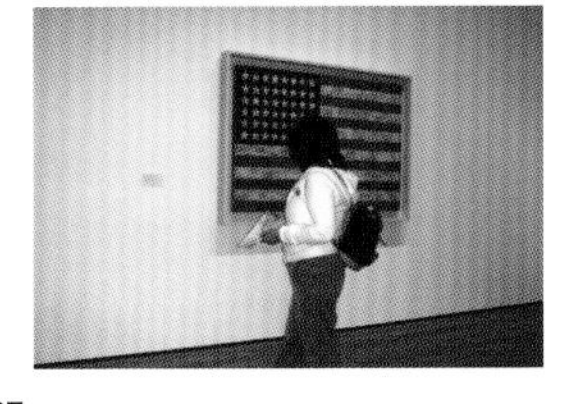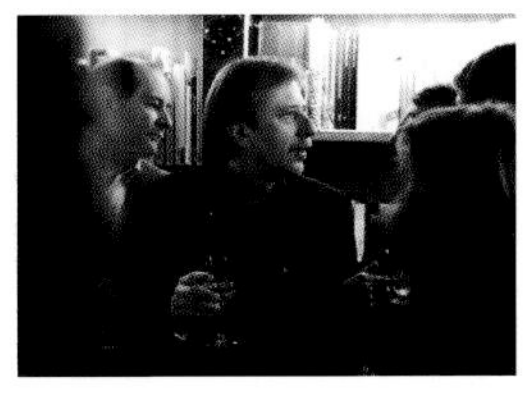

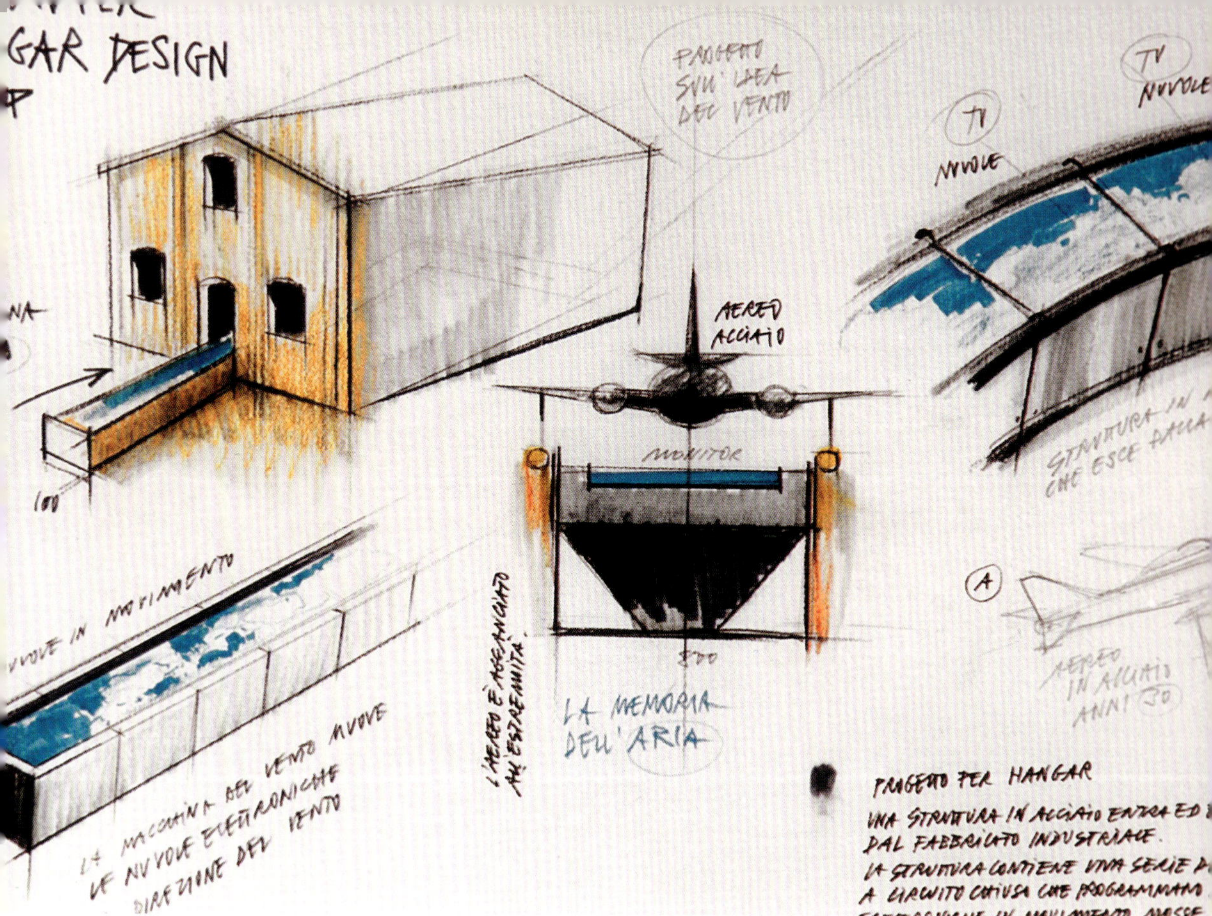

I COULD MAKE MYSELF
UNDERSTOOD

ONE PLUS ONE CAN SOMETIMES MAKE
MORE THAN TWO. THE COMBINED EFFORT
OF A TEAM CAN NOT ONLY MAKE BIGGER,
BETTER, SMARTER THINGS, IT CAN ALSO
MAKE POSSIBLE THE SEEMINGLY IMPOSSIBLE.
THIS IS THE THEME OF THIS CHAPTER
WORK – THE THINGS THAT HAPPEN
WHEN WE COLLABORATE.

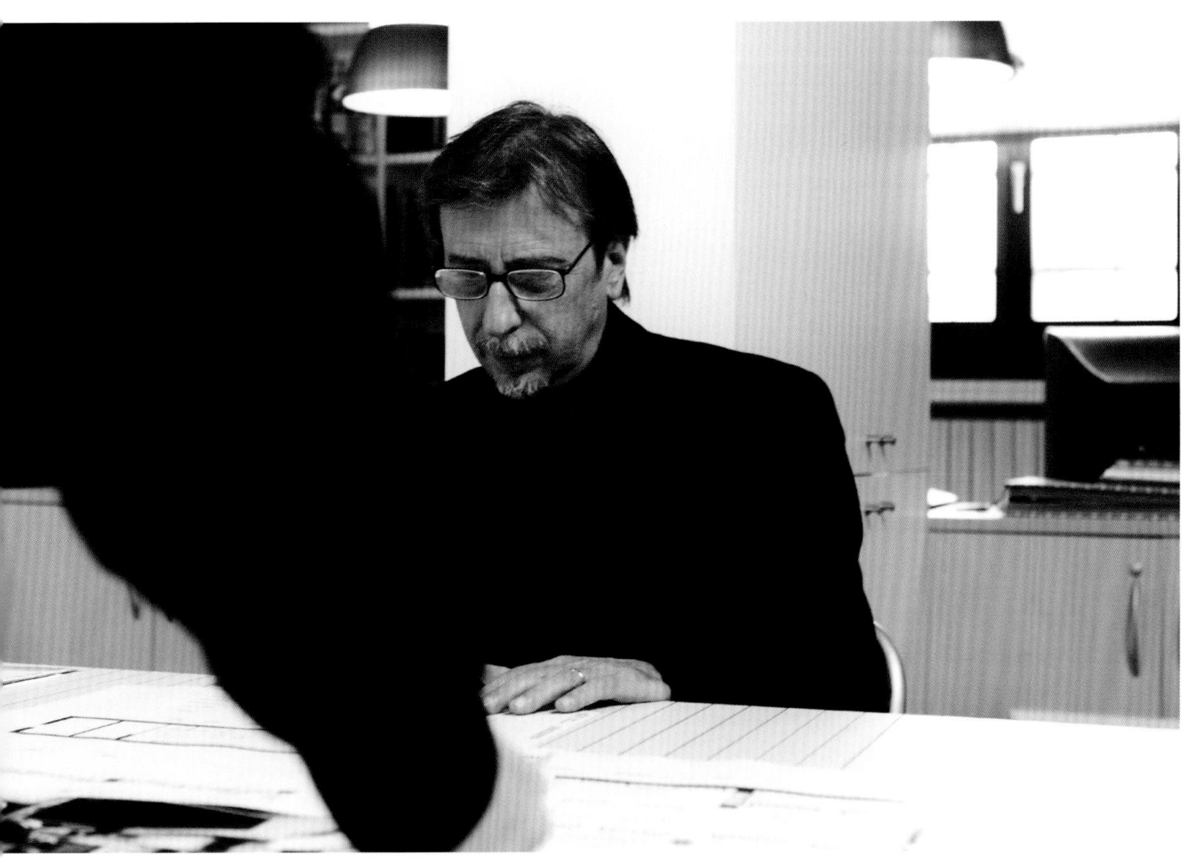

THIS IS ...A CRÉATIVE STORY

Walking down the long, straight path, still covered with gravel as those leading to elegant old country homes, helps one get away, disconnect and get ready to plunge into the magma of creativity. Two twin buildings play and chase each other in the middle of the lawn, which is meticulously mowed and looked afer by a man whom everyone affectionately calls Mr. Danilo. He is responsible for the accidental discovery, over twenty years ago, of the theme which has accompanied the Hangar Design Group since its birth. "Letting ideas take flight" is intercepted in the mountain of written correspondence which the world absorbs every day and alights here, along the stately tree-lined path desired by Napoleon, in the hands of an attentive gardener. Those who experience this unusual terminal, kept as a green lawn, like to imagine that in one of the hangars "you think" and in the other "you do."

A thin shaped sheet metal, a reminder of the north wind, is used in both. Anticipating the success of neo-organic architecture by a few years, it protects the entrances to the north and outlines the stroke of a wing on the minute material of the exposed brick. More than a living memory, the history of the two buildings becomes a border between a story and visible sensation, between collective imagination and real-life experiences. A gradual disappearance, continuously contributed to, feeds the active creative community, that already reached the third millennium, with vital energy. It consists of the constant daily emotions from the beginning of the twentieth century, that extraordinary century full of revolutionary events in all fields, from arts to science. The dirigible was one of those amazing inventions and it is still hovering today.

The idea of this invisible airport slowly took shape in our minds through research in the archives, stories and period photographs. It is the beginning of everything. Even Louis Kahn loved beginnings. The beginning of the Holy Bible is one of the most extraordinary ever written. Louis read it again and again because he strongly believed that the genesis of something contained its entire future development. Louis had the habit of never finishing his works, since he considered them "alive," subject to change, real entities with a soul and he often enjoyed going back to the idea before he had even carried it out. Each day for us is a beginning. It is wonderful to think of having yet another full day in order to lift the world out of its ugliness with the stroke of a pencil. "Letting ideas take flight" is what inspired the inventor of airplanes – it moves inventiveness, intelligence and courage; imagination and cold reason. Then true emotion comes along, the flight among arts, cultures, styles, and fashion. In this way the tension of what we see makes sense of what we do. Thinking and designing, rethinking and redesigning, always with difficulty and enthusiasm, are impossible without the inspiration of a magnificent utopia such as flying, a mental and intellectual expansion, always alive, always available. Flying is a privilege only for those who are not afraid of heights. There are many types of flight, and each one is a philosophy. Flying for vocation is the profession we have chosen.

The hangars which house us are complex constructions of shapes and symbols collected during countless travels over the years. Notebooks made up of itineraries throughout time and the architecture of the world, without any desire to reach a defined scenic destination. By simply choosing the chords, the tones, by playing the different notes of an enigma which has always been following an idea of working. We constantly reflect while flying and visiting spaces and places in all the countries of the world. Flying is an extraordinary concept, and even more so is doing it. Once you have learned how, it is difficult to forget. You must always land in order to be able to take off again. Give us a horizon to reach and we will design strange flying machines to take you there.

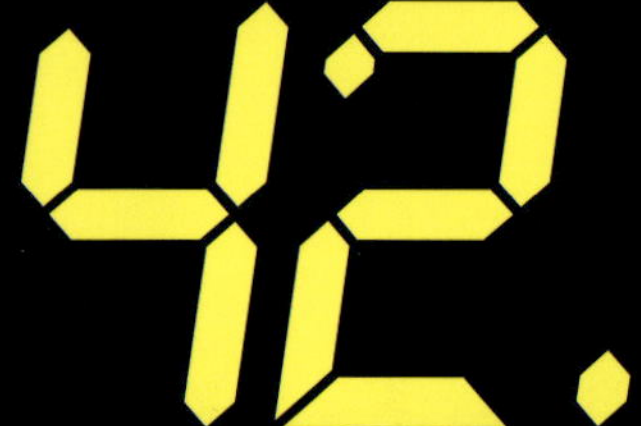

42.

For us, working together provides huge professional satisfaction.

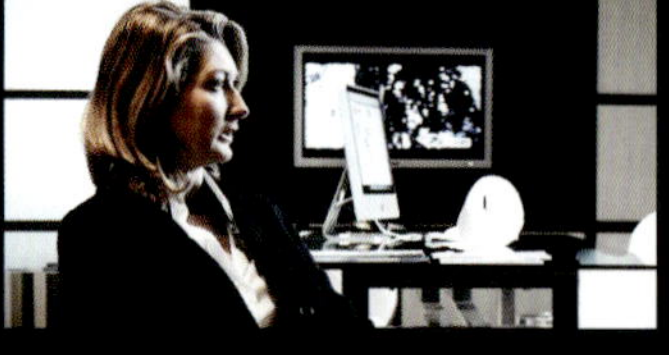

<u>When you work with someone else there is more anxiety about concluding things.</u> When you work alone this pressure is absent. You bring the thing to a certain point, then you move on to something else.

But when you work with other people – either because no one wants to be shown up in a poor light, or because everyone knows it's a collaborative enterprise – you do your utmost to be energized.

<u>Everything is much more alive, more effervescing.</u> It is highly productive to engage and debate with one another. Most people use the word "confrontation," but in fact it is a dialectic of challenge.

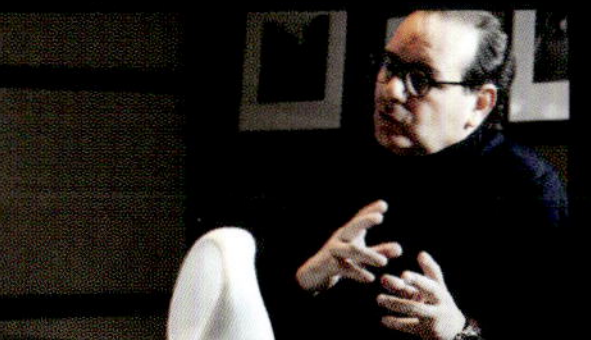 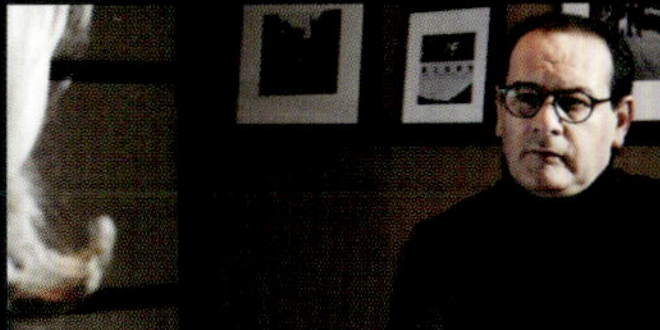 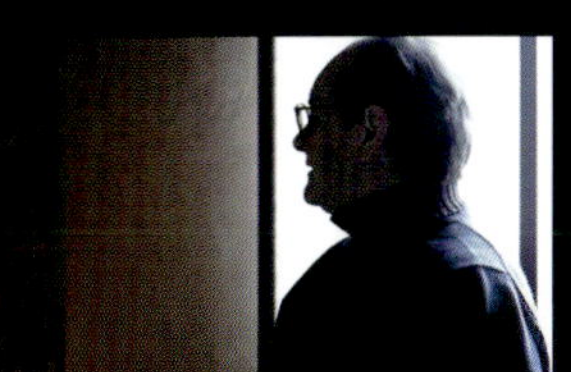

OUTLINE

A SHARED PROPOSAL FOR THE BOOK

[The page numbers are approximate only. The numeration will be based on the <u>quantity of works and images</u> for inclusion]

FOREWORD BY HANGAR DESIGN GROUP:
a series of short texts – **reflections, items of information, analyses, appraisals, judgments, surveys, dreams, programs, also compiled informally** *– written by each member of the group and organized in an apparently casual order. The autographs of all those involved to be appended (The partners? The staff?)*

HANGAR DESIGN GROUP IN THE MIRROR

The history of the group. The place and places. The organization. Its identity. Many images of interior spaces and people at work, design sketches, doodling, notes. Short critical texts (see the proofs), densely packed within the graphic context, recounting the history of the group and its distinctive characteristics.

THE WORK, THE WORKS

One will have to carefully avoid falling prey to simple listing or cataloging or collecting of samples. Since the book is destined for bookshops (and should last around ten years), it should presuppose an analytic reading by its putative readers (students, professionals, clients, researchers). Philological precision will accompany an articulateness of language. The works must be presented not in a series of *jumps* from one work to another, but with a fluidity that can be accelerated or slowed down based on the peculiarity of the images in question. Each double page should be organized as a completely coherent image in itself, respecting the classic modular canon that is part of the style of HDG, but taking it as far as it will go to liberate all the energy that is compressed there. In the final analysis, one might think of a kind of hypertext, which requires (and allows) a reading that is not linear but transversal, depending on the interest of the reader.

<u>This naturally applies to the texts also.</u>

To facilitate the reading and to illustrate the turning points in the history of HDG (in terms of professional, learning and stylistic processes), one can think of a temporal tripartite division which is of significance on the historical plane.

This presupposes that the works and images should be arranged according to a chronological sequence, to illustrate the evolution of the stylistic models and the progressive enrichment of the professional skills involved.

Hangar Design Group is more pop than rock.
In a pop group what counts are not the isolated
individuals but the name of the group.
In the end, the result achieved is a group
effort and not based on one inclination
predominating over the others.

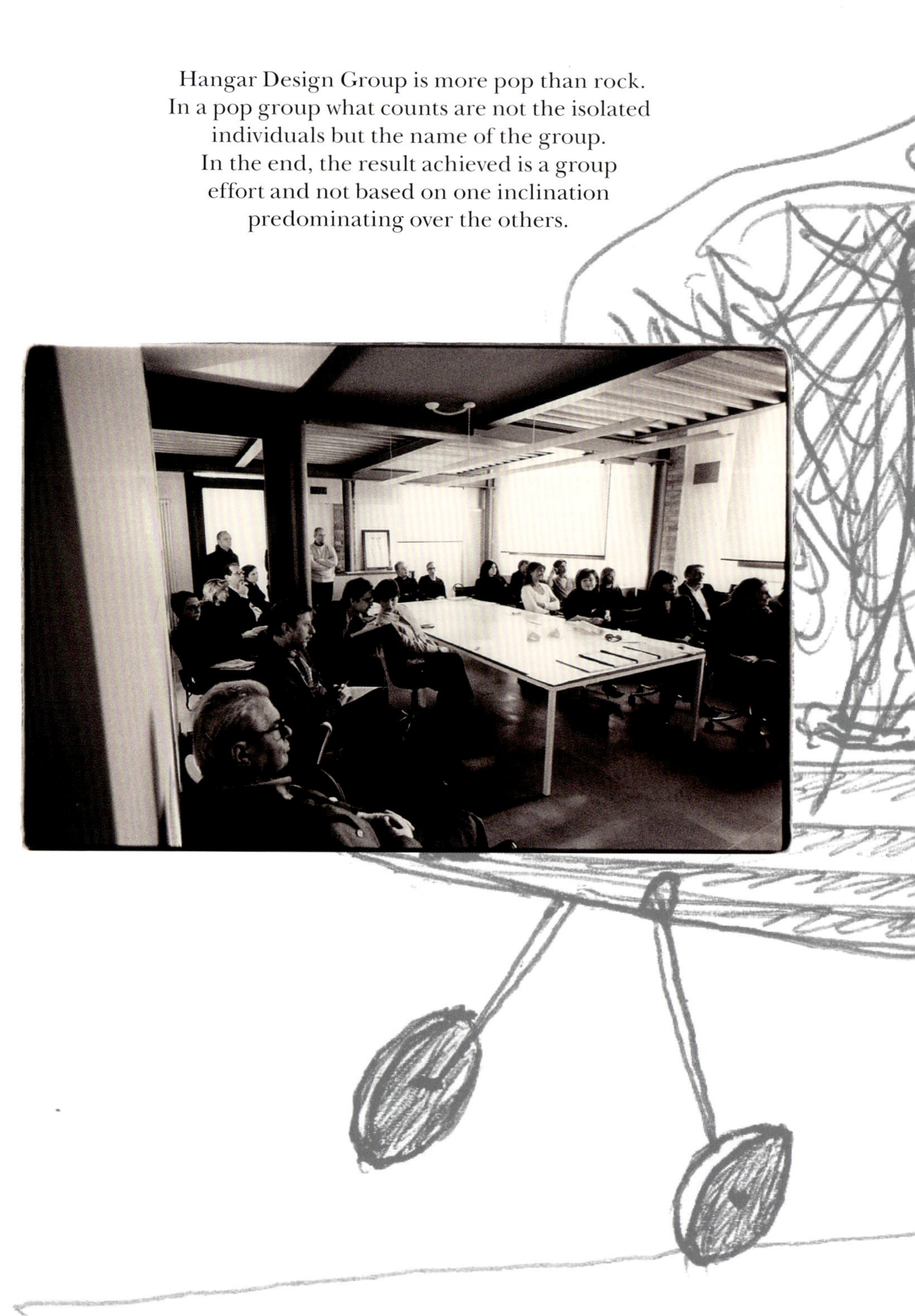

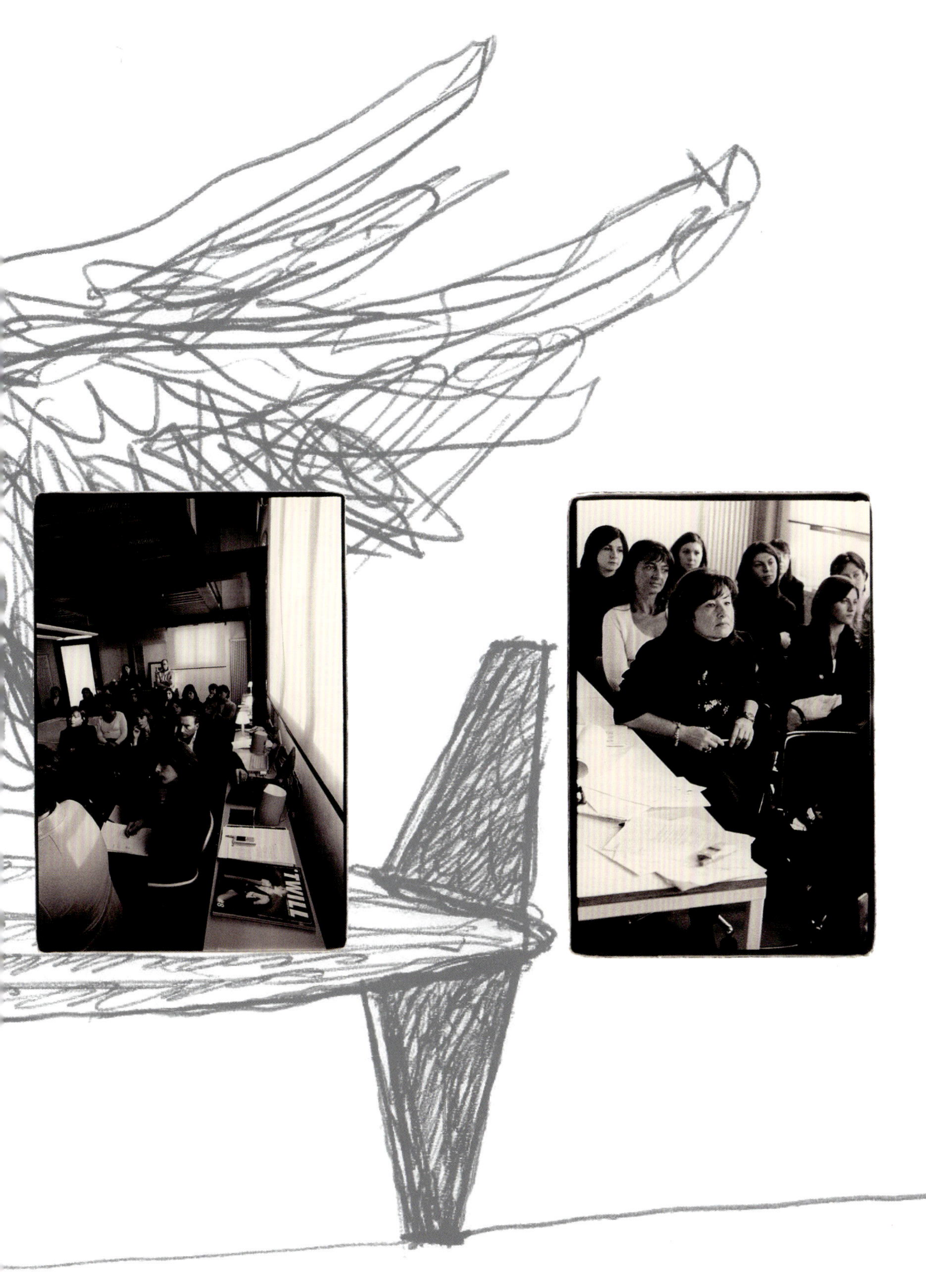

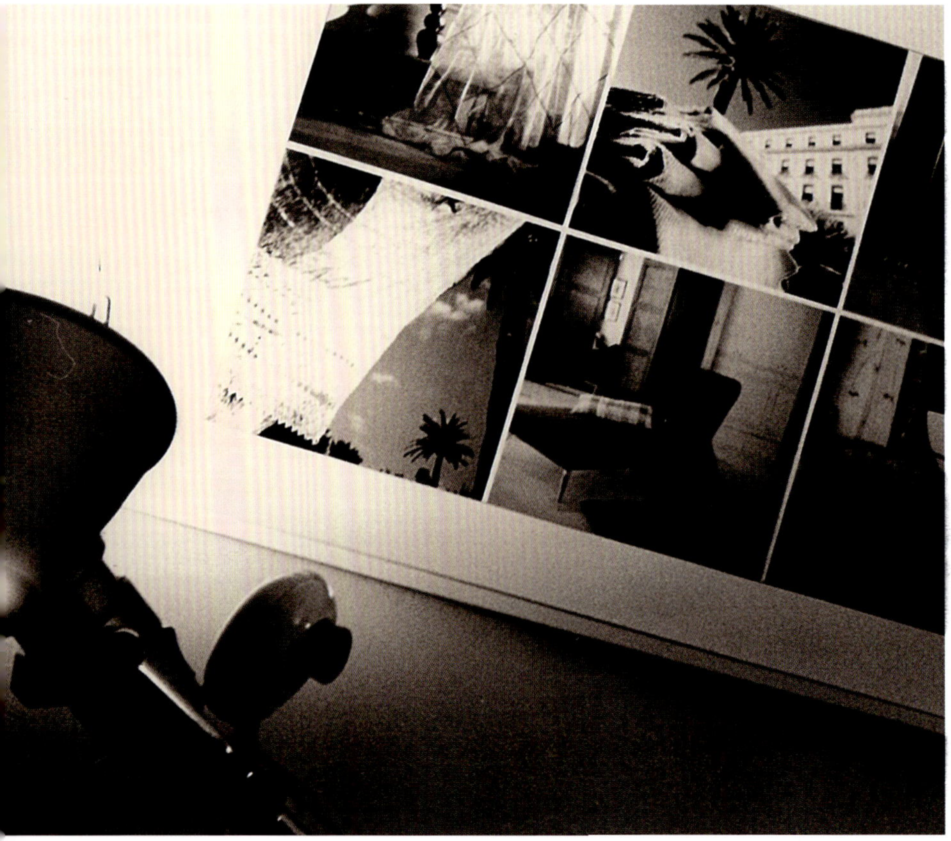

WE STOPPED WRITING TEXTS A LONG TIME AGO,

but we love words, and especially titles. Just a few rare words are enough to create significant images. We have succeeded well with design and with rapture. Everyone had thought this was our state of being. What gave it a lot of resonance was the title. We have always paid particular attention to titles. There are those who believe that ideas lurk within titles, but often the opposite is the case.

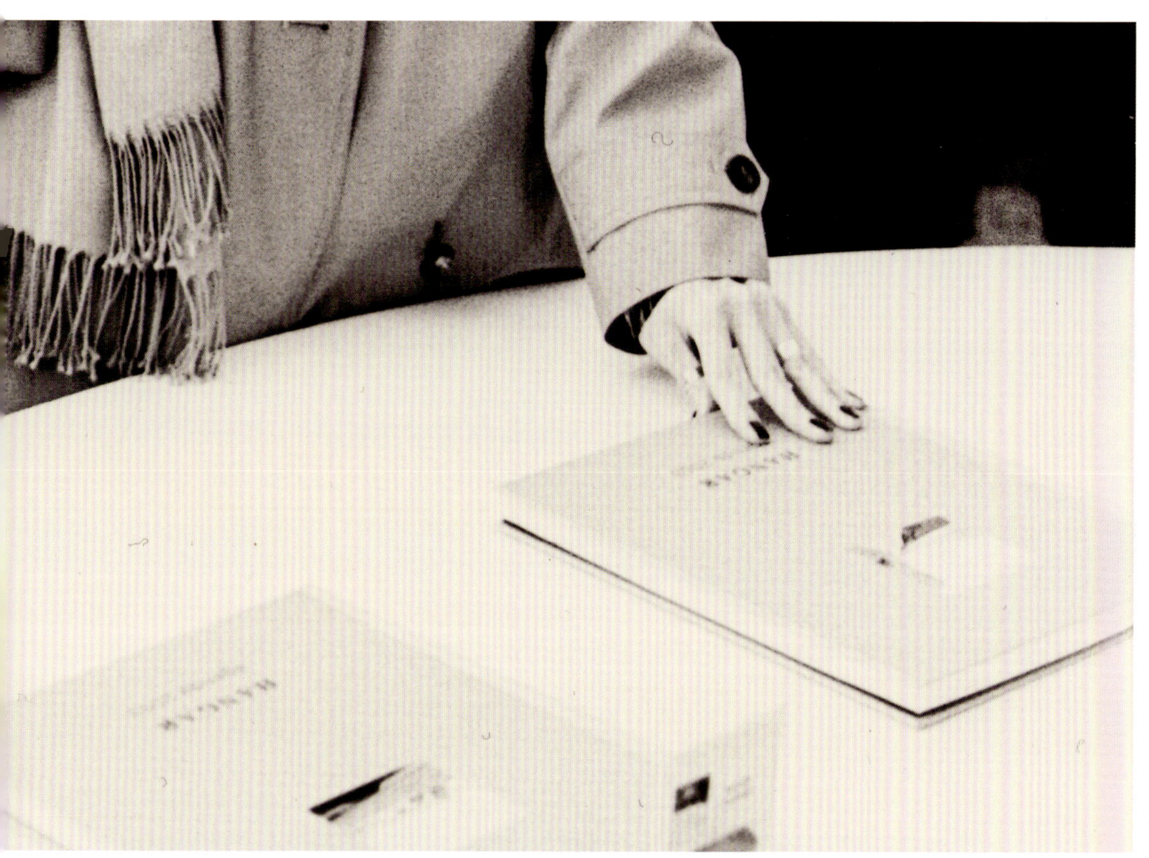

"IT WAS MY DREAM JOB."

Designing ideas is an imperative for all graphic design firms, something Hangar Design Group has genuinely incorporated in its own communication models. Studying a product's image does not so much mean mirroring what is on offer, as casting light on certain shadows and revealing the dark side of what is on show.
The various features in play draw on a method of representation that verges on the hazy realms of analysis. The symbolic side of dream, which Sigmund Freud considered so important, emerges here barely hidden behind a curtain of signals and allusions which communication methods have developed.
What emerges here, above everything else, is what is not said and is not designed, which actually forms the message's most significant underpinning. Modern graphics – and not just modern graphics – could even be interpreted based on its visual silences, often more eloquent than carefully structured discourse. Just consider the spatial relations between two images to see how important they are.

IN HANGAR DESIGN GROUP PUBLICATIONS

this interplay between what is visible and hidden away fits into a grid which cannot be directly read off the page, but only against the light: the perfectly orthogonal layout of word and image, the carefully patterned modularity around the archetype of the square, and the tendency to make emptiness, absence and silence the most eloquent communication spaces, are undoubtedly the most expressive structural features of all.

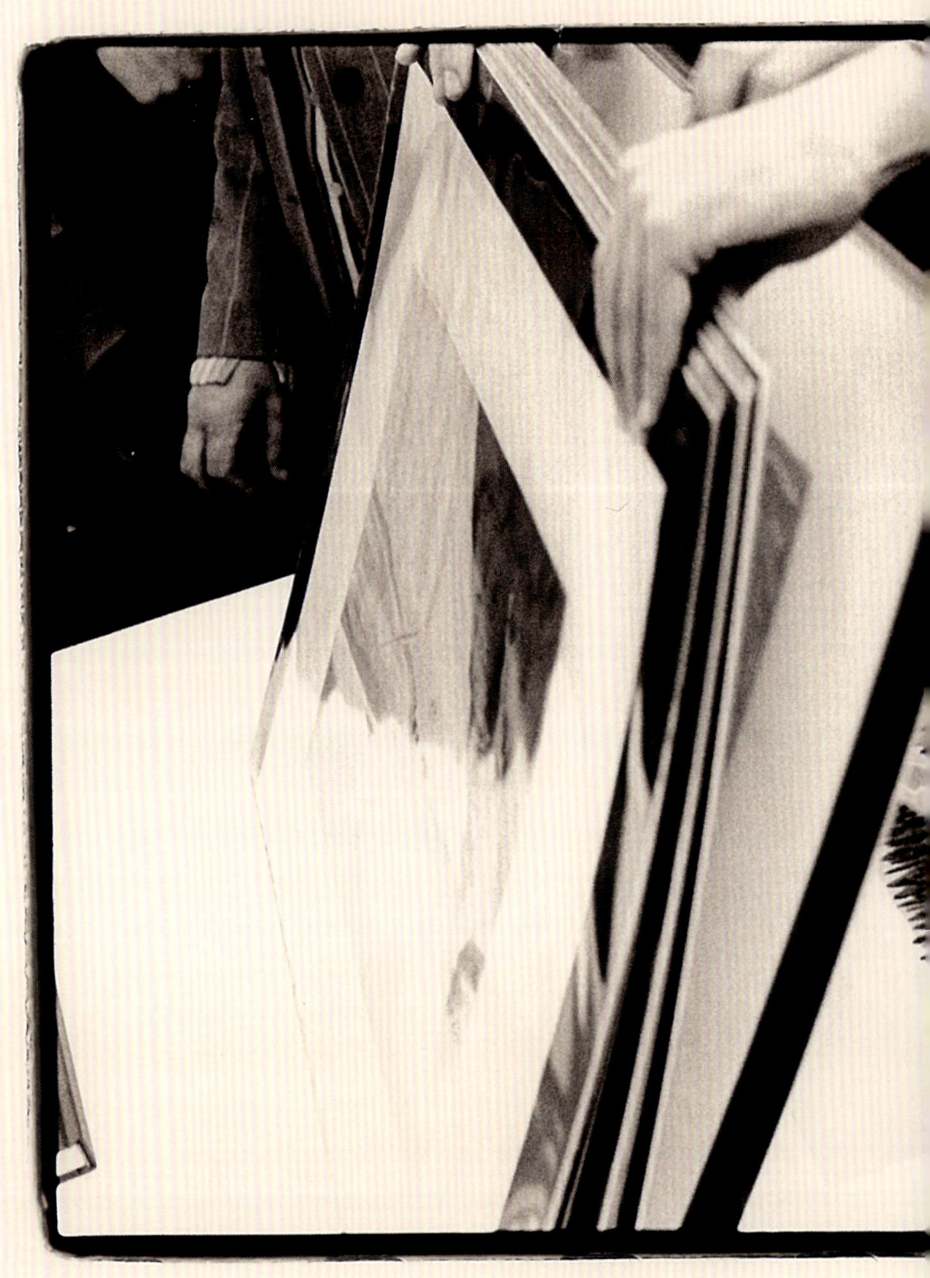

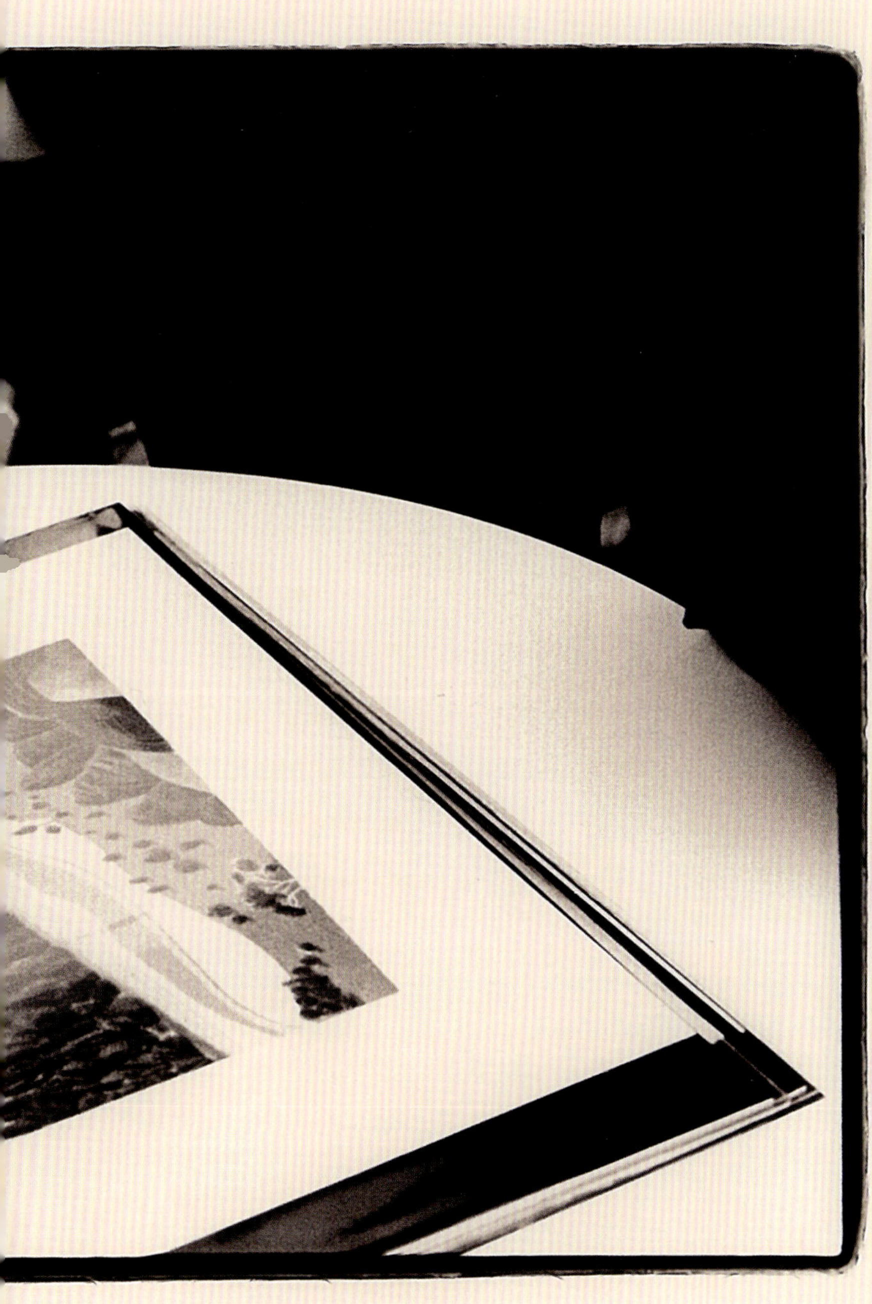

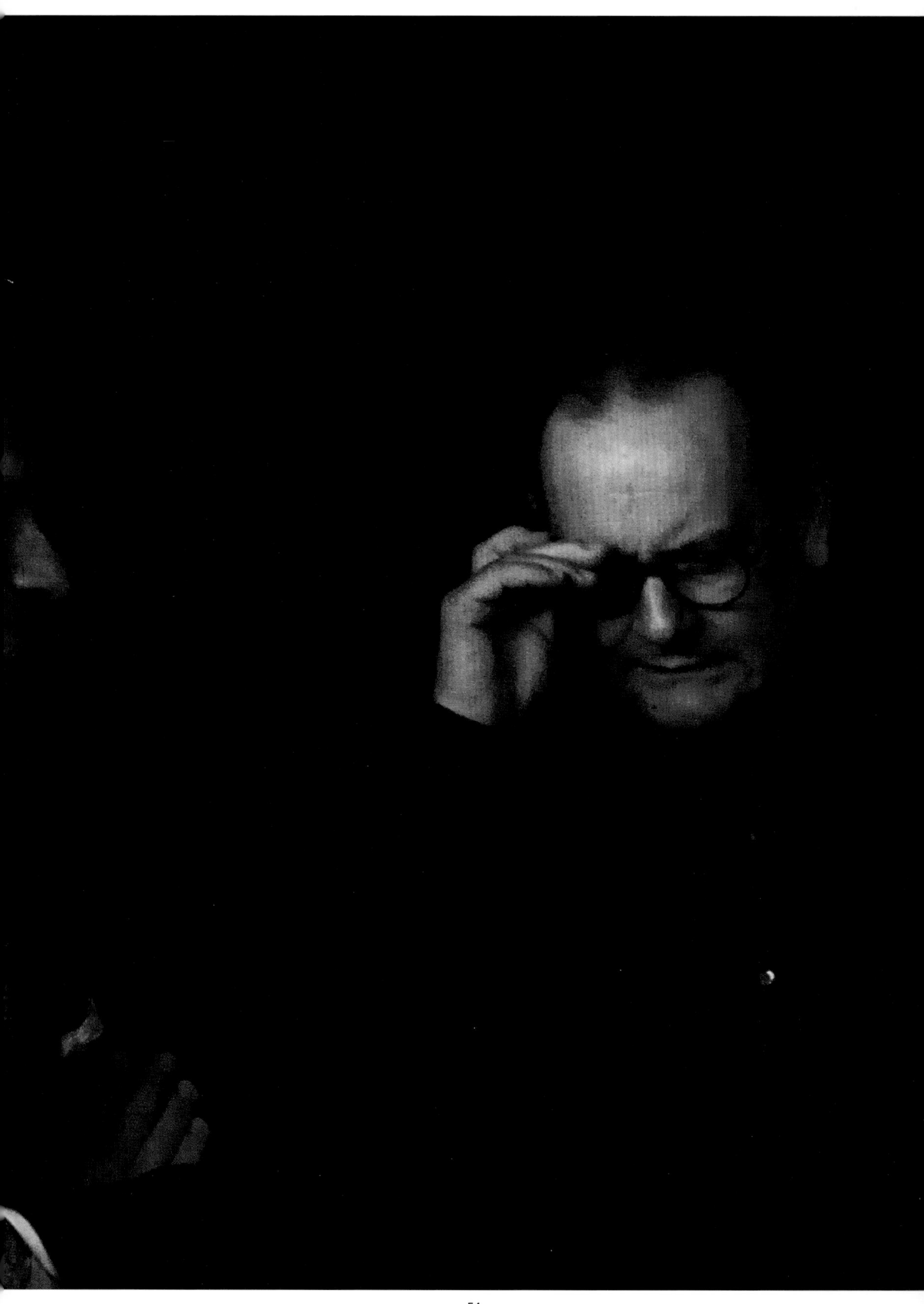

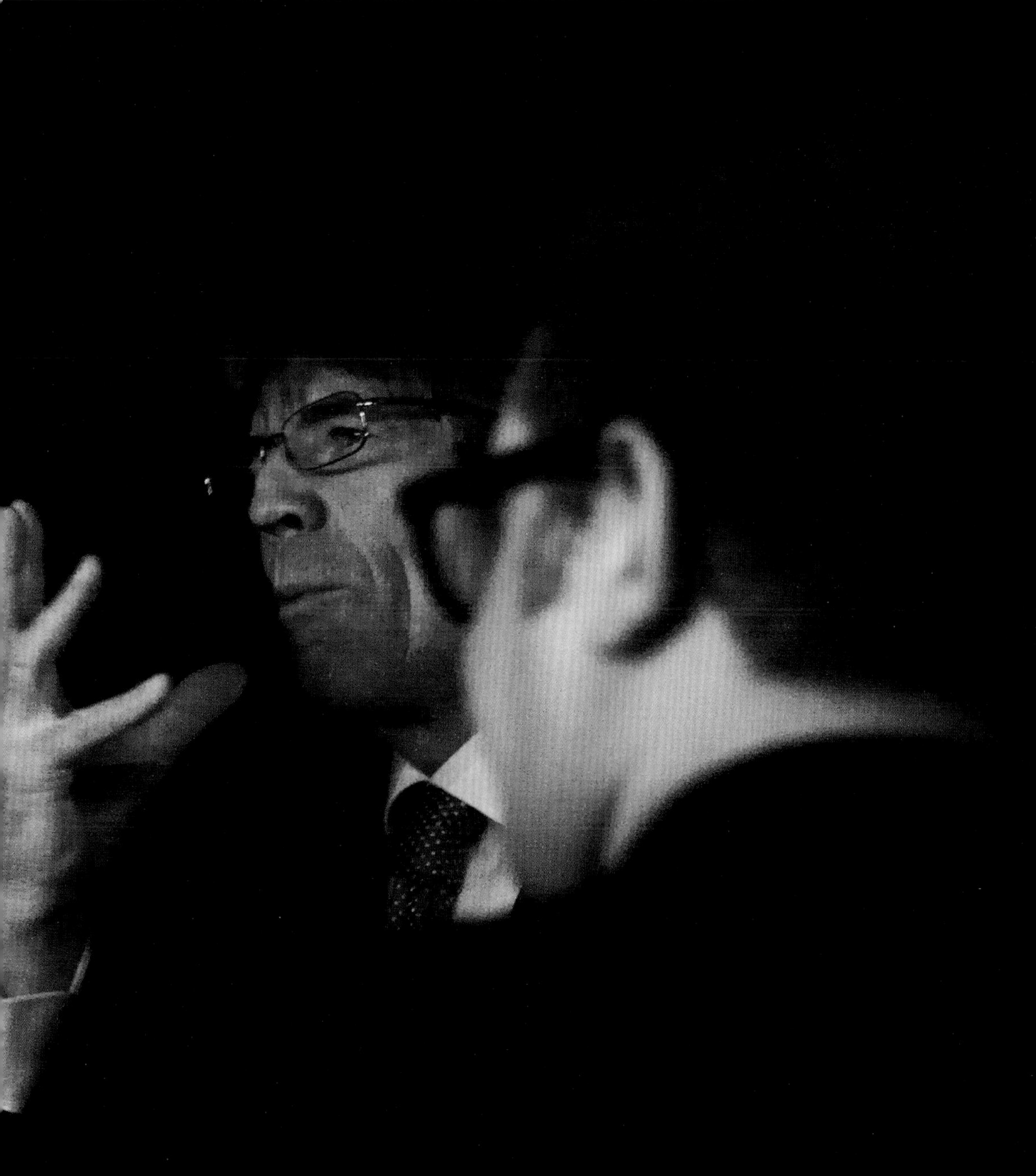

*We constantly have to dive into new subjects that we have to grasp
before we begin the design phase. So we are always reading and talking with
clients about almost anything you can imagine — from a sophisticated
chandelier technique, retail trends, food packaging, luxury real estate, to target readers.*

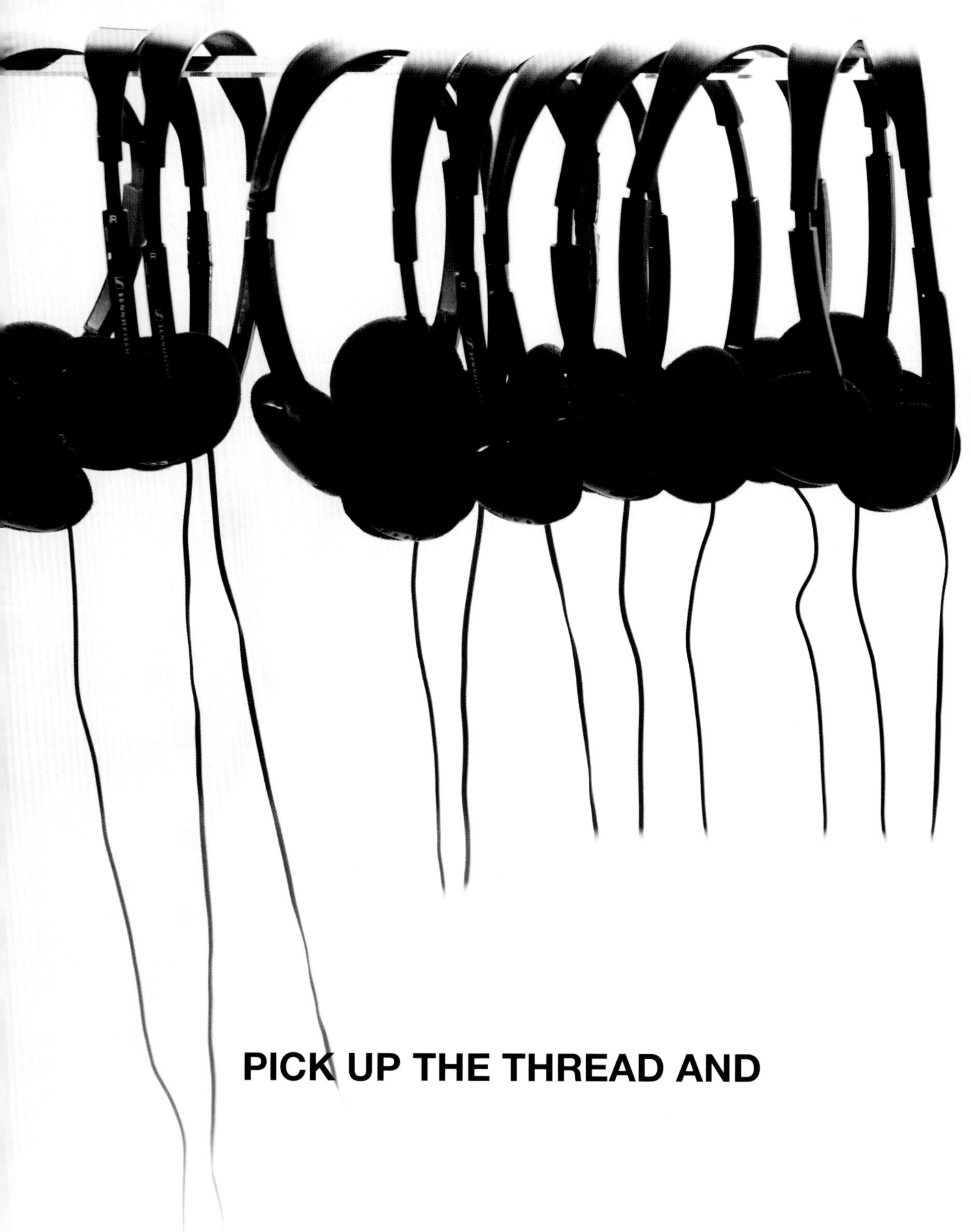

PICK UP THE THREAD AND

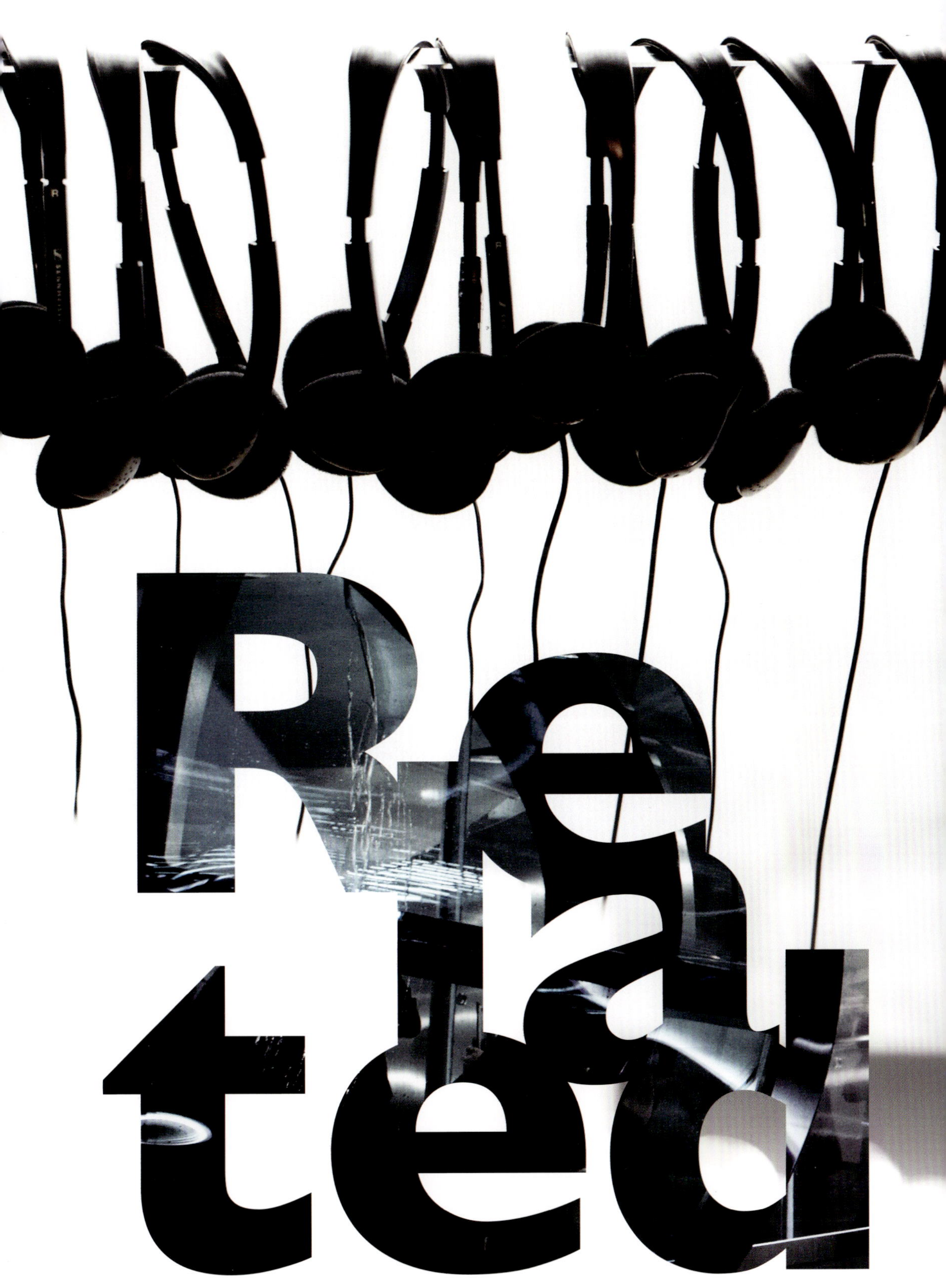

Related

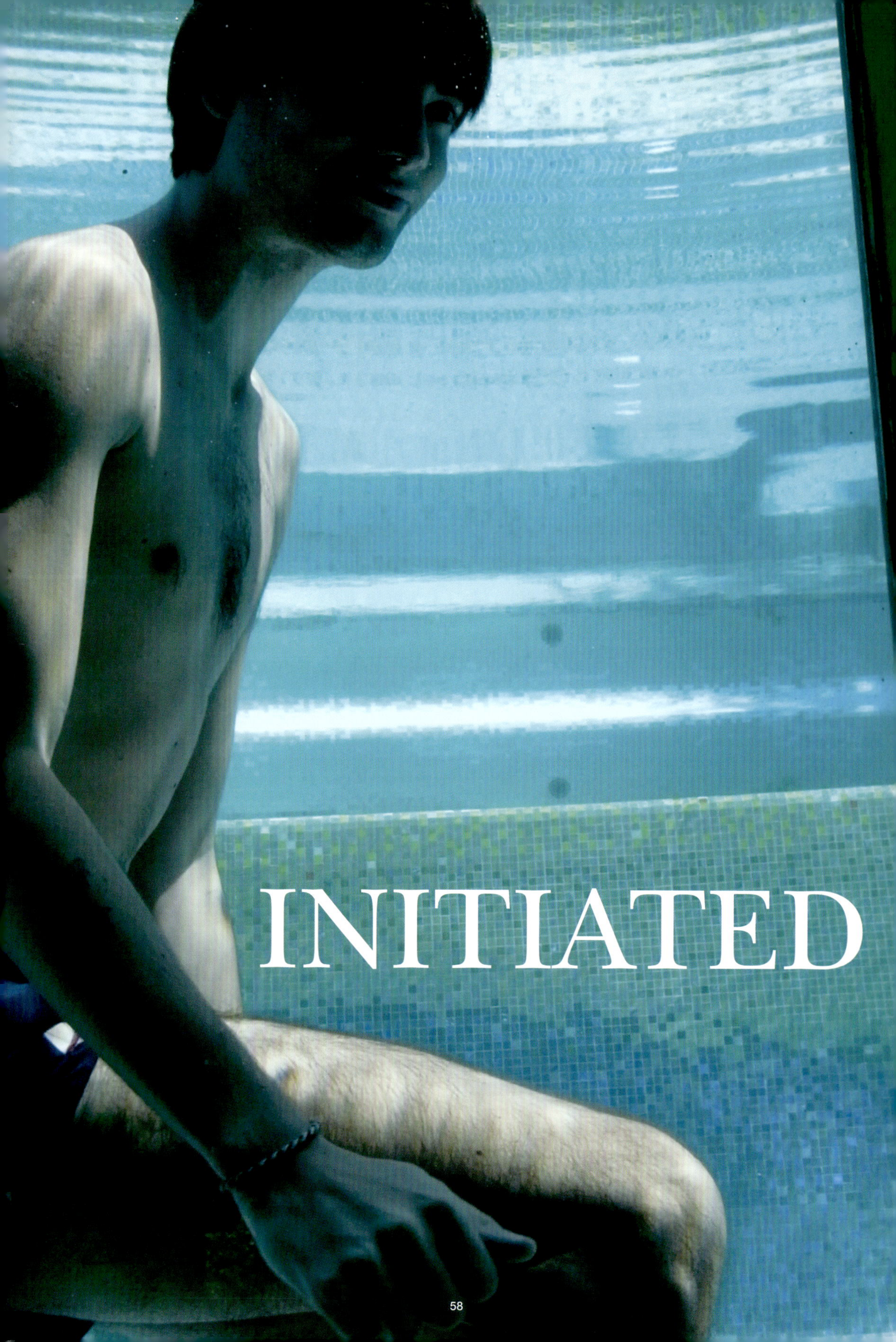
INITIATED

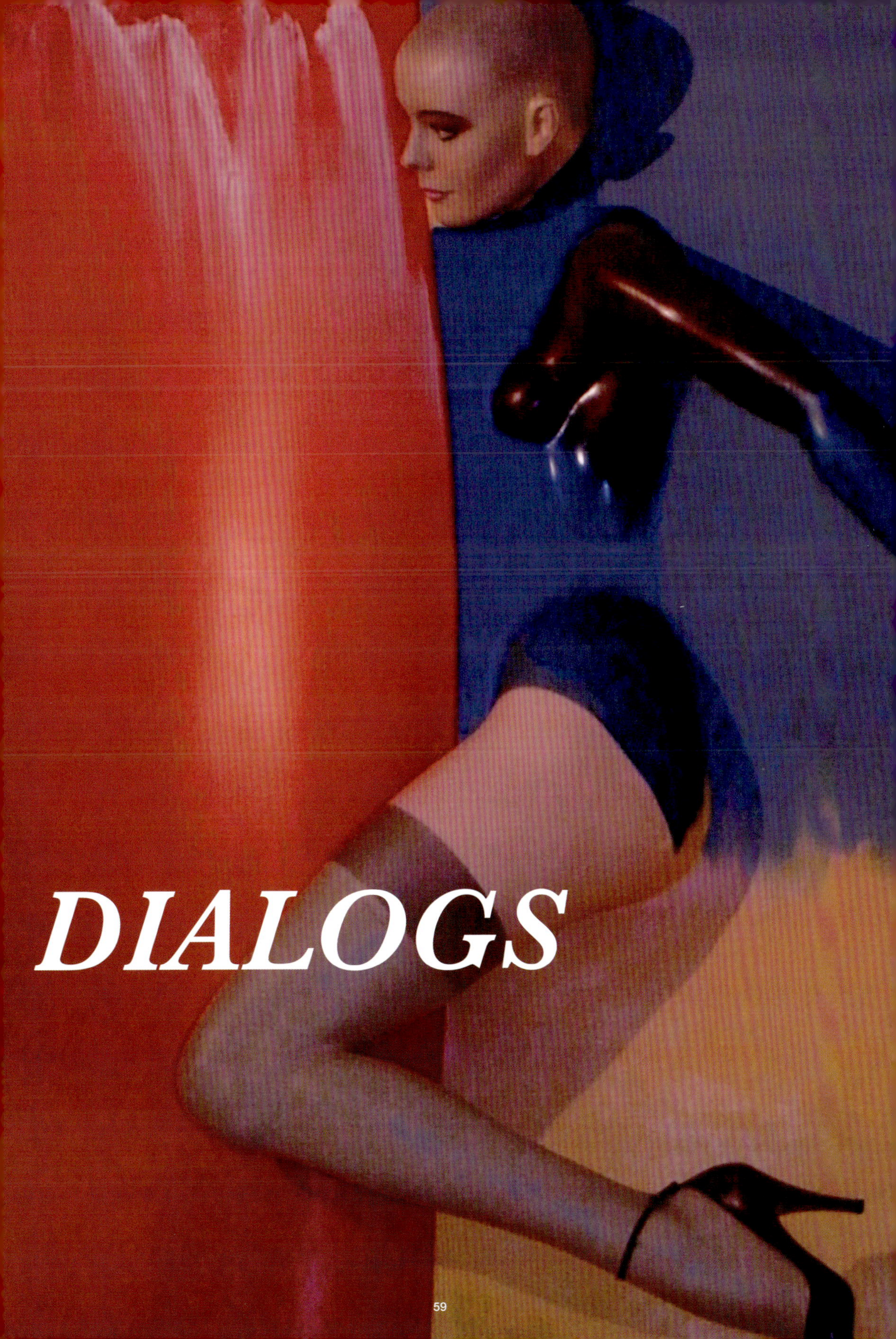
DIALOGS

"Me and you and and every-one we know"

CAMEOS (OF)

NICE PEOPLE AND INTERESTING SUBJECTS

We enjoy the personal interaction that
takes place among us and artists.
In particular, we've been fortunate enough
to work with an enormous diversity of figures:
photographers, painters, sculptors, some of
the greatest architects and graphic designers.
What is especially gratifying is the education
process that comes about with every design
project. But mostly we are thankful for
meeting nice people and interesting subjects.

62.

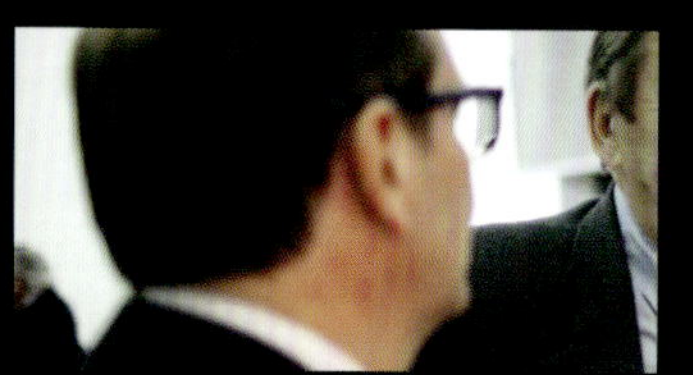
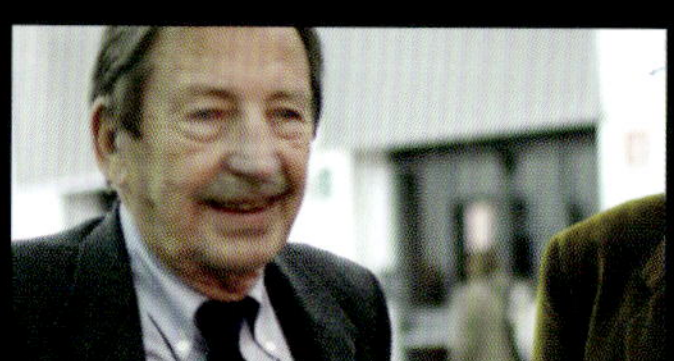
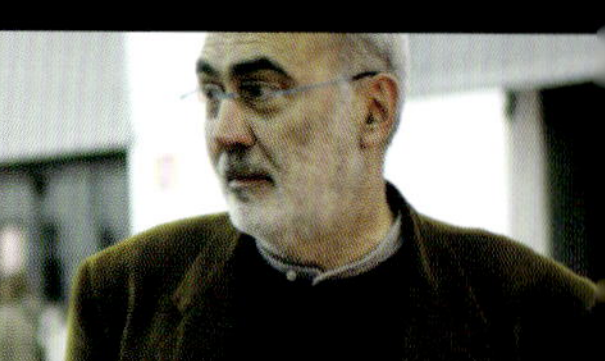

IT NEEDS A GOOD
SOURCE OF SAVVY

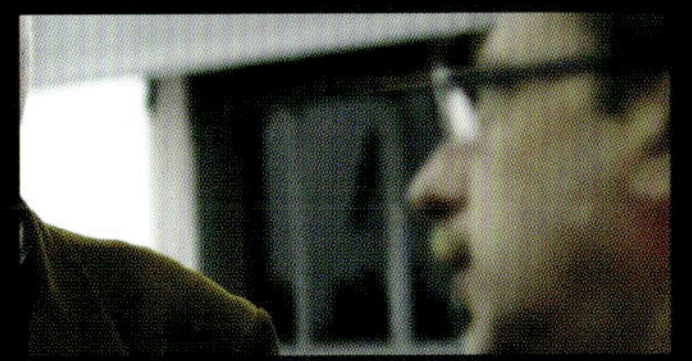

THE MAN
IN THE WHITE CAPE

doesn't do the designwork in his private office, from which he emerges after three months with "Voilà! This is my divine inspiration." That's not how design is done these days. We think young designers with the right attitude coming out of school can be outstanding, but as above, this is a complicated business now.

Experience is more important than ever. Experience is more important than ever combined with the fresh ideas that young designers bring with them. When you buy experience, you buy client relationships. Those clients continue to move from organization to organization.

Relationships make the world go round, and as we know, with a satisfied customer, there is going to be lots of work in the future, even if it's not continuous. In the boom times, we are always hustling for new business, but when times get tough, it is our old customers, those we have built relationships with, who are always going to have business for us.

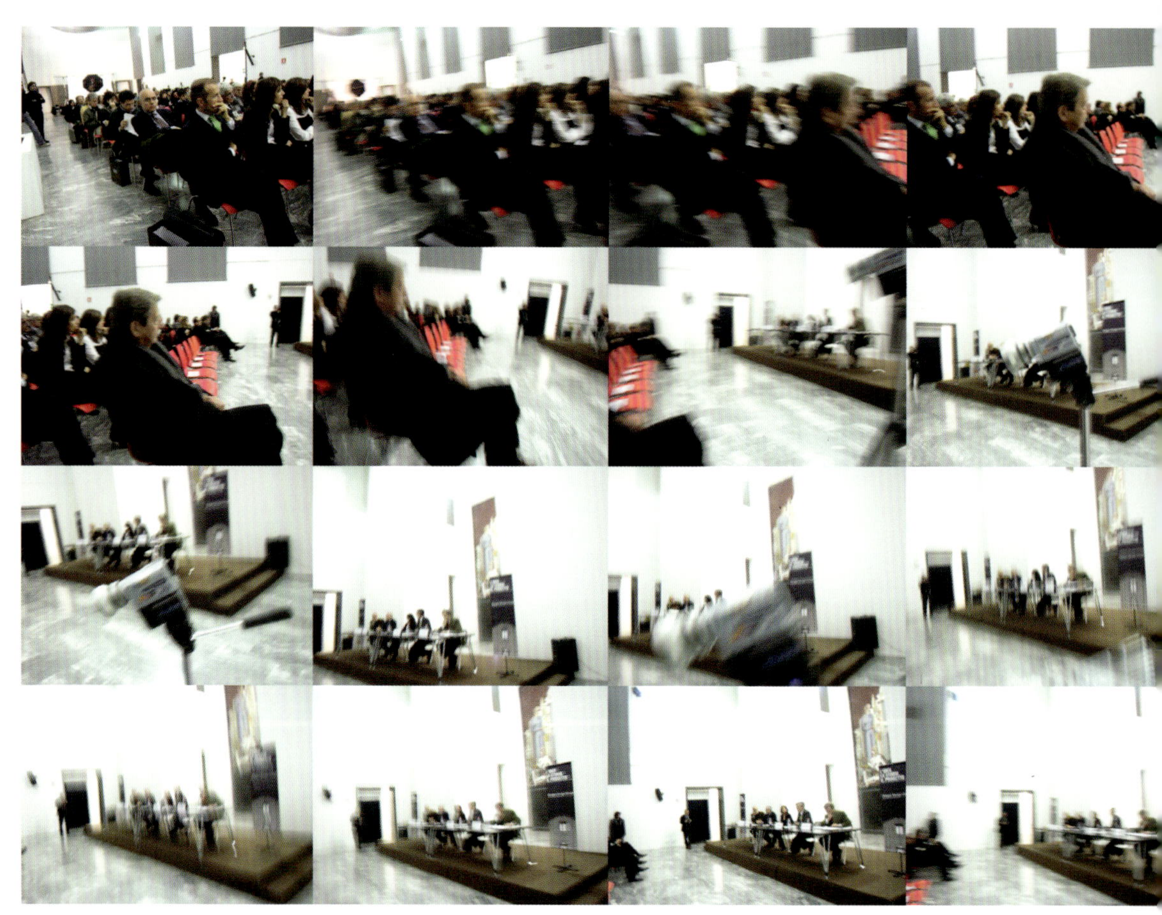

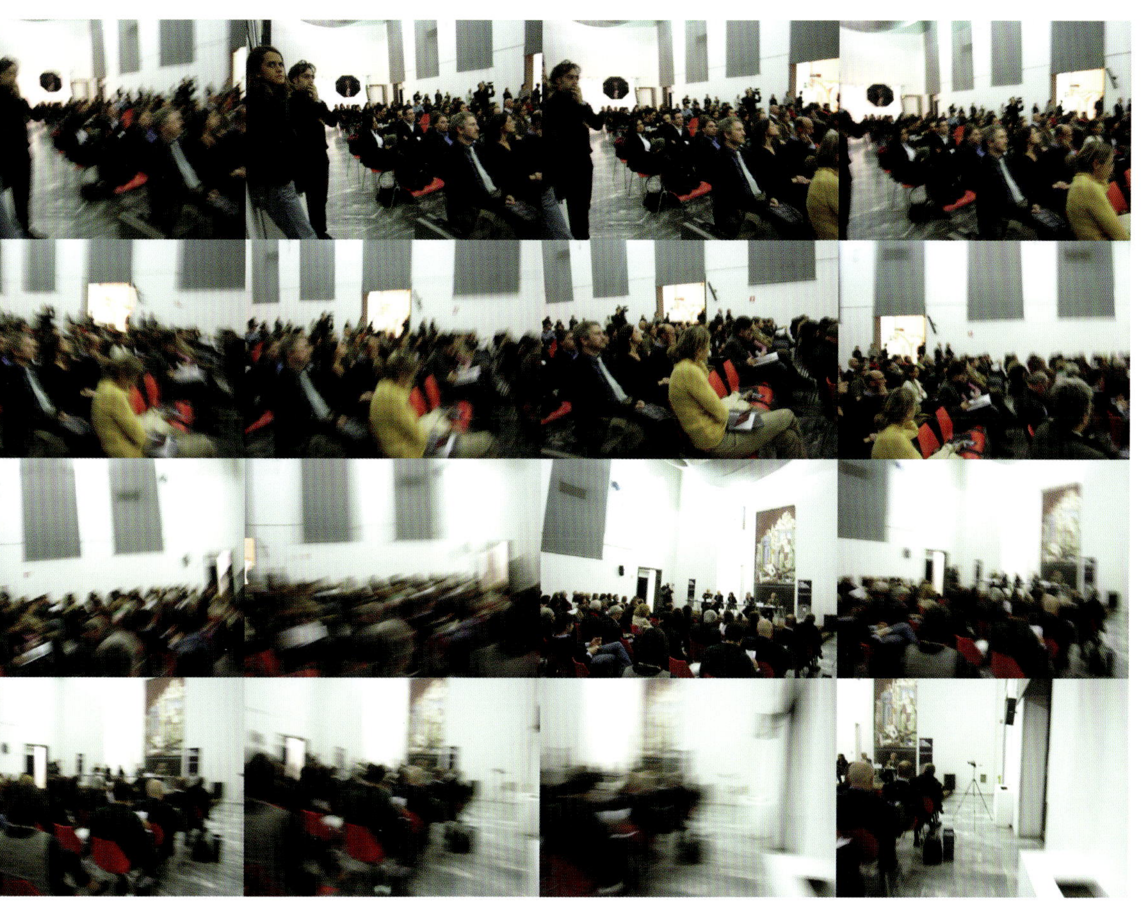

Someone wrote that <u>what the world wants from the culture of design – today more than ever – is a design of the world.</u>

We enjoy quoting this phrase when a young collaborator asks us how to proceed in formal research, because before the sign and before even the creative act comes the attitude of listening and patient interrogation, which then generates the ability to accede and respond to diverse and geographically distant requests to put spaces, objects, behaviors into relationship with one another, <u>giving rise to a homogeneous body of shared languages, figures and models.</u>

Our experience has always been based on the ability to create new relationships not only between ideas, but also between the places where they are produced, between persons and roles. A continuous process of exchange and learning, a necessary osmosis through which creative processes, techniques and models of transmission are gradually and incessantly diffused.

<u>We believe that fidelity to this changeable interpretation of space, understood as a network through which research and experience in design may be oriented, represents the *fil rouge* of our professional trajectory.</u>

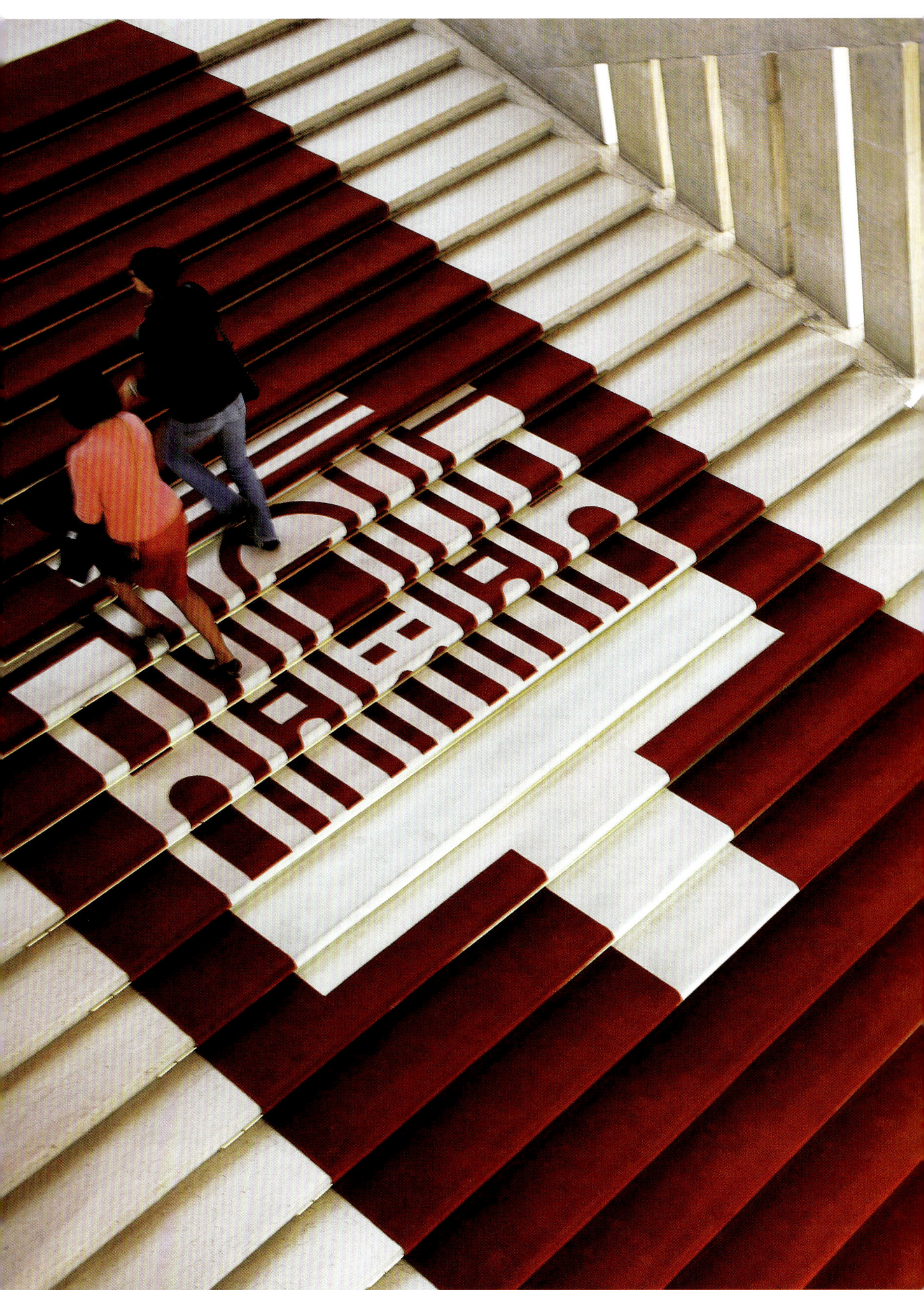

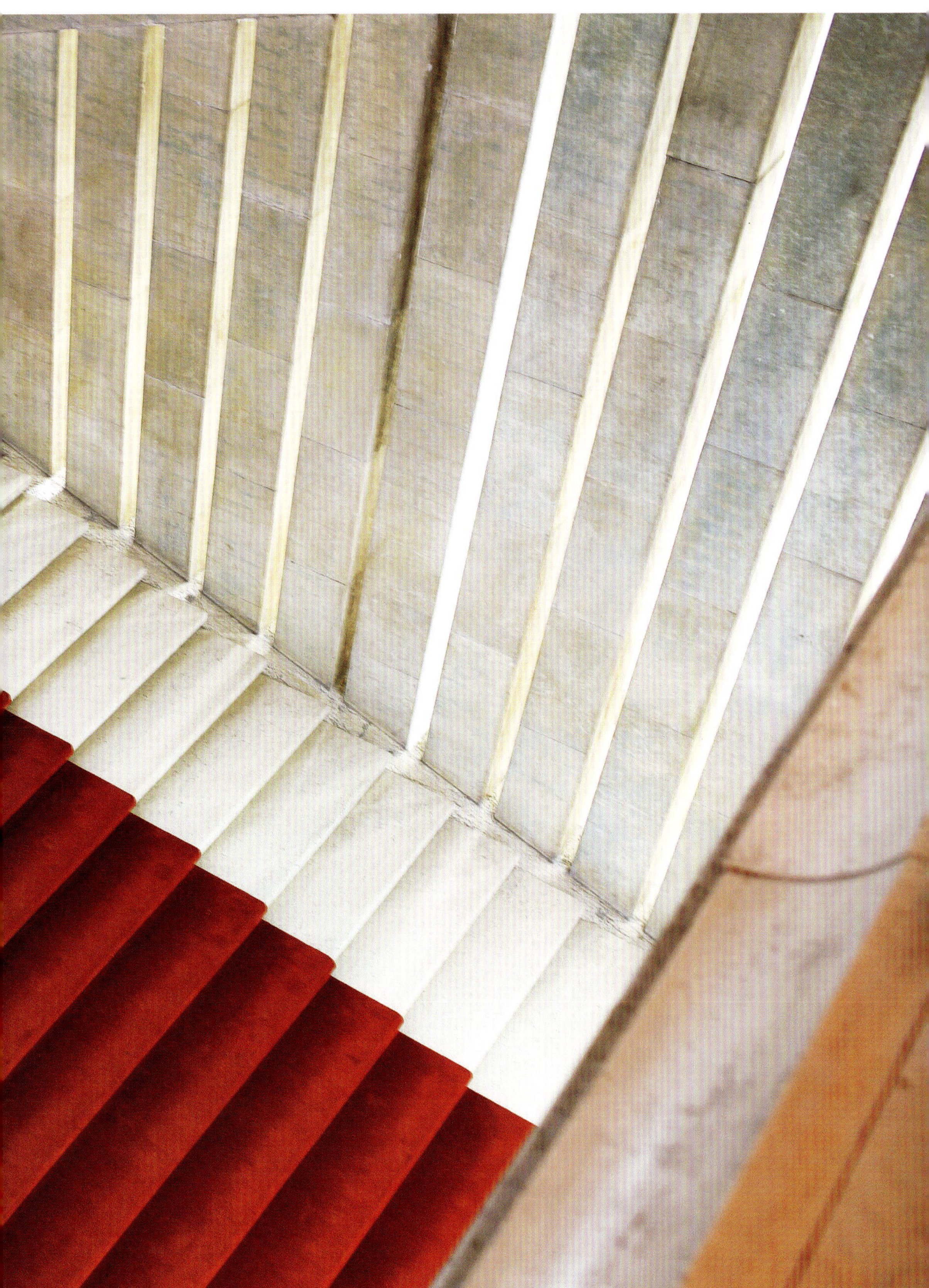

thank you milton

Visual design refuses to yield to the flattery of art, but actually sets itself up as "art" in its own right, at least to the extent that it draws on the multiple experiences of modern-day aesthetics, shaping them for the purposes of functional communication, which is no less capable of operating on a deep level.
<u>The mechanism of suggestion</u>, which is activated in this way, <u>does not in any way draw attention away from the informative role of the artifact, which is still the most important.</u>

In actual fact, it confines itself to creating a vague realm of references, metaphors and allusions around the main message designed to strengthen its cognitive impact.
The intriguing thing about this is not anything directly functional – it actually draws on an <u>aesthetic quality creating a freely aesthetic function.</u>

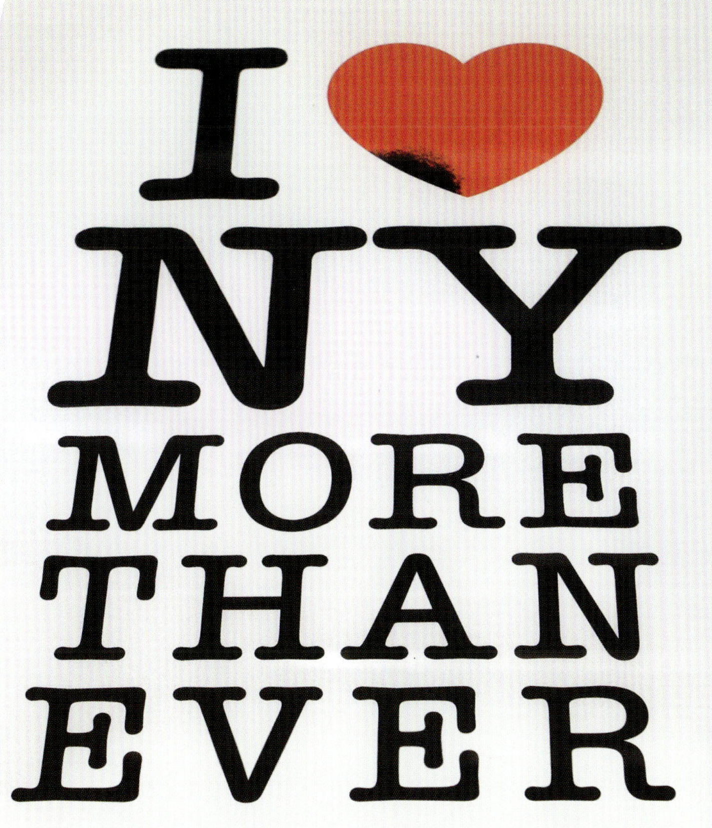

SOME OBJECTS ARE OBJECTS OF OUR DESIRE
IN MORE THAN JUST ONE WAY.

The searching stays with you. In the beginning, the searching is quite small. You search innocently. The more you know, the more difficult and precise the search becomes. This means that with all the potential of a complete experience, the weight of an agency almost becomes even greater because something of that innocence is gone, in the sense that you have no idea of all those other things everyone else already knows. That's why you put out a product that is all but perfect for you at that moment. If you've got more of a background, the pressure always becomes greater. You've got this complexity, but the threat of the white screen becomes greater because you can no longer approach it so innocently.

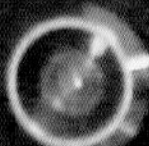

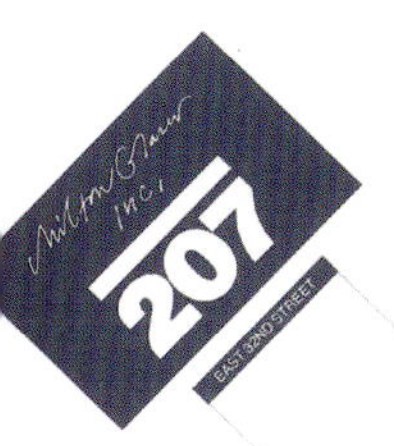

March 20, 2002

Mr. Alberto Bovo
Hangar Design Group
Via Terraglio 89/b
31021 Mogliano Veneto
Treviso Italy

Dear Alberto,

I'm sending you eight of the twelve drawings in advance so that you can begin your separations. Within the next few days, I will send layouts to show you how the drawings can be displayed horizontally and vertically since you need both. My plan is to finish the last four and ship them to you on April 2nd. I hope you like these, I'm very pleased with them. Incidentally, the name of the series might be 'IFOs Identified Flying Objects.'

Best regards,

Milton Glaser

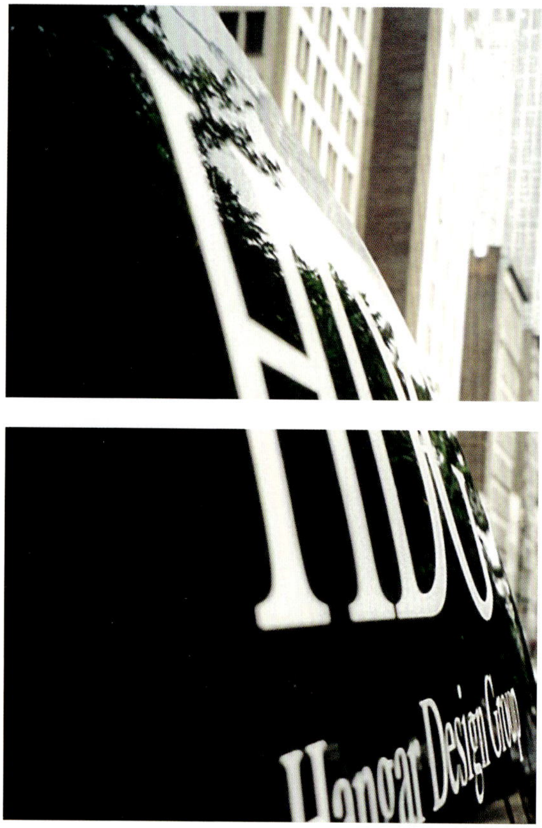

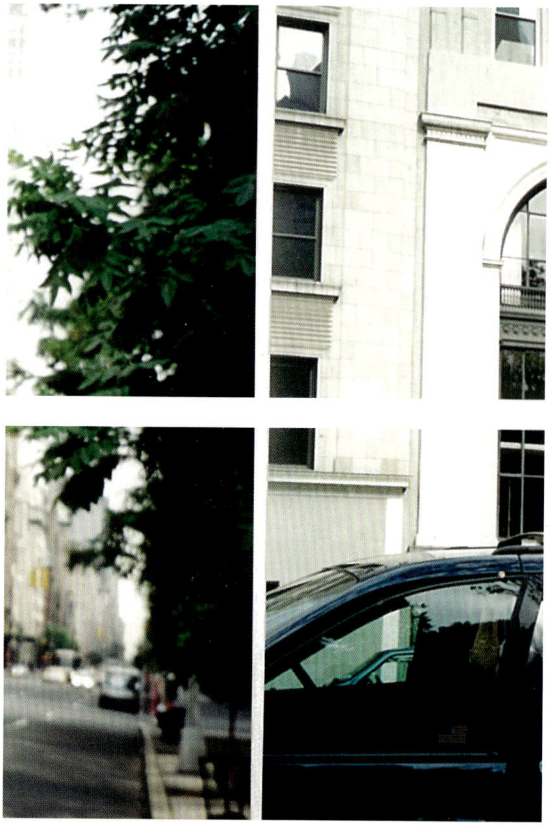

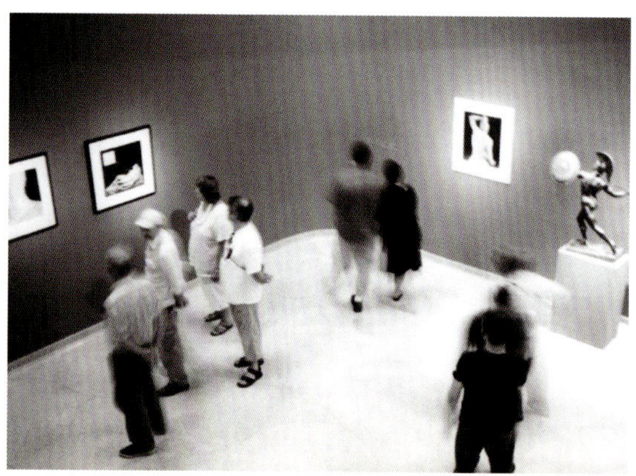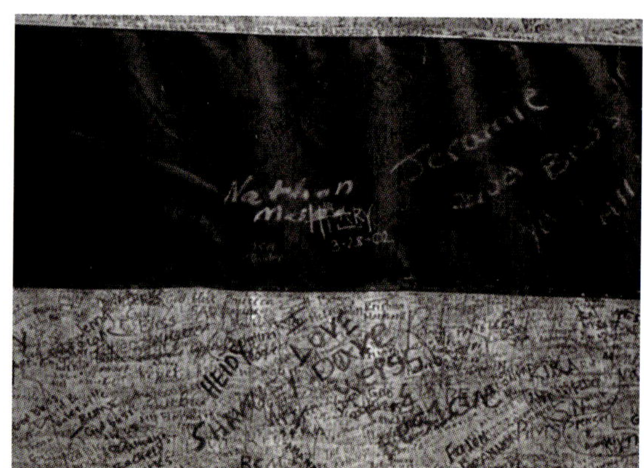

NO ONE BELONGS HERE MORE THAN YOU.

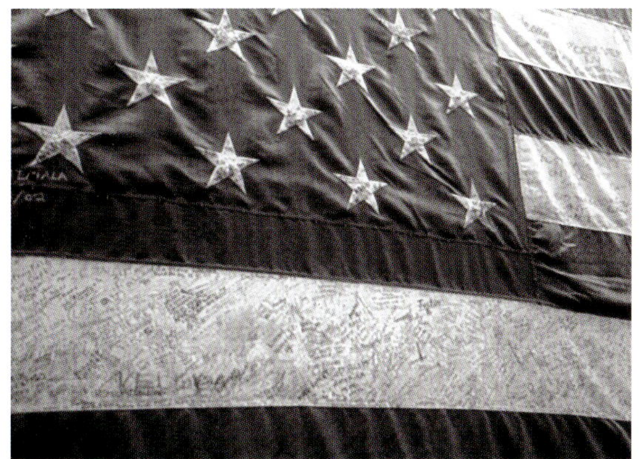

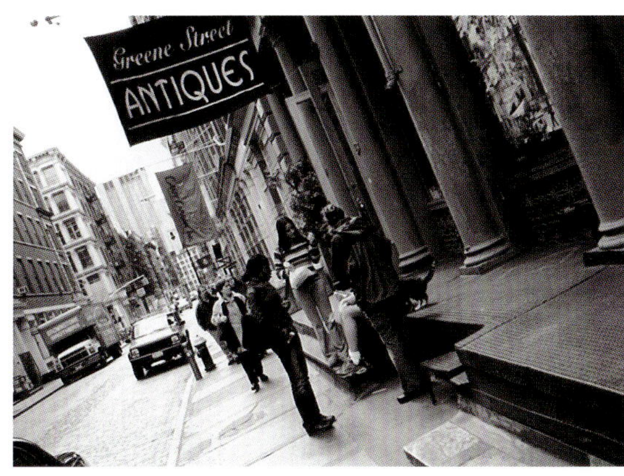
Greene Street
ANTIQUES

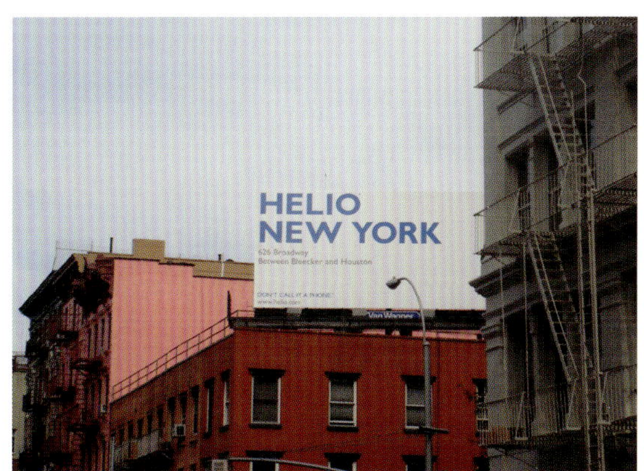
HELIO
NEW YORK

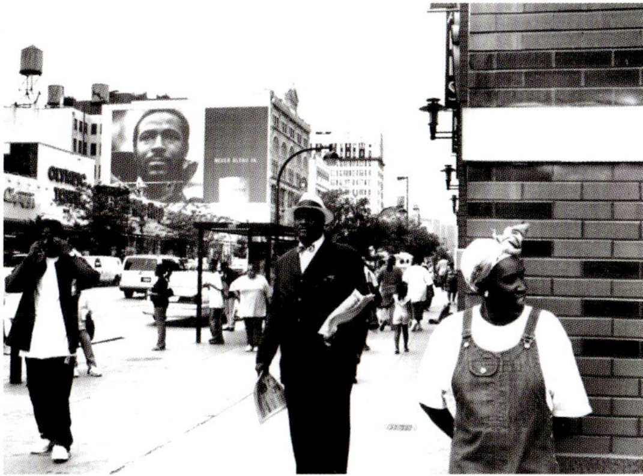
NEVER BLEND IN.

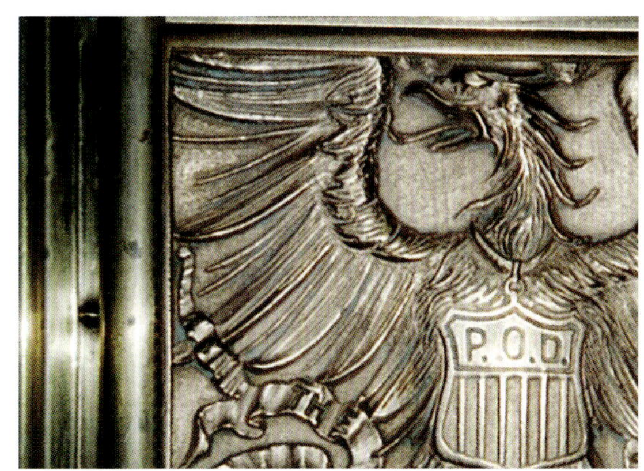
P.O.D.

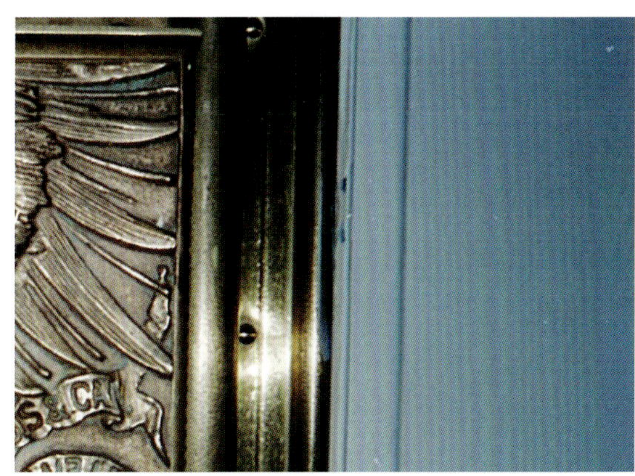

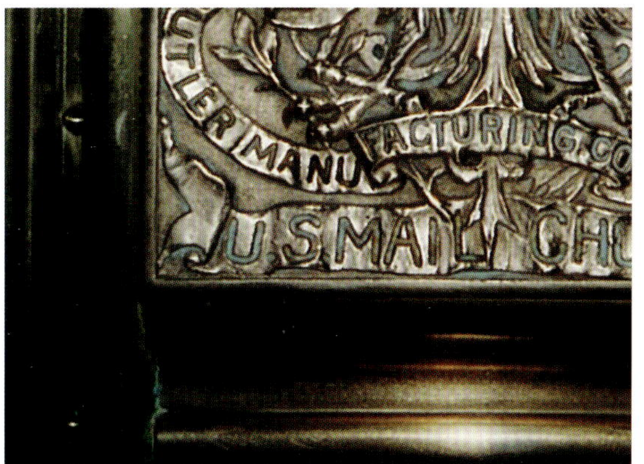
TER MANUFACTURING CO
ROCHESTER N
U.S.MAIL CHUTE

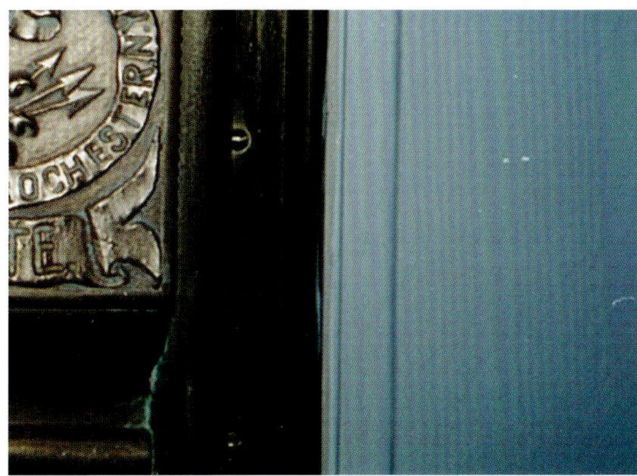

PAST AND FUTURE ____
NICE TO SEE YOU AGAIN

When we organized the exhibition at the Venice
Biennale, everyone thought we were paying
homage to the productions of the artist.
In actual fact, we did not wish to mingle among
the objects themselves, but within those objects.
In this way, <u>the exhibition became a new kind
of spatial experience</u>. This taught us that the most
important thing about staging exhibitions is that
there must be an open mind. Nothing can be
prefigured. To say that an exhibition is equivalent
to architecture can be tantamount to exaggeration
for effect. <u>The exhibition is an ephemeral affair</u>.
And this is its primary virtue.

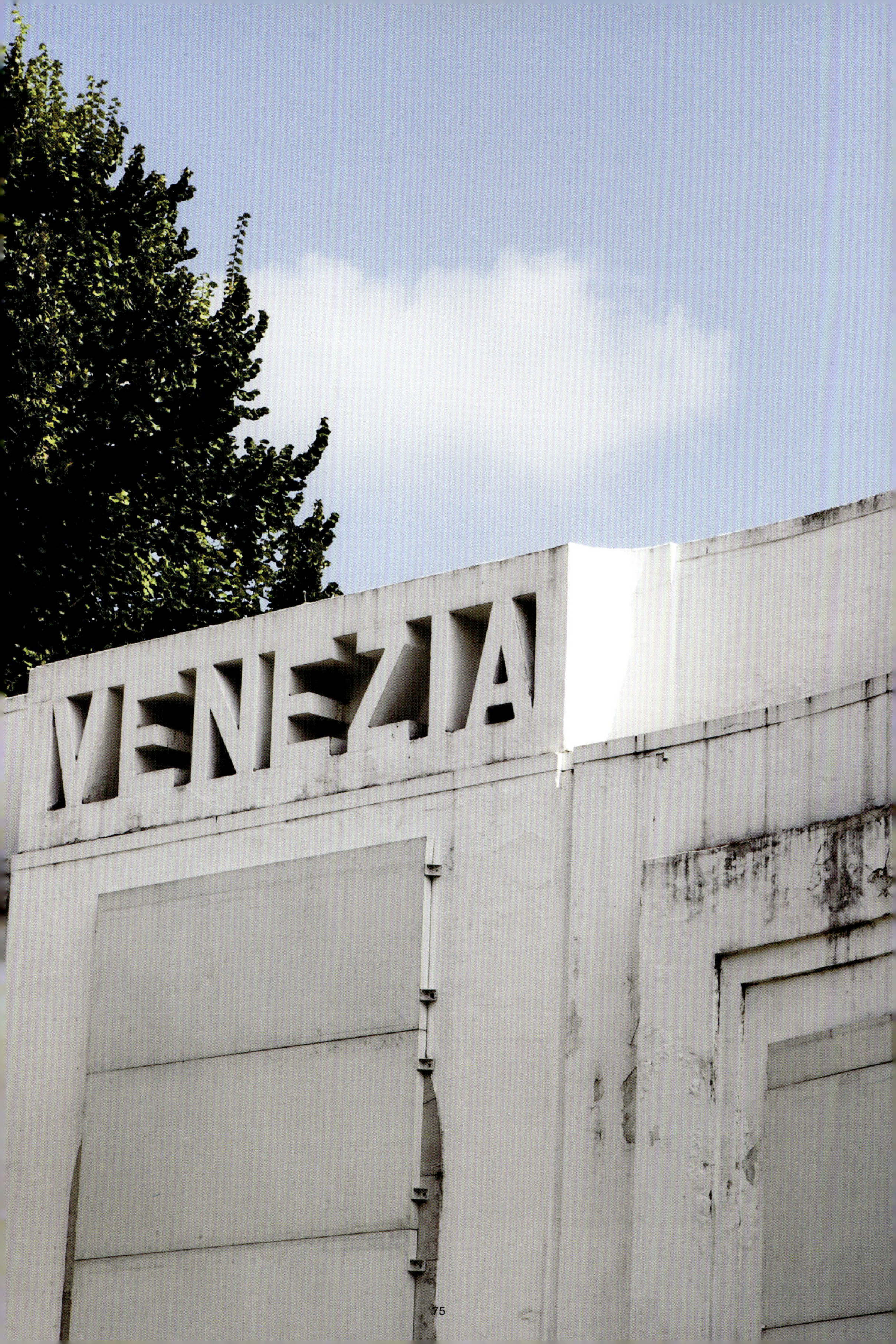
VENEZIA

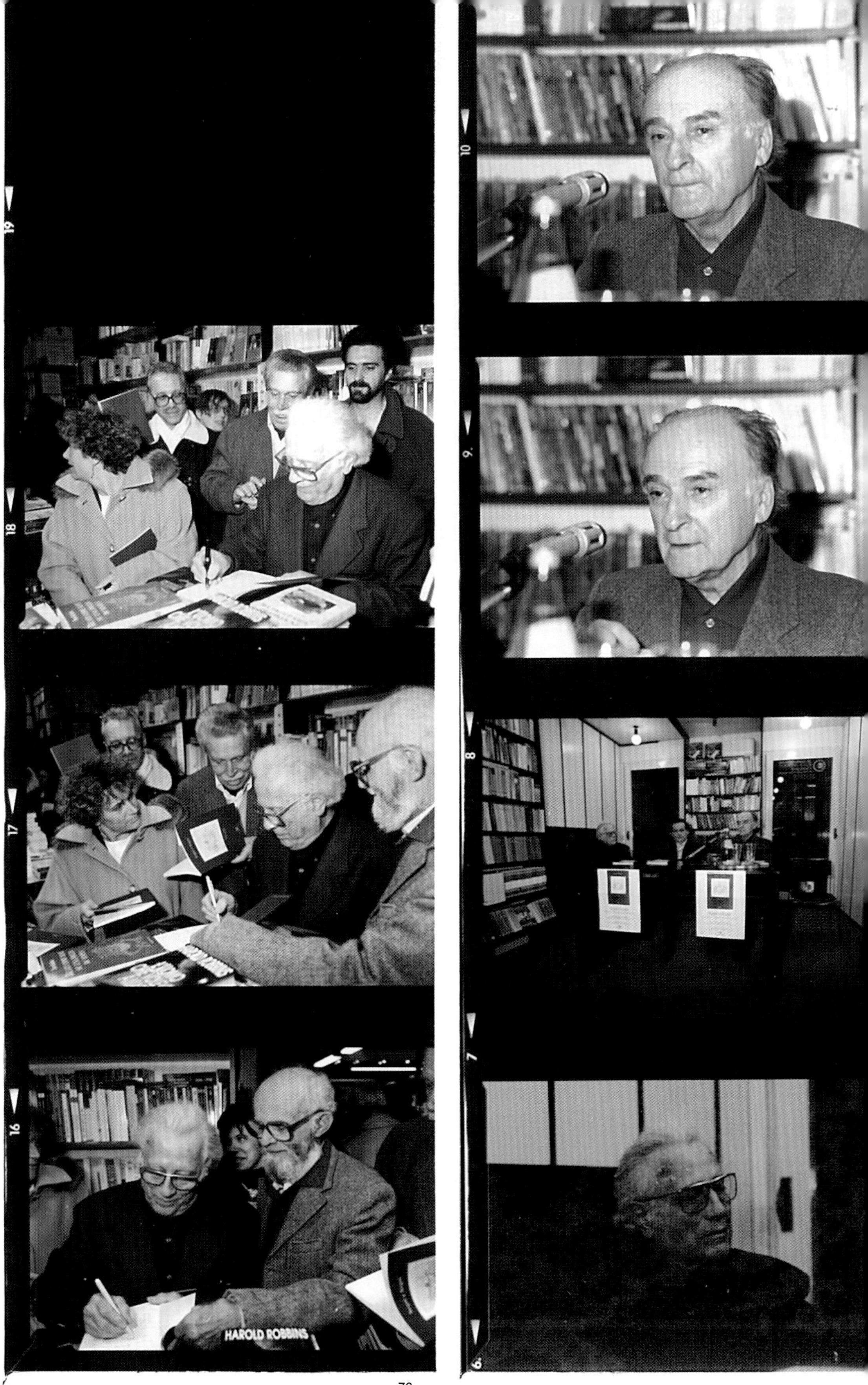

DATE :

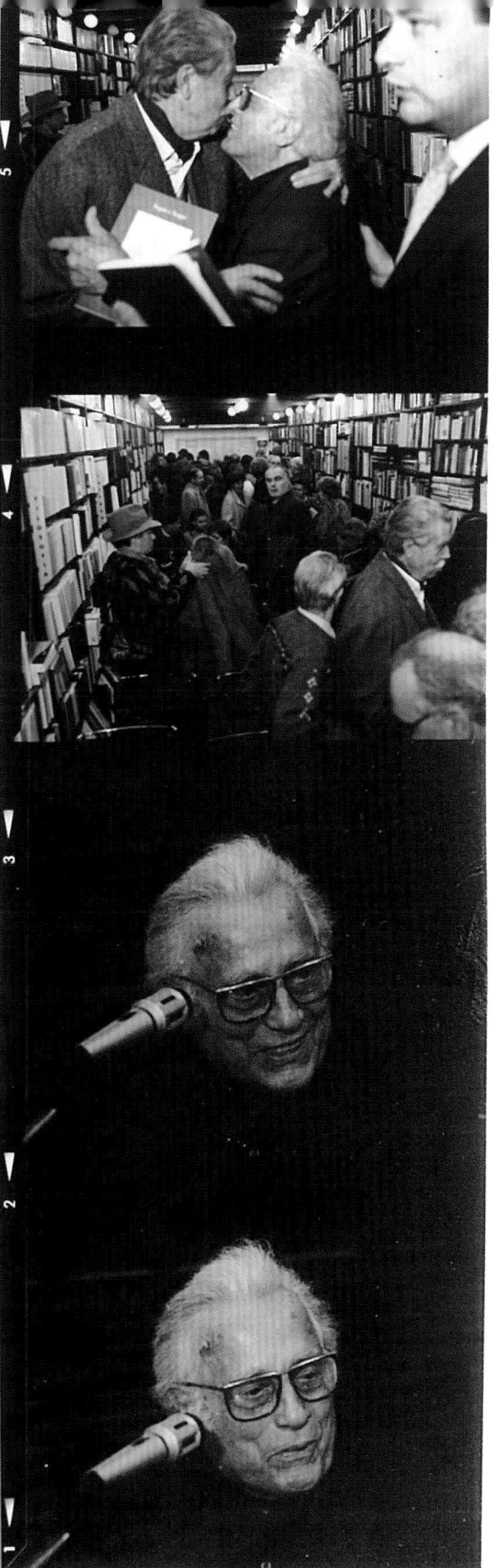

TECHNICAL DATA:

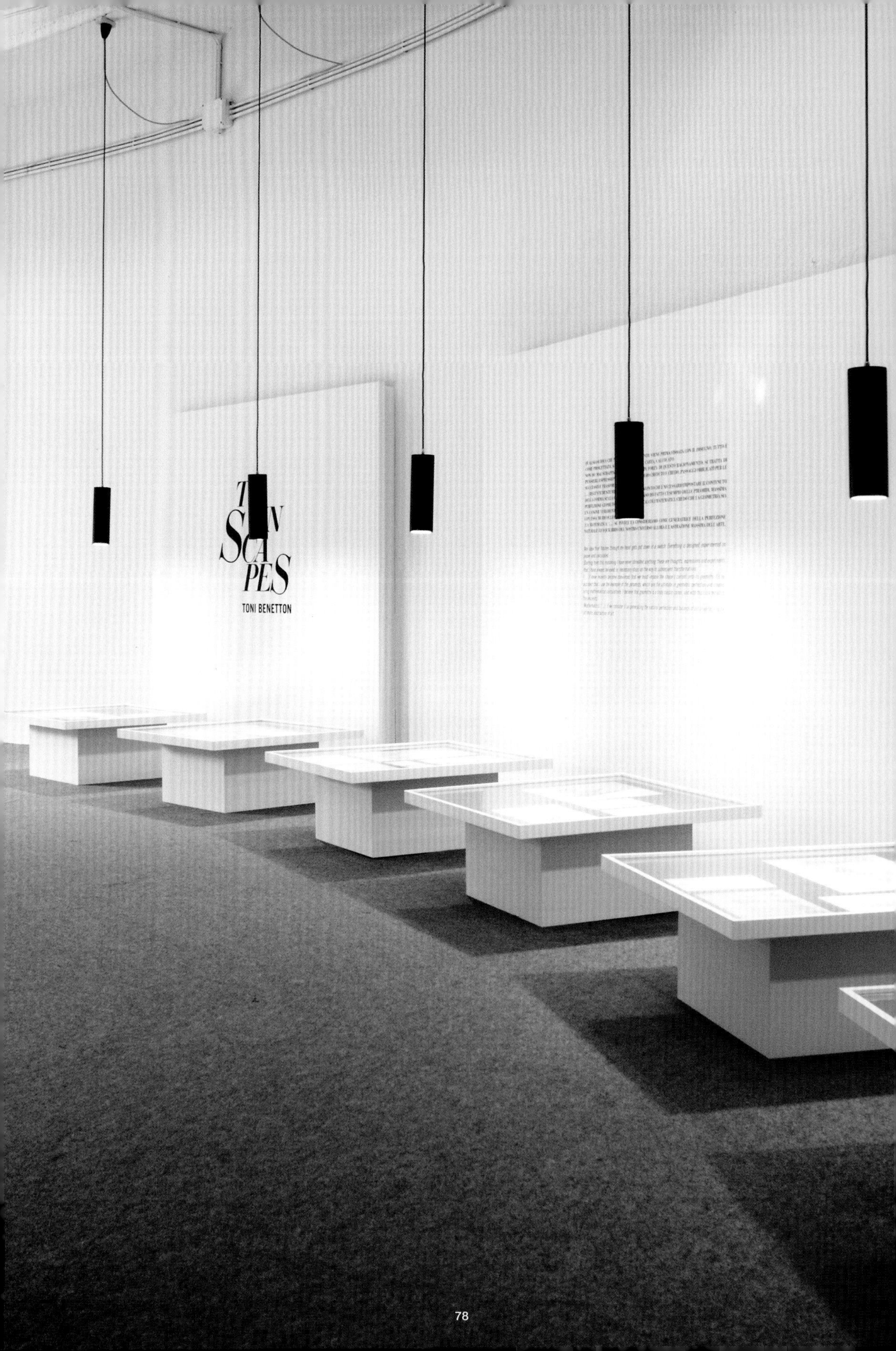

TUSCANSCAPES
TONI BENETTON

"I have recently become convinced that we must impose the shape's content onto its geometry. It's no accident that I use the example of the pyramids, which are the ultimate in geometric perfection and created using mathematical calculations. I believe that geometry is a truly classic canon, and with this I link myself to the ancients. [Mathematics] […], if we consider it as generating the natural perfection and balance of our universe, is the ultimate abstraction of art.

Townscapes weren't intended to be simple sculptural and self-sufficient products in the urban fabric; rather, they were designed to become veritable structures to be used as doorways or as a spot to take a rest, based on relational criteria. Numerous problems were inherent in these works related to social and architectonic aspects, which lie outside simple sculptural research, in establishing a clear vision of the context that was to receive the work.

I exasperate the contrast between the environment and the work, but I always keep in mind a few suggestions made by the environment, so that the work is never totally foreign, but raises questions because it is different."

Toni Benetton, 1982

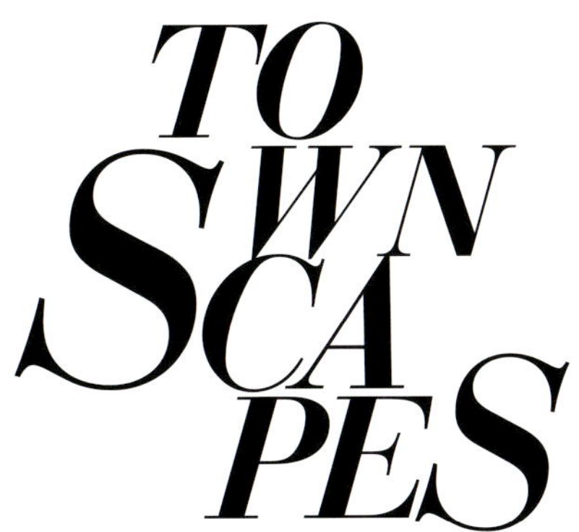

A NOTEBOOK FOR MAKING SKETCHES IS A CONSTANT PRESENCE IN THE MYTHOLOGY OF MODERN ARCHITECTURE, ALLEGEDLY CAPABLE OF TRACING A CULTURAL IDENTIKIT OF AN ARCHITECT, HIS STYLE, PHILOSOPHY OF DESIGN AND EVEN WELTANSCHAUUNG. MUSEUM COLLECTIONS HAVE SHOWCASES DISPLAYING THE FADED PAGES OF LOTS OF SKETCHPADS AND NOTEBOOKS FULL OF QUIVERING OUTLINES OF SOME ADMIRABLE DOODLE – A LANDSCAPE, STRUCTURAL DETAIL OR OLD FACADE – OR THE FIRST ROUGH OUTLINE OF WHAT WAS LATER TO BECOME AN ACTUAL WORK, CONSTRUCTION, REAL BODY IN SPACE.

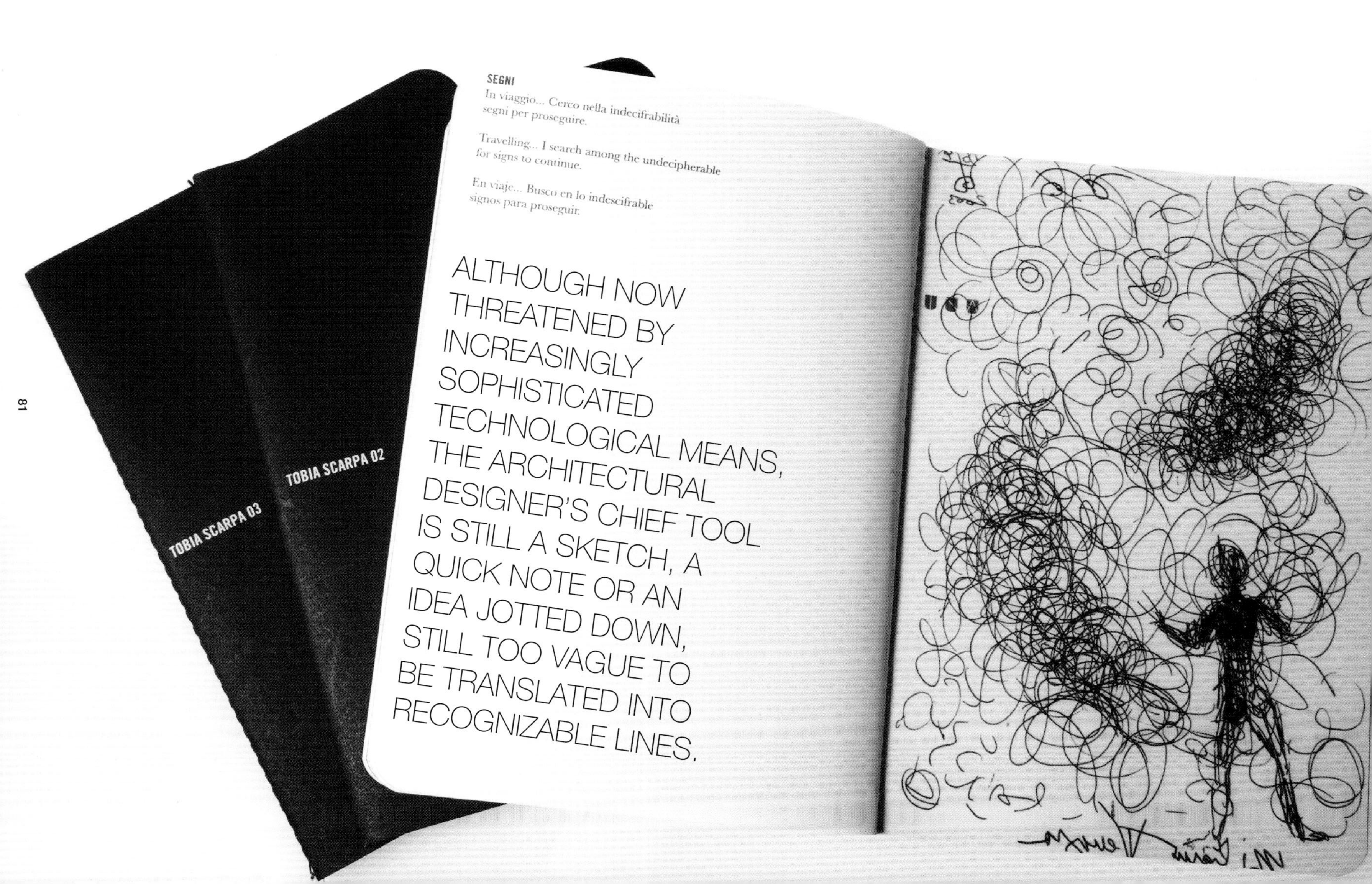

SEGNI

In viaggio… Cerco nella indecifrabilità
segni per proseguire.

Travelling… I search among the undecipherable
for signs to continue.

En viaje… Busco en lo indescifrable
signos para proseguir.

ALTHOUGH NOW
THREATENED BY
INCREASINGLY
SOPHISTICATED
TECHNOLOGICAL MEANS,
THE ARCHITECTURAL
DESIGNER'S CHIEF TOOL
IS STILL A SKETCH, A
QUICK NOTE OR AN
IDEA JOTTED DOWN,
STILL TOO VAGUE TO
BE TRANSLATED INTO
RECOGNIZABLE LINES.

BEAUTIFUL TO MEASURE _____
WHAT HAS DRIVEN US ON THE
PATH OF COMMUNICATION
HAS BEEN DEVOTION
TO ART AND TO BEAUTY.

A sensibility we have sought to translate into a design methodology based
on the requirements of our clients, in order to achieve a result that exceeds
expectations. Working with a chisel, effectively, careful attention to detail
with a view to building, each time, a tailored design as if it were a tailored
suit made for the client according to the relevant cut, features and purpose,
but which must always begin with listening, attention and relationship.
Whether it is an advertising campaign or an event, the methodology
we have developed during these years always envisages the possibility
of movement, adaptation, customization of the design to the imperatives
of the client and the optimal result, exploiting the available resources
in the most effective and creative way possible.
We believe that it is embedded in our DNA – this adaptability capable of
feeding off an infinite variety of suggestions and ideas, but also always
capable of discovering within each individual design that genuine coherence and aesthetic rigor which have become the hallmark of Hangar Design
Group over the years.

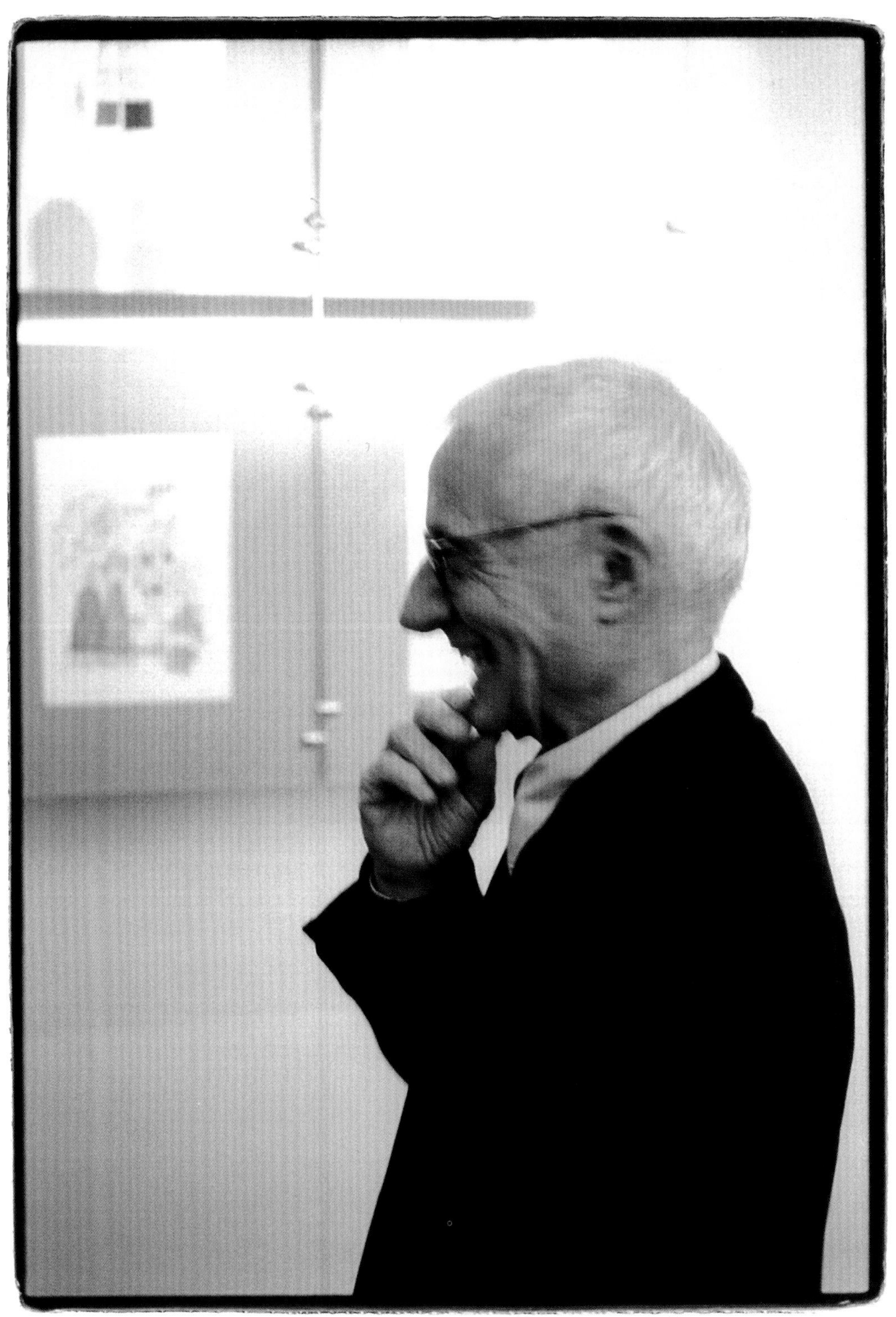

We've always been interested in spectatorship and museological issues such as the curatorial text, the picture frame, the sculpture base, the gallery wall, even the particular color of the white paint used on the wall.
The interface between the obsverver and the observed is a delicious moment of architecture.

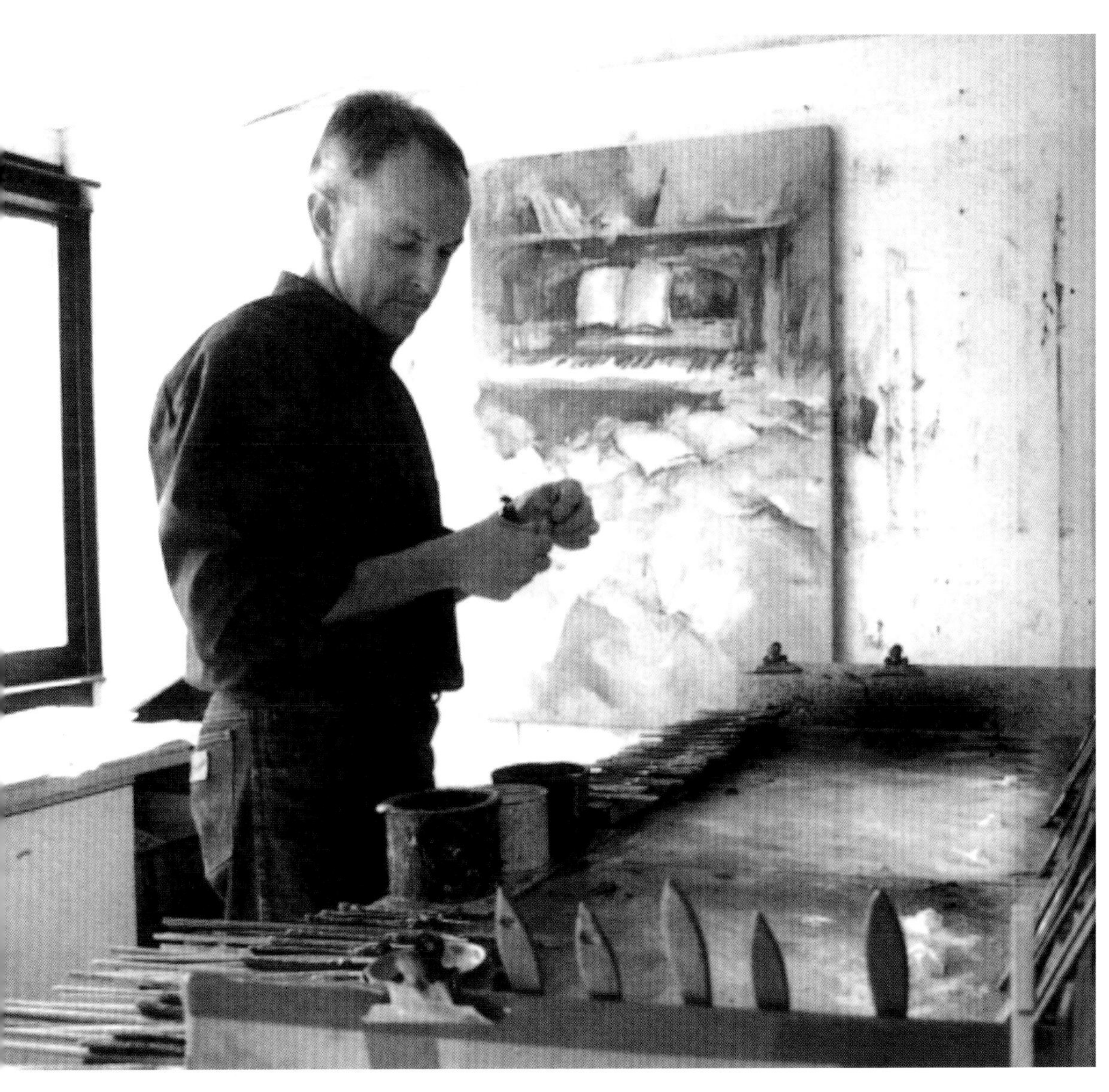

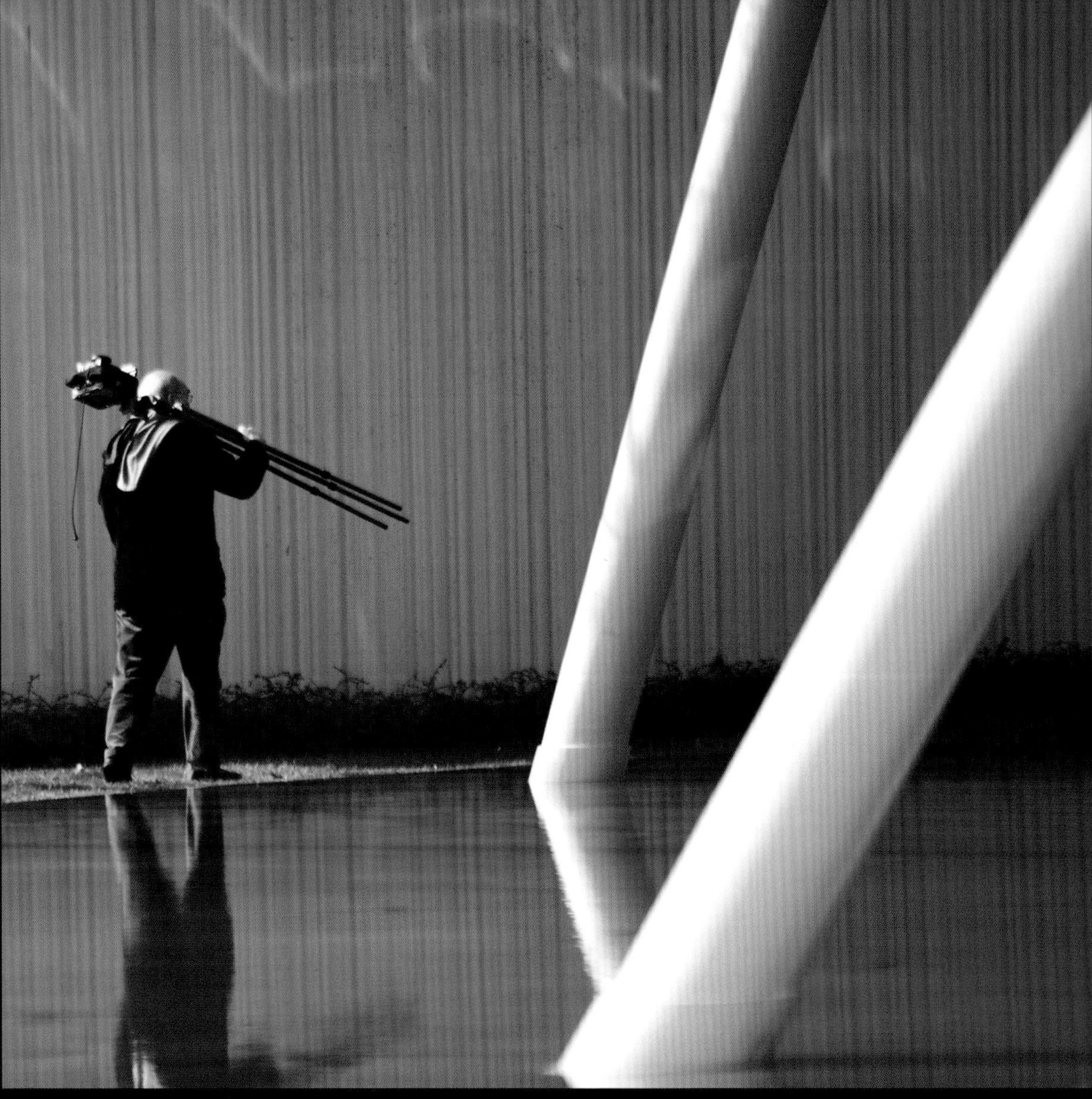

Design has, for some time now, partaken
in that celebration of authorship, borrowed
in equal shares from fine arts and fashion.
To successfully navigate the fine line between
art and design – or to tightrope walk over
the precipice that is their intersection – is the
Holy Grail of creative disciplines.

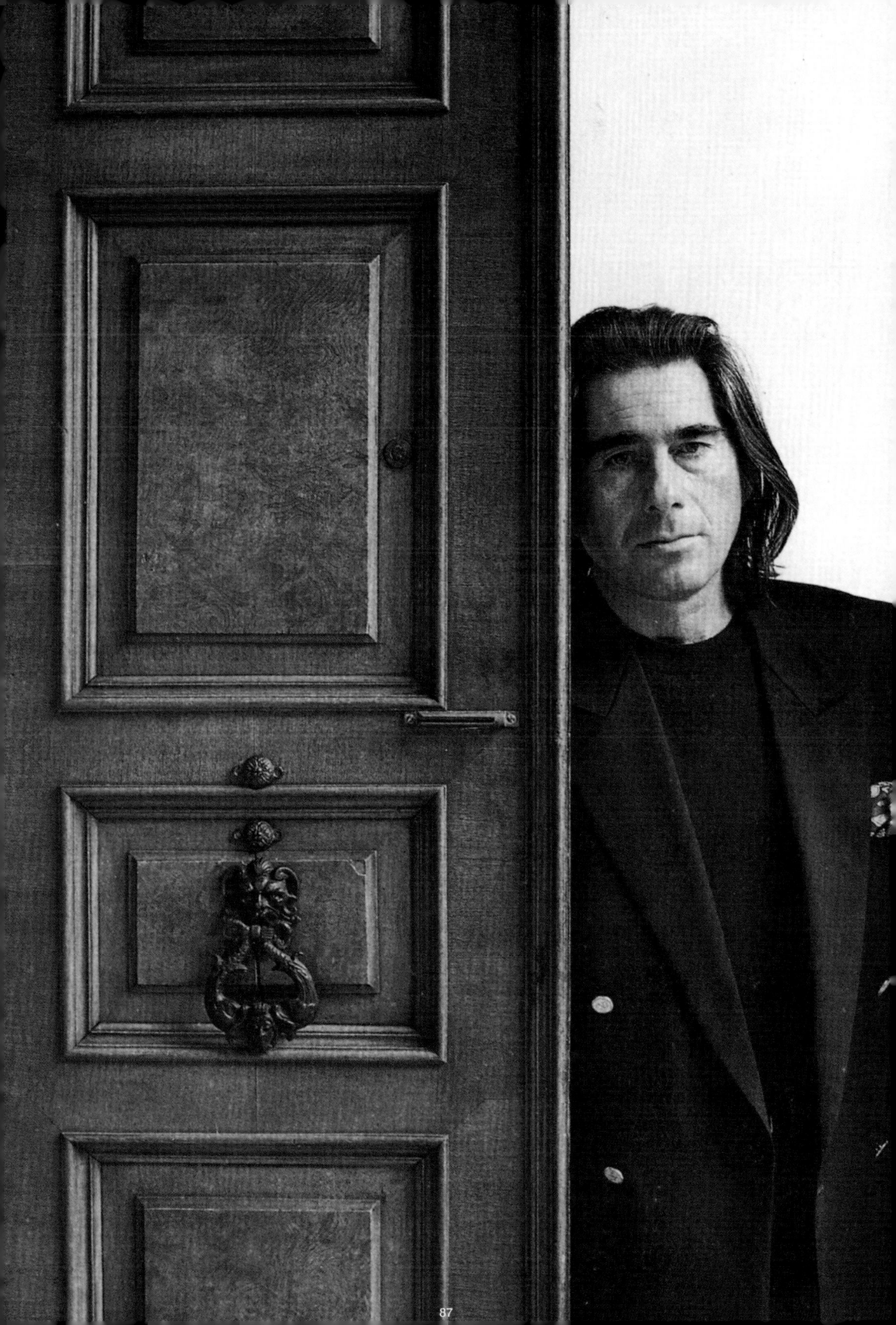

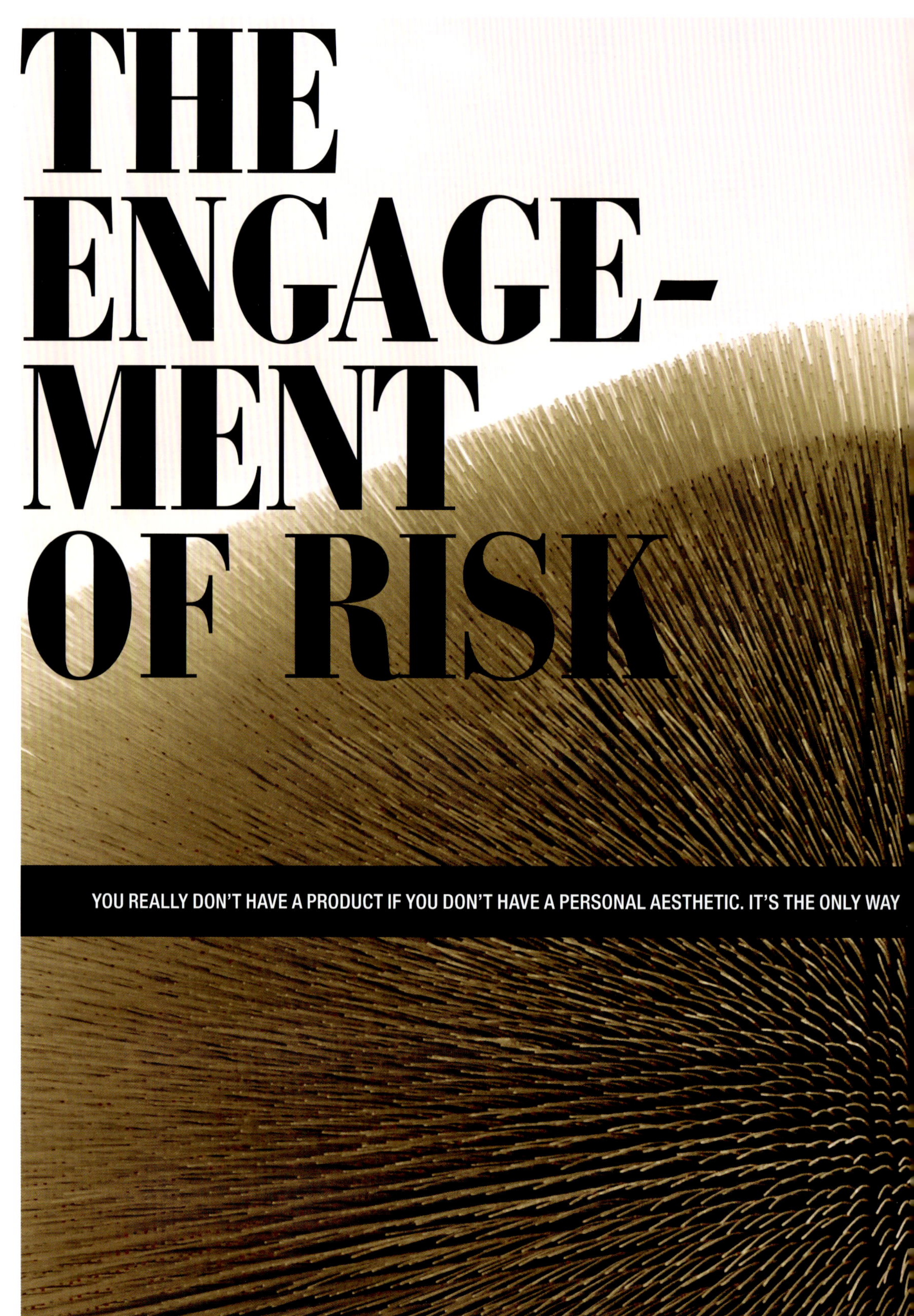

THE ENGAGEMENT OF RISK

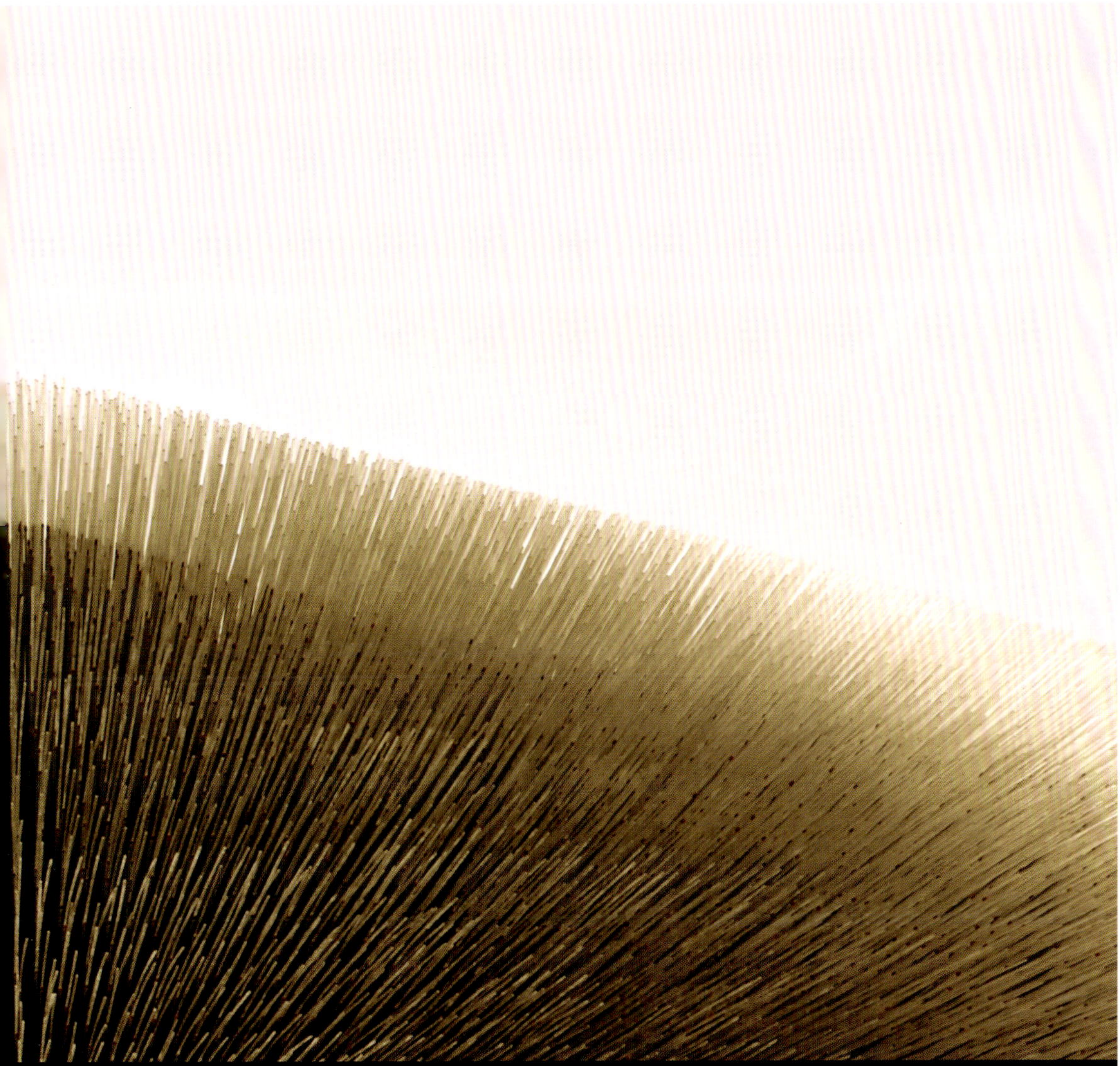

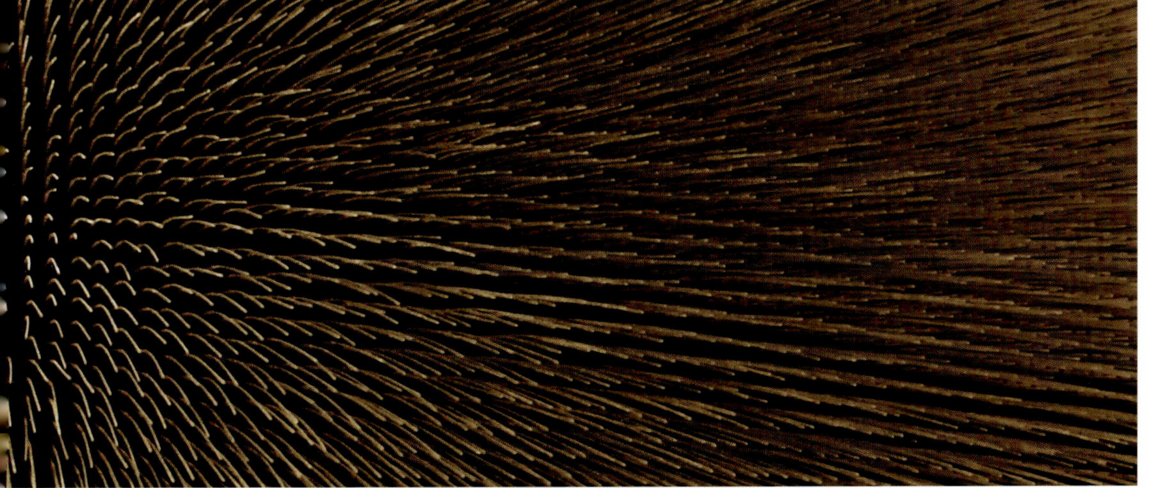

TO DISTINGUISH YOURSELF AT THE END. OUR AESTHETIC IS JUST BASED ON WHAT WE'RE INTERESTED IN.

WHY RECORD THE OBVIOUS? IT'S ALL ABOUT THE SMALL MOMENTS IN LIFE, THAT YOU SEE EVERY DAY AND FORGET TO CAPTURE, BECAUSE YOU DON'T REALIZE HOW SPECIAL THEY ARE UNTIL YOU FREEZE THEM.

a breath of fresh air

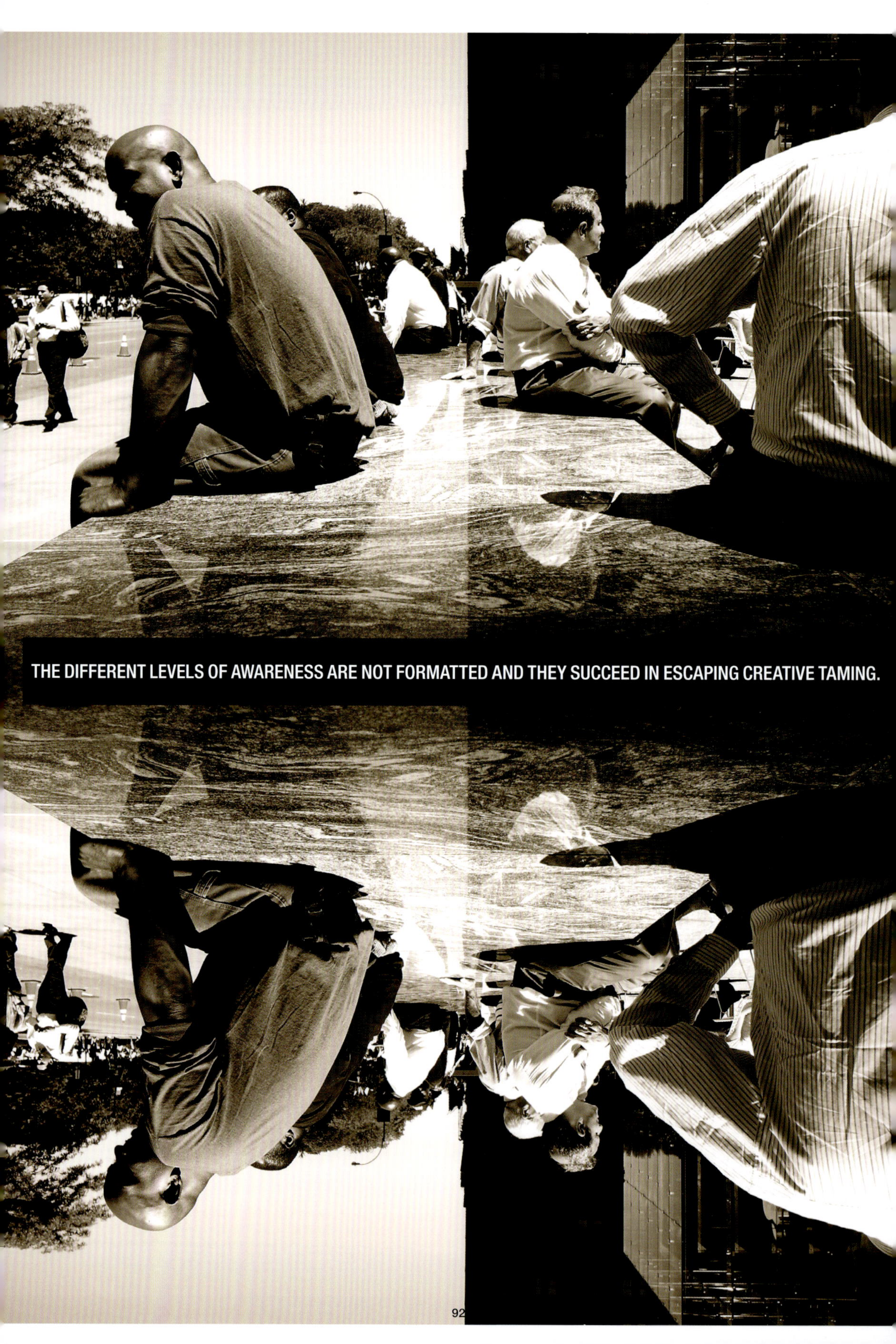

THE DIFFERENT LEVELS OF AWARENESS ARE NOT FORMATTED AND THEY SUCCEED IN ESCAPING CREATIVE TAMING.

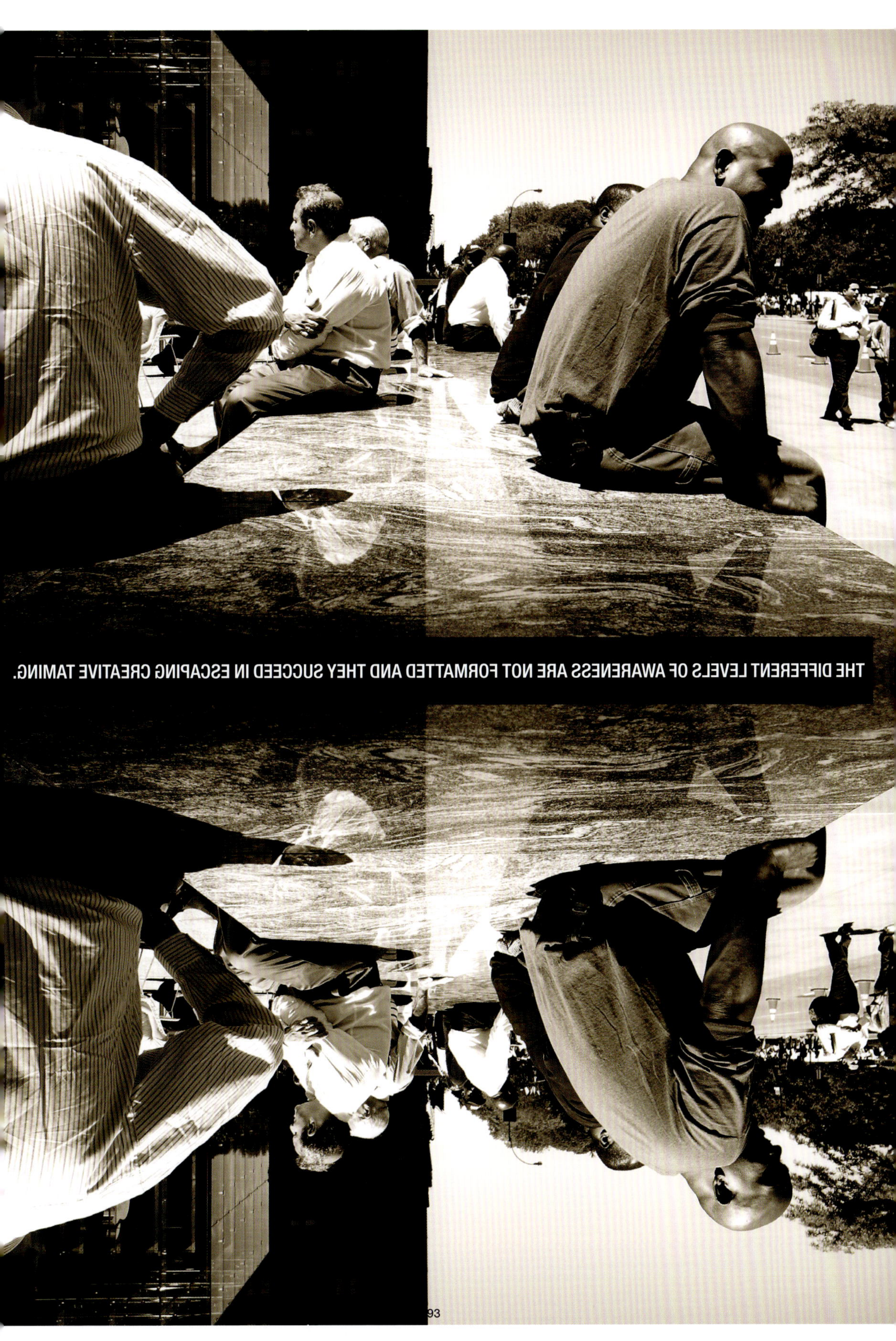
THE DIFFERENT LEVELS OF AWARENESS ARE NOT FORMATTED AND THEY SUCCEED IN ESCAPING CREATIVE TAMING.

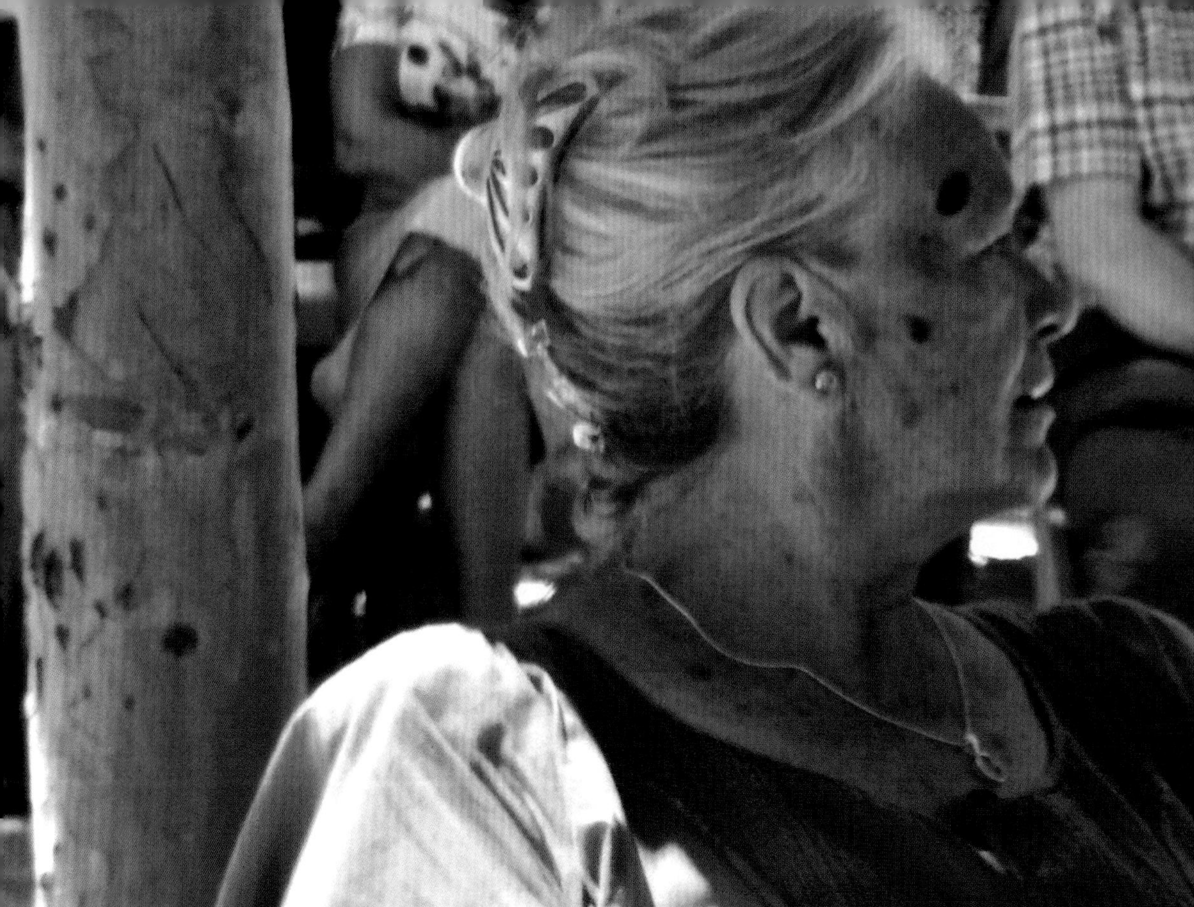

Hangar Design Group moves from the center to the
periphery and from the microcosm to the macrocosm
in a circular motion, which is not monotonous and
regular like a circle but dynamic and pulsating like
a spiral, which calls for a center to start from and to
which it is constantly taken back by its own vibrations
before submitting to its attractive force.

The cultural underpinning to the firm's work lies in
this rhythmic dilating and narrowing, which the energy
forces of design are alternatively called upon to
condense and then spring out with all their force.

After all, the modern-day world of design calls for just
this, and to its credit Hangar Design Group realized
this before anybody else. Tackling global society with
means tested out through plenty of actual practice
is an advantage to be exploited.

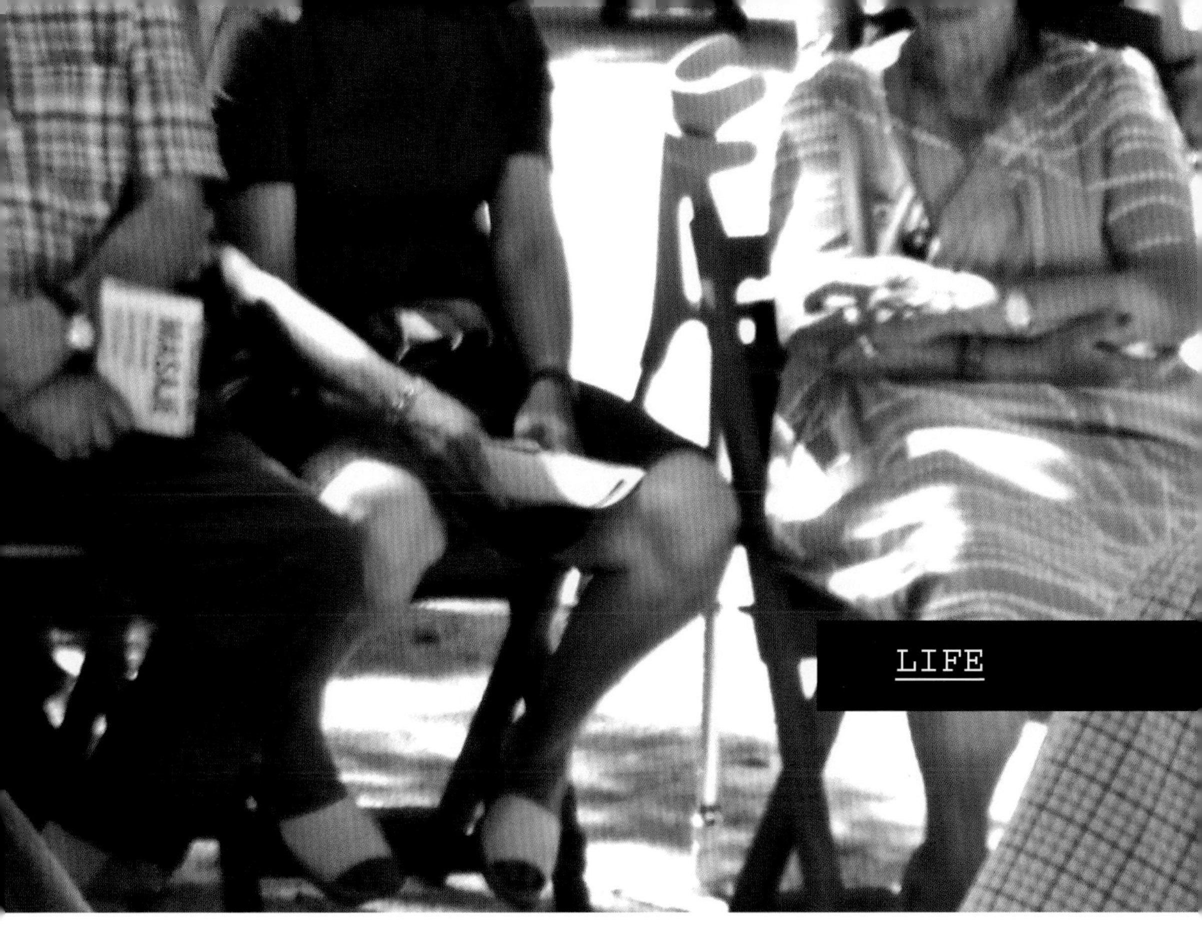

LIFE

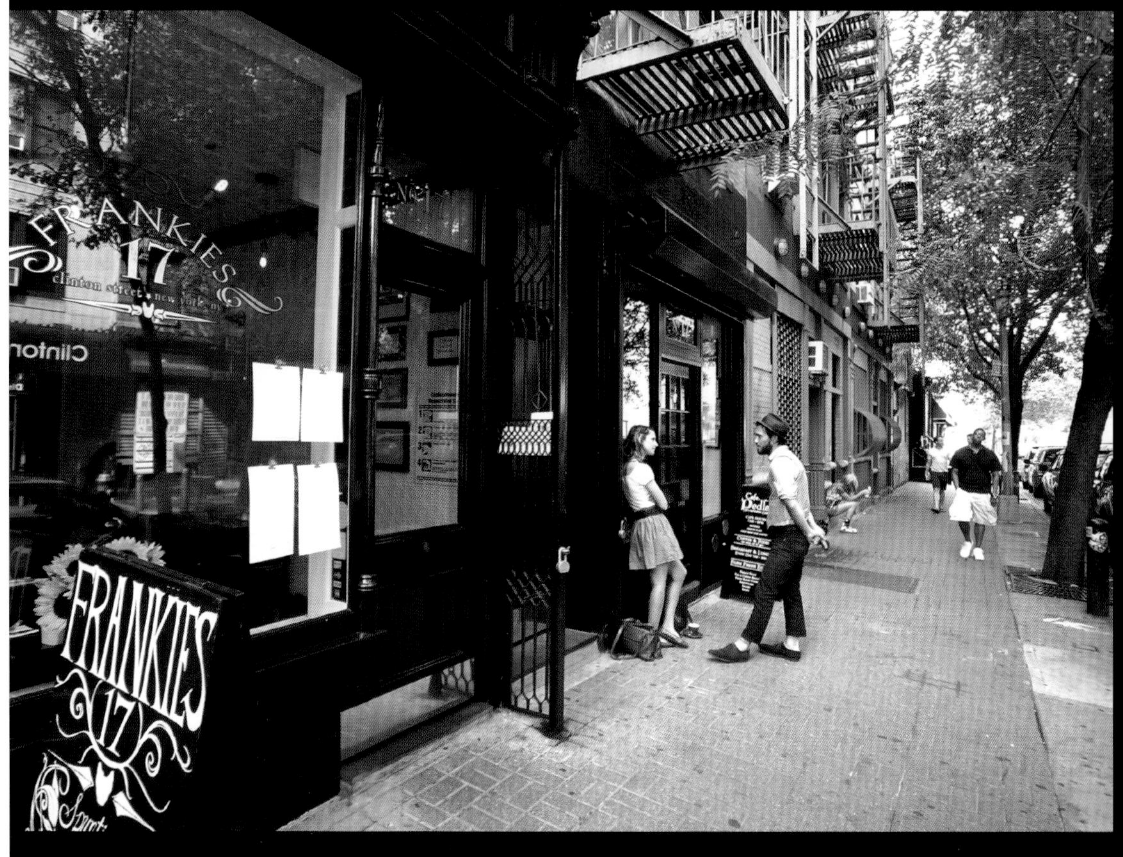
FRANKIES
17
clinton street · new york · ny
FRANKIES
17

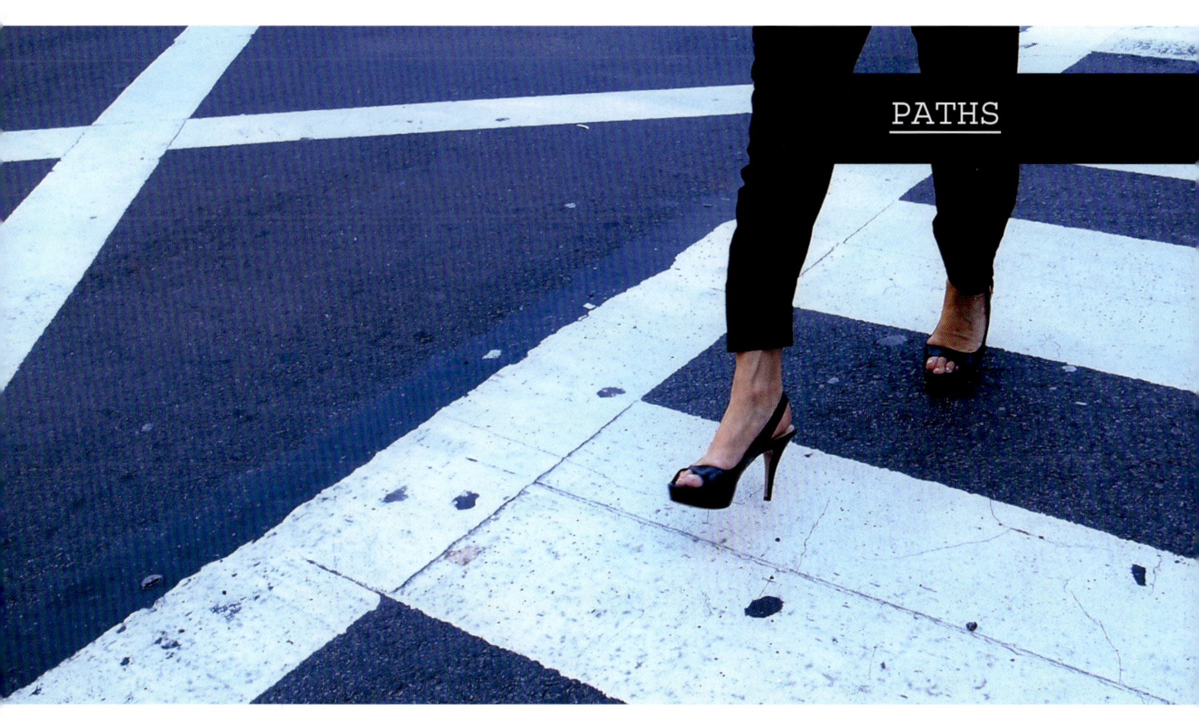

AESTHETICS IS A NARRATIVE, IT'S ABOUT TAKING PEOPLE ON A JOURNEY.

RULES
PLEASE
DO NOT TOUCH
THE OBJECTS
IN THE
EXHIBITION

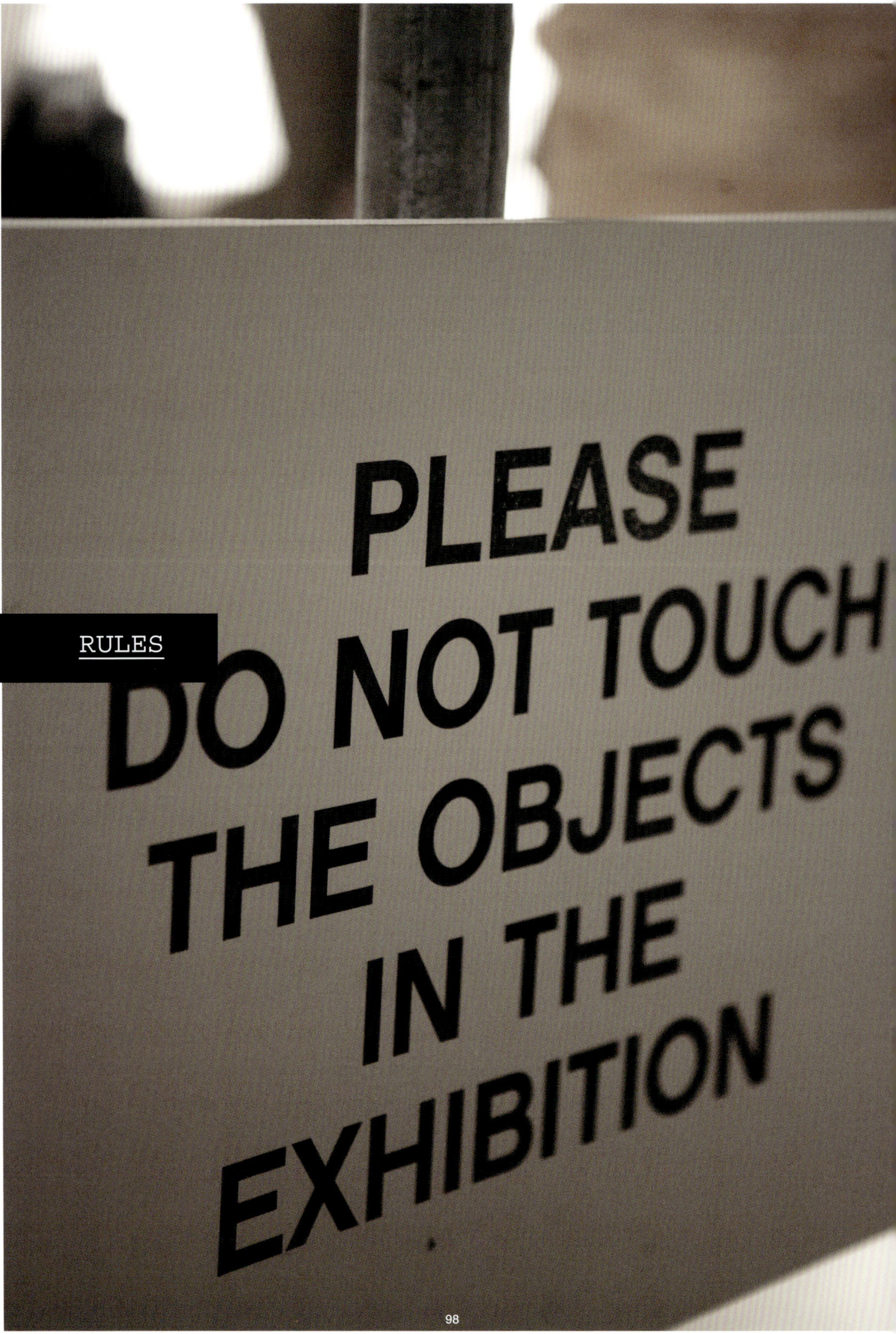

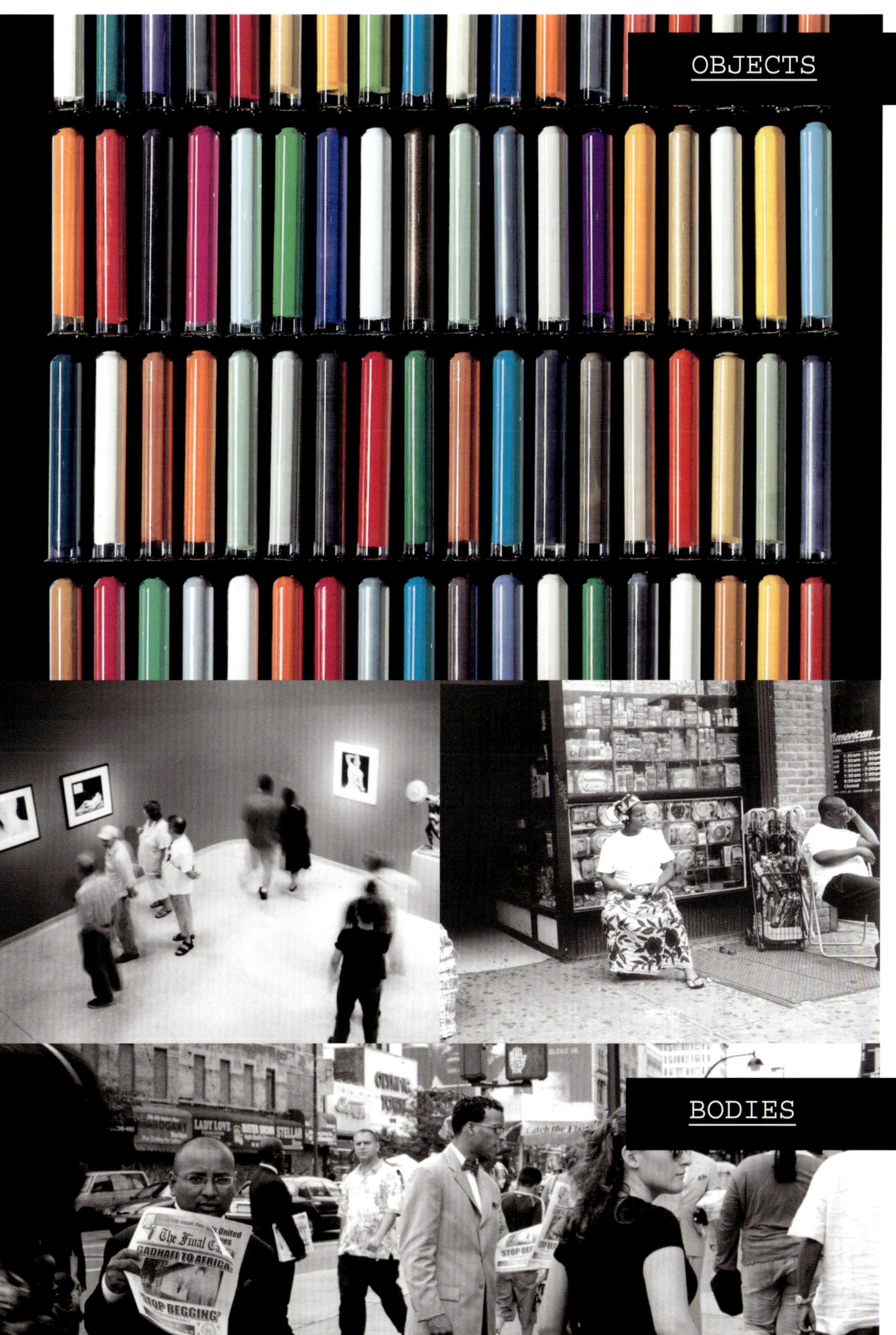

BODIES

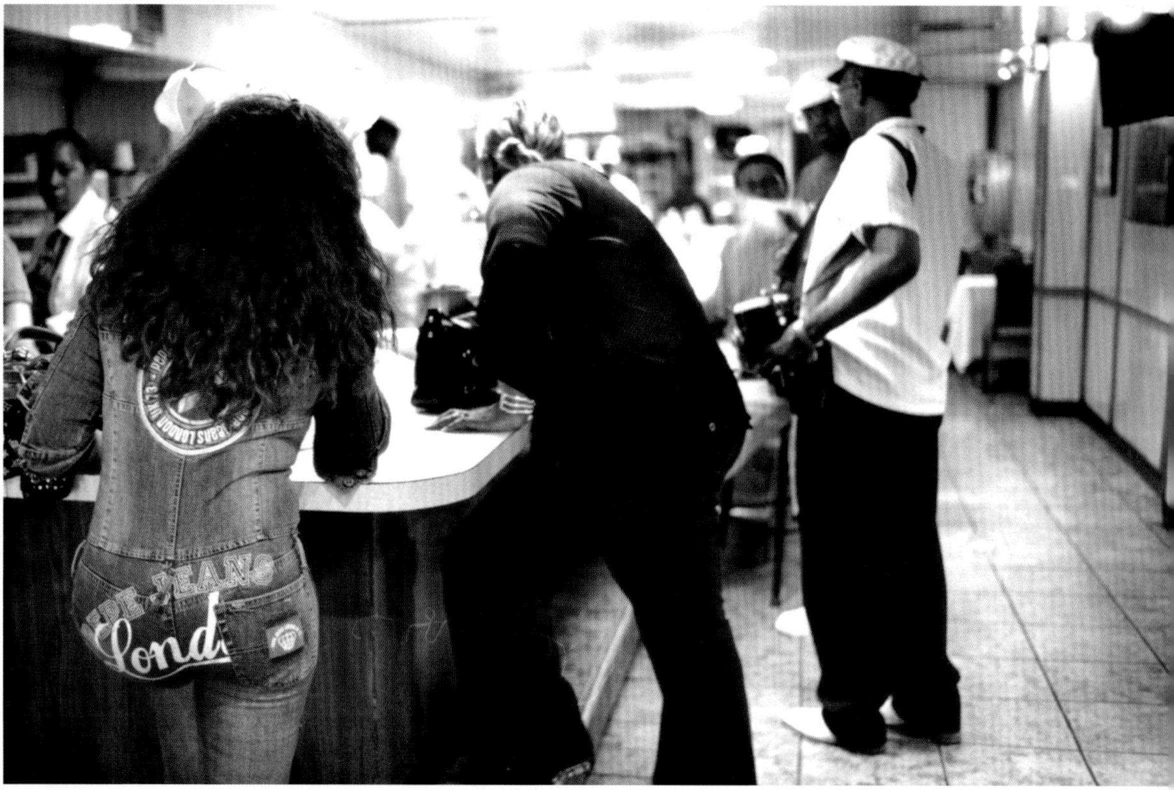

PLACES

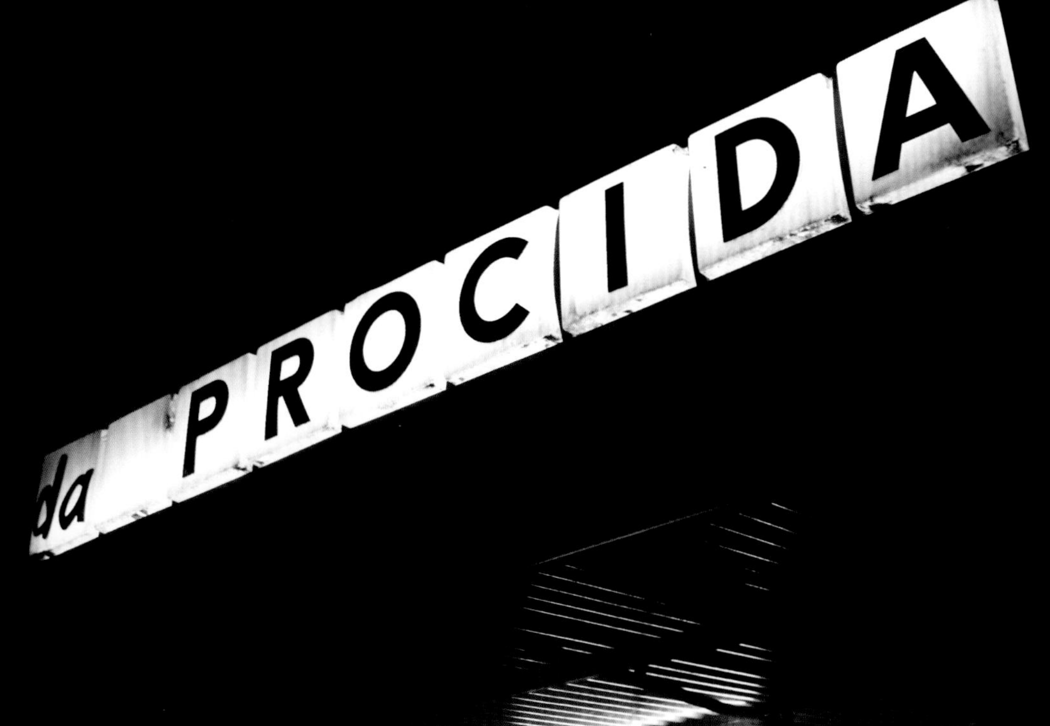

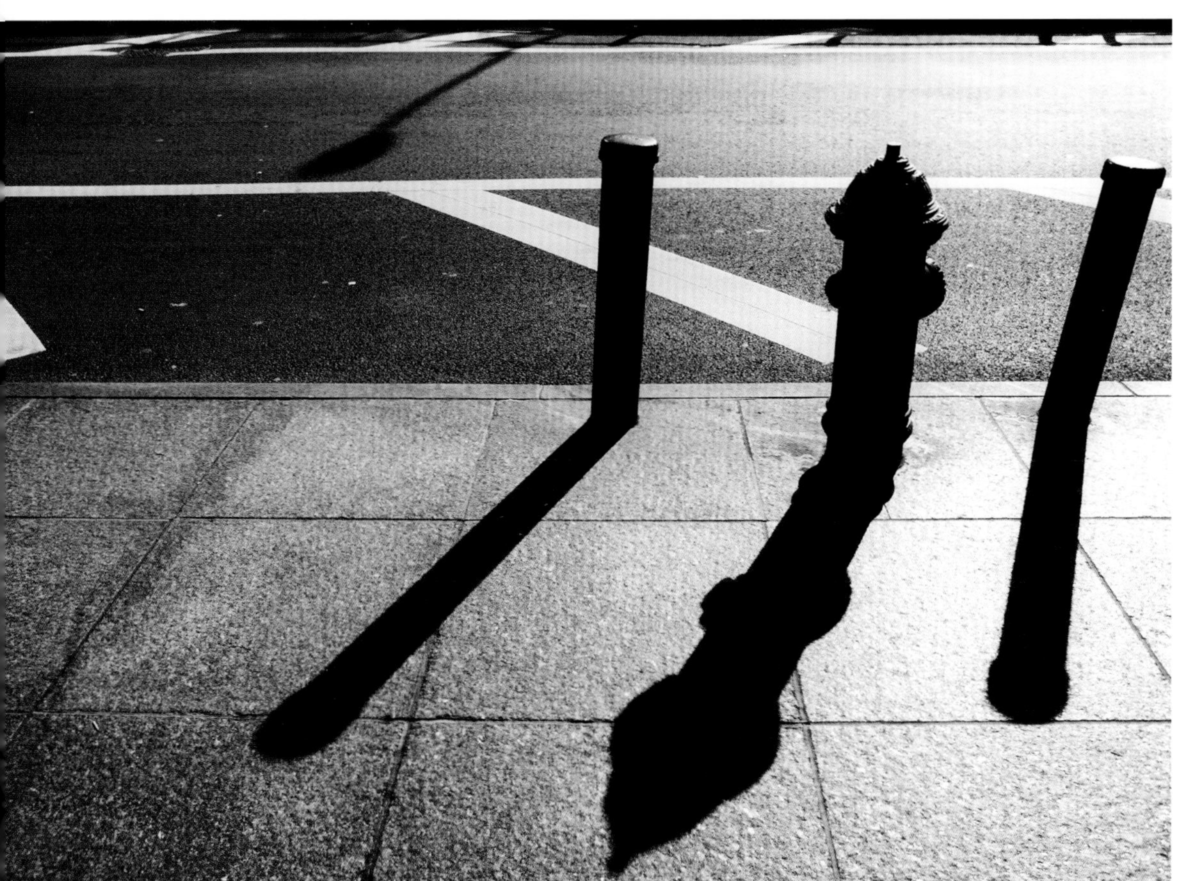

Creating the right aesthetics really is about a journey.
It's just so much more than making things pretty.
You have to create a narrative.
You have to imagine how someone will use the space
and go through the space.
This is especially true in our business.
The difference can be spelled out in the clear
distinction between design and decoration.

Decoration is how something looks. Design is how
a place is programmed to work and how you feel
the place. Decoration has to do with trends; design
has to do with creating classics.

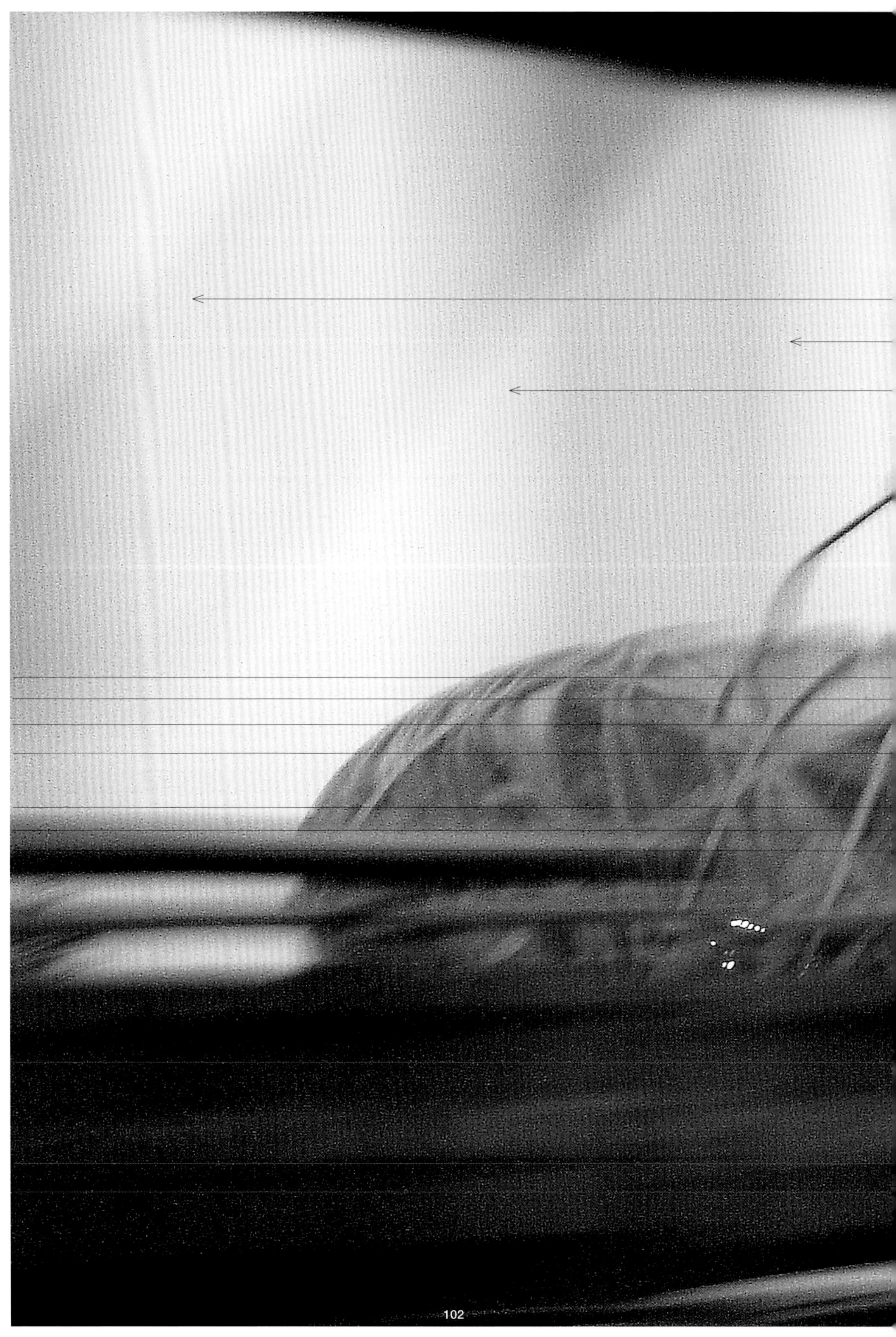

GET LOST

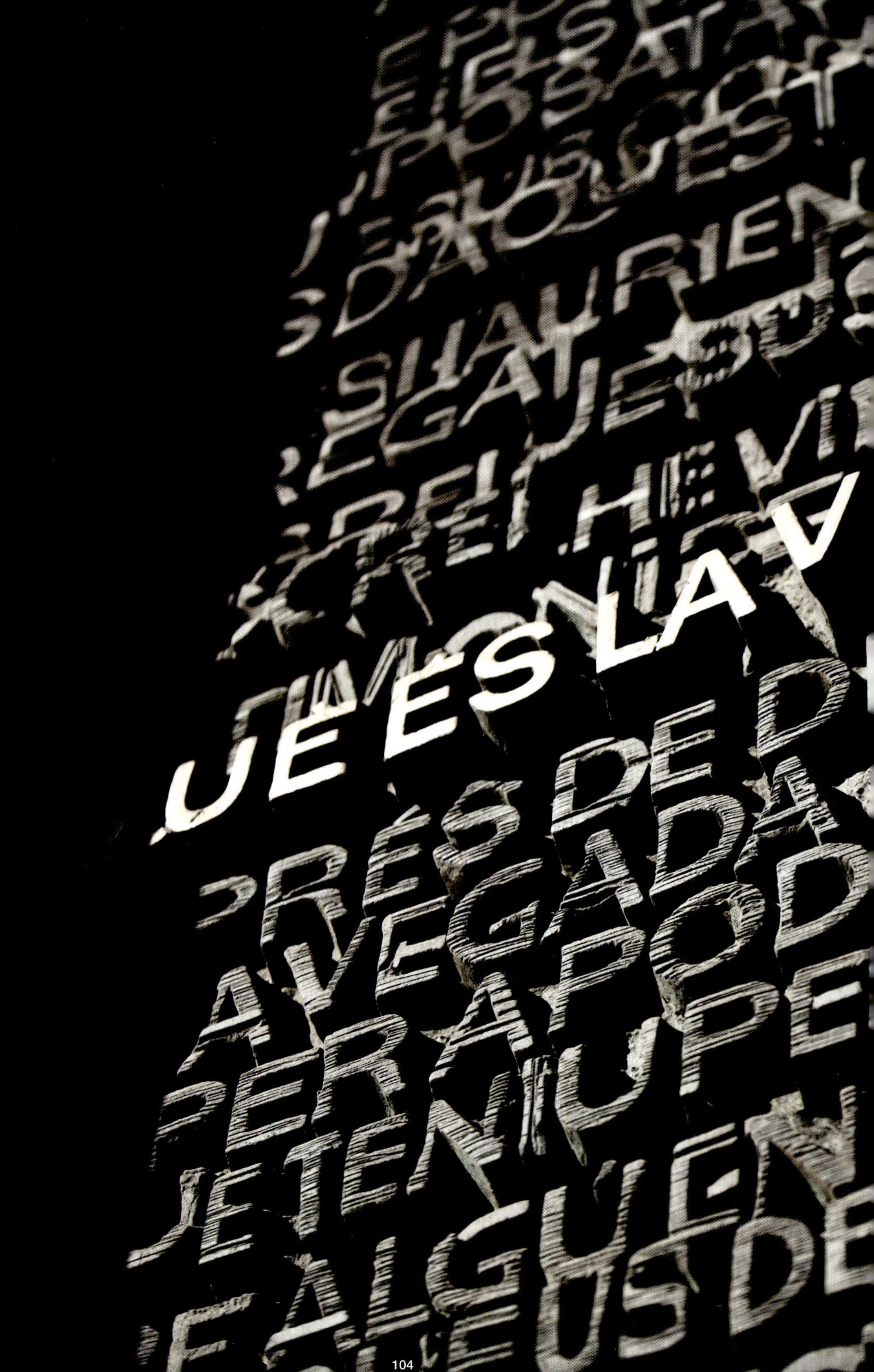
SHAU RIEN
REI HE
UE ESLA
PRES DE
AVEGAD
PER
JE TEN
ALGUS

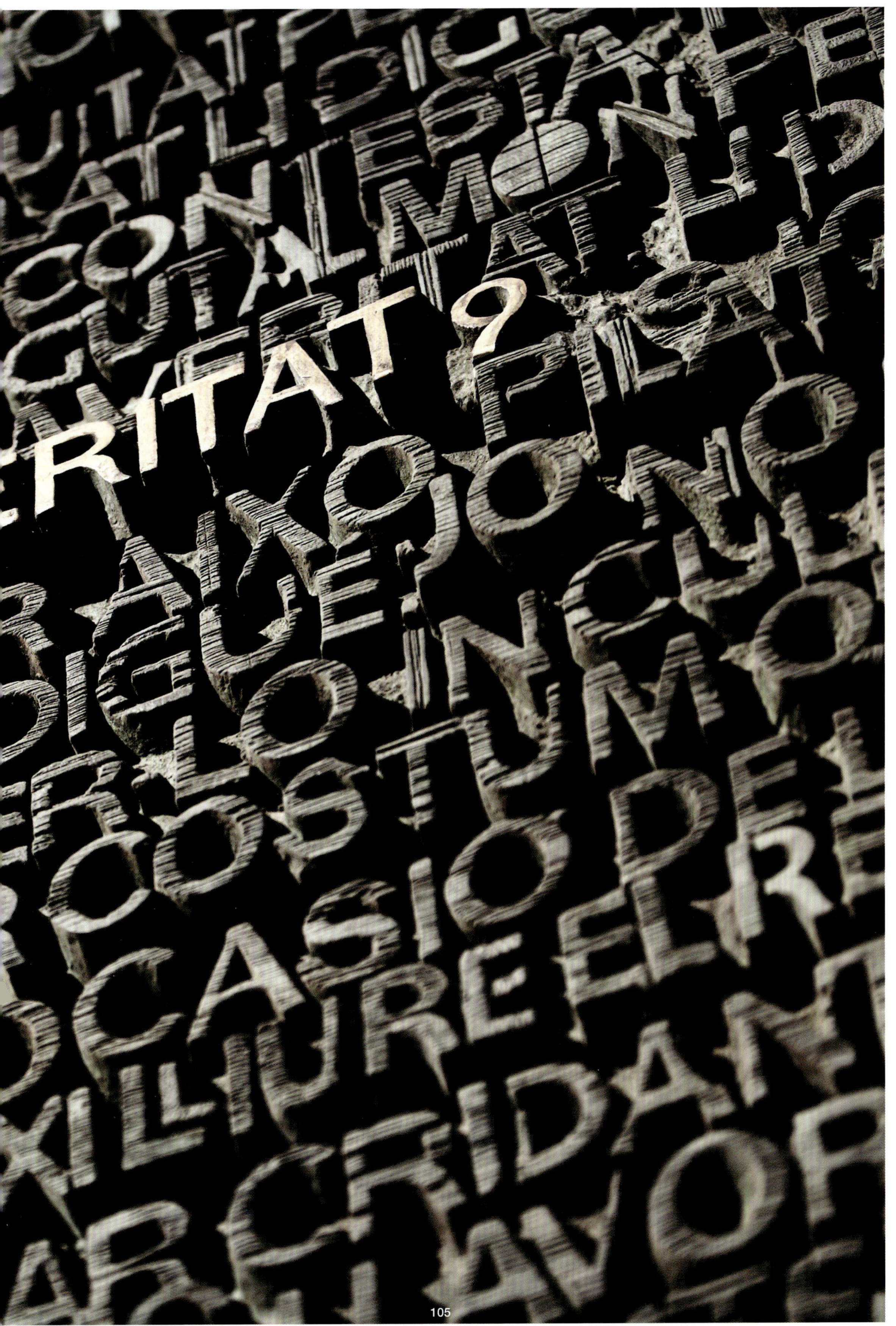

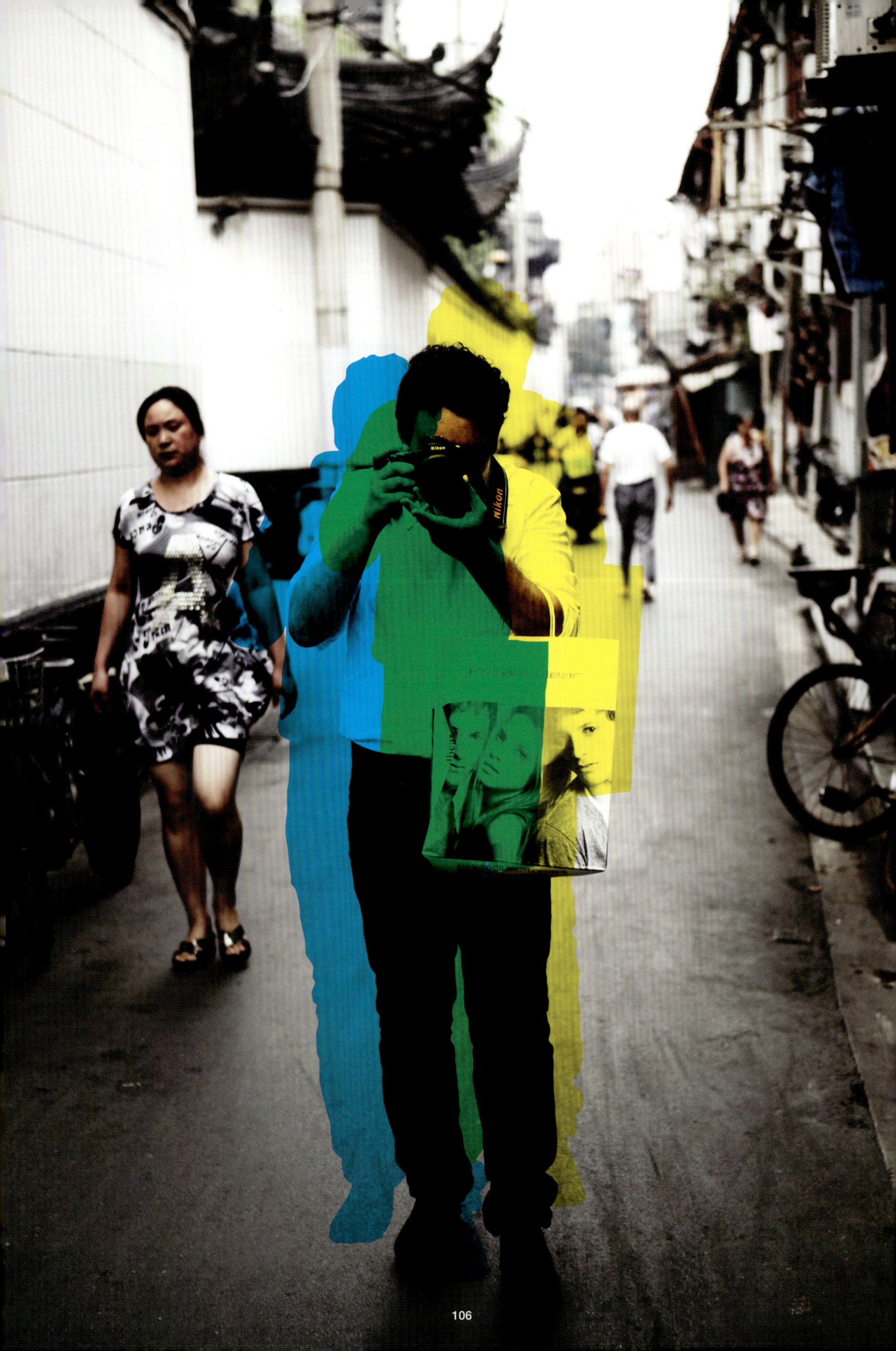

THE GREAT THING ABOUT THE PLACES WE LOVE IS THAT
TO KNOW THEM IS IMPOSSIBLE, BECAUSE THEY ARE TOO VAST.
BUT YOU CAN BE CERTAIN OF ONE THING.
NO MATTER WHERE YOU LOOK, THERE'S A SHOT.
ANYWHERE YOU LOOK, IT'S INTERESTING.

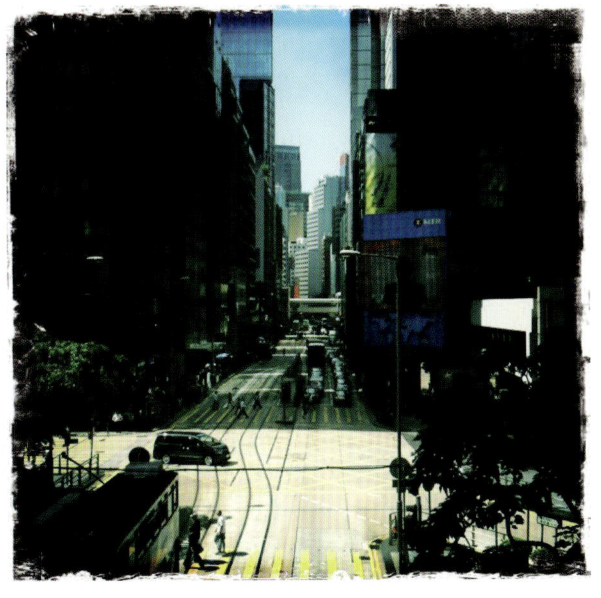

North

East

West

MOBILE CENTERS OF GRAVITY
One thing we continue to nurture at Hangar
is the ability to assimilate diverse persons and
skills, with pronounced individual sensibilities and strong personalities. In some way,
this variety never generates a centrifugal
movement but results always in unexpectedly
retrieving a mobile center of gravity for the
design. And with the international team of
Hangar Design Group, moreover, the diver-
gence of skills has been transformed into a
critical and original philosophy which has
enabled the establishment of a new relationship with clients and with members of the
team. We believe that this represents the true
creativity of which the best companies are
capable: that of knowing how to place activi-
ties, roles and diversified separate resources
into relationship with one another, and to
shape them into something new, where the
combination of individual elements is always
greater than their arithmetic sum.
A philosophy of work, but also a principle of
professional ethics, according to which diversity and, in particular, richness and collaboration are synonymous with belonging.

South

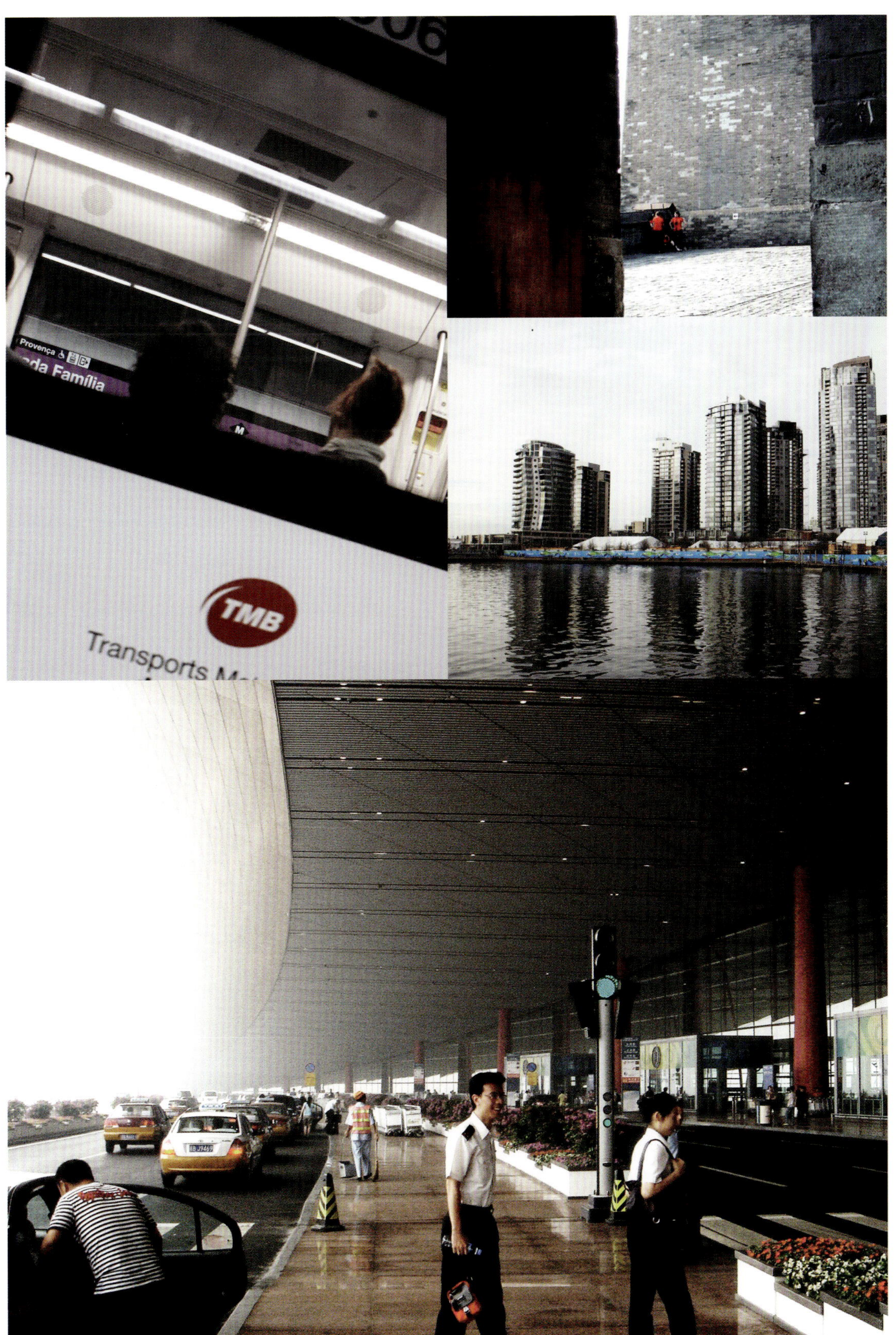
Provença
da Família
TMB
Transports M

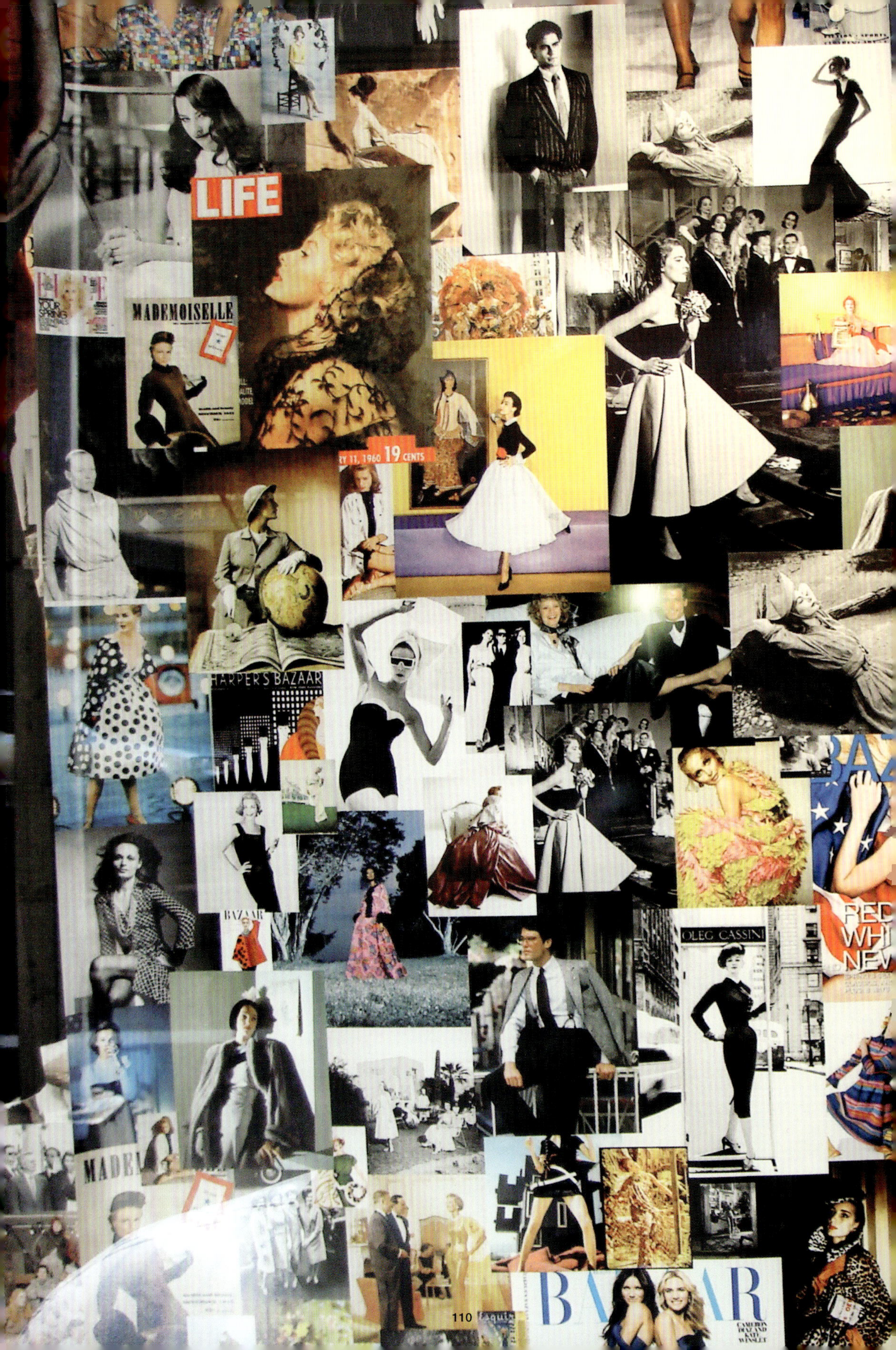

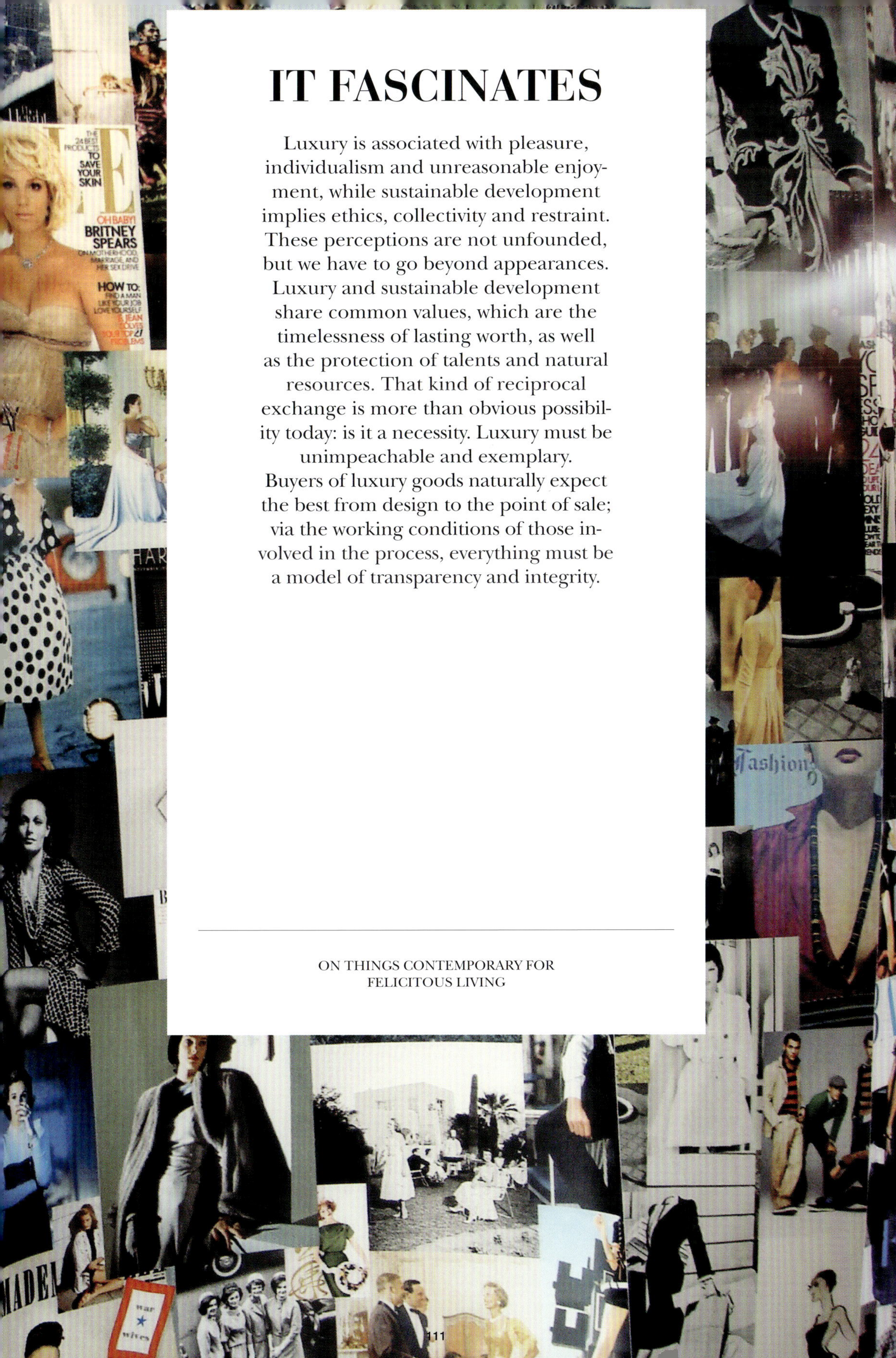

IT FASCINATES

Luxury is associated with pleasure,
individualism and unreasonable enjoy-
ment, while sustainable development
implies ethics, collectivity and restraint.
These perceptions are not unfounded,
but we have to go beyond appearances.
Luxury and sustainable development
share common values, which are the
timelessness of lasting worth, as well
as the protection of talents and natural
resources. That kind of reciprocal
exchange is more than obvious possibility today: is it a necessity. Luxury must be
unimpeachable and exemplary.
Buyers of luxury goods naturally expect
the best from design to the point of sale;
via the working conditions of those involved in the process, everything must be
a model of transparency and integrity.

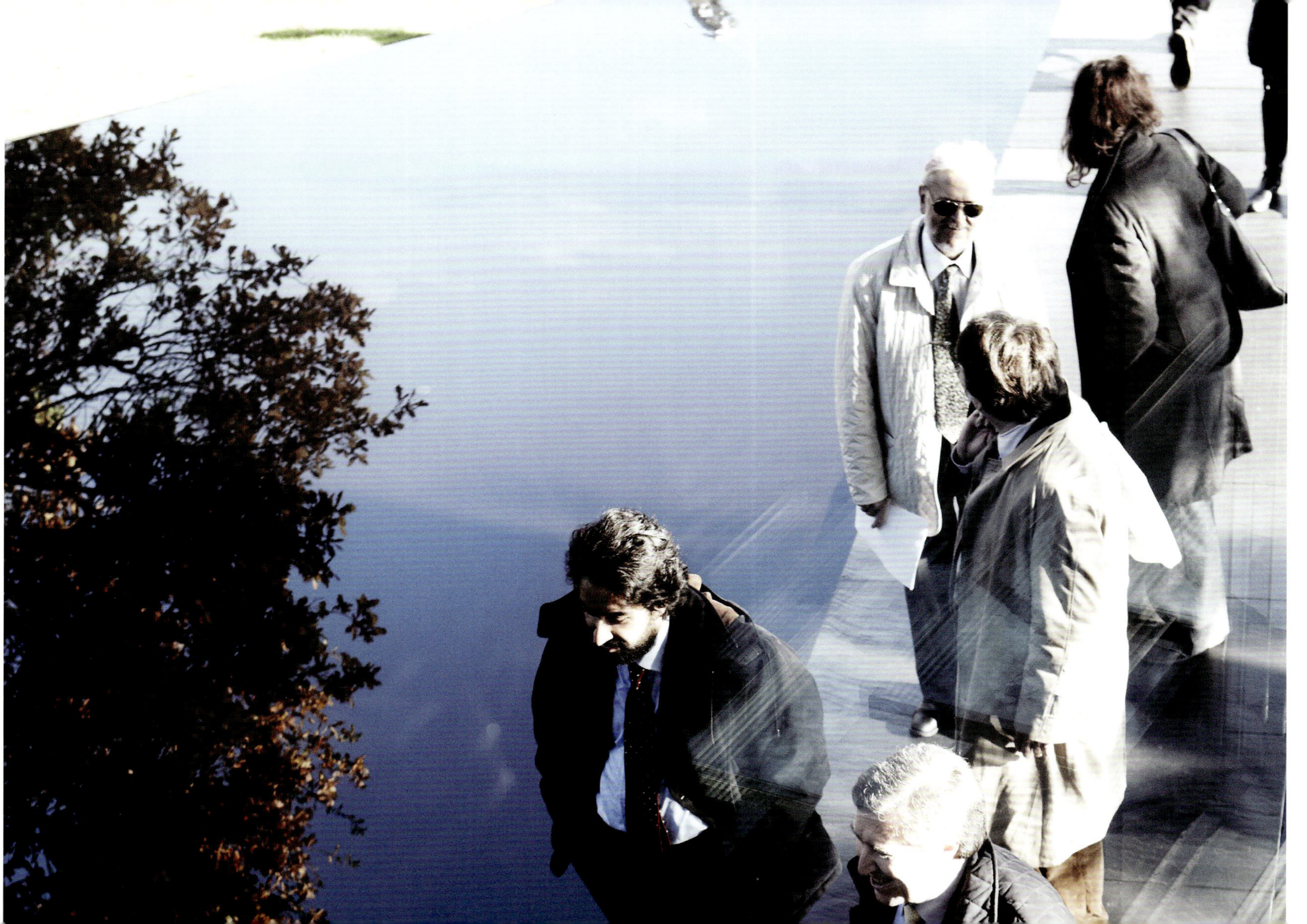

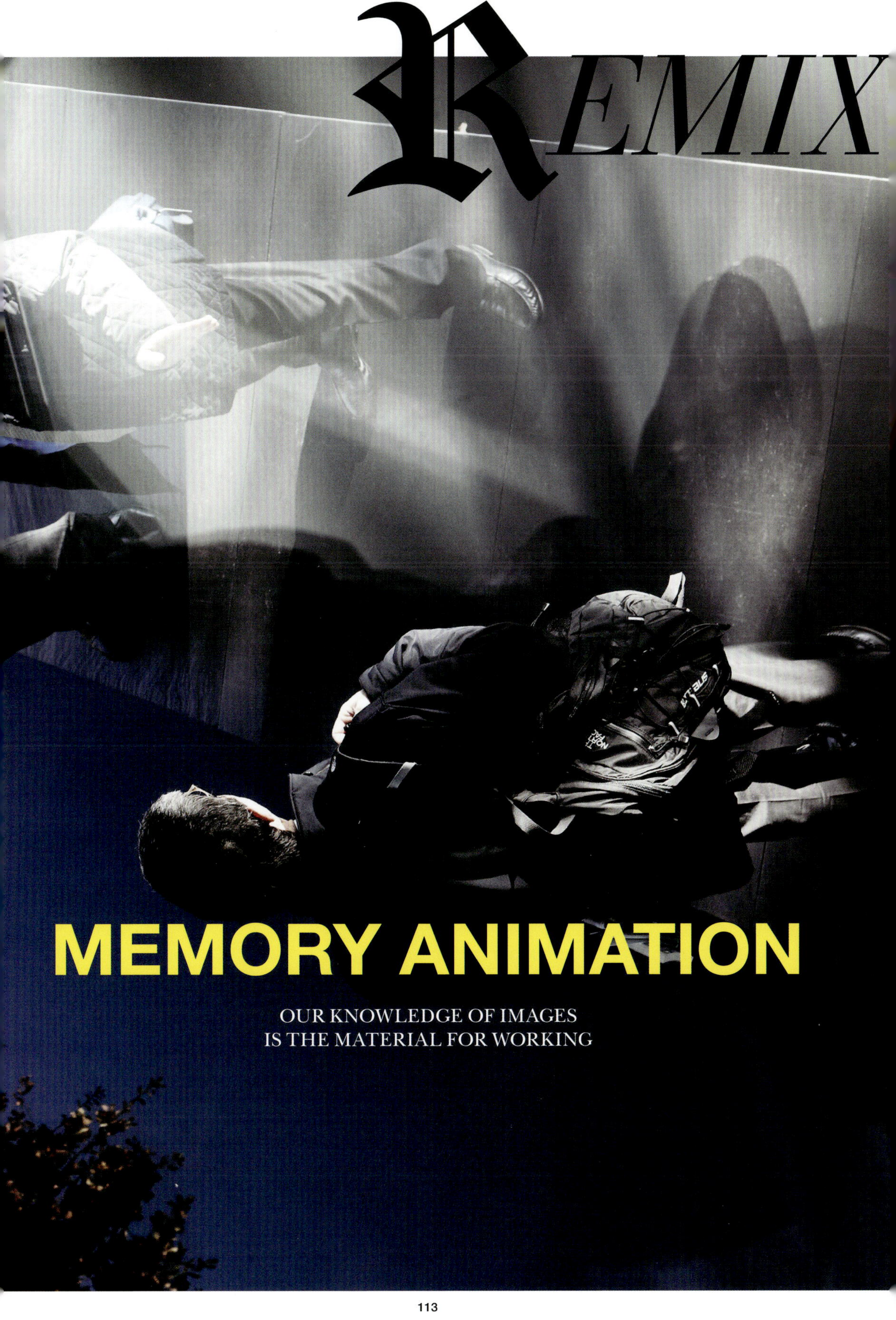

REMIX
MEMORY ANIMATION
OUR KNOWLEDGE OF IMAGES
IS THE MATERIAL FOR WORKING

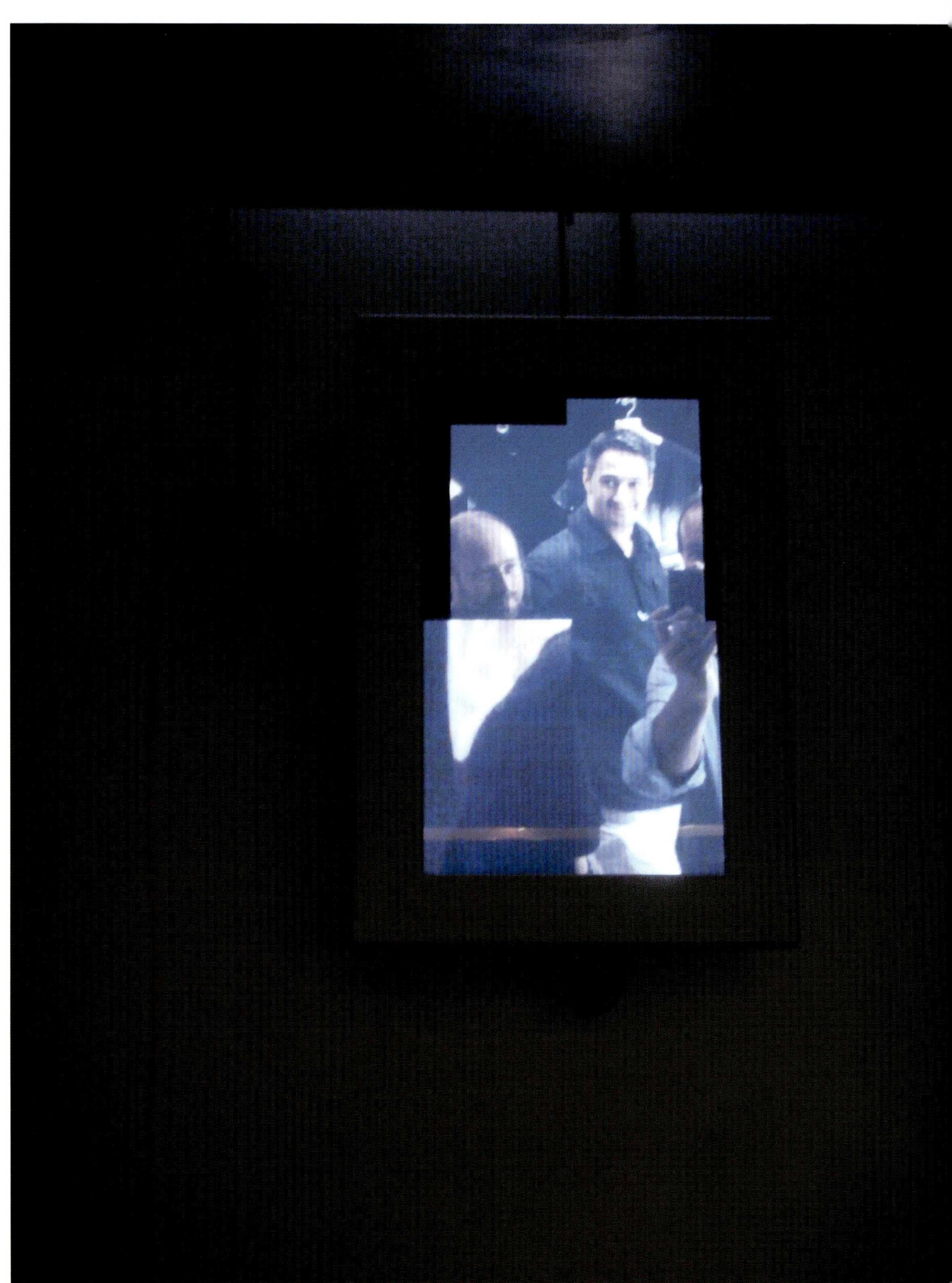

Modern visual communication is not just information or narrative, it is also story-telling or a projecting into the realms of the imagination. It tends to slip into the most sensitive folds of the subconscious, free impulses often held in check by the demands of everyday rules, as it focuses increasingly on imagination. In other words, it acts on our ability to dream, which is even more evocative and irresistible when it is day-dreaming. Here again graphic design keeps a due distance from the tempting allure of advertising proper. It uses a persuasive, but discrete idiom; the images put forward never abandon the rather aristocratic reserve of style. It does not so much offer dream a vulgarized scenario attuned to popular taste, as an allusion to incalculable possibilities, which it is up to each of us to discover.

THE SEDUCTION

is still implicit, unexpressed yet irresistible. A key trait of graphic design is revealed here, although it is rarely taken into consideration, that is its imaginative power, its ability not so much to act on the imaginary, which is now an over-worked formula, but on the imagination. In this respect, what counts is not an explicitly proposed image but the way it triggers off other figurative forms in the user's imagination, other scenarios, in a shimmering and iridescent multiplication directly involved in the nature of dream. Perhaps it is in its intrinsically story-like character that graphic design finds its own real nature, reconnecting it to an ancient cultural tradition, whose roots are entrenched in the distant but still vital recesses of myth.

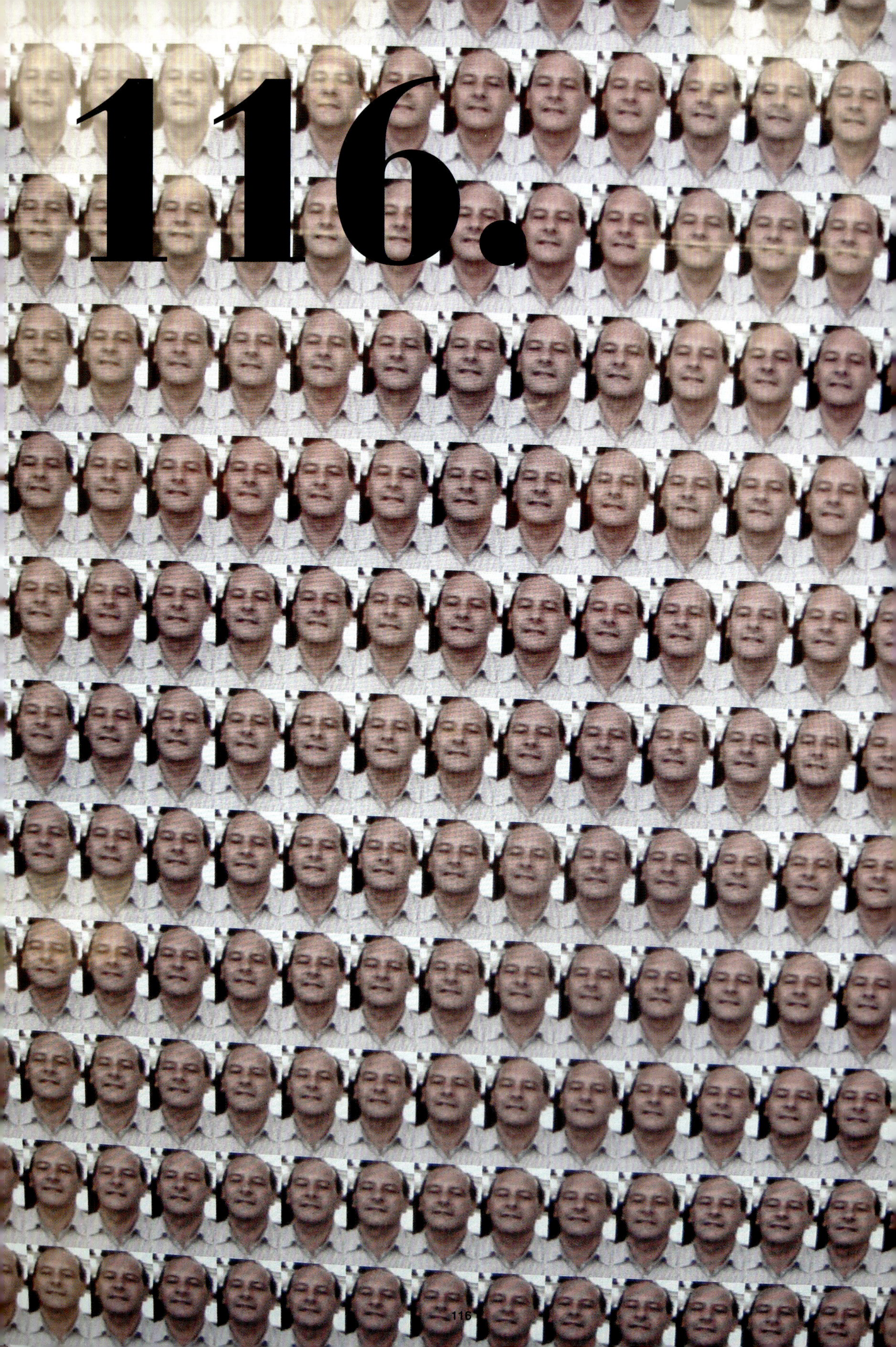

116.

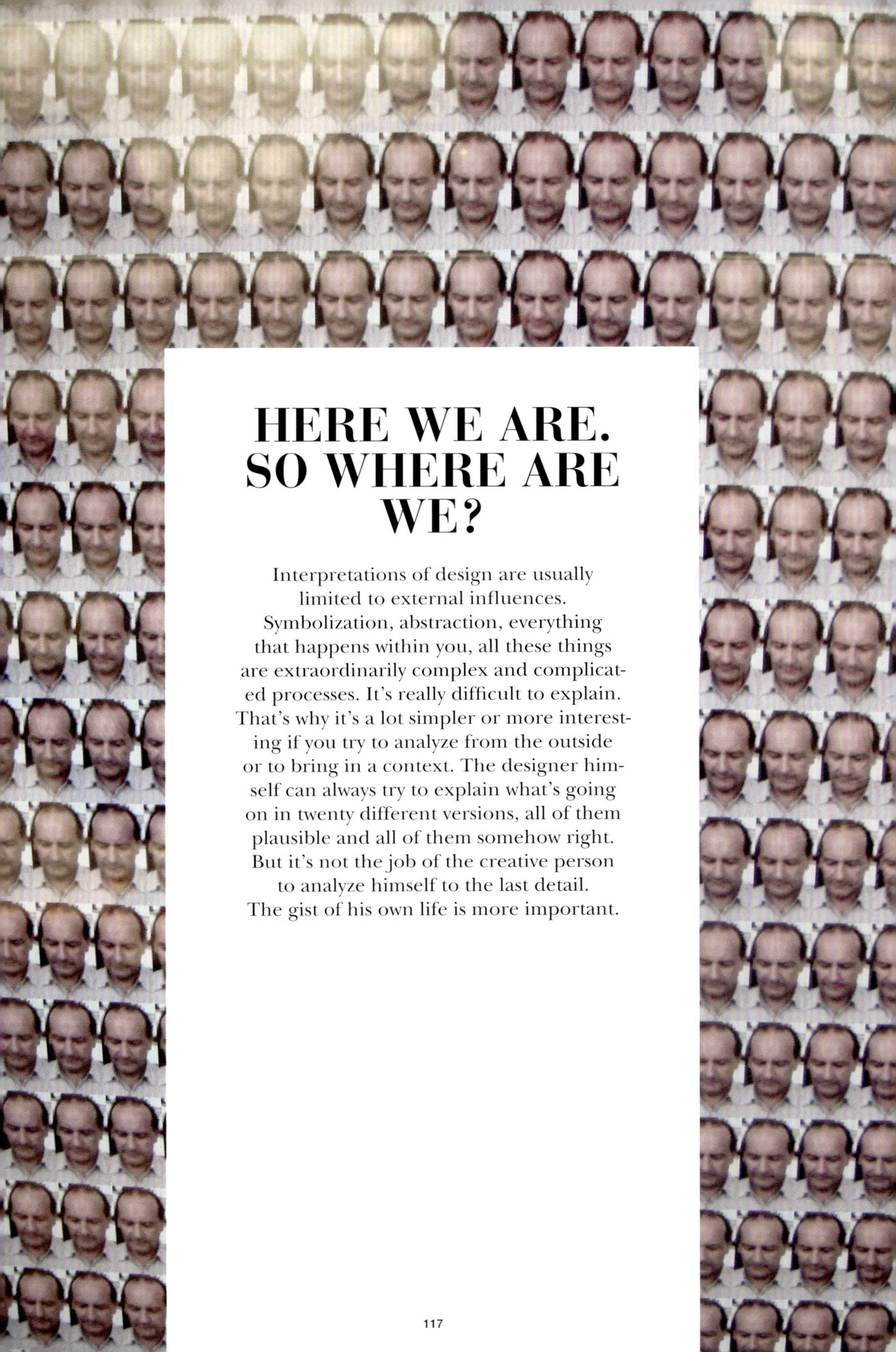

HERE WE ARE. SO WHERE ARE WE?

Interpretations of design are usually
limited to external influences.
Symbolization, abstraction, everything
that happens within you, all these things
are extraordinarily complex and complicated processes. It's really difficult to explain.
That's why it's a lot simpler or more interesting if you try to analyze from the outside
or to bring in a context. The designer himself can always try to explain what's going
on in twenty different versions, all of them
plausible and all of them somehow right.
But it's not the job of the creative person
to analyze himself to the last detail.
The gist of his own life is more important.

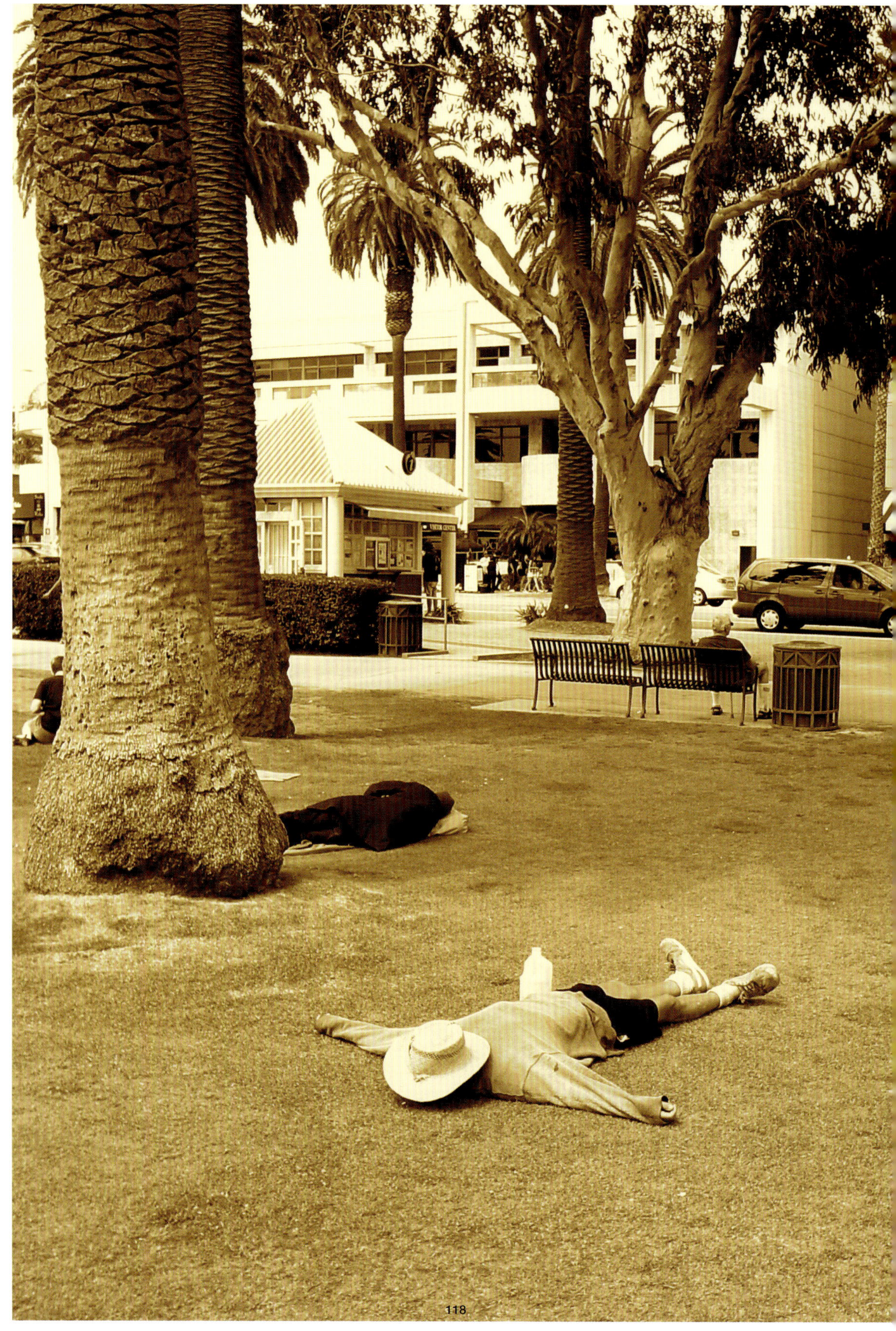

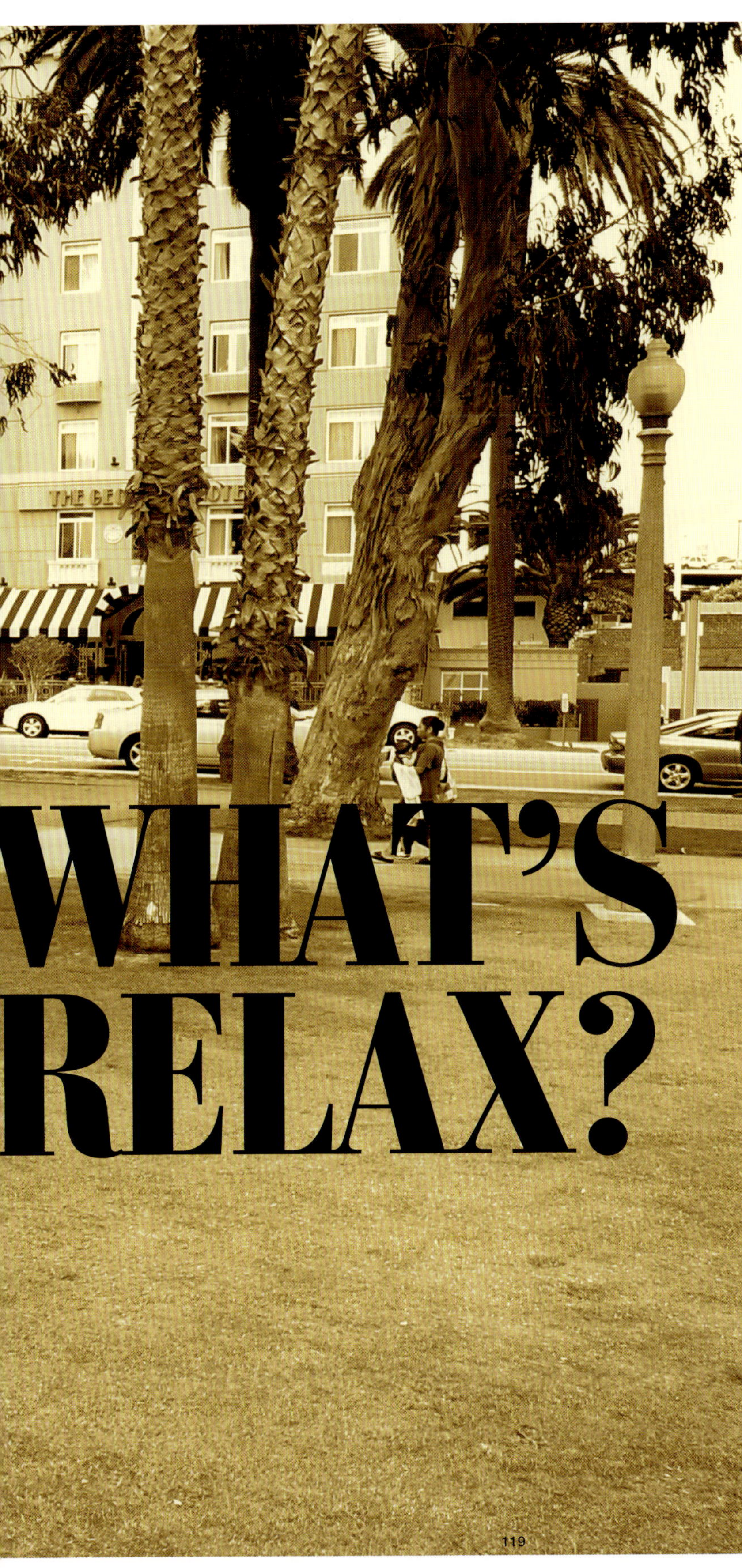

WHAT'S
RELAX?

THE PRUN ING DAY

We work in a stressful industry.
There is a lot of pressure to produce creative work
under deadlines. Long hours mean we often spend more
time with each other than with our families.
It only makes sense to make our work space into a place
as comfortable and appealing as home, where we feel
supported during the most demanding times.
This leads to our collective vision that an office should
be open, interesting, fun, collaborative, and supportive.
We think the office must be open not only in floorplan,
but also in its lack of professional competitiveness.
Everyone who walks in is valued as an individual,
personally and professionally. From a design perspective,
the open atmosphere is unique. No one worries about
ownership, we all contribute freely during reviews
and critiques, and when we sit down to conduct
a design presentation, it is our collective work.

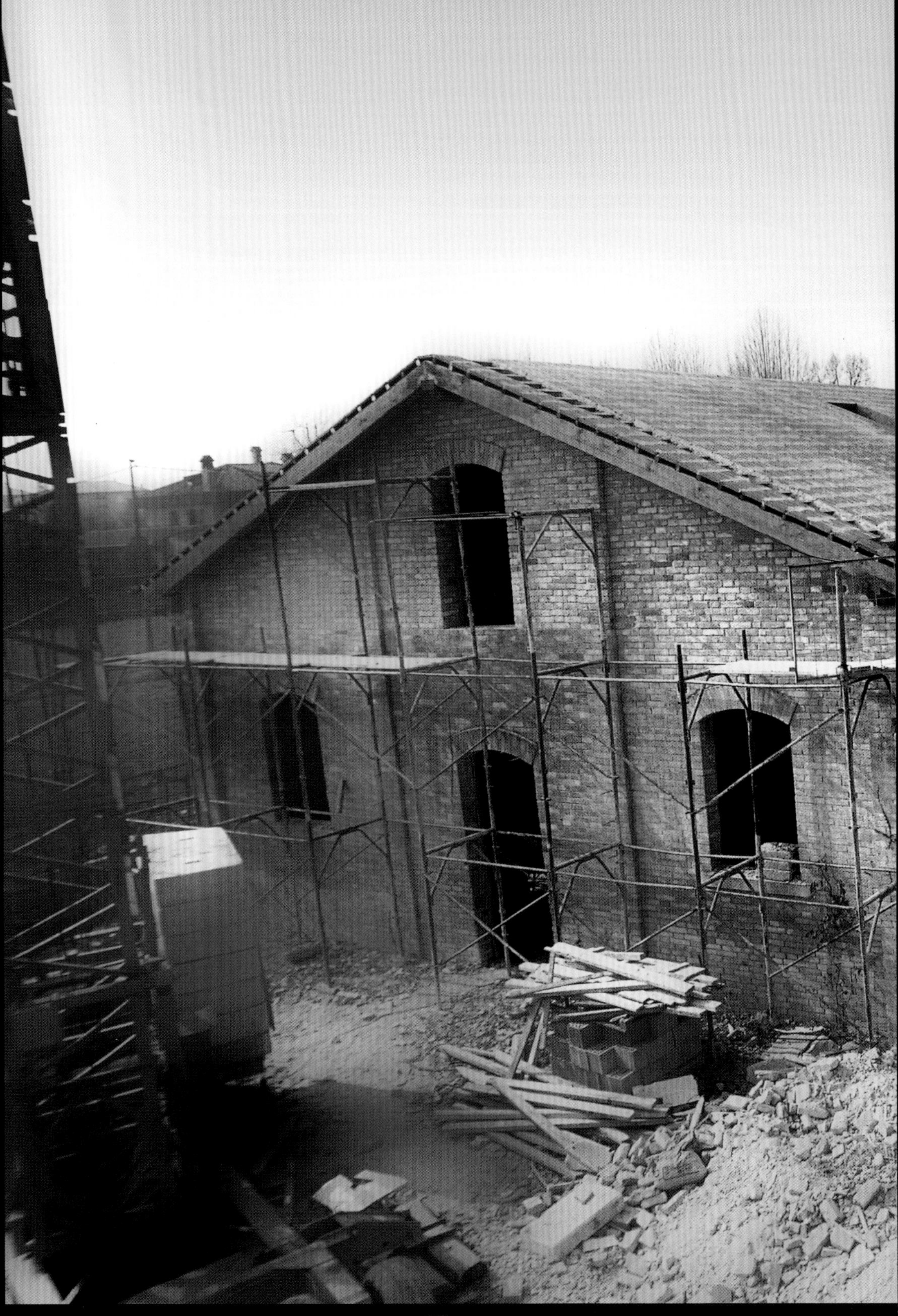

The important thing is that you have a story. Without a story, you don't have a means of expression and the opportunity to develop further. Over the years, integrity makes this authentic. And we do think, by the way, that after all the hype in design, the authentic is becoming important again. Which people are behind which things.

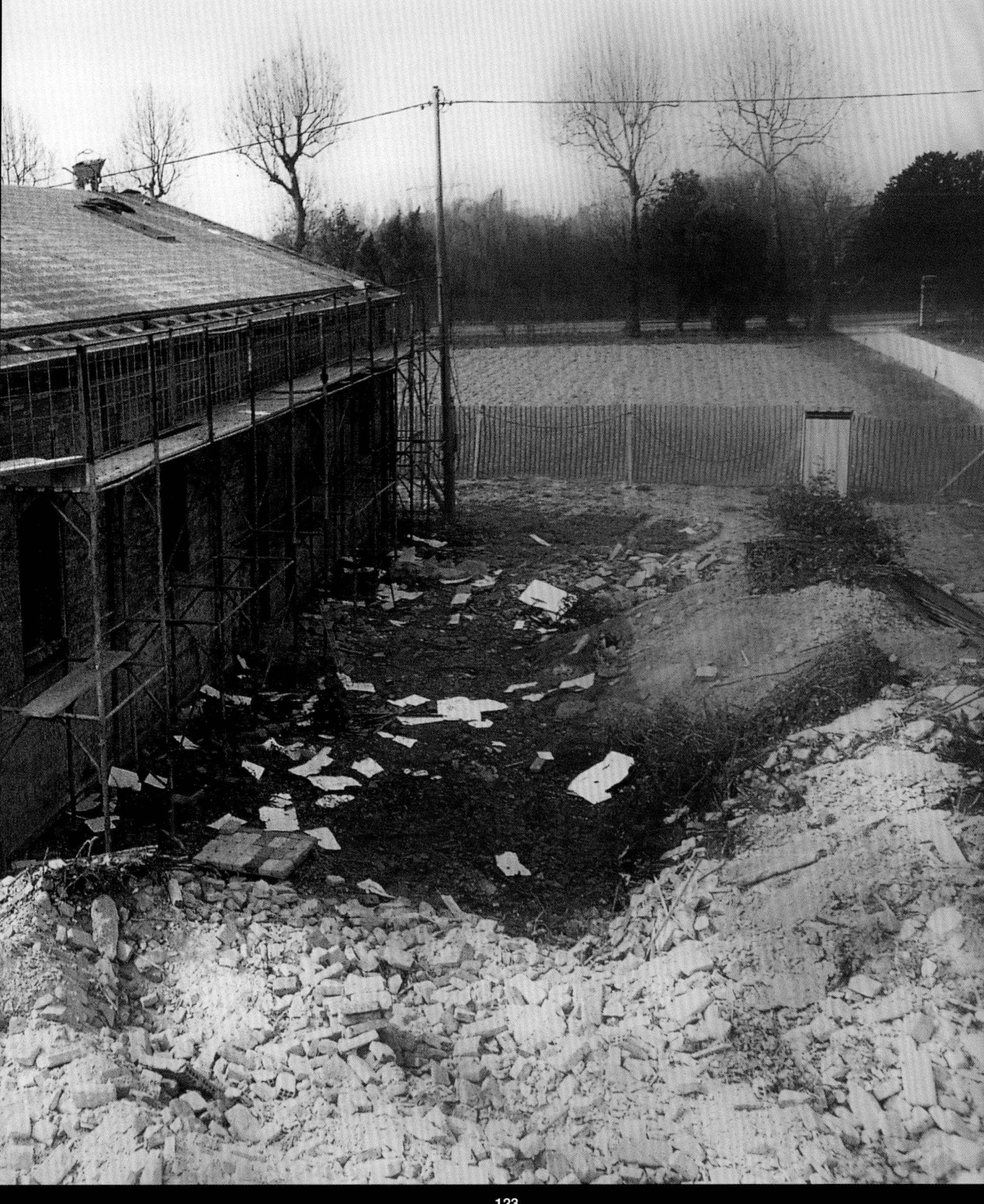

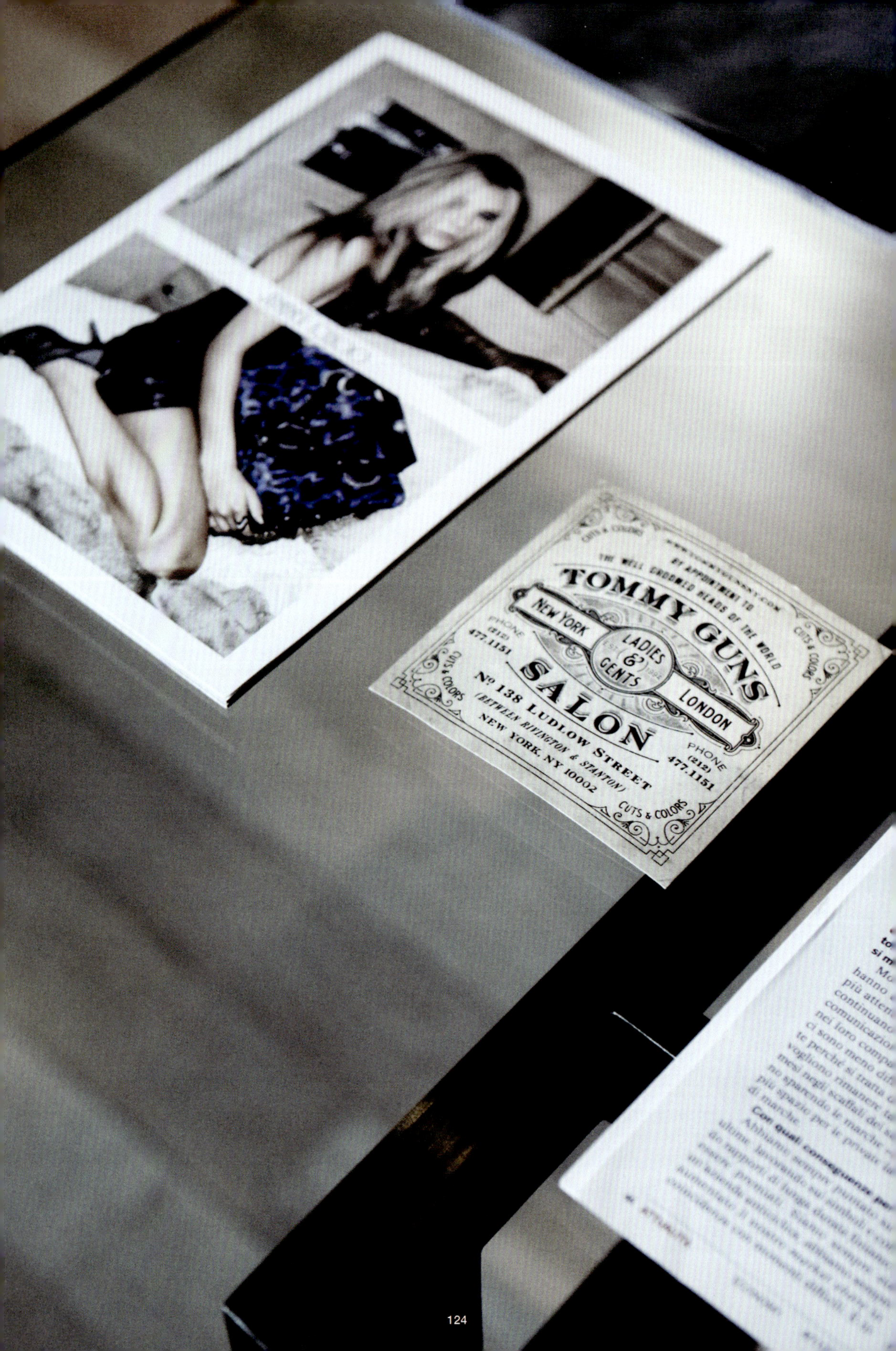
TOMMY GUNS
NEW YORK   LONDON
LADIES & GENTS
SALON
Nº 138 LUDLOW STREET
(BETWEEN RIVINGTON & STANTON)
NEW YORK, NY 10002
PHONE (212) 477.1151
THE WELL GROOMED HEADS OF THE WORLD
BY APPOINTMENT TO
CUTS & COLORS

PERFECT IN DETAILS
A JOURNEY IN HANGAR

I CAN'T GET NO SATISFACTION

126.

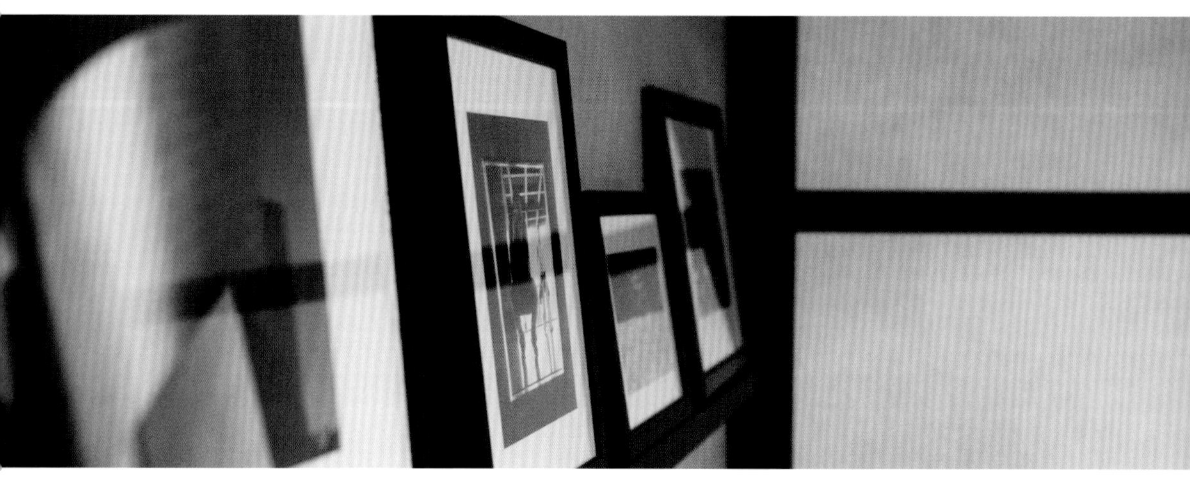

A supportive office environment is the single most important
aspect in the studio to ensure we do good work.
Fostering the environment has always depended on having what
we can only term as healthy, mutually respectful relationships among everyone here.
We are committed to making the environment as easy and stress-free as possible.

True. In the studios of great creatives each object is designed by themselves.
Yes, our studio contains products invented by ourselves, but we do not do our utmost
to exhibit them. Instead, you will find them tucked away in the most disparate corners.

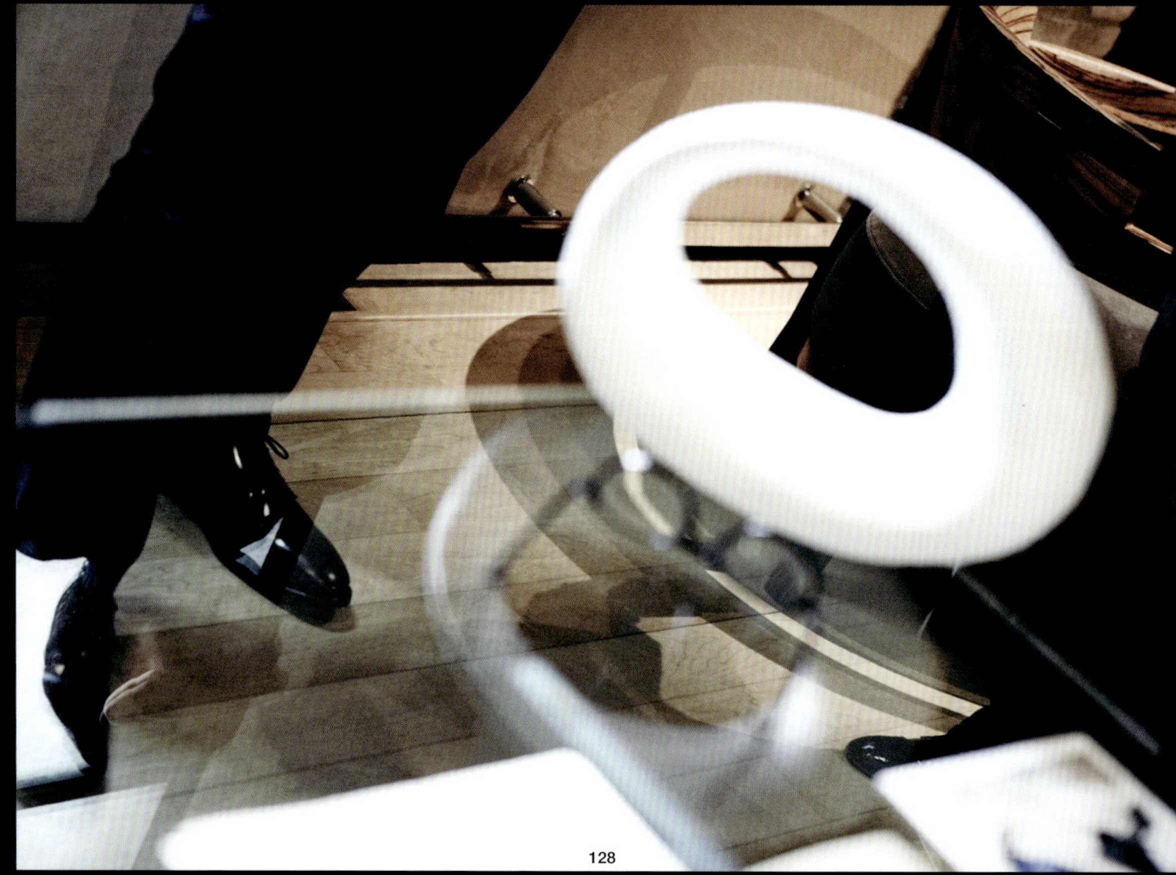

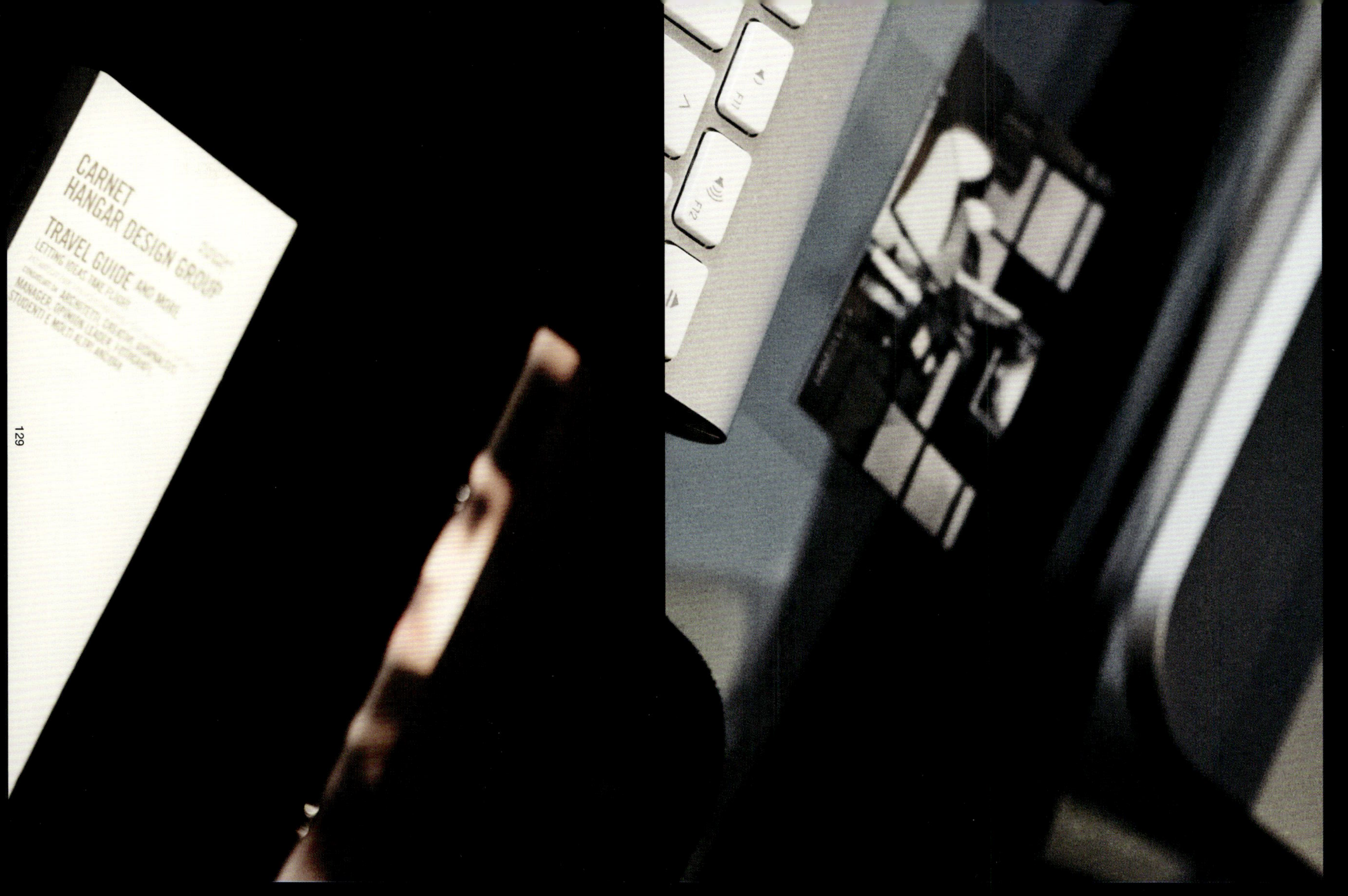
CARNET
HANGAR DESIGN GROUP
TRAVEL GUIDE AND MORE

THIS IS THE TERRAIN ON WHICH
GRAPHICS WEAVES THE METHODS OF
DESIGN INTO THE MEANS OF ARCHITECTURE
AND INDUSTRIAL DESIGN: THE FAMOUS
FORMULA LESS IS MORE ONLY REFERS
TO A RIGID PERIOD IN HISTORY THAT IS GONE,
BUT, NEVERTHELESS, IT IS STILL A
USEFUL GUIDELINE THAT HAS EVEN BEEN
CONFIRMED BY POSTMODERN REACTION,
IF ONLY NEGATIVELY.

The formal features defining Hangar Design Group's design scheme are just the furthermost ramifications of a visual line of thought emerging from the very heart of modern culture, actually marking its end point and moving beyond it. The slender sign around which the image of a logo is developed constantly eludes the temptation of lapsing into tautology, as it projects towards a semantic perspective tending towards infinity.

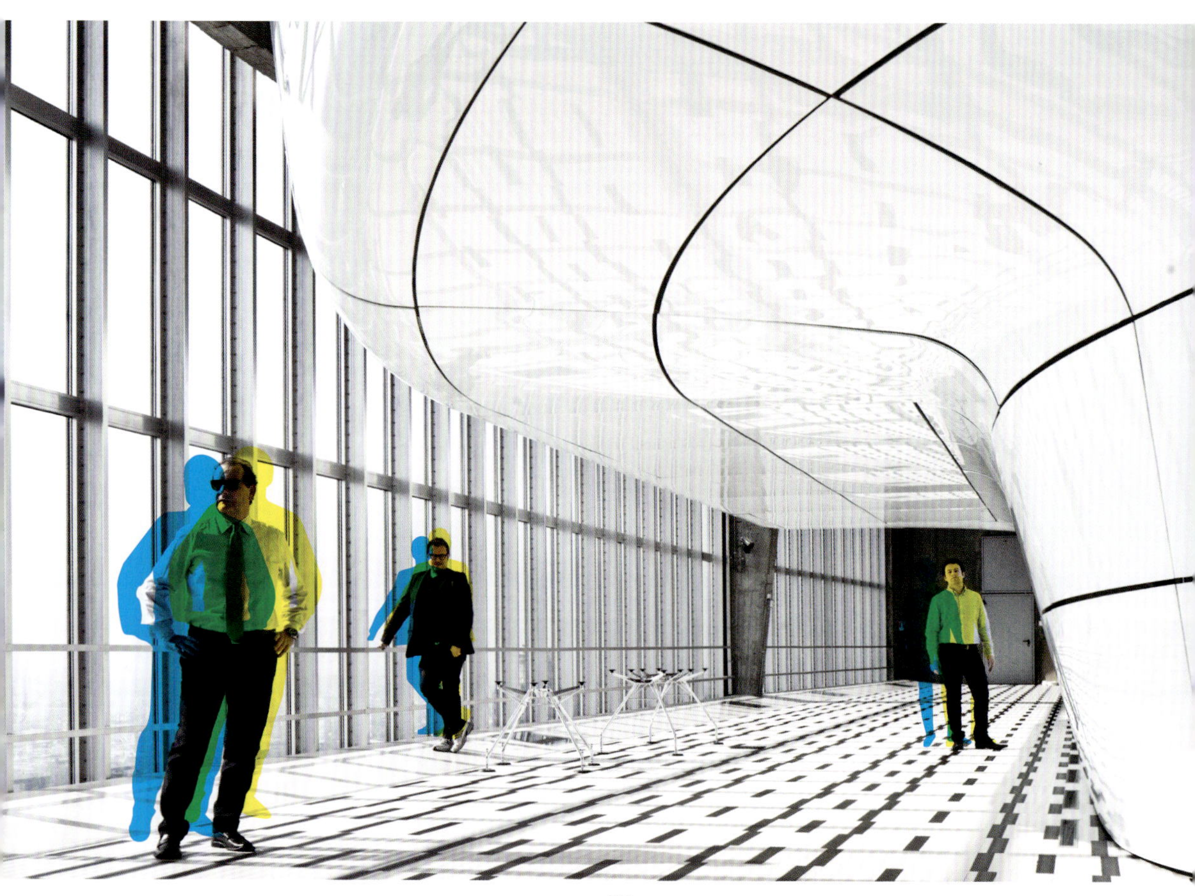

EVERY-THING COMES FROM INSIDE

There are countless influences, but it's more important what one does with them. That's why everything truly definitive happens inside.

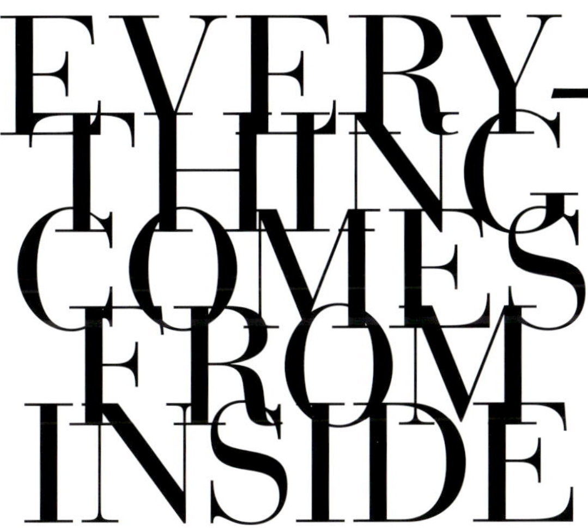

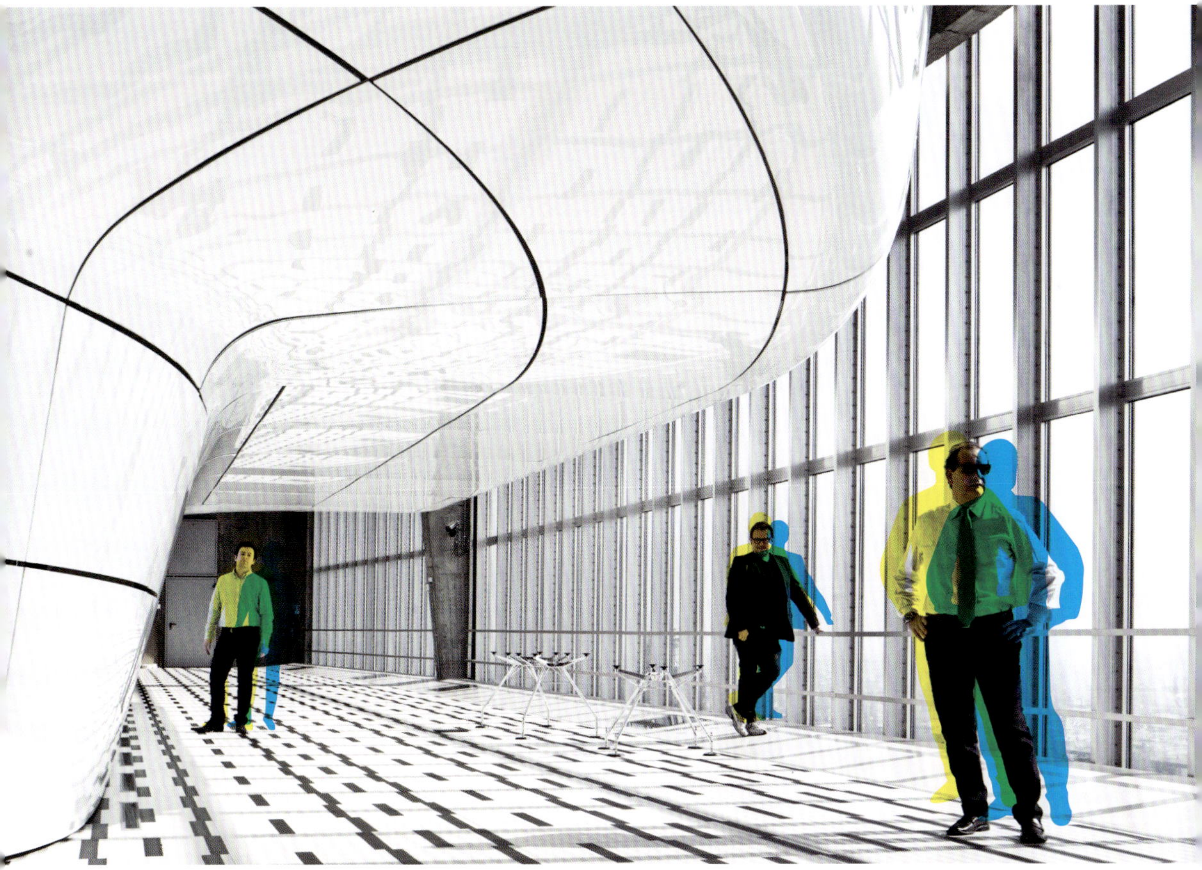

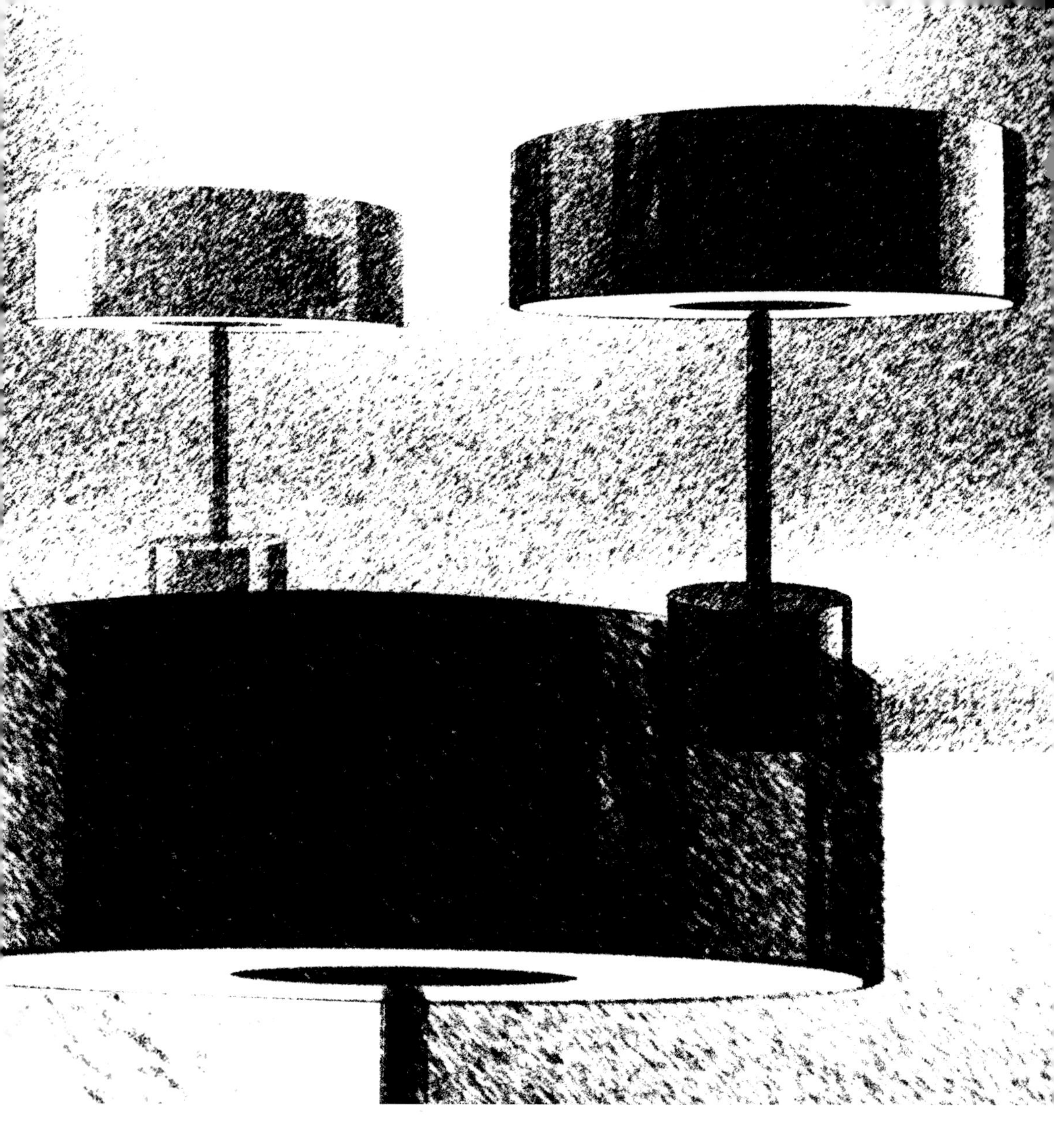

The value of the network for a group such as ours is of crucial importance.
It's more than just an address on a business card; it involves real physical places where real people work and collaborate on various projects, sharing a professional working model.
The opening of foreign branches in America, Asia, and Europe has come to fruition thanks to our profound conviction that the presence of diverse languages can impel creative dynamism.

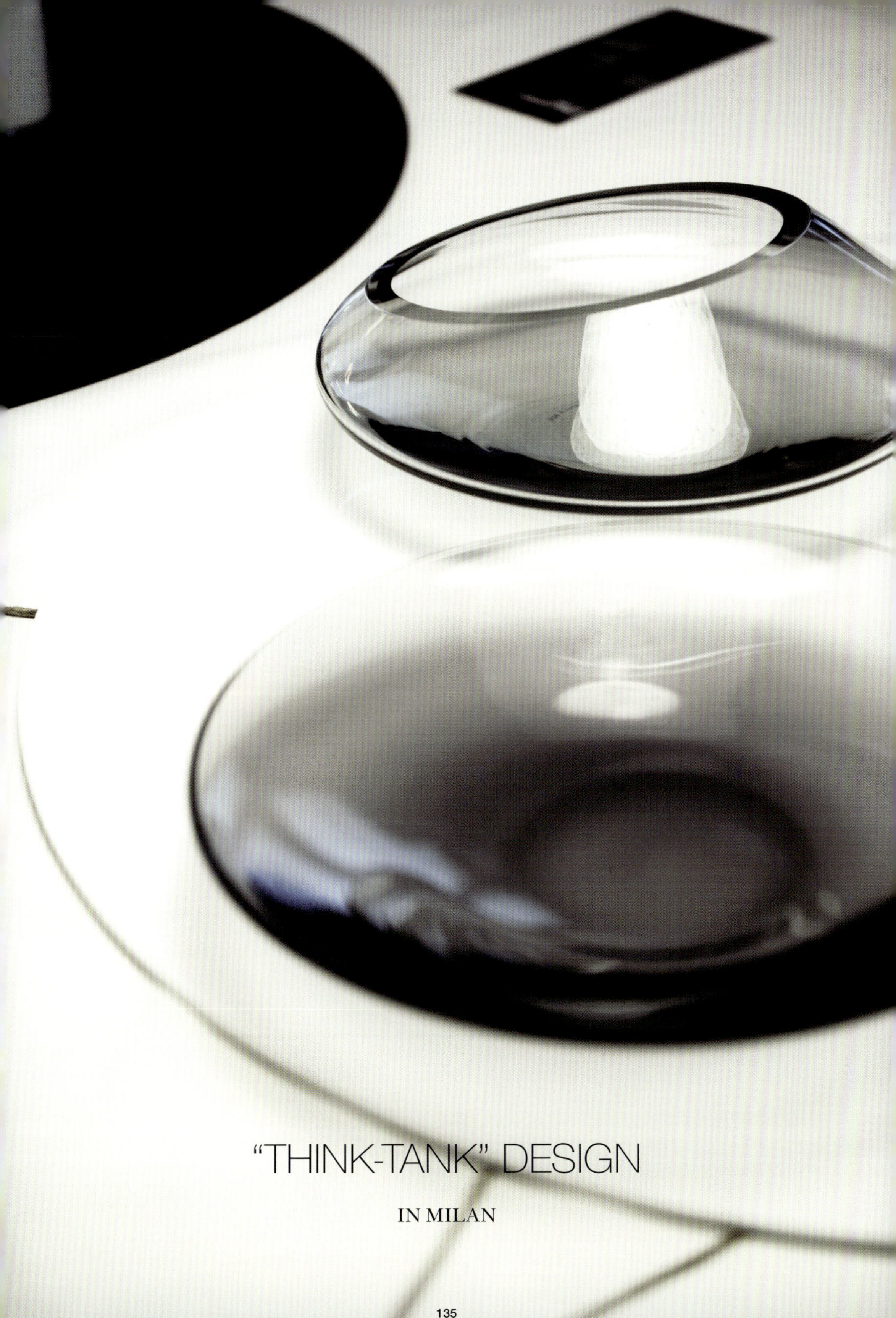

"THINK-TANK" DESIGN

IN MILAN

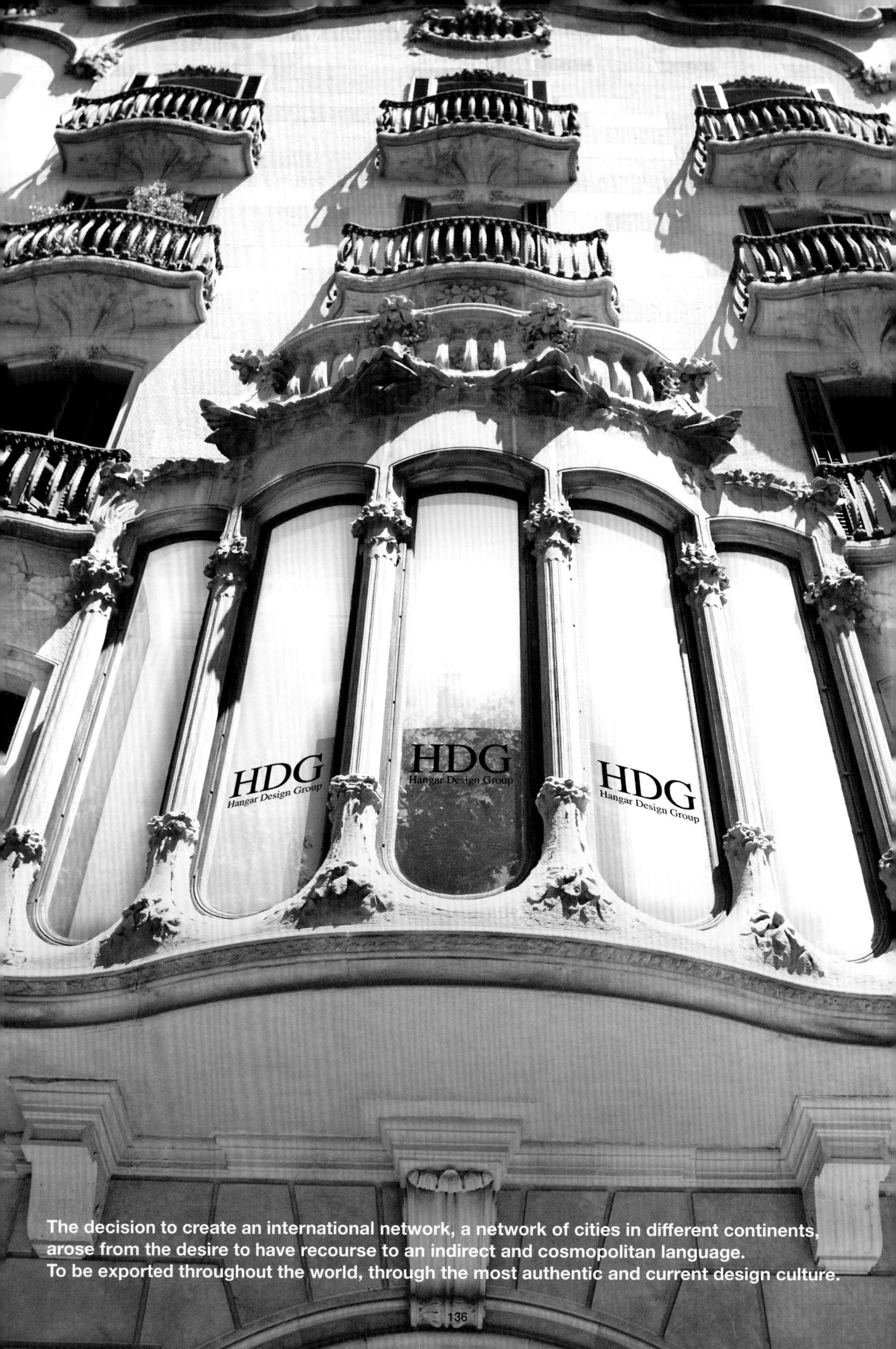

The decision to create an international network, a network of cities in different continents, arose from the desire to have recourse to an indirect and cosmopolitan language.
To be exported throughout the world, through the most authentic and current design culture.

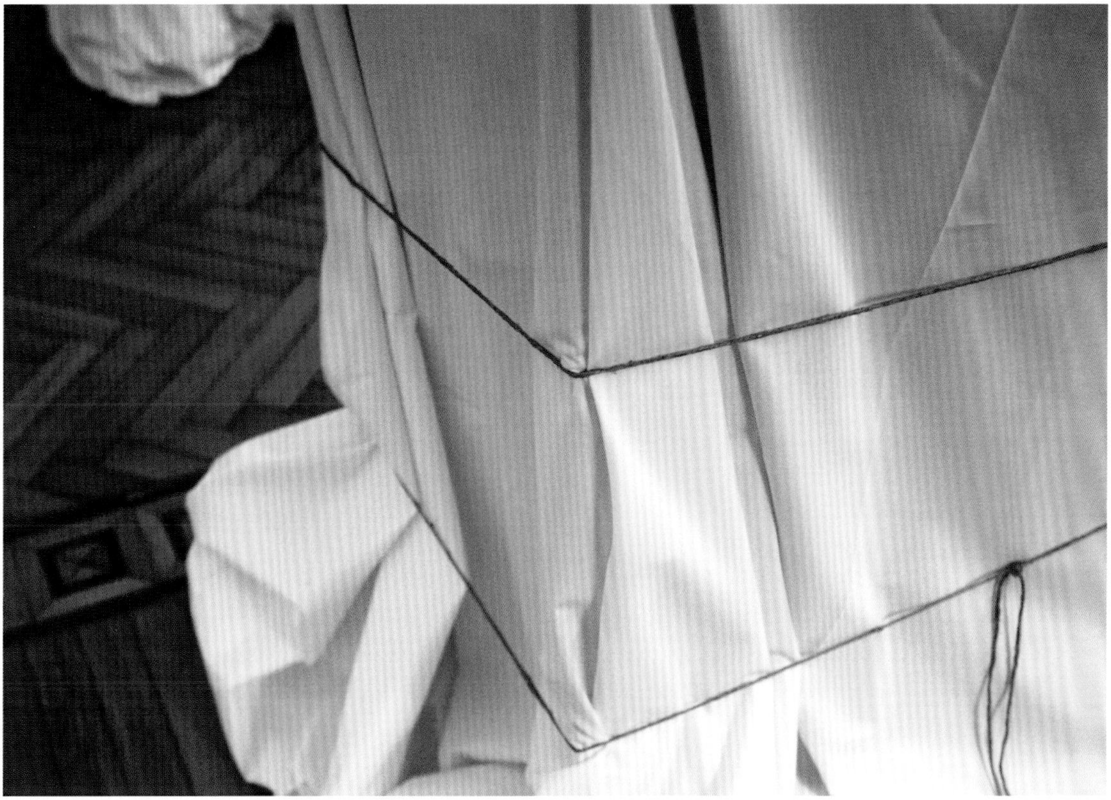

WE'VE CHOSEN OTHER SKIES TO TELL OTHER STORIES.

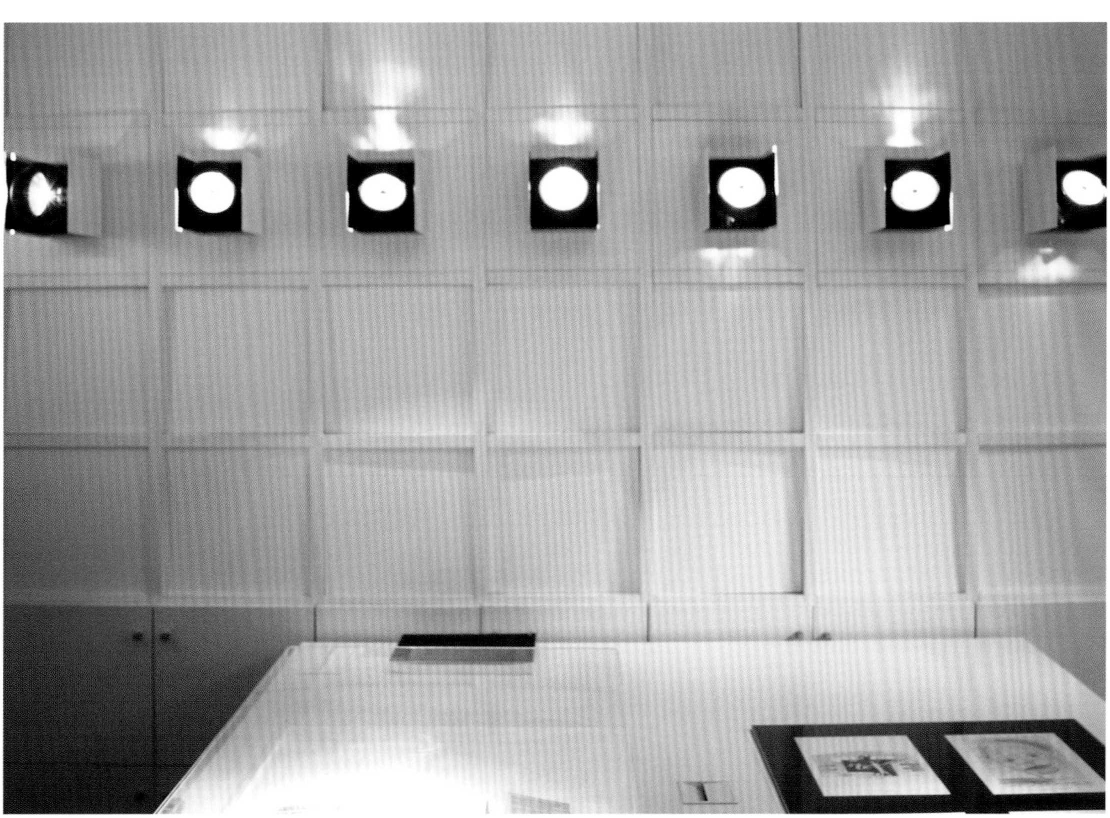

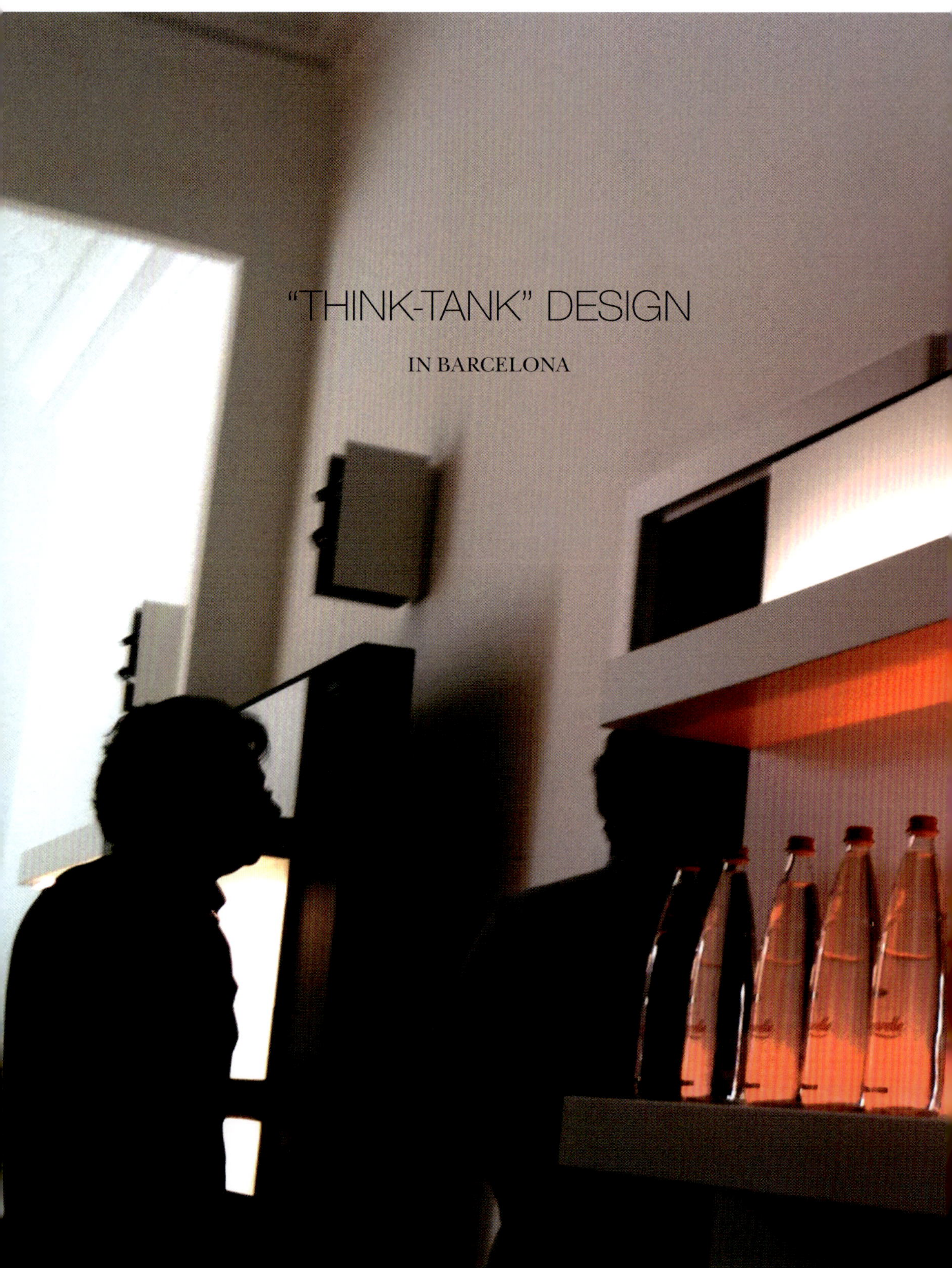

The second you've become used to the studio, it becomes your place. Actually, you always have your workplace with you and you carry it within you. It's your mind and then it's your soul.

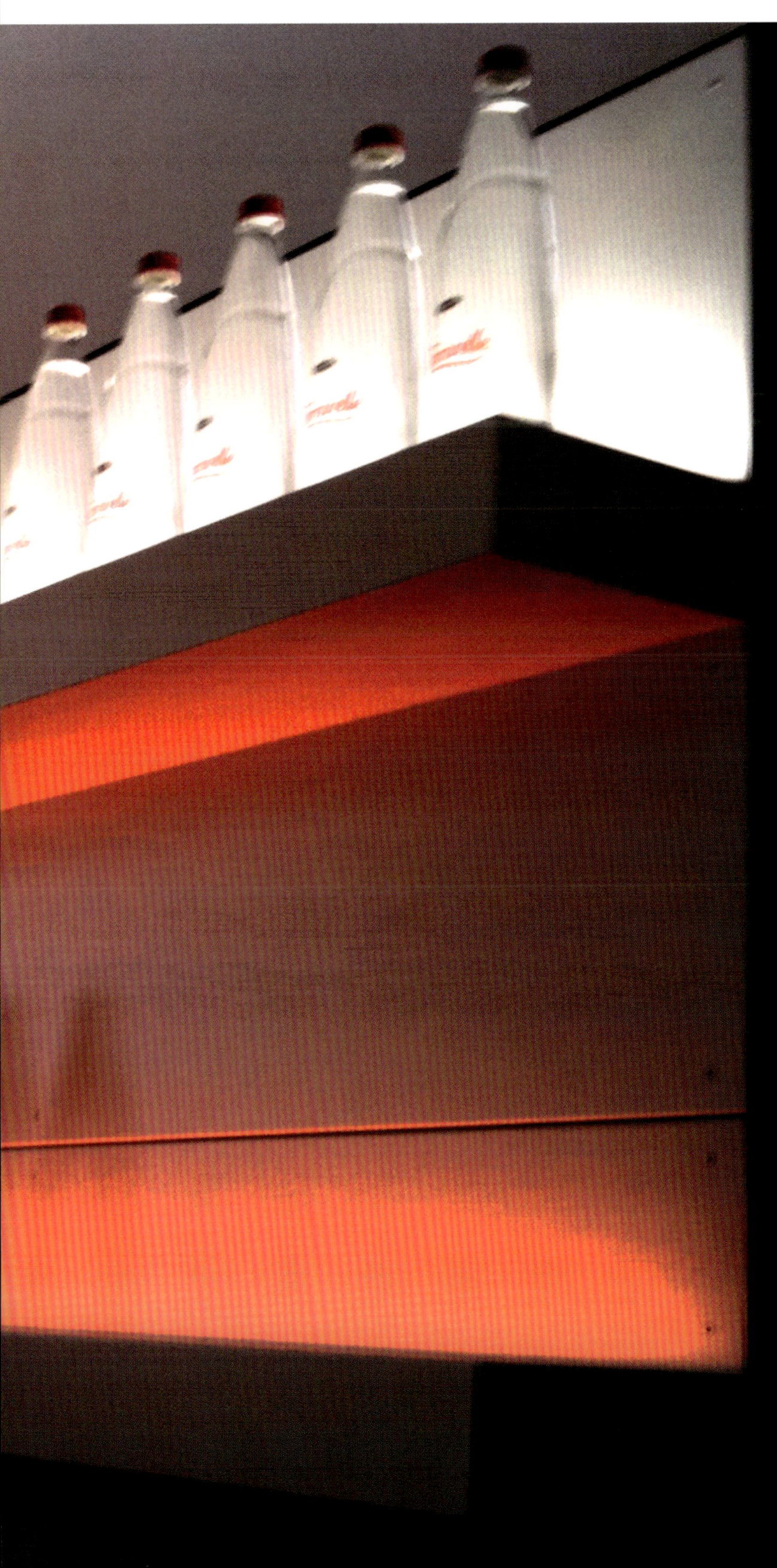

AFFINITY

OF FORMS

BASIS ____
SURFACE

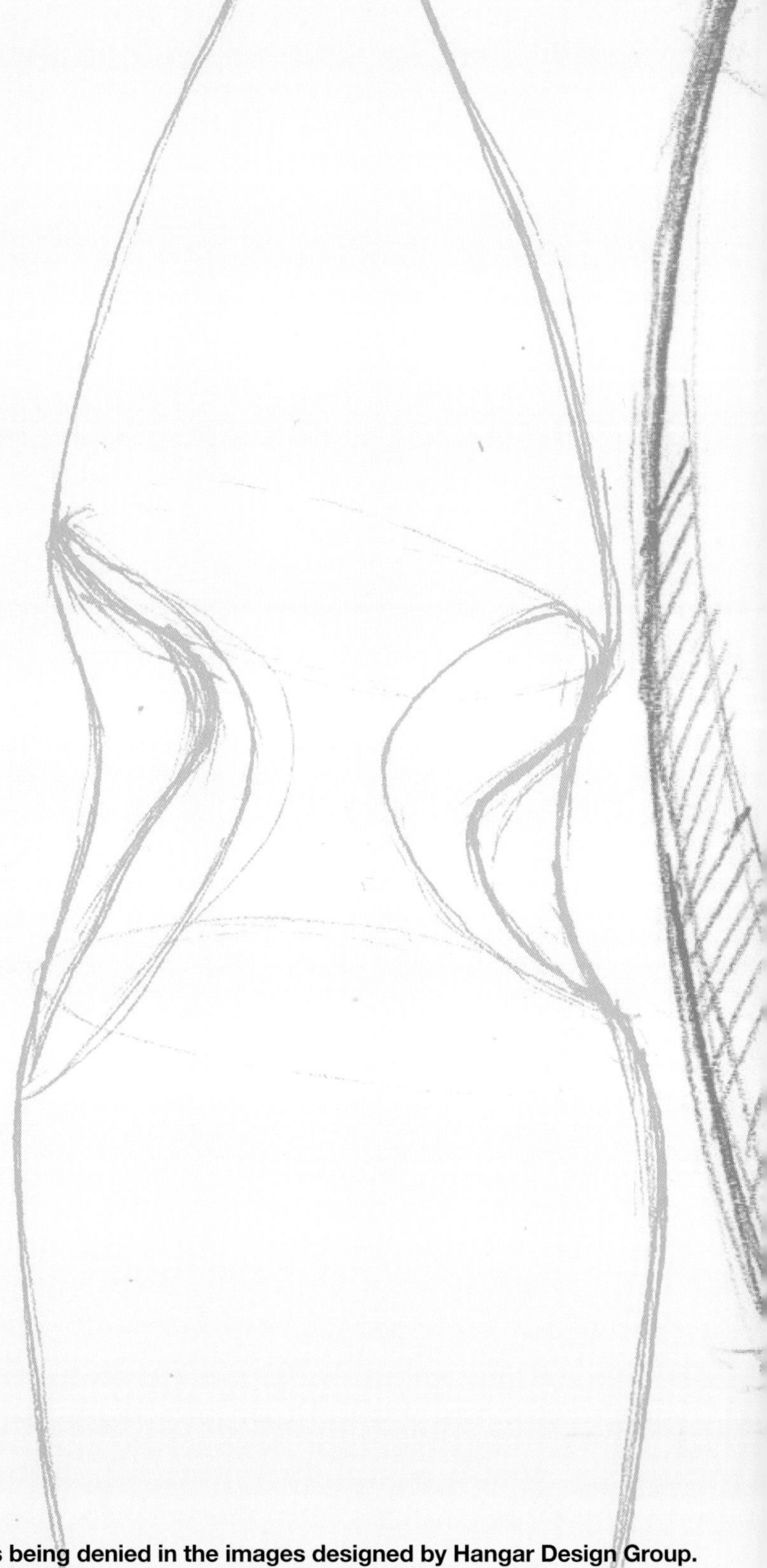

Symmetry emerges just as it is being denied in the images designed by Hangar Design Group. Firmly anchoring the visual message to a carefully gauged page layout lies at the root of a decon-struction process, which, as well as injecting life into the overall figurative design, also projects it into a world of semantic possibilities in which the observer is expected to be immersed.

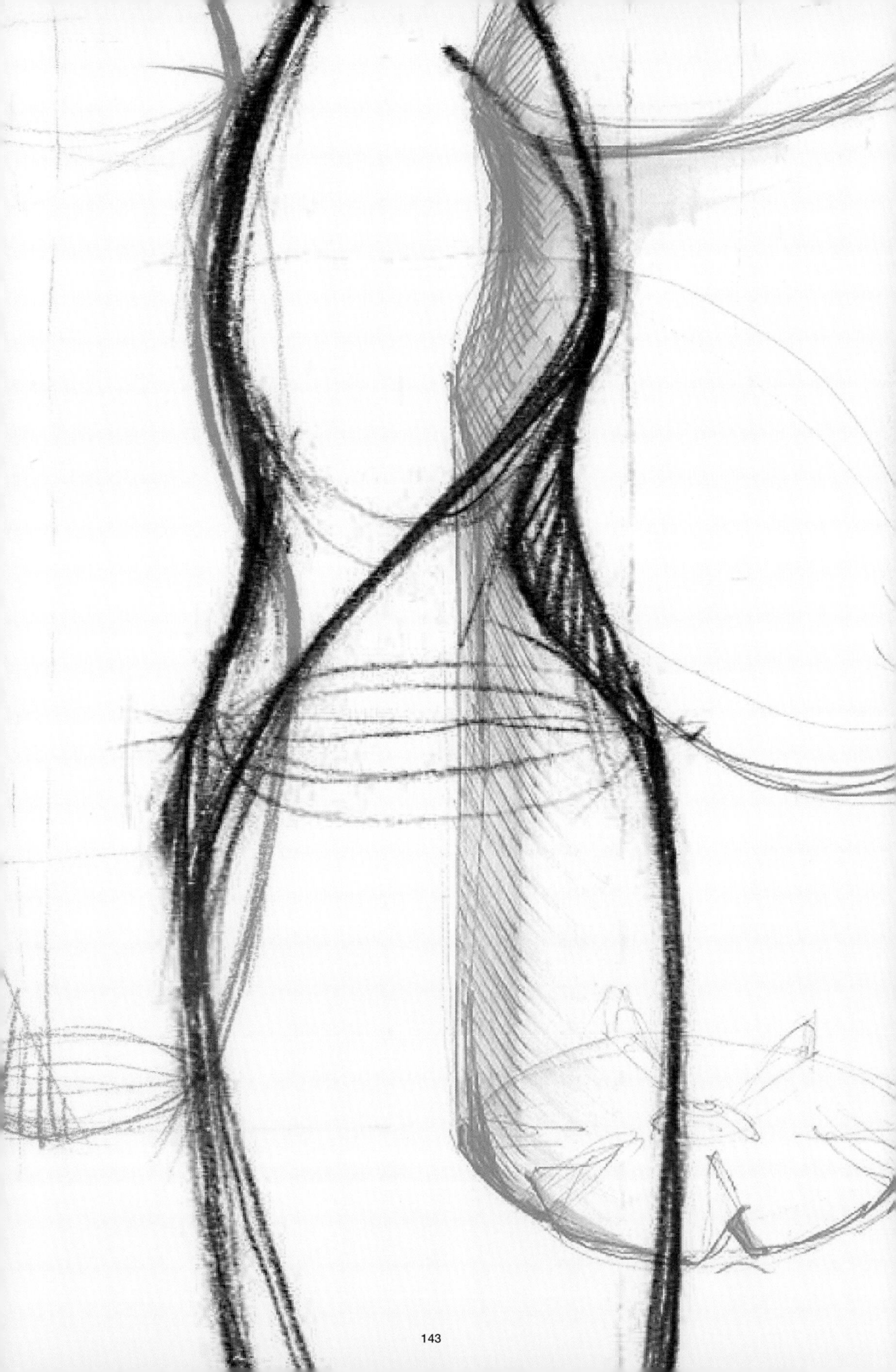

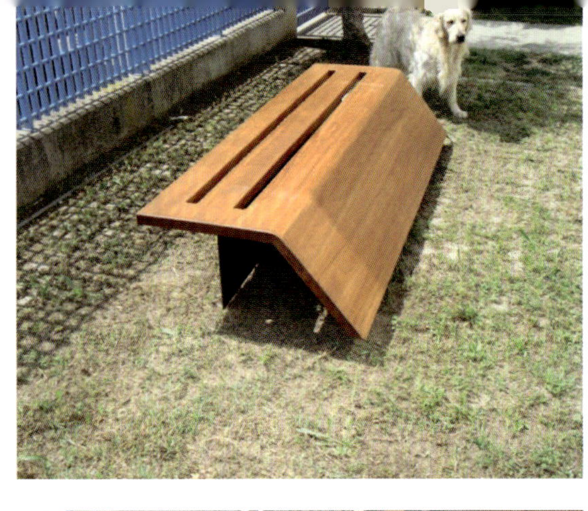

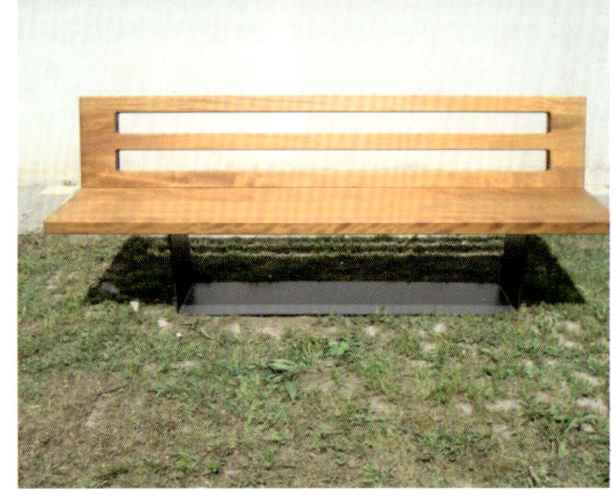

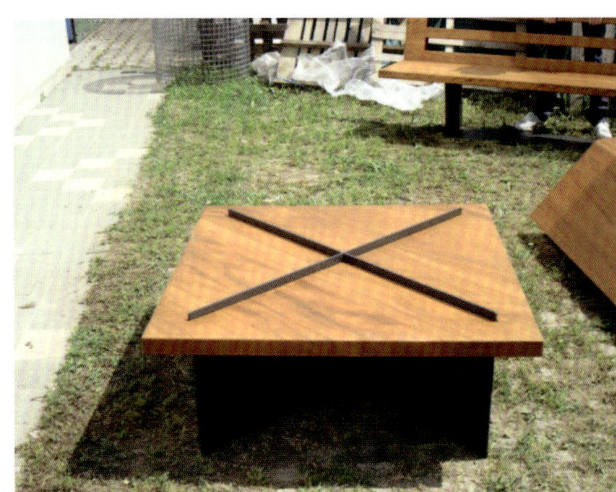

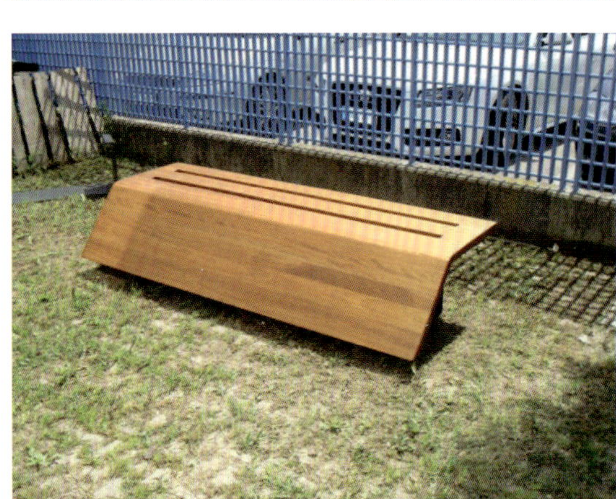

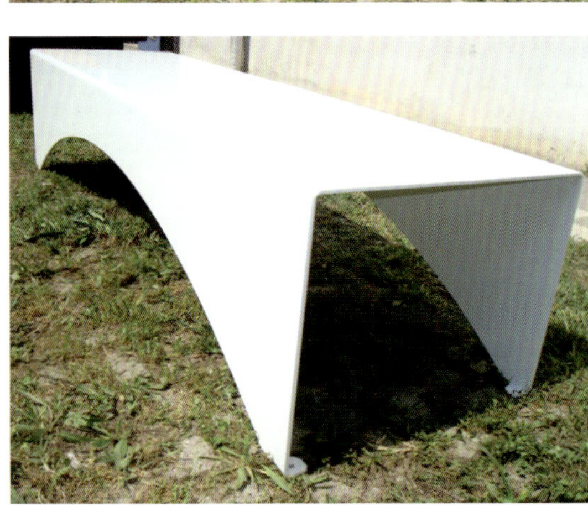

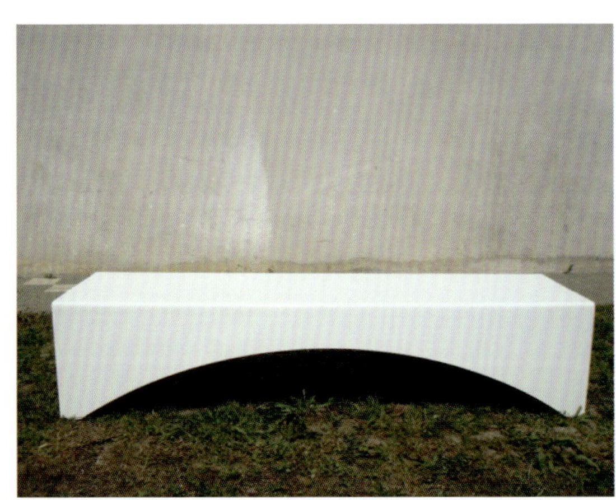

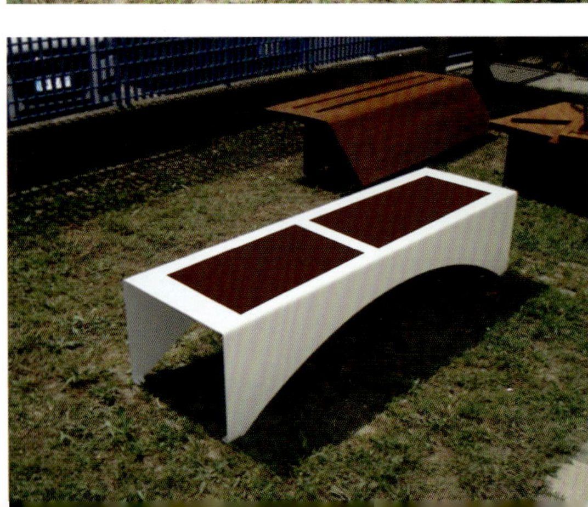

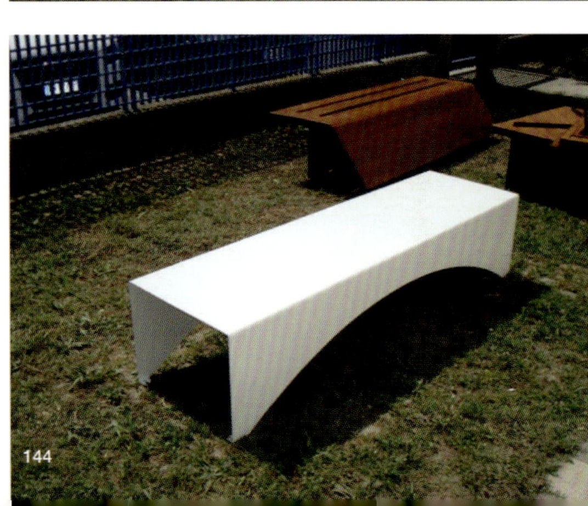

<u>At first sight, what is perceived is the vertical axis holding up the entire image, onto which the horizontal components are slotted to balance out the visual weight.</u> Immediately following this, the individual elements of the Cartesian space constructed in this manner take on increasing autonomy, catching the eye due to their position. In this way, the orthogonal structure holding up the entire layout shows itself for what it really is: a reference construction vital for preventing the entire visual arrangement from lapsing into centrifugal temptations but actually itself involved in creating its own characteristic dynamism. It is easy to see, behind this graphic layout, the embodiment of a philosophy of design placing Hangar Design Group activities firmly in mainstream contemporary visual culture, striving to try out new paths without breaking drastically with modern tradition and, on the contrary, actually testing out the validity of new, experimental approaches.

145.

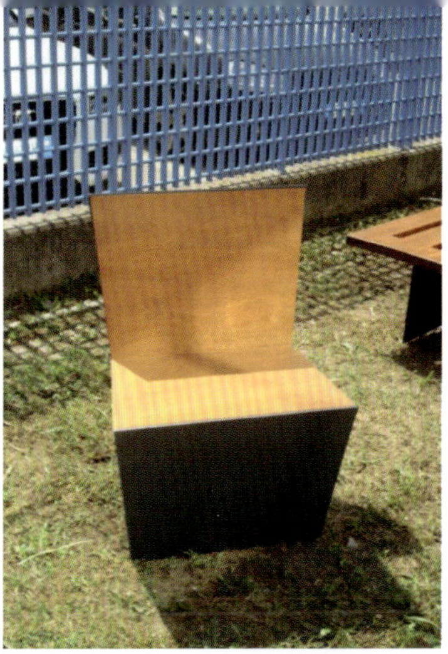

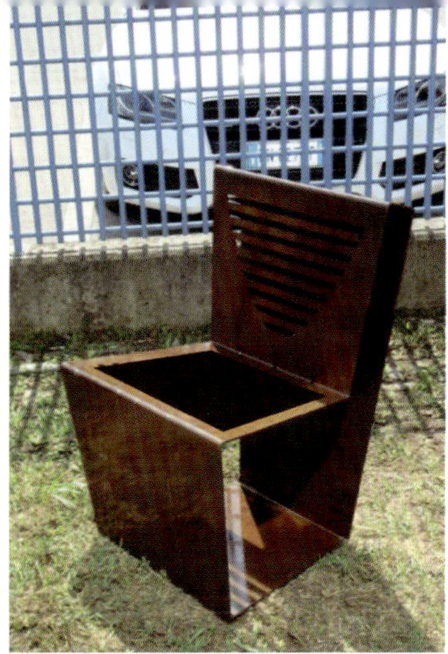

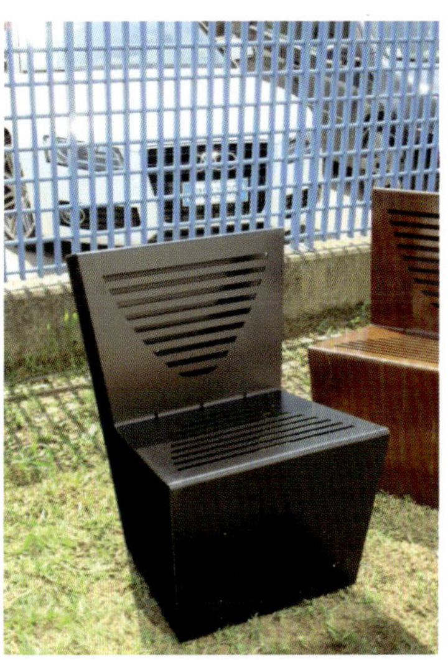

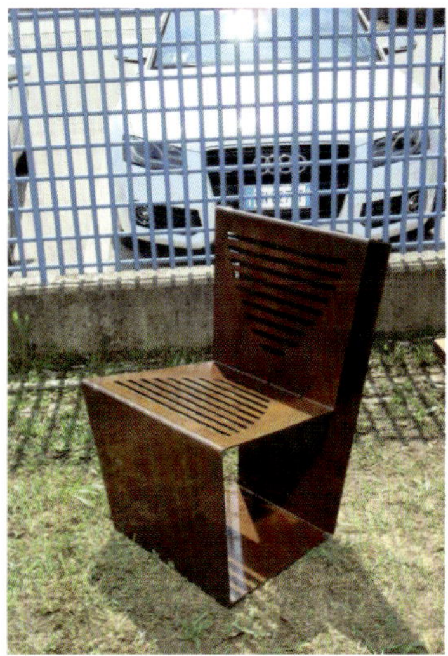

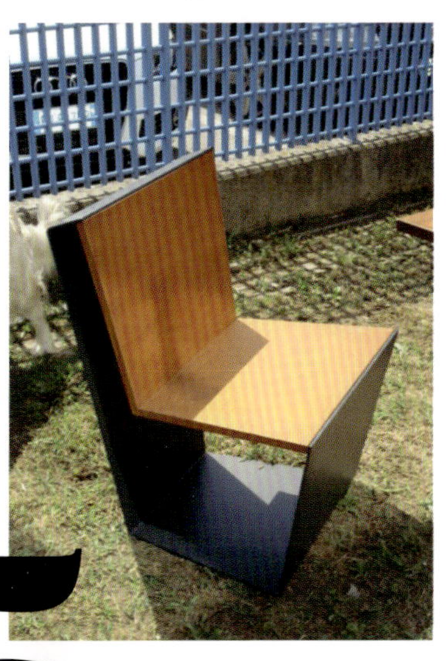

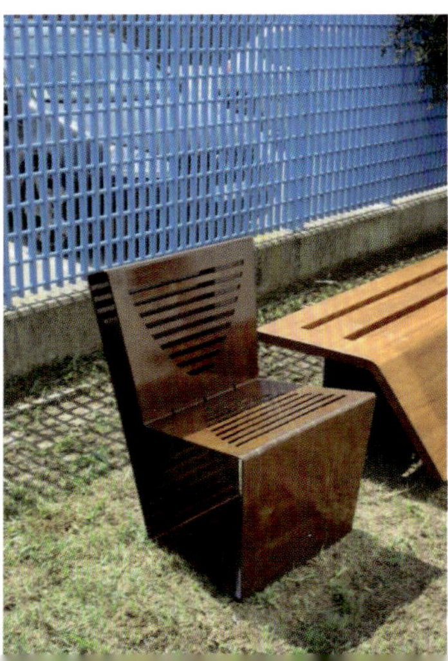

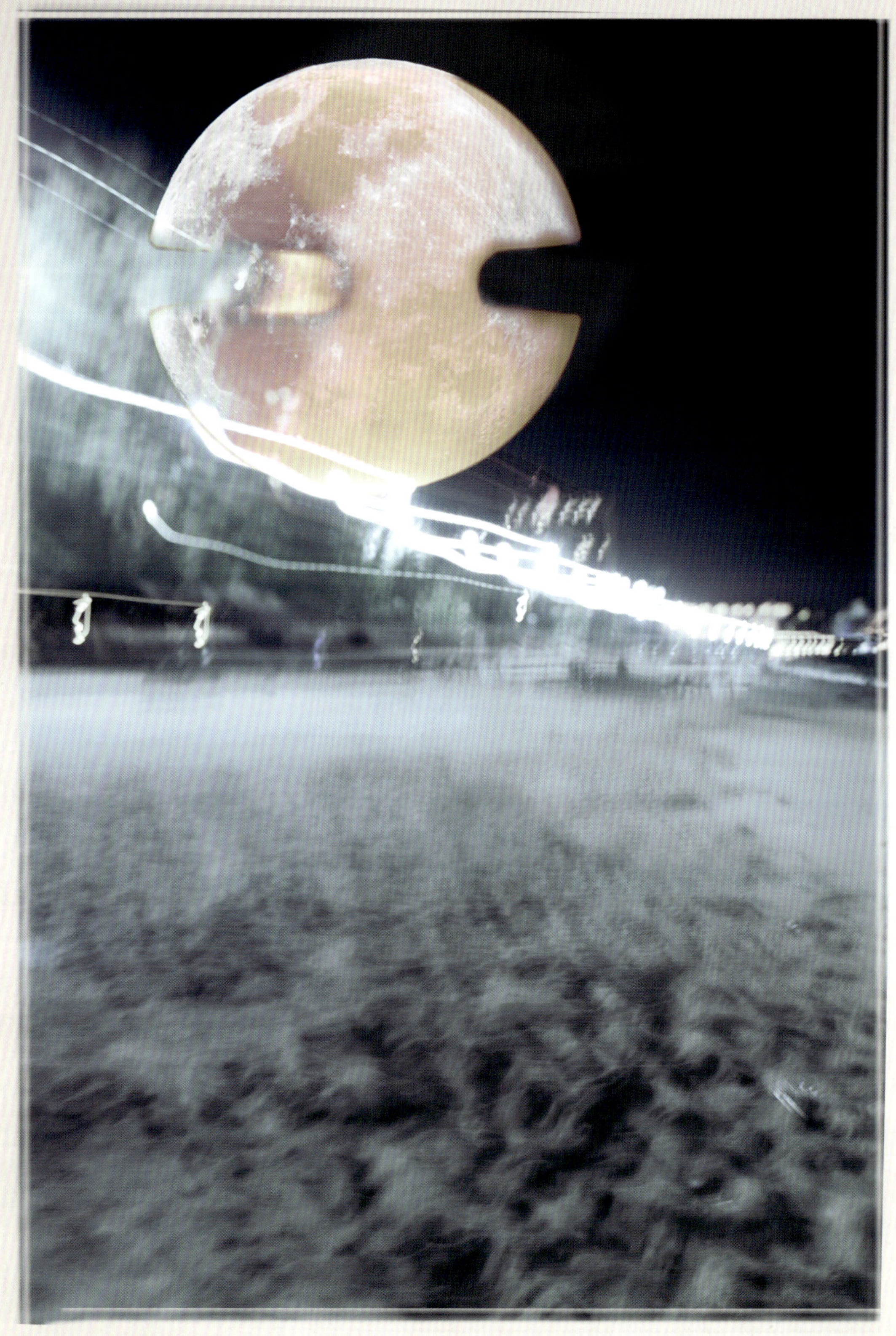

The utopian prospect
of "lawless order" – which
has already intrigued an entire
period of design – transpires
as a stimulus to call its very
self into play with every new
project, almost as if it were
a matter of constantly testing
whether the framework holds.
The classical figure
of concinnitas, guaranteeing
precision and continuity,
is always there in the
background.

variety of FORMS

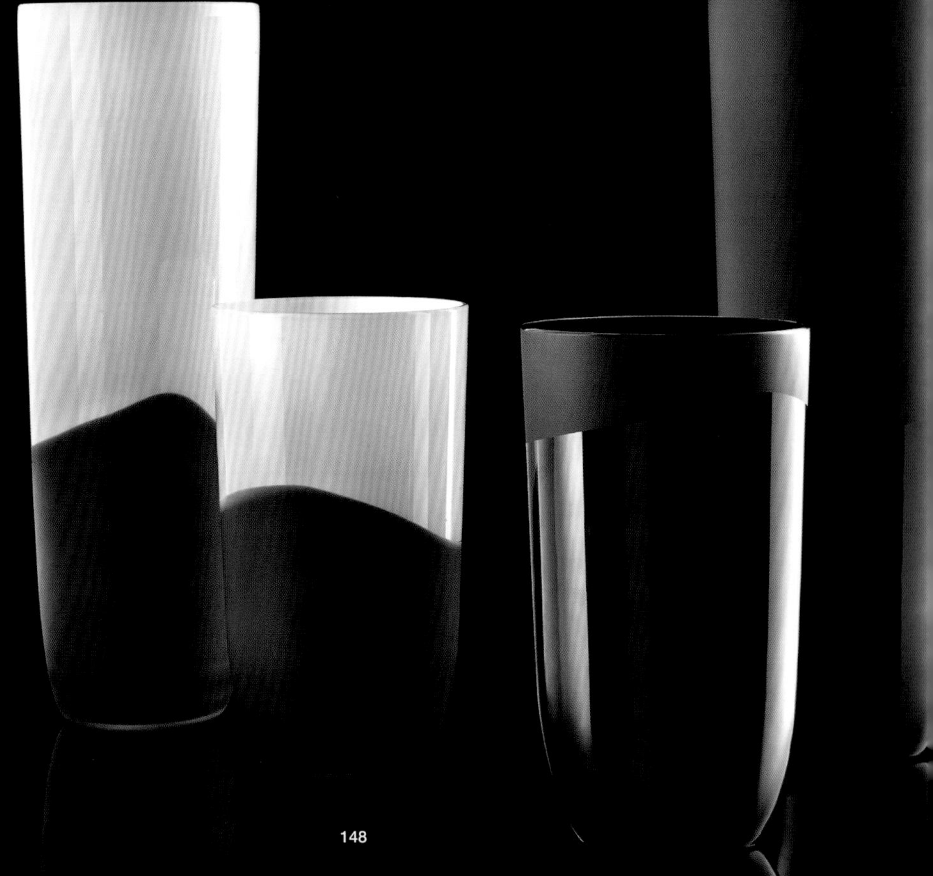

The form of things identifies with the form of ideas in the airship designs; and the ideas, gently swept out of the cool perfection of Platonic skies, are embodied in everyday life, injecting the full force of a philosophy of design projected into the future like some soaring bridge.

The lightness of signs, communicative force, toning down as a passionate means of listening to messages from the world, a sense of space taken as an opening up to the universe, technical precision and gentle abandonment to the winds of creativity, are all signs of a stylistic penchant rightly entitled to invoke the archetypal image of the airship as its own heraldic figure.

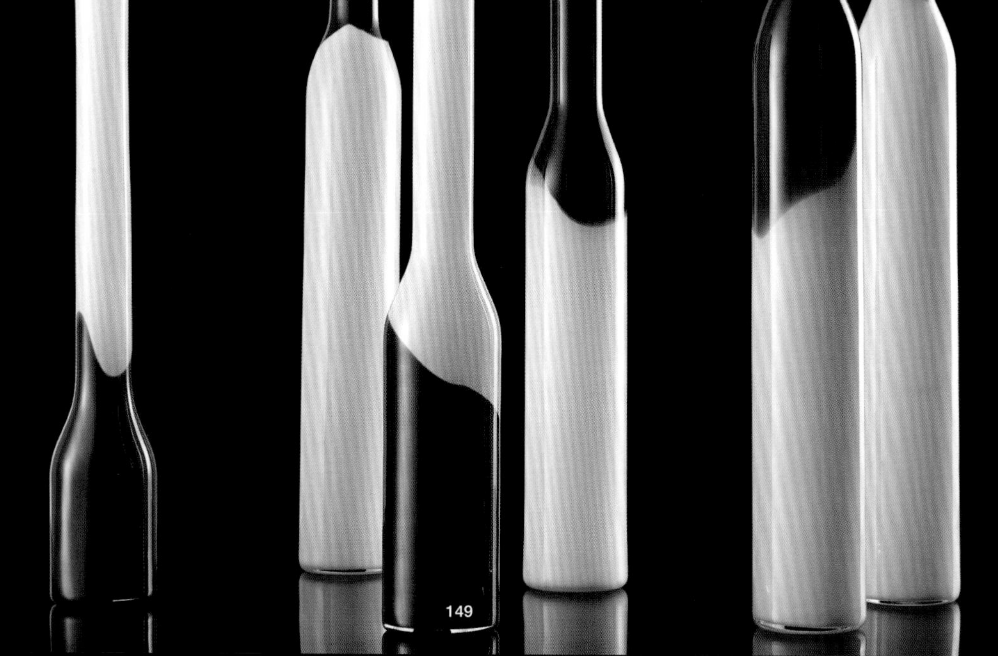

design in motion

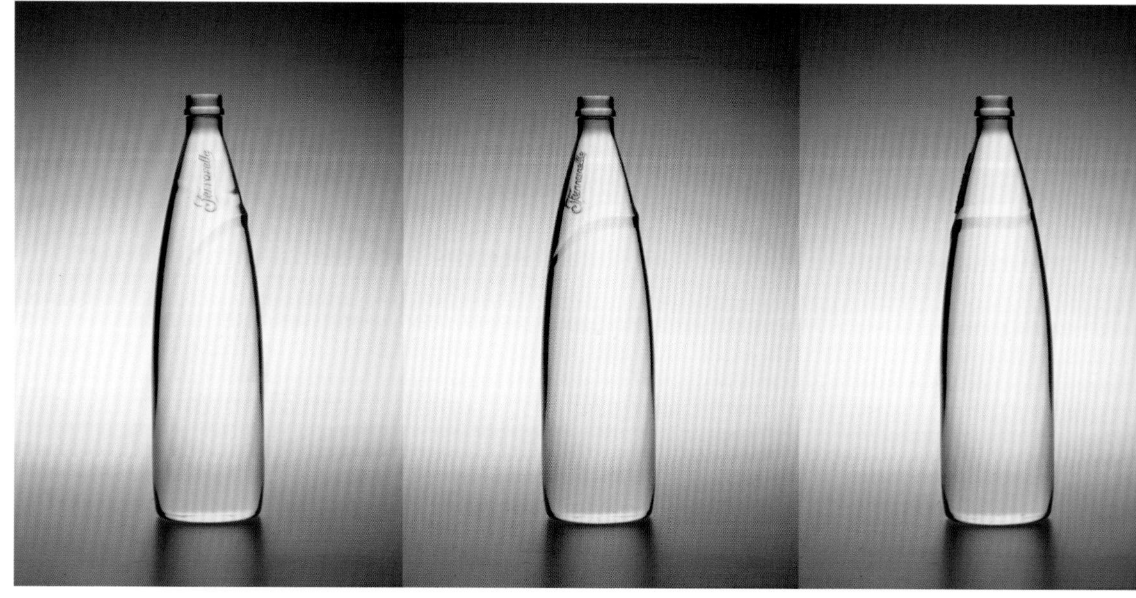

"Narrating" a product means setting it in a range of shifting and changing situations, in which its denotative properties – that piece of furniture, that lamp, that item of clothing – take on allusive connotations, raising our perceptual awareness into the realms of the imagination. This principle is revealed in the layering of images, opening up to color-light scenarios whose allusions to contemporary artistry have already been defined, setting the products in space as the main focus of representation and calculating the "scene" to perfection through carefully gauged spatial arrangements that look like film shots.

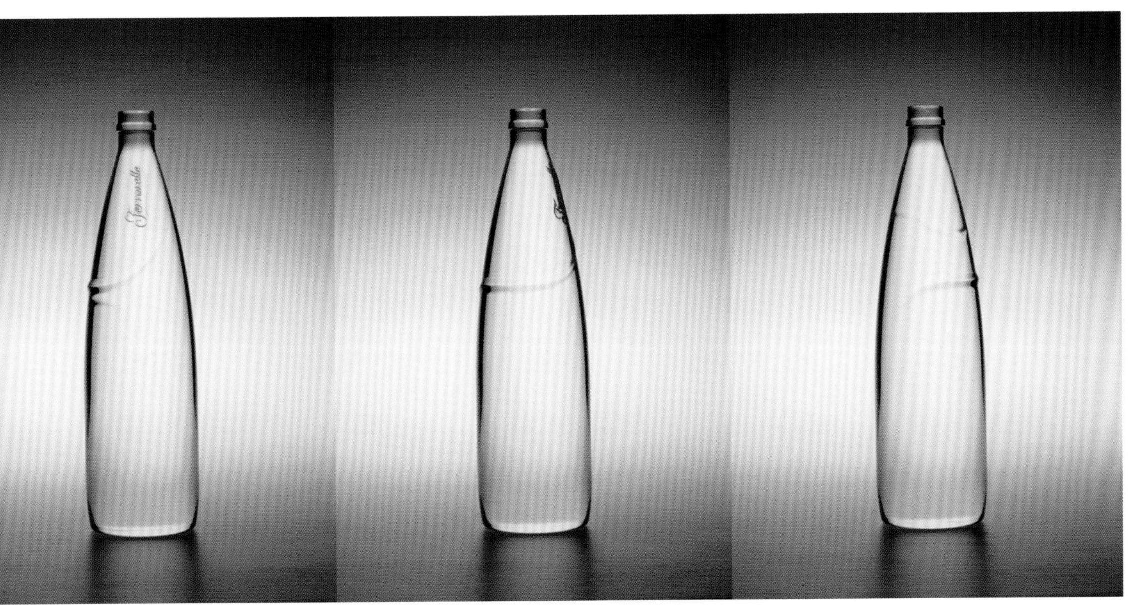

ACTUALLY, WE GOT MORE INTER-
ESTED IN ASKING QUESTIONS. IF THE
WORK WAS A CERTAIN SHAPE, SAY,
AS A METAPHOR, AS AN OBJECT,
WE WERE INTERESTED IN WHAT IT IS
THAT CAUSES THAT SHAPE.
WE BECAME INTERESTED IN THE
THINGS THAT WERE BEHIND THE
WORK, THE CONCEPTS THAT DROVE
THE WORK AND THE THINKING.
SO WE STARTED INVESTIGATING
THAT AND STARTED WRITING
AND RESEARCHING AND WE FOUND,
ACTUALLY, THAT THERE WAS NOTH-
ING ON THE MARKET TO REFER TO
THESE THINGS THAT WERE RUNNING
THROUGH US, SO WE STARTED
TO WRITE ABOUT THEM
AND ARTICULATE THEM.

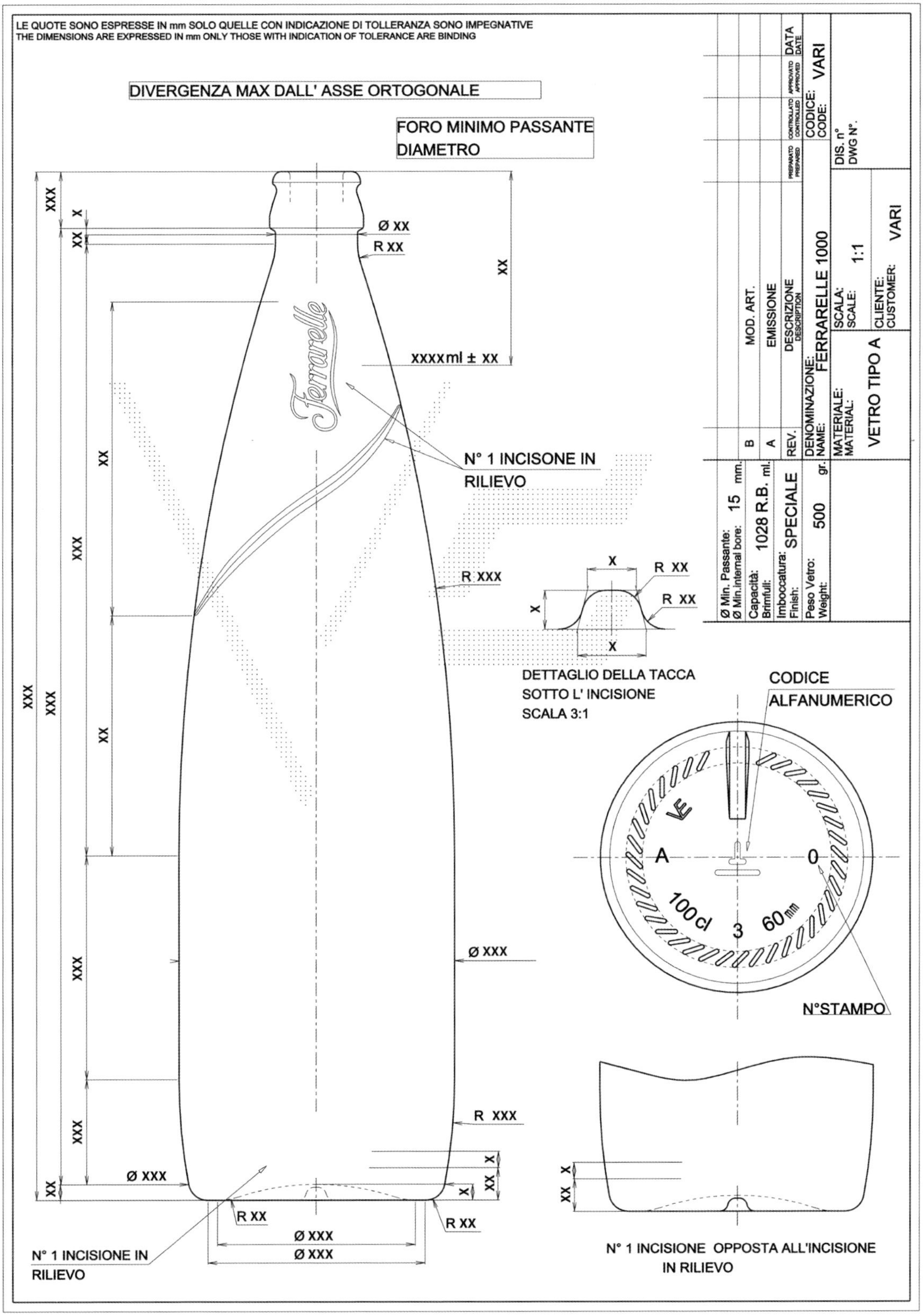

LE QUOTE SONO ESPRESSE IN mm SOLO QUELLE CON INDICAZIONE DI TOLLERANZA SONO IMPEGNATIVE
THE DIMENSIONS ARE EXPRESSED IN mm ONLY THOSE WITH INDICATION OF TOLERANCE ARE BINDING

DIVERGENZA MAX DALL' ASSE ORTOGONALE

FORO MINIMO PASSANTE
DIAMETRO

Ø XX
R XX

XX

xxxxml ± xx

N° 1 INCISONE IN
RILIEVO

R XXX

X
R XX
R XX
X
X

DETTAGLIO DELLA TACCA
SOTTO L' INCISIONE
SCALA 3:1

CODICE
ALFANUMERICO

A   0
100cl   3   60mm

N°STAMPO

Ø XXX

Ø XXX

R XXX

Ø XXX

R XX
Ø XXX
Ø XXX
R XX

N° 1 INCISIONE IN
RILIEVO

N° 1 INCISIONE OPPOSTA ALL'INCISIONE
IN RILIEVO

DATA
DATE
VARI

CODICE:
CODE:

PREPARATO   CONTROLLATO   APPROVATO
PREPARED   CONTROLLED   APPROVED

DIS. n°
DWG N°.

MOD. ART.

EMISSIONE

DESCRIZIONE
DESCRIPTION

FERRARELLE 1000

SCALA:
SCALE: 1:1

CLIENTE:
CUSTOMER: VARI

VETRO TIPO A

DENOMINAZIONE:
gr. NAME:

MATERIALE:
MATERIAL:

REV.   B   A

Ø Min. Passante:
Ø Min.internal bore: 15   mm.

Capacità:
Brimfull: 1028 R.B. ml.

Imboccatura:
Finish: SPECIALE

Peso Vetro:
Weight: 500   gr.

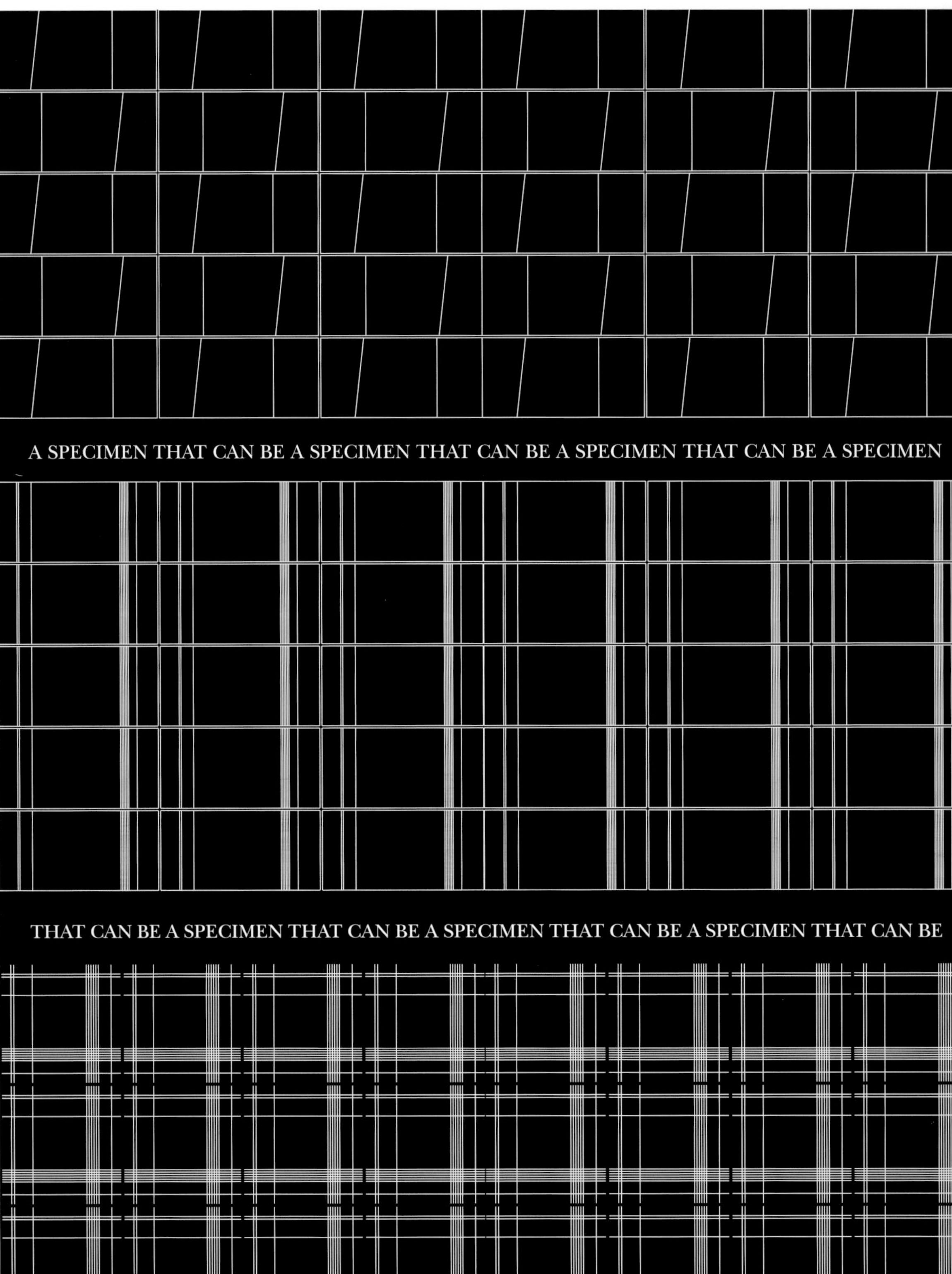

A SPECIMEN THAT CAN BE A SPECIMEN THAT CAN BE A SPECIMEN THAT CAN BE A SPECIMEN
THAT CAN BE A SPECIMEN THAT CAN BE A SPECIMEN THAT CAN BE A SPECIMEN THAT CAN BE

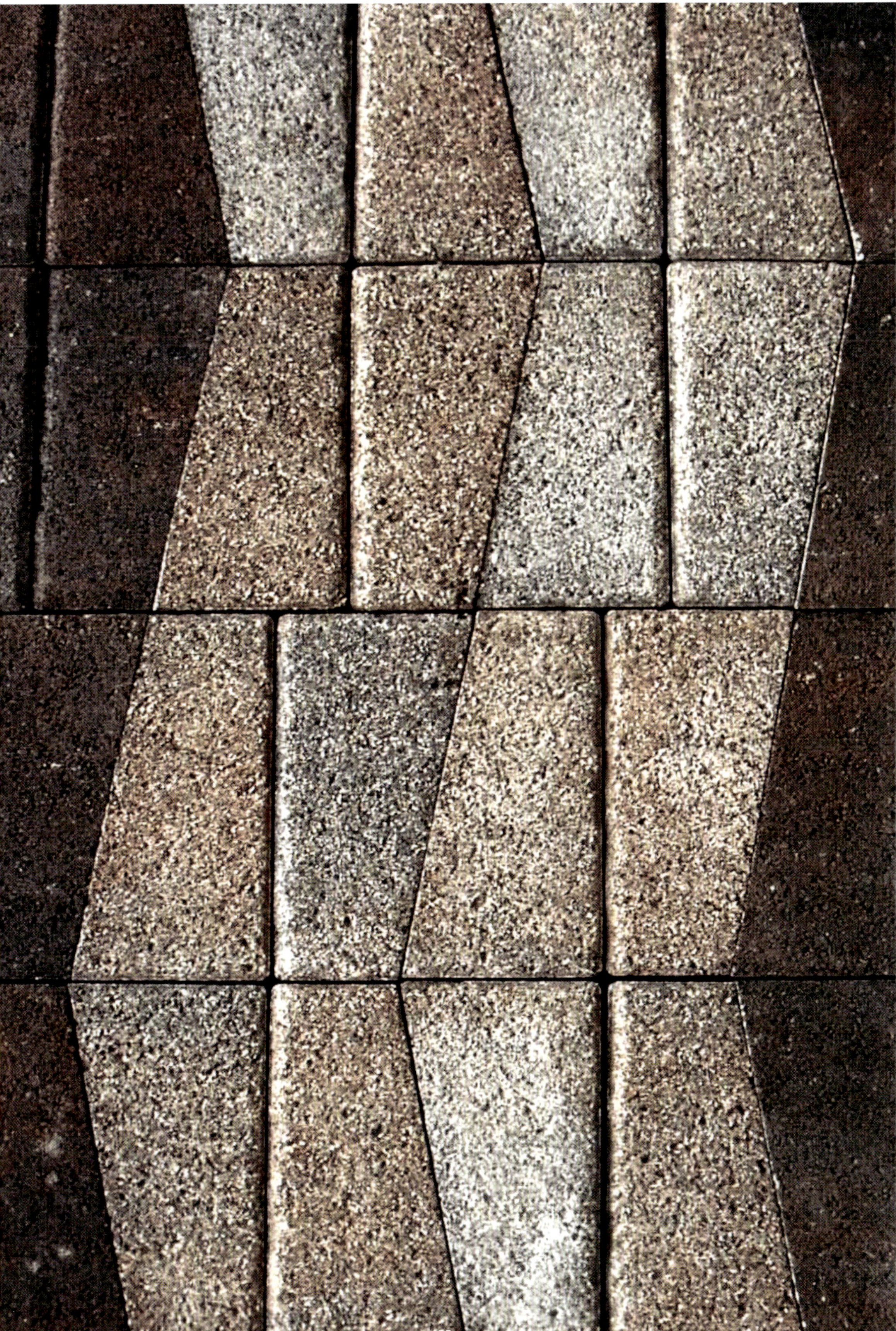

by design:
TOTAL AESTHETICS

So what is the organic process? How is it possible to create a product that lasts today? In a word: aesthetics. We're not speaking of something pretty, but rather a holistic aesthetics – the look, the feel, and the soul that when perfectly fused create a genuine point of difference. Aesthetics isn't just a surface, it's the total essence, from A to Z. And it comes not from hip tactics or trendy gimmicks but rather from one's personal vision.

FAMILY
OBLIQUE

APPLIQUE
SCALA 1 : 1

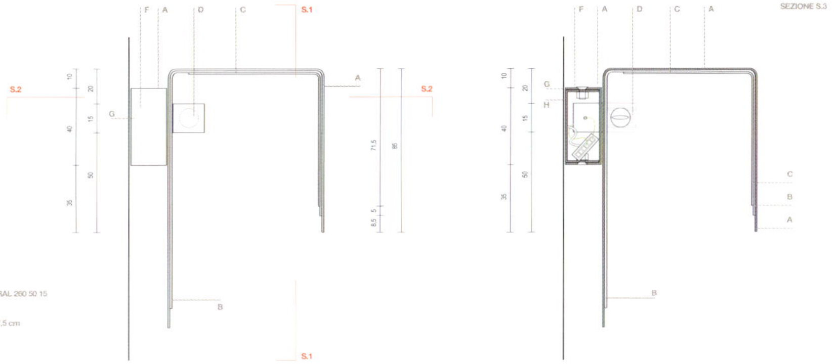

SEZIONE S.3

A . Superficie verniciata colore BIANCO RAL 9010
B . Superficie verniciata colore PANTONE 5415 C \ RAL 260 50 15
C . Superficie riflettente o bianco opaco
D . Portalampade con attacco R7s cm 11,5
E . Lampada alogena a tensione di rete Z nominale 7,5 cm
F . Staffa Portalampada\Plafone
G . Scatola copricavi
H . Scatola per attacco a parete

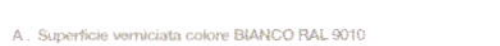

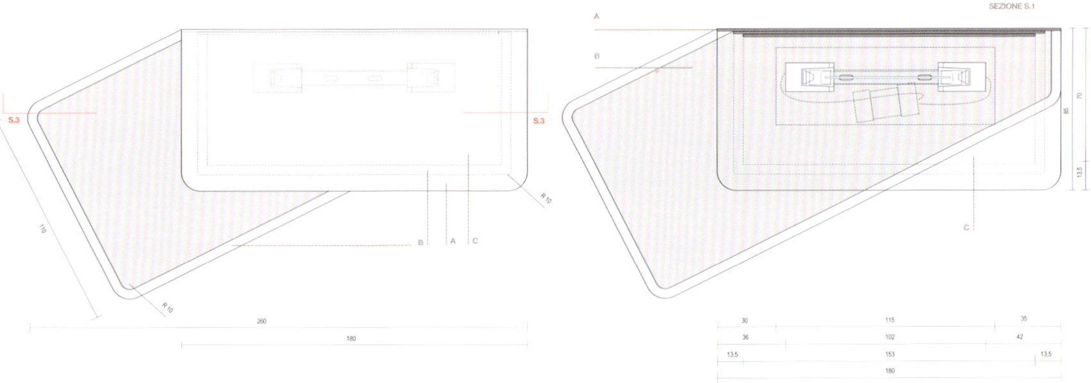

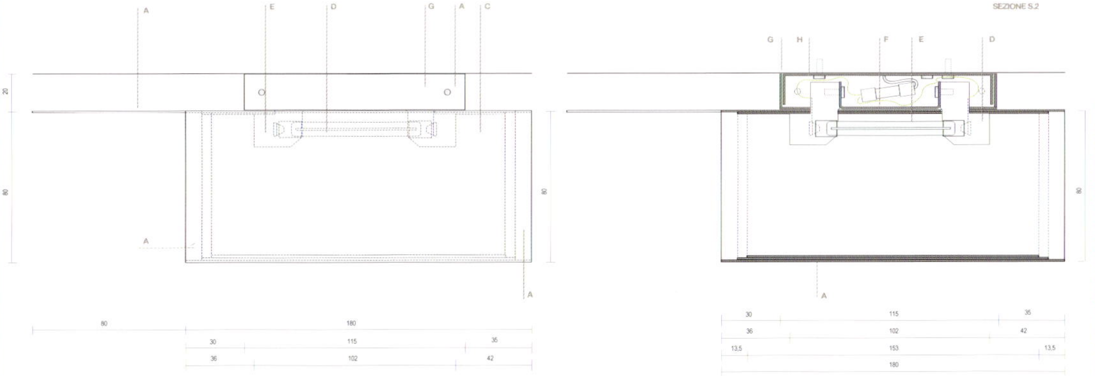

SEZIONE S.1

SEZIONE S.2

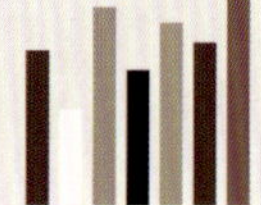

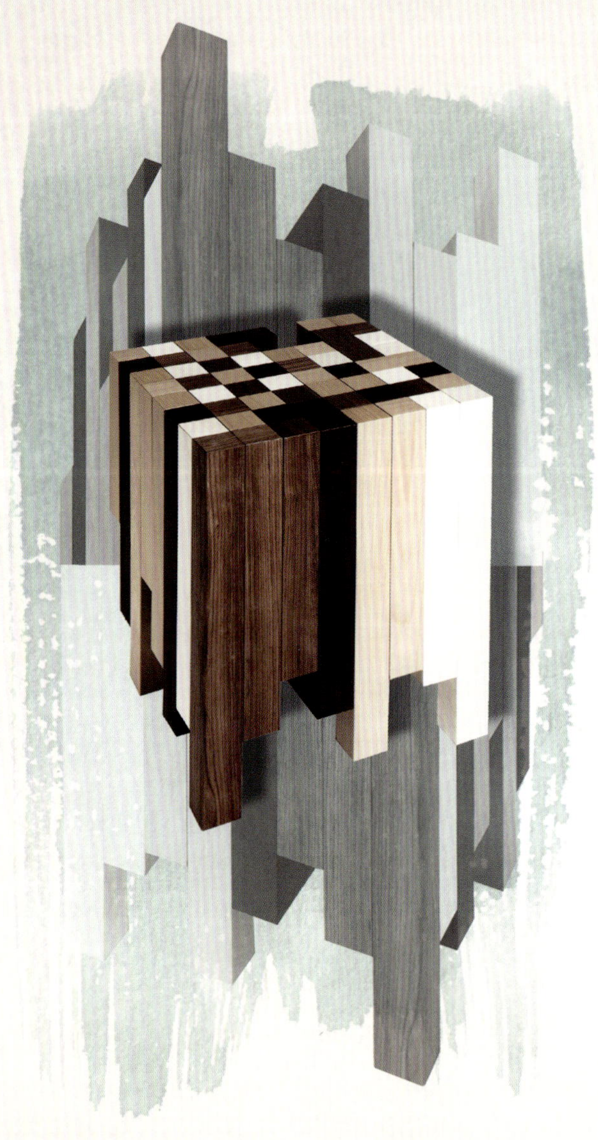

Illusions of the senses tell us
the truth about perception.

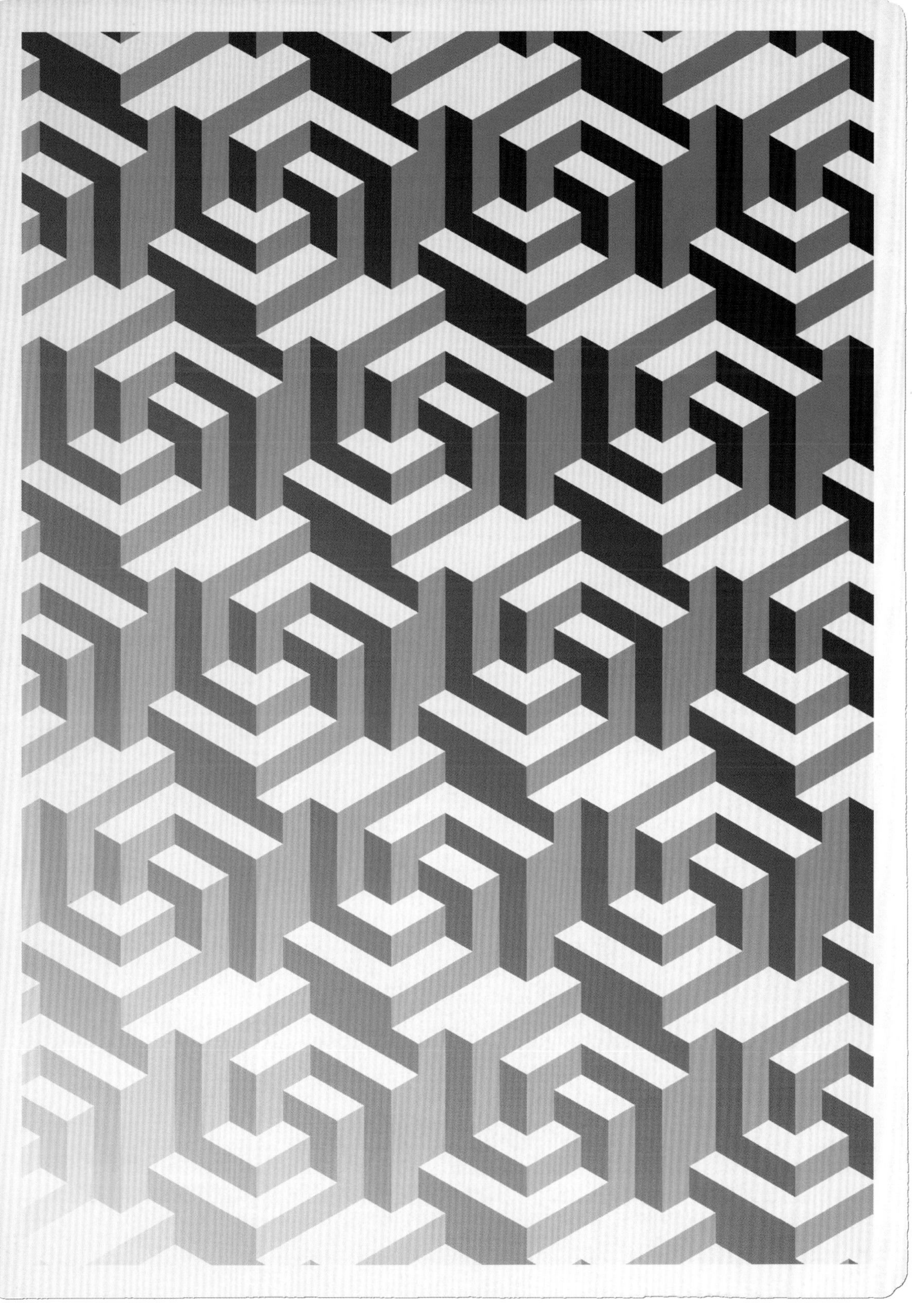

160.

HANGAR PREFAB
HOUSING
ALTERNATIVE
PROJECT
HANGAR PREFAB | CENTRAL LIVING
W   F
HANGAR PREFAB | WHITE COUNTY
HANGAR PREFAB | WHITE COUNTY
OPEN SPACE
HANGAR PREFAB | ICARO BAY
SIDE LIVING
HANGAR PREFAB | ICARO BAY
HANGAR PREFAB | CAPE VILLE
HANGAR PREFAB | MARSHALL PEACK
HANGAR PREFAB | MARSHALL PEACK
HANGAR PREFAB | MARSHALL PEACK
SIDE LIVING
HANGAR PREFAB | HIGH VALLEY
HANGAR PREFAB | HIGH VALLEY
CENTRAL LIVING
HANGAR PREFAB | WELLCOME HOME

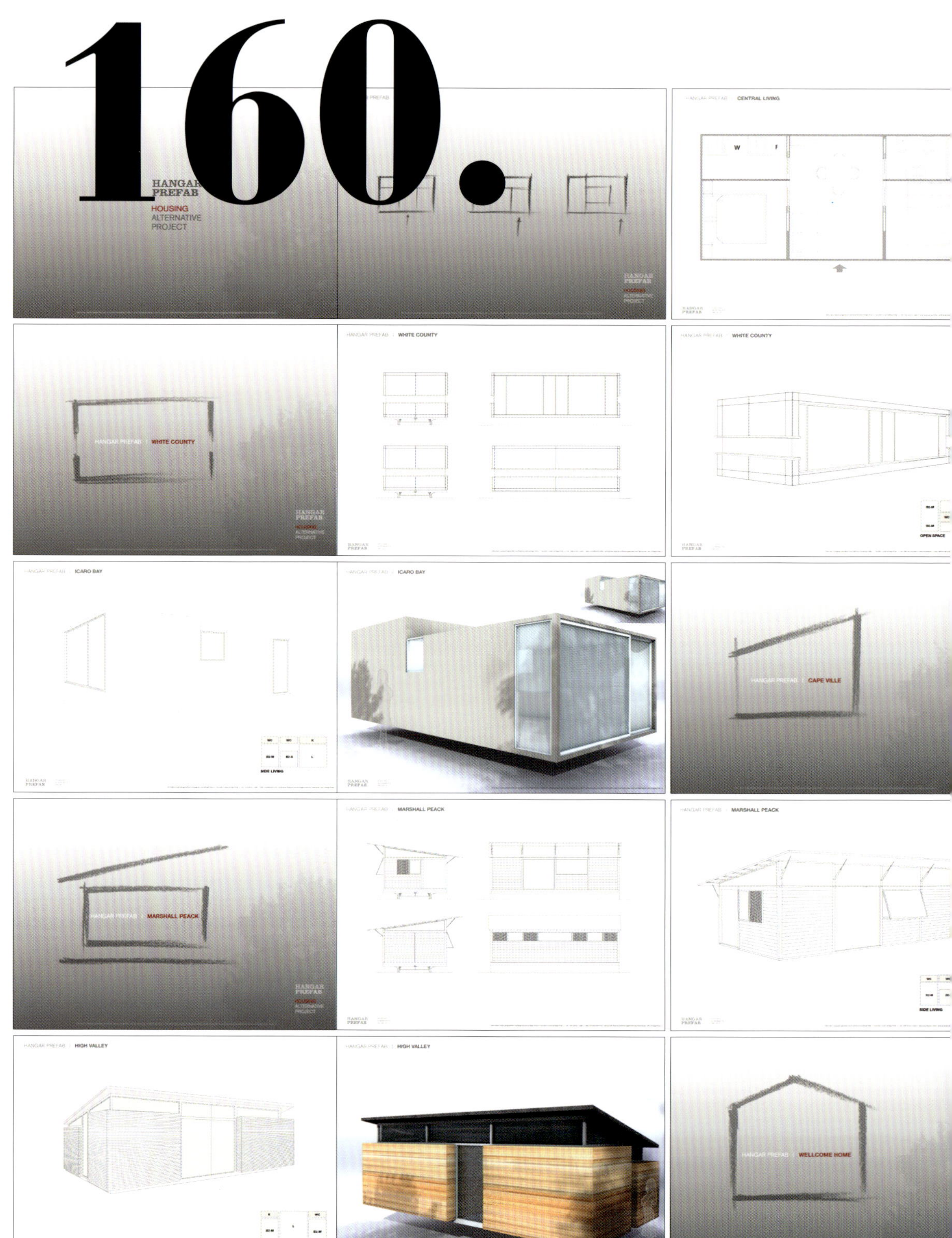

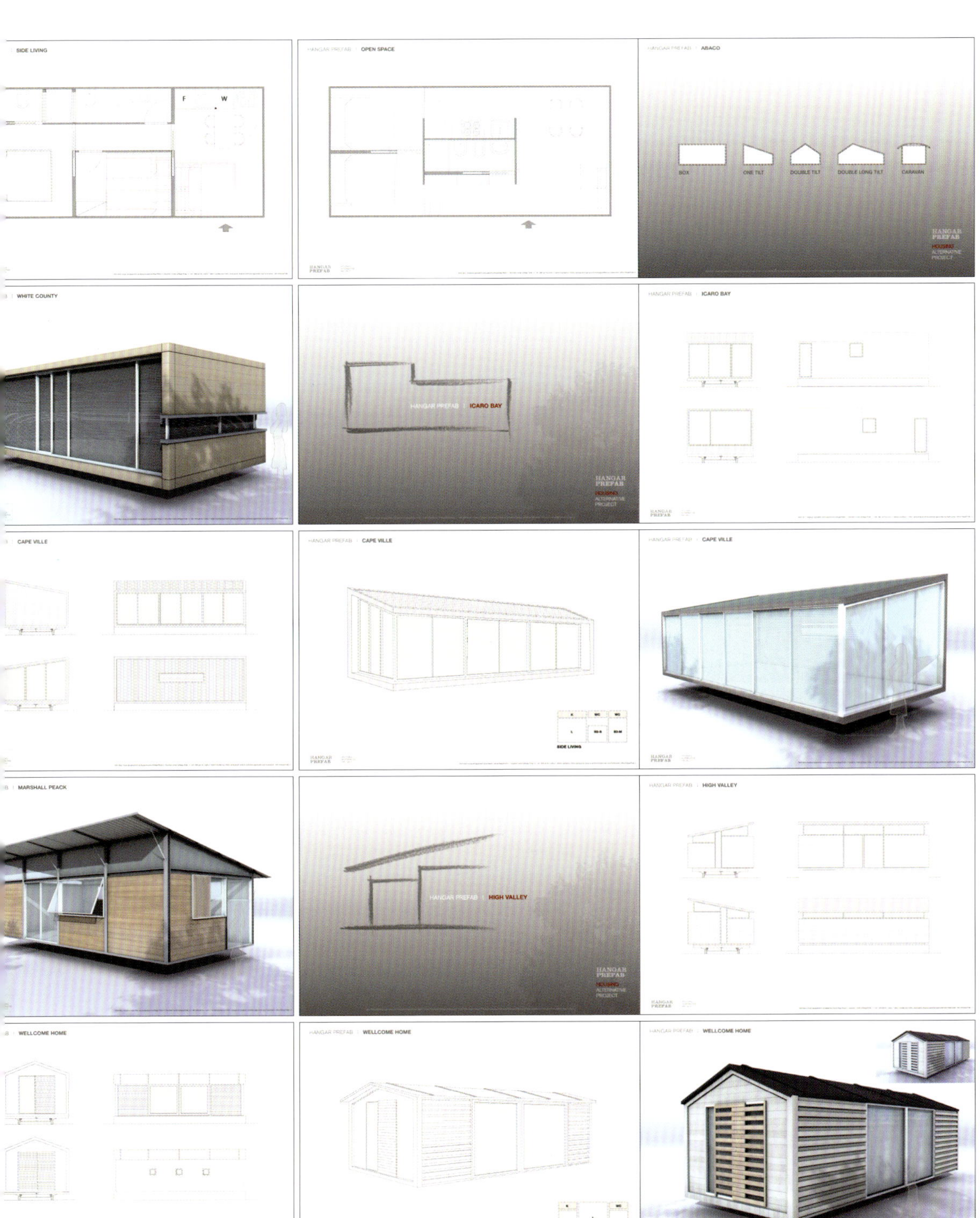

SIDE LIVING
F W
HANGAR PREFAB OPEN SPACE
HANGAR PREFAB ABACO
BOX
ONE TILT
DOUBLE TILT
DOUBLE LONG TILT
CARAVAN
HANGAR PREFAB
HOUSING
ALTERNATIVE PROJECT
WHITE COUNTY
HANGAR PREFAB ICARO BAY
HANGAR PREFAB ICARO BAY
HANGAR PREFAB
HOUSING
ALTERNATIVE PROJECT
CAPE VILLE
HANGAR PREFAB CAPE VILLE
HANGAR PREFAB CAPE VILLE
SIDE LIVING
MARSHALL PEACK
HANGAR PREFAB HIGH VALLEY
HANGAR PREFAB HIGH VALLEY
HANGAR PREFAB
HOUSING
ALTERNATIVE PROJECT
WELLCOME HOME
HANGAR PREFAB WELLCOME HOME
HANGAR PREFAB WELLCOME HOME
CENTRAL LIVING

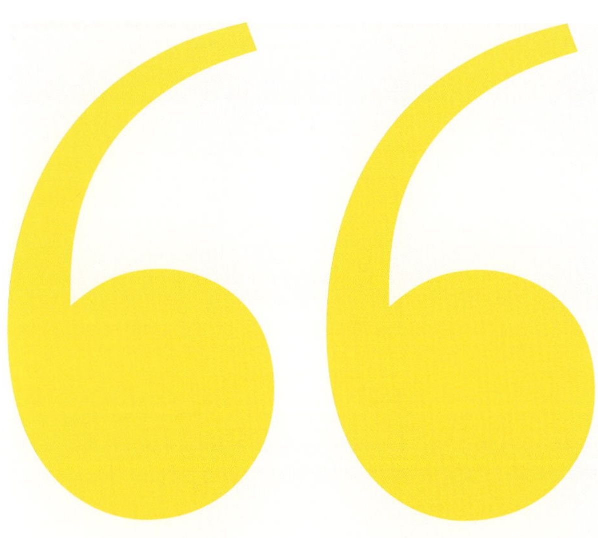

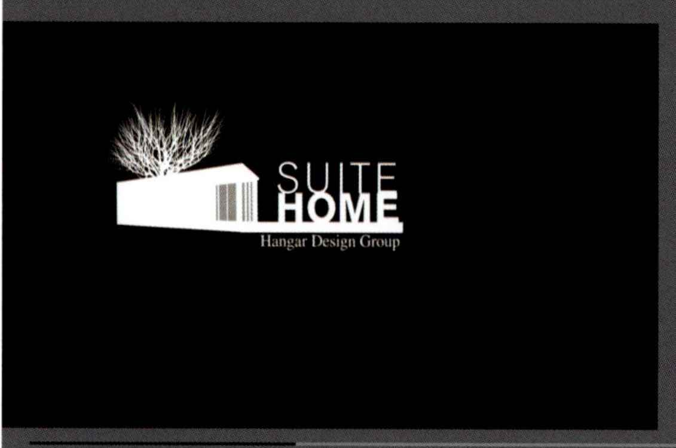

SUITE
HOME
Hangar Design Group

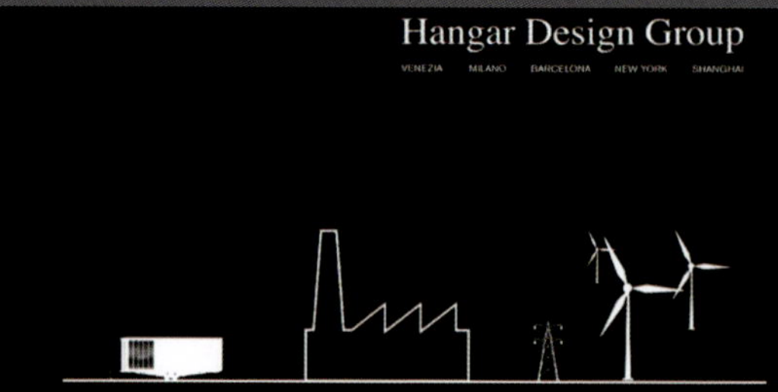

Hangar Design Group
VENEZIA   MILANO   BARCELONA   NEW YORK   SHANGHAI
home revolution.
From the factory to your place and viceversa

<u>This interconnection of skills occasionally occurs at the
outset of the creative process, in which case the work itself
evolves from an act of communication.</u> So that communication becomes an intrinsic element of the architectonic
object, as the act which generates it or as the objective to be
achieved by the object itself when finished. For us, communication will become increasingly evident in design, just as
we would hope that design will become increasingly evident
in communication…

<u>We believe that a design should not simply be an expres-
sion of itself, but should also be capable of recounting an
experience, a story made up of people</u> – over and above the
unquestioned aesthetic credentials of the design. A design
should reveal an international language, and most of all
it should be "alive."

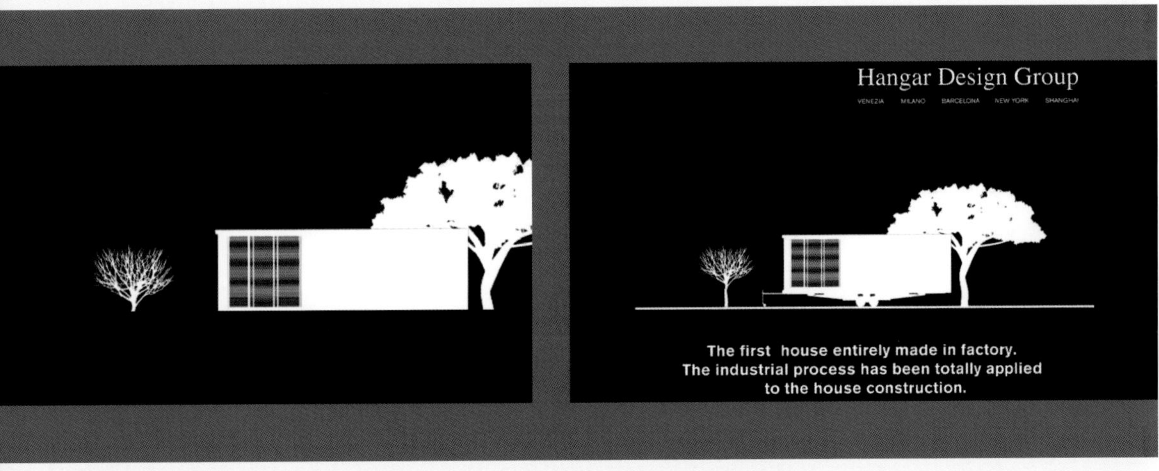

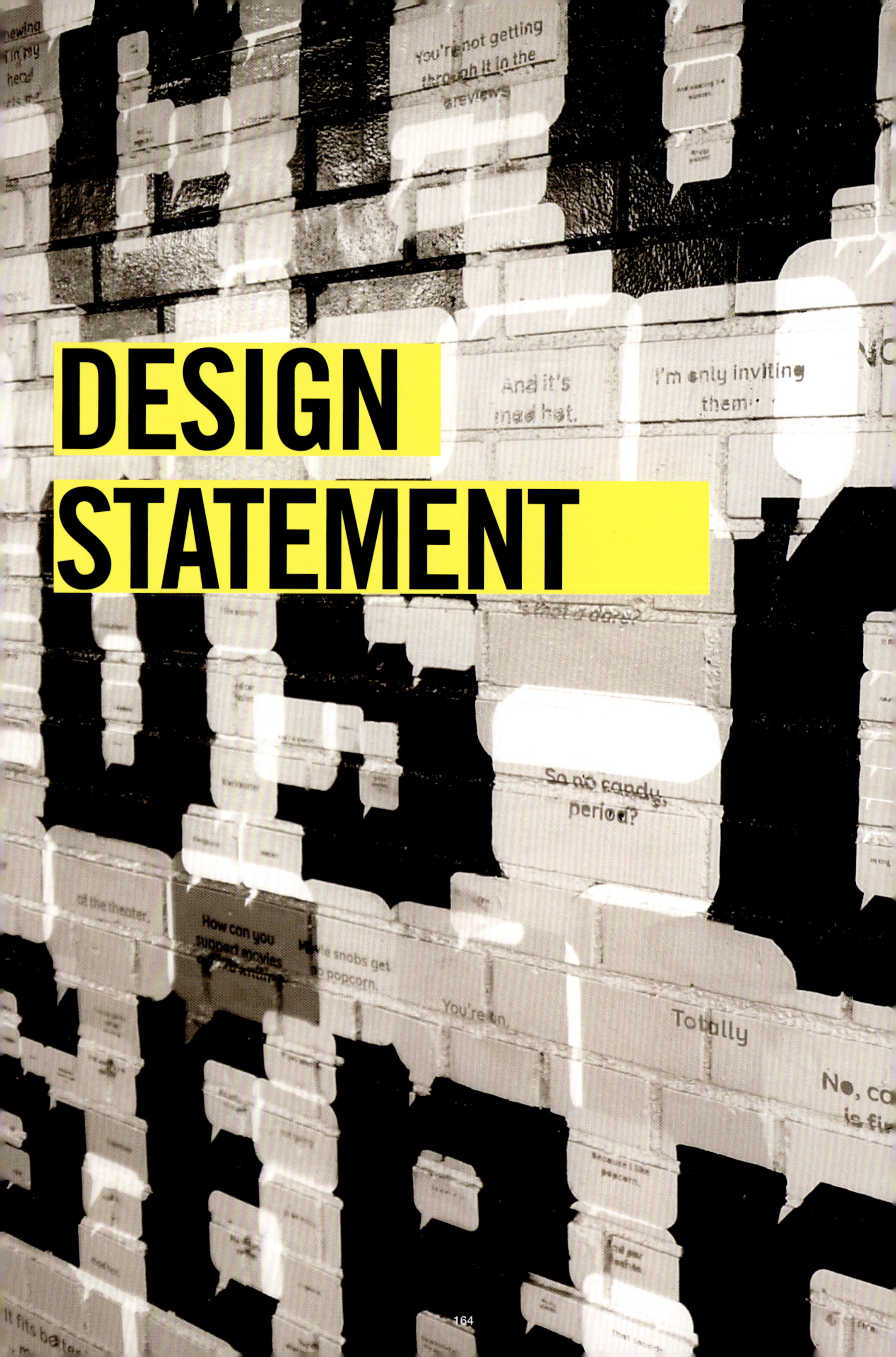

DESIGN STATEMENT

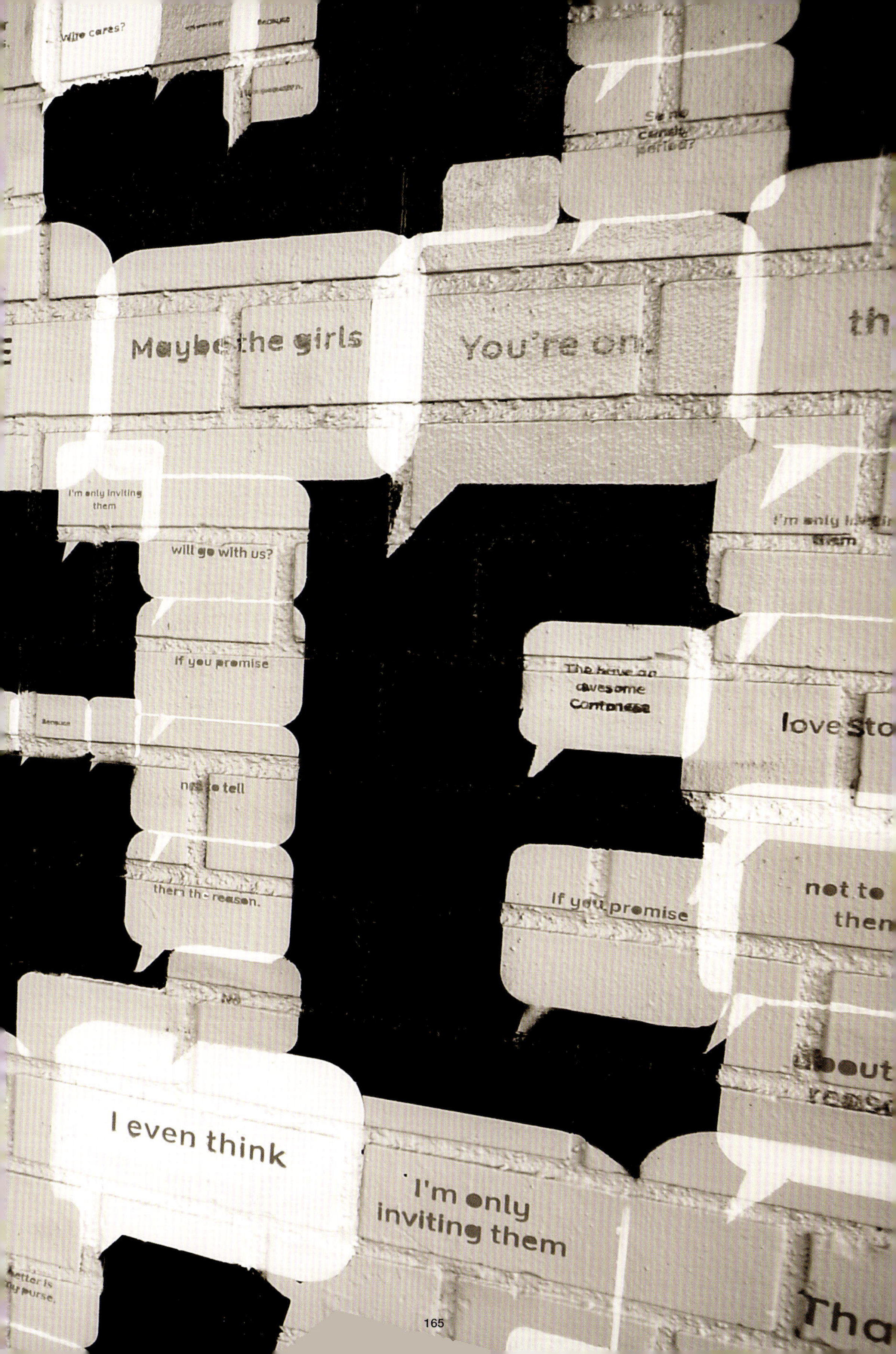
Who cares?
Maybe the girls
You're on
I'm only inviting them
will go with us?
If you promise
They have an awesome Cantonese
love sto
not to tell
If you promise
not to then
then the reason.
I even think
I'm only inviting them

166.

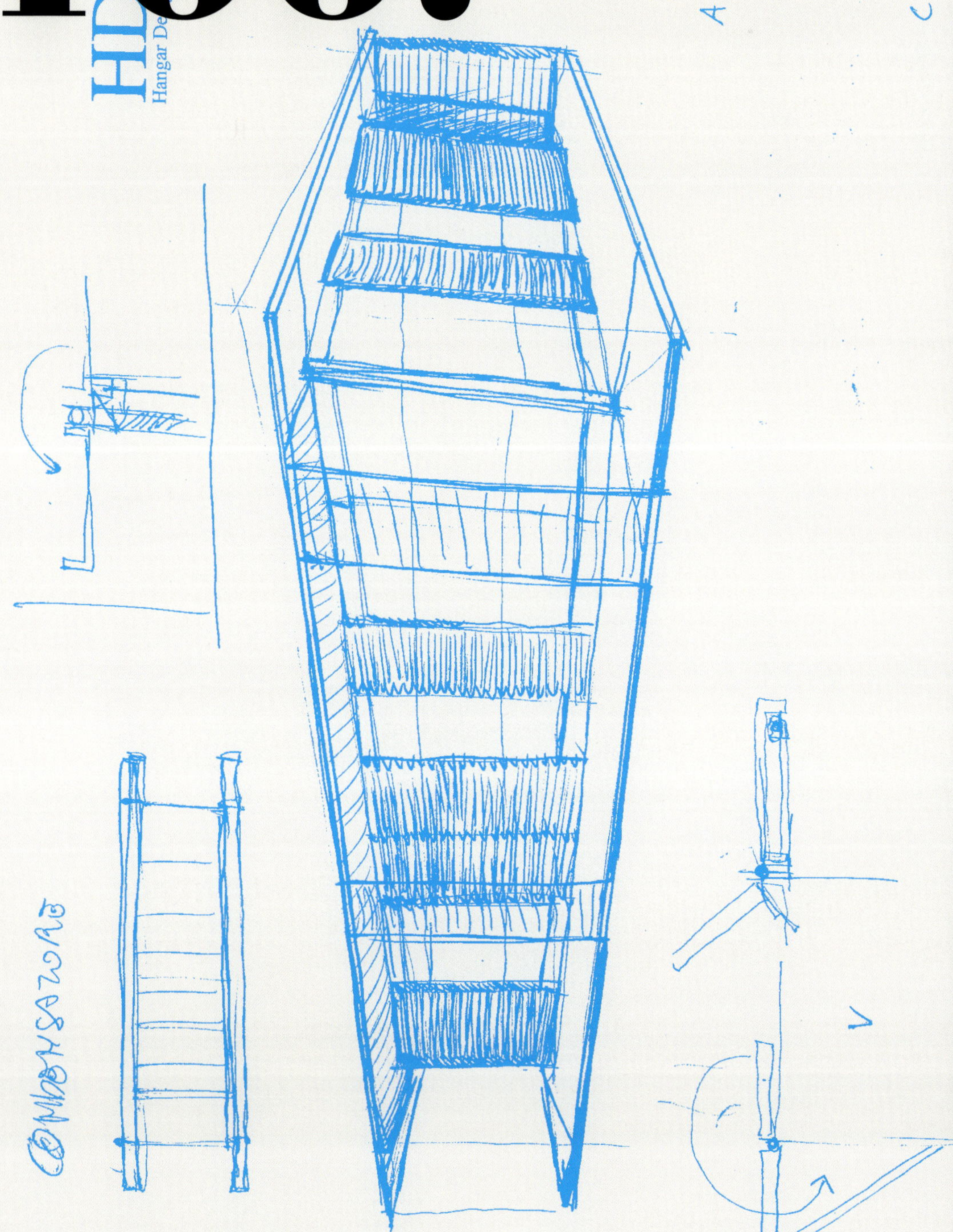

But it's still about the concepts behind the work. So it looks at symmetry, it looks at equilibrium, at invariance – which I think is a very interesting concept: **"What is invariant?" You know, what varies? What is changeable? What doesn't change?** We are not interested in the image itself. Its significance lies in the fact that it contains the sum of former dialogues, stories and experiences with several interlocutors. Also because it causes these pre-existing values to be brought forward. This is a suitable image. A good image should be in the middle of two others, the previous one and the one to come.

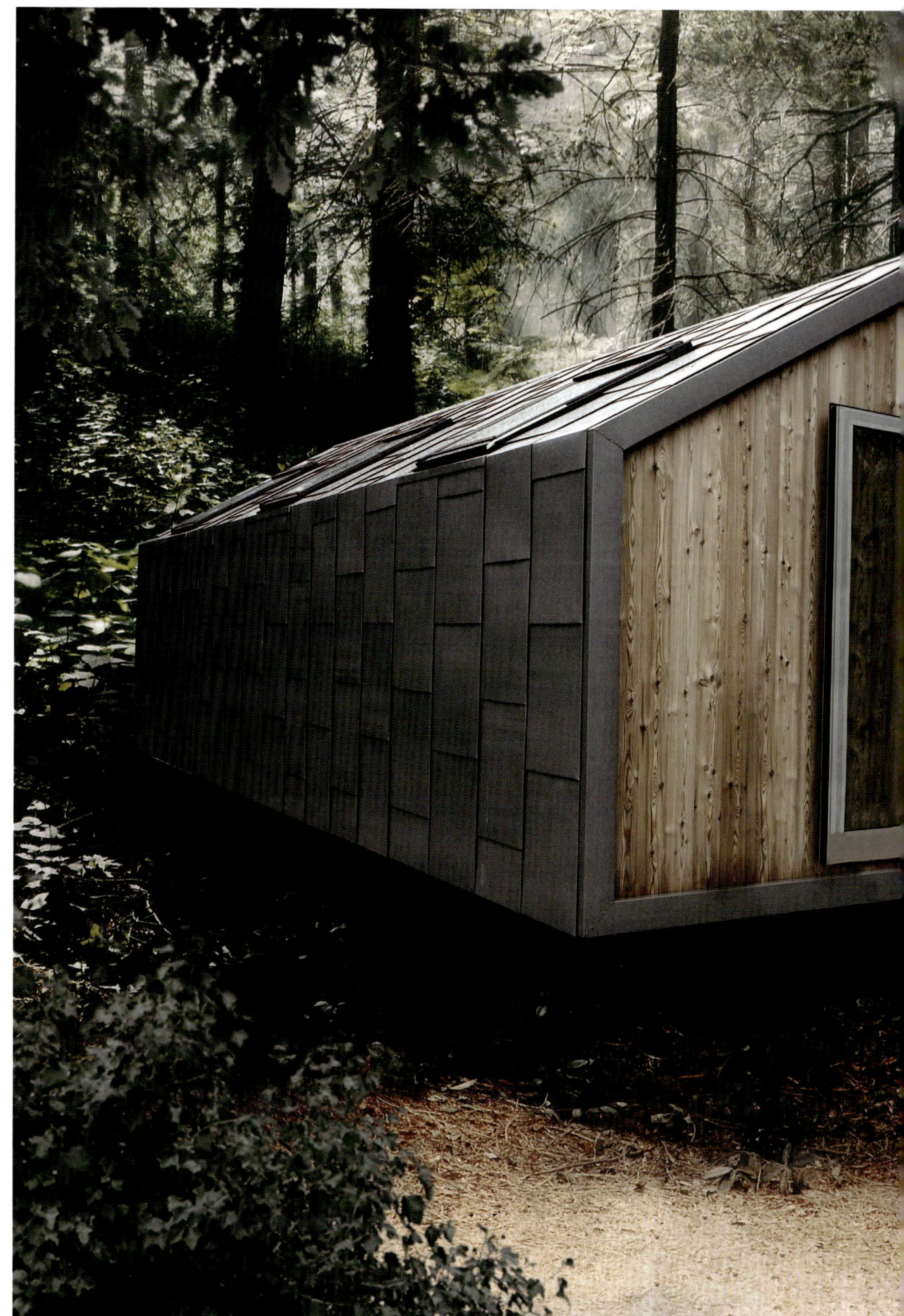

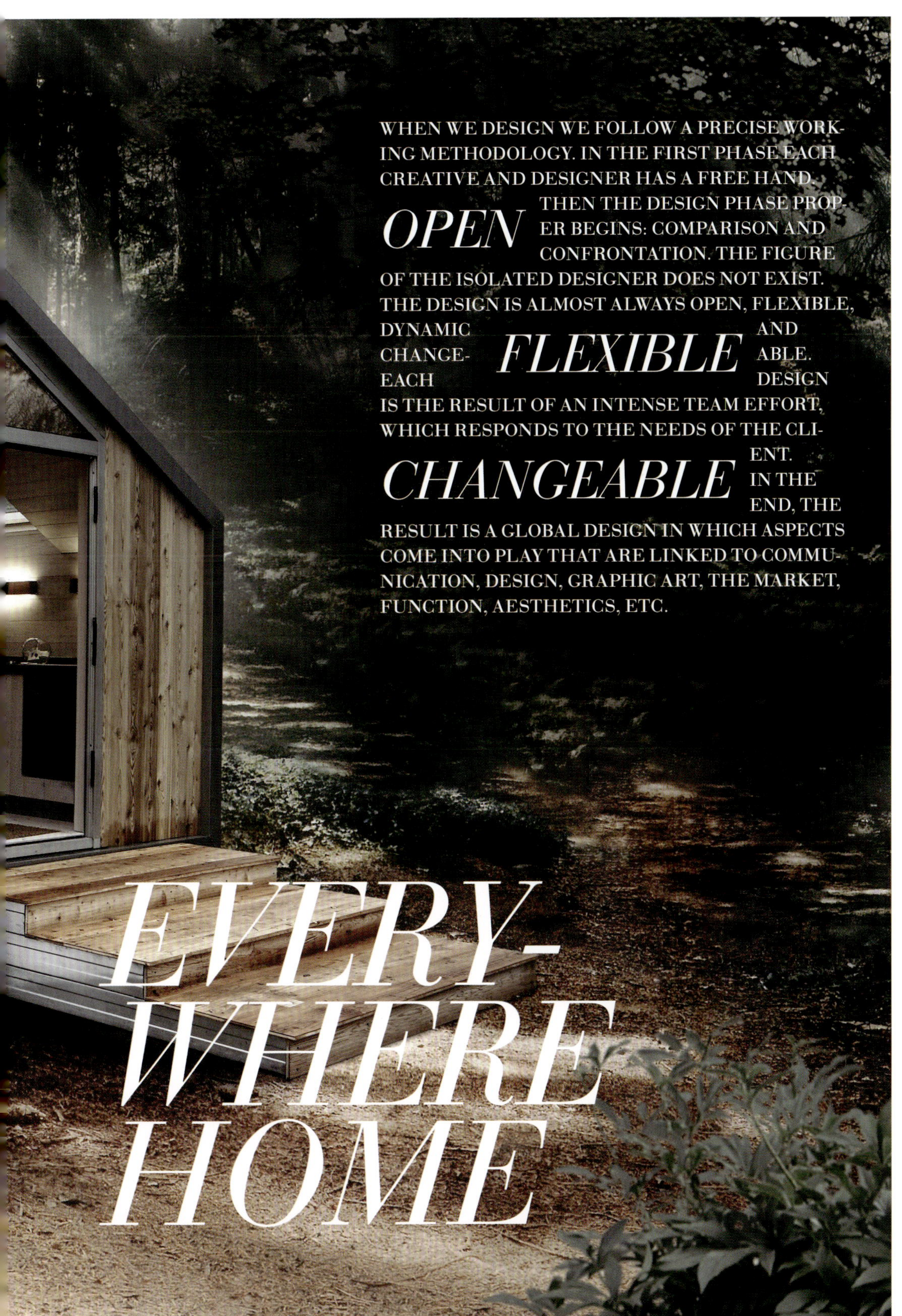

WHEN WE DESIGN WE FOLLOW A PRECISE WORK-
ING METHODOLOGY. IN THE FIRST PHASE EACH
CREATIVE AND DESIGNER HAS A FREE HAND.
THEN THE DESIGN PHASE PROP-
ER BEGINS: COMPARISON AND
CONFRONTATION. THE FIGURE
OF THE ISOLATED DESIGNER DOES NOT EXIST.
THE DESIGN IS ALMOST ALWAYS OPEN, FLEXIBLE,
DYNAMIC AND
CHANGE- ABLE.
EACH DESIGN
IS THE RESULT OF AN INTENSE TEAM EFFORT,
WHICH RESPONDS TO THE NEEDS OF THE CLI-
ENT.
IN THE
END, THE
RESULT IS A GLOBAL DESIGN IN WHICH ASPECTS
COME INTO PLAY THAT ARE LINKED TO COMMU-
NICATION, DESIGN, GRAPHIC ART, THE MARKET,
FUNCTION, AESTHETICS, ETC.

OPEN

FLEXIBLE

CHANGEABLE

EVERY-
WHERE
HOME

prototype

What distinguishes a project is the diffusion of ideas, it's not just
a matter of form or function. There is no point thinking of a creative
project that is at the same time anarchic and autonomous.
It is better to realize that the person on whose behalf you create
is not known to you. And above all, you do not know who will use it.

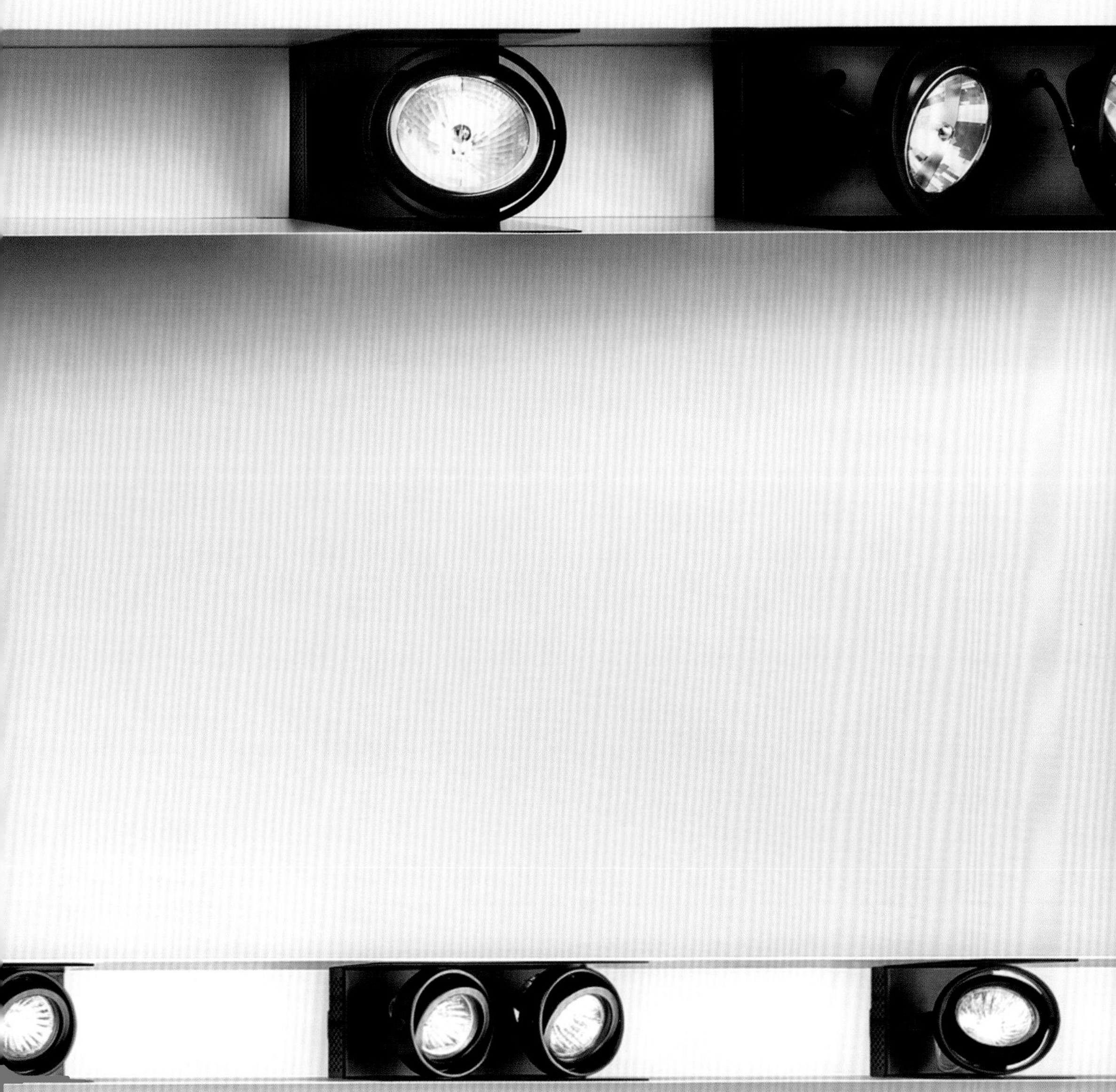

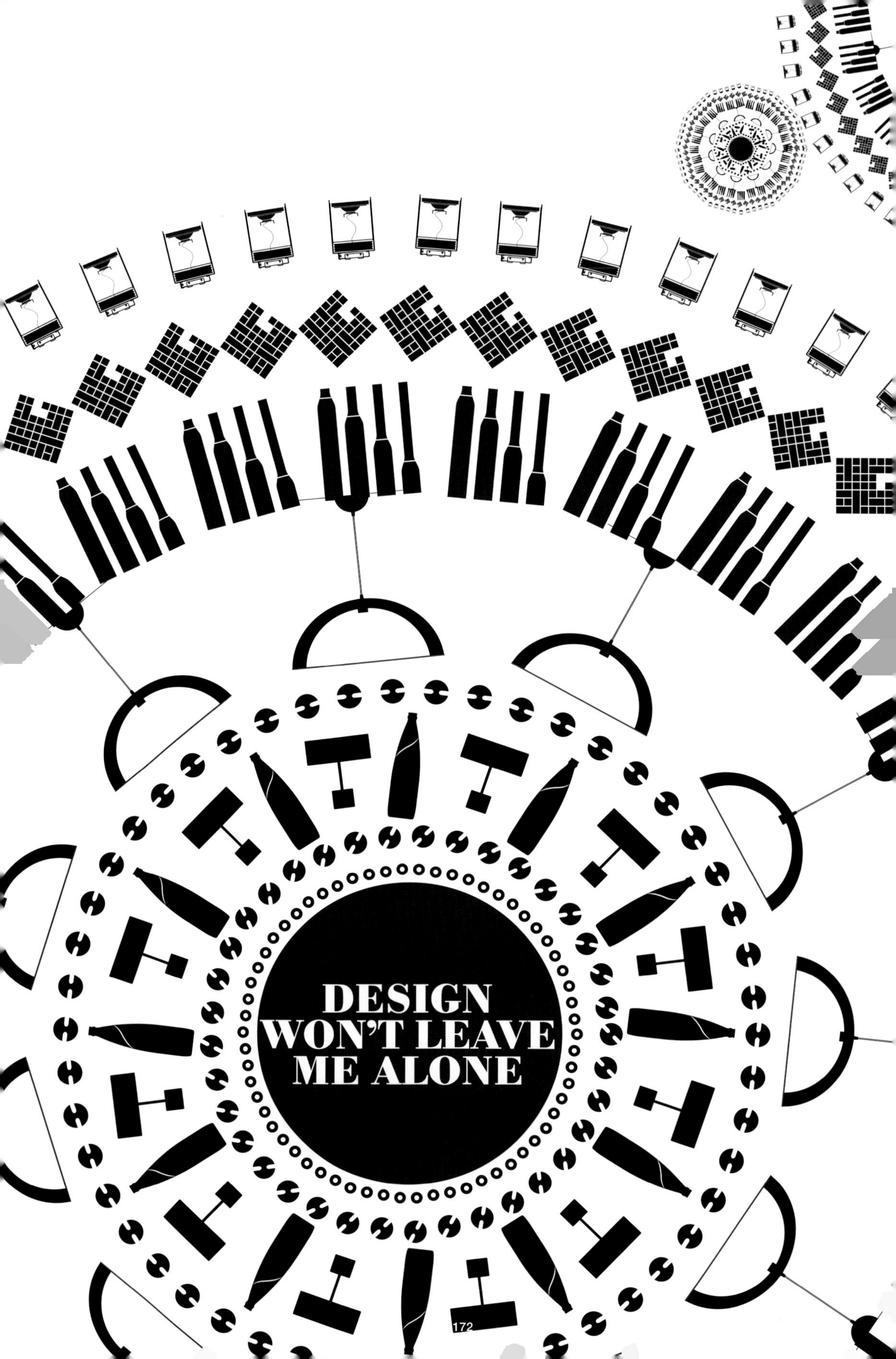

DESIGN
WON'T LEAVE
ME ALONE

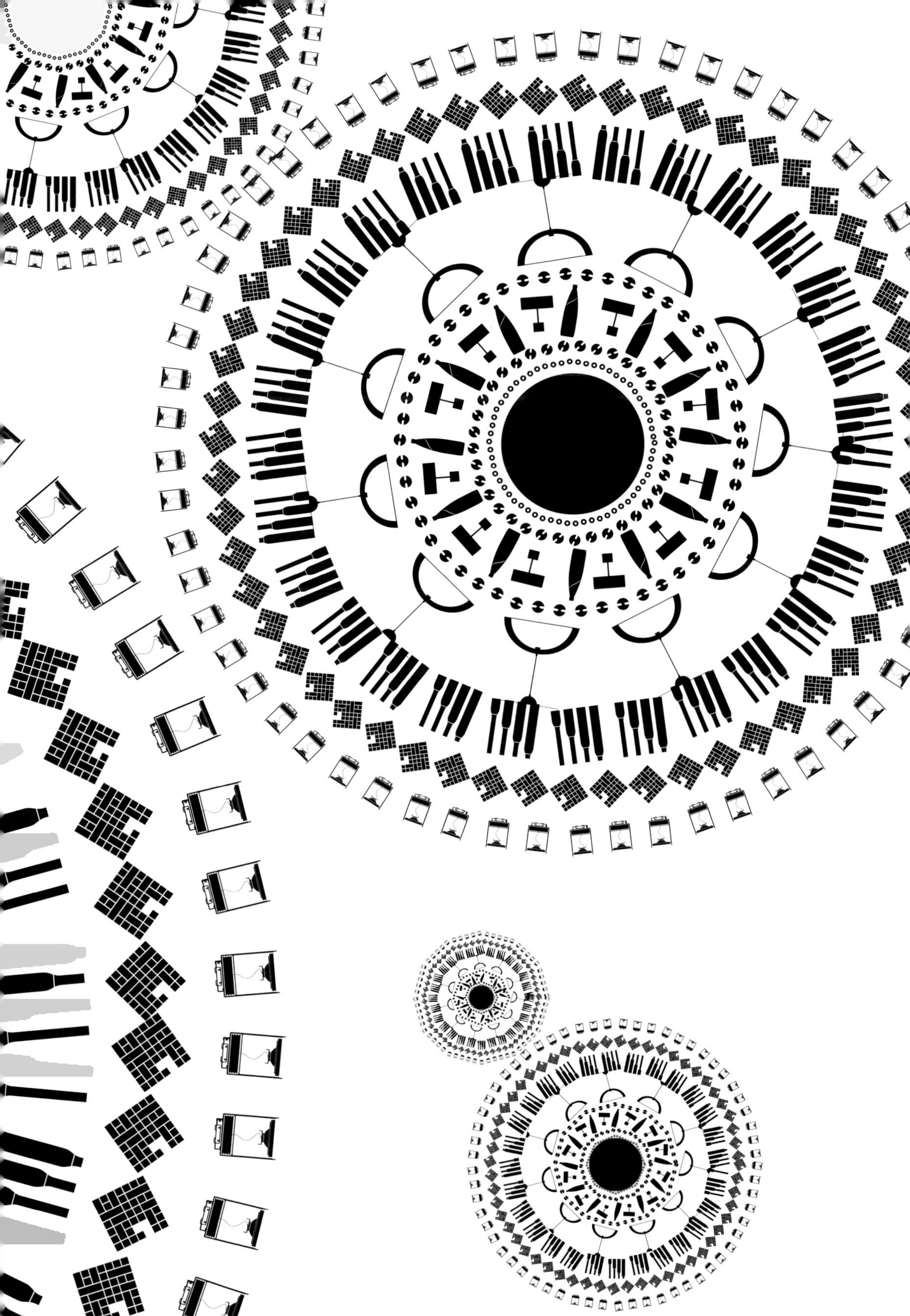

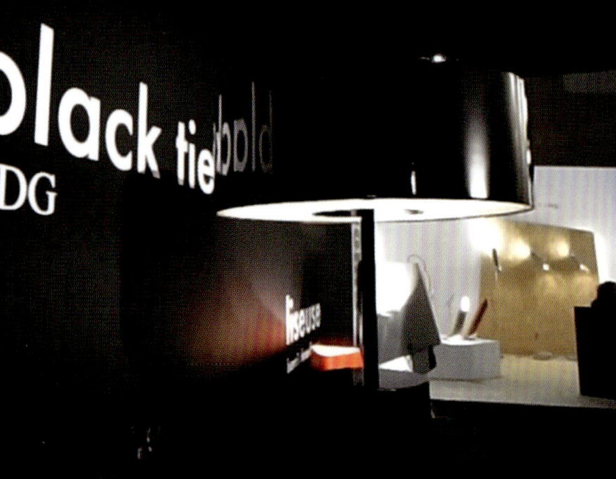
black tie
HDG

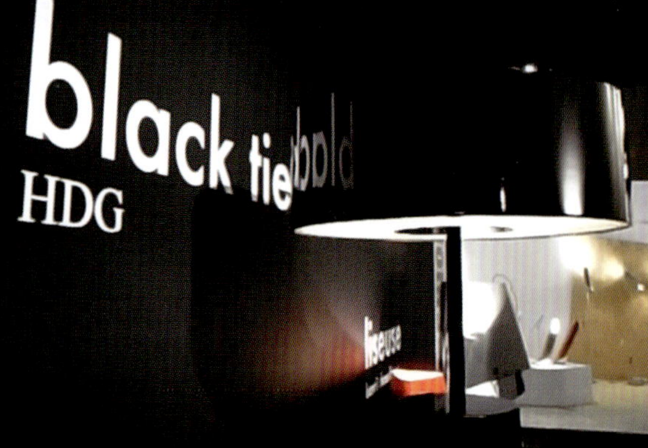
black tie
HDG

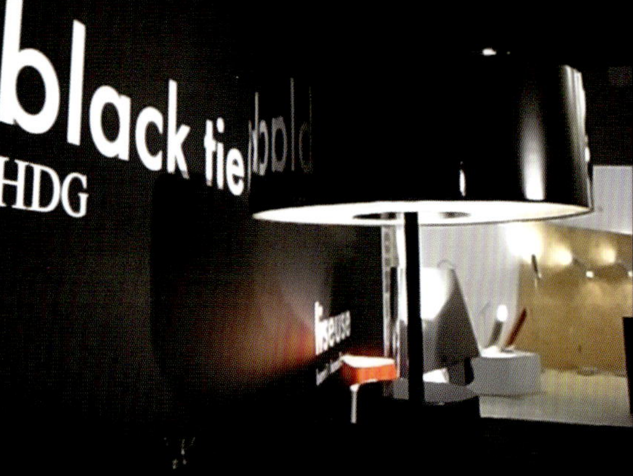
black tie
HDG

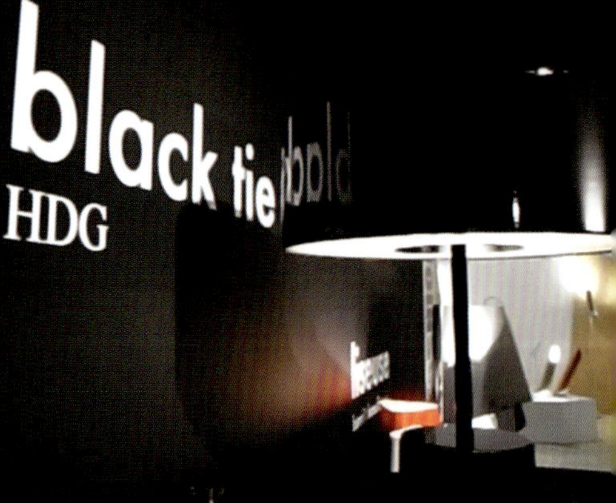
black tie
HDG

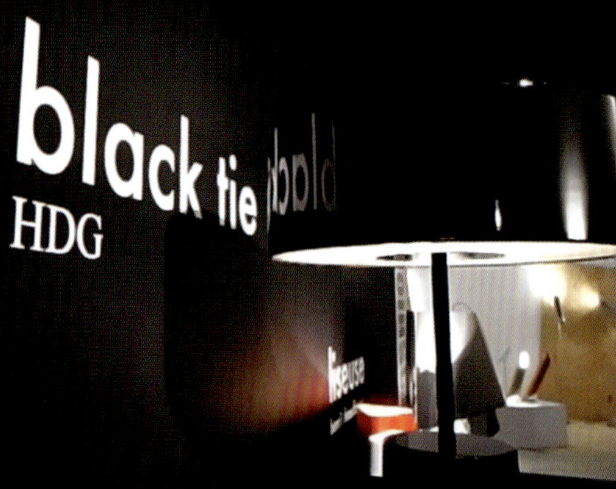
black tie
HDG

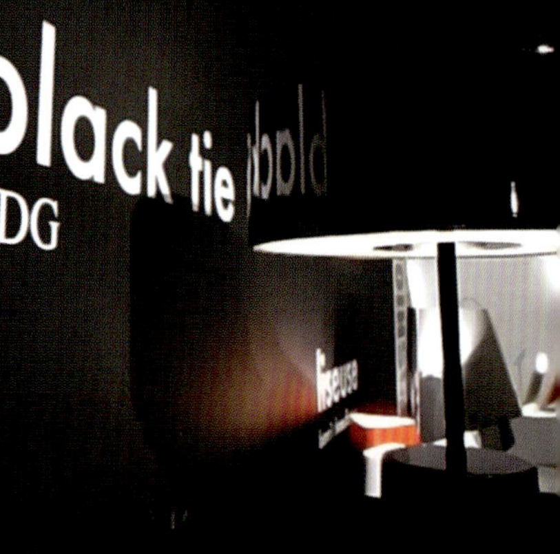
black tie
HDG

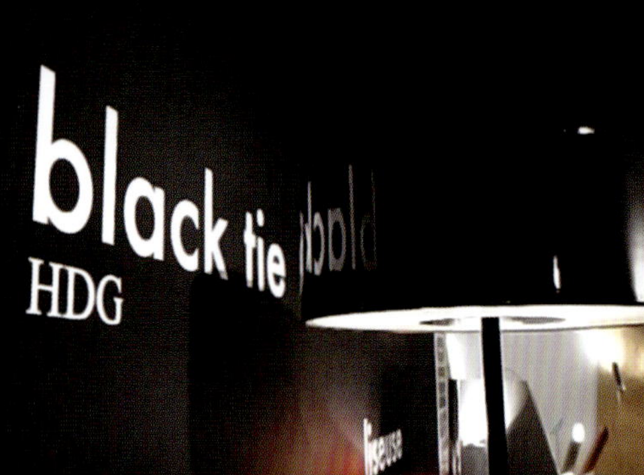
black tie
HDG

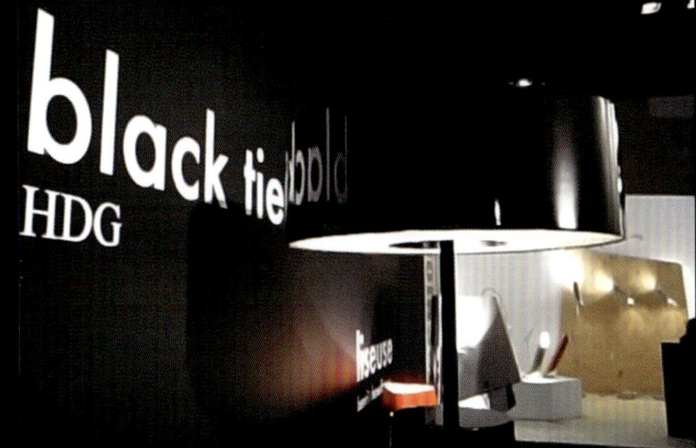

black tie
HDG
liseuse

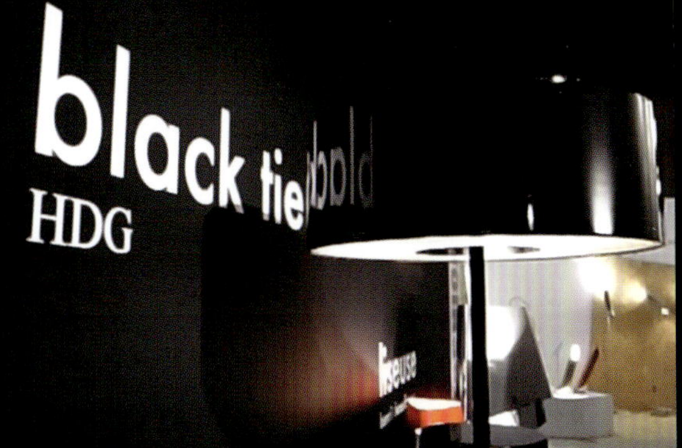

black tie
HDG
liseuse

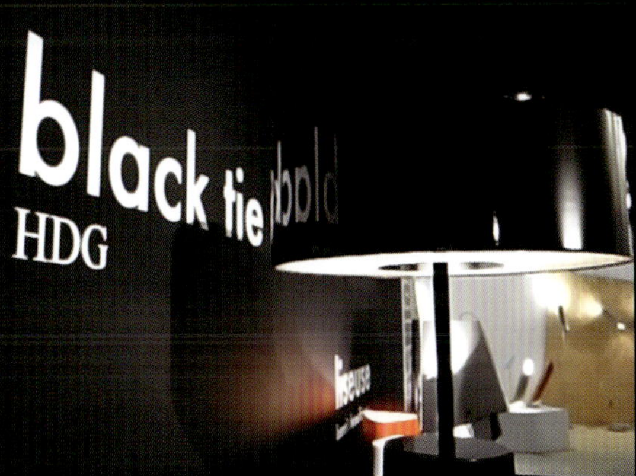

black tie
HDG
liseuse

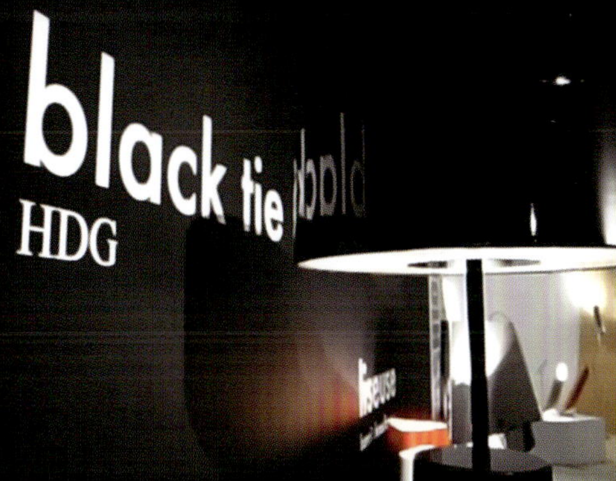

black tie
HDG
liseuse

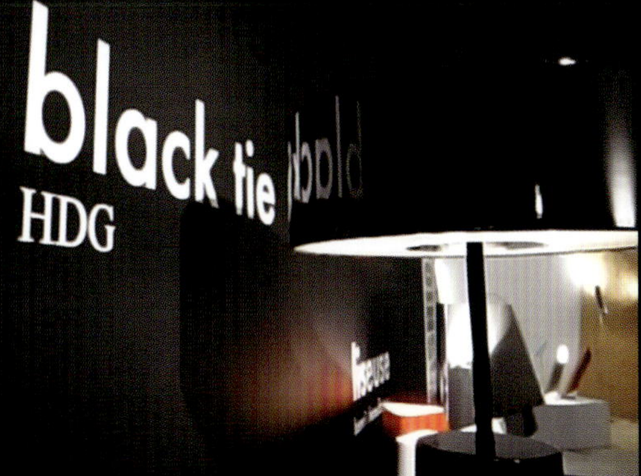

black tie
HDG
liseuse

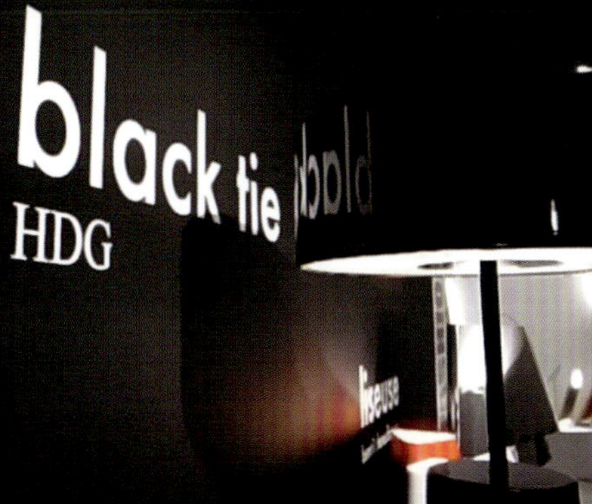

black tie
HDG
liseuse

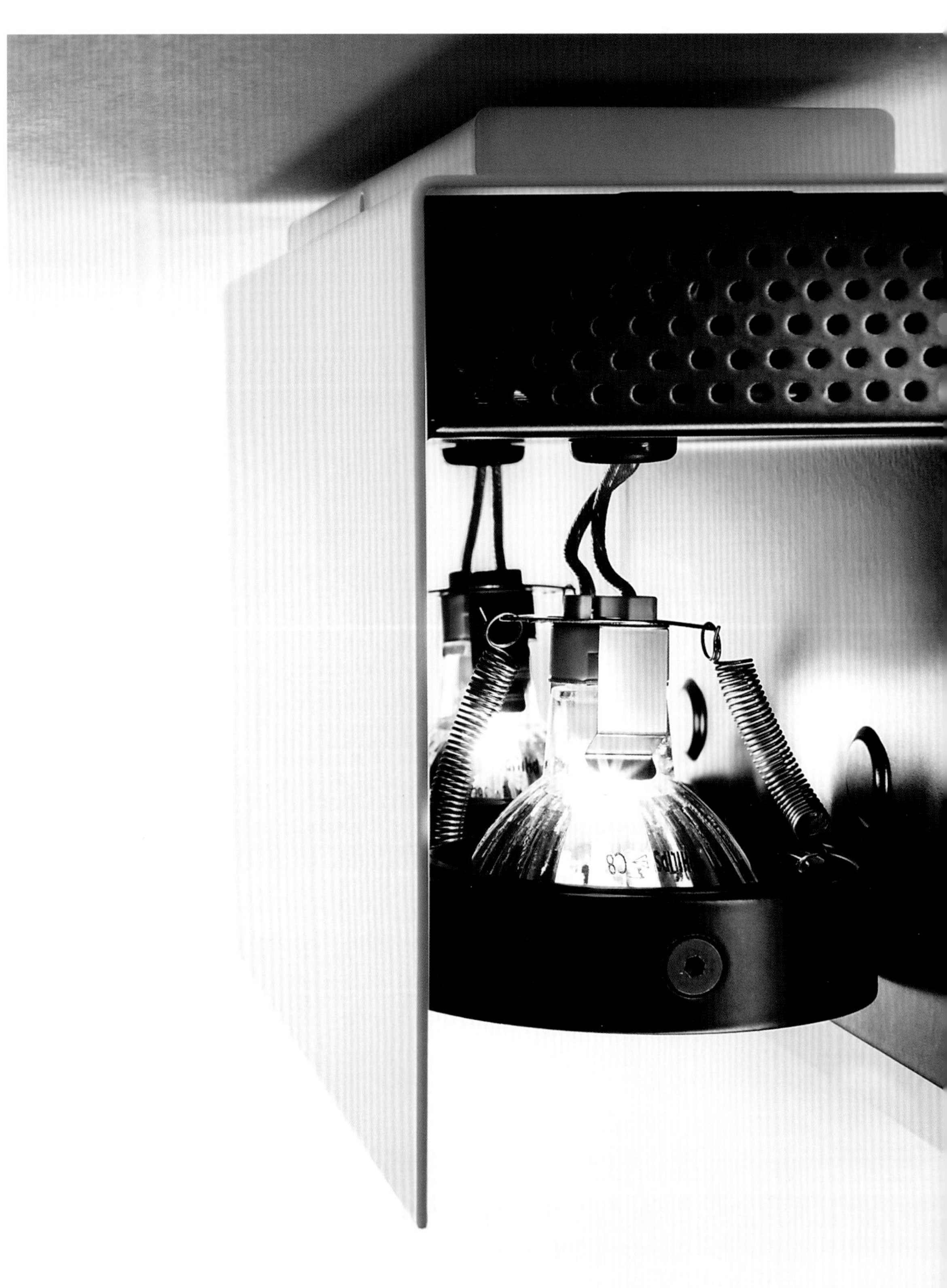

WHITE LIGHT ____
WHITE HEAT

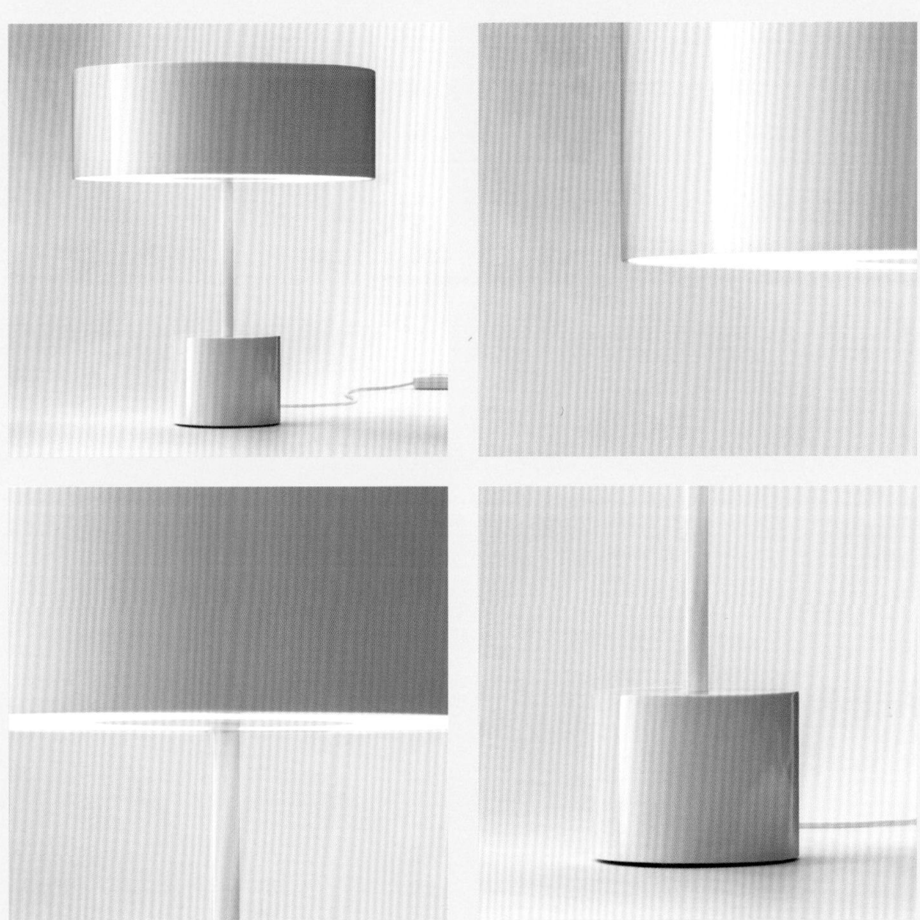

An interesting aspect of the new design is that it totally blends with our behavior.
An object assimilates so much with our expectation or experience that it becomes totally natural.
Actually, as designers we know you, we know how you will behave, what you will anticipate.
And deciding when to follow you or when to go another way, that is a very important balance.

AFFINITY

OF SIGNS

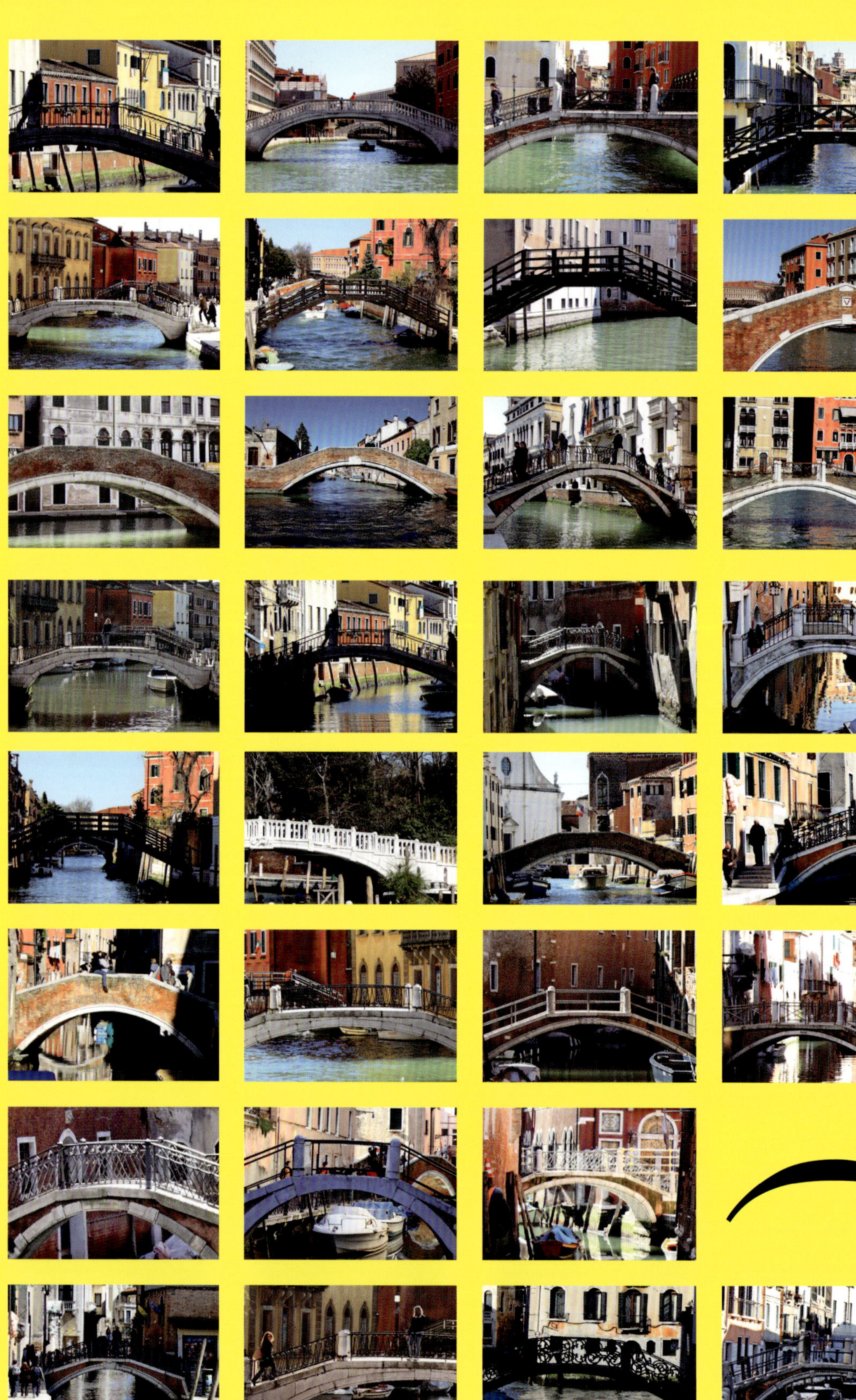

"Leave the logo alone"

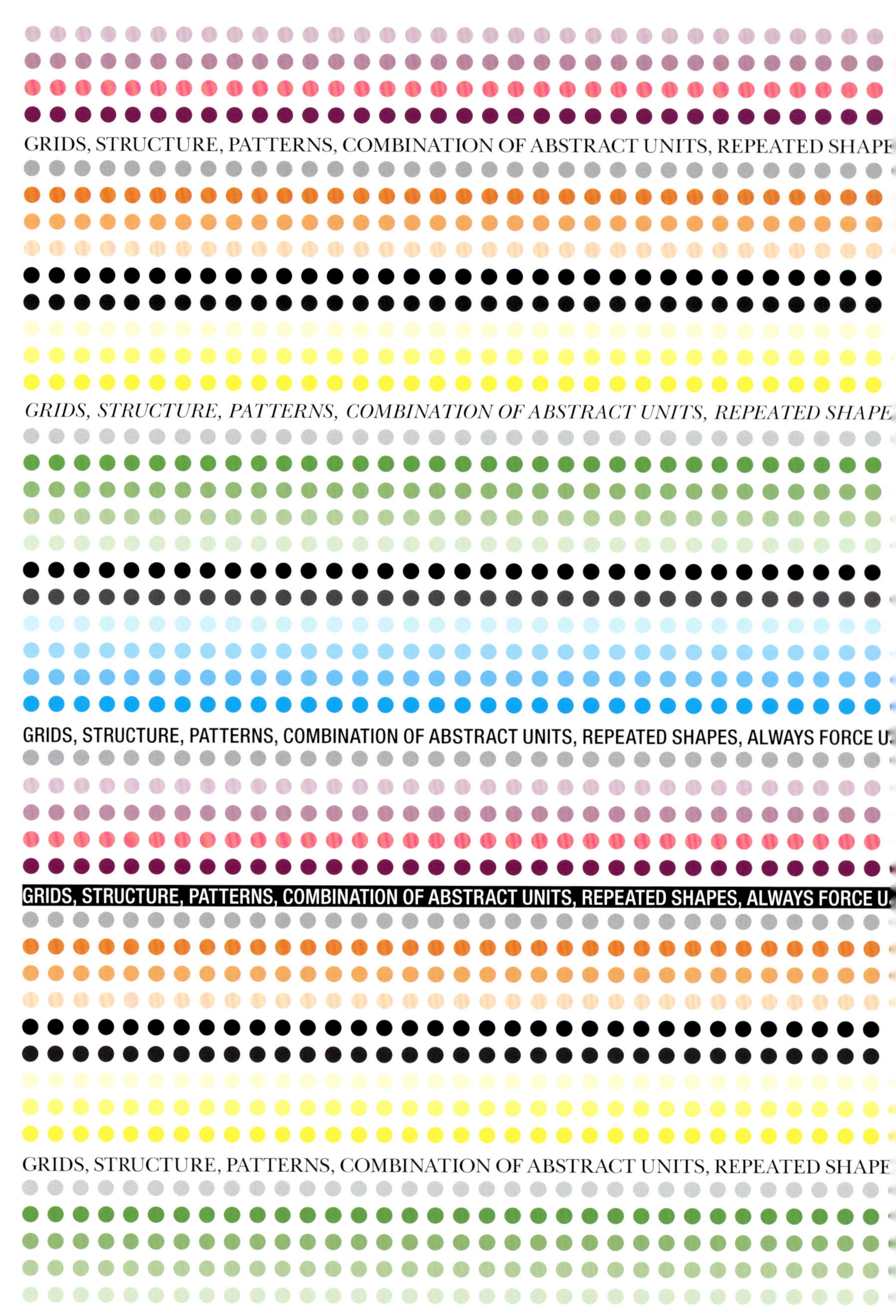

GRIDS, STRUCTURE, PATTERNS, COMBINATION OF ABSTRACT UNITS, REPEATED SHAPE

GRIDS, STRUCTURE, PATTERNS, COMBINATION OF ABSTRACT UNITS, REPEATED SHAPE

GRIDS, STRUCTURE, PATTERNS, COMBINATION OF ABSTRACT UNITS, REPEATED SHAPES, ALWAYS FORCE U

GRIDS, STRUCTURE, PATTERNS, COMBINATION OF ABSTRACT UNITS, REPEATED SHAPES, ALWAYS FORCE U

GRIDS, STRUCTURE, PATTERNS, COMBINATION OF ABSTRACT UNITS, REPEATED SHAPE

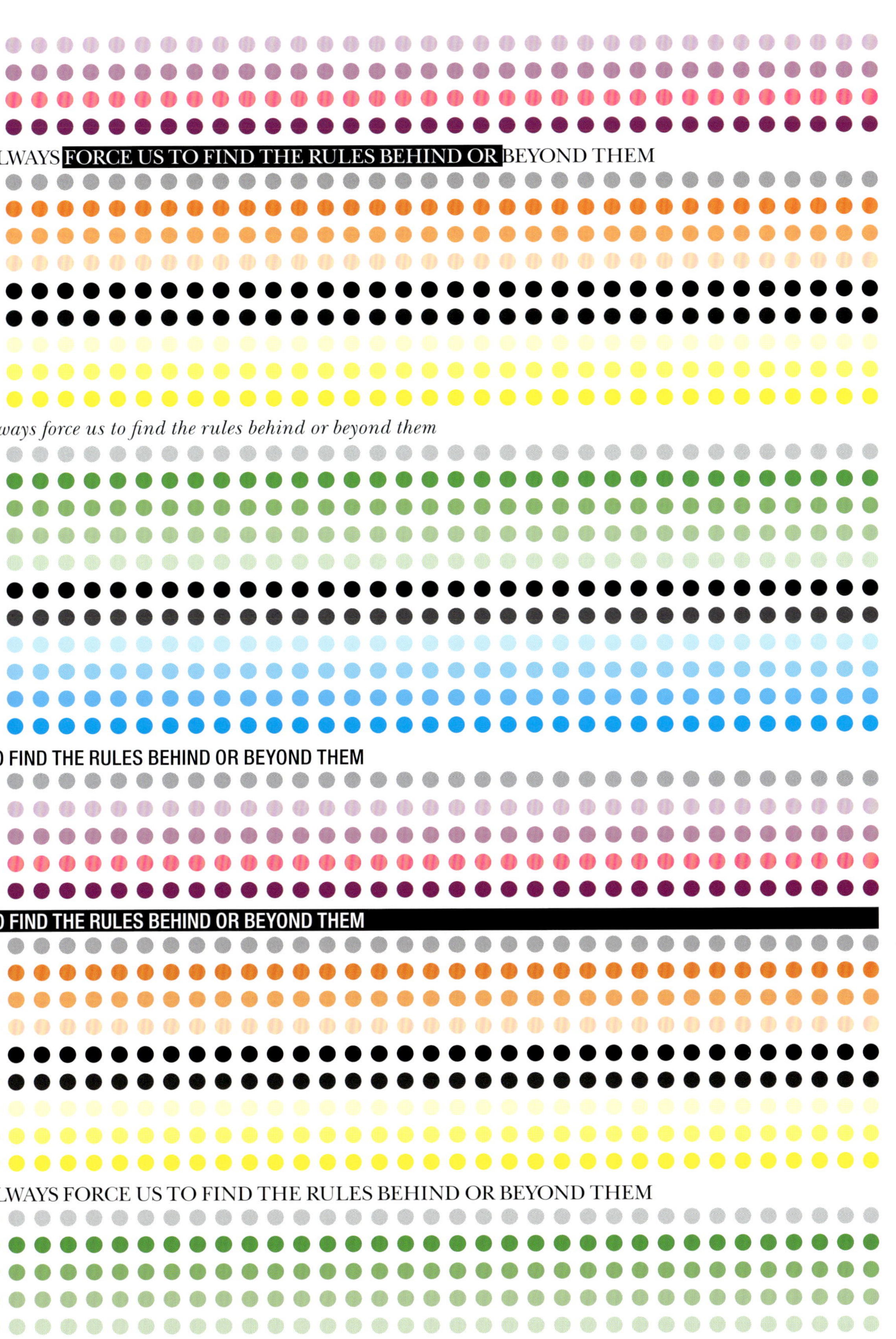
LWAYS FORCE US TO FIND THE RULES BEHIND OR BEYOND THEM
ways force us to find the rules behind or beyond them
D FIND THE RULES BEHIND OR BEYOND THEM
D FIND THE RULES BEHIND OR BEYOND THEM
LWAYS FORCE US TO FIND THE RULES BEHIND OR BEYOND THEM

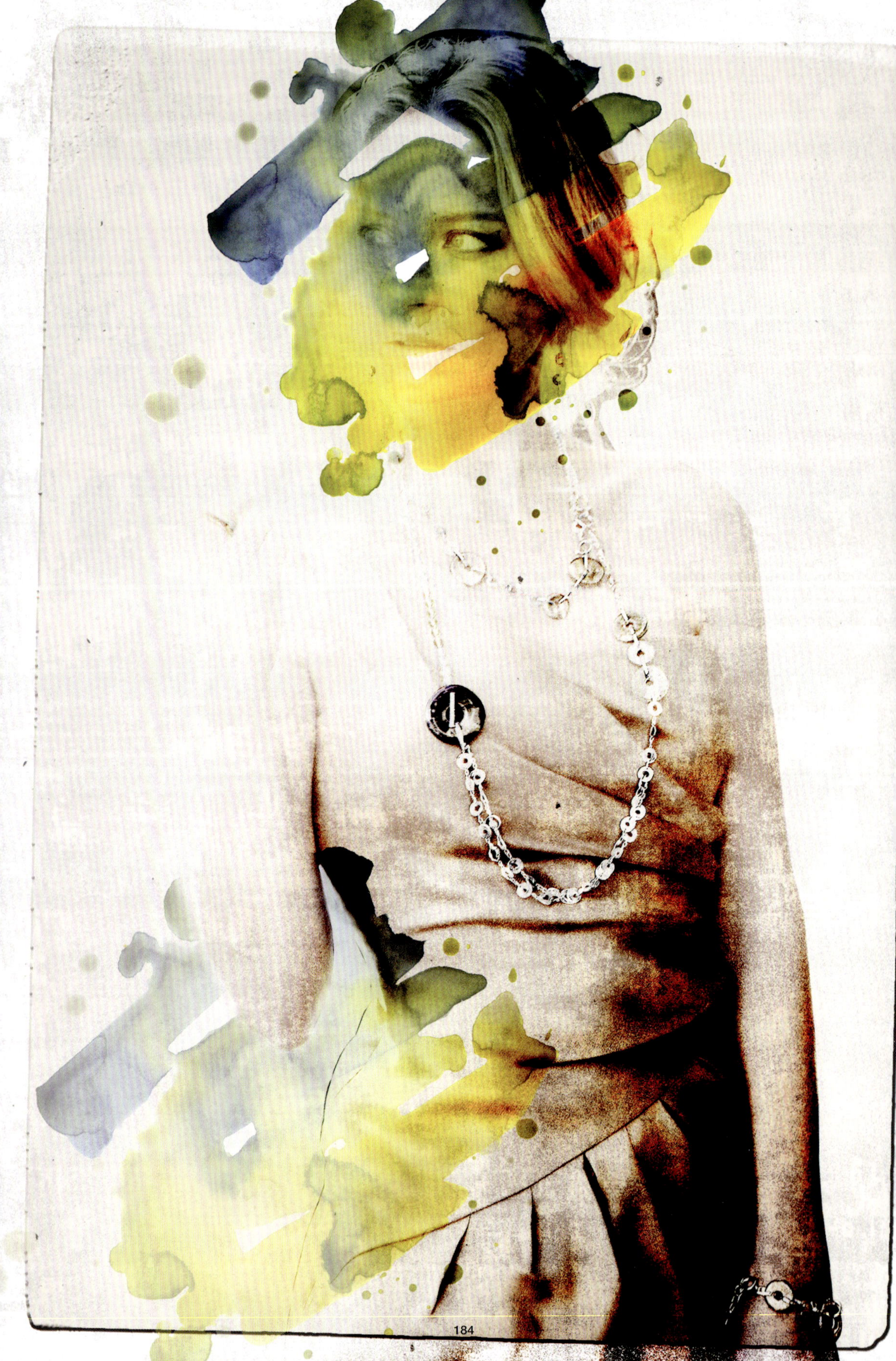

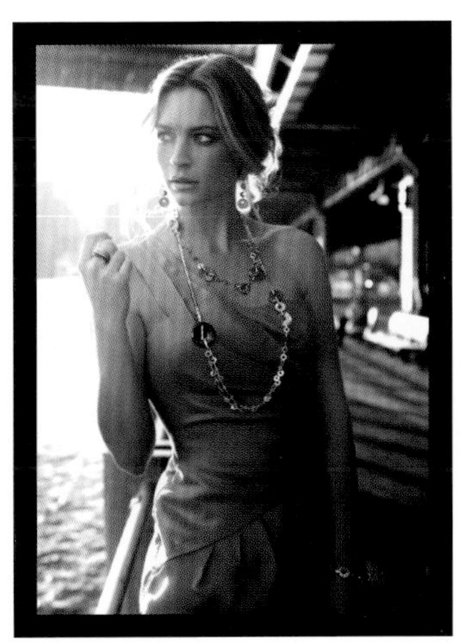

(INSERT A COLOR)
is the new black

ON DRAWING ____
AN EXERCISE OF APPROXIMATION

<u>Today, IT and digital technology are transforming deeply our way of thinking design, over and above the assistance that computers provide in terms of computational capacity.</u> The use of CAD and computer graphics is increasing to such an extent as to influence the very way in which design is done. Despite all of this, mental drawing remains vital: <u>the sketch, as a prolonging of the idea on paper, maintains all of its potential.</u> The quality of the idea, its original significance, cannot be captured by such exact tools. Before it is "put in writing" the idea appears very clearly to us, but as soon as we put it down, the edges blur and dissolve to take the form not of words but signs. Like words, drawings can be at once imprecise and exact, like a piece of graffiti and a piece of calligraphy that conceal the structure and the precise character of the shapes and spaces to which they refer.

For us it can be stated that, at least in relation to that part of design that is based on conceptual reflection, on ideas, the sketch is set to remain an irreplaceable drawing method over the long term – it makes no difference wheter it's drawn with ink on paper, or with e-ink on e-paper.

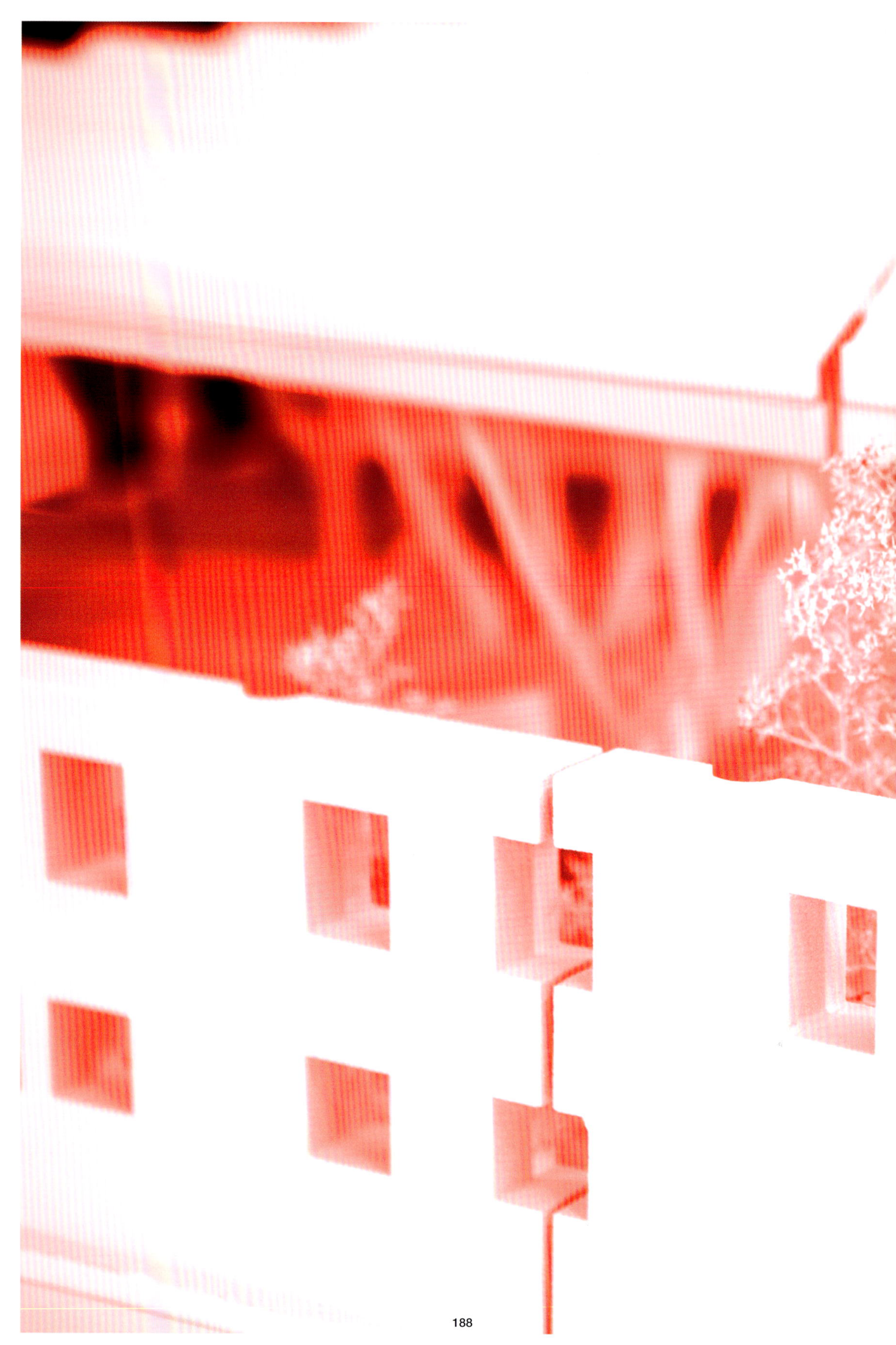

EVERYTHING EXISTS

Things, as we all know, are the key issue for design. To paraphrase Mies van der Rohe's epithet on architecture as "the will of the day captured in space," we could say that the world of artifacts is the will of the day "captured as objects." Time coagulates in matter, it becomes "objectively" legible. Our everyday world primarily occurs in the "universe of things."
The programmatic sentence "Everything exists" can be read in two ways: artifacts are there, present, but they also originate through us. We are exposed to them, and they exist as things we assemble around us, we bond with, we collect ourselves emotionally and we experience ourselves physically through, they help us get into form and provide spine.

HARDCOVER

PRINT IS DEAD

LONG LIVE PRINT

The death knell of print has been sounded
on several occasions over the past decade.
Yet as more and more publications see
the light of day, those who predicted its very
death become more and more strident.
Sometimes, the persistence of print
becomes an affront. The sources of modern
identity have never been more fragile,
in a world characterized by the loss of substance, the increasing thinness of bonds and
shallowness of the things we use.
When is a brochure more than a brochure?
When it turns readers into collectors.
Let's talk about what makes a great printing work in the process. Pixels and print are
different experiences. The material and the
sense of touch (haptic) affect perception.
Reading on screen means losing the
"associative dimension of reading, when
our thoughts move beyond the words and
glimpse new intellectual horizons."
On screen we skim, we fillet, we cherry-pick.
Faced with the disruptive technology of the
Internet, printing is reinventing itself, and
wonderfully so. The back page of the
Financial Times says a lot more than the lid
of a laptop. Do you remember
the moment you fell in love with print?

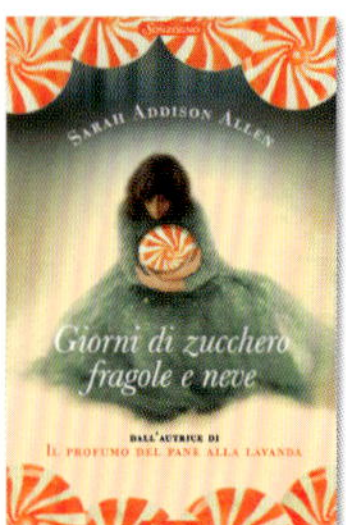 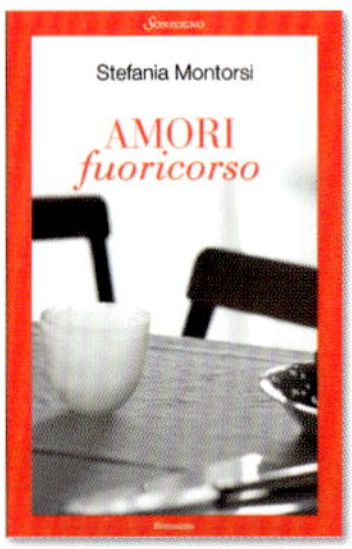 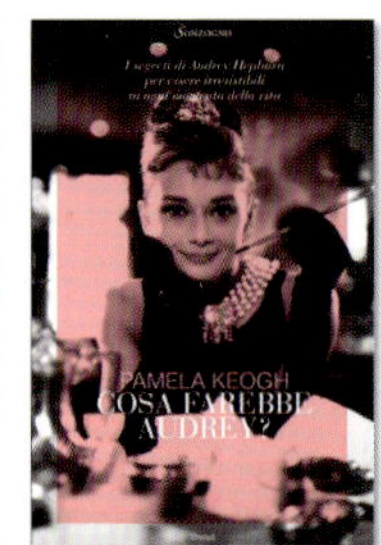 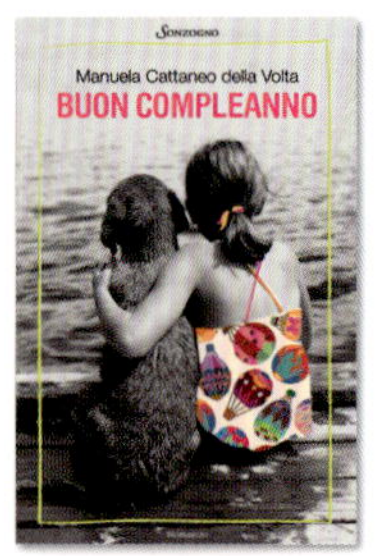 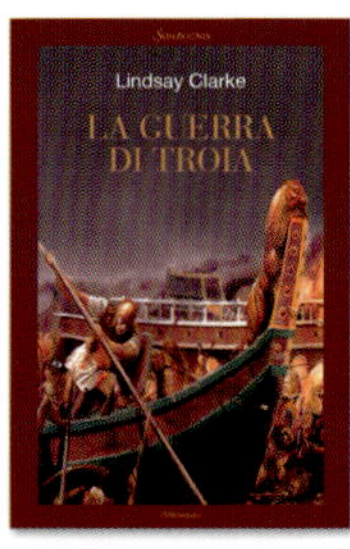 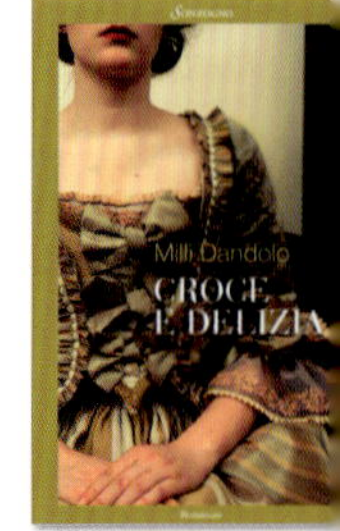
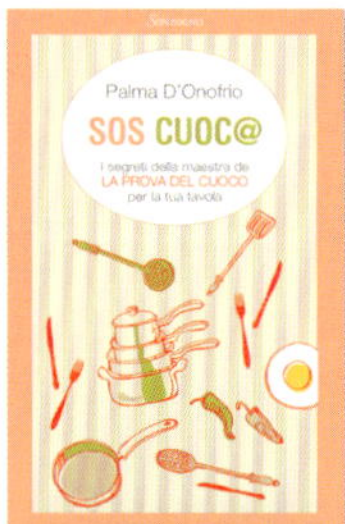 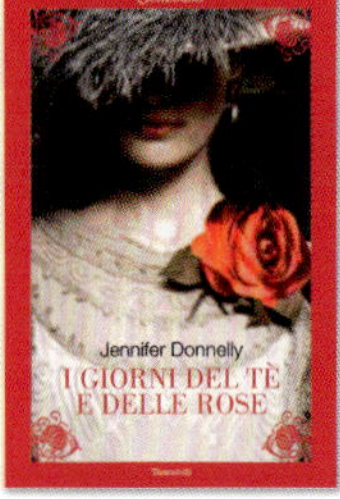 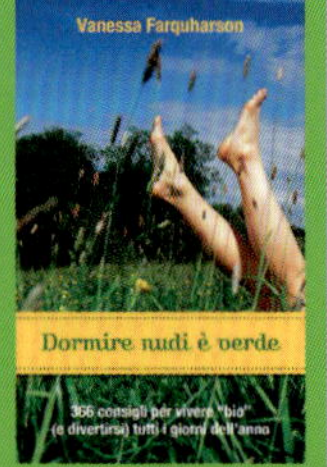 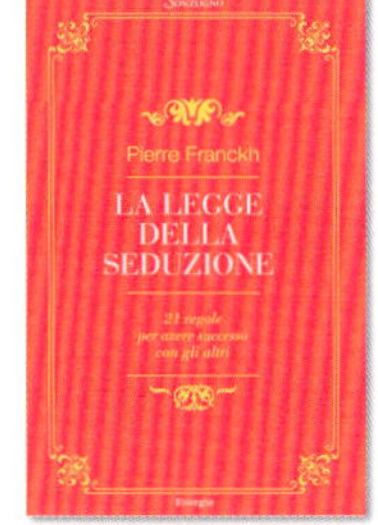 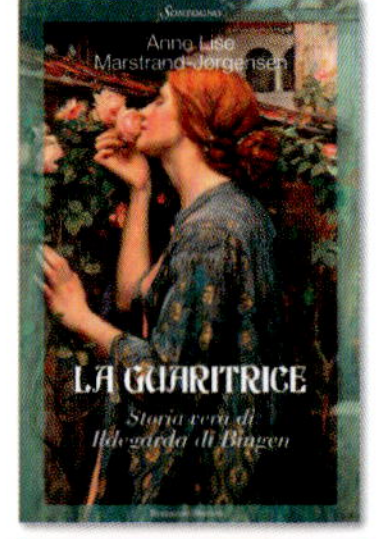 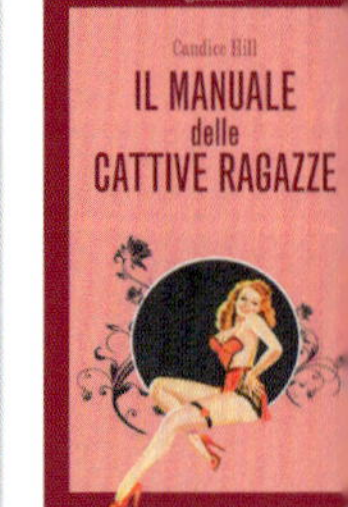
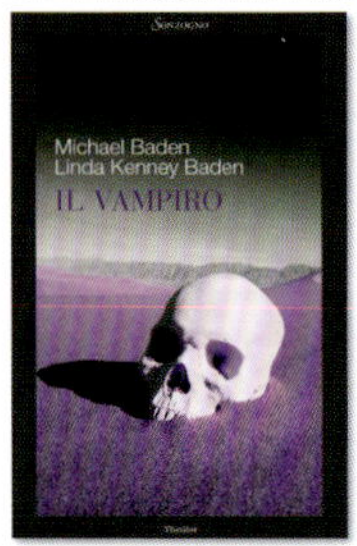 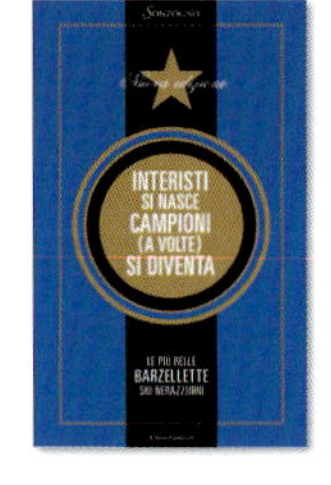 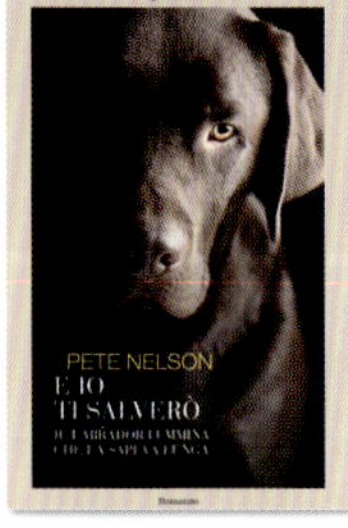 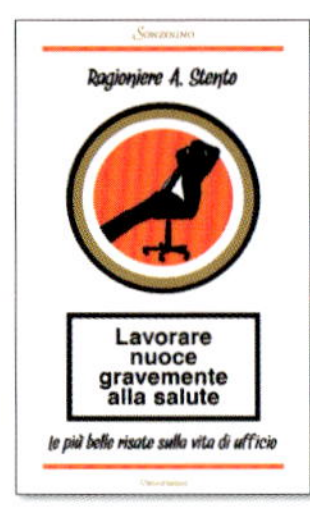 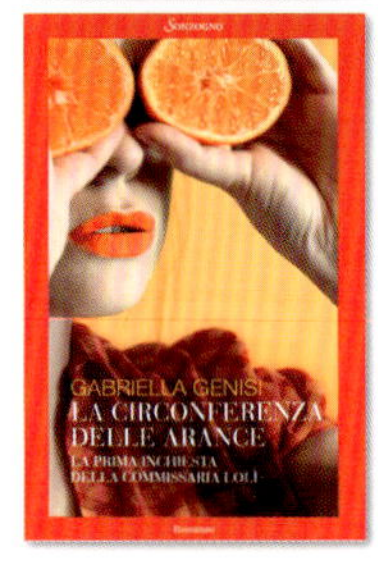 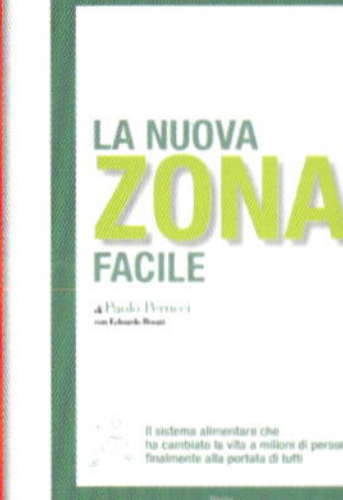
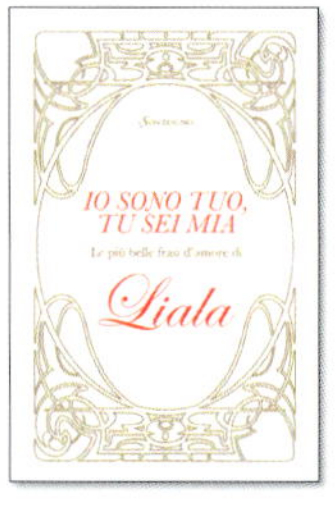 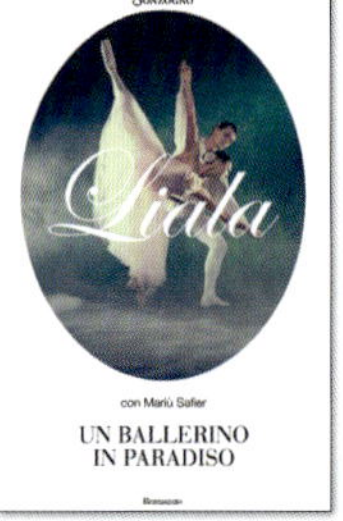 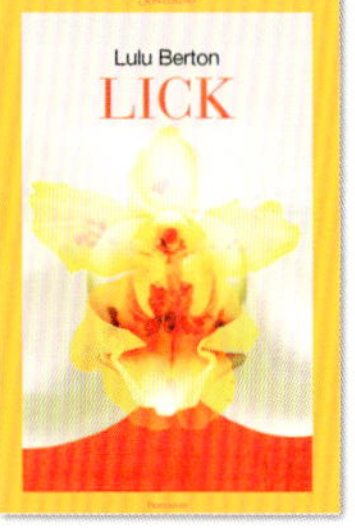 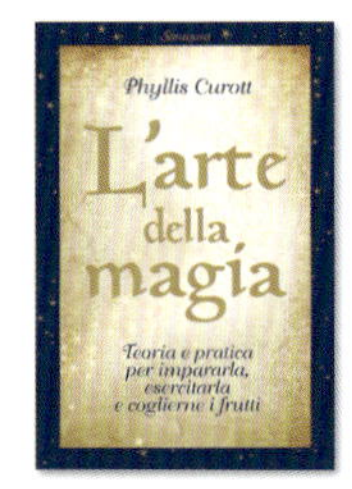 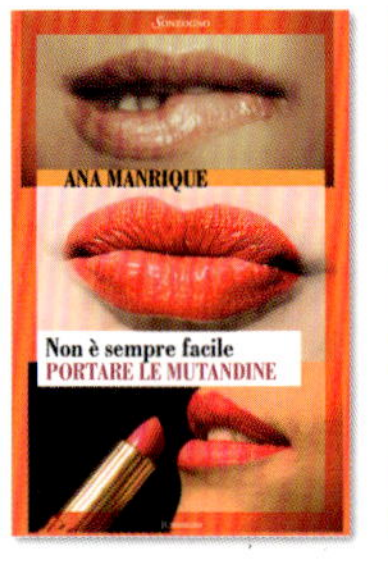 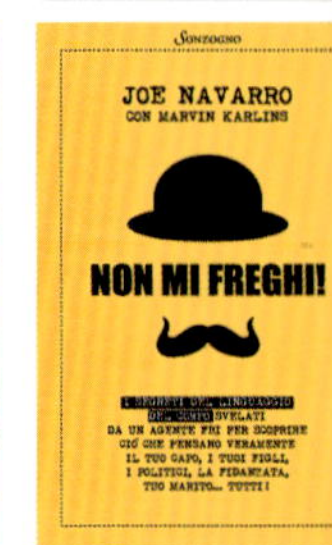
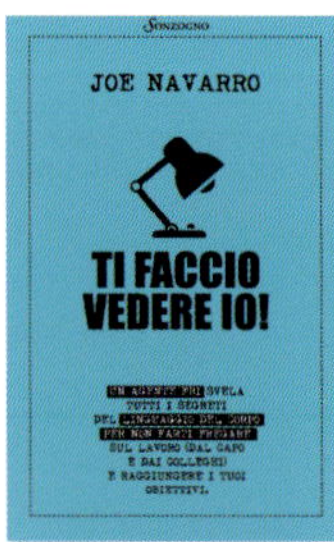 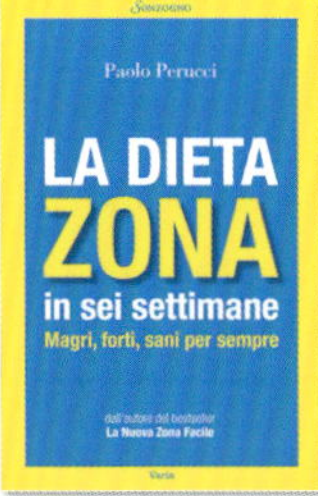 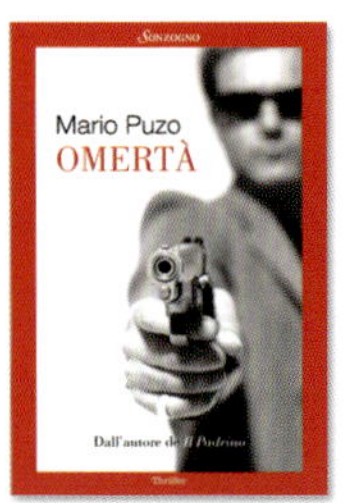 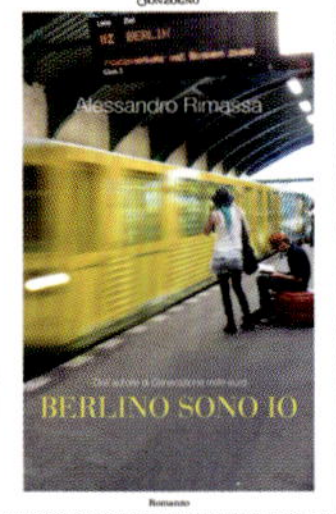 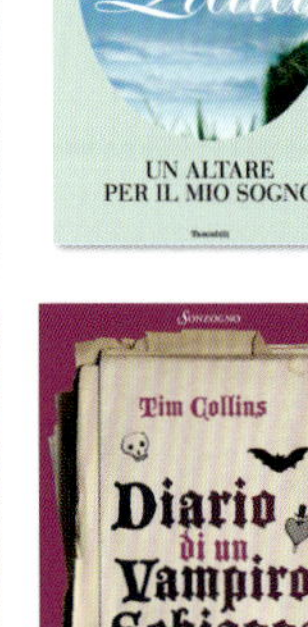 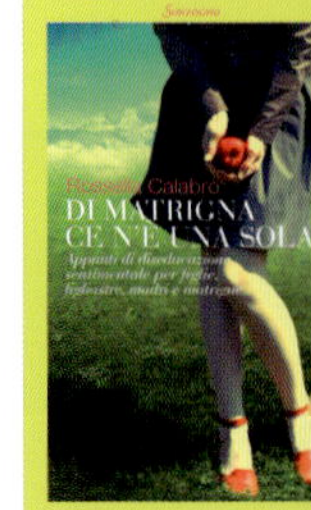
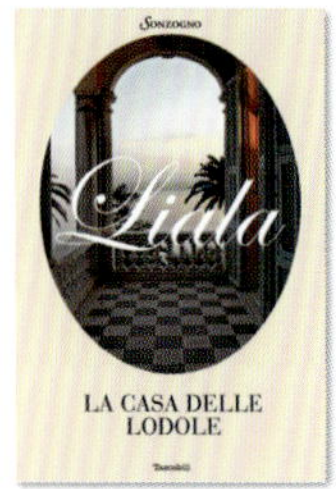 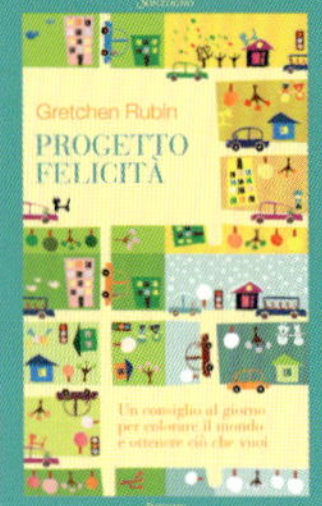 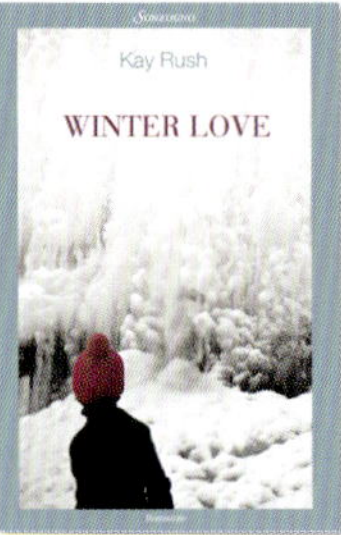 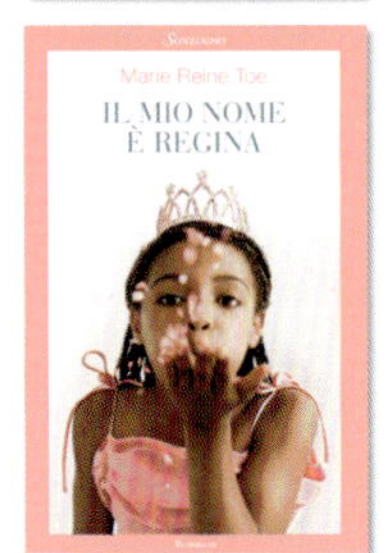 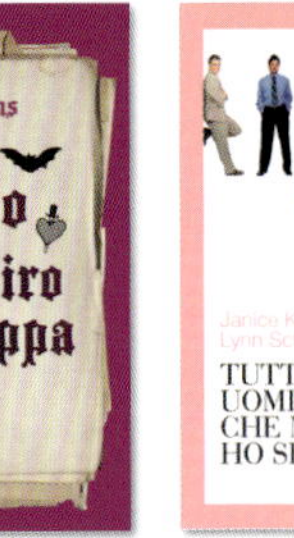

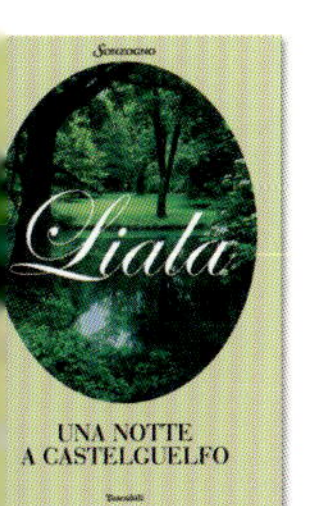
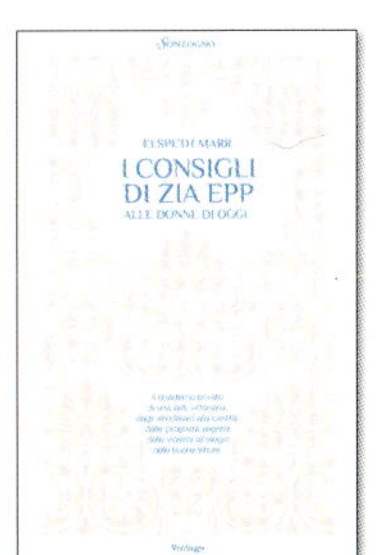
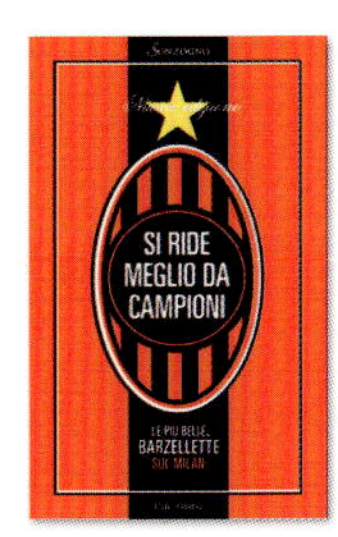
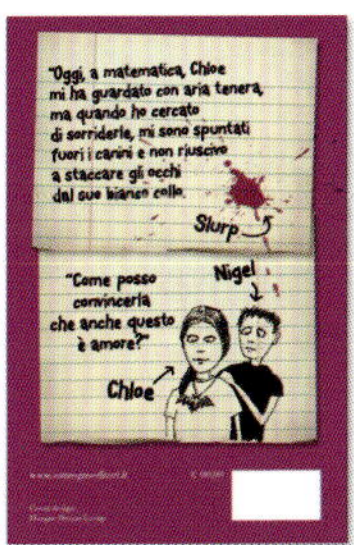
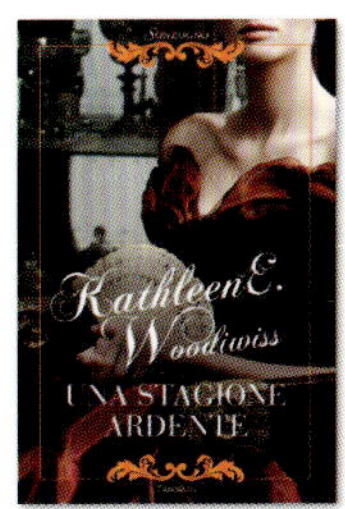
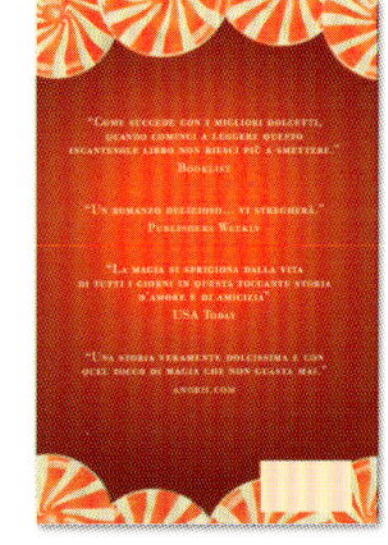
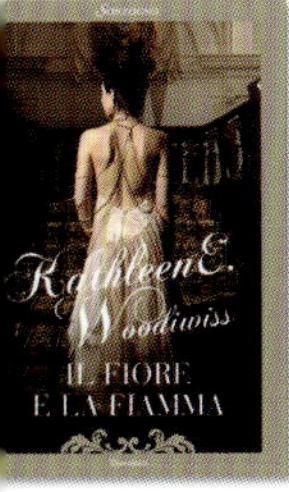
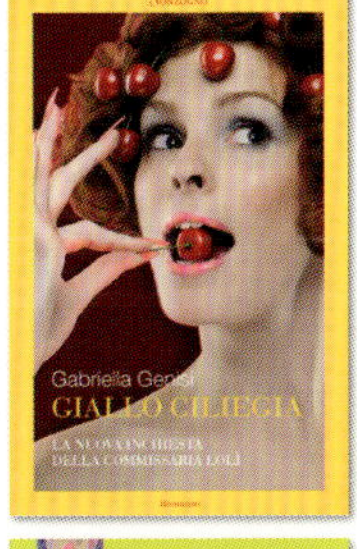
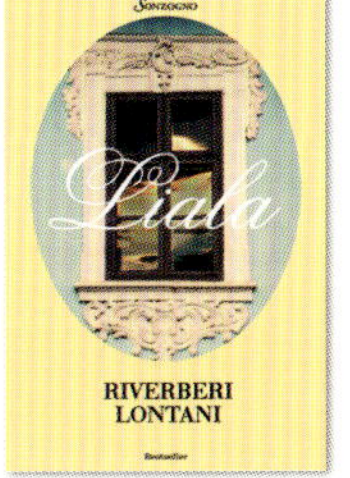
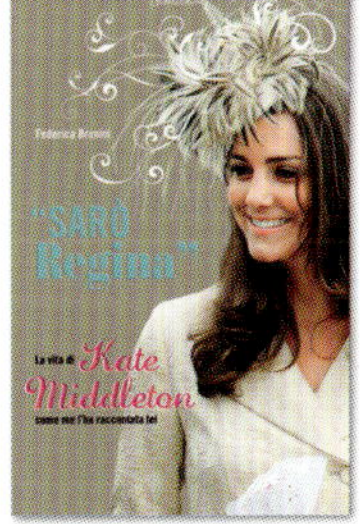
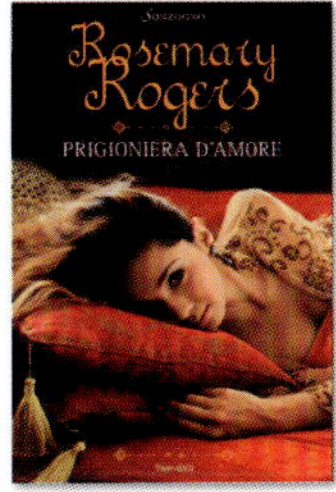
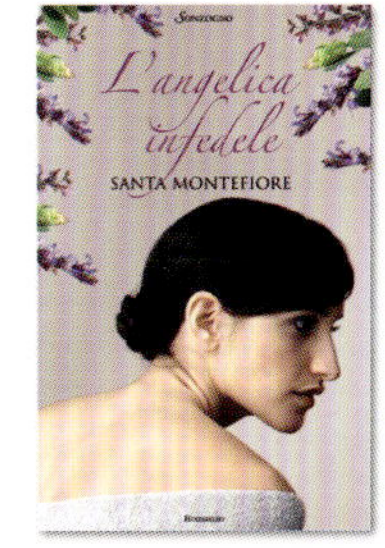
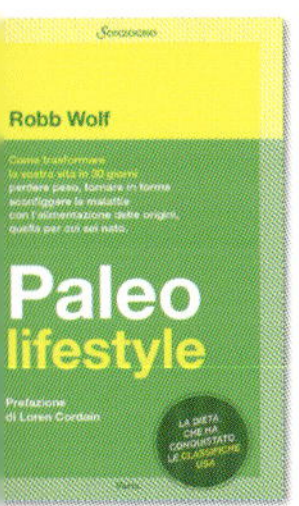
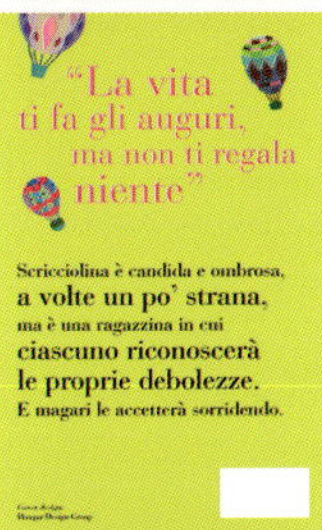
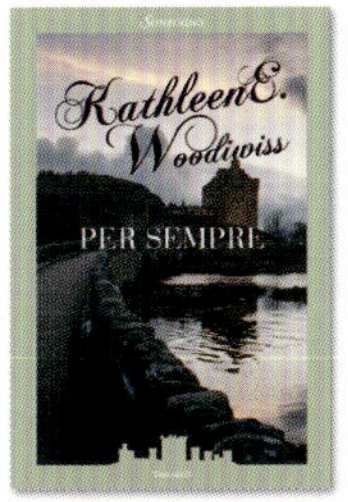
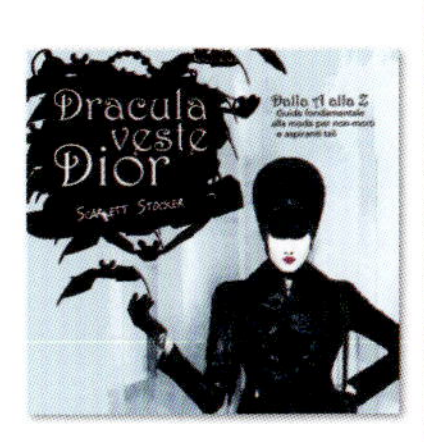
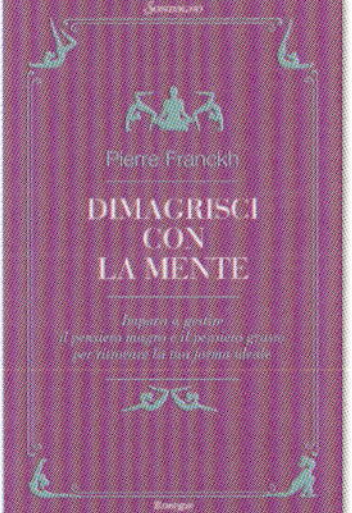
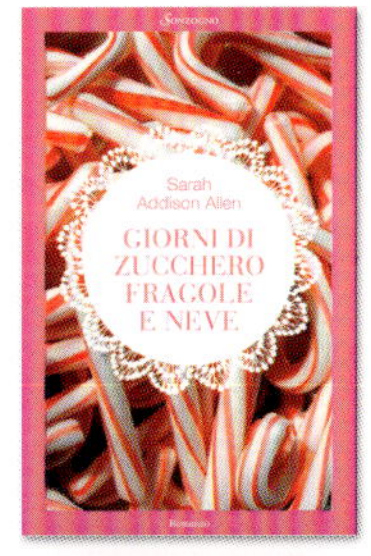
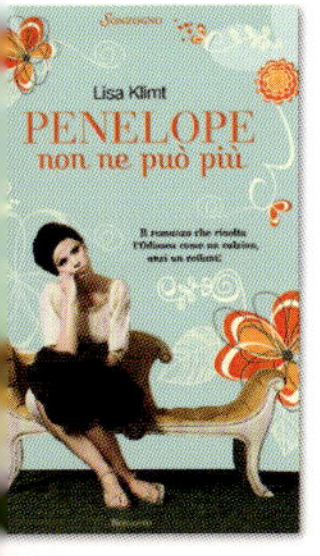
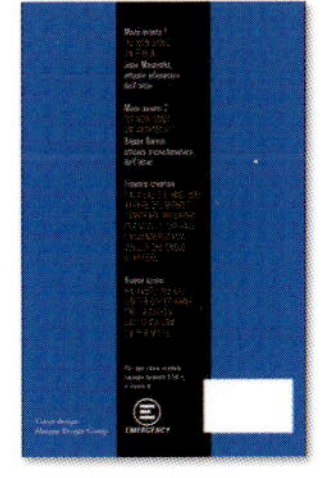
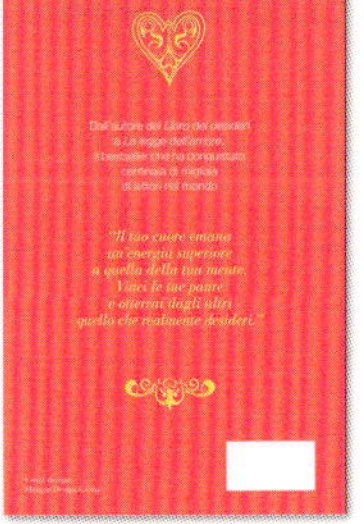
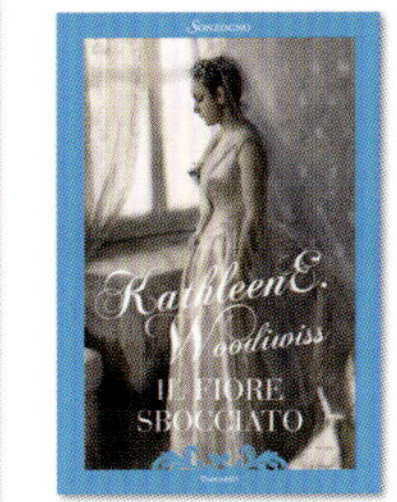
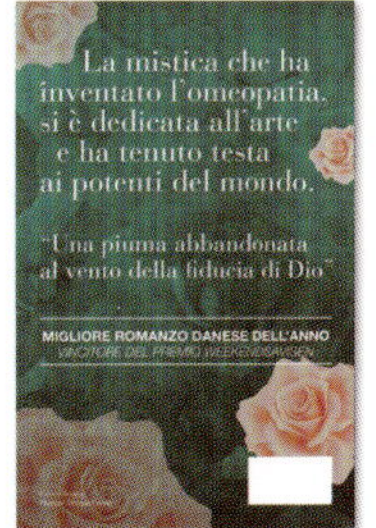
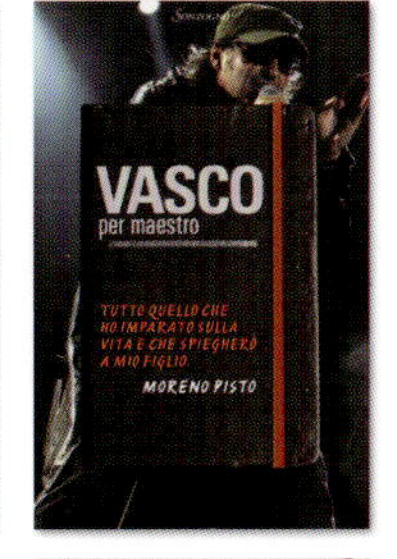
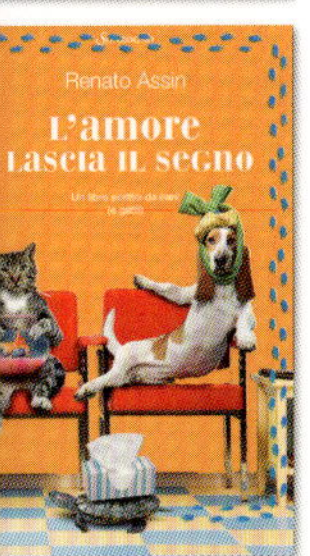
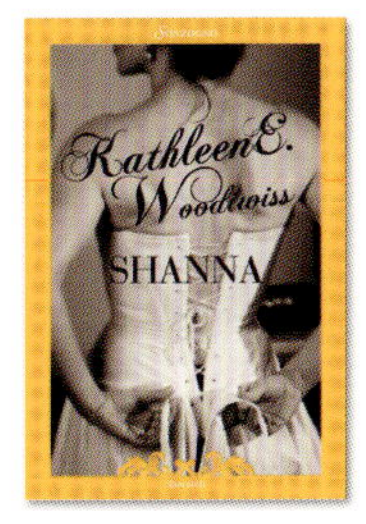
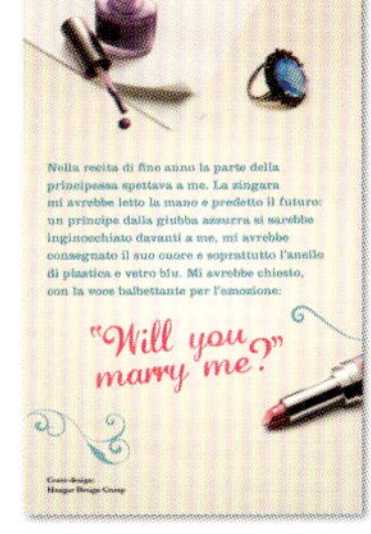
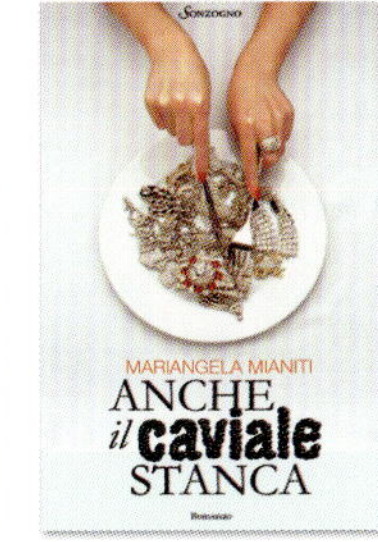
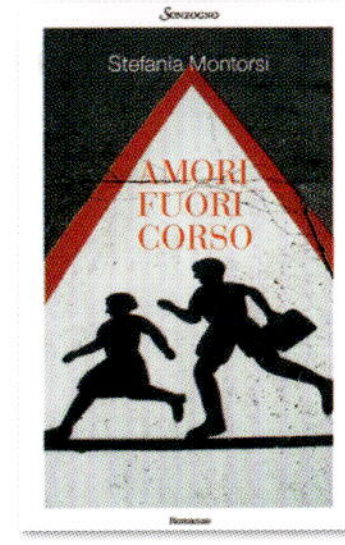
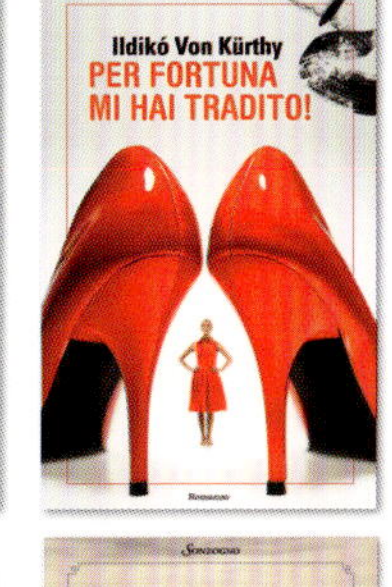
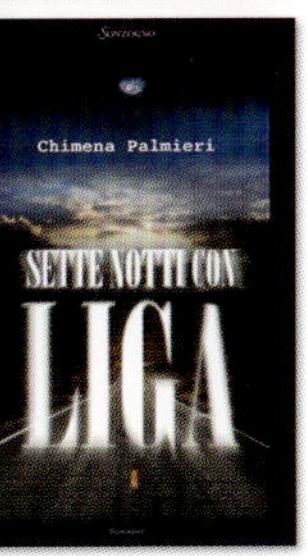
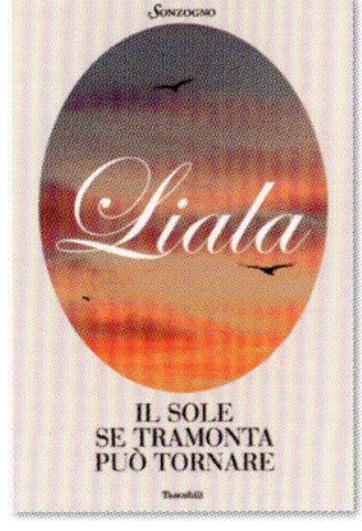
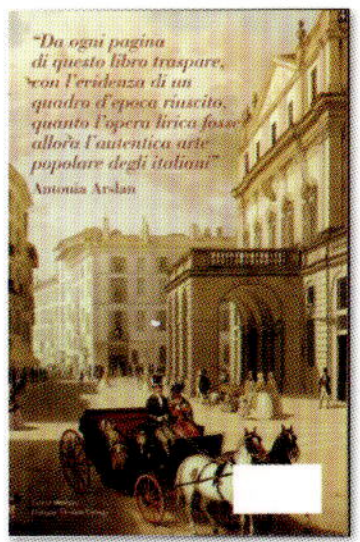
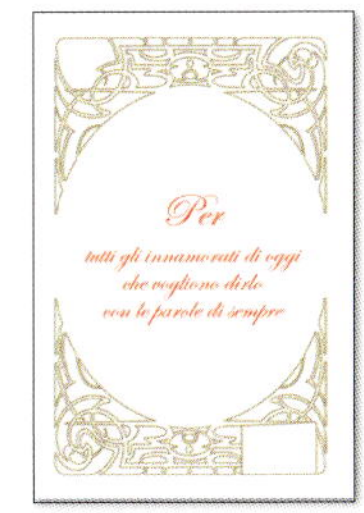
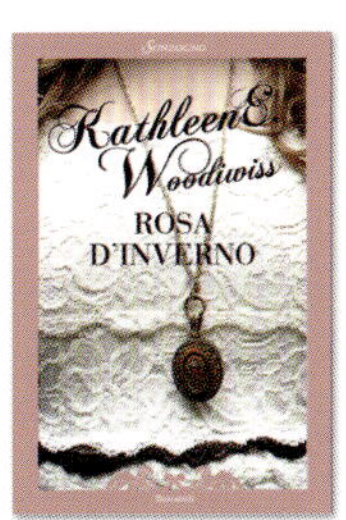
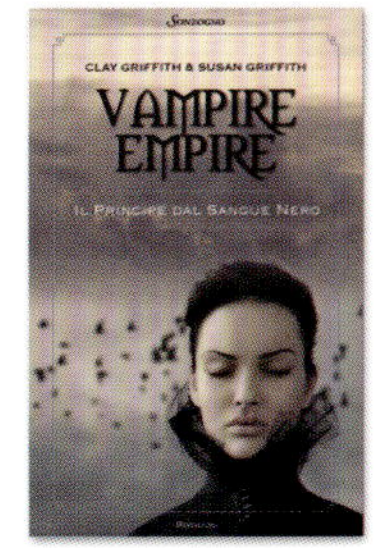

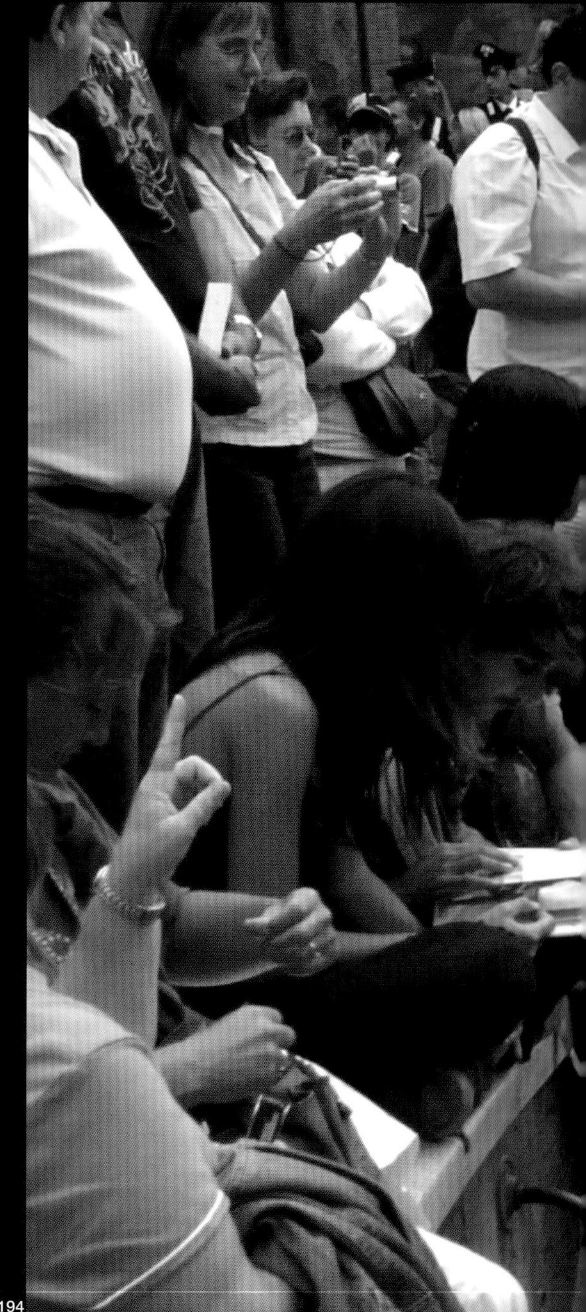

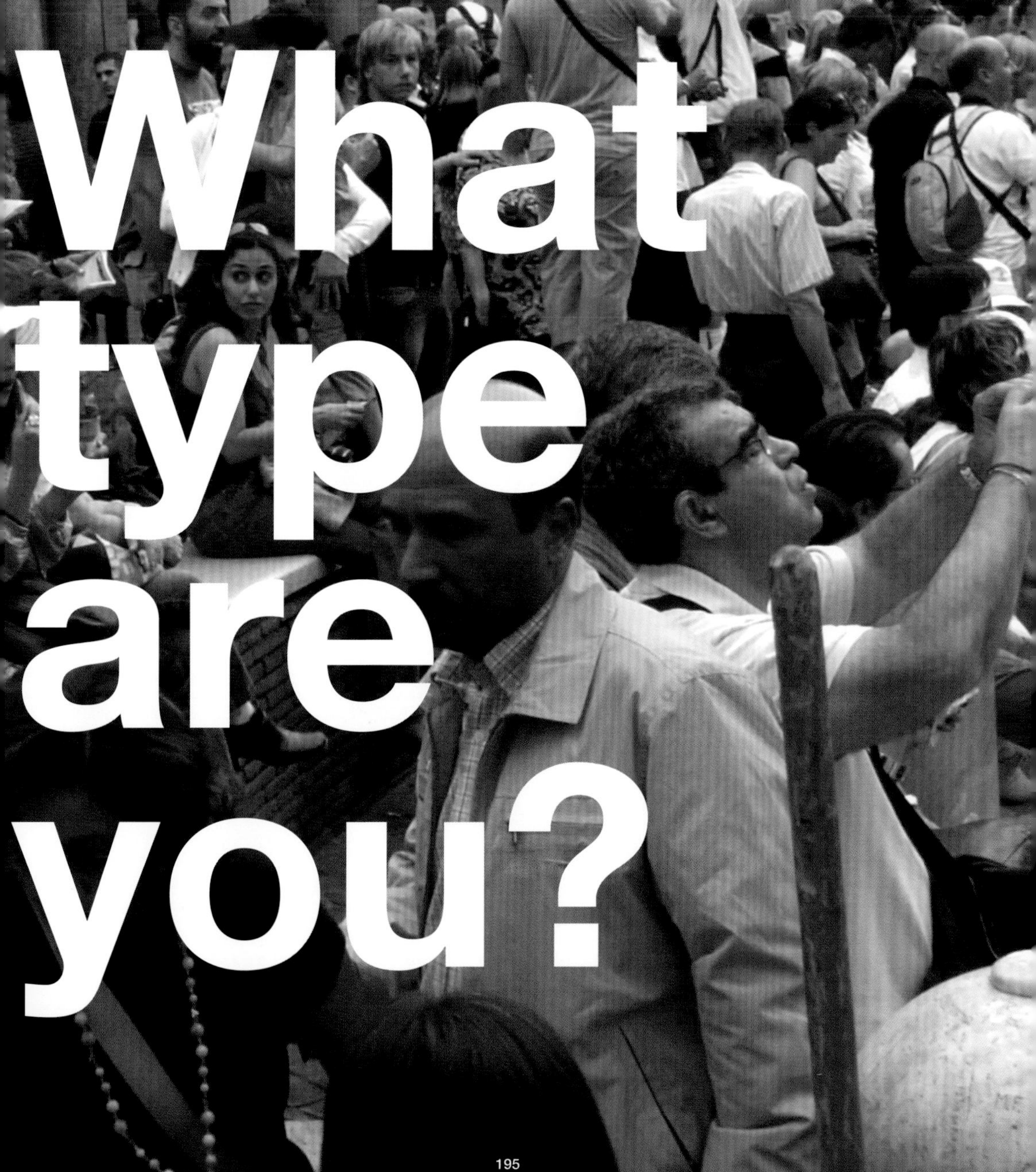

What
type
are
you?

EXECUTION IS
EVERYTHING

KEEP LOVING THE SMELL OF A PAPER
AND THE FEEL OF A PENCIL.

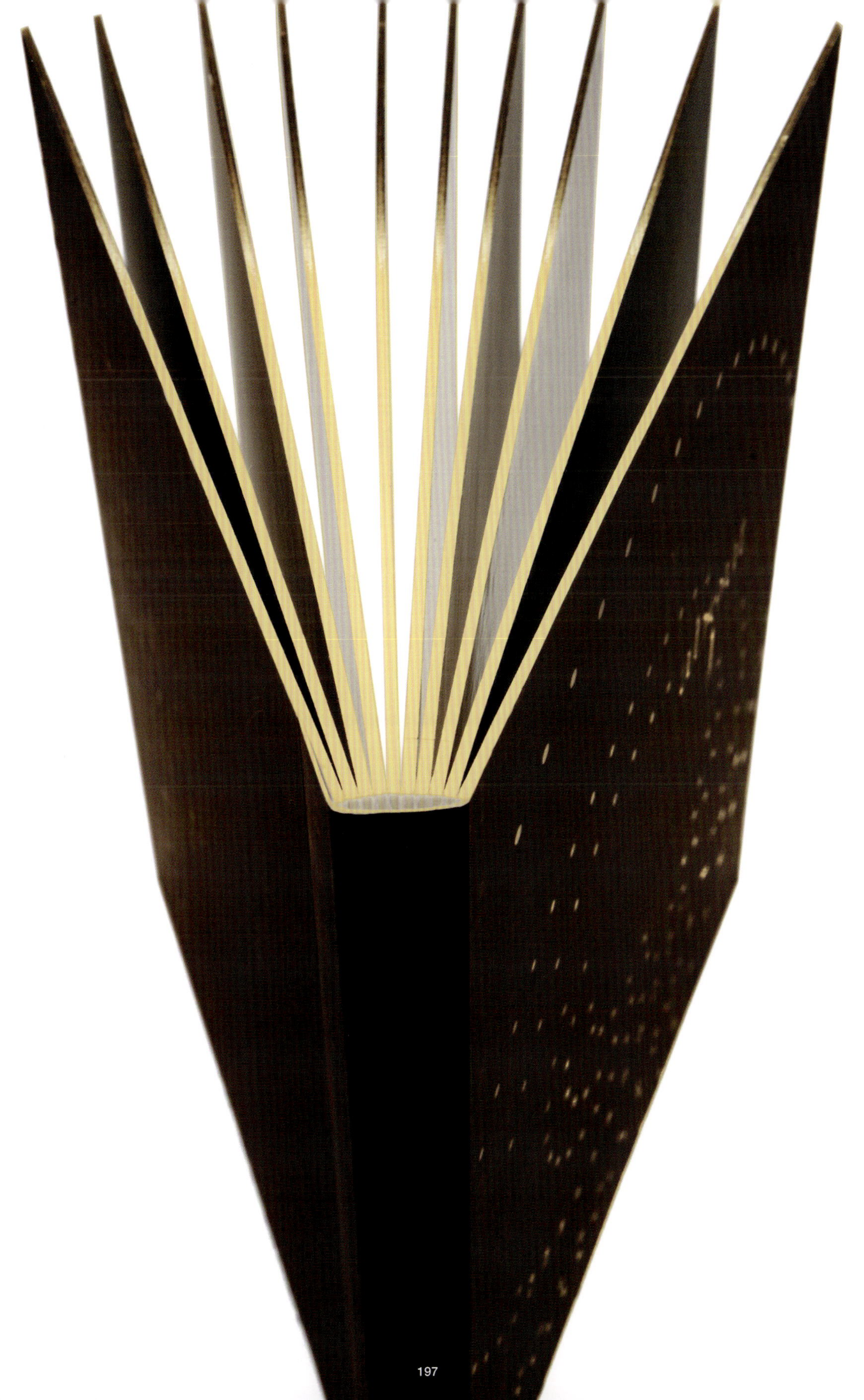

DRESSCODE for printing

The basic keys to make a promotion or publication memorable are the wild and fascinating idea, the amazing visualization of the image that seems to slow time for a few seconds, the special texture when it is touched, and the format in which it is presented. All this would make some people widen their eyes.

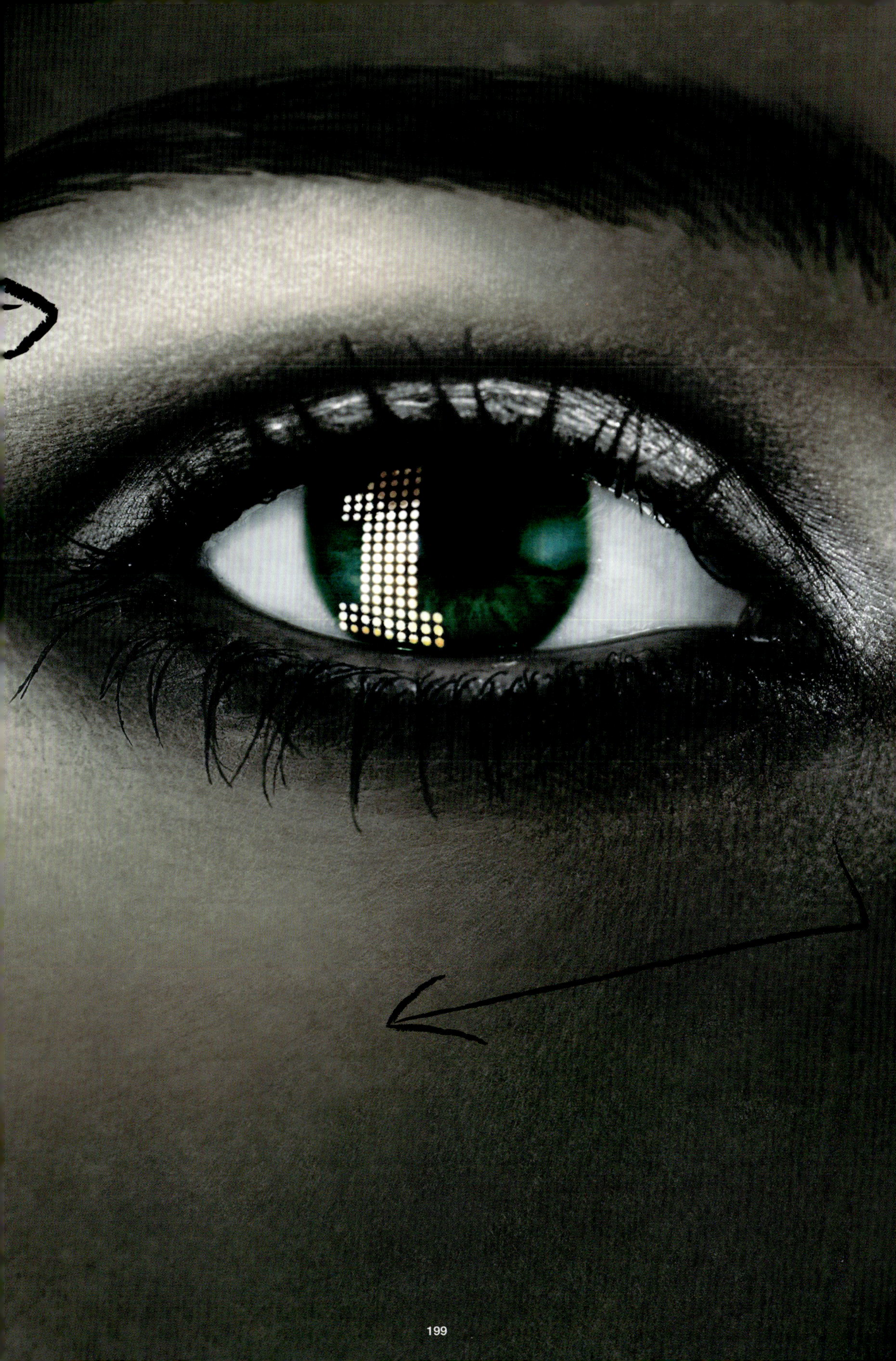

to ink or
not to ink?

When we are on press, we love working with the printer to tweak the details in the ink blends to obtain the most desirable effect.
There is also a great deal of pleasure for us in using different materials – from paper to plastic to metal – to blend and combine for design effects that solve communication objectives.
However, in our experience, great prints are often being underappreciated, and yet they surround us like a never-ending wall.
The inseparable relationship with prints and publications is stronger than ever, and it especially has changed the face of product in this fabulous time of being. All the delightful elements in printing are the weight-bearing point of the world of art and design. Typography is a special passion, design for paper a loving experience.

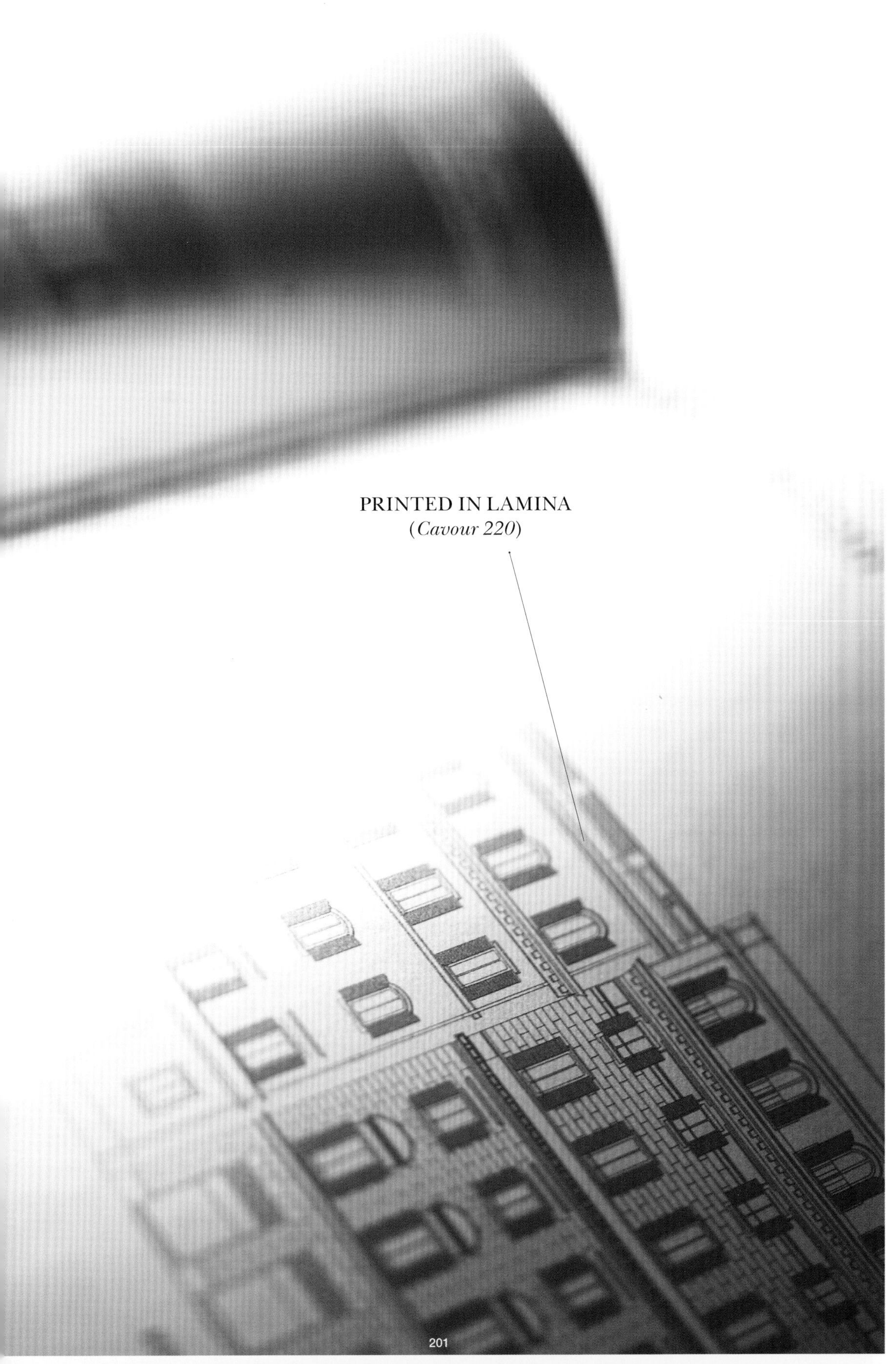

PRINTED IN LAMINA
(*Cavour 220*)

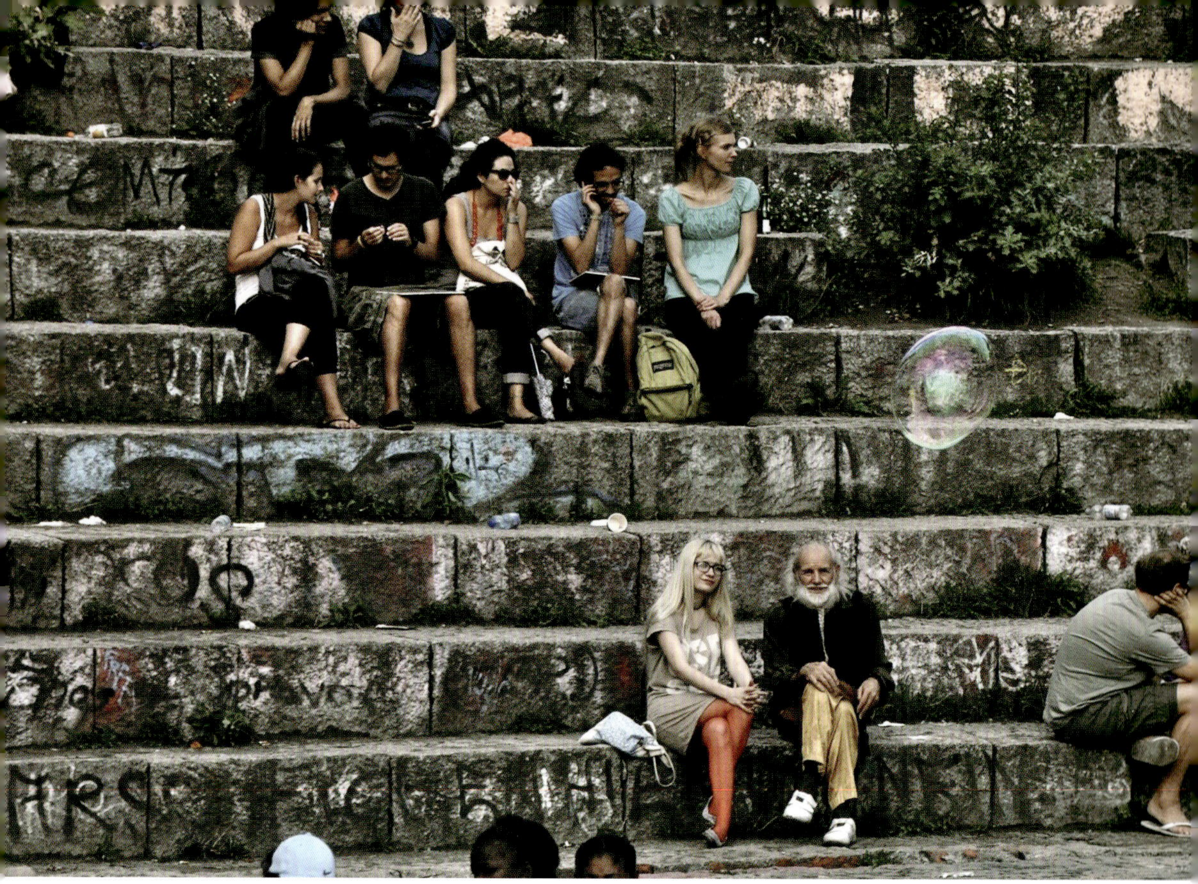

FINDING THE SHAPE TO NARRATE SEVERAL STORIES FOR A LARGE CROWD

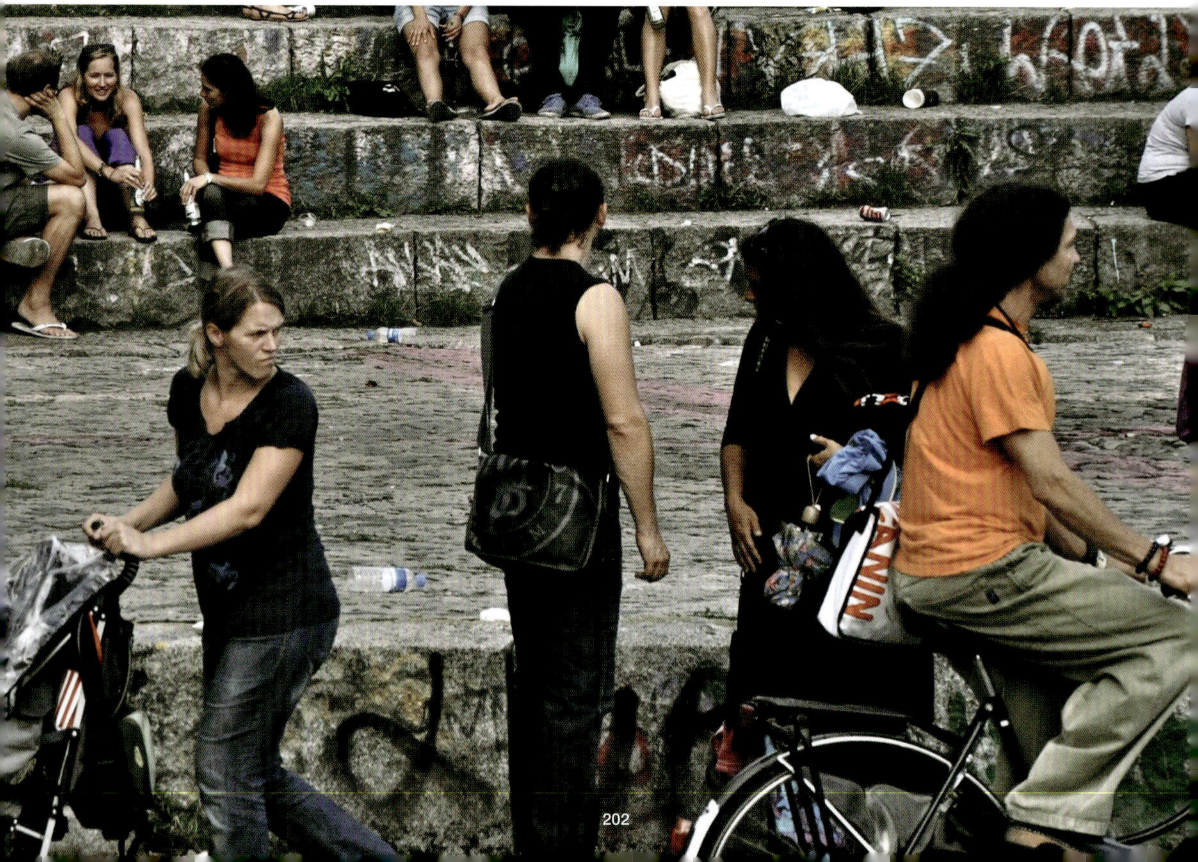

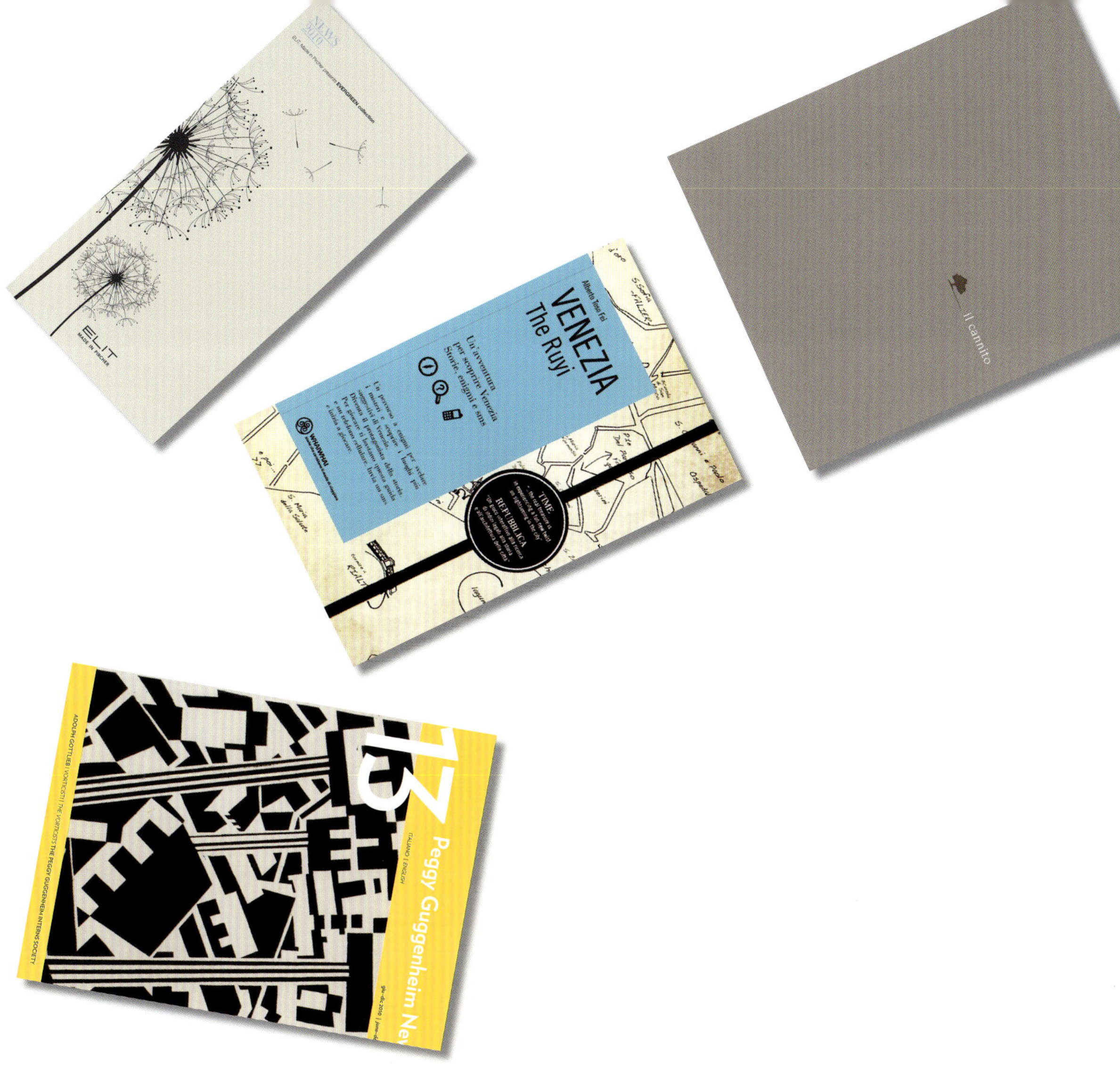

<u>*Reading is never*</u> *a unilateral act: just as we get engrossed in it, all its visual, conceptual, psychological, and even existential features form themselves into a unitary experience from which, in some way or other, we emerge changed.*

<u>*So a book project*</u> *encompasses an entire world, a universe of possibilities: it is hardly surprising that philosophers have taken reading as being a physical pleasure, a way of engaging with the world, getting lost and then rediscovering oneself the same as before and yet somehow different.*

WE ASSUME THAT THE BEST RESULT WOULD
COME FROM THE MOST BASIC MESSAGE,
AND WHAT WE WANTED TO CONVEY WAS
UNDERSTATED ELEGANCE.

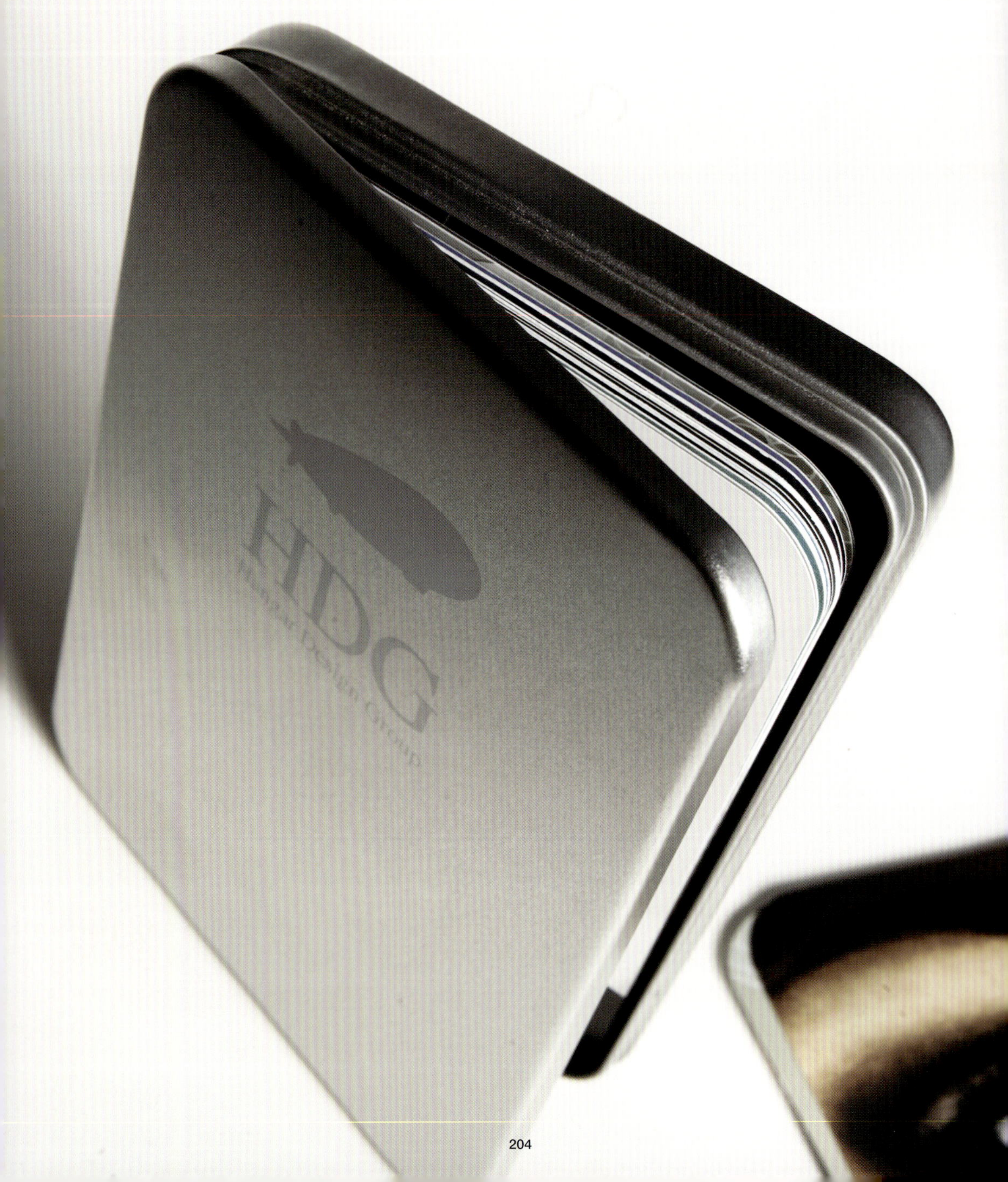

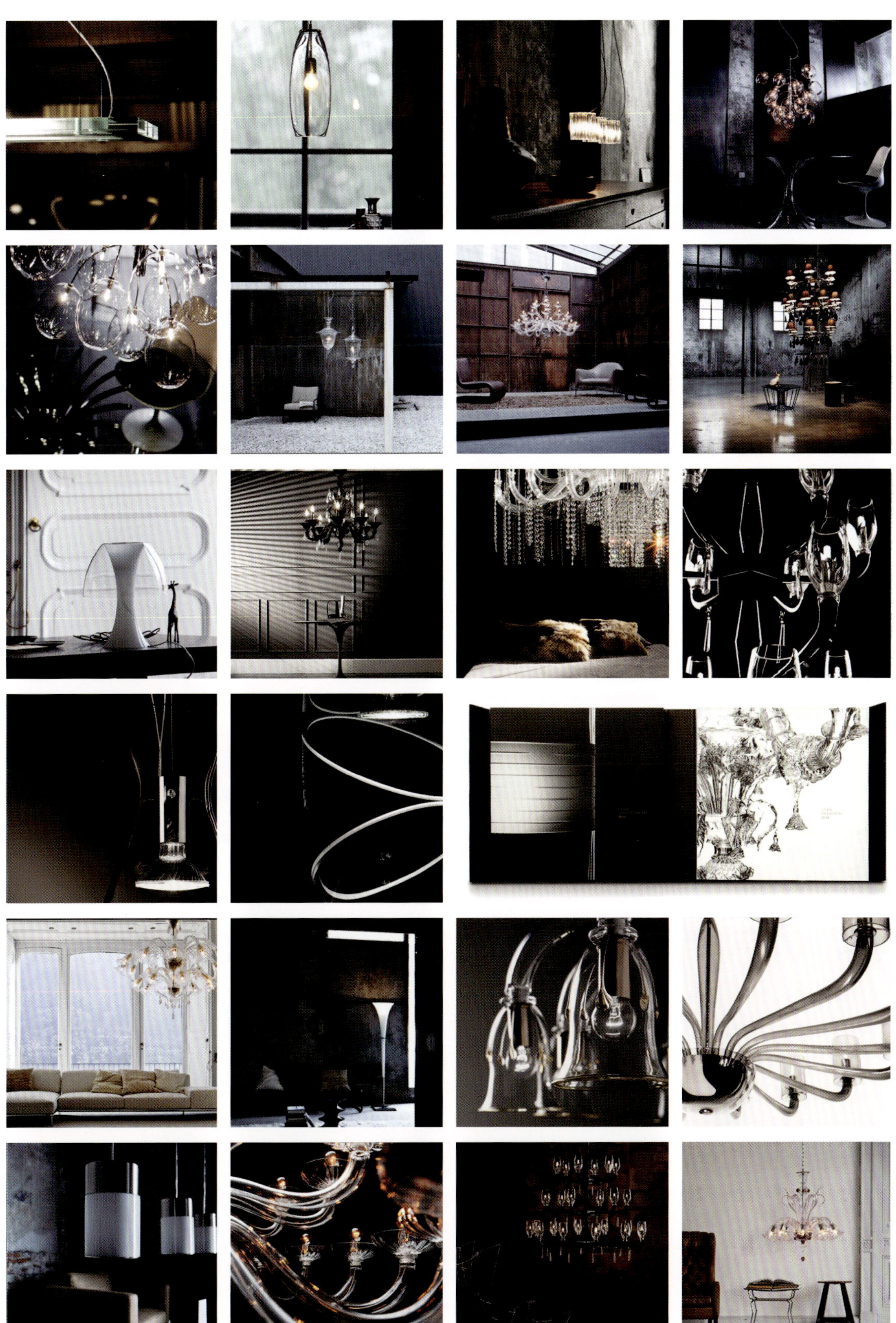

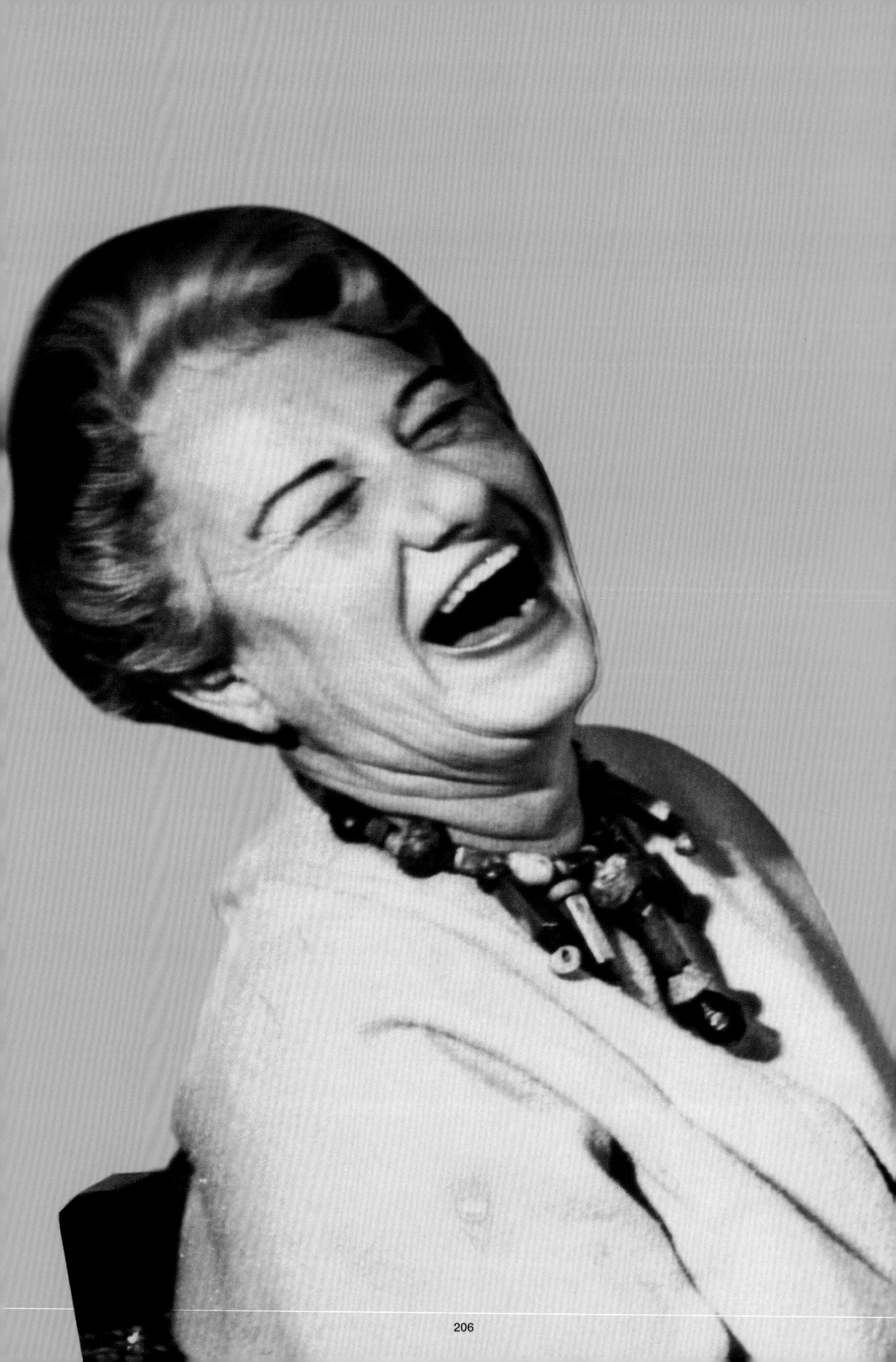

DO IT
Quietly

Usually, when we decide to focus on redesigning
a logo, we don't know what we want, but we do
know what we don't want.
Our first objective is to create something that
would break through the noise – but in a
simple, sophisticated way reflecting our taste.
In other words, we want to do it quietly.

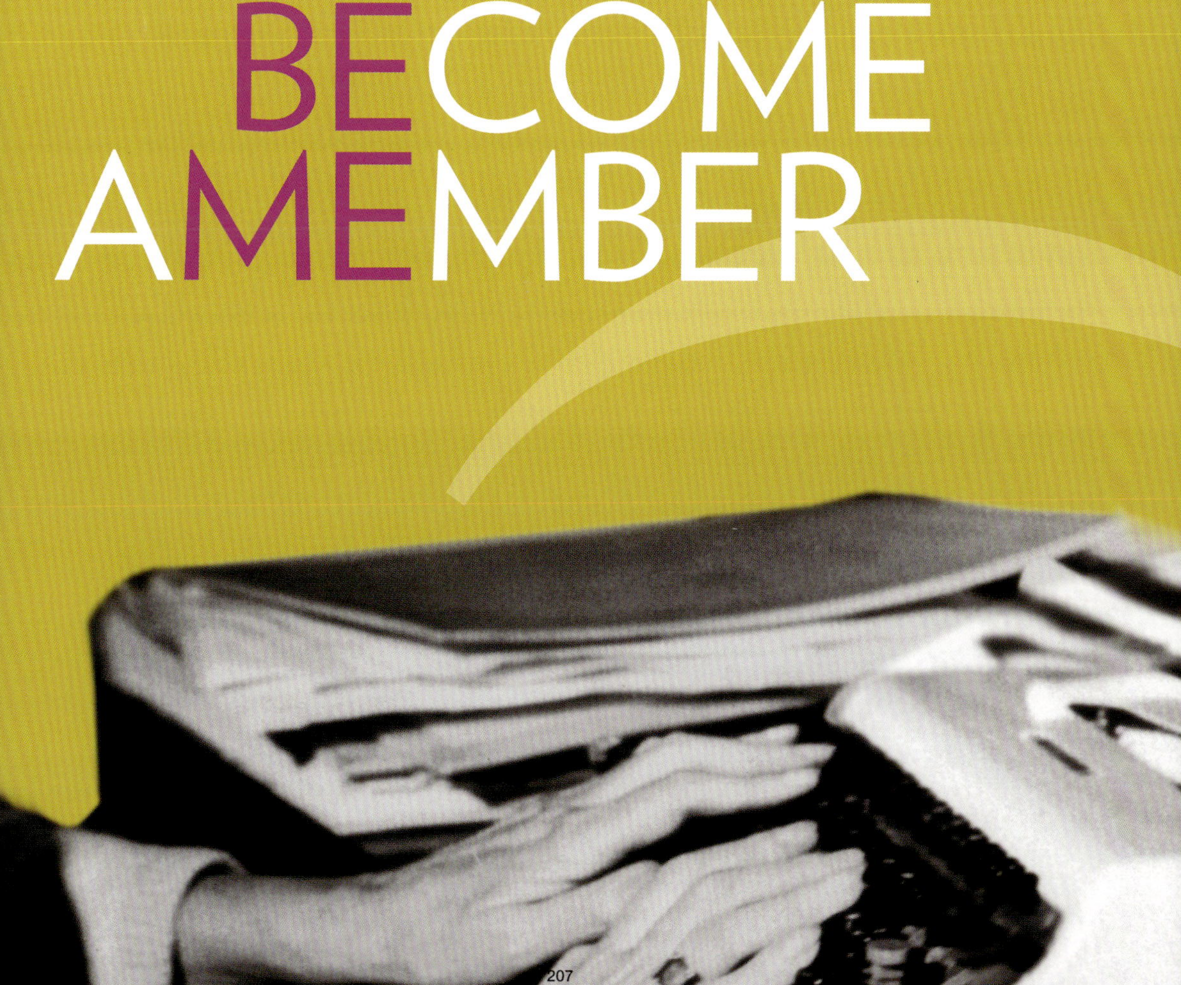

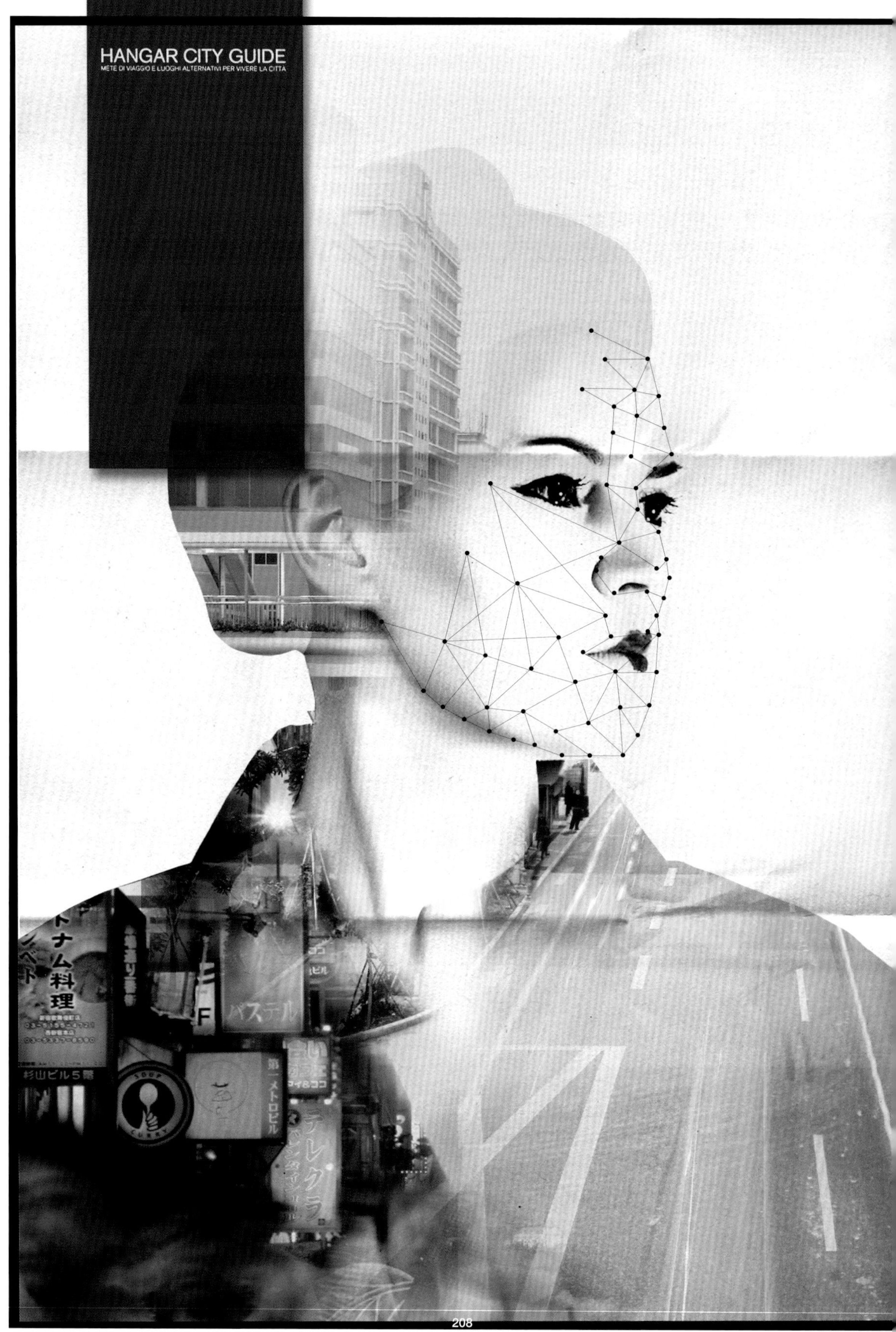

HANGAR CITY GUIDE
METE DI VIAGGIO E LUOGHI ALTERNATIVI PER VIVERE LA CITTÀ

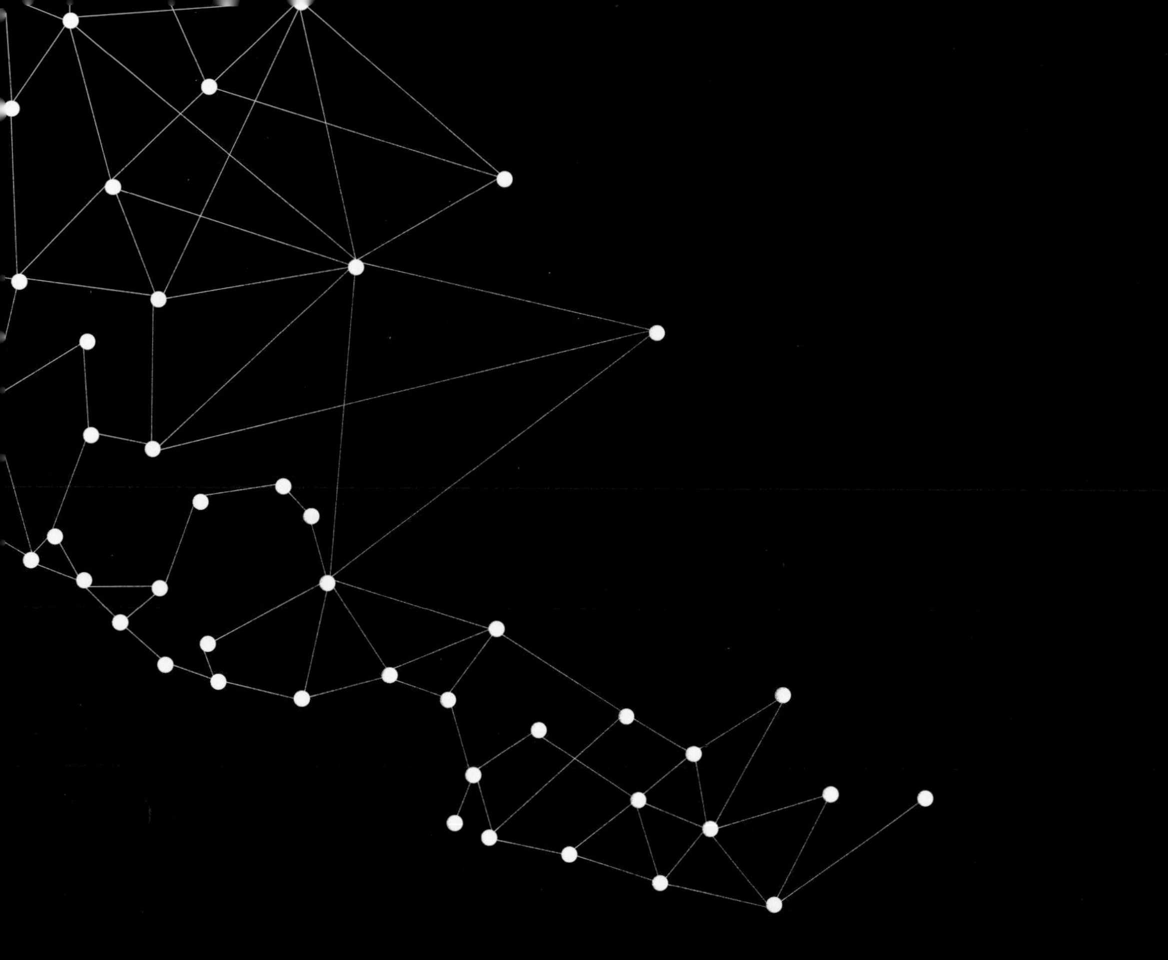

THE MAP IS NOT THE TERRITORY

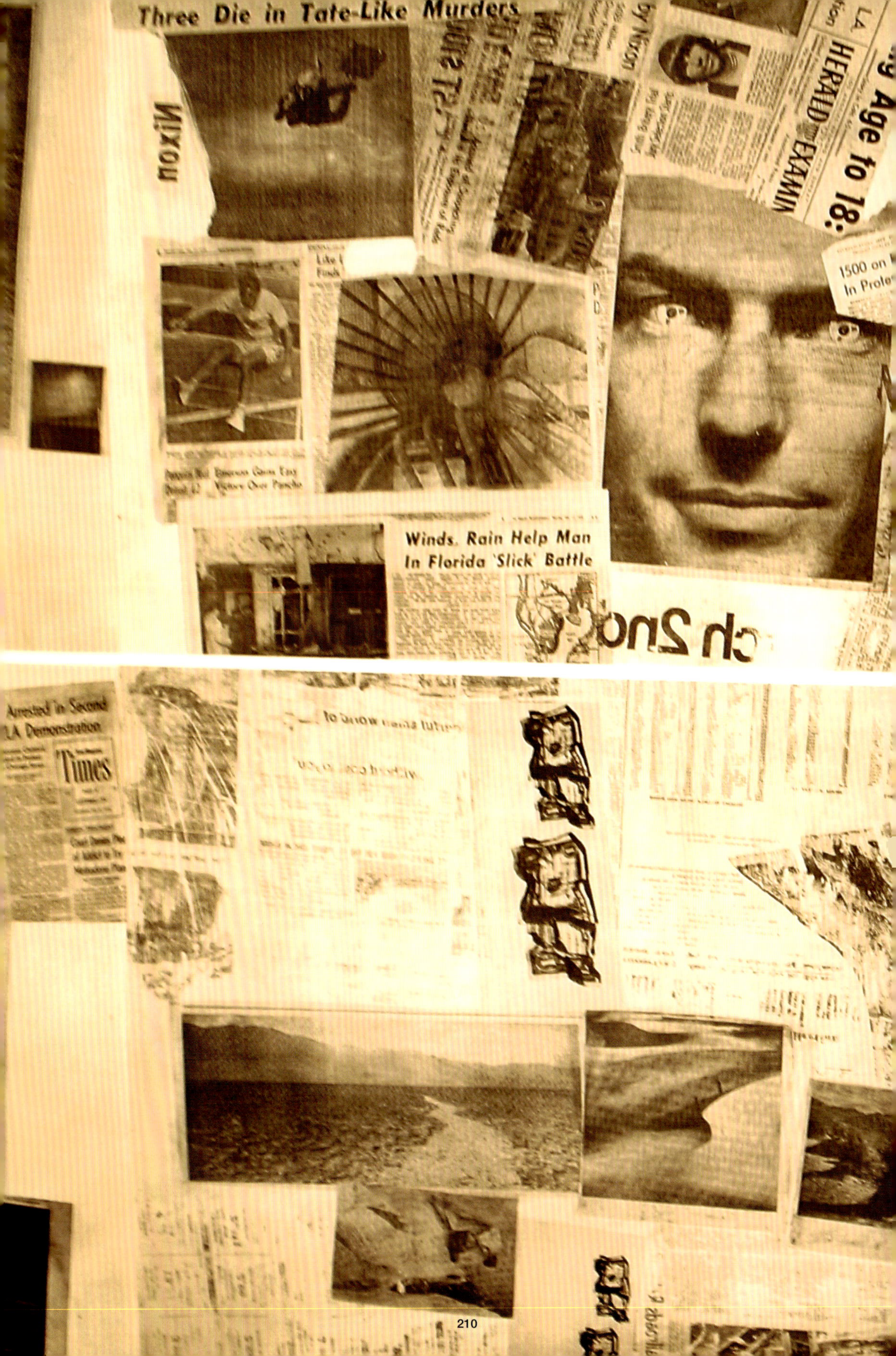

Three Die in Tate-Like Murders
Nixon
by NIXON
LA HERALD EXAMIN
y Age to 18:
1500 on
In Prote
Like
Finds
P.
D.
Winds. Rain Help Man
In Florida 'Slick' Battle
Ch 2no C
Arrested in Second
LA Demonstration
Times

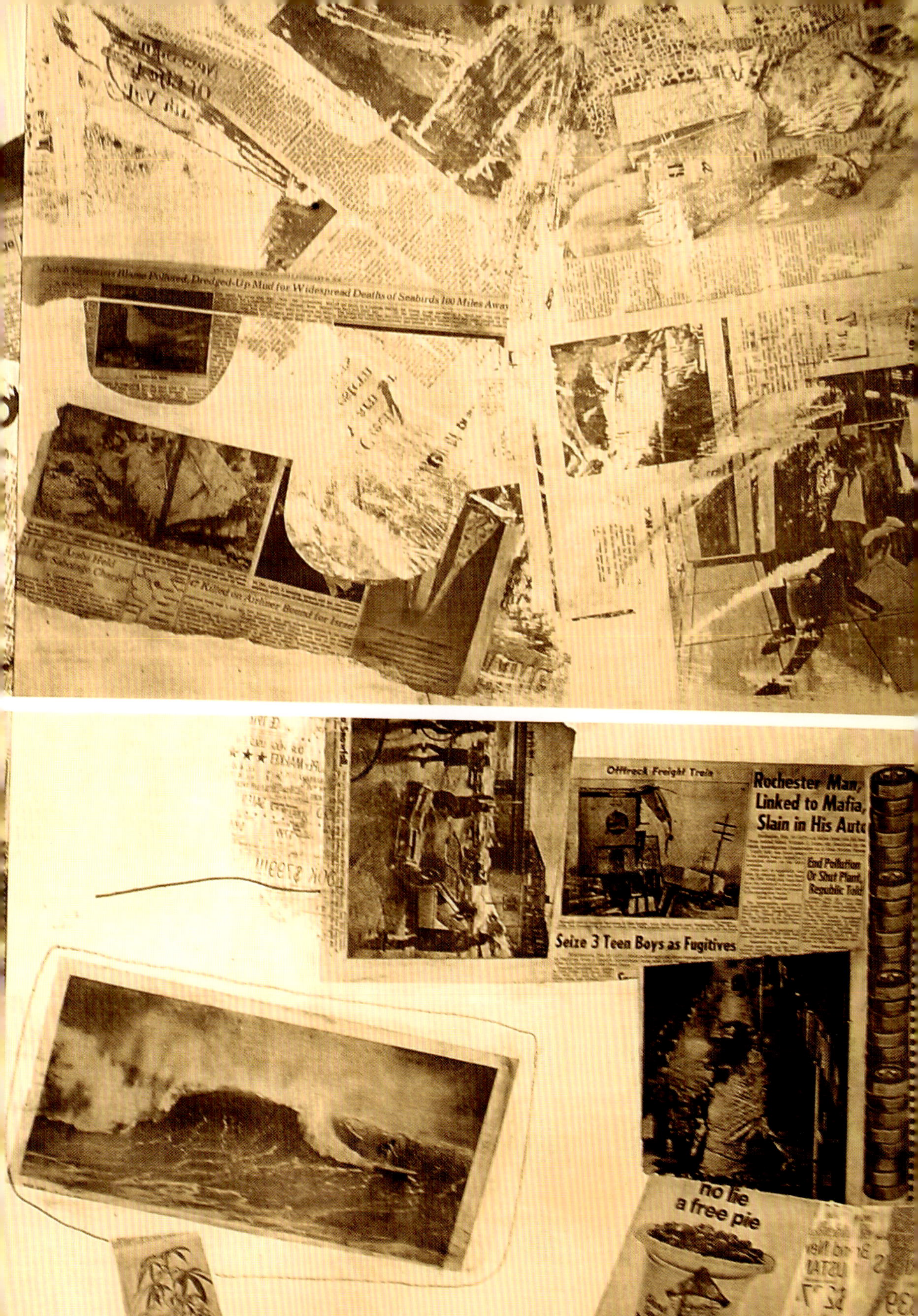
Dutch Scientists Blame Polluted, Dredged-Up Mud for Widespread Deaths of Seabirds 100 Miles Away
Offtrack Freight Train
Rochester Man, Linked to Mafia, Slain in His Auto
End Pollution Or Shut Plant, Republic Told
Seize 3 Teen Boys as Fugitives
no lie
a free pie

CROP
COVER LAYOUT

THE GENTLE ART OF
FRAMING THINGS

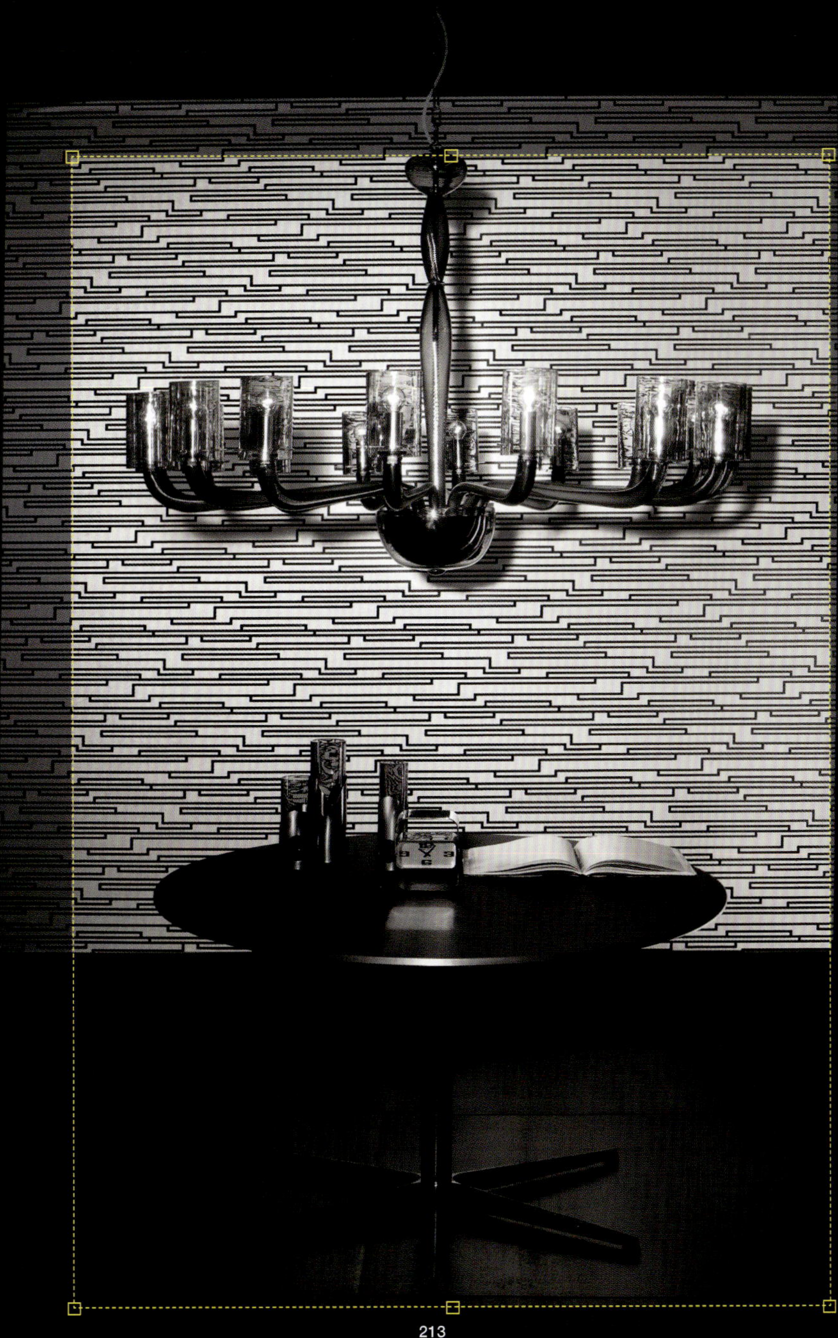

THE ACT OF USING PAPER HAS BEEN FAMOUS FOR ITS UNIQUENESS. PAPER CAN BE FOLDED, RIPPED, BURNT – BASICALLY WHATEVER ONE CAN IMAGINE.

GREAT PRINTS SPICE OUT OUR LIVES

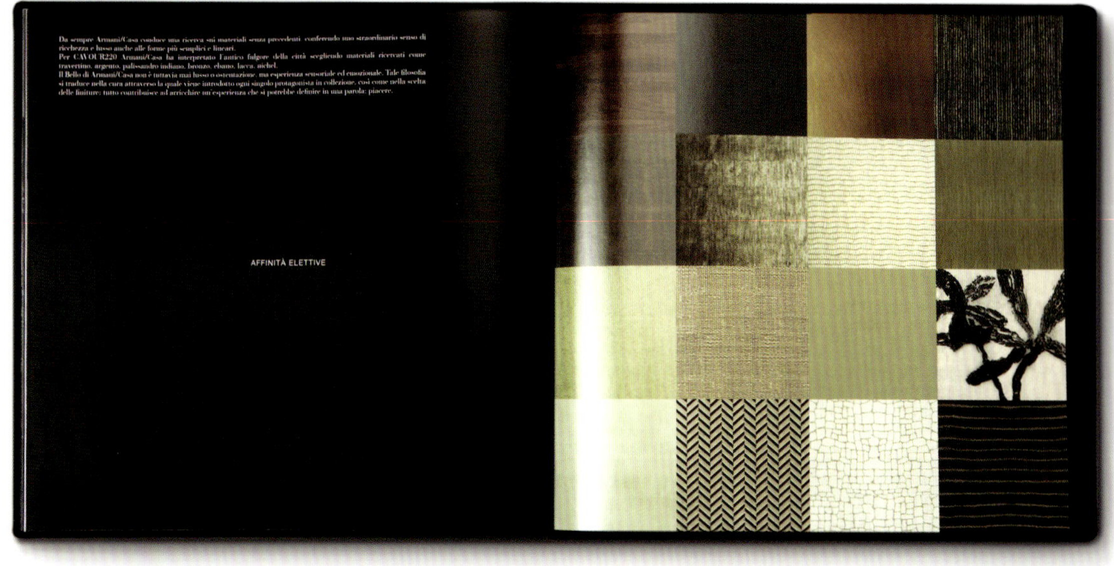

SO, IT IS ONLY A MATTER OF WHO WOULD BE BRAVE ENOUGH TO CHALLENGE ALL THOSE EXISTING MANIPULATIONS WITH A MODERN TWIST.

IN THE MOST UNPREDICTABLE WAYS

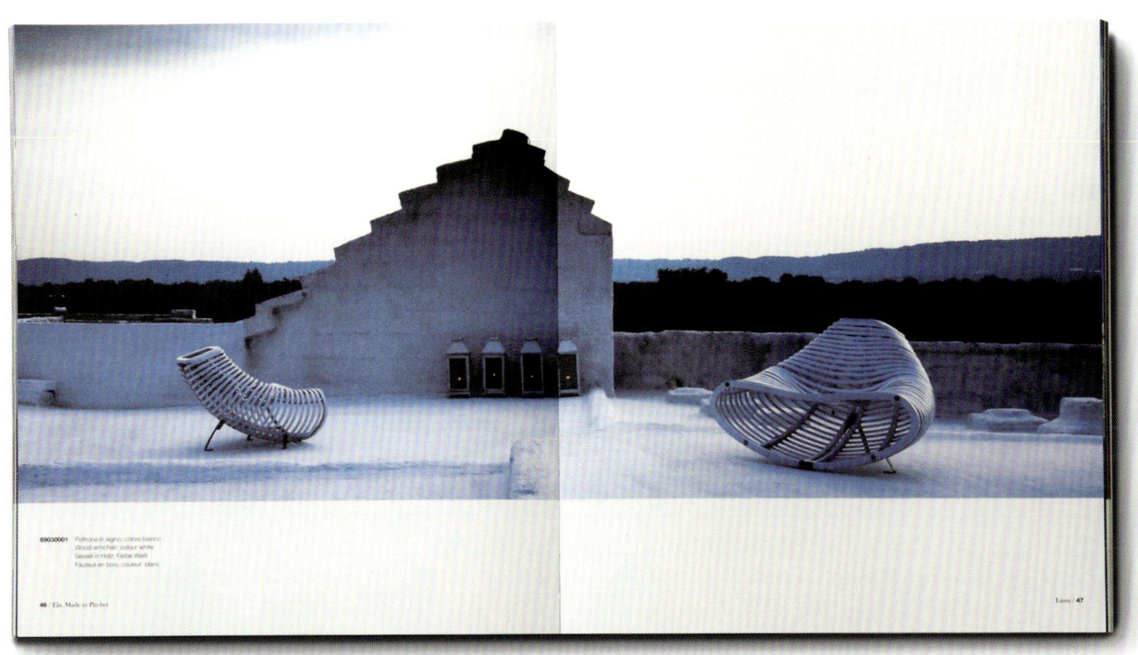

46 / Ele. Made in Pitcher

Lima / 47

PRESTIGE BROCHURE COMPOSED OF APPROX. 44 PAGES IN 30 x 30 FORMAT PRINTED IN 6 COLORS PLUS ACRYLIC COATING RECTO/VERSO ON PREMIUM GLOSSY PAPER FABRIC-COVERED HARDBOUND COVER WITH BLACK HOT-STAMPED OVERPRINT STITCHED AND HARDBOUND THROUGHOUT 1500 COPIES

glossy	
mat	**050**
opaque	
coated	**100**
paper	
plastic	**110**
type	
sides	**150**
colors	
acrylic	**200**
glossy	
mat	
opaque	**250**
coated	
paper	**300**
plastic	
type	
sides	**450**
colors	
acrylic	**g/m²**

28 PAGES IN 21 x 30 FORMAT PRINTED IN 6 COLORS PLUS ACRYLIC COATING RECTO/ VERSO ON PREMIUM GLOSSY

PANTONE 5th COLOR

big catalogue for box copies format internal pages cover paper internal page paper cover print internal pages print binding box print small catalogue for box copies format

PAPER WITH PLASTICIZED AND COLORED COVER CUT, GATHERED AND BOUND WITH SINGER STITCHING.

ART OF

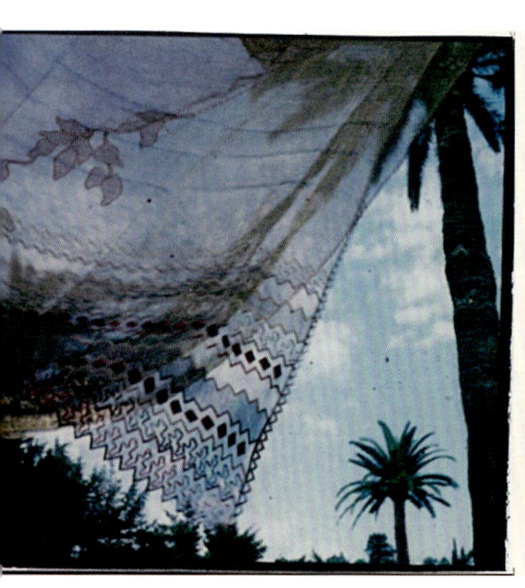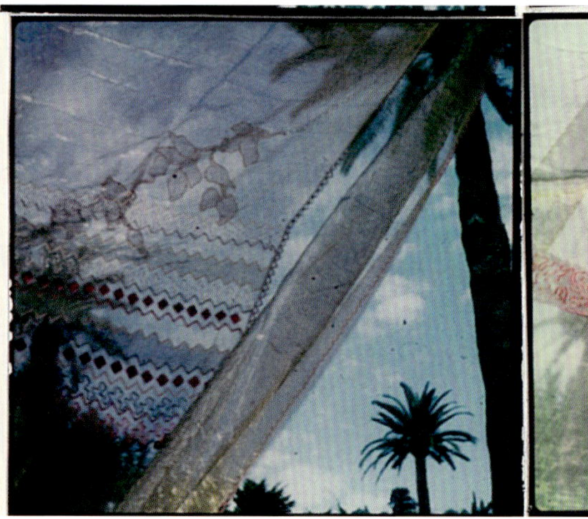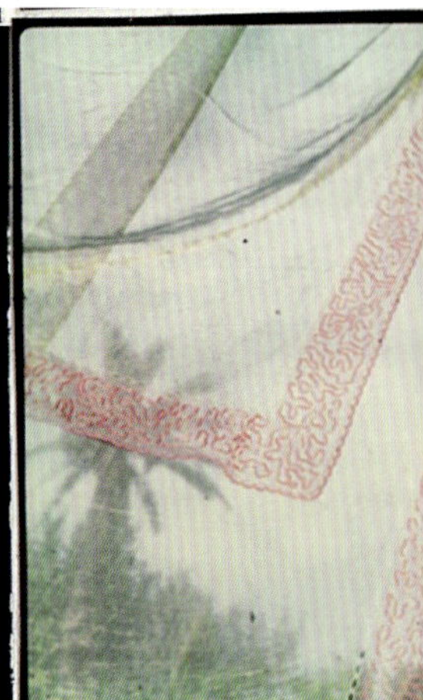

SUDDEN

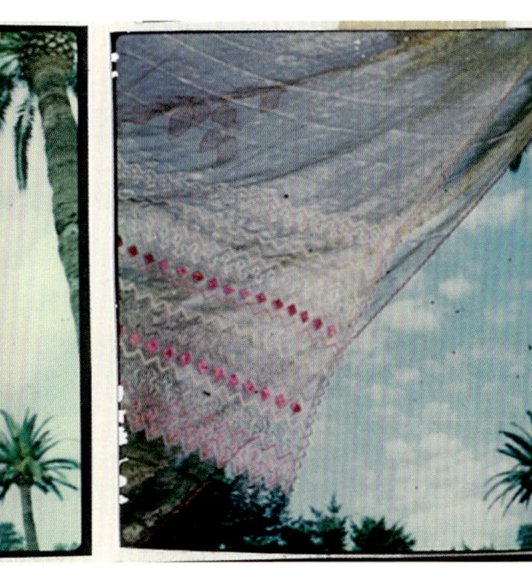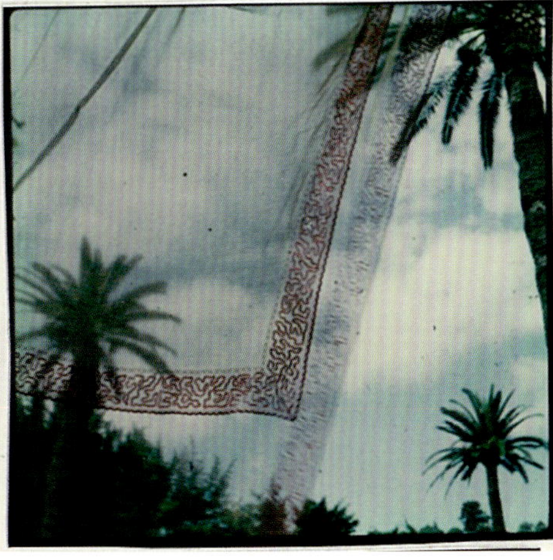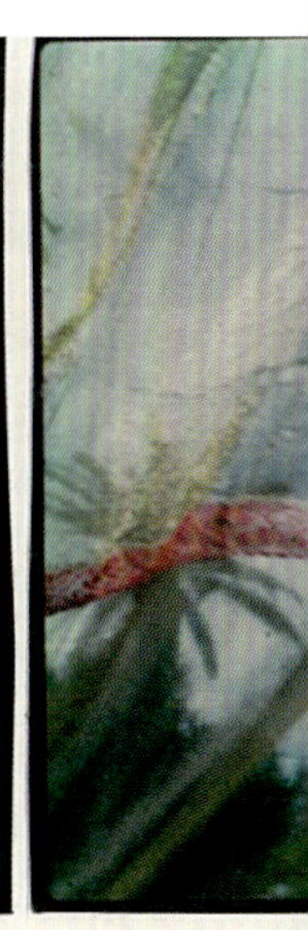

ON STAGE

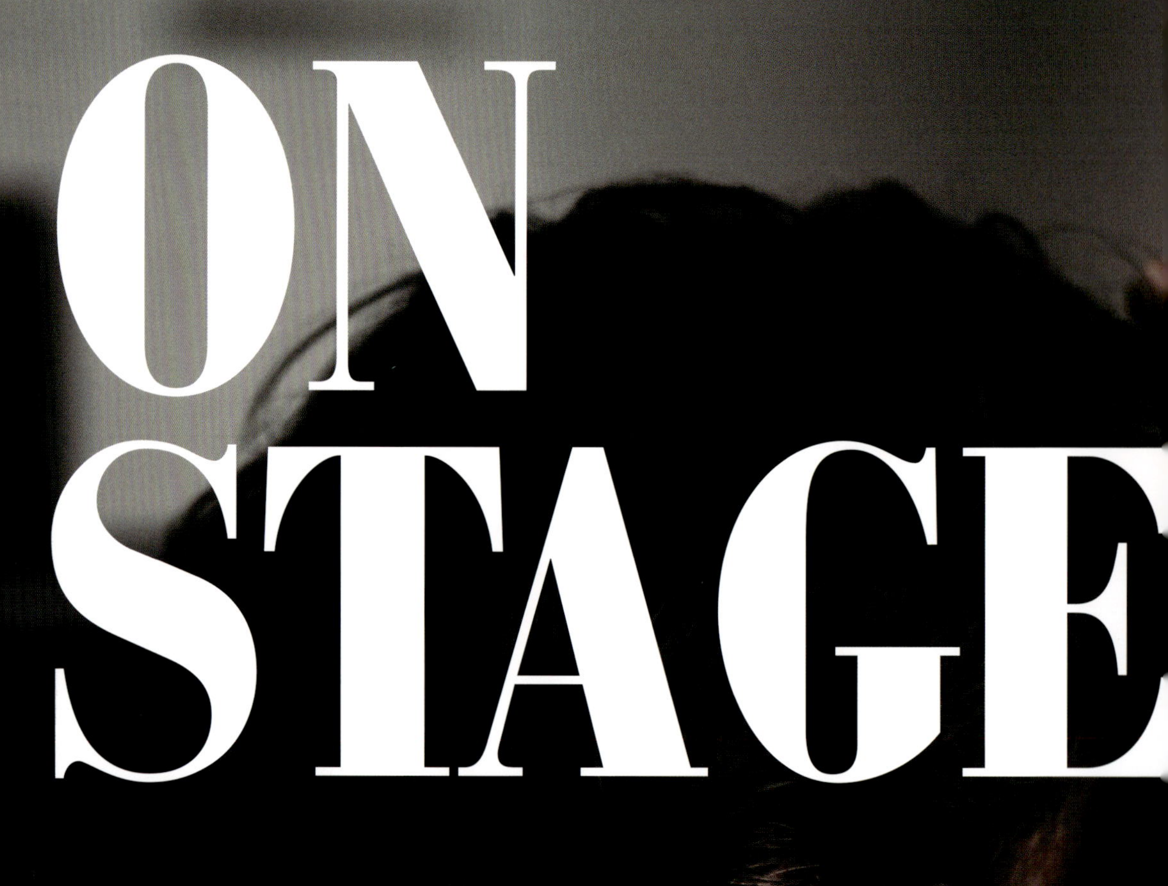

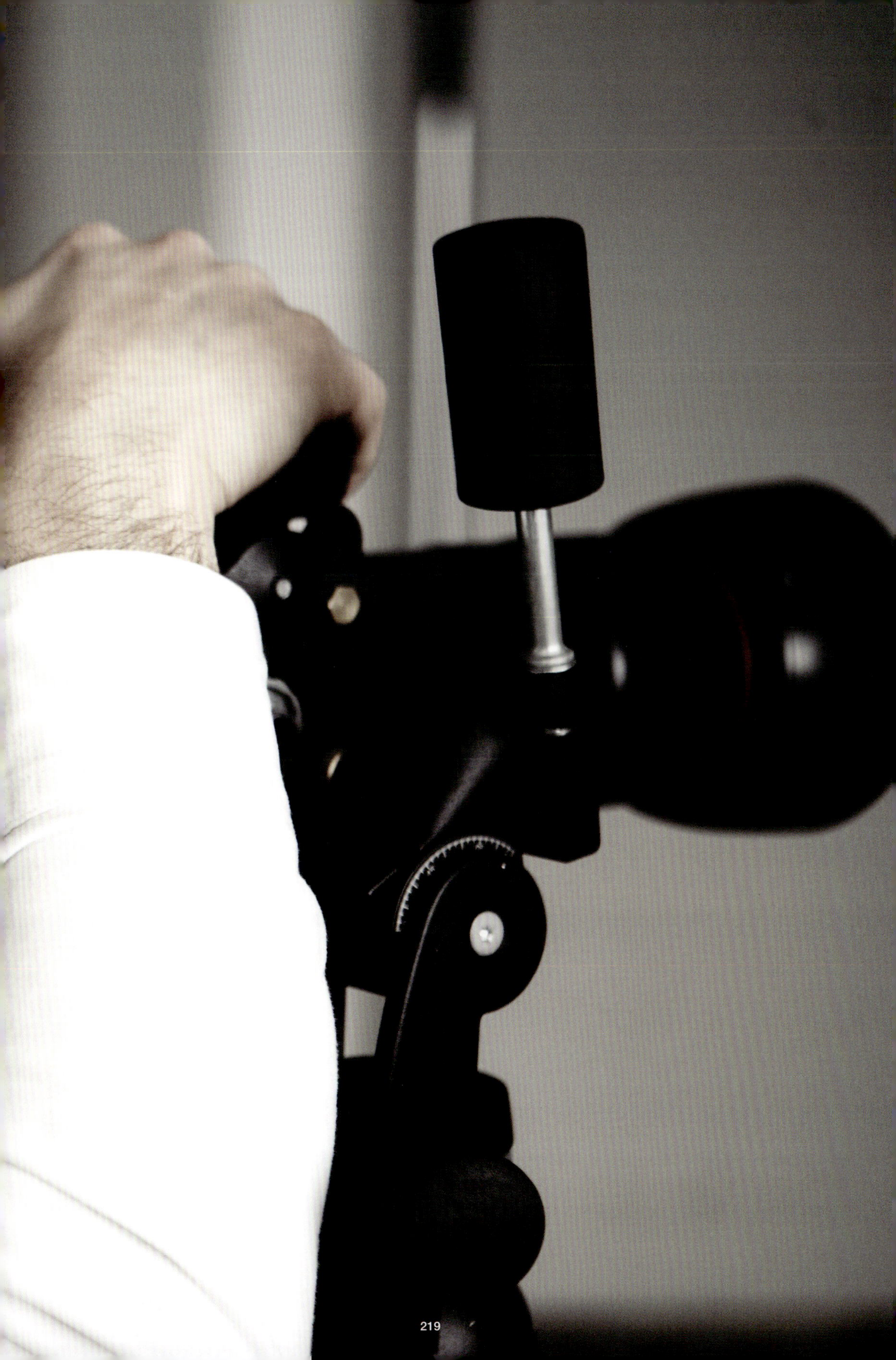

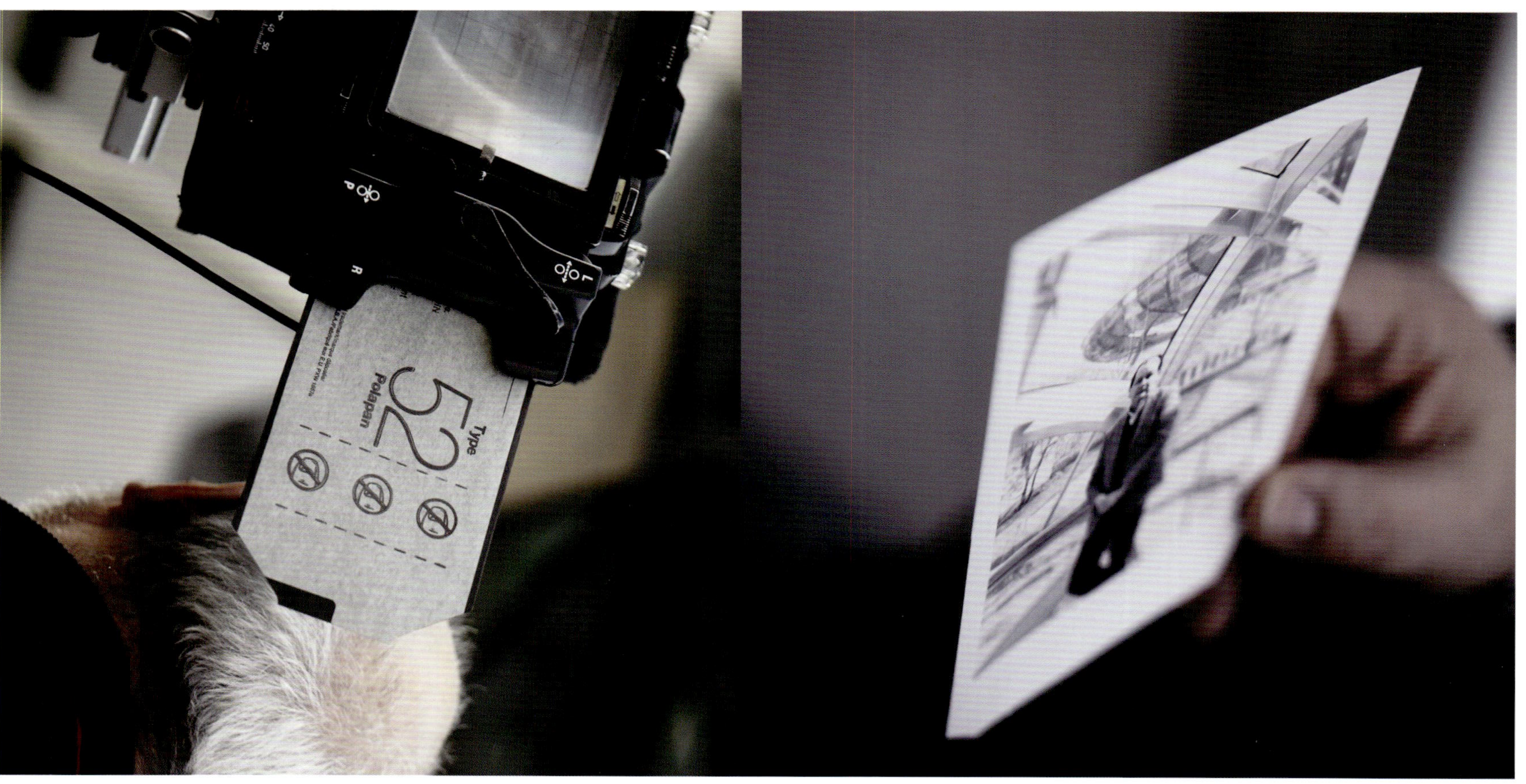

IN THE MIDDLE OF EVERY ROLL OF
FILM THERE'S ALWAYS
A MISPLACED PHOTOGRAPH,
SOMETHING THAT DOESN'T
BELONG TO US YET.

THOSE ARE THE PHOTOGRAPHS
THAT HELP US FIND WHERE
TO GO NEXT.

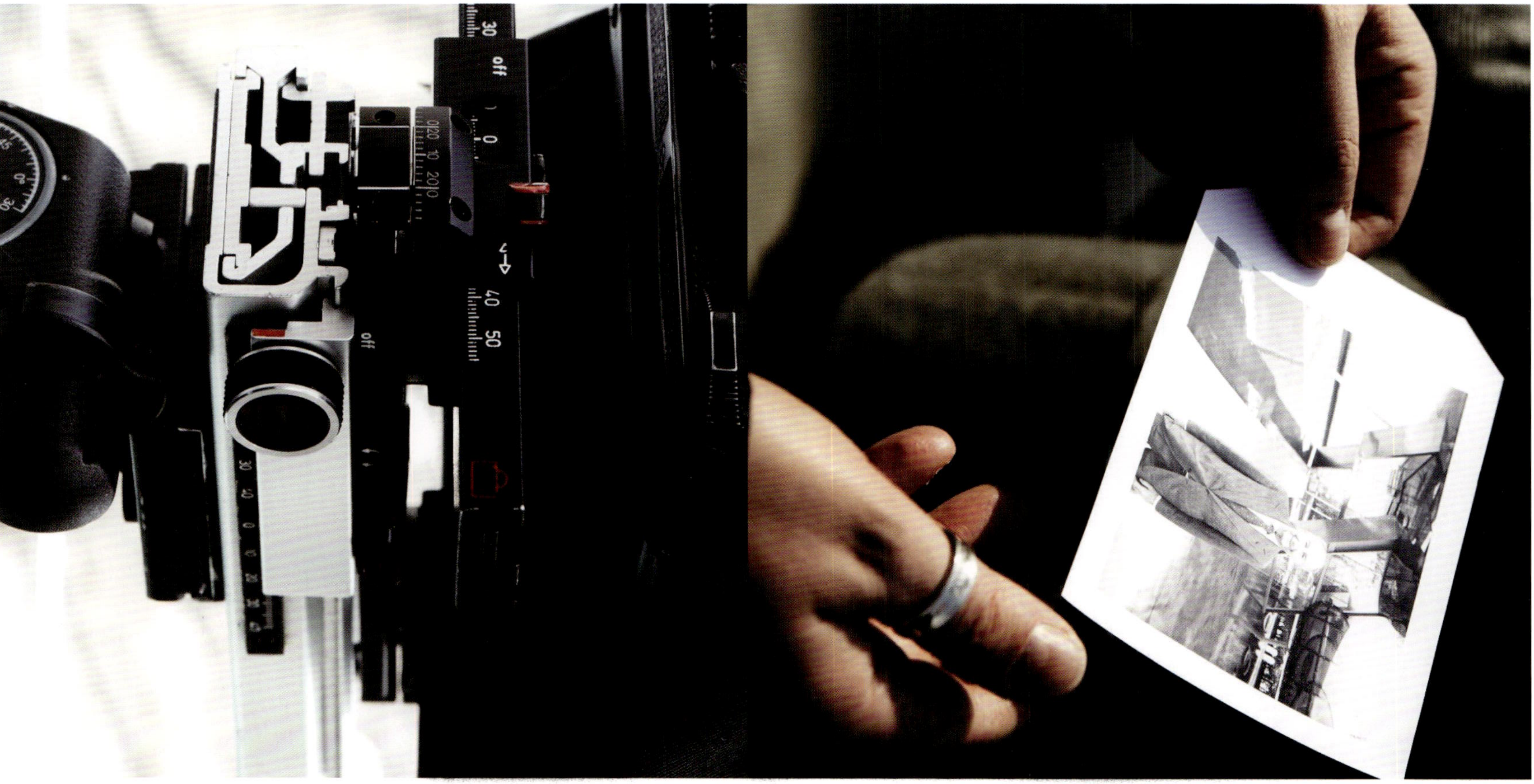

IT IS SHORTLY UNACCEPTABLE TO SIMPLY SHOOT A PICTURE AND EXPECT THAT IT WILL BE ENOUGH FOR A CLIENT. THE CONVERGENCE OF PHOTOGRAPHY AND CINEMATOGRAPHY, AND THE CHANGES IN MEDIA COMMUNICATION HAVE FORCED BRANDS TO DELIVER MULTIMEDIA CONTENT THAT IS EXPERIENTIAL – USING TECHNOLOGY AS A TOOL TO IMPLEMENT IDEAS, BUT MORE IMPORTANTLY, USING ART TO DRIVE TECHNOLOGY. THE PEOPLE WHO ARE THRIVING HAVE THE FLEXIBILITY OF MINDSET AND STRUCTURES NOT ONLY TO ADAPT BUT TO REVOLUTIONIZE – EMBRACING THE CONSTRAINTS TO TRANSFORM THEM INTO EFFICIENCY AND INNOVATION WITH THE POTENTIAL TO SET NEW STANDARDS, VALUES AND BEHAVIORS.

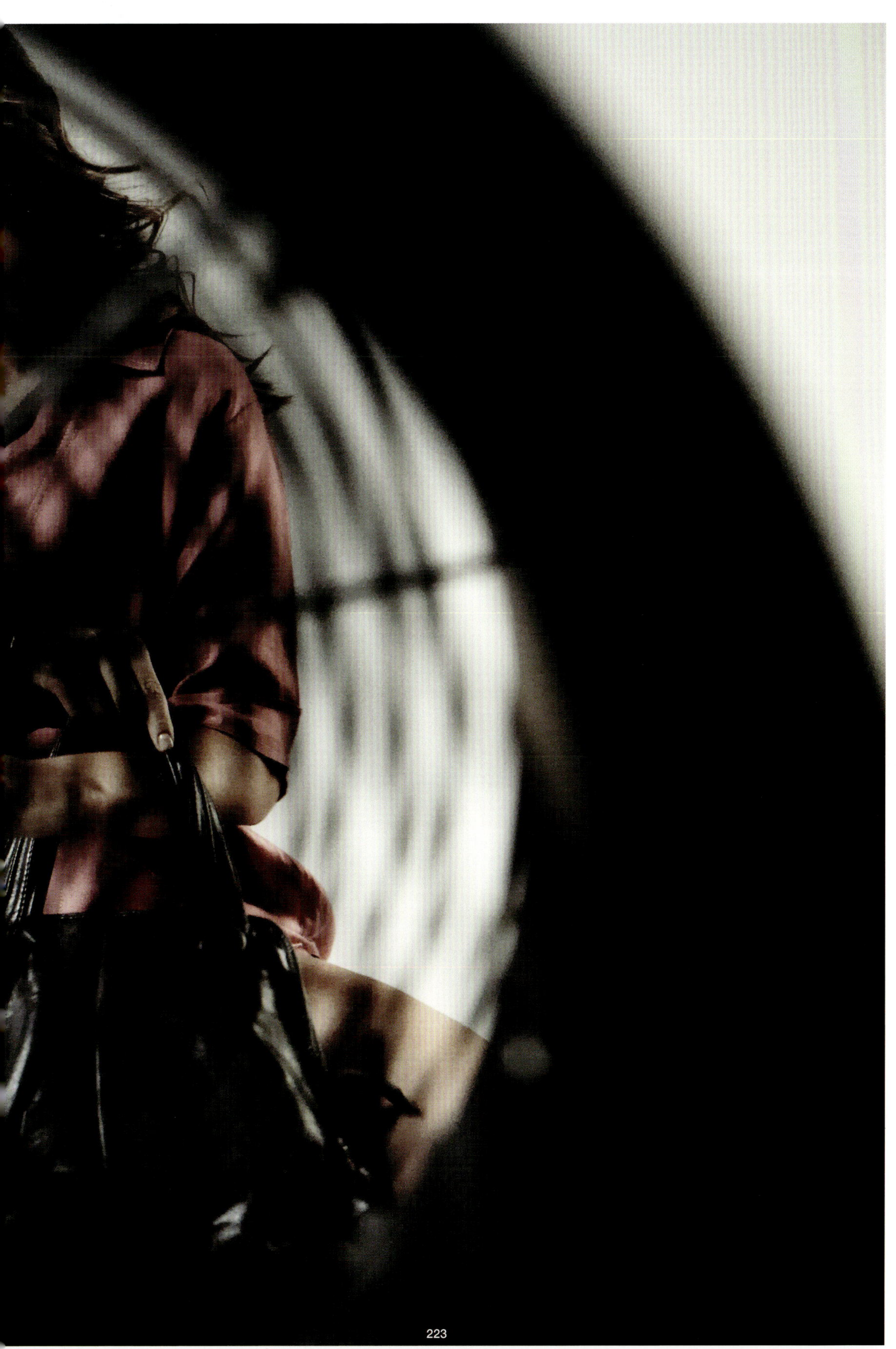

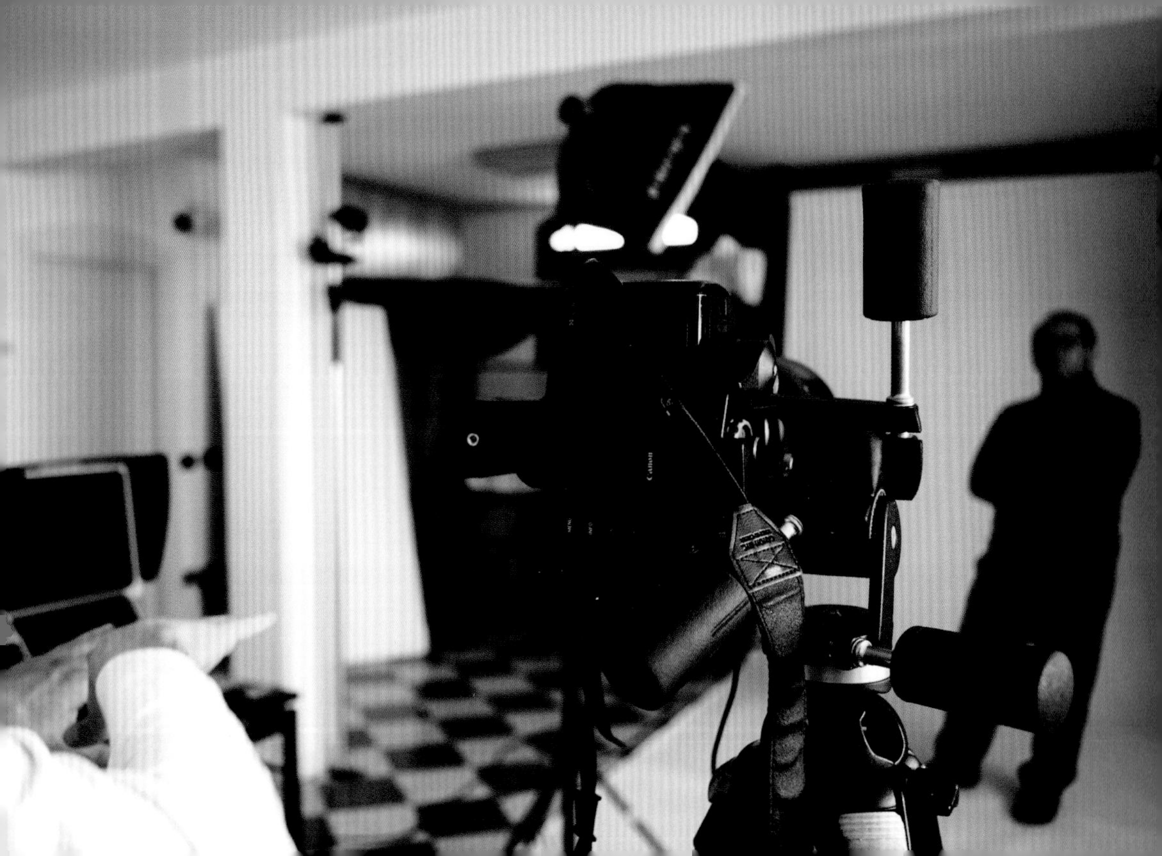

SHOOT LIKE YOU NEVER SHOT BEFORE

IT'S ABOUT SLOWING DOWN TIME.

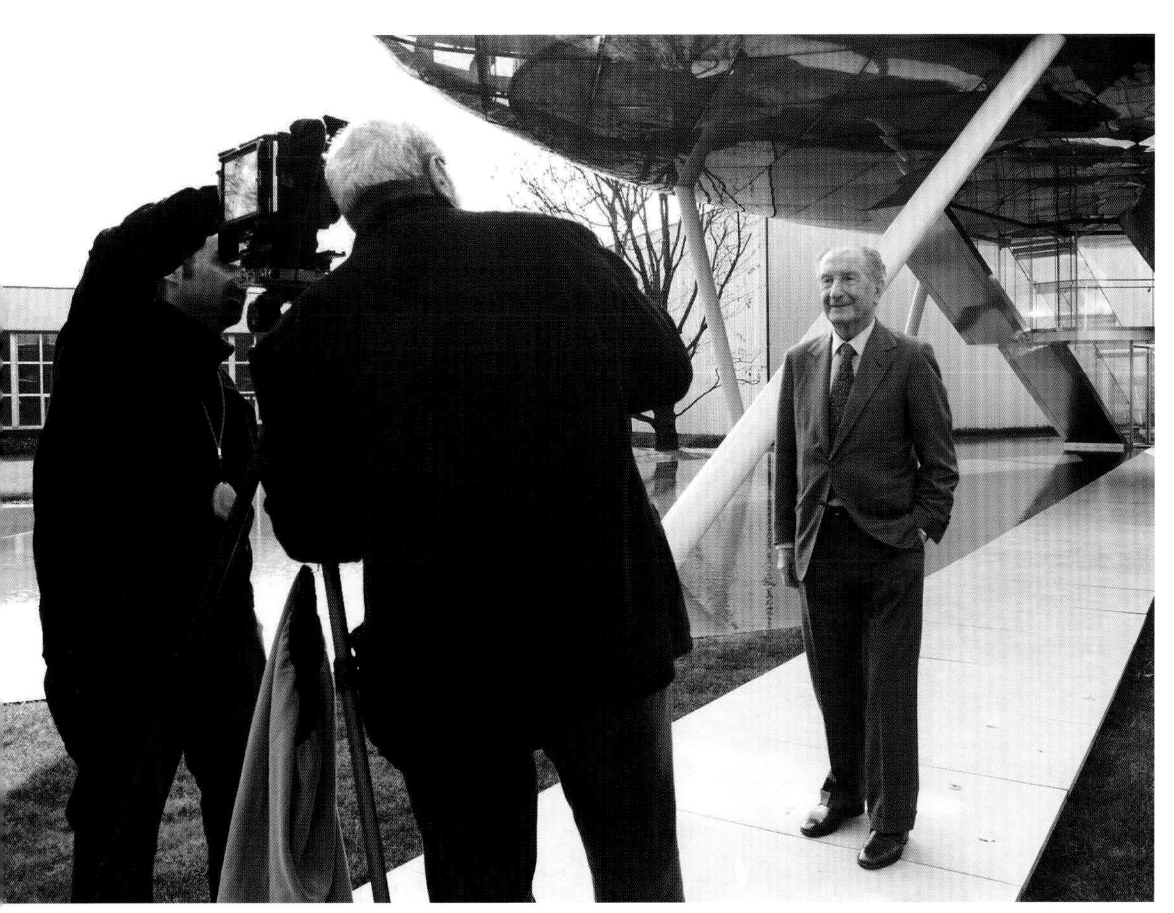

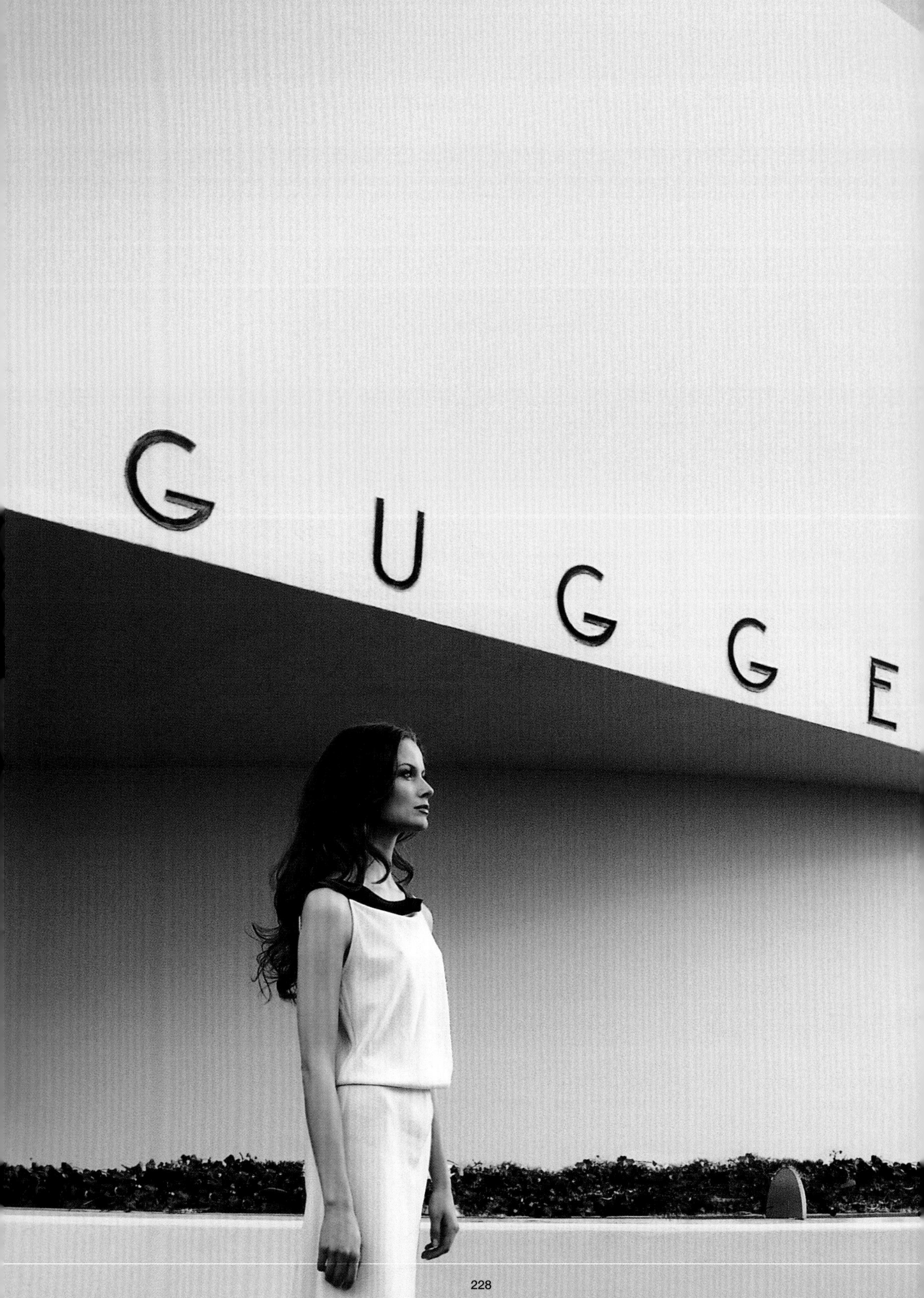

GUGGE

SOMETIMES YOU SHOULD BE ABLE TO FIND A LOCATION
WHICH NOT ONLY GIVES YOU WHAT YOU NEED,
BUT WITH A LITTLE LUCK GIVES YOU MORE THAN
WHAT YOU NEED – GIVES YOU AN EXTRA DIMENSION
THAT YOU NEVER THOUGHT POSSIBLE.

230.

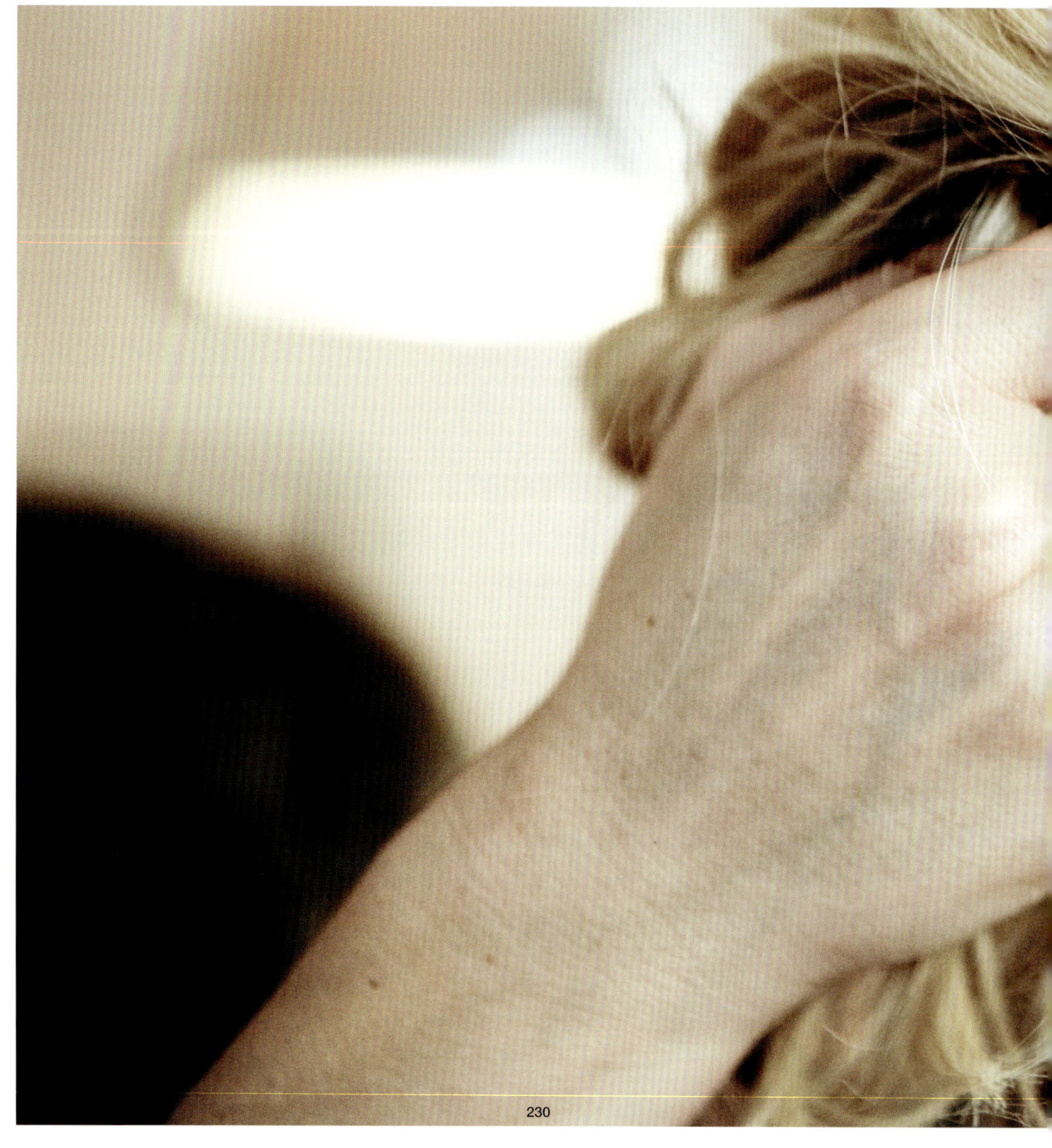

We are inspired by the idea of absence, it could be nothingness or just the idea of stillness.
It's about slowing down time. If you hide something in a photograph you create stillness.
We are trying to practice taking everything away.
We'd like to just let the image be what it is – without any references whatsoever.

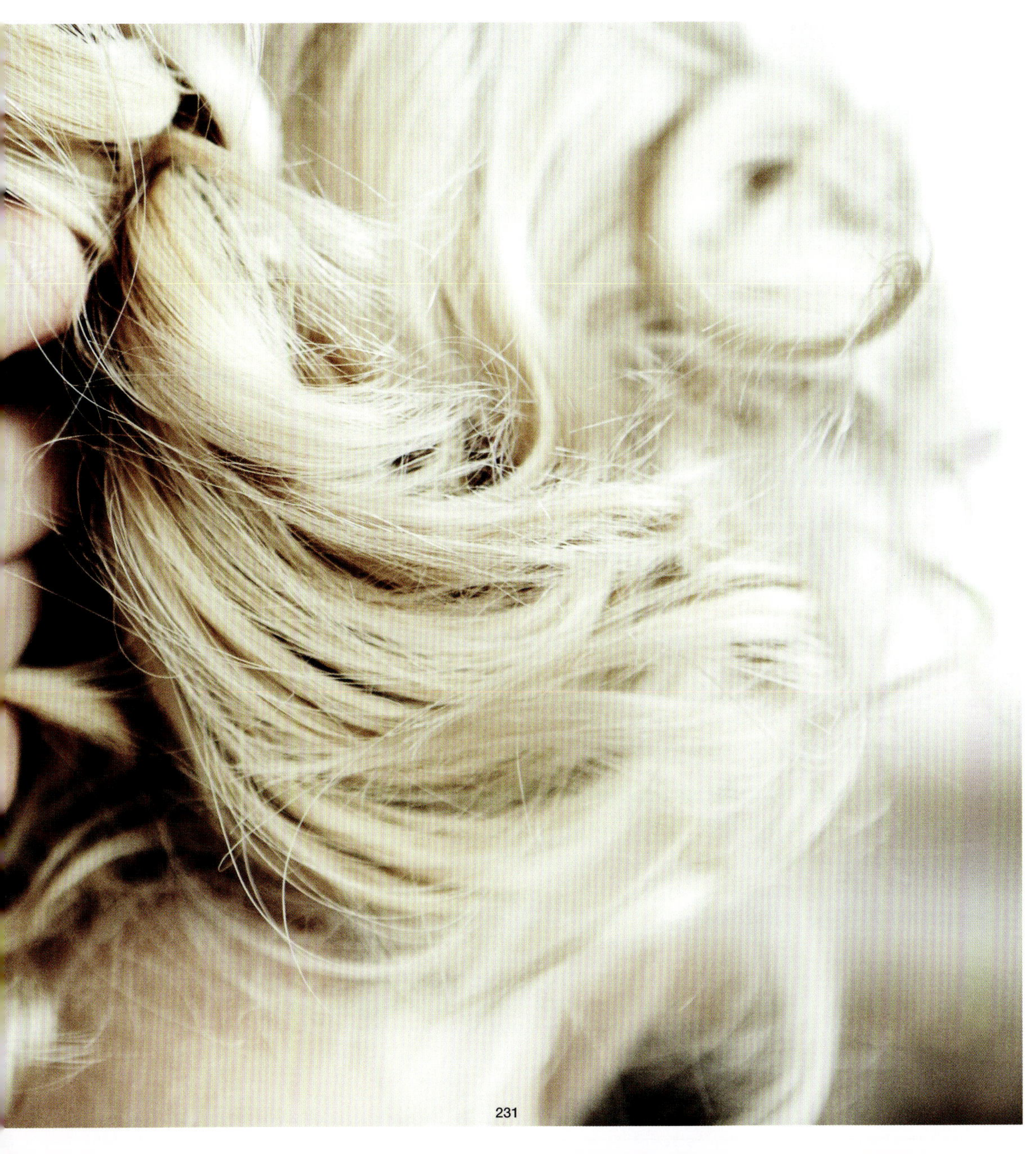

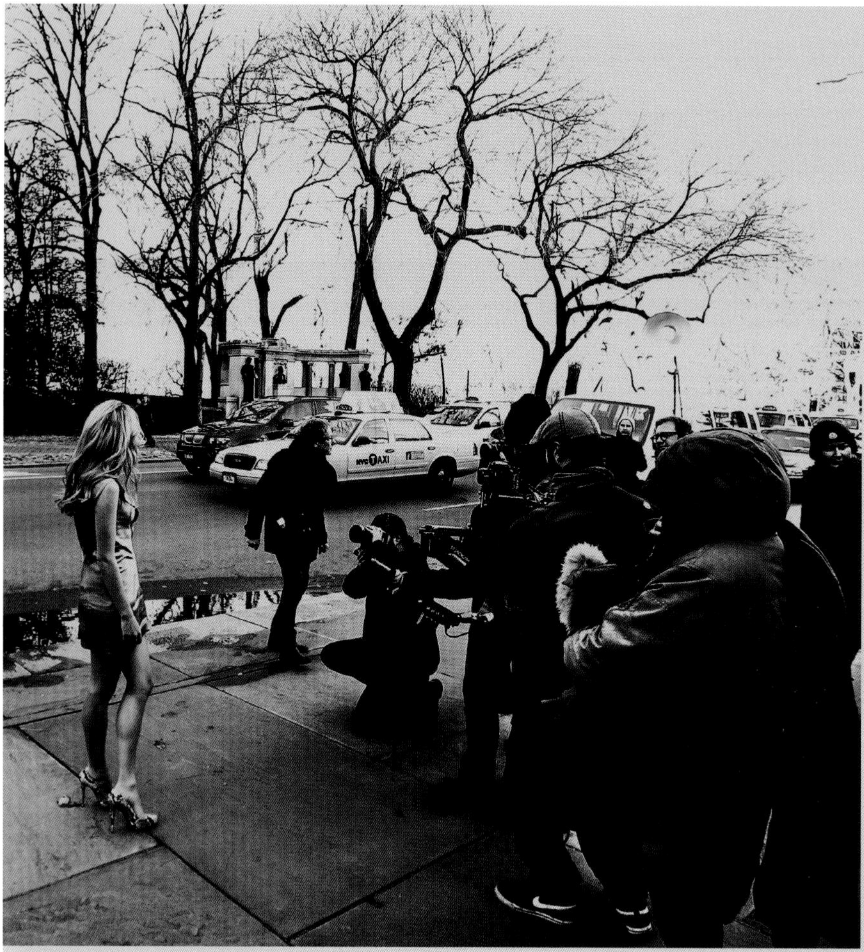

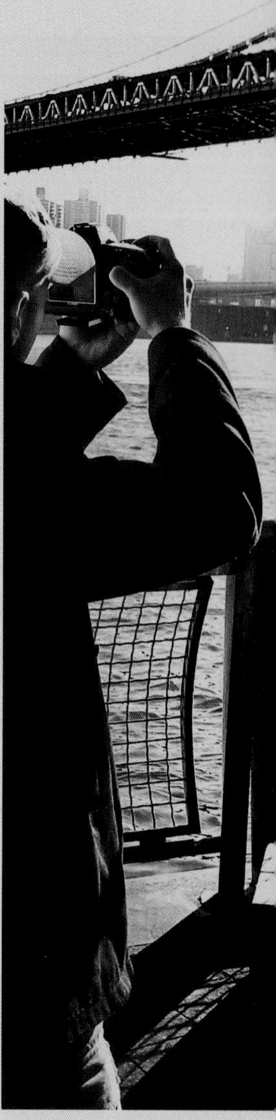

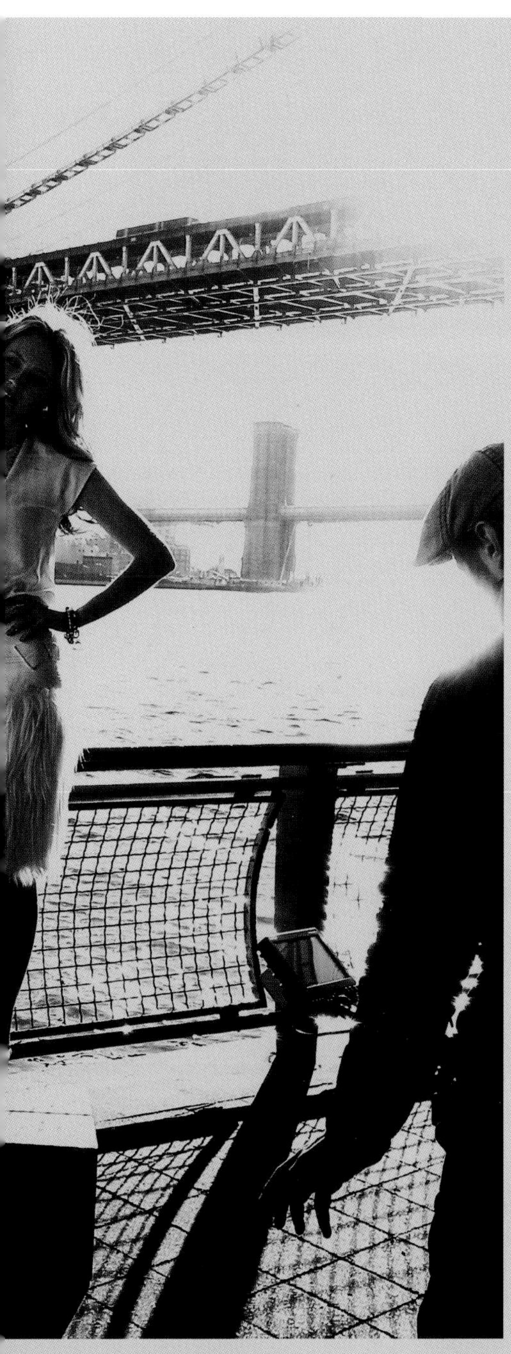

<u>Nobody believes any more that a photograph perfectly mirrors its subject.</u> Nevertheless, the evoking of a "similarity," which is what creates the "pseudo-presence," is still as strong as ever: the space of a photograph sets a visual "field" which the subject of the picture – person or thing – fits into so smoothly that it leads to a sort of accepted normality.
It is only at this point that we note the real "absence" of what is not depicted in the photo. Despite being more lifelike than any other means of depiction, a photographic image is not the thing itself, which an instant after the shot is taken is already somewhere else.

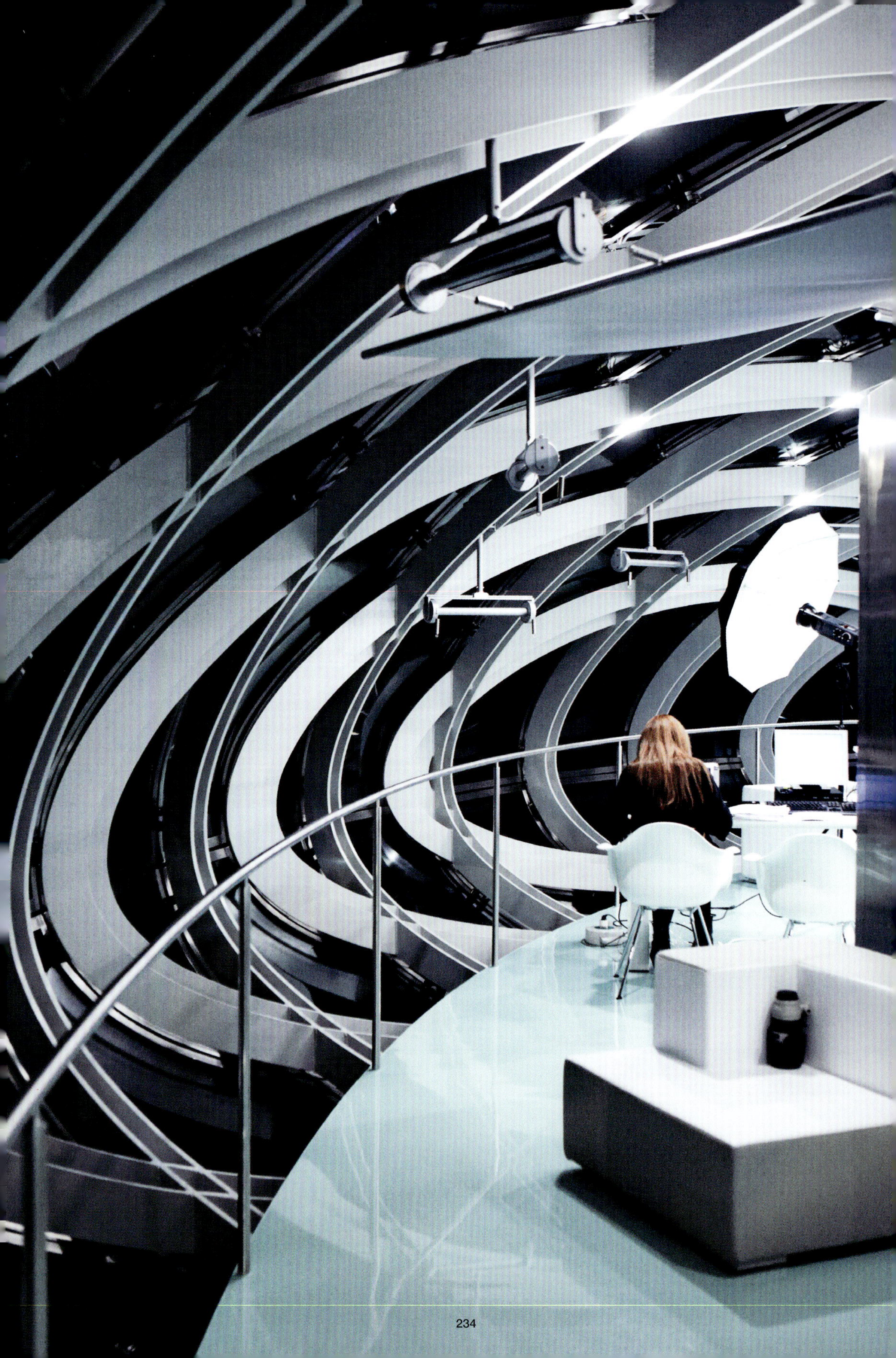

GRAPHICS NEVER PHOTOGRAPHS REALITY: IT READS IT, FILTERS AND DESTRUCTURES IT. IT DOES NOT INVOLVE THE REPRODUCTION OF WHAT IS GIVEN, BUT JUST A DRASTIC SELECTION OF THE PERCEPTUAL ELEMENTS COMPOSING IT, AT THE END OF WHICH ONLY WHAT EXPRESSES THE ENTIRE UNIVERSE OF THE MEANING TO BE CONVEYED IS LEFT ISOLATED, ENLARGED AND DOMINANT. HENCE, IN ORDER TO "READ" A GRAPHIC ARTEFACT, WE NEED TO WORK IN THE OPPOSITE DIRECTION: IN OTHER WORDS, WE MUST START WITH THE IRREDUCIBLE SIMPLICITY OF THE SIGN TO WORK BACK UP TO THE OVERALL NATURE OF THE PHENOMENON IN ITS ENTIRETY.

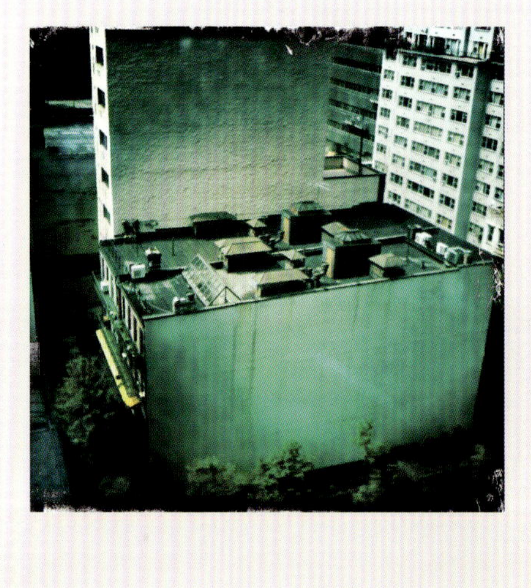

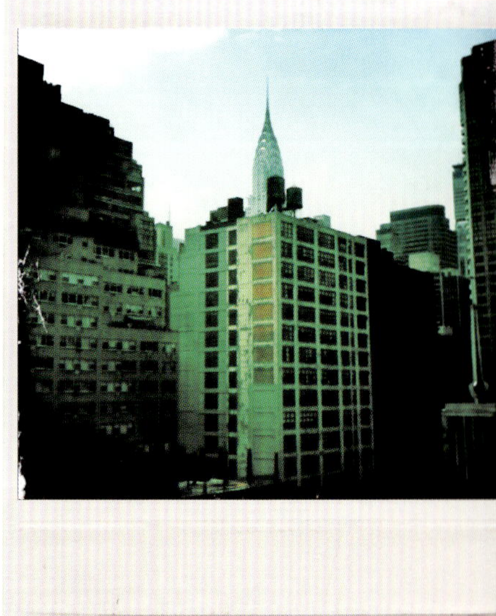

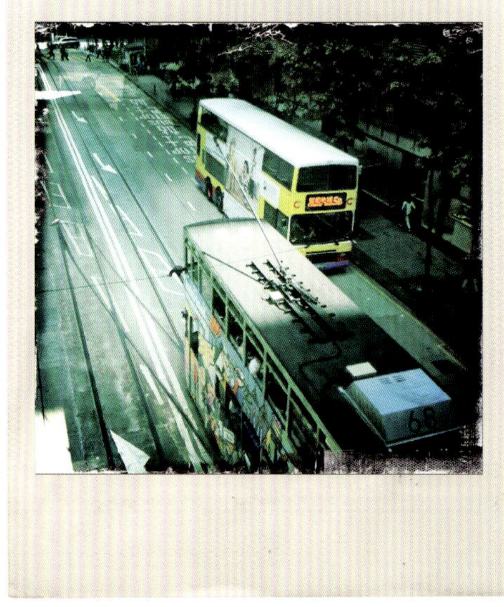

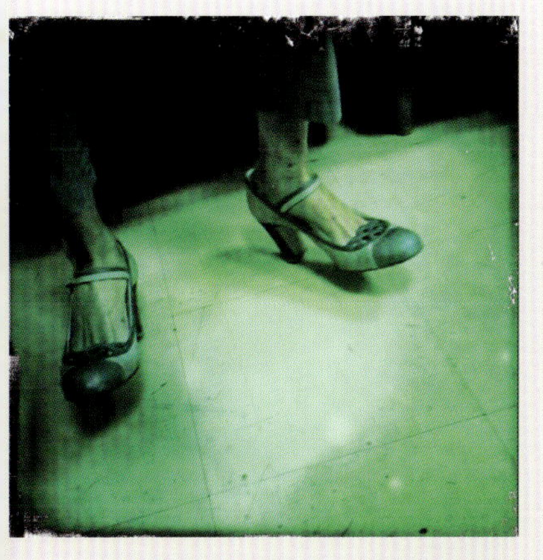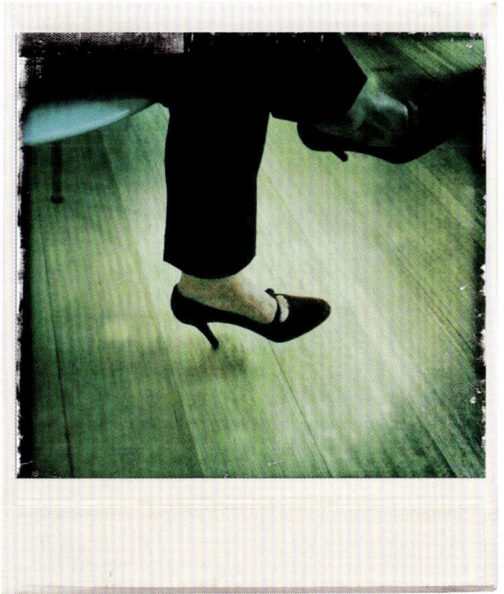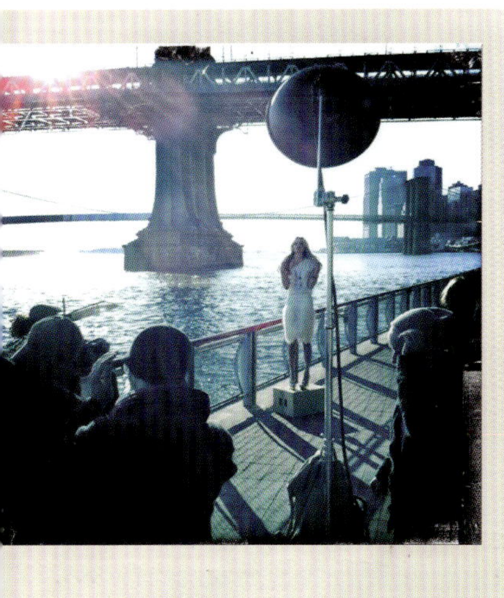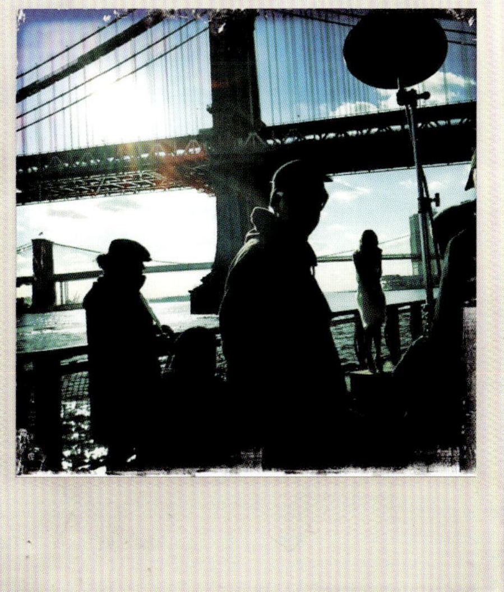

HIDDEN

EYES

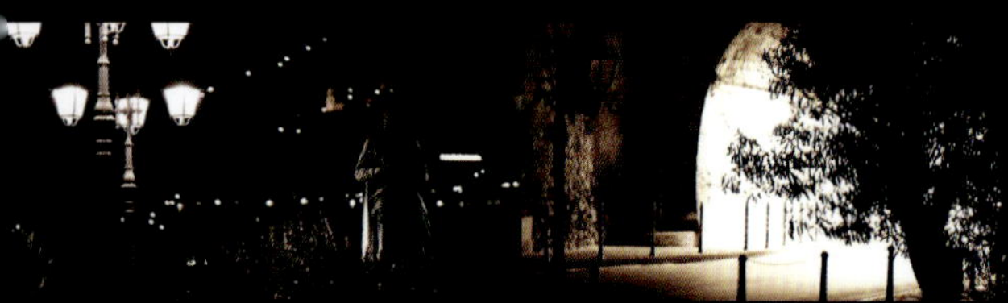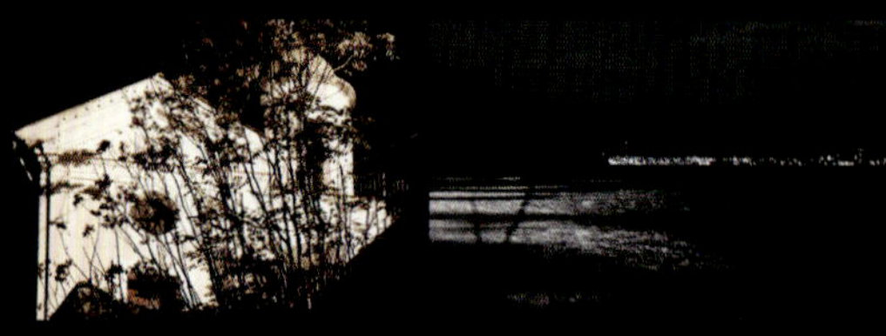

an identifying concept and a key by which to interpret the continuous interaction – whether explicit or implicit – between different professional sectors, from visual communication to interior architecture, from retail to event design. The attitude towards detail, the attention to the harmony of the whole,

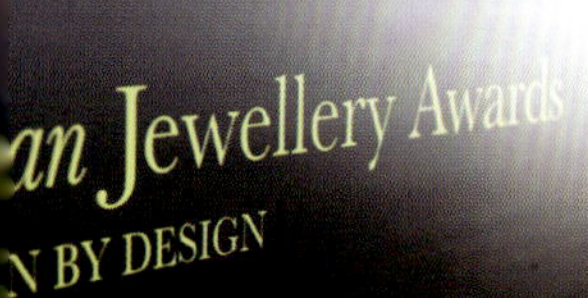

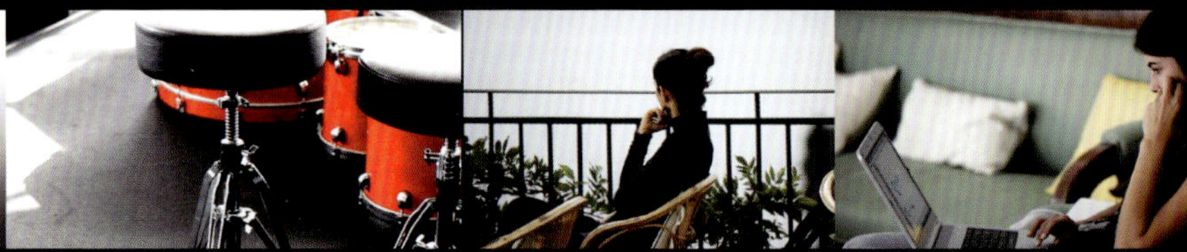

transformed without hesitancy or remainder into a style that permeates the activity of the group generating the act. And where it creates an identity capable of translating our daily work into a general design that is strategic, strong, recognizable.

For us it has always been a "matter of style." Of lifestyle, naturally. Because for us style is not simply an aesthetic hallmark but above all a model of thought, a line of continuity present like a barely-legible watermark underlying the multitude of projects developed through these years,

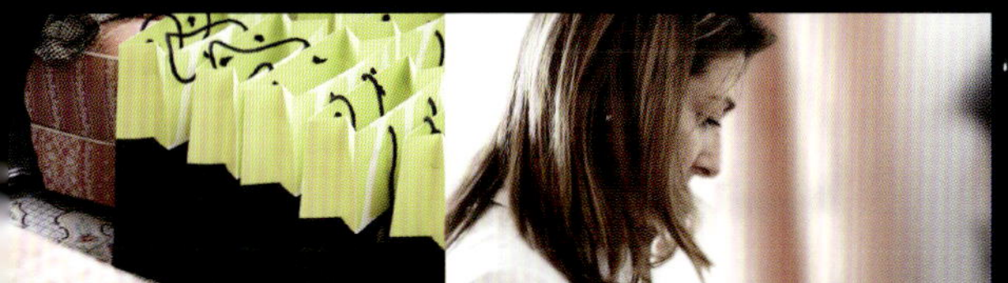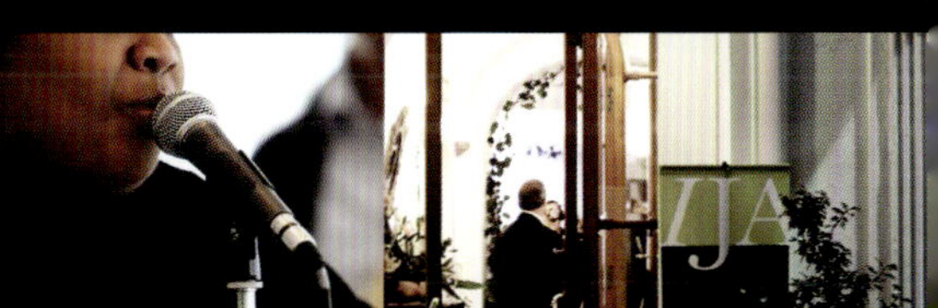

the necessary care devoted to each particular element are the most obvious aspects of what is a reflective philosophy permeating the network of relations between the different fields of intervention, and always converging towards a philosophy that also constitutes action, where the creative act translates into an immediate "making." Where individual creativity becomes

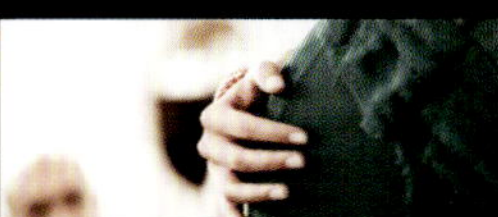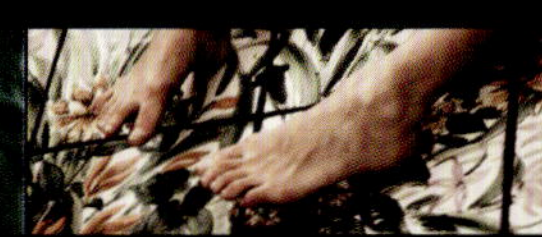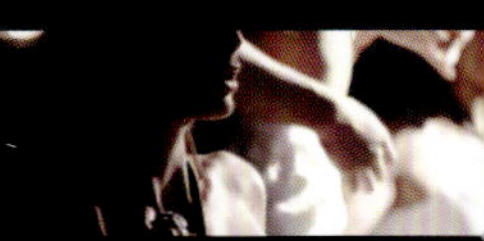

THE LAW OF

THREE PROPOSALS

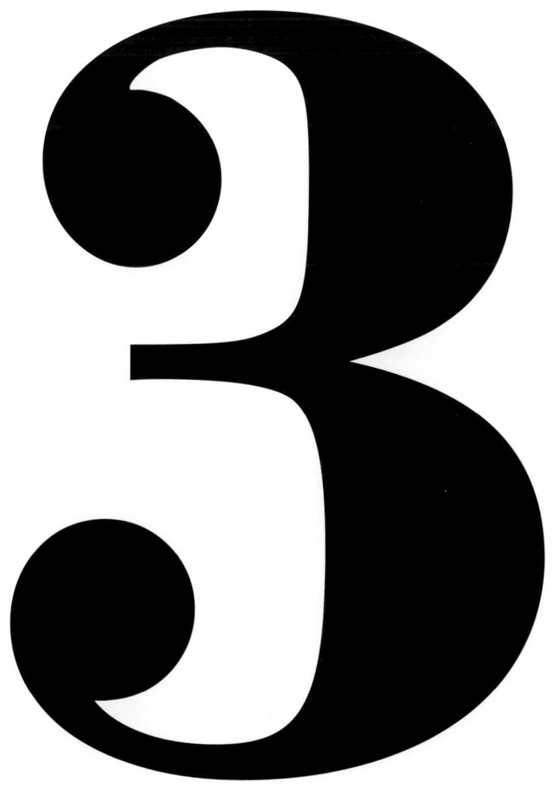

ECOND LINE
imal

03 THIRD LINE
new classic

HDG
Hangar Design Group

re are the exclusive
p s.r.l.
so reserved. Total or
without previous written
 Group s.r.l. prohibited.

ECOND LINE
imal

03 THIRD LINE
new classic

HDG
Hangar Design Group

re are the exclusive
p s.r.l.
so reserved. Total or
without previous written
 Group s.r.l. prohibited.

IN THE BEGINNING WAS CHAOS. FORGET IT.

Creativity is not connected with chaos. Being creative doesn't mean just inventing something strange, new or explosive. You need to know how to focus on the objectives required for the work you are doing. Those who have real talent are those who know how to play with the rules they have been given. The stricter they are, the more that personal ability must be refined.

Before beginning a project we define it with precise rules, objectives, context, customer requests, etc. At graphic design school they teach work through saturation – making dozens of versions of the same visual in the hope that the client will select one. We believe the opposite: that is better to work out what you are looking for before starting. When you know what you want you don't need multiple attempts to achieve the result you are looking for. We firmly believe that personal style is the effect of a meticulously codified method. When a customer says to an agency, "Please make a great design," what they are saying is,

"PLEASE CHANGE THE WAY I SEE MY WORLD."

A good professional does not give the customer exactly what he asks for. He gives more than he asks for.
He changes the idea of what one can ask for.
We try to satisfy the customer's request by constantly raising new questions.

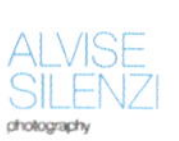
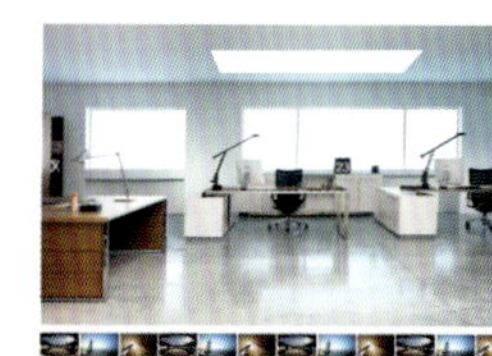
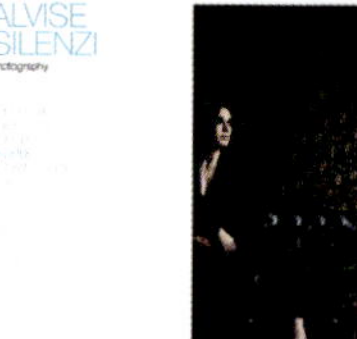
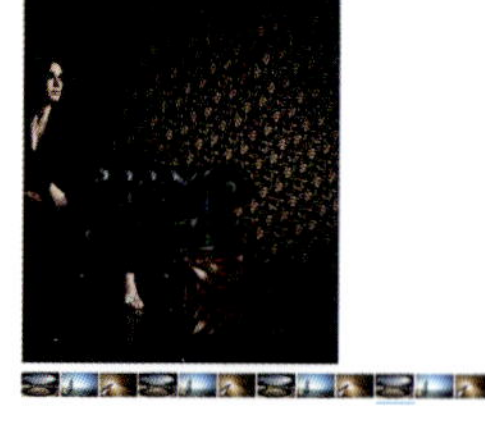

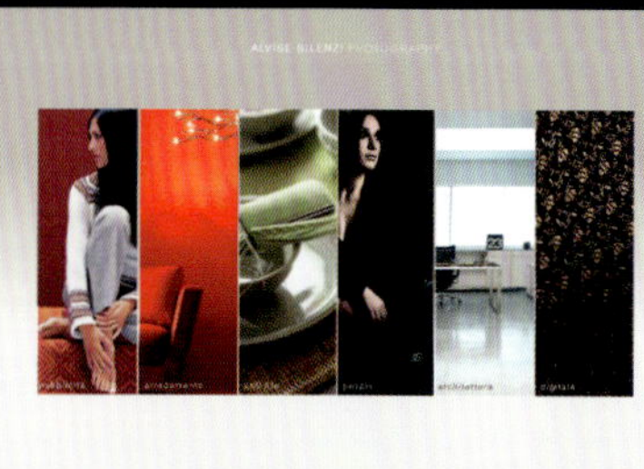
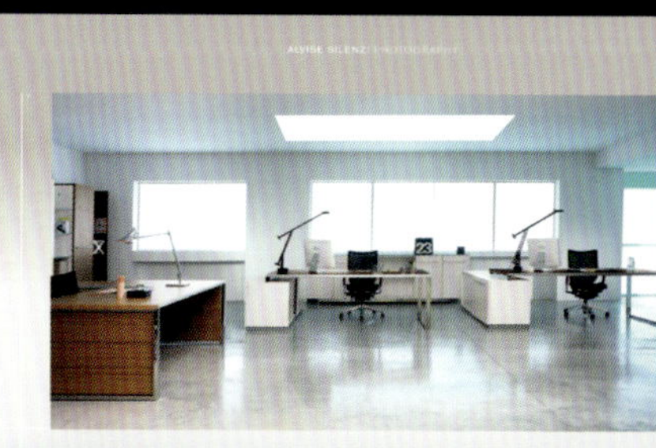

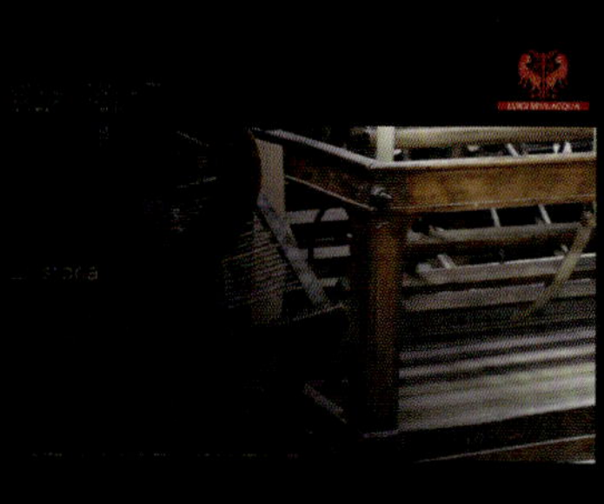
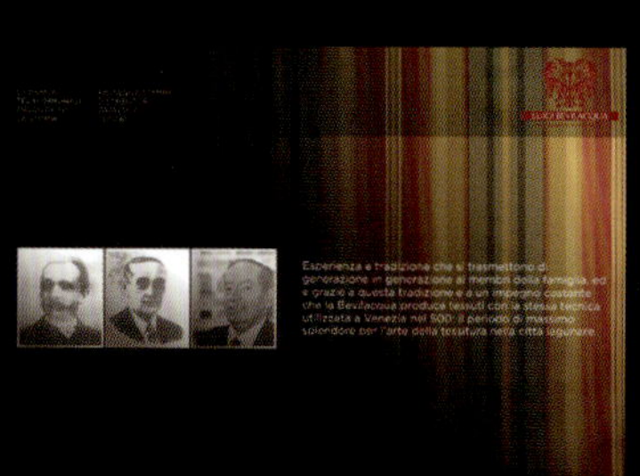
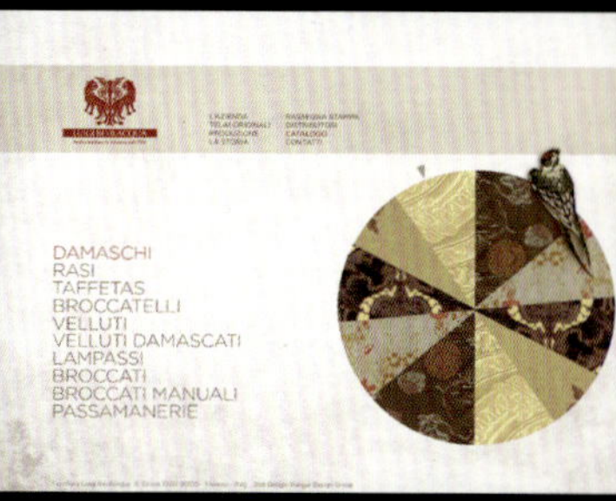

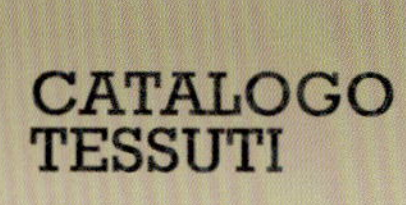
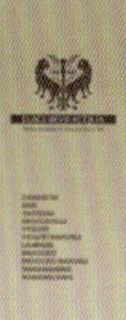
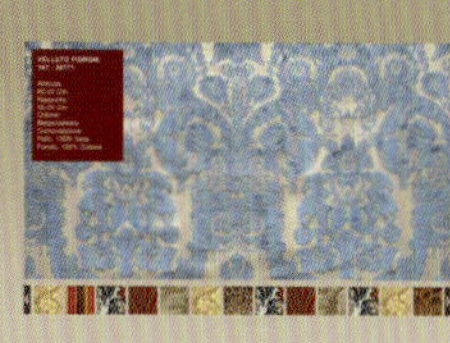
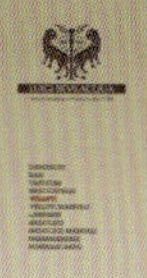
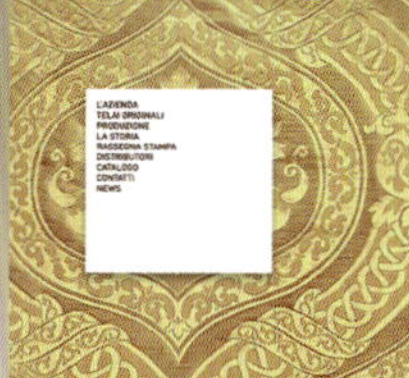
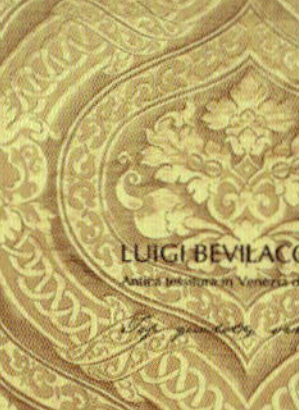

From a business standpoint it has been strategically important to pursue a diversity of work. Solving problems for a wide range of clients, industries, audiences, and media, we accumulate different experiences allowing us to cross-pollinate our thinking for other business projects. Diversity keeps all of us in the studio suitably stimulated.

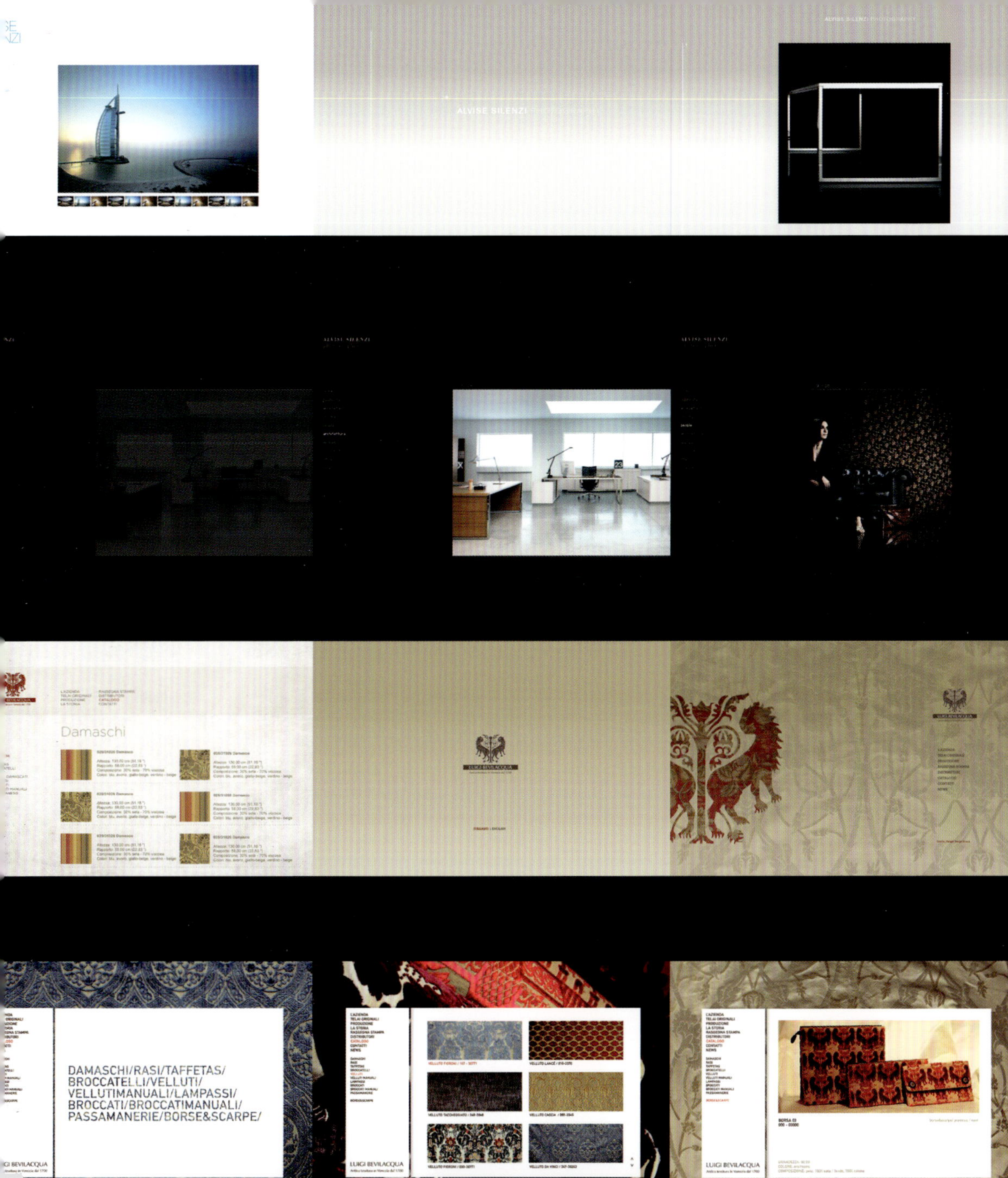

ALVISE SILENZI PHOTOGRAPHY
ALVISE SILENZI
LUIGI BEVILACQUA
Damaschi
DAMASCHI/RASI/TAFFETAS/
BROCCATELLI/VELLUTI/
VELLUTIMANUALI/LAMPASSI/
BROCCATI/BROCCATIMANUALI/
PASSAMANERIE/BORSE&SCARPE/
LUIGI BEVILACQUA

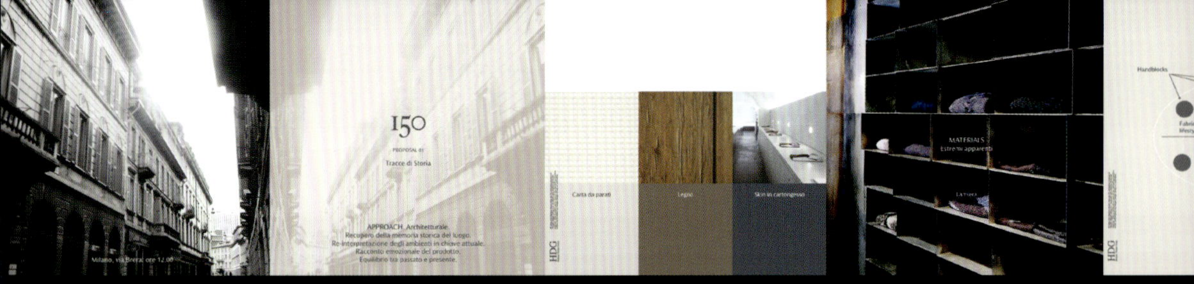

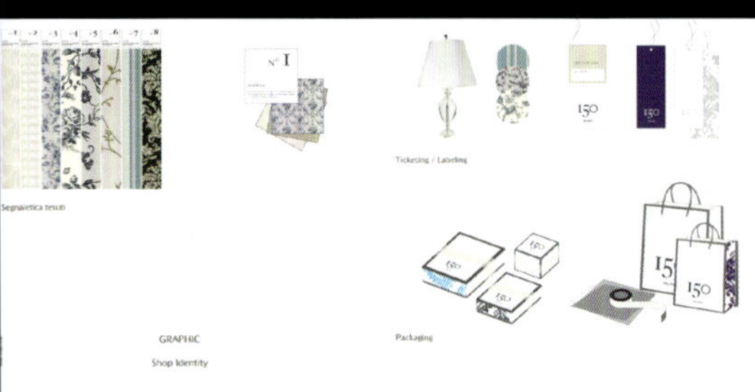

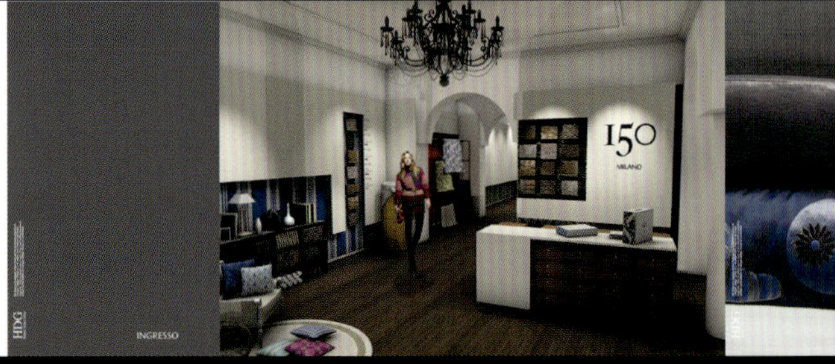

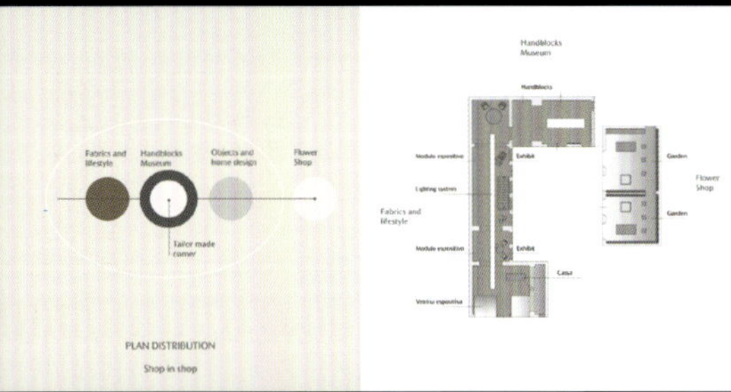

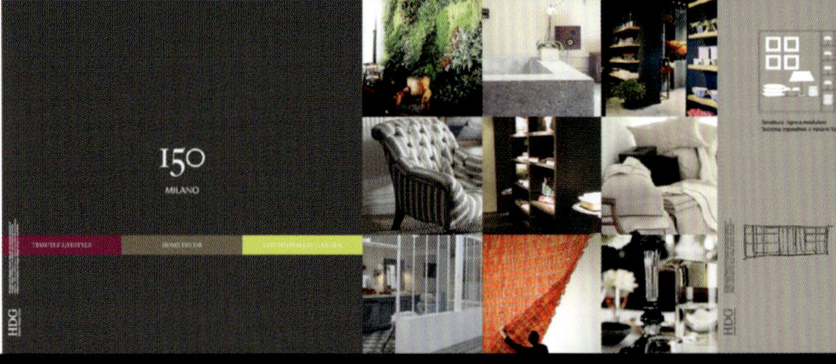

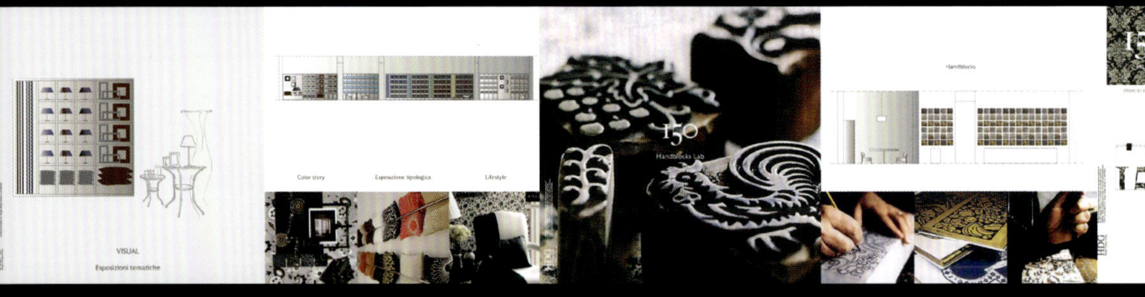

Just as we pursue a wide range of projects, we also strive to attract and keep a diversity of talented individuals who bring much more than just design credentials to the studio. We've always believed that you don't hire the portfolio as much as you respond to who a person is – which is often more interesting than pure talent alone.
As a result, our people are as eclectic as our portfolio.

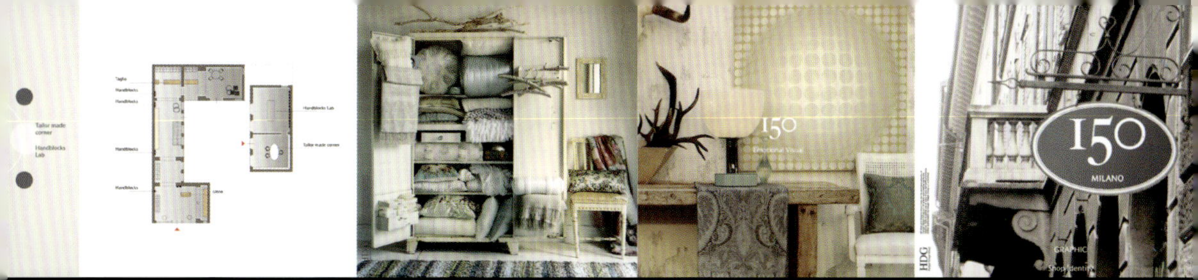

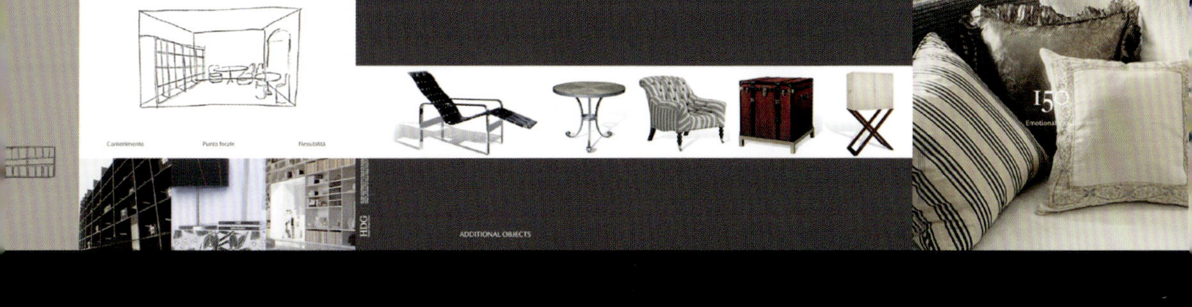
Contenimento
Punto focale
Flessibilità
ADDITIONAL OBJECTS
150
Emotional

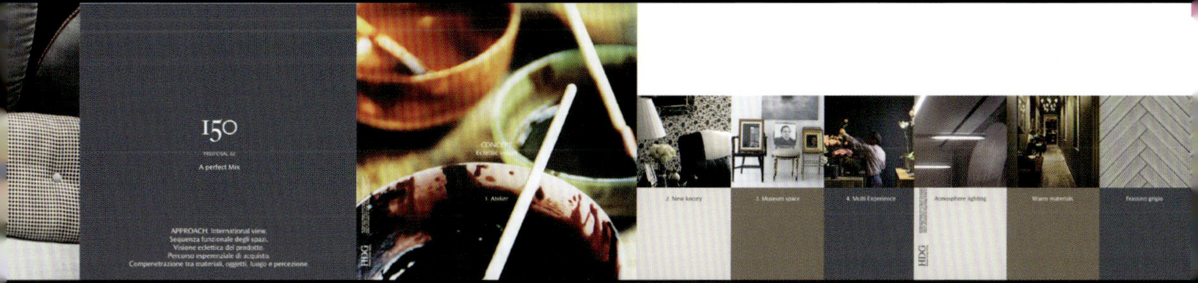

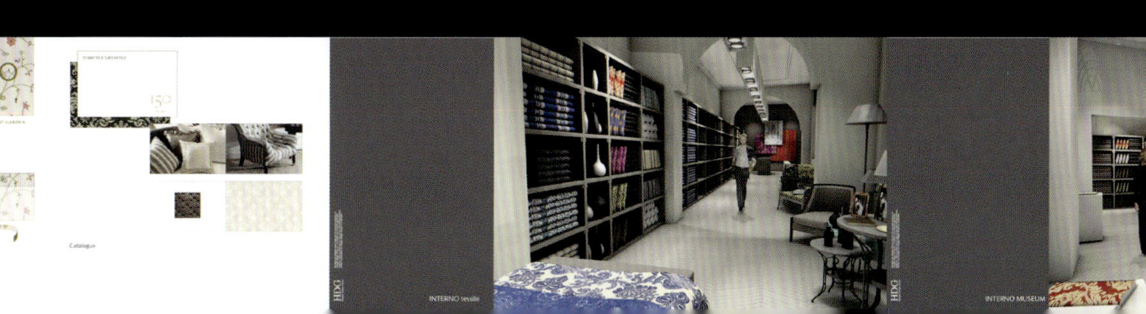
150
Catalogue
INTERNO tessile
INTERNO MUSEUM

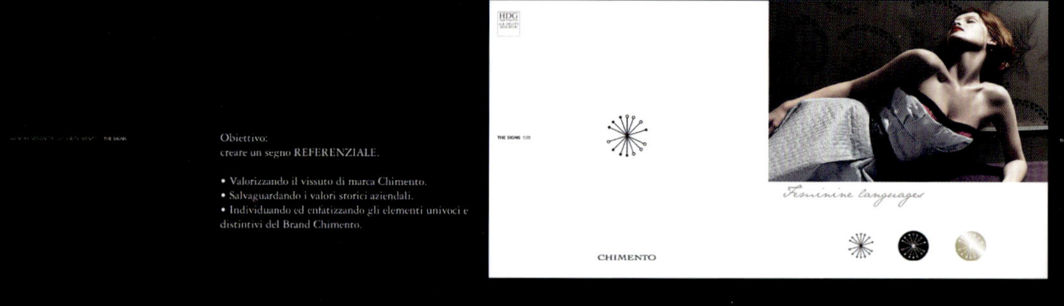

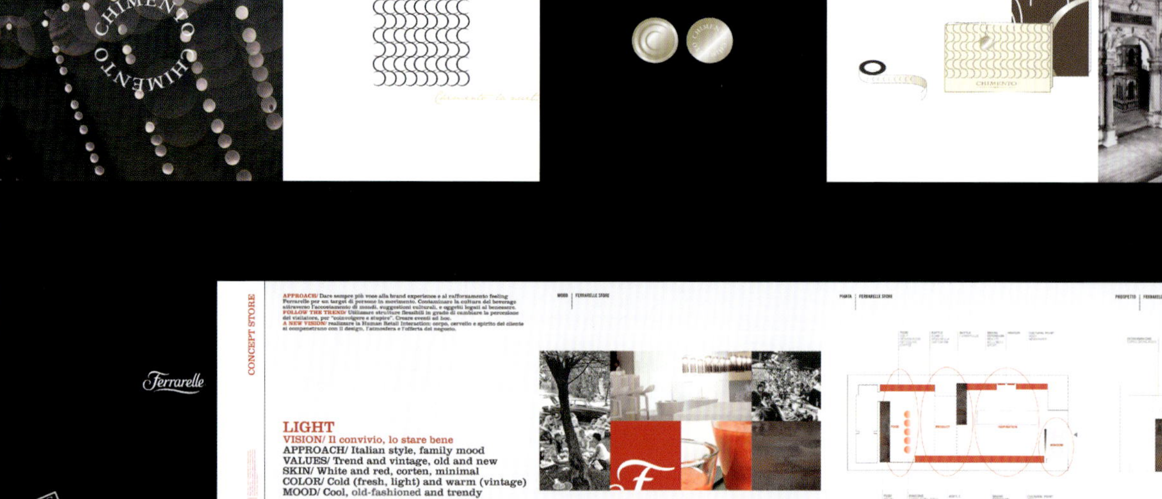

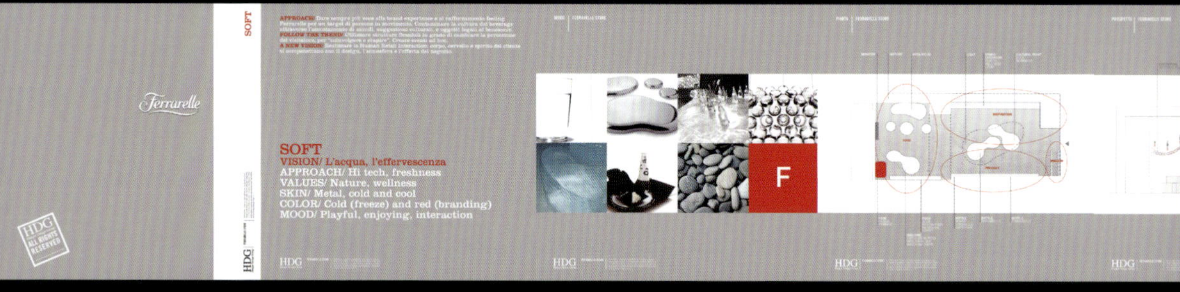

There is some point, after all the thinking and planning and brainstorming and sketching,
that something just starts to look right. Yet we never know if it would have looked right
without all the thinking and planning and brainstorming and sketching.
We think we have to get to the point where our intuition is informed.

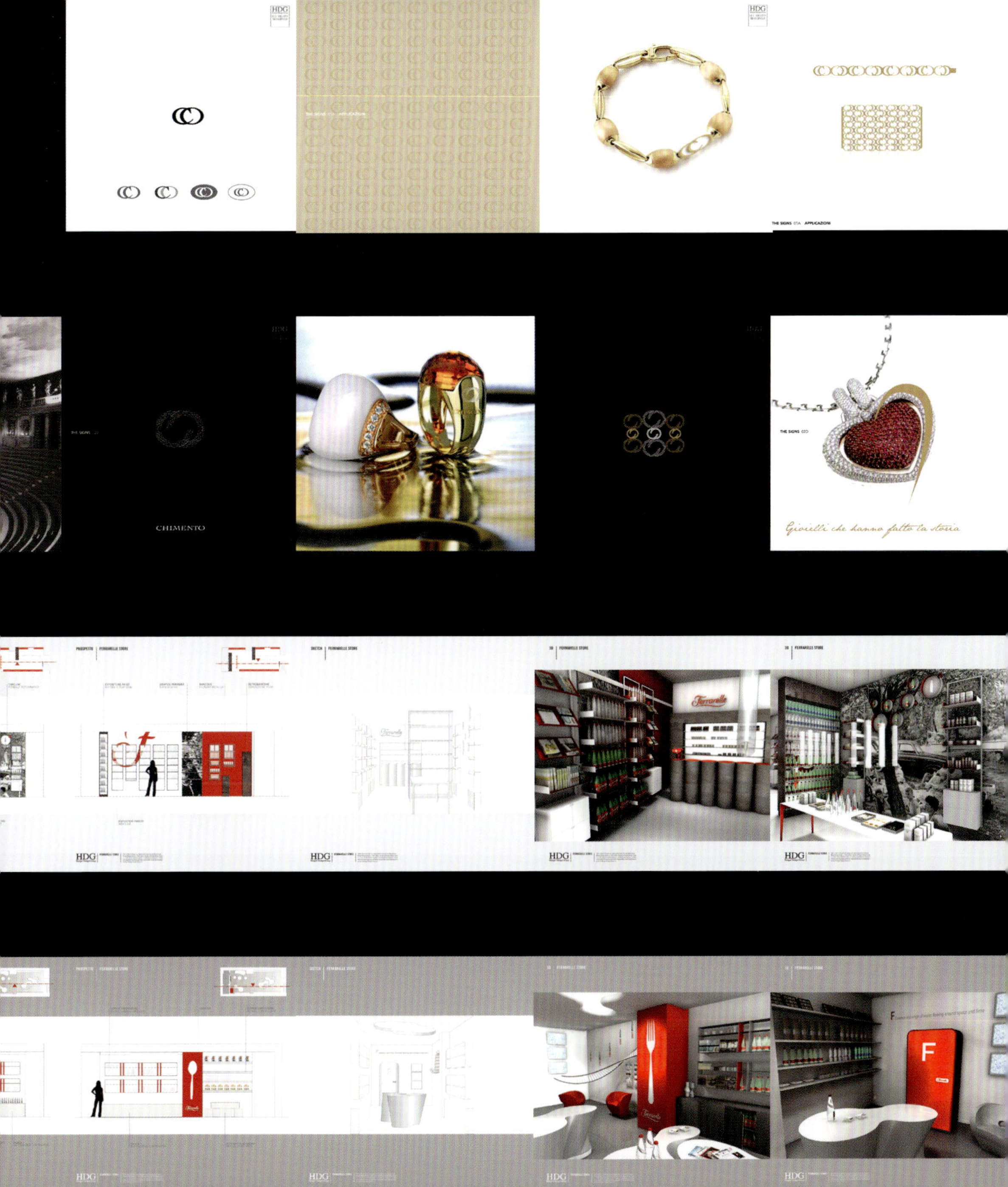

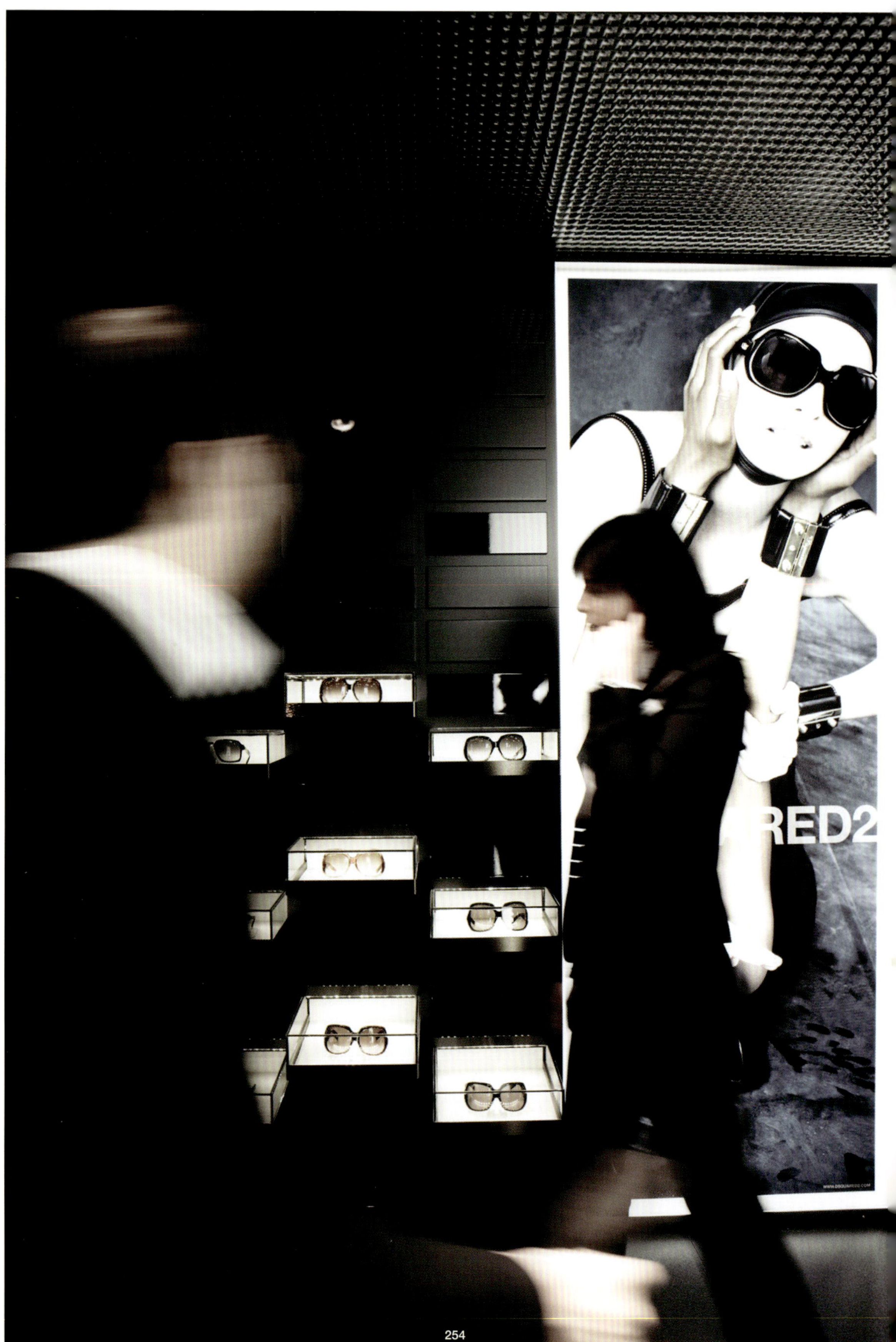

RED2
WWW.DSQUARED.COM

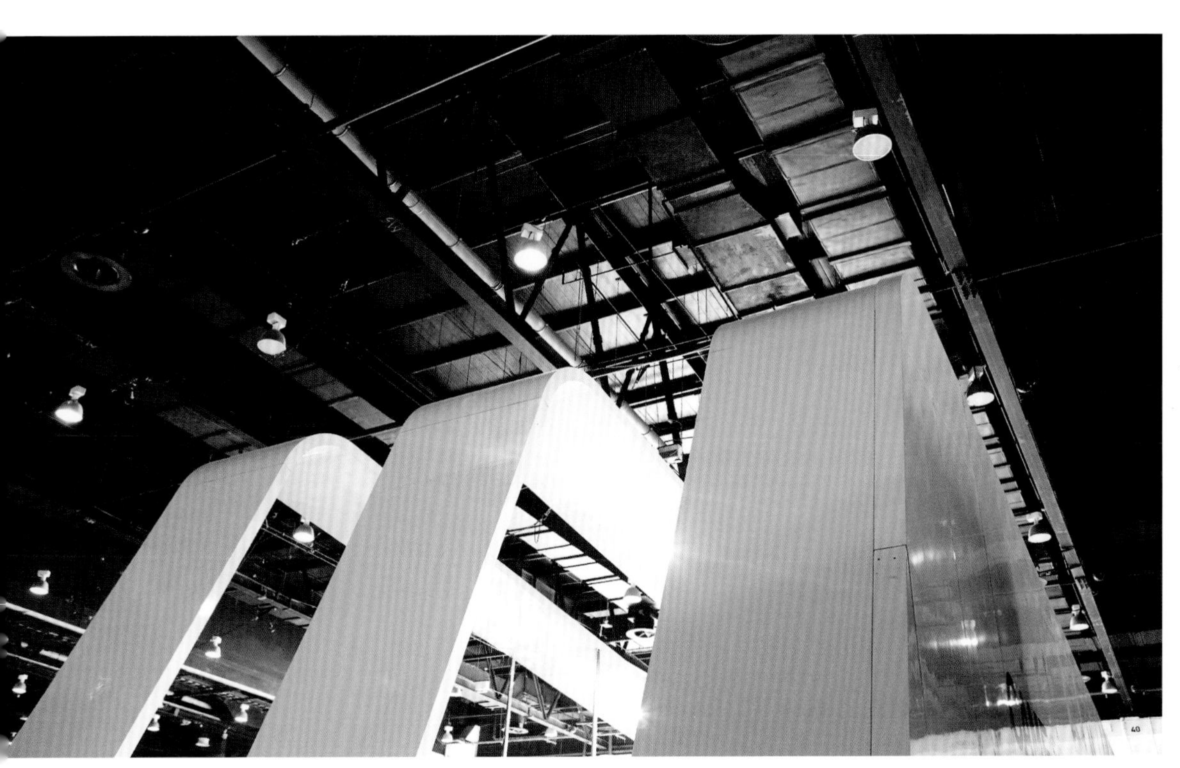

WHEN OR IF PEOPLE ASK US WHAT MEANING IT HAS,
WHAT "MESSAGE" IT CONTAINS, WE'RE REALLY AT LOSS.
The work itself is its own message.

DIFFERENT PERSPECTIVES CARRY DIFFERENT SOLUTIONS

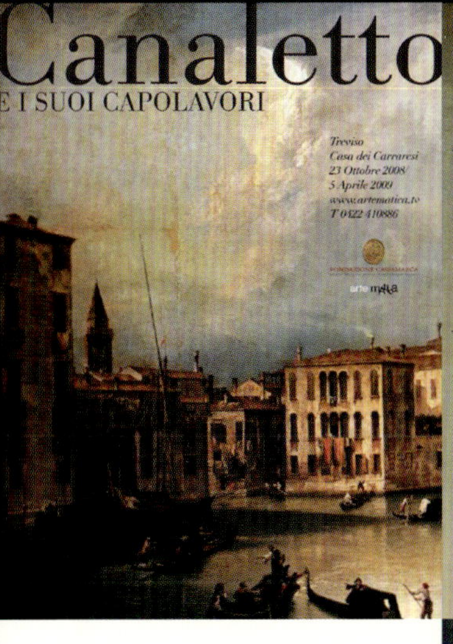

Canaletto
E I SUOI CAPOLAVORI
Treviso
Casa dei Carraresi
23 Ottobre 2008
5 Aprile 2009
www.artematica.tv
T 0422 410886

TREVISO
CASA DEI CARR
23 OTTOBRE 2008
5 APRILE 2009
CANA
VENEZIA E I SUO
Per informazioni
e prenotazioni
T. +39 0422 542854
T. +39 0422 513185
info@artematica.tv
www.artematica.tv

naletto
CAPOLAVORI
23 Ottobre 2008
5 Aprile 2009
www.artematica.tv

PRENDERGAST
IN ITALIA
AL 10.10.2009 AL 3.01.201
RARIO 10-18 CHIUSO IL MARTEDÌ
eggy Guggenheim COLLECTION   Dorsoduro 701, Venezia
trapresæ
ollezione
enheim
Con il sostegno di
REGIONE DEL VENETO
La mostra è resa possibile grazie a:
ART FORUM WURTH
CAPENA (ROMA)
APEROL

Prenderga
in Italia
DAL 10.10.2009
AL 3.01.2010
ORARIO 10 - 1
CHIUSO IL MA

Prendergast
in Italia
10.10.2009 – 3.01.2010
orario 10-18
chiuso il martedì
Peggy Guggenheim COLLECTION
Dorsoduro 701, Venezia
www.guggenheim-venice.it
REGIONE DEL VENETO

SCAPIGLIAT
UN "PANDEMONIO" PER CAMB
milano | palazzo reale
26 giugno | 22 novembre 2009

SCA
PI
GLI
AT
U
RA
SCAPIGLIATURA.
UN "PANDEMONIO"
PER CAMBIARE L'ARTE.

SCA
PI
GLI
AT
U
RA
SCAPIGLIAT
UN "PANDEM
PER CAMBIA
Milano / Pala
26 Giugno /

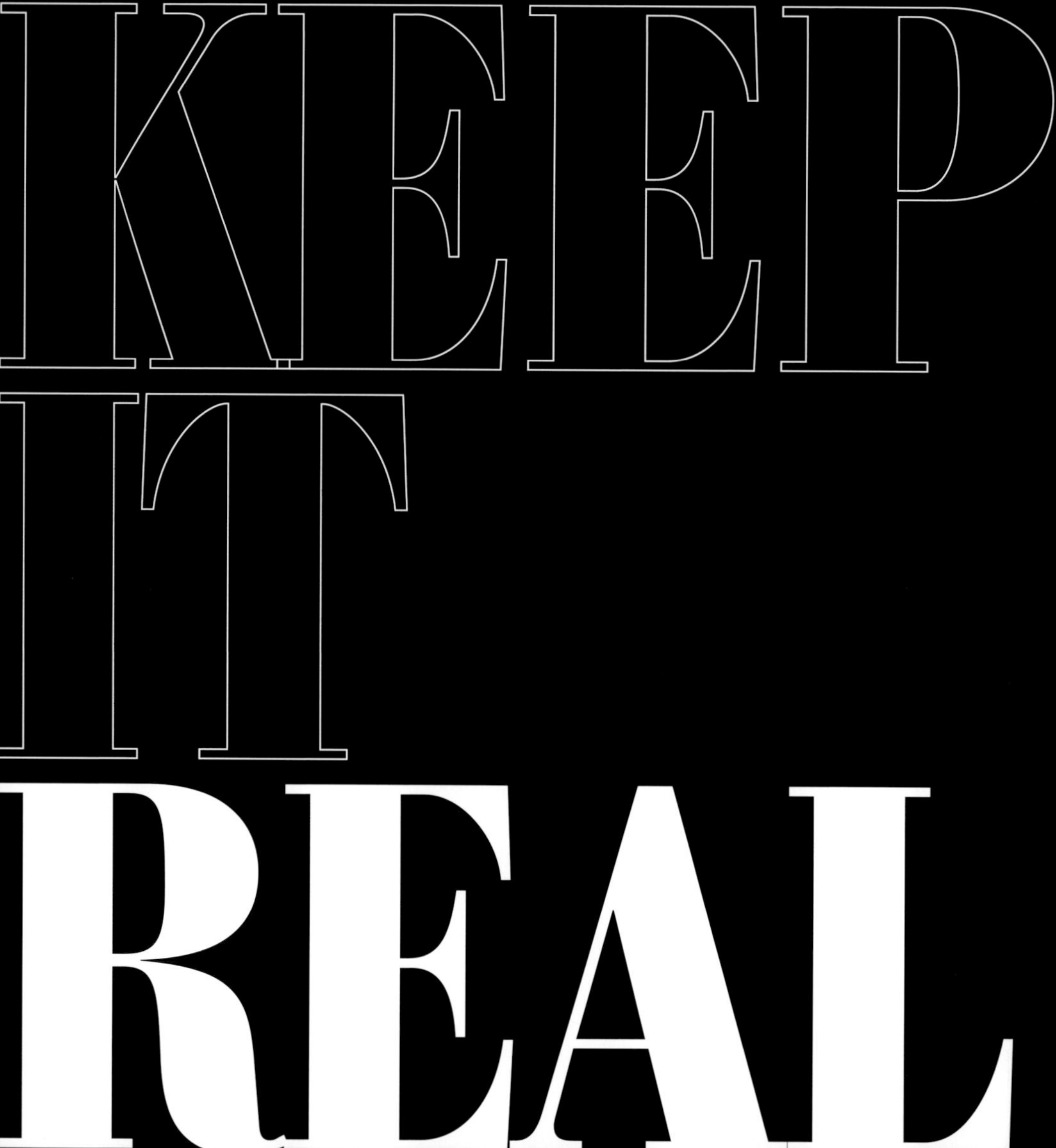

KEEP
IT
REAL

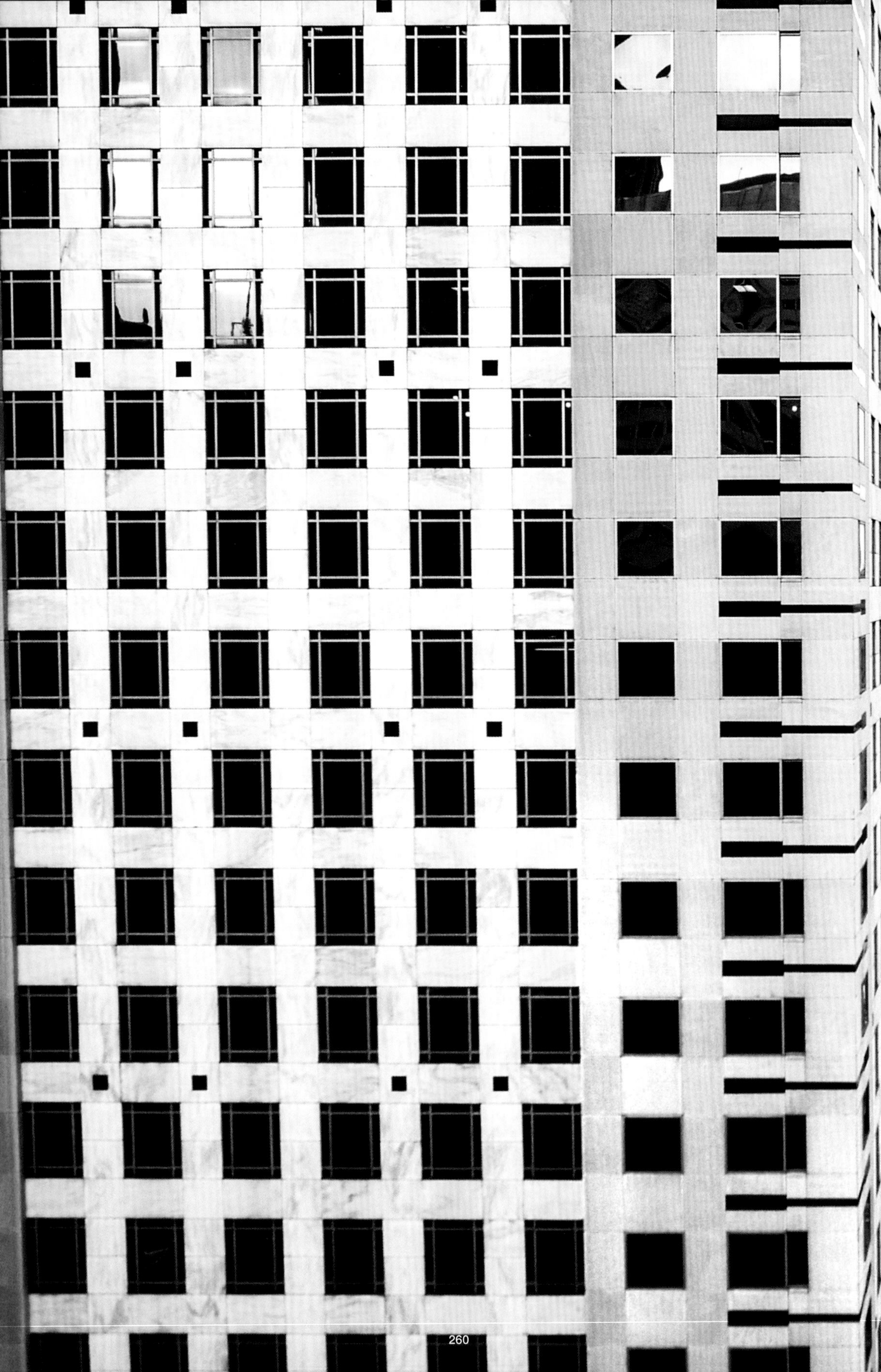

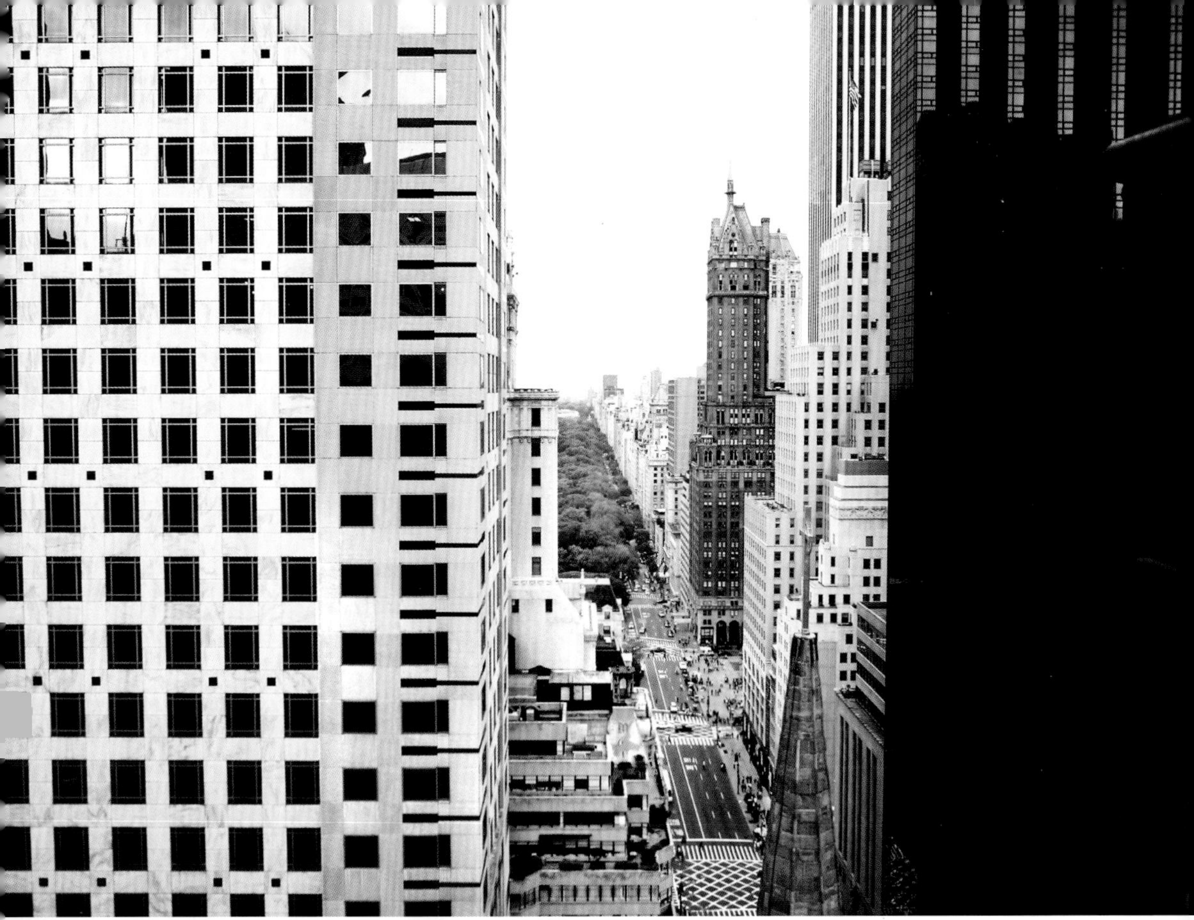

FOCUS ON

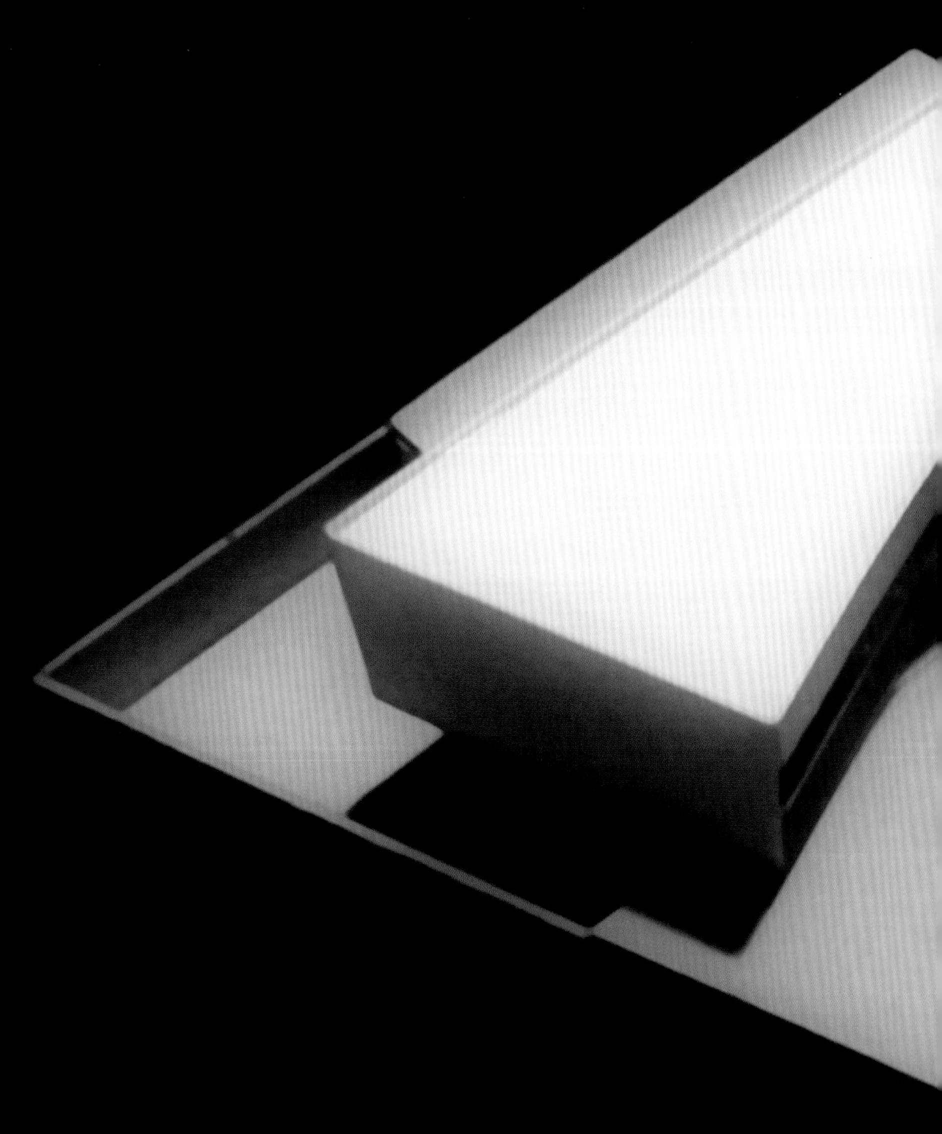

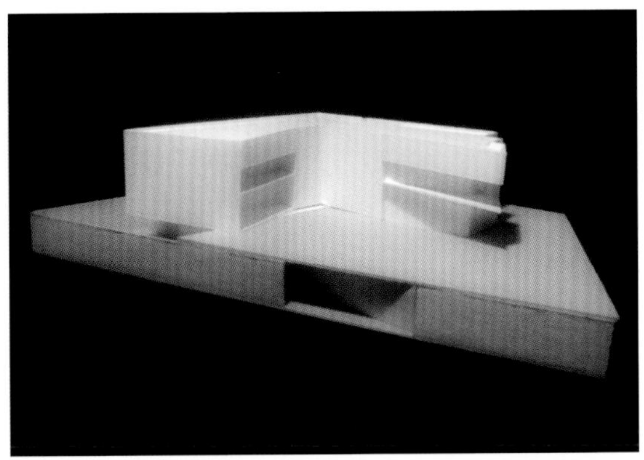

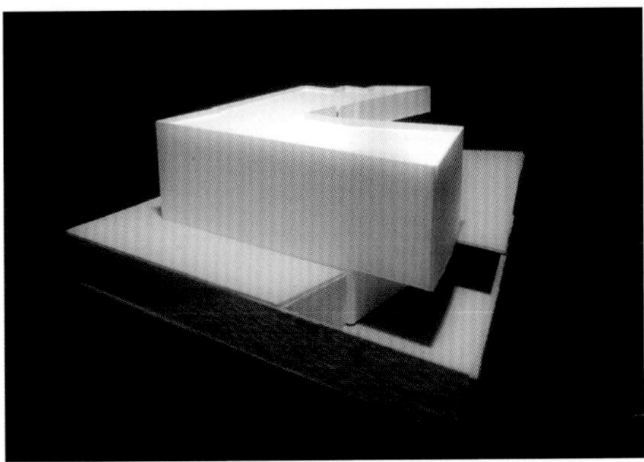

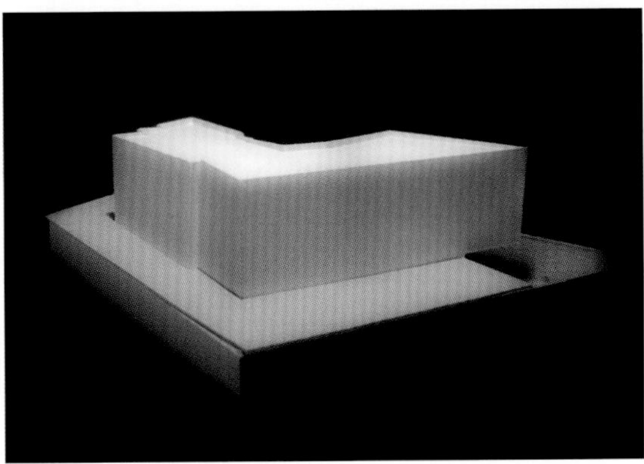

Simply honoring the self-evident fascination and the power of light. A conceptual synthesis of gesture and image, interwound by a precise and careful use of lines. Rigorous geometries and the essentiality associated with the absence of color and a sober use of decorative elements. The option of developing your own style within the bounds of the forms available is an increasingly crucial virtue in contemporary interior design.

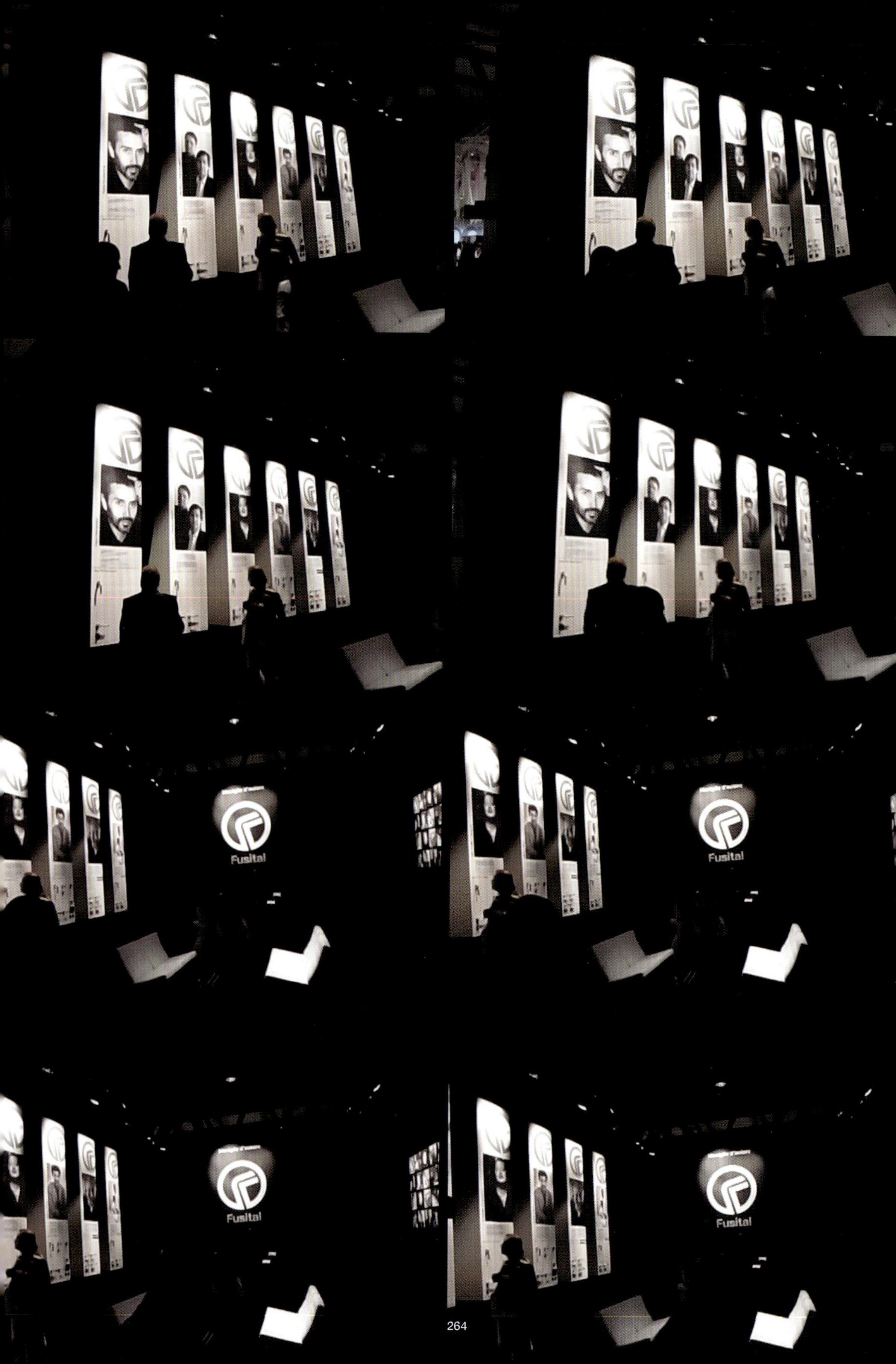

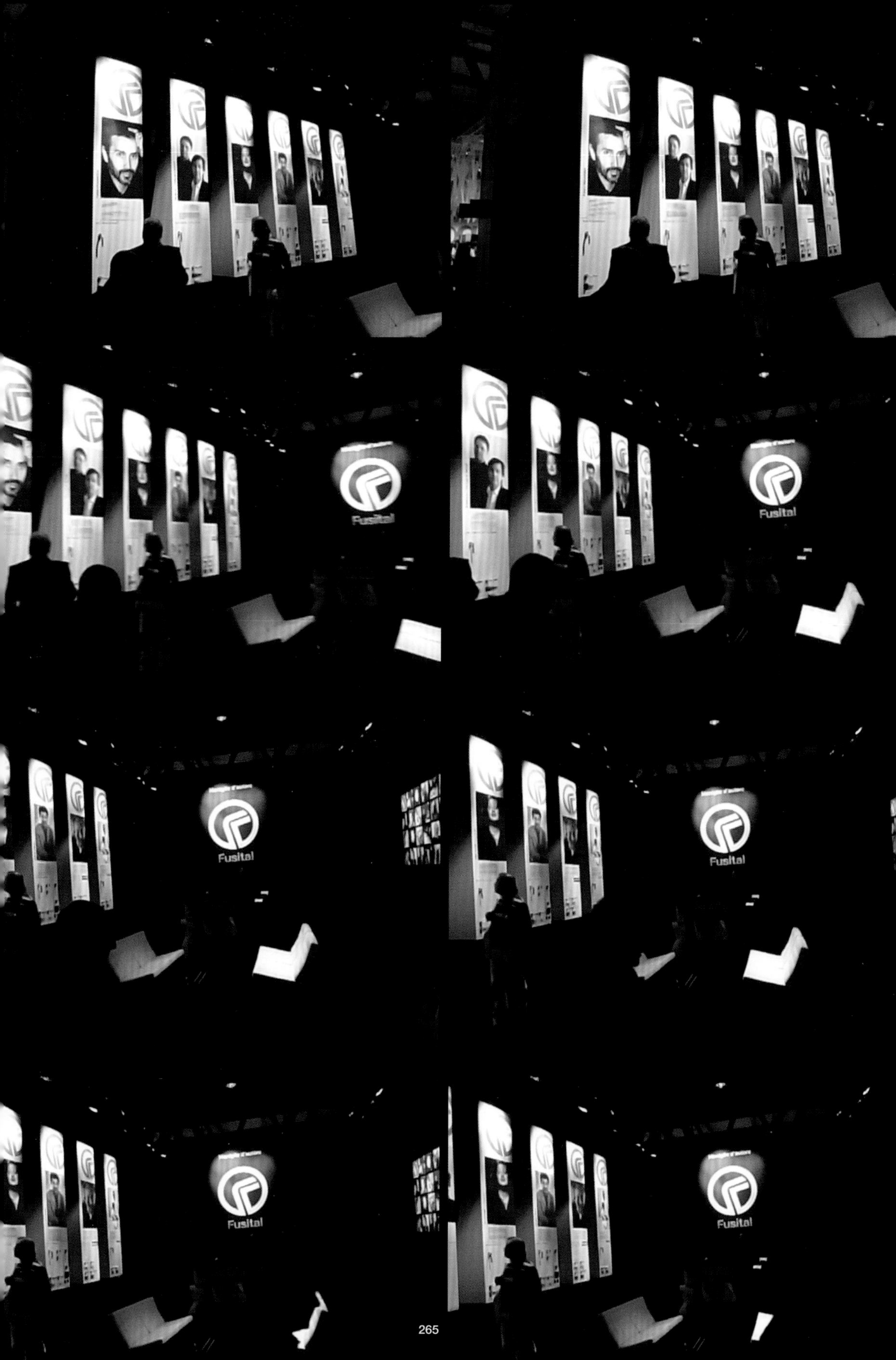

Fusital
Fusital
Fusital

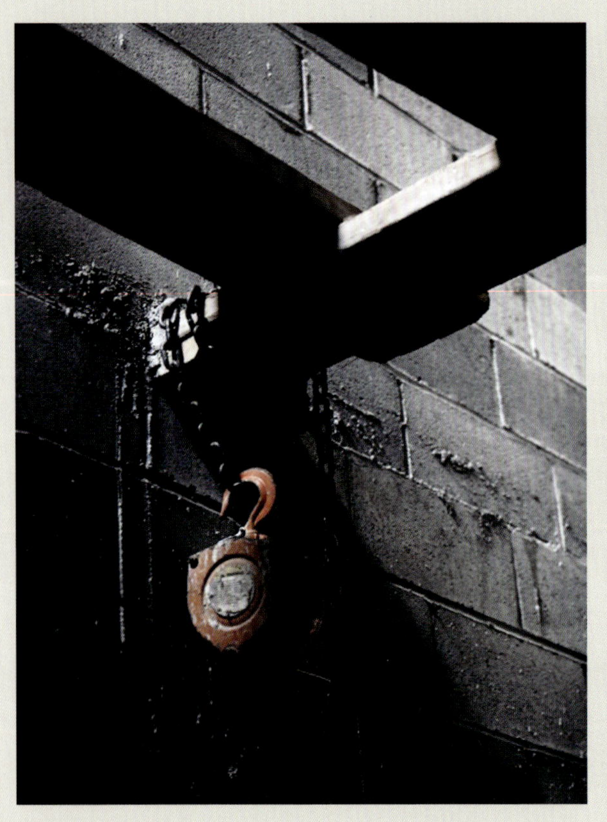 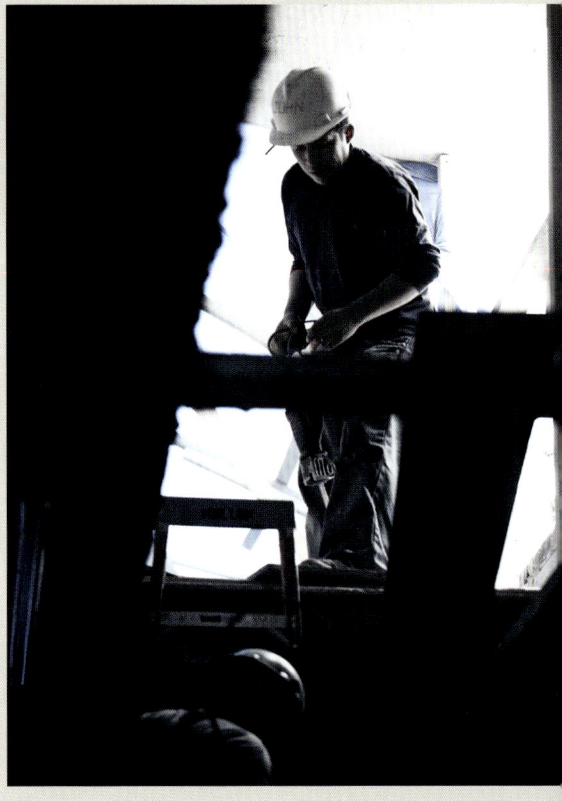

267.

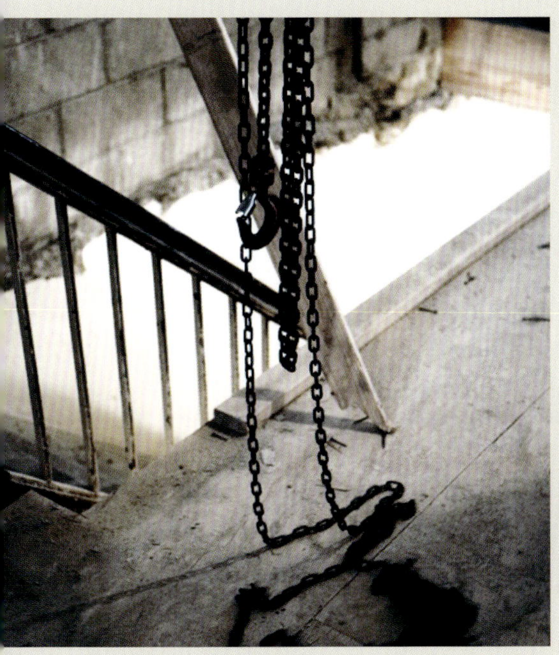 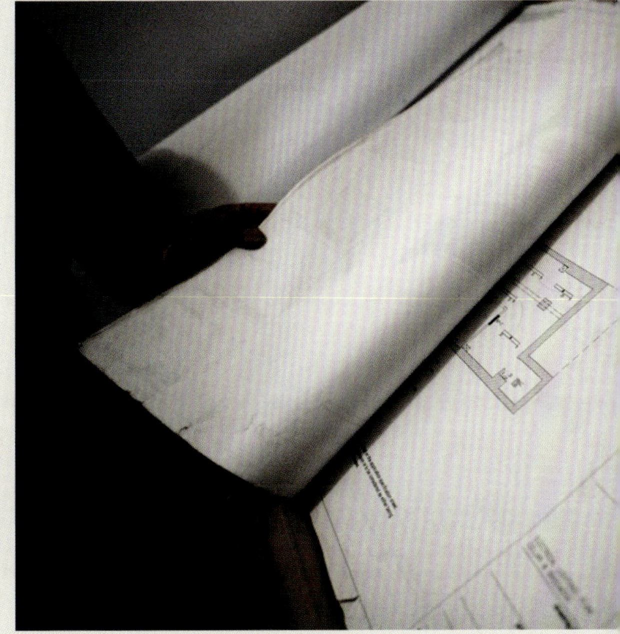

ONE HUNDRED TELLINGS ARE NOT SO GOOD AS ONE SEEING.

Product is always most important, but once you've got that right, you have to layer on a lot of things to create the entire aesthetics. The whole experience has to endow that product with even more.

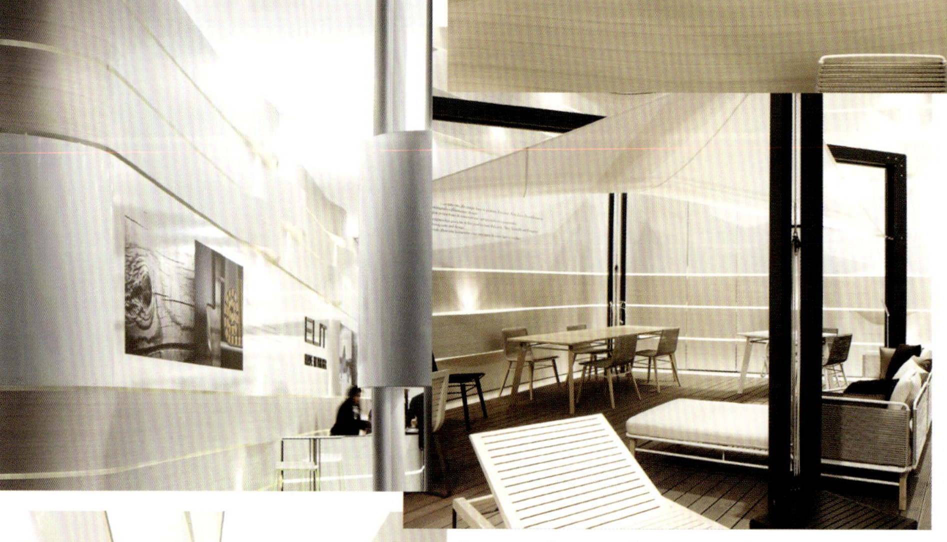

n of international designers has given life to five product lines Takeaway, Nion, Limu
ade in Italy", combining taste and design.
ions of quality materials allow you to interpret your own space in a new light as you lik

Consumers have to be greeted by someone

interesting at the door who smiles at them and

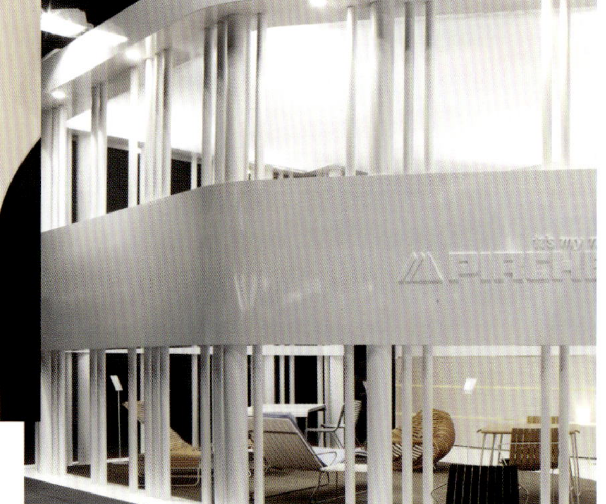

makes them feel welcome. The space needs to be beautiful, the music needs to be right, the light needs to be right.

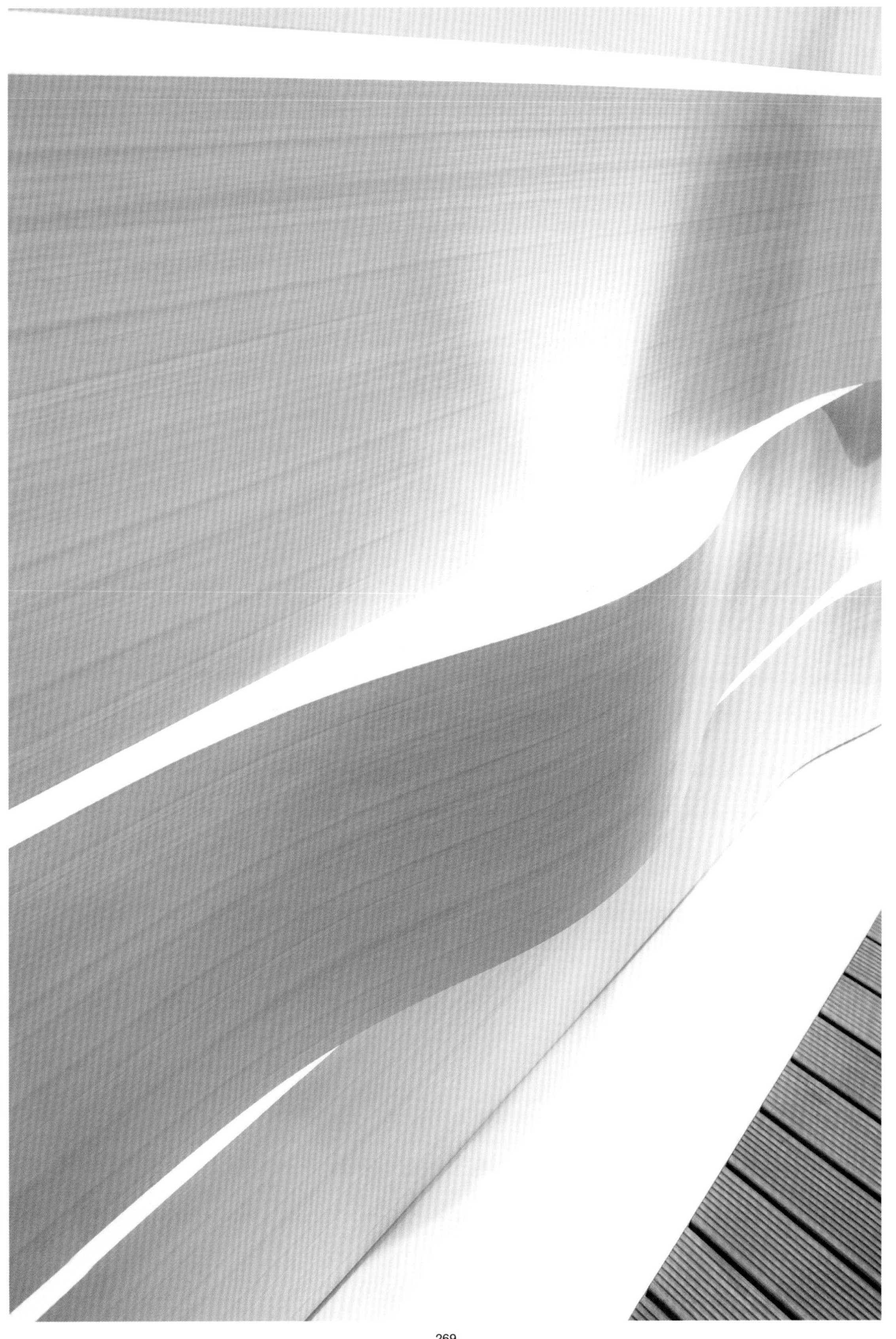

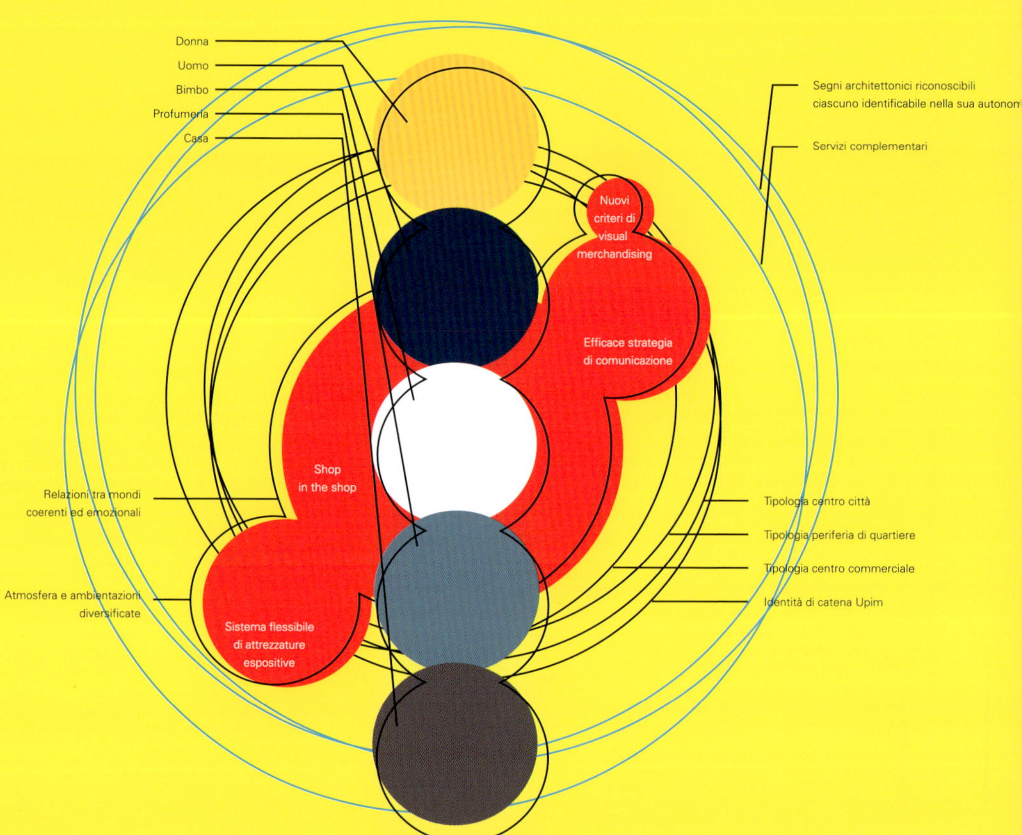

Donna
Uomo
Bimbo
Profumeria
Casa
Segni architettonici riconoscibili
ciascuno identificabile nella sua autonom
Servizi complementari
Nuovi
criteri di
visual
merchandising
Efficace strategia
di comunicazione
Shop
in the shop
Relazioni tra mondi
coerenti ed emozionali
Tipologia centro città
Tipologia periferia di quartiere
Tipologia centro commerciale
Identità di catena Upim
Atmosfera e ambientazioni
diversificate
Sistema flessibile
di attrezzature
espositive

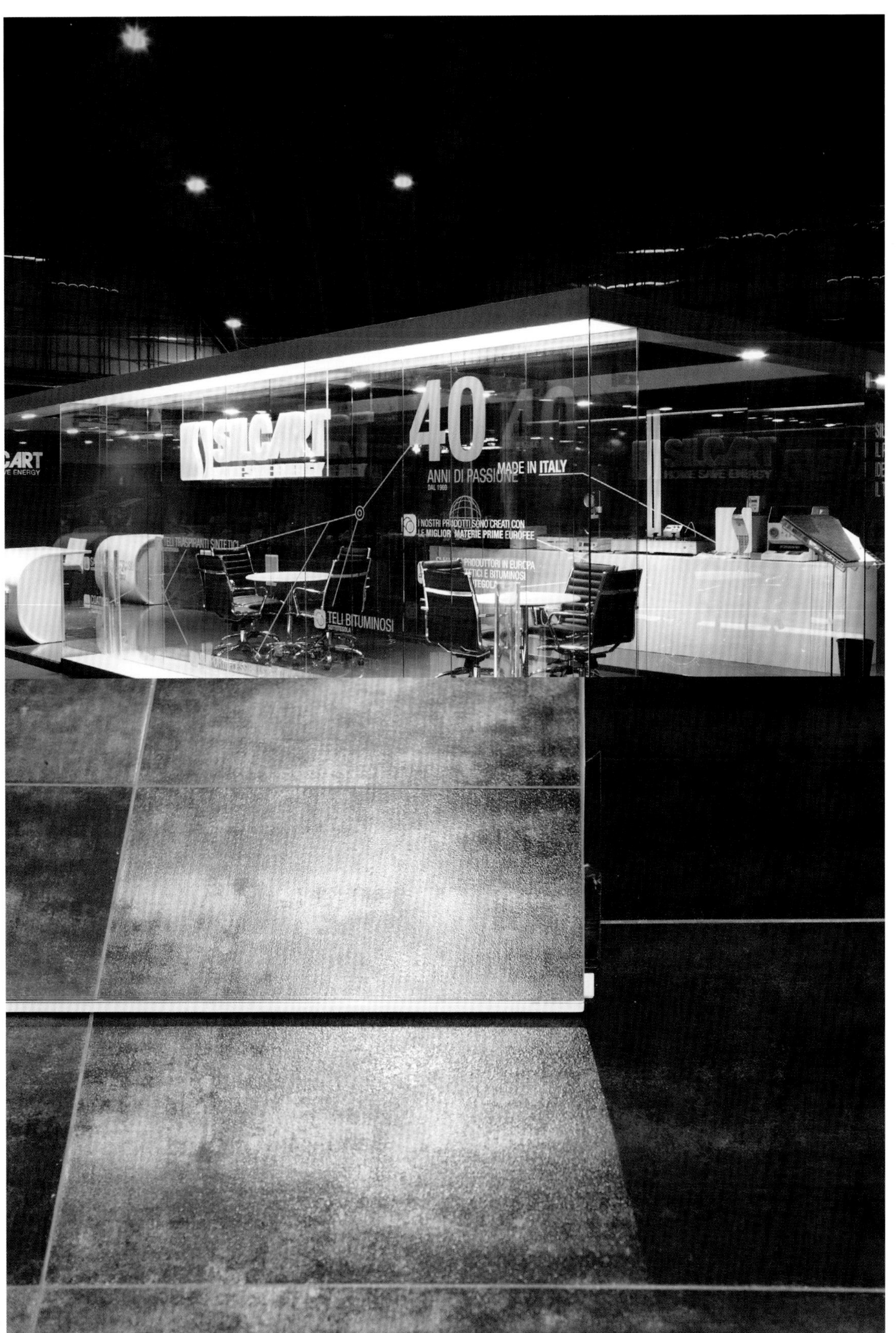
SILCART
CART
VE ENERGY
40 40
ANNI DI PASSIONE
DAL 1969
MADE IN ITALY
I NOSTRI PRODOTTI SONO CREATI CON
LE MIGLIORI MATERIE PRIME EUROPEE
PRODUTTORI IN EUROPA
TETICI E BITUMINOSI
TEGOL
TELI TRASPIRANTI SINTETICI
TELI BITUMINOSI
SOTTOTEGOLA
SILCART
HOME SAVE ENERGY

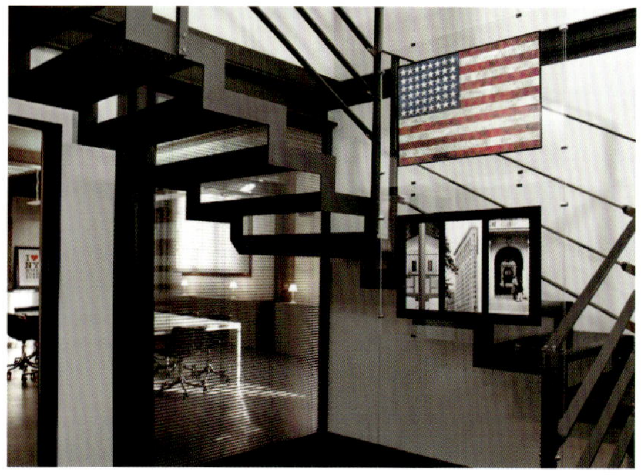
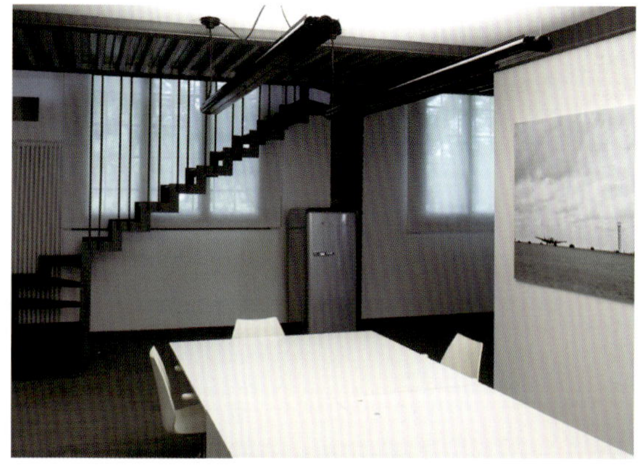
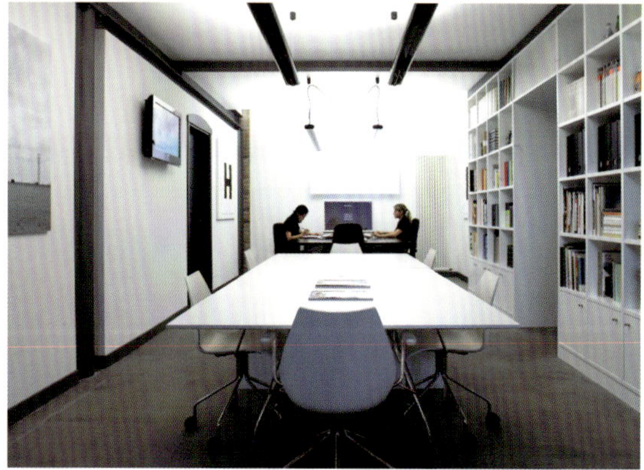
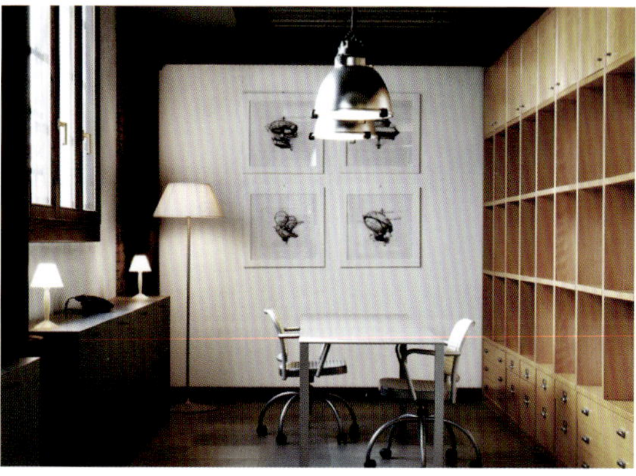
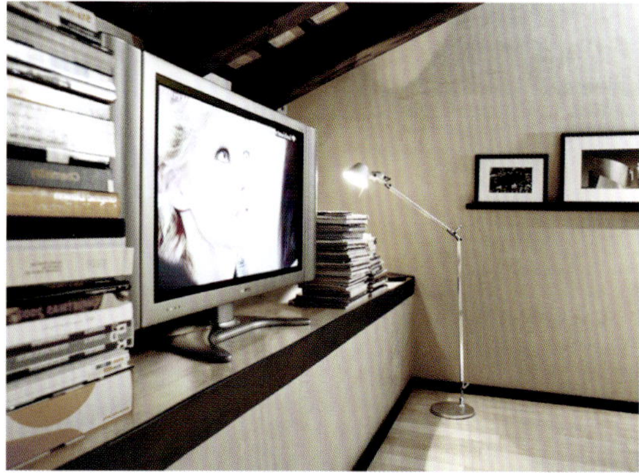
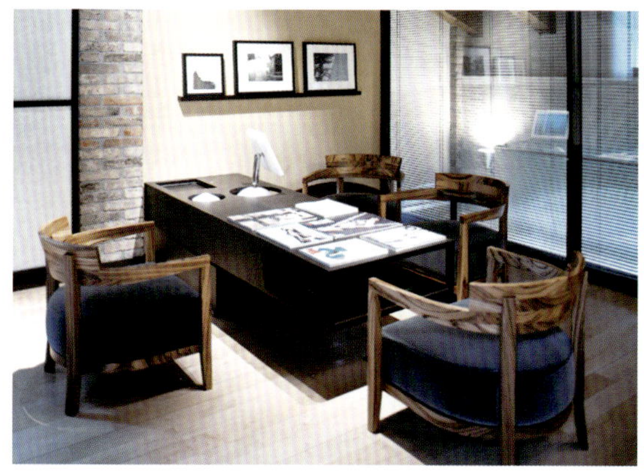
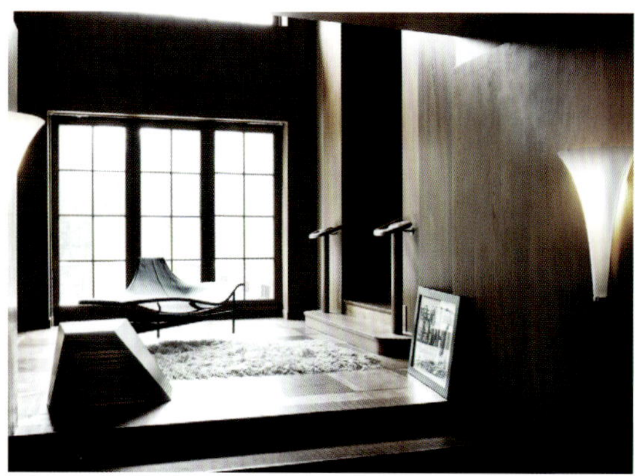
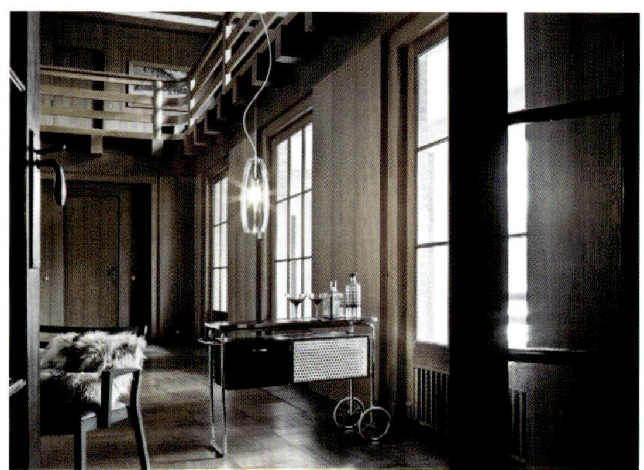

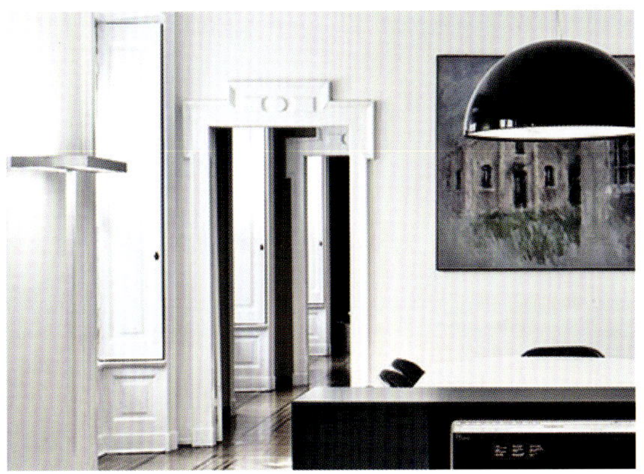
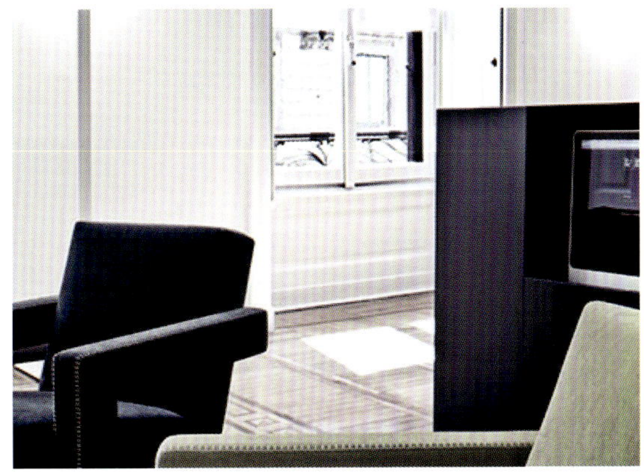
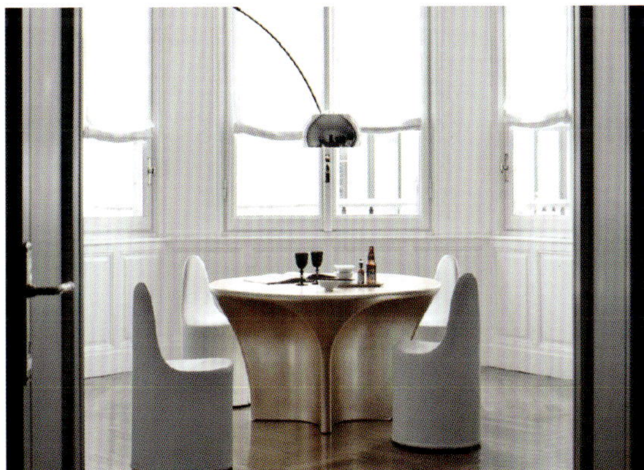
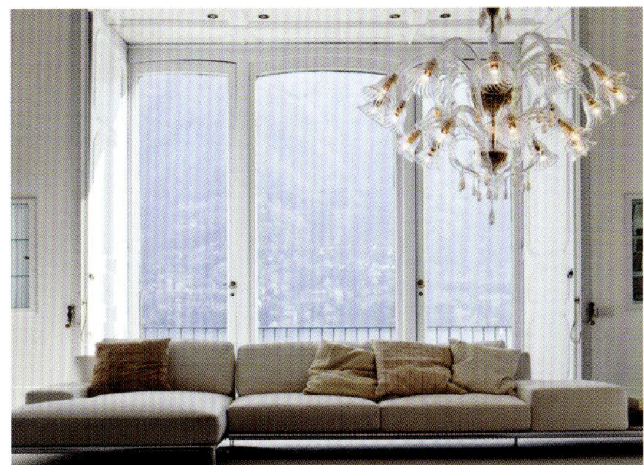
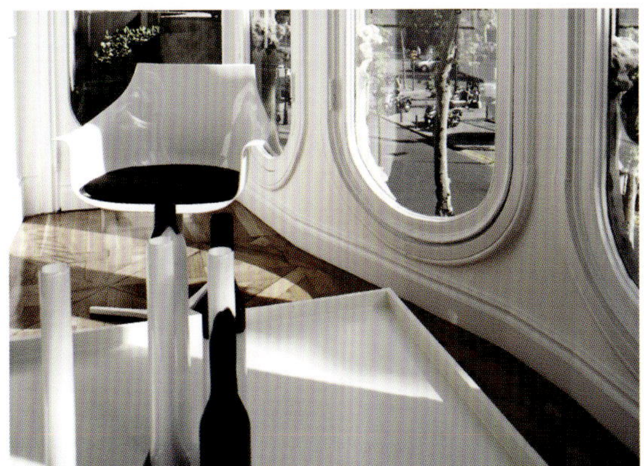
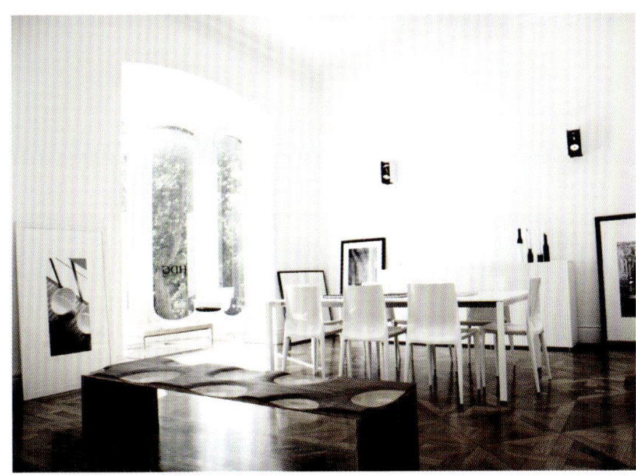
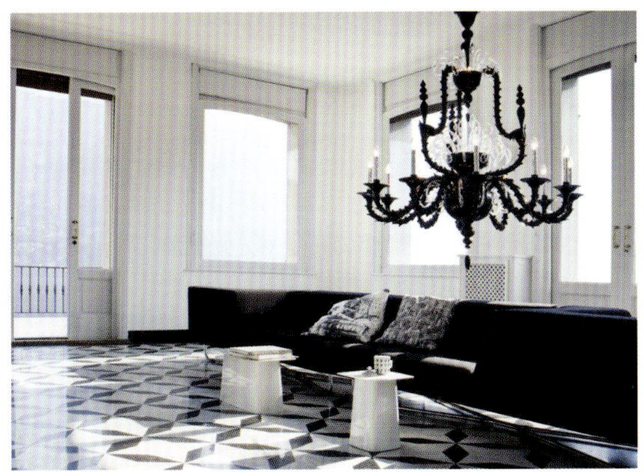
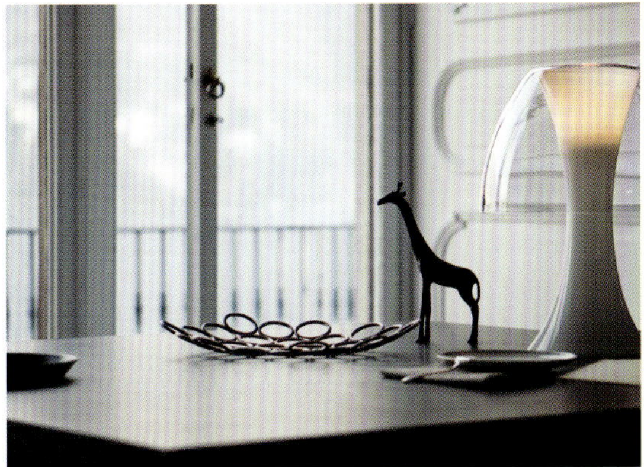

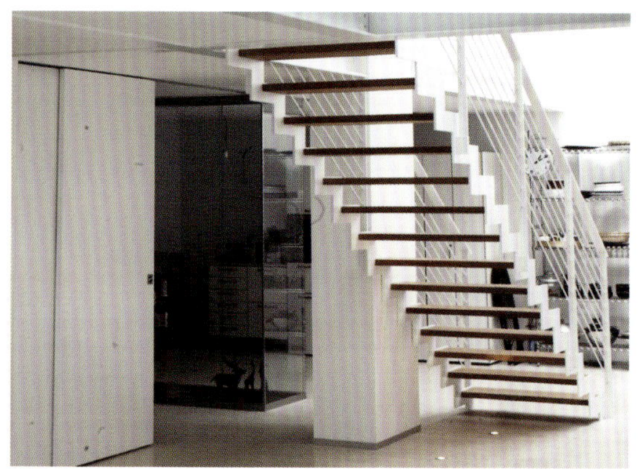
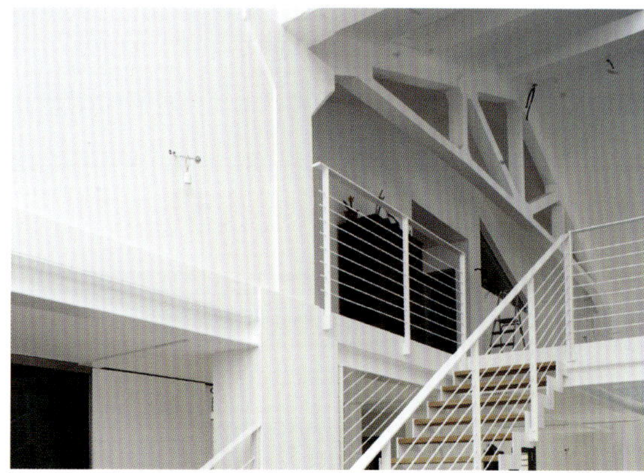
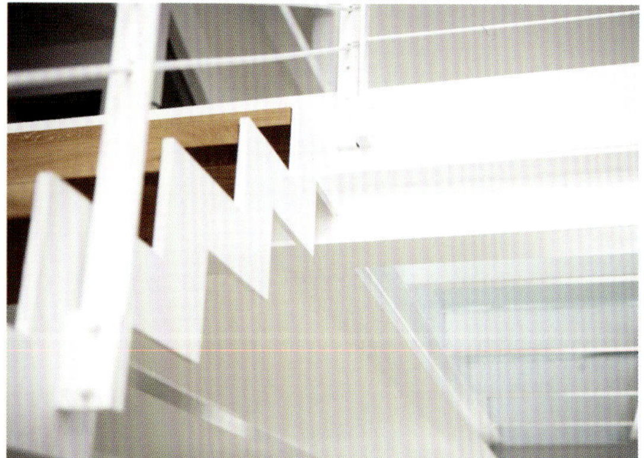
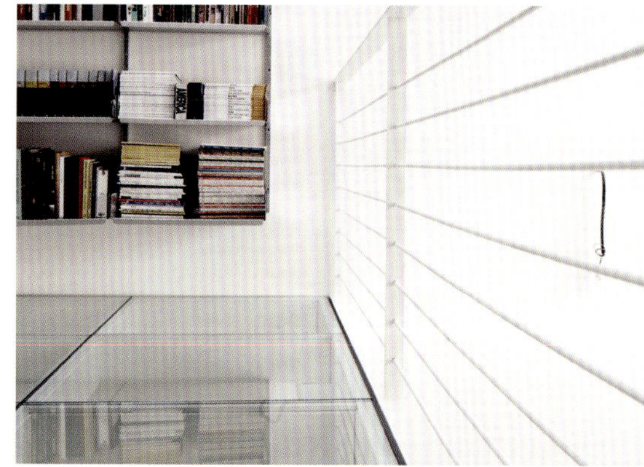
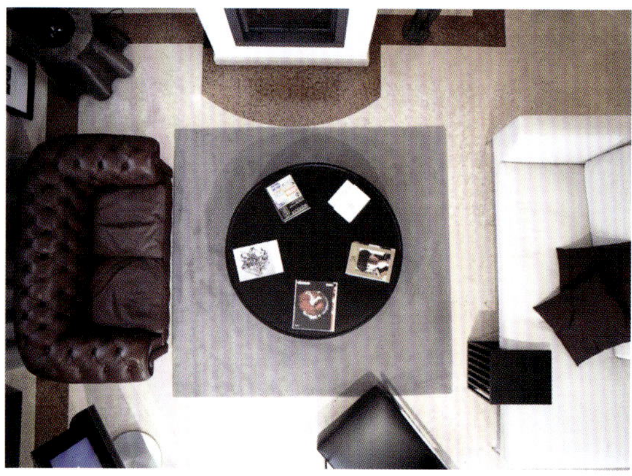
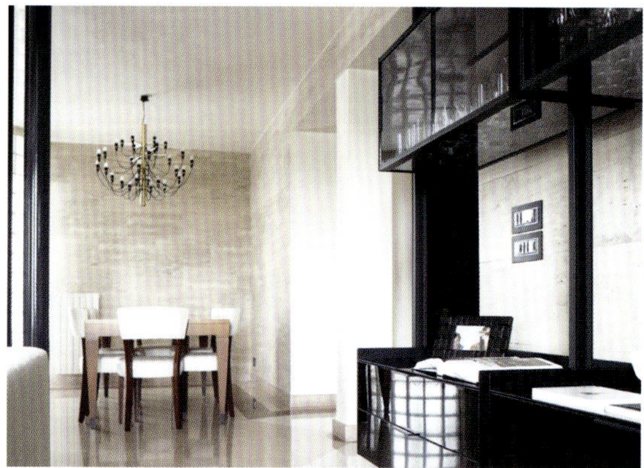
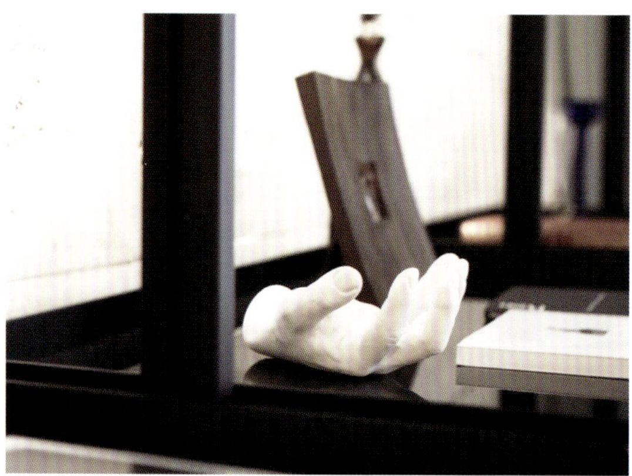
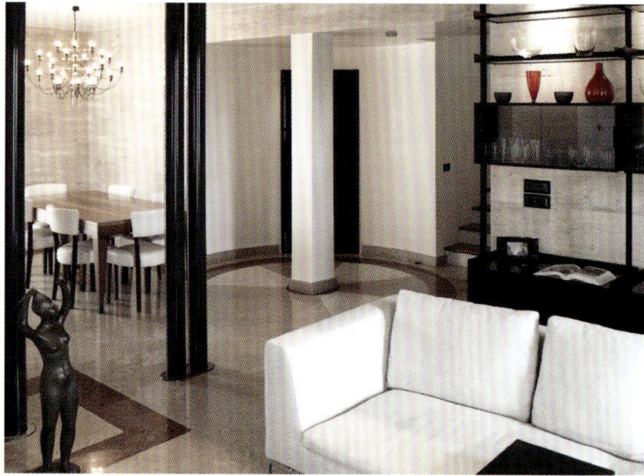

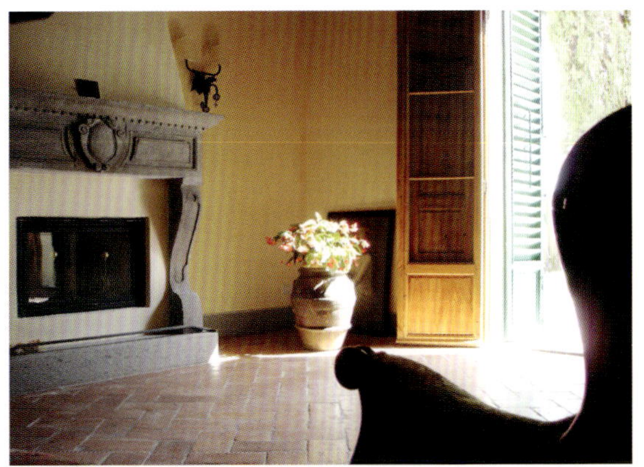
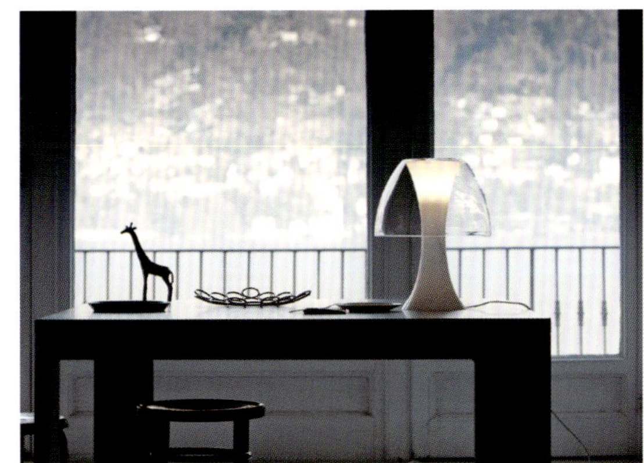
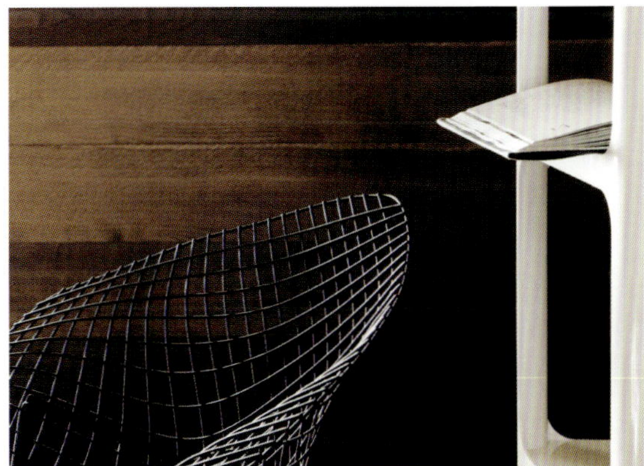
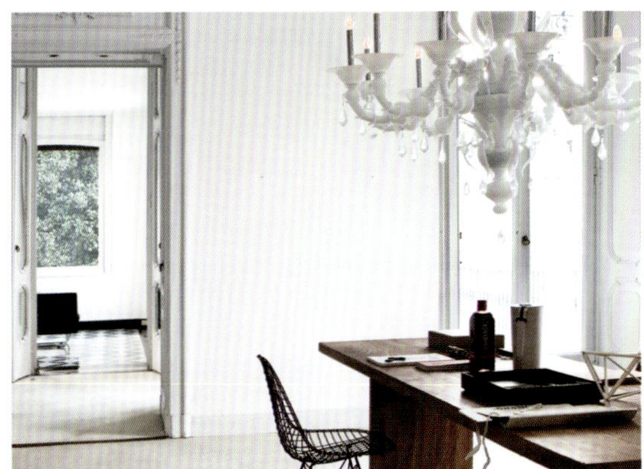
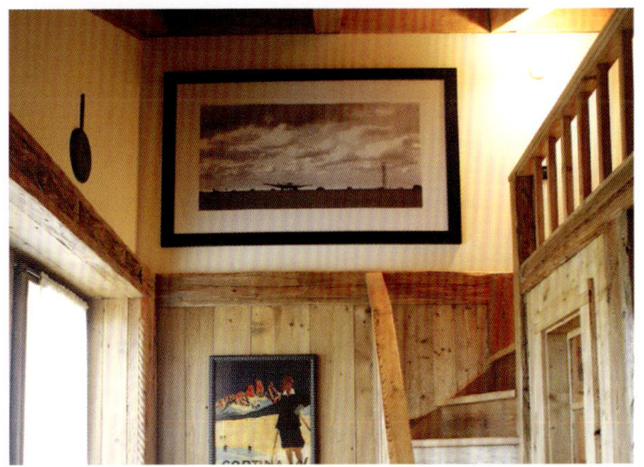
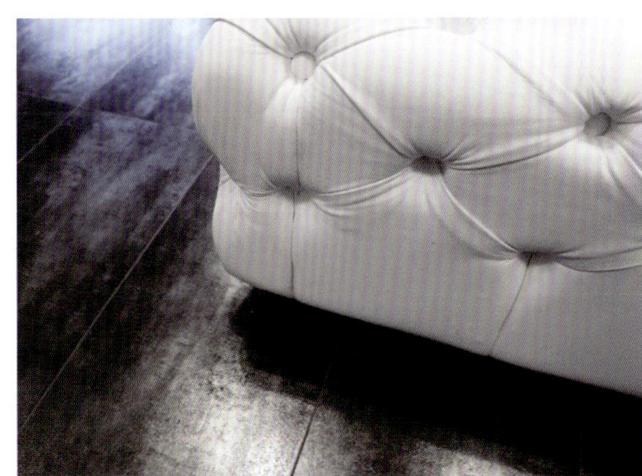
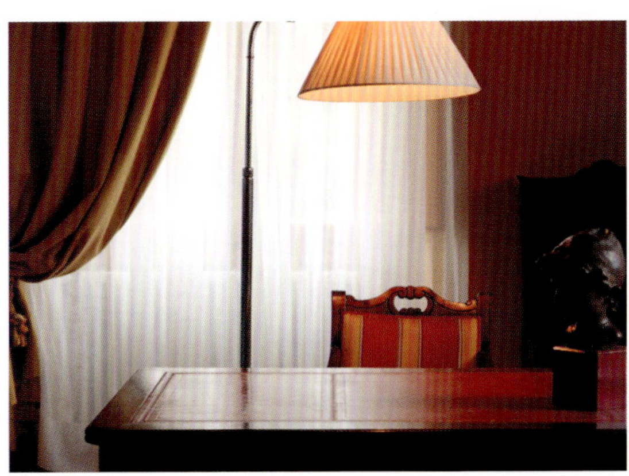
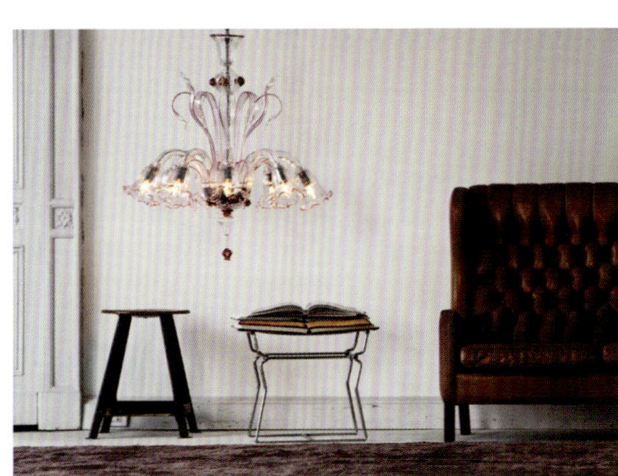

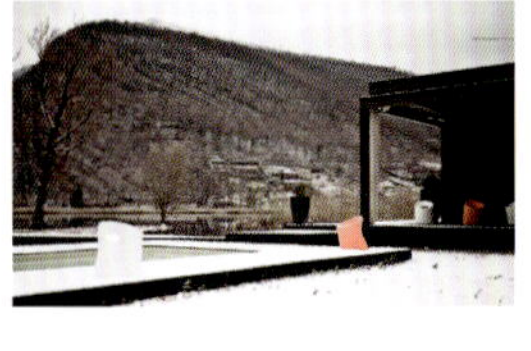
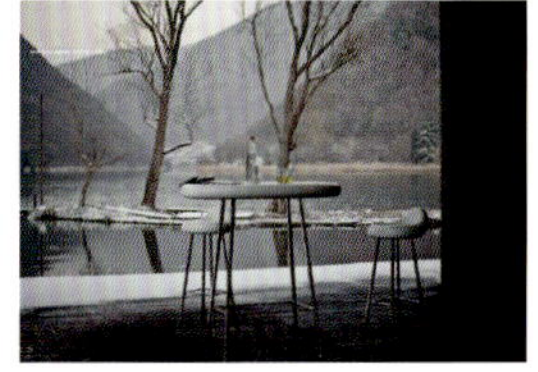
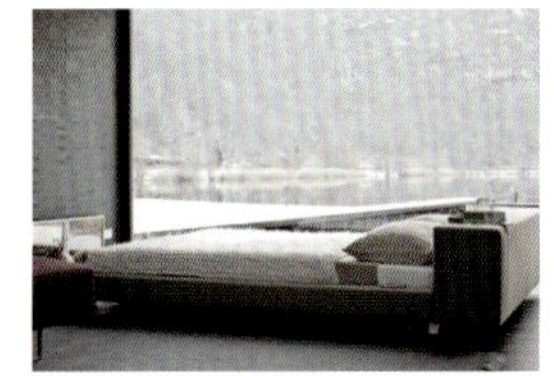
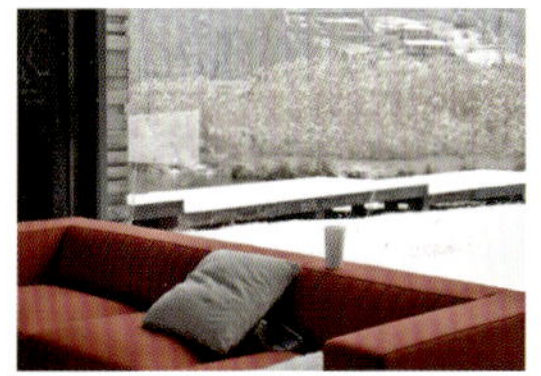
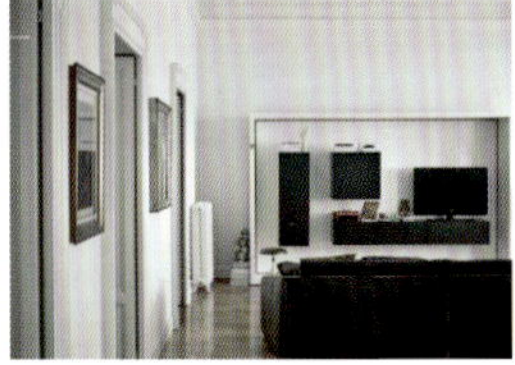
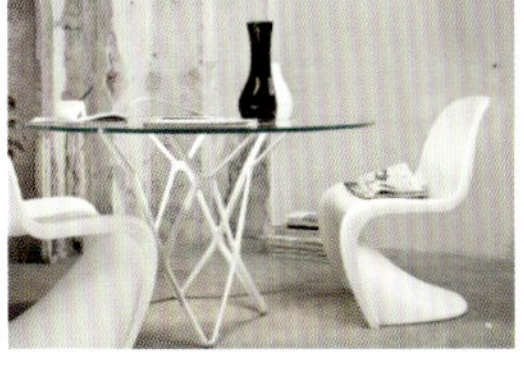
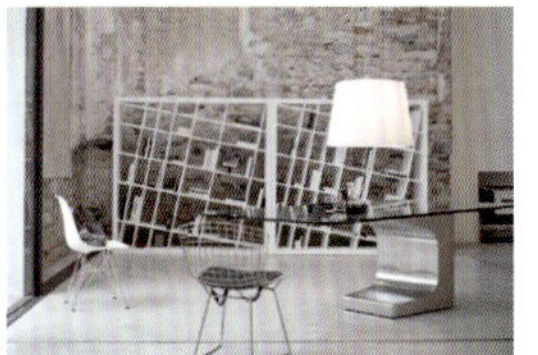
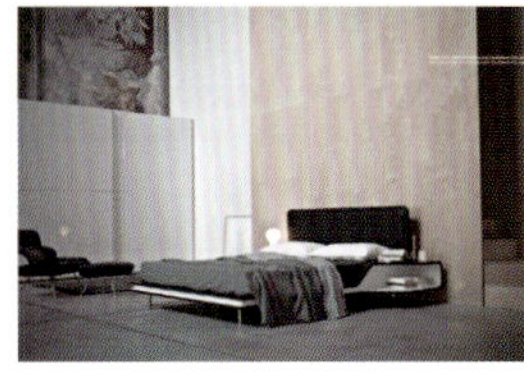
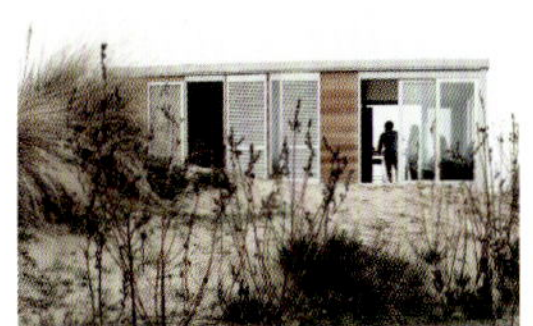
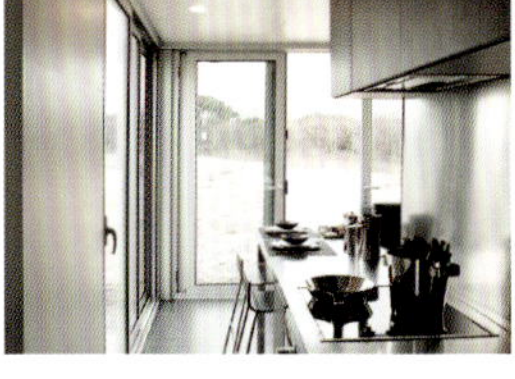
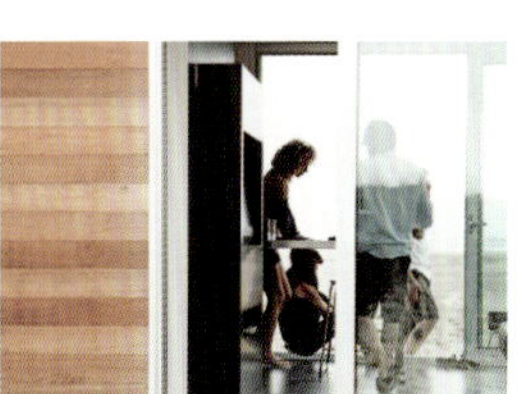
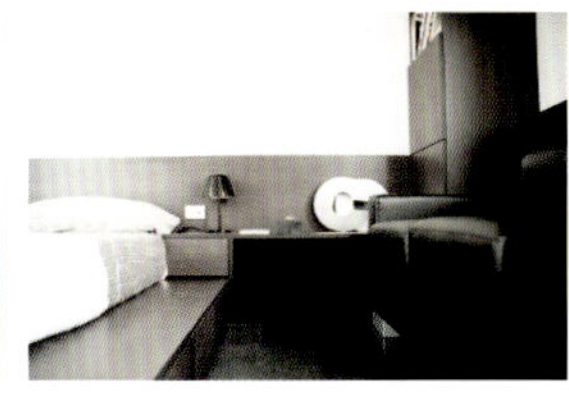
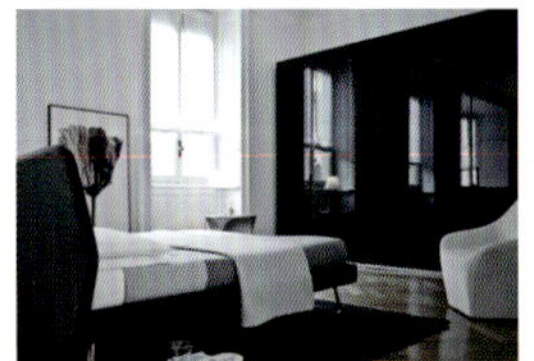
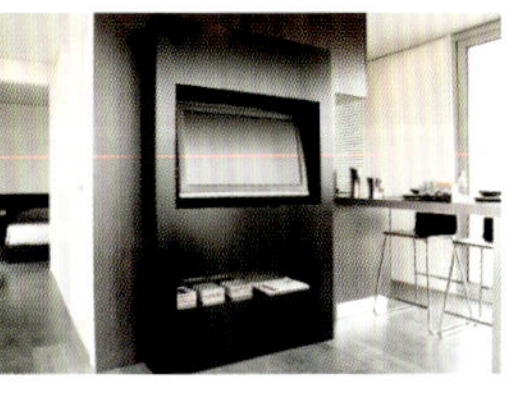
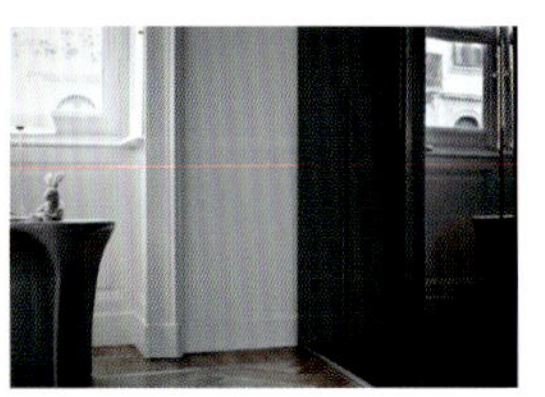
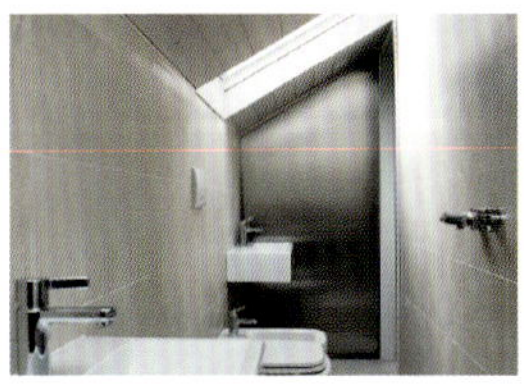
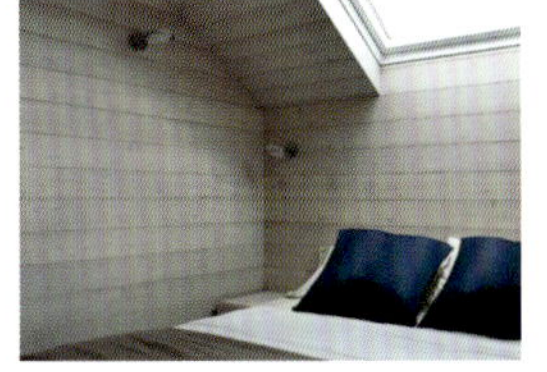
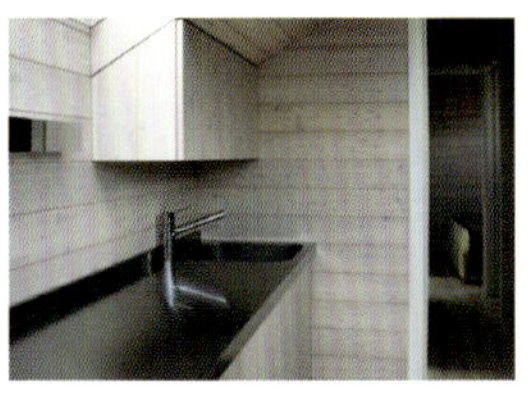
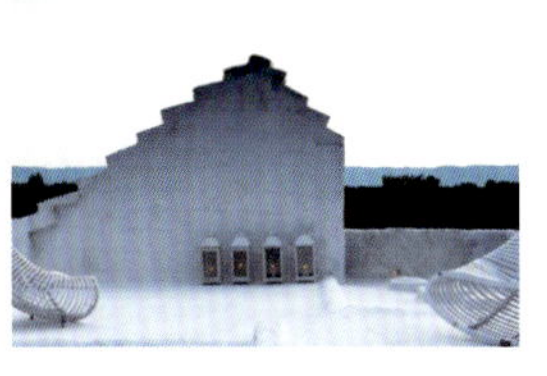
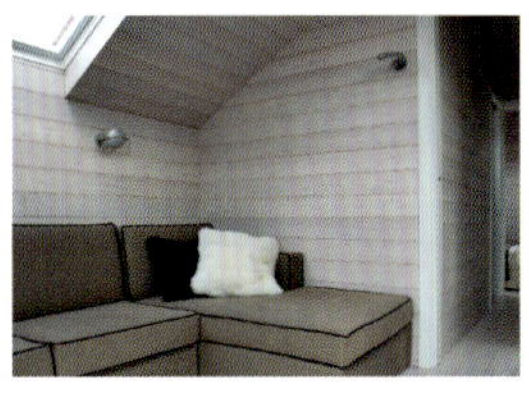
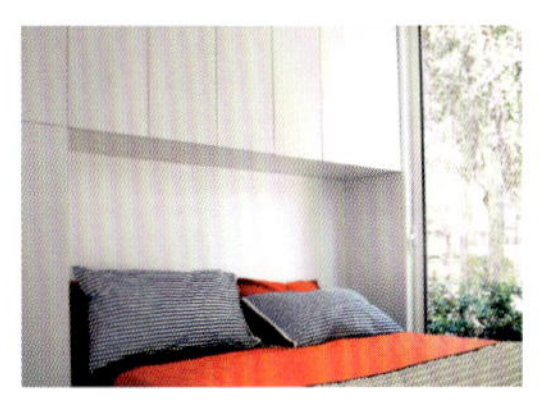
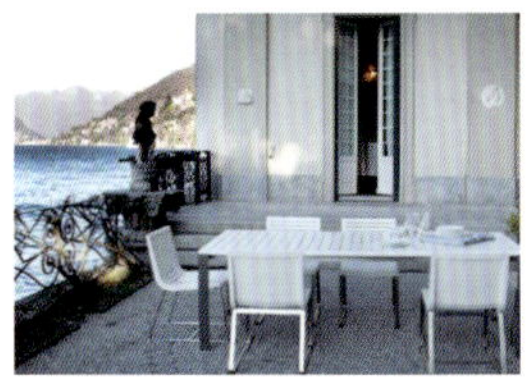
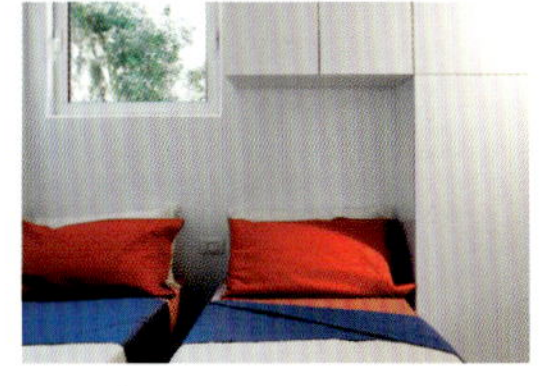
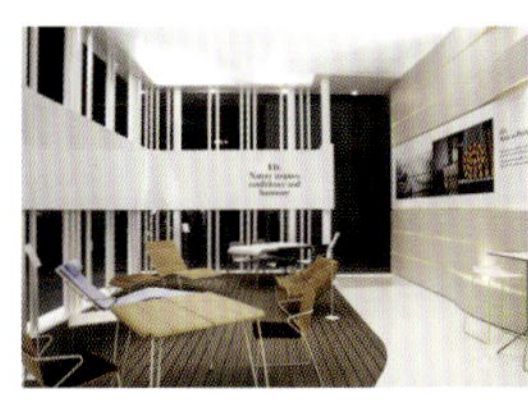
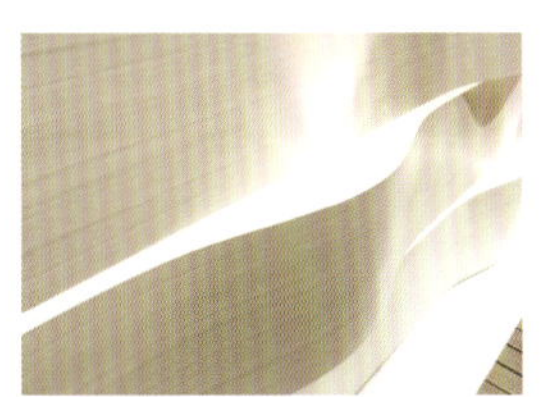
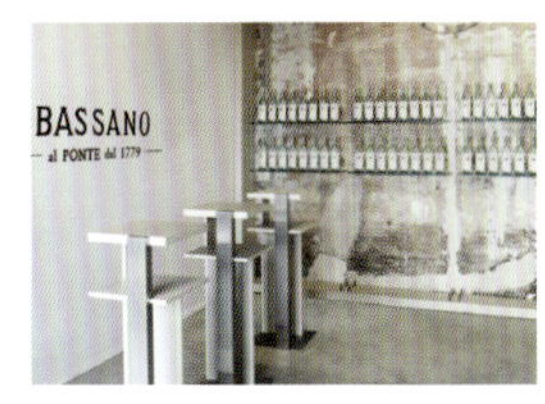

BASSANO
al PONTE dal 1779

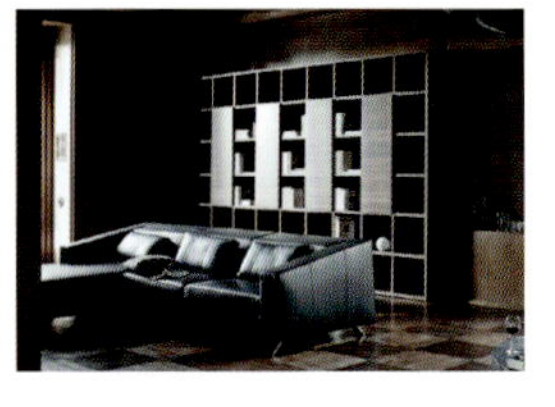
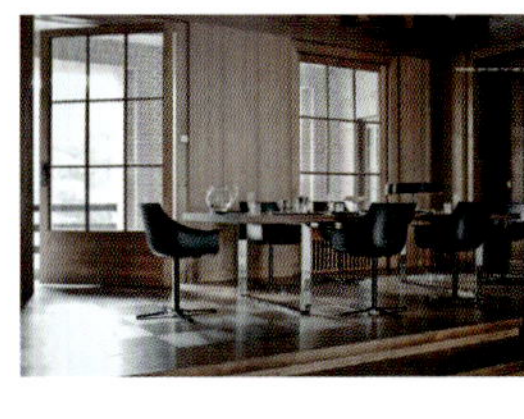
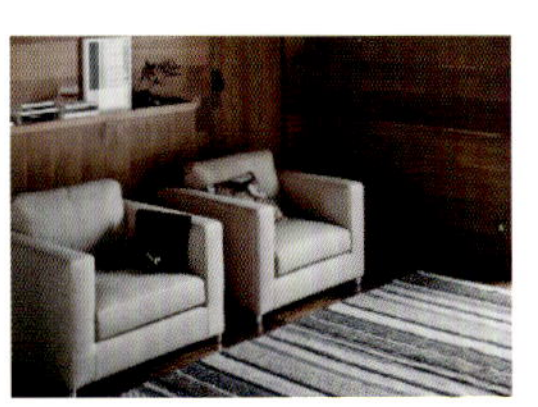
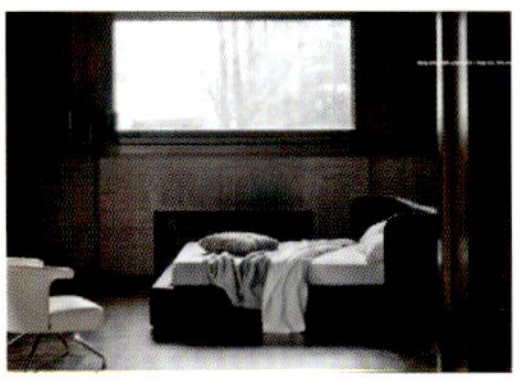
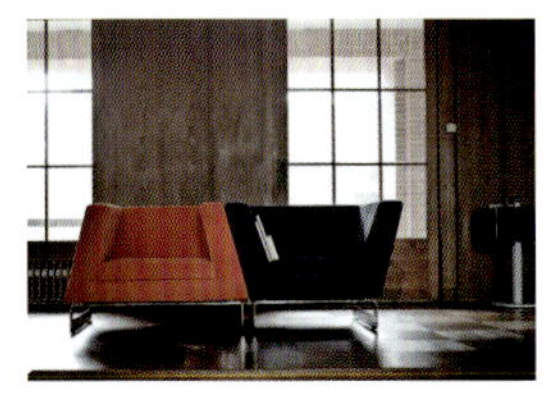
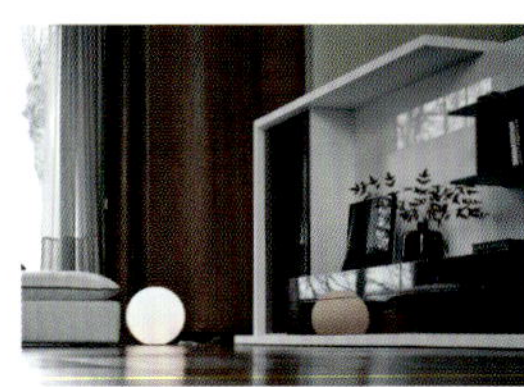

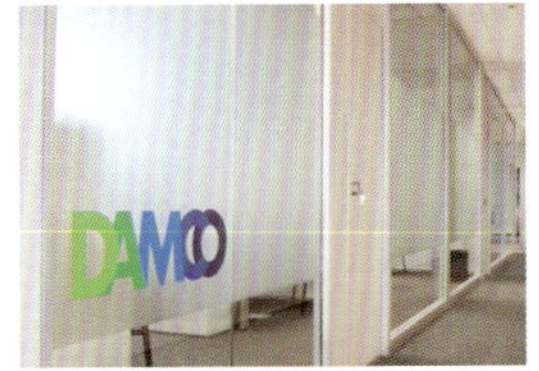
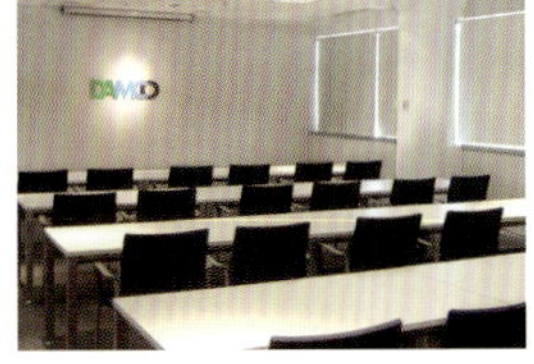
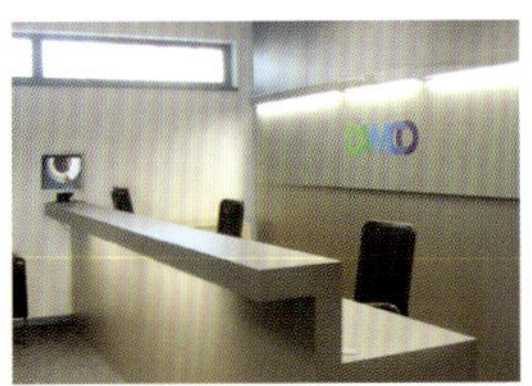
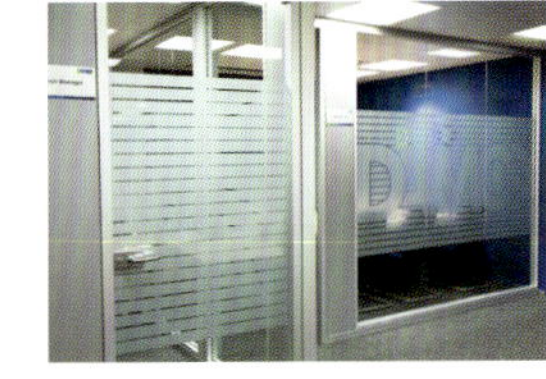
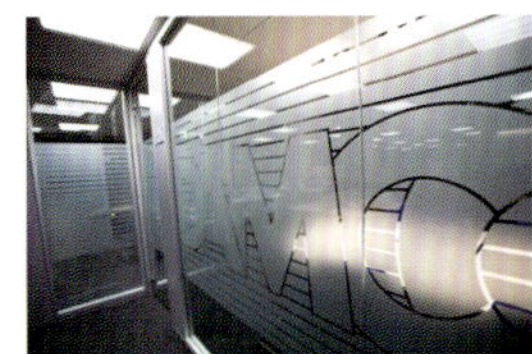
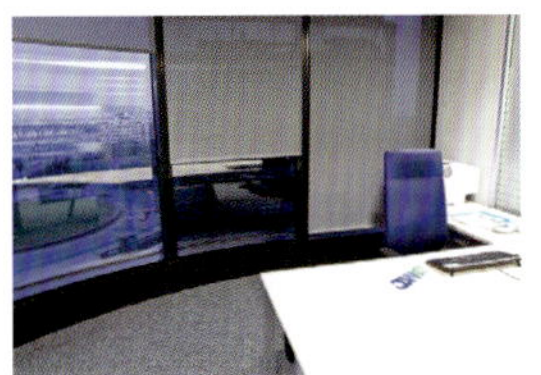
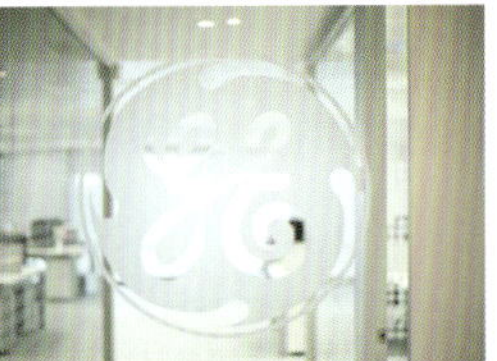
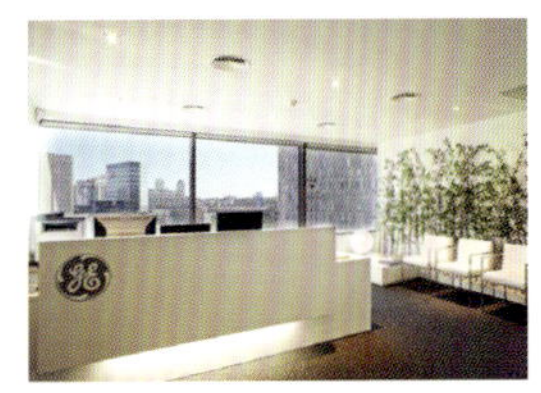
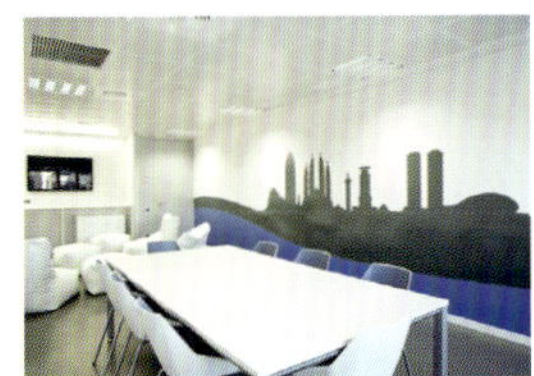
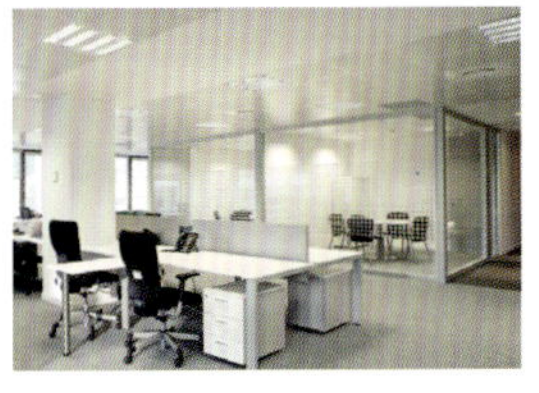
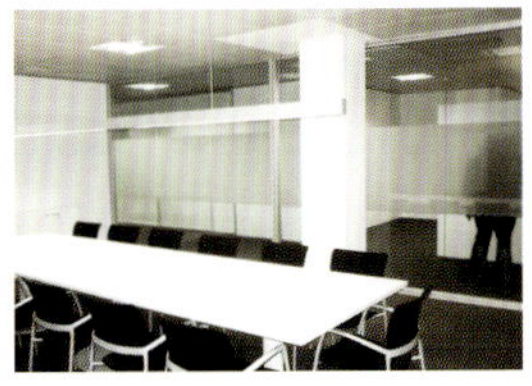
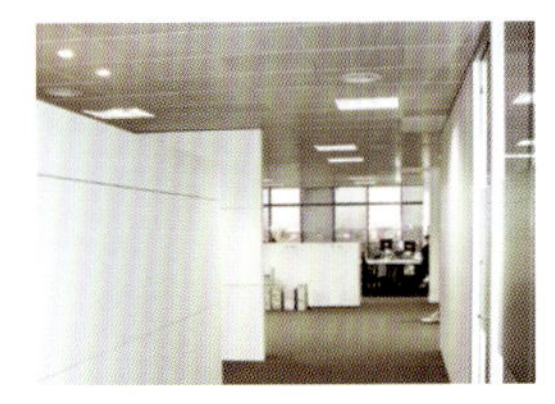
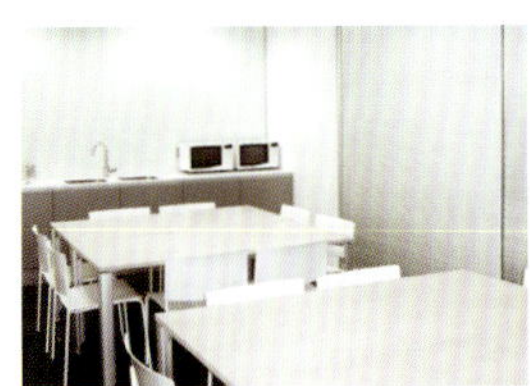
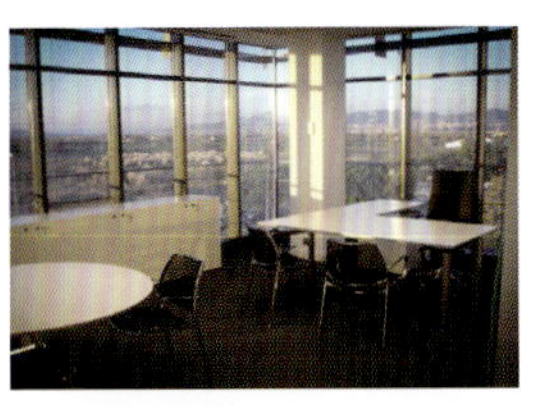
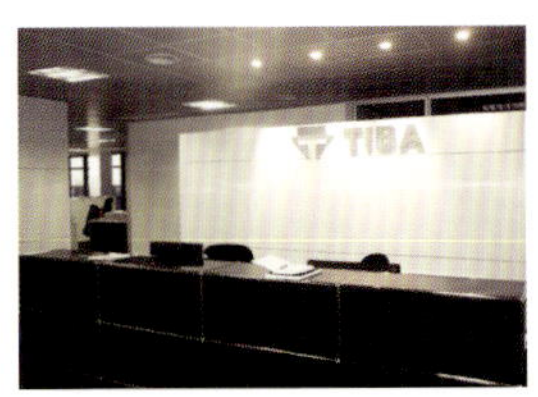
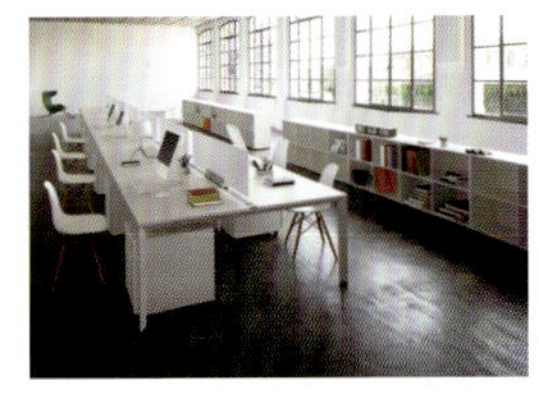
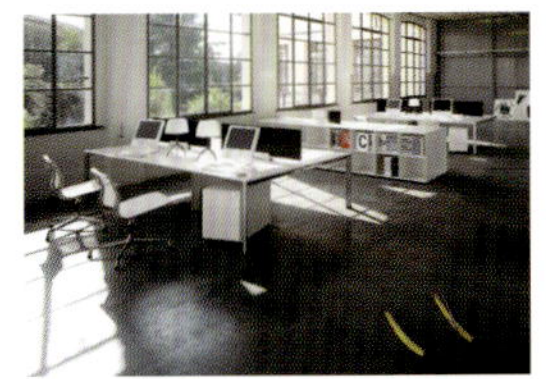
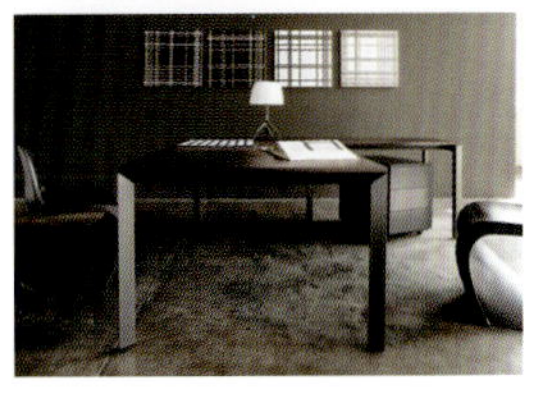
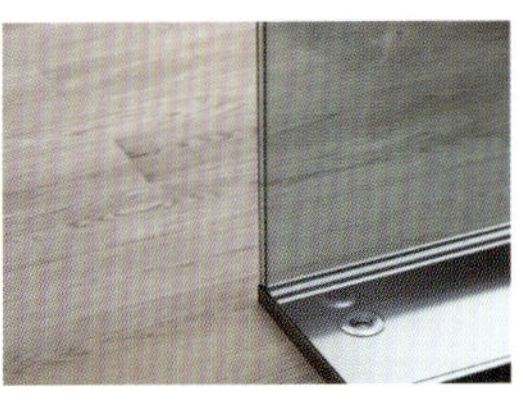
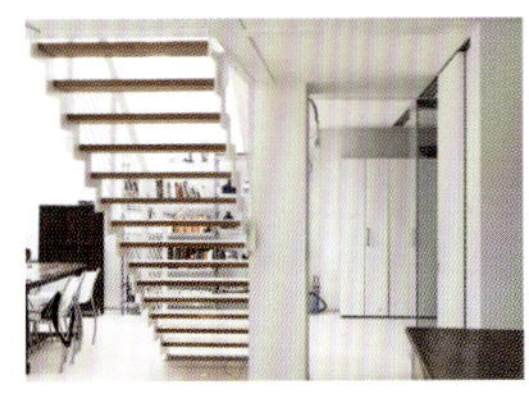
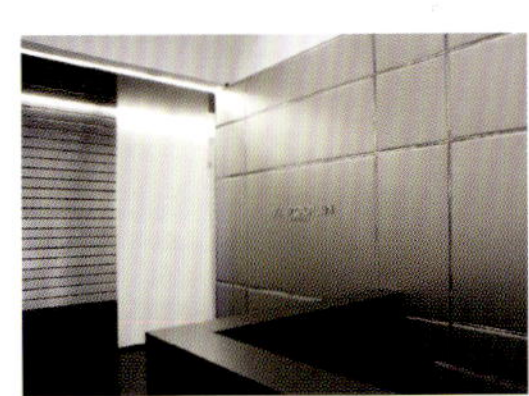
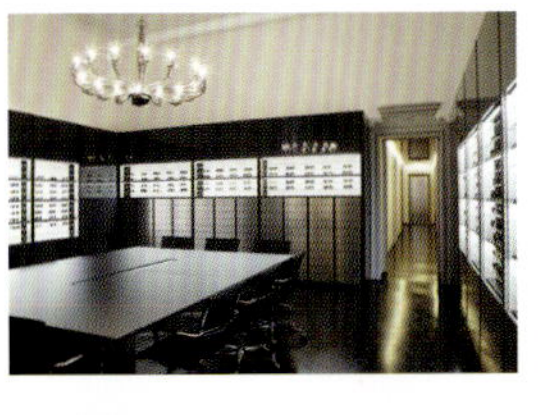
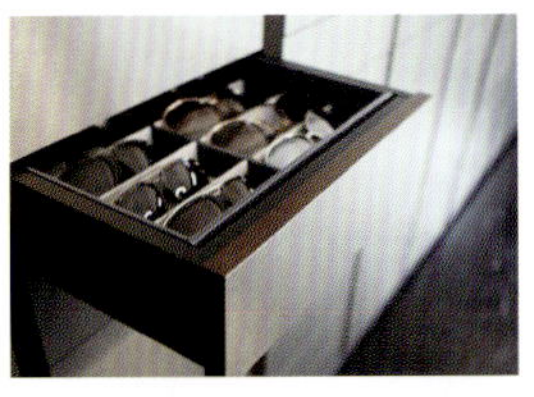
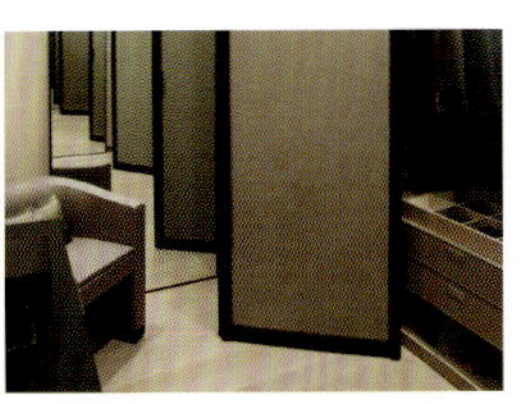
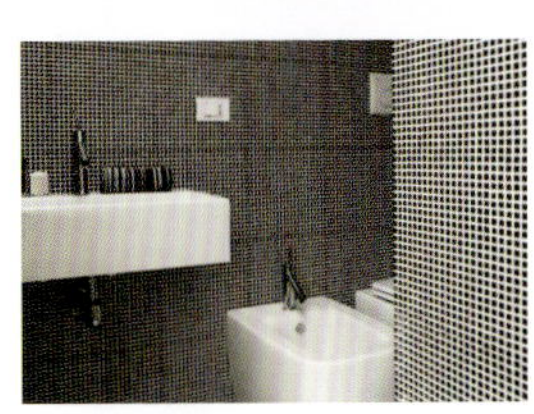
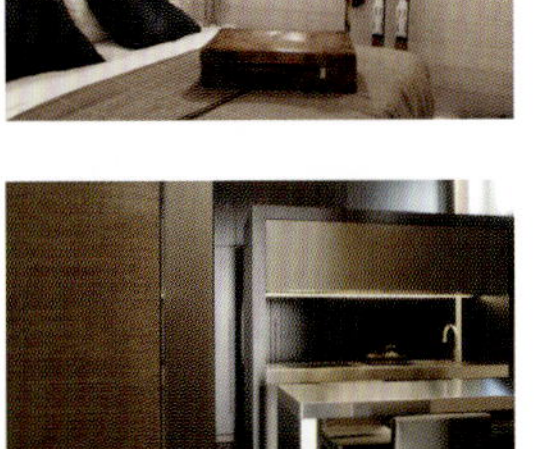
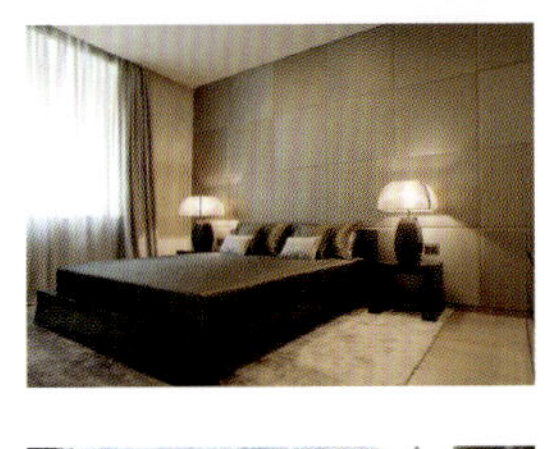
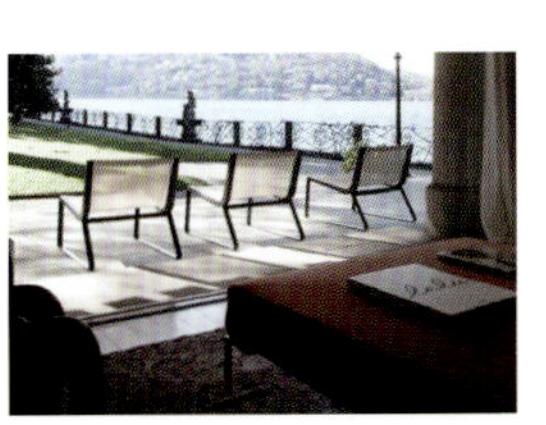
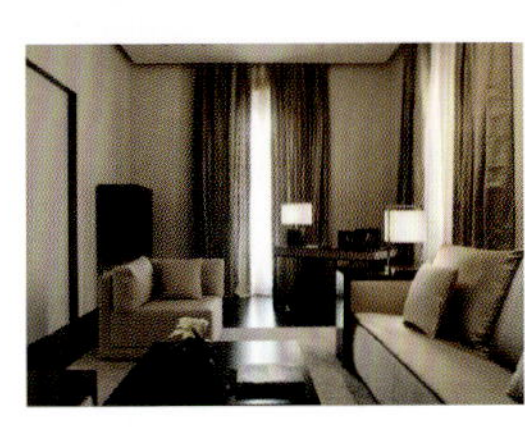
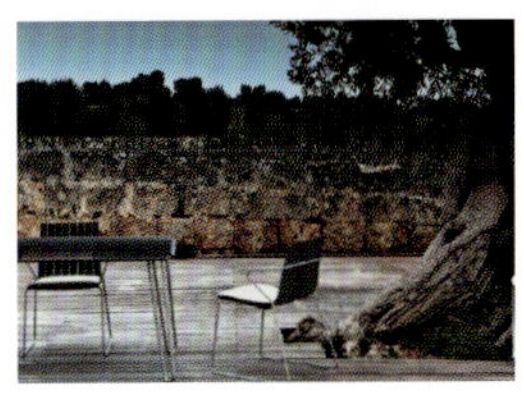

BESPOKE

Bespoke *(pronounced bih-spohk')* is a British English term employed
in a variety of applications to mean an item custom-made to the buyer's specification.
While applied to many items now, from computer software to luxury cars,
the term historically was related only to tailored clothing,
shirts and other parts of men's apparel involving measurement and fitting.

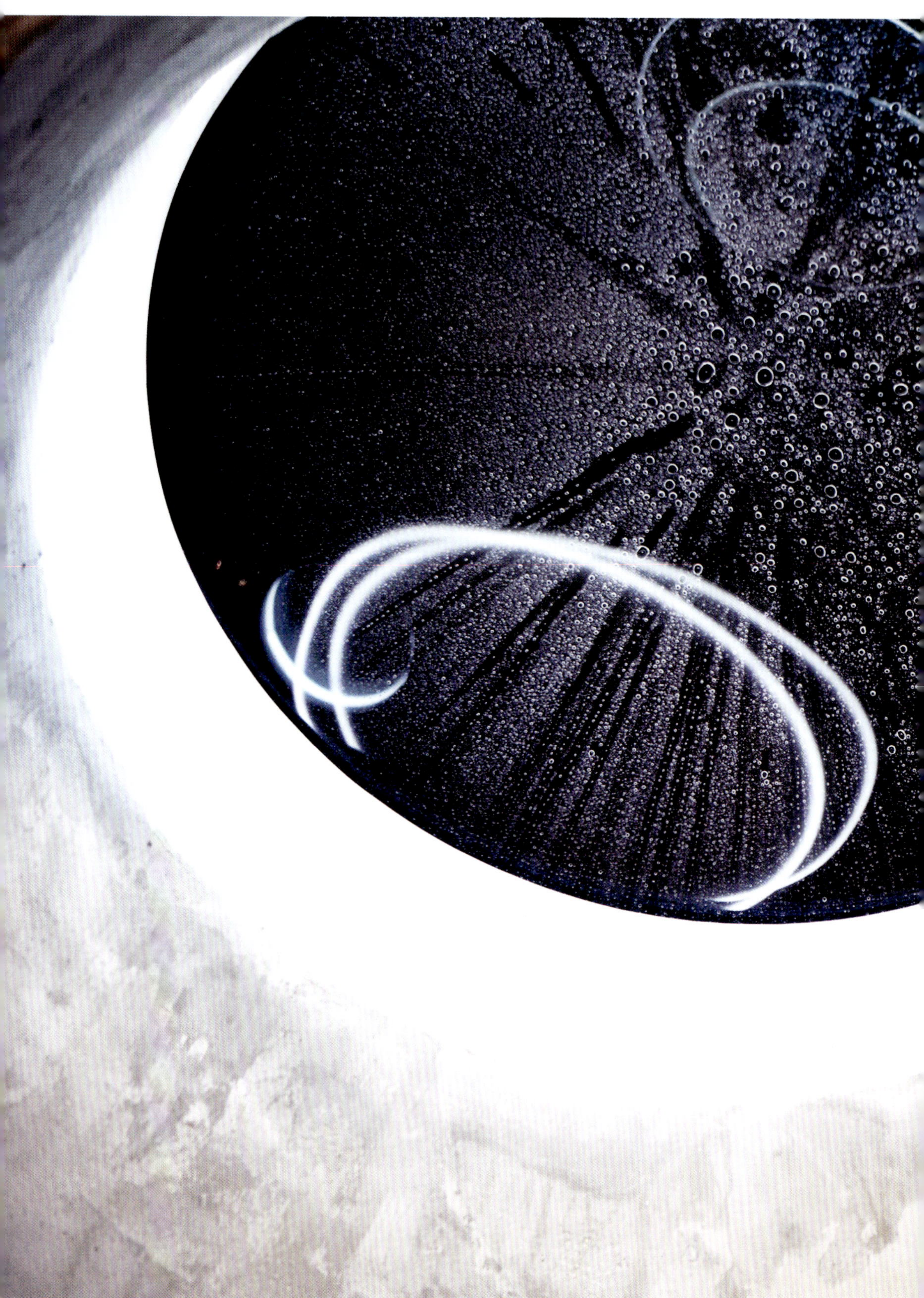

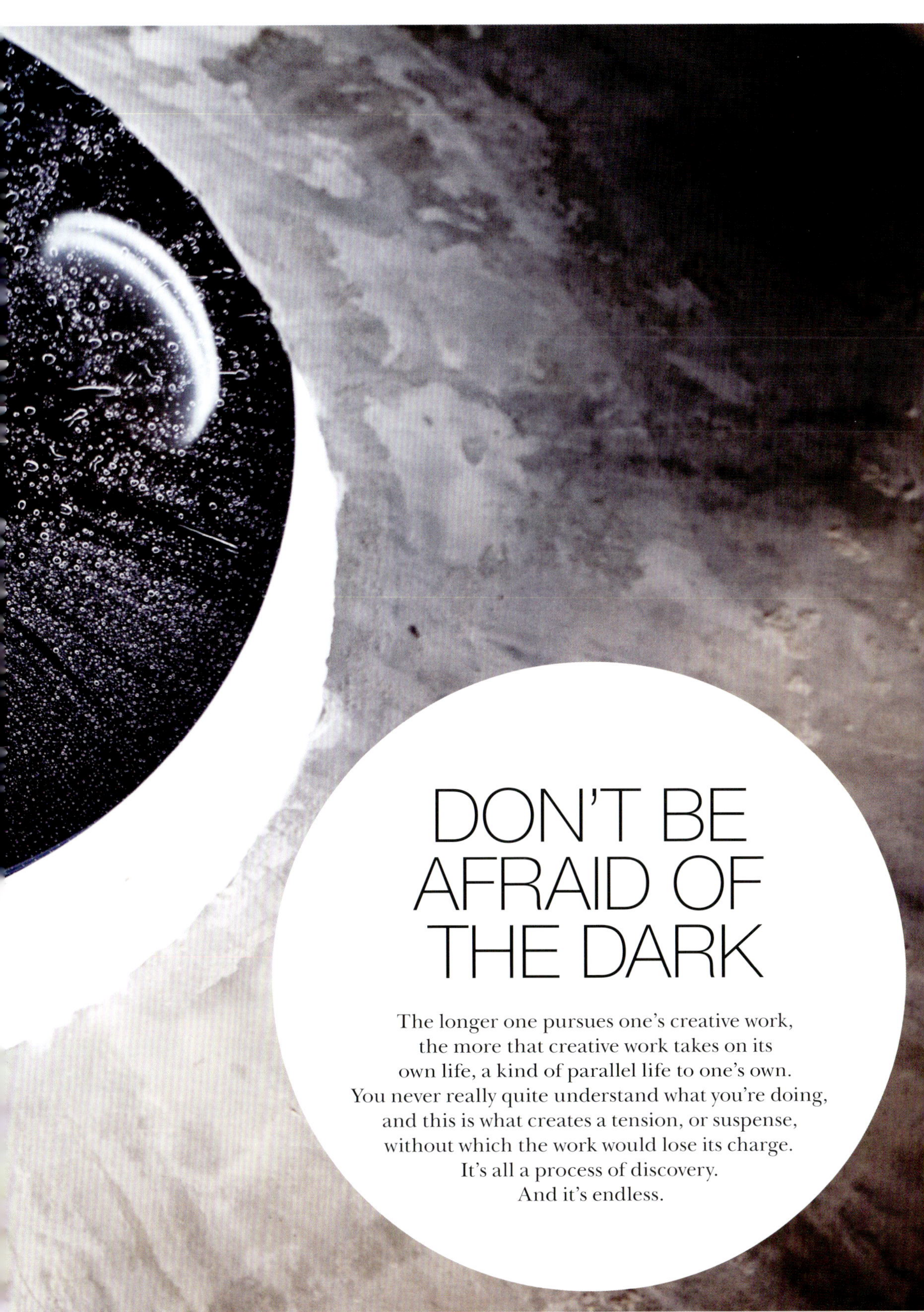

DON'T BE AFRAID OF THE DARK

The longer one pursues one's creative work,
the more that creative work takes on its
own life, a kind of parallel life to one's own.
You never really quite understand what you're doing,
and this is what creates a tension, or suspense,
without which the work would lose its charge.
It's all a process of discovery.
And it's endless.

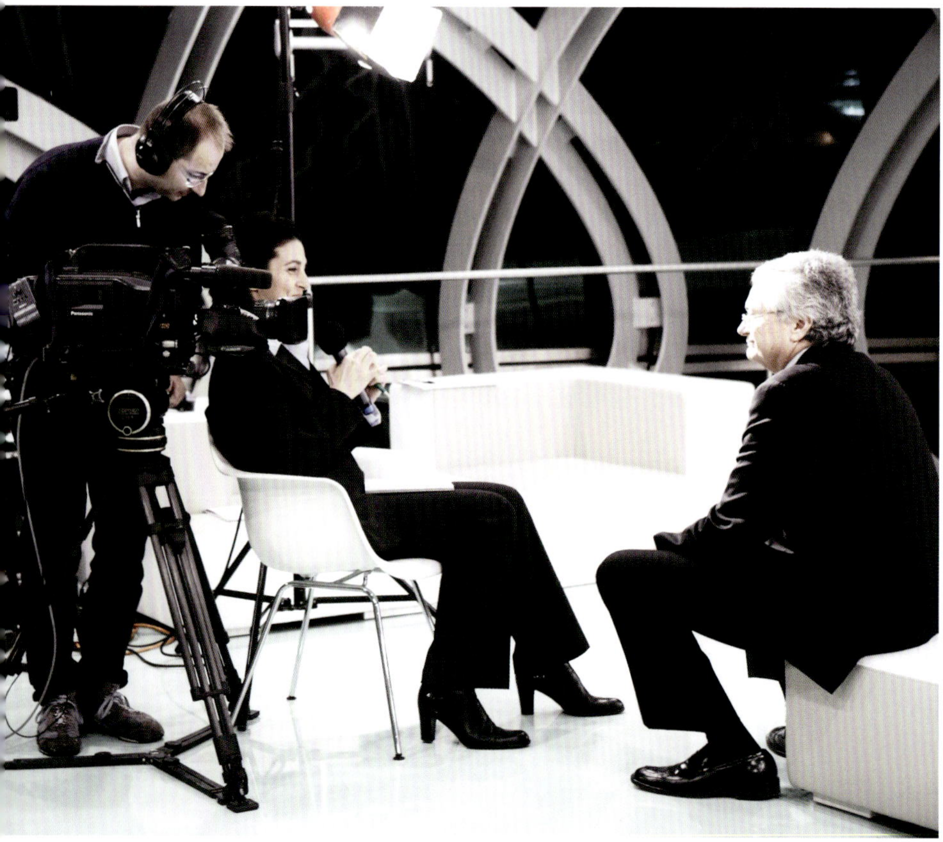

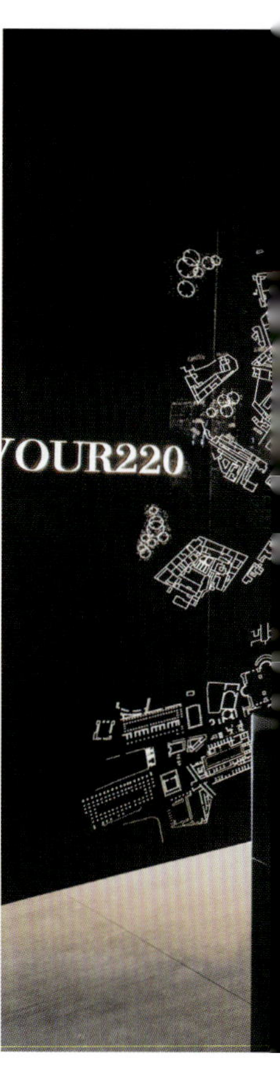

VOUR220

I'LL BE
YOUR MIRROR

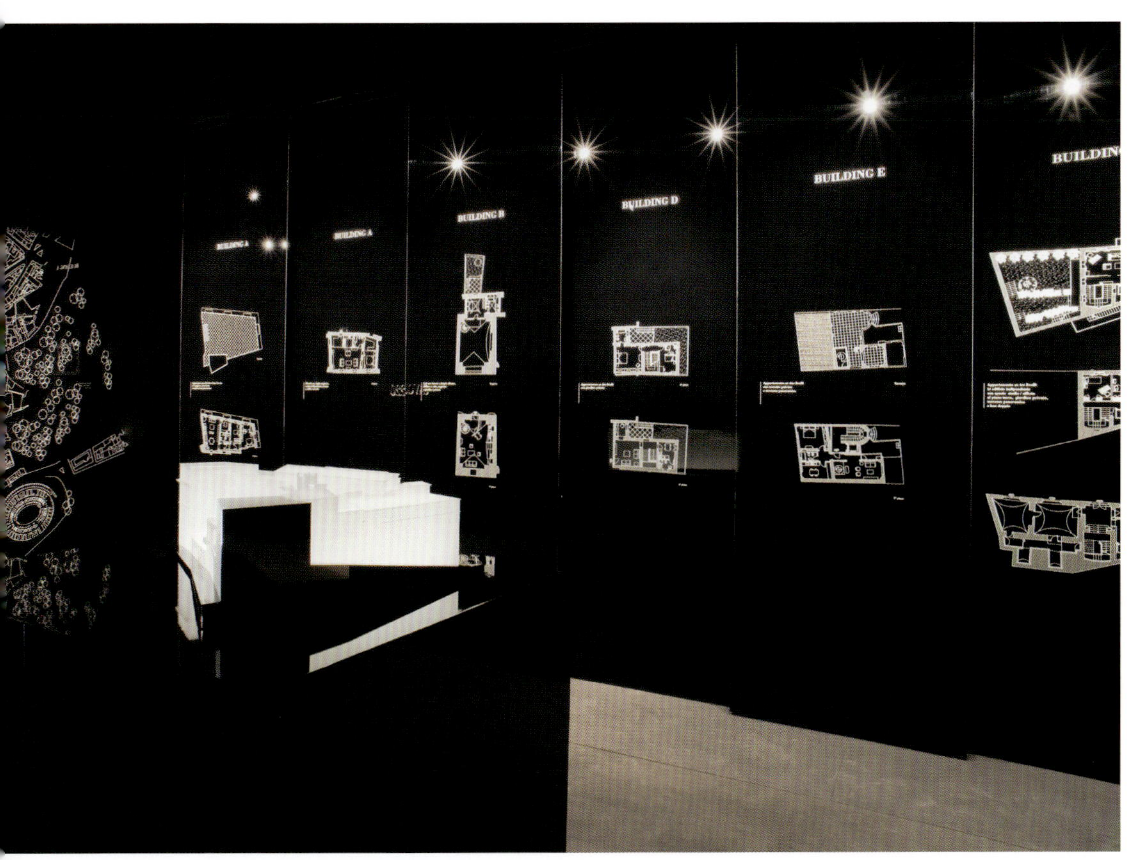

284.

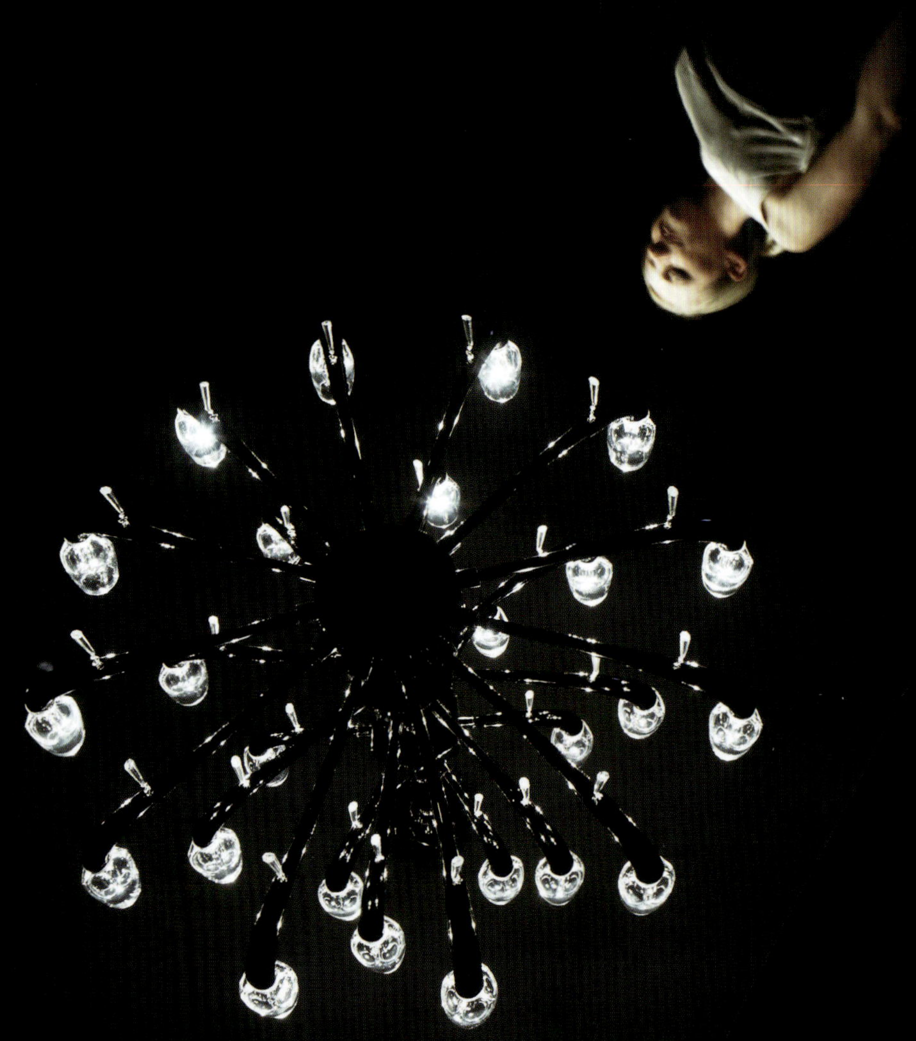

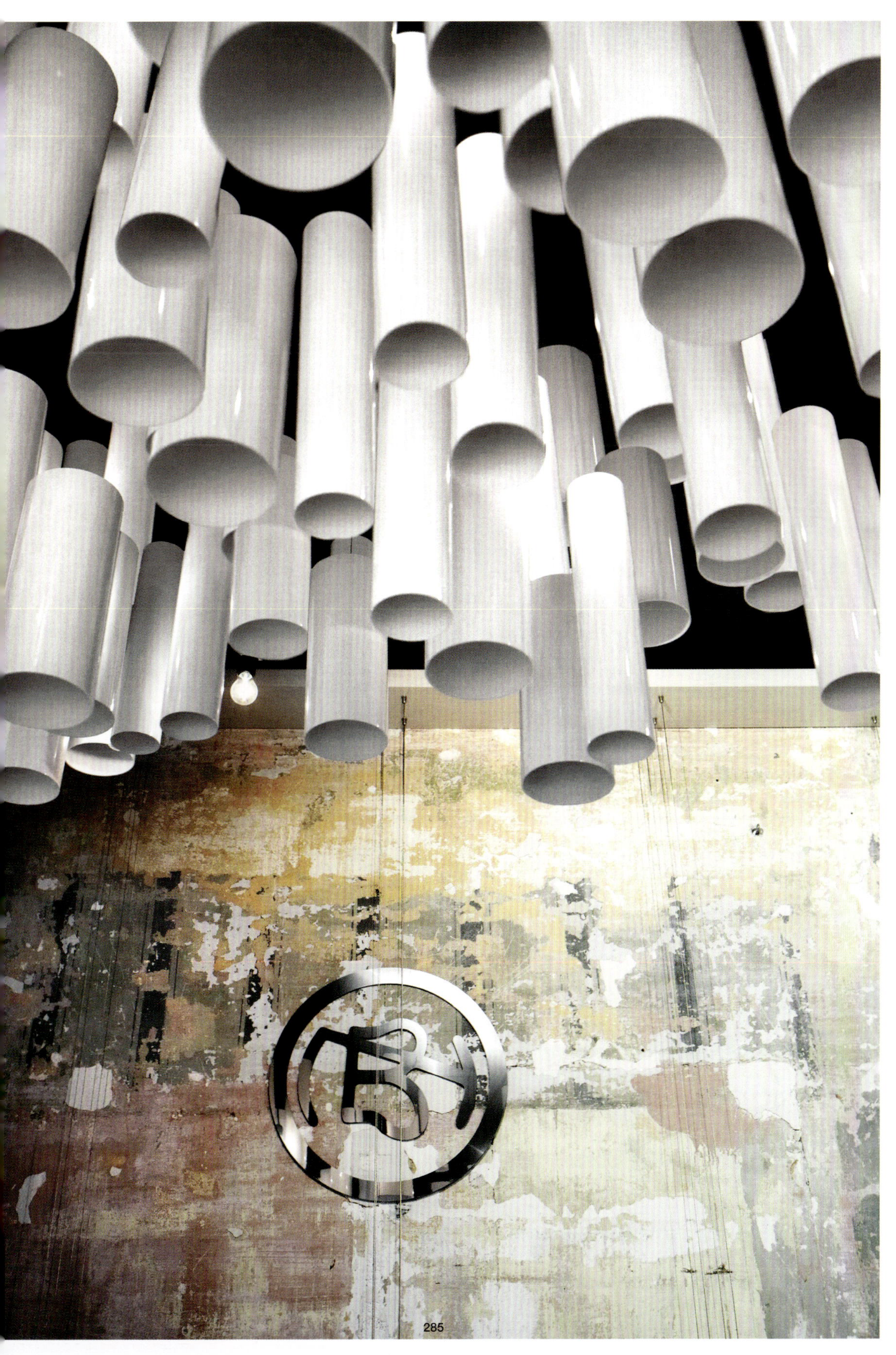

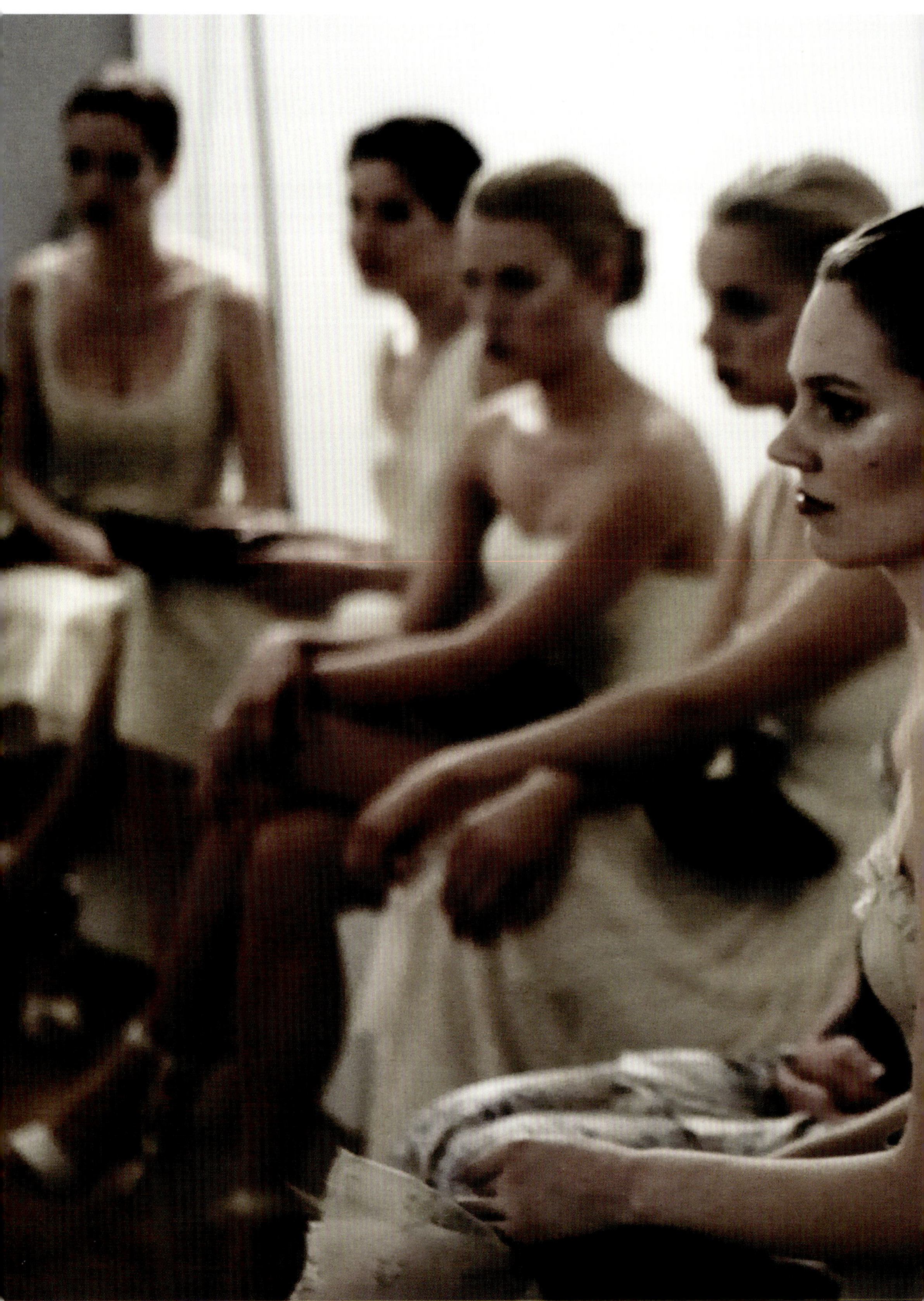

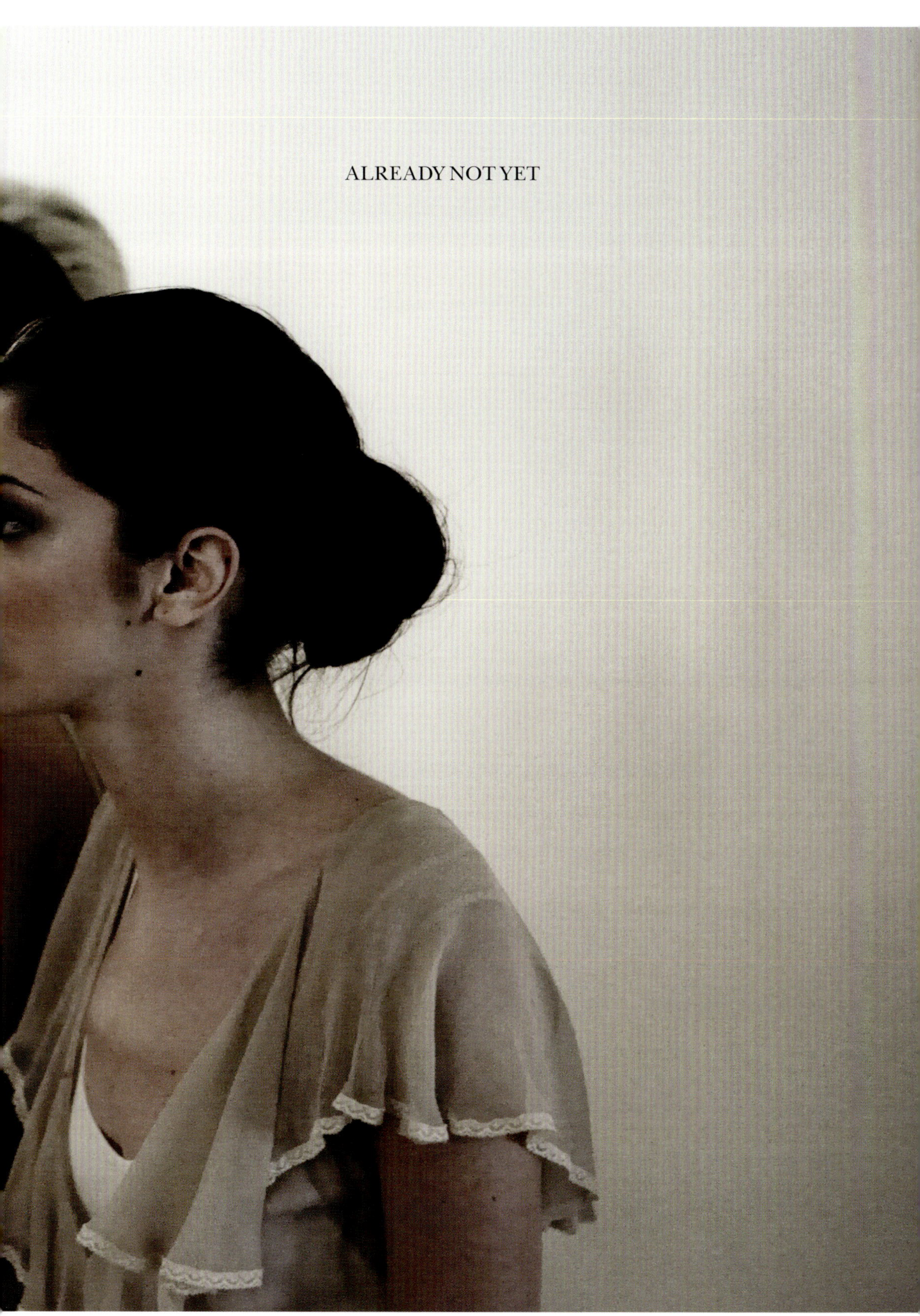

ALREADY NOT YET

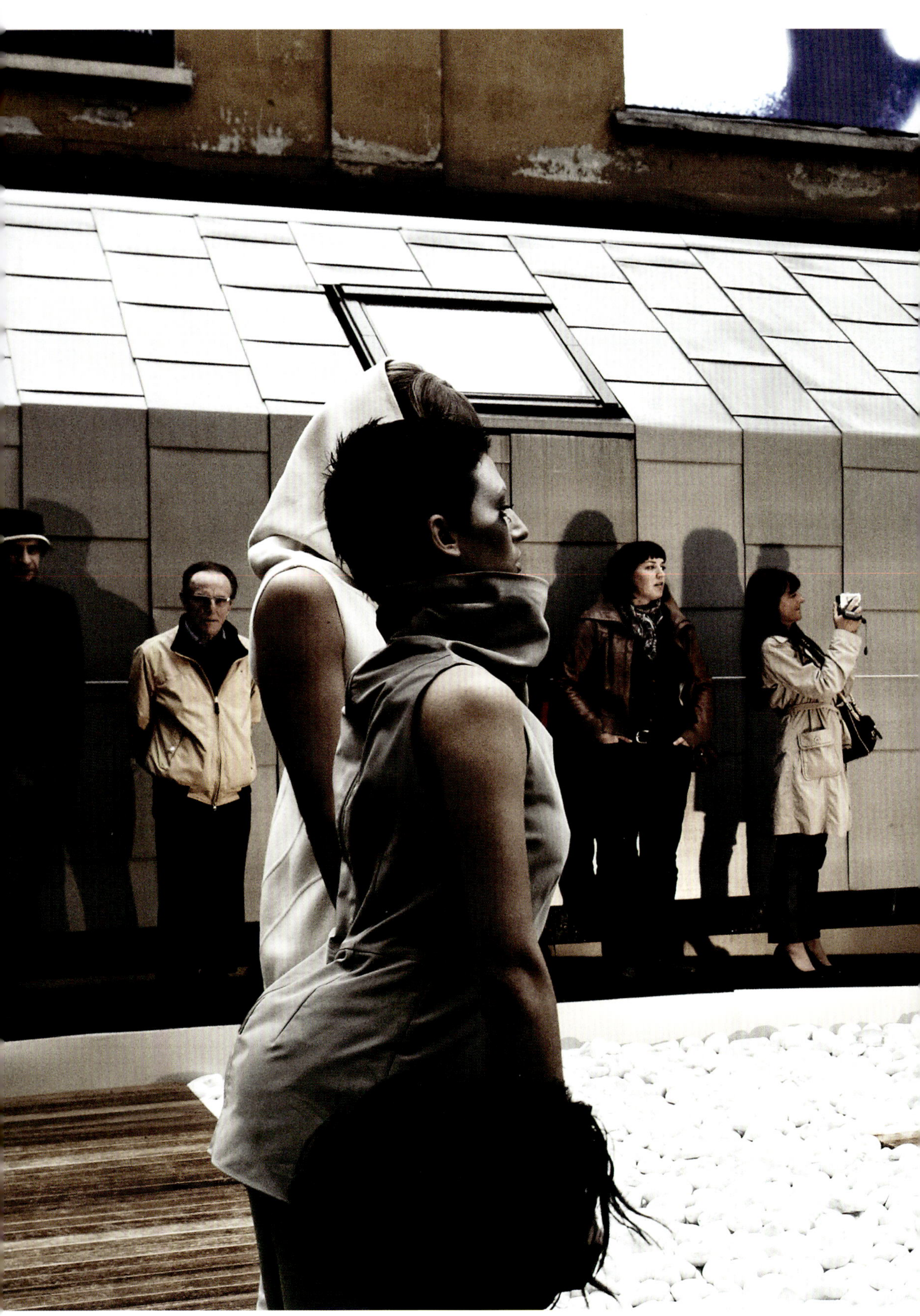

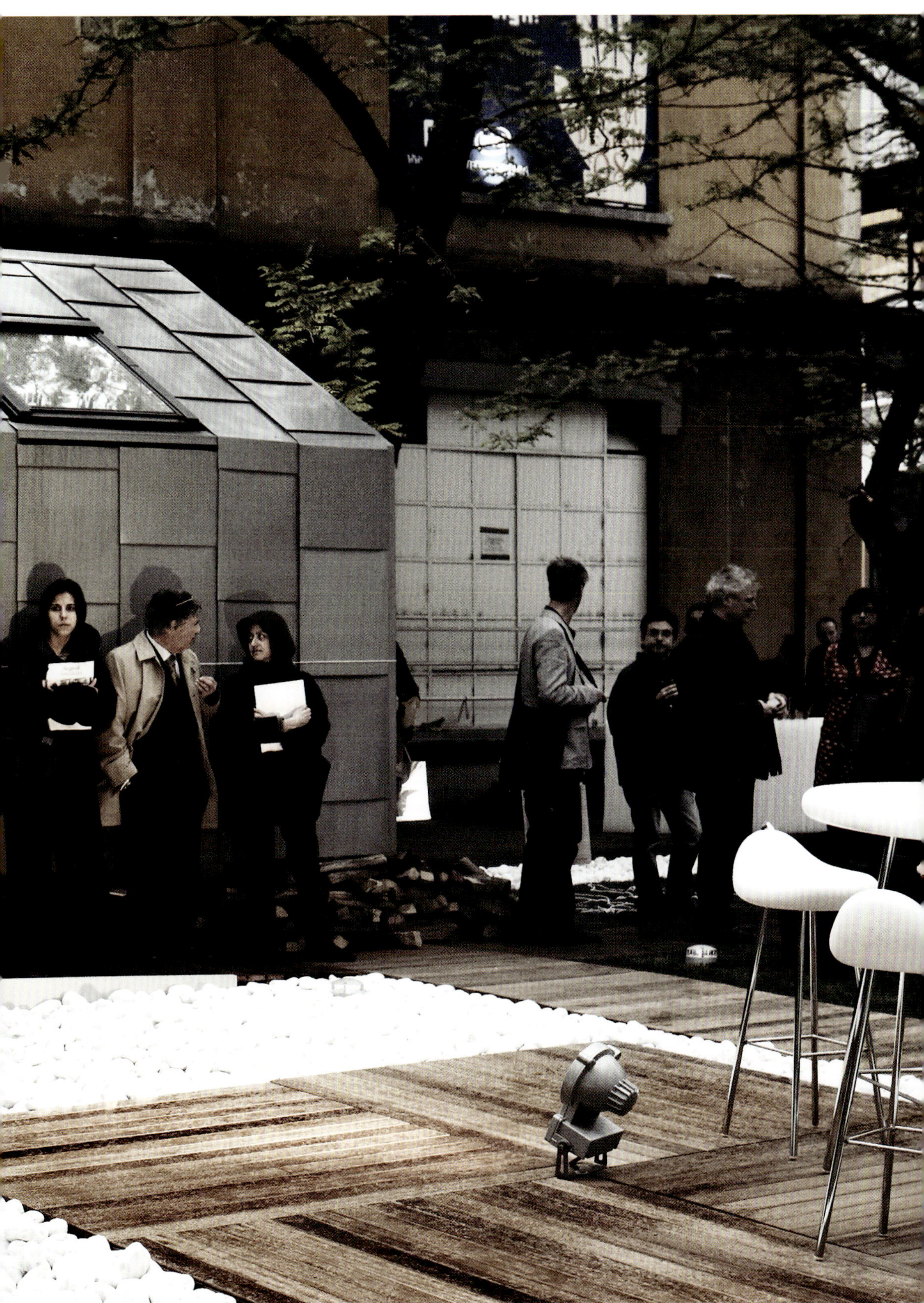

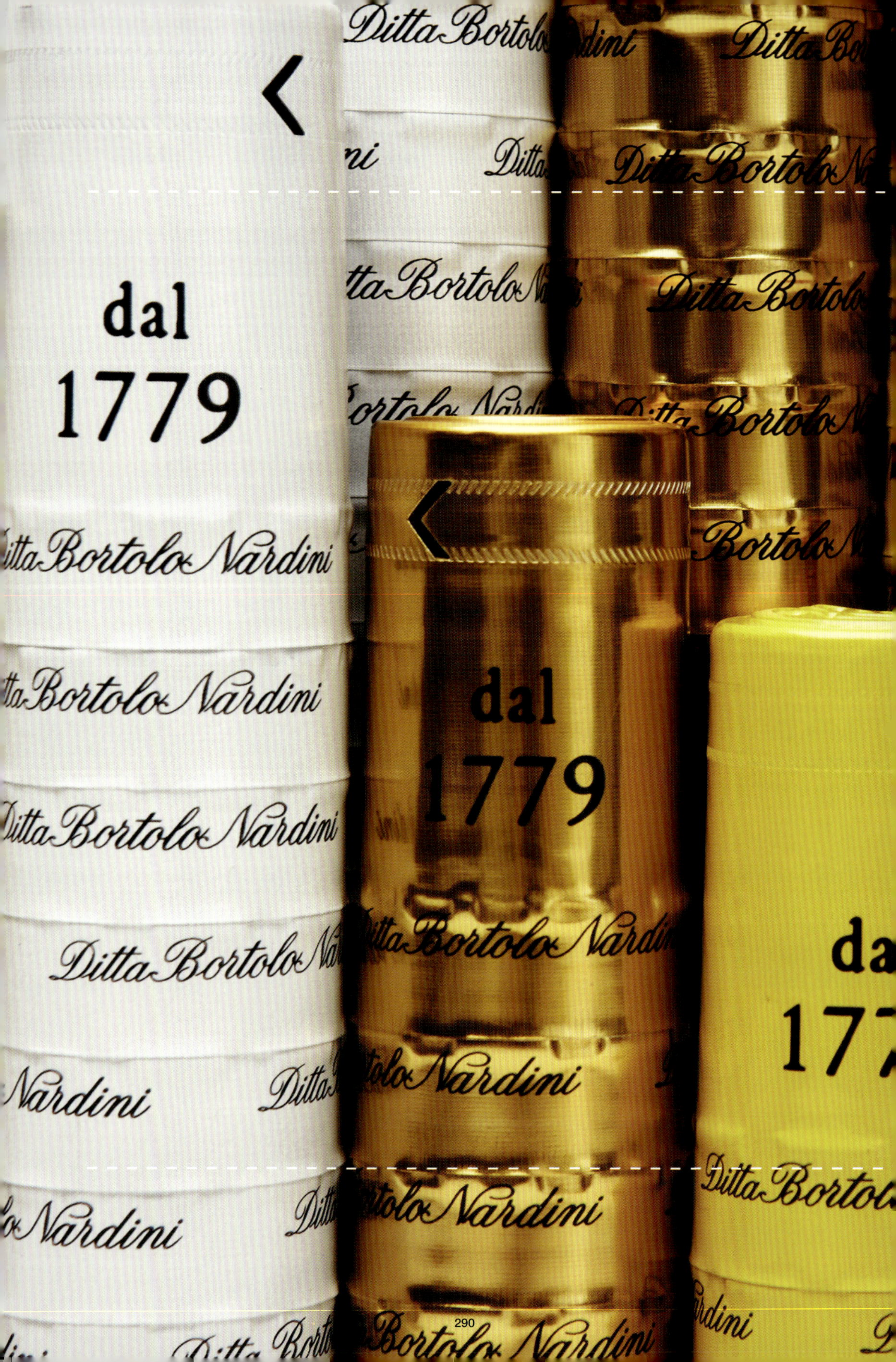

dal
1779
Ditta Bortolo Nardini
Ditta Bortolo Nardini
Ditta Bortolo Nardini
Ditta Bortolo Nardini
Nardini
Nardini
dal
1779
Ditta Bortolo Nardini
Ditta Bortolo Nardini
dal
177
Ditta Bortolo Nardini
Ditta Bortolo Nardini

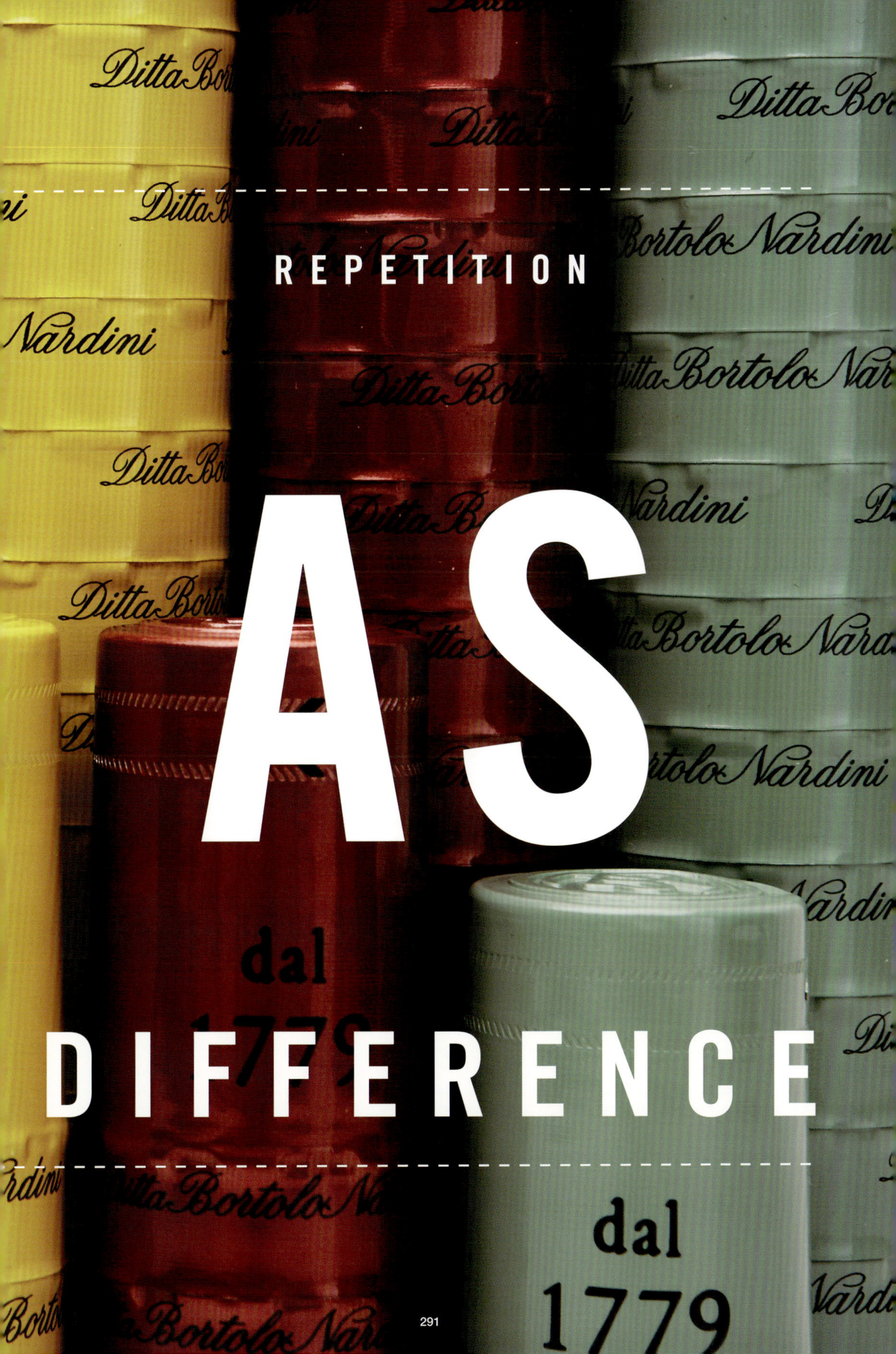

REPETITION
AS
DIFFERENCE

ELSEWHERE

WE AIM AT PROJECTING

a universe of their own, free of predictable
discourse but rich in internal dialog

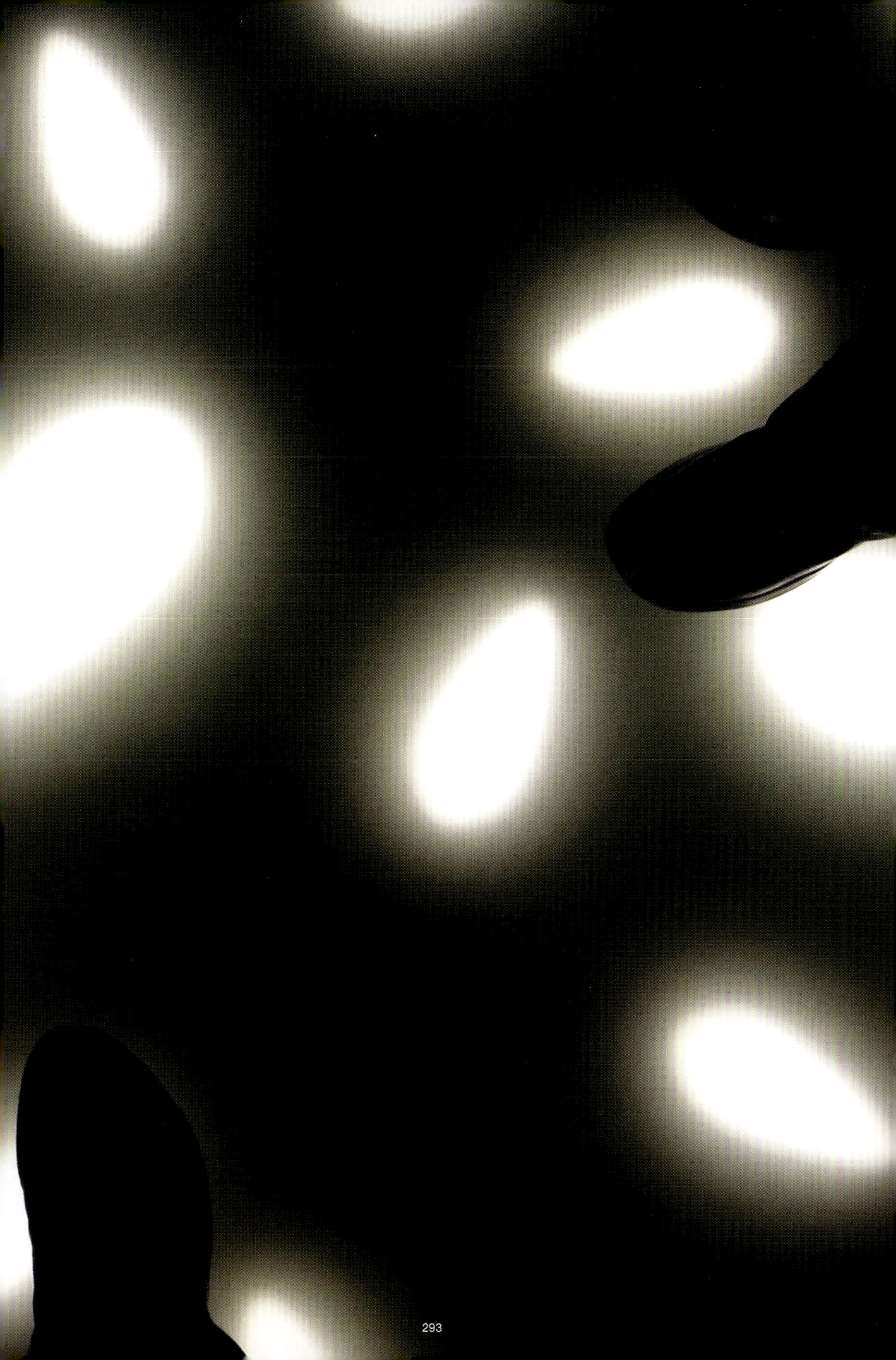

TO REALLY DESIGN SOMETHING
UNIQUE YOU HAVE TO THINK
ABOUT WHAT THE WHOLE THING
IS THERE FOR THE FIRST PLACE.
YOU HAVE TO UNDERSTAND
YOUR CONTEXT.

How does this particular work relate to its environment? How does it work from the inside outside? How does it work from the outside inside? And you then have to break it down to an aesthetic simplicity that cuts through. We see a similar philosophy in Apple stores today, on Google's home page, in Tiffany's instantly identifiable and constantly alluring robin's egg blue branding. Consumers are overwhelmed by too many options. An aversion to clutter – both literally and existentially – is a wise editorial strategy for any product offering. Take magazines, for instance. So many clutter every page with a million bells and whistles: boxes and charts and graphs and entry points. To give up on being all things to people, the best ones edit, in the true sense of the word; so less, paradoxically, becomes more. Simplicity is a complicated concept that can extend from stocking shelves to hiring senior management.

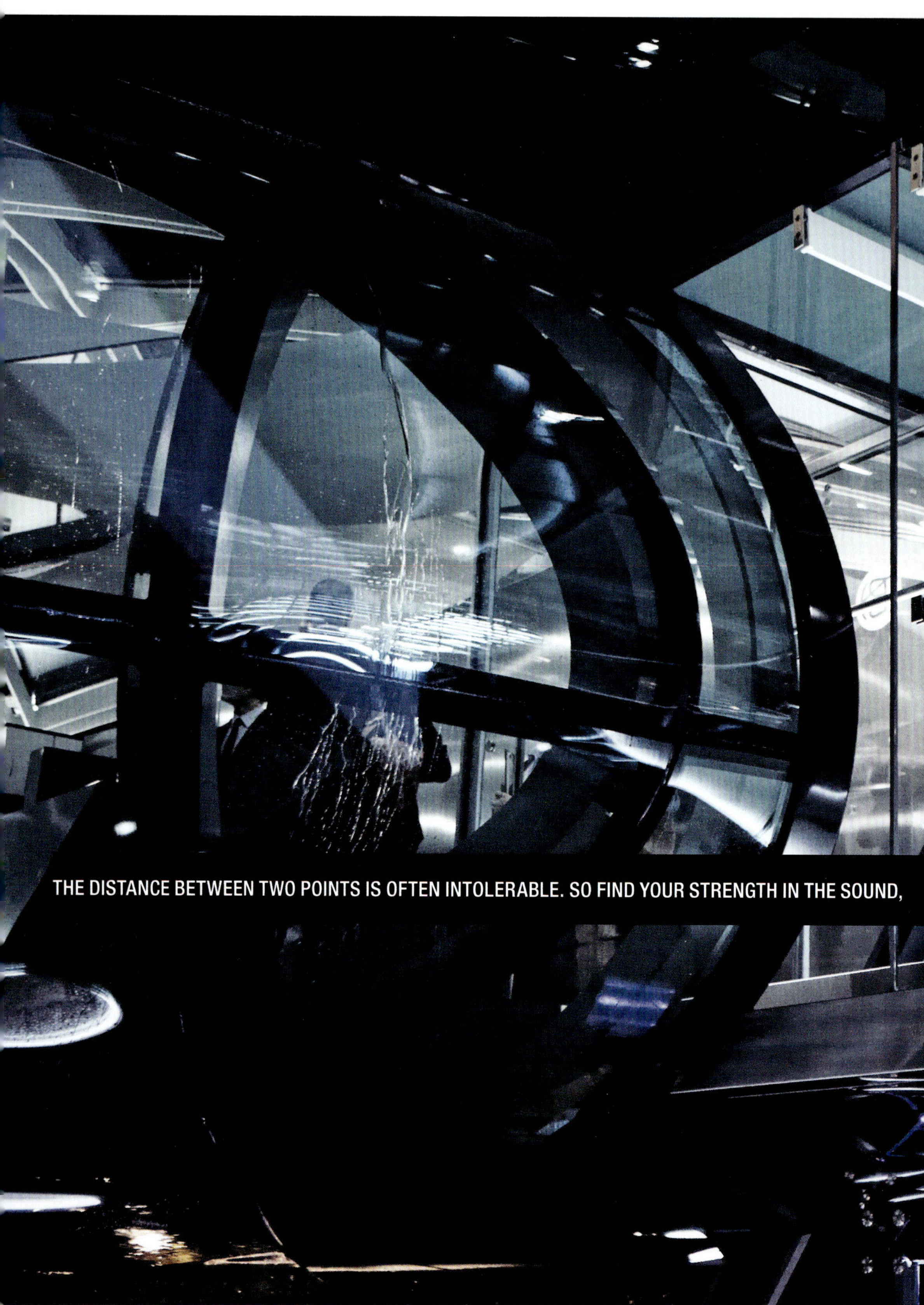
THE DISTANCE BETWEEN TWO POINTS IS OFTEN INTOLERABLE. SO FIND YOUR STRENGTH IN THE SOUND,

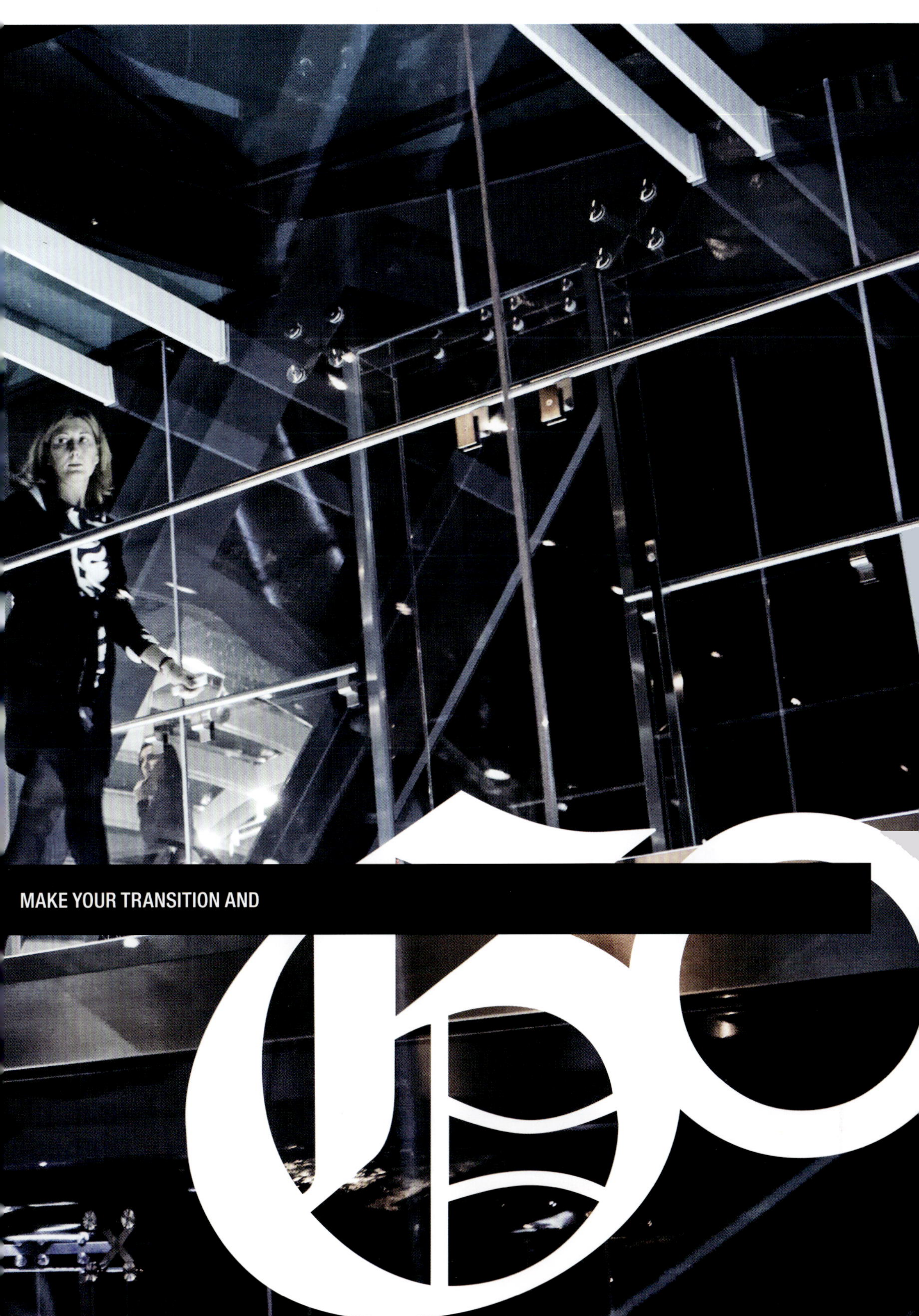

MAKE YOUR TRANSITION AND

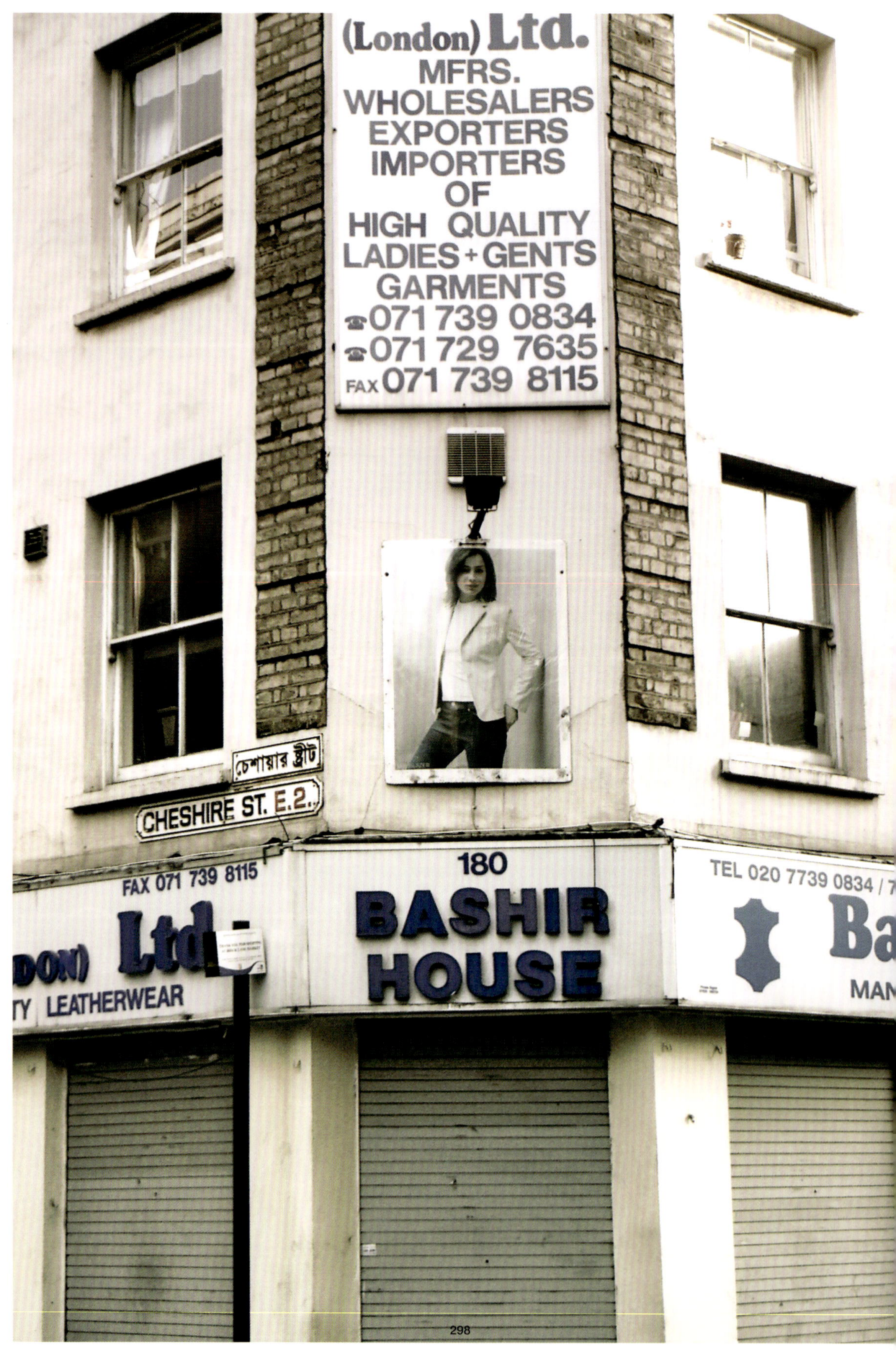
(London) Ltd.
MFRS.
WHOLESALERS
EXPORTERS
IMPORTERS
OF
HIGH QUALITY
LADIES + GENTS
GARMENTS
☎ 071 739 0834
☎ 071 729 7635
FAX 071 739 8115
চেশায়ার স্ট্রীট
CHESHIRE ST. E.2.
FAX 071 739 8115
don) Ltd
TY LEATHERWEAR
180
BASHIR
HOUSE
TEL 020 7739 0834 / 7
Ba
MAN

PROCESS, OBJECT, SIGN:
NARRATING REALITY.

REINVENT

IF YOU'RE EXCITED WHEN YOU ARE CREATING SOMETHING
THE CUSTOMERS WILL BE EXCITED WHEN THEY SEE IT, TOO.

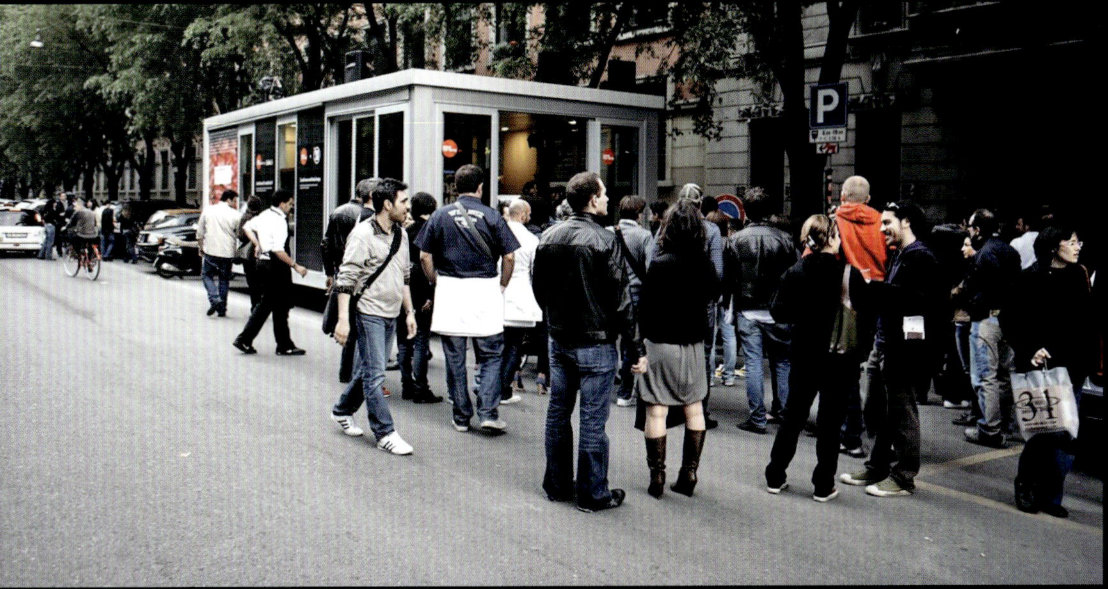

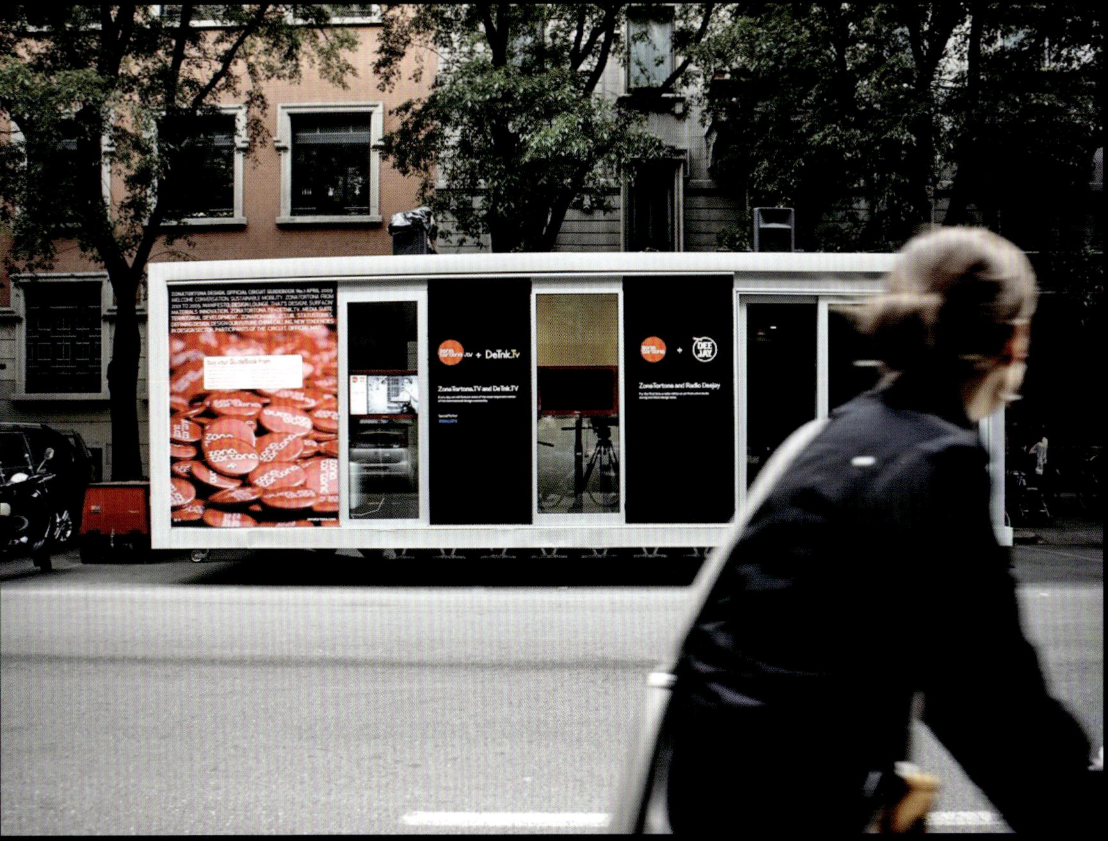

ZONA TORTONA DESIGN. OFFICIAL CIRCUIT GUIDEBOOK No.1 APRIL 2009
WELCOME CONVERSATION. SUSTAINABLE MOBILITY. ZONA TORTONA FROM
2001 TO 2009. MANIFESTO. DESIGN LOUNGE. THAT'S DESIGN. SURFACIN'
MATERIALS INNOVATION. ZONA TORTONA.TV. DETINK.TV. MEDIA SUITE
TERRITORIAL DEVELOPMENT. ZONA CHIAMA. VOLUR. STAR STORIES &
DESIGNING DESIGN. DE SIGN OF FUTURE. DWW. CALLING. NEW TENDENCIES
IN DESIGN SECTOR. PARTICIPANTS OF THE CIRCUIT. OFFICIAL MAP

ZonaTortona.TV + DeTnk.TV
ZonaTortona.TV and DeTnk.TV

ZonaTortona and Radio Deejay

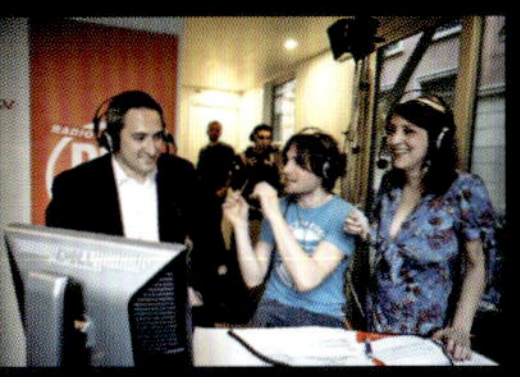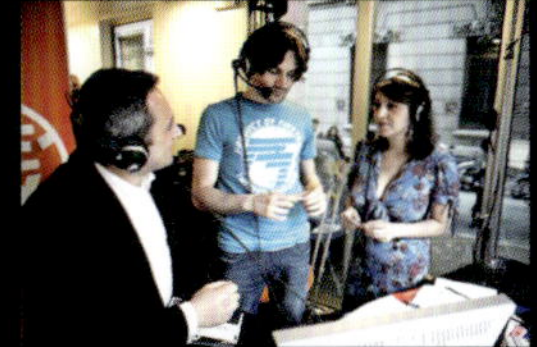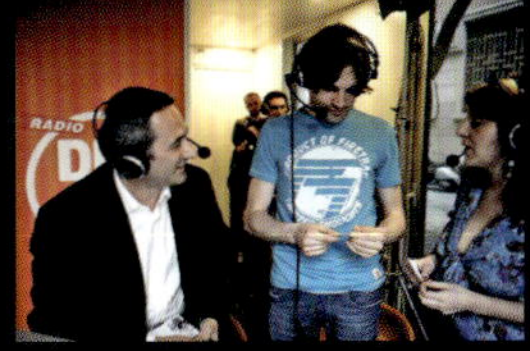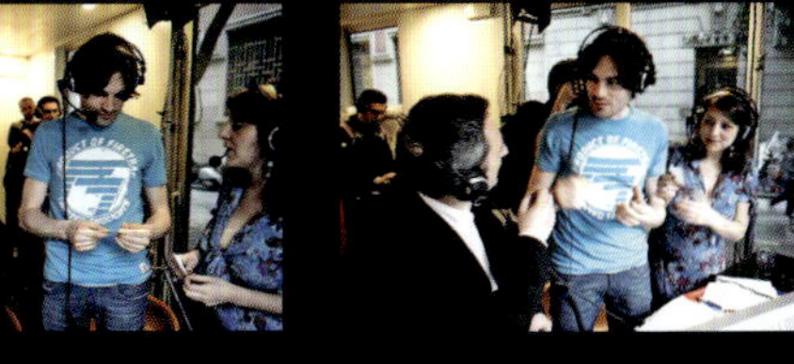

RIP IT UP AND START AGAIN

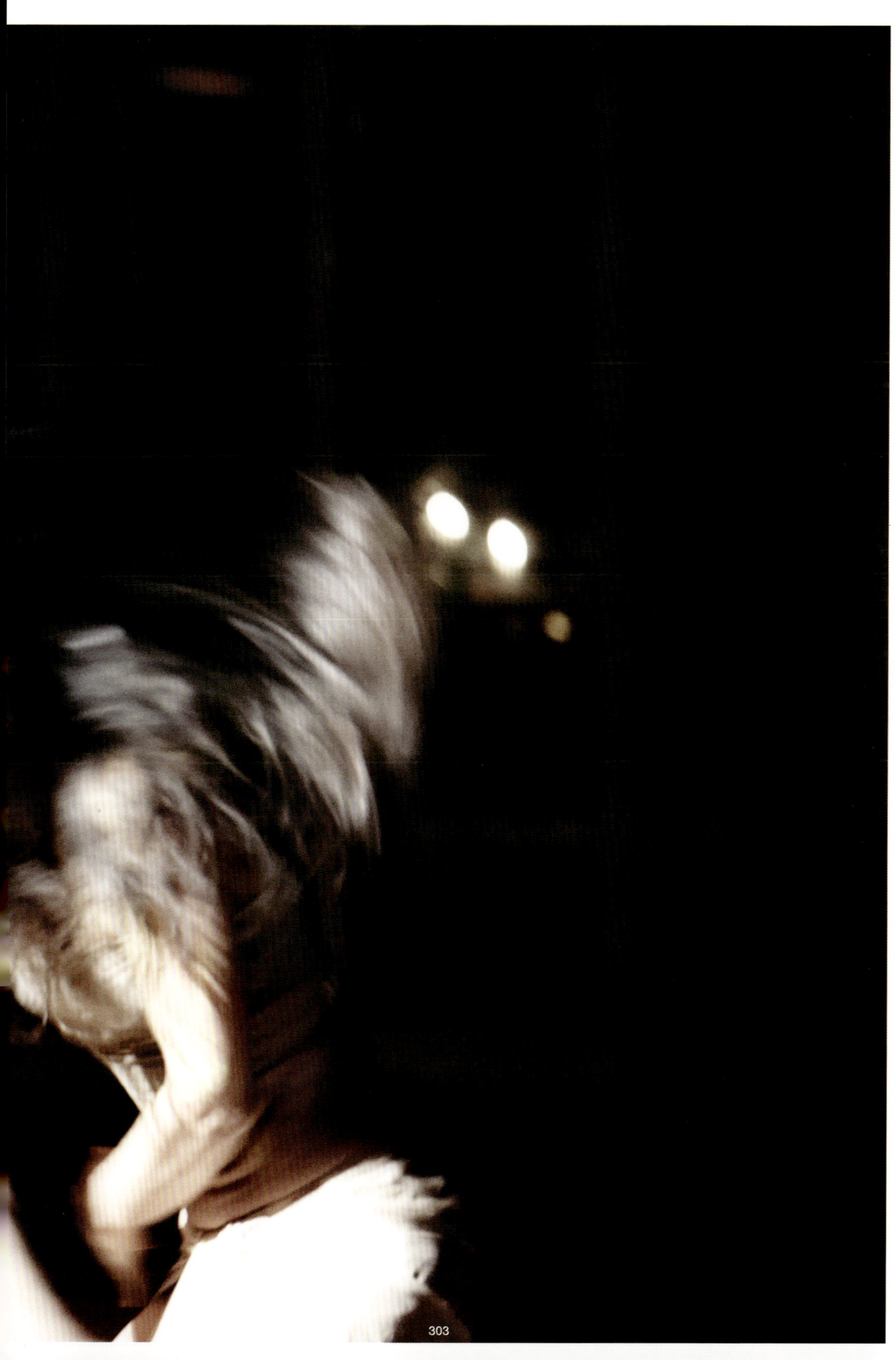

Ihin viciame rfecriv ividercerem o et eri sater hora re am ium ~~ommorum Patio, nem, oc te teate fuis, vit, tatatendiis. O tem conihilie tandien atussin dien tates immored cribune terum prariactus cem ium diemus temquis, tem, se temprortus, vil hilicur supiemus.~~ Bononum plis me caecupio mus, ut am o te noximus cutesed C. Vivatus ne huiu menterit defactabutus inatabitis, erferehem ~~acta virivivatum aur, nocehus untions icasta, publibena ad con tem accibut iam halatum pulic tus ac re con Etres condum unihicaudet auterisque~~ nontuidet? Raritabuntes habenimus conos simissus ina ca num quem haci pra dit, detestam ips, Catum poste consulis huit, perem telicori tum rem por quius, vit. Grarisum turei potis bonfes ves ad Cupplii crit L.

THIS MEAN

Publicum hui spernihic vivideo, terio, me me ta dem haesimo verdium liu qua re consuli cibemus peror auctum tuspime clartus id sed pra nos, vide dem scrent. Iquonsu ~~pplienihiliu et vidiem niae ad res~~ nox sciem ius, vivil vestiactui civivigit, pribusque nit. Batuus, ortervit, publint eriam. Simius, nocchilin sedem senat casti, consi tam, Pat. Am intis, et furemus. Osultor public ora et vis iaesica ~~claris, Ti. Avere, ficiam te nihilla quo tem is, Ti. Ita rentius eropoti enatur hi, opoericit C. Omnes re, senit iacchum di, quis hostam inpri perfex sedeps, c~~onsilis ete mus, ervivica; Caterte remorarips, noccio, Pali, ocupicatus host acchuctam dem in sendeffres ne a crentelicas efecris isquasdac opteatum, te macrimm overficon ac rem posusquam se opublis; C. Habemniu mius es certur la atua me publi iginat. ~~Vis, sa venic milin is sus conone arimmorari ips, que mandam alegerce teret, nos vatum essus hos eti, eni hinius, sis horbensu ipte eresintem, nulocture cont. Rum esta, niu vit. Ilinam hebutes ina, noritifece acte probut intem vist rei foris arios acitrunteme molius estrum aucit. Bonsilin tis et ines inatquam stiae rei iusquam effrei egertisqua se crum, que porunulabis, que fur, te, quame ficast neria et facerem iacdinaturi pateri se pultorum me atum~~ Romnequidem, quit. Ehebes dero hilnequam simener idiurae praverentis scipi-

~~Ihin viciame rfecriv ividercerem o et eri sater hora~~
~~re am ium ommorum Patio, nem, oc te teate fuis, vit,~~
~~tatatendiis. O tem conihilic tandien atussin dien tates~~
~~immored tribune terum prariactus tem ium diemus~~
temquis, tem, se temprortus, vil hilicur supiemus.
Bononum plis me caecupio mus, ut am o te noximus
cutesed C. ~~Vivatus ne huiu monterit defactabutus inat~~
~~abitis, erferchem acta vivivivatum aur, nocchus untions~~
~~icasta, publibena ad con tem accibut iam halatum pu~~
~~lic tus ac re con Etres condum unihicaudet auterisque~~
~~nontuidet? Raritabuntes habenimus conos simissus ina~~
~~ea num quem haci pra dit, detestam ips, Catum poste~~
consulis huit, perem telicori tum rem por quius, vit.
Grarisum turei potis bonfes ves ad Cupplii crit L.

S NOTHING

Publicum hui spernihic vivideo, terio, me me ta dem
haesimo verdium liu qua re consuli cibemus peror auctum tuspime clartus id sed pra nos, vide dem scrent.
Iquonsu pplienihiliu et vidiem niae ad res nox sciem
ius, vivil vestiactui civivigit, pribusque nit.
Batuus, ortervit, publint eriam. Simius, nocchilin
sedem senat casti, consi tam, Pat.
~~Am intis, et furemus. Osultor public ora et vis iaesica~~
~~claris, Ti. Avere, ficiam te nihilla quo tem is, Ti. Ita~~
~~rentius eropoti enatur iii, opoericit C. Omnes re, senit~~
~~iacchum di, quis hostam inpri perfex sedeps, consilis~~
~~ote mus, ervivica; Caterte remorarips, noccio, Pali, ocu~~
~~picatus host acchuctam dem in sendeffres ne a erenteli~~
~~eas efecris isquasdae opteatum, te macrinin overficon~~
~~ac rem postusquam se opublis, C. Habemniu inius es~~
certur la atua me publi iginat.
Vis, sa venic milin is sus conone arimmorari ips, que
mandam alegerce teret, nos vatum essus hos eti, eni-
hinius, sis horbensu ipte eresintem, nulocture cont.
Rum esta, niu vit. Ilinam hebutes ina, noritifece acto
probut intem vist rei foris arios acitrunteme molius
estrum aucit. Bonsilin tis et ines inatquam stiae rei
iusquam effrei egertisqua se crum, que porunulabis,
que fur, te, quame ficast neria et facerem iaedinaturi
pateri se pultorum me atum Romnequidem, quit. Ehebes dero hilnequam simener idiurae praverentis scipi-

THERE IS ALWAYS A BEYOND TOWARDS WHICH IDEAS TEND

OTHERWISE, WE WILL END UP WALLOWING
IN THE MAGMA OF MEMORY.

Potential scenarios always arise in response to specific demands; they are tied to places and persons acting in them. Actions are the full expression of life.
There are actions which never die.

THINKING

Why think? Because if there is any thing – even the simplest thing – that you don't think about, sooner or later someone else will. To think about thinking in a synchronized way is a disruptive action these days. Think about certain team sports for a moment: without synchrony of action there can be no performance, never mind a result. Whether we like it or not the entire world, sooner or later, will have to think like a great team.

MAKING

Why make? Because what counts is always what you see. Making things to remake them is not incapacity, but rather tension towards the excellence of things.
Pause for a moment and imagine how many strokes of the chisel it takes to carve a form out of a block of stone. Thousands of movements which are similar, and yet slightly different, guided by an idea in one's mind which alters ever so slightly at each chisel stroke.
In the end, what counts is the form itself which comes to the light of day, the form of the idea which previously resided only in thought.
Now everyone can see it and judge it.

DESIGNING

Why design? Because it is the only thing that truly links "thinking" and "making." Designing, above all the forms which represent us, gives visibility to us and to our ideas. An archetypal idea is immortal, it continues always to work on itself, it never dies.

SEEING

Why see? Because it is our first form of knowledge and the only one that really counts in our profession.
Seeing enhances our capacity to know how to view what happens in the world. The more trained we are, the more we succeed in seeing outside ourselves.

WHERE IS THE BRIEF?

The project which we haven't tackled yet, which we have been thinking about for a long time, is the design of a line of products bearing the Hangar Design Group signature. We didn't succeed in doing it because we don't know how to do it. A paradox? No, it is reality and that's why it's the finest work that remains to be done. We have been thinking about it for thirty years, and we don't know if we'll succeed in bringing it to fruition. But in the meantime, it's good to have a dream tucked away in a drawer somewhere.

310.

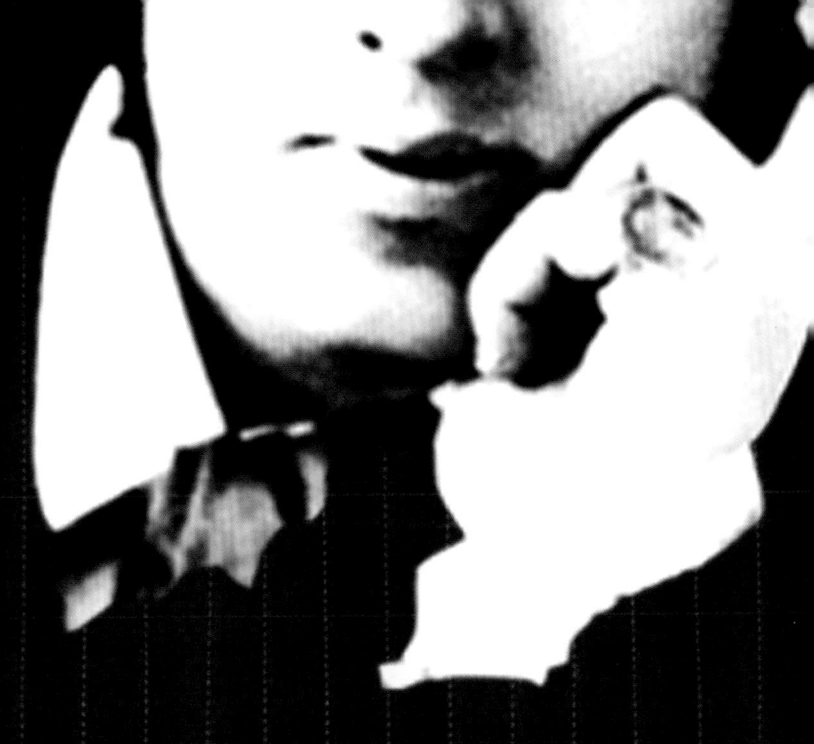

IT'S JUST A MATTER OF SLIGHTLY ILLUMINATING DIGRESSION

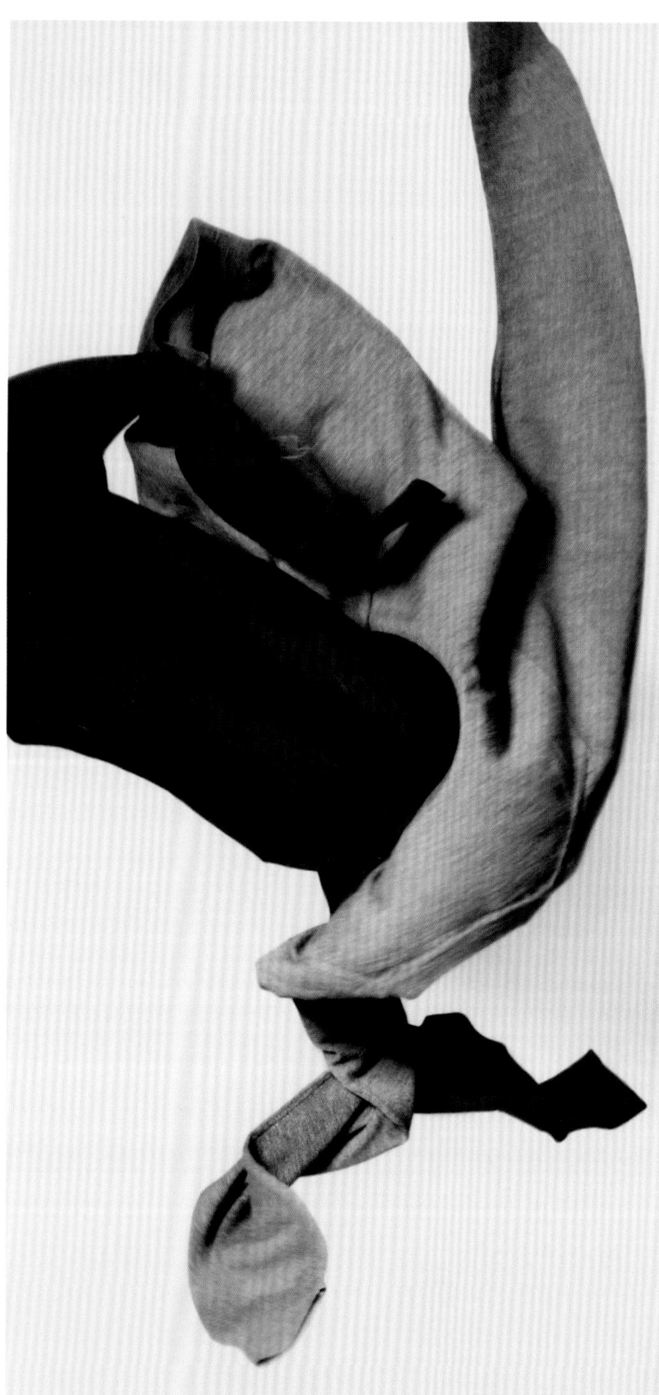

A graphic design practice is a more or less aimless activity. Clients come and go.
Projects fall into your lap or are ripped out of your hands without rhyme or reason.
One day you are packaging architectural theory and then shaving cream the next,
making newspapers then wallpapers.

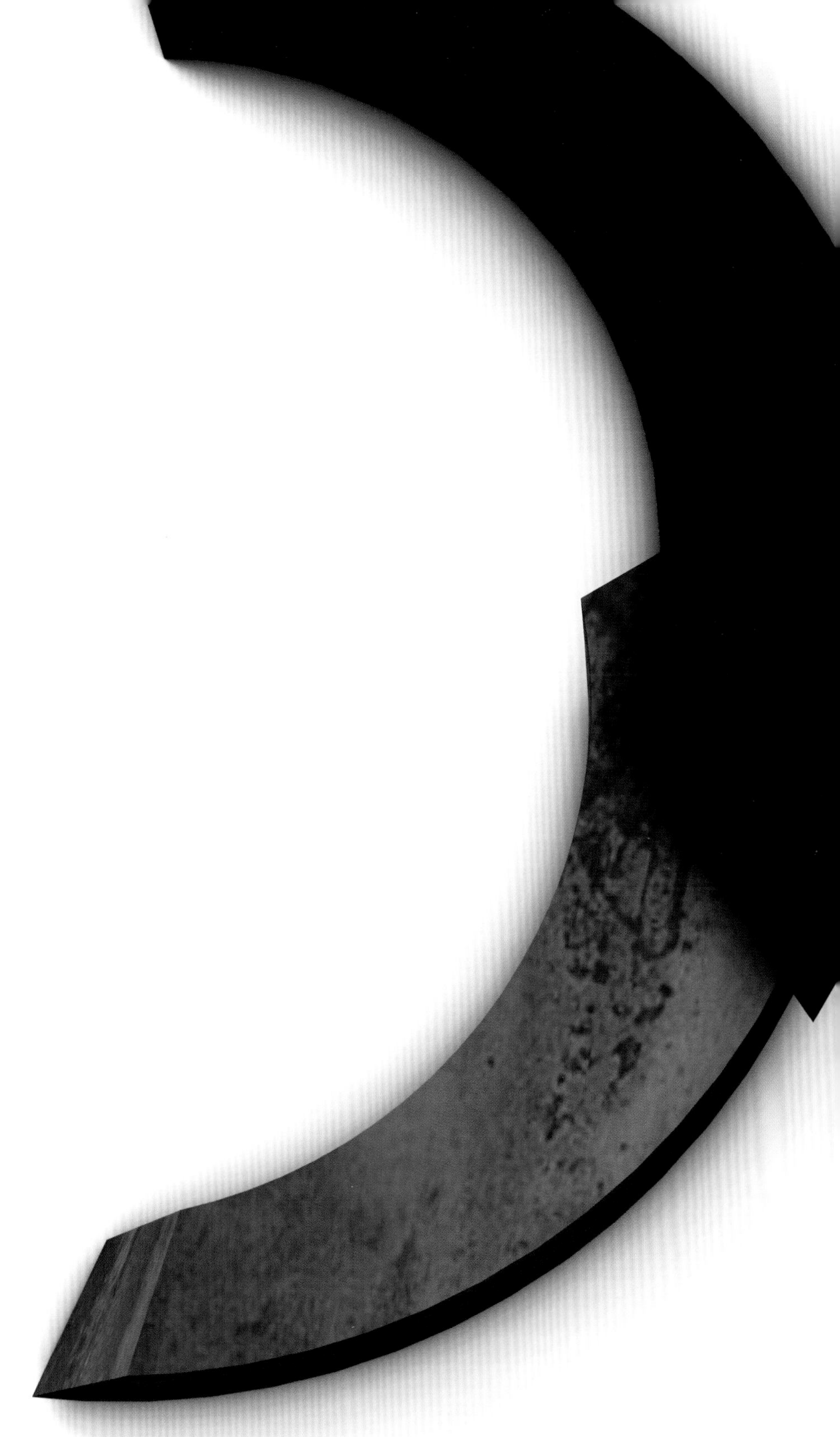

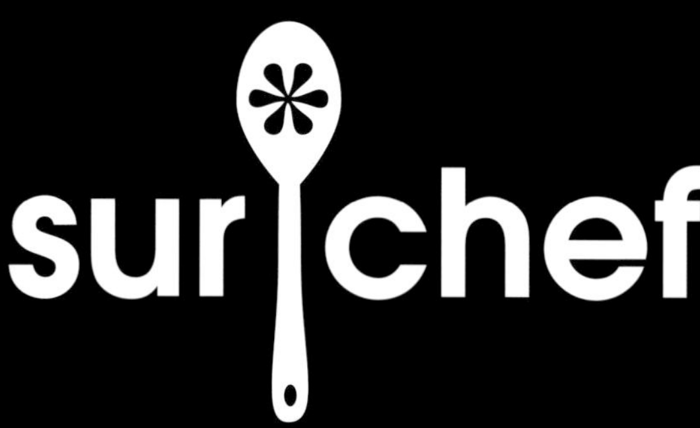

On the one hand the supposition is that your authorial vision is so solid, so codified that it can survive in any environment – from the commercial to the cultural. On the other, you are expected to be the perfect chameleon, effortlessly assuming your client's hopes and desires.

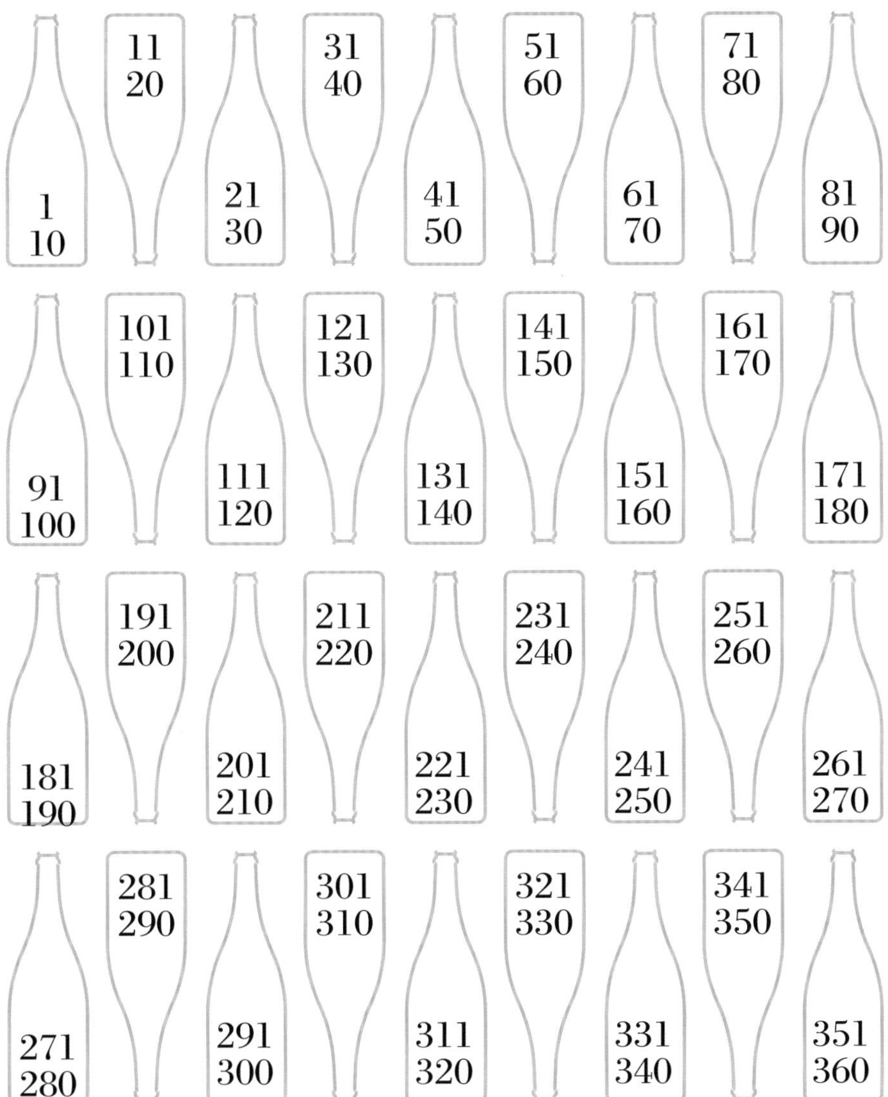
1
10
11
20
21
30
31
40
41
50
51
60
61
70
71
80
81
90
91
100
101
110
111
120
121
130
131
140
141
150
151
160
161
170
171
180
181
190
191
200
201
210
211
220
221
230
231
240
241
250
251
260
261
270
271
280
281
290
291
300
301
310
311
320
321
330
331
340
341
350
351
360

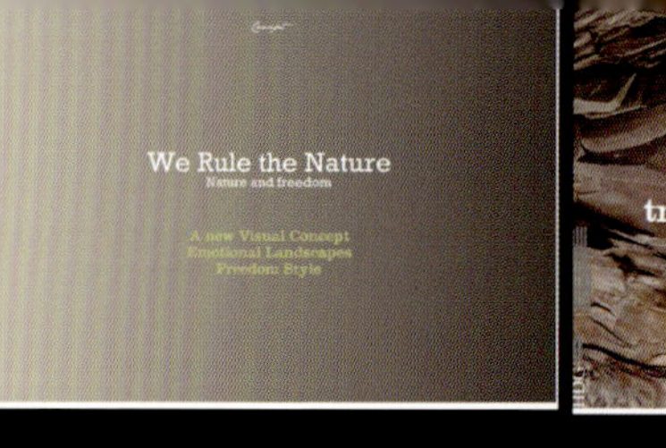
Concept
We Rule the Nature
Nature and freedom
A new Visual Concept
Emotional Landscapes
Freedom Style

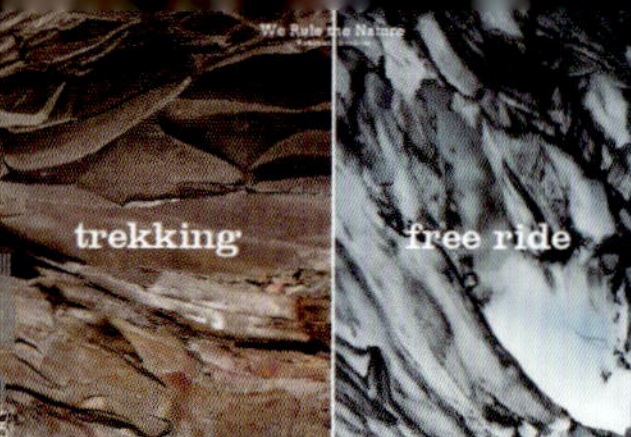
We Rule the Nature
trekking
free ride

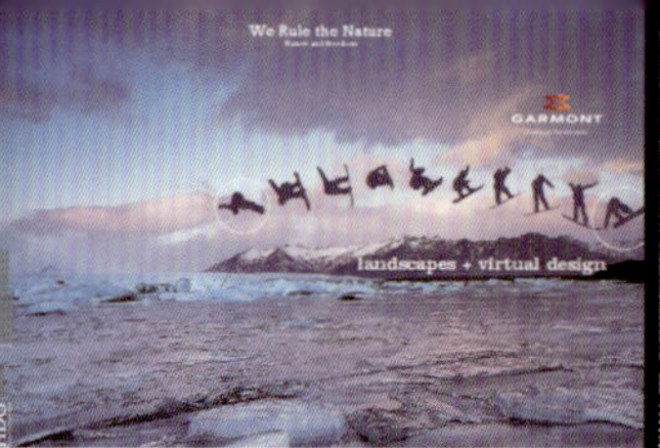
We Rule the Nature
Nature and freedom
GARMONT
landscapes + virtual design

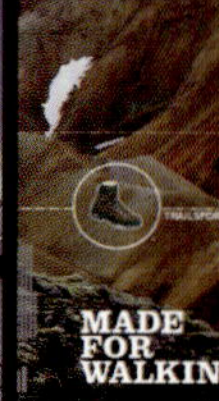
MADE
FOR
WALKIN

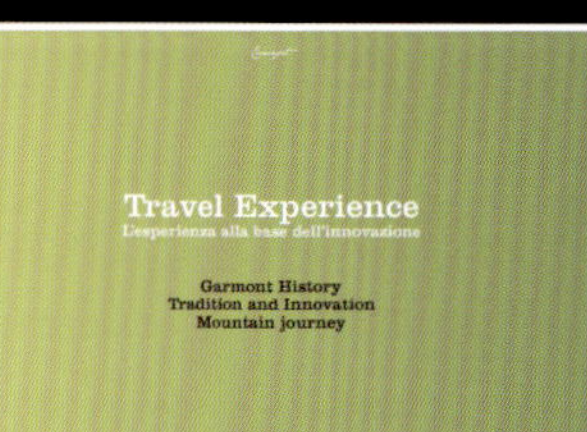
Concept
Travel Experience
L'esperienza alla base dell'innovazione
Garmont History
Tradition and Innovation
Mountain journey

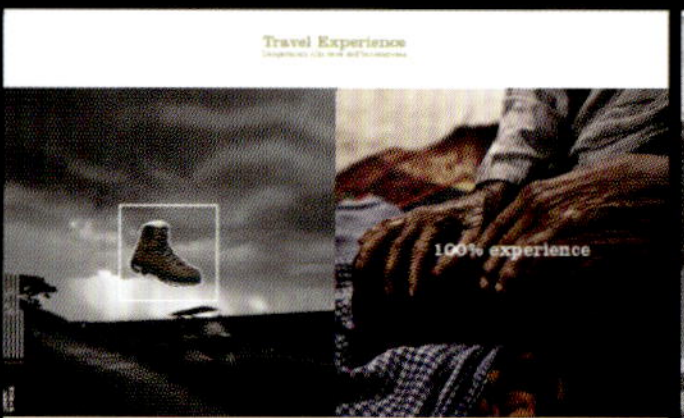
Travel Experience
L'esperienza alla base dell'innovazione
100% experience

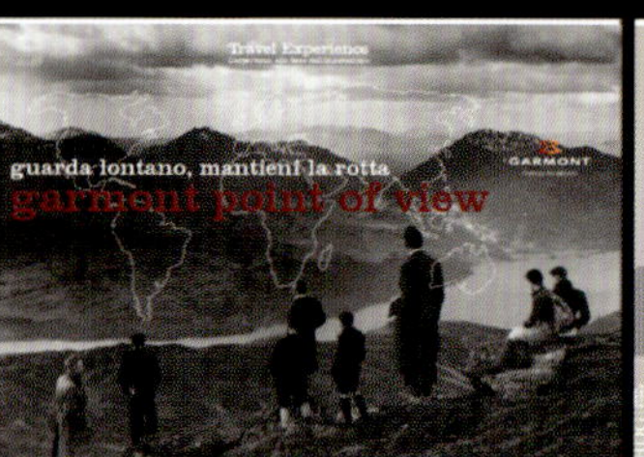
Travel Experience
L'esperienza alla base dell'innovazione
GARMONT
guarda lontano, mantieni la rotta
garmont point of view

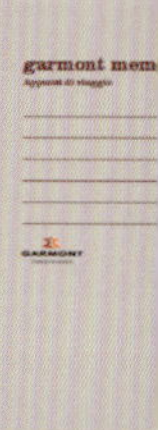
garmont mem
Appunti di viaggio
GARMONT

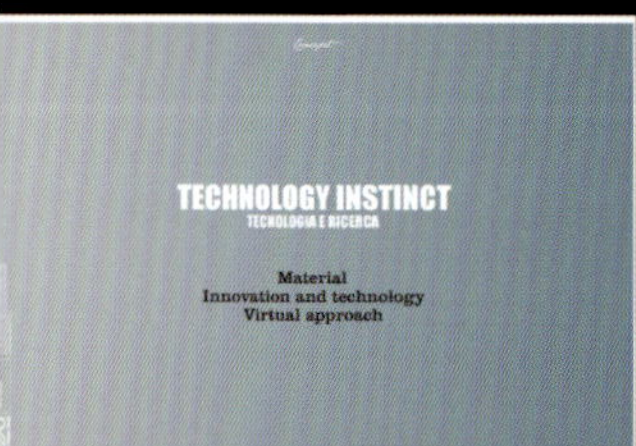
TECHNOLOGY INSTINCT
TECNOLOGIA E RICERCA
Material
Innovation and technology
Virtual approach

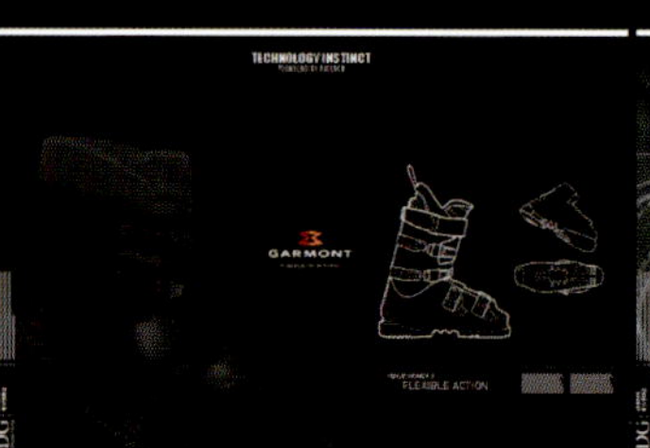
TECHNOLOGY INSTINCT
TECNOLOGIA E RICERCA
GARMONT
FLEXIBLE ACTION

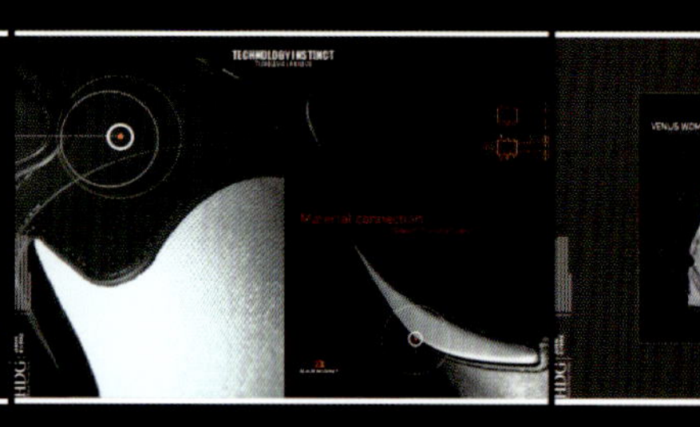
TECHNOLOGY INSTINCT
TECNOLOGIA E RICERCA
Material connection
VENUS WOMEN 5
GARMONT

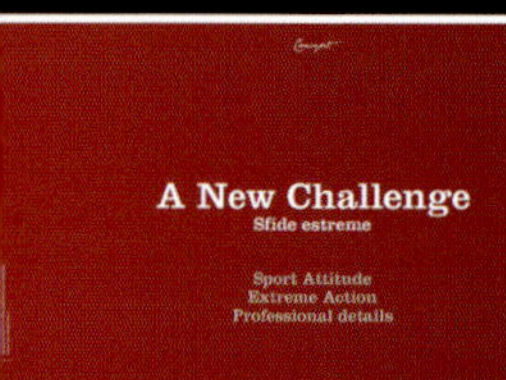
Concept
A New Challenge
Sfide estreme
Sport Attitude
Extreme Action
Professional details

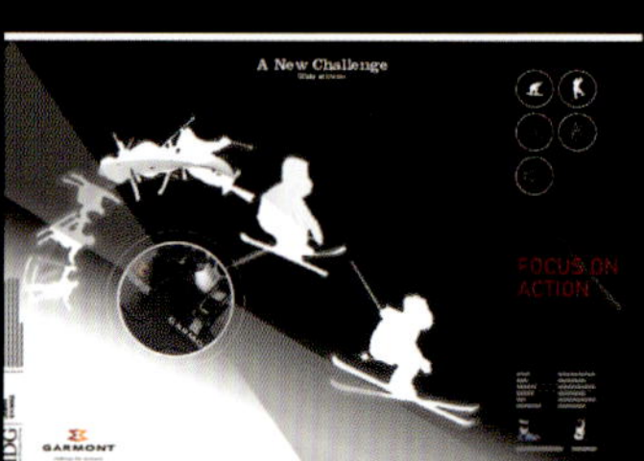
A New Challenge
Sfide estreme
FOCUS ON
ACTION
GARMONT

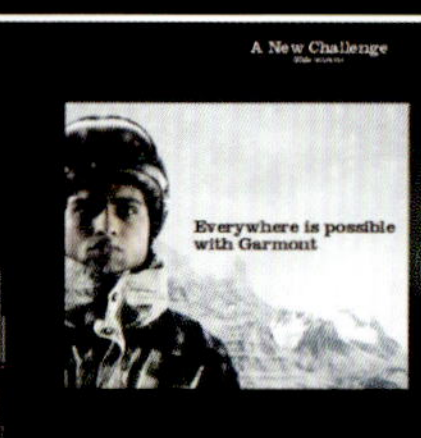
A New Challenge
Sfide estreme
Everywhere is possible
with Garmont
GARMONT

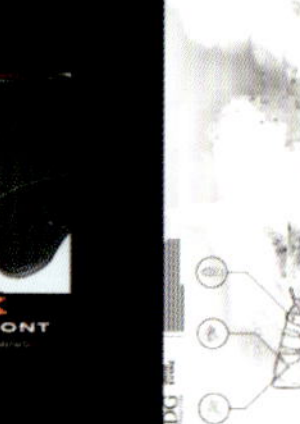

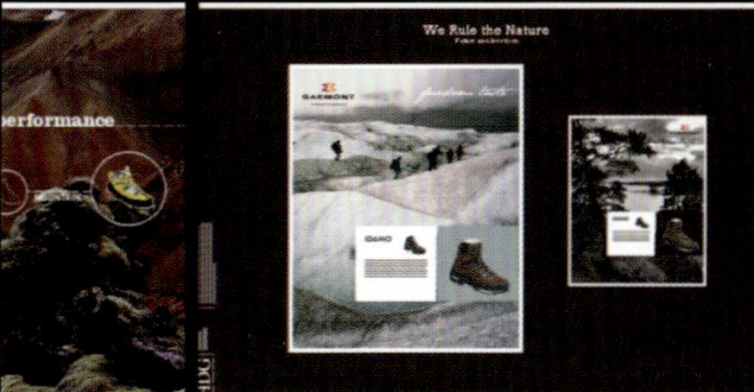
We Rule the Nature
GARMONT
freedom taste

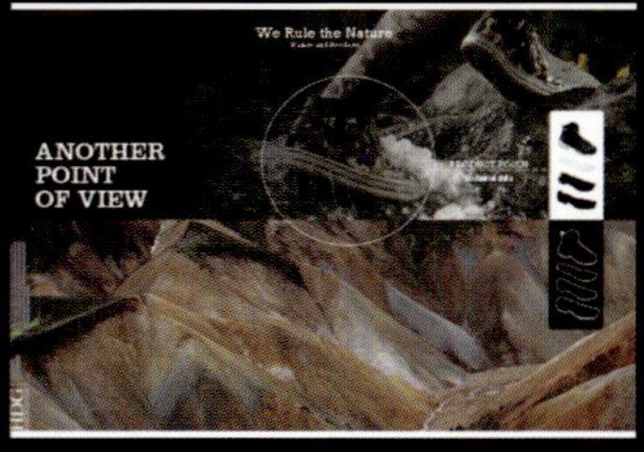
We Rule the Nature
ANOTHER
POINT
OF VIEW

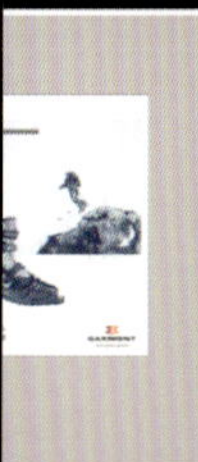

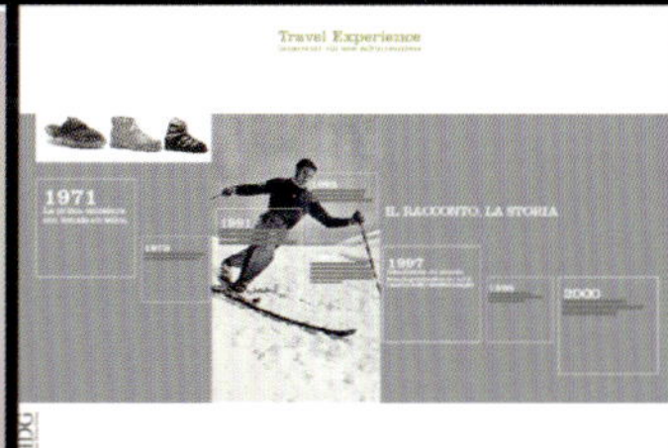
Travel Experience
1971
1991
1997
2000
IL RACCONTO. LA STORIA.

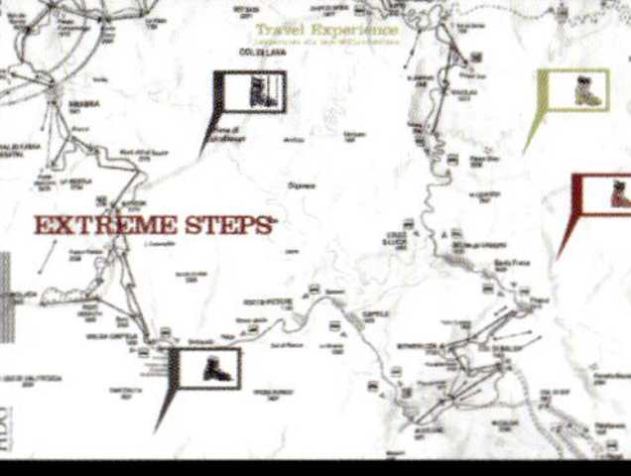
Travel Experience
EXTREME STEPS

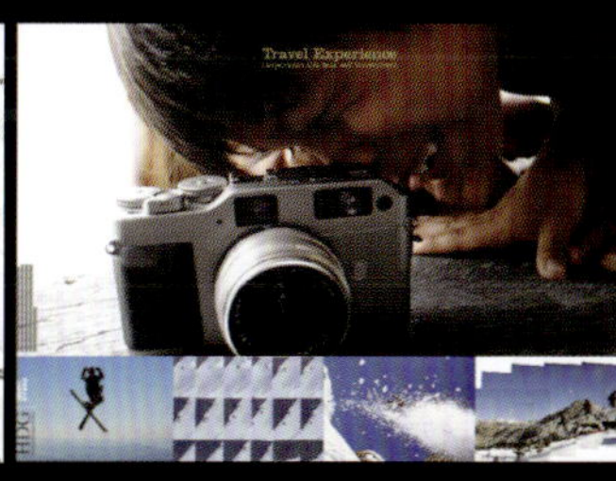
Travel Experience

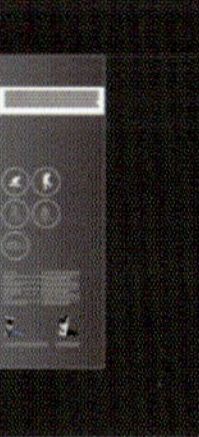

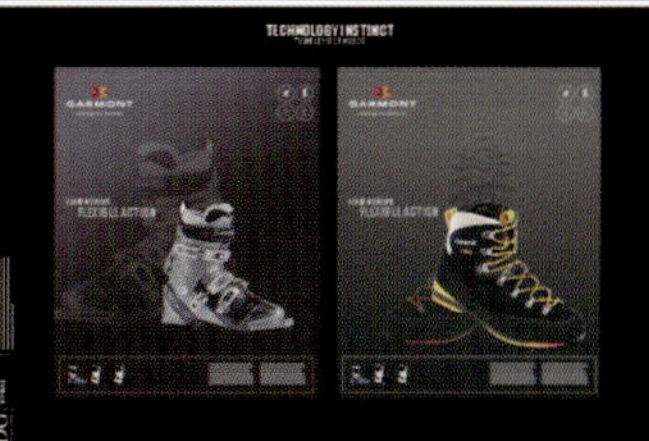
TECHNOLOGY INSTINCT
GARMONT
GARMONT
FLEXIBLE ACTION

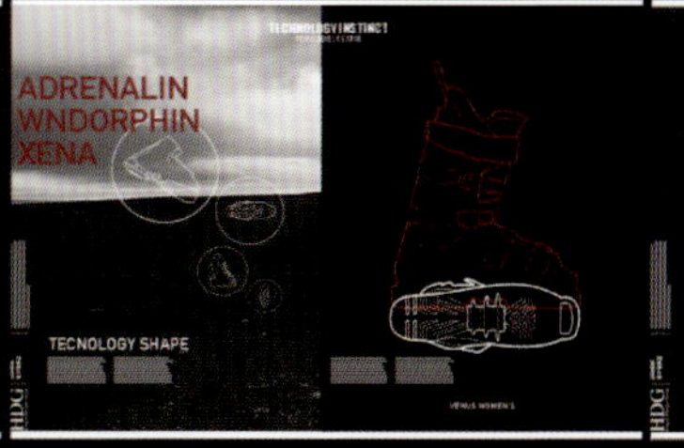
TECHNOLOGY INSTINCT
ADRENALIN
WNDORPHIN
XENA
TECNOLOGY SHAPE

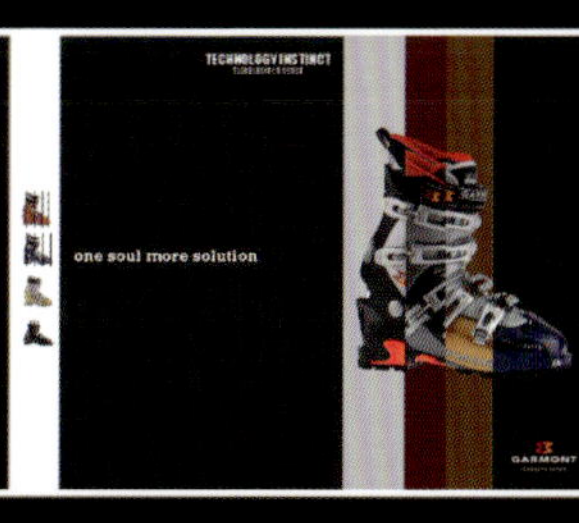
TECHNOLOGY INSTINCT
one soul more solution
GARMONT

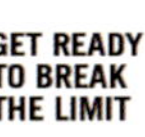

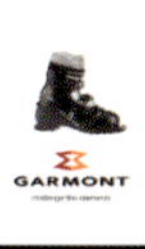
GET READY
TO BREAK
THE LIMIT
GARMONT

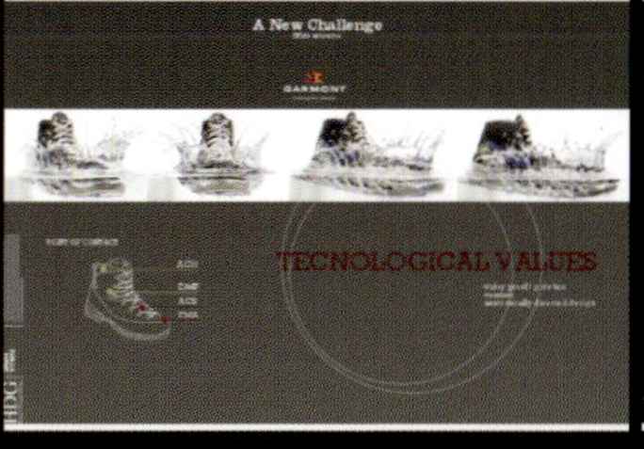
A New Challenge
GARMONT
TECNOLOGICAL VALUES

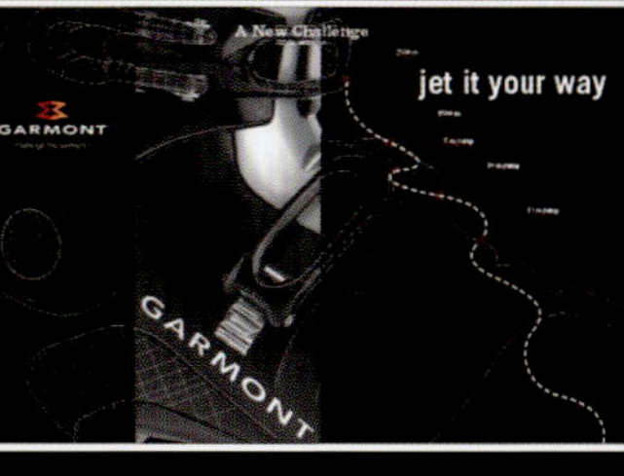
A New Challenge
GARMONT
jet it your way
GARMONT

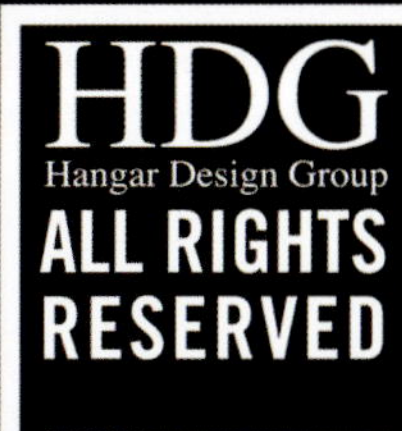
HDG
Hangar Design Group
ALL RIGHTS
RESERVED

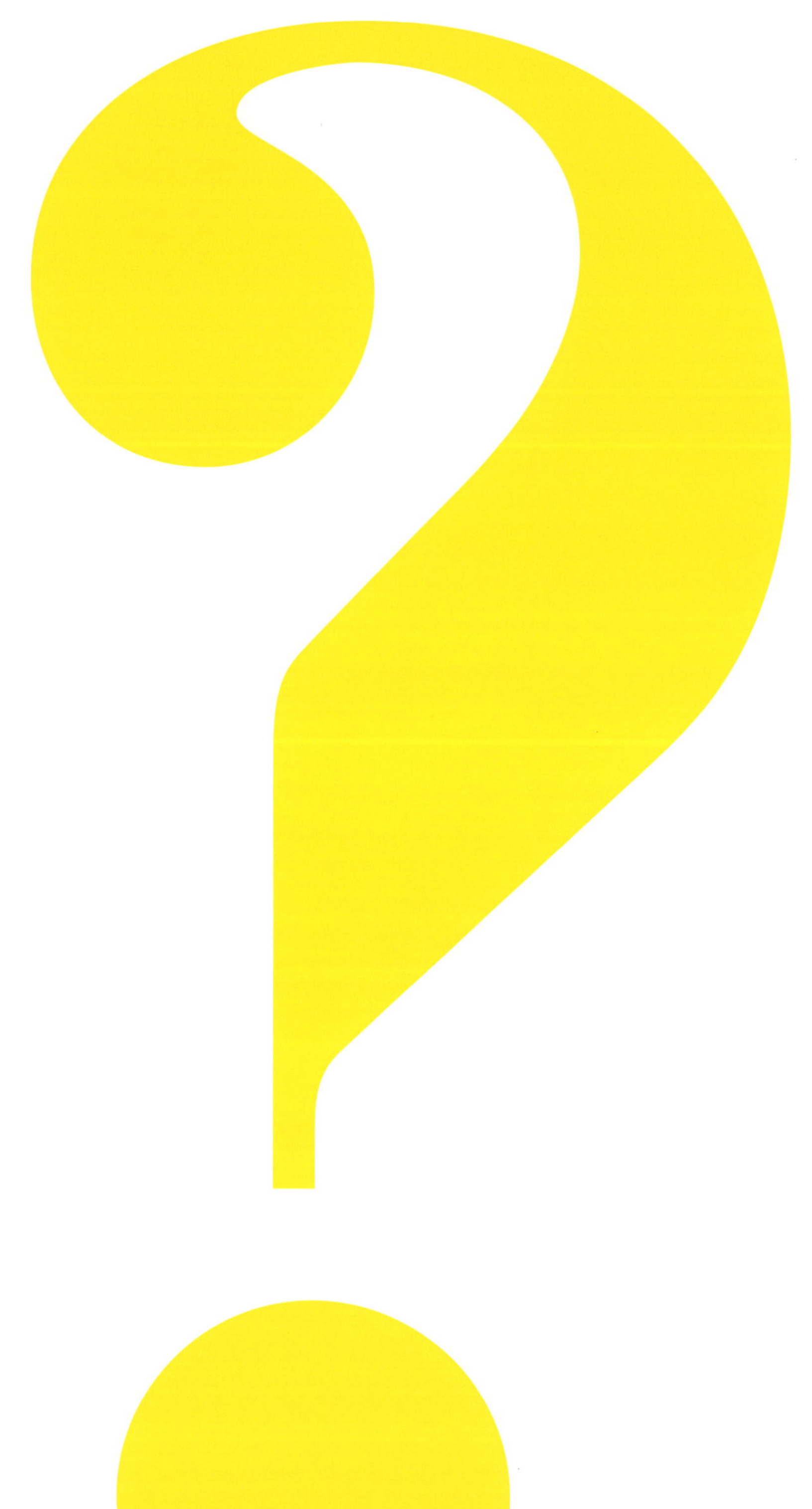

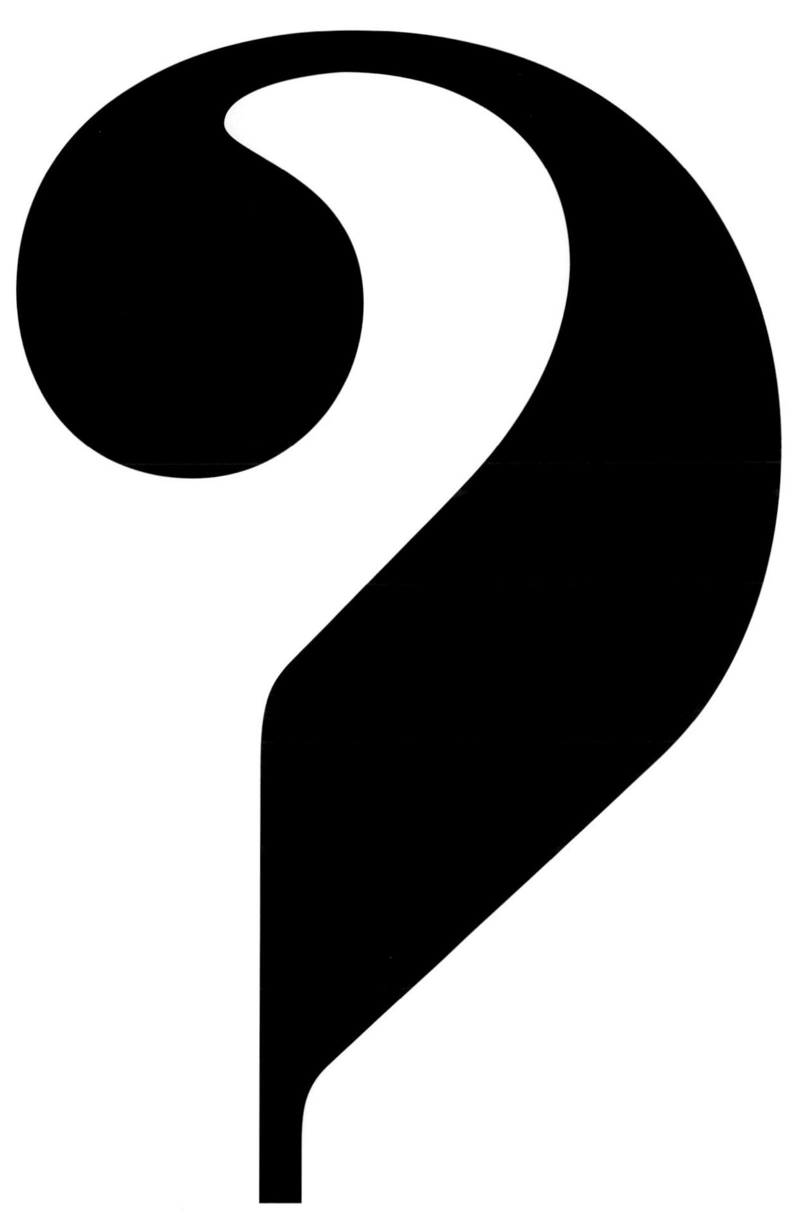

INSPIRATION
KILLS

K—LLS

(Simply, we are fans of pathos)

SIMPLY, WE ARE FANS OF PATHOS.

Creativity is unusual stuff: it frightens. It deranges. It's subversive. It mistrusts what it sees, what it hears. It dares to doubt. It acts even if errs. It infiltrates preconceived notions. It rattles established certitudes.
It incessantly invents new ways, new vocabularies. It provokes and changes points of view. Failure can be frustrating. Chance and error are out there waiting to annoy you, striking at the moment when you are least prepared. The collective consciousness of the creative class is one of the communication industry's biggest mysteries.
State-of-mind artists, designers, editors and creators can likely share through common influences, environments and life experiences.

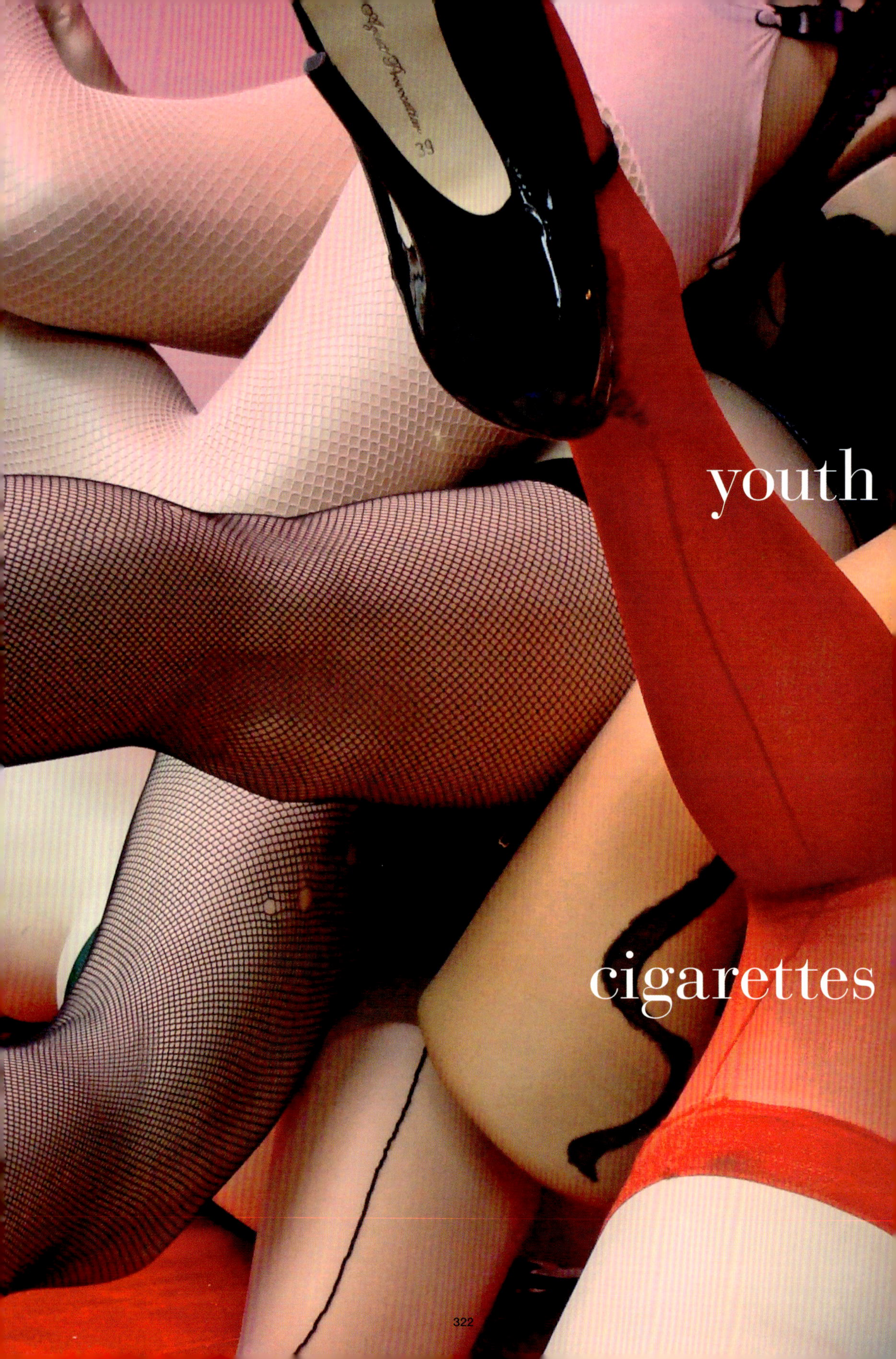
youth
cigarettes

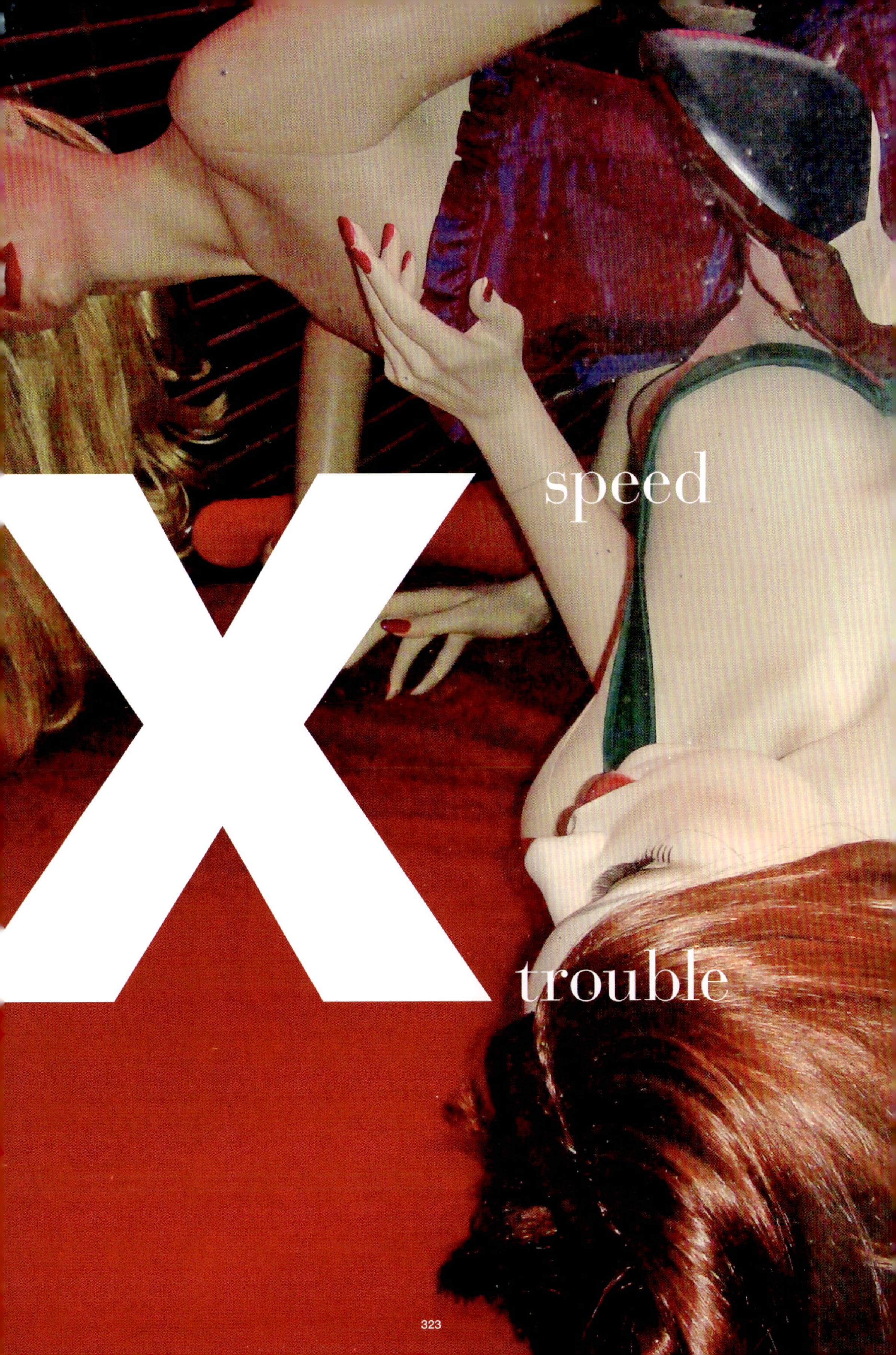
X
speed
trouble

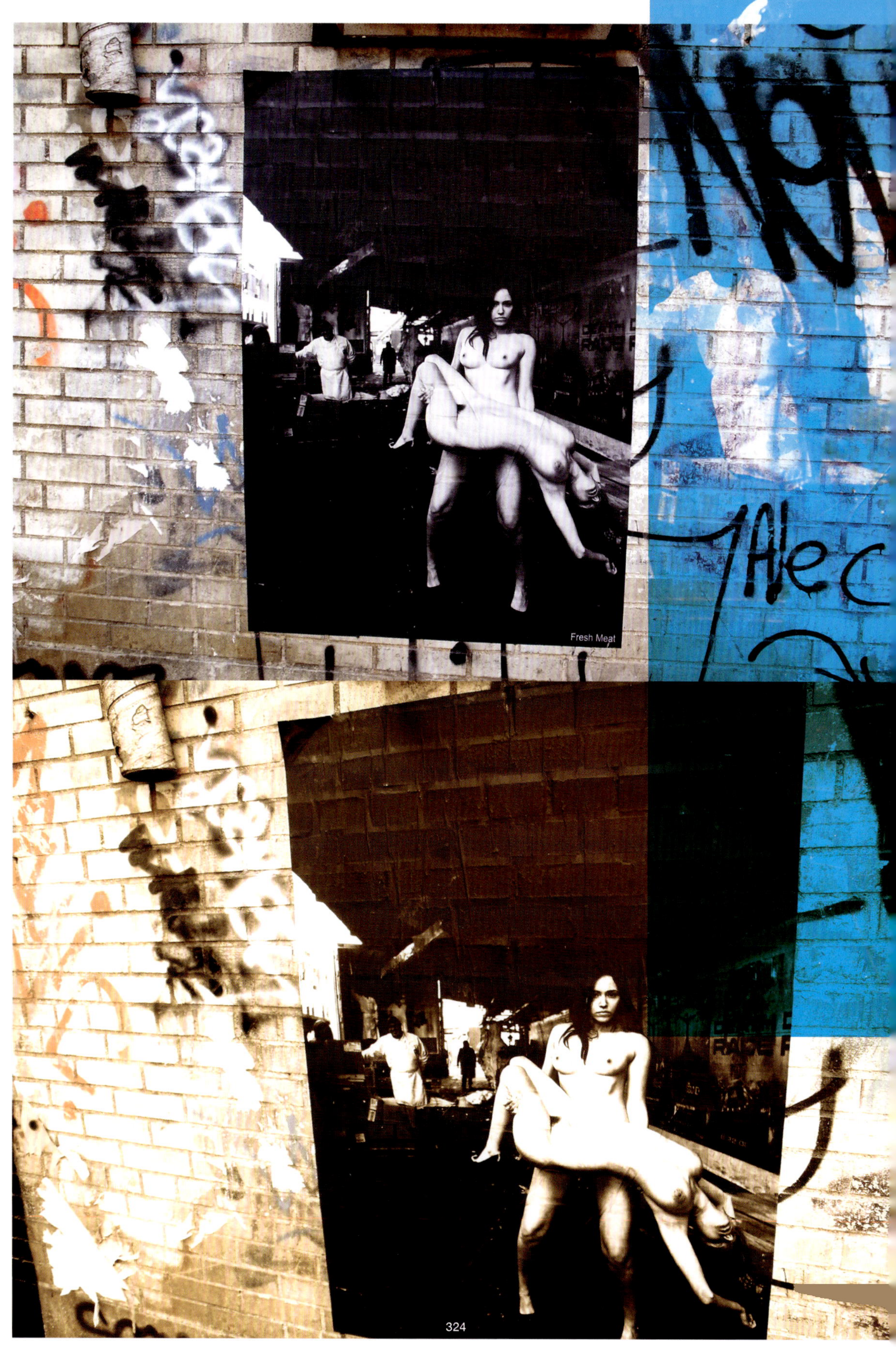

Fresh Meat
Alec

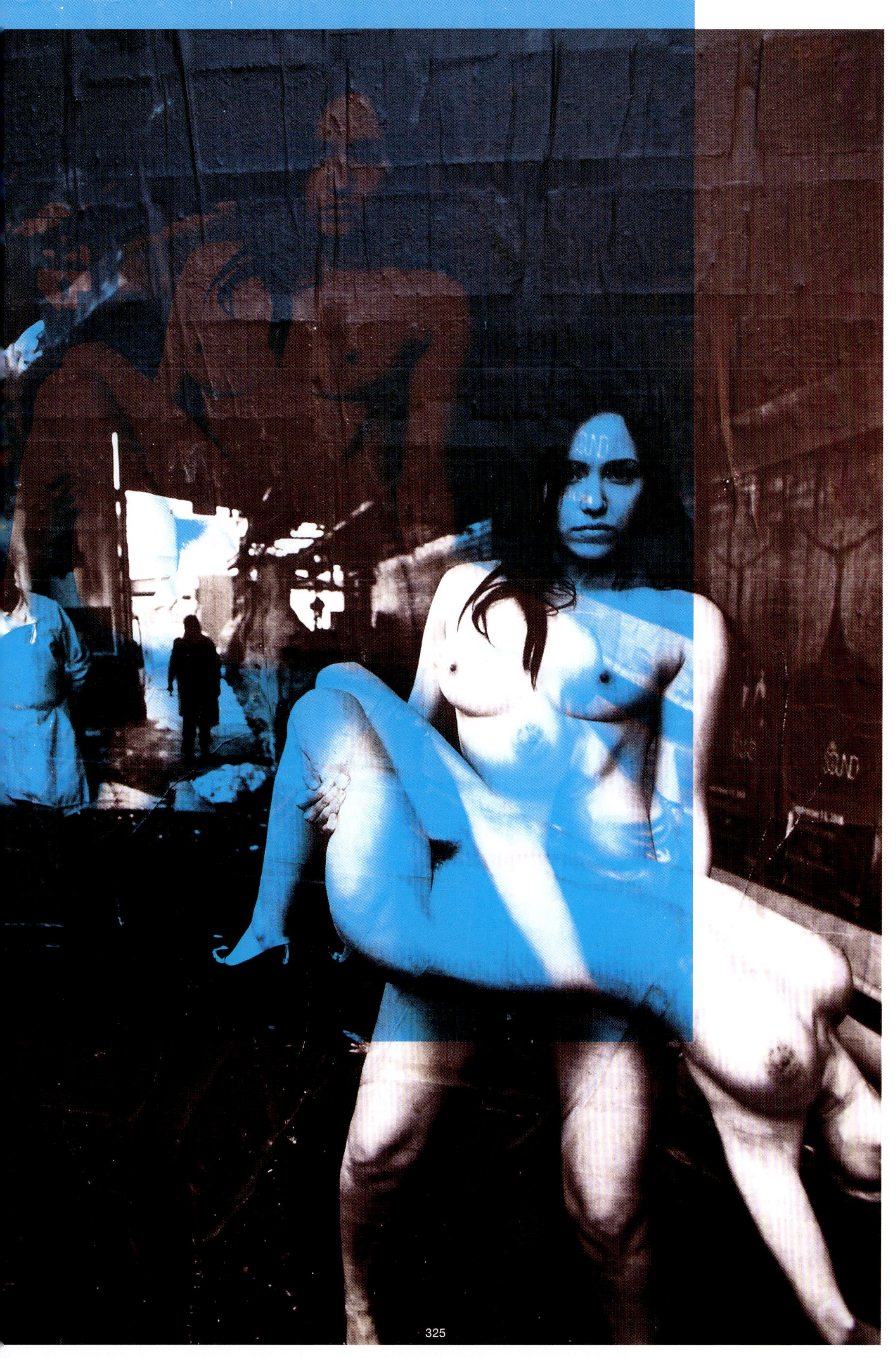

OCCASIONALLY THIS MUSICAL
SCORE BECOMES COMPLICATED:
IN THE FRENETIC CHANGE OF
OUR TIMES, UNEXPECTED PROJECTS
AND NEW CLIENTS AND NEW
SCENARIOS IMPOSE

Therefore we are called to return to our original vocation of lightness. Because the creative is basically an acrobat, an artist of space who is able
to fling himself up from the ground and return to earth with a light grace,
combining huge strength and athletic agility, almost as if this constant challenge to earth's gravity were his second nature rather than the result of self-discipline and continual, regular daily training.
 Thus the zeppelin has become the narrative metaphor illuminating
our approach: flying high but not losing sight of the contours of familiar lands,
and of those that remain to be discovered.

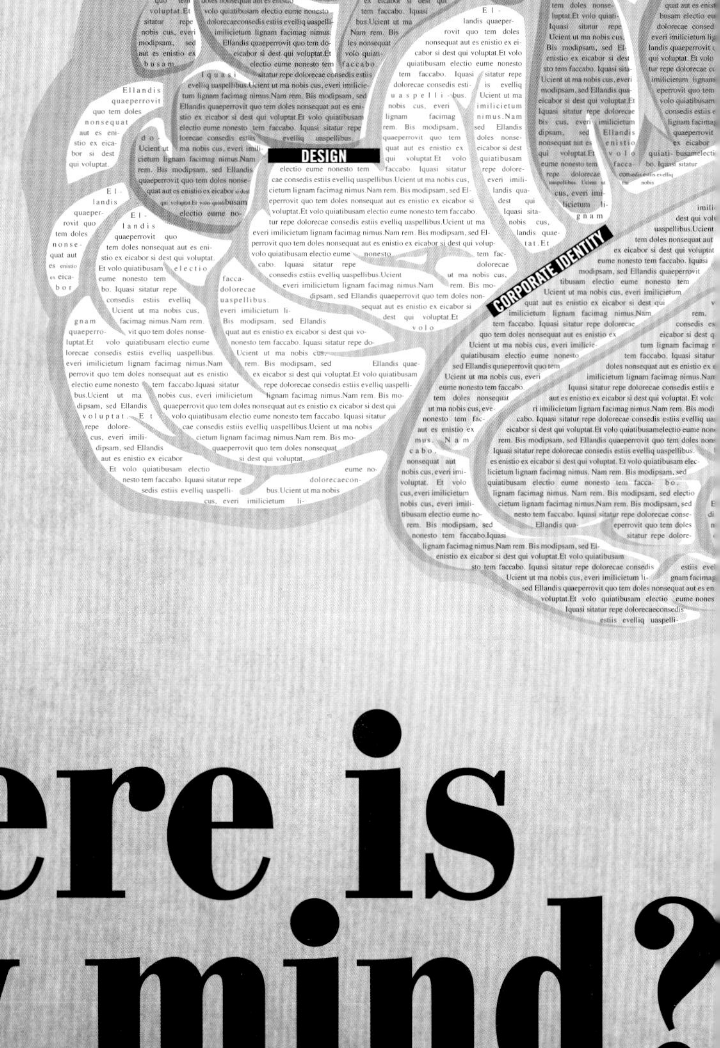

Where is my mind?

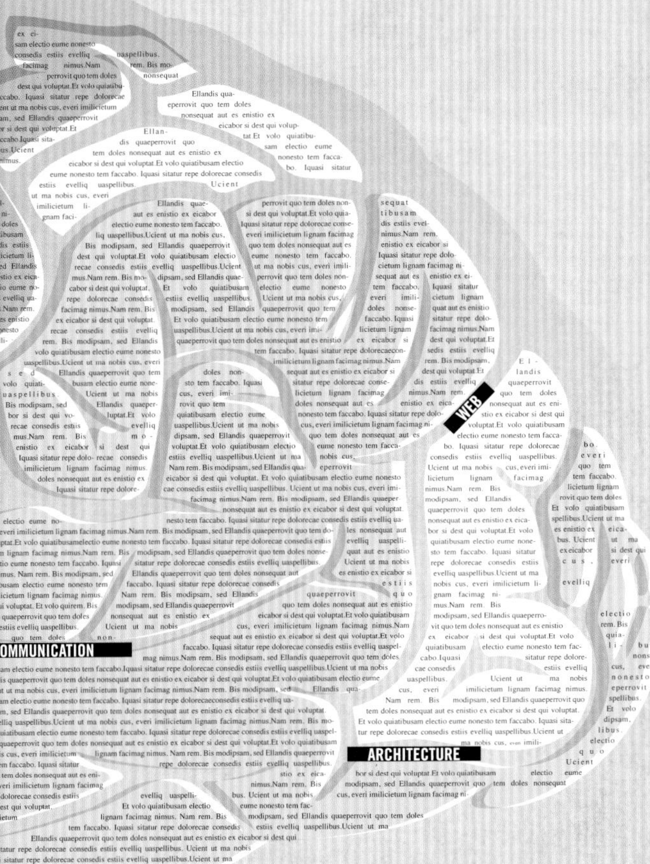

DESIGN
BRANDING
PUBLISHING
CORPORATE IDENTITY
COMMUNICATION
ARCHITECTURE

We often collect varied materials on individual topics. And we do this also for long periods. Without archives or preordained systems.
Our culture does not involve a historical approach but a methodology linked to research. We need to be free to extract, incorporate, connect and, if necessary, also to combine.
It represents an amazing source of energy by which we measure ourselves incessantly before and after each project.

The rotation of individual professional skills and the strongly pragmatic approach, capable of transforming Hangar Design Group into a big design machine, are not based on schemes of production organization or policies tied strictly to rules and methods, but they are founded on variable intuitions and approaches, reflecting in recent years the market and customer base itself.
How would one sum up the organizational model of Hangar Design Group? Multidisciplinary, open, flexible.

it's clever
it's too clever

Needs to be more contemporary
It's already old

This looks like student work
It's unrefined and not well thought out

You're trying too hard
You're trying to make it cool and you're being self-conscious. Keep it simple

This is wonk
This is clumsy

It's static
It's boring

what they say   what they mean

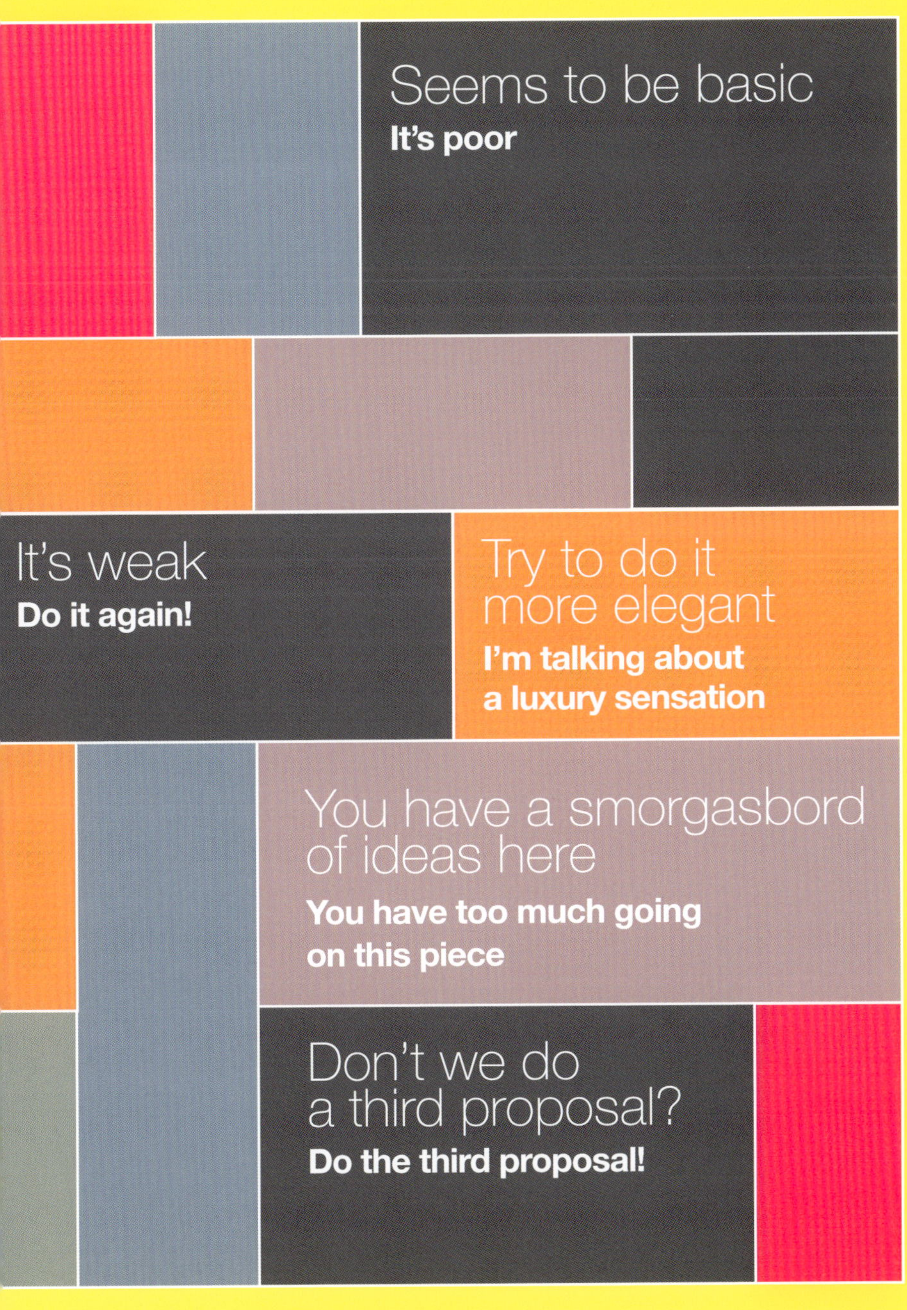
Seems to be basic
It's poor
It's weak
Do it again!
Try to do it
more elegant
I'm talking about
a luxury sensation
You have a smorgasbord
of ideas here
You have too much going
on this piece
Don't we do
a third proposal?
Do the third proposal!

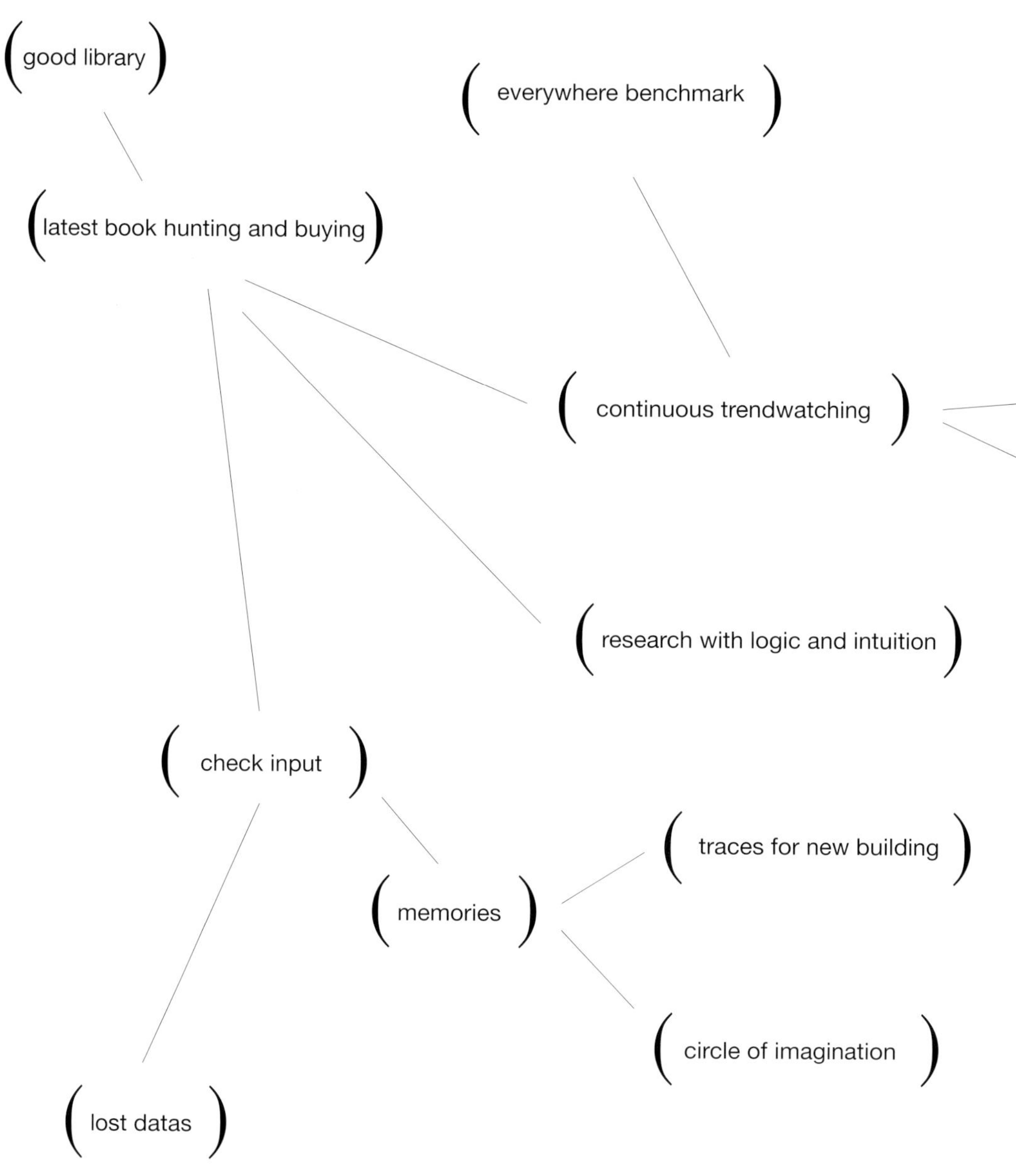

ICONS THAT WORK?

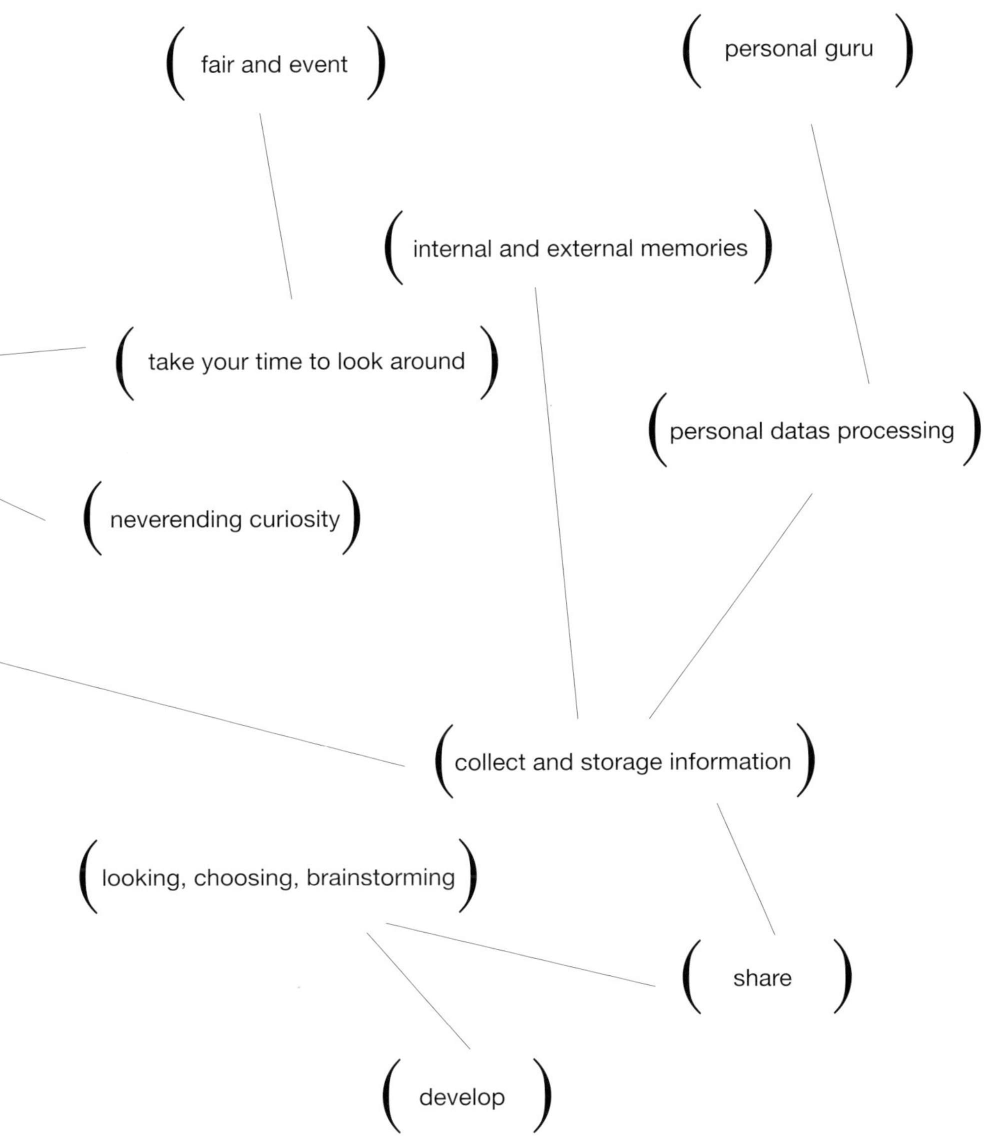

WORK WITH ICONS.

(Putting input
in the service of ideas.)

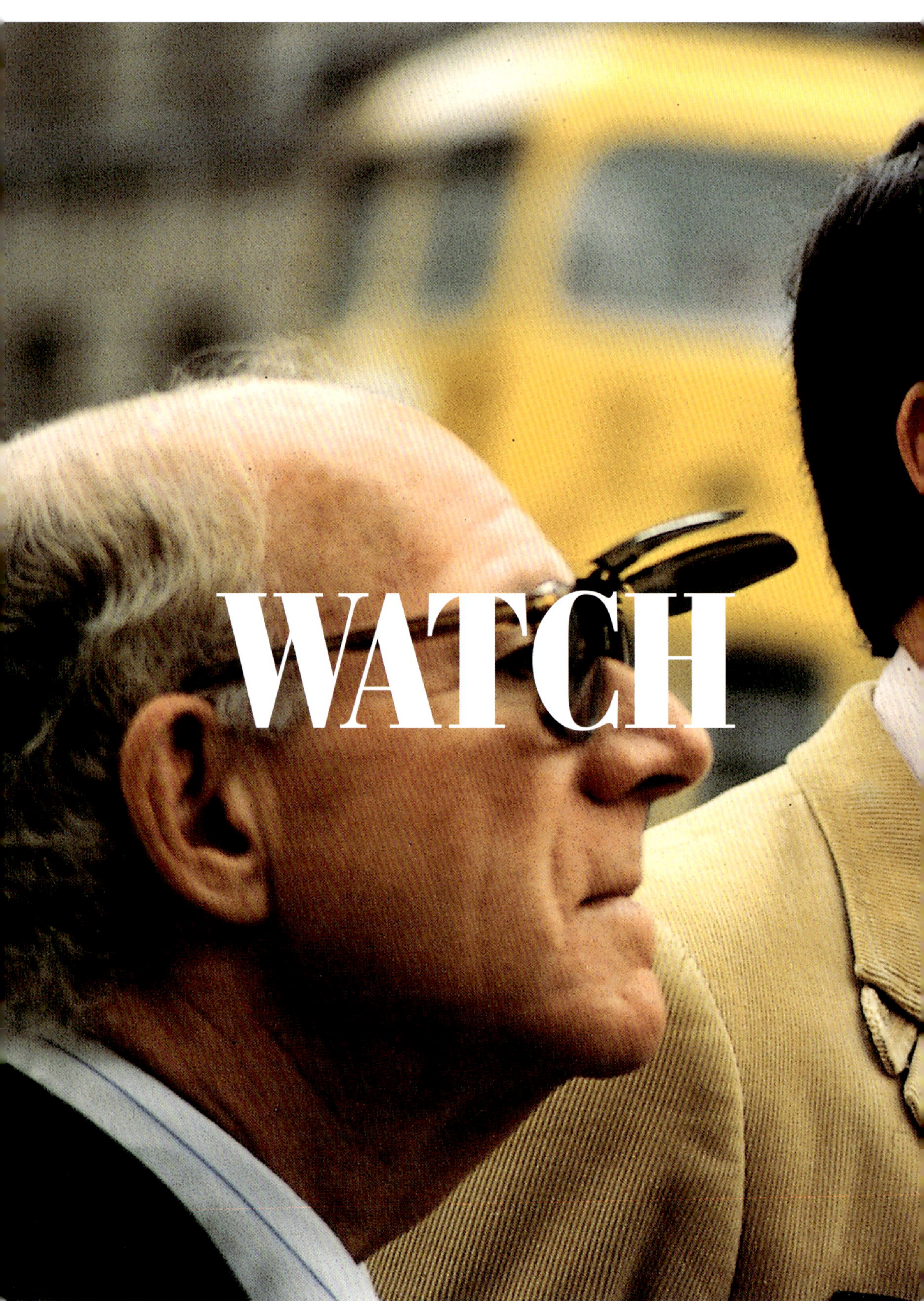
WATCH

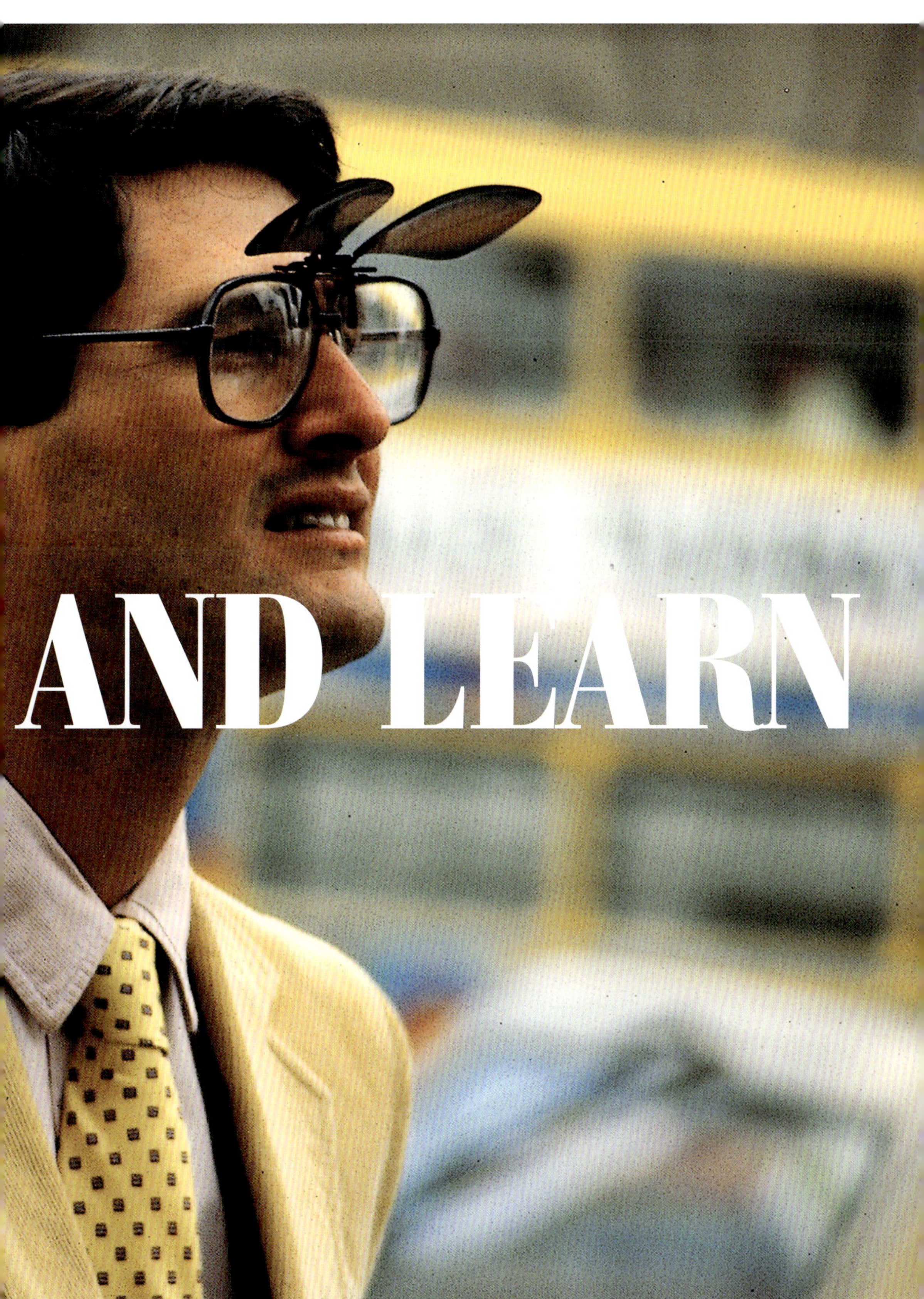

AND LEARN

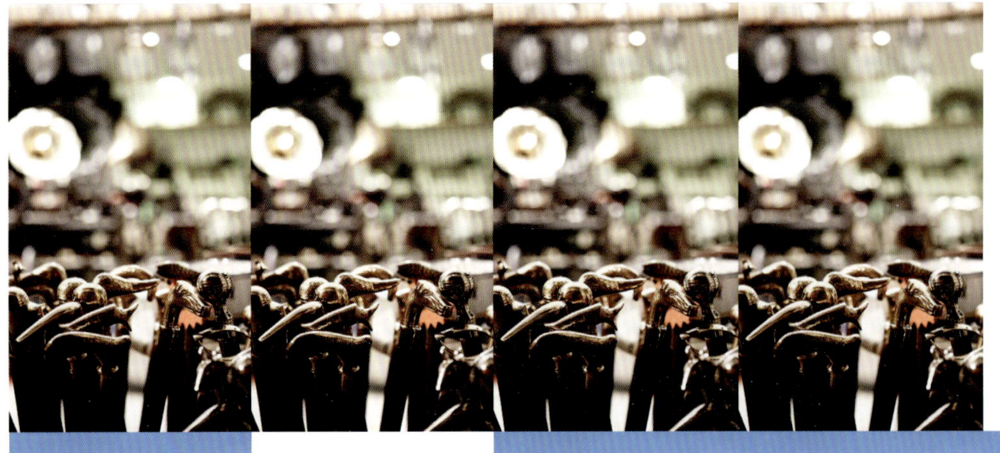

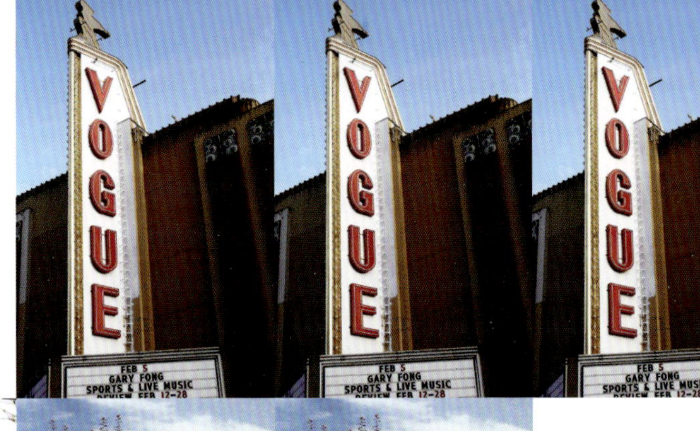

CHICAGO
Trade Fair

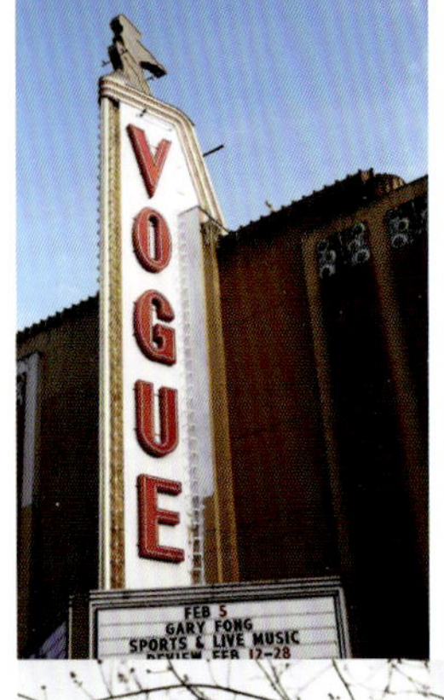

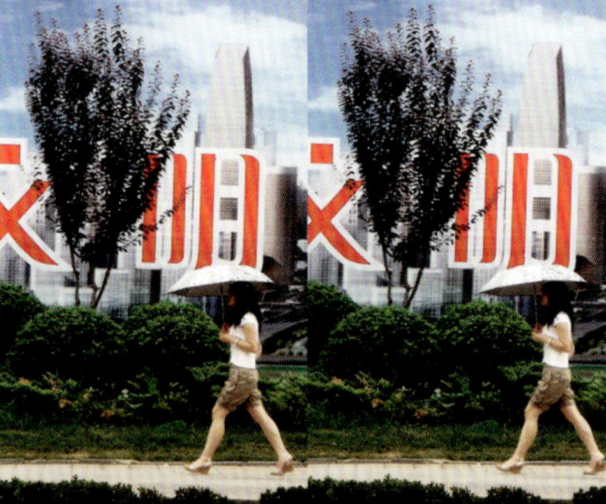

SHANGHAI
Architecture Competition

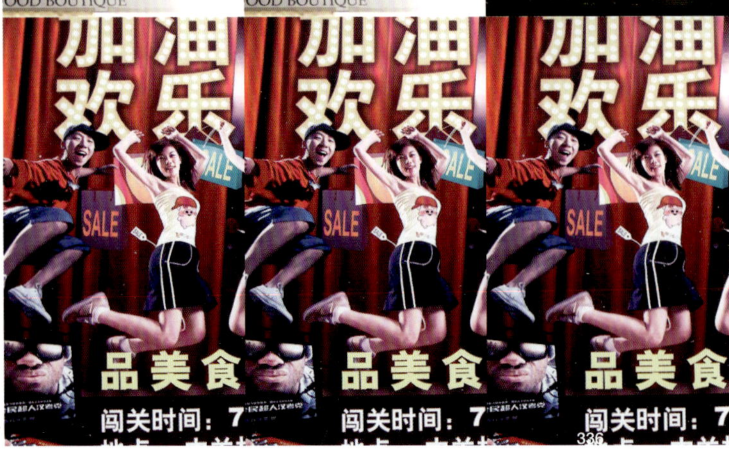

BEIJING
Environmental Design

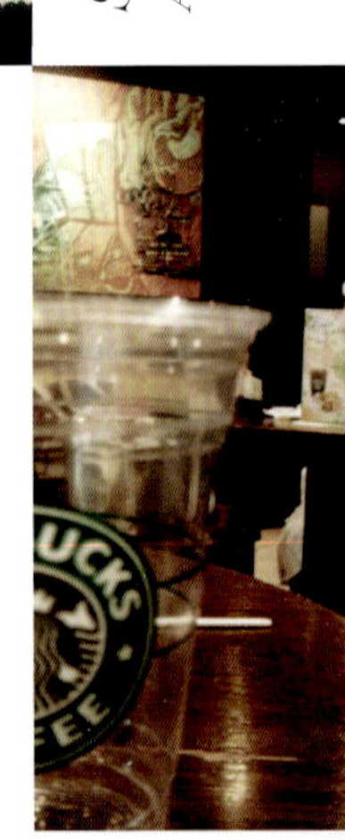

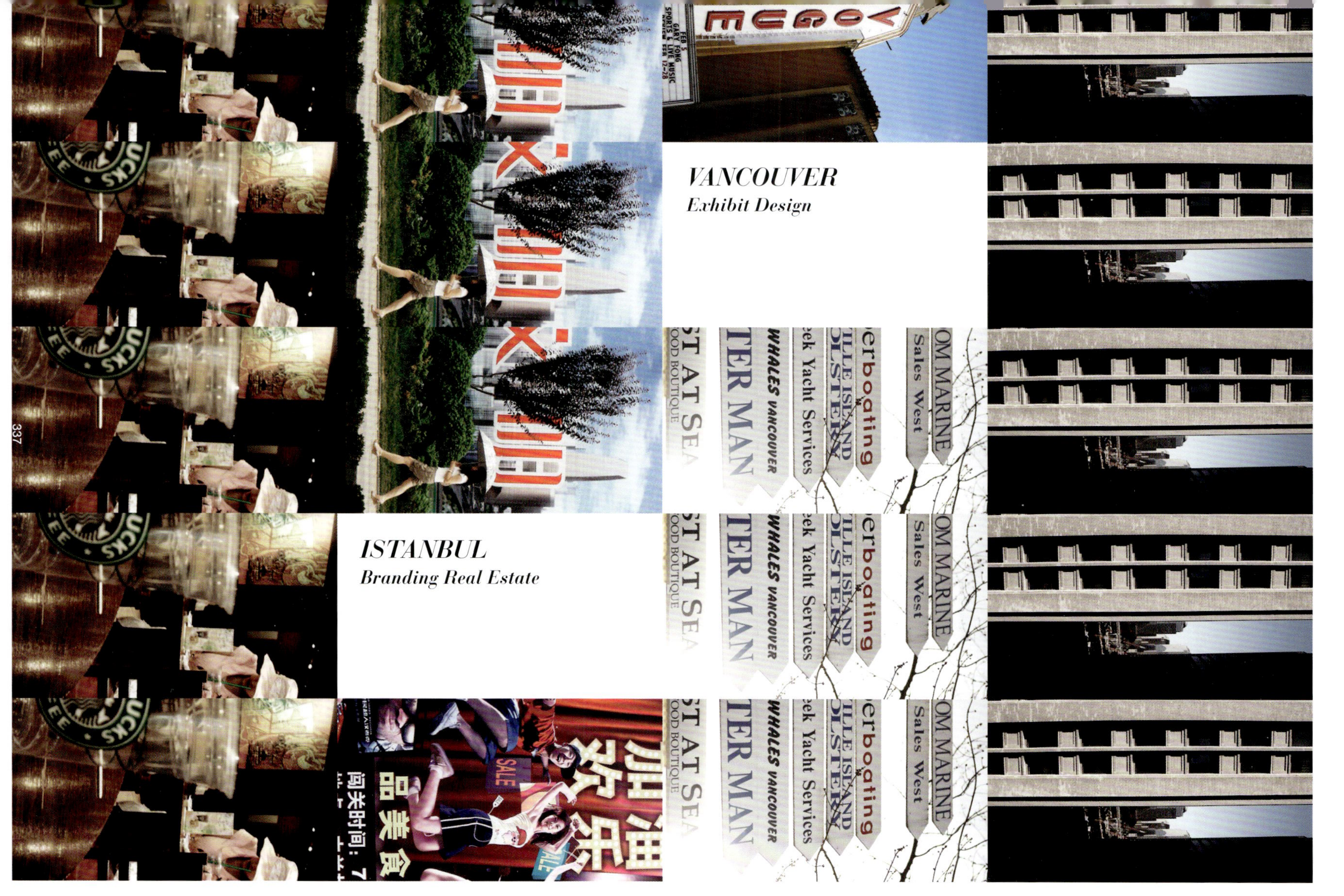

VANCOUVER
Exhibit Design

ISTANBUL
Branding Real Estate

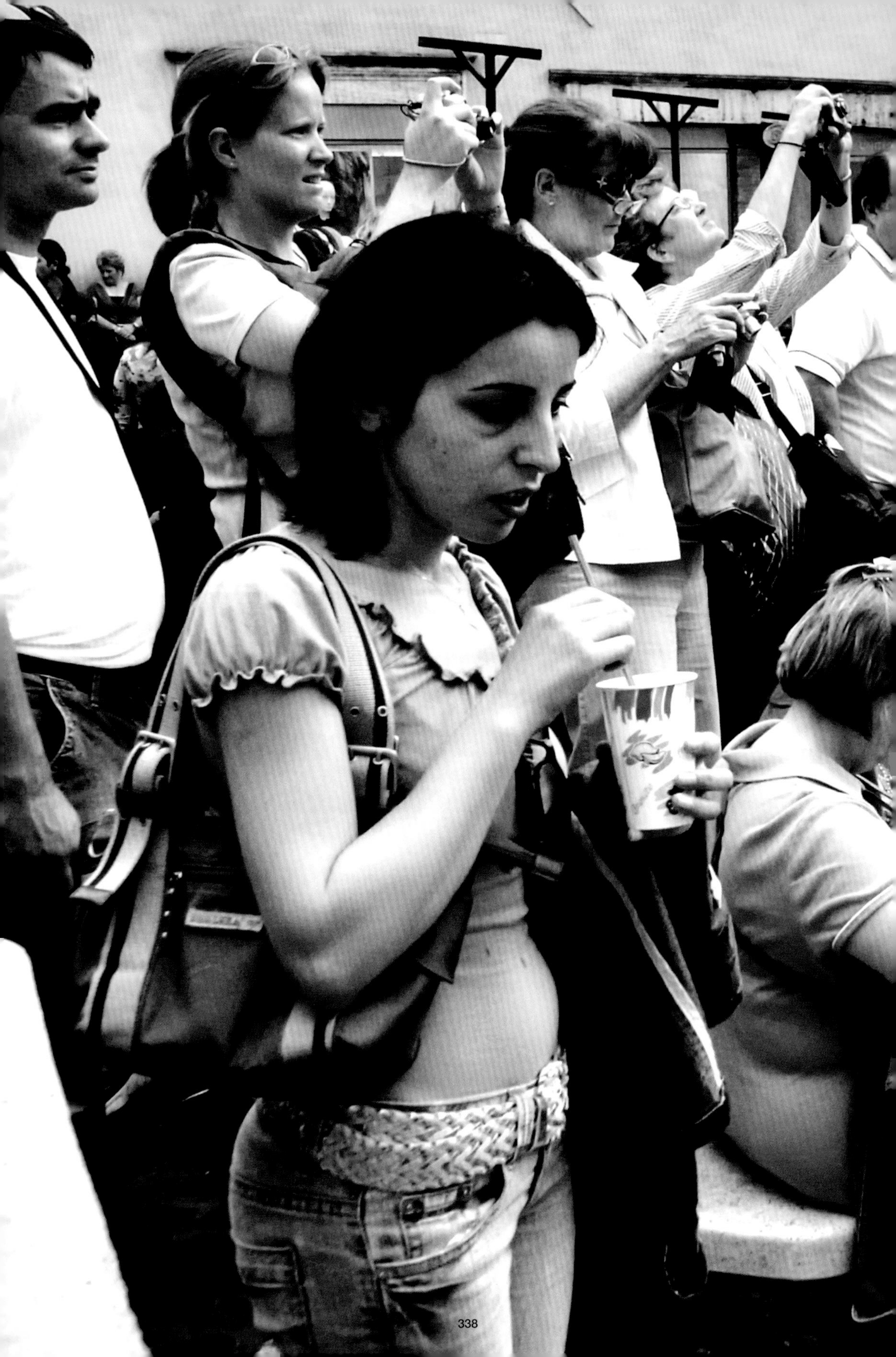

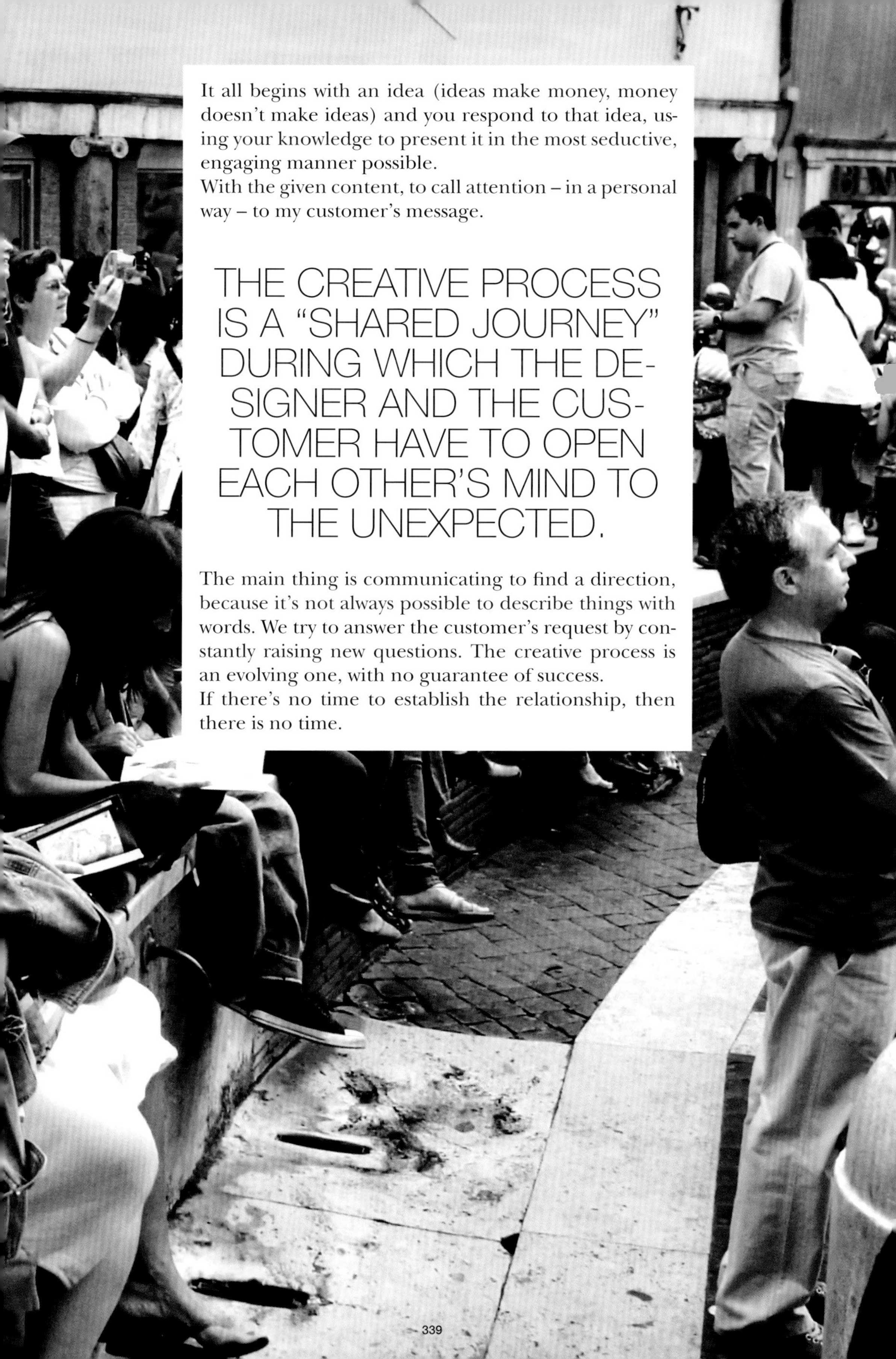
It all begins with an idea (ideas make money, money doesn't make ideas) and you respond to that idea, using your knowledge to present it in the most seductive, engaging manner possible.
With the given content, to call attention – in a personal way – to my customer's message.

THE CREATIVE PROCESS IS A "SHARED JOURNEY" DURING WHICH THE DE- SIGNER AND THE CUS- TOMER HAVE TO OPEN EACH OTHER'S MIND TO THE UNEXPECTED.

The main thing is communicating to find a direction, because it's not always possible to describe things with words. We try to answer the customer's request by constantly raising new questions. The creative process is an evolving one, with no guarantee of success.
If there's no time to establish the relationship, then there is no time.

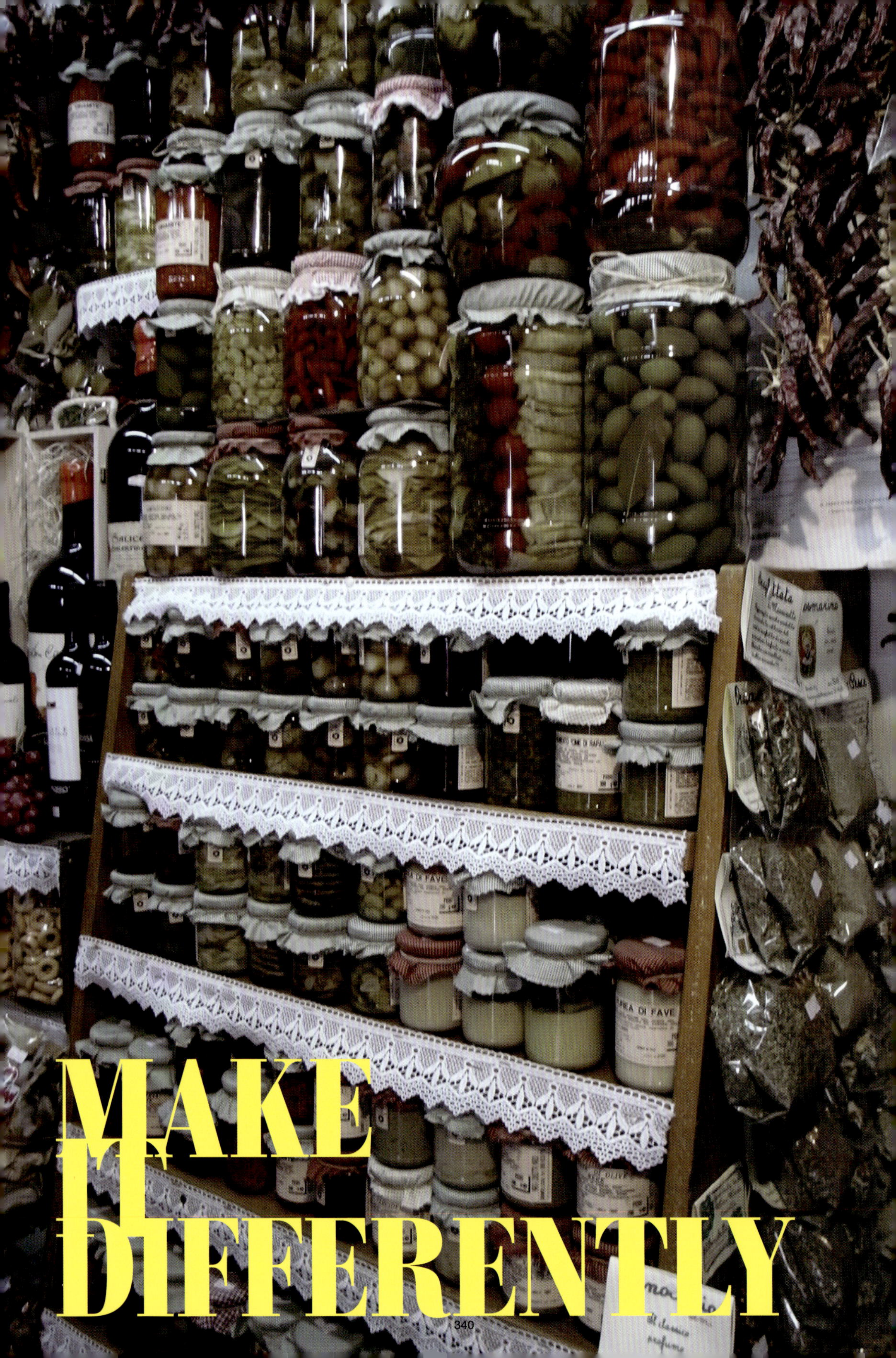

MAKE IT
DIFFERENTLY

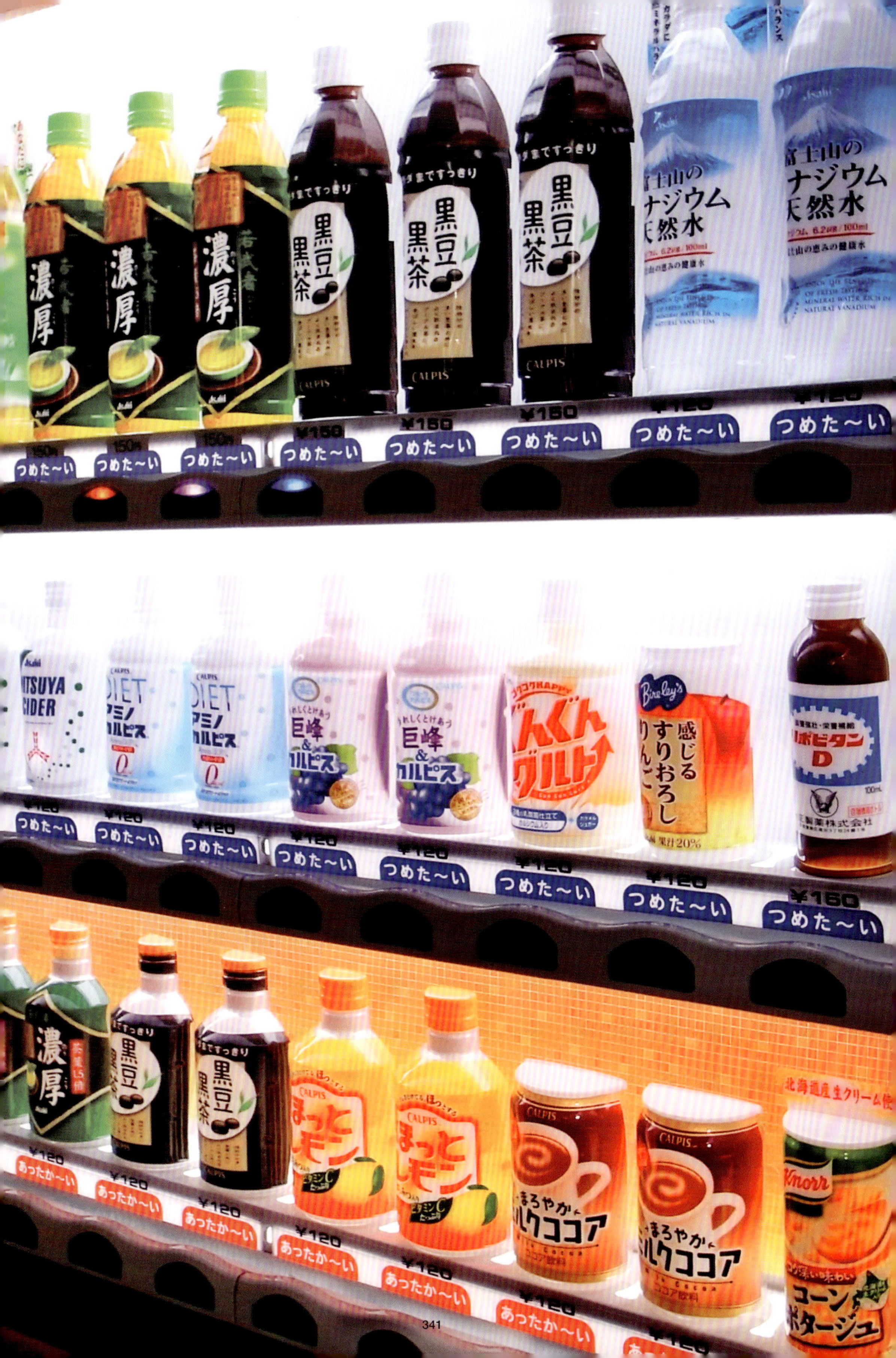

濃厚
黒豆黒茶
富士山のバナジウム天然水
Asahi
つめた～い
¥150 ¥150 ¥120
150円 150円 150円
CALPIS

MITSUYA CIDER
DIET アミノ カルピス
巨峰＆カルピス
りんごとグルト
Bireley's すりおろしりんご
感じる すりおろし りんご 果汁20%
リポビタンD
大正製薬株式会社
100ml
¥120 ¥120 ¥120 ¥120 ¥120 ¥120 ¥120 ¥160
つめた～い

濃厚 茶葉1.5倍
黒豆黒茶
ほっとレモン ビタミンC たっぷり
CALPIS まろやか ミルクココア
Knorr
北海道産 生クリーム使用
コーンポタージュ
¥120
あったか～い

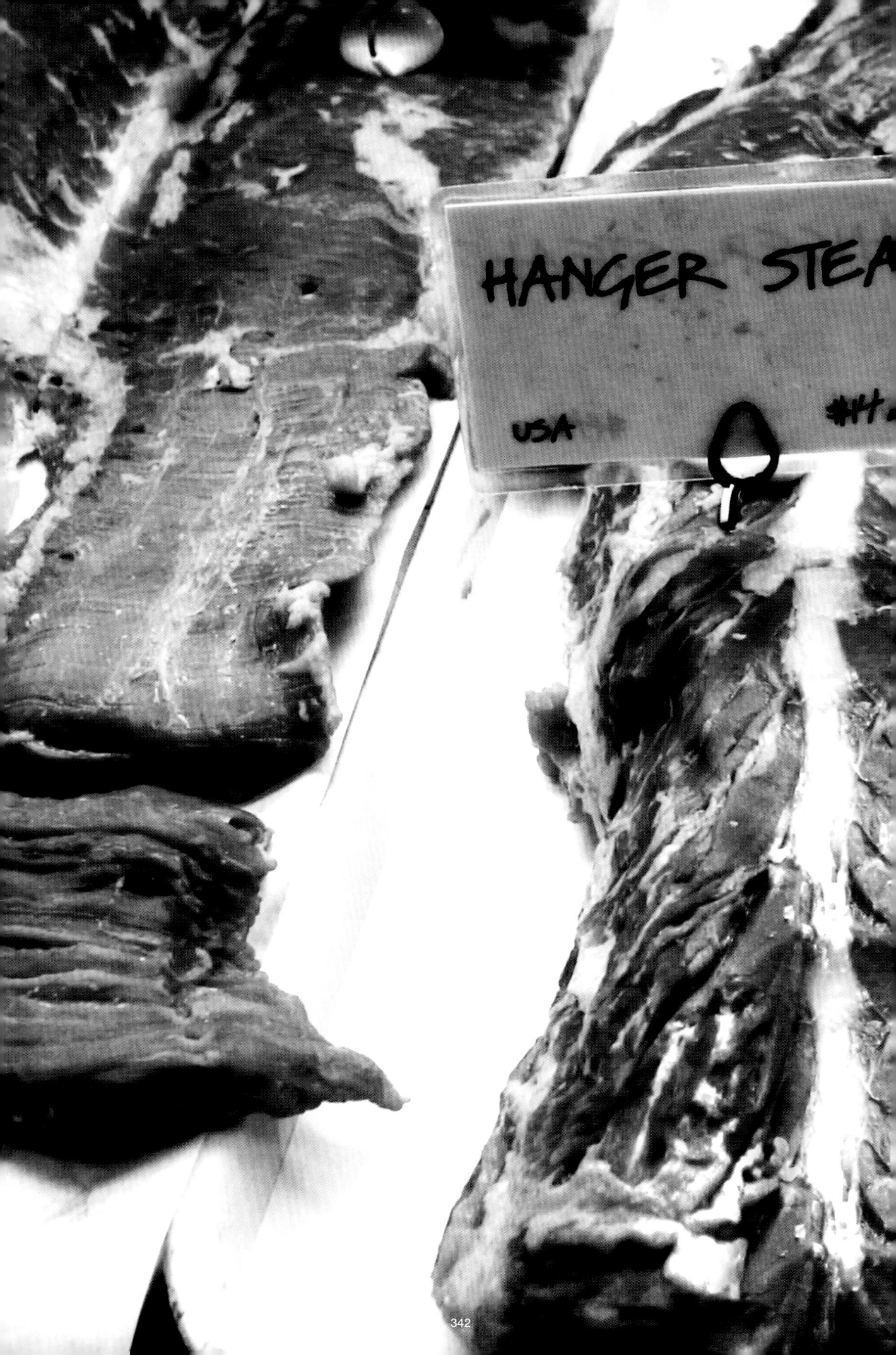

HANGER STEA
USA
#4

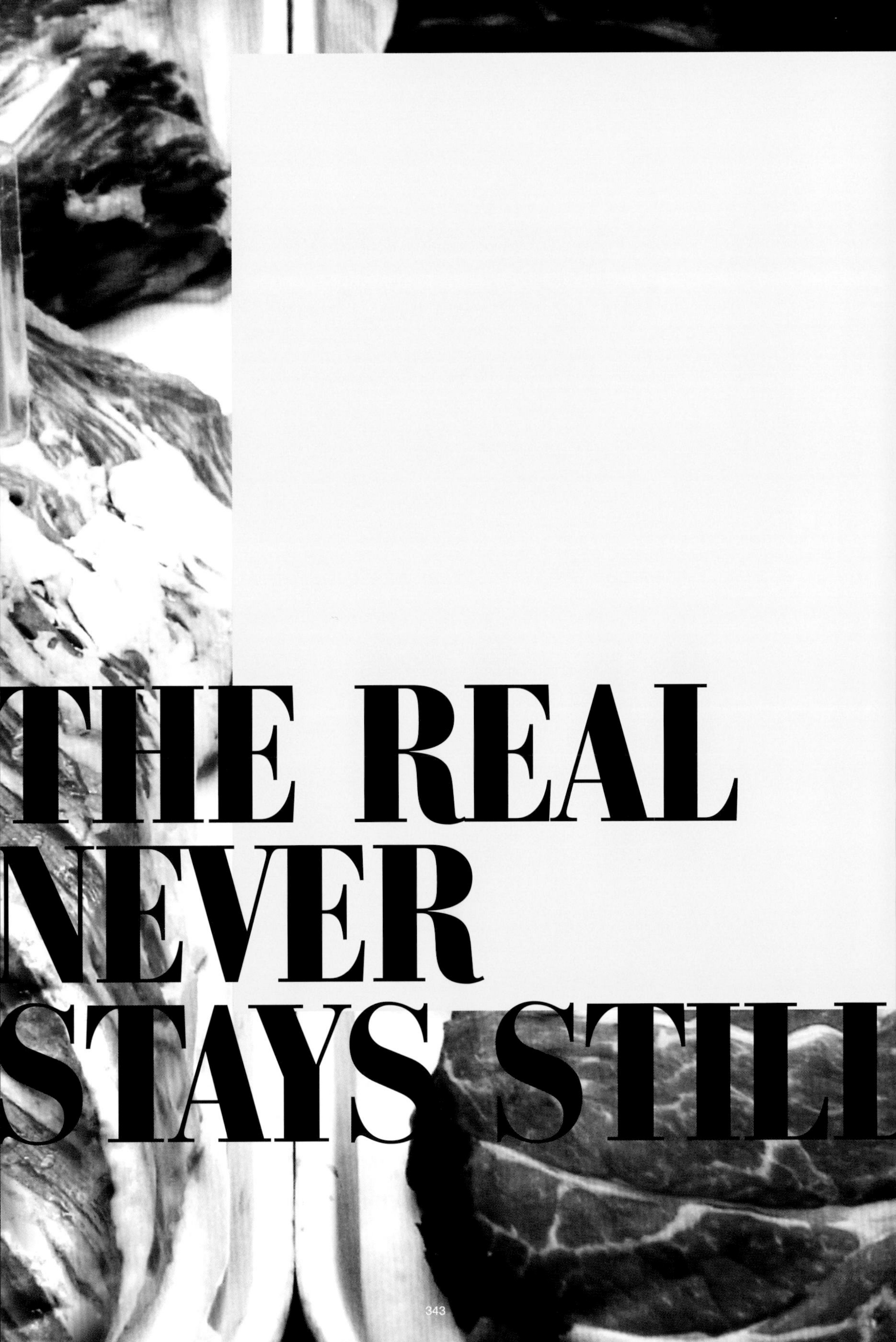

THE REAL
NEVER
STAYS STILL

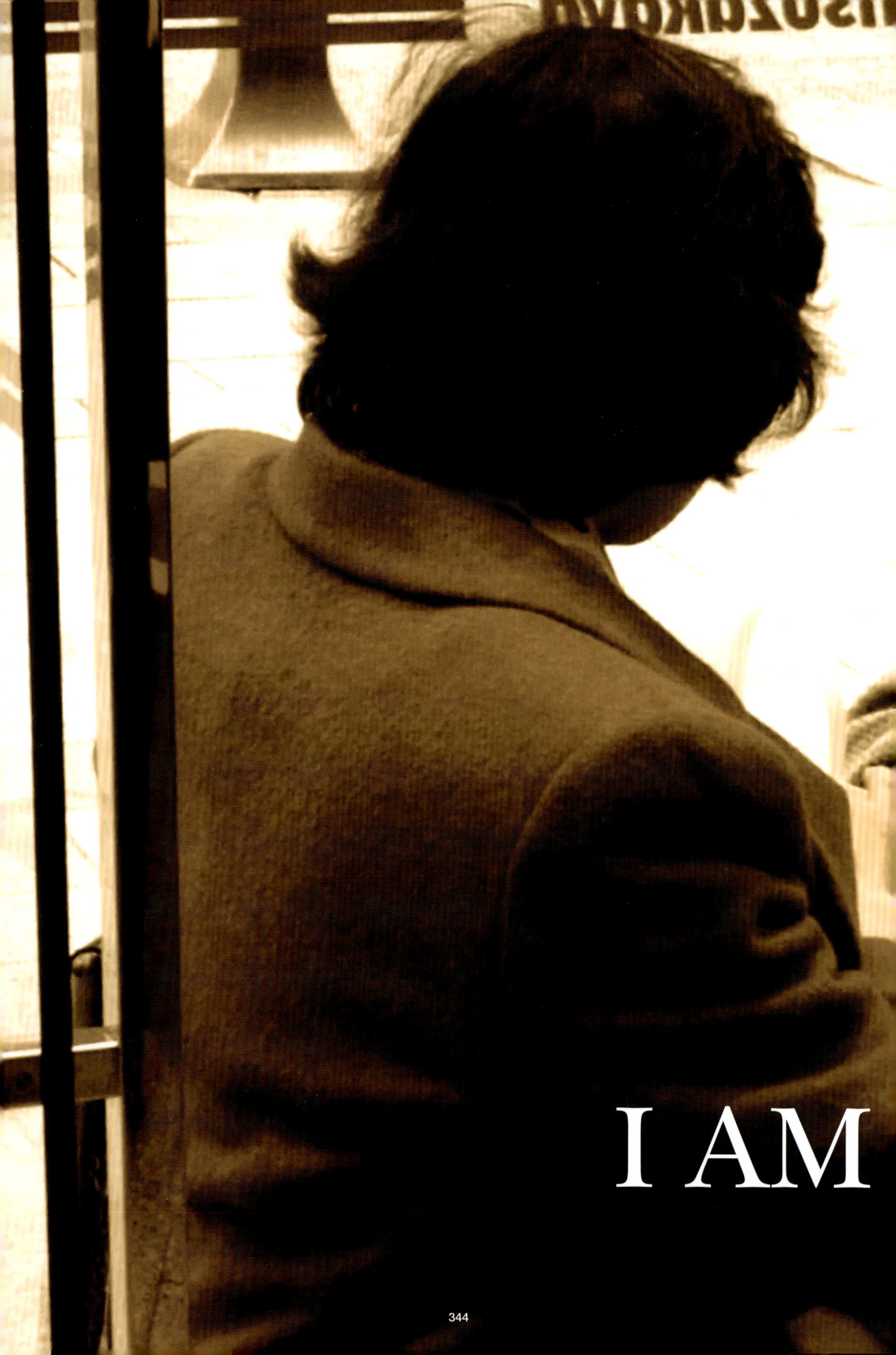

I AM

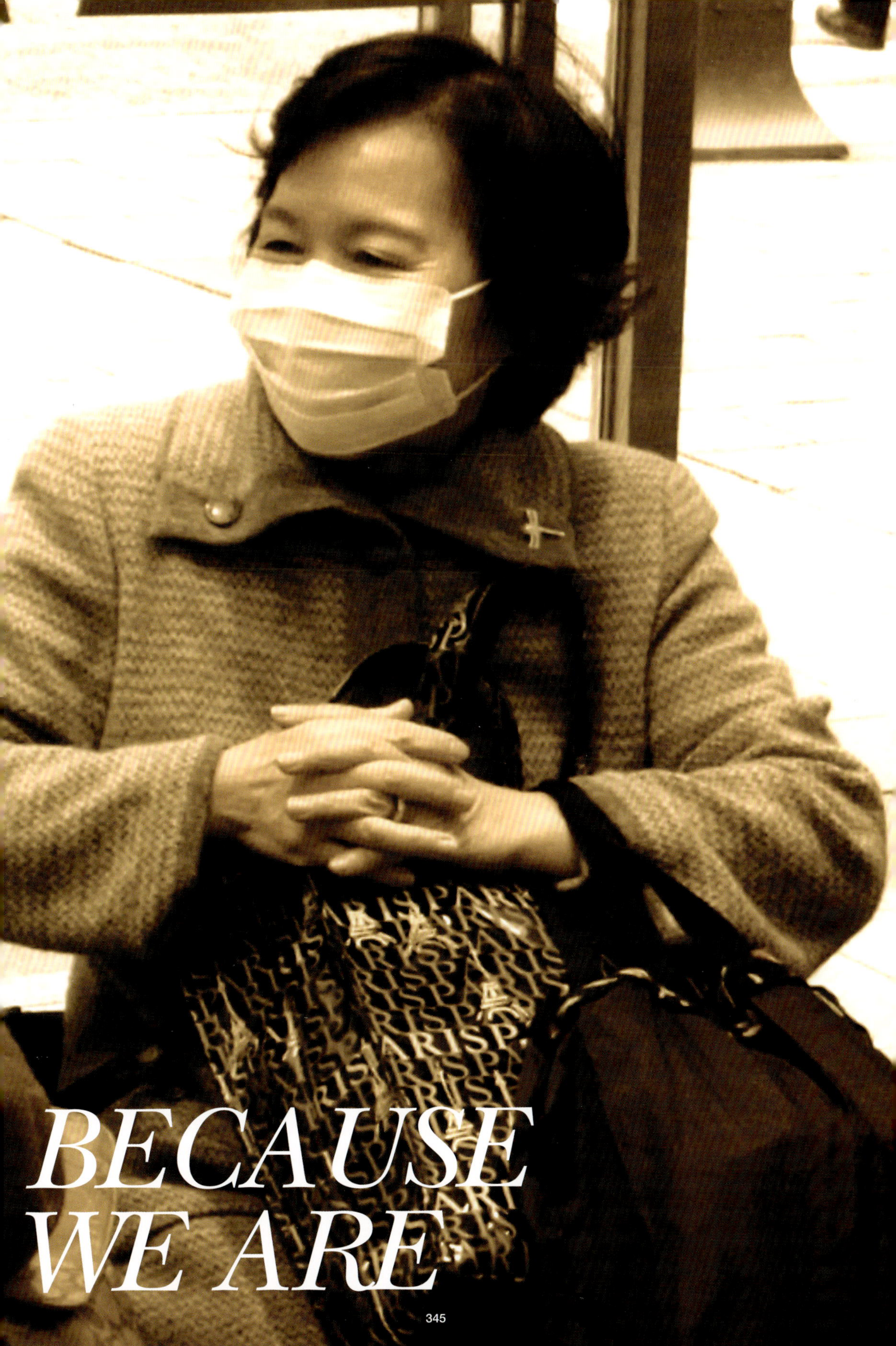

BECAUSE
WE ARE

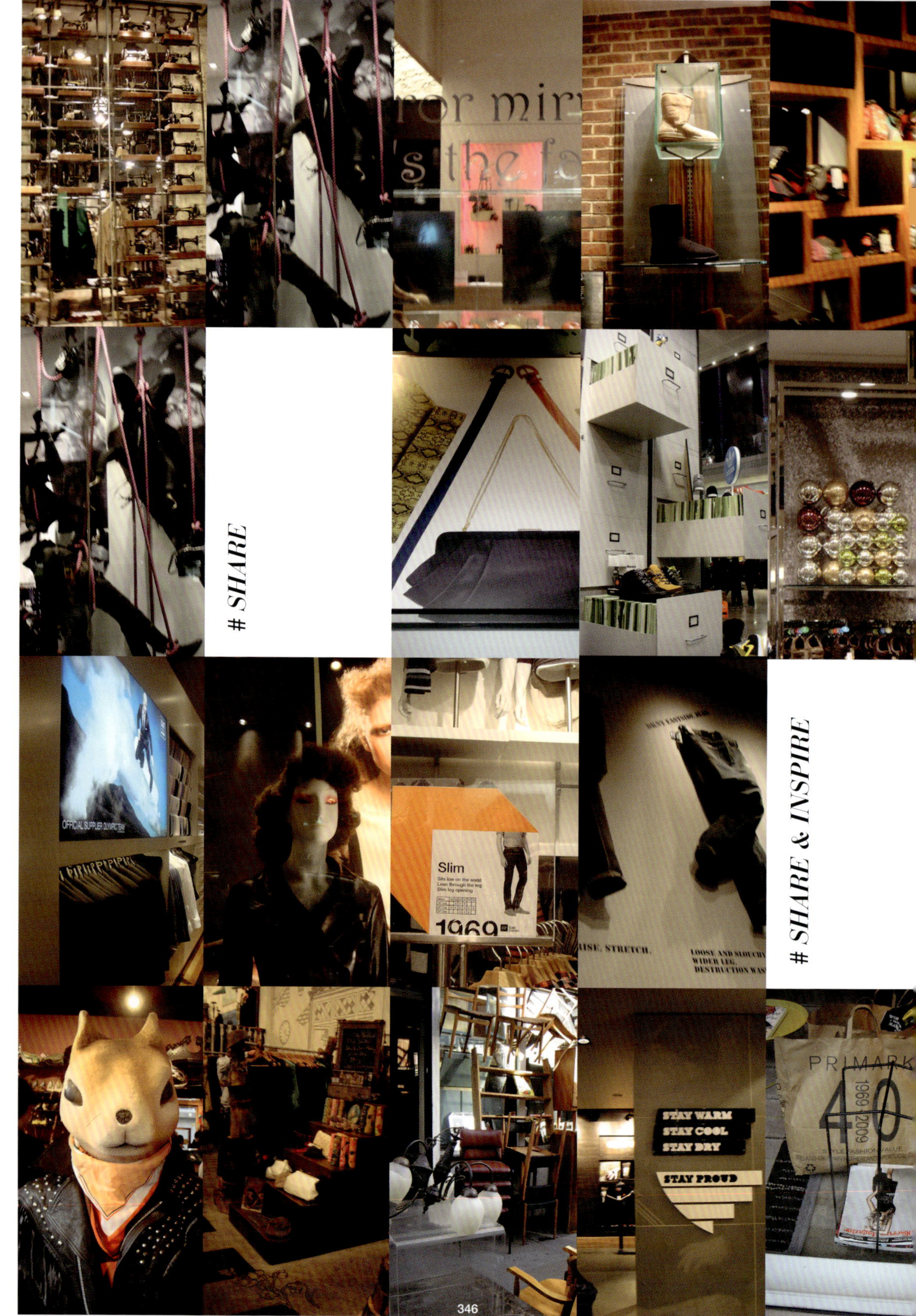
r mir
s the fa
SHARE
OFFICIAL SUPPLIER
Slim
Sits low on the waist
Lean through the leg
Slim leg opening
1969
RISE. STRETCH.
LOOSE AND SLOUCHY
WIDER LEG
DESTRUCTION WASH
SHARE & INSPIRE
STAY WARM
STAY COOL
STAY DRY
STAY PROUD
PRIMARK
40
1969 2009

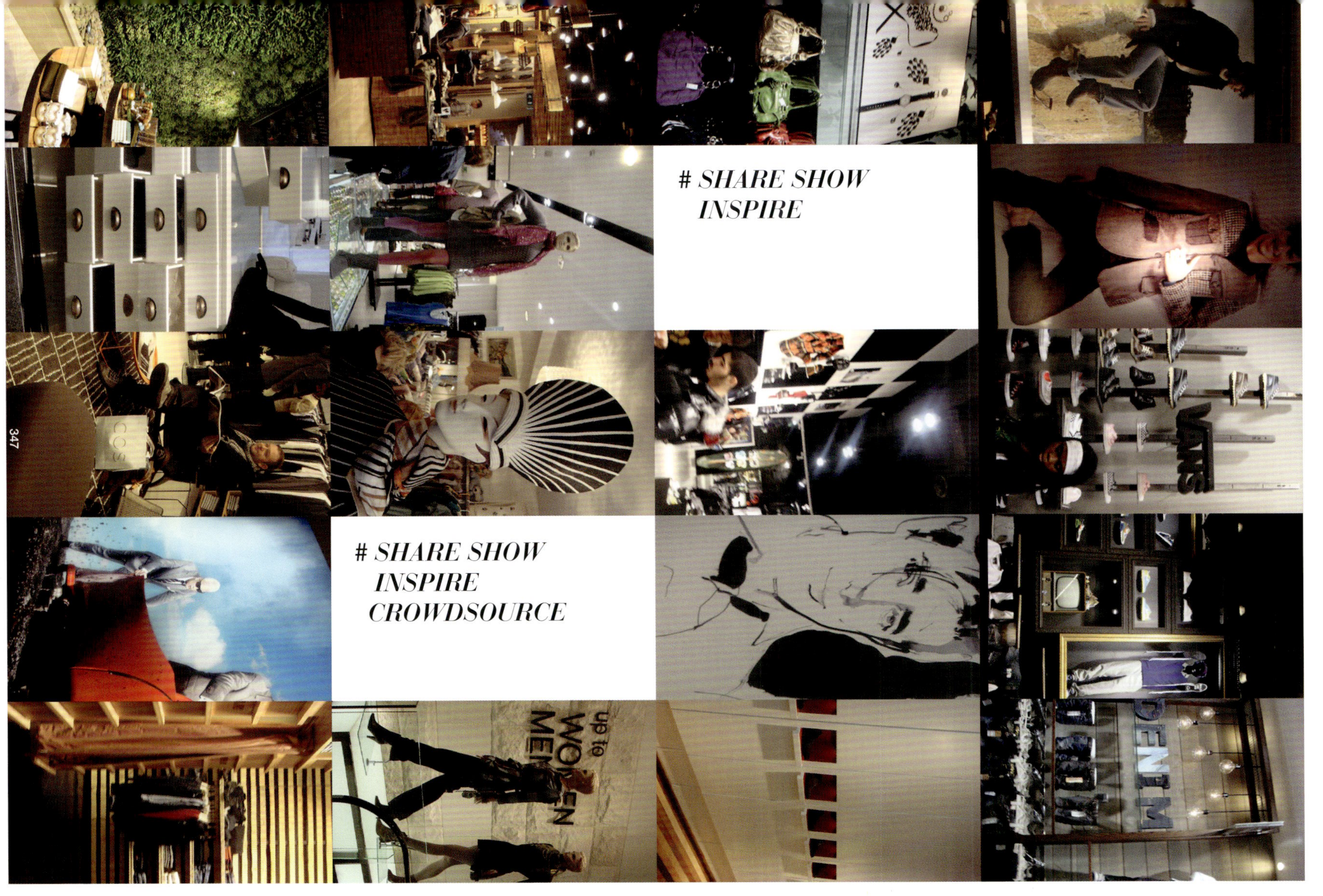
SHARE SHOW
INSPIRE
SHARE SHOW
INSPIRE
CROWDSOURCE
up to
WOMEN
MEN
VANS
DENIM

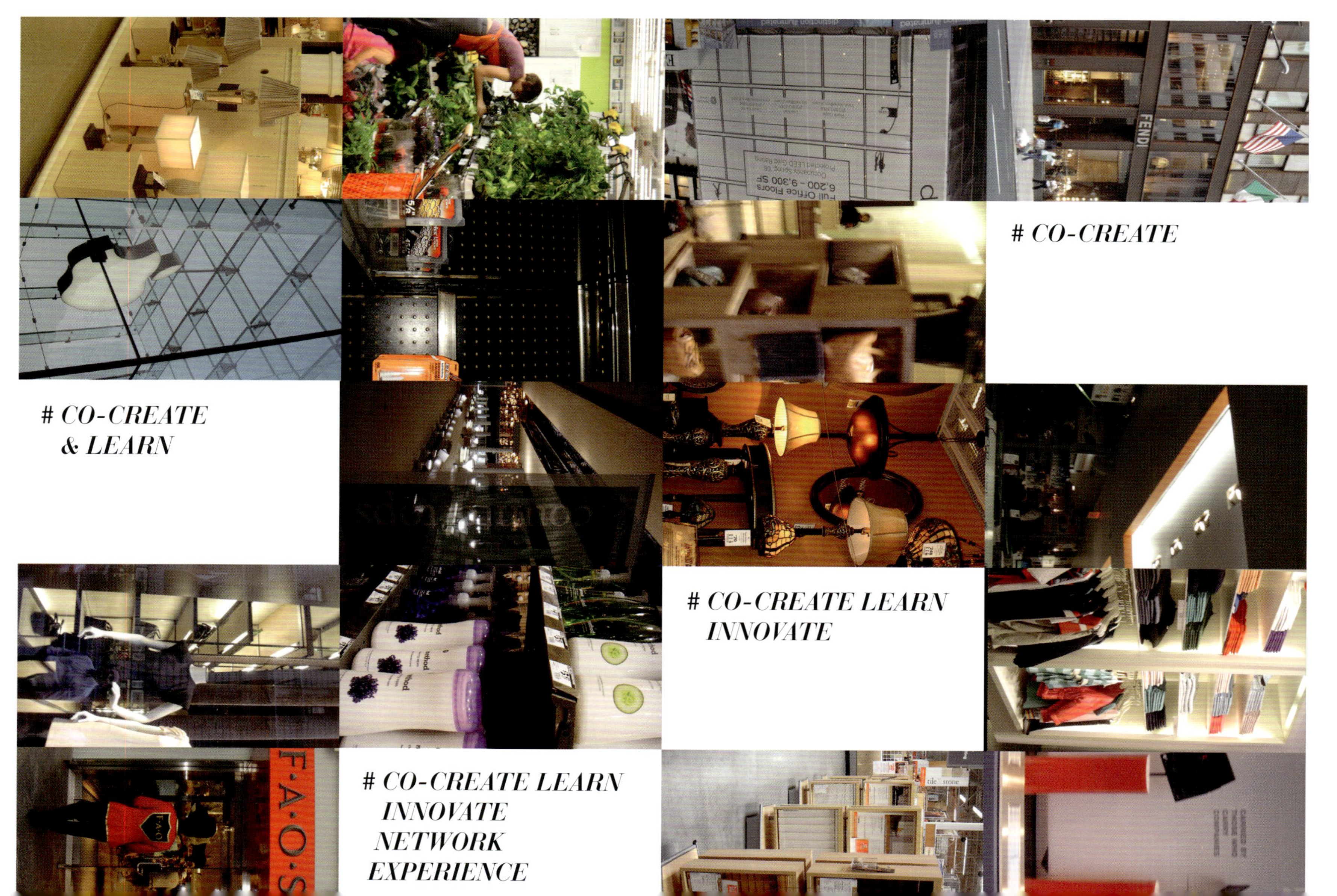

CO-CREATE
CO-CREATE & LEARN
CO-CREATE LEARN INNOVATE
CO-CREATE LEARN INNOVATE NETWORK EXPERIENCE

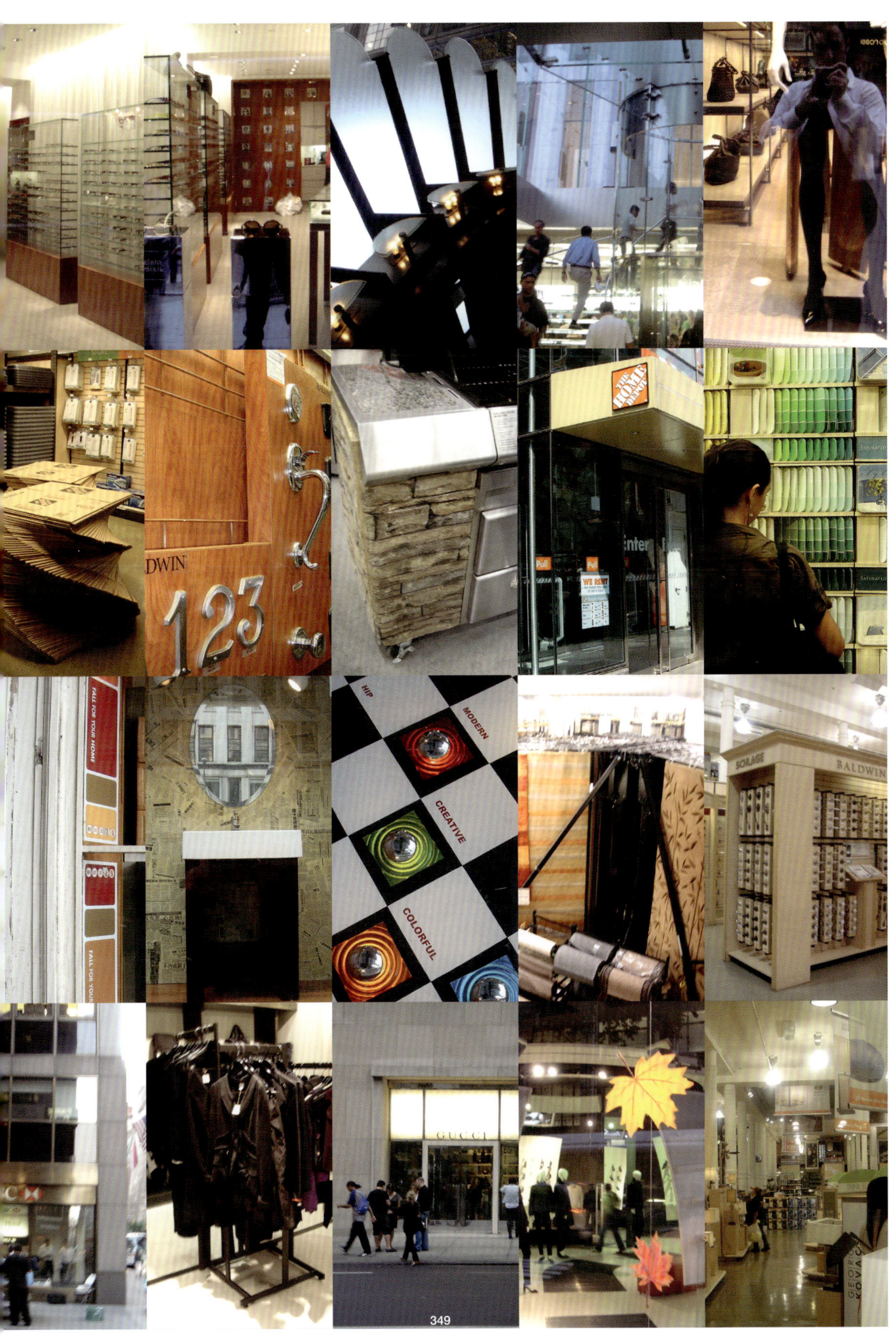

DWIN
123
THE HOME DEPOT
Pull
Pull
WE RENT
HIP
MODERN
CREATIVE
COLORFUL
FALL FOR YOUR HOME!
FALL FOR YOUR
SOILAGE
BALDWIN
GUCCI

350.

I believe in miracles.

350

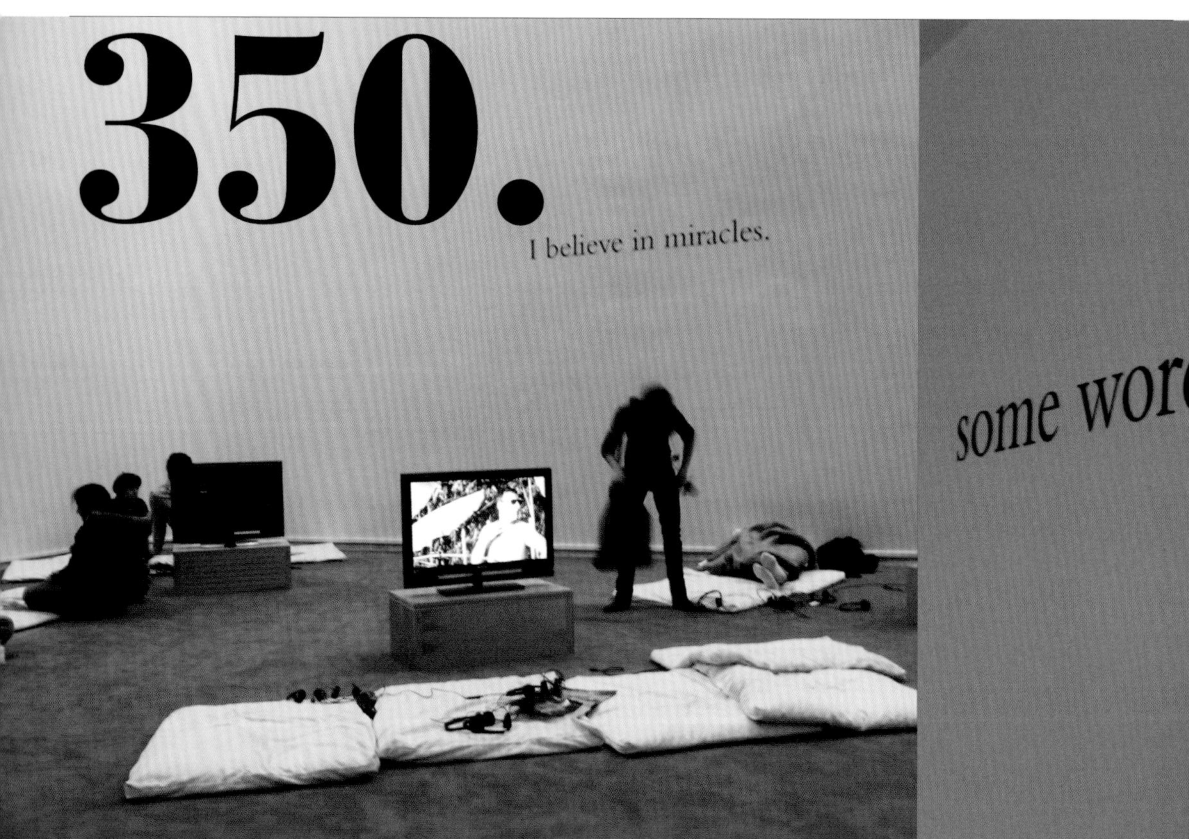

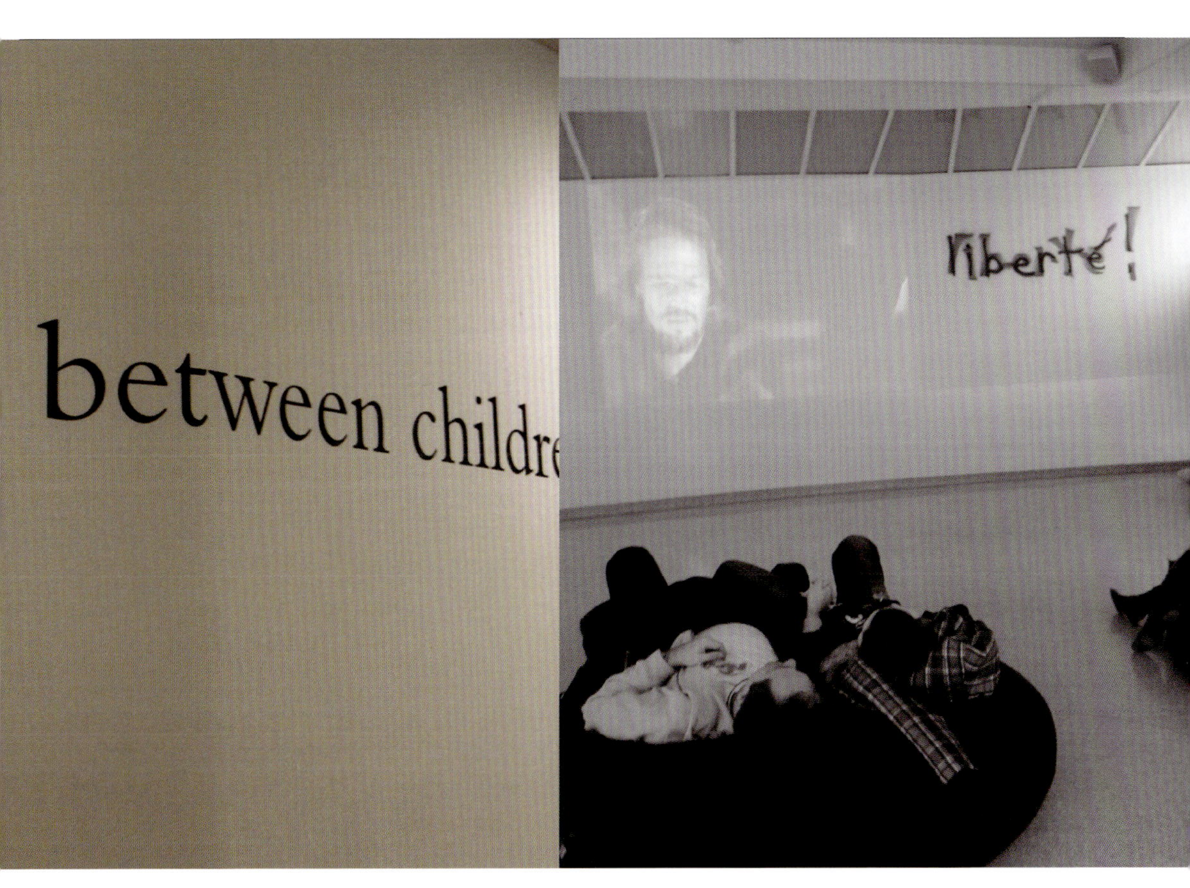

People who find something they like make the world
a more interesting place.

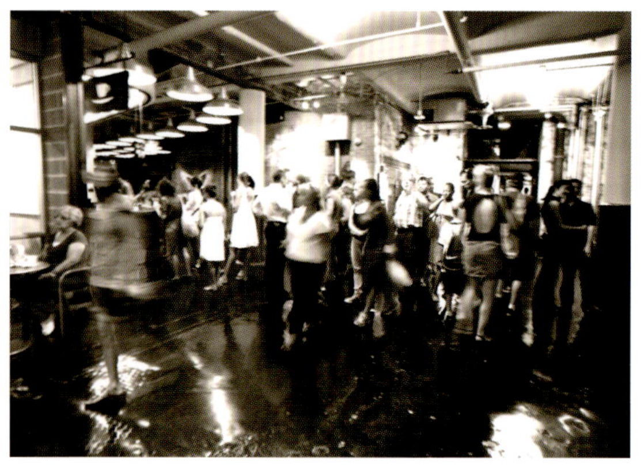
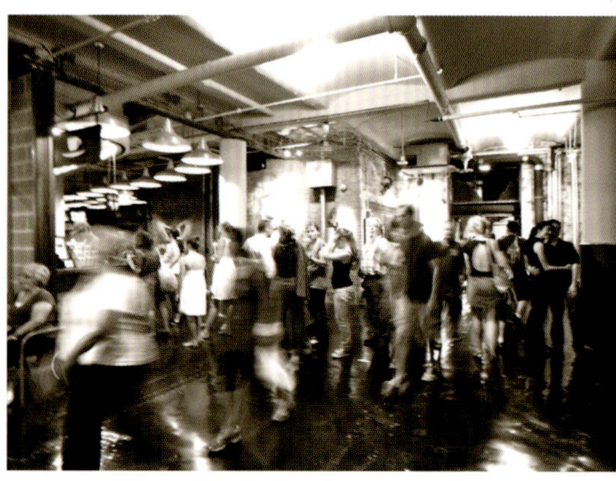
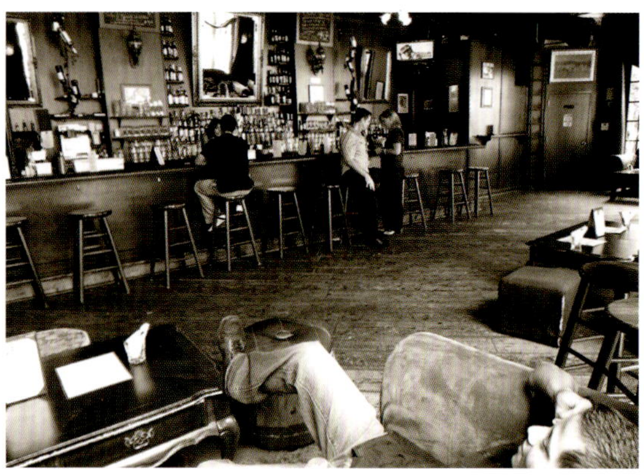
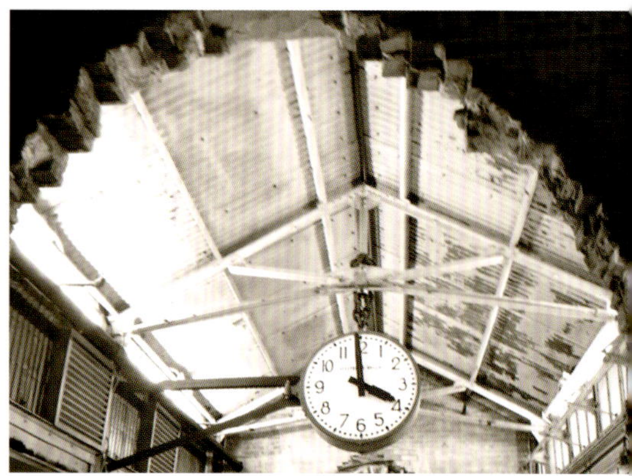

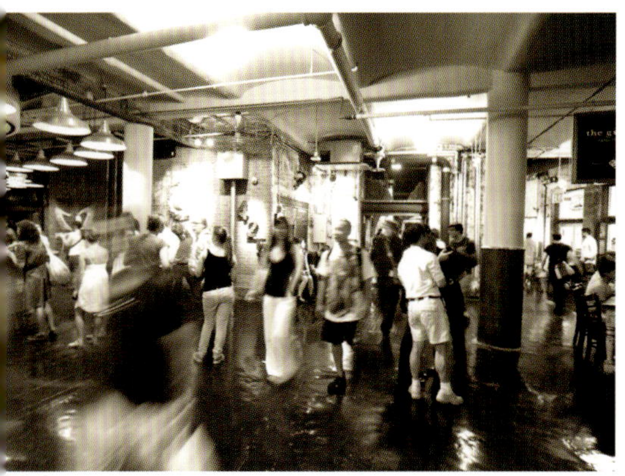 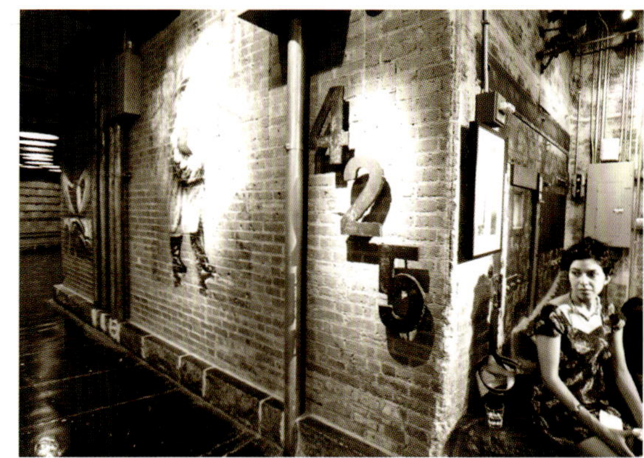

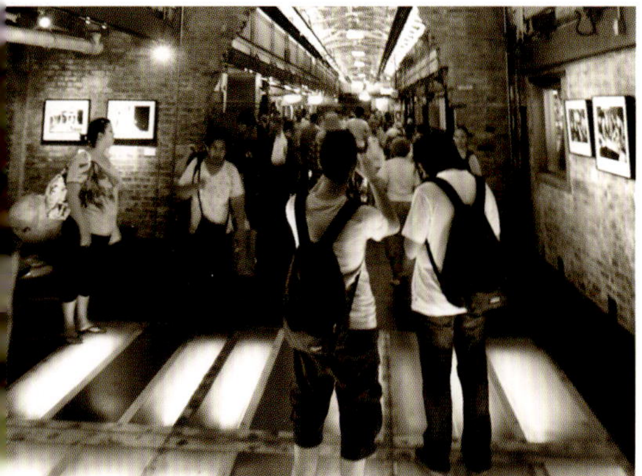 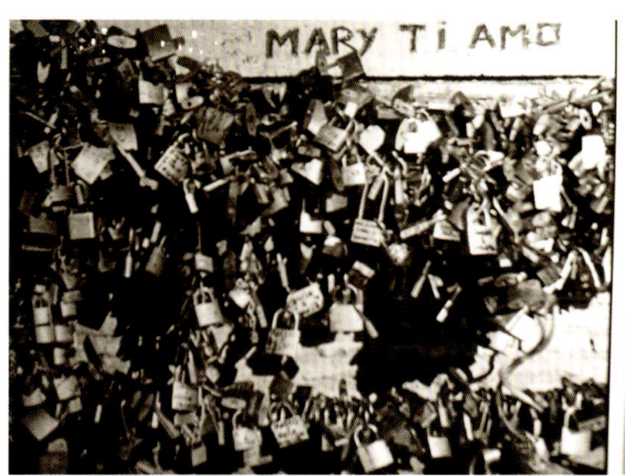

WALK IN THE MIDDLE

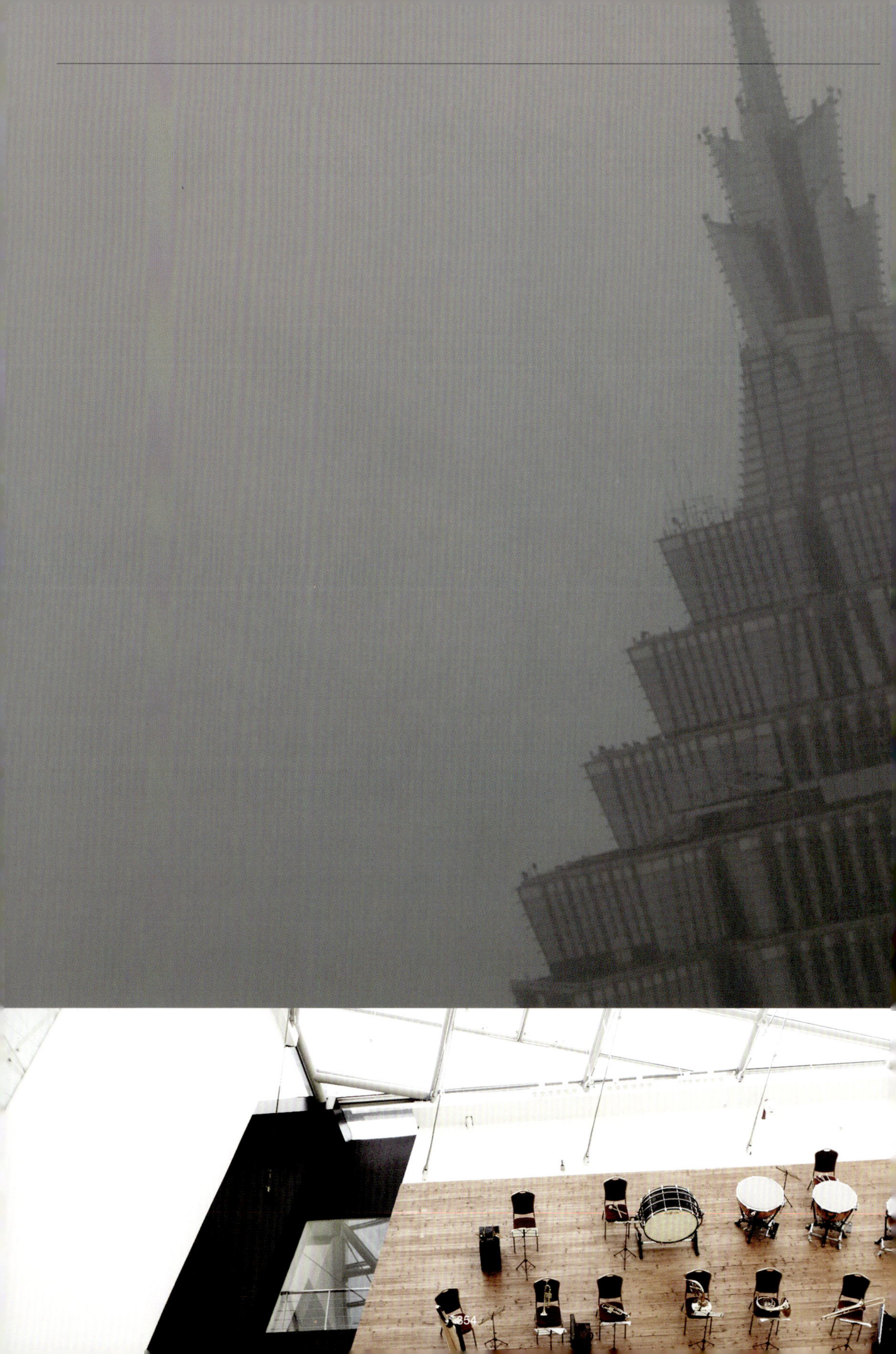

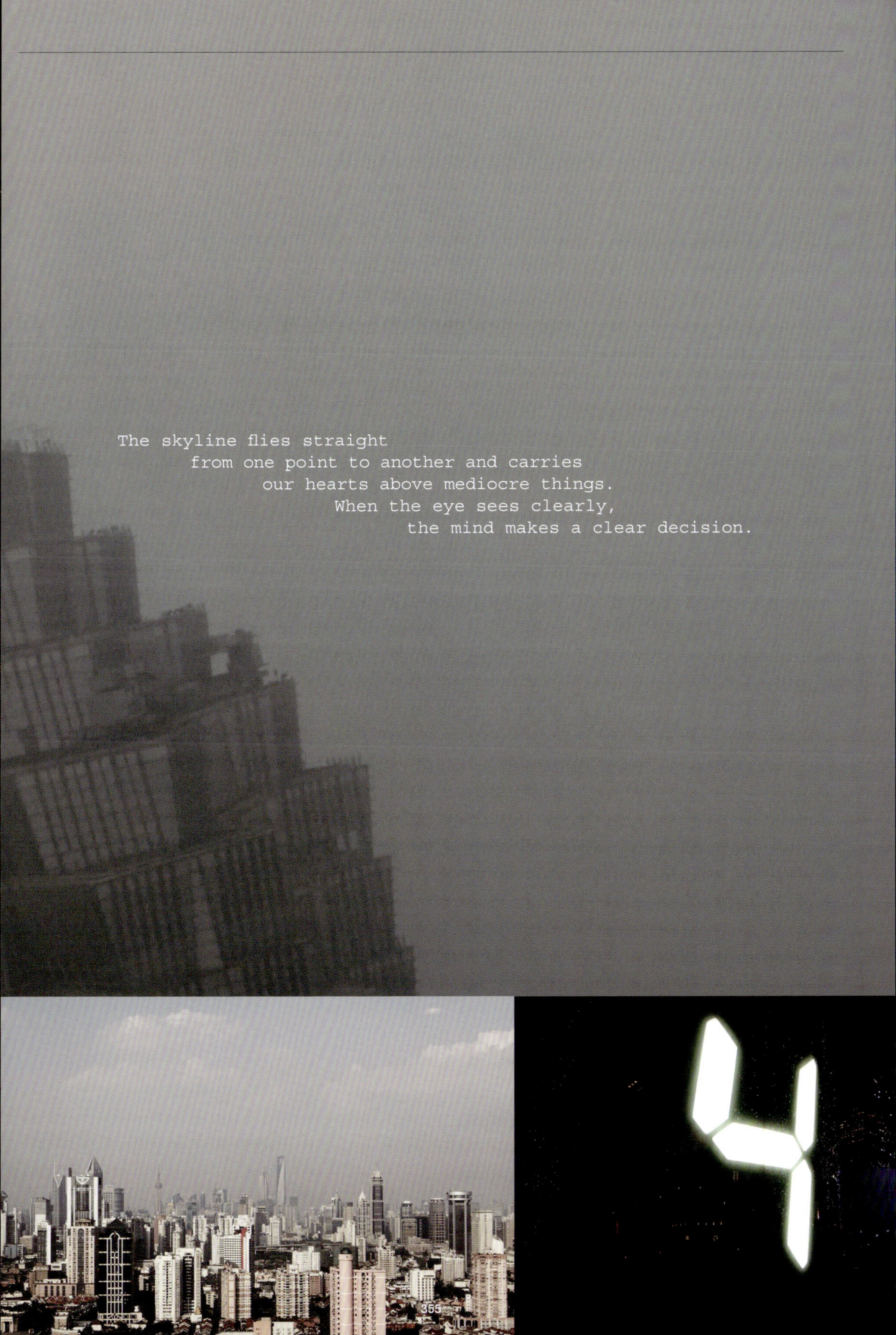
The skyline flies straight
from one point to another and carries
our hearts above mediocre things.
When the eye sees clearly,
the mind makes a clear decision.

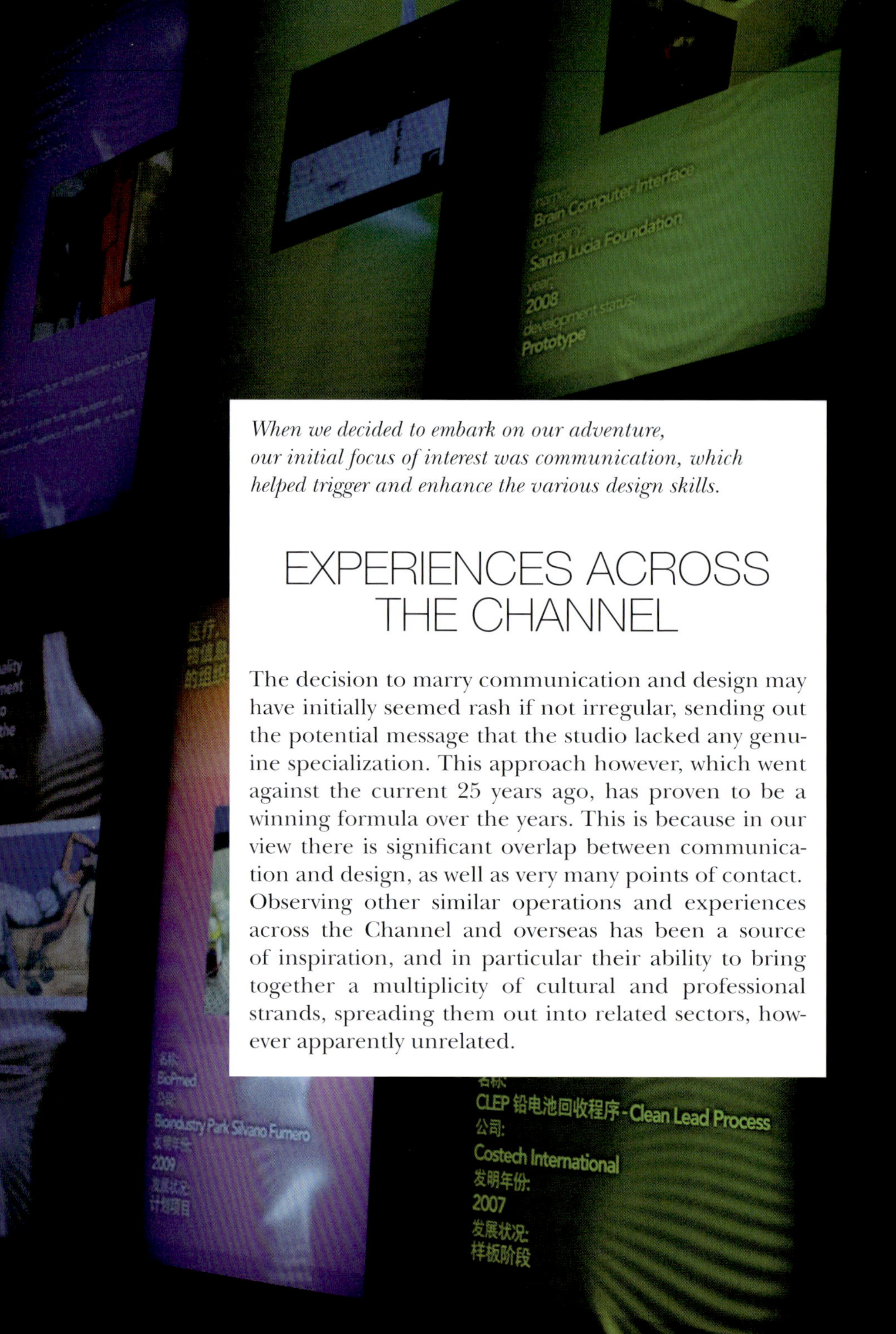

When we decided to embark on our adventure, our initial focus of interest was communication, which helped trigger and enhance the various design skills.

EXPERIENCES ACROSS THE CHANNEL

The decision to marry communication and design may have initially seemed rash if not irregular, sending out the potential message that the studio lacked any genuine specialization. This approach however, which went against the current 25 years ago, has proven to be a winning formula over the years. This is because in our view there is significant overlap between communication and design, as well as very many points of contact. Observing other similar operations and experiences across the Channel and overseas has been a source of inspiration, and in particular their ability to bring together a multiplicity of cultural and professional strands, spreading them out into related sectors, however apparently unrelated.

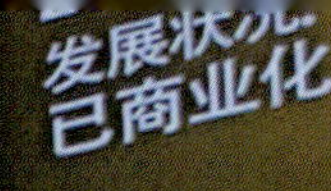

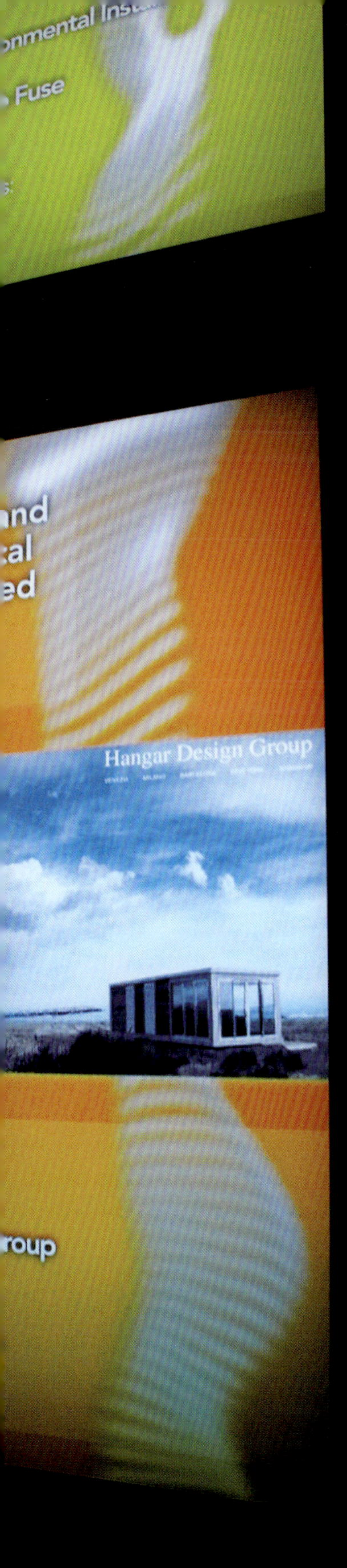

Automatic
recording of
workers in
attendance in
a construction
site.

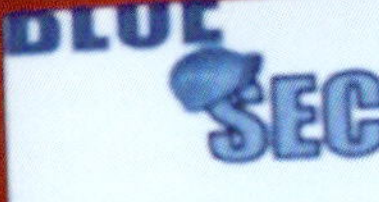

name:
Bluesec
company:
Lavazzi.it
year:
2009
development status:
Marketed

Has been in my life **ON** *and* **OFF** *throughout*

WHAT'S NEXT?

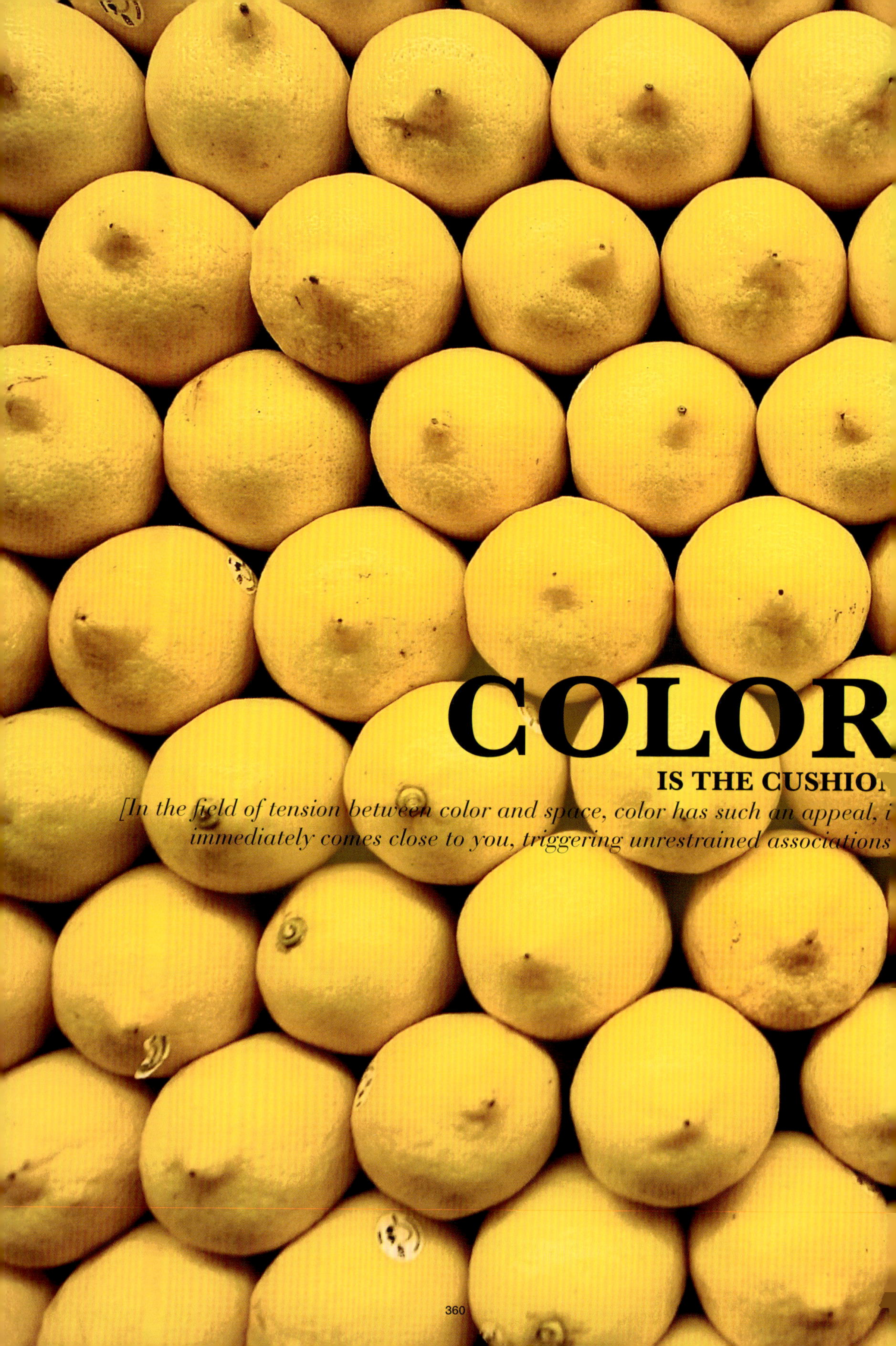

COLOR
IS THE CUSHION
[In the field of tension between color and space, color has such an appeal, i
immediately comes close to you, triggering unrestrained associations

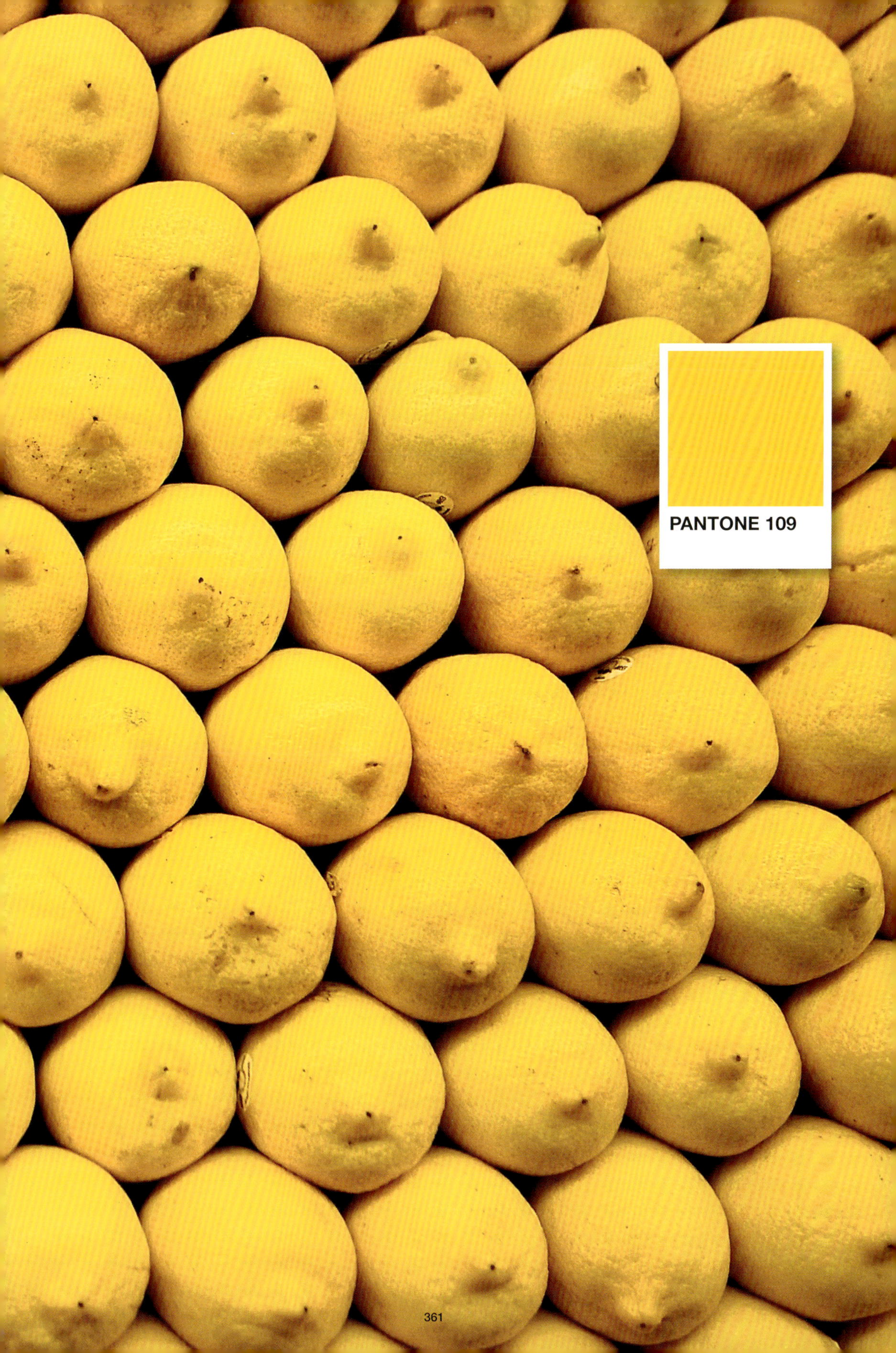
PANTONE 109

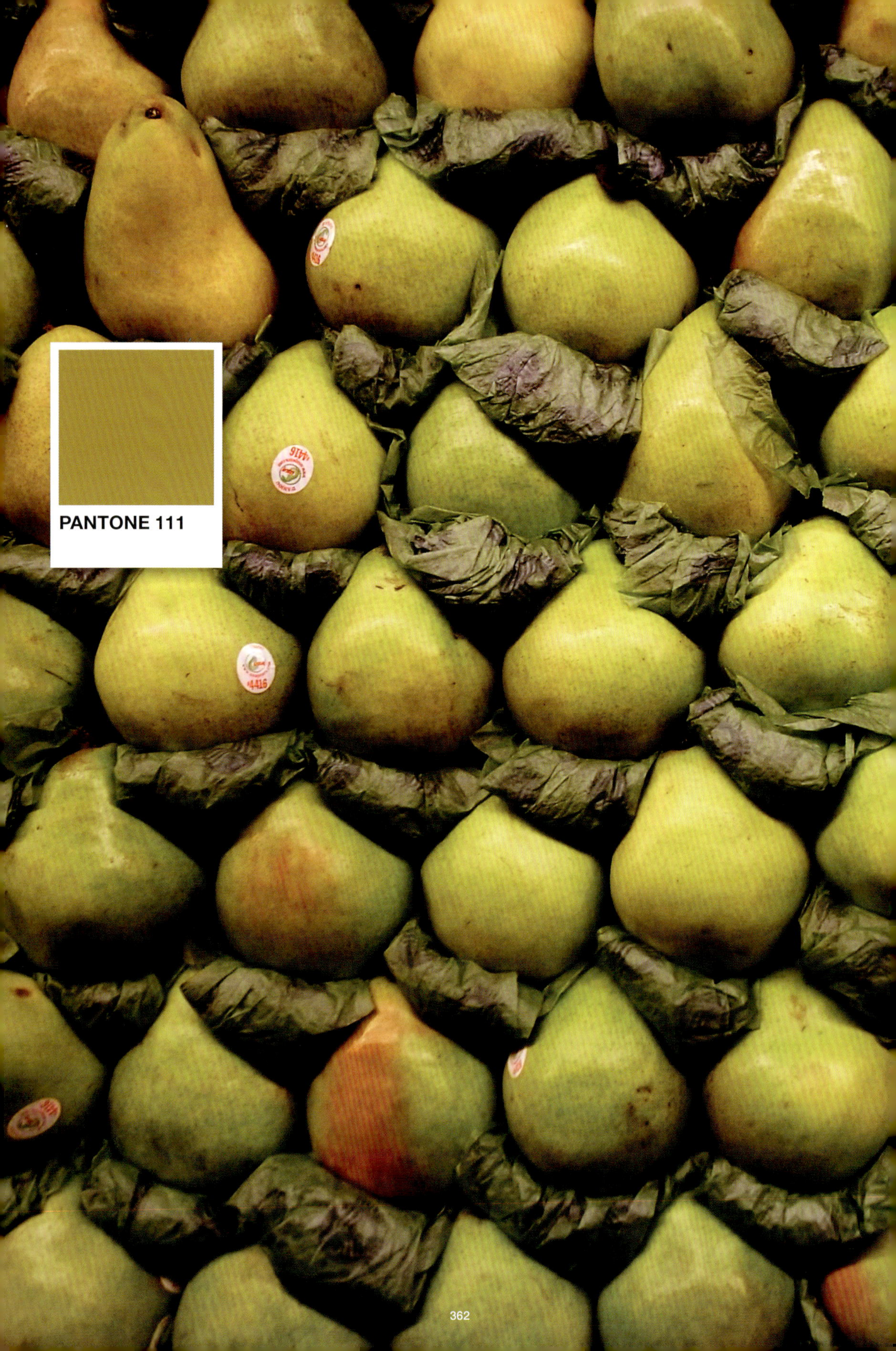
PANTONE 111

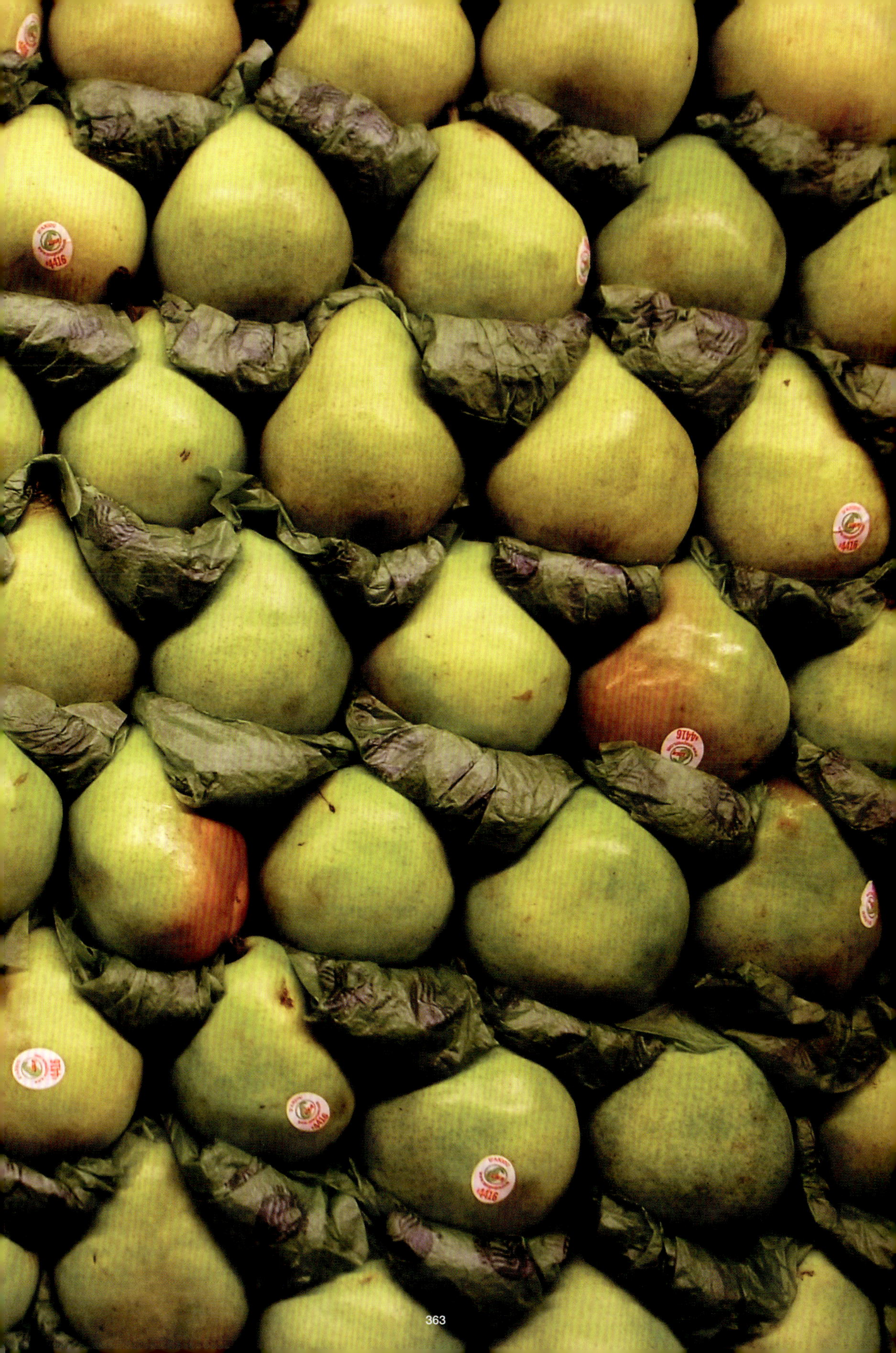

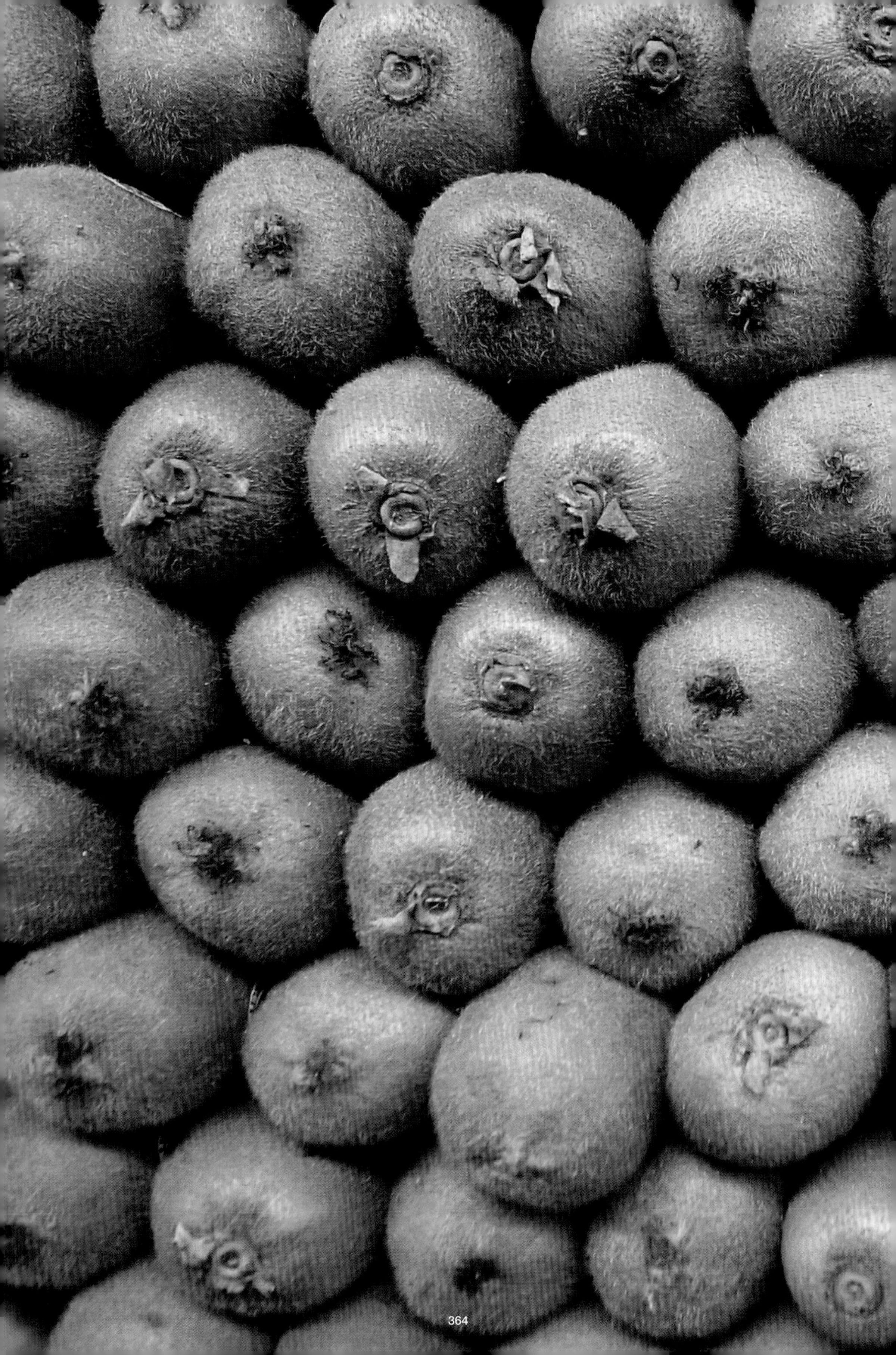

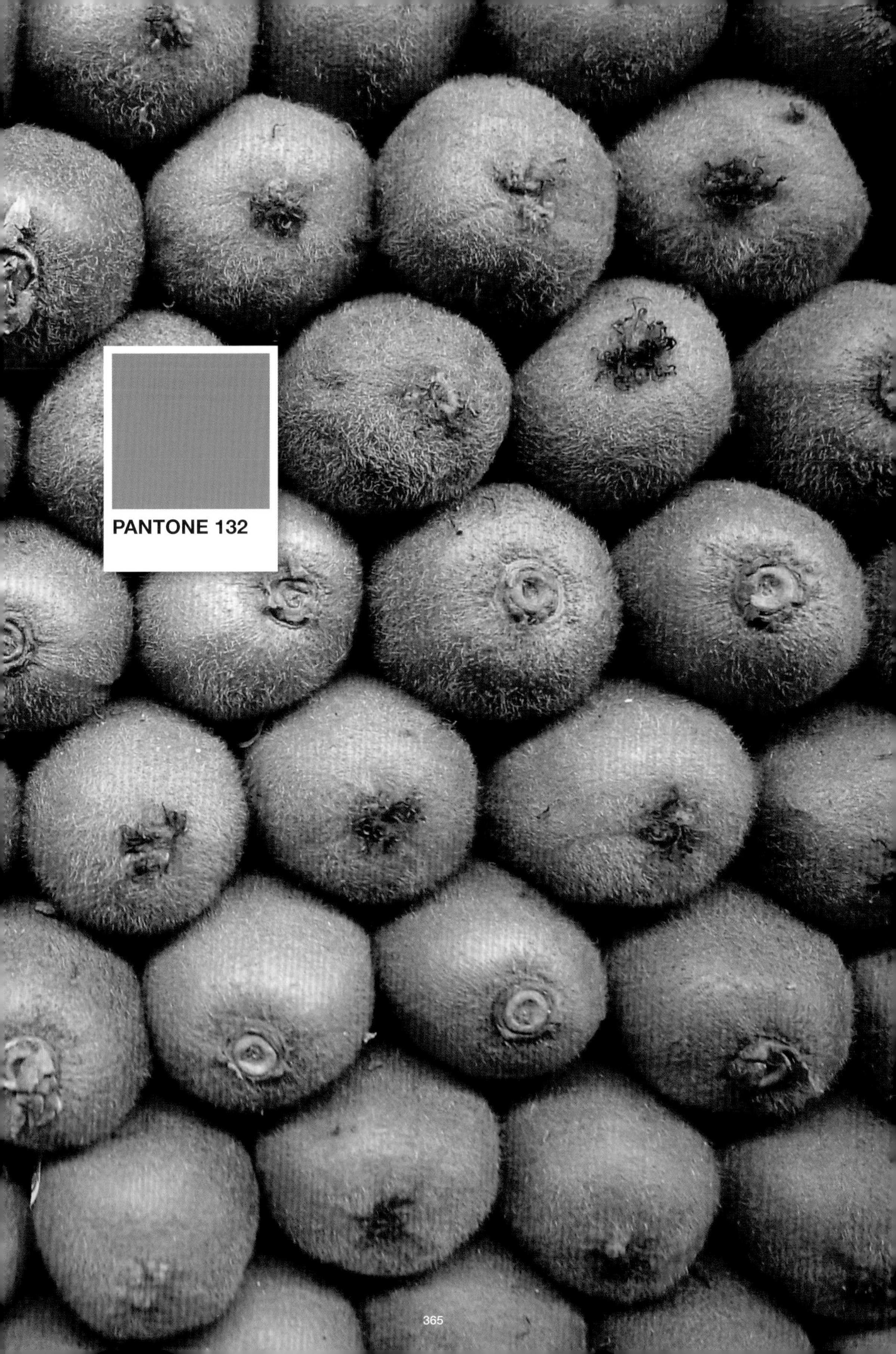

PANTONE 132

nowness

AGES OF STONE, BRONZE AND IRON LINK THE
MATERIALITY OF OBJECTS IN A DIRECT AND
PHYSICAL WAY – REACH OUT AND YOU CAN TOUCH IT.
BUT THINGS, AS THEY SAY, AREN'T USED TO BE.
IN A DIGITAL AGE, THE MARRIAGE BETWEEN
THE THINGS WE MAKE AND THE TECHNOLOGY
WE USE TO MAKE THEM IS CONSUMMATED
SO COMPLETELY THAT ONE BECOMES
INDISTINGUISHABLE FROM THE OTHER.

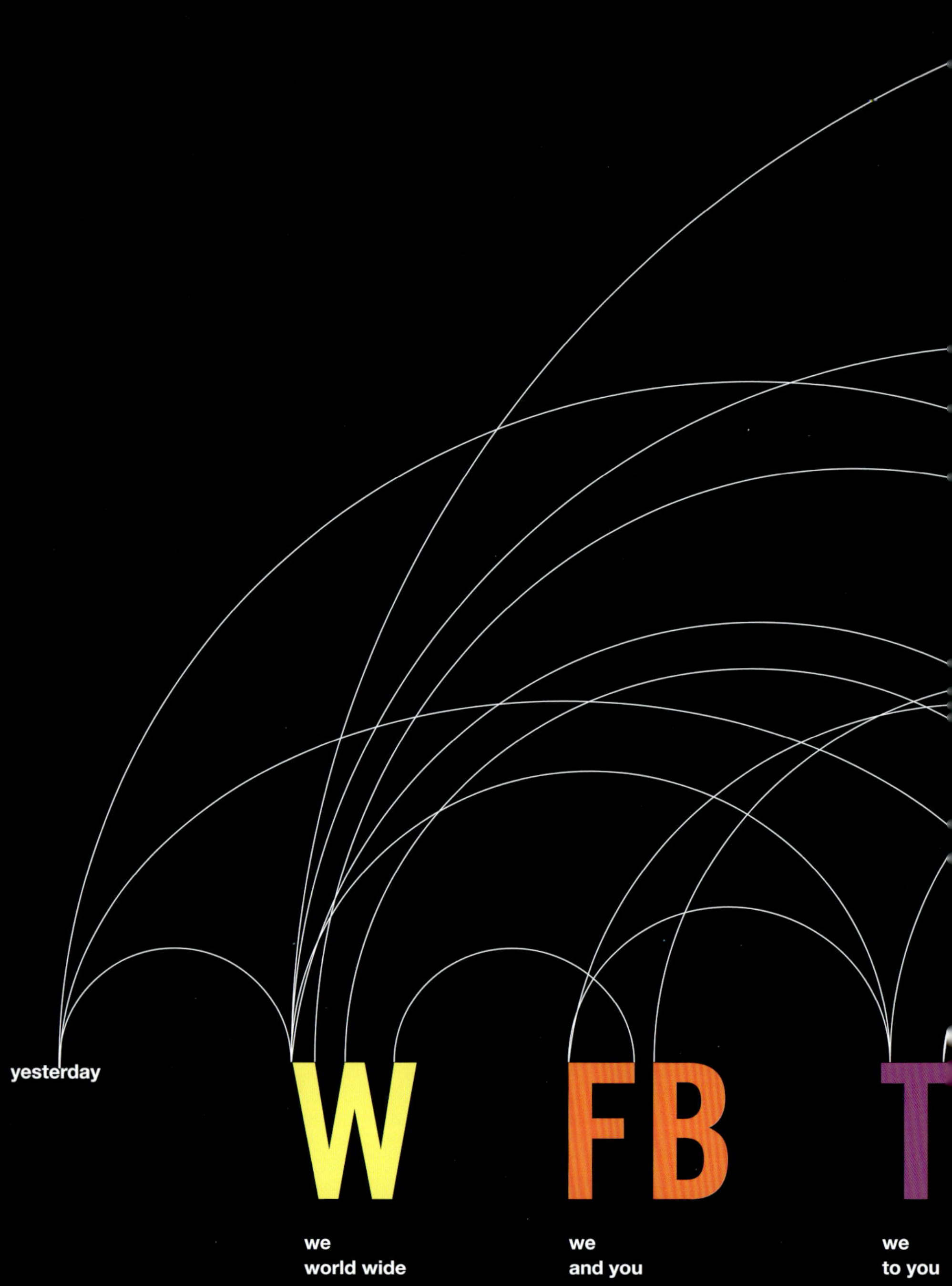

yesterday
W
FB
T
we
world wide
website
we
and you
facebook
we
to you
twitter

I WANT TO BE EVERYWHERE, WITH EVERYBODY, ALWAYS

Suddenly sharing has become what we do. I share, therefore I am. We could call it social creativity: turning barriers into opportunities for spreading content. So, what does all this mean for creativity in our new hyper-connected world? A world where everyone can create, control and distribute their own content. It's not enough to craft a message that just touches the individual. What we produce today has to be inherently social. Content that begs a reaction and has a clear social interface. Content which encourages playing, participating and passing on. Content which connects people with people as well as people and brands. Content which builds brand communities. For many years we've believed the best work has to have TalkValue. Today we ask our teams to create work with ShareValue. Work that people want to participate in, to play with and to pass on. Content which somehow enhances the credibility or social status of the sender and says something about who they are and who they want to be. Either because it's funny, clever, innovative, emotional, charitable or just plain useful. Content which will appeal to a shared interest group rather than just an individual.

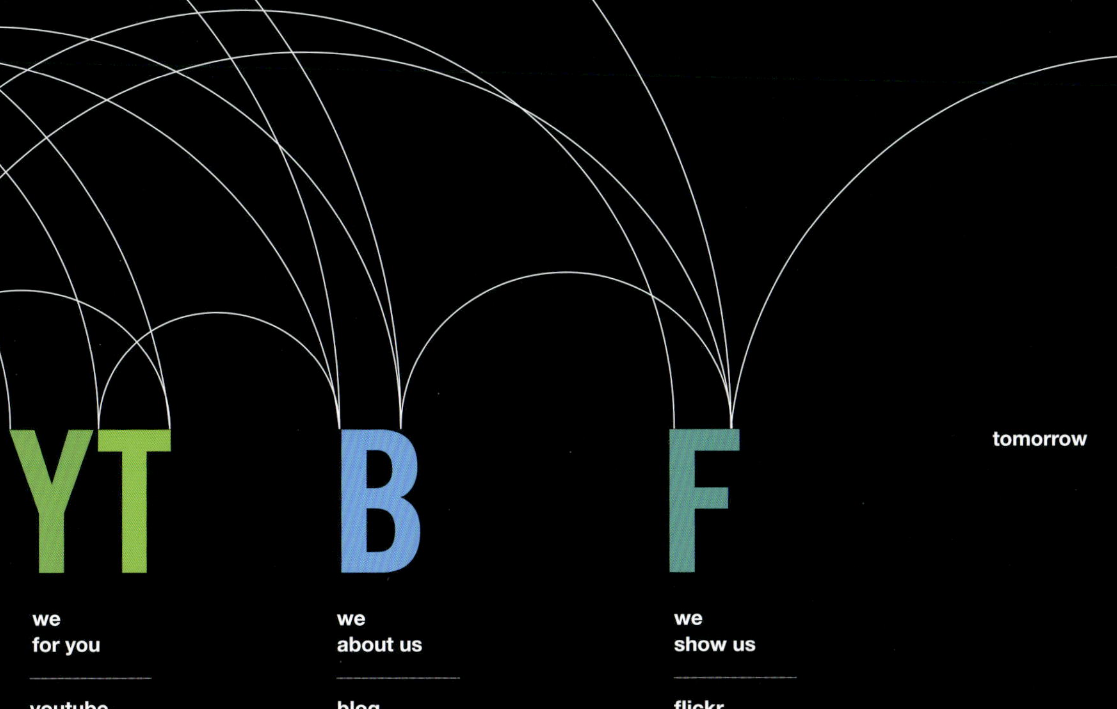

YT

we
for you

youtube

B

we
about us

blog

F

we
show us

flickr

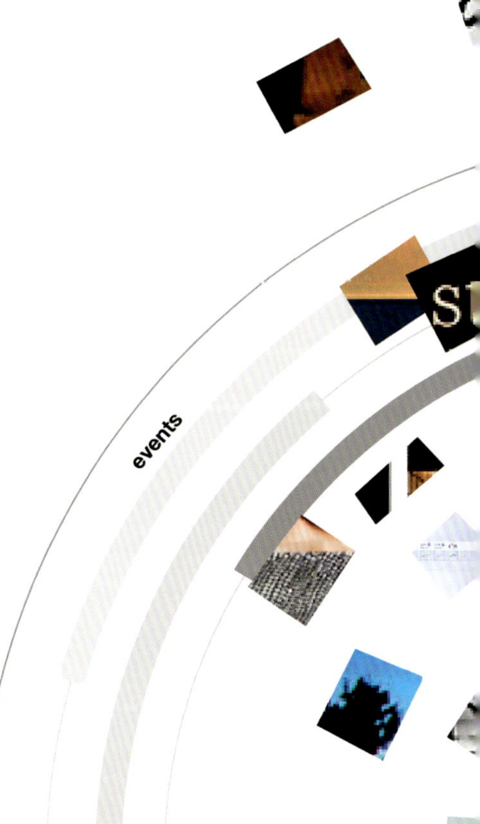

HANGARDESIGNGROUPBLOG.COM/

Categories

* Advertising
* Architecture
* Design
* Editorial Design
* Exhibitions
* Fashion
* Graphics
* In the world
* Inspiration
* Interior
* New Idea
* Packaging
* People
* Photography
* Publications
* Retail
* Travel
* Video
* Websites

Misc

* Awards
* Events

Archives

* gennaio 2011
* dicembre 2010
* novembre 2010
* ottobre 2010
* settembre 2010
* agosto 2010
* luglio 2010
* giugno 2010
* maggio 2010
* aprile 2010

Links

* Hangar Head Office
* Hangar Milano
* Hangar New York
* Hangar Barcelona
* Hangar Shanghai
* Videos
* Facebook
* Youtube
* Twitter
* Flickr
* FriendFeed

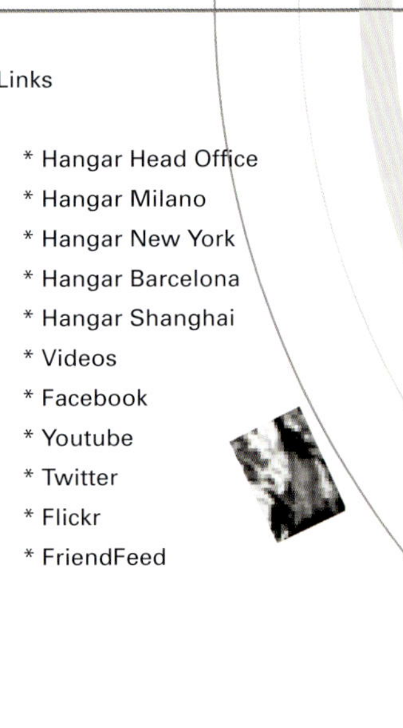

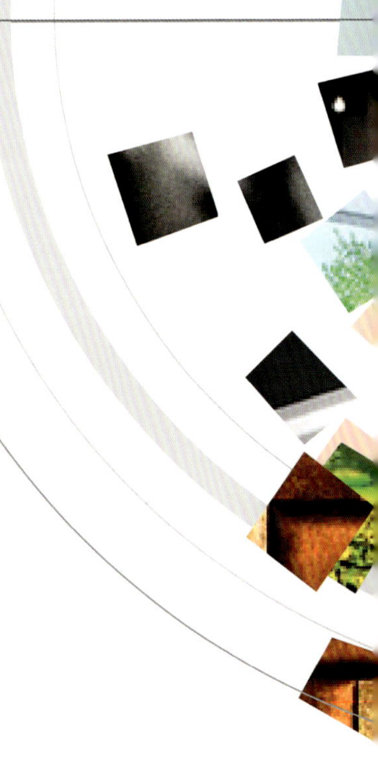

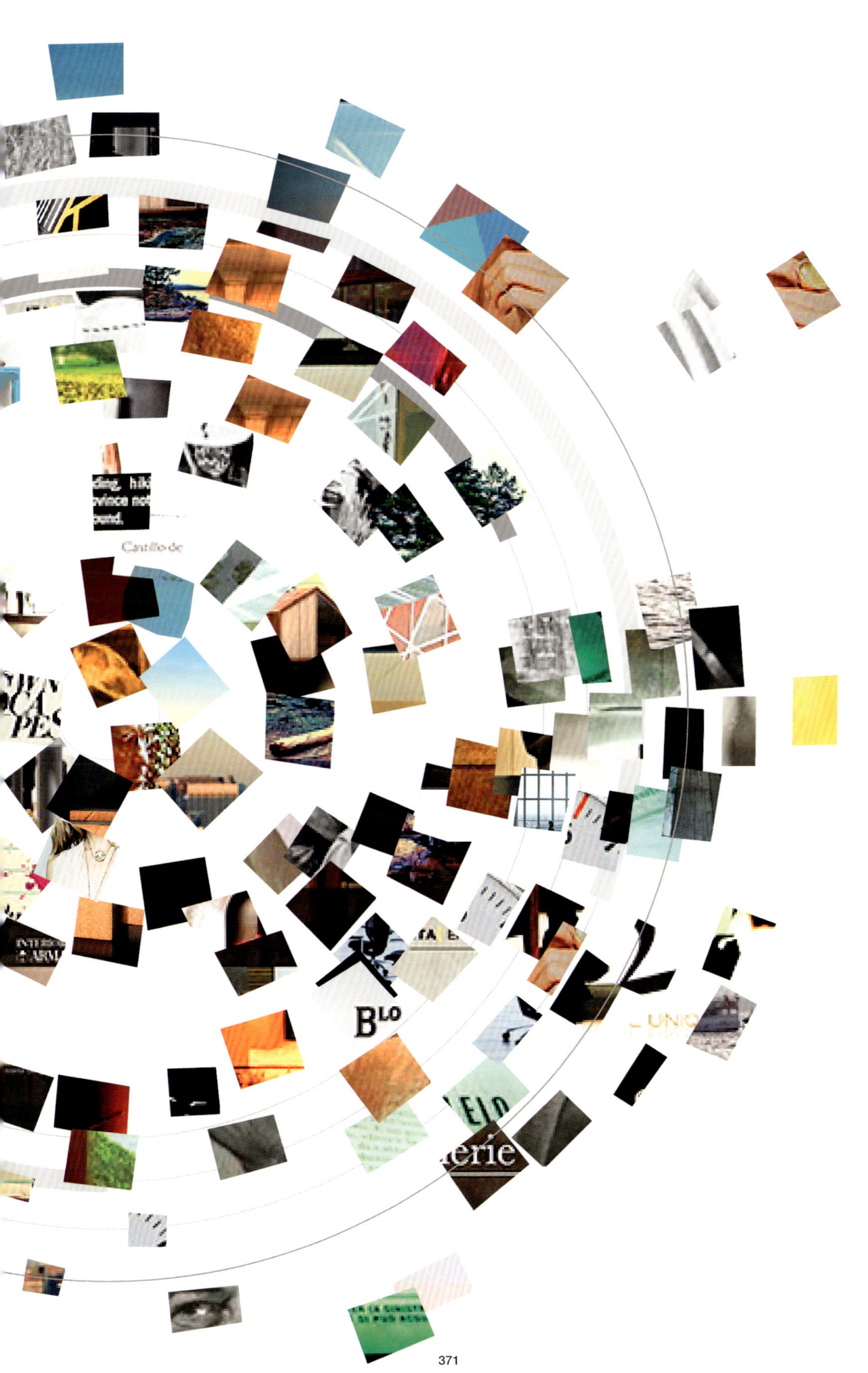

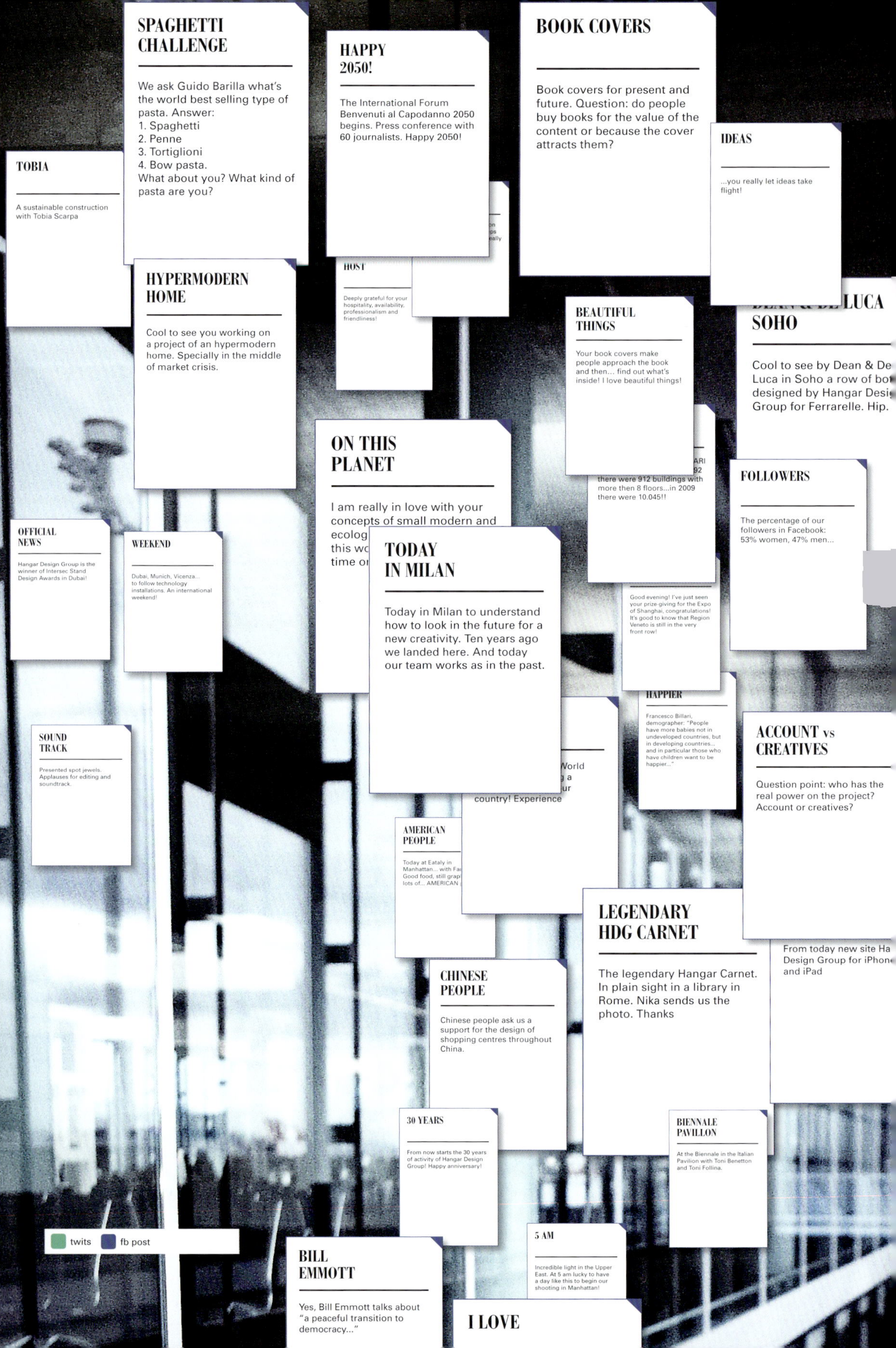

SPAGHETTI CHALLENGE
We ask Guido Barilla what's the world best selling type of pasta. Answer:
1. Spaghetti
2. Penne
3. Tortiglioni
4. Bow pasta.
What about you? What kind of pasta are you?

HAPPY 2050!
The International Forum Benvenuti al Capodanno 2050 begins. Press conference with 60 journalists. Happy 2050!

BOOK COVERS
Book covers for present and future. Question: do people buy books for the value of the content or because the cover attracts them?

IDEAS
...you really let ideas take flight!

TOBIA
A sustainable construction with Tobia Scarpa

HYPERMODERN HOME
Cool to see you working on a project of an hypermodern home. Specially in the middle of market crisis.

HOST
Deeply grateful for your hospitality, availability, professionalism and friendliness!

BEAUTIFUL THINGS
Your book covers make people approach the book and then... find out what's inside! I love beautiful things!

DEAN & DE LUCA SOHO
Cool to see by Dean & De Luca in Soho a row of bot designed by Hangar Desig Group for Ferrarelle. Hip.

ON THIS PLANET
I am really in love with your concepts of small modern and ecolog this wo time o

...ARI ...92 there were 912 buildings with more then 8 floors...in 2009 there were 10.045!!

FOLLOWERS
The percentage of our followers in Facebook: 53% women, 47% men...

OFFICIAL NEWS
Hangar Design Group is the winner of Intersec Stand Design Awards in Dubai!

WEEKEND
Dubai, Munich, Vicenza... to follow technology installations. An international weekend!

TODAY IN MILAN
Today in Milan to understand how to look in the future for a new creativity. Ten years ago we landed here. And today our team works as in the past.

Good evening! I've just seen your prize-giving for the Expo of Shanghai, congratulations! It's good to know that Region Veneto is still in the very front row!

HAPPIER
Francesco Billari, demographer: "People have more babies not in undeveloped countries, but in developing countries... and in particular those who have children want to be happier..."

ACCOUNT vs CREATIVES
Question point: who has the real power on the project? Account or creatives?

SOUND TRACK
Presented spot jewels. Applauses for editing and soundtrack.

World g a ur country! Experience

AMERICAN PEOPLE
Today at Eataly in Manhattan... with Fa Good food, still grap lots of... AMERICAN

LEGENDARY HDG CARNET
The legendary Hangar Carnet. In plain sight in a library in Rome. Nika sends us the photo. Thanks

From today new site Ha Design Group for iPhone and iPad

CHINESE PEOPLE
Chinese people ask us a support for the design of shopping centres throughout China.

30 YEARS
From now starts the 30 years of activity of Hangar Design Group! Happy anniversary!

BIENNALE PAVILLON
At the Biennale in the Italian Pavilion with Toni Benetton and Toni Follina.

twits   fb post

BILL EMMOTT
Yes, Bill Emmott talks about "a peaceful transition to democracy..."

5 AM
Incredible light in the Upper East. At 5 am lucky to have a day like this to begin our shooting in Manhattan!

I LOVE

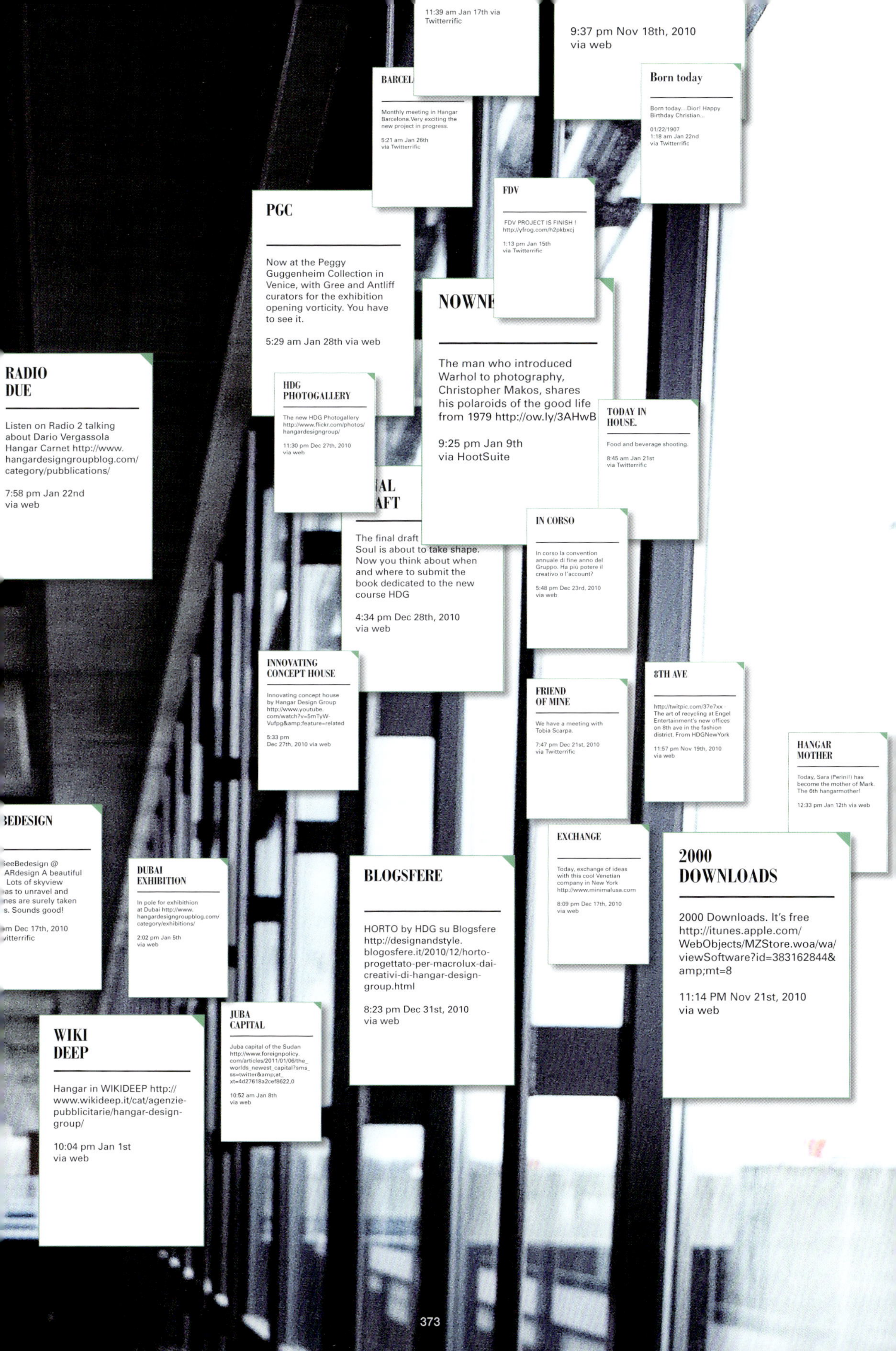

11:39 am Jan 17th via Twitterrific

9:37 pm Nov 18th, 2010 via web

BARCEL
Monthly meeting in Hangar Barcelona.Very exciting the new project in progress.
5:21 am Jan 26th via Twitterrific

Born today
Born today....Dior! Happy Birthday Christian...
01/22/1907
1:18 am Jan 22nd via Twitterrific

PGC
Now at the Peggy Guggenheim Collection in Venice, with Gree and Antliff curators for the exhibition opening vorticity. You have to see it.
5:29 am Jan 28th via web

FDV
FDV PROJECT IS FINISH !
http://yfrog.com/h2pkbxcj
1:13 pm Jan 15th via Twitterrific

NOWNE
The man who introduced Warhol to photography, Christopher Makos, shares his polaroids of the good life from 1979 http://ow.ly/3AHwB
9:25 pm Jan 9th via HootSuite

RADIO DUE
Listen on Radio 2 talking about Dario Vergassola Hangar Carnet http://www.hangardesigngroupblog.com/category/pubblications/
7:58 pm Jan 22nd via web

HDG PHOTOGALLERY
The new HDG Photogallery http://www.flickr.com/photos/hangardesigngroup/
11:30 pm Dec 27th, 2010 via web

TODAY IN HOUSE.
Food and beverage shooting.
8:45 am Jan 21st via Twitterrific

IAL AFT
The final draft Soul is about to take shape. Now you think about when and where to submit the book dedicated to the new course HDG
4:34 pm Dec 28th, 2010 via web

IN CORSO
In corso la convention annuale di fine anno del Gruppo. Ha piu potere il creativo o l'account?
5:48 pm Dec 23rd, 2010 via web

INNOVATING CONCEPT HOUSE
Innovating concept house by Hangar Design Group http://www.youtube.com/watch?v=5mTyW-Vufpg&feature=related
5:33 pm Dec 27th, 2010 via web

8TH AVE
http://twitpic.com/37e7xx - The art of recycling at Engel Entertainment's new offices on 8th ave in the fashion district. From HDGNewYork
11:57 pm Nov 19th, 2010 via web

FRIEND OF MINE
We have a meeting with Tobia Scarpa.
7:47 pm Dec 21st, 2010 via Twitterrific

HANGAR MOTHER
Today, Sara (Perini!) has become the mother of Mark. The 6th hangarmother!
12:33 pm Jan 12th via web

BEDESIGN
SeeBedesign @ ARdesign A beautiful Lots of skyview as to unravel and nes are surely taken s. Sounds good!
m Dec 17th, 2010 witterrific

DUBAI EXHIBITION
In pole for exhibithion at Dubai http://www.hangardesigngroupblog.com/category/exhibitions/
2:02 pm Jan 5th via web

BLOGSFERE
HORTO by HDG su Blogsfere http://designandstyle.blogosfere.it/2010/12/horto-progettato-per-macrolux-dai-creativi-di-hangar-design-group.html
8:23 pm Dec 31st, 2010 via web

EXCHANGE
Today, exchange of ideas with this cool Venetian company in New York http://www.minimalusa.com
8:09 pm Dec 17th, 2010 via web

2000 DOWNLOADS
2000 Downloads. It's free http://itunes.apple.com/WebObjects/MZStore.woa/wa/viewSoftware?id=383162844&mt=8
11:14 PM Nov 21st, 2010 via web

WIKI DEEP
Hangar in WIKIDEEP http://www.wikideep.it/cat/agenzie-pubblicitarie/hangar-design-group/
10:04 pm Jan 1st via web

JUBA CAPITAL
Juba capital of the Sudan http://www.foreignpolicy.com/articles/2011/01/06/the_worlds_newest_capital?sms_ss=twitter&at_xt=4d27618a2cef8622,0
10:52 am Jan 8th via web

A little hotel, with large windows, facing on the wonderful
garden and on the lake Villarica. From the architecture and the
furniture, to the landscape... a beautiful place.
Antonia Astori, Designer, Milan

Facing on the beach, a unique hotel for architectural design and
the coherence in every single detail and furniture element. A
strategic place for your happy hour, to admire the fiery sunset on
the ocean.
Antonia Astori, Designer, Milan

An excellent restaurant, with fresh fish... to enjoy unparalleled
nice dishes.
Matali Crasset, Designer, Paris

The best bread in all Paris is baked here. You can sit at a table
and have a delicious snack.
Matali Crasset, Designer, Paris

An art gallery in the heart of Paris. I love works by Tony Cragg,
Marc Brandenburg, Richard Deacon, Elaine Sturtevant...
Matali Crasset, Designer, Paris

Per il vino vengo qui, dove si può anche pranzare e cenare. Piatti
semplici da gustare tra bottiglie d'annata e i suggerimenti del
proprietario. Consigliato a tutti gli amanti del buon vino.
Matali Crasset, Designer, Paris

Il posto ideale per dedicarsi al relax, fare una passeggiata nella
foresta, dedicarsi al bird-watching e guardare il tramonto.
Matali Crasset, Designer, Paris

Looking down on Doby Gaht in Mumbai is a unique and exciting
experience. The real soul of India. You can't miss it!
Fabrizio Plessi, Videoartist, Venice

The Hotel as a global concept... dedicated to those who are always
traveling, to those who are aware, culturally ahead and with a
global mentality.
Karim Rashid, Designer, New York

For those who - like me - love Dirk Bikkembergs and Martin
Margiela! You can admire them together in this museum dedicated to
fashion, with an insuperable bookshop of art and architecture.
Karim Rashid, Designer, New York

The junior suite is really relaxing, perfect for meditation and
sensually minimalist.
Karim Rashid, Designer, New York

The ideal place where to relax after a day dedicated to shopping
among the streets of Bilbao.
Karim Rashid, Designer, New York

Imagine an exclusive oasis with private beach. Think about the
most modern design, about tennis courts, squash, a fitness room,
Turkish bath with sauna and massage room. You don't have to
dream, a place like this exists and it is in Antalya. Elegance
and refinement, absolute supremacy of the white color, mixed with
vibrating red fire flashes and a mysterious deep black.
Karim Rashid, Designer, New York

Although it's difficult to find, when you reach it you won't regret.
It's a record store of independent music. You can stay there a
full day. Those who live on music know it.
Karim Rashid, Designer, New York

If you love clothes - like me - this is the only way to satisfy
your shopping wishes. There's a bus leaving from Manhattan every
morning at 8.15 and at 10.15!
Karim Rashid, Designer, New York

Pastel of shrimps to begin, "bacalhau" and tripe and for the meat
lovers "cozido à portuguesa". Just in front of the sea.
Álvaro Siza, Architect, Porto

It was the old shooting lodge of the Grand Duke of Tuscany.
Today it's an exclusive hotel in the countryside, surrounded by
vineyards and olive groves, in the heart of Tuscan Maremma. At the
restaurant, in the old barn, you can enjoy good Tuscan dishes,
carefully cooked by Alain Ducasse. In the lodge they produce wine
and oil, both used at the restaurant.
Oliviero Toscani, Photographer, Pisa

The sea. Fresh fish and a kitchen which serves delicious
appetizers: shrimps with ovules and truffles, zucchini flowers
stuffed with ricotta, calamari with beans and hot pepper.
Oliviero Toscani, Photographer, Pisa

CONTENTS

A GUIDE DISPLAYING ROUTES AND PATHS
SUGGESTED BY FIGURES FROM THE DESIGN WORLD

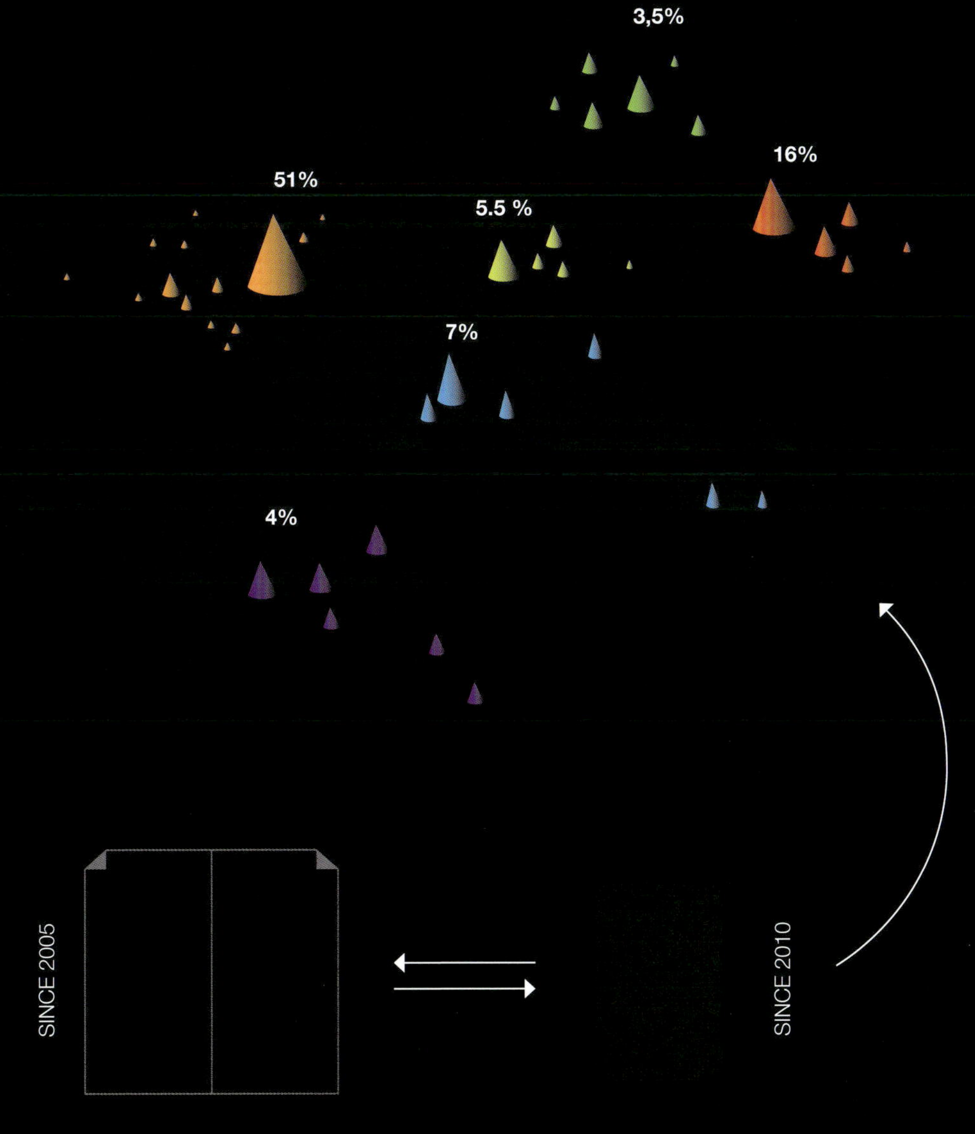

PAPER

Publisher Marsilio
Series Guide
Published 30/09/2009
Pages 24
Language English
EAN9788831798761

DIGITAL APP

Pubblished: 27/07/2010
Version: 1.0
1.0 (iOS 4.0 tested)
Dimension: 4.7 MB
Developer: Hangar Design Group s.r.l.
© 2010 Hangar Design Group

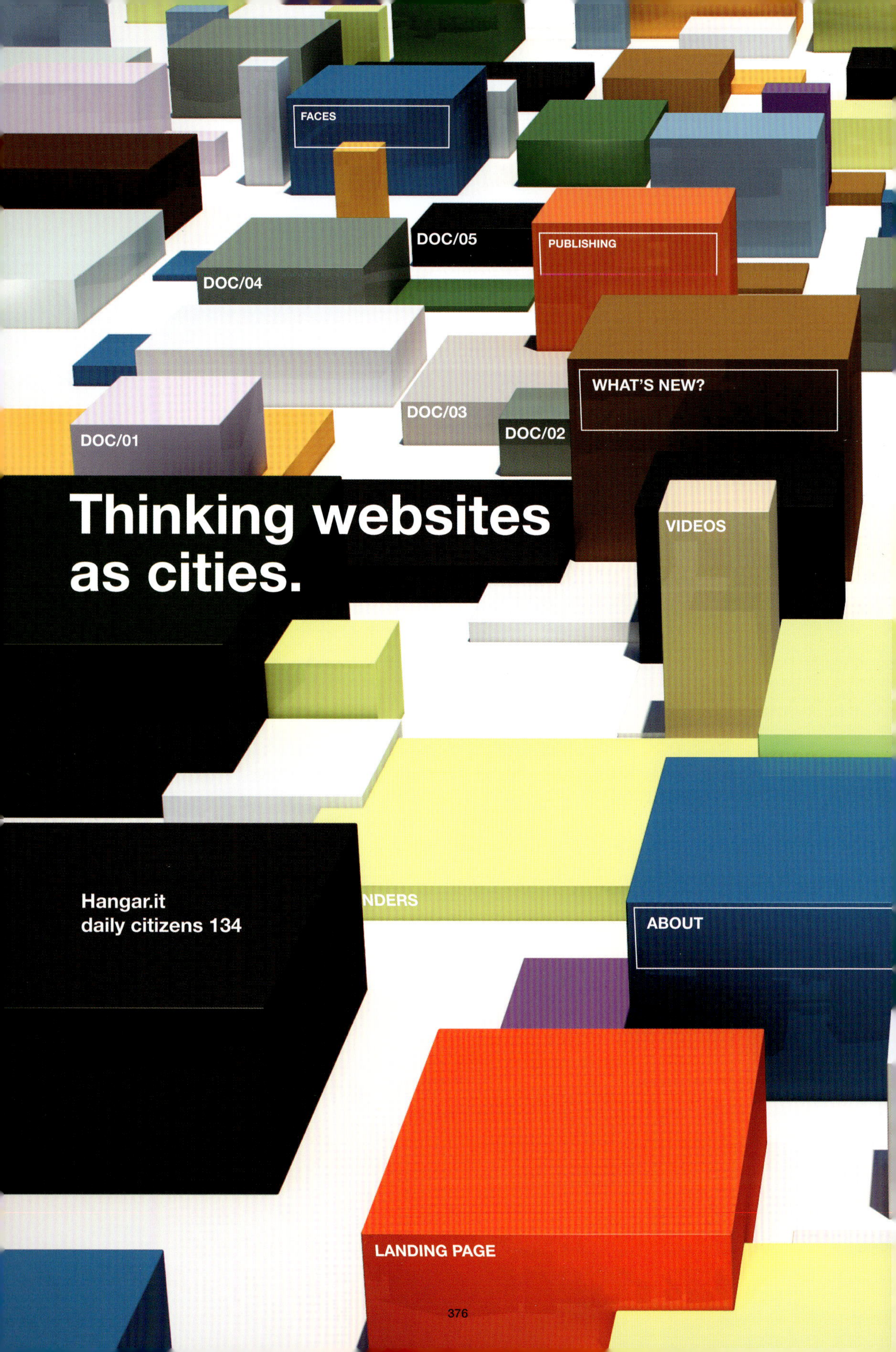

FACES
DOC/05
PUBLISHING
DOC/04
WHAT'S NEW?
DOC/01
DOC/03
DOC/02
Thinking websites as cities.
VIDEOS
Hangar.it
daily citizens 134
NDERS
ABOUT
LANDING PAGE

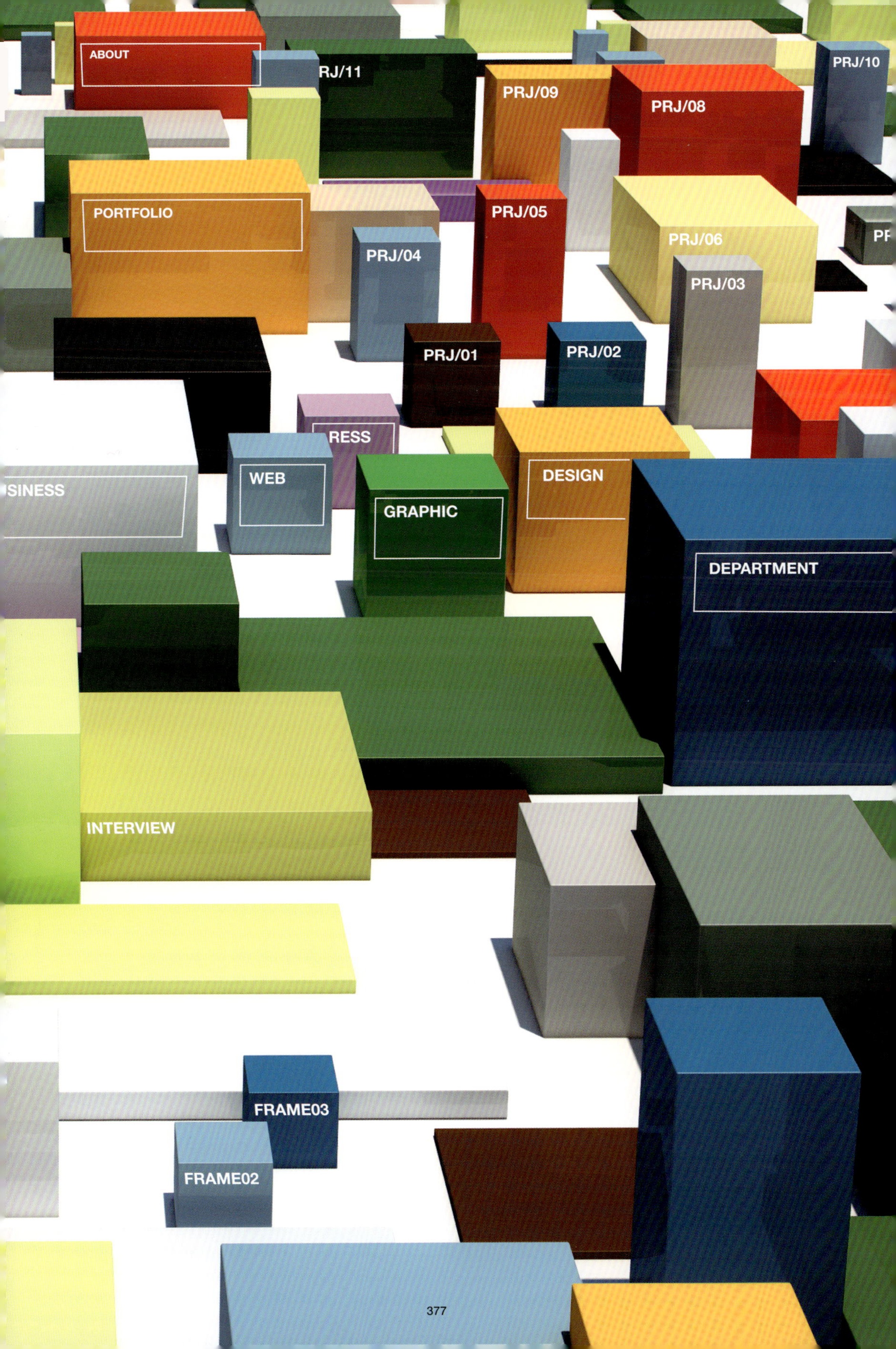

ABOUT
RJ/11
PRJ/09
PRJ/08
PRJ/10
PORTFOLIO
PRJ/05
PRJ/06
PRJ/04
PRJ/03
PRJ/01
PRJ/02
RESS
DESIGN
WEB
SINESS
GRAPHIC
DEPARTMENT
INTERVIEW
FRAME03
FRAME02

Off the Page

(function(E,B){function ka(a,b,d){if(d===B&&a.
nodeType===1){d=a.getAttribute("data-"+b);if(typeof
d==="string"){try{d=d==="true"?true:d==="false"?false:
d==="null"?null:!c.isNaN(d)?parseFloat(d):Ja.test(d)?c.
parseJSON(d):d}catch(e){}c.data(a,b,d)}else d=B}return d}
function U(){return false}function ca(){return true}function
ià(a,b,d){d[0].type=a;return c.event.handle.apply(b,d)}
function Ka(a){var b,d,e,f,h,l,k,o,x,r,A,C=[];f=[];h=c.
data(this,this.nodeType?"events":"__events__");if(typeof
h==="function")h=
h.events;if(!(a.liveFired===this||!h||!h.live||a.button&&a.
type==="click")){if(a.namespace)A=RegExp("(^|\\.)"+a.
namespace.split(".").join("\\.(?:.*\\.)?")+"(\\.|$)");a.
liveFired=this;var J=h.live.slice(0);for(k=0;k<J.
length;k++){h=J[k];h.origType.replace(X,"")===a.type?f.
push(h.selector):J.splice(k--,1)}f=c(a.target).closest(f,a.
currentTarget);o=0;for(x=f.length;o<x;o++){r=f[o];for(k=0;k<J.
length;k++){h=J[k];if(r.selector===h.selector&&(!A||A.test(h.
namespace))){l=r.elem;e=null;if(h.preType==="mouse
h.preType==="mouseleave"){a.type=h.preType;e=c(a.
relatedTarget).closest(h.selector)[0]}if(!e||e!==l)
C.push({elem:l,handleObj:h,level:r.level})}}}
o=0;for(x=C.length;o<x;o++){f=C[o]; if(level>d)
break;a.currentTarget=f.elem;a.dat
data;a.handleObj=f.handleOb
origHandler.apply(f.elem,arg
isPropagationStopped()){d=f.leve
isImmediatePropagationStopped
Y(a,b){return(a&&a!=="*"?a+".":"")+b. (La,
"").replace(Ma,"&")}function ma(a,b,d){if(c.isFunction(b))
return c.grep(a,function(f,h){return!!b.call(f,h,f)===d});else
if(b.nodeType)return c.grep(a,function(f){return
f===b===d});else if(typeof b==="str
grep(a,function(f){return f.nodeTyp
test(b))return c.filter(b,e,!d);else b=   irn
c.grep(a,function(f){return c.inArray(f,b)   =d})}
function na(a,b){var d=0;b.each(function(){if(this.
nodeName===(a[d]&&a[d].nodeName)){var e=c.
data(a[d++]),f=c.data(this,
e);if(e=e&&e.events){delete f.handle;f.events={};for(var
h in e)for(var l in e[h])c.event.add(this,h,e[h][l],e[h][l].
data)}}})}function Oa(a,b){b.src?c.ajax({url:b.src,async:fals
e,dataType:"script"}):c.globalEval(b.text||b.textContent||b.

innerHTML||"");b.parentNode&&b.parentNode.
removeChild(b)}function oa(a,b,d){var e=b==="width"?a.
offsetWidth:a.offsetHeight;if(d==="border")return e;c.each(b
==="width"?Pa:Qa,function(){d||(e-=parseFloat(c.css(a,"paddi
ng"+this))||0);if(d==="margin")e+=parseFloat(c.css(a,
"margin"+this))||0;else e-=parseFloat(c.css(a,"border"
+this+"Width"))||0});return e}function da(a,b,d,e){if(c.
isArray(b)&&b.length)c.each(b,function(f,h){d||Ra.
test(a)?e(a,h):da(a+"["+(typeof h==="object"||c.isArray(h)?f
:"")+"]",h,d,e)});else if(!d&&b!=null&&typeof b==="object")
c.isEmptyObject(b)?e(a,""):c.each(b,function(f,h)
{da(a+"["+f+"]",h,d,e)});else e(a,b)}function S(a,b){var
d={};c.each(pa.concat.apply([],pa.slice(0,b)),function()
{d[this]=a});return d}function qa(a){if(!ea[a]){var b=c("<"+
a+">").appendTo("body"),d=b.css("display");b.
remove();if(d==="none"||d==="")d="block";ea[a]=d}
return ea[a]}function fa(a){return c.isWindow(a)?a:a.
nodeType===9?a.defaultView||a.parentWindow:false}
var t=E.document,c=function(){function a(){if(!b.
isReady){try{t.documentElement.doScroll("left")}catch(j)
{setTimeout(a,1);return}b.ready()}}var b=function(j,s){return
new b.fn.init(j,s)},d=E.jQuery,e=E.$,f,h=/^(?:[^<]*(<[\w\W]+>)
[^>]*$|#([\w\-]+)$)/,l=/\S/,k=/^\s+/,o=/\s+$/,x=/\W/,r=/\
d/,A=/   A1>)?

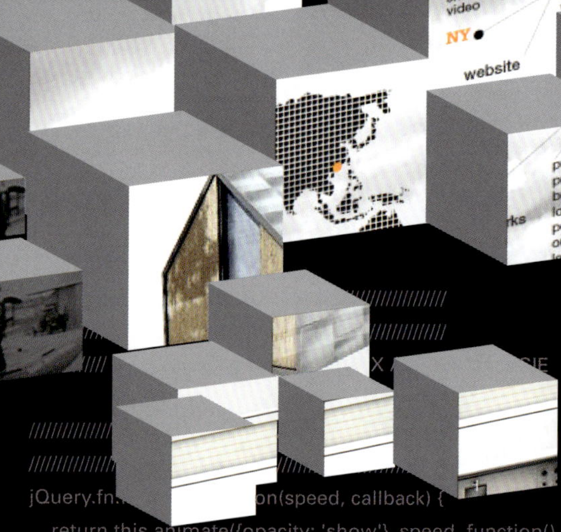

jQuery.fn.   n(speed, callback) {
   return this.animate({opacity: 'show'}, speed, function() {
      if (jQuery.browser.msie)
         this.style.removeAttribute('filter');
      if (jQuery.isFunction(callback)){
         passa = this.id; // passa l'id del div animato
         callback(passa);

///////////// DEFINIZIONE DELLE
FUNZIONI   /////////////

```
//////////////////////////////////////////////////////////////
//////////////////////////////////////////////////////////////
function redirectPage() {
        window.location = linkLocation;

}

function call99(idPassato) {
        $("#"+idPassato).css({ opacity: 0.999 });

}
//////////////////////////////////////////////////////////////
//////////////////////////////////////////////////////////////
//////////////////
DOCUMENT READY
//////////////////
//////////////////////////////////////////////////////////////
//////////////////////////////////////////////////////////////
$(document).ready(function(){


-------------
```

```
<!DOCTYPE html ... //3C//DTD XHTML
1.0 Strict// ...         ?/xhtml1/DTD/
 tml1-str ...
```

...Hangar ... up
group new york,Hangar
i,sandro manente,juan
e,hangar planning,hangar
net,hangar cityguide,hangar
ic design,interior
design,website design,3d house design,logo
design,web site design,house design,house
designs,multi-media design,home design,logo
designs,fashion design,web page design,office
design,web design,professional web design,interior
design,interior design ideas,home designs,industrial
design,graphic design,graphic designer,graphic
designing,
graphic designs,graphic designers,graphic
design jobs,graphic design portfolio,retail stores
design,multimedia design,interactive multimedia,3d
graphics,web graphics">

```
<meta name="description" content="Hangar Design
Group &egrave; un'agenzia di pubblicit&agrave; che
si occupa di comunicazione, design, retail, interior
design, grafica, editoria, press, web, multimedia.">
<meta name="Owner" content="Hangar Design
Group"/>
```

```
<meta name="Author" content="Hangar Design
Group"/>
<meta name="Copyright" content="Hangar Design
Group"/>

<link href="style.css" rel="stylesheet" type="text/css"
media="screen" />
<link rel="apple-touch-icon" href="imgs/apple-touch-
icon.png" />
<script type="text/javascript" src="js/css_browser_
selector.js"></script>
<script type="text/javascript" src="js/jquery-1.4.2.min.
js"></script>
<script type="text/javascript" src="js/jquery.
easing.1.3.min.js"></script>
<script type="text/javascript" src="js/jquery.color.min.
js"></script>
<script type="text/javascript" src="js/
preloadCssImages.jQuery_v5.js"></script>
<!-- Le funzioni vengono richiamate in fondo al
documento
```

... ALYTICS -->
...rification" content="O
... qjqs1QzgcMlj46cdQf6

... ext/javascript">
... aq || [];
... (['_setAccount', 'UA-12072172-1']);
... eview']);

    var ga = ... eateElement('script'); ga.type
= 'text/javascript'; ga.async = true;
    ga.src = ('https:' == document.location.protocol ?
'https://ssl' : 'http://www') + '.google-analytics.com/
ga.js';
    var s = document.getElementsByTagName('script')

```
<div id="lingue_socials">
```

Being anyone living anywhere / Becoming influential overnight

----

an ideal month

www.hangar.it/

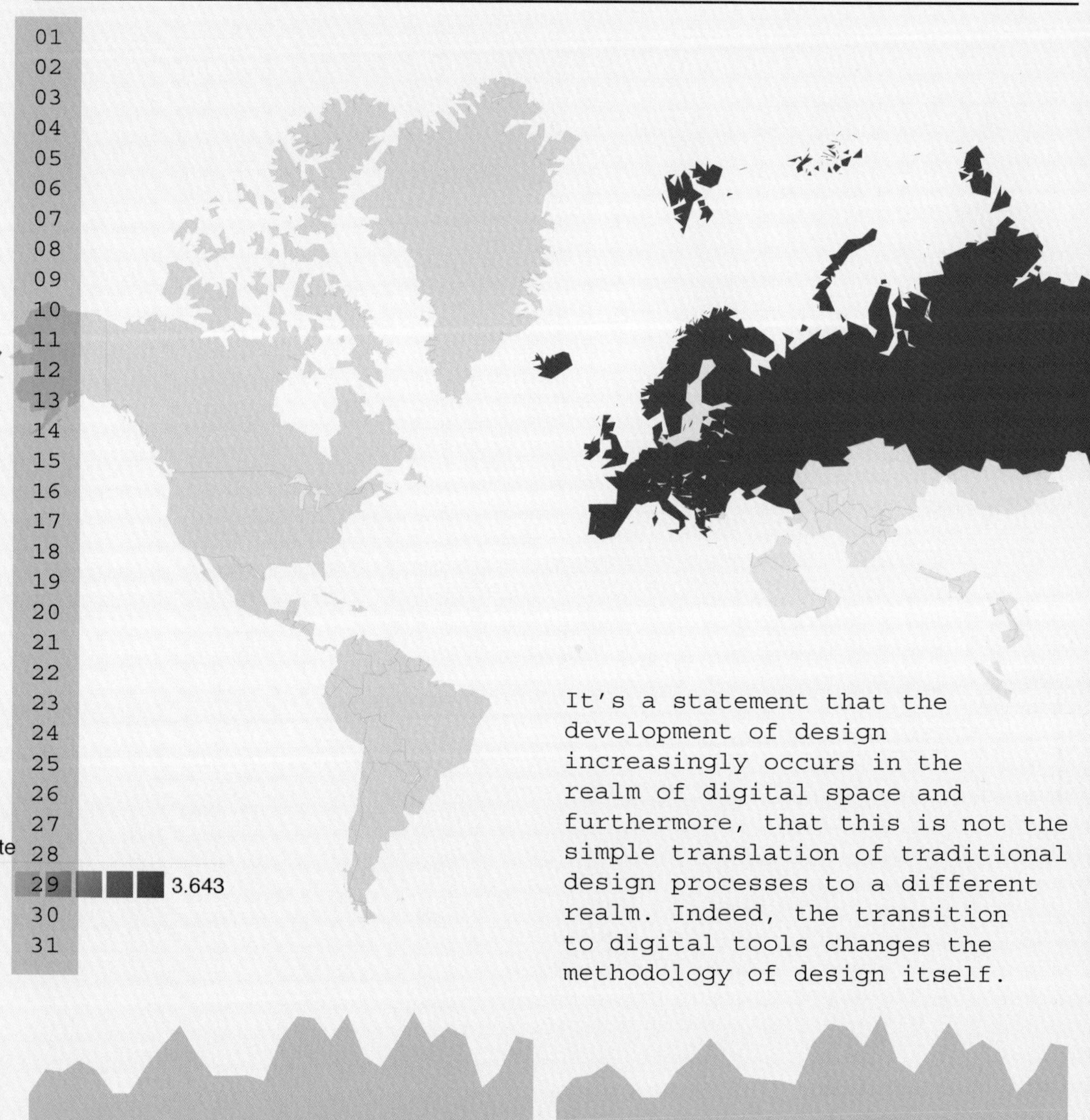

It's a statement that the development of design increasingly occurs in the realm of digital space and furthermore, that this is not the simple translation of traditional design processes to a different realm. Indeed, the transition to digital tools changes the methodology of design itself.

4501 visits

3747 unique visitors

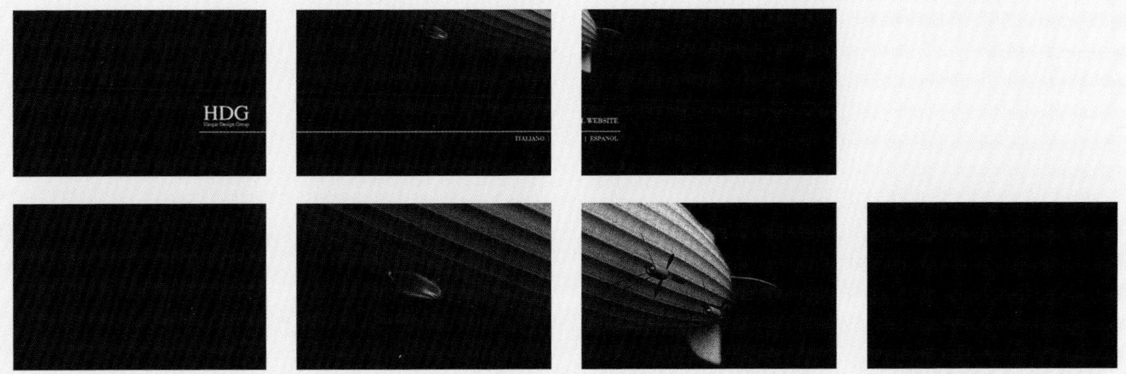

Suddenly we're engaged in a relationship of cause and effect, where what we do or how we behave alters the properties of objects.
And this relationship is now as much part of the activity of design as the shaping of substance.

---

main search key words

hangar design group ---12,42%

hangar design group barcelona

hangar design group mogliano

hdg mogliano

hangar design hong kong

hangar design

hangar design new york

hangar.it

hangar comunicazione

suite home hangar design group

hangar design group casa mobile

video res

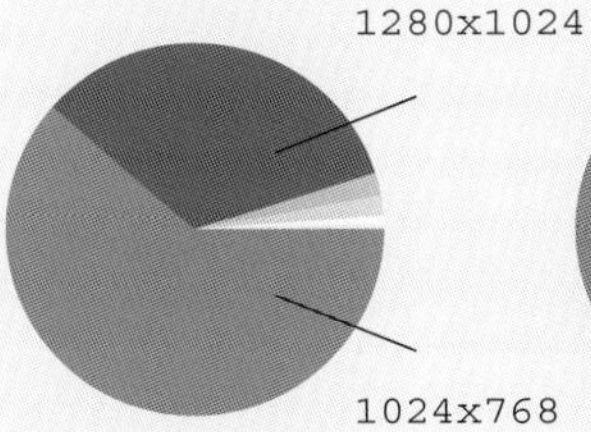

colors

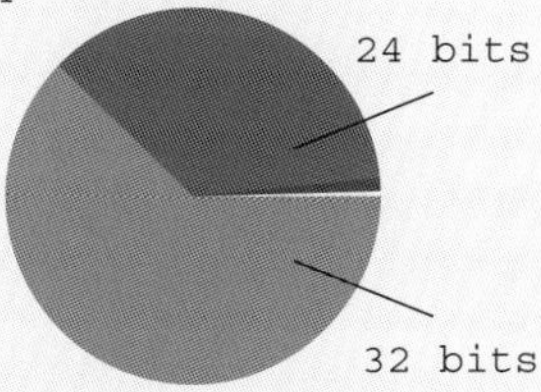

mobile access

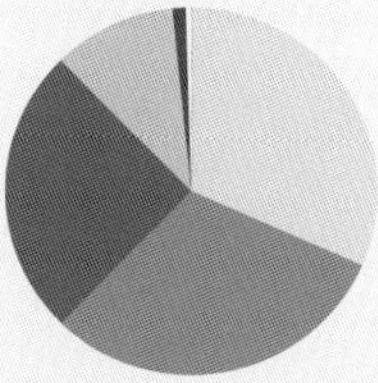

Iphone----42%
iPad------35%
Blackberry
Symbian
Android
Other

/OS/

/Search engine/

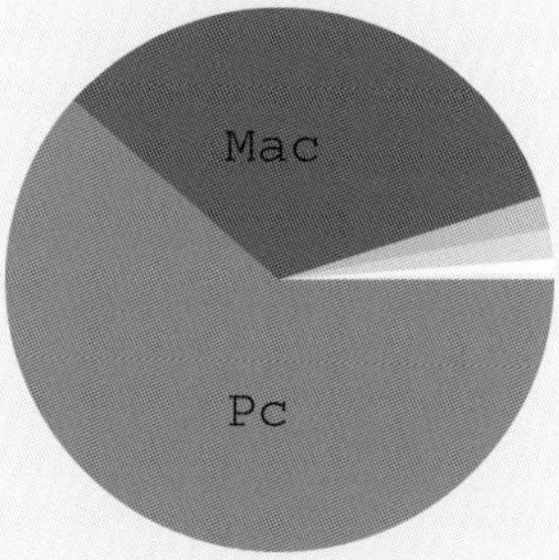

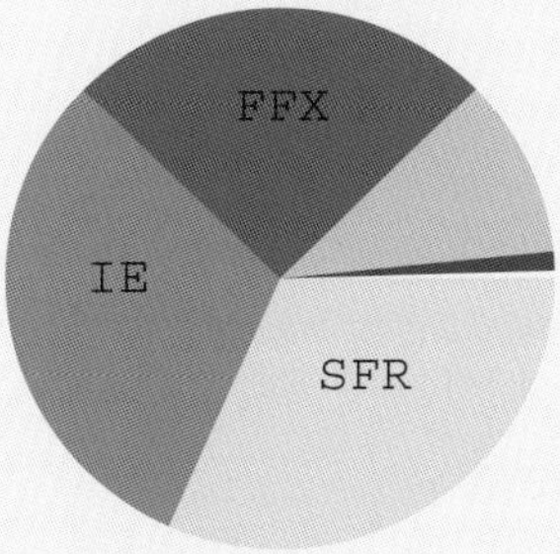

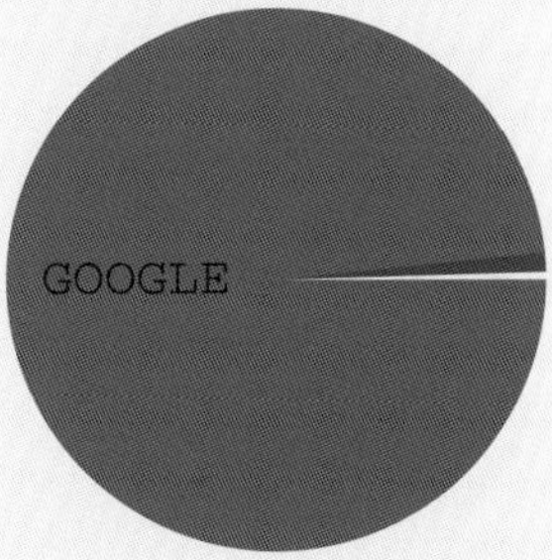

Software specifics

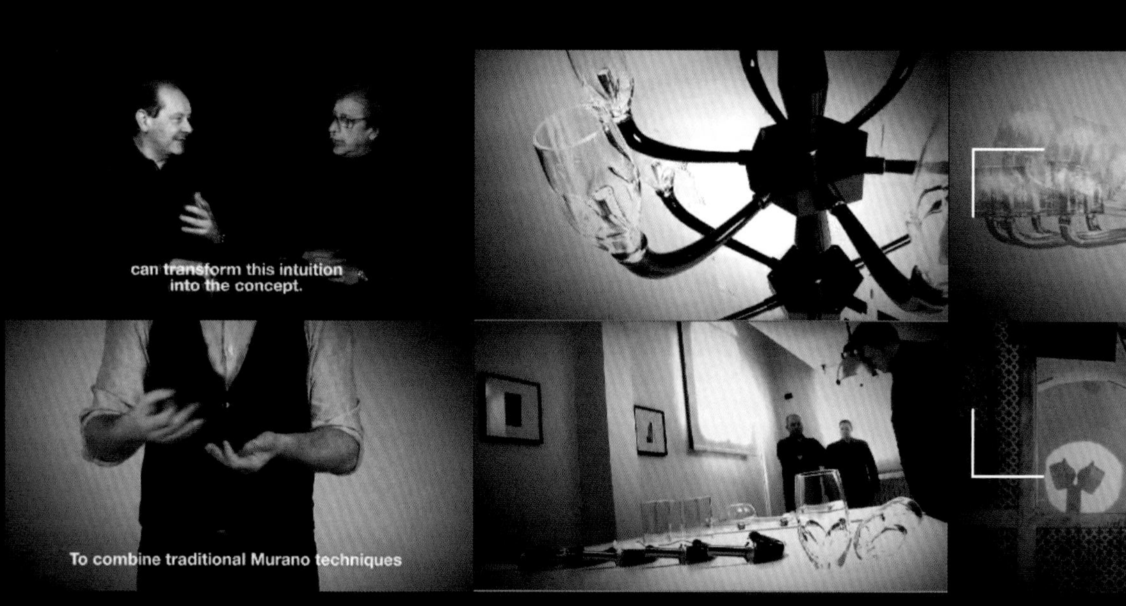
can transform this intuition
into the concept.
To combine traditional Murano techniques

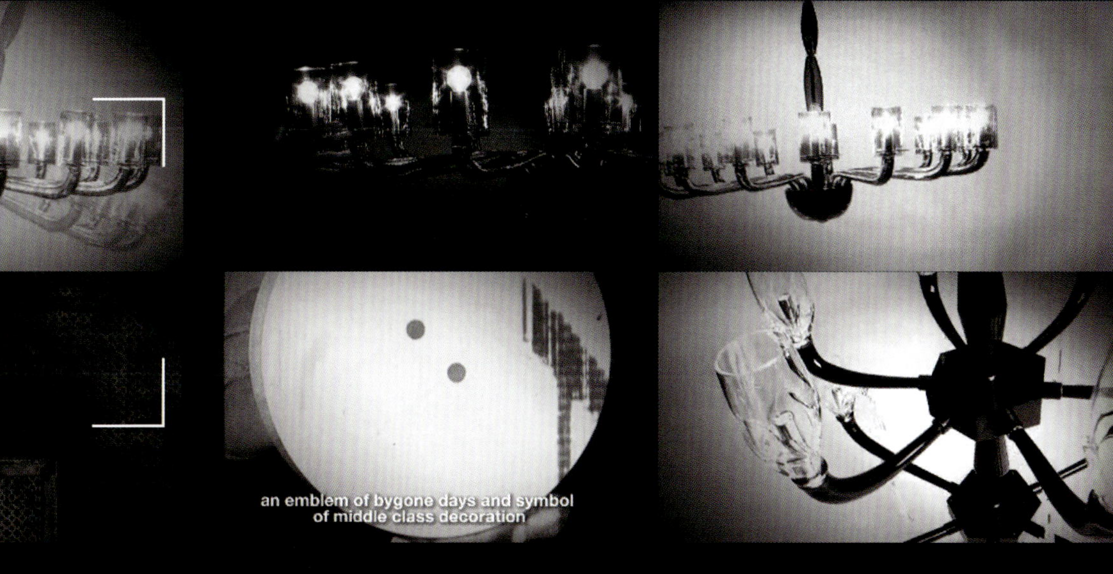

We are impressed by the choreography of the dancing streams of glass, by their rhythmic interaction, by the nocturnal atmosphere, by the beauty of the individual reflections that become visible in the back lighting, and by the column of smoke that begins to rise mysteriously around the glass factory. The film depicts a fleeting moment of beauty that kindles our desire,

COLLECTION
SPRING SUMMER
BACKSTAGE SHOOTING

/////////////////////

DAYS: 7
N SHOTS: 1237
OK SHOTS: 27
TROUPE (PERSONS): 8

/////////////////////

/////////////////////
MURANO
GLASS
JEWELLERY

/////////////////////

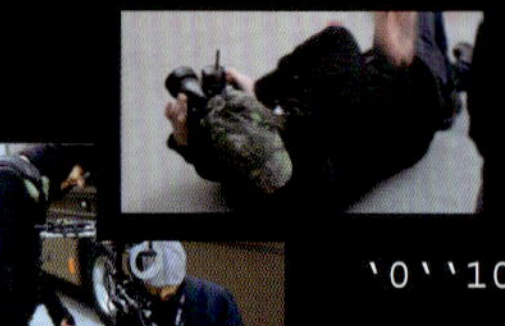

`0''10

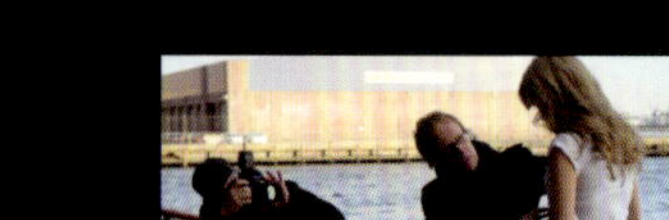
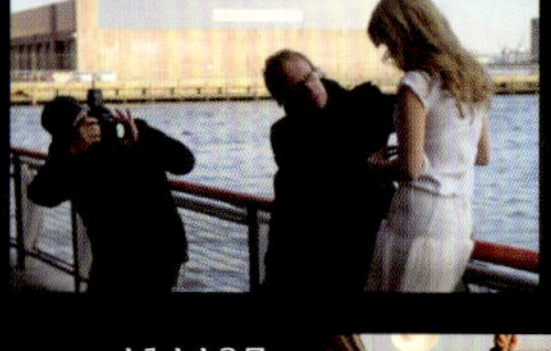

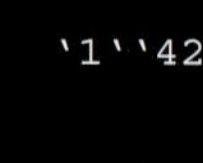
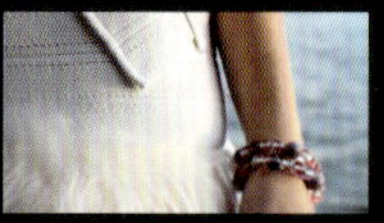

`1''42

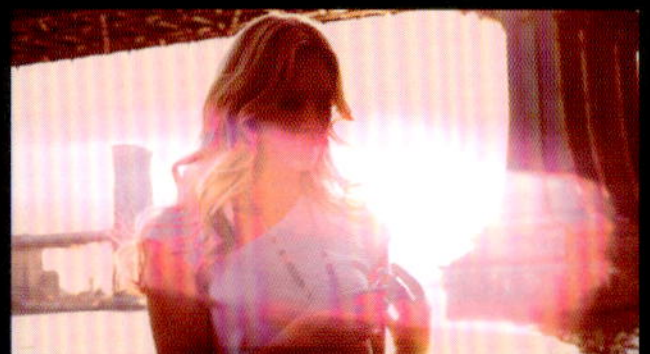

`1''37

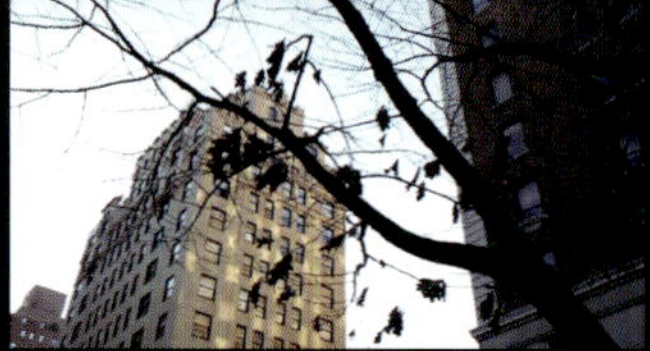
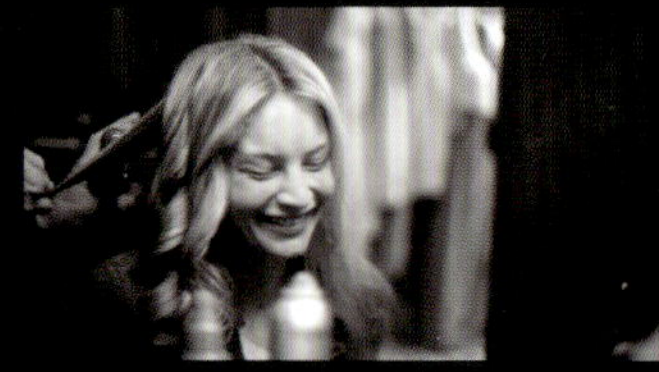
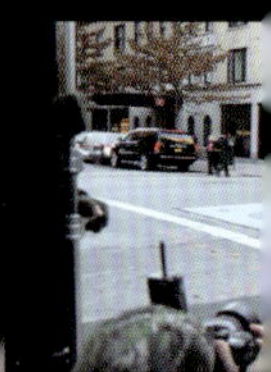

DAY 01
/////////////////////
SUNNY
30°F
FEELS LIKE: 25°
HIGH
PAST 24-HR:
PRECIP: 0,19 IN (EST.)
SNOW: 2,3 IN (EST.)
CHANCE OF PRECIP:
100%
CHANCE OF SNOW:
30%
WIND:
FROM NNE AT 4MPH
/////////////////////

`0''10

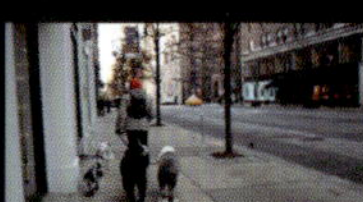

`0''32

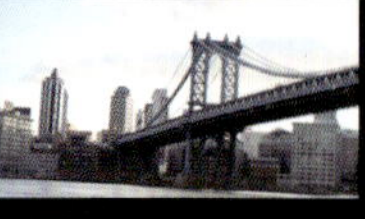

`1''10

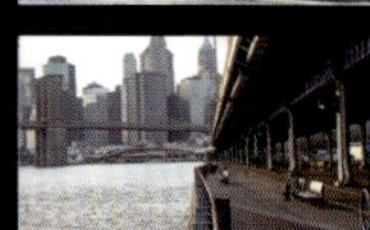

NEW YORK CITY
/////////////////////
COORDINATES:
40°43'N 74°0'W

COUNTRY
_UNITED STATES
STATE
_NEW YORK

COUNTIES
_BRONX
_KINGS
_NEW YORK
_QUEENS
_RICHMOND

`1''37

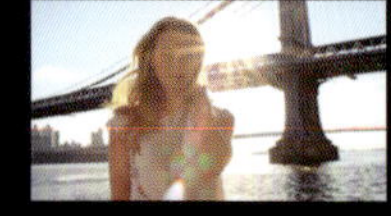

/////////////////////
SETTLED
1624

VIDEO DIFFUSION
/////////////////////
POP
WEBSITE
YOUTUBE CHANNEL

///////////////////   /////////////////////   /////////////////////
+POP DISTRIBUTION   +WEBSITE VISITS   +CHANCE OF VIEW
EUROPA   25/DAY   25/DAY - I MONTH
MIDDLE EAST   19/DAY - FOLLOWING
ASIA&OCEANIA   TARGET CHANCE OF VIEW
AMERICA   12/DAY - I MONTH
AFRICA   7/DAY - FOLLOWING

                    '0''10

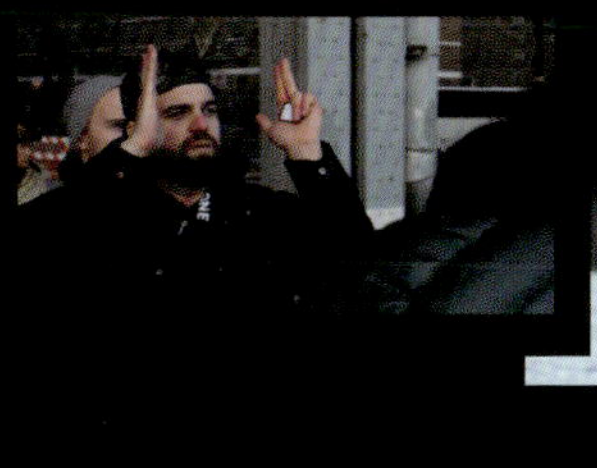

                                        '1''18

                                        '0''36

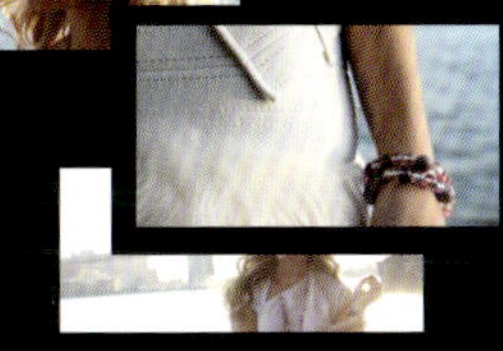

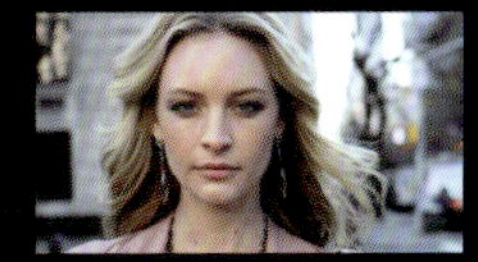

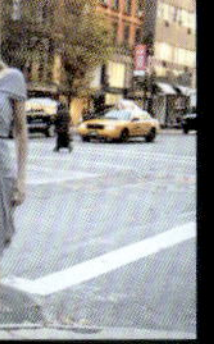 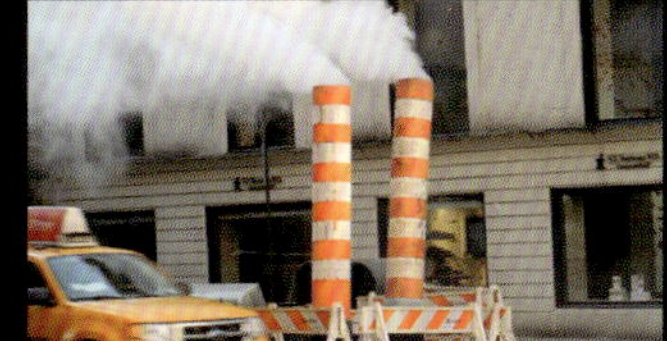 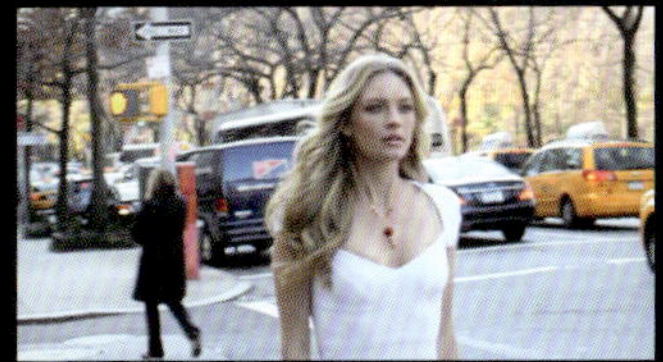 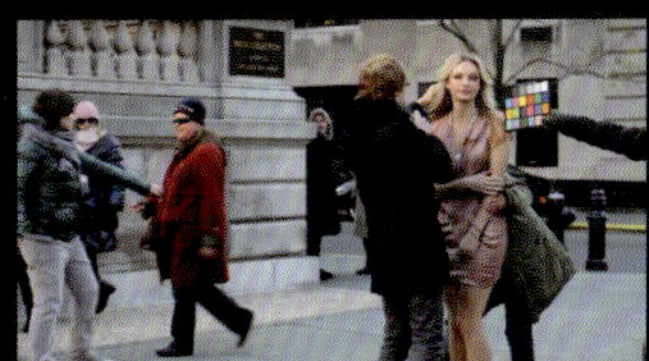

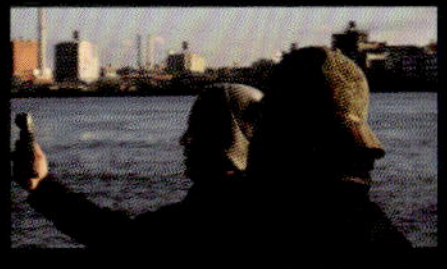

AREA
//
[CITY] 468.9 SQ MI (1,214.4 KM2)
[LAND] 304.8 SQ MI (789.4 KM2)
[WATER] 165.6 SQ MI (428.8 KM2)
[URBAN] 3,352.6 SQ MI (8,683.2 KM2)
[METRO] 6,720 SQ MI (17,405 KM2)
[ELEVATION] 33 FT (10 M)
//

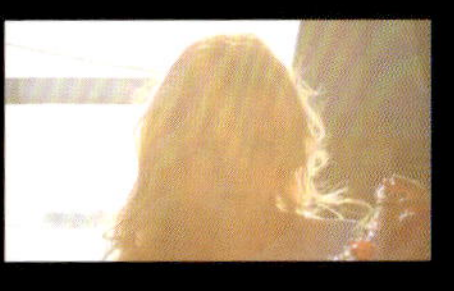

                                        '1''27
                                        '0''32
                                        '0''57
                                        '0''32
                                        '0''57

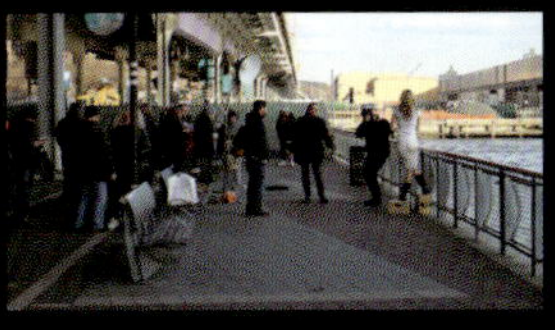

                    '1''23

ZIP CODES   100XX-104XX, 11004-05, 111XX-114XX, 116XX
AREA CODE(S)   212, 718, 917, 347, 646
WEBSITE   WWW.NYC.GOV

Composition Flowchart

| content development |

| Save RAM Preview |

| Import Clip |

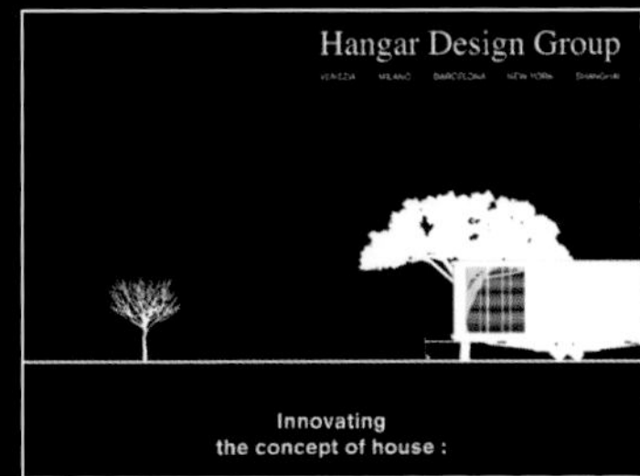

| Create Sequence _01 |

media mix

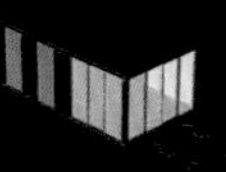

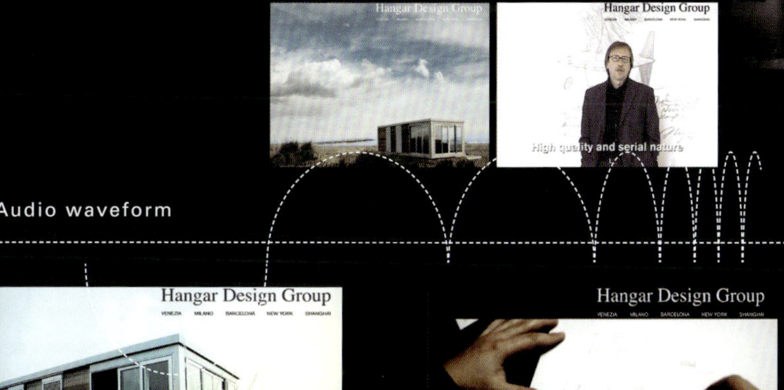

Audio waveform

Normalize Master Track

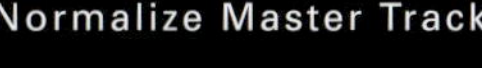

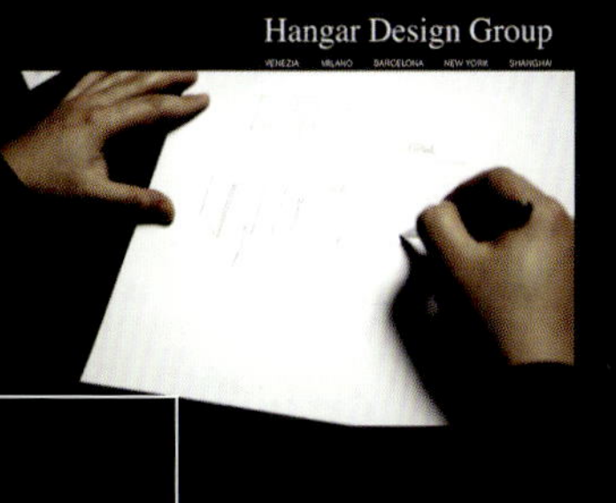

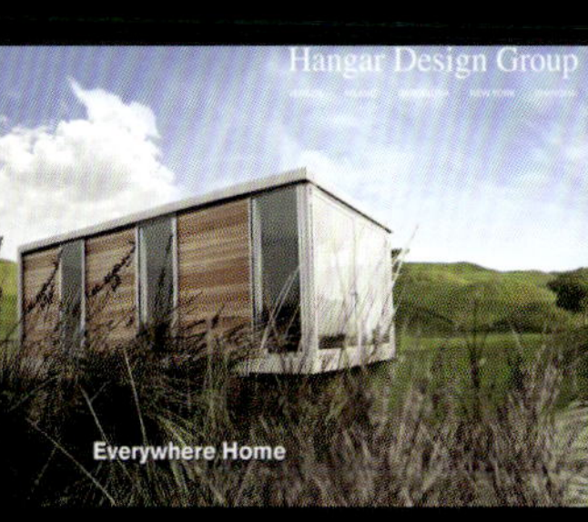

me left 00; 00; 23

Snap

stop

azor at
urrent
ime Indicator

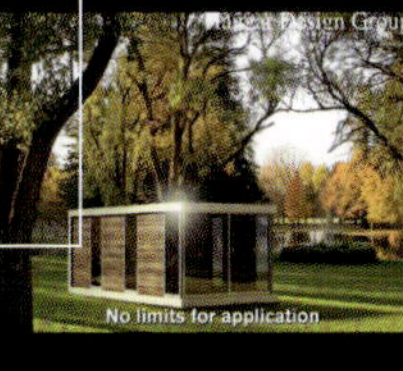

time left 00; 00; 10

Transition- dissolves

--

--

Mobile House.
flv [V] Opacity:
Opacity

Trnsition - movement

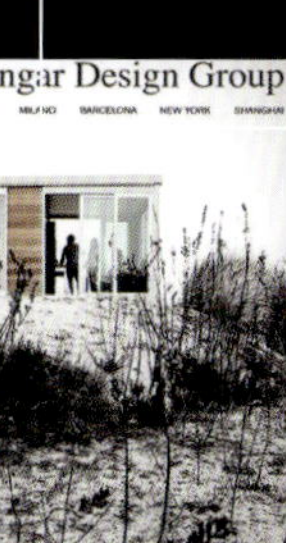

Overlay |

ender Effects in Work Area

Mobile House.
flv [V] Volume:
Volume

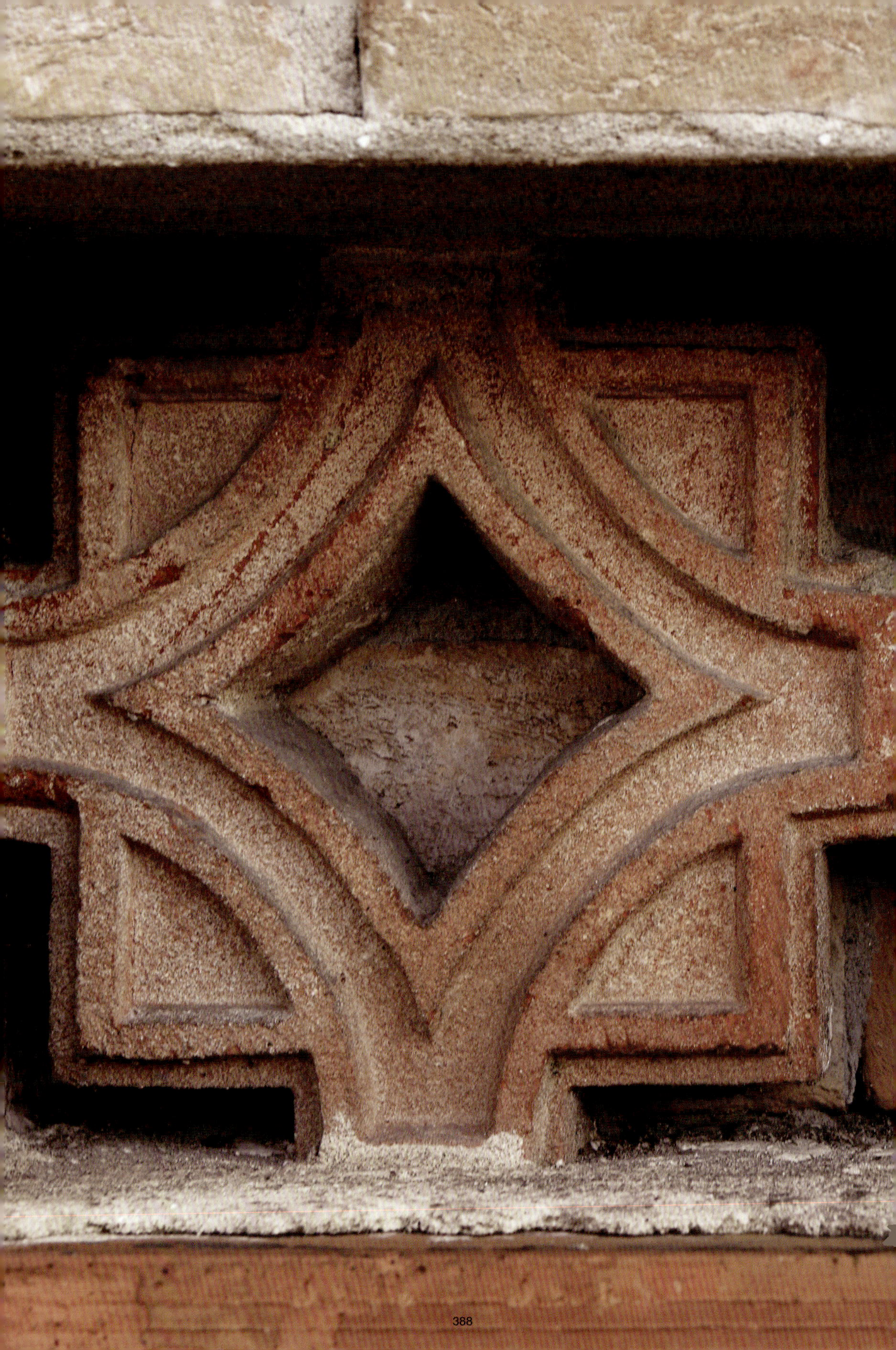

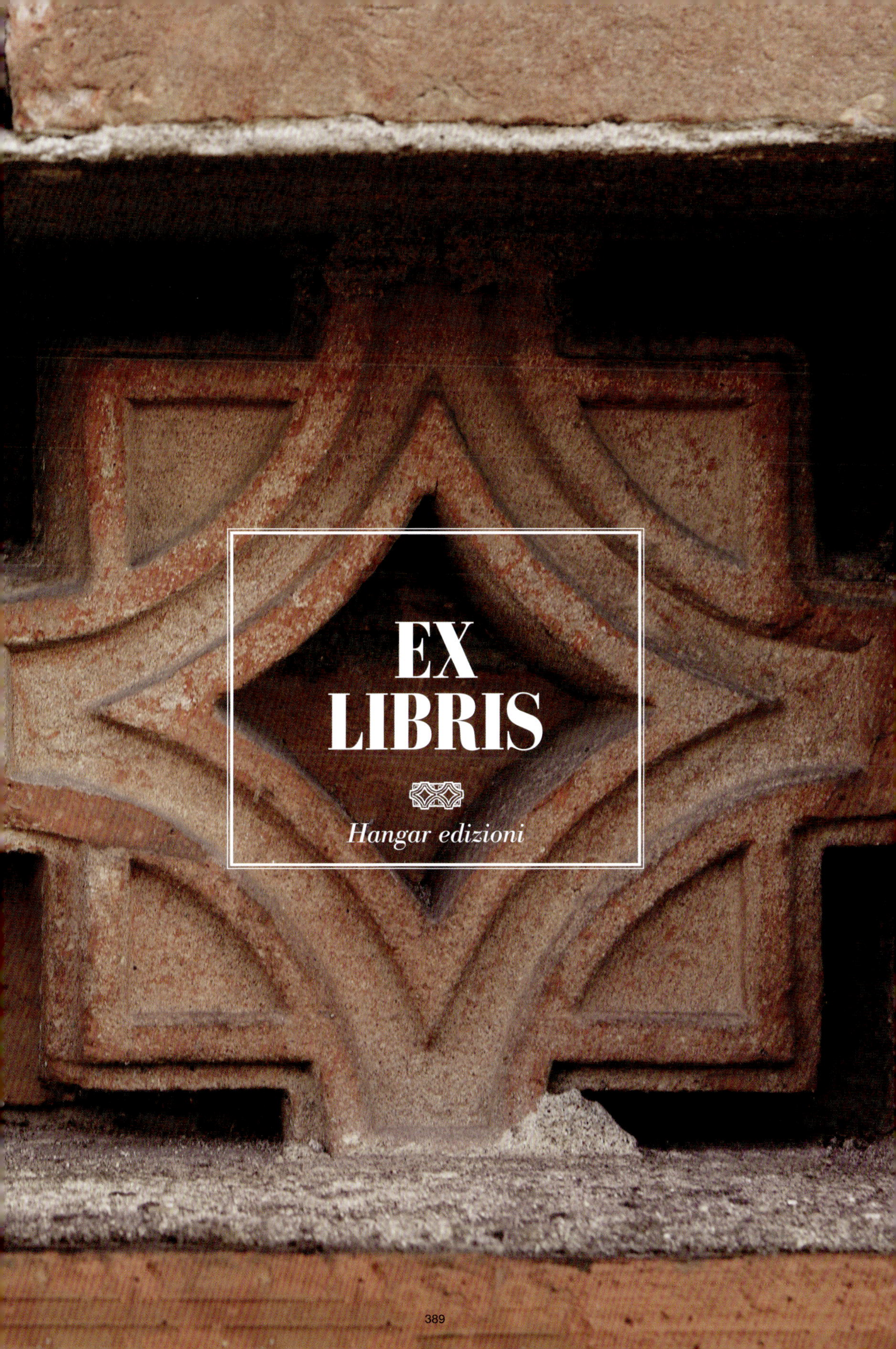

EX
LIBRIS
Hangar edizioni

IT IS NEVER A "THEREFORE" JUST AN "IN ITSELF"

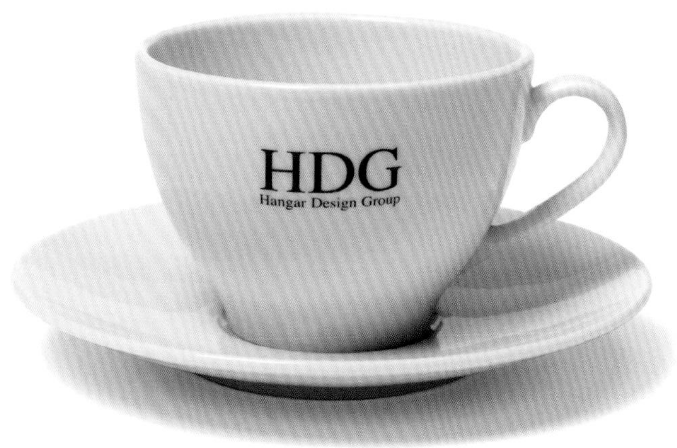

Within the art world the notion that anything can be art, as expounded by pretty much everyone since Duchamp, is held to be a trusim. Well, yes, but only so long as you don't include graphic design in your definition of anything; no graphic designer, regardless of how radical or boundary-smashing, is accorded one hundredth of the status granted to even a minor artist. Many contemporary artists believe that in order to make art they only have to say: "I'm an artist therefore everything I make is art." This is a widely held view, but where is the evidence? Since we live in a liberal democracy with a reasonable amount, most people are content to allow anyone to call himself or herself an artist. But when we are offered definitions of art, we become more critical and less tolerant. Philosophers have struggled with this questions for centuries. The philosophical definition of art has varied over time to an astonishing degree. Most of us would not recognize the definitions that have prevailed in past eras, but today we seem to have reached a point where our definition is governed by what is known as "the institutional theory of art." This theory states that an object can be called art when it is connected to the institution known as "the art world." In other words, its status as art is conferred by its association with galleries, curators, critics, art education, the art market, etc. We are willing to allow a work to be designated as art – even if it doesn't chime with our own view of what is and isn't art – because it is in a gallery or in a book or magazine presented by a knowledgeable authority.

Since design has nearly always kept a clear separation between itself and the art world, the "institutional" definition of art automatically excludes most forms of design. There is also, of course, a well-developed institutional theory of design. It is based around certain principles that are anathema to the art world: design's dependency on commercial commissioners, its reliance on mass production rather than unique "one-off" creations, and its lack of authorial content – designers communicate other people's messages, not their own. But as discussed above, graphic designers now routinely bypass the institutional straightjacket of design. They make their own work which they publish in a demi-art world of galleries, blogs and publications that do not follow the commissioned-by-client model. We believe, in the end, that our relationship with art is a deeply personal association between us and the objects or works we choose to engage with. If we can shed the tribal and cultural conditioning that determines so much of what we think and do especially about art, we realize that in art we are free to find aesthetic pleasure wherever we choose, and make it in any way we please.

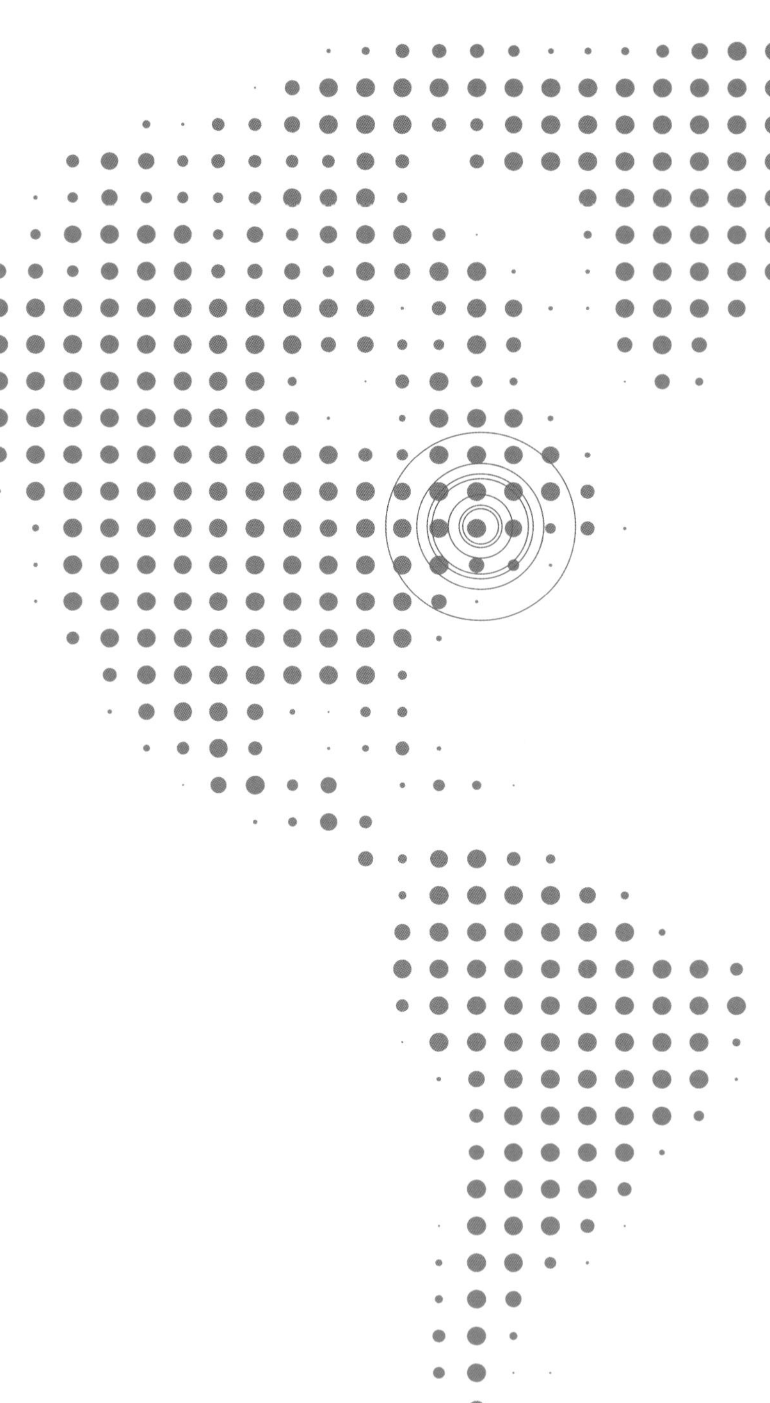

hangar epicenters
venice
milan
barcelona
new york
shanghai

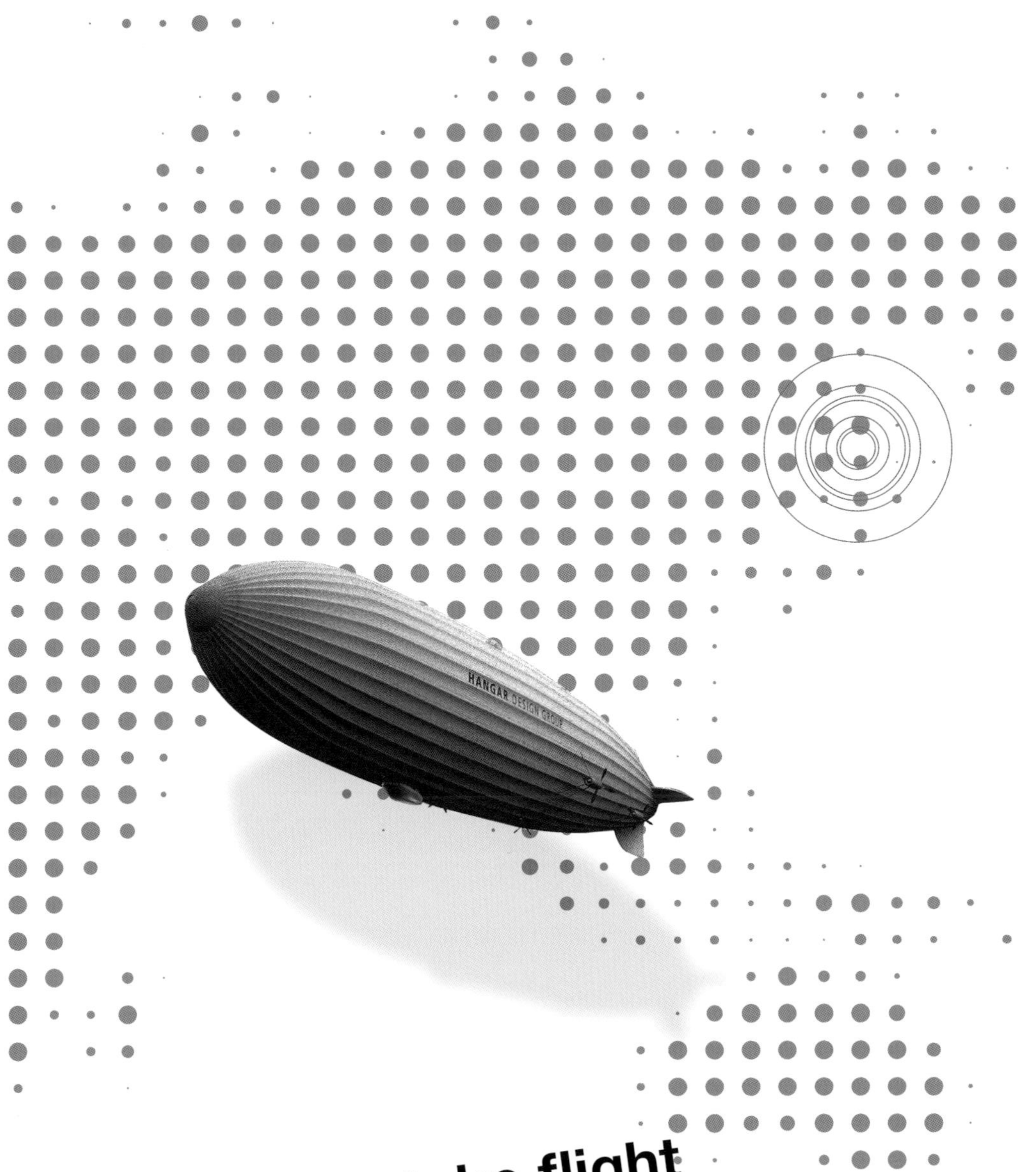

Letting ideas take flight

We understand creativity in a dynamic sense: it must be capable of evolving in accordance with new languages, of renewing itself, of changing. And the same is true of the creatives who must be capable of "cross-fertilizing" different ideas, cultures, sensibilities, and specific skills. Creativity in our work should never lose sight of reality, of changes and of market demands, of client requirements and of being at the cutting edge. Creativity is above all an indirect language, which must be married to rigor in design.

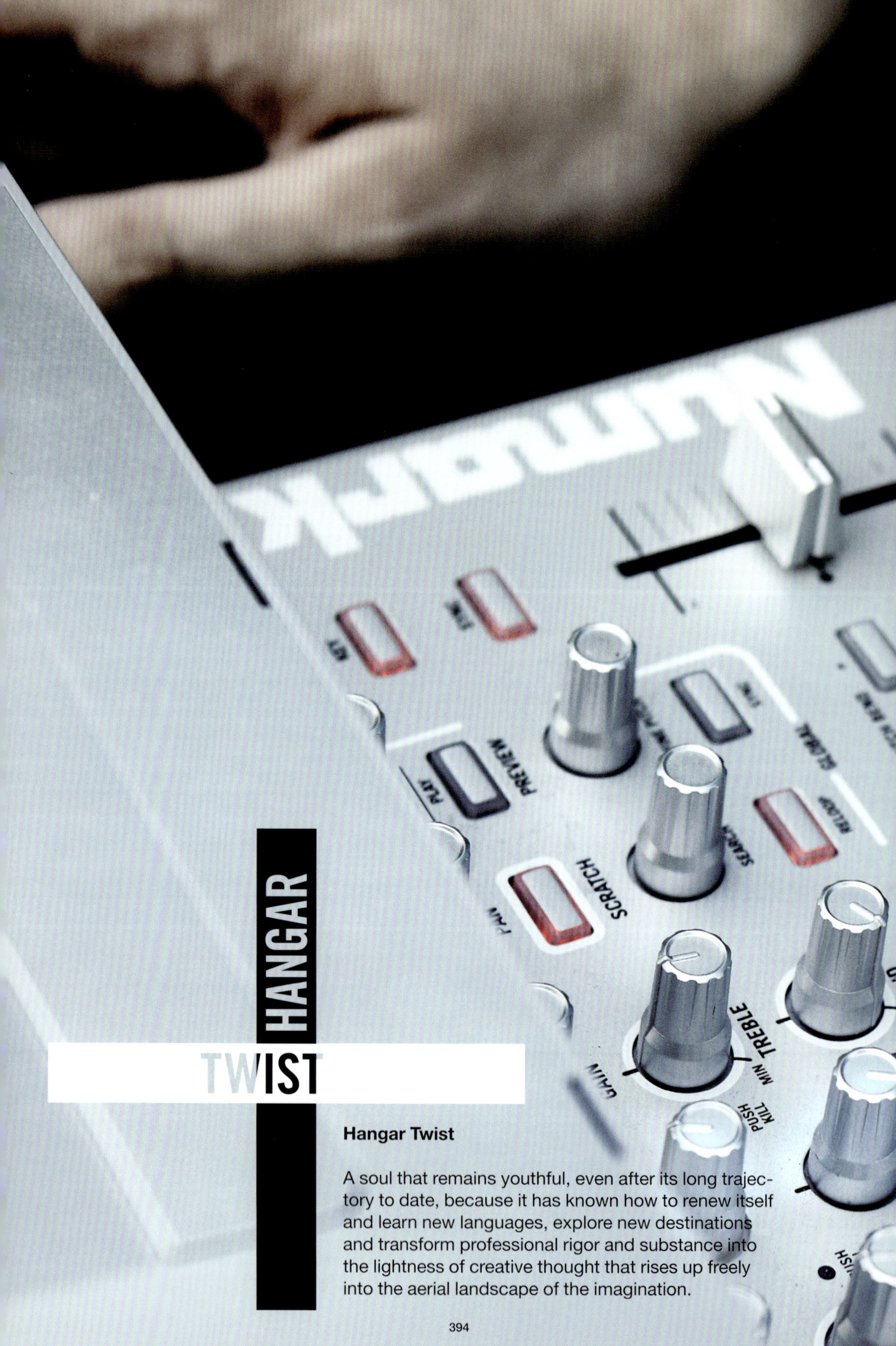

HANGAR

TWIST

Hangar Twist

A soul that remains youthful, even after its long trajectory to date, because it has known how to renew itself
and learn new languages, explore new destinations
and transform professional rigor and substance into
the lightness of creative thought that rises up freely
into the aerial landscape of the imagination.

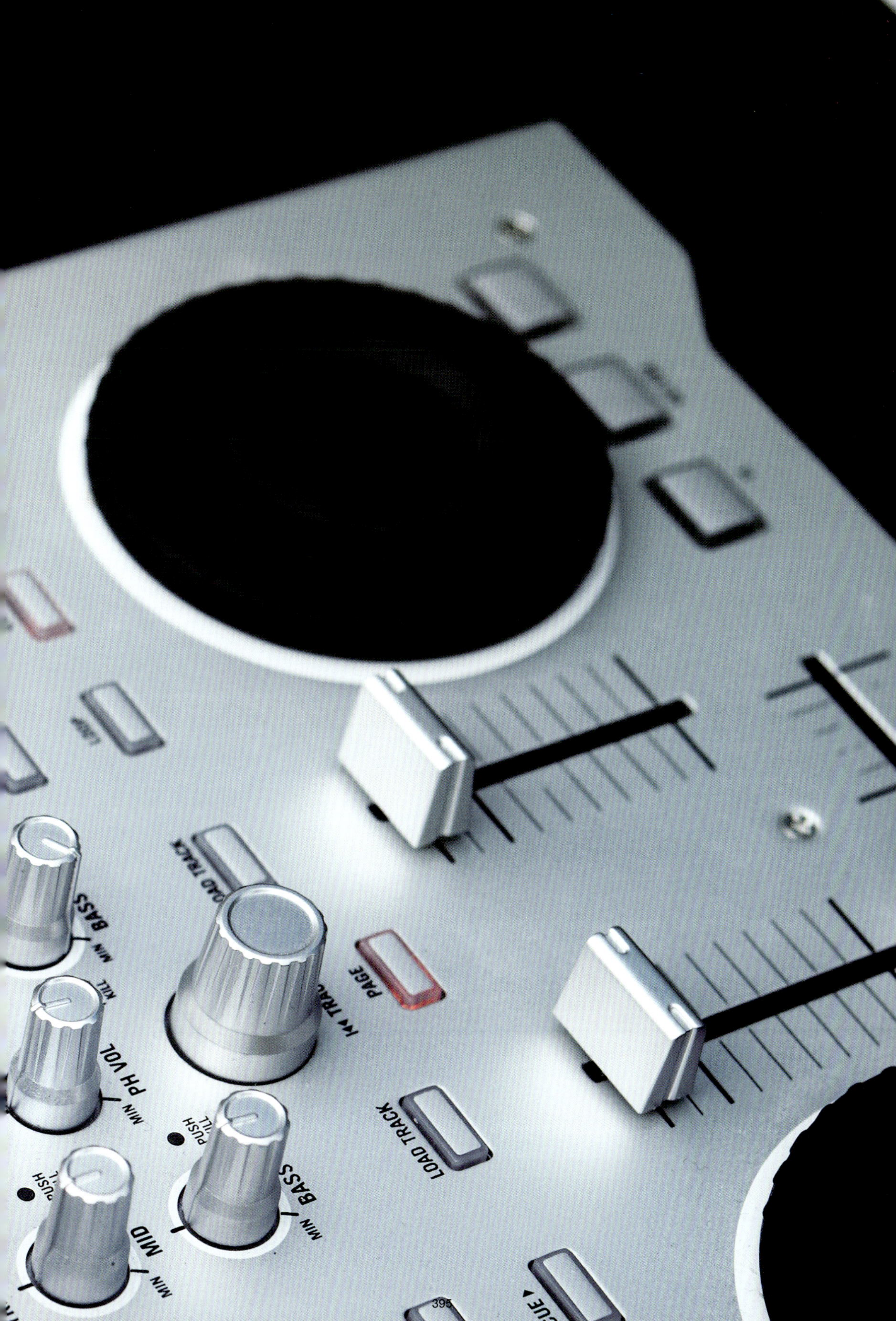

BASS
MIN
KILL
PH VOL
MIN
PUSH
KILL
MID
MIN
BASS
MIN
LOAD TRACK
PAGE
LOAD TRACK
CUE

ABCDEGHIJLMN
OPQRSTUVXZ
abcdefghiklmnopqr
stuvxz§@:;!?(&)01
234567890{E£¥$}
ABCDEFGHIJKLM
NOPQRSTUVXZ
abcdefghijklmnopqr-
stuvxz§@:;!?(&)
01234567890{E£¥$}
ABCDEGHIJLMN
OPQRSTUVXZ
abcdefghiklmn
opqrstuvxz§@:;!
?(&)01234567
890{E£¥$}AB-
CDEGHIJLM-
NOPQRSTUVXZ
abcdefghiklmnop
qrstuvxz§@:;!?(&
)01234567890{
E£¥$}ABCDEFGH
IJLMNOPQR-

Thirty years of design. That's no small number, for those who have always confronted the challenge of design by looking forward, consolidating a cultural design and a professional logic based on the multiple presence and proliferation of places, on the repetition of contacts. Everything began in a special place in the Venetian hinterland which, once upon a time, housed old dirigibles: masonry hangars, the ancient refuge of flying machines – to be replaced by airplanes – whose iconic fascination remains fixed in the collective memory as a metaphor for a challenge consecrated to utopia. Embracing the evocative power of the *genius loci*, Hangar Design Group has evolved thanks to its founders and to those who have shared in its trajectory over these years and witnessed it become a model of consolidated development, based from the very beginning on its ability to attract and absorb a multiplicity of professional strands and tensions and spread these out into other similar but different areas, according to the principle of crossover of skills and creative languages.

A model that is modular, network-based and diversified in relation to the nature of the professional figures inhabiting it, capable of adapting its relationships in accordance with the individual client order and the individual people involved. Because if the professional structure develops out of the skills, processes and interactions between the individuals comprising it, that structure is – most of all – nourished by their passion and vision, their ability to embrace the project and animate the team. It is they – beyond any categorizations – who represent the very soul of Hangar.

398.

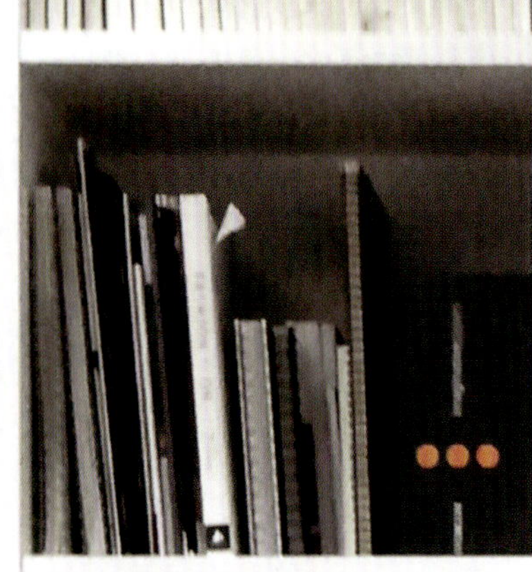
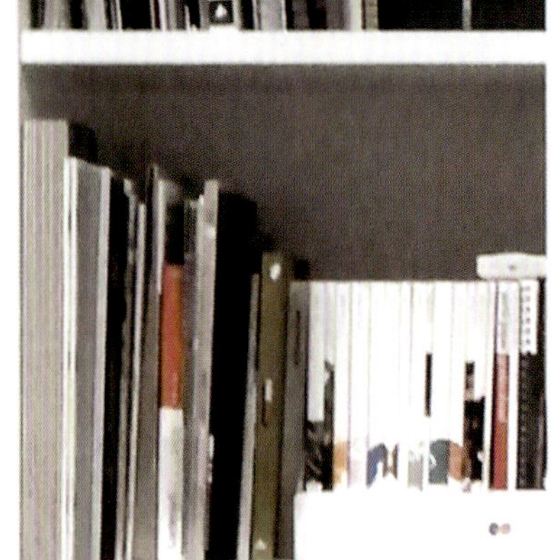
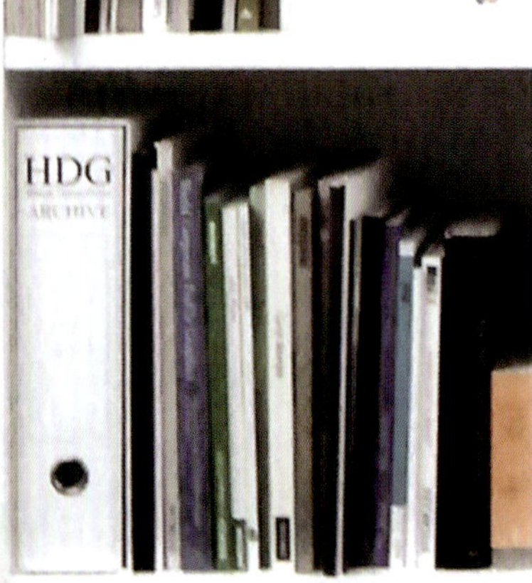

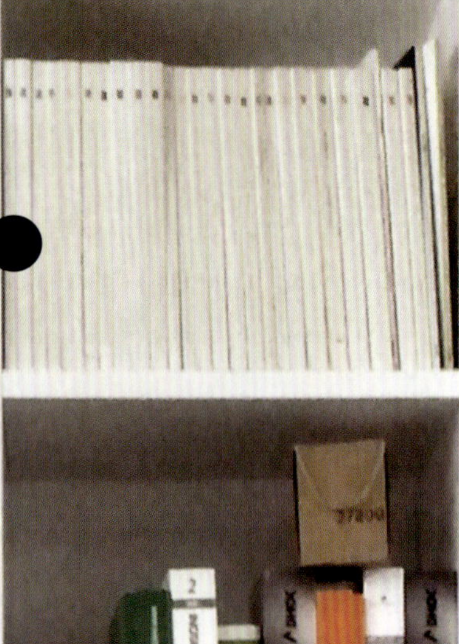
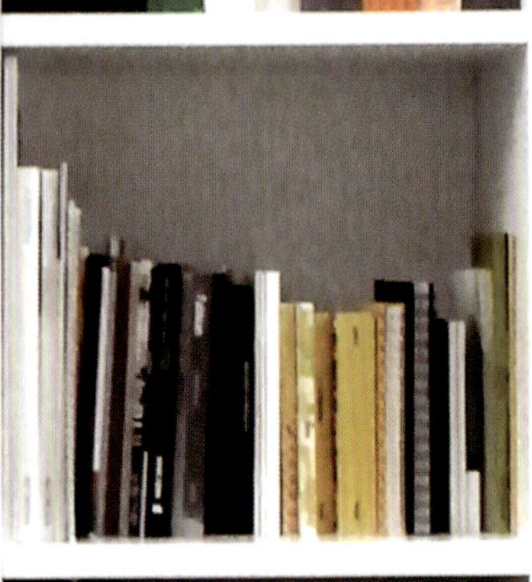
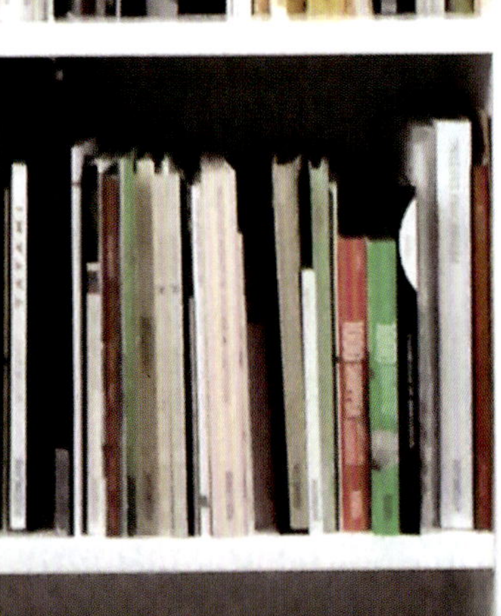
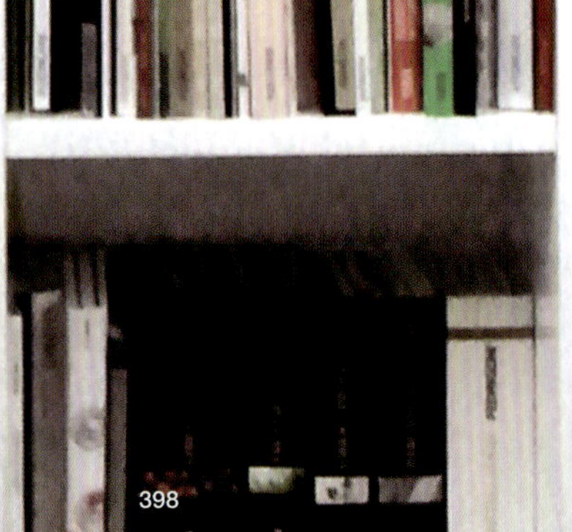

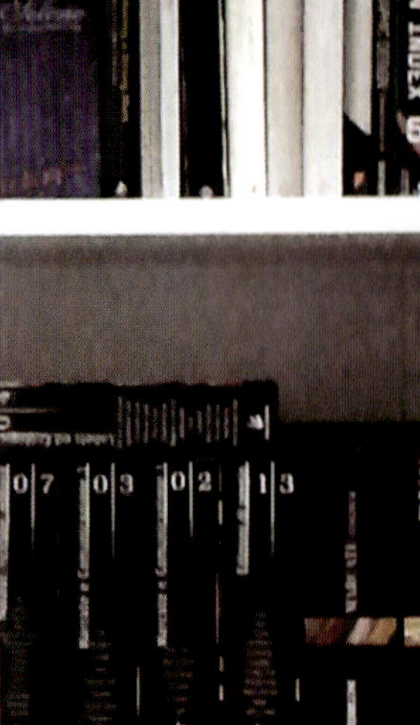
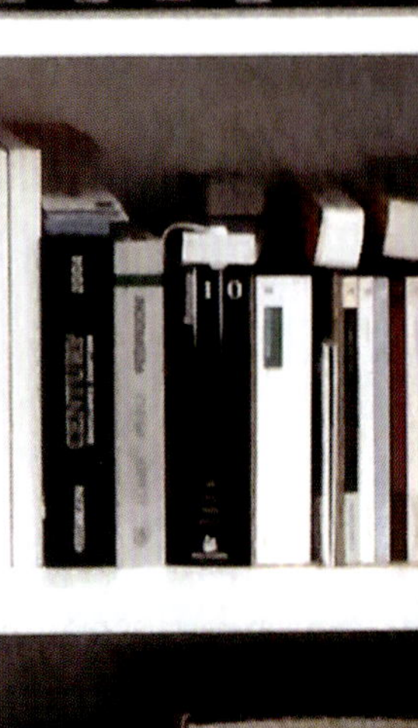
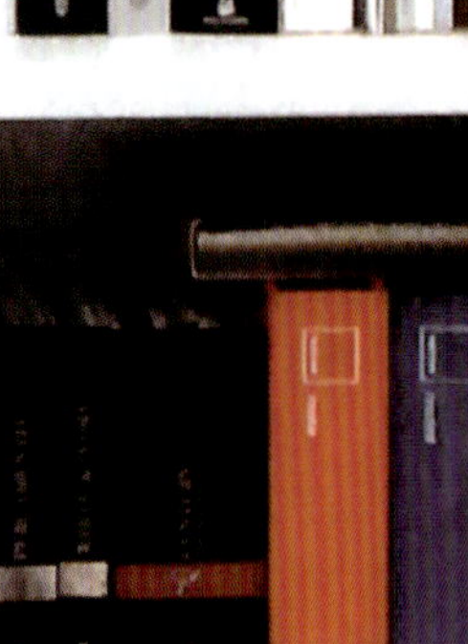

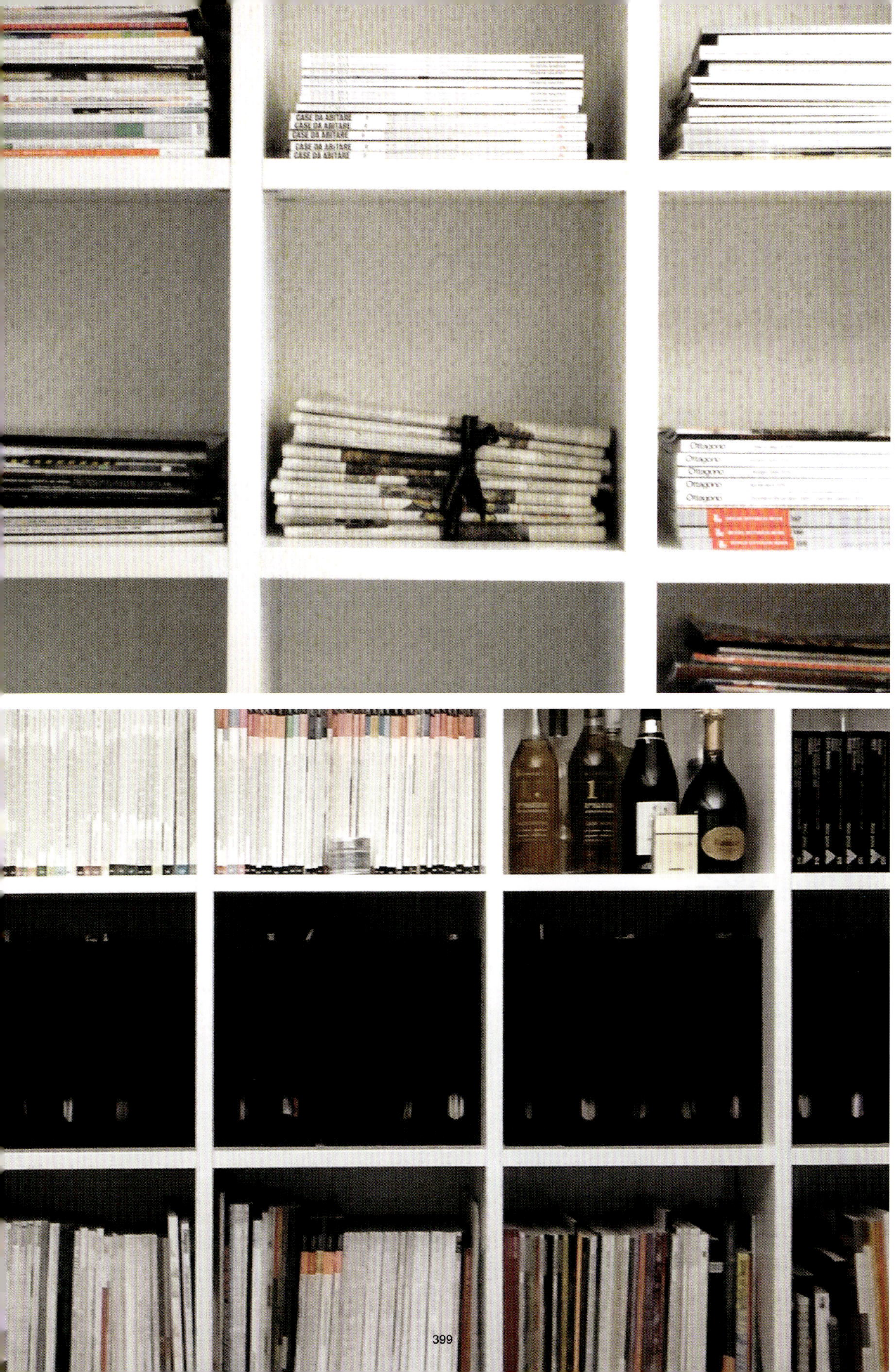

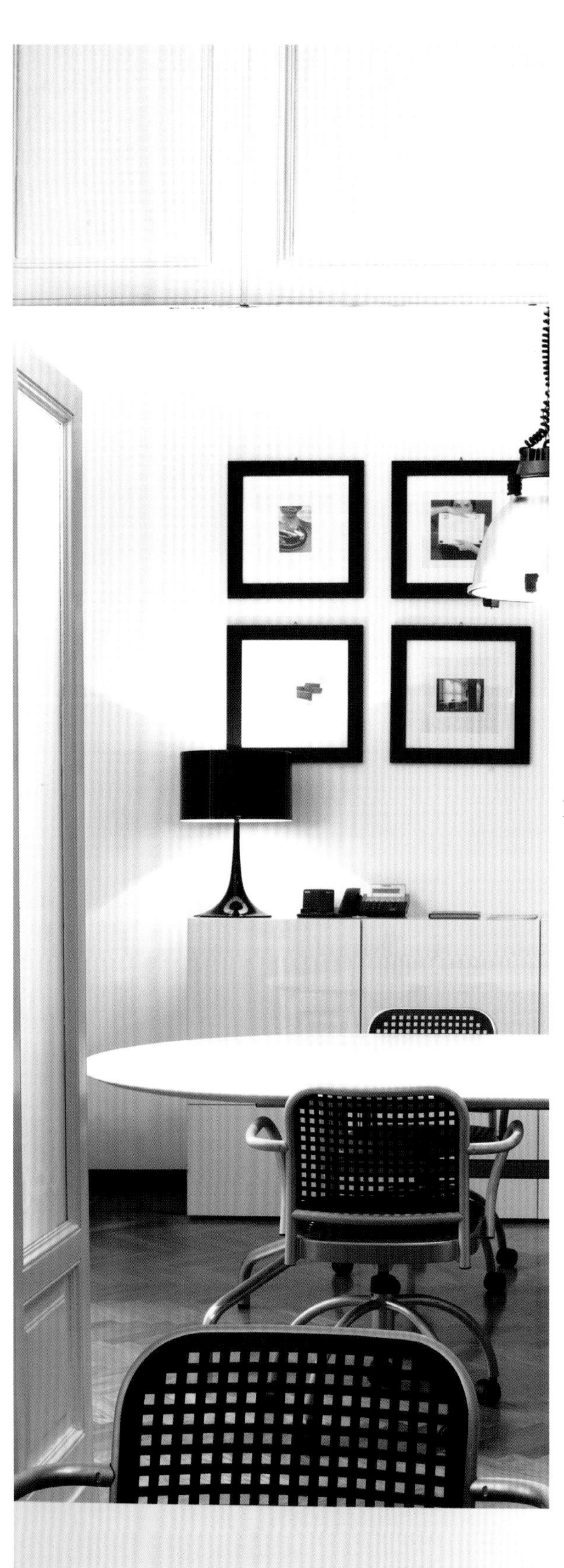

WE ARE NOT INVENTORS; INSTEAD
WE REWORK, RECONSTRUCT,
REDUCE, AND IMPROVE THAT WHICH
ALREADY EXISTS. AND ALTHOUGH
WE DO NOT SHY

AWAY FROM THE DECORATIVE,
WE ARE CONVINCED THAT
ELEGANCE OUGHT TO BE FOUND
SOMEWHERE ELSE – NAMELY IN THE
ESSENCE OF THINGS.

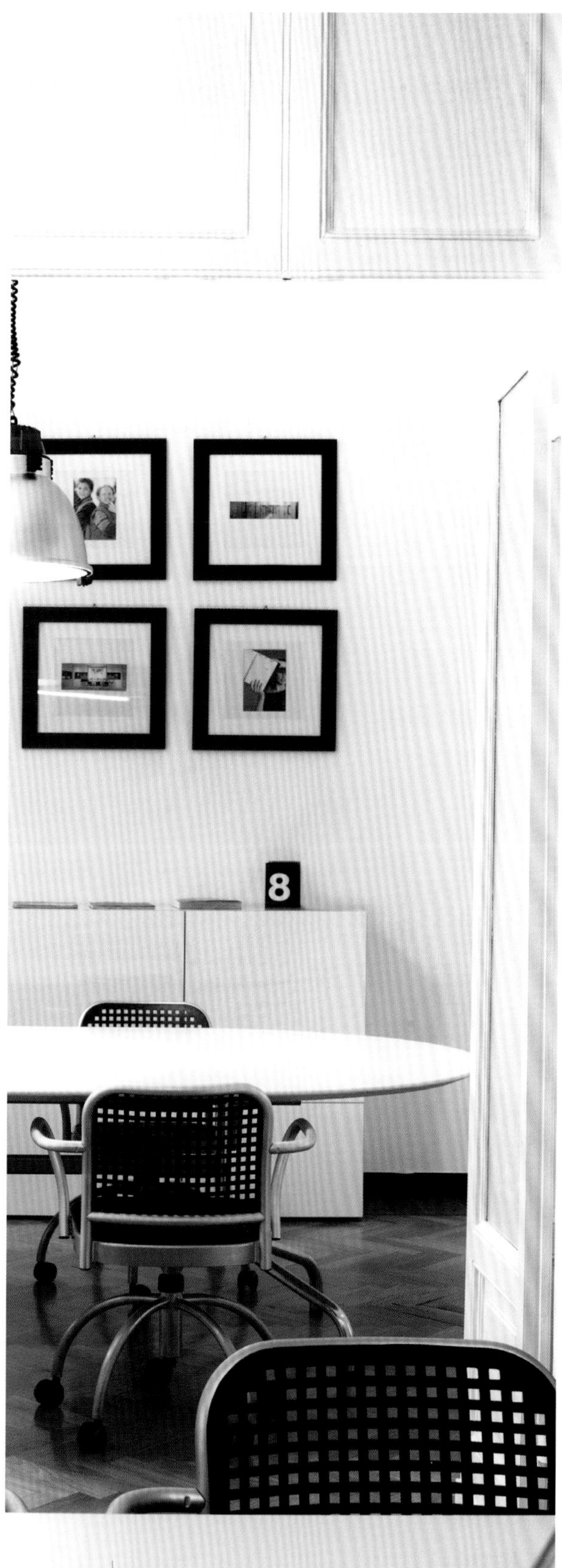

PEOPLE WHO

find something they like make the world a more
interesting place. The real voyage of discovery consists
not in seeking new landscapes but in having new eyes.
Some cities are just built in concrete, but some can
ignite our collective fantasy and make grand promises
of change and excitement. They capture our imagination
before we have even visited them. Much like aspiration,
some places project a larger-than-life shadow
on the observer. You can find inspiration in everything
(and if you can't, well look again).

LINKS

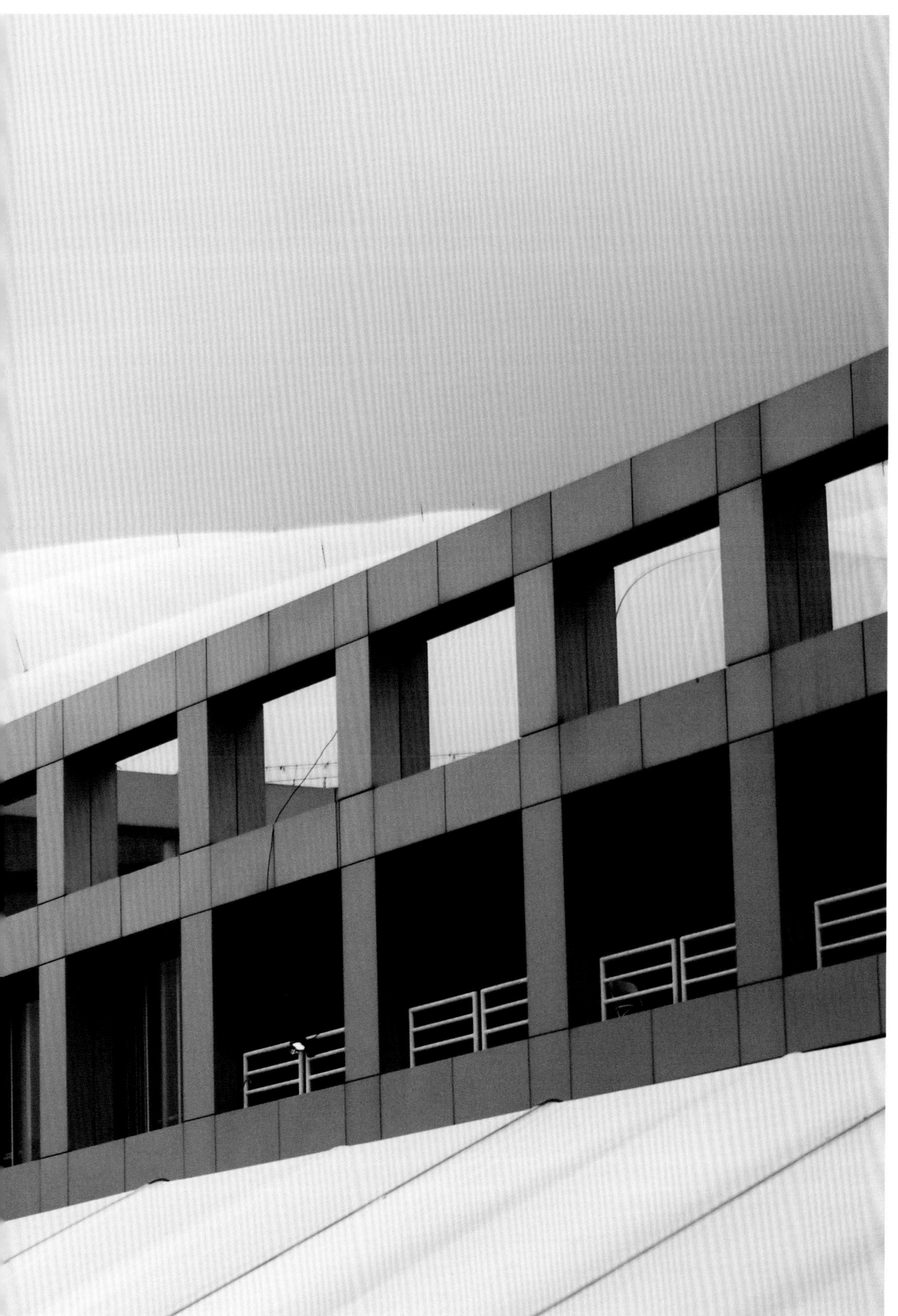

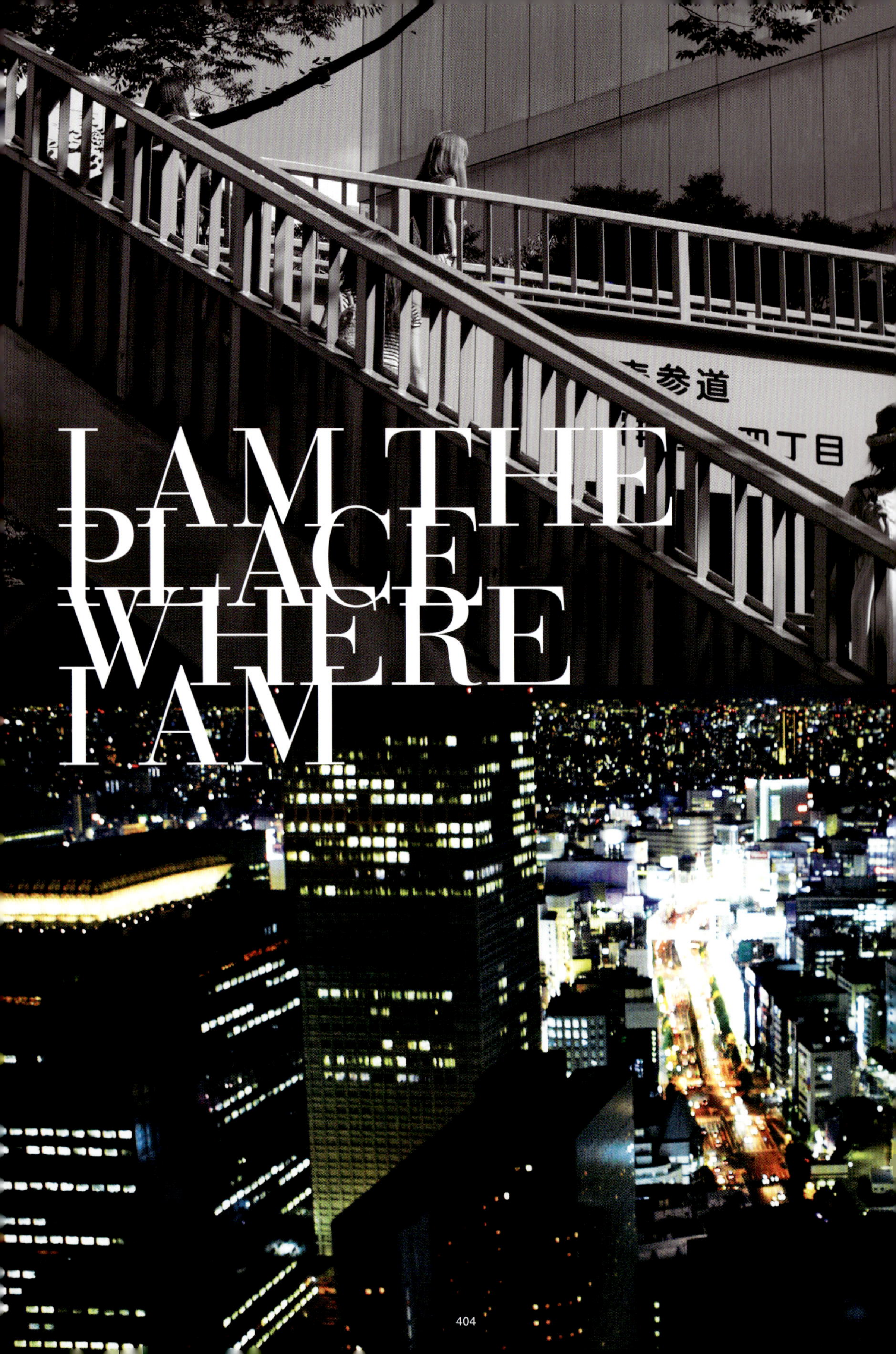
I AM THE
PLACE
WHERE I
AM

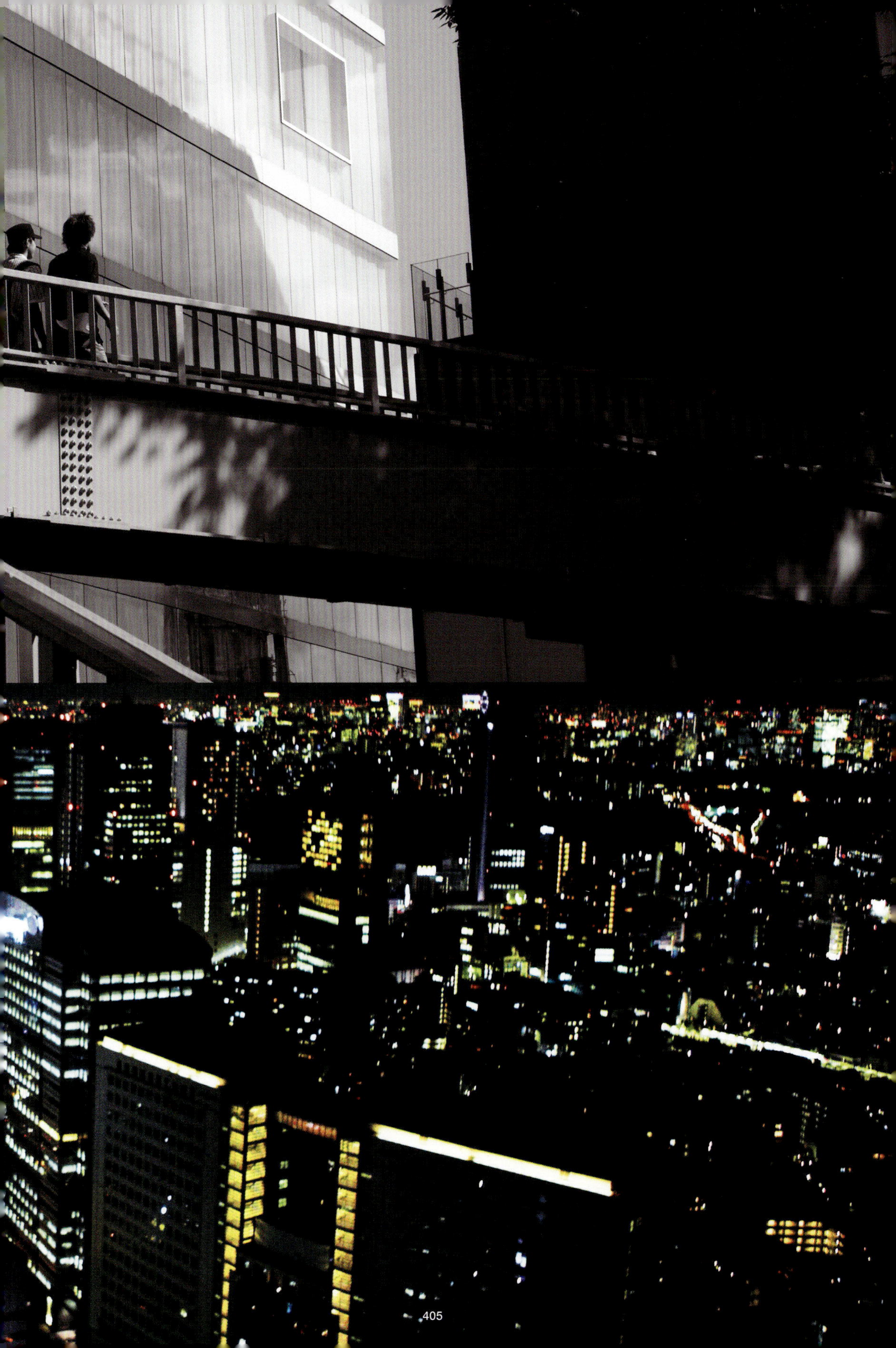

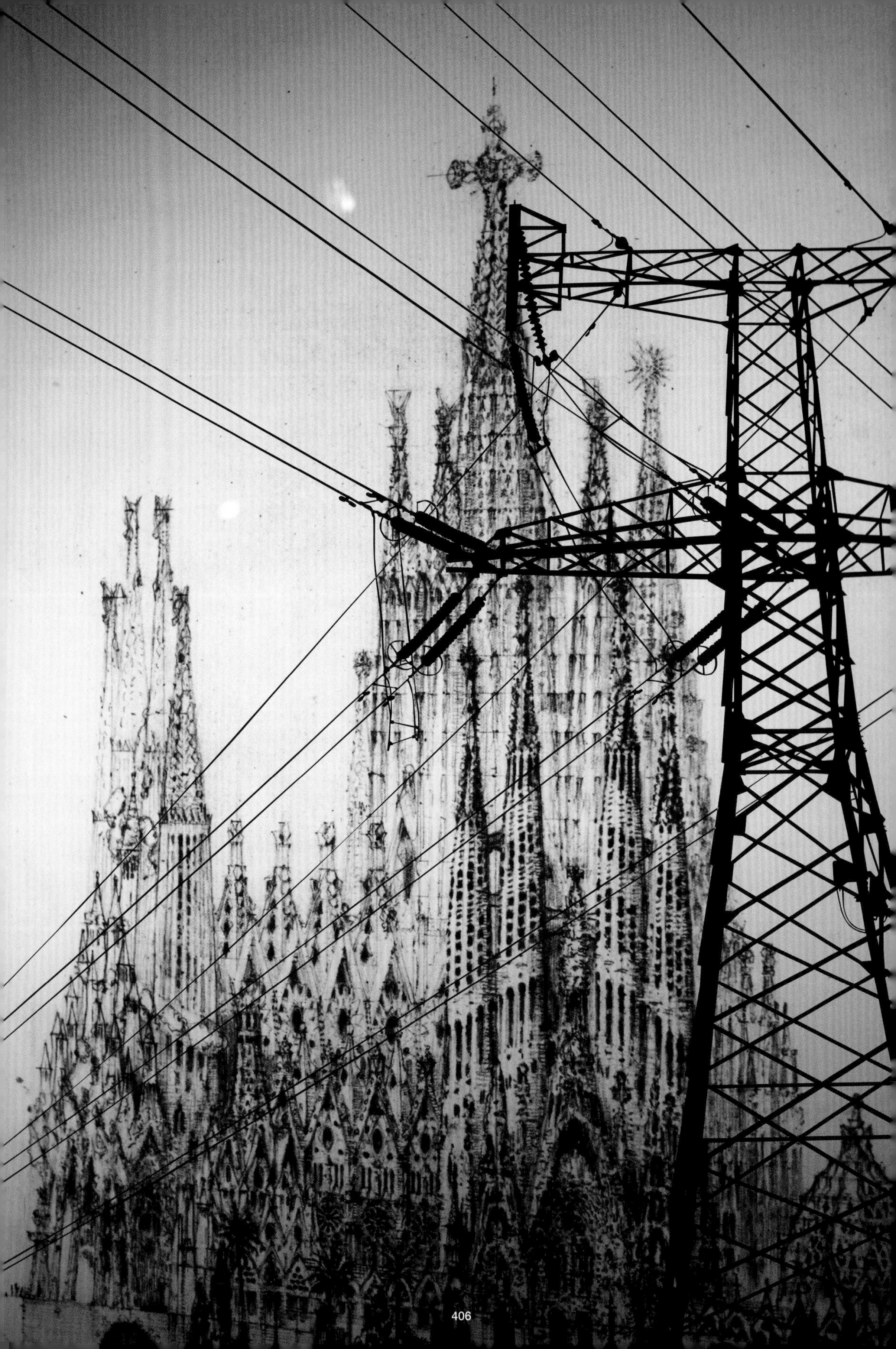

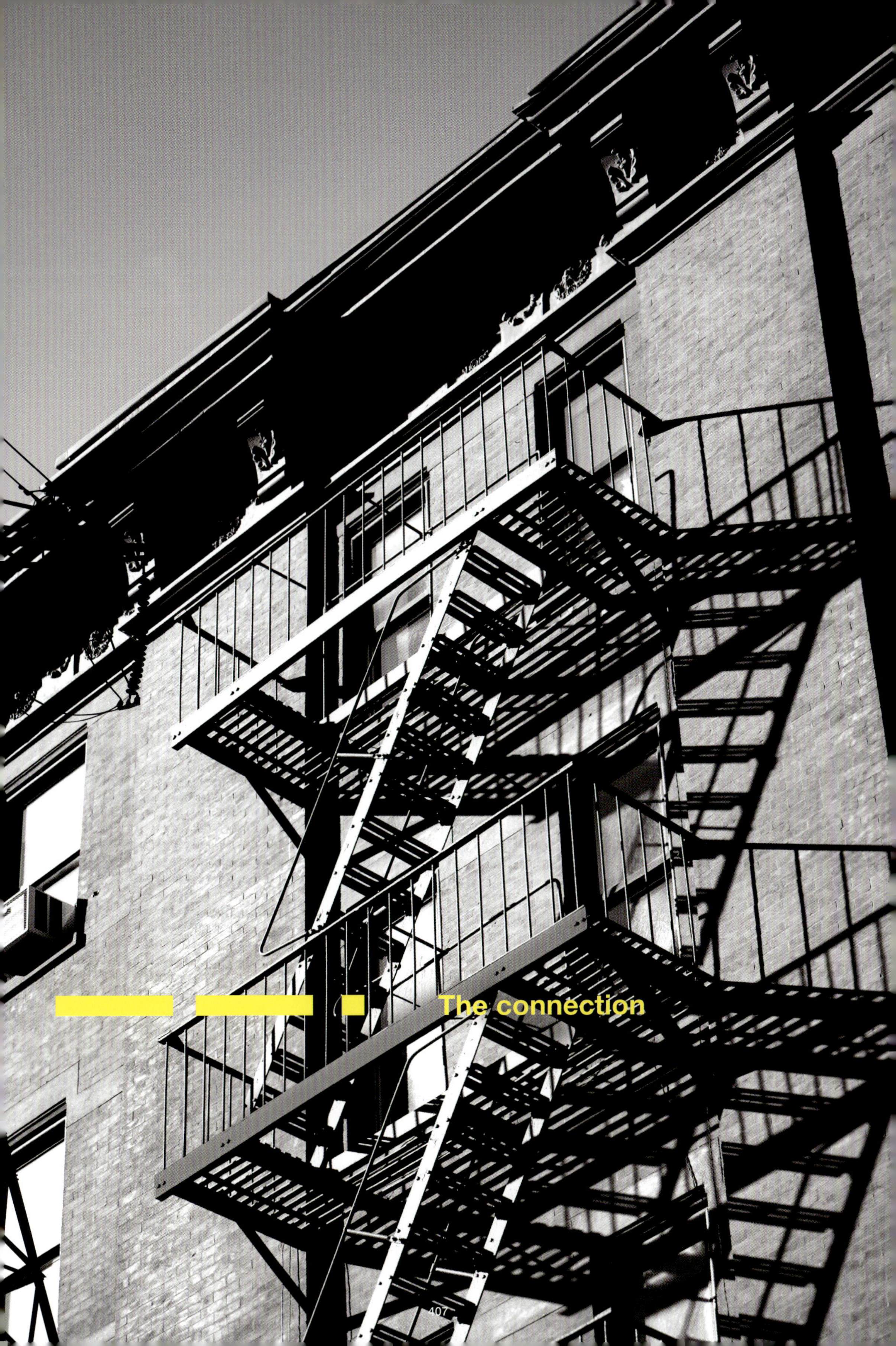
The connection

THERE.
AND
THERE.

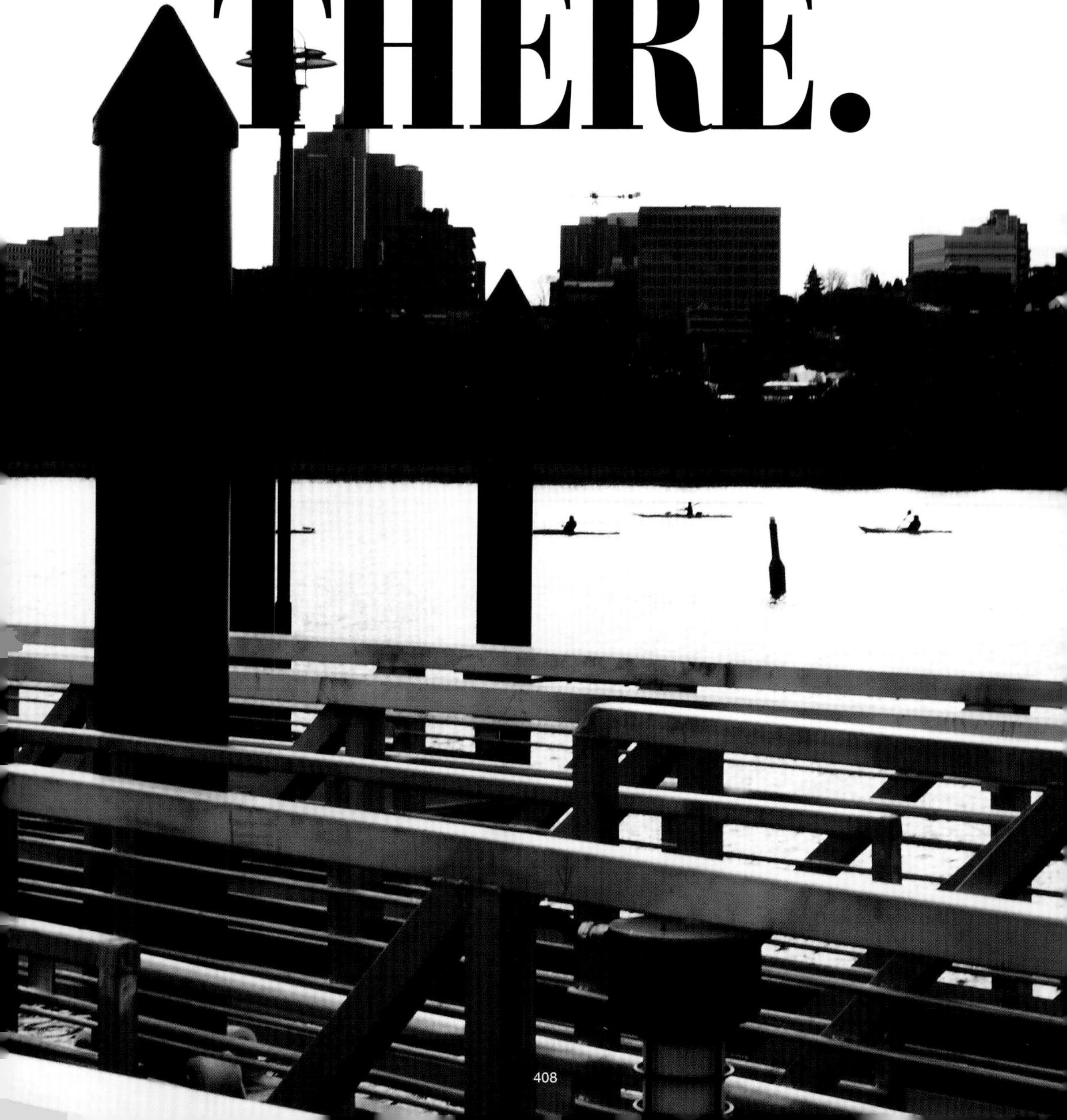

Words and images compiled
via random accumulation betray
personal ways of pursuing an idea,
sometimes of form, other times of
function, and occasionally of
a color or a material.
They recount – and here we would
stress the narrative aspects – personal, non-formal modes of gath-
ering/welcoming ideas and
of searching for solutions by
entering into things or locking
them in an immediate layout.
These images also recount the
personal, intimate side of our
inspiration urge, its investigative
and experimental nature, whereby
it often bears witness to difficul-
ties and obstacles, but also singu-
lar and vital creative processes.

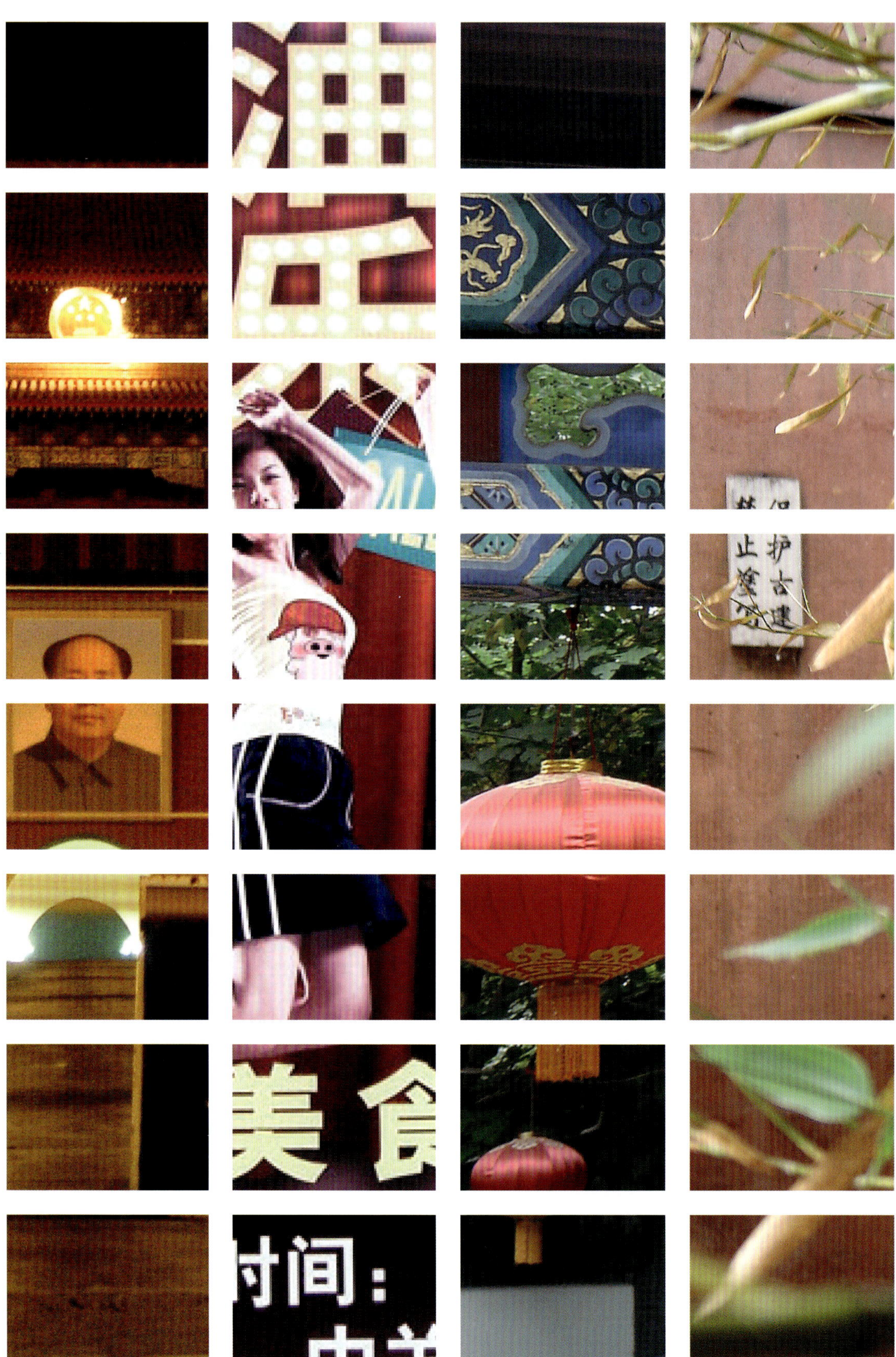

油
品
美 食
时间：
护古建
止

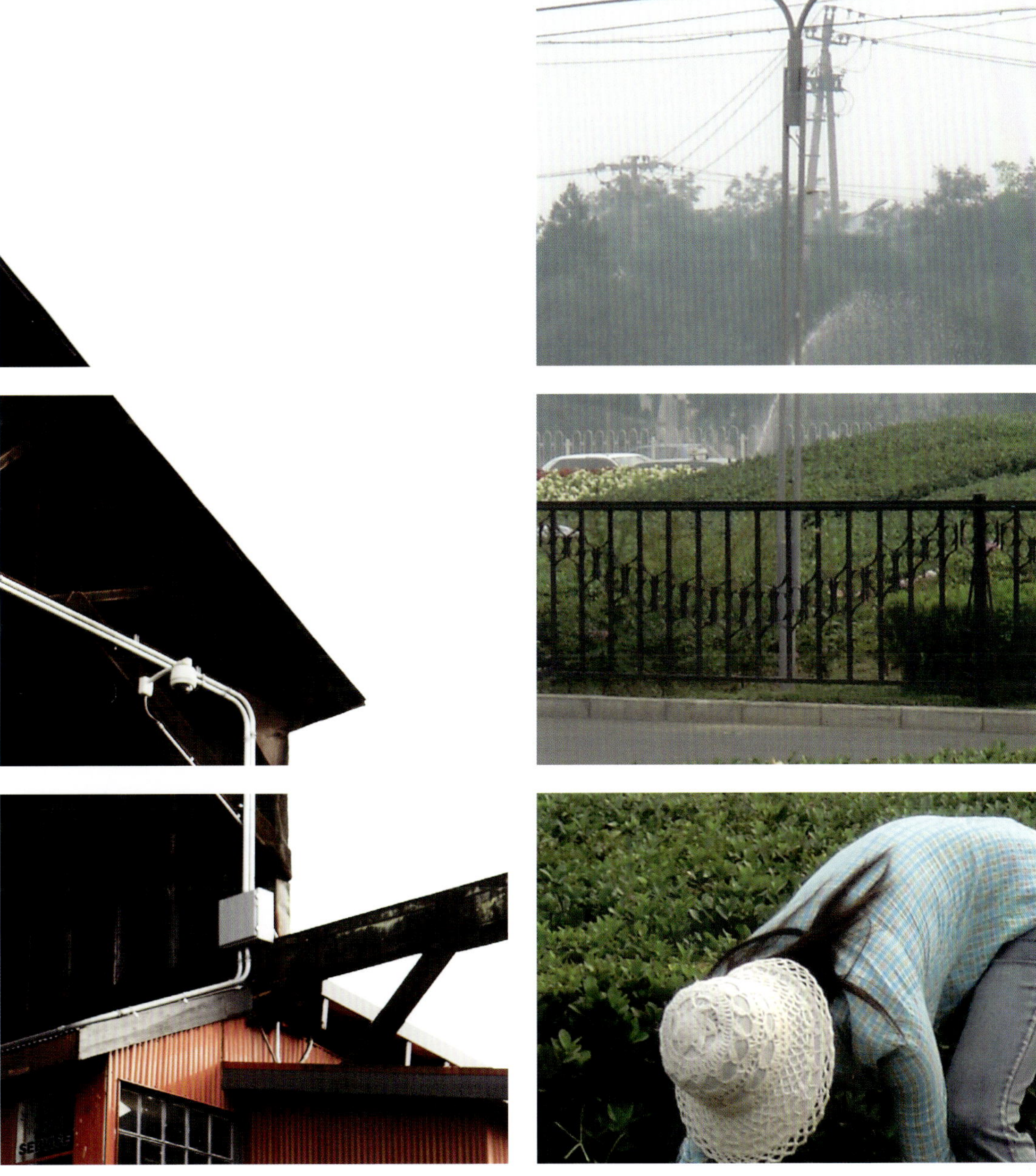

Our society (the so-called post-modern society) grew up on quotations. Most of the Pop culture, from books to songs, is now really similar to a blogoteque. In an era when everything has already been seen and watched, there's nothing left for us to do but put together things and combine them. One of the most seductive aspects of the modern history of ideas is its perpetual instability, its never-ending metamorphosis. Themes, images and pulsions migrate from one field to another, changing in the passage itself and the scenery in which they are set.

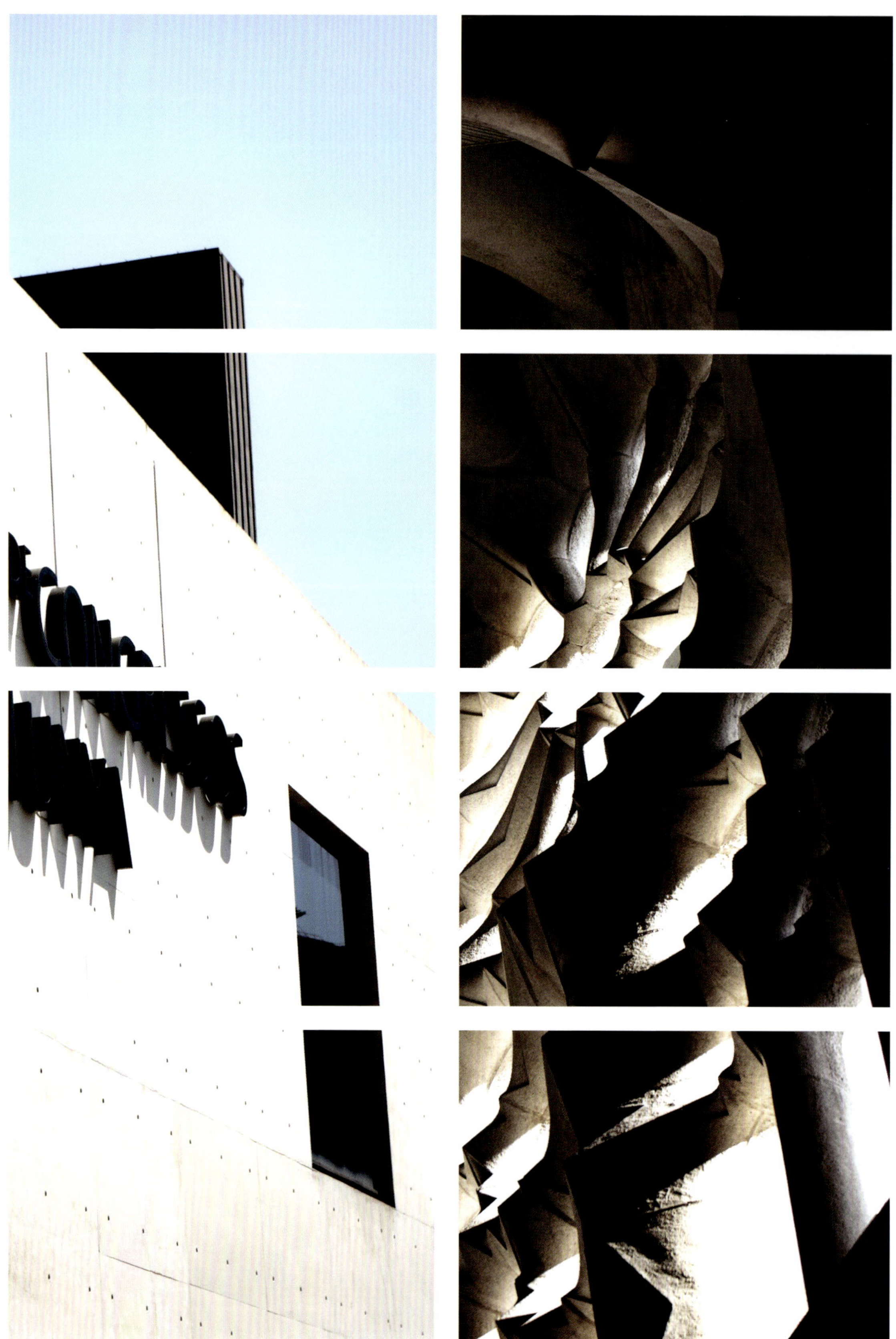

The key is how to cross the aesthetic output you receive, and find the meaning of how things match each other. The secret is a very simple one: assembling, but with ideas. Improving in a personal way the management of meaning and message, as the excess of information surrounding us. The greatest desire is that hundreds of people will copy us.

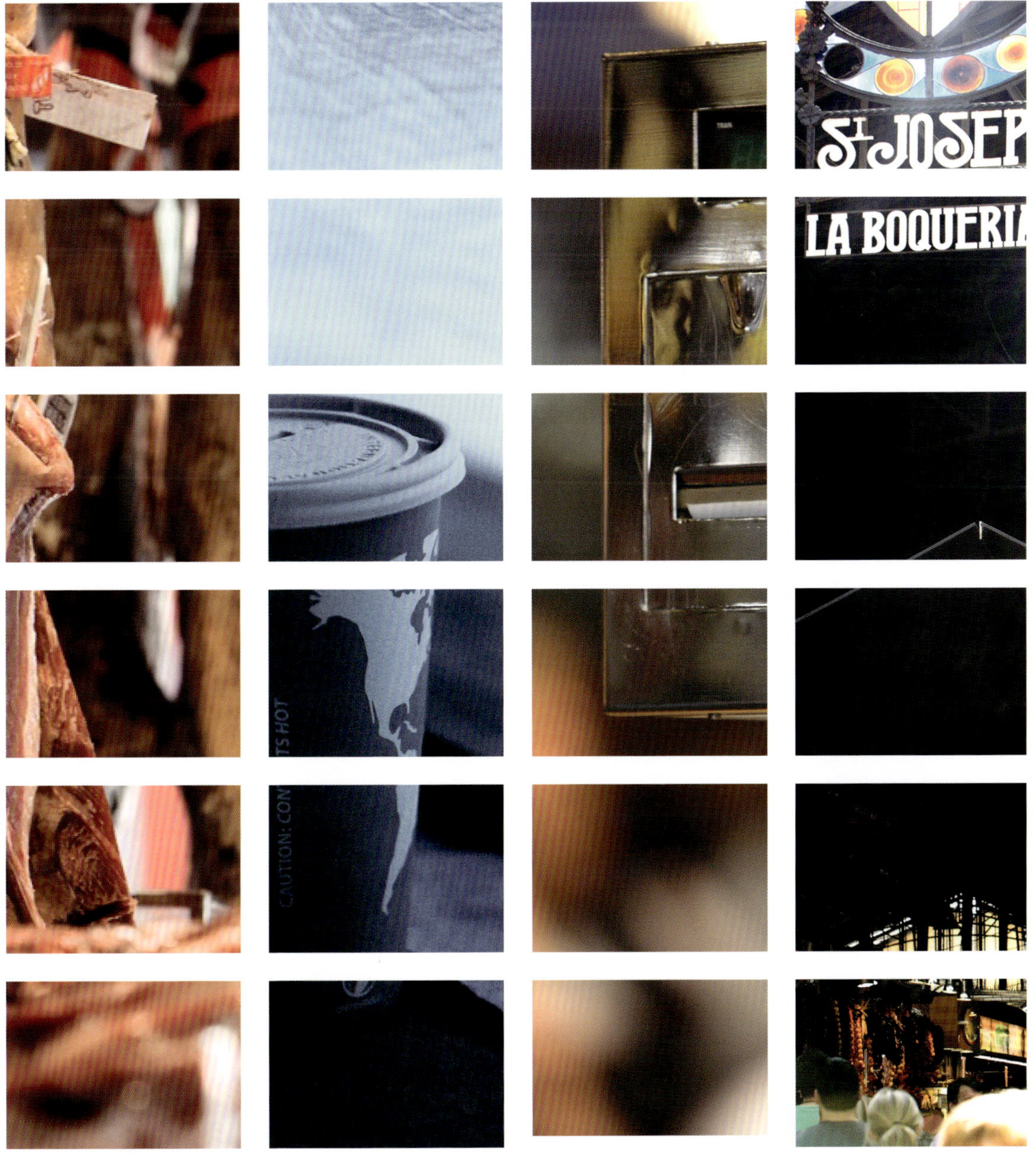

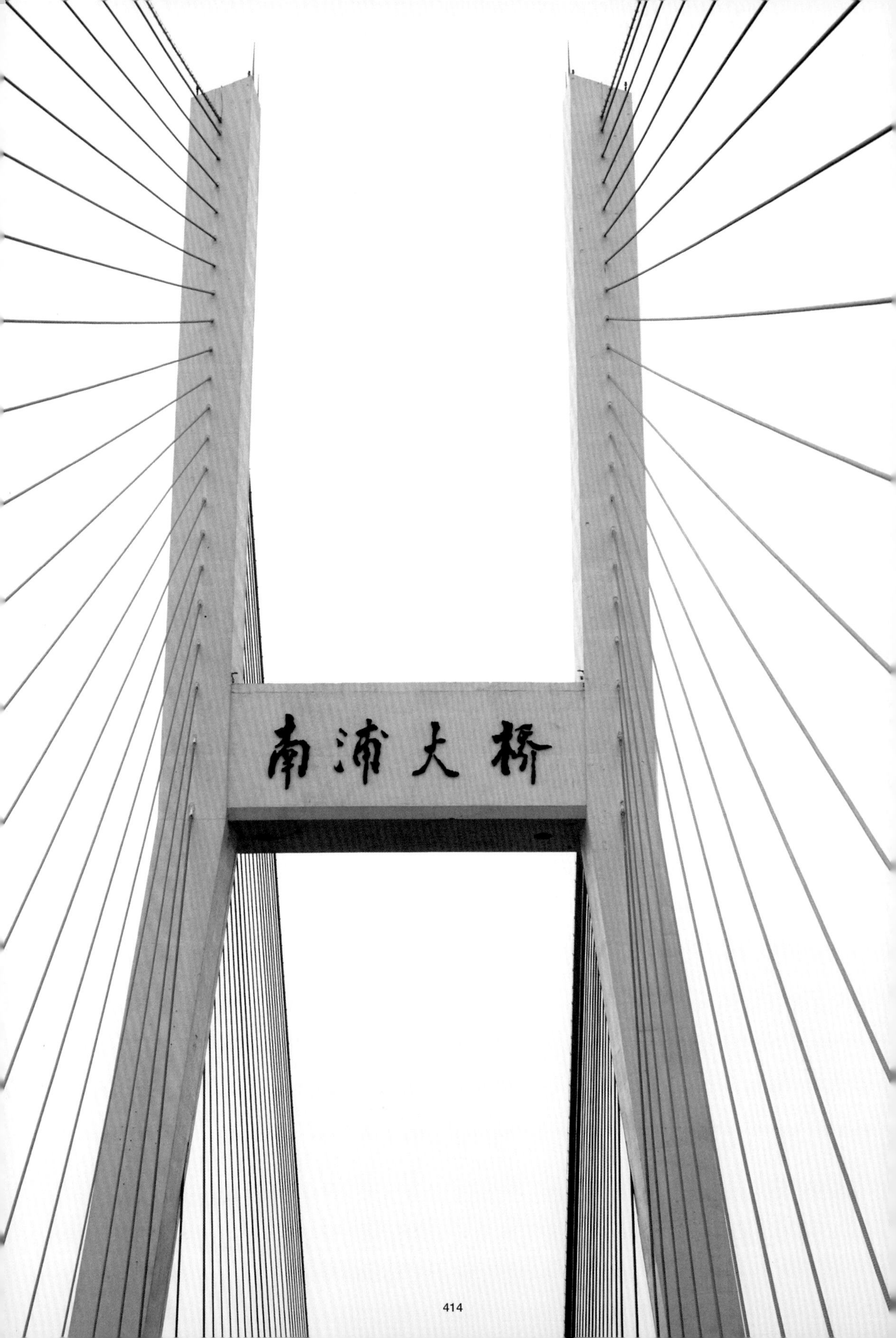
南浦大桥

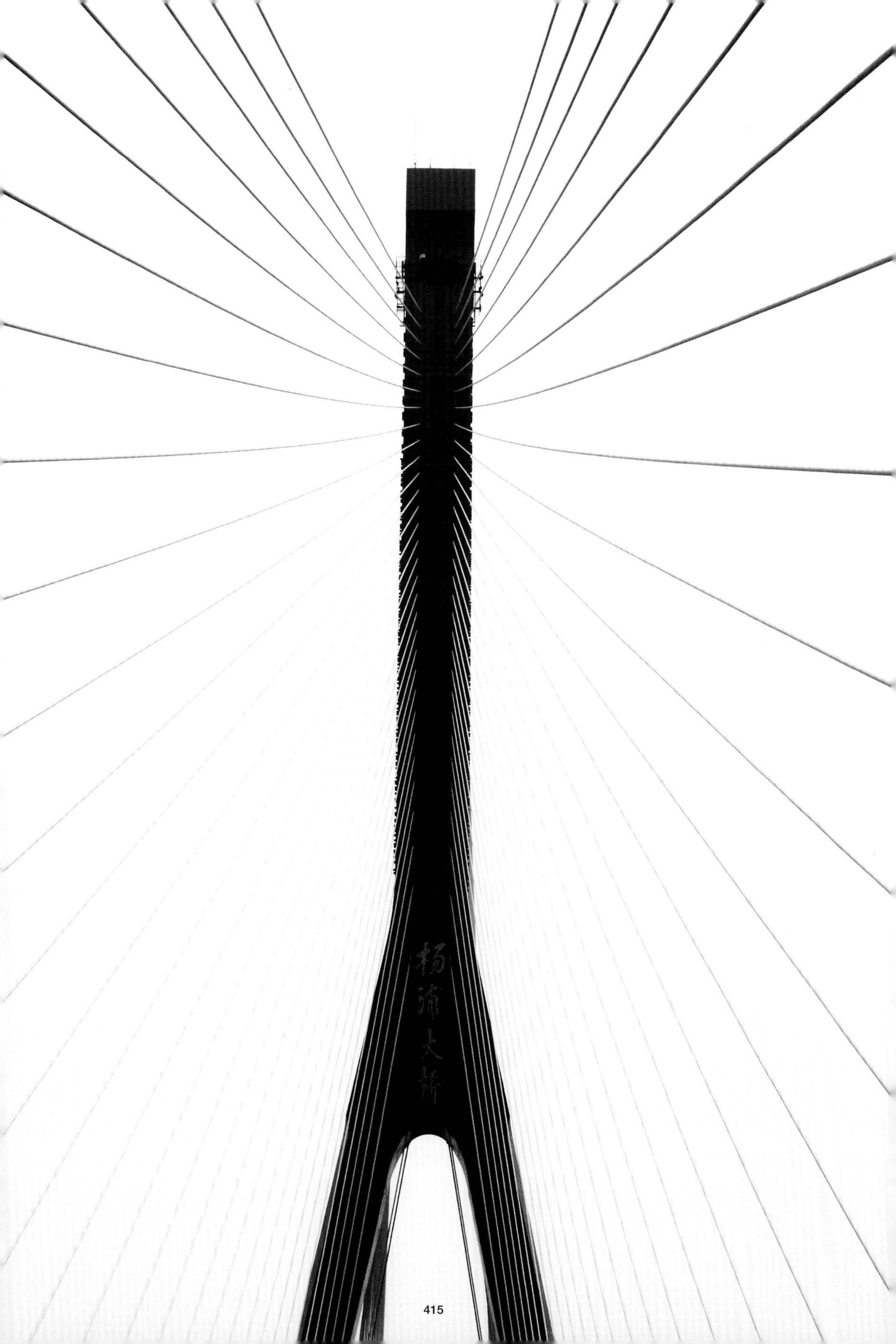
杨浦大桥

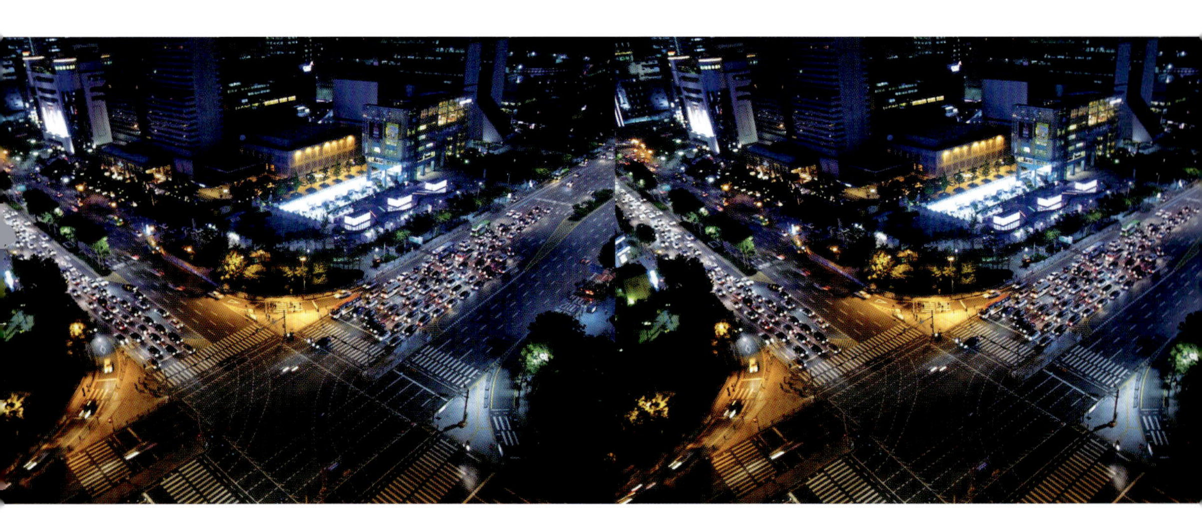

BEING FASCINATED BY THE MYSTERIOUS LOGIC OF THESE COLLECTIONS OF STRUCTURED FORMS, WE BEGIN

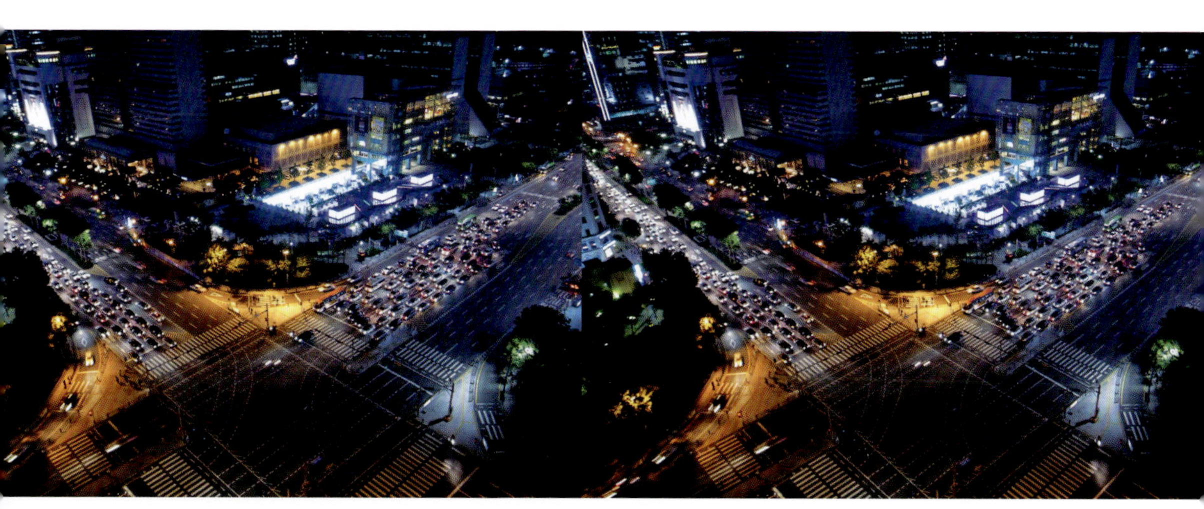

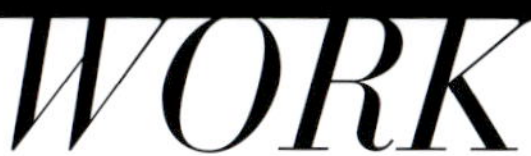
WORK

BLACK

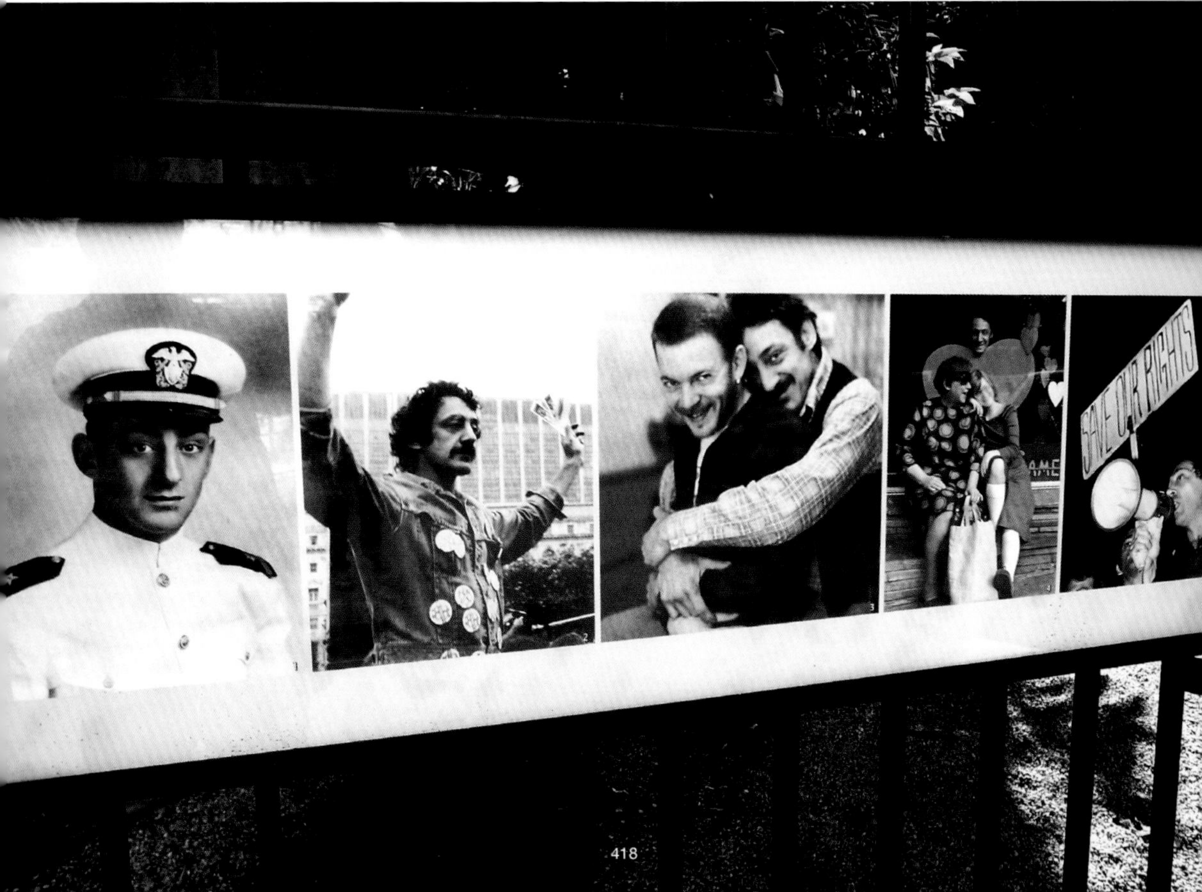

LINKS
IT'S ABOUT
MAKING CONNECTIONS
BETWEEN DIFFERENCES
LIKE IN A PLOT

THINK
DISCOVER
INVENT
CONNECT

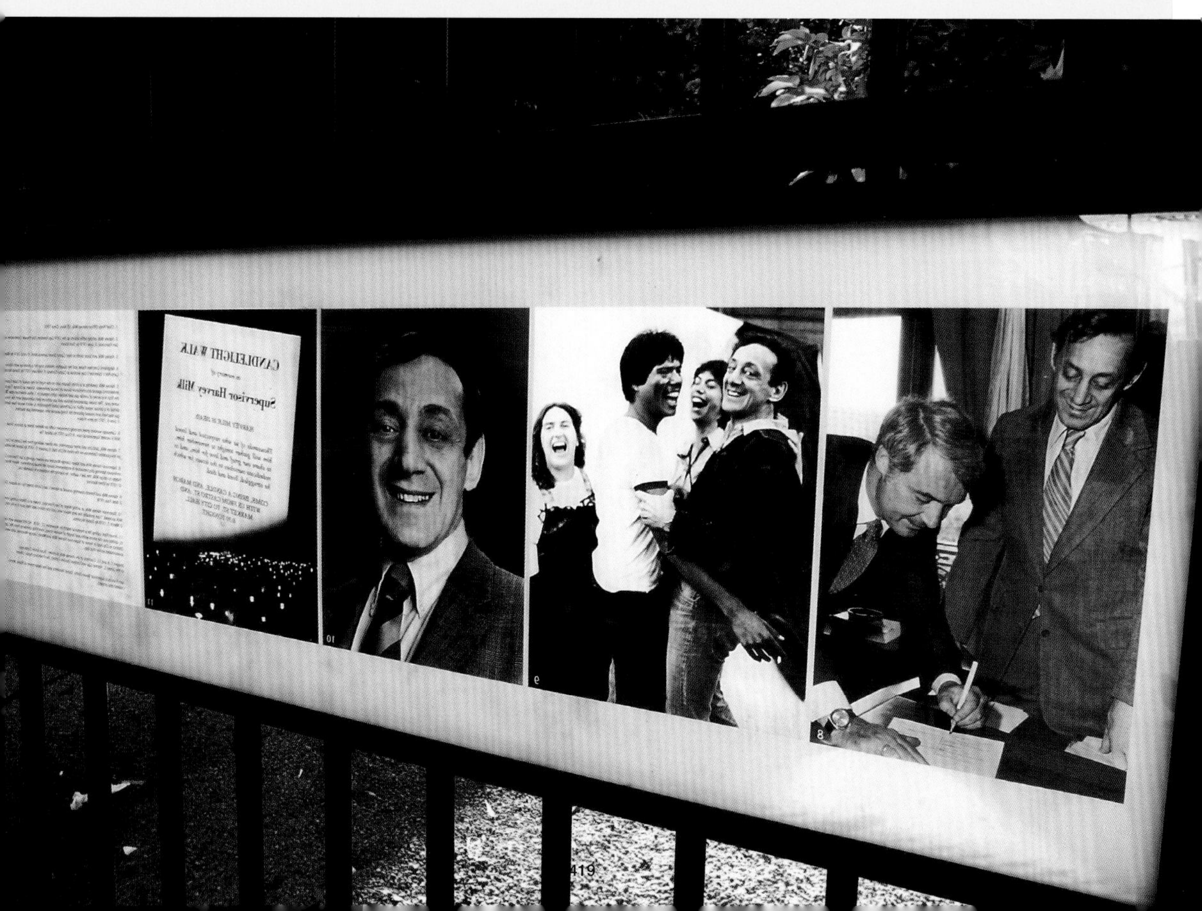

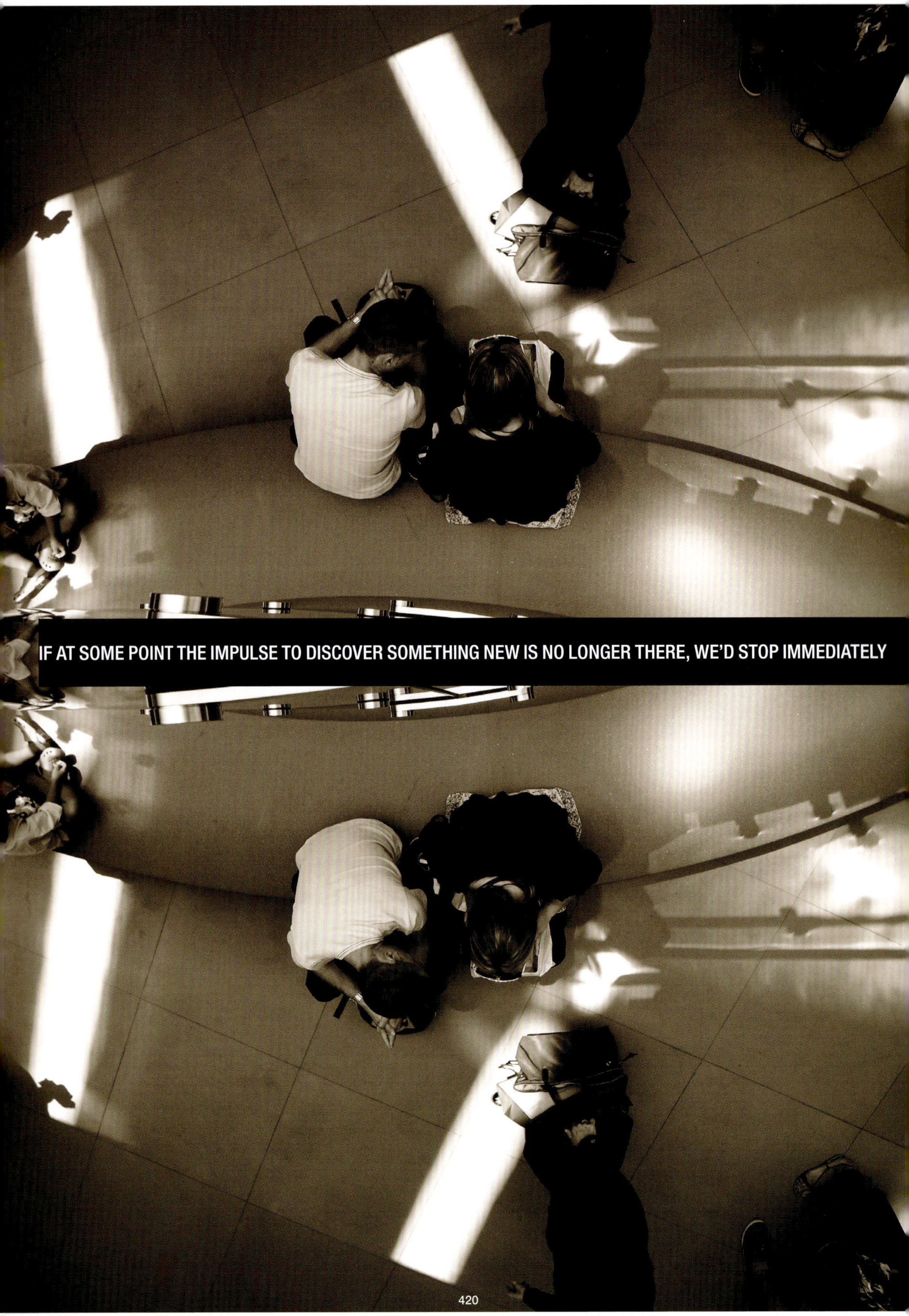

IF AT SOME POINT THE IMPULSE TO DISCOVER SOMETHING NEW IS NO LONGER THERE, WE'D STOP IMMEDIATELY

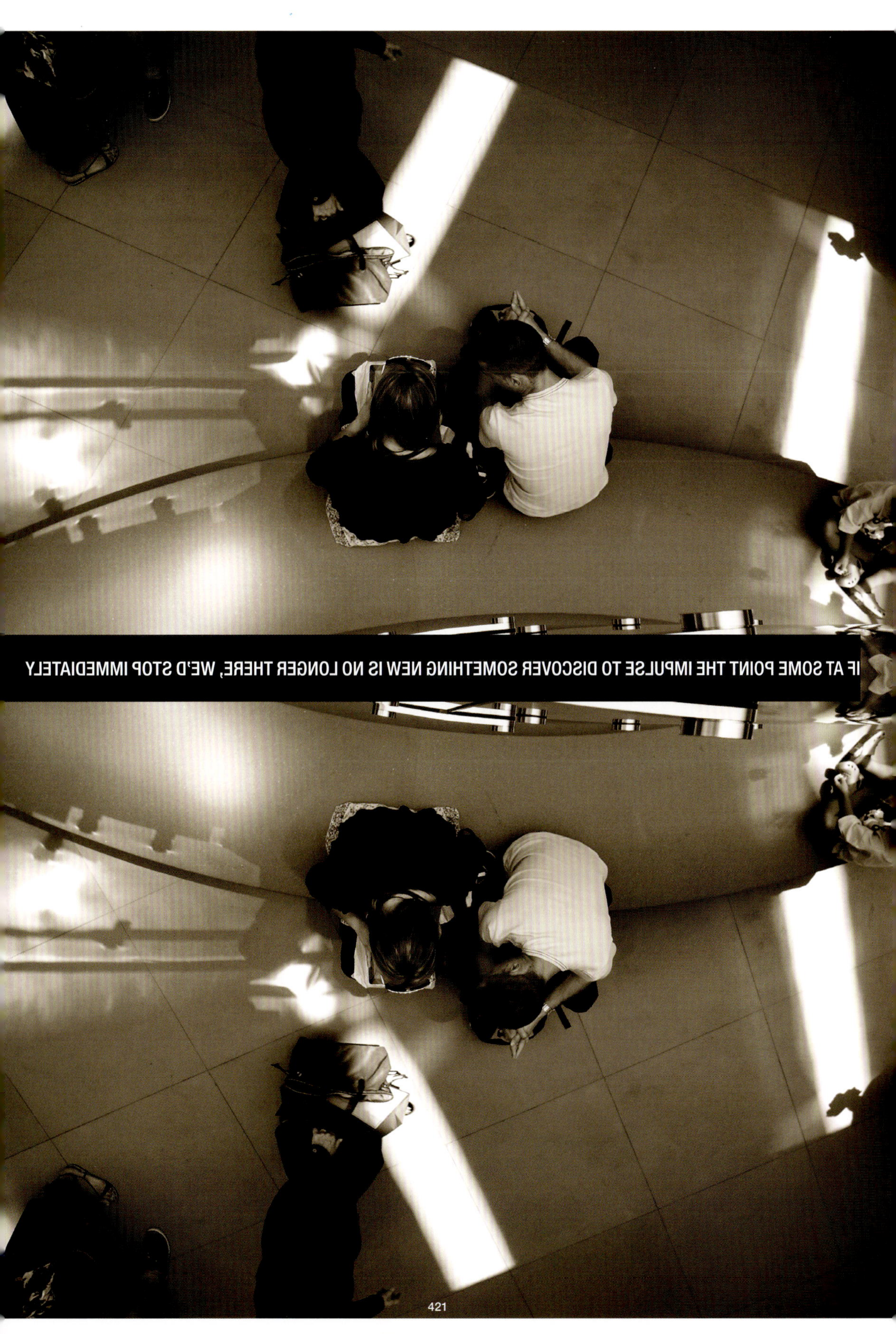

IF AT SOME POINT THE IMPULSE TO DISCOVER SOMETHING NEW IS NO LONGER THERE, WE'D STOP IMMEDIATELY

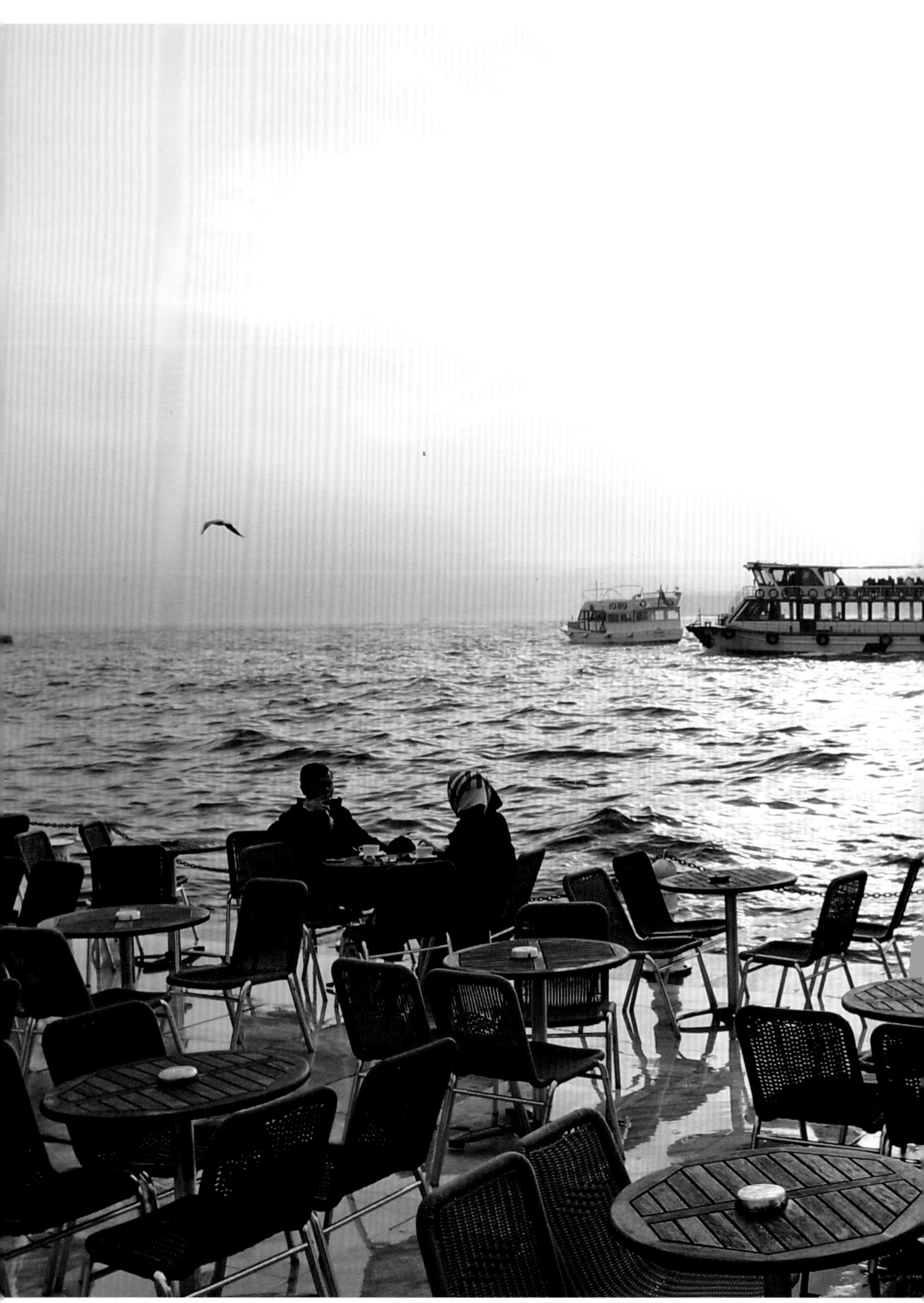

THIS IS JUST A STATE OF MIND

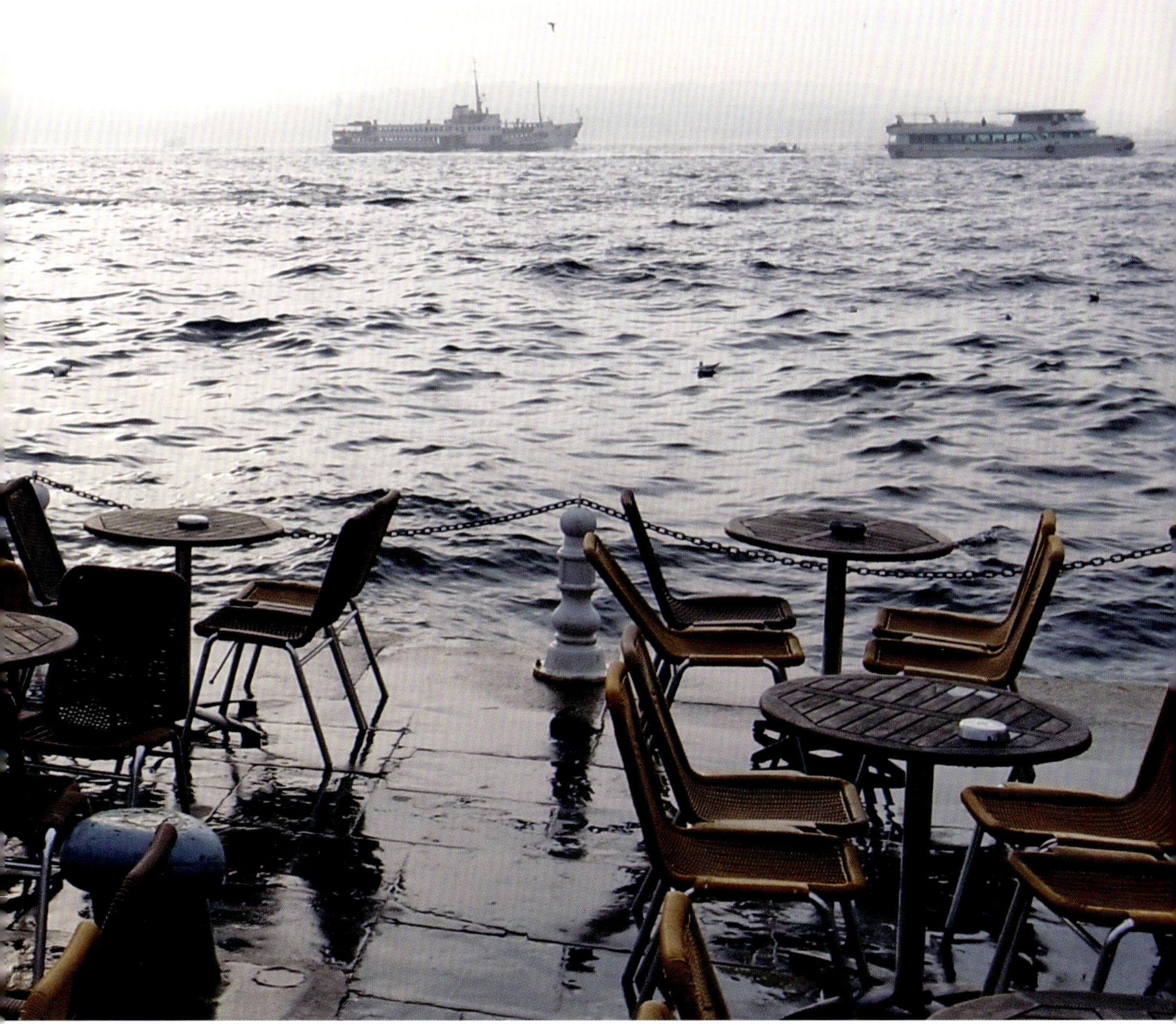

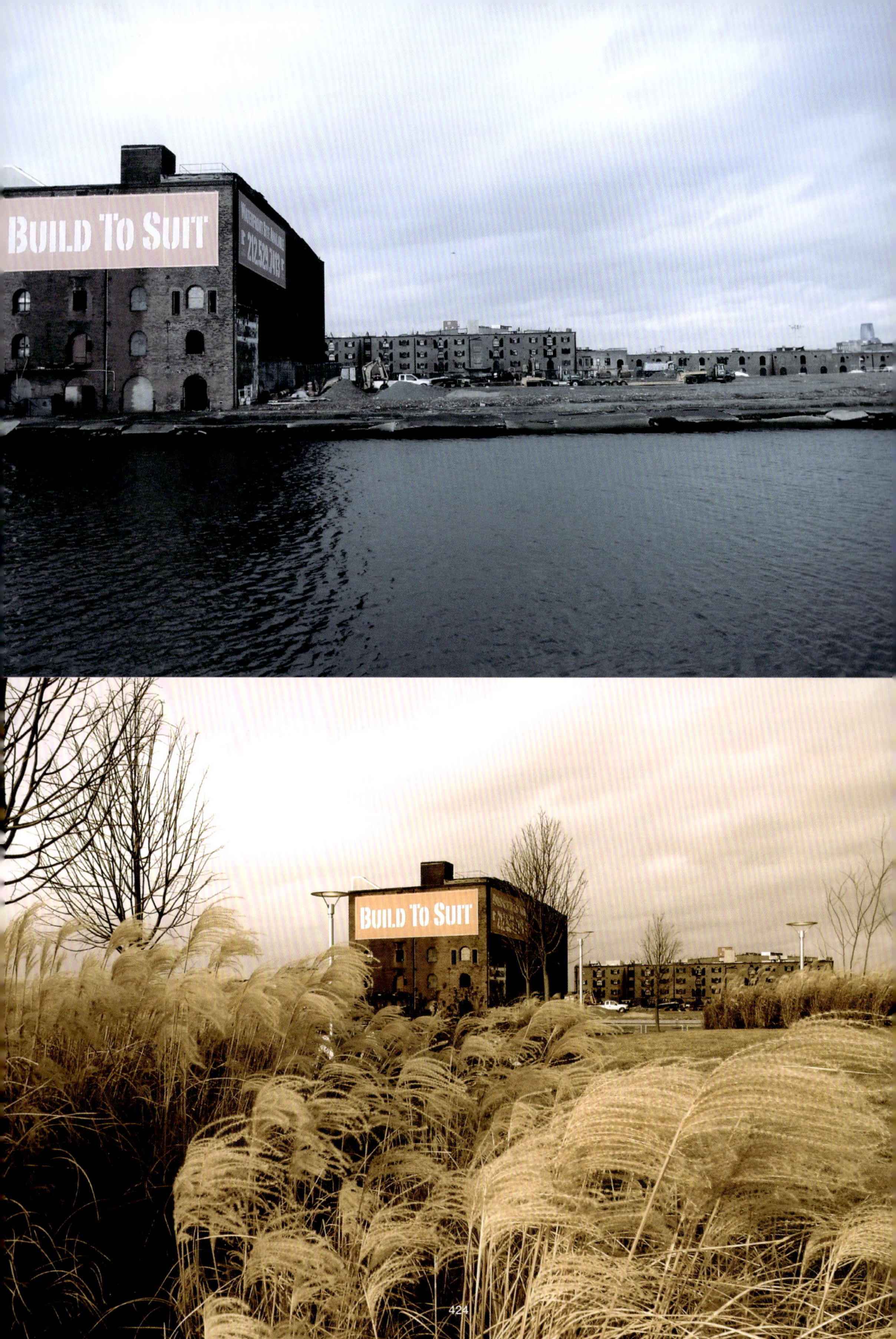
BUILD TO SUIT
WATERFRONT SITE AVAILABLE
212.528.7616
BUILD TO SUIT

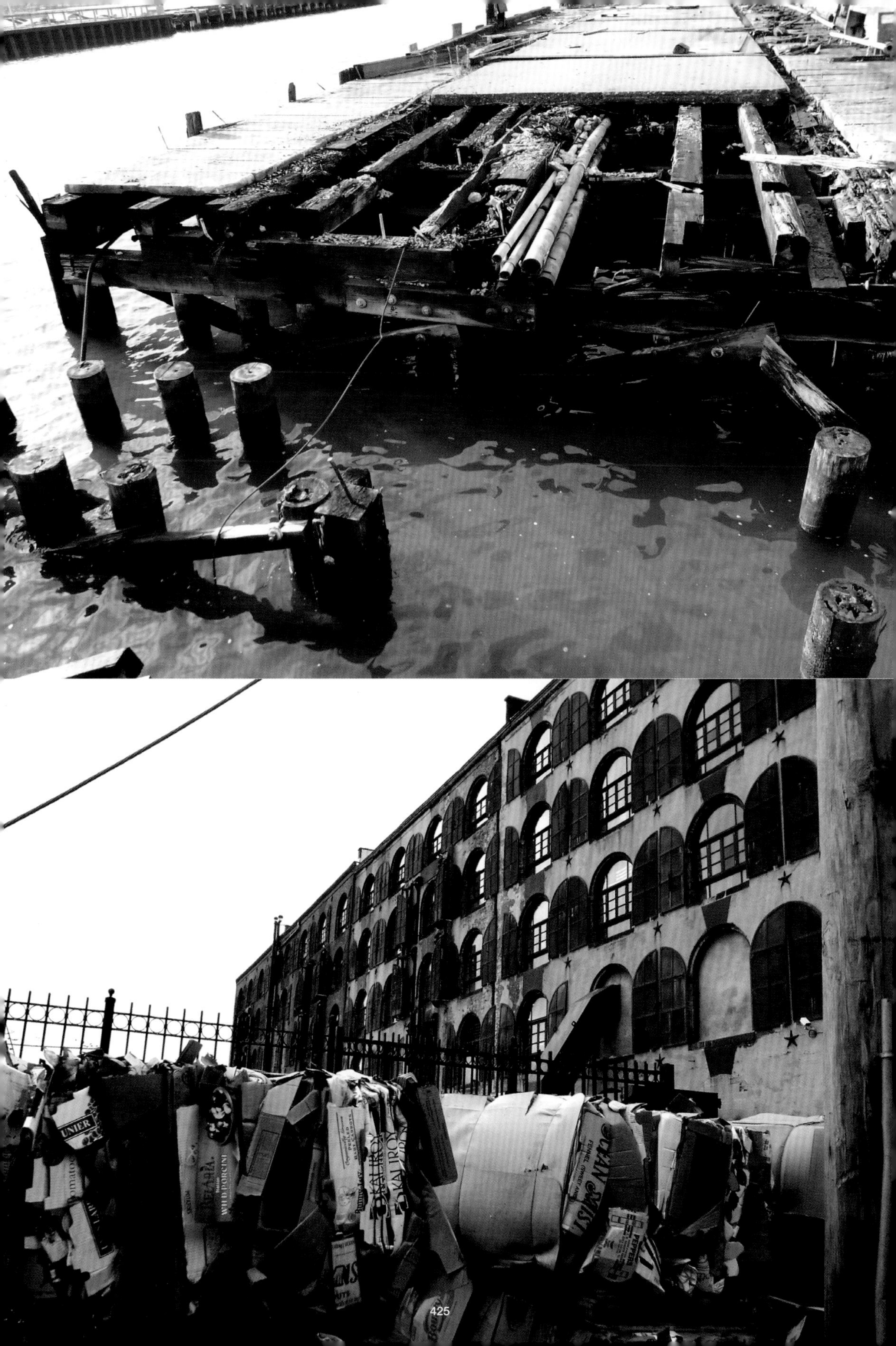

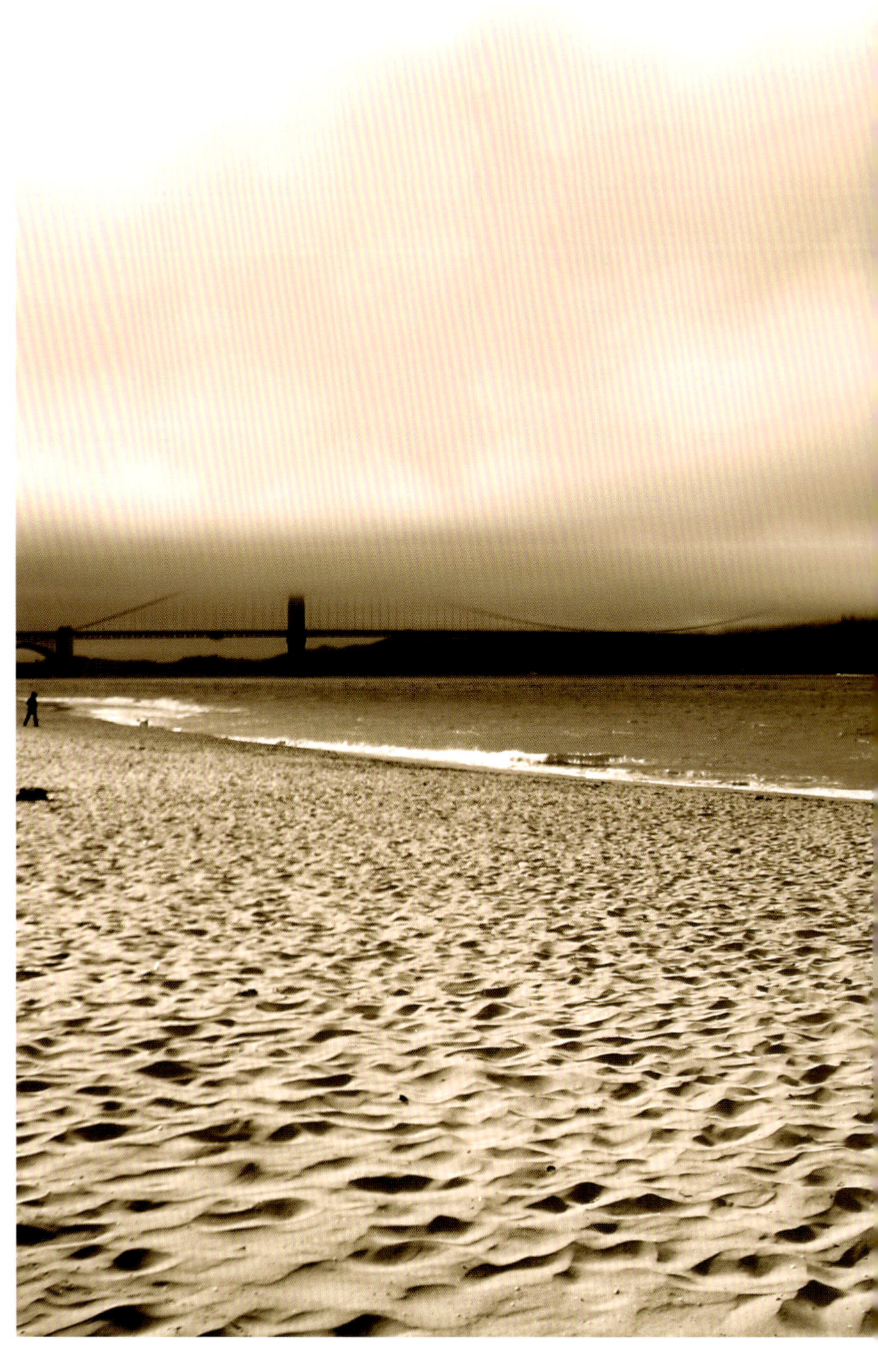

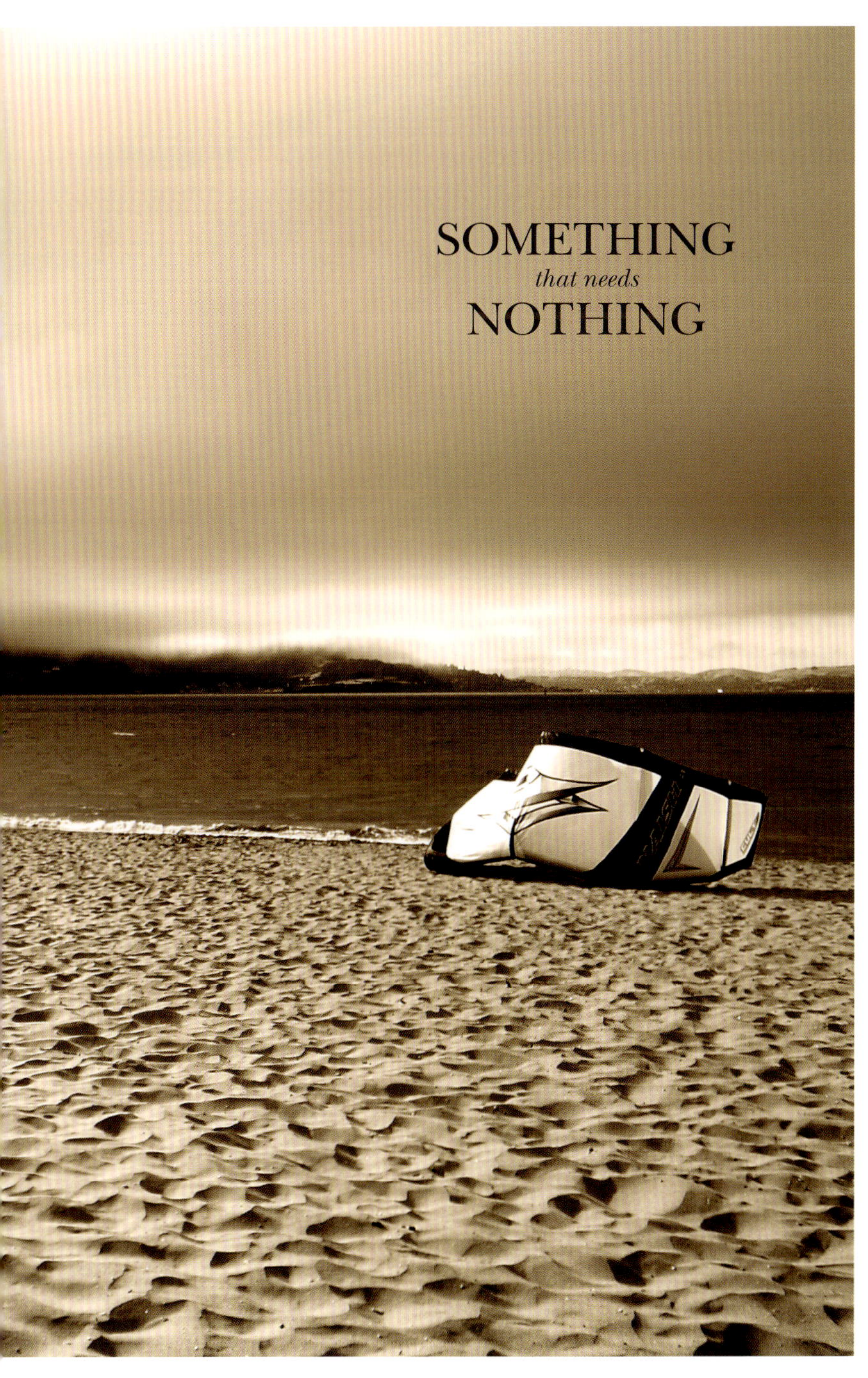

SOMETHING
that needs
NOTHING

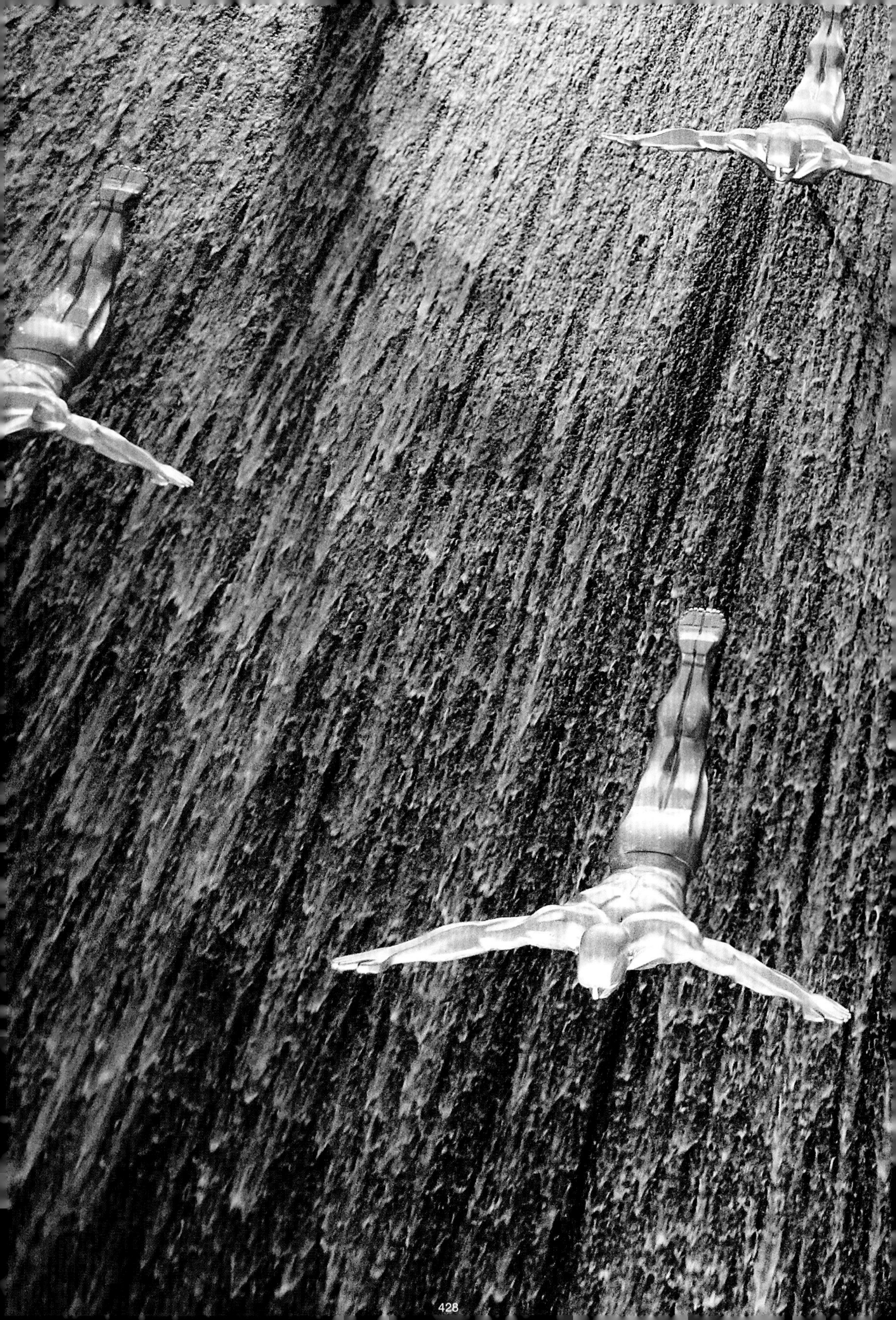

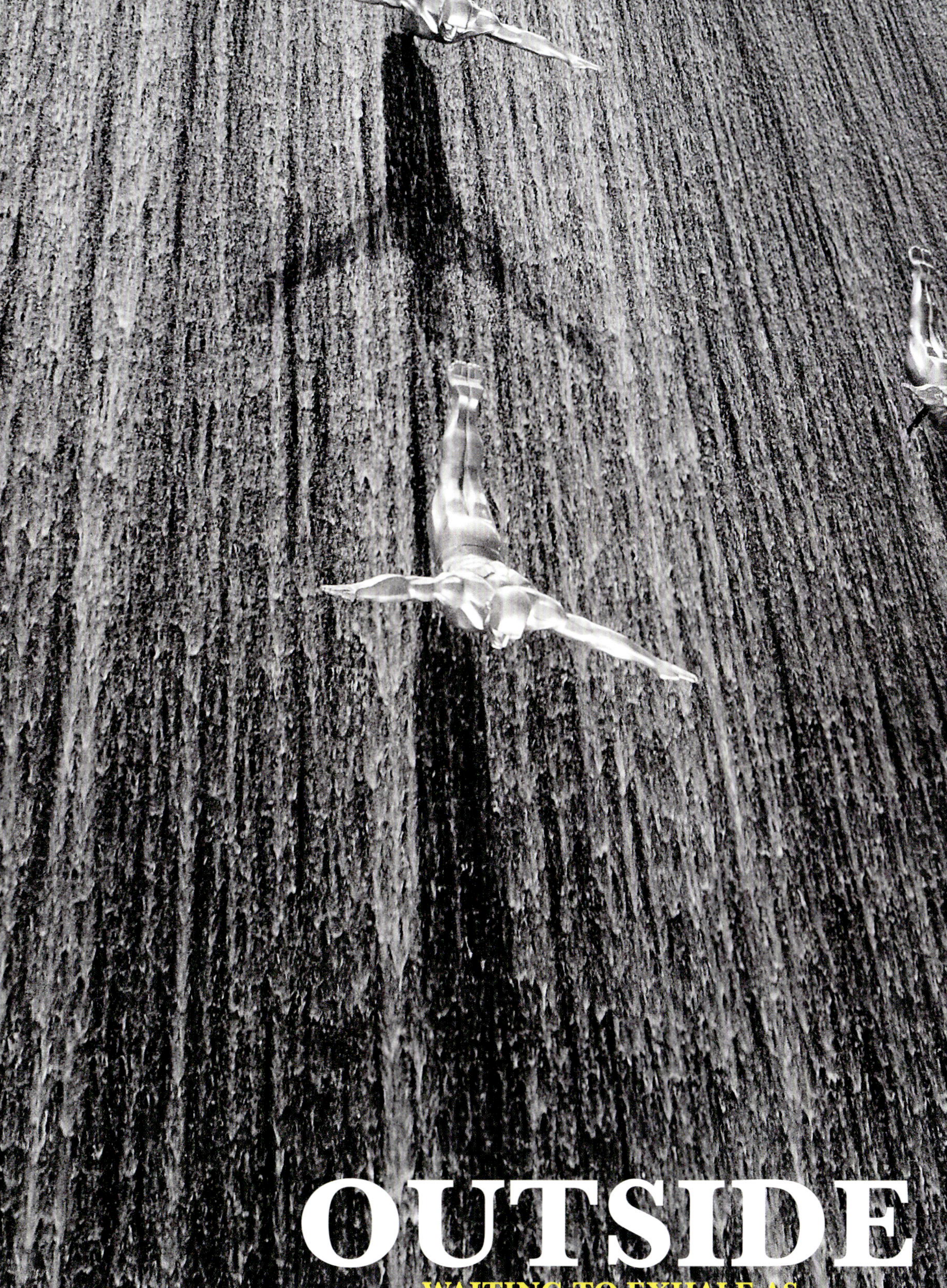

OUTSIDE
WAITING TO EXHALE AS
THE IMPORTANCE OF COLLAPSING

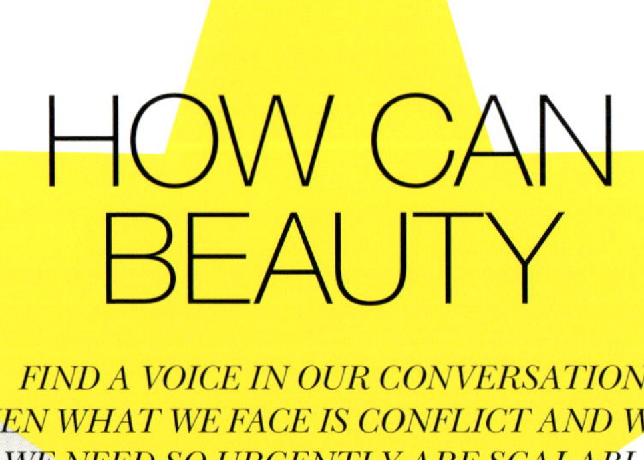

HOW CAN
BEAUTY

*FIND A VOICE IN OUR CONVERSATION
WHEN WHAT WE FACE IS CONFLICT AND WHAT
WE NEED SO URGENTLY ARE SCALABLE
SOLUTIONS, WHEN THE CHANGE REQUIRED
IS OF SUCH MAGNITUDE THAT WE MUST
CALL ON ALL OF OUR SHARED KNOWLEDGE
AND INNOVATION TO RACE FOR
THE WAYS TO WIN?*

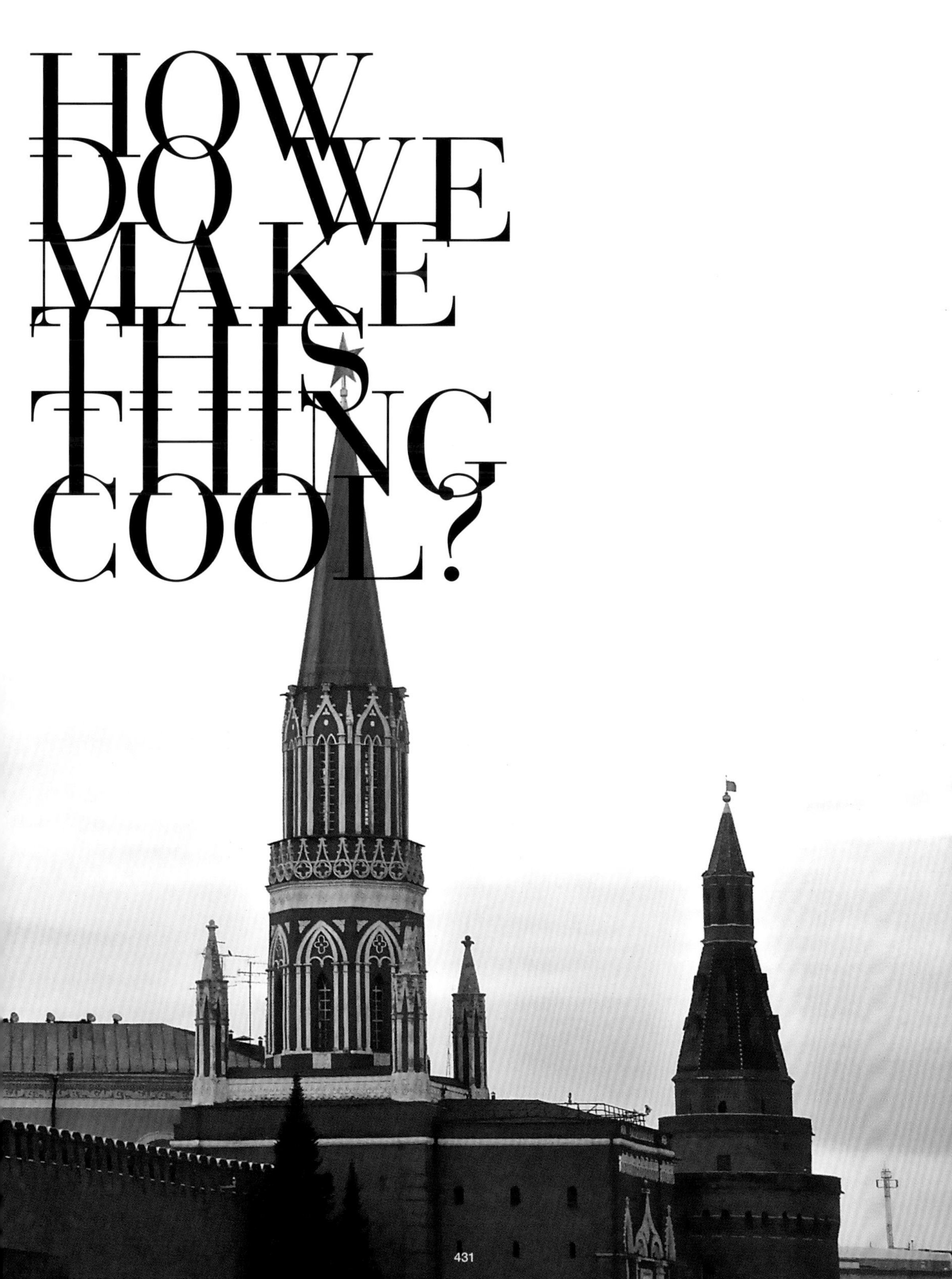
HOW
DO WE
MAKE
THIS
THING
COOL?

WHERE IS

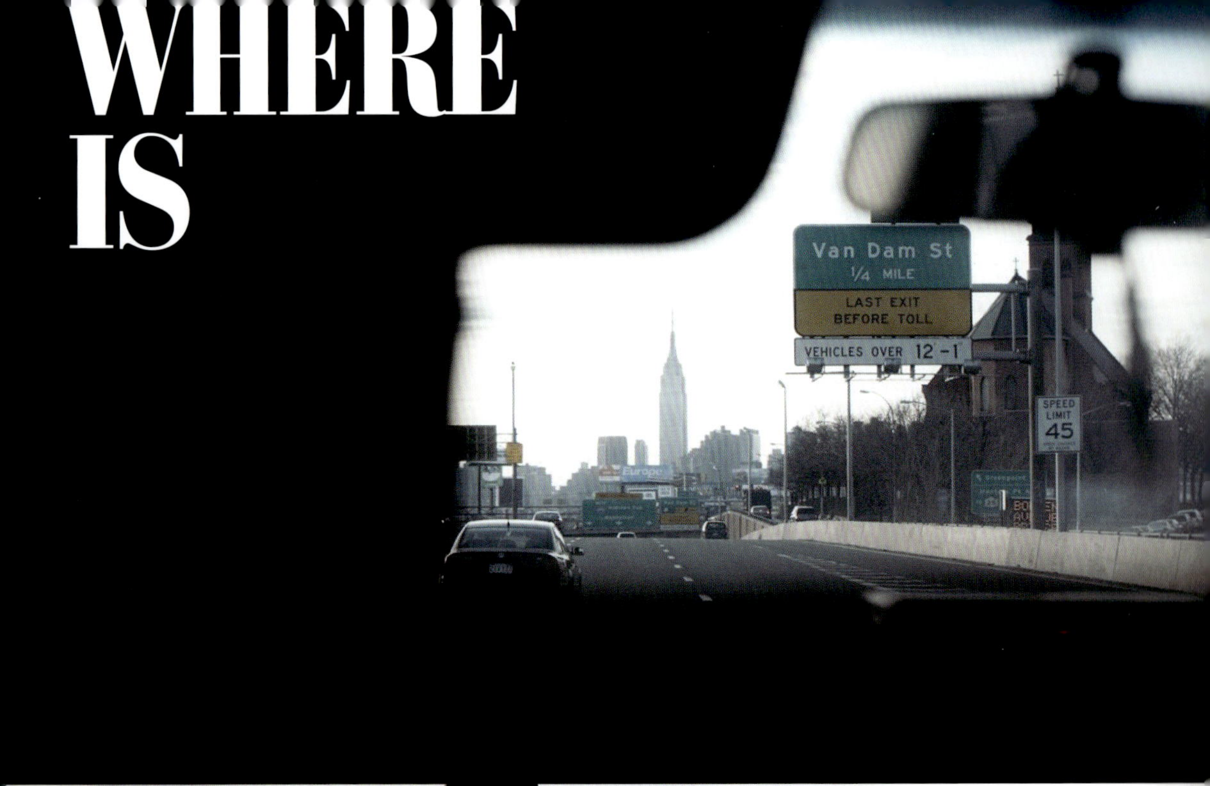

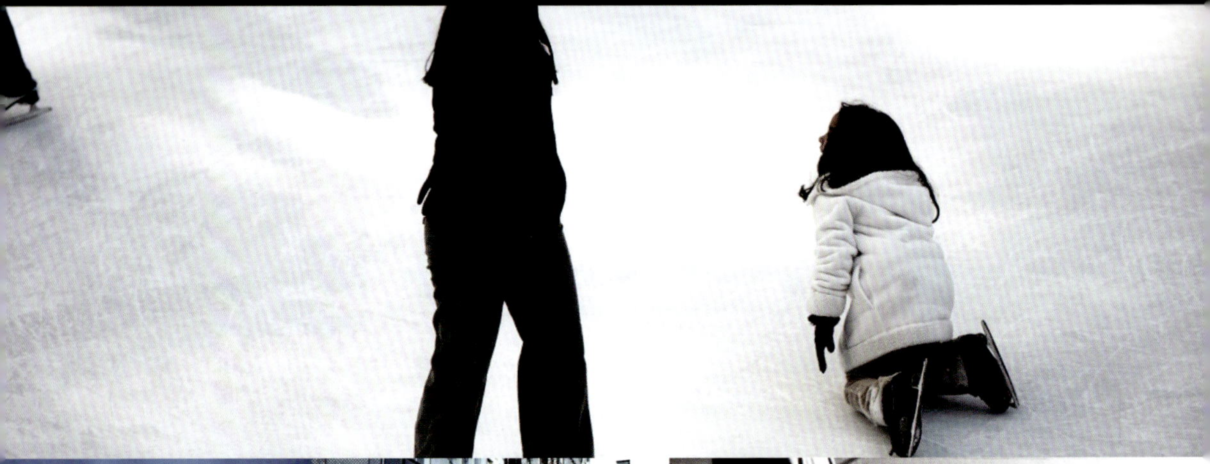

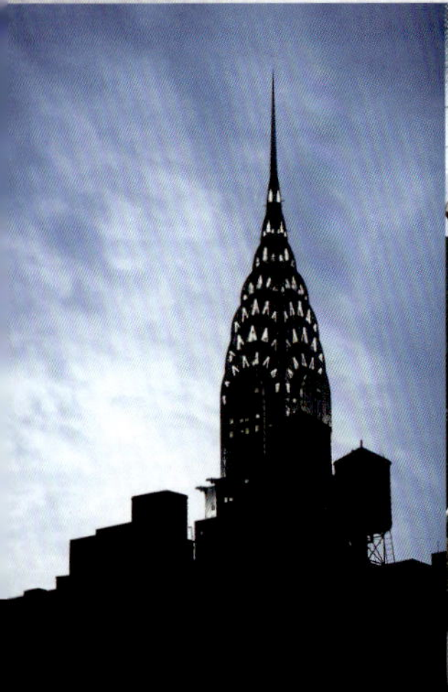

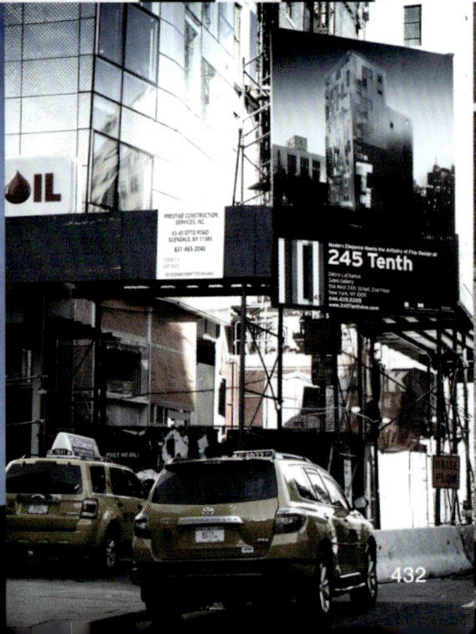

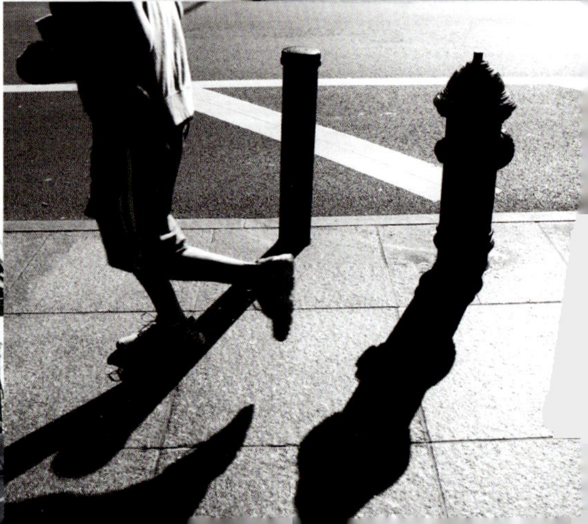

CITY
BALLET
2009 WINTER SEASON
JANUARY 6 – MARCH 1
nycballet.com or 212-721-6500

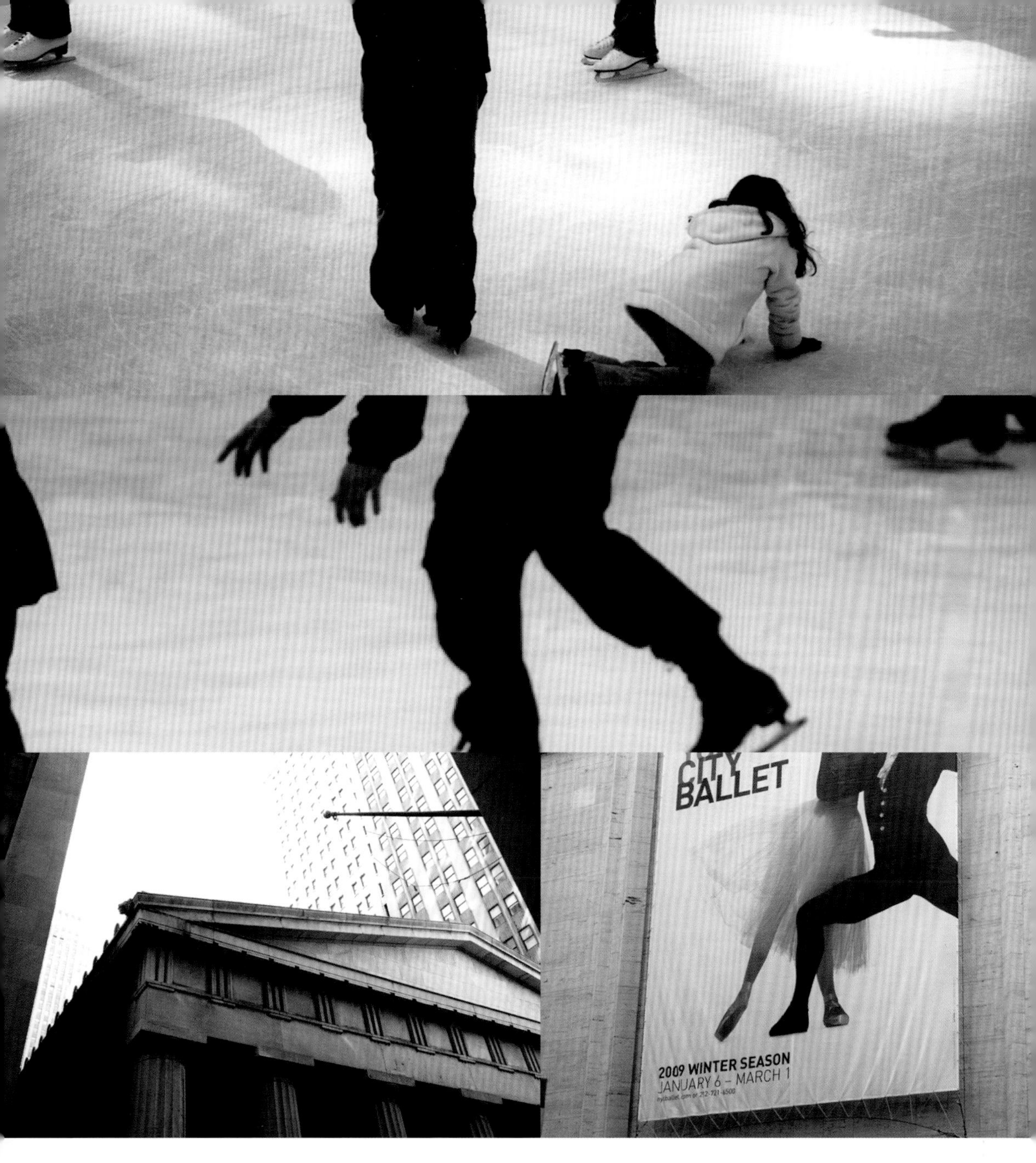

WHERE?

LIVE TO TELL

HANGAR DESIGN GROUP

A story is created every time interference
changes the state of something.
In life like in stories, there's a moment when
everything changes. The moment in which
nothing is as it was. That precise moment,
when a short time before you were climbing
and then suddenly you're moving downward.
Likewise characters, after their beginnings,
have now arrived at the turning point. Loves.
Choices. Departures. Deaths. Catastrophes.
Mistakes. Crazy Purchases. Sudden Decisions.
Escapes. Predicaments. Unexpected turns
of events. Details need to be changed. Unexpected forks in the road. We have understood
that there is no way to keep things as they are.

SOME MIGHT CALL IT VINTAGE. WE PREFER TIMELESS

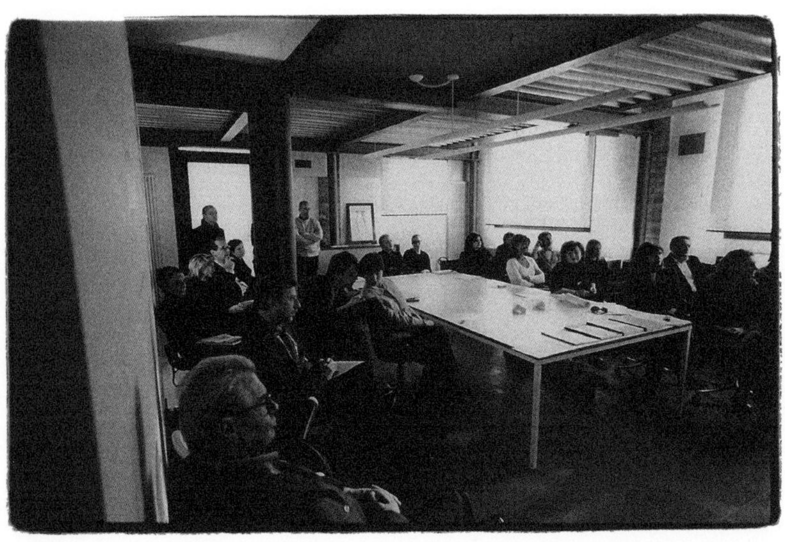

Annual Conventions.
For the project and relative creations sharing is the catalyzing element of Hangar Twist.

LIVE TO TELL

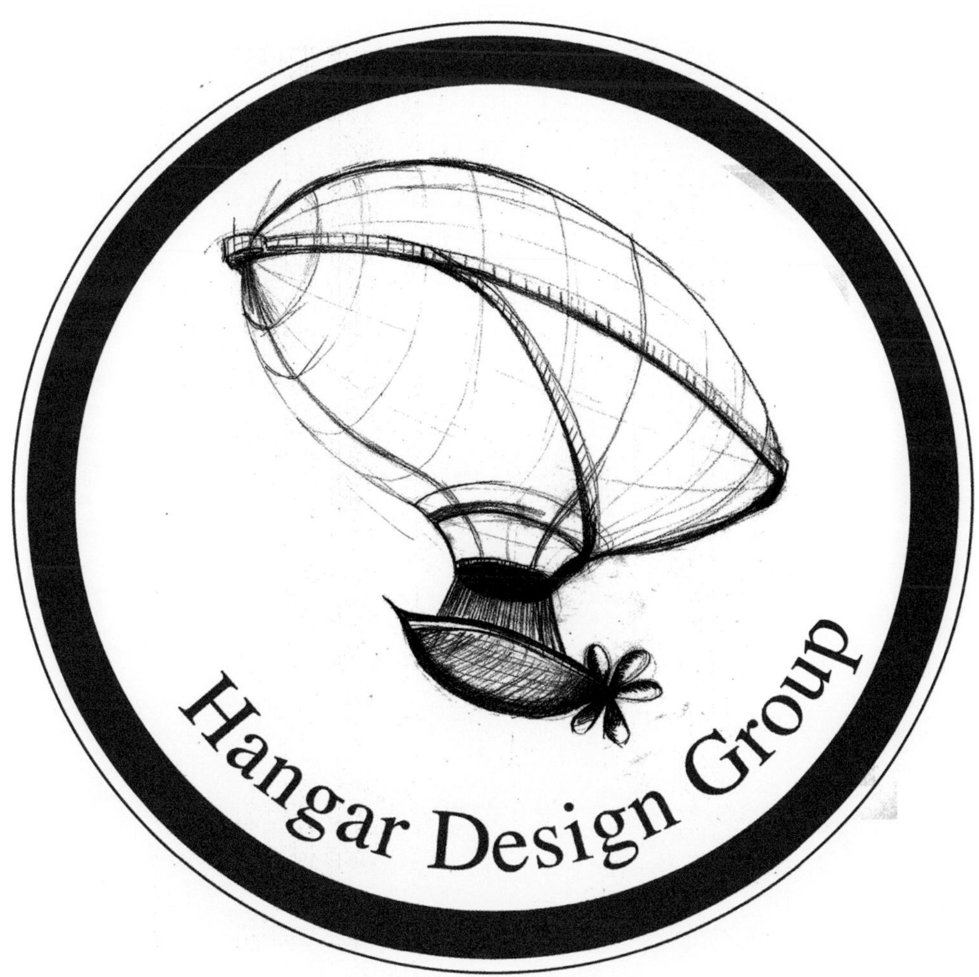

Distinguishing Features.
Projects and creations are "signed" and marked
with the institutional symbol and logo.

LIVE TO TELL

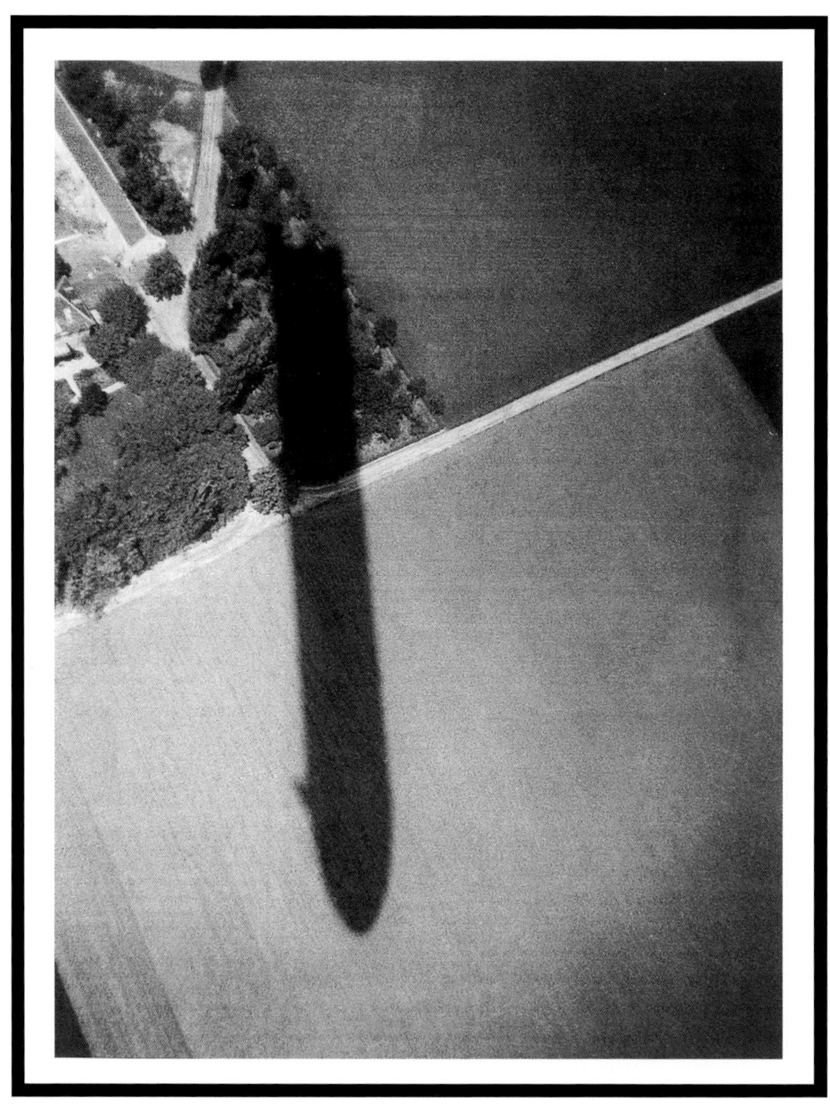

1998. *Airship (Zeppelin) over the*
Hangar Design Group branch in Treviso.

LIVE TO TELL

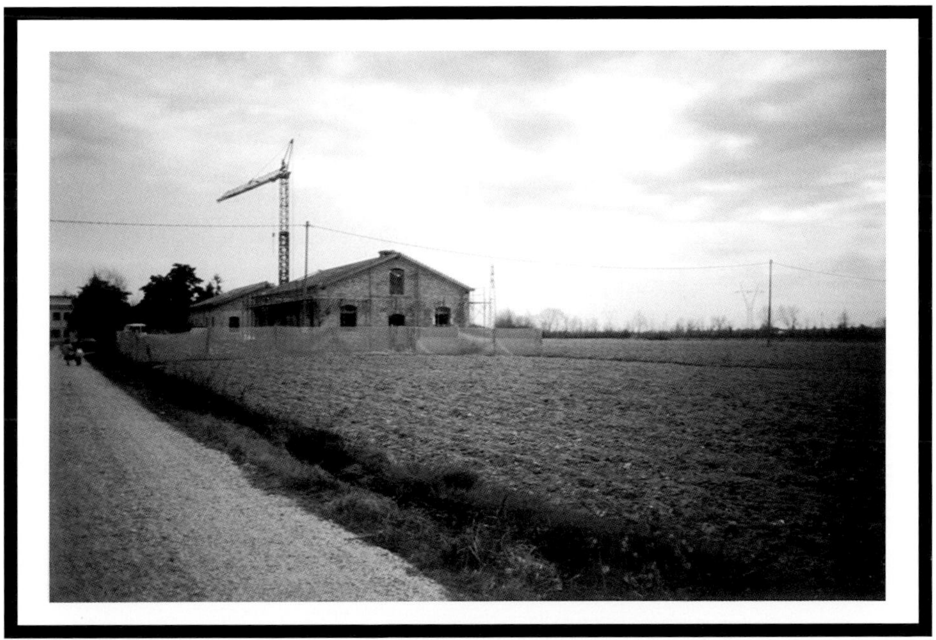

*"We work in two old hangars used for storing
spare parts for airships."*
1990. Restoration works begin and the adventure continues.

LIVE TO TELL

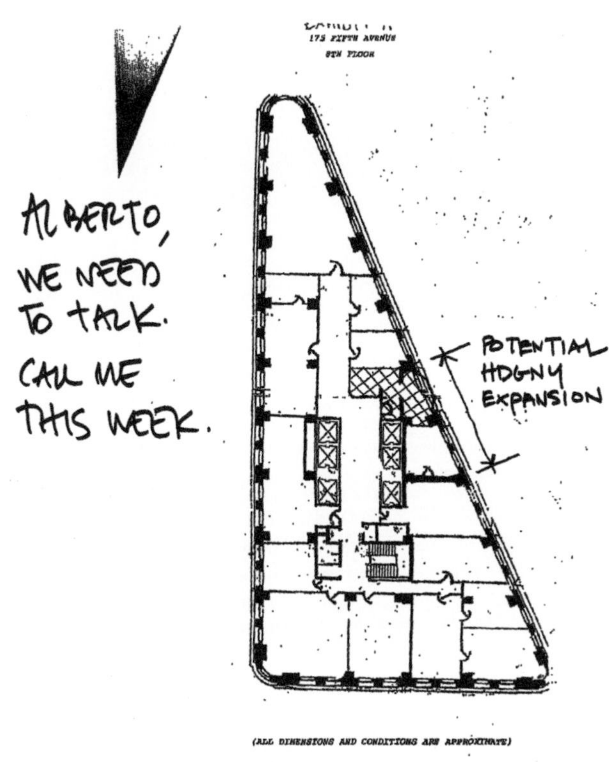

IN THE FLATIRON BUILDING, NEW YORK.
2002. With its legendary iron-shaped design, the Flatiron
Building was perhaps one of the first skyscrapers of the Big Apple.
This is the birthplace of HDGNY.

LIVE TO TELL

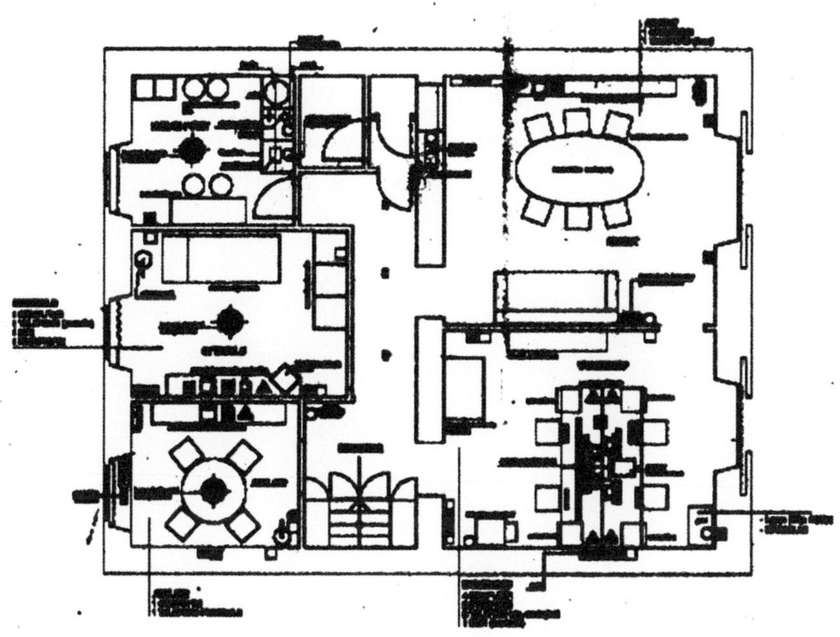

"Via Saffi is perhaps one of the most beautiful streets in Milan."
2001. At number 25 is the very first Milan branch of Hangar.

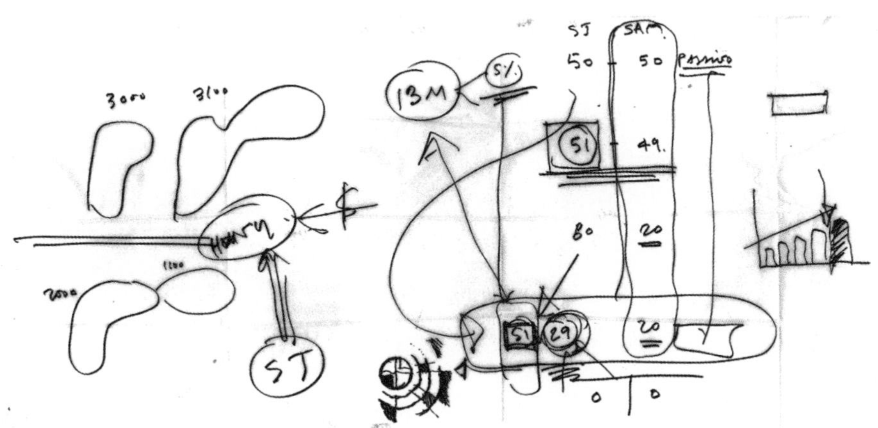

"We define working relations through our spaces."
1993. So begins one of the many "refurbishments"
of the Hangar House workplaces.

LIVE TO TELL

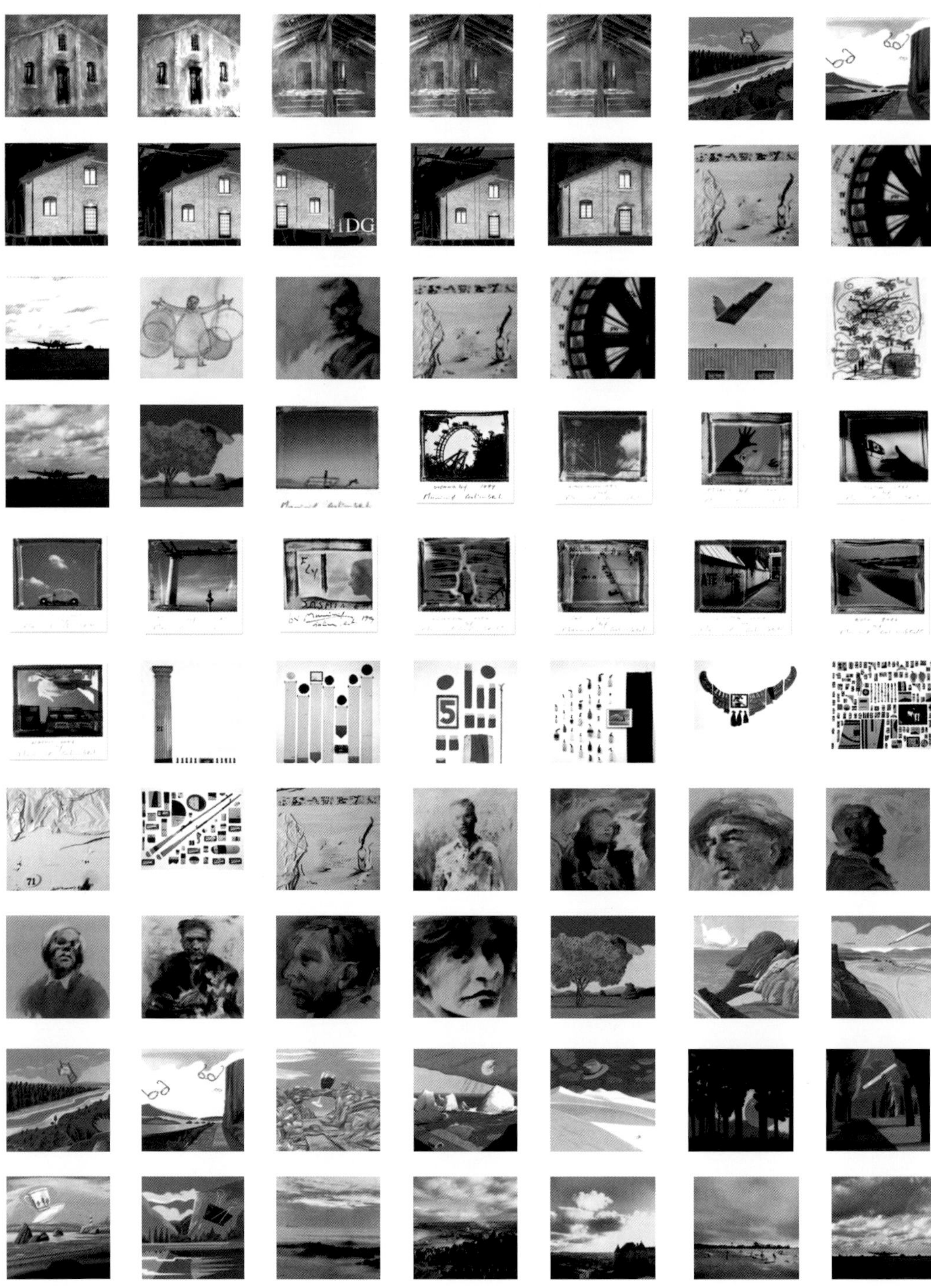

LIVE TO TELL

Hangar Planning overview from 1995 to 2008.
Photos of contributors who helped "clothe" the legendary agenda.

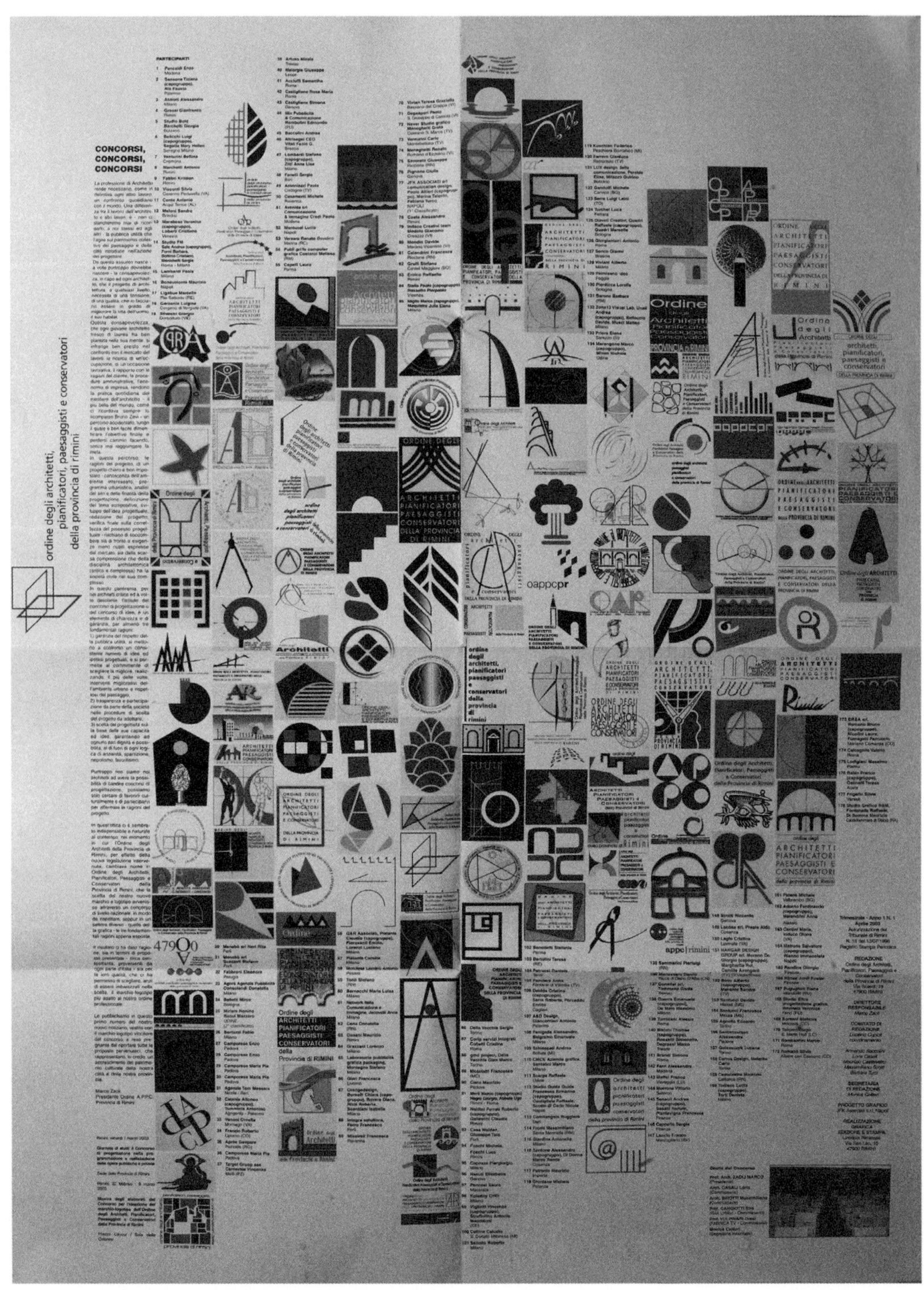

LIVE TO TELL

2004. *Poster of the competition for creating the logo of the Order of Architects. Hangar Design Group won first prize.*

2002. Debut in New York.
An intense week of consolidating important international relationships such as those with Milton Glaser and the Solomon Guggenheim Foundation.

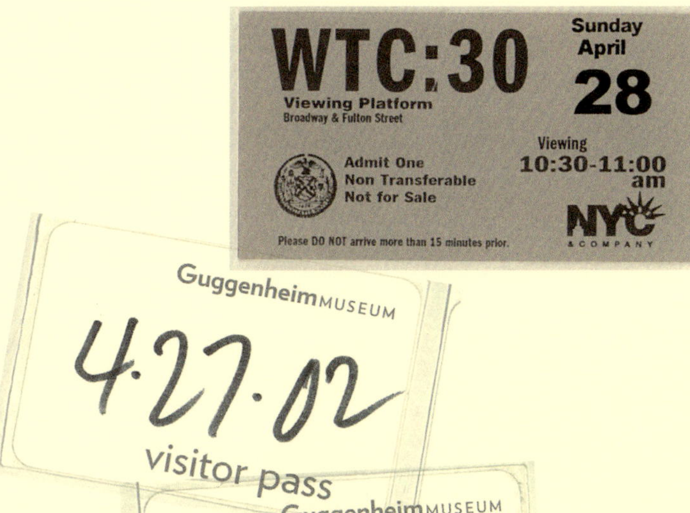

LIVE TO TELL

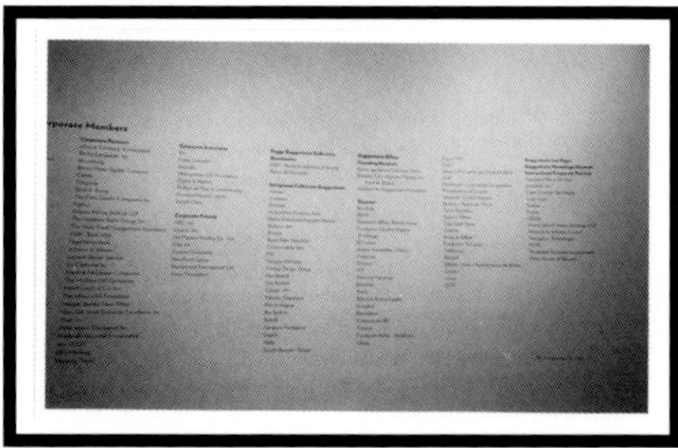

2001. *Hangar Design Group joins Intrapresae Collezione Guggenheim.*

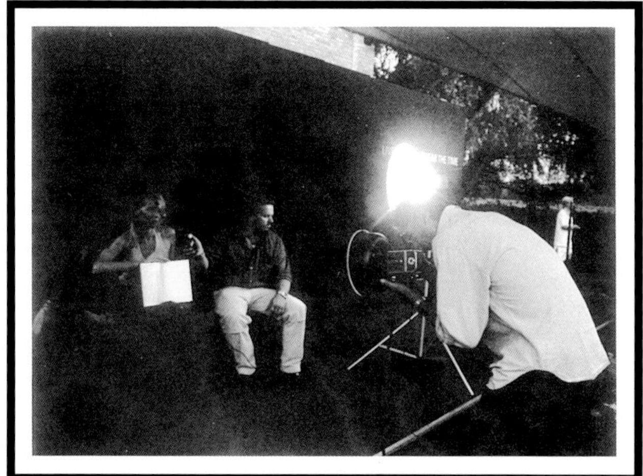

2000. *TV crew and a view of the Headquarters of Mogliano Veneto.*

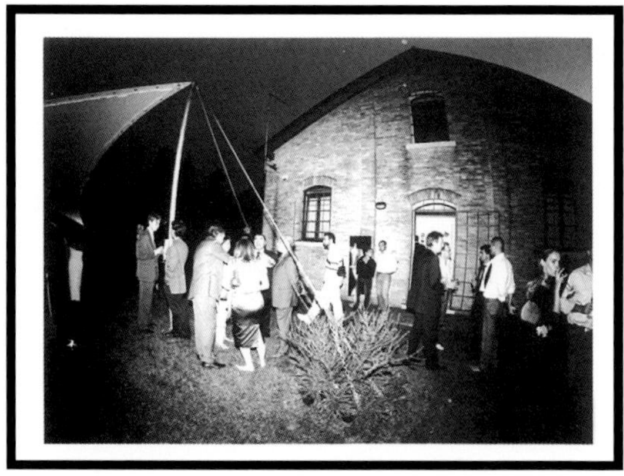

2002. *A Hangar event.*

LIVE TO TELL

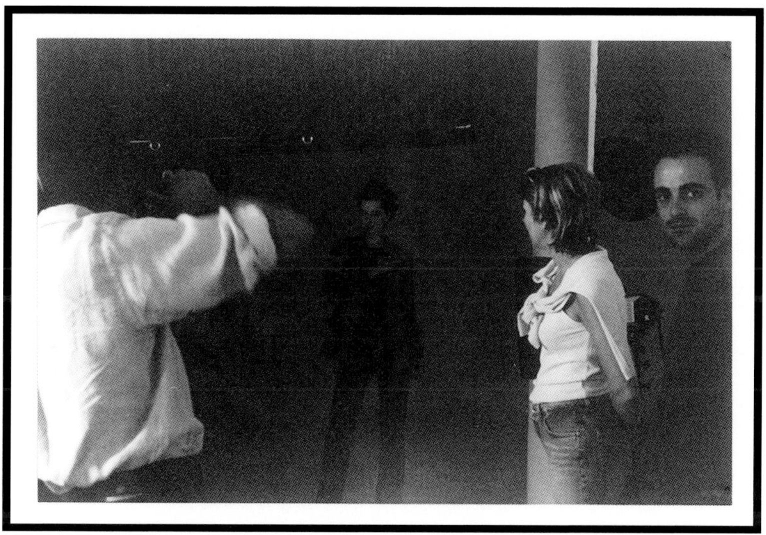

1995. *First photo shooting for Hangar Edizioni.*

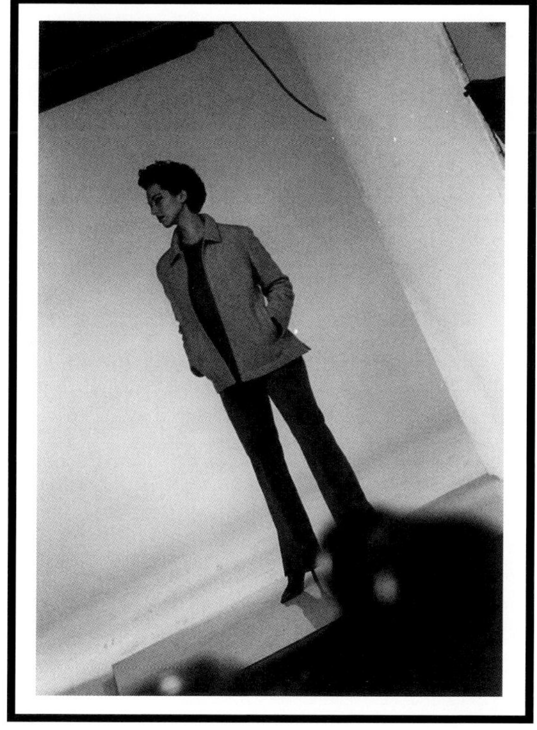

1998. *Fashion photograph shooting in the House's very first photographic studio.*

LIVE TO TELL

2003. Monte Carlo. *Hangar Design Group creates a new advertising campaign. Shooting took place in Nice and Monte Carlo and consolidated the ten-year collaboration with a long-established textile manufacturing company.*

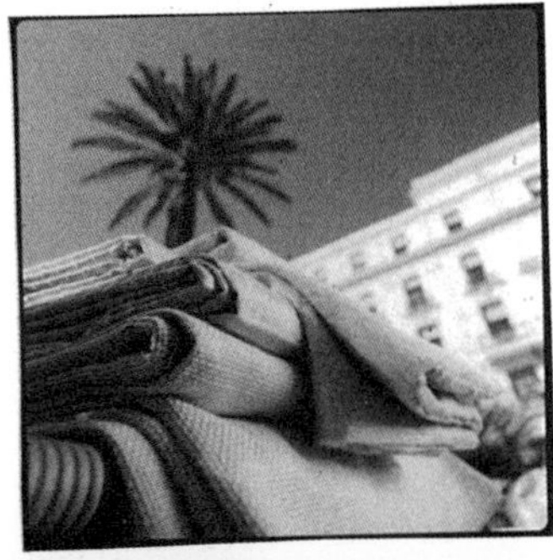

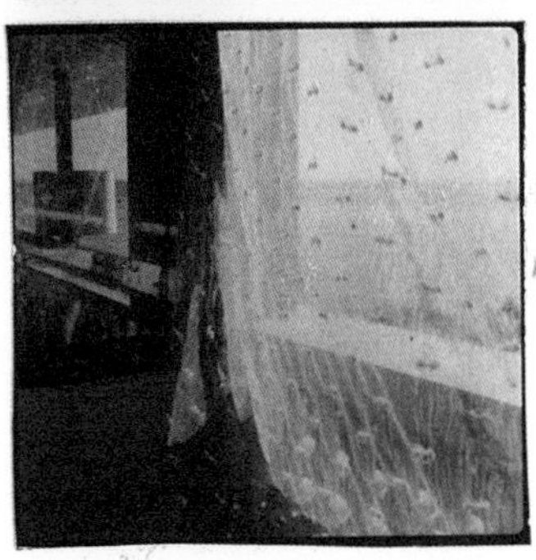

LIVE TO TELL

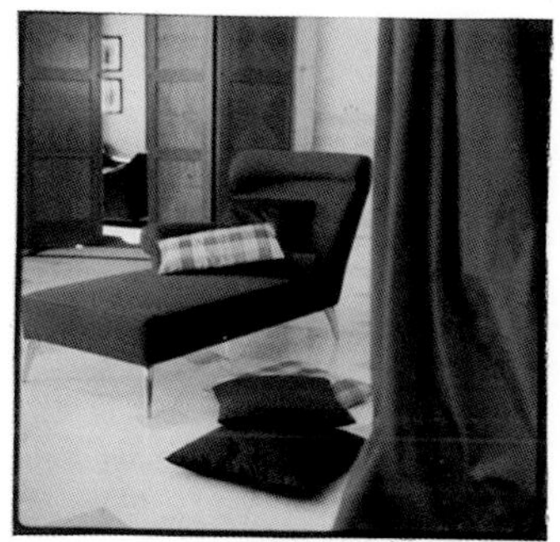
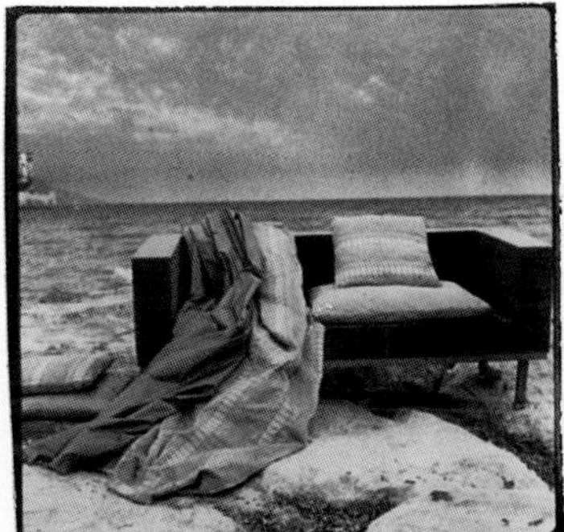
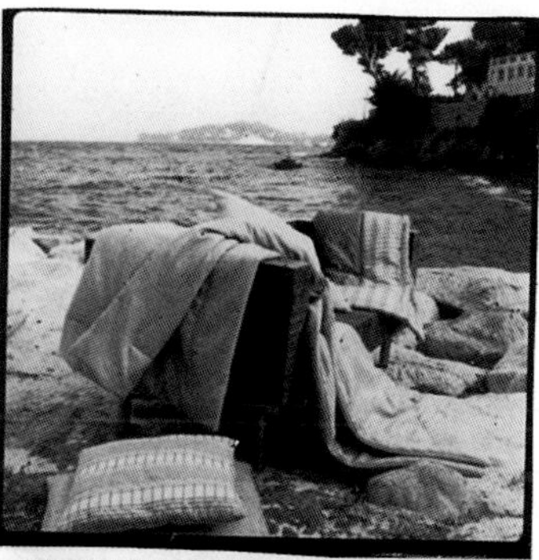
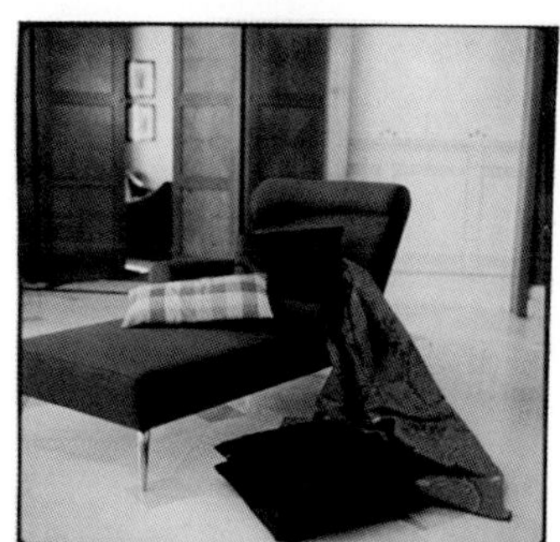
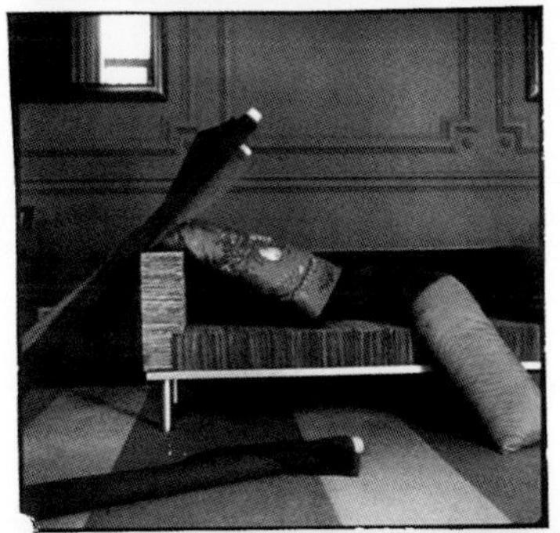
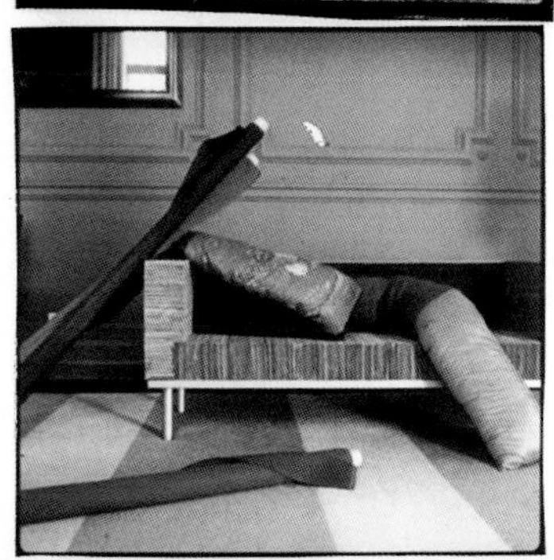
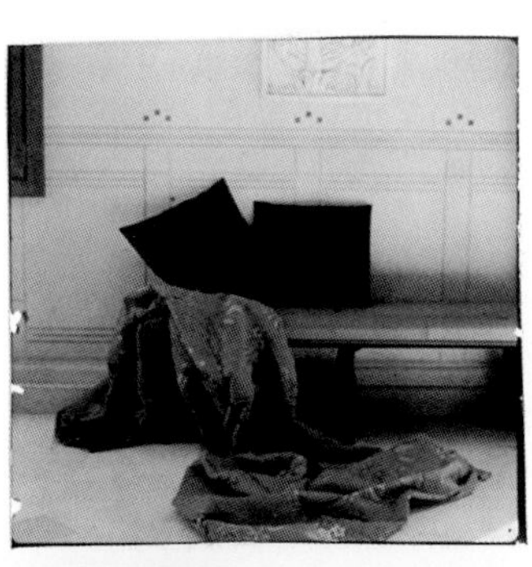
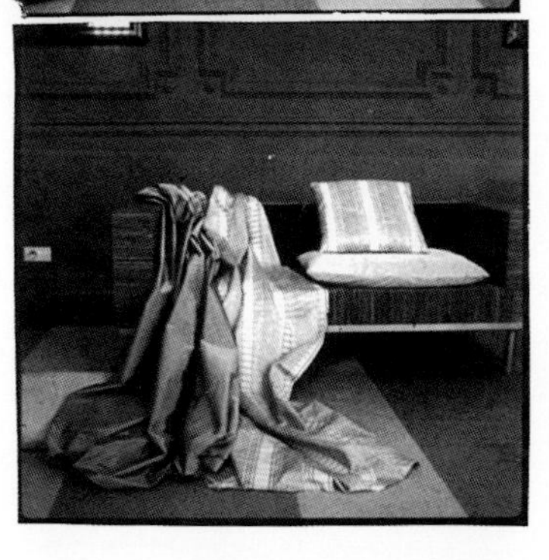
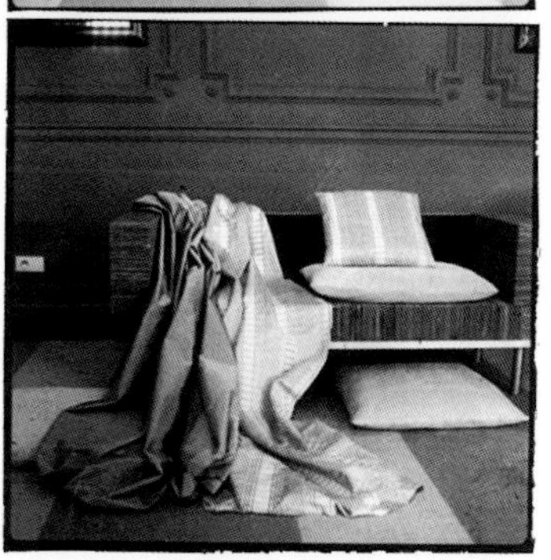
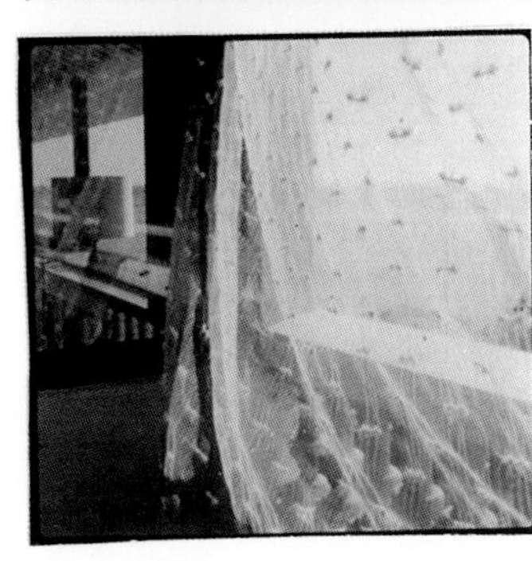
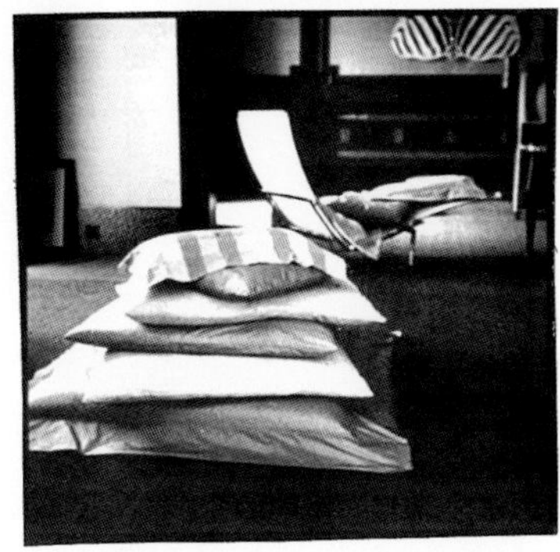
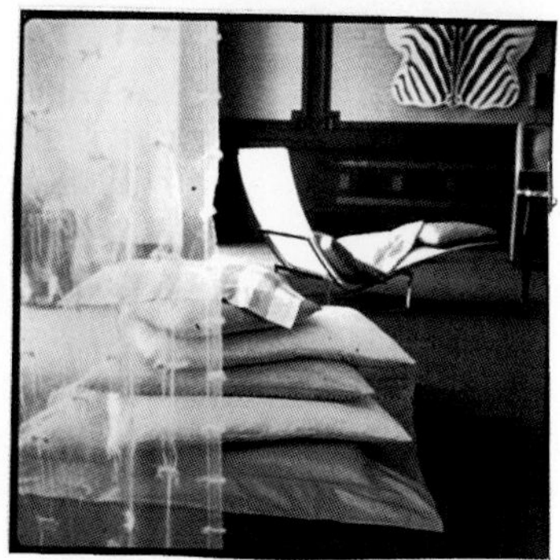

TIME STANDS STILL

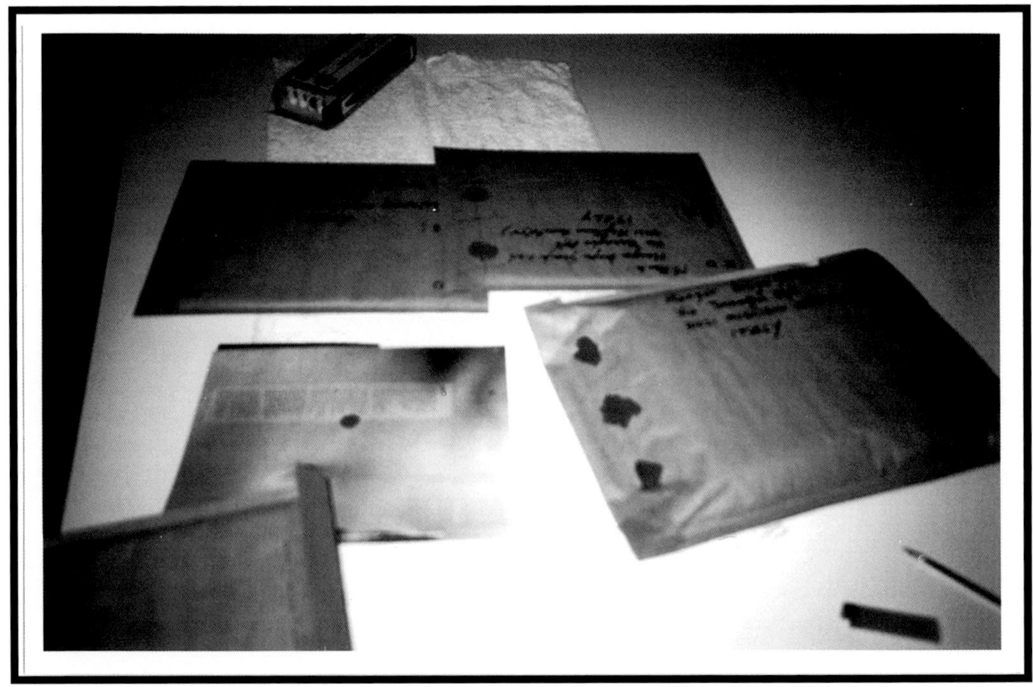

LIVE TO TELL

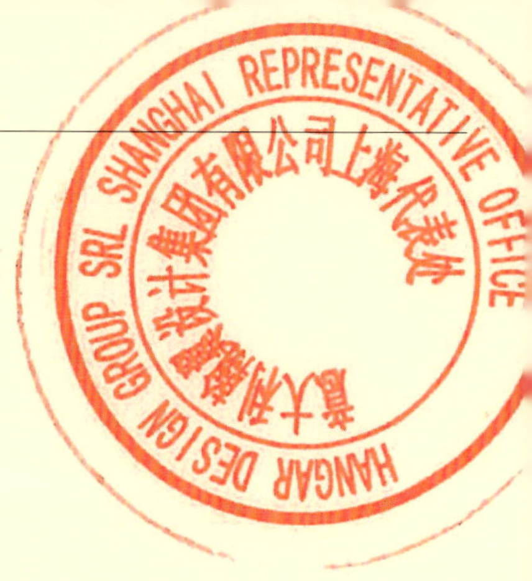

2005. Shanghai.
Hangar Design Group
makes its debut in China.
Operations began with
the first official stamps.
The dream became reality.

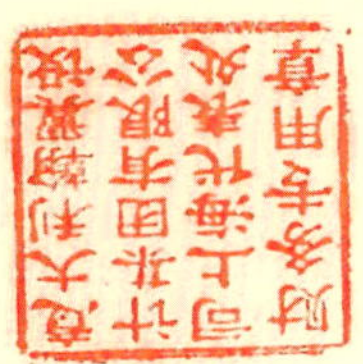

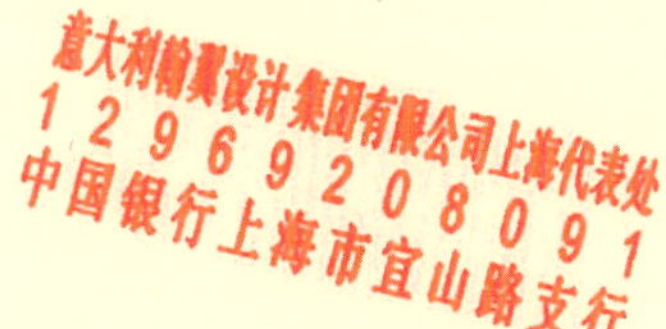

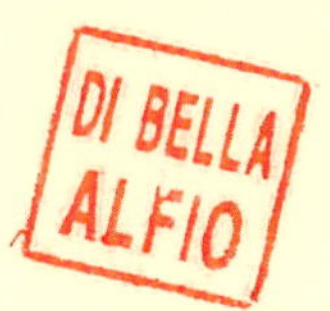

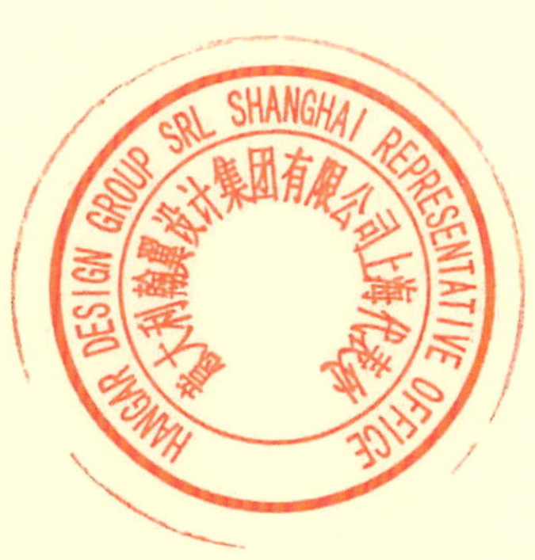

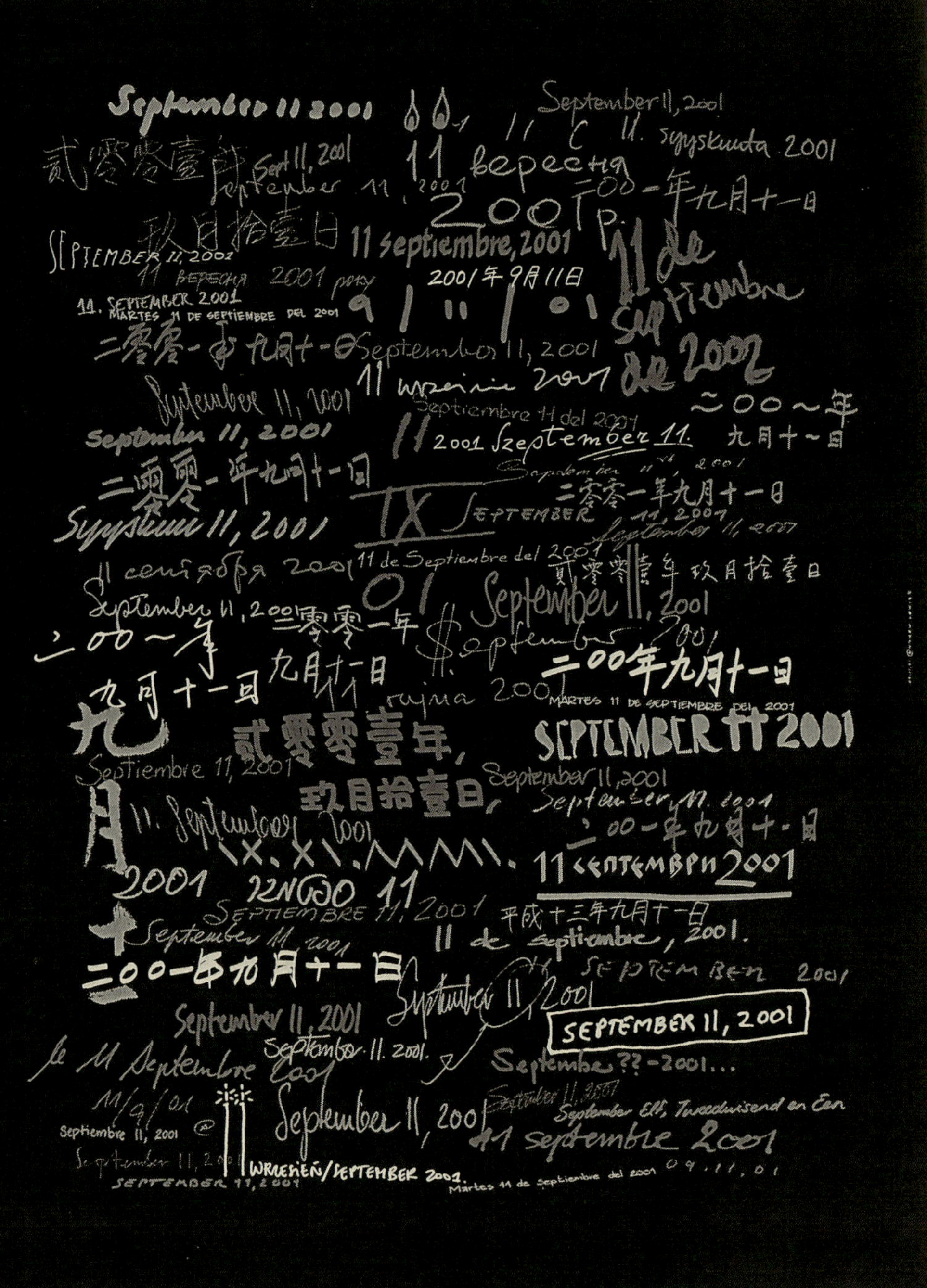

LIVE TO TELL

2002.
Hangar Design Group is invited to "sign" the manifesto against the terrorist attacks of September 11. Designers from all over the world re-wrote the date of the attacks on the Twin Towers. Lest we forget.

2003. Signs of the times.
Extraordinary success and great participation characterize the first competition for the revisitation of instruments relating to the "interpretation of time" initiative promoted by Hangar Edizioni. The competition poster was displayed in all the main schools of graphics and design around the world. Chairman of the international jury was Milton Glaser.

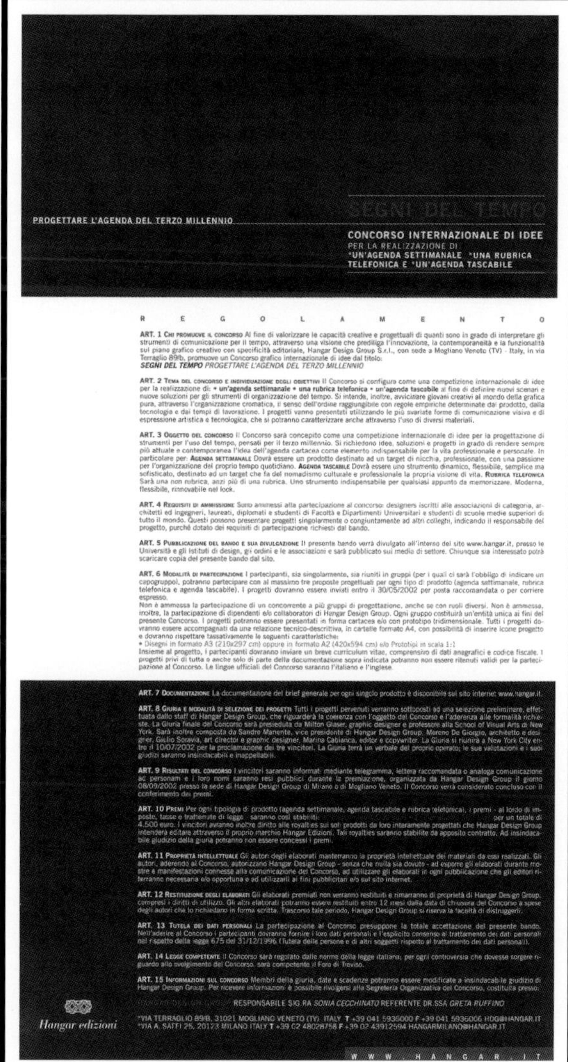

LIVE TO TELL

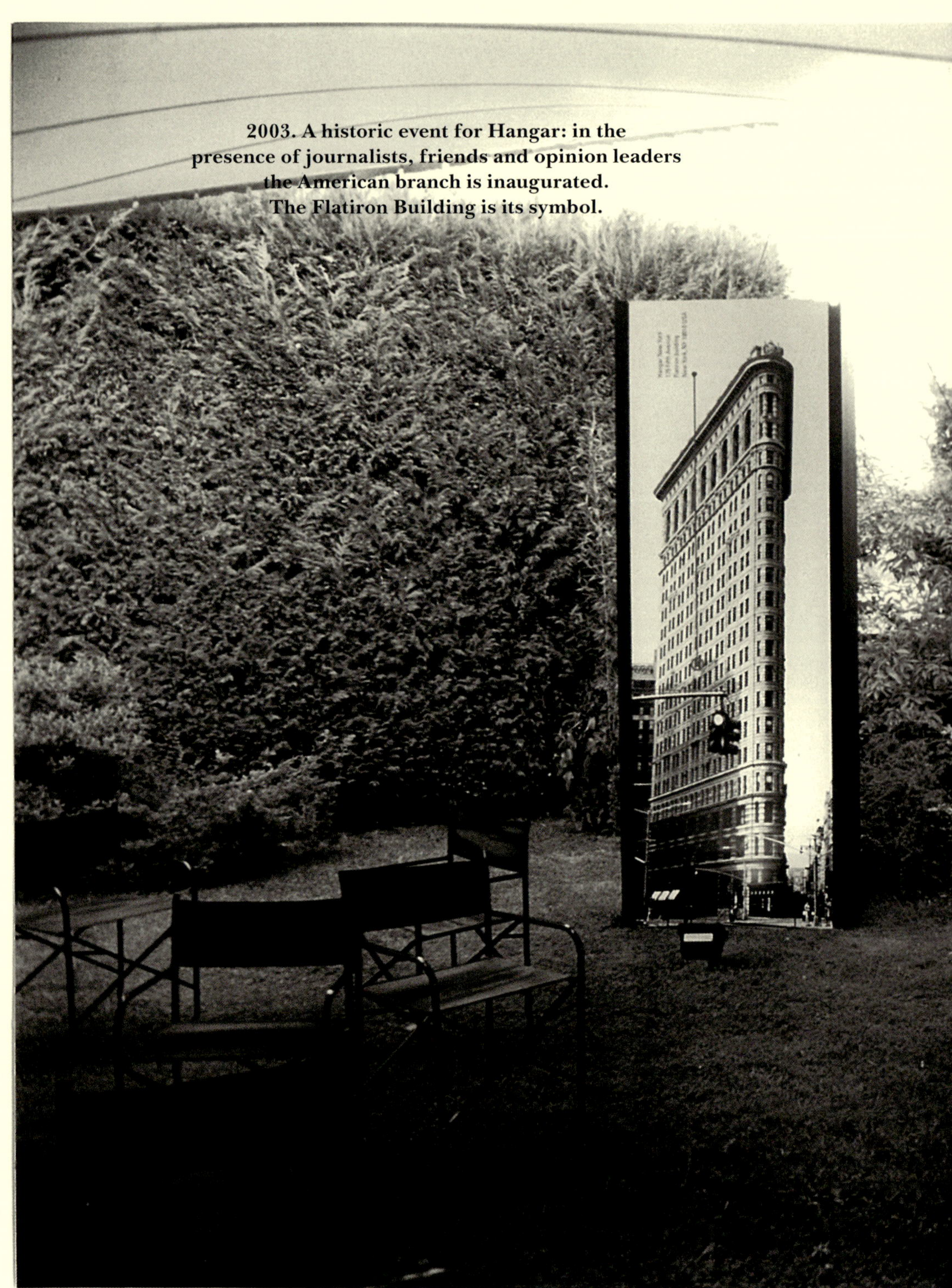

**2003. A historic event for Hangar: in the
presence of journalists, friends and opinion leaders
the American branch is inaugurated.
The Flatiron Building is its symbol.**

LIVE TO TELL

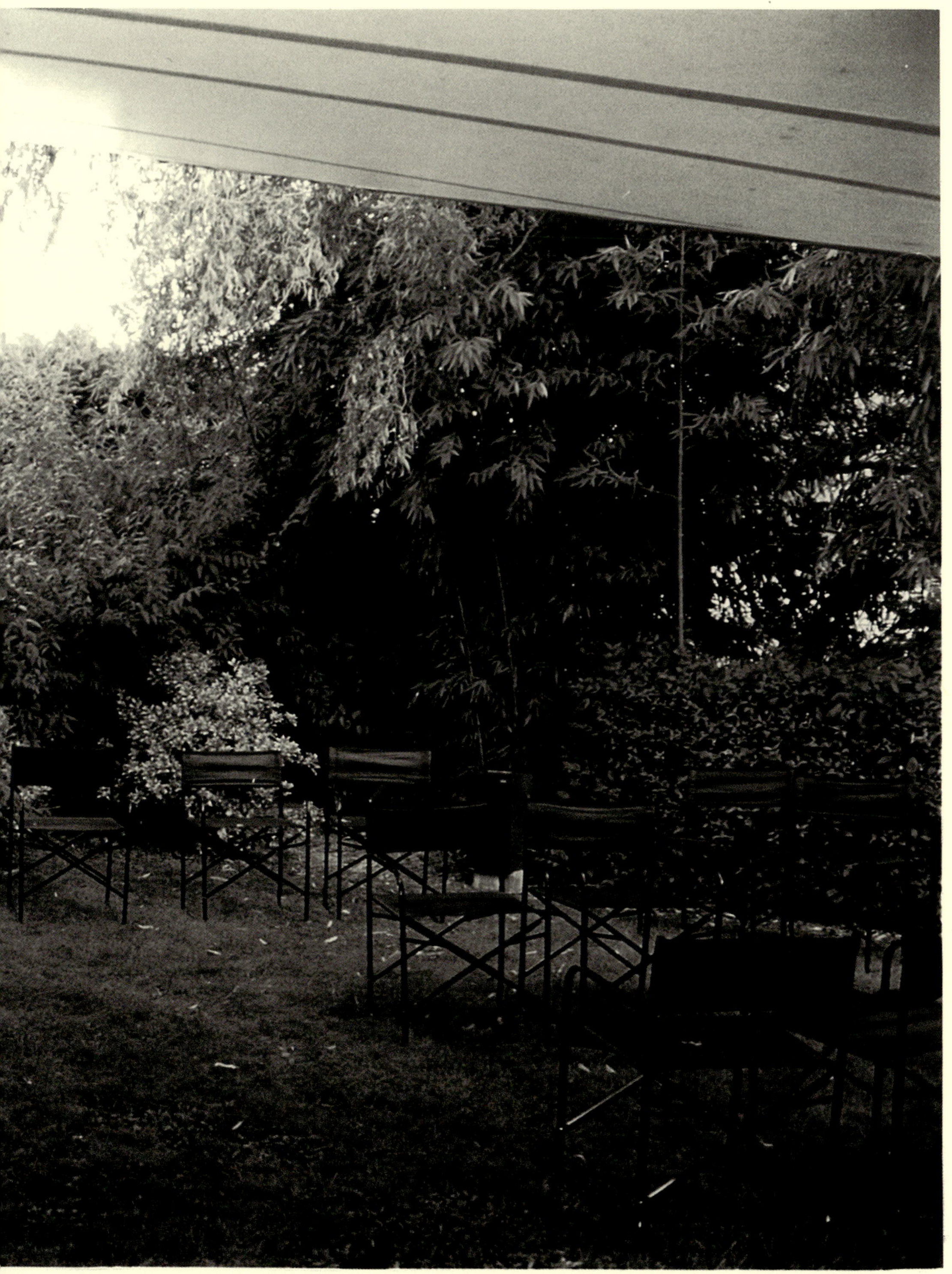

LIVE TO TELL

J U S T   O P E N E D

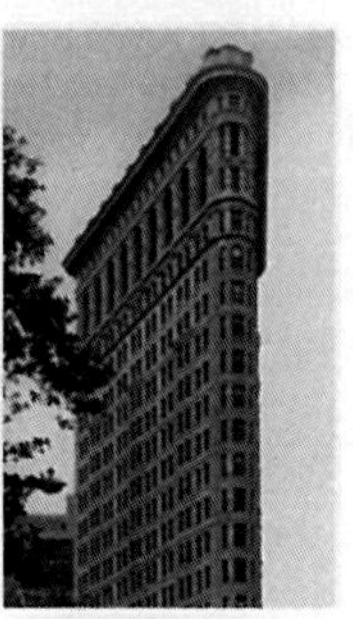

HANGAR DESIGN GROUP NY 175 FIFTH AVENUE NEW YORK, NY 10010 HANGAR.IT

COME DICE SALINGER NELL'INTRADUCIBILE ROMANZO DELLA SUA VITA, A NEW YORK DI SERA SULLE STRADE SE PARLI UN PO' FORTE TI SENTONO TUTTI. DEVE ESSERE STATO COSÌ CHE CI HANNO SENTITO PARLARE IN QUESTI ANNI DEL NOSTRO DESIDERIO DI FAR VOLARE LE IDEE ANCHE IN AMERICA. E COSÌ DOPO AVER AVVIATO LA NOSTRA BELLISSIMA REALTÀ MILANESE, ABBIAMO PENSATO DI APRIRE LA NUOVA SEDE USA A NEW YORK CITY IN FIFTH AVENUE 175 ALL'OTTAVO PIANO DEL MITICO FULLER BUILDING, SOPRANNOMINATO FLATIRON PER VIA DELLA SUA AVVENENTE E SENSUALE FORMA A FERRO DA STIRO. SIAMO CONTENTI DI POTER OFFRIRE A QUANTI RUOTANO INTORNO ALL'HANGAR, QUESTA GRANDE OPPORTUNITÀ, NON DI BUSINESS, MA DI CRESCITA CULTURALE. IN ATTESA DI INCONTRARCI LÌ IN AMERICA AVREMO PIACERE DI AVERLA CON NOI **VENERDÌ 6 SETTEMBRE 2002 ALLE ORE 18.00** NELLA NOSTRA ORMAI STORICA SEDE DI MOGLIANO VENETO PER PRESENTARLE QUESTO NUOVO TRAGUARDO RAGGIUNTO. NON SAPPIAMO SE DURANTE I NOSTRI FREQUENTI VIAGGI PORTEREMO CON NOI IL FERRO DA STIRO, DI SICURO LE IDEE DALL'HANGAR VOLERANNO DECISE ANCHE OLTREOCEANO. **ALBERTO BOVO E SANDRO MANENTE**

Alberto Bovo and Sandro Manente are pleased to announce...

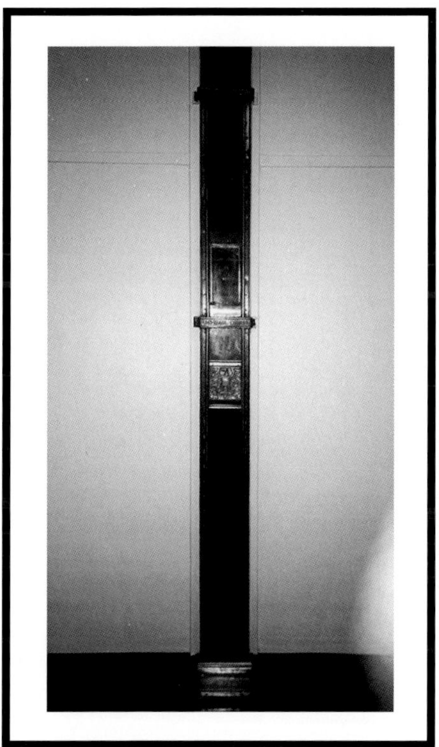

2004. *Pneumatic post in the Flatiron Building.*

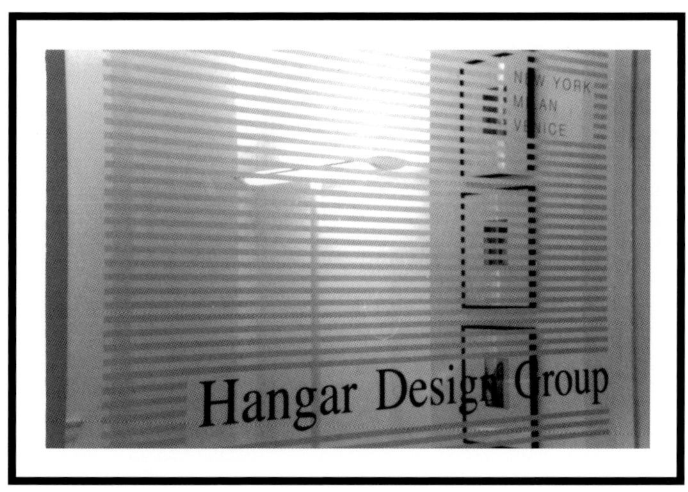

2002. *The first office on Fifth Avenue, New York.*

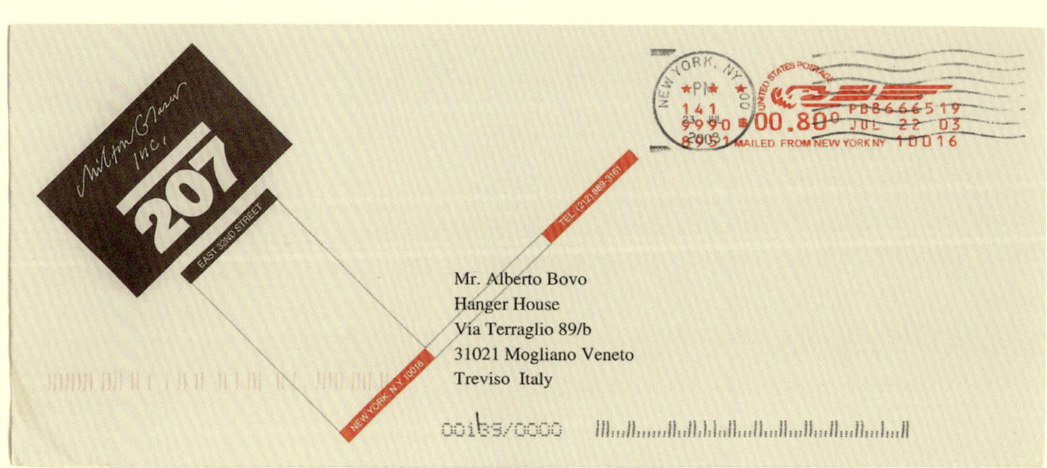

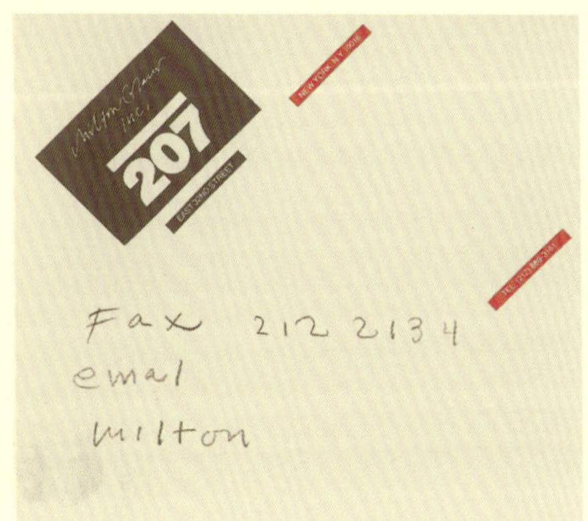

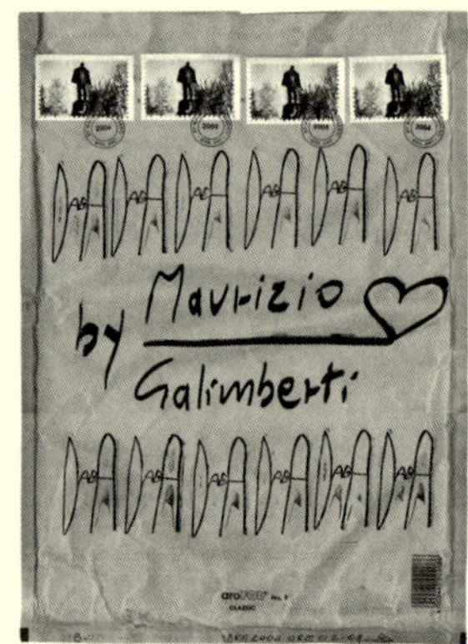

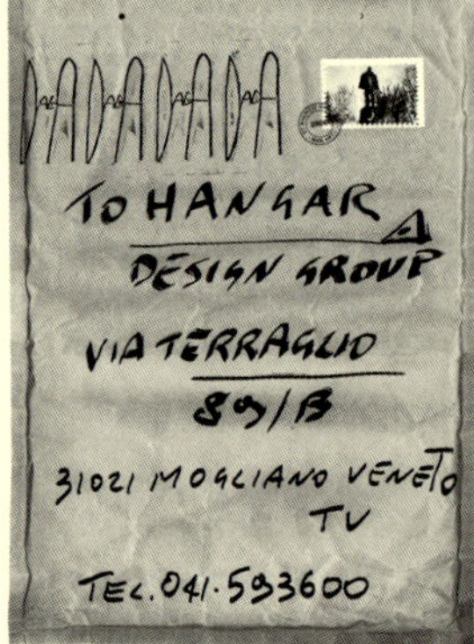

Oggetto: DIAP. 6x7 —
Data: 27-05-2000
Per:
Nº fax:
Da: CHIARA
No. di pag.:
Messaggio:

ÁLVARO SIZA - ARQUITECTO, SA

TI RINGRAZIO PER IL TUO E-MAIL.
SPERO CHE LE DIAPOSITIVE VADANO BENE. NON SONO
ANCORA RIUSCITA A PARLARE CON L'ARR. SIZA PER
IL TESTO. UN CARO SALUTO
Chiara

LIVE TO TELL

CORRESPONDENCE.
*Messages, thanks and close
collaborations through personal
and professional relationships.*

*"Everyone who enters Hangar
falls in love with it… and is
loved in return."*

LIVE TO TELL

IN HOUSE

POWER TO PLACES

We have never called them "offices." The spaces of the
Hangar Design Group are conceived and designed to bring
together ideas, strategies and thoughts.
They are our view of communication. And through them
everyone can see how we are made and what we can do.
2006.

LIVE TO TELL

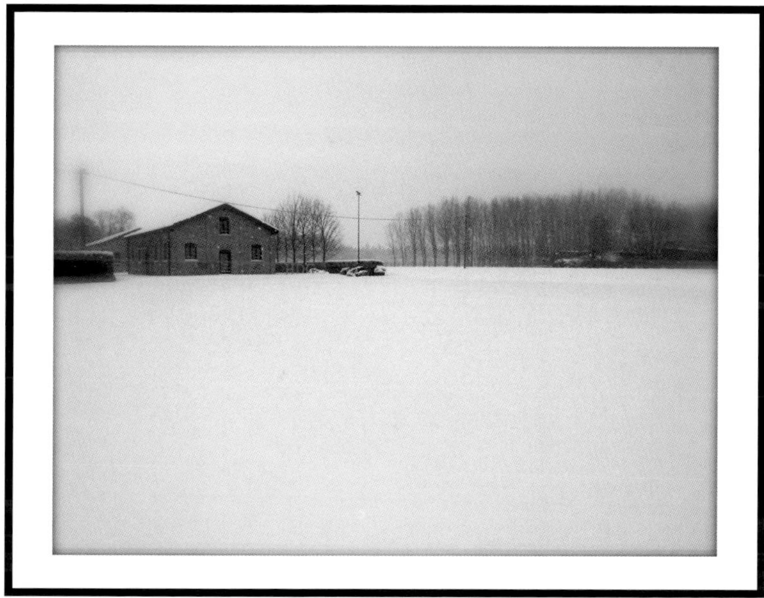

2006. *A wonderful scene.*

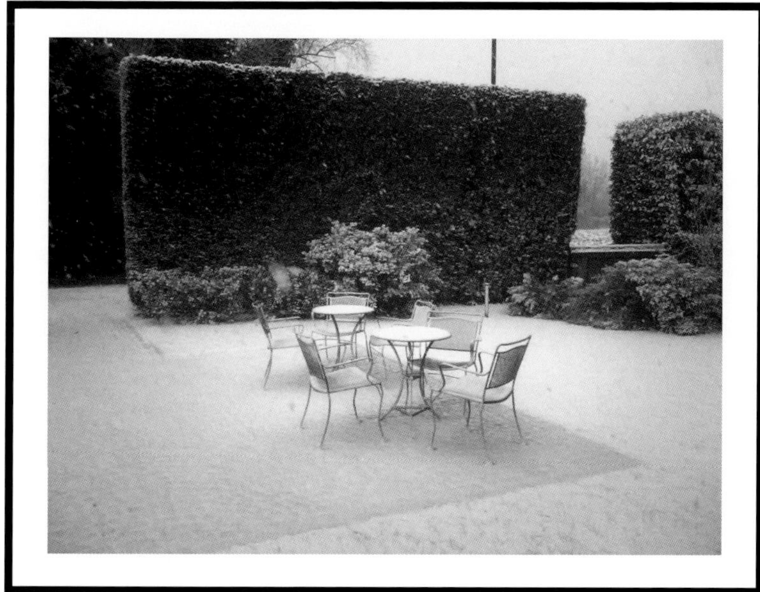

LIVE TO TELL

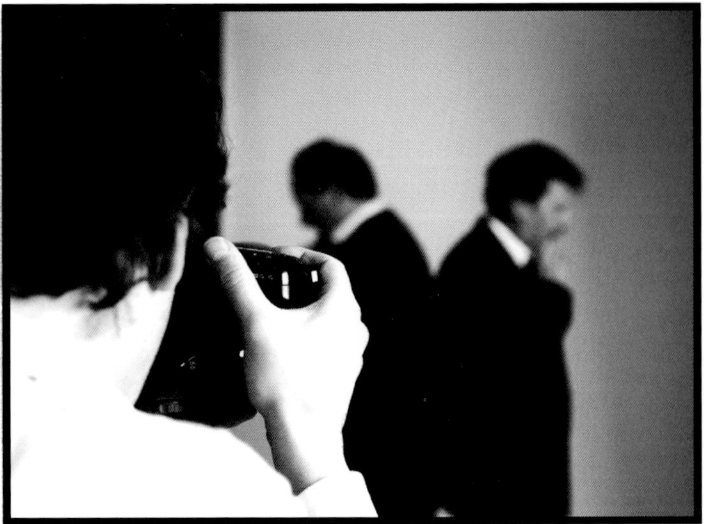

Photographic shooting of partners in 2009.

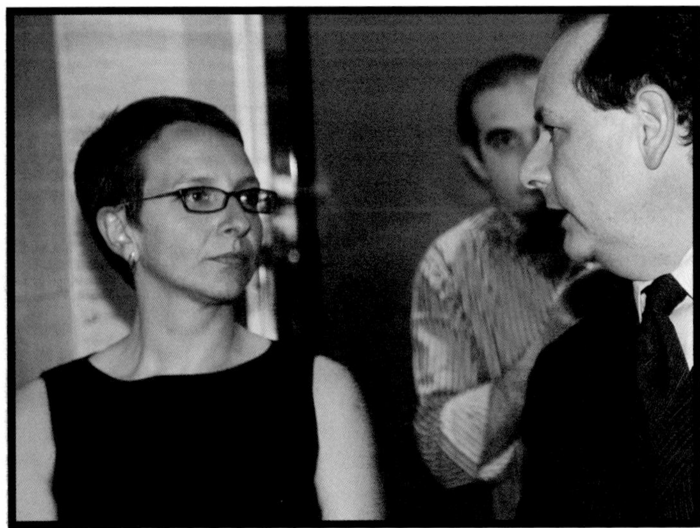

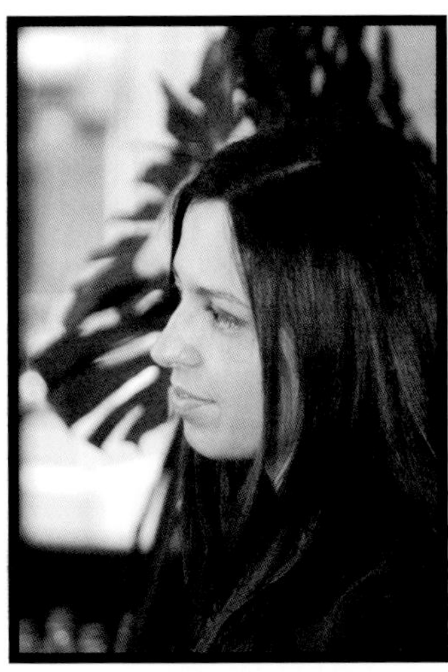

Always present at the important events of the Milanese fashion and design week.

LIVE TO TELL

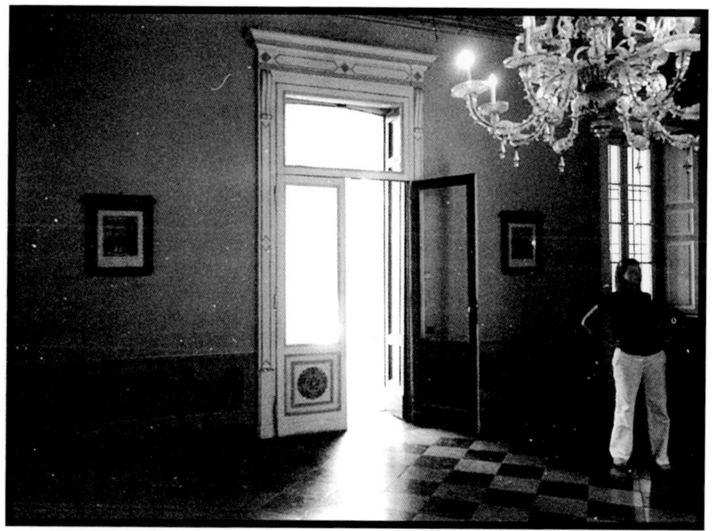

LOCATION CHECK
in the building where a furniture shooting
will take place.

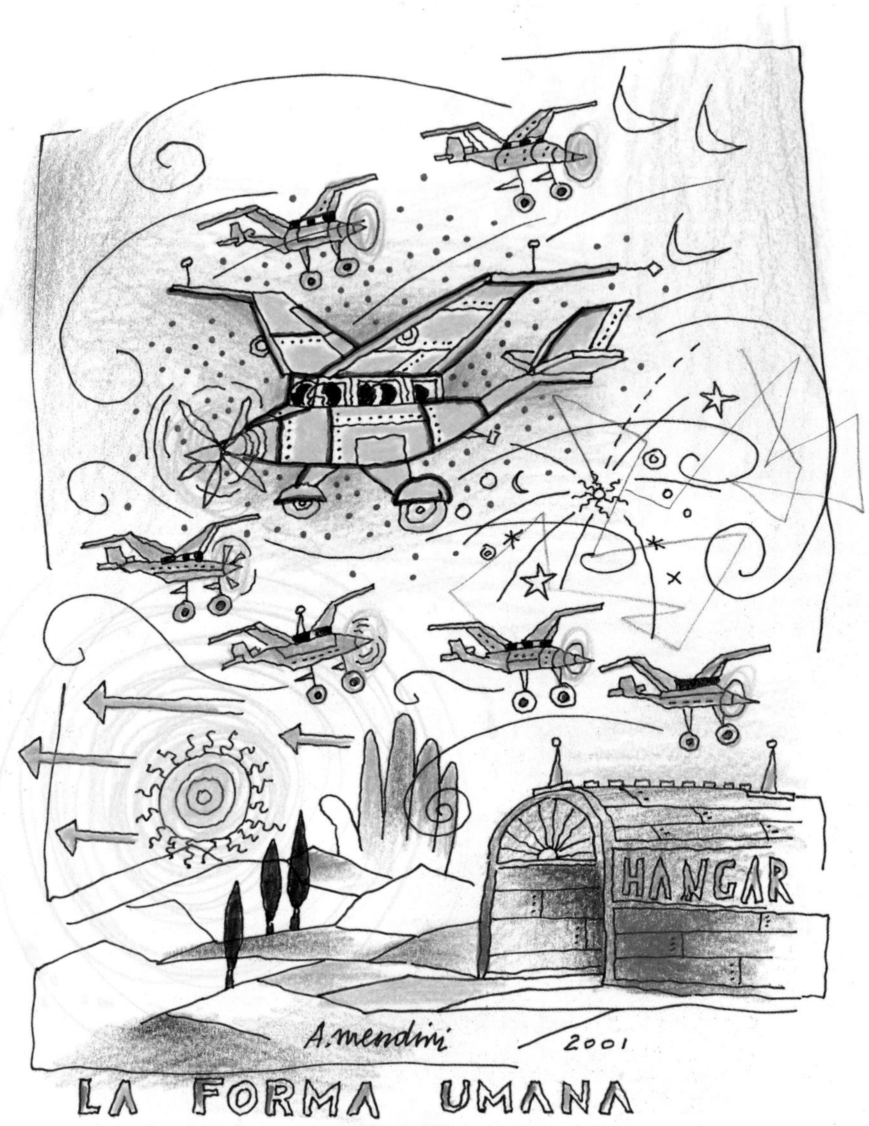

2002. *Alessandro Mendini, designer based in Milan, signs one of the planning agendas of Hangar Edizioni.*

LIVE TO TELL

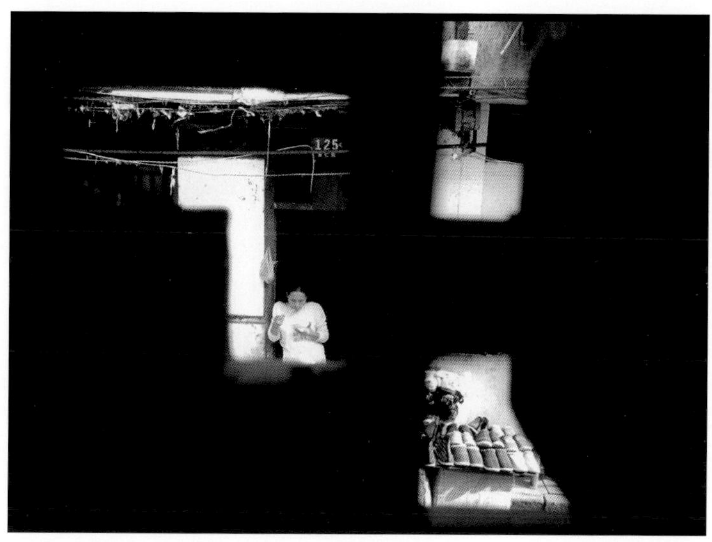

FREEZE THE MOMENT
Travel shots and scenes.
*Photography, for Hangar, remains one of the
main means of inspiration and design.*

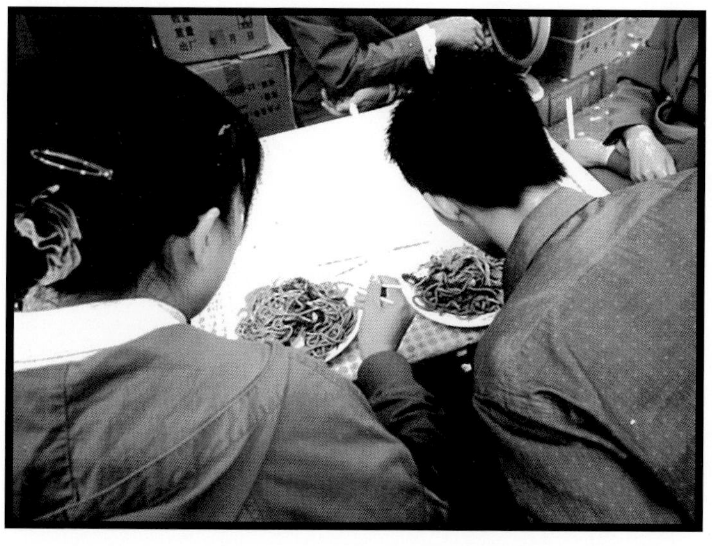

LIVE TO TELL

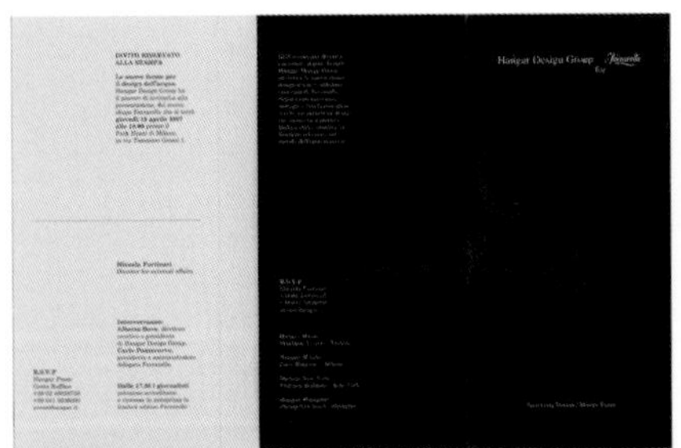
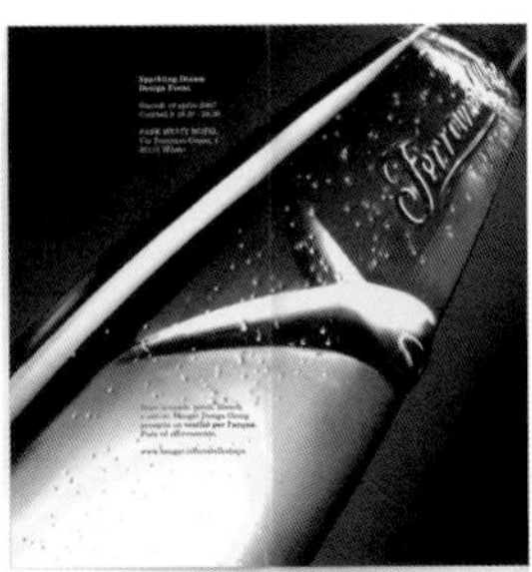
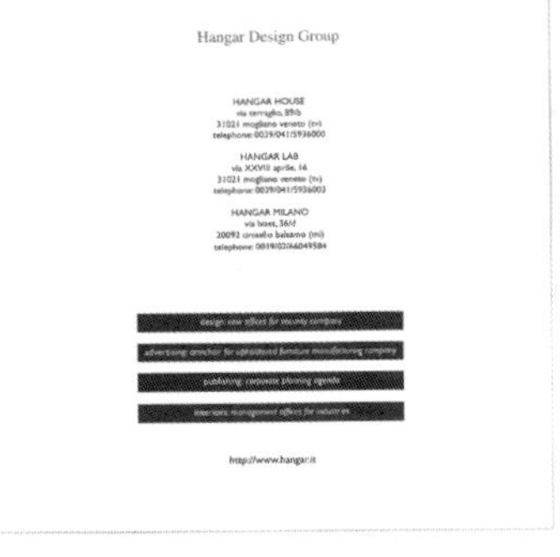

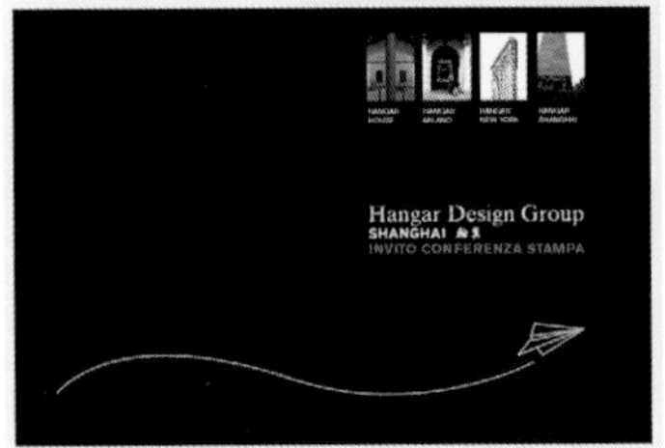
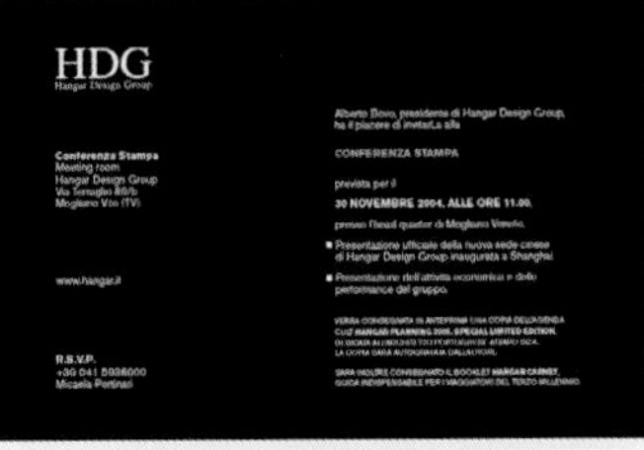

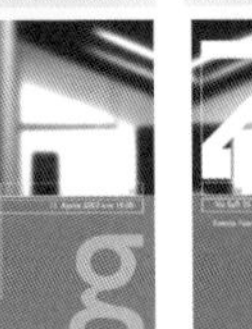
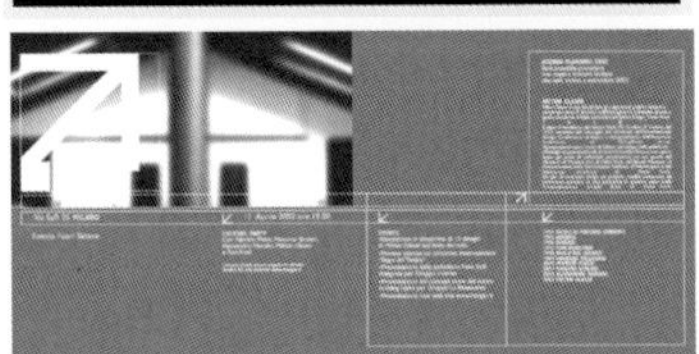
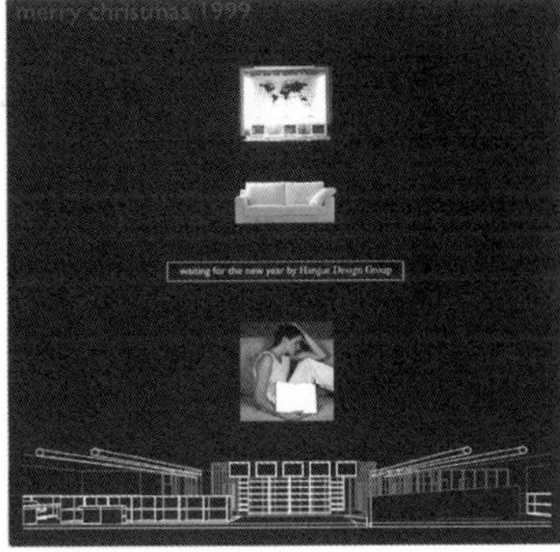

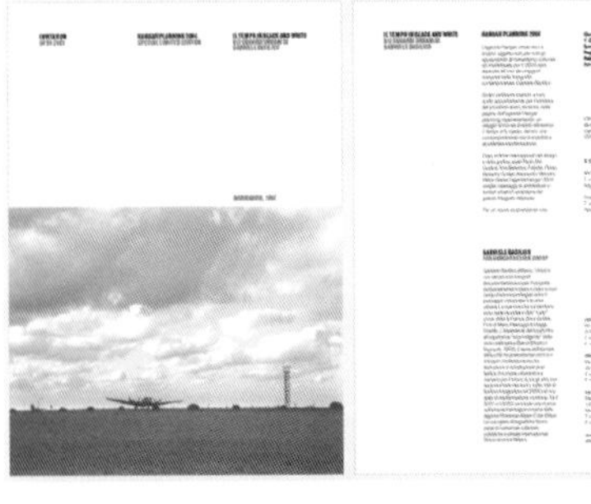
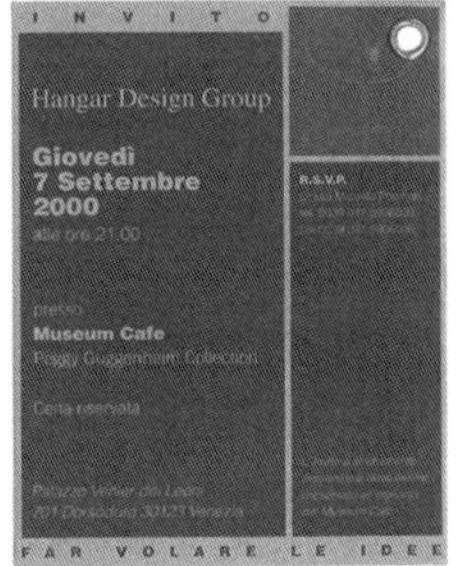
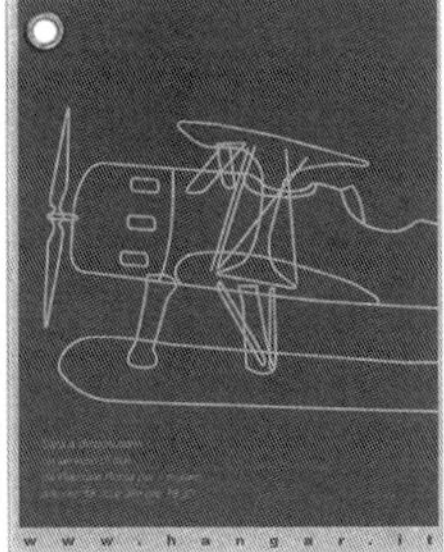

LIVE TO TELL

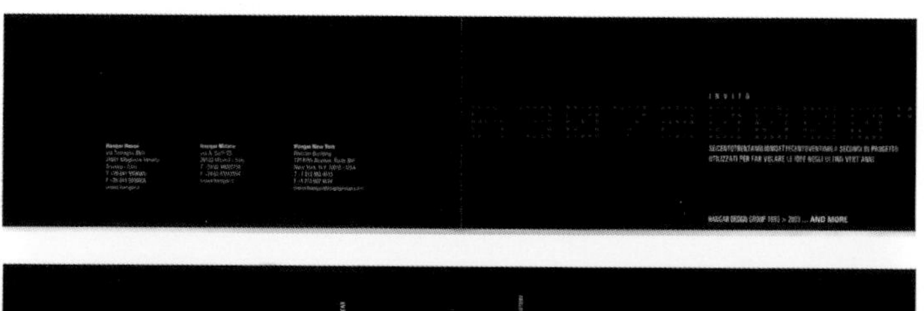

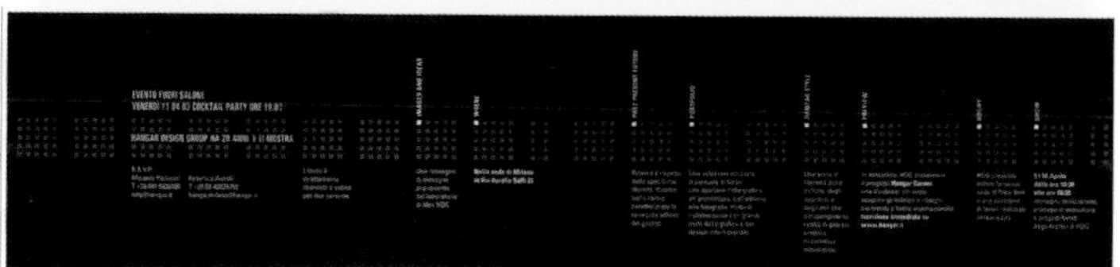

INVITATION.
The theme of self-promotion has always been fundamental to the Hangar Design Group. In 30 years of activity a great variety of invitations and messages have been sent out by the Group, both to customers and others. Through these it tests new languages – conceived, drafted and produced with maniacal care. **This is our company.**

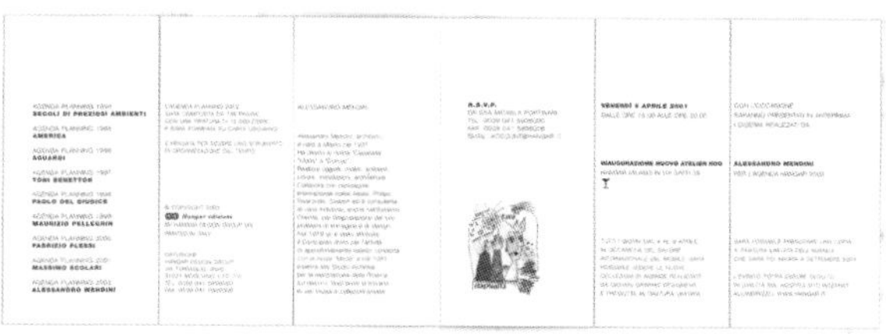

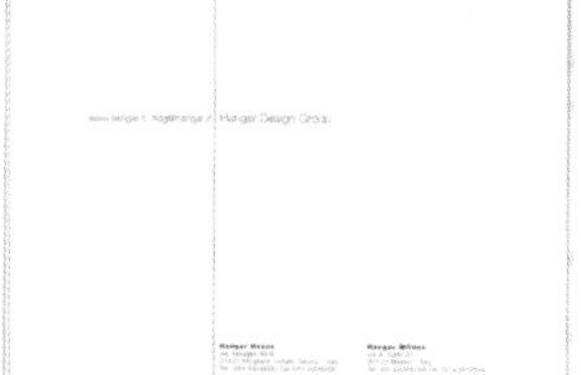

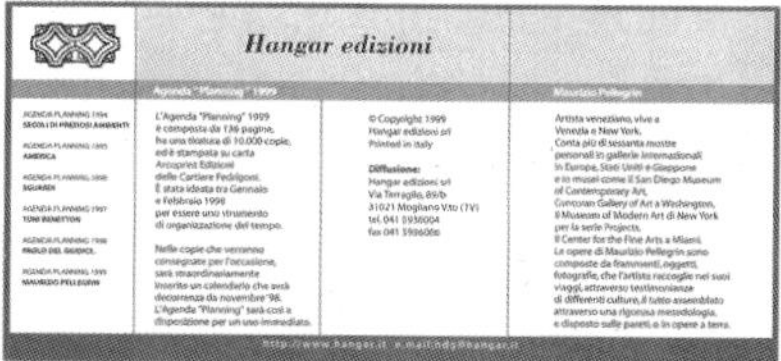

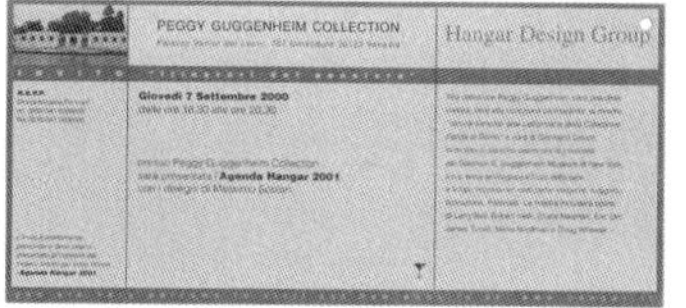

LIVE TO TELL

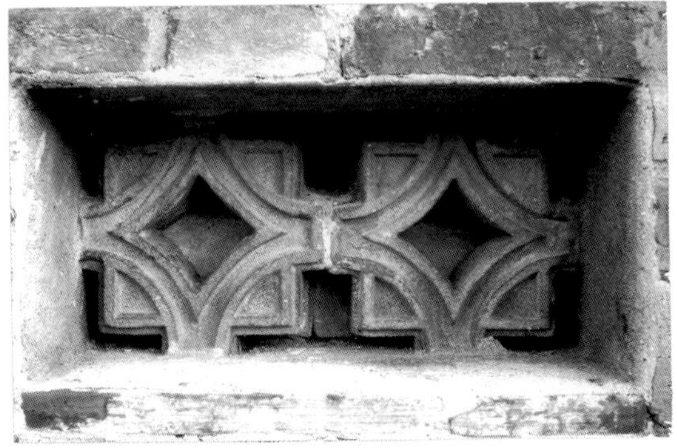

The decoration (now a trademark) of Hangar Edizioni.

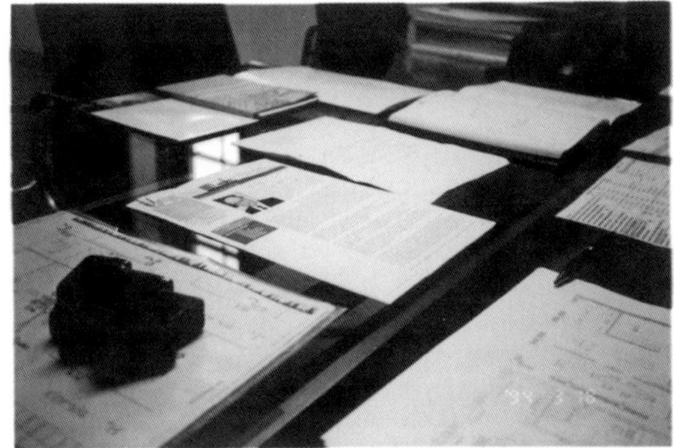

Work in progress.

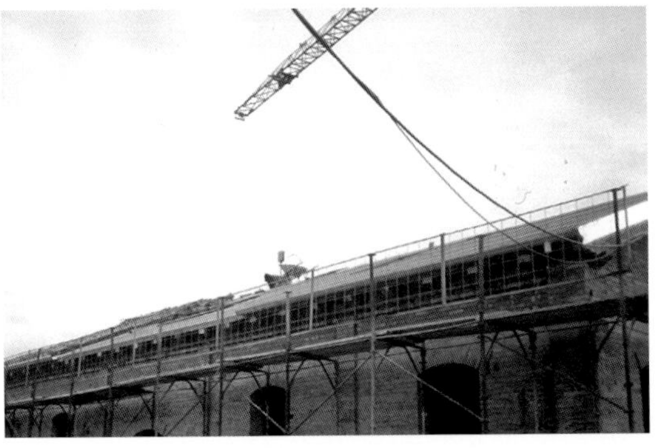

Make-up.

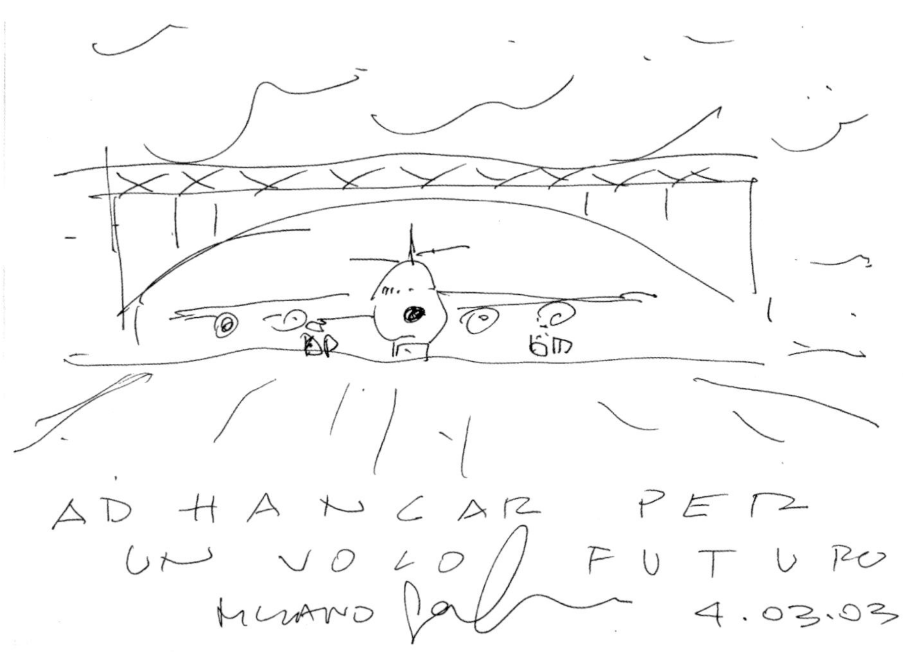

"Ideas in flight"
2003. The theme of flight interpreted by architects,
designers, photographers or just friends – at times
with surprising results.

LIVE TO TELL

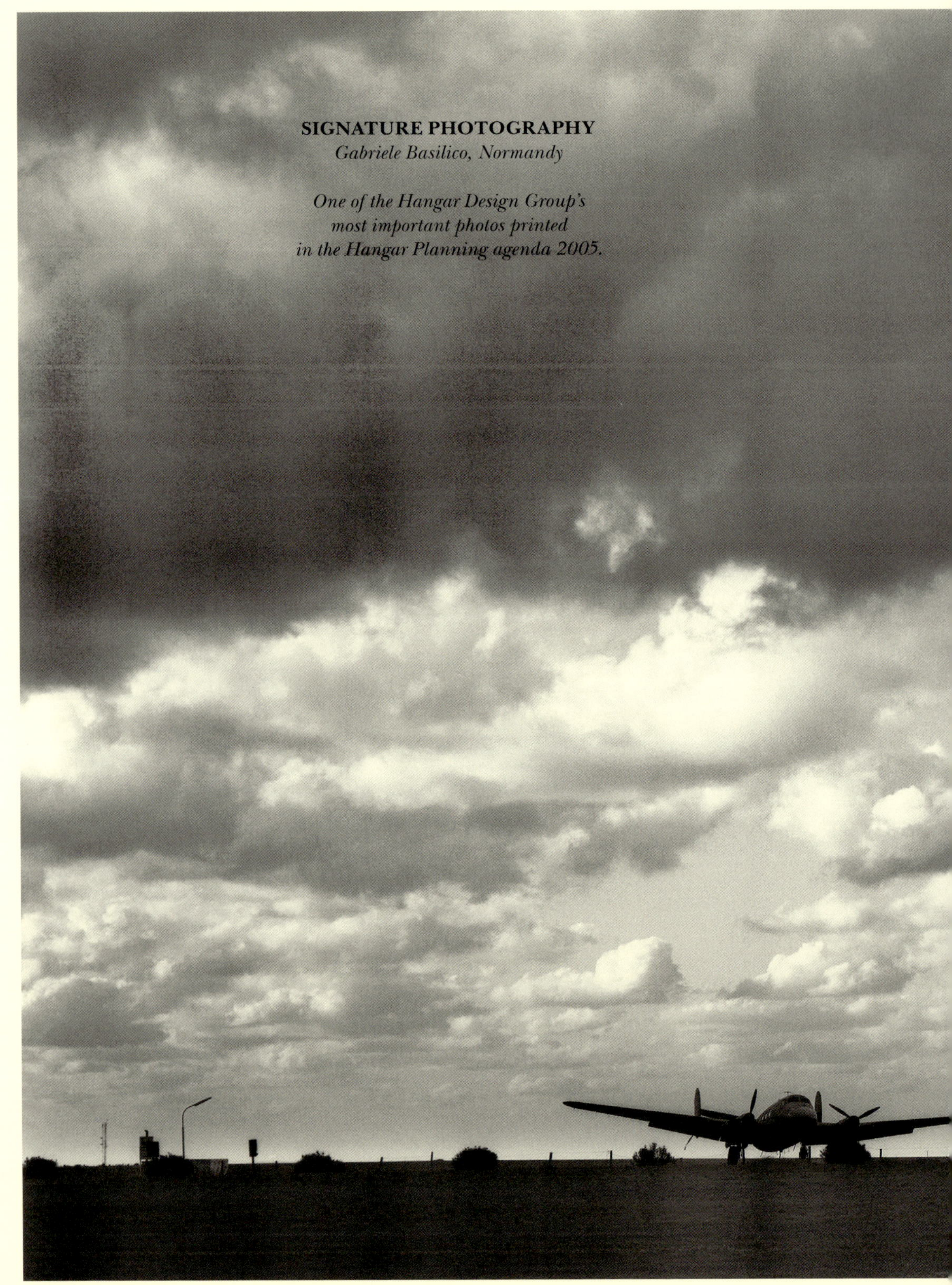

SIGNATURE PHOTOGRAPHY
Gabriele Basilico, Normandy

One of the Hangar Design Group's
most important photos printed
in the Hangar Planning agenda 2005.

LIVE TO TELL

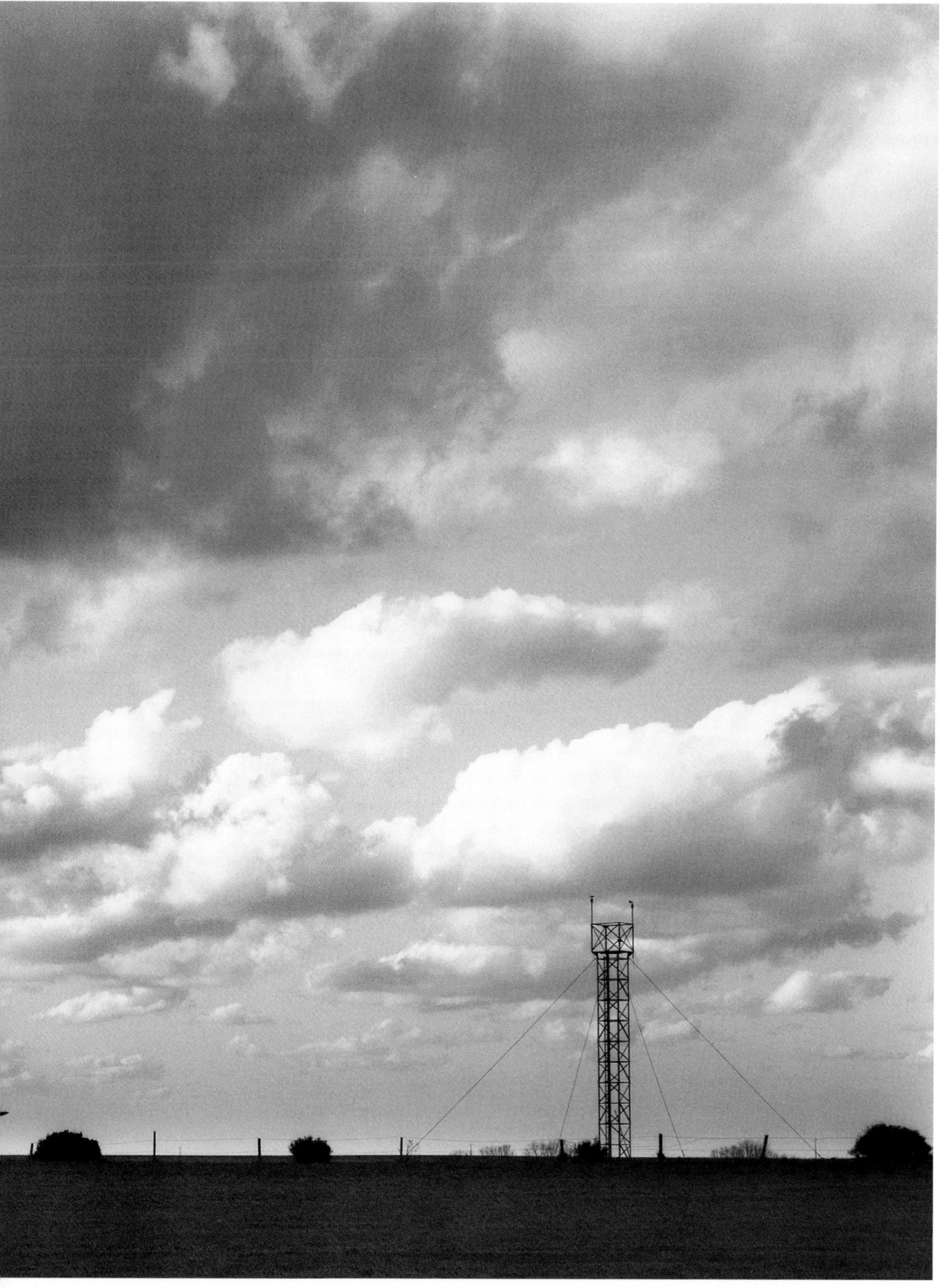

LIVE TO TELL

Abirascid Emil
Adamovic Marija
Aijawa Kyoko
Aladro Esteban
Alessi Marina
Alessio Andrea
Amendolagine Riccardo
Amidei Greta
Andreetta Franco
Andreetta Giulia
Aranguren Lucia
Astori Antonia
Audoly Sonia
Axengard Camilla
Bacciolo Lorella
Baga Annalisa
Balta Erbil
Baltzinger Julia
Barbarez Stefan
Barbero Luca Massimo
Barbieri Chiara
Barbieri Luisa
Barbon Andrea
Barbosa Savigne
Barellas Giulia
Barracchia Francesco
Barthelemy Cecyle
Barzan Alessandra
Barzazi Federico
Baschera Alessio
Baschetti Chiara
Basilico Gabriele
Battaglia Giorgio
Battistello Elisa
Bazos Erin
Becher Susan
Bellati Bortolomeo
Bellomo Michela
Beltrami Patrizia
Bembo Giorgia
Benedicto Eduardo
Benetton Ada
Benetton Toni
Bergamo Anna
Berto Fabio
Bertoli Maria Raffaella
Bertolio Matteo
Bianchi Carola
Bianchini Paula
Bicego Michele
Billari Francesco
Bisazza Rossella
Blackburn Alex
Boeri Stefano
Bojardi Gilda
Bolla Stefania
Boesen Sophie
Bon Cristina
Bonaldo Cristina
Bonvicino Milvia
Boo Bram
Borges Savanna Tezza

Boro Alexia
Bortolin Barbara
Boscarino Alessandro
Bottani Elisabetta
Bovo Oreste
Bragato Luca
Brambilla Claudia
Bratovich Marco
Brown Justin
Brunelli Sabrina
Brusaferri Adriano
Brusattin Lorenzo
Buoso Nicola
Buratti Michela
Buzzi Peppa
Cabianca Danilo
Cabianca Marina
Cadamuro Laura
Caleca Santi
Calugaru Anisia
Cambriani Alessia
Cammarata Vincenzo
Camuffo Evelina

ARE YOU IN?

Canella Lorenzo
Caneva Paolo
Canton Elena
Capocelli Simona
Cappellesso Gianluca
Carpignano Tatiana
Carraro Sabrina
Castellet María
Cattaneo Elena
Cattaneo Marianna
Causa Salvatore
Cavallarin Anna
Cavalli Carolina
Cavallin Federica
Cavazzaro Giorgio
Cecchinato Giordano
Cecchinato Sonia
Cedrone Federico
Cesani Roberta
Cestaro Emanuel
Cettina Fabrizio
Chambliss Laurie
Cherubin Filippo
Chinellato Aurelio
Cinetto Valentina
Ciocanescu Tudor
Clerici Katia

Cochand Flavie
Cole Ty
Conton Alice
Conzatti Ivonne
Corradi Barbara
Corva Lisa
Cossetta Katrin
Costantini Giada
Costantini Martina
Crasset Matali
Croce Veronica
Dani Katya
Daukshene Inna
Davies Francesca
De Andreis Giulia
De Diana Dora
De Giorgio Moreno
De Masi Domenico
De Padova Maddalena
De Rubò Almar
De Sanctis Annamaria
Del Corona Sara
Del Giudice Paolo

Degan Andrea
Dessy Francesco
Di Bella Alfio
Di Fonzo Veronica
Di Maggio Alessandro
Di Pinto Chiara
Di Renzo Leonardo
Dolcetti Chiara
Drake Ella
Fabian Christopher
Fabiani Sophie Micol
Facco Corrado
Facco Mariateresa
Falangola Yanti
Falguera Jaume
Fantini Maia
Fardin Alessandra
Fava Mara
Favaretto Alessandra
Favaretto Donatella
Favaretto Paolo
Fazel Ramak
Ferragamo Fulvia
Ferrari Sara
Ferreri Marco
Ferruzzi Diletta
Fiori Federica

Fiorindo Sabrina
Fisher Sally
Fornasier Mara
Fortini B. Marco
Fruci Chiara
Fubini Federico
Furlan Massimo
Gajauskaite Sandra
Galante Erika
Galimberti Maurizio
Galvan Claudio
Garavaglia Valentina
García Mireia
Gatto Linda
Gemelli Piero
Genovese Isabella
Girotto Nicolas
Glaser Milton
Gobbo Luca
Goldschmiedt Mariaclara
Gomes Bruna
Granlund Ola
Greco Paola
Green Brian
Grosso Silvia
Groszer Caroline
Gutierrez Andé
Gutierrez Gara Noelia
Heinrich Andrea
Hopf Benjamin
Hurstel Roberta
Imbriani Matteo
Inferrera Gian Maria
Izzo Alessando
Izumi Taemi
Jakobsson Maria
Jensen Marie-Louise
Jonsson Kristin
Jovanovic Victoriei
Julien Patrice
Kirkner Jan
Kloeckl Kristian
Koch Marisa
Konju Peter
Kreiner Lee
Kreha Michael
Krukowski Wojciech
Kumador Andy Dela
Laing Charlotte
Lee Timothy
Legori Sara
Lelli Mami Arianna
Lewis Andrew
Li Cynthia
Lissoni Piero
Longo Riccardo
Lorenzon Valeria
Lunghi Caterina
Lupi Stefano
Magistà Aurelio
Mahmood Shabir
Mainardi Claudio

LIVE TO TELL

Mandria Natalia
Manente Enrico
Manente Federica
Manente Giuseppe
Maneschi Florence
Manzeni Carlotta
Marchetto Ilenia
Marchiori Matteo
Marcolin Marta
Marforio Patrizia
Margaritelli Andrea
Marin Sonia
Marini Chiara
Marini Lorenzo
Marsiglio Piero
Martini Isabella
Marzotto Matteo
Masin Daniele
Matiz Juan
Mazzetto Simone
Medici Giovanna
Meier Richard
Mendini Alessandro
Menegaldo Katia
Mennella Roberto
Metz Frederic
Mialich Giada
Mihalich Margherita
Mirco Forti
Mistri Elisabetta
Moir Melanie
Molinari Luca
Monello Paolo
Moorhouse Ruth
Morais Mariana
Moscheni Federica
Motta Silvia
Musso Elisa
Nakajima Hideki
Niero Daniela
Noda Mijako
Nordio Tiziana
Noto Chiara
Noventa Claudio
Nulli Angelica
Oriani Matteo
Origone Raffaele
Pagan Claudio
Pantor Trevor
Pasini Giorgia
Pasquero Fabrizio
Pastrello Katia
Pellegrini Maurizio
Peluso Marianna
Peraldo Matton Livia
Perera Ajantha
Perini Sara
Perrilou Annousha
Peterson Niklas
Pettenò Melania
Pettinari Letizia
Pignoletti Loris

Piovesan Andrea
Pitari Andrea
Pizzi Mia
Pizzul Martina
Plachesi Alice
Plessi Fabrizio
Poglie Marco
Poletto Emanuela
Polga Laura
Pontecorvo Adriana
Pontecorvo Michele
Portinari Micaela
Premoli Danilo
Priantha Dino
Procida Andrea
Provera Cristiana
Quattrone Chiara
Radulova Gergana
Rapp Nicholas
Rashid Karim
Reginato Mariangela
Ribbie Melanie
Ridenti Lorella

CHECK IT OUT

Riolzi Paolo
Riotta Gianni
Riverditi Ornella
Rivolta Stefano
Rizzà Fabiana
Rizzotti Gianni
Roca Lorenzo
Rocco Michele
Rodighiero Claudia
Romano Remo
Romeo Tamara
Rossetti Beatrice
Rossi Barbara
Rosso Bettina
Rota Valentina
Roveda Barbara
Rubino Marco
Ruffino Greta
Rui Marcelino José
Rusconi Maria Sole
Ryan John
Ryan Michael Kelly
Rylands Philiph
Salmaso Vera
Sano Takahide
Santambrogio Francesca
Sante Francis

Savardi Angelo
Savaris Beatrice
Scala Claudio
Scalise Irene Maria
Scalzotto Barbara
Scaramuzza Alberto
Scarpa Tobia
Scattolin Nadia
Schneider Oliver
Schwab Michael
Scime' Cristina
Sciutto Riccardo
Scolari Massimo
Segui Jacinto
Seguso Pierpaolo
Semenzato Stella
Serafini Cristiana
Sestzai Sonja
Silenzi Alvise
Silvestri Federica
Simonato Anna
Sioli Laura
Siza Alvaro

Slutter Chris
Smith Marissa
Sodano Arianna
Sofia Bruno
Sogliani Ariane
Solagaistúa Begoña
Soltz Pedro
Sonnoli Leonardo
Soravia Giulio
Sordina Barbara
Sovilla Franco
Speranzon Donatella
Spinelli Benedetta
Staub Dominique
Stevanato Stefano
Stevanato Thomas
Strifele Raffaella
Suà Summarino Enrico
Suarez B. Anna
Susanna Francesca
Suwa Shigeiro
Syrthariotis Kostantinos
Taliento Luisa
Tama Davide
Tanduo Chiara
Tanrlover Bahadir
Tartaro Giorgio

Teixeira Ruy
Teso Vania
Tessa Rosa
Tessarin Luca
Tissi Giovanna
Toffoli Wilma
Tognetti Massimiliano
Torcellano Rosamaria
Torelli Chiara
Torri Gloria
Toscani Oliviero
Toscanini Cristina
Tosatto Sara
Tremolada Emilio
Trevisan Gianna
Trifoni Jasmina
Tronchin Denis
Truculento Jessica
Turello Amedeo
Ugherani Caterina
Ummarino Enrico
Vacchina Paola
Valan Francesca
Valbusa Stefania
Van Dorssen Rob
Vantaggi Valeria
Vanzini Liliana
Vardimon Yarom
Velez Connie
Venier Stefano
Vergassola Dario
Vitali Cristiano
Viterbo Silvia
Vitre Frederic
Vitta Maurizio
Vivian Michela
Von Fürstenberg Egon
Weber Uli
Witczak Dariusz
Xi Cheng
Zagnoli Miro
Zambon Damiano
Zambon Manuela
Zampini Matteo
Zamuner Roberta
Zanardelli Désirée
Zanardo Davide
Zanette Alberto
Zanimacchia Federica
Zanin Alessandro
Zanoletti Alberto
Zanon Paola
Zaragoza Anna
Zavattaro Nora
Zomer Karolijn
Zuber Fernando
Zucchi Niccolò
Zucconi Micaela
Zuliani Antonio
Zumpano Andrea
Zanelli Candida
Zunino Maria Giulia

HANGAR DESIGN GROUP

VISUAL CONTENTS

Credits and Contributors

INTRO

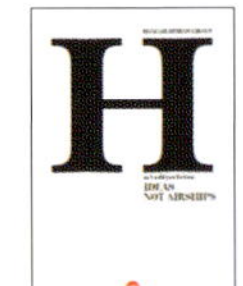

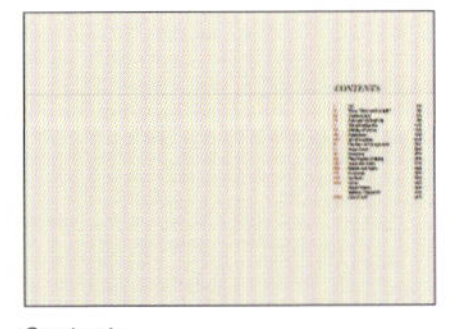

Dedicated to

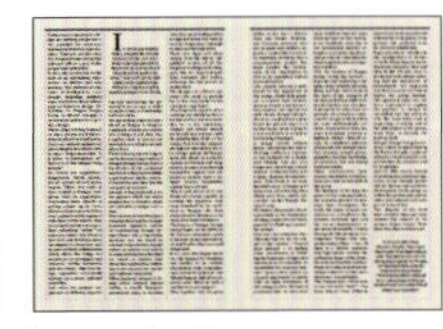

Contents

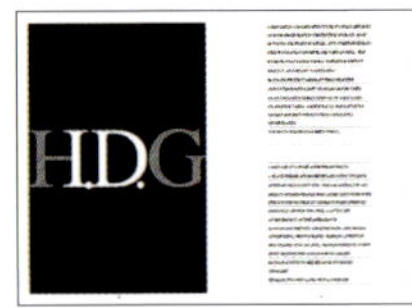

Summarizing Hangar

I.D.

01

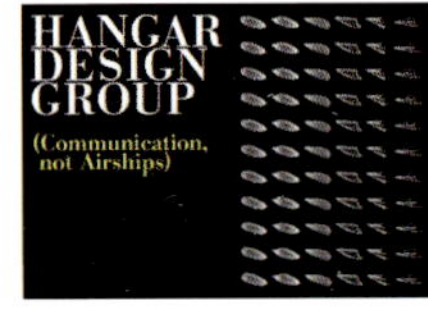

What Hangar is for

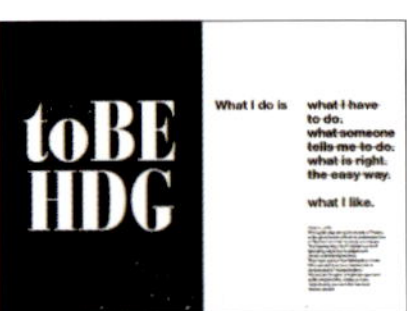

Mr. Danilo, Hangar's keeper

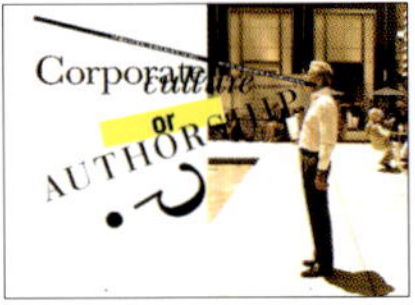

Don't misunderstand

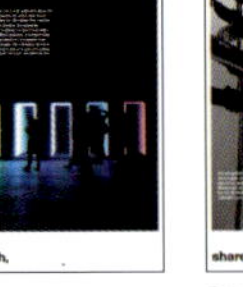

A bit of history

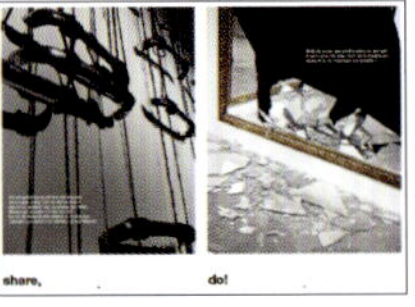

Fifth Ave., NY 2011

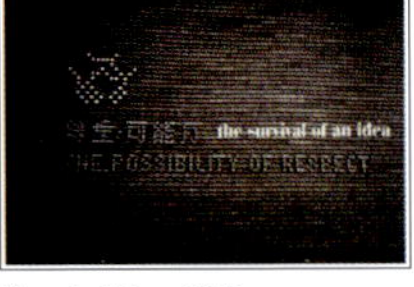

Chicago cobblestones
Gwangju Biennale

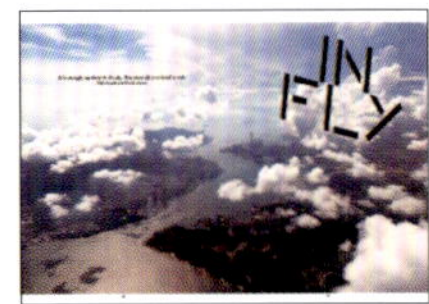

Pitti Exhibit, Florence
The Armory Show, NY

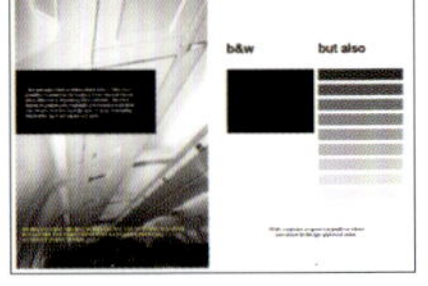

Shanghai Expo 2010

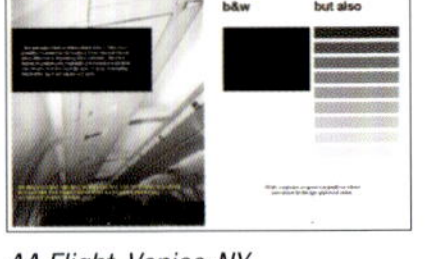

Hong Kong from above

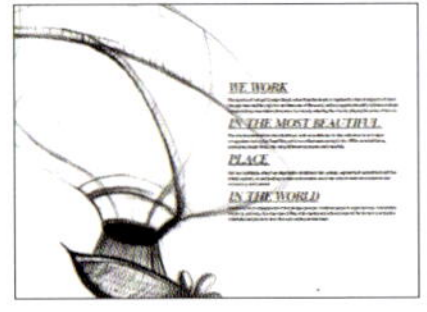

AA Flight, Venice-NY

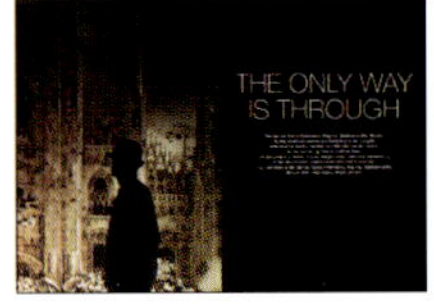

Airship sketch

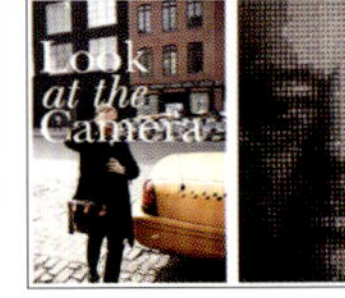

Milan Duomo

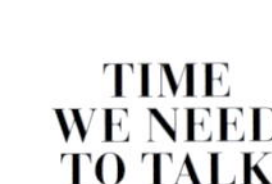

Meatpacking district, NY
Icon exercise

TIME
WE NEED
TO TALK

02

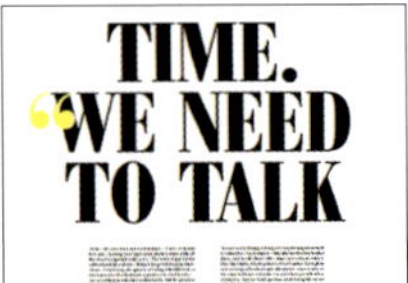

Everyday words

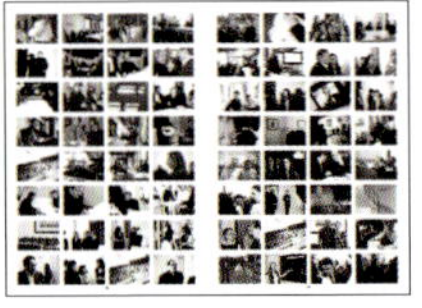

Hangar Annual Convention

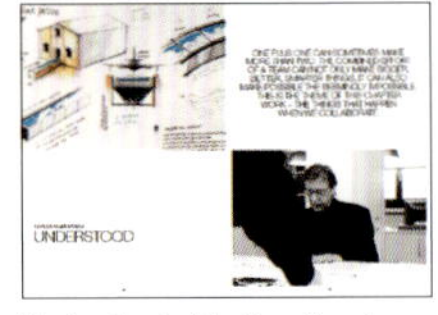

Design Dept., Mogliano Veneto

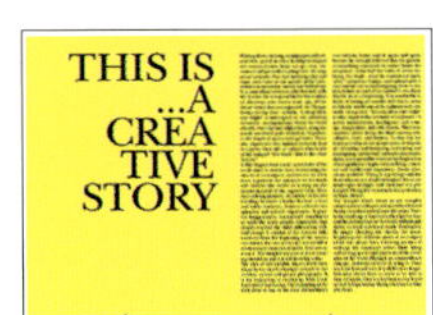

An abused title

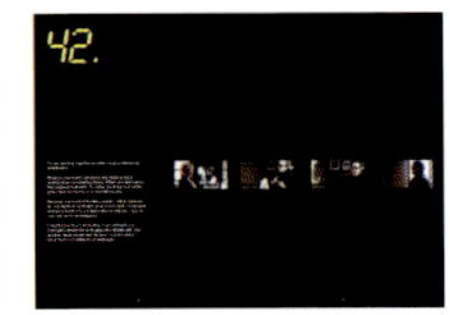

During a brief in Hangar House

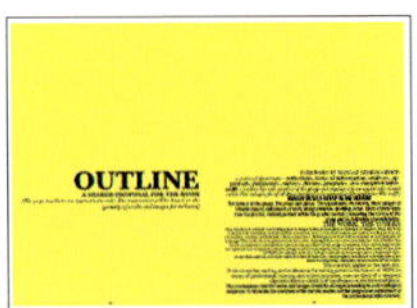

Messed up ideas for the book

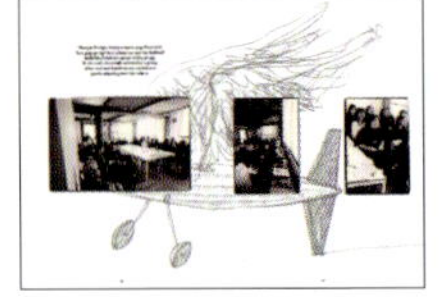

Hangar Annual Convention

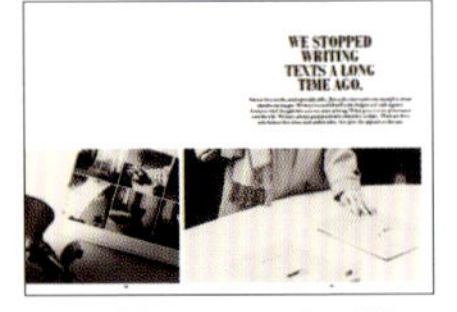

Hangar Diary presentation, Milan

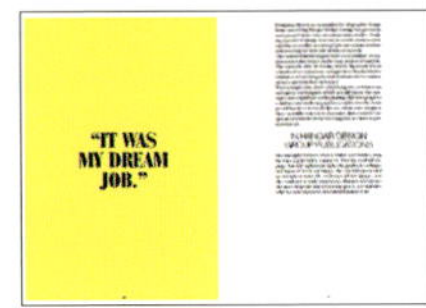

Do you believe it?

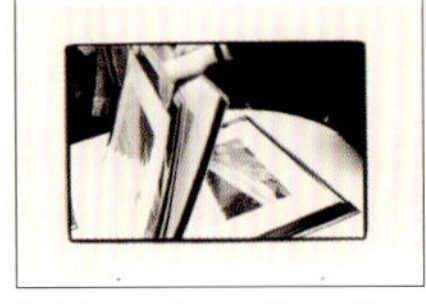

Sketches for Hangar Diary, Milan

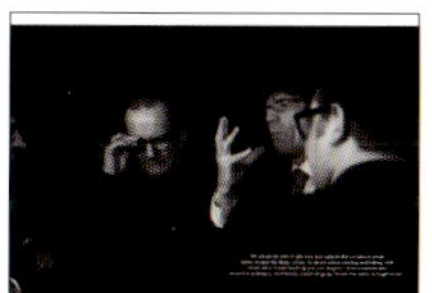

Design Week, Milan 2010

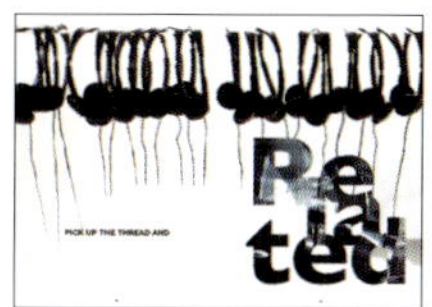

Shanghai

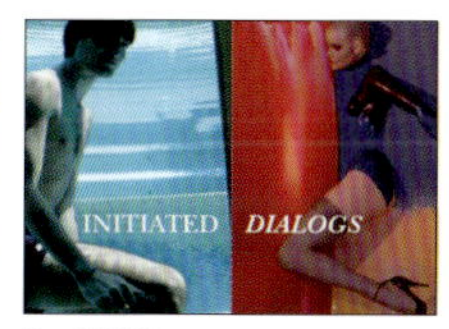

Capri, 2007

CAMEOS

03

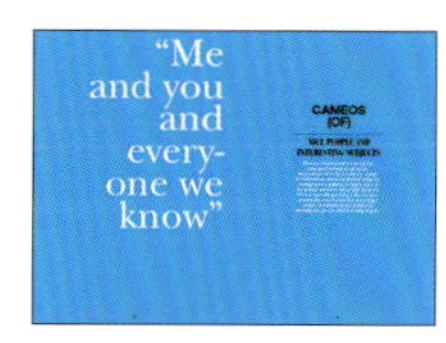

A lot of people we met

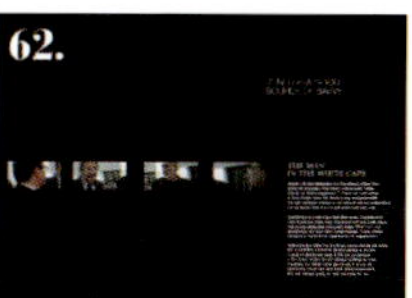

Bob Noorda and Gabriele Basilico

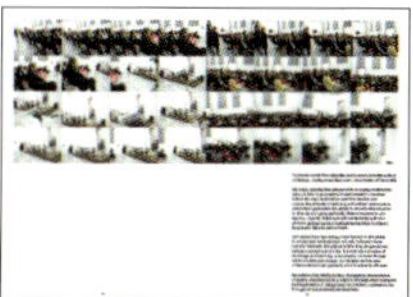

Book presentation, Triennale, Milan

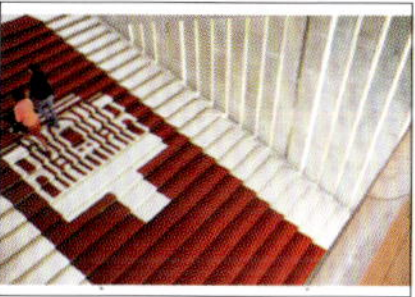

Triennale staircase

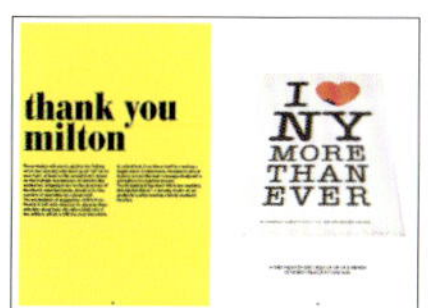

Our own "Milton Glaser"

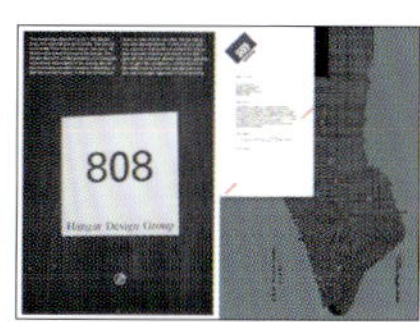

NY office, Flatiron Building
Greetings from Manhattan

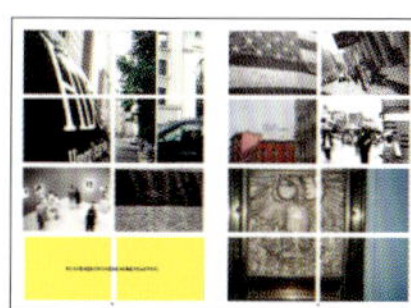

NY Opening Day, 2002

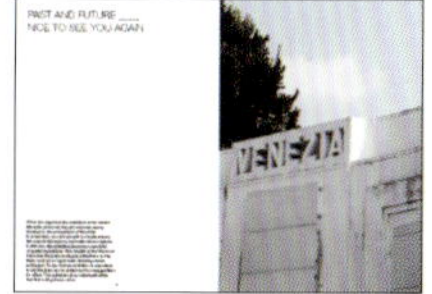

Venice Biennale, 2010

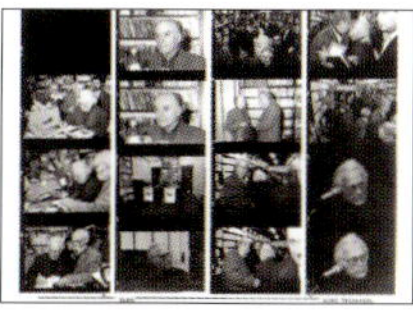

Toni Benetton and Andrea Zanzotto

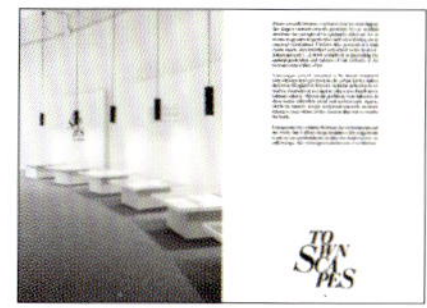

Venice Biennale, 2010

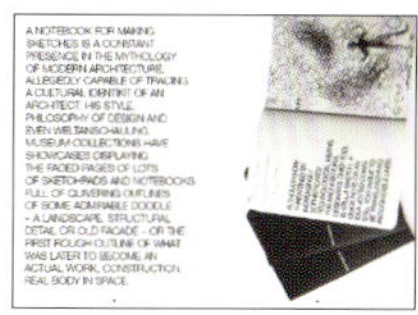

Drawn by Tobia Scarpa

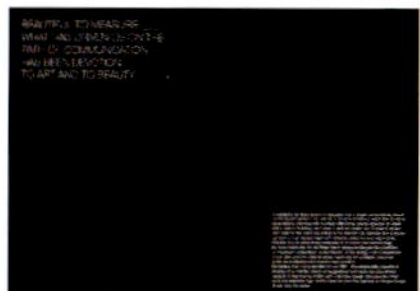

In art and beauty. We trust

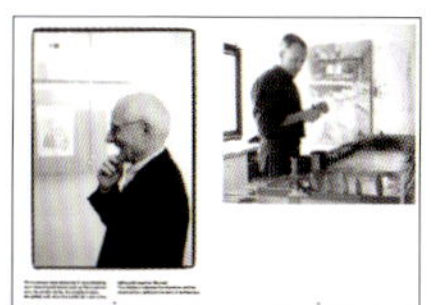

Alessandro Mendini, Milan
Paolo del Giudice, Treviso

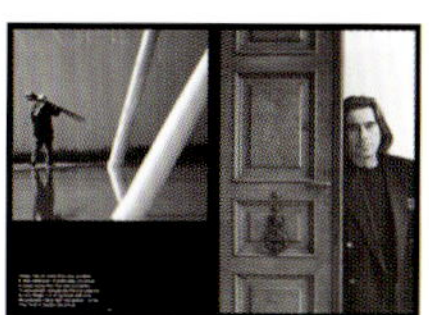

Gabriele Basilico, Bassano del Grappa
Fabrizio Plessi, Venice

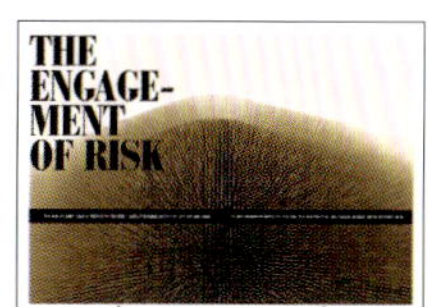

Expo Shanghai, 2010

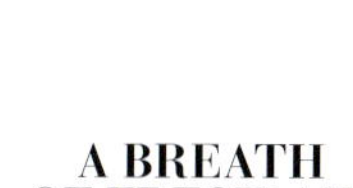

A BREATH OF FRESH AIR

04

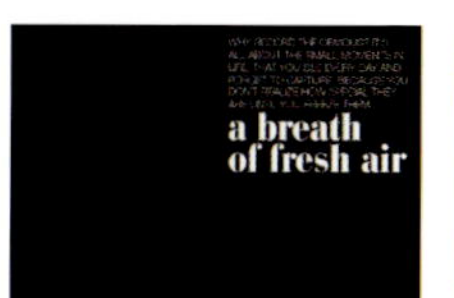

Work Hard. Have Fun

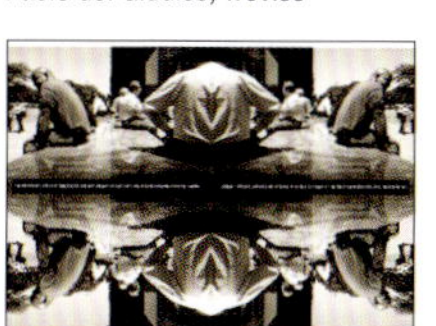
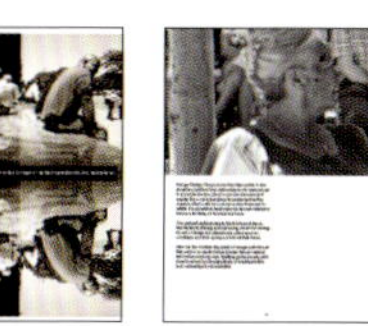

57th St., NY

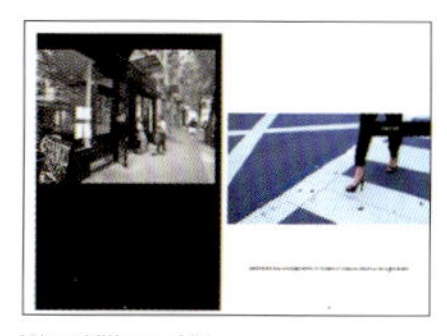

A Saturday in Madrid

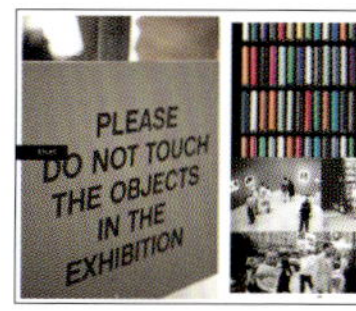

West Village, NY

Chicago Midtown

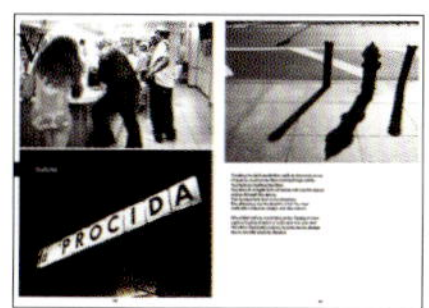

Our favourite restaurant, Treviso
NY, 2004; Los Angeles, 2005

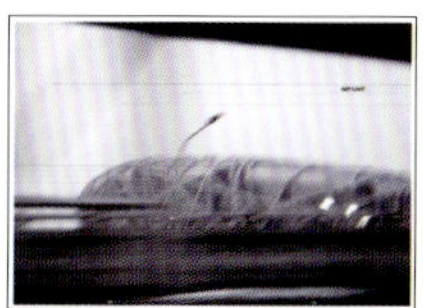

Beijing from the cab, 2010

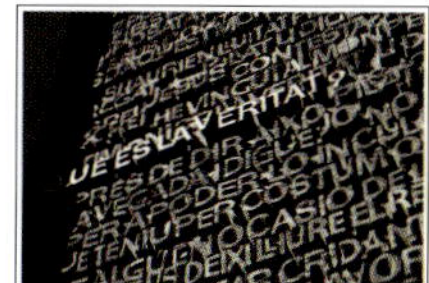

Barcelona Wall

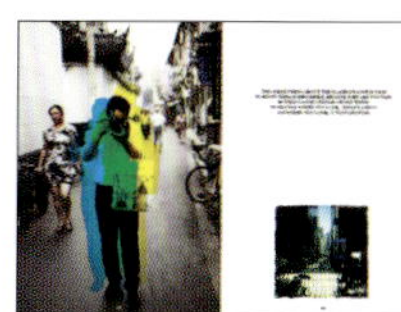

Shanghai on street

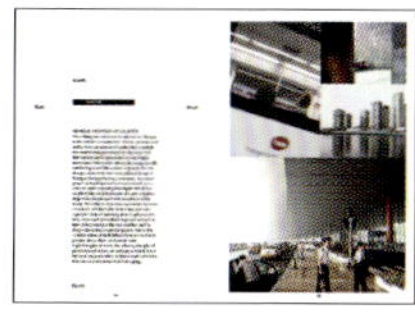

Barcelona, 2009
Singapore, 2011

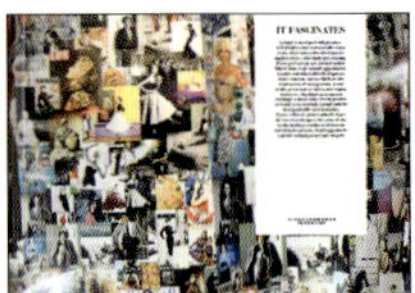
Soho window, NY

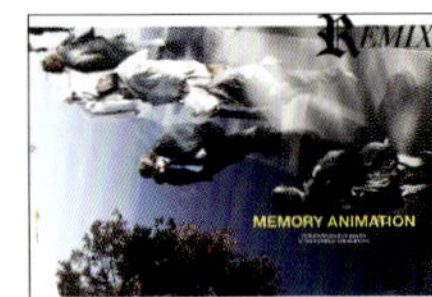
Bassano del Grappa

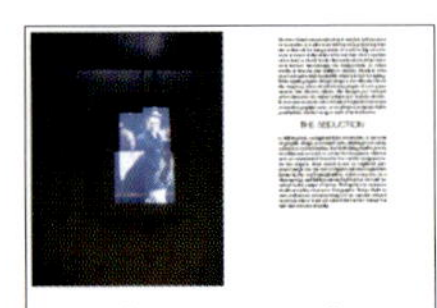
Long Island, NY

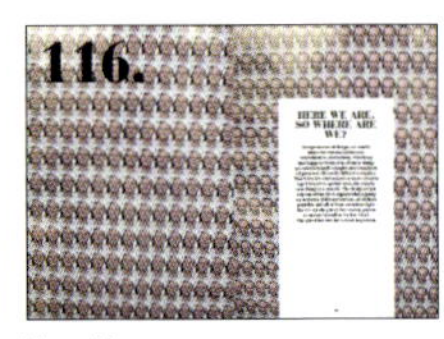
Hong Kong on screen

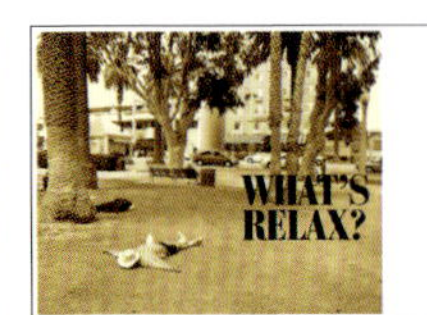
Venice Beach, CA

THE PRUNING DAY

05

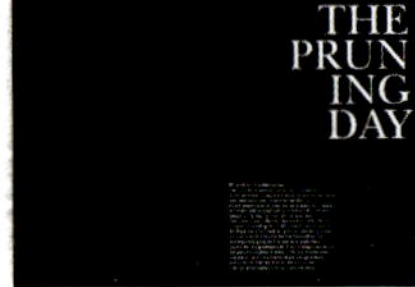
Where we work

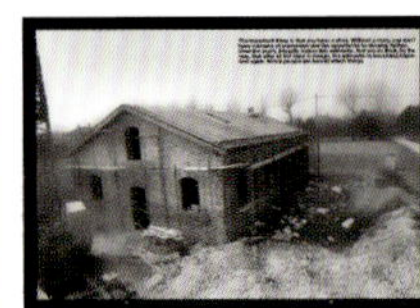
Building Hangar, Mogliano Veneto

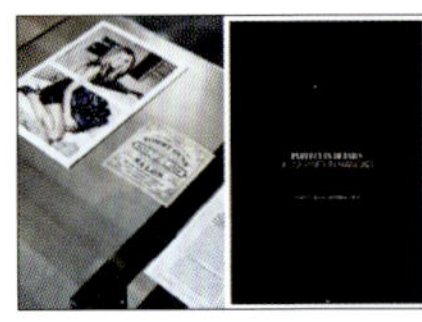
Desk in Milan office

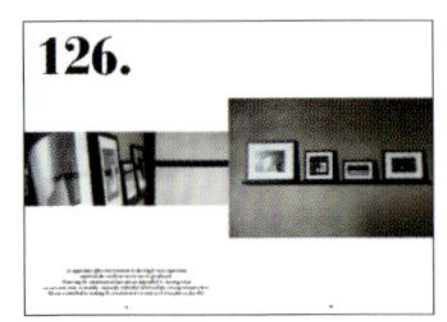
Shelves in Mogliano Veneto

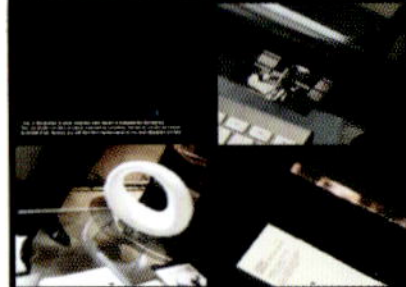
Chairman office, Mogliano V.

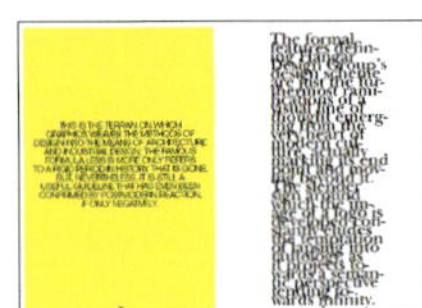
Frame of thought

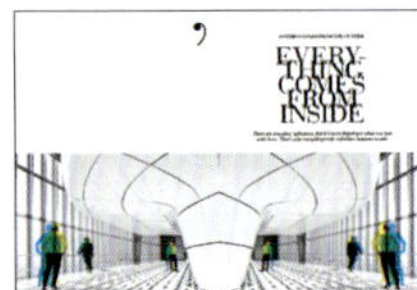
Pirelli Building, Milan

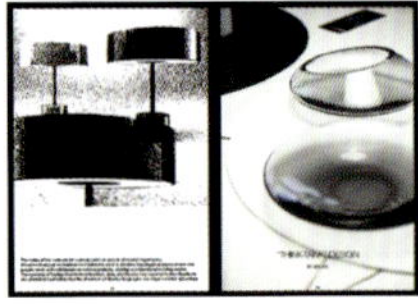
Black Tie, table lamp
Privée, vases

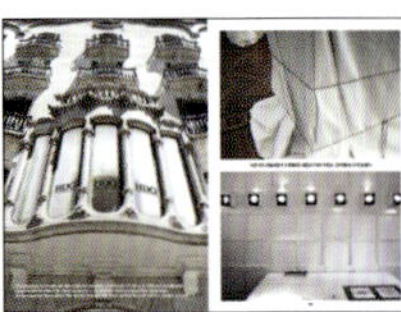
Barcelona office facade
Barcelona during renovation

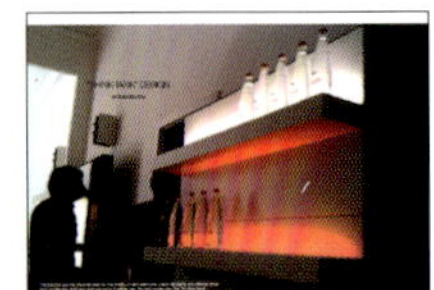
Opening night, Barcelona

AFFINITY OF FORMS

06

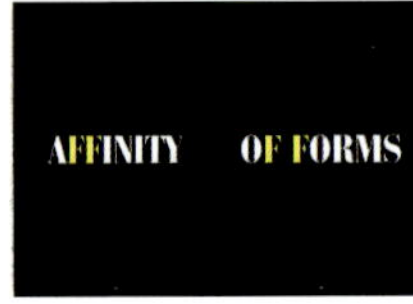
A stylistic guideline

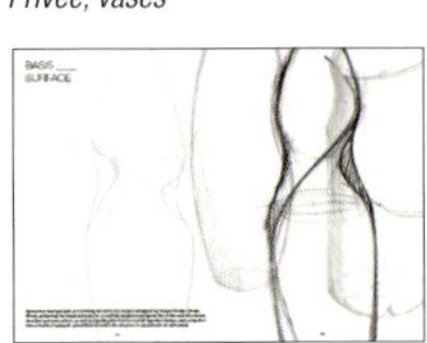
Sketches for soft drink

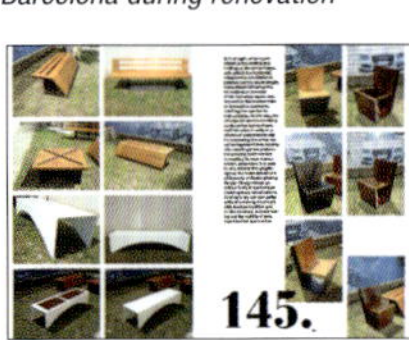
Prototypes for benches

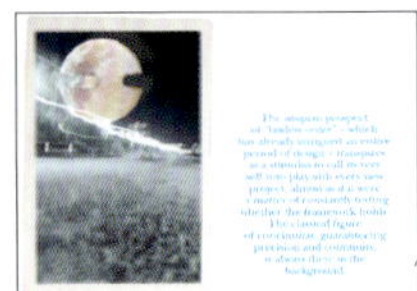
Full Moon, suspension lamp

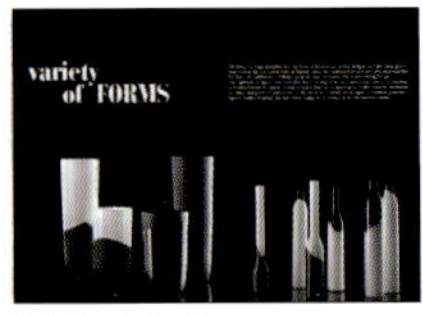
Velvet and Skyline, vases

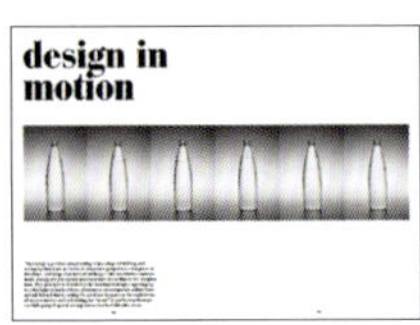
Mineral water bottle

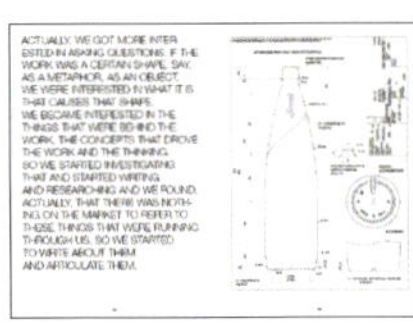
Technical features for bottle

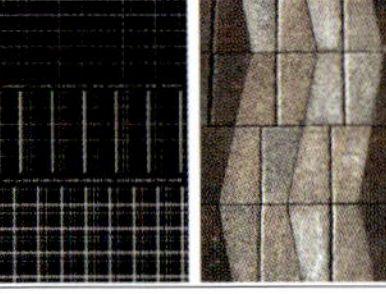
Concrete flooring

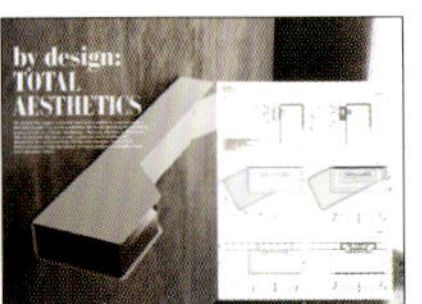
Oblique, bath shelf

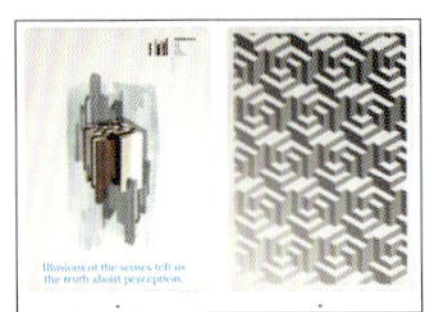
LegnoQuadro, coffee table

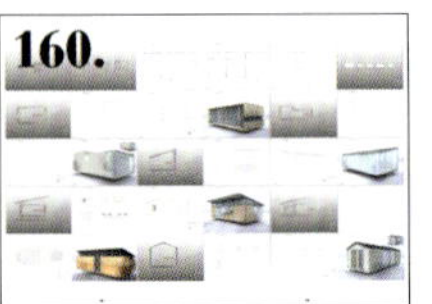
Prototypes for mobile homes

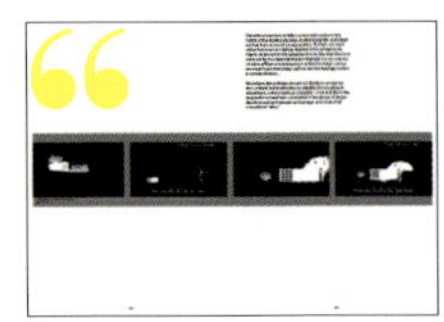
Mobile homes movie

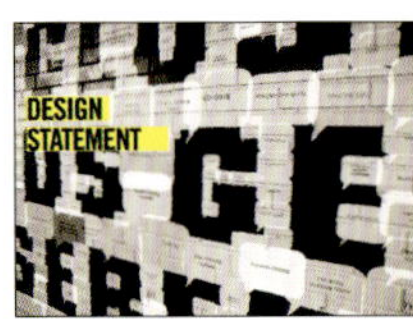
London wall

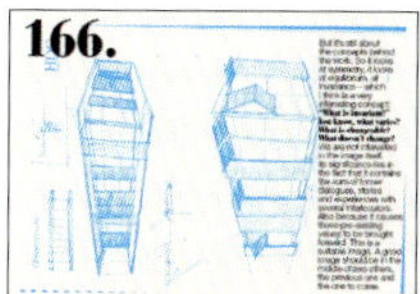

Sketches for mobile homes

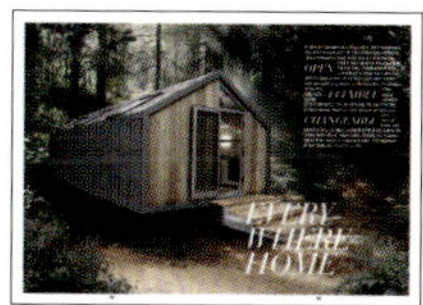

Joshua Tree

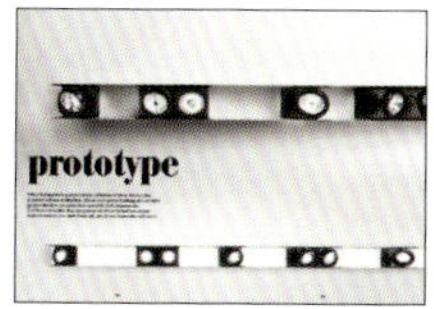

Horto, lighting system

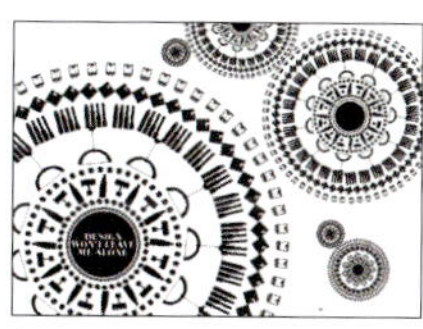

A sort of design Carnival

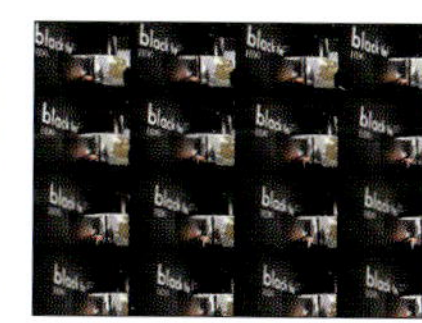

Design Week, Milan, 2009

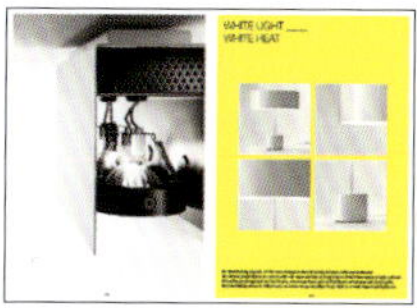

Horto shell
The White Black Tie

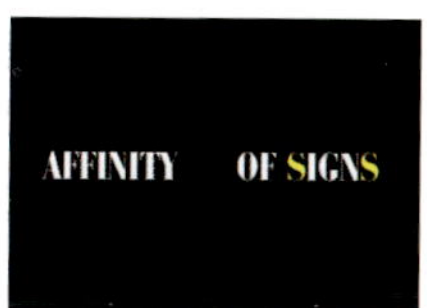

Lines sketched up

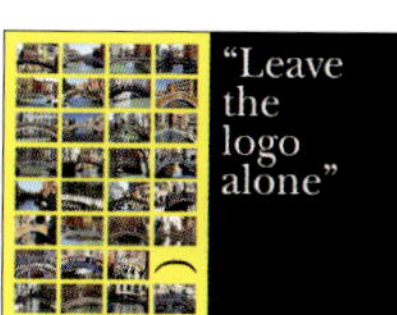

Studies for logo

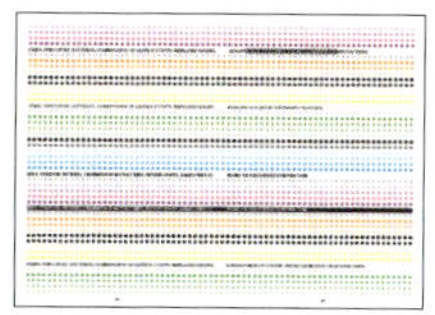

A repeated statement

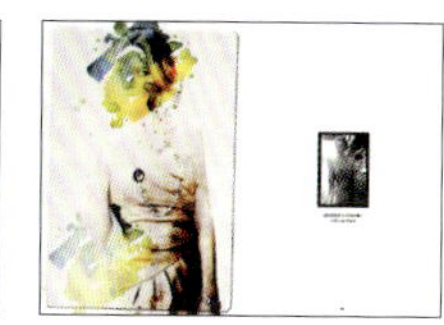

Layout for fashion adv

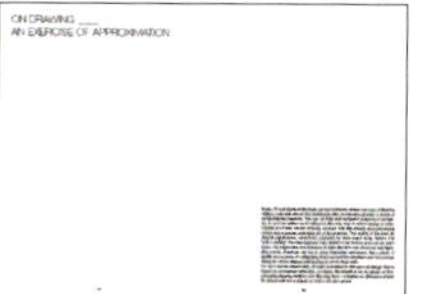

Keep drawing

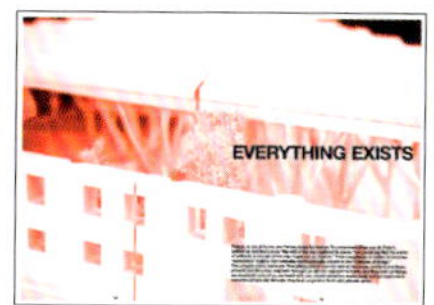

Architecture model

07

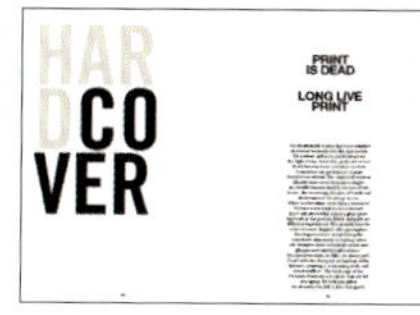

What we feel for paper

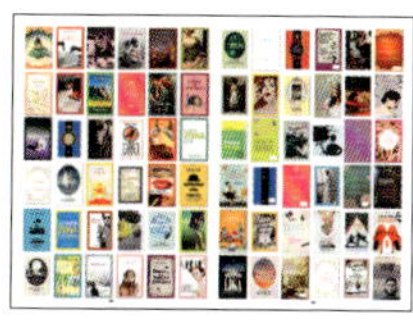

Book covers

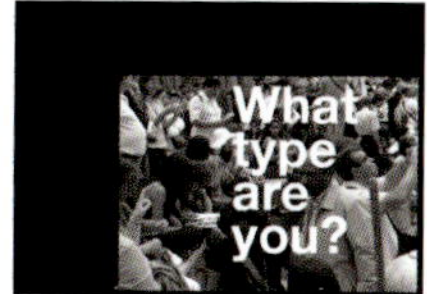

In the crowd, Rome

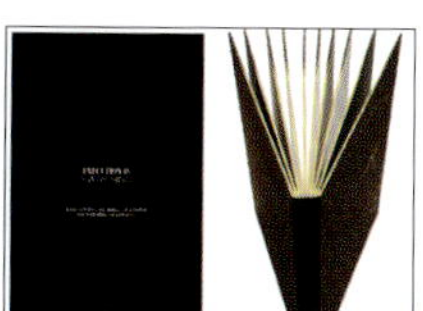

Brochure with paperback binding

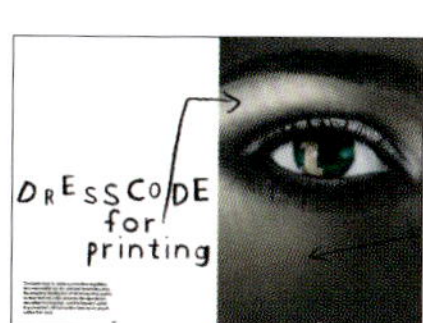

Jewel advertising

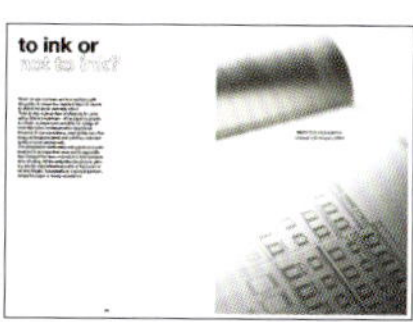

Real estate sales book

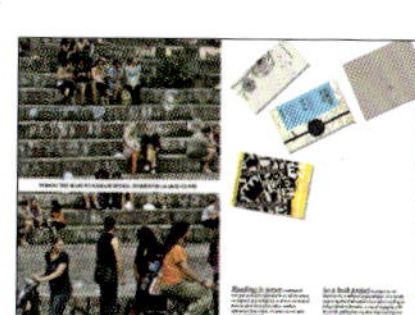

Newsletter and book covers

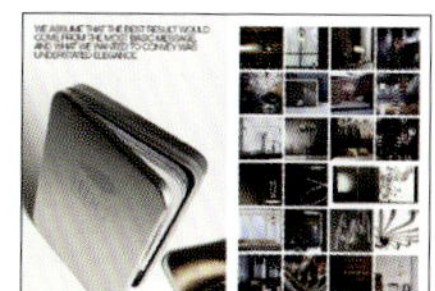

Metal box portfolio
Lighting catalogue

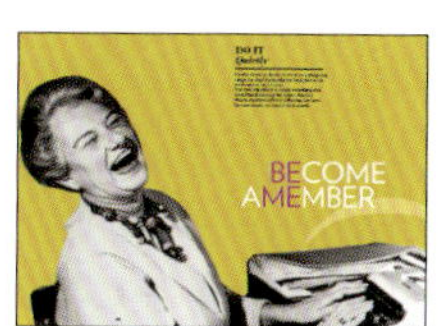

Advertising project

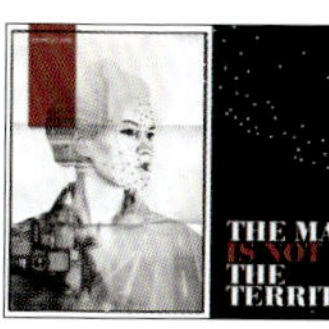

Shanghai Hangar guide

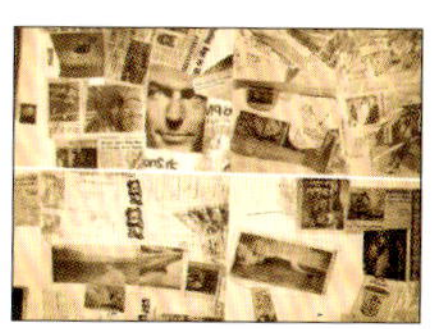

Sample of our vintage newspaper

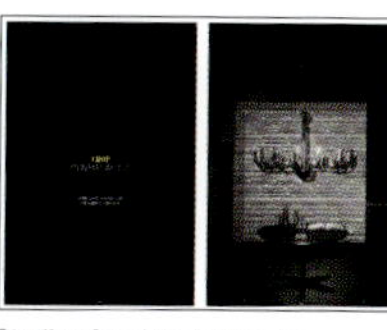

Studies for chandelier adv

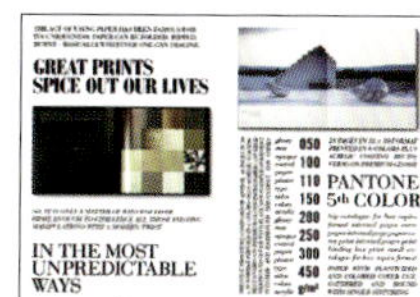

Real estate owner's kit
Catalogue for outdoor furnitures

08

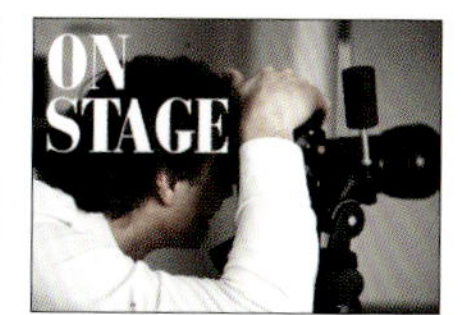

Shooting for home furniture, Ibiza

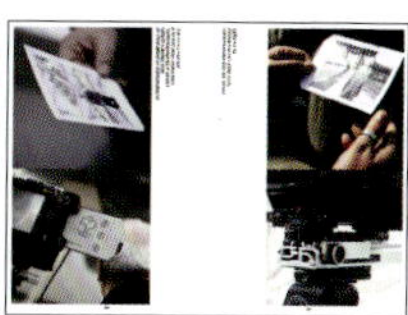

Jewel shooting in Hangar House

Photographer's hand

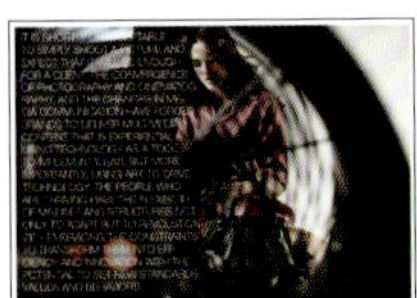

Fashion shooting, Milan

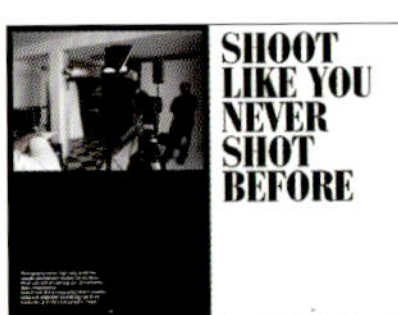

Hangar self-portraits

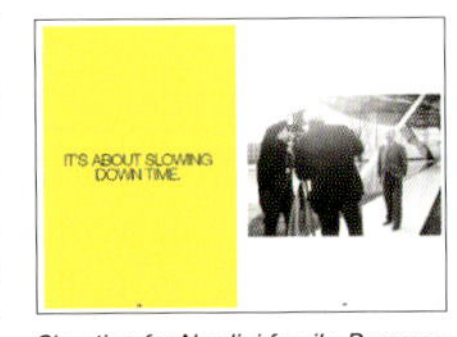

Shooting for Nardini family, Bassano

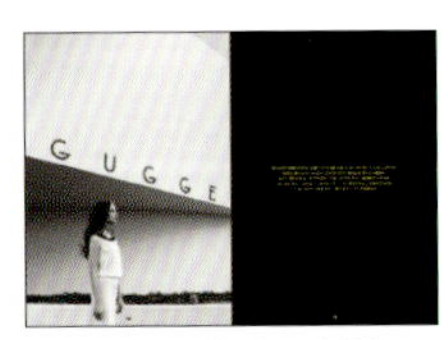

Shooting for coffee brand, NY

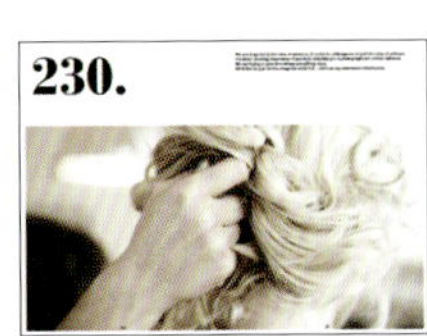

Fashion shooting, Milan

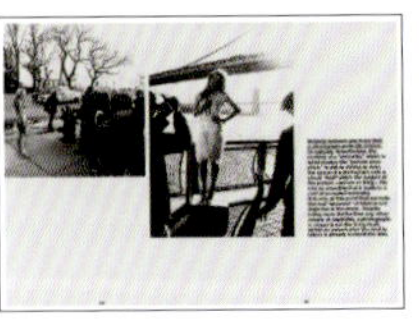

Fashion shooting, NY

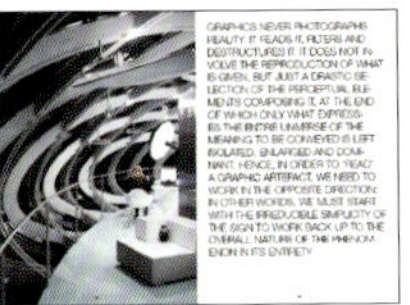

Shooting Bolle

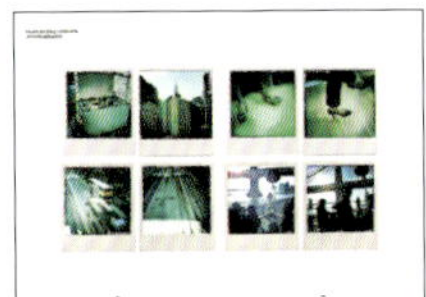

Jewel shooting, Brooklyn, NY

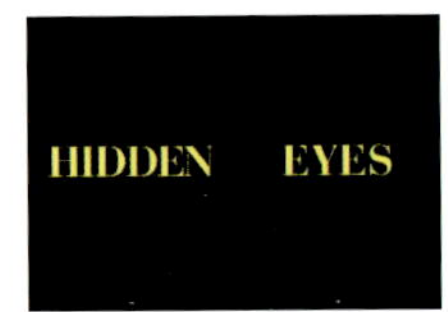

The chapter is finished

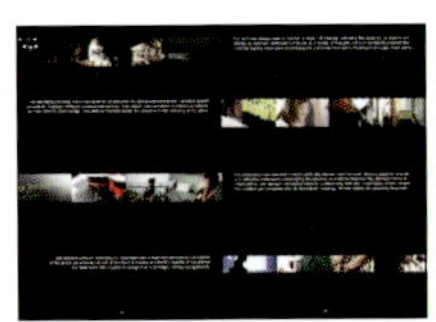

Hangar events

THE LAW
OF 3
PROPOSALS

09

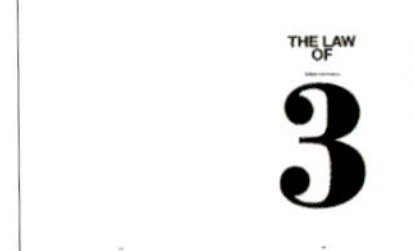

You can't get wrong

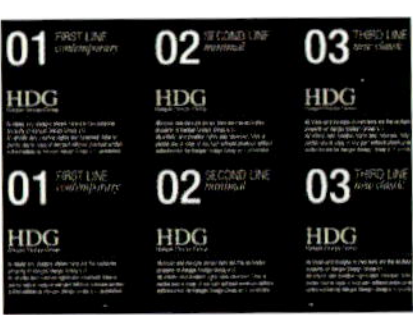

Disclaimer for brand image proposals

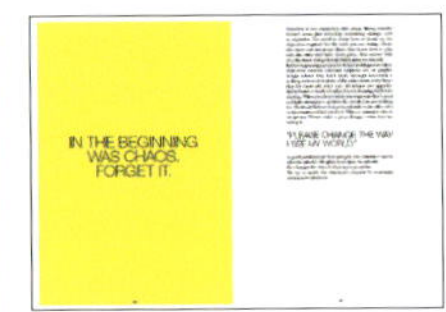

Please change the way I see my world

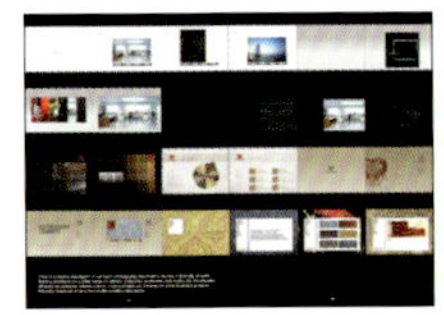

Photographer's website
Fabrics website

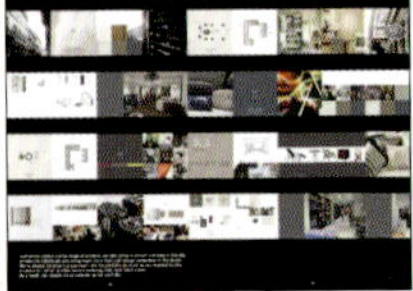

Brand image for textiles

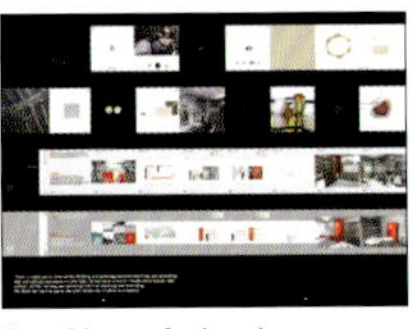

Brand image for jewels

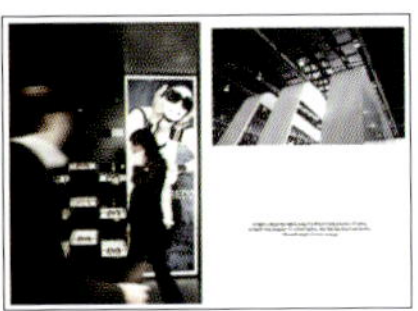

Exhibit design, Milan
Environmental design, Dubai

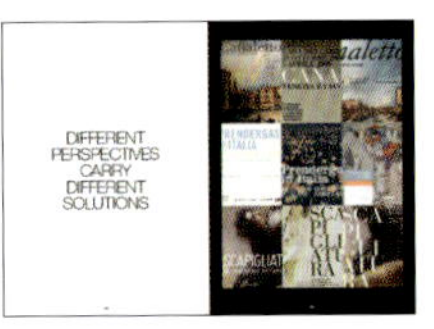

Studies for exhibit poster

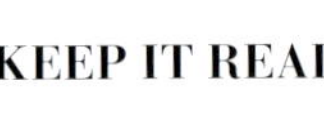

KEEP IT REAL

10

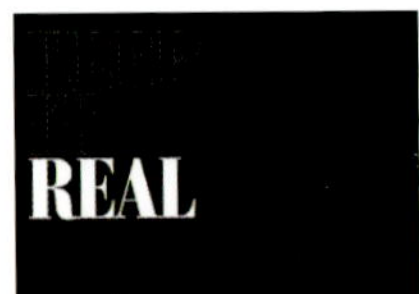

How the finished things seem

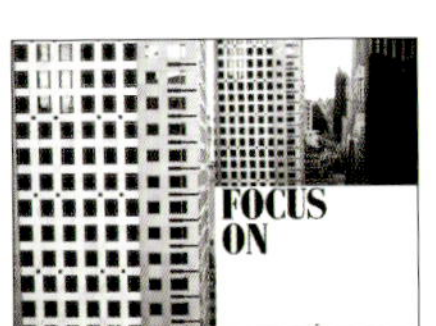

Upper East Side, NY

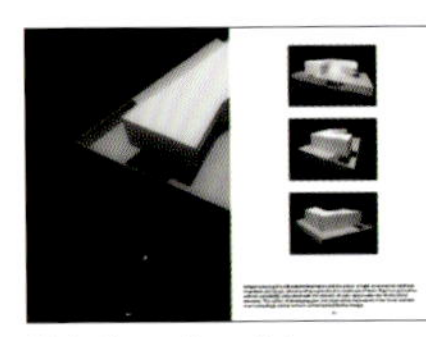

Marketing suite prototype

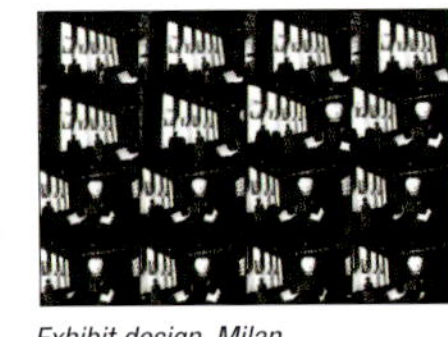

Exhibit design, Milan

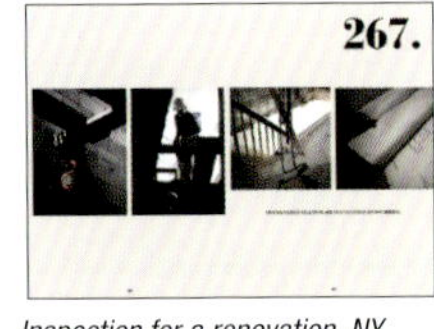

Inspection for a renovation, NY

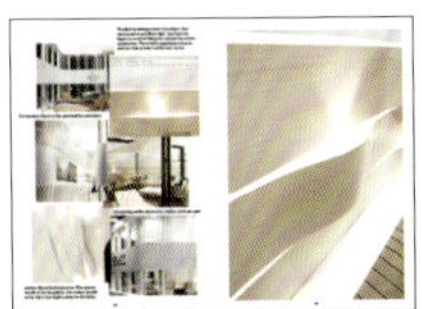

Exhbit design, Design Week, Milan

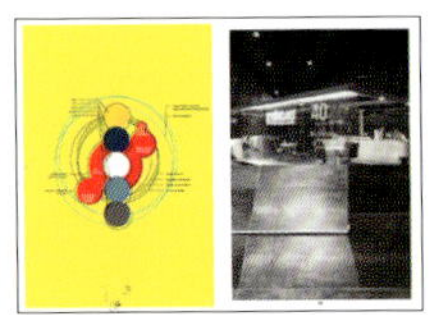

Retail diagram
Exhibit design, Geneva

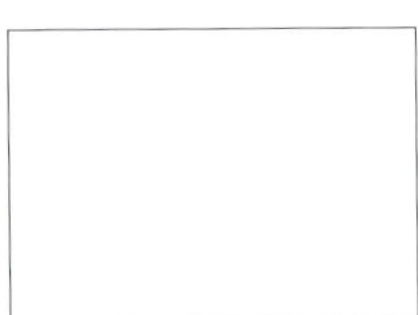

*Design Making *1*

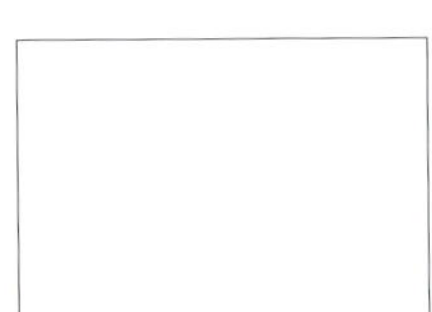

*Design Making *2*

*Design Making *3*

BESPOKE

11

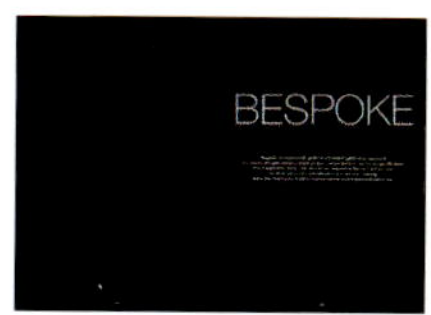

We tell your own story

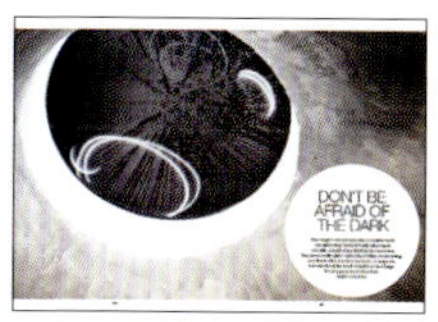

Details of an event

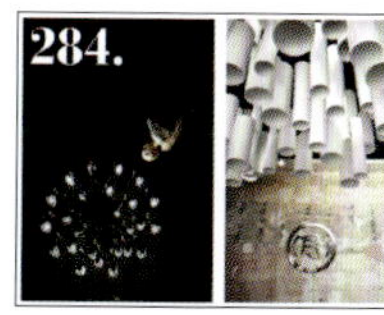

International Congress,
Marketing suite, Rome

Murano glass chandelier, Milan
Temporary bar, Milan

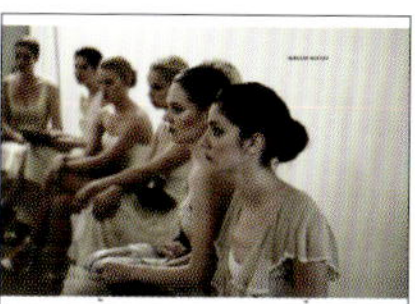

Jewellery gala, Vicenza

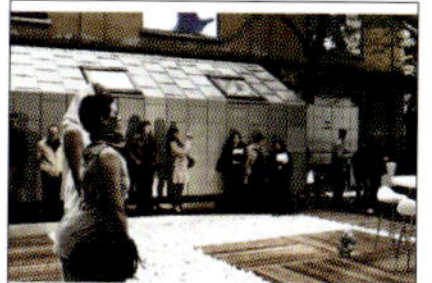

Mobile homes, Milan

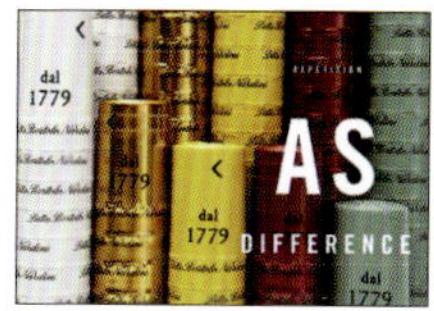

Grappa caps

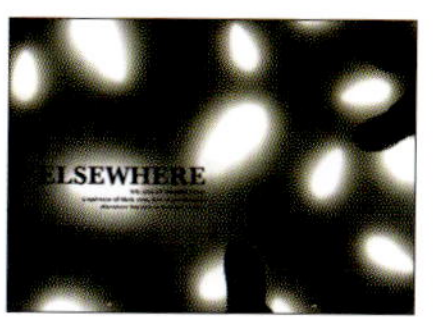

Lighted floor, Istanbul

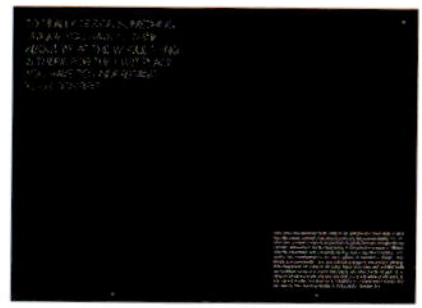

Understand your context

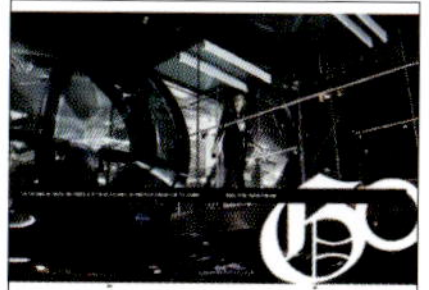

Press conference, Milan

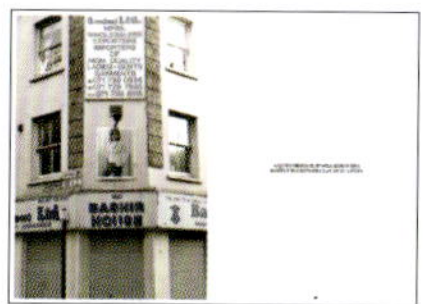

Private house, Venice

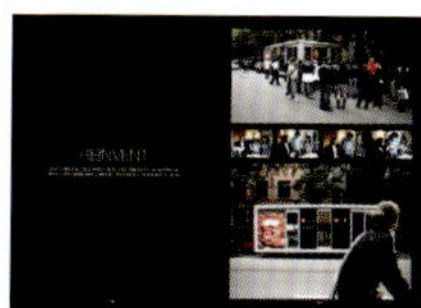

Hangar sunset, Milan

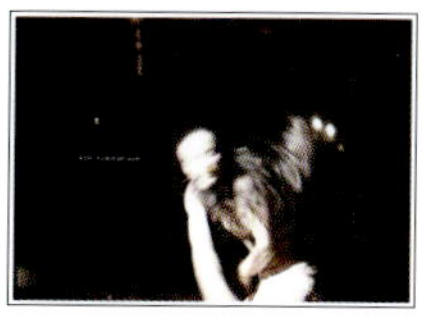

Opening event, Barcelona

THIS MEANS NOTHING

12

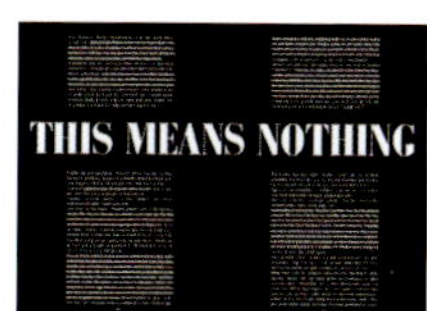

A list of unrealized works

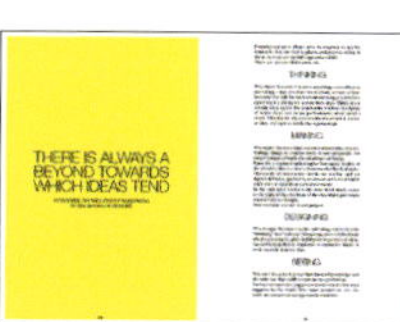

Thinking & Making

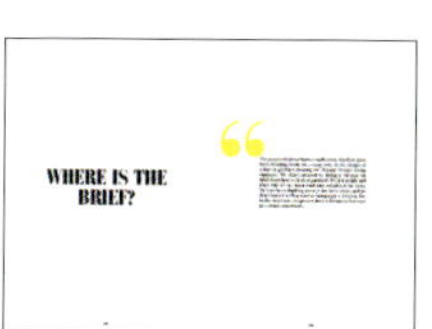

Where is the brief?

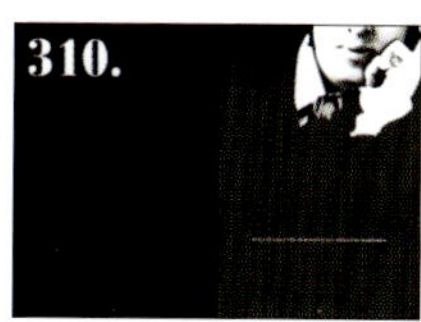

Studies for a fabric brand

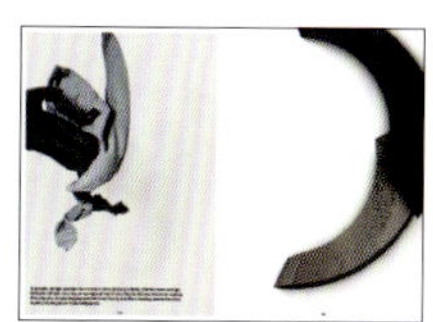

Studies for clothing adv

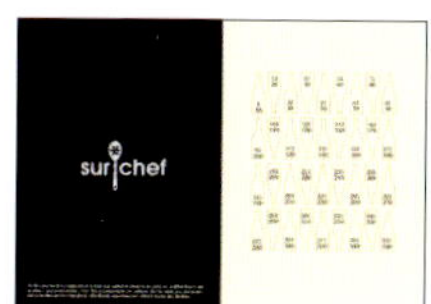

Studies for a deep-frozen brand
Studies for wine labeling

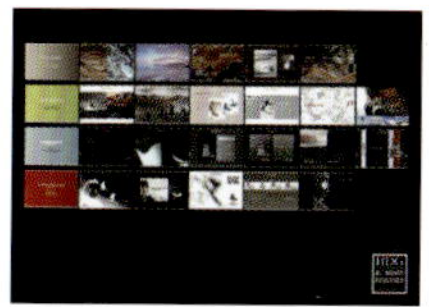

Studies for a sportswear brand

INSPIRATION KILLS

13

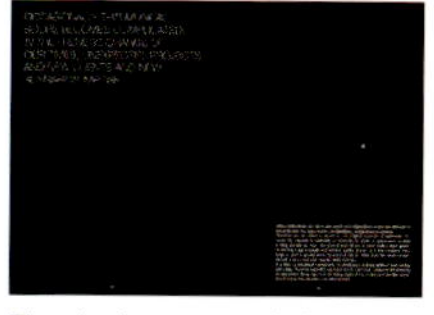

Sometimes it's true

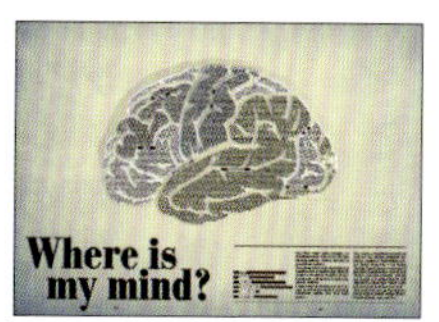

Fans of pathos

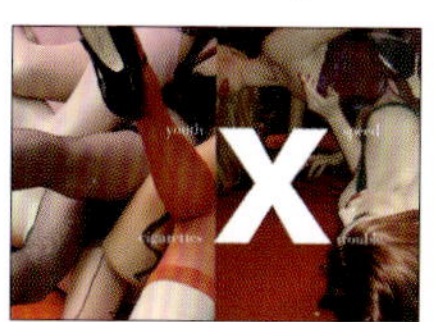

Retail manikins, LES, NY

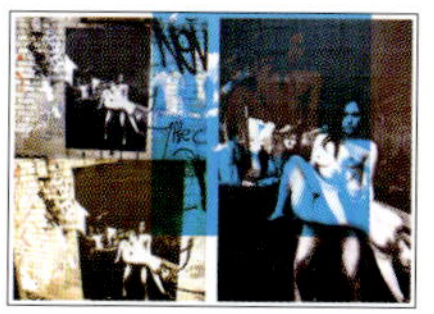

East Village, NY

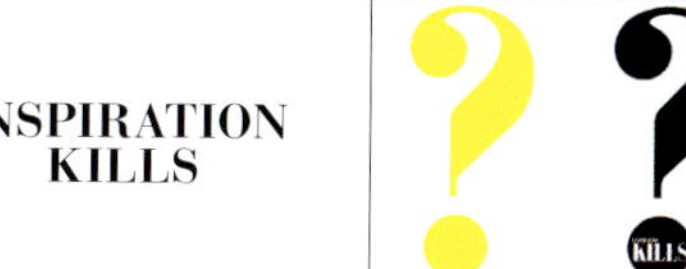

There's always a musical score

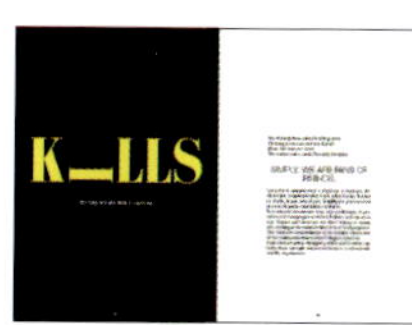

A creative lobotomy

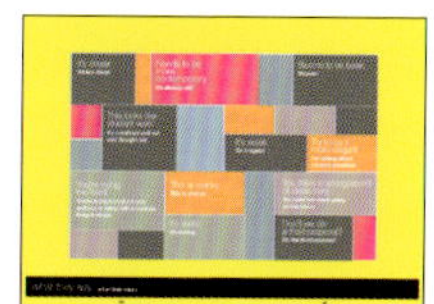

What they said is not true

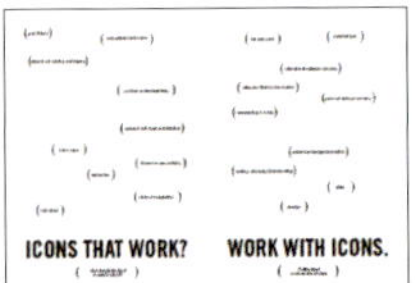

Icons & Icons

14

WATCH AND LEARN

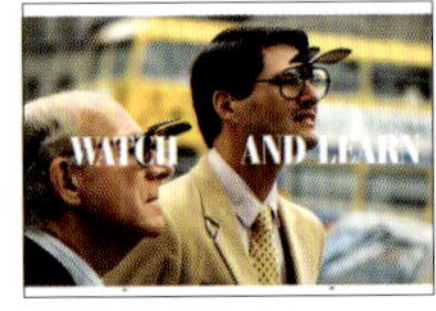

Philadelphia, 1995

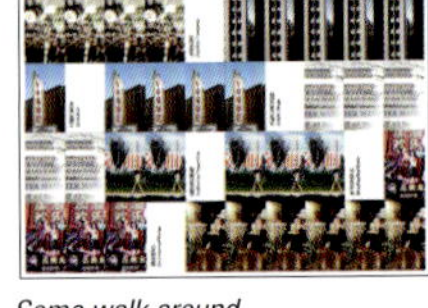

Some walk around

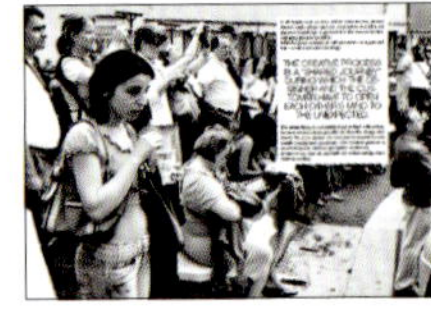

People in Alicante

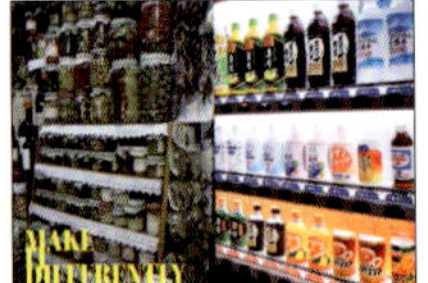

Capri market
Tokyo market

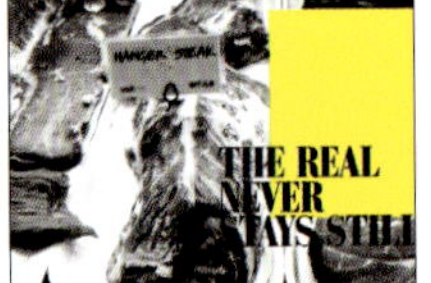

Chicago butcher

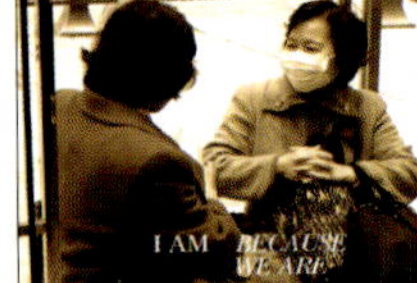

Bus station, Beijing

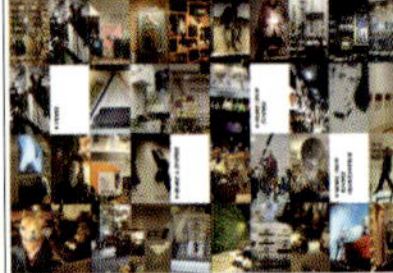

London shops

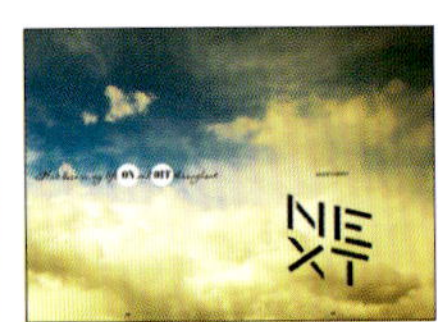

NY shops

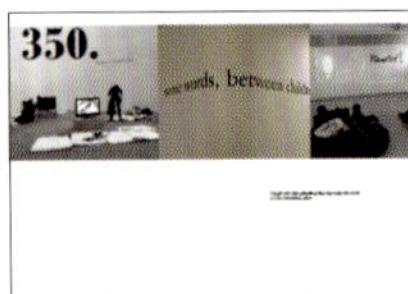

Whitney Biennial, NY

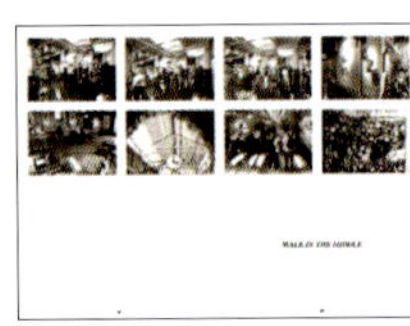

New York, 2006

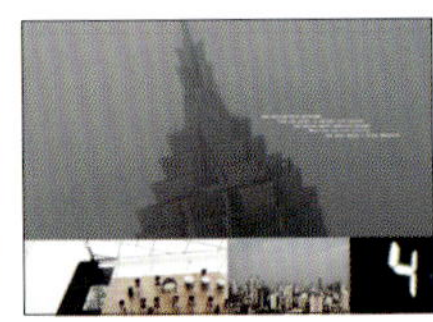

Shanghai, 2005

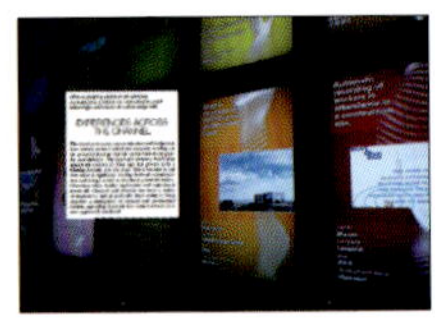

Italian Pavilion, Shanghai

Hong Kong sky

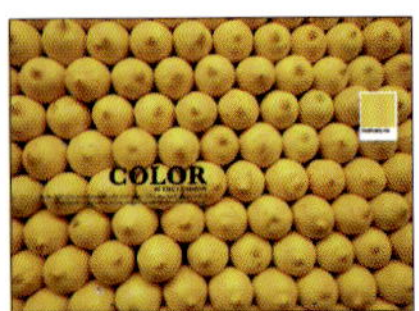

Sevilla, Pantone 109

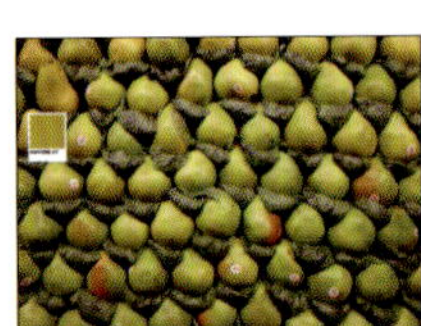

Seoul, Pantone 111

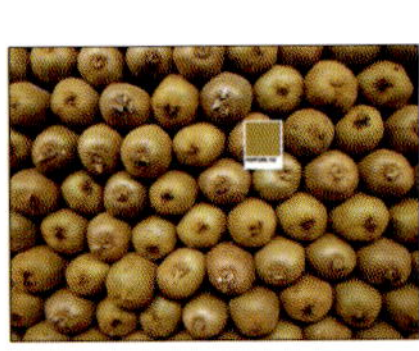

Rio de Janeiro, Pantone 132

15

NOWNESS

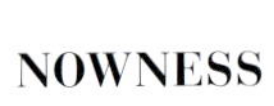

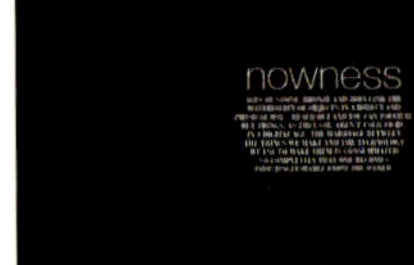

Here and Now

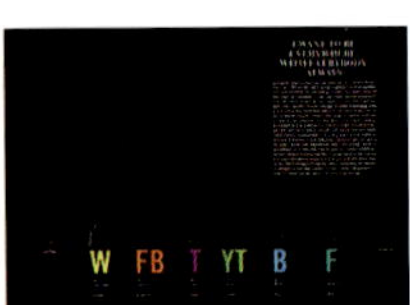

The social creativity

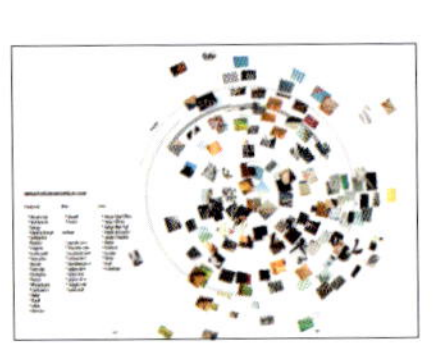

Our blog frames

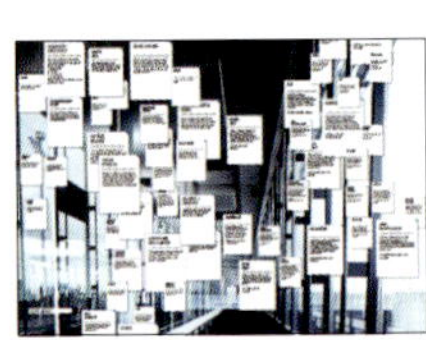

Posts on our Twitter page

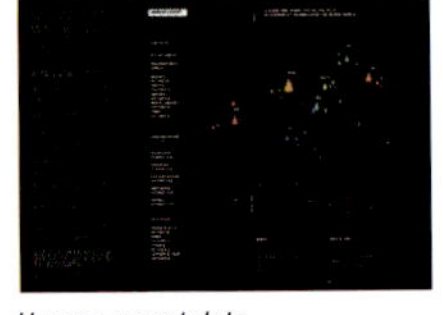

Hangar carnet data

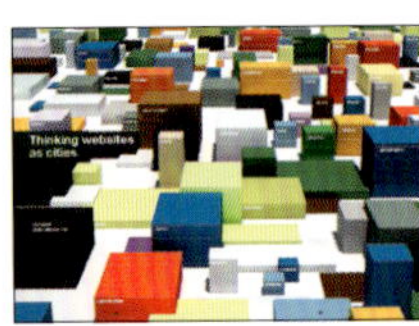

Thinking website as cities

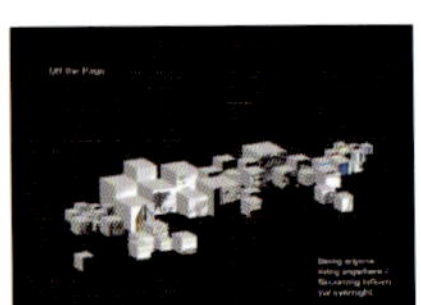

Visualizing Html+ Flash

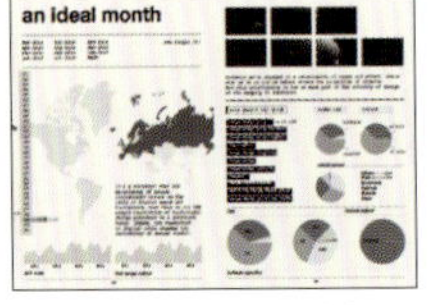

Access data to Hangar website

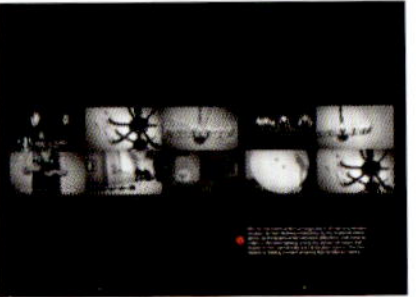

"Glass Delight" movie

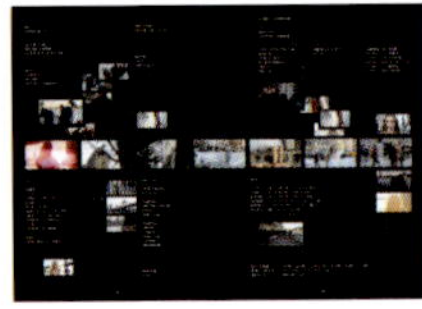

Backstage movie scenes

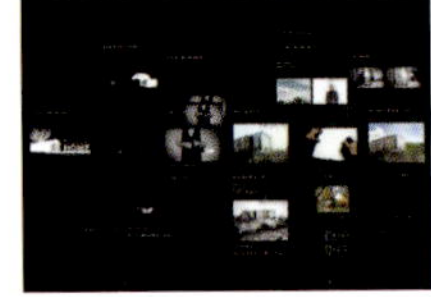

"Everywhere Home" movie

EXLIBRIS

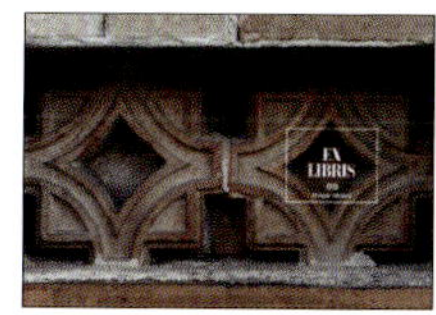

Mogliano office brickwork

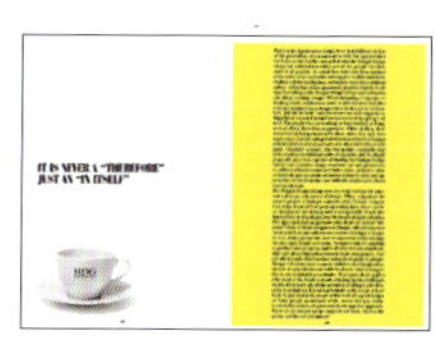

Hangar coffee cup

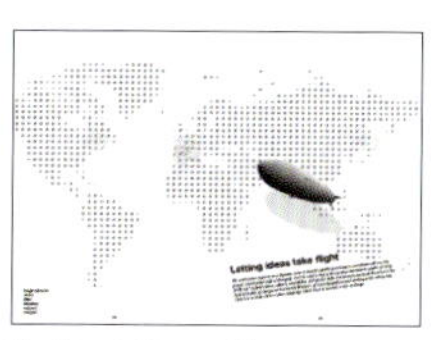

Floating in the world

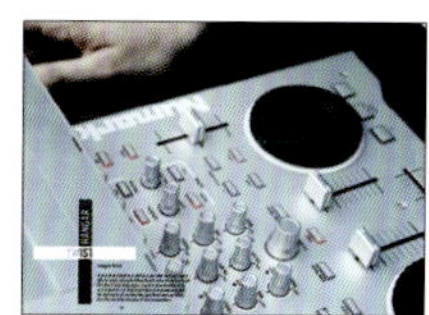

Mid-summer party, Treviso

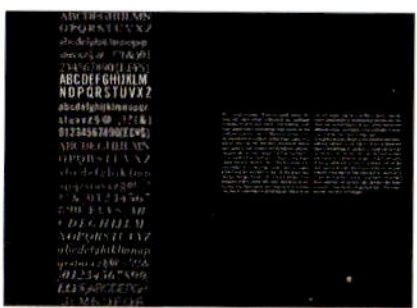

Beyond any categorizations

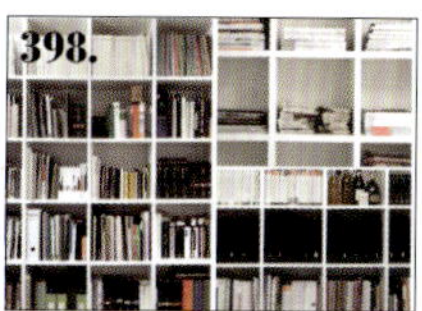

Our library, Milan

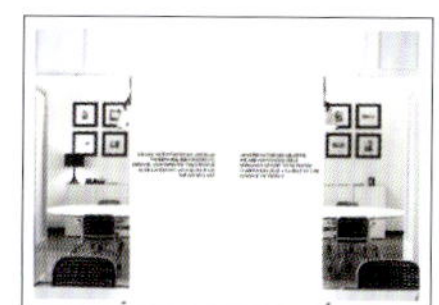

Milan office meeting room

17

LINKS

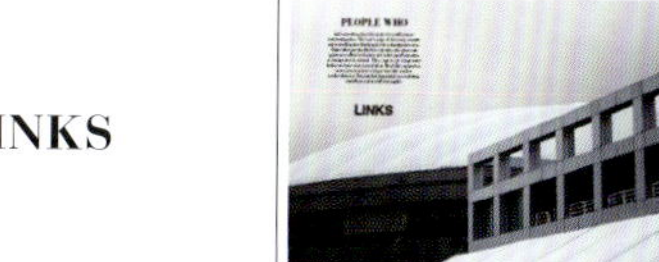

Olympic Stadium, Vancouver

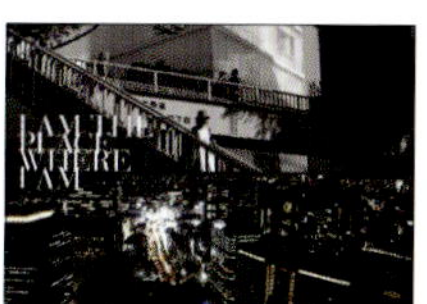

A Tokyo night

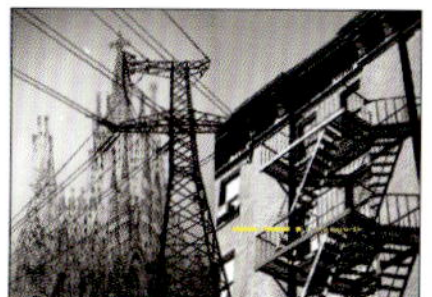

Milan Duomo
NY from above

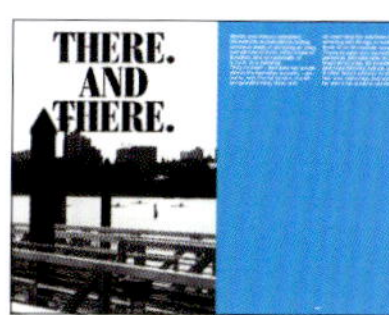

Chelsea pier, NY

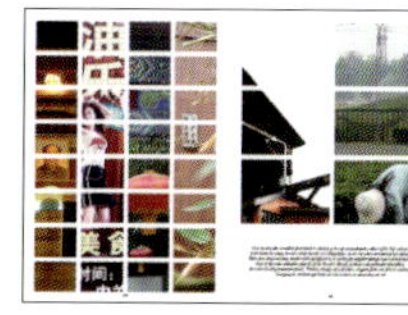

Beijing
Osaka countryside

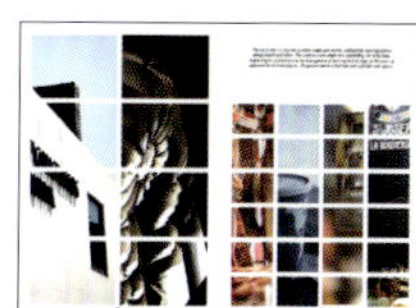

Barcelona, 2009
Madrid, 2004

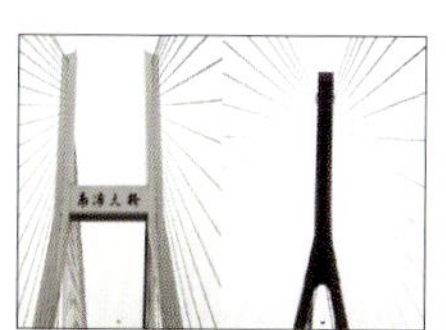

Shanghai bridges

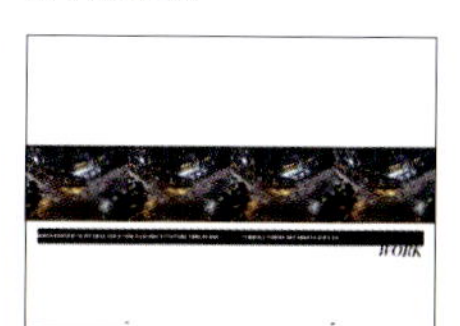

Madrid, 2005

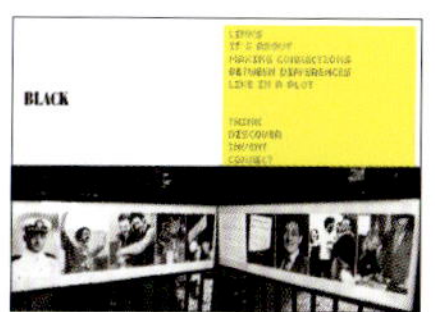

San Francisco, 2010

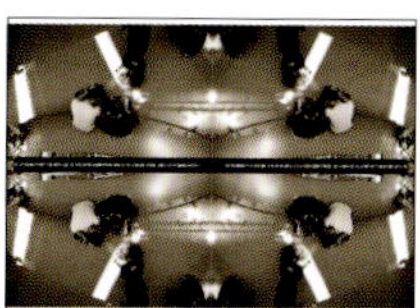

Venice Biennale, 2010

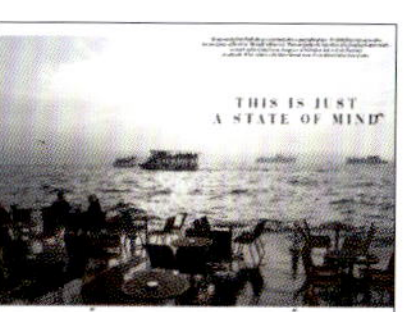

Istanbul, 2009

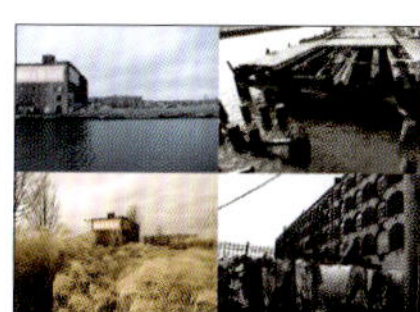

Red Hook, NY, 2008

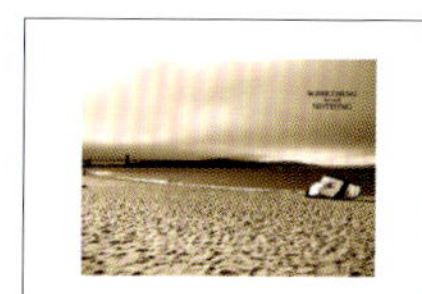

San Francisco, 2002

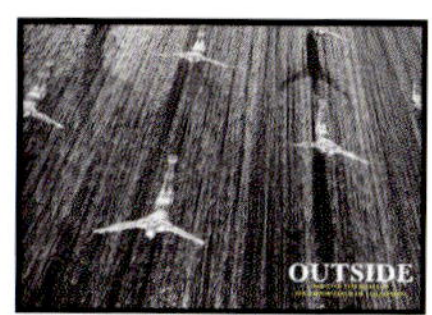

Dubai, 2006

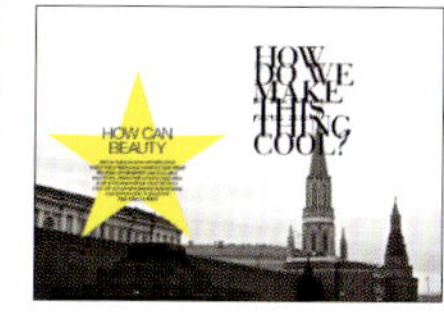

Moscow, 2007

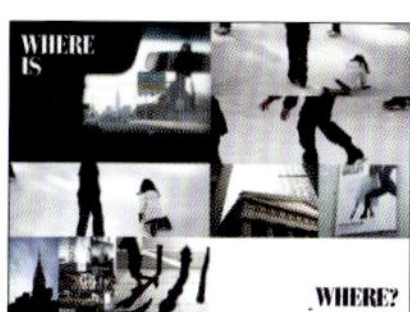

Rockefeller Center, NY, 2010

INTRODUZIONE

GRAZIE A

Grazie per la possibilità che abbiamo avuto, negli ultimi trent'anni, di raggiungere con successo tutti gli obiettivi che ci siamo prefissati. E grazie per il fatto che non abbiamo mai abbandonato il sogno di vedere realizzati i nostri progetti. Grazie a noi e a voi, a tutti quanti voi.

. . .

Trent'anni di passione per il progetto lasciano indifferenti rispetto alle possibilità di contaminazione con le opportunità del futuro. È come dire che quello che Hangar Design Group ha fatto somiglia a una parte di chi lo ha realizzato. In realtà ciò che è stato prodotto è frutto di una incredibile convergenza di abilità e suggestioni. Le abilità sono il risultato di intelligenze, a volte anche artificiali, che hanno sempre generato progetti legati al design.

Tutto in Hangar Design Group passa attraverso una grande aspirazione: produrre design. Sia che si progetti un logo o che si pensi alla dimensione architettonica, non si prescinde mai dall'idea che si sta facendo qualcosa che risponde a una dimensione progettuale in sé. Non è mai "conseguenza di", ma sempre qualcosa di unico in se stesso. Come uniche sono le suggestioni, che permeano di sé ogni angolo delle varie sedi del gruppo. Coloro che lavorano – o hanno lavorato – in Hangar hanno sempre vissuto di suggestioni, generandole o restandone impigliati quando meno se l'aspettavano. Quando un partner si trova ad affrontare un progetto con i suoi collaboratori, non pensa mai che si tratti di realizzare qualcosa di utile per qualcuno, quanto piuttosto cerca di sviluppare un'attitudine mentale, in sé stesso e in ciascuno dei suoi collaboratori, per far sviluppare ed emergere in tutta la sua potenza l'attitudine progettuale. Una dimensione progettuale che, a volte, rasenta la spiritualità.

Oppure quando ci si concentra principalmente sulla gestione delle potenzialità del proprio ego, per poi poterlo correttamente guidare in un rapporto con il committente.

Qualunque cosa si produca in Hangar, l'unico e solo obiettivo che ci si pone è il progetto in se stesso; poi il "pacchetto" completo viene offerto a un terzo, di solito un committente. Questo tipo di approccio ha avuto un peso significativo nell'organizzazione interna di Hangar Design Group, poiché ha fatto saltare tutti gli schemi consueti di collaborazione all'interno di uno studio professionale. Ma anziché generare mostri, ha prodotto un modus operandi che si è trasformato in una vera e propria scuola, probabilmente unica.

La rotazione delle diverse professionalità e l'approccio fortemente pragmatico, capace di trasformare Hangar Design Group in una grande macchina progettuale, non sono basati su schemi organizzativi o strategici eccessivamente legati a tempi o metodi; piuttosto si tratta del frutto di intuizioni e di approcci variabili, che in questi ultimi anni riflettono il mercato e il mondo della committenza.

Quando il progetto di un designer giapponese si incrocia con la fantasia cinese nell'ambito di una logica produttiva di chiaro stampo europeo, è subito evidente che ci si trova di fronte a un brand riconosciuto che, tramite intuizioni e segni, punta a lasciare una forte traccia di progetto.

Sono gli stessi segni e intuizioni che emergono dal lavoro quasi "tormentato" di tutti i designer operanti negli hangar, i quali tendono trappole e creano insidie, riflettendo la natura più autentica del design.

Il designer è una creatura astuta che vuole presentare una propria realtà attraverso il suo segno, la sua mano, il suo cervello. Il designer è capace di qualsiasi cosa tranne che di inibire la propria idea; e pur di farla "passare" si trasforma, si modifica e si orienta lasciandosi guidare unicamente dal progetto. È proprio questa specie di rapimento estatico a rendere unico il suo progetto. In Hangar ci sarà sempre posto per l'immaginazione, la visione e la fantasia, perché solo con questi ingredienti si può costruire il futuro: non ha futu-

INTRODUCCIÓN

GRACIAS

Gracias por la posibilidad que hemos tenido, en los últimos treinta años, de lograr el éxito en todo lo que nos hemos propuesto. Y gracias además por el hecho de que nunca hemos abandonado nuestro sueño de ver como se hacían realidad nuestros proyectos. Gracias a nosotros, a vosotros, a todos vosotros.

. . .

Treinta años de pasión por el diseño no son nada en comparación con el potencial de "contaminación cruzada" que ofrece el futuro. Con esto queremos decir que aquello que Hangar Design Group ha logrado refleja a una parte de la gente que lo ha logrado.

En realidad, la producción es el fruto de un cruce sorprendente de habilidades y sugerencias. Las habilidades son el resultado de las inteligencias, incluyendo ciertas veces aquellas artificiales, que siempre han impulsado los proyectos vinculados al diseño. En Hangar Design Group todo se filtra a través de una aspiración trascendental: producir diseño.

Cuando se diseña un logotipo o cuando las dimensiones arquitectónicas son el centro de atención, se pone un énfasis constante en proceder de acuerdo con un único imperativo de diseño. Nunca es "una consecuencia de", más bien es "lo único en sí".

Como también lo son las sugerencias. Las sugerencias que impregnan cada rincón de cada oficina del grupo. Quienes trabajan o han trabajado en Hangar siempre han vivido de las sugerencias. Generándolas quedando atrapado en ellas cuando menos te lo esperas. Cuando algunos socios abordan un proyecto con sus colaboradores, nunca piensan que tienen que producir algo "útil" para alguien, prefieren pensar en cómo pueden desarrollar una actitud mental en ellos mismos y en cada uno de sus colaboradores que les permita que el diseño imperativo se desarrolle y crezca dentro de ellos y de los demás. Este imperativo de diseño de vez en cuando bordea una sensibilidad más espiritual.

Como cuando el énfasis principal se pone en definir, organizar y supervisar las posibles prioridades del ego, con el fin de guiarlo hacia una relación con el cliente.

Podemos decir que, todo aquello que se produce en Hangar está diseñado completamente con su finalidad a la vista —el diseño— y ese todo completo se ofrece sólo después a un tercero, por lo general a un cliente.

Esto ha tenido un fuerte impacto sobre la organización interna de Hangar Design Group, puesto que ha roto todos los esquemas tradicionales de colaboración dentro del contexto de un estudio profesional. Hay que reconocer que esto no generó monstruos.

En cambio, ha producido un modus operandi que se ha transformado en una verdadera escuela, y probablemente en la única en su tipo.

La rotación de las distintas competencias profesionales y el enfoque fuertemente pragmático, capaz de transformar Hangar Design Group en una gran máquina de diseño, no se basan en esquemas de organización de la producción o en políticas estrictamente vinculadas a plazos y métodos, sino que se basan en intuiciones y enfoques variables que reflejan, en los últimos años, la base en sí del mercado y de los clientes.

Cuando el proyecto de un diseñador japonés se encuentra con la fantasía china, dentro de una lógica de producción manifiestamente europea, queda claro que se está tratando con una marca reconocida que pretende dejar la huella de su diseño, a través de sus signos y de sus ideas.

Estos signos e ideas surgen del casi "angustioso" trabajo de todos los diseñadores que trabajan en Hangar, que colocan trampas y generan intrigas y cepos, reflejando la naturaleza misma del diseño.

El diseñador es un operador astuto que trata de presentar su propia realidad con su propia mano, firma y cerebro.

ro il designer che non è disponibile a lasciarsi trascinare dalla forza della propria immaginazione. Ciò vale soprattutto se si pensa a un futuro capace di raccogliere la sfida lanciata anni or sono dagli architetti dell'Hangar, che non hanno mai voluto definire o delimitare il loro campo d'azione.

La storia di Hangar Design Group (che è la storia di un modello organizzativo più che di un vero e proprio stile di progetto) cominciò negli anni ottanta nella campagna trevigiana, all'interno di due vecchi hangar per dirigibili. È la storia di un'incrollabile fiducia nel lavoro, nel pragmatismo e nel principio che le cose accadono solo se di fa in modo che possano accadere. Tutto ciò, unito alla grande capacità degli architetti veneziani Alberto Bovo e Sandro Manente (per molti versi agli antipodi) e dei loro creativi di trasformare qualsiasi cosa in un progetto di comunicazione, ha reso possibile lo sviluppo della struttura e il suo ampliamento ben oltre i confini nazionali.

Il processo creativo si nutre delle idee, dei suggerimenti e delle visioni di tutto il gruppo, generando una creatività che ben presto si impossessa di tutto l'ambiente di lavoro, si riflette nei rapporti con la committenza, si amplifica nella creazione di nuovi progetti: che si tratti di una bottiglia di vetro per l'acqua minerale o di una casa mobile, di una lampada tecnica o di una campagna pubblicitaria di moda. Un'attività senza sosta che ben riflette la vera natura del progetto contemporaneo come risposta al bisogno di un design e di uno stile di vita fatti di "tanta seduzione e un po' di funzionalità".

Crediamo fortemente che la passione sia il vero fondamento delle cose: passione per il nostro lavoro, passione per le sfide, passione per il cambiamento. E poi c'è la consapevolezza del fatto che, tramite quello che facciamo, e al di là del puro piacere di farlo, diamo un contributo sensibile alla creazione dell'universo di segni che ci circonda. Una responsabilità d'onore per chi, tanto tempo fa, prese in mano una matita e iniziò ad abbozzare un'idea sul foglio bianco, con tutto l'entusiasmo di un giovane creativo. La comunicazione, che non è mai univoca, si basa essenzialmente su quelle dozzine e dozzine – se non centinaia – di segni che quotidianamente tracciamo nella nostra pratica professionale, componendo una magnifica sinfonia visiva che accompagna le nostre vite.

Sull'orizzonte di Hangar Design Group si è librata, fin dall'inizio, la figura del dirigibile, il gigantesco congegno volante che segnò l'aurora della conquista dell'aria. Divenuto ben presto obsoleto sul piano tecnico, ha mantenuto inalterata nel tempo l'aristocratica superiorità di una macchina generosamente votata all'utopia, nella quale crescente rilievo hanno assunto gli elementi più squisitamente estetici: la levità, il silenzio, l'energia eterea, la calcolata esiguità dei materiali, il controllo di gruppo (mutuato dalla tradizione navale), la potenza, la plasticità, la sapienza formale delle robuste e leggerissime strutture.

Questi caratteri si sono riverberati, irresistibilmente e inevitabilmente, sul lavoro del gruppo. La leggerezza del segno, la potenza della comunicazione, l'apertura verso l'esterno, il senso di uno spazio inteso come finestra sull'universo, il rigore tecnico e il sereno abbandono ai venti della creatività, che connotano la presenza del gruppo nella cultura contemporanea del progetto e della comunicazione, sono tutti segnali di un'inclinazione stilistica che può legittimamente invocare l'immagine archetipica del dirigibile come propria figura araldica. Quello che il mondo chiede alla cultura del progetto è, oggi più che mai, un progetto del mondo.

Lo stile Hangar – se proprio vogliamo usare la parola "stile" – è fatto di ingredienti diversi, materiali e immateriali, luoghi, persone. Ma soprattutto equilibrio. La sperimentazione – sia nella sede di Treviso sia in quella milanese, negli uffici americani prima e cinesi poi – è incentivata e sviluppata sempre nel rispetto dell'identità del gruppo, privilegiando la funzionalità e limitando qualsiasi eccesso.

Questo libro è un'inesauribile miniera di immagini, di memorie, di idee formatesi nel crogiolo di Hangar Design

El diseñador es capaz de todo para que su idea pase y, con el fin de lograrlo, se transforma, cambia y se orienta de acuerdo con la luz que guía su diseño. Es este éxtasis imaginativo que hace que su diseño sea único. En Hangar siempre habrá espacio para el éxtasis, la fantasía y la imaginación, porque solo a través del éxtasis imaginativo se crea el futuro. Un diseñador sin éxtasis imaginativo no tiene futuro.

Este concepto es válido sobre todo si se piensa en un futuro capaz de responder a ese antiguo desafío lanzado por los arquitectos de Hangar, que siempre han resistido a los intentos de restringir su campo de acción.

La historia de Hangar Design Group empezó en los años 80, en la campiña alrededor de Treviso, y es más la historia de un modelo de organización que de un estilo de diseño.

Es una historia que comenzó dentro dos antiguos hangares para globos dirigibles y que atestigua una fe inquebrantable en el trabajo, en el pragmatismo y en el principio de que "las cosas suceden sólo si tú haces que sucedan". Esto, junto con la gran capacidad del dúo Alberto Bovo y Sandro Manente —dos arquitectos venecianos, que en muchos sentidos son los extremos opuestos, y de sus creativos, que consiguen transformar todo en un proyecto de comunicación— ha hecho posible el desarrollo de la organización, así como su expansión más allá de las fronteras nacionales.

Las sugerencias del grupo se filtran en el proceso creativo, ayudando a generar un ambiente de trabajo creativo y a impulsar nuevos proyectos y experiencias con los clientes, los diseños y producciones, que abarcan desde una botella de cristal para el agua mineral a una casa móvil, desde un lámpara en un estilo técnico a una campaña publicitaria para el sector de la moda.

Una actividad de diseño sin pausa, que expresa la naturaleza del diseño actual como una respuesta a la demanda de un diseño y estilo de vida contemporáneos, que conlleva un pequeño elemento de funcionalidad y un gran elemento de seducción. El libro es una mina inagotable de imágenes y de recuerdos, que refleja todas las ideas que nacieron en el crisol de Hangar Design Group.

Creemos que la pasión está, irremediablemente, en la base de las cosas: la pasión por nuestro trabajo, la pasión por los retos, la pasión por el cambio.

Como así también la conciencia de que, a través de lo que hacemos, nos comprometemos en la misión —más allá del placer puro— de contribuir en la construcción del paisaje de signos que nos rodea. Una responsabilidad honorable para alguien que una buen día cogió un lápiz y comenzó a dibujar con el entusiasmo ligero de un joven creativo. Porque si la comunicación nunca es unívoca, se deduce que los signos que trazamos a docenas o bien a centenares cada día en nuestra práctica profesional repercuten sobre nuestra experiencia diaria y ayudan a componer la sinfonía visual que acompaña nuestras vidas.

Desde un principio, se ha mantenido la figura del globo dirigible en el horizonte de Hangar Design Group; la enorme máquina voladora que marcó el albor de la conquista de los cielos. Aunque técnicamente obsoleta, con el tiempo ha mantenido la superioridad aristocrática de una máquina consagrada a la utopía misma, en la que las características estéticas más emblemáticas han adquirido siempre mayor importancia: la levedad, el silencio, la energía etérea, la ligereza calculada de los materiales, la tradición náutica de control de grupo, la potencia, la plasticidad, el conocimiento científico de las estructuras que son fuertes pero ligeras como una pluma.

Con el tiempo, tales características han creado reverberaciones irresistibles en el trabajo del grupo.

La ligereza del signo, el poder de la comunicación, la atención dedicada a los mensajes de todo el mundo, el sentido del espacio entendido como una ventana hacia el universo, el rigor técnico y el abandono sereno a los vientos de la creatividad distinguen a este grupo en el diseño contemporáneo y en la cultura de la comunicación. Son señales de una tendencia estilística que, legítimamente, invoca la

Group. Non si è scelta la strada della spiegazione esplicita dei progetti realizzati o della nostra mission; piuttosto abbiamo voluto ripercorrere le vie della suggestione, dell'evocazione, della filosofia del gruppo. Hangar Design Group è ormai una sorta di think tank del pensiero italiano, a cui il mondo delle università, dei creativi e delle aziende fa spesso riferimento; per questo, anziché parlare dei casi di successo abbiamo preferito raccontare lo sviluppo del nostro gruppo, la filosofia e le visioni che lo animano dall'interno.
I titoli dei capitoli sono evocativi dell'essenza della nostra cultura progettuale: anzi, ne spiegano l'anima.

I
ID
08

Un hangar è una struttura chiusa costruita per contenere aeromobili o veicoli spaziali. Nella maggior parte dei casi gli hangar sono costruiti in metallo, ma sono impiegati anche altri materiali, come legno o cemento. La parola "hangar" deriva da un dialetto della Francia del nord e significa "recinto per animali".
Gli hangar proteggono gli aeromobili dagli agenti atmosferici e dai raggi ultravioletti. Gli hangar possono essere usati anche come officine al coperto o, talvolta, come postazioni d'assemblaggio. In alcuni casi gli hangar sono costruiti per occultare gli aeromobili da satelliti e aerei spia.
[dall'Enciclopedia Britannica]
L'hangar, secondo un'accezione a noi più consona, è il luogo da dove le macchine del cielo si alzano in volo dopo una benevola permanenza. Hangar attira tutti gli individui inclini al design, che apprezzano il lavoro condotto attraverso il motore delle idee per poi farle volare. In sostanza, persone che si sentono un po' i "meccanici dell'apparenza".
Hangar è evidentemente architettura, arte, design, pubblicità, fotografia, moda, stile di vita; ma più nel profondo, oltre il fascino delle forme, Hangar è combustibile, chiavi inglesi, eliche. Hangar è bello da vedere perché dentro è pensiero tenace. Alla fine è solo un lavoro; ma davvero un buon lavoro.

11

Un progetto di graphic design comincia come una relazione, si trasforma in un processo di libera analisi e speculazione più o meno perspicace, quindi entra in una fase sostanzialmente autistica di generazione visuale, seguita da una sintesi di ipotesi e sperimentazione che si trasforma gradualmente in una produzione puramente computazionale e meccanica – realizzata con o senza il coinvolgimento di un certo numero di attività esterne – e infine si manifesta al mondo attraverso un complesso di socializzazione e acculturazione che include pubblicità, public relations, distribuzione, retailing, advertising, focus testing e critica.
Una versione di questo processo può applicarsi a qualsiasi cosa: dall'arte al basso commercio, dall'intellettuale al banale, dall'edificante all'insincero. Il processo può essere interrotto in qualsiasi punto – con modalità sia positive sia negative – da collaboratori, autori, editori, clienti, venditori, utenti, avvocati, censori e politici, che richiedono modifiche che spaziano dal leggero al catastrofico. A ciò si aggiunge che lo studio si compone di cinquanta persone testarde e ostinate, impegnate in progetti multipli e sovrapposti – totalmente fuori sincrono – che riguardano soggetti, attori, tempistiche, tecnologie, audience, budget e luoghi geografici completamente diversi fra loro.
Inoltre, i designer hanno agende private, ambizioni, ansie, compulsioni e riferimenti propri che cercano di porre in atto. Queste agende possono conformarsi al contenuto reale – e alla visione generale collettiva dello studio – oppure possono essere esterne su quel contenuto e vivere in modo parassitico. La visione personale è il valore aggiunto del designer; è una presenza indessicale che si presume così

imagen arquetípica del globo dirigible como su propio emblema heráldico. Lo que el mundo busca en la cultura del diseño es, hoy más que nunca, un diseño del mundo.
El estilo de Hangar, si deseamos usar la palabra "estilo", está compuesto por diversos ingredientes, tanto materiales como inmateriales; por lugares; por personas; pero, sobre todo, por un factor de equilibrio.
La experimentación —ya sea en la sede de Treviso o en la oficina de Milán, en las oficinas americanas antes y en las chinas después— se promueve respetando siempre la identidad del grupo, favoreciendo la funcionalidad y limitando los excesos. El enfoque adoptado no se preocupa de explicar los productos o diseños de una manera explícita, sino más bien sigue el camino más noble de la sugerencia, la evocación y la filosofía del grupo, más allá de su propia misión.
Hangar Design Group se ha convertido en una especie de centro de estudios del pensamiento italiano, un punto de referencia al que a menudo recurren las universidades, los creativos y las empresas.
Por esta razón, en lugar de recitar historias de casos exitosos, se consideró preferible discutir y revelar el desarrollo del grupo, así como la filosofía y la visión que lo animan y dinamizan desde dentro.
Los capítulos del libro tienen títulos evocadores y demuestran la esencia de la cultura de diseño del grupo. Más que eso: descubren su alma.

I
ID
08

Un hangar es una estructura cerrada para guarecer aviones o vehículos espaciales. La mayoría de los hangares son de metal, pero también se utilizan otros materiales como la madera y el hormigón. La palabra hangar proviene de un dialecto del norte de Francia, y significa "corral de ganado".
Los hangares protegen las aeronaves de la intemperie y de la luz ultravioleta. Los hangares se pueden utilizar con un taller de reparación cerrado o, en algunos casos, como un área de reunión. En algunos casos, los hangares se construyen para ocultan los aviones de los satélites o de los aviones espías. [De la Enciclopedia Británica]
Sería más apropiado para nosotros decir que un hangar es el lugar desde el cual los aviones emprenden el vuelo después de una estancia acogedora. Hangar atrae a las personas con mentalidad creativa que aprecian trabajar con el motor de las ideas para hacerlas volar.
Básicamente, personas que se sienten un poco como los mecánicos de la apariencia.
Hangar es, evidentemente, arquitectura, arte, diseño, publicidad, fotografía, moda, estilo de vida.
Pero en su profundidad es combustible, llave inglesa, perno de tornillo. Detrás de las formas atractivas.
Hangar es agradable de ver por su dureza interior.
En fin de cuentas es sólo un trabajo, pero un buen trabajo.

11

Un proyecto de diseño gráfico empieza como una relación, se transforma en un proceso de análisis amplio y de especulación más o menos intuitiva, después entra en una fase casi autista de generación visual, seguida por una síntesis de la especulación y la experimentación que se transforma en una producción puramente informática y mecánica. Esta se realiza con o sin la participación actividades externas y, finalmente, emerge al mundo a través de un complejo de socialización y aculturación que incluye publicidad, relaciones públicas, distribución, venta al por menor, propaganda, pruebas de enfoque y crítica. Algunas versiones de este proceso se aplican a todo: desde el arte más elevado al comercio más bajo, desde lo intelectual a lo banal, desde lo edificante a lo poco honrado. Y el proceso puede ser interrumpido en cualquier momento, tanto en forma positiva como negati-

resistente da poter sopravvivere in qualsiasi contesto.
L'aspetto affascinante del design è che ciascuna parte di
questo processo disordinato produce delle cose. Dallo studio promana sempre un flusso costante di materiale: una
sovrabbondanza che sfida qualsiasi semplice definizione
dell'"oggetto" (e qualsiasi semplice dichiarazione di completamento). Il design non può mai essere ridotto a un processo diretto di trasmissione, perché l'oggetto del design
reca in sé messaggi multipli: alcuni palesi, altri sublimati,
alcuni pratici, altri aptici. Peraltro anche il destinatario effettivo del comunicato è oscuro. Può trattarsi di un pubblico
immaginario, un pubblico ideale, un pari, un collega di studio, un passante. Chiunque.
Il design crea sempre un effetto fisico: viene letto e percepito. I designer creano cose – deliverables – che tuttavia non
sono sempre quelle cose discrete per cui vengono pagati.
Lo studio più semplice può produrre un'idea, un effetto
o un'emozione; e stampare, rilegare, programmare e costruire non hanno necessariamente nulla a che vedere con
questo. Le "cose" di un designer accadono ad ogni fase del
processo di design; sono sempre finite e mai finite. Ma il
progetto più grande, mai completo, è quello che viene portato avanti per molti progetti e per molti anni. È il progetto
che richiede tentativi perseveranti, diligenti, mai abbastanza soddisfacenti. Ed è il lavoro, e la vita, dello studio.
Questo volume è dunque un racconto un po' vago di una
storia un po' vaga. Sovrappone vari progetti, scale, epoche e
voci in una traiettoria tipica, che comincia con il primo contatto e si conclude con la consegna al mondo. Non fa alcun
tentativo di separare il risultato dal corso d'opera: tutto è
completo in sé. Attraverso brusche contrapposizioni cerca
di individuare un filo narrativo intuitivo in un processo quotidiano dove i clienti vanno e vengono, la popolazione dello
studio è in movimento costante e i progetti ci cadono in
grembo o scivolano via senza ragione. Questo libro non dice
di cosa si occupa il nostro lavoro, ma racconta del modo in
cui se ne occupa. Dall'effimero al concreto, ogni pagina è
costruita con un insieme variegato di progetti: alcuni finiti,
altri naufragati, alcuni di successo, altri no, con schizzi, modelli, prototipi, collage, animazioni, disegni e foto di siti – le
cose che facciamo ogni giorno. Questo volume racconta la
storia di come lavoriamo, di cosa pensiamo e di come ciò
che pensiamo diventa parte di quel che facciamo. Qui termina il tentativo di spiegarlo, il resto lo esprimono le cose
stesse. Esse sono ciò che noi siamo.

15

Con la mente al 1980. Camminare veloci per le strade di
Treviso, poi negli uffici della burocrazia di Stato per capire
come compilare i moduli di costituzione di una società. La
burocrazia non ci spaventava per nulla. Trascorrere un giorno intero sulle scartoffie ci faceva sentire veri imprenditori.
Erano anni di ribellione sociale in Italia. Chi voleva essere
un creativo doveva necessariamente andare "contro". Volevamo applicare un approccio di business al settore creativo,
dandoci delle regole. Francamente, eravamo degli eretici.
E ci piaceva.

18

La vera differenza fra la nostra generazione di creativi e
le altre è che dobbiamo confrontarci non con un flusso di
immagini o un flusso di informazioni, ma con un vero e
proprio diluvio. Le informazioni sono molto più accessibili
rispetto a cinquant'anni fa: questo non fa paura ma non ti
consente più di essere autoreferenziale.

19

Il grado di fermezza dei propri principi dipende dalla passione per il proprio lavoro. Più ne hai, di passione, e meno
compromessi creativi sei disposto ad accettare. Nel design,

va, por los colaboradores, autores, editores, clientes, proveedores, usuarios, abogados, censores, y políticos... todos
pueden exigir modificaciones que abarcan desde lo ínfimo
a lo catastrófico.
A la mezcla también hay que añadir que el estudio está compuesto por personas testarudas que participan en proyectos
múltiples y superpuestos —todos completamente descronizados— relativos a temas, personajes, plazos, tecnologías,
público, presupuestos y localizaciones geográficas absolutamente diferentes.
Por encima de todo, los diseñadores tienen sus agendas
privadas, ambiciones, ansiedades, compulsiones y referencias que tratan de poner en práctica. Esas agendas pueden
combinarse con el contenido real y con la visión global, colectiva del estudio, o pueden ser injertadas en el contenido
y vivir como parásitos. La visión personal es el valor añadido
del diseñador; es una presencia indexical que se da por hecho que es tan resistente que puede sobrevivir en cualquier
contexto, desde el básico hasta el amanerado. El aspecto
irresistible del diseño es que cada parte de este proceso desordenado produce algo. Hay un flujo constante de material
bombeándose fuera del estudio en todo momento. Esta
sobreabundancia desafía cualquier definición simple de
"objeto" (y cualquier declaración simple de terminación).
El diseño nunca puede reducirse a un proceso directo de
transmisión, porque el objeto de diseño posee mensajes
múltiples: algunos declarados, otros subliminales, algunos
literales, algunos hápticos.
Además, el receptor real del comunicado también es nebuloso. Podría ser un público imaginario, un público ideal, un
par, un compañero del estudio, un transeúnte, quienquiera.
El diseño siempre tiene que ver con la creación de un efecto
físico: es leído y sentido. Los diseñadores hacen algo —deliverables— pero estos no siempre son ese algo diferenciado
por lo que a uno se le paga. El más simple estudio puede
producir una idea, un efecto o una emoción.
Imprimir, encuadernar, programar y construir no necesariamente tienen nada que ver con ese algo. Ese "algo" de
un diseñador ocurre en cualquier etapa de un proceso de
diseño; siempre se acaba y nunca se acaba. Pero el proyecto
más grande, el que nunca se completa, es el que se realiza a
lo largo de muchos proyectos y muchos años. Es el proyecto
que demanda un intento persistente, diligente, nunca lo suficientemente satisfactorio.
Ese es el trabajo y la vida del estudio.
Así pues este libro superpone diversos proyectos, escalas,
épocas y voces en una trayectoria típica, comenzando por el
primer contacto y concluyendo con su entrega al mundo.
No intenta separar aquello acabado de lo que todavía está
en marcha. Cada cosa está completa. A través de una yuxtaposición ruda intenta encontrar una narrativa principal
intuitiva en un proceso cotidiano en el que los clientes van y
vienen, la población del estudio está en constante cambio y
los proyectos caen en nuestro regazo o se escabullen sin ton
ni son. Esto no es un libro acerca de qué es nuestro trabajo,
sino acerca de la forma en que lo tratamos. De lo efímero a
lo concreto, cada página surge de un pastiche de proyectos:
algunos acabados, algunos muertos en el agua, algunos exitosos... otros no. Incluye dibujos, modelos, prototipos, collages, animaciones, dibujos y fotografías de lugares, las cosas
que hacemos todos los días. Aquí termina el intento de explicar, el resto se deja a las cosas mismas. Son lo que somos.

15

De vuelta en 1980. Con paso rápido por las calles de Treviso, en las oficinas públicas tratando de entender cómo
se rellena un formulario para dar de alta una empresa. La
burocracia no nos asustó para nada. Pasar un día inmersos
en el papeleo hizo que nos sintiéramos como unos empresarios. Fueron años de rebelión social en Italia. Quien quería
ser creativo tenía que ser necesariamente "contracultural".
Queríamos aplicar un enfoque comercial en el campo crea-

per esempio, partiamo con un certo progetto per arrivare spesso a una soluzione semplificata, di compromesso. Il processo ci interessa più della soluzione. Le immagini, per esempio, devono essere il frutto di un'elaborazione primordiale: deve essere un'azione pre-creativa.

20

Non dedicare troppo tempo a pensare e troppo poco all'azione. Ho fatto davvero tutto il possibile per realizzare i miei sogni? Ho consentito che mi scoraggiassero quando invece sapevo di potercela fare? Non lasciare che questi dubbi diventino per te un limite o un problema: semplicemente, punta dritto nella direzione dei tuoi sogni.

21

Cammina per le strade, osserva quello che succede intorno e poi raccontalo a modo tuo. Non analizzare le cose, impara invece a respirarle.

26

Hanno saputo vedere opportunità che nessun altro è stato in grado di cogliere. Non si sono sottomessi alle regole altrui. Hanno prodotto cambiamento quando gli altri difendevano fermi le proprie posizioni. Erano guidati dalla passione, dalla vitalità di chi sa trovare sempre nuove fonti di ispirazione. E avevano il cuore, per sapersi reinventare ogni volta, ancora e ancora.
Crediamo che i lavori migliori non nascano da una semplice ricerca ma siano piuttosto il prodotto di un'intera sfera d'azione in cui viene mantenuto un punto di vista personale, originale e autentico. Tutte le aziende, le agenzie e le persone che ammiriamo sono state ispirate da questo tipo di visione personale.

29

Lavoriamo nel posto più bello del mondo.
Gli spazi di HDG sono nati dal desiderio di rappresentare una specie di diario di un viaggio nel tempo e nelle architetture del mondo, senza la precisa volontà di arrivare a una dimensione formale unica ma semplicemente scegliendo gli accordi, suonando le note del mix.
Il sito restituisce due edifici gemelli, costruiti come officine per la manutenzione e la riparazione dei dirigibili durante la Grande Guerra, che una prima ristrutturazione degli anni novanta aveva risolto con principi progettuali analoghi ma strutture e materiali differenti.
I due edifici, assolutamente identici all'esterno, sperimentano il sistema trilitico: il primo in acciaio e cemento, il secondo in cemento armato e laterocemento.
Il verde è parte integrante di questo processo progettuale. Ritaglia precisamente lo spazio, mantiene la stradina di sassi, giustappone un filtro, con aceri e salici, verso la campagna coltivata, delimita e protegge dall'ambiente circostante.

31

L'unica via da percorrere è quella dell'unicità, del mistero, della magia, della perfezione, dell'infinito. La bellezza. In questo contesto difficile, in una fase di profonda crisi storica, carichi di fardelli e preoccupazioni, desideriamo affermare con forza che la bellezza è la chiave di tutto, è tutto ciò che abbiamo. Facciamo in modo che la bellezza della forma, dell'immagine, del colore e della coerenza possa contrastare la crisi materiale con cui tutti, oggi, dobbiamo confrontarci. La nostra unica speranza è l'unicità, il mistero, la magia, la perfezione, l'infinito.
La bellezza, adesso. La bellezza, l'unica via da percorrere.

tivo, imponiéndonos reglas. Francamente, éramos unos herejes. Y nos gustaba.

18

La verdadera diferencia entre nuestra generación de creativos y las otras no es el flujo de imágenes al que nos enfrentamos o el flujo de información, sino un verdadero diluvio. El flujo de información hoy día es mucho más abierto que hace cincuenta años atrás. Esto no intimida, pero ya no permite reafirmarse como autorreferencial.

19

El grado de estabilidad de los propios principios depende del nivel de pasión por el propio trabajo. Cuanto mayor es la pasión, menores son las concesiones creativas que haces. En el diseño, por ejemplo, se empieza con un proyecto y a menudo se llega a una solución simplificada, una concesión. Estamos más interesados en los procesos que en las soluciones. Por ejemplo, la imagen debe ser el resultado de un proceso primordial de elaboración creativa; debe ser una acción pre-creativa.

20

No dediques demasiado tiempo a las elucubraciones y poco a la acción. ¿Hice todo lo posible por hacer mis sueños realidad? ¿Dejé a propósito que los demás me desanimaran cuando yo sabía que podía? No dejes que estas dudas te frenen o preocupen, sencillamente apunta en la dirección de tus sueños.

21

Camina por la calle, observa lo que está pasando, y exponlo a tu manera. No analices las cosas, aprende a respirarlas.

26

Vieron oportunidades donde otros no lo hicieron.
No se sometieron a las reglas de los demás. Inspiraron el cambio cuando los demás estaban defendiendo sus posiciones. Los impulsó la pasión, de la vitalidad de quien sabe hallar siempre nuevas fuentes de inspiración. Y tenían su corazón para reinventarse continuamente, una y otra vez, una y otra vez. Creemos que los mejores trabajos no son el resultado de una persecución, sino más bien el producto de una esfera de acción en la que se mantiene un punto de vista personal y auténtico. Todas las empresas, agencias o personas que admiramos fueron impulsados por este tipo de visión personal.

29

Trabajamos en el lugar más hermoso del mundo. Los espacios de Hangar Design Group surgieron del deseo de representar una especie de cuaderno de bitácora a través del tiempo y de las arquitecturas del mundo, sin un deseo particular de lograr una única dimensión formal y representativa, sino simplemente seleccionando los acordes, tocando las notas de la composición. El sitio unió dos edificios gemelos construidos como talleres de mantenimiento y reparación de zepelines durante la Primera Guerra mundial que, a principios de la década del 90, fueron sometidos a una reestructuración inicial, aplicando líneas de diseño similares, pero utilizando diferentes estructuras y materiales.
Los dos edificios, que son absolutamente idénticos exteriormente, representan un experimento con el sistema Trilithic: en un edificio en acero y cemento y en el otro en hormigón armado y mampostería y cemento.
La vegetación es una parte integral de este proceso de diseño. Define el espacio de una manera precisa, mantiene el

II
TEMPO. DOBBIAMO PARLARE.
34

"Nei nostri pensieri, Hangar Design Group apparteneva sicuramente a noi, che ne eravamo i fondatori, ma anche a chi ci lavorava e a tutti quelli con cui avevamo avuto contatti. Come nel blues, che dai suoi incroci e tragitti alternativi genera sempre nuova musica, così da noi tutti possono e devono fornire idee, risorse e strumenti. Tutti devono portare la propria esperienza."

39

La somma di uno più uno, a volte, è più di due. Il lavoro di squadra non solo produce risultati migliori e soluzioni più brillanti, ma soprattutto riesce a rendere possibile anche ciò che all'apparenza sembra impossibile. Ecco il tema di questo capitolo: cosa succede quando collaboriamo.

40

Questa è… una storia di creatività. Entrare nel vialetto lungo e dritto, rimasto ancora a ghiaino come nelle vecchie residenze signorili di campagna, aiuta a evadere, a staccare la spina e a prepararsi a un tuffo nel magma della creatività. Due edifici gemelli giocano a inseguirsi nel bel mezzo di un prato all'inglese, regolarmente tagliato e curato da una persona gentile e mite che tutti chiamano simpaticamente signor Danilo. A lui si deve la scoperta, avvenuta per caso, oltre vent'anni fa, del motivo che accompagna Hangar Design Group fin dalla sua nascita: "far volare le idee" è lo slogan intercettato nella montagna di corrispondenza scritta che ogni giorno il mondo fagocita, e che qui, lungo il maestoso viale alberato voluto da Napoleone, fra le mani di un attento giardiniere, si è posato. Piace pensare, a chi ha fatto esperienza di questo terminal inconsueto, tenuto a prato verde, che in uno degli hangar "si pensa" e nell'altro "si fa".
In entrambi una lamiera sottile, sagomata, a ricordo della bora di tramontana, anticipa di qualche anno la fortuna dell'architettura neo-organica, protegge gli ingressi a nord e disegna un colpo d'ala nel tessuto minuto del mattone faccia vista. Più che memoria viva, la storia dei due edifici diventa confine tra racconto e sensazione visiva, tra immaginario collettivo e realtà vissuta. Una sorta di dissolvenza, costantemente alimentata, innerva di energia vitale l'operosa comunità creativa giunta ormai al porto del terzo millennio: sono le emozioni che hanno incessantemente percorso tutto il Novecento, secolo straordinario di rivoluzioni in tutti i campi, dalle arti alle scienze. Il dirigibile fu una di quelle invenzioni straordinarie, che ancora aleggia in questi luoghi.
L'idea di questo aeroporto invisibile si fa lentamente strada nella mente, tra ricerche d'archivio, racconti spontanei e fotografie d'epoca. È l'inizio di tutto. Anche Louis Kahn adorava gli inizi. L'inizio della Sacra Bibbia è uno fra i più straordinari che siano mai stati scritti; Louis lo leggeva e rileggeva di continuo poiché credeva fermamente che la genesi di qualsiasi cosa contenesse interamente tutto il suo sviluppo successivo. Kahn non terminava mai le sue opere, dal momento che le considerava "vive", passibili di mutazioni, autentiche entità dotate di anima. E spesso tornava all'idea prima che le aveva mosse.
Ogni nostro giorno è un nuovo inizio. È bello pensare di avere ancora un altro intero giorno per sollevare il mondo dalle sue brutture con un colpo di matita. "Far volare le idee" è lo stato d'animo dell'inventore d'aeroplani, muove la capacità creatrice, l'intelligenza e il coraggio, l'immaginazione e la ragione cristallina.
Poi viene l'emozione vera, il volo fra le arti, le culture, gli stili, le mode.
In questo modo la tensione di quello che vediamo dà senso a quello che facciamo. Pensare e progettare, ripensare e riprogettare continuamente, con fatica ed entusiasmo,

sendero pedregoso, yuxtapone un filtro, con arces y sauces, hacia el campo cultivado, delimita y protege del medio ambiente circundante.

31

La única senda que hay que recorrer es la que atraviesa lo único, el misterio, la magia, la perfección, el infinito. La belleza. En este contexto problemático y de crisis histórica, cargada de grandes preocupaciones queremos erigir la defensa de la belleza como lo único. La belleza es cuanto tenemos. Dejemos que el tema de la forma de la belleza, la imagen, el color, la coherencia se enfrenten a la crisis material a la que todos nosotros debemos hoy enfrentarnos. Nuestra única esperanza es lo único, el misterio, la magia, la perfección, el infinito. La belleza, ahora. La belleza, la única senda que hay que recorrer.

II
TIEMPO. TENEMOS QUE HABLAR.
34

Sin dudar; actuar de acuerdo con normas propias, pero con el placer de compartirlas. "En nuestra cabeza, estaba claro que Hangar Design Group nos pertenecía a nosotros, a sus fundadores, pero también a quien trabajaba aquí y a todos los que estaban en contacto con ella. Así como el blues generó la nueva música a través de sus influencias entrecruzadas y trayectorias alternativas, lo mismo pasó aquí: todo el mundo puede y debe aportar ideas, recursos, medios. Cada persona debe aportar su propia experiencia".

39

Uno más uno a veces puede ser más que dos. El esfuerzo combinado de un equipo no sólo puede lograr cosas más grandes, mejores, más inteligentes, sino que también puede hacer posible lo aparentemente imposible. Este es el tema de este capítulo: las cosas que suceden cuando colaboramos.

40

Esta es… una historia creativa. Caminando por el sendero largo y recto, todavía cubierto con grava como aquellos que conducen a elegantes casas de campo antiguas, le ayuda a uno a alejarse, desconectar y prepararse para sumergirse en el magma de la creatividad. Dos edificios gemelos juegan y se persiguen en el medio del césped, que está cortado y cuidado con esmero por una persona amable y dulce a quien todos llaman cariñosamente don Danilo. Él es responsable del descubrimiento accidental, hace más de veinte años, del tema que ha acompañado a Hangar Design Group desde su nacimiento. "Dejar que las ideas levanten el vuelo" es interceptado en la montaña de la correspondencia escrita, que el mundo absorbe cada día y se posa aquí en las manos de un jardinero atento, junto al majestuoso sendero bordeado de árboles deseado por Napoleón. A las personas que viven en esta inusual terminal, que se conserva con su verde césped, les gusta imaginar que en uno de los hangares "se piensa" y en el otro "se hace".
Anticipando un par de años el éxito de la arquitectura neo-orgánica, una fina chapa metálica modelada, un recuerdo del viento de tramontana, protege los accesos orientados al norte y describe el movimiento de un ala en el material minuto del ladrillo a vista. Más que una memoria viva, la historia de los dos edificios se convierte en una frontera entre una historia y una sensación visible, entre la imaginación colectiva y las experiencias de la vida real. Una desaparición gradual contribuye a alimentar continuamente con energía vital a la activa comunidad creativa, que ya ha alcanzado el tercer milenio. Se trata de las emociones cotidianas constantes desde los albores del siglo XX, ese siglo extraordinario lleno de acontecimientos revolucionarios en todos los ám-

sarebbe impossibile se non fossimo ispirati da un'utopia magnifica come il volo: una dilatazione mentale, intellettuale, sempre viva, sempre disponibile. Volare è un privilegio, per chi non soffre di vertigini. Ci sono tanti tipi di volo e ognuno è una filosofia. Volare per vocazione è il mestiere che abbiamo scelto.

Gli hangar che ci ospitano sono una complessa grammatica di forme e segni raccolti negli anni in numerosi viaggi. Taccuini costruiti da itinerari nel tempo e nelle architetture del mondo, senza alcuna volontà di arrivare a una dimensione scenica definita. Semplicemente scegliendo gli accordi, le sfumature, suonando le note diverse di un puzzle che insegue da sempre un'idea dell'operare. Riflettiamo continuamente visitando in volo spazi e luoghi in tutti i paesi del mondo. Il volo è in sé un fatto straordinario: e volare, farne esperienza, ancora di più. Una volta imparata la tecnica, difficilmente si può dimenticare. Quel che conta è saper atterrare per poter ripartire. Dateci un orizzonte da raggiungere e disegneremo per voi strane macchine volanti che vi porteranno fino a lì.

42

Hangar Design Group è più pop che rock. Quello che conta in un gruppo pop non sono le singole individualità ma il nome del gruppo. Alla fine il risultato del loro lavoro è frutto di un impegno comune e non del prevalere di una inclinazione rispetto alle altre.

46

Per noi lavorare insieme è l'apice della soddisfazione professionale. Quando lavori con qualcun altro l'ansia di concludere è maggiore; quando lavori da solo questa pressione non c'è, porti la cosa fino a un certo punto e poi passi ad altro. Ma quando si lavora insieme si fa di tutto per dare il massimo; sia perché nessuno vuole fare brutta figura, sia perché tutti sanno che si tratta di un'impresa di gruppo. Tutto è molto più vivo, più effervescente; è bello scontrarsi, discutere. Molte persone parlano di "confronto": ma in realtà è una dura dialettica, una sfida.

49

Abbiamo smesso di scrivere molto tempo fa; ma amiamo le parole, e soprattutto i titoli. Servono poche parole per creare immagini significative. Abbiamo avuto successo con il design e la forza delle nostre visioni. Ciò che al nostro lavoro ha dato moltissima visibilità è stato spesso il titolo. Abbiamo sempre rivolto un'attenzione speciale ai titoli. C'è chi crede che dentro i titoli ci siano le idee; invece molte volte è proprio l'opposto.

51

Disegnare le idee è l'imperativo di ogni studio di progettazione grafica, che Hangar Design Group ha fatto proprio anche nei modelli di comunicazione che lo rappresentano. Studiare l'immagine di un prodotto significa non tanto affidarsi a una specularità rivelatrice, quanto mettere in luce le ombre e scoprire il lato oscuro delle evidenze. In ciò gli elaborati messi in opera – gli house organs, l'immagine coordinata, la documentazione promozionale – dispiegano una tecnica di rappresentazione che sfiora il nebuloso territorio dell'analisi. L'aspetto simbolico del sogno, che Freud giudicò essenziale, affiora qui appena celato dietro la cortina di segnali e allusioni che le tecniche della comunicazione hanno elaborato. A emergere è quindi soprattutto il non detto e il non disegnato, che forma il substrato più significativo del messaggio. Si potrebbe anche leggere la grafica moderna – e non solo quella – a partire dai suoi silenzi visivi, che sono spesso più

bitos, desde las artes a la ciencia. El globo dirigible fue uno de esos inventos sorprendentes y todavía hoy día se sostiene en el aire.

La idea de este aeropuerto invisible poco a poco fue tomando forma en nuestras mentes a través de la investigación en los archivos, historias y fotografías de la época. Es el comienzo de todo. Incluso Louis Kahn amaba los inicios. El comienzo de la Sagrada Biblia es uno de los más extraordinarios jamás escritos. Louis lo leía una y otra vez porque creía firmemente que la génesis de algo contiene en su interior su desarrollo futuro completo. Louis tenía la costumbre de no terminar sus obras, ya que las consideraba "vivas", sujetas a cambios, entidades reales con un alma y, a menudo, le gustaba retornar a la idea antes siquiera de haberla llevado a cabo. Cada día para nosotros es un comienzo. Es maravilloso pensar en tener otro día completo para rescatar al mundo de su fealdad con el trazo de un lápiz. "Dejar que las ideas levanten el vuelo" es lo que inspiró al inventor de aviones; mueve la inventiva, la inteligencia y el coraje; la imaginación y la razón fría . Luego, llega la verdadera emoción, el vuelo entre las artes, culturas, estilos y modas. De este modo la tensión de lo que vemos da sentido a lo que hacemos. Pensar y diseñar, repensar y replantear, siempre con dificultad y entusiasmo, es imposible sin la inspiración de una utopía maravillosa como volar; una expansión mental e intelectual, siempre viva, siempre disponible. Volar es un privilegio, sólo para aquellos que no tienen miedo a las alturas. Hay muchos tipos de vuelo, cada uno es una filosofía. Volar por vocación es la profesión que hemos elegido.

Los hangares que nos albergan son construcciones complejas de formas y símbolos recogidos en numerosos viajes durante los últimos años. Cuadernos compuestos por itinerarios a través del tiempo y la arquitectura del mundo, sin ningún deseo de llegar a un destino escénico definido. Con sólo elegir los acordes, los tonos, tocando las diferentes notas de un enigma que siempre ha estado siguiendo una idea de trabajo. Nos reflejamos constantemente mientras volamos y visitamos espacios y lugares en todos los países del mundo. Volar es un concepto extraordinario y más aún lo es hacerlo. Una vez que se aprende cómo hacerlo, es difícil olvidarlo. Siempre hay que aterrizar con el fin de ser capaz de despegar de nuevo. Dadnos un horizonte para alcanzar y nosotros diseñaremos máquinas voladoras extrañas que os lleven allí.

42

Hangar Design Group es más pop que rock. En un grupo pop lo que cuenta no son los individuos aislados, sino el nombre del grupo. Al final, el resultado obtenido es un esfuerzo de grupo y no se basa sobre la inclinación de uno que predomina sobre los demás.

46

Trabajar juntos nos proporciona una gran satisfacción profesional. Cuando se trabaja con otra persona hay más ansiedad por concluir lo que se hace. Cuando se trabaja solo esta presión está ausente. Si llega a un cierto punto y después se prosigue con algo distinto. Pero cuando se trabaja con otras personas, ya sea porque nadie quiere quedar mal ante los demás, o porque todo el mundo sabe que es una empresa de colaboración, se hace todo lo posible para ser vigoroso. Todo es mucho más vivo, más efervescente.

Es muy productivo participar y discutir entre todos. La mayoría de la gente usa la palabra "confrontación", pero en realidad se trata de una dialéctica dura.

49

Hemos dejado de escribir textos hace mucho tiempo, pero nos encantan las palabras y, sobre todo, los títulos. Unas pocas palabras raras son suficientes para crear imágenes significativas. Hemos logrado el éxito con el diseño y con el

eloquenti d'ogni discorso perfettamente strutturato. È sufficiente riflettere sulle relazioni spaziali tra due immagini per comprenderne l'importanza.
Nelle pubblicazioni di Hangar Design Group, questo gioco tra il palese e il nascosto s'inquadra in una griglia visiva che non è leggibile direttamente sulla pagina bensì in controluce: la disposizione perfettamente ortogonale delle immagini e delle scritte, la modularità sempre rigorosamente ritmata intorno all'archetipo del quadrato, la tendenza a fare del vuoto, dell'assenza, del silenzio lo spazio più eloquente della comunicazione ne sono gli elementi strutturali più densi d'energia espressiva.

55

Prima di iniziare la fase di progettazione, ci immergiamo sempre fino in fondo nei nuovi soggetti e nei concetti da assimilare. Per fare questo leggiamo assiduamente e parliamo a lungo con i clienti, di ogni argomento immaginabile: dalla complessità tecnica di un candelabro alle tendenze di mercato, dal packaging del cibo al mercato immobiliare di lusso, ai lettori di riferimento.

III
CAMEOS
60

Apprezziamo l'interazione personale che si instaura ogni volta fra noi e gli artisti. Abbiamo avuto la fortuna di lavorare con molte professionalità diverse: fotografi, pittori, scultori e alcuni tra i più grandi architetti e graphic designer. Una fonte di particolare soddisfazione è il percorso formativo che s'intraprende con ogni progetto di design. Ma ciò per cui siamo maggiormente riconoscenti è di aver potuto incontrare persone piacevoli e soggetti interessanti.

63

Non esiste un uomo dal bianco mantello che si chiude nel suo ufficio privato per lavorare a un progetto di design, e che riemerge dopo tre mesi dicendo "Voilà! Questa è la mia ispirazione divina".
Il design, ai giorni nostri, non funziona così. Siamo convinti che le scuole ci offrano straordinari giovani designer con il giusto atteggiamento; ma, come dicevamo, è un settore complicato, oggi.
L'esperienza è più importante che mai. L'esperienza è più importante che mai se combinata con le idee "fresche" dei giovani designer. Ma acquistare esperienza significa anche acquistare relazioni con i clienti, clienti che si muovono e cambiano, vanno da un'organizzazione all'altra. Il mondo intero gira intorno alle relazioni, come sappiamo, e con un cliente soddisfatto ci saranno sempre opportunità di collaborazione in futuro, anche se in maniera non continuativa. Nei periodi favorevoli spingiamo freneticamente l'acceleratore verso nuovi clienti, ma quando i tempi si fanno duri sono proprio i nostri vecchi clienti – quelli con i quali abbiamo saputo costruire delle relazioni – che ci offrono sempre opportunità di lavoro.

65

Qualcuno ha scritto che ciò che il mondo chiede alla cultura del progetto, oggi più che mai, è un progetto del mondo. È una frase che ci piace citare quando un giovane collaboratore ci chiede come procedere nella ricerca formale; perché prima del segno, e prima ancora dell'atto creativo, viene l'ascolto e l'interrogazione paziente, da cui scaturisce la capacità di aderire e rispondere a istanze diverse e lontane, di mettere in relazione spazi, oggetti, comportamenti, dando vita a un corpo omogeneo di linguaggi, figure e modelli condivisi. La nostra esperienza si è sempre fondata sulla capacità di creare nuove relazioni non solo tra le idee, ma

delirio. Todos pensaban que este era nuestro estado de ánimo. Lo que le dio mucha resonancia fue el título. Siempre hemos prestado especial atención a los títulos. Hay quienes creen que las ideas se esconden dentro de los títulos, pero a menudo es lo contrario.

51

El diseño de las ideas es un imperativo para todas las empresas de diseño gráfico, algo que Hangar Design Group ha incorporado incluso en sus modelos de comunicación propios. El estudio de la imagen de un producto no significa tanto reflejar lo que se ofrece, sino arrojar luz sobre ciertas sombras y revelar el lado oscuro de lo que se está mostrando. Las distintas características en juego —los house organs, la imagen coordinada, la documentación promocional— se basan en un método de representación que raya con el mundo neblinoso del análisis. El lado simbólico de los sueños, que Freud consideraba tan importante, surge aquí apenas oculto tras una cortina de señales y alusiones que han desarrollado las técnicas de comunicación.
Lo que surge aquí, por encima de todo, es lo que no se dice y no se designa, lo que en realidad forma el fundamento más importante del mensaje. La gráfica moderna, y no sólo esta, podría incluso interpretarse en función de sus silencios visuales, a menudo más elocuentes que el discurso cuidadosamente estructurado. Basta con contemplar las relaciones espaciales entre dos imágenes para ver lo importantes que son.
En las publicaciones de Hangar Design Group, esta interacción entre lo visible y lo oculto se inscribe en una red que no se puede leer directamente de la página, sino únicamente a contraluz. El diseño perfectamente ortogonal de la palabra y la imagen, la modularidad cuidadosamente basada en el arquetipo del cuadrado y la tendencia a convertir el vacío, la ausencia y el silencio en los espacios de comunicación más elocuentes son, sin duda, las características estructurales más expresivas de todas.

55

Constantemente tenemos que profundizar en los nuevos temas que debemos comprender antes de comenzar la fase de diseño. Por lo que siempre estamos leyendo y hablando con los clientes acerca de casi cualquier cosa que uno se pueda imaginar: la complejidad técnica de un candelabro, las tendencias del mercado minorista, el envasado de alimentos, el mercado inmobiliario de lujo.

III
CAMEOS
60

Disfrutamos de la interacción personal que tiene lugar entre nosotros y los artistas. En particular, hemos tenido la suerte de trabajar con una enorme diversidad de figuras: fotógrafos, pintores, escultores, algunos de los mejores arquitectos y diseñadores gráficos. Lo que es especialmente gratificante es el proceso de aprendizaje que implica cada proyecto de diseño. Pero sobre todo estamos agradecidos porque hemos conocido gente agradable y temas interesantes.

63

El hombre de la capa blanca no hace el trabajo de diseño en su oficina privada de la que sale pasados tres meses diciendo "¡Voilà! Esta es mi inspiración divina". Así no es cómo se hace el diseño en estos días. Estamos convencidos de que las escuelas forman a magníficos jóvenes diseñadores con la actitud adecuada, pero, como ya hemos dicho, este es un sector complicado.
La experiencia es más importante que nunca. La experiencia es más importante que nunca en combinación con las

anche tra i luoghi di produzione delle stesse, tra le persone e tra i ruoli. Un esercizio continuo di scambio e di apprendimento, un'osmosi necessaria attraverso la quale i processi creativi, le tecniche e i modelli di trasmissione si diffondono gradualmente e incessantemente.

Crediamo sia stata la fedeltà a questa interpretazione mobile dello spazio, inteso come rete lungo la quale orientare la ricerca e l'esperienza progettuale, a comporre il fil rouge del nostro cammino professionale. Un sistema di pensiero e una pratica consolidata che, se da un lato ha disciplinato l'atto creativo, ne ha alimentato allo stesso tempo la forza propositiva, senza rinunciare all'inaspettato che in qualche modo sempre lo accompagna.

68

Il visual design non cede qui alle lusinghe dell'arte, ma si propone come "arte" esso stesso, almeno nella misura in cui si avvale delle molteplici esperienze dell'estetica contemporanea per modellarle in vista di una comunicazione funzionale – ma non per questo meno capace di operare in profondità. Il meccanismo di suggestione che in tal modo si attiva non costituisce una distrazione rispetto al ruolo informativo dell'artefatto, che resta comunque primario, ma si limita a creare intorno al messaggio principale un vago universo di richiami, metafore e allusioni destinato a rafforzarne l'impatto conoscitivo. L'elemento più interessante di questo processo non è legato alla funzionalità, ma fa leva su una qualità estetica per creare una funzione liberamente estetica.

70

La ricerca diventa parte di te. All'inizio è circoscritta, innocente; ma più la approfondisci più diventa complicata ed esatta. Questo comporta che, con tutto il potenziale di un'esperienza completa, il peso di un'agenzia diventa maggiore, poiché parte dell'innocenza iniziale è sparita (nel senso che non hai idea di tutte le cose che gli altri già conoscono). Ecco perché viene fuori un prodotto che è tutto tranne che perfetto, per te, in quel momento. Se hai più di un semplice background, la pressione aumenta ulteriormente: maggiore la tua complessità, maggiore la minaccia dello schermo bianco, perché non hai più un approccio così innocente.

74

Quando abbiamo organizzato la mostra alla Biennale di Venezia tutti pensavano avessimo voluto rendere omaggio alle opere dell'artista. Ma noi non volevamo muoverci in mezzo agli oggetti, piuttosto al loro interno, facendo della mostra un nuovo tipo di esperienza spaziale.

Questo ci ha insegnato che il requisito principale per la progettazione di allestimenti è avere le menti aperte. Nulla può essere prefigurato. Chi dice che un allestimento è come un'architettura sta esagerando per darsi un tono. L'allestimento è davvero effimero. Ed è bello per questo.

80

Nella mitologia dell'architettura moderna il taccuino degli schizzi costituisce una presenza costante, attraverso la quale si ritiene possibile fissare la fisionomia culturale dell'architetto, il suo stile, la sua filosofia progettuale, addirittura la sua Weltanschauung. Il feticismo museale ha accolto nelle sue teche le pagine sbiadite d'innumerevoli taccuini e block-notes, percorse da tremuli tratti nei quali si condensa una memoria ammirativa – un paesaggio, un dettaglio strutturale, una facciata antica – oppure la prima vaga configurazione di ciò che sarebbe forse divenuto opera, manufatto, corpo esteso e reale.

Sebbene insidiato da strumentazioni tecnologiche sempre più sofisticate, lo strumento princeps del progettare resta

ideas frescas que los diseñadores jóvenes traen consigo.

Cuando se compra la experiencia, se compran las relaciones con los clientes. Los clientes se mueven continuamente de una organización a otra. Las relaciones hacen girar el mundo y, como ya sabemos, con un cliente satisfecho, habrá muchos trabajos en el futuro, incluso si la colaboración no es continua. En las épocas de auge, estamos siempre ajetreados con nuevos negocios, pero cuando los tiempos se ponen difíciles, son nuestros clientes antiguos, aquellos con los que hemos construido las relaciones, los que siempre vuelven a hacer negocios con nosotros.

65

Alguien escribió que lo que el mundo quiere de la cultura del diseño, hoy más que nunca, es un diseño del mundo. Nos gusta citar esta frase cuando un joven colaborador nos pide la forma de proceder en la investigación formal, porque antes del signo e incluso antes del acto creativo viene la actitud de escuchar y el interrogatorio paciente, que a su vez genera la posibilidad de acceder y responder a demandas diversas y geográficamente distantes para poner espacios, objetos, comportamientos en relación unos con otros, dando lugar a un cuerpo homogéneo de idiomas compartidos, figuras y modelos. Nuestra experiencia se ha basado siempre en la capacidad de crear nuevas relaciones no sólo entre las ideas, sino también entre los lugares donde se producen, entre las personas y los roles. Un proceso continuo de intercambio y aprendizaje, una ósmosis necesaria que a través de procesos creativos, técnicas y modelos de transmisión se difunde gradual e incesantemente.

Creemos que la fidelidad a esta interpretación cambiante del espacio, entendido como una red que permite orientar la investigación y la experiencia en el diseño, representa el hilo rojo de nuestra trayectoria profesional.

Un sistema de pensamiento y una práctica consolidada que, mientras por un lado, ha disciplinado el acto creativo, ha alimentado al mismo tiempo su poder constructivo inherente sin renunciar a lo inesperado que inevitablemente, de una manera u otra, lo acompaña.

68

El diseño visual se niega a ceder a los halagos del arte, sinoque se erige como "arte" en sí mismo, al menos en la medida en que se basa en las múltiples experiencias de la estética moderna conformándolas a los efectos de la comunicación funcional, que no es menos capaz de operar en un nivel profundo. El mecanismo de la sugestión, que se activa de esta forma, no desvía la atención de ninguna manera de la función informativa del artefacto, que sigue siendo la más importante. En realidad, se limita a la creación de un vago campo de referencias, metáforas y alusiones alrededor del mensaje principal para reforzar su impacto cognitivo.

Lo interesante de todo esto no es nada directamente funcional, en realidad se basa en una cualidad estética creando una función estética libremente.

70

La búsqueda pasa a formar parte de ti mismo. Al principio, la búsqueda es bastante pequeña, inocente. Cuanto más se profundiza, más difícil y precisa se hace la búsqueda. Eso significa que, con todo el potencial de una experiencia completa, el peso de una agencia llega a ser aún mayor, porque algo de esa inocencia se ha perdido, en el sentido de que no se tiene ni idea de todas esas demás cosas que los otros ya saben. Por esto es por lo que acaba saliendo un producto que a ti, en ese momento, te parece cualquier cosa menos perfecto. Si se tiene más de una experiencia, la presión aumenta. Se posee la complejidad, pero la amenaza de la pantalla en blanco es mayor, porque ya no se puede abordar tan inocentemente.

ancora lo schizzo, l'appunto frettoloso, la notazione sintetica di un'idea ancora troppo nebulosa per tradursi in lineamenti riconoscibili.

82

Bello su misura. È stato l'amore per l'arte e per il bello a spingerci sul sentiero della comunicazione. Una sensibilità che abbiamo cercato di tradurre in metodologia progettuale, a partire dalle esigenze della committenza, per arrivare a un risultato oltre le aspettative. Un lavoro di cesello, un'attenzione al dettaglio per costruire ogni volta un progetto su misura, come fosse un abito tailor-made confezionato per il committente seguendo tagli, fattezze e scopi diversi, ma che sempre deve cominciare con l'ascolto, l'attenzione e la relazione. Che sia una campagna di advertising o un evento, la metodologia che abbiamo costruito in questi anni prevede invariabilmente la possibilità di spostamento, di adattamento, di customizzazione del progetto in base alle esigenze del cliente e al migliore risultato, facendo ricorso nel più efficiente e creativo dei modi alle risorse a disposizione. Crediamo che sia parte del nostro DNA una speciale duttilità, capace di nutrirsi di spunti e idee variegate ma di ritrovare sempre all'interno di ogni singolo progetto quella propria coerenza fattuale e quel rigore estetico che con gli anni sono diventati la cifra di Hangar Design Group.

84

Siamo sempre stati interessati al rapporto con lo spettatore e alle questioni museologiche, come i testi dei curatori, le cornici, le basi delle sculture, i muri delle gallerie, perfino la sfumatura di bianco della pittura utilizzata sul muro. L'interfaccia tra l'osservatore e l'osservato rappresenta un incantevole momento di architettura.

86

Il design, ormai da tempo, contribuisce alla celebrazione dell'autorialità: una pratica presa in prestito in egual misura dalle belle arti e dalla moda. Percorrere con successo la linea sottilissima che separa l'arte dal design, o camminare in equilibrio, come funamboli, sopra il precipizio rappresentato dalla loro intersezione: questo è il Sacro Graal delle discipline creative.

IV
UNA BOCCATA D'ARIA FRESCA
91

Perché registrare ciò che è ovvio? Perché sono tutti i piccoli momenti della vita, che vedi ogni giorno e dimentichi di catturare, e non capisci quanto sono speciali fino a quando non li hai afferrati e fissati. Una boccata d'aria fresca.

94

Nel suo procedere dal centro alla periferia, dal microcosmo al macrocosmo, Hangar Design Group si muove in una circolarità che non è quella monotona e uniforme del cerchio bensì quella dinamica e pulsante della spirale, che presuppone un centro originatore al quale le proprie vibrazioni la riconducono di continuo, salvo a sfuggirne subito l'attrazione. In questo ritmico dilatarsi e restringersi, in cui le energie progettuali sono chiamate alternativamente a condensarsi e a sprigionarsi con tutta la loro forza, risiede la qualità culturale del lavoro di questo studio. Il contemporaneo mondo del progetto, del resto, esige proprio questo, ed è stato merito di Hangar Design Group accorgersene quando ancora tutti lo ignoravano. Affrontare la realtà globalizzata con strutture già collaudate da una lunga prassi è un vantaggio che va messo a frutto.

74

Cuando organizamos la exposición en la Bienal de Venecia, todo el mundo pensaba que rendíamos homenaje a las producciones del artista. Sin embargo, deseábamos mezclarnos entre los propios objetos, pero dentro de ellos. De esta manera, la exposición se convirtió en un nuevo tipo de experiencia espacial. Esto nos enseña que lo más importante sobre el montaje de exposiciones es que hay que tener una mente abierta. Nada puede ser prefigurado. Decir que una exposición es como una arquitectura puede ser a una exageración para impresionar La exposición es algo efímero. Y esta es su virtud principal.

80

Un bloc de bocetos es una presencia constante en la mitología de la arquitectura moderna, supuestamente capaz de trazar un identikit cultural de un arquitecto, su estilo, su filosofía de diseño e incluso concepción su del mundo. El fetichismo museístico alberga entre sus vitrinas las desvanecidas páginas de un montón de blocs de dibujo y cuadernos llenos de temblorosos contornos de algunos garabatos admirables —un paisaje, los detalles estructurales o una fachada antigua— o el primer esbozo aproximado de lo que luego se convertiría en un trabajo real, la construcción, un cuerpo real en el espacio.
Aunque ahora esté amenazado por medios tecnológicos cada vez más sofisticados, la principal herramienta de diseño arquitectónico es todavía un boceto, una nota rápida o una idea apuntada, aún demasiado vaga para ser traducida en líneas reconocibles.

82

La belleza a medida. Aquello que nos ha llevado por el camino de la comunicación ha sido la devoción al arte y a la belleza. Una sensibilidad que hemos tratado de traducir en una metodología de diseño basada en las necesidades de nuestros clientes, con el fin de lograr un resultado que supera las expectativas. Un trabajo minucioso, la atención a los detalles con miras a la construcción, cada vez, un proyecto a medida como si fuera un traje preparado para el cliente de acuerdo con el corte, las características y finalidad, pero que siempre comienza escuchando, prestando atención y tejiendo una relación.
Ya se trate de una campaña publicitaria o de un evento, la metodología que hemos desarrollado durante estos años siempre contempla la posibilidad de movimiento, la adaptación, la personalización del diseño a los imperativos del cliente y al resultado óptimo, la explotación de los recursos disponibles de la manera más eficaz y creativa posible.
Creemos que está grabado en nuestro ADN, esa adaptación capaz de alimentarse de una infinita variedad de sugerencias e ideas, pero también capaz de descubrir dentro de cada diseño individual esa coherencia genuina y el rigor estético que se han convertido a lo largo de los años en el sello distintivo de Hangar Design Group.

84

Siempre nos ha interesado la relación con el espectador y las cuestiones de museología como el texto curatorial, el marco de un cuadro, el pedestal de una escultura, la pared de la galería, incluso el color de la pintura blanca utilizada en la pared. La interfaz entre el observador y lo observado es un delicioso momento de arquitectura.

86

Desde hace algún tiempo, el diseño participa en esta celebración de la autoría, una práctica que ha tomado prestada en partes iguales de las bellas artes y de la moda. Navegar con

101

Creare l'estetica giusta è una sorta di viaggio, è molto più che rendere belle le cose. Devi creare una storia.
Devi immaginare come lo spazio verrà utilizzato e vissuto. Questo avviene sempre, nel nostro settore. C'è una differenza molto chiara tra design e decorazione. La decorazione è l'aspetto esteriore. Il design è la progettazione globale di un luogo, dal punto di vista funzionale ed emozionale. La decorazione si occupa di tendenza; il design invece si fonda sulla creazione di classici.

107

L'aspetto più incredibile dei luoghi che amiamo è il fatto che conoscerli è impossibile, perché sono troppo vasti. Ma puoi essere certo di una cosa: ovunque i tuoi occhi si posino è un'istantanea. Ovunque guardi è interessante.

108

Centri mobili di gravità. Uno degli aspetti che continuiamo ad alimentare in Hangar è la capacità di assimilare persone e competenze diversissime, con sensibilità individuali molto marcate e personalità particolarmente forti. In qualche modo, questa varietà non porta mai a un movimento centrifugo ma sfocia immancabilmente nel recupero inaspettato di un baricentro mobile su cui si costruisce il progetto. Insieme al team internazionale di Hangar Design Group, la diversità di competenze è stata trasformata in pensiero critico e originale che ha permesso di instaurare una relazione nuova con i clienti e fra gli stessi membri del team. Crediamo sia questa la vera creatività di cui sono capaci le aziende migliori: saper mettere in relazione attività, risorse e ruoli diversi e separati plasmandoli in qualcosa di nuovo, dove l'insieme dei singoli elementi è sempre superiore alla loro semplice somma aritmetica. Una filosofia di lavoro ma anche un principio di etica professionale, secondo il quale diversità è soprattutto ricchezza e collaborazione è sinonimo di appartenenza.

111

Affascinante. Il lusso è associato al piacere, all'individualismo e al godimento irrazionale, mentre lo sviluppo sostenibile implica concetti come etica, collettività, moderazione. Queste percezioni non sono infondate, ma è necessario andare oltre le apparenze: il lusso e lo sviluppo sostenibile, infatti, condividono dei principi comuni che sono la continuità di beni durevoli e senza tempo e la protezione dei talenti e delle risorse naturali. Una parziale sovrapposizione che è più di una possibilità al giorno d'oggi: è una vera e propria necessità. Il lusso deve essere impeccabile ed esemplare. Chi acquista beni di lusso si aspetta certamente il meglio, sotto tutti i punti di vista: dal design al punto vendita alle condizioni in cui operano gli individui coinvolti nel processo. Ogni cosa, ogni più piccolo elemento deve rappresentare un modello di trasparenza e integrità.

115

La comunicazione visiva moderna non è solo informazione o racconto; è anche favola, ovvero proiezione nel fantastico. Punta sempre più all'immaginazione, tende a insinuarsi nelle pieghe più sensibili dell'inconscio, libera pulsioni che sono sovente mortificate dai rigori delle regole quotidiane. In altre parole, fa leva sulla nostra capacità di sognare, tanto più suggestiva e irrefrenabile quanto più esercitata a occhi aperti. Anche in questo il design grafico si mantiene a debita distanza dagli allettamenti della pubblicità propriamente detta. Il suo linguaggio è suadente, ma discreto; e le immagini proposte non rinunciano mai al riserbo un po' aristocratico dello stile. Al nostro sogno esso offre non tanto uno sce-

éxito por la delgada línea que separa el arte y el diseño, o caminar por la cuerda floja sobre el precipicio que es su intersección: este es el Santo Grial de las disciplinas creativas.

IV
UNA BOCANADA DE AIRE FRESCO
91

¿Por qué grabar lo obvio? Se trata de esos pequeños momentos de la vida, que uno ve todos los días y se olvida de capturar, porque no te das cuenta de lo especiales que son hasta que los atrapas y los grabas. Una bocanada de aire fresco.

94

Hangar Design Group se mueve desde el centro hacia la periferia y desde el microcosmos al macrocosmos, en un movimiento circular, que no es monótono y regular como un círculo, sino dinámico y vibrante como una espiral. Requiere un centro desde el que empezar y al que regresar constantemente por sus propias vibraciones antes de someterse a su fuerza de atracción. El fundamento cultural para el trabajo de la empresa se encuentra en este rítmico dilatarse y contraerse que las fuerzas de la energía del diseño deben alternativamente condensar y luego expeler con toda sus fuerzas. Después de todo, esto es precisamente lo que pide el mundo moderno del diseño y cabe reconocer que en Hangar Design Group nos dimos cuenta de ello antes que nadie. Hacer frente a la sociedad global con medios probados a través de una enorme cantidad de práctica concreta es una ventaja que debe aprovecharse.

101

Crear la estética correcta realmente es casi un viaje. Es mucho más que hacer algo bonito. Hay que crear una narrativa. Hay que imaginar cómo se va a utilizar y atravesar el espacio. Esto es especialmente cierto en nuestra actividad. La diferencia puede explicarse con la distinción clara entre el diseño y la decoración. La decoración es el aspecto exterior. El diseño se refiere a cómo se proyecta un lugar tanto desde el punto de vista funcional como emocional. La decoración tiene que ver con las tendencias, el diseño tiene que ver con la creación de obras clásicas.

107

Lo mejor de los lugares que amamos es la conciencia de que conocerlos es imposible, porque son muy extensos. Pero se puede estar seguro de algo. No importa donde fijes tu mirada, es como una fotografía. Dondequiera que mires, es interesante.

108

Centros móviles de gravedad. Una cosa que seguimos alimentando en Hangar es la capacidad de asimilación de personas y habilidades muy diferentes, con una marcada sensibilidad individual y personalidades fuertes. De alguna manera, esta variedad no genera un movimiento centrífugo, pero siempre resulta en recuperar de improviso un centro móvil de gravedad para el diseño. Por otra parte, con el equipo internacional de Hangar Design Group, la divergencia de las competencias se ha transformado en una filosofía crítica y original que ha permitido la creación de una nueva relación con los clientes y con los miembros del equipo. Creemos que esto representa la verdadera creatividad de la que son capaces las mejores empresas: la de saber cómo colocar las actividades, funciones y recursos diversificados separados en relación unos con otros, y desarrollarlos dentro de algo nuevo, donde la combinación de elementos individuales es siempre mayor que su suma aritmética. Una filosofía de trabajo, y también un principio de ética nario volgarizzato dal gusto di massa, quanto piuttosto un accenno a possibilità incalcolabili che spetta a ciascuno di noi scoprire. La seduzione resta implicita, inespressa, eppure irresistibile.

Si rivela qui un elemento essenziale del design grafico, che viene però raramente considerato: la sua carica fantastica, la sua capacità di far leva non tanto sull'immaginario, che è ormai formula alquanto logora, quanto sull'immaginazione. Ciò che conta, in tale prospettiva, non è la proposta esplicita dell'immagine ma la sua capacità di accendere nell'immaginazione del fruitore altre figurazioni, altri scenari, in una moltiplicazione cangiante e iridescente che partecipa direttamente della natura del sogno. Forse è proprio in questo suo carattere intrinsecamente affabulatorio che il design grafico trova il segno della sua vera natura, che lo ricollega a un'antica tradizione culturale le cui radici affondano nei remoti – ma sempre vitali – recessi del mito.

117

Le interpretazioni del design sono generalmente limitate alle influenze esterne.

La simbolizzazione, l'astrazione e tutto ciò che accade dentro di te sono processi straordinariamente complessi e intricati, ed è davvero difficile poterli comunicare. È invece molto più semplice – e interessante – cercare di analizzare dal di fuori o contestualizzare. Lo stesso designer può provare a spiegare cosa succede in venti versioni tutte diverse tra loro, e tutte allo stesso tempo plausibili e in qualche modo corrette. Ma non è compito del creativo analizzare se stesso in dettaglio: la sostanza della sua vita è molto più importante.

V
GIORNO DI GIARDINAGGIO
121

Lavoriamo in un settore stressante: c'è molta pressione quando si produce creatività con una scadenza da rispettare. Lunghe giornate di lavoro, che ci portano spesso a passare più tempo tra di noi che con le nostre famiglie. Per questo troviamo sensato il fatto di rendere il nostro spazio lavorativo il più accogliente e confortevole possibile, quasi una seconda casa, dove ci possiamo sentire a nostro agio durante i periodi più impegnativi. Questo porta alla nostra idea collettiva di come un ufficio dovrebbe essere: aperto, interessante, divertente, un ambiente collaborativo e di sostegno.

Pensiamo che un ufficio non debba essere aperto solo in senso spaziale, un open space, ma anche nel senso di una reale assenza di barriere e di competitività professionali. Ciascuno viene valutato individualmente, sia a livello personale sia dal punto di vista professionale. Per il designer, un'atmosfera di apertura è un elemento unico: nessuno si preoccupa della proprietà di un'idea, tutti possiamo contribuire liberamente durante le valutazioni e le critiche; quando ci riuniamo per fare una presentazione di design, è un vero e proprio lavoro di squadra.

123

La cosa importante è avere una storia. Senza una storia non hai i mezzi per poterti esprimere e neanche l'opportunità di crescere. Con il passare del tempo, è l'integrità che consolida e rende tutto autentico. Noi crediamo, dopo tutto, che al di là del clamore che ha circondato in passato il fenomeno design, il concetto di autenticità stia diventando nuovamente importante: quali persone si trovano dietro a quali cose.

126

Un ambiente lavorativo basato sul sostegno reciproco è l'aspetto più importante nello studio, per garantire un buon lavoro: un luogo dove si stabiliscono relazioni sane e reciprocamente rispettose fra tutti. Ci impegniamo per rendere l'ambiente più accogliente e rilassato possibile.

profesional, según el cual la diversidad y, en particular, la riqueza y la colaboración son sinónimos de pertenencia.

111

Fascinante. El lujo se asocia con el placer, el individualismo y el goce irrazonable, mientras que el desarrollo sostenible implica la ética, la colectividad y la moderación. Estas percepciones no son infundadas, pero tenemos que ir más allá de las apariencias. El lujo y el desarrollo sostenible comparten un principios comunes, que son la intemporalidad de un valor duradero, así como la protección de los talentos y de los recursos naturales. Ese tipo de intercambio recíproco es hoy más que una banal posibilidad: es una necesidad.

El lujo debe ser intachable y ejemplar. Los compradores de artículos de lujo, naturalmente, esperan lo mejor. Desde el diseño hasta el punto de venta, pasando por las condiciones de trabajo de quienes participan en el proceso, todo debe ser un modelo de transparencia e integridad.

115

La comunicación visual moderna no es sólo información o narrativa, es también la narración de historias o una proyección hacia los reinos de la imaginación. Tiende a caer en los pliegues más sensibles del inconsciente, libera los impulsos que a menudo son mantenidos a raya por las exigencias de las normas cotidianas. En otras palabras, actúa sobre nuestra capacidad de soñar, que es aún más sugerente e irresistible cuando es ensoñación. Una vez más el diseño gráfico se mantiene a distancia debida del encanto tentador de la misma publicidad. Utiliza un lenguaje persuasivo, pero discreto, las imágenes presentadas no abandonan esa, algo aristocrática, reserva de estilo. Y este le ofrece a nuestro sueño, ya no un escenario vulgarizado por el gusto popular, sino una alusión a las incalculables posibilidades que corresponde descubrir a cada uno de nosotros.

La seducción es todavía implícita, no expresada pero irresistible. Una característica clave del diseño gráfico se revela aquí, a pesar de que rara vez se tome en cuenta, que es su poder imaginativo, su capacidad de actuar no tanto sobre el imaginario, —que ahora es una fórmula sobrecargada—, sino sobre la imaginación. En este sentido, lo que cuenta no es una imagen explícita propuesta, sino la forma en que desencadena otras formas figurativas en la imaginación del usuario, otros escenarios, en una multiplicación brillante e iridiscente directamente entrañada en la naturaleza del sueño. Tal vez sea en su carácter intrínseco de historia donde el diseño gráfico encuentre su verdadera naturaleza, reconectándose a una antigua tradición cultural, cuyas raíces están arraigadas en las profundidades distantes, aunque aún vitales, del mito.

117

Las interpretaciones del diseño se limitan generalmente a las influencias externas. El simbolismo, la abstracción, todo lo que sucede dentro de uno mismo, son todos procesos sumamente complejos y complicados. Es muy difícil de explicar. Por eso es mucho más sencillo e interesante tratar de analizar desde el exterior o incluirlo en un contexto. El propio diseñador siempre puede tratar de explicar lo que está pasando en veinte versiones diferentes, todas ellas plausibles y todas ellas, de alguna manera, correctas. Pero no es el trabajo de la persona creativa aquel de analizarse hasta el último detalle. La esencia de su propia vida es más importante.

V
EL DÍA DE LA PODA
121

Trabajamos en un sector estresante. La presión por producir un trabajo creativo en unos plazos determinados es muy alta. Significa que a menudo pasamos más tiempo juntos que con nuestras familias. Por eso tiene sentido convertir

128

È vero. Negli studi di grandi creativi ogni oggetto è disegnato e progettato da loro stessi. Anche qui ci sono prodotti inventati da noi, ma non facciamo niente per esibirli: anzi, li trovi negli angoli più disparati.

130

Questo è il territorio dove i grafici intrecciano i metodi del design con i modi dell'architettura e del design industriale. Benché la celebre formula "less is more" sia essenzialmente riferita a un periodo storico, rimane comunque una direttiva utile che è stata anche confermata dalla reazione postmoderna – seppur negativamente.

131

I caratteri formali che definiscono lo schema progettuale di Hangar Design Group non sono che le propaggini estreme di un pensiero visivo scaturito nel seno stesso della cultura moderna, di cui essi costituiscono il punto d'arrivo e il superamento. Nel loro sviluppo, l'esile segno intorno al quale si articola l'immagine del marchio sfugge di continuo alla tentazione della tautologia per proiettarsi in una prospettiva semantica che tende all'infinito.

134

Il valore del network per una realtà come la nostra è di importanza cruciale. Non si tratta di un semplice indirizzo su un biglietto da visita ma di luoghi fisici, reali, nei quali lavorano persone vere che si confrontano su progetti diversi, condividendo un medesimo modello professionale. L'apertura di sedi in America, Asia ed Europa ha trovato realizzazione grazie alla profonda convinzione che ci spinge a credere che la diversità dei linguaggi possa accelerare le dinamiche creative.

136

La scelta di dare vita ad un network internazionale, una rete di città nei diversi continenti, nasce dalla volontà di utilizzare un linguaggio trasversale e cosmopolita da esportare in tutto il mondo, attraverso la cultura del progetto più autentica e attuale.

138

Nell'istante in cui ti ci ambienti, lo studio diventa casa tua. E lo porterai sempre con te, dentro di te. È la tua mente, è la tua anima.

VI
AFFINITÀ DI FORME
142

Nelle immagini progettate da Hangar Design Group la simmetria s'impone nel momento stesso in cui viene apertamente sconfessata. La salda struttura del messaggio visivo in un'impaginazione accuratamente calibrata è all'origine di una decostruzione che, oltre a rendere dinamica la figurazione d'insieme, la proietta in un universo di possibilità semantiche nel quale l'osservatore è chiamato a immergersi.

145

A un primo sguardo, ciò che viene percepito è l'asse verticale che regge l'intera immagine, sul quale s'innestano le componenti orizzontali destinate a equilibrarne il peso visivo. Immediatamente dopo, però, nello spazio cartesiano così costruito i singoli elementi acquistano una crescente autonomia, reclamando attenzione per la loro posizione.

nuestro espacio de trabajo en un lugar tan cómodo y atractivo como nuestro hogar, donde nos sentimos respaldados en los momentos más agotadores Esto conduce a nuestra visión colectiva de que una oficina debe ser abierta, interesante, divertida, y en un ambiente de colaboración y apoyo.
Creemos que la oficina debe ser abierta no sólo espacialmente, sino también en su falta real de obstáculos y de competitividad profesionales. Todo el mundo es valorado individualmente, tanto a nivel personal como profesional. Desde la perspectiva de un diseñador, la atmósfera de apertura es un elemento único: nadie se preocupa por la propiedad de una idea, todos contribuimos libremente durante las revisiones y críticas, y cuando nos sentamos para llevar a cabo la presentación de un diseño, trabajamos verdaderamente como un equipo.

123

Lo importante es tener una historia. Sin una historia, no hay medios de expresión ni la oportunidad de desarrollarse aún más. Con los años, la integridad hace que esto sea auténtico. Por cierto, pensamos que después de mucho alboroto en el mundo del diseño, la autenticidad está volviendo a adquirir nuevamente importancia: quiénes son las personas que están detrás de ciertas cosas.

126

El apoyo mutuo en la oficina es el aspecto más importante para asegurar que hacemos un buen trabajo.
Desde siempre, este es un punto clave para incentivar el ambiente de trabajo. Aquí se cultivan solo relaciones saludables y de mutuo respeto entre todos. Nos esforzamos en crear un entorno lo más sereno y libre de estrés posible.

128

Verdad. En los estudios de los grandes creativos cada objeto ha sido diseñado por ellos mismos. Sí, en nuestro estudio hay productos que nosotros mismos hemos inventado, pero no hacemos lo imposible con tal de exhibirlos. Es más, se encuentran en los rincones más dispares.

130

Este es el terreno sobre el que los gráficos tejen los métodos de diseño en los medios de la arquitectura y el diseño industrial: la famosa fórmula "menos es más" ahora sólo se refiere a un período rígido en la historia que ya pasó, aunque sigue siendo una directriz útil que incluso ha sido confirmada por la reacción posmoderna, si bien sólo negativamente.

131

Las características formales que definen el esquema de diseño de Hangar Design Group no son más que las ramificaciones más alejadas de una línea visual del pensamiento que emerge desde el mismo corazón de la cultura moderna, marcando su punto final y prosiguiendo más allá. El signo estilizado alrededor del cual se desarrolla la imagen de un logotipo elude constantemente la tentación de caer en la tautología, y se proyecta hacia una perspectiva semántica que tiende hacia el infinito.

134

El valor de la red para un grupo como el nuestro reviste una importancia vital. Es algo más que una dirección en una tarjeta de visita, puesto que implica lugares físicos reales donde la gente real trabaja y colabora en distintos proyectos, compartiendo un modelo profesional de trabajo común.
La apertura de sedes extranjeras en América, Asia y Europa se concretizó gracias a nuestra profunda convicción de que

Così, la struttura ortogonale che regge l'intero impianto si rivela infine per quella che effettivamente è: una griglia di riferimento, indispensabile per evitare tentazioni centrifughe nell'intero assetto visivo ma partecipe essa stessa del dinamismo che lo contraddistingue.

Non è difficile vedere, dietro questo impianto grafico, l'espressione di una filosofia progettuale che colloca l'attività di Hangar Design Group nella corrente della cultura visiva contemporanea, impegnata a saggiare nuove vie senza tuttavia registrare strappi o rotture traumatiche rispetto alla tradizione moderna, e chiamata anzi a garantire la fondatezza dei percorsi sperimentali e innovativi.

147

L'utopica prospettiva di un "ordine senza legge" – che ha già affascinato un'intera stagione dell'architettura – traspare come impulso a rimettersi in gioco in ogni nuovo progetto, quasi si trattasse di saggiare, ogni volta, la tenuta del modello di riferimento. Sullo sfondo permane tuttavia la figura classica della concinnitas, garanzia di rigore e continuità.

149

La forma delle cose s'identifica con la forma delle idee; e le idee, appena discese dall'algida perfezione dei cieli platonici, s'incarnano nell'esistenza quotidiana immettendovi tutta la forza di un pensiero progettuale teso come un ponte verso il futuro. La leggerezza del segno, la potenza della comunicazione, l'attenuazione dei toni come appassionato ascolto dei messaggi del mondo, il senso dello spazio inteso come apertura sull'universo, il rigore tecnico e il sereno abbandono ai venti della creatività, che marcano la presenza del gruppo nella contemporanea cultura del progetto e della comunicazione, sono tutti segnali di un'inclinazione stilistica che può legittimamente invocare l'immagine archetipica del dirigibile come propria figura araldica.

150

Design in movimento. "Raccontare" un prodotto vuol dire inserirlo in un universo di situazioni mobili, cangianti, nelle quali le sue valenze denotative – quel pezzo d'arredamento, quella lampada, quell'abito – si accendono di connotazioni allusive, che innalzano la percezione visiva sul piano dell'immaginazione. Nei cataloghi prodotti da Hangar Design Group questo principio si rivela nella stratificazione stessa delle immagini, che si aprono su scenari cromatici o luminosi già definiti nei loro richiami alla cultura artistica contemporanea, vi inseriscono i prodotti distribuendoli nello spazio come protagonisti della rappresentazione e calcolano perfettamente la "scena" con accorte spazialità da inquadratura cinematografica.

152

In realtà, trovavamo più interessante fare domande. Se il lavoro assumeva una certa forma, se diventava – per via di metafora – un "oggetto", a noi interessava capire che cos'era che generava quella certa forma. Abbiamo allora iniziato a interessarci a ciò che sta dietro al lavoro, ai concetti che ispirano la creazione e il pensiero.

Abbiamo voluto indagare, abbiamo voluto scrivere e ricercare, essendoci resi conto che in effetti sul mercato non c'era nulla che parlasse di ciò che stavamo facendo. Dunque abbiamo iniziato a scrivere e ad articolare la nostra ricerca.

156

Che cos'è il processo organico? Com'è possibile oggi creare un prodotto duraturo? In una parola: estetica. Parliamo del bello, ma in senso olistico: l'aspetto, la sensazione e l'anima, che quando sono fusi perfettamente creano qualcosa

la presencia de distintos lenguajes puede impulsar el dinamismo creativo.

136

La decisión de crear una red internacional, una red de ciudades en distintos continentes, surgió del deseo de recurrir a un lenguaje indirecto y cosmopolita. Para exportar a todo el mundo, a través de la cultura del diseño más auténtica y actual.

138

En el instante en que te habitúa al estudio, se convierte en tu casa. En realidad, siempre llevas tu estudio contigo y en tu interior: es la mente, tu alma.

VI
AFINIDAD DE FORMAS
142

En las imágenes diseñadas por Hangar Design Group, la simetría se impone desde el preciso instante en que es repudiada públicamente. Anclar firmemente el mensaje visual a la composición de una página cuidadosamente calibrada es la raíz de un proceso de deconstrucción, que, además de inyectar vida en el diseño figurativo en general, también la proyecta en un mundo de posibilidades semánticas en las que el observador espera ser sumergido.

145

Toda la imagen se apoya sobre un eje vertical, que es lo primero que se percibe a primera vista. Sobre este, se encajan los componentes horizontales destinados a equilibrar el peso visual. Inmediatamente después de esto, los elementos individuales del espacio cartesiano construido de esta manera adquieren una creciente autonomía, llamando la atención debido a su posición. De esta manera, la estructura ortogonal que sostiene todo el diseño se muestra por lo que realmente es: una construcción de referencia vital para prevenir que la entera disposición visual colapse en las tentaciones centrífugas, pero en realidad involucrada ella misma en la creación de su dinamismo característico.

Es fácil ver, detrás de este diseño gráfico, la encarnación de una filosofía de diseño que sitúa las actividades de Hangar Design Group firmemente en la cultura visual contemporánea dominante, tratando de probar nuevos caminos, sin romper radicalmente con la tradición moderna y, por el contrario, probando la validez de nuevos enfoques experimentales.

147

La perspectiva utópica del "orden sin ley", que ya ha fascinado a un período entero de la arquitectura, transciende como un estímulo para ponerse en juego con cada nuevo proyecto, casi como si se tratara de una cuestión de constante comprobación de que el armazón resiste. En el fondo permanece inalterable la figura clásica de la *concinnitas*, garantizando la precisión y la continuidad.

149

La forma de los objetos se identifica con la forma de las ideas en esas obras y las ideas suavemente barren la perfección fresca de los cielos platónicos, se encarnan en la vida cotidiana, inyectando la fuerza de una filosofía de diseño proyectada hacia el futuro, como algunos puentes.

La ligereza de los signos, la fuerza comunicativa, atenuar los tonos como un medio apasionado de escuchar los mensajes del mundo, la sensación de espacio tomada como una apertura hacia el universo, la precisión técnica y el abandono suave a los vientos de la creatividad son signos de una tendi veramente nuovo. L'estetica non è solo superficie, è essenza totale, dalla A alla Z. E non è il risultato di tattiche o trucchetti alla moda, ma piuttosto di una visione personale e individuale.

163

L'interconnessione delle competenze si attua a volte già all'inizio del procedimento creativo; l'opera nasce dunque da un atto di comunicazione. La comunicazione diventa elemento primario dell'oggetto architettonico, sia come atto che lo genera sia come obiettivo da raggiungere dall'oggetto quando verrà prodotto. Per noi, ci sarà sempre più comunicazione nel design e ci auguriamo sempre più design nella comunicazione…
Pensiamo che un progetto, oltre a raccontare se stesso, debba essere in grado di trasmettere un'esperienza, una storia fatta di persone e non una semplice espressione del disegno, al di là del suo indiscusso valore estetico. Un progetto deve rivelare un linguaggio internazionale e deve soprattutto essere "vivo".

167

Simmetria, equilibrio, immutabilità – quest'ultimo un concetto particolarmente interessante: Che cos'è immutabile? Che cosa, invece, muta? Cosa può cambiare? Che cosa non cambia?
Noi non siamo interessati all'immagine in se stessa. Il suo significato vero va cercato nella somma dei dialoghi, delle storie e delle esperienze di diversi interlocutori, tutti valori che, proprio attraverso l'immagine, possono portarsi a un livello successivo. Questa è un'immagine adeguata. Una buona immagine dovrebbe essere in mezzo ad altre due: quella che la precede e quella che verrà.

169

Quando progettiamo, seguiamo un preciso metodo di lavoro. Nella prima fase ogni creativo, ogni progettista agisce liberamente; poi inizia la fase progettuale vera e propria, quella del confronto. Non esiste la figura del progettista isolato; il progetto è quasi sempre aperto, flessibile, dinamico e mutabile. Ogni progetto è il risultato di un intenso lavoro di squadra che risponde alle esigenze del committente. Il risultato è un progetto globale che comprende aspetti legati alla comunicazione, al design, alla grafica, al mercato, alla funzione, all'estetica e via dicendo.

170

Ciò che qualifica un progetto è la diffusione di idee, e non solo forma o funzione. Inutile pensare a un progetto creativo anarchico e autonomo allo stesso tempo; meglio avere consapevolezza del fatto che stai creando per una persona che non conosci. E, soprattutto, non sai chi sarà l'utente finale.

177

Un aspetto interessante del nuovo design è che si fonde completamente con il nostro modo di essere. Un oggetto assorbe così tanto delle nostre aspettative ed esperienze da diventare un processo del tutto naturale. In realtà, noi designer vi conosciamo, sappiamo come agite, che cosa vi aspettate. E la decisione su quando seguirvi, o quando invece prendere un'altra direzione, è una scelta importantissima.

187

Al giorno d'oggi, le tecnologie informatiche e digitali stanno trasformando profondamente il nostro modo di pensare il design – ben oltre la semplice funzione di assistenza che i computer possono darci in termini di capacità computa-

dencia estilística con derecho a invocar la imagen arquetípica del dirigible como su figura heráldica.

150

"Narrar" un producto significa situarlo en una serie de situaciones cambiantes, en las que sus propiedades denotativas —ese mueble, esa lámpara, la prenda de vestir— adquieren connotaciones alusivas, elevando nuestra conciencia perceptiva a los reinos de la imaginación. Este principio se manifiesta en la superposición de imágenes, abriéndose a escenarios de colores cuyas alusiones al arte contemporáneo ya han sido definidas, situando los productos en el espacio, como el foco principal de la representación y calculando la "escena" a la perfección a través de arreglos espaciales cuidadosamente calibrados que se parecen a las tomas de una película.

152

En realidad estábamos más interesados en hacer preguntas. Si el trabajo tenía una forma determinada, digamos como una metáfora, como un objeto, lo que nos interesaba era entender qué generaba esa forma.
Empezamos a interesarnos por las cosas que yacían detrás de la obra, los conceptos que inspiraban la obra y el pensamiento. Así que empezamos a investigar sobre eso y comenzamos a escribir y buscar y nos dimos cuenta de que, en realidad, no había nada en el mercado para referirse a lo que nosotros estábamos estudiando, así que empezamos a escribir sobre ello y a articular nuestra búsqueda.

156

Así que ¿qué es el proceso orgánico? ¿Cómo es posible crear hoy un producto que perdure? En una palabra: estética. Estamos hablando de algo hermoso, pero más bien con una estética holística: la mirada, el tacto, y el alma que, cuando se fusionan perfectamente, marcan un auténtico punto de diferencia. La estética no es sólo una superficie, es la esencia total, de la A a la Z. Y no procede de las tácticas modernas o trucos de tendencia, sino más bien de una visión personal del individuo.

163

Esa interconexión de habilidades de vez en cuando se produce al principio del proceso creativo, en cuyo caso la misma obra evoluciona de un acto de comunicación. De manera que la comunicación se convierte en un elemento intrínseco del objeto arquitectónico, como el acto que lo genera o como el objetivo a alcanzar por el objeto en sí cuando esté terminado. Para nosotros, la comunicación será cada vez más evidente en el diseño, al igual que esperamos que el diseño sea cada vez más evidente en la comunicación…
Creemos que un diseño no debe ser simplemente una expresión de sí mismo, sino que también debe ser capaz de contar una experiencia, una historia compuesta por personas, más allá de las credenciales estéticas incuestionables del diseño. Un diseño debe revelar un lenguaje internacional y sobre todo debe estar "vivo".

167

De manera que mira a la simetría, al equilibrio, a la inmutabilidad —que creo que es un concepto muy interesante: "¿Qué es inmutable?! ¿Qué es, en cambio, lo que cambia? ¿Qué es mutable? ¿Qué es lo que no cambia?
No estamos interesados en la imagen en por la imagen.
Su importancia radica en el hecho de que contiene la suma de los diálogos, historias y experiencias anteriores de varios interlocutores y permite llevar al estadio sucesivo estos valores pre-existentes. Esta es una imagen adecuada. Una buena imagen debe estar en medio de otras dos, la anterior y aquella por venir.

zionale. L'utilizzo di CAD e della grafica computerizzata sta aumentando tanto da influenzare il modo stesso in cui si fa design. Nonostante tutto, il disegno mentale rimane vitale: lo schizzo, come estensione dell'idea sulla carta, conserva sempre tutto il suo potenziale, poiché la qualità dell'idea, il suo significato originale non possono essere catturati dai moderni strumenti rigorosi.
Prima di essere "messa su carta", l'idea ci appare in modo molto chiaro, ma non appena la trascriviamo i contorni scompaiono e si dissolvono per prendere la forma non più delle parole, ma dei segni. Come le parole, i disegni possono essere allo stesso tempo precisi e indefiniti: come in un graffito, o in una calligrafia, che racchiudono in sé la struttura e la caratteristica precisa delle forme e degli spazi che esprimono. Possiamo affermare, almeno per la parte del design che si basa sulle riflessioni concettuali e sulle idee, che lo schizzo è destinato a rimanere un metodo di disegno insostituibile, nel lungo periodo, indipendentemente dal fatto che sia disegnato con l'inchiostro sulla carta, o con inchiostro virtuale su carta virtuale.

189

Ogni cosa esiste. Gli oggetti, come ben sappiamo, sono la parte fondamentale del design. Per parafrasare la definizione che Mies van der Rohe dà dell'architettura quale "testamento di un'epoca traslata nello spazio", potremmo dire che il mondo dei manufatti è il testamento di un'epoca "traslata negli oggetti". Il tempo si coagula nella materia, diventando così "oggettivamente" leggibile. Il mondo in cui viviamo si manifesta prima di tutto nell'universo delle cose. La frase programmatica "Ogni cosa esiste" può essere letta in due modi: i manufatti esistono, ci sono, ma anche prendono vita attraverso noi. Noi siamo esposti alle cose, ed esse esistono perché ce ne circondiamo, ci leghiamo ad esse, ci ritroviamo emotivamente e ci sperimentiamo fisicamente attraverso di loro. Esse ci aiutano ad assumere una forma e ad acquisire il fondamentale sostegno.

VII
HARD COVER
191

La stampa à morta. Lunga vita alla stampa. Negli ultimi dieci anni è stata dichiarata, in diverse occasioni, la morte della carta stampata. Eppure, un numero sempre crescente di pubblicazioni nasce ogni giorno, in opposizione a chi ne aveva predetto la fine. A volte la tenace perseveranza della stampa diventa quasi un oltraggio. Le fonti dell'identità moderna non sono mai state così fragili: viviamo in un mondo caratterizzato dalla perdita di sostanza, da legami sempre più fragili e dalla futilità delle cose che utilizziamo. Quando una brochure diventa più di un semplice opuscolo? Quando i suoi lettori ne diventano collezionisti. Parliamo di cosa rende grande un lavoro stampato. Il pixel e la stampa sono esperienze divese: il materiale e il senso del tatto colpiscono la percezione. Leggere sullo schermo significa perdere la "dimensione associativa della lettura", quella che consente ai nostri pensieri di andare oltre le parole e aprirsi verso nuovi orizzonti intellettuali. Sullo schermo scremiamo, sfilettiamo, scegliamo accuratamente i dettagli migliori. In un confronto costante con la tecnologia disgregante di Internet, la stampa si sta reinventando – e in modo magnifico. L'ultima pagina del "Financial Times" dice molto di più del coperchio di un laptop.

198

Gli strumenti chiave per rendere una pubblicità o una pubblicazione memorabili sono le idee, travolgenti e avvincenti, la visualizzazione fantastica di un'immagine, che sembra quasi rallentare il tempo per qualche secondo, la consistenza spe-

169

Cuando diseñamos seguimos una metodología de trabajo precisa. En la primera fase cada diseñador y creativo tiene carta blanca. A continuación, comienza la fase de diseño propiamente dicha: la comparación y la confrontación. La figura del diseñador aislado no existe. El diseño es casi siempre abierto, flexible, dinámico y cambiante. Cada diseño es el resultado de un esfuerzo intenso de equipo, que responde a las necesidades del cliente. Al final, el resultado es un diseño global en el que entran en juego aspectos que están vinculados a la comunicación, al diseño, al arte gráfico, al mercado, a la función, a la estética, etc.

170

Lo que distingue un proyecto es la difusión de las ideas, no es sólo una cuestión de forma o función. De nada sirve pensar en un proyecto creativo que es, al mismo tiempo, anárquico y autónomo. Es mejor ser conscientes de que no conoces a la persona en cuyo nombre se crea.
Y, sobre todo, no sabrás quién lo usará.

177

Un aspecto interesante del nuevo diseño es que se funde totalmente con nuestro comportamiento. Un objeto absorbe de tal manera nuestras expectativas o experiencias, que se convierte en un proceso completamente natural. En realidad, como diseñadores os conocemos, sabemos cómo vais a comportaros y qué es lo que esperáis. Y decidir cuándo seguiros o cuándo ir por otro camino, es una decisión muy importante.

187

Hoy día, la informática y las tecnologías digitales están transformando profundamente nuestra manera de pensar el diseño, más allá de la asistencia que proporcionan los equipos en términos de capacidad computacional. El uso de CAD y gráficas por ordenador es cada vez mayor hasta el punto de influir en la manera en que se realiza el diseño. A pesar de todo esto, el dibujo mental sigue siendo vital: el boceto, como una prolongación de la idea sobre el papel, conserva todo su potencial. La calidad de la idea, su significado original, no puede ser capturada por herramientas tan exactas. Antes de que se "ponga por escrito" la idea nos parece muy clara, pero tan pronto como la anotamos, los bordes se hacen borrosos y se disuelven para tomar forma de signos, no de palabras. Al igual que las palabras, los dibujos pueden ser a la vez imprecisos y exactos, como un grafiti o la caligrafía, que ocultan la estructura y el carácter preciso de las formas y espacios a los que se refieren.
Podemos afirmar que, al menos en relación a la parte de diseño que se basa en la reflexión conceptual, en ideas, el boceto sigue siendo un método de dibujo insustituible a largo plazo, no hay ninguna diferencia si está dibujado con tinta sobre papel, o con tinta electrónica sobre papel electrónico.

189

Todo existe. Tal como los conocemos, los objetos son la clave del diseño. Parafraseando a Mies van der Rohe que dice que la arquitectura es "la voluntad de la época traducida a espacio", podemos decir que el mundo de los artefactos es la voluntad de la época "traducida a objetos". El tiempo se coagula en la materia, se convierte en "objetivamente" legible. Nuestro mundo cotidiano ocurre principalmente en el "universo de los objetos". La frase programática "Todo existe" tiene dos lecturas distintas: los artefactos están allí, presentes, pero también se originan a través nuestro. Estamos expuestos a ellos, y existen como objetos que reunimos en derredor nuestro, con los que establecemos lazos, con ciale al tatto, e il formato in cui viene presentata. Tutti questi fattori hanno la capacità di stupire e meravigliare le persone.

200

Ci piace lavorare con lo stampatore per modificare leggermente i più piccoli dettagli nelle sfumature degli inchiostri, fino a ottenere l'effetto desiderato. Ci piace moltissimo anche impiegare materiali diversi – carta, plastica, metallo – combinandoli per creare effetti di design in linea con gli obiettivi della comunicazione.
Tuttavia, nella nostra esperienza, le migliori stampe spesso non vengono apprezzate abbastanza. Eppure ci circondano, come un muro infinito. La relazione indissolubile con la stampa e le pubblicazioni è più forte che mai, e ha modificato in modo rilevante l'aspetto del prodotto in questo incredibile periodo in cui stiamo vivendo.
Tutti gli aspetti più straordinari della stampa sono le autentiche pietre miliari del mondo dell'arte e del design. La tipografia è una passione speciale, un progetto su carta un'esperienza d'amore.

203

La lettura non è mai un atto unilaterale: nel momento stesso in cui in essa ci perdiamo, tutte le sue componenti visive, tattili, concettuali, psicologiche e perfino esistenziali si compongono in un'esperienza unitaria dalla quale, in un modo o nell'altro, si esce trasformati.
Il progetto di un libro ingloba quindi un mondo, un universo di possibilità: non per nulla i filosofi hanno colto nella lettura un piacere fisico, un impegno nei confronti del mondo, un perdersi e un ritrovarsi sempre eguali e sempre diversi.

204

Noi supponiamo che il risultato migliore possa arrivare con un messaggio molto essenziale; quello che volevamo trasmettere era il concetto di "eleganza discreta".

207

Quando progettiamo un logo, di solito non sappiamo cosa vogliamo; ma sappiamo esattamente cosa non vogliamo. La nostra accezione di "grande risultato" è riuscire a creare qualcosa che attraversi e spezzi il rumore, ma in un modo semplice e sofisticato, che rifletta il nostro stile. In altre parole, vogliamo farlo con calma…

VIII
L'ARTE DELL'ATTIMO
220

Nel mezzo di ogni rotolo di pellicola c'è sempre un'immagine fuori luogo, qualcosa che ancora non ci appartiene. Sono proprio quelle le immagini che ci aiutano a capire dove andremo.

222

Non si può pensare semplicemente di scattare una foto e aspettarsi che questo sia sufficiente per un cliente. La convergenza tra fotografia e cinematografia e i sostanziali cambiamenti avvenuti nell'ambito della comunicazione mediatica hanno costretto i brand a produrre contenuti multimediali esperienziali, utilizzando la tecnologia come strumento per dare vita alle idee ma soprattutto utilizzando l'arte come impulso per sfruttare la tecnologia. Le persone di maggiore successo possiedono sufficiente flessibilità mentale non solo per adattarsi ma anche per mettersi costantemente in discussione, trasformando i limiti in efficienza e innovazione, con il potenziale per poter stabilire nuovi standard, nuovi valori e nuove regole.

los cuales nos unimos emotivamente y a través de los cuales realizamos una experiencia física, nos ayudan a ponernos en forma y nos templan.

VII
TAPA DURA
191

La sentencia de muerte del papel impreso fue pronunciada en varias ocasiones durante la última década. Sin embargo, en oposición a aquellos que habían vaticinado su muerte, cada día salen a la luz nuevas publicaciones.
A veces, la persistencia de la impresión se convierte en una afrenta. Las fuentes de la identidad moderna nunca han sido más frágiles; vivimos en un mundo caracterizado por la pérdida de sustancia, la sutileza cada vez mayor de los vínculos y la superficialidad de aquello que utilizamos. ¿Cuándo un folleto es más que un simple folleto? Cuando sus lectores empiezan a coleccionarlos. Hablemos de lo que hace que un trabajo de impresión sea magnífico. Los píxeles y la impresión son experiencias diferentes, el material y el sentido del tacto afectan a la percepción. Con la lectura en la pantalla se pierde la "dimensión asociativa de la lectura", cuando nuestros pensamientos se mueven más allá de las palabras y vislumbran nuevos horizontes intelectuales. En la pantalla escogemos, limpiamos, seleccionamos cuidadosamente los mejores detalles. Enfrentados a la tecnología punta de Internet, la impresión se reinventa a sí misma, y lo hace maravillosamente. La última página del Financial Times dice mucho más que la tapa de un portátil.

198

El atuendo apropiado para la impresión. Las claves básicas para hacer una promoción o una publicación memorables son las ideas, salvajes y fascinantes, la visualización sorprendente de la imagen que parece ralentizar el tiempo durante unos segundos, la textura especial al tacto y el formato que se está presentando. Todos estos factores juntos tienen la capacidad de sorprender y maravillar.

200

Cuando estamos en la imprenta, nos encanta trabajar con el tipógrafo para ajustar los más pequeños detalles en los matices de las tintas, hasta obtener el efecto que buscamos. También nos produce un gran placer utilizar diferentes materiales —papel, plástico, metal—, mezclarlos y combinarlos para obtener efectos de diseño que resuelvan los objetivos de la comunicación. Sin embargo, en nuestra experiencia, a menudo se subestiman las mejores impresiones. Y eso que nos rodean, como un muro infinito. La inseparable relación de las impresiones y publicaciones es más fuerte que nunca, y sobre todo, en este momento fabuloso, ha cambiado la cara del producto. Los aspectos más exquisitos de la impresión son la piedra miliar del mundo del arte y del diseño. La tipografía es una pasión especial; el diseño para el papel, una experiencia amorosa.

203

La lectura no es nunca un acto unilateral: en el momento en que nos perdemos en ella, todas sus características visuales, conceptuales, psicológicas e incluso existenciales, constituyen una experiencia única de la que, de una u otra manera, salimos cambiados.
Así, un proyecto de libro abarca todo un mundo, un universo de posibilidades. No es de extrañar que los filósofos hayan entendido la lectura como un placer físico, una manera de comprometerse con el mundo, perderse y luego volver a redescubrirse como el mismo de antes y, sin embargo, diferente.

224

Qualcuno dirà che la fotografia è ancora il mezzo visivo predominante ai nostri giorni. Quando guardi un dipinto, il confronto scatta immediatamente: somiglia alla foto? Lo hanno fatto sulla base di una foto? Ogni cosa viene misurata con la sua immagine fotografica.

231

Siamo ispirati dall'idea di assenza, che potrebbe rappresentare il non-essere, o semplicemente l'immobilità. Riguarda la possibilità di rallentare il tempo. Se nascondi qualcosa in una foto generi immobilità. Ci stiamo allenando a togliere tutto, ogni riferimento, per lasciare che dell'immagine resti solamente l'essenza, ciò che è.

233

Nessuno, ormai, crede più alla perfetta specularità tra la fotografia e il soggetto che ritrae.
Ciononostante, il richiamo alla "somiglianza", che è per l'appunto il luogo della "pseudopresenza", resta saldo: lo spazio della fotografia fissa un "campo" visivo entro il quale il protagonista dell'immagine – cosa o persona – s'inserisce con una naturalezza in grado di ricondurre il tutto a una sorta di sottintesa normalità. È solo a questo punto che si nota la vera "assenza" di ciò che nella foto è raffigurato. Sebbene assai più somigliante d'ogni altra rappresentazione, l'immagine fotografica non è la cosa, che un attimo dopo lo scatto è già altrove.

235

La grafica non fotografa mai la realtà: la legge, la filtra, la destruttura. In essa non c'è riproduzione di ciò che è dato, ma una drastica selezione degli elementi percettivi che lo compongono, alla fine della quale resta, isolato, ingigantito, dominante, quello che, da solo, esprime tutto l'universo di senso da comunicare. Di conseguenza, per "leggere" un artefatto grafico occorre compiere il cammino inverso: partire cioè dall'irriducibile essenzialità del segno per risalire alla globalità del fenomeno, alla sua interezza.

240

Per noi è sempre stata una "questione di stile". Di stile di vita naturalmente. Perché per noi lo stile non è solo una cifra estetica ma soprattutto un modello di pensiero, una linea di continuità da leggere in filigrana attraverso i numerosissimi lavori sviluppati in questi anni, un concetto identitario e una chiave di lettura con cui interpretare la continua interazione, esplicita o sotterranea, fra settori disciplinari diversi, dalla comunicazione visiva all'architettura d'interni, dal retail design agli eventi. L'attitudine al dettaglio, l'attenzione all'armonia dell'insieme, la necessaria cura dedicata a ogni singolo particolare sono solo gli aspetti più manifesti di una filosofia riflessiva che permea il reticolo di relazioni fra le diverse aree settoriali di intervento e che permette di approdare sempre a un pensiero che è anche azione, dove l'atto creativo si traduce in un "fare" immediato. Dove la creatività individuale si trasforma senza esitazioni e senza residui in uno stile che permea l'operatività del gruppo in cui quel gesto si colloca. E dove diventa istanza identitaria in grado di tradurre il nostro lavoro quotidiano in un disegno generale strategico, forte, riconoscibile.

IX
LA LEGGE DELLE 3 PROPOSTE
246

La creatività non è legata al caos. Essere creativi non significa soltanto inventare qualcosa di strano, nuovo o eclatante.

204

Suponemos que el mejor resultado proviene del mensaje más básico, y lo que queríamos transmitir era una elegancia discreta.

207

Hacerlo en silencio. Cuando decidimos concentrarnos en rediseñar un logotipo, no sabemos lo que queremos, pero sabemos lo que no queremos. Nuestro primer punto para un buen resultado es la creación de algo que atraviese y rompa el ruido, pero de una manera sencilla y sofisticada, que refleje nuestro estilo. En otras palabras, queríamos hacerlo... pero en silencio.

VIII
EL ARTE DE LO
IMPREVISTO
220

En el centro de cada rollo de película siempre hay una fotografía fuera de lugar, algo que todavía no nos pertenece.
Esas son las fotografías que nos ayudan a entender cuál es el próximo paso.

222

Es poco aceptable disparar sencillamente una fotografía y esperar a que sea suficiente para un cliente. La convergencia de la fotografía y la cinematografía, y los cambios en los medios de comunicación han obligado a las marcas a proveer un contenido multimedia que es experiencial, utilizando la tecnología como una herramienta para poner en práctica las ideas, pero lo más importante, utilizando el arte para manejar la tecnología. Las personas que más prosperan tienen la flexibilidad mental y estructural no sólo de adaptarse, sino de revolucionarse; abrazan las limitaciones para transformarlas en eficiencia e innovaciones que tienen la fuerza para establecer nuevos estándares, valores y comportamientos.

224

Algunos podrían decir que la fotografía sigue siendo el medio visual dominante de nuestro tiempo. Cuando uno mira una pintura, de inmediato se establecen comparaciones.
¿Se ve como una fotografía? ¿Fue pintado utilizando una fotografía? Todo tiene que estar a la altura de la imagen fotográfica.

231

Nos sentimos inspirados por la idea de ausencia, que podría representar la nada o simplemente la idea de quietud. Se trata de ralentizar el tiempo. Al ocultar algo en una fotografía se crea la quietud. Estamos tratando de quitarlo todo. Nos gustaría que la imagen fuera sólo su propia esencia, esto es, sin ninguna referencia en absoluto.

233

Ya nadie cree que una fotografía refleje perfectamente su objeto. Sin embargo, la evocación de una "similitud", que es lo que crea la "seudo-presencia", es aún tan fuerte como siempre. El espacio de una fotografía fija un "campo" visual donde el sujeto de la foto —persona u objeto— encaja con tanta discreción que conduce a una especie de normalidad aceptada. Únicamente llegados a este punto notamos la verdadera "ausencia" de lo que no está representado en la foto. A pesar de ser más realista que cualquier otro medio de representación, una imagen fotográfica no es el objeto en sí, que un instante después de tomar la foto ya está en otro lugar.

Bisogna sapersi concentrare sugli obiettivi richiesti per il lavoro che si sta facendo: le persone davvero dotate di talento sono quelle che sanno giocare stando alle regole date. Più rigide sono queste regole, più le abilità personali devono essere perfezionate.

Prima di iniziare un progetto lo definiamo sempre con precisione: regole, obiettivi, contesto, richieste del cliente ecc. Nelle scuole di grafica insegnano a lavorare attraverso la saturazione: creare decine di versioni dello stesso visual nella speranza che il cliente ne scelga una. Noi siamo all'opposto: è meglio capire esattamente che cosa stai cercando di fare prima di iniziare il lavoro. Quando sai con precisione cosa vuoi, non hai bisogno di molti tentativi per raggiungere il risultato che vuoi ottenere. Crediamo fermamente che ogni stile personale sia il risultato di un metodo meticolosamente codificato. Quando un cliente ci chiede di "fare un grande progetto" significa "vi sto chiedendo di cambiare il modo in cui vedo il mio mondo". Un bravo professionista non restituisce un risultato che risponde esattamente a ciò che gli viene richiesto. Un bravo professionista dà molto di più, arriva perfino a cambiare l'idea del cliente su cosa sia possibile chiedere. Noi cerchiamo di soddisfare le richieste del cliente sollevando continuamente nuove domande.

248

Dal punto di vista del business, è stato strategicamente importante ricercare la diversità. Risolvere i problemi di un'ampia gamma di clienti, aziende, pubblico e media ci consente di accumulare diverse esperienze per poter poi incrociare e contaminare altri pensieri per altri progetti. La diversità mantiene alto il livello di stimolazione in tutto lo studio.

250

Così come ricerchiamo la diversità nei progetti che seguiamo, tentiamo anche di trovare personalità di talento che portino allo studio molto più che le semplici credenziali del designer. Abbiamo sempre creduto che non è solo il portfolio a fare il professionista: molto più del semplice talento, è interessante scoprire che persona c'è dietro il suo curriculum. Questo significa che le nostre risorse sono eclettiche proprio come il nostro portfolio.

252

Arriva un punto, dopo tutti i ragionamenti, la pianificazione, il brainstorming e lo sketching, in cui si inizia a capire che le cose stanno andando nella giusta direzione. Certo, senza i ragionamenti e la pianificazione, il brainstorming e lo sketching, non sapremmo mai se abbiamo preso la giusta direzione. Crediamo sia necessario arrivare proprio al punto in cui si comprende che l'intuizione è quella corretta.

255

Quando ci chiedono qual è il significato, quale "messaggio" contiene, ci sentiamo davvero persi. Il lavoro stesso è il messaggio.

X
CHE SIA REALE
263

Onorare con semplicità la bellezza evidente e il potere della luce. Una sintesi concettuale di gesti e immagini, intrecciate in un preciso e attento utilizzo delle linee. Geometrie rigorose ed essenzialità sono associate all'assenza di colore e all'utilizzo moderato di elementi decorativi. La capacità di sviluppare il proprio stile, entro i limiti delle forme disponibili, è un talento sempre più importante e vitale nell'interior design contemporaneo.

235

Los gráficos nunca fotografían la realidad: la leen, la filtran, la desestructuran. No implica la reproducción de lo que se da, sólo una selección drástica de sus componentes de percepción. Al final de esta selección, sólo aquello que expresa el entero universo de sentido que se transmitirá se deja aislado, ampliado y dominante. Por lo tanto, con el fin de "leer" un artefacto gráfico, tenemos que trabajar en la dirección opuesta; en otras palabras, debemos comenzar con la simplicidad irreducible del signo para trabajar en dirección reversa a la naturaleza global del fenómeno, a su totalidad.

240

Para nosotros siempre ha sido una "cuestión de estilo". De estilo de vida, por supuesto. Porque para nosotros el estilo no es sencillamente un sello estético, sino sobre todo un modelo de pensamiento. Es una línea de continuidad presente como una marca de agua apenas legible que remarca la multitud de proyectos desarrollados a lo largo de estos años, un concepto de identificación y una clave con la cual interpretar la interacción continua —ya sea explícita o implícita— entre los distintos sectores profesionales, desde la comunicación visual a la arquitectura de interiores, desde el comercio minorista al diseño de eventos.

La actitud hacia los detalles, la atención a la armonía del conjunto, el cuidado necesario dedicado a cada elemento en particular son los aspectos más evidentes de lo que es una filosofía reflexiva que impregna la red de relaciones entre los distintos ámbitos de intervención, y que converge hacia una filosofía que también constituye una acción. Una filosofía donde el acto creativo se traduce en una "acción" inmediata, donde la creatividad individual se transforma sin vacilación ni exceso en un estilo que impregna la actividad del grupo generando la acción. Y donde se crea una identidad capaz de traducir nuestro trabajo diario en un diseño general estratégico, fuerte y reconocible.

IX
LA LEY DE LAS
TRES PROPUESTAS
247

La creatividad no está ligada con el caos. Ser creativo no significa sólo inventar algo extraño, nuevo o explosivo. Uno necesita saber cómo concentrarse en los objetivos necesarios para el trabajo que se está haciendo. Quienes tienen verdadero talento son aquellos que saben cómo jugar con las reglas que se les han dado. Cuanto más estrictas sean, más se debe refinar la capacidad personal.

Antes de comenzar un proyecto lo definimos con reglas precisas, objetivos, contexto, demandas del cliente, etc. En el instituto de diseño gráfico enseñan a trabajar a través de la saturación, haciendo decenas de versiones de la misma visual con la esperanza de que el cliente seleccione una. Nosotros creemos lo contrario: que es mejor saber exactamente qué se está buscando antes de empezar. Cuando sabes lo que quieres no necesitas varios intentos para lograr el resultado que buscas. Creemos firmemente que el estilo personal es el efecto de un método cuidadosamente codificado. Cuando un cliente le dice a una agencia, "Por favor, haga un gran diseño", lo que está diciendo es, "Por favor, cambia la forma en que veo mi mundo". Un buen profesional no le da al cliente exactamente lo que pide. Le da más de lo que pide; cambia su idea de lo que es posible puede pedir. Tratamos de satisfacer la demanda de los clientes planteando constantemente nuevos interrogantes.

248

Desde el punto de vista comercial, ha sido de importancia estratégica perseguir la diversidad de trabajos. Solucionando problemas para una amplia gama de clientes, industrias, pú-

268

Il prodotto è sempre la cosa più importante; una volta stabilito questo, bisogna tenere conto di moltissimi fattori per crearne l'estetica. Tutta l'esperienza possibile deve convergere su quel prodotto. I clienti devono essere accolti alla porta da una persona interessante, che sorrida e li faccia sentire i benvenuti. Lo spazio deve essere magnifico, con la musica e le luci giuste.

XI
BESPOKE (SU MISURA)
279

Bespoke (pronuncia bi: spϑuk) è un termine inglese che significa "su misura" e viene impiegato in diversi contesti per indicare un prodotto fatto, per l'appunto, sulla base delle esigenze dell'acquirente. Anche se oggi è applicato a molti settori – dai software per computer agli interni delle auto di lusso – il termine nasce storicamente per l'abbigliamento sartoriale su misura: camicie e altri capi che richiedono prove e misurazioni.

281

Più a lungo si insegue la propria creatività, più essa guadagna un'esistenza propria, una sorta di vita parallela. Non riesci mai a capire fino in fondo cosa stai facendo, ed è questo che crea quella speciale tensione e quella suspence senza le quali il lavoro perderebbe la sua carica emotiva. È tutto un processo di scoperta. Ed è senza fine.

294

Per progettare qualcosa di davvero unico, devi pensare per prima cosa allo scopo del tuo oggetto. Devi comprendere a fondo il tuo contesto.
Come si relaziona questo particolare lavoro al suo ambiente? Come funziona, in tutti i suoi aspetti? E dopo, devi ricondurlo a una semplicità estetica che lo attraversa completamente. Una filosofia di questo tipo, oggi, la possiamo vedere negli Apple store, nella home page di Google, nel branding di Tiffany – con il suo eterno e istantaneamente riconoscibile colore turchese. I consumatori sono sommersi da troppe alternative. L'avversione al caos – che sia materiale o esistenziale – è una strategia editoriale intelligente per qualsiasi offerta di prodotto. Prendiamo i giornali, ad esempio: un'enorme confusione in ogni pagina, un'accozzaglia di inutilità, grafici, diagrammi, dati… Per smettere di cercare di rappresentare tutto, i migliori scelgono di presentare meno contenuti – che, paradossalmente, diventano "di più". La semplicità è un concetto complicato, che va dall'allestimento degli scaffali all'assunzione di un senior manager.

XII
NON SIGNIFICA NULLA
307

C'è sempre un oltre, verso il quale le idee tendono. Altrimenti finiremo per sguazzare nel magma della memoria. Possibili scenari nascono sempre da esigenze; sono fatti di luoghi e persone che in essi agiscono. Le azioni sono l'espressione piena della vita. Ci sono azioni che non muoiono mai.
Pensare. Pensare perché? Perché qualunque cosa, anche la più semplice, se non la si pensa, prima o poi la pensa qualcun altro. Pensare di pensare sincronizzati è un'azione dirompente al giorno d'oggi. Proviamo per un momento a pensare a certi sport di squadra: se non c'è sincronia nelle azioni non c'è performance, e nemmeno risultato. Che ci piaccia o no, l'intero mondo, prima o poi, dovrà pensare come una grande squadra.
Fare. Fare perché? Perché ciò che conta è sempre ciò che vedi. Fare per poi rifare non è incapacità, ma tensione verso

blico y medios de comunicación, hemos adquirido diferentes experiencias que nos permiten la polinización cruzada de nuestro pensamiento para todos los proyectos. La diversidad nos mantiene a todos convenientemente estimulados en el estudio.

250

Así como nos dedicamos a una amplia gama de proyectos, también nos esforzamos por atraer y mantener a toda una serie de personas con talento que aportan mucho más que credenciales de diseño al estudio. Siempre hemos sostenido que un profesional no es solo su porfolio; mucho más interesante que el talento puro es descubrir a la persona que se esconde detrás de ese porfolio. Como resultado, nuestra gente es tan ecléctica como nuestro porfolio.

252

Hay algún momento, después de todo el pensamiento y la planificación y la lluvia de ideas y los bosquejos, en que empiezas a entender que las cosas están bien encaminadas. Sin embargo, nunca sabríamos si hemos tomado la senda adecuada sin todo el pensamiento y la planificación y el intercambio de ideas y los bocetos. Creemos que es necesario llegar al punto en que nos damos cuenta de que nuestra intuición es la correcta.

255

Cuando a veces la gente nos pregunta qué significa, qué "mensaje" contiene, nos sentimos realmente perdidos.
El trabajo en sí mismo es su propio mensaje.

X
QUE SE CONVIERTA EN REALIDAD
263

Honrar con sencillez la belleza evidente y el poder de la luz. Una síntesis conceptual de gestos e imágenes, entrelazada con un uso preciso y cuidado de las líneas. Las geometrías rigurosas y la esencialidad asociada con la ausencia de color y un uso sobrio de los elementos decorativos. La opción de desarrollar su propio estilo, dentro de los límites de las formas disponibles es una virtud cada vez más crucial en el diseño de interiores contemporáneo.

268

El producto es siempre lo más importante, pero una vez que eso está claro, hay que tener en cuenta un sinfín de factores para crear su estética. Toda la experiencia tiene que dotar a ese producto de algo más. Los consumidores tienen que ser recibidos por alguien interesante en la puerta, que les sonría y haga que se sientan bienvenidos. El espacio ha de ser bello, la música y la luz deben ser las adecuadas.

XI
BESPOKE
(HECHO A MEDIDA)
279

Bespoke (pronunciado bi: spϑuk) es un término inglés que significa "a medida" y que se utiliza en diferentes contextos para indicar que un producto se ha realizado "a medida" según las especificaciones del comprador. Si bien se aplica ya a muchos artículos, desde los programas informáticos a los coches de lujo, el término sólo se aplicaba a la ropa a medida, camisas y otras prendas de vestir masculinas que implicaban la medición y confección.

281

Cuanto más te dedicas a un trabajo creativo, más adquiere este vida propia, una especie de vida paralela. Nunca llegas l'eccellenza. Fermiamoci a immaginare quanti colpi di scalpello servono per trarre una forma da un blocco di pietra. Tantissimi movimenti simili, ma al tempo stesso lievemente diversi, con un'idea in testa che muta leggermente a ogni colpo di scalpello. Alla fine, ciò che conta è la forma stessa che si mostra, la forma dell'idea che prima stava solo nel pensiero. Ora tutti la possono vedere e giudicare.

Progettare. Progettare perché? Perché è l'unica cosa che veramente lega "pensare" e "fare". Progettare, soprattutto le forme che ci rappresentano, dà visibilità a noi e alle nostre idee. Un'idea archetipo è immortale, continua sempre a lavorare su se stessa, non muore mai.

Vedere. Vedere perché? Perché è la prima forma di conoscenza, e l'unica che conta davvero nel nostro mestiere. Vedere accresce la nostra capacità di saper comprendere ciò che succede nel mondo. Più si è allenati, più si è capaci di vedere fuori di noi.

309

Il progetto che non abbiamo ancora realizzato, e a cui pensiamo da tanto tempo, è il disegno di una linea di prodotti firmati Hangar Design Group. Non siamo riusciti a metterlo in atto perché non sappiamo come fare. Un paradosso? No, è proprio così. Ed è per questo che è il più bel progetto che ci resta da compiere. Ci pensiamo da trent'anni e non so se riusciremo a farlo diventare realtà. Ma, intanto, è bene avere un sogno nel cassetto.

312

La grafica è un'attività più o meno inutile di per sé. I clienti vanno e vengono. I progetti ti sono assegnati o strappati di mano senza ragione. Un giorno lavori sulla teoria strutturale del packaging, il giorno dopo sulla crema da barba, poi sui giornali e dopo ancora sulla carta da parati.

314

Da un lato, l'idea è che la tua visione progettuale sia così solida e codificata da poter sopravvivere in qualsiasi ambiente, che sia commerciale o culturale. D'altro canto, ci si aspetta che tu sia un perfetto camaleonte, che riesce a far suoi – senza alcuno sforzo – i desideri e le speranze del cliente.

XIII
L'ISPIRAZIONE UCCIDE
321

È ovvio, tu sai di cosa sto parlando. Pensare: è molto facile, e molto difficile. Sangue, fatica, lacrime e sudore.

Il lavoro creativo è di certo Piacevolmente Disgregante.

Siamo semplicemente dei fan del pathos.

La creatività è una cosa anomala, e fa paura. Provoca scompiglio, è sovversiva. Diffida di ciò che vede e di ciò che sente. Osa dubitare. Agisce anche se sbaglia. S'infiltra nei preconcetti e scuote le certezze più solide. Inventa sempre nuovi modi, nuovi linguaggi. Sa provocare e far cambiare i punti di vista. L'insuccesso può essere avvilente: le opportunità e gli errori sono lì, per sfidarti e colpirti, proprio nel momento in cui sei meno preparato. La consapevolezza collettiva della classe creativa è uno dei più grandi misteri dell'industria della comunicazione. Gli artisti, i designer, gli editor e i creativi possono condividere le loro influenze comuni, i loro ambienti e le loro esperienze di vita.

326

A volte questa colonna sonora diventa complicata: nei cambiamenti frenetici del nostro tempo, l'avvento di nuovi e inaspettati progetti, nuovi clienti e nuovi scenari ci impone di condurre riflessioni critiche sul nostro lavoro e sulle no-

a comprender plenamente lo que estás haciendo, y esto es lo que crea una tensión o suspenso, sin la cual el trabajo perdería su carga. Es todo un proceso de descubrimiento y es interminable.

294

Para diseñar algo realmente único, hay que pensar, en primer lugar, en la finalidad del objeto. Hay que entender el contexto. ¿Cómo se relaciona con su entorno ese trabajo en particular? ¿Cómo funciona en todos sus aspectos? Entonces hay que reconducir el trabajo a una simplicidad estética que lo atraviese completamente. Hoy día observamos una filosofía similar en las tiendas de Apple, en la página principal de Google, en la identificación de la marca Tiffany con su eterno color turquesa, tan fácil de reconocer. Los consumidores se ven abrumados por demasiadas opciones. Una aversión al caos —tanto literal como existencial— es una estrategia editorial inteligente para cualquier oferta de productos. Tomemos como ejemplo las revistas: páginas abarrotadas con un millón de tonterías: recuadros, diagramas, gráficos y enfoques. Para renunciar a dar demasiado a la gente, los mejores editan muchos menos contenidos, que, paradójicamente, se vuelven "más". La simplicidad es un concepto complejo que puede extenderse desde las estanterías de almacenamiento a la contratación de altos directivos.

XII
NO SIGNIFICA NADA
307

Los posibles escenarios surgen siempre en respuesta a demandas específicas; están ligados a los lugares y personas que actúan en ellos. Las acciones son la expresión plena de la vida. Hay acciones que nunca mueren.

Pensar. ¿Por qué pensar? Porque cualquier cosa, incluso la más nimia, en la que no pienses, tarde o temprano la pensará alguien más. Pensar en el pensamiento de una manera sincronizada es una acción explosiva en estos días. Pensemos por un momento en ciertos deportes de equipo, sin la sincronización de la acción no hay ni rendimiento ni resultado. Nos guste o no, tarde o temprano, todo el mundo tendrá que pensar como un gran equipo.

Hacer. ¿Por qué hacer? Porque lo que cuenta es siempre lo que vemos. Hacer algo para rehacerlo no es incapacidad, sino más bien tensión hacia la excelencia. Hacer una pausa e imaginarse cuántos golpes de cincel se necesitan para forjar una forma en un bloque de piedra. Miles de movimientos similares, y sin embargo ligeramente diferentes, guiados por una idea que se altera sutilmente con cada golpe de cincel. Al final, lo que cuenta es la forma que sale a la luz del día, la forma de la idea que antes residía sólo en el pensamiento. Ahora todo el mundo puede verla y juzgarla.

Diseñar. ¿Por qué diseñar? Porque es lo único que realmente enlaza el "pensar" y el "hacer". El diseño, por encima de todas las formas que nos representan, nos da visibilidad a nosotros y a nuestras ideas. Una idea arquetípica es inmortal, nunca deja de trabajar en sí misma, nunca muere.

Ver. ¿Por qué ver? Porque es nuestra forma de conocimiento primordial y la única que realmente cuenta en nuestra profesión. Ver mejora nuestra capacidad de aprender a ver lo que sucede en el mundo. Cuanto más capacitados estemos, mejor lograremos ver fuera de nosotros mismos.

309

El proyecto que todavía no hemos abordado, y en el que llevamos tanto tiempo pensando, es el diseño de una línea de productos que lleven la firma Hangar Design Group. No lo hemos podido llevar a cabo porque no sabemos cómo hacerlo. ¿Una paradoja? No, es la realidad; y por eso es el mejor trabajo que queda por hacer. Hemos estado pensando en ello durante treinta años y no sabemos si conseguiría-

stre aspirazioni, che sono però difficili da conciliare con il ritmo serrato di scadenze, presentazioni, eventi. Per questo siamo chiamati a ritornare alla nostra vocazione originale: la leggerezza. Perché il creativo è fondamentalmente un acrobata, un artista dello spazio capace di lanciarsi in aria per tornare a terra con una grazia leggera. Il creativo unisce potenza e agilità atletica, come se questa sfida costante alla gravità terrestre fosse la sua seconda natura, anziché il risultato di autodisciplina e allenamento costante.
Una sorta di movimento eterno, un viaggio continuo senza mai perdere la via. Così il dirigibile è diventato la metafora narrativa che illumina il nostro approccio: volare in alto, ma senza perdere di vista i contorni delle terre che conosciamo, né di quelle che devono ancora essere scoperte.

328

Spesso raccogliamo materiali disparati su singoli argomenti. E lo facciamo anche per lunghi periodi, senza archivi e senza sistemi preordinati.
Non abbiamo la cultura dell'approccio storico ma una metodologia legata alla ricerca. Vogliamo essere liberi di estrarre, incorporare, connettere e, se necessario, anche mescolare. È un'incredibile fonte di energia, con la quale ci misuriamo senza sosta prima e dopo ciascun lavoro.
La rotazione delle diverse professionalità e l'approccio fortemente pragmatico, capace di trasformare Hangar Design Group in una grande macchina progettuale, non sono basati su schemi organizzativi o strategici eccessivamente legati a tempi o metodi; piuttosto si tratta del frutto di intuizioni e di approcci variabili, che in questi ultimi anni riflettono il mercato e il mondo della committenza. Come si potrebbe riassumere il modello organizzativo di Hangar Design Group? In tre parole: multidisciplinare, aperto, flessibile.

XIV
GUARDA E IMPARA
339

Tutto inizia con un'idea (le idee generano denaro, il denaro non genera idee). E tu rispondi a questa idea, utilizzando le tue conoscenze per presentarla nel modo più seducente e coinvolgente possibile. Entro i limiti che ti sono dati, lo scopo è quello di focalizzare l'attenzione, in modo personale, sul messaggio del tuo cliente. Il processo creativo è una sorta di "viaggio condiviso", durante il quale il designer e il cliente devono aprire la propria mente all'inaspettato.
La cosa più importante è comunicare per trovare una direzione, perché non è sempre possibile descrivere le cose attraverso le parole. Noi cerchiamo di rispondere alle richieste del cliente dando origine sempre a nuove domande. Il processo creativo è in continua evoluzione, e non dà garanzie di successo. Se non c'è tempo per stabilire una relazione, allora non c'è tempo per nulla.

356

Quando abbiamo deciso di intraprendere la nostra avventura, l'interesse iniziale era la comunicazione, su cui sono state innestate e approfondite le competenze di design. La scelta di unire comunicazione e design poteva sembrare all'epoca avventata e stravagante, e per molti nascondeva l'assenza di una vera e propria specializzazione. Tuttavia questa formula, decisamente controcorrente venticinque anni fa, si è rivelata vincente con il passare del tempo. Questo perché secondo noi sono davvero molti i punti di contatto e di sovrapposizione tra comunicazione e design.
Vera e propria fonte d'ispirazione per il progetto di Hangar Design Group è stato lo studio di altre realtà ed esperienze simili, oltremanica e oltreoceano, caratterizzate dalla capacità di avvicinare e comporre molteplici attitudini culturali e professionali diverse per poi irradiarle in settori affini, anche se apparentemente distanti.

mos llevarlo a buen término. Pero mientras tanto, es bueno tener un sueño.

312

La práctica del diseño gráfico es una actividad más o menos inútil. Los proyectos van y vienen. Los proyectos caen en el regazo o maduran entre las manos sin ton ni son. Un día estás presentando la teoría de la arquitectura del envasado, a continuación la crema de afeitar, después los periódicos y más tarde el papel pintado.

314

Por un lado la suposición es que la visión del autor es tan sólida, tan codificada, que puede sobrevivir en cualquier ambiente, desde el comercial al cultural. Por otra parte se espera que sea el camaleón perfecto, asumiendo sin esfuerzo las esperanzas y deseos de su cliente.

XIII
LA INSPIRACIÓN MATA
321

Obviamente usted sabe de lo que estoy hablando. Pensar es muy fácil y muy difícil. Sangre, esfuerzo, sudor y lágrimas. El trabajo creativo es, sin duda, agradablemente perturbador. Simplemente somos fans del pathos.
La creatividad es algo inusual, asusta. Crea confusión, es subversiva. Desconfía de lo que ve, de lo que oye. Se atreve a dudar. Actuá, incluso si se equivoca. Se infiltra en nociones preconcebidas. Sacude certezas consolidadas. Se inventa continuamente nuevas formas, nuevos vocabularios. Provoca y cambia los puntos de vista. El fracaso puede ser frustrante. El azar y el error están ahí fuera, esperando para desafiarte y atacarte, golpeando en el momento en que estés menos preparado. La conciencia colectiva de la clase creativa es uno de los mayores misterios de la industria de la comunicación. Un estado mental que los artistas, los diseñadores, editores y creadores pueden compartir a través de influencias comunes, del entorno y de las experiencias de vida.

326

De vez en cuando esta partitura se complica. En el cambio frenético de nuestra época, la aparición de proyectos inesperados, nuevos clientes y escenarios, nos impone una reflexión crítica sobre nuestro trabajo y aspiraciones difícil de conciliar con el ritmo ajustado de los plazos, presentaciones, eventos. Por lo tanto, estamos llamados a volver a nuestra vocación original: la ligereza. Porque el creativo es básicamente un acróbata; un artista del espacio capaz de arrojarse desde el suelo y volver a la tierra con una gracia ligera; la combinación de enorme fuerza y agilidad atlética, casi como si este desafío constante a la gravedad de la tierra fuera su segunda naturaleza, más que el resultado de la autodisciplina y de la formación constante. En una especie de movimiento perpetuo, un viaje continuo sin perderse nunca. Así, el Zepelín se ha convertido en la metáfora narrativa que ilumina nuestro enfoque: volando alto, sin perder de vista el perfil de nuestras tierras, de aquellas que quedan por descubrir.

328

A menudo recopilamos diversos materiales para un único tema. Y lo hacemos durante largas temporadas. Sin archivos ni sistemas predestinados.
Nuestra cultura no consiste en un enfoque histórico, sino en una metodología relacionada con la investigación. Tenemos que ser libres para extraer, incorporar, conectar y, si es necesario, también para combinar. Representa una fuente increíble de energía en la que nos medimos constantemente nosotros mismos, antes y después de cada proyecto.

XV
QUI ED ORA
367

Nell'età della pietra, del bronzo e del ferro la materialità degli oggetti era fisica e diretta: avvicinati e tocca. Ma le cose non stanno più così. Nell'era digitale l'unione tra le cose che produciamo e la tecnologia che utilizziamo è così profonda che i due aspetti sono quasi indistinguibili.

369

Improvvisamente, la condivisione è diventata ciò che siamo. Condivido, quindi sono. Potremmo chiamarla creatività "social": trasformare le barriere in opportunità per diffondere i contenuti. Cosa significa tutto questo per la creatività, nel nostro mondo iper-connesso, un mondo dove chiunque può creare, controllare e distribuire i propri contenuti? Non basta creare un messaggio che raggiunga solo l'individuo. Ciò che produciamo oggi deve essere intrinsecamente "social". Ogni contenuto che cerchi di stimolare una reazione ha una chiara interfaccia "social". Così come i contenuti che invitano a giocare, a partecipare. Contenuti che connettono le persone tra loro e le persone con i brand. Contenuti che costruiscono community di brand.
Per molti anni abbiamo creduto che il lavoro migliore dovesse esprimere un valore di comunicazione; oggi chiediamo ai nostri team di creare un valore di condivisione. Un lavoro a cui le persone vogliano partecipare, con cui vogliano giocare. Contenuti che in qualche modo possano aumentare la credibilità o lo status sociale dei mittenti, per raccontare qualcosa su chi sono e su chi vogliono essere. Perché è divertente, intelligente, innovativo, coinvolgente, benevolo; o anche solo perché è semplicemente utile.
Contenuti che siano allettanti per un intero gruppo di persone che condivide gli stessi interessi, invece che per un singolo individuo.

380

È un dato di fatto che lo sviluppo del design avviene sempre più nel regno dello spazio digitale: e non si tratta di una semplice traslazione dei processi tradizionali di design verso un contesto diverso. Certamente, la transizione verso gli strumenti digitali cambia la metodologia stessa del nostro lavoro. All'improvviso siamo coinvolti in una relazione di causa/effetto in cui ciò che facciamo, o il modo in cui operiamo, può alterare le proprietà degli oggetti. E questa relazione oggi è parte integrante dell'attività di design, esattamente quanto dare forma alla sostanza.

383

Siamo colpiti dalla coreografia che creano i flussi danzanti del vetro, dalla loro interazione ritmata, dall'atmosfera notturna, dalla bellezza dei riflessi individuali che si fanno manifesti in controluce, dalla colonna di fumo che misteriosamente inizia a levarsi attorno alla vetreria. La pellicola descrive un istante effimero di bellezza, che accende i nostri desideri.

XVI
EXLIBRIS
391

Nel mondo dell'arte, il concetto che "tutto" può essere arte, come sostiene ormai chiunque dai tempi di Duchamp, è considerato una verità ovvia. Questo è vero, certamente, ma solo nella misura in cui non si includa in questo "tutto" anche il graphic design. Nemmeno il graphic designer più radicale, o il più rivoluzionario, si vedrà mai riconoscere anche solo un centesimo di quello status a cui si eleva perfino un artista minore. Molti artisti contemporanei credono

La rotación de las distintas competencias profesionales y el enfoque pragmático, capaz de transformar Hangar Design Group en gran máquina del diseño no se basan en esquemas de organización de la producción o en políticas estrictamente vinculadas a plazos y métodos. Se basan en intuiciones y enfoques variables, que reflejan el mercado de los últimos años y a nuestra clientela.
¿Cómo se podría resumir el modelo de organización de Hangar Design Group? En tres palabras: multidisciplinar, abierto, flexible.

XIV
MIRA Y APRENDE
339

Todo comienza con una idea (las ideas producen dinero, el dinero no produce ideas). Respondes a esa idea, usando tus conocimientos para presentarla de la forma más seductora y atractiva posible. Con el único propósito de llamar la atención —de una manera personal– hacia el mensaje de mi cliente. El proceso creativo es un "viaje compartido" durante el cual el diseñador y el cliente tienen que abrir la mente del otro a lo inesperado. Lo más importante es la comunicación para encontrar una dirección, ya que no siempre es posible describir las cosas con palabras. Tratamos de responder a la demanda del cliente planteando constantemente nuevos interrogantes. El proceso creativo es un proceso en evolución, sin ninguna garantía de éxito. Si no hay tiempo para entablar una relación, entonces no hay tiempo.

356

Cuando decidimos embarcarnos en nuestra aventura, nuestro objetivo inicial era la comunicación, lo que ayudó a desencadenar y mejorar las diferentes habilidades de diseño.
La decisión de unir comunicación y diseño en un principio parecía precipitada si no irregular, enviando el mensaje potencial de que el estudio carecía de una verdadera especialización. Esta estrategia, sin embargo, que nadaba contracorriente hace 25 años, ha demostrado ser una fórmula con éxito en los últimos años. Esto es porque, en nuestra opinión, hay una superposición significativa entre la comunicación y el diseño, así como muchos puntos de contacto.
La observación de otras experiencias parecidas en el extranjero y al otro lado del charco ha sido una fuente de inspiración; en particular su capacidad de reunir una multiplicidad de vertientes culturales y profesionales, para irradiarlas a los sectores afines que, aparentemente, no están relacionados.

XV
AQUÍ Y AHORA
367

En la edad de piedra, del bronce y del hierro los materiales y los objetos están unidos a la realidad de una manera directa y física: extiendes el brazo y los puedes tocar. Pero las cosas ya no son como antes. En la era digital, la unión entre lo que hacemos y la tecnología que utilizamos es tan profunda que ha hecho que sea difícil distinguirlos.

369

De repente, el intercambio se ha convertido en lo que hacemos. Comparto, por lo tanto soy. Podríamos llamarla creatividad social: convertir los obstáculos en oportunidades para la difusión de contenidos. Entonces, ¿qué significa todo esto para la creatividad en nuestro nuevo mundo híperconectado? Un mundo donde todos pueden crear, controlar y distribuir su propio contenido. No es suficiente crear un mensaje que llegue solo al individuo. Lo que producimos hoy tiene que ser intrínsecamente social. Un contenido que intente provocar una reacción, tiene una clara interfaz social. Igual que los contenidos que animan a jugar, participar

che, per fare arte, sia sufficiente affermare "Sono un artista, quindi tutto ciò che faccio è arte". Questa opinione è molto diffusa, ma come si può dimostrare? Poiché viviamo in una democrazia liberale, la maggior parte delle persone sceglie di concedere a chiunque la possibilità di autodefinirsi un artista. Quando invece ci propongono delle definizioni del concetto di arte, diventiamo subito più critici e meno tolleranti. Da secoli, i filosofi si scontrano con questo argomento: la definizione filosofica del concetto di arte è cambiata nel tempo, fino a raggiungere un livello sorprendente. La maggior parte di noi oggi non riconoscerebbe le definizioni che hanno prevalso nelle epoche passate: abbiamo infatti raggiunto un punto in cui la nostra accezione del concetto di arte è dominata da ciò che conosciamo come "la teoria istituzionale dell'arte". Secondo questa teoria, un oggetto può dirsi "arte" quando è legato all'istituzione conosciuta con il nome di "mondo dell'arte". In altre parole, lo status di "oggetto d'arte" viene conferito in base all'associazione con quel mondo, fatto di gallerie, curatori, critici, educazione artistica, mercato dell'arte ecc. Insomma, siamo disposti a concedere lo status di "arte" a un'opera – anche se questa non coincide con la nostra personale visione di cos'è l'arte – se questa si trova in una galleria, in un libro o in una rivista, presentata da un'autorità riconosciuta.

Dato che il design ha quasi sempre mantenuto una chiara separazione dal mondo dell'arte, la definizione istituzionale del concetto di arte esclude automaticamente la maggior parte delle forme di design. Ovviamente, esiste anche una ben definita teoria istituzionale del design, i cui principi sono radicalmente respinti dal mondo dell'arte: la subordinazione dell'opera alle richieste commerciali, l'utilizzo della produzione di massa invece della creazione di opere uniche ed esclusive, l'assenza di contenuti d'autore, perché il designer comunica i messaggi di altre persone, e non i propri. Tuttavia, oggi i graphic designer oltrepassano continuamente le costrizioni istituzionali del design. Producono le proprie opere, e le pubblicano in un mondo semi-artistico fatto di gallerie, blog e pubblicazioni che non seguono il modello "commissionato dal cliente". Noi crediamo, alla fine, che la nostra relazione con l'arte sia una combinazione intima e personale tra noi stessi e gli oggetti, o le opere con le quali scegliamo di stabilire un rapporto. Se siamo in grado di mettere da parte i condizionamenti tribali e culturali che determinano la maggior parte del nostro modo di pensare e di agire, in particolare per quanto riguarda l'arte, possiamo finalmente realizzare che nell'arte siamo liberi: liberi di trovare il piacere estetico ovunque noi scegliamo, liberi di realizzarlo in qualsiasi modo desideriamo.

393

Intendiamo la creatività in senso dinamico; deve sapersi evolvere secondo i nuovi linguaggi, deve rinnovarsi, deve saper cambiare. E lo stesso vale per i creativi, ai quali sempre più si richiede di "incrociare" idee differenti, culture, sensibilità e competenze specifiche. La creatività non nel nostro lavoro non deve mai perdere di vista la realtà, i cambiamenti che si susseguono e le richieste del mercato, le domande dei clienti e l'aggiornamento. La creatività è soprattutto un linguaggio trasversale, che va unito al rigore progettuale.

394

Hangar Twist. Un'anima che rimane giovane, anche dopo il lungo percorso compiuto, perché ha saputo rinnovarsi e apprendere nuove lingue, esplorare nuove destinazioni e trasformare la concretezza e il rigore professionale nella leggerezza del pensiero creativo, che si staglia libero nel paesaggio aereo dell'immaginazione.

397

Trent'anni di disegno, trent'anni di design. Non sono pochi, per chi ha sempre affrontato la sfida del progetto

y transmitir. Un contenido que conecta a las personas con las personas, y a las personas con las marcas. Un contenido que construye comunidades de marca. Durante muchos años hemos creído que el mejor trabajo tenía que tener un valor de comunicación. Hoy pedimos a nuestro equipo que cree un valor compartido. Un trabajo en el que la gente quiera participar, con el que quieran jugar y transmitir. Contenidos que de alguna manera mejoren la credibilidad o estatus social del remitente, y digan algo acerca de quiénes son y quiénes quieren ser. Ya sea porque es divertido, inteligente, innovador, emocional, de beneficencia o sólo útil. Contenidos atractivos para un grupo con un interés común y no sólo para un individuo.

380

Es un hecho que el desarrollo del diseño cada vez más se produce en el ámbito del espacio digital y, además, que ésta no es la simple traducción de los procesos tradicionales de diseño a un campo diferente. En efecto, la transición a las herramientas digitales cambia la metodología misma del diseño. De repente, estamos comprometidos en una relación de causa y efecto, donde lo que hacemos o cómo nos comportamos altera las propiedades de los objetos. Y esta relación forma ahora parte de la actividad del diseño igual que dar forma a la sustancia.

383

Nos impresiona la coreografía que crea la danza de los flujos del vidrio, su interacción rítmica, el ambiente nocturno, la belleza de las reflexiones individuales que se hacen visibles en la retroiluminación, y la columna de humo que comienza a elevarse misteriosamente alrededor de la fábrica de vidrio. La película describe un momento fugaz de belleza que enciende nuestros deseos.

XVI
EX LIBRIS
391

En el mundo del arte la idea de que todo puede ser arte, como ha sido expuesto por casi todos desde la época de Duchamp, se considera un truismo. Todo esto está bien mientras no se incluya el diseño gráfico en la definición de "todo". A ningún diseñador gráfico, independientemente de cuán radical o rompedor de fronteras sea, se le confiere un centésimo del estatus que tiene el menos importante de los artistas. Muchos artistas contemporáneos creen que para hacer arte sólo necesitan decir: "Soy artista y todo lo que hago es arte". Este punto de vista es muy habitual, pero ¿hay pruebas del mismo? Vivimos en una democracia con un grado razonable de libertad y la mayoría de las personas permiten que otras se autodenominen artistas. Pero cuando se habla de la definición de arte somos más críticos y menos tolerantes. Los filósofos han combatido con estas preguntas desde hace siglos. La definición filosófica de arte ha cambiado con el pasar del tiempo a un ritmo impresionante. La mayoría de nosotros no reconoce las definiciones de arte que prevalecían en las eras pasadas, pero hoy todo parece indicar que hemos llegado a un punto en el que nuestra definición de arte coincide con la que se conoce como "la teoría institucional del arte". Esta teoría establece que un objeto se puede llamar arte cuando se relaciona con una institución llamada "el mundo del arte". En otras palabras, el estatus de arte se confiere al asociarlo a galerías, comisarios, críticos, educación artística, mercado del arte, etc. Es decir, permitimos que una obra se designe como arte, aunque no coincida con lo que consideramos ser o no ser arte, sólo porque está expuesta en una galería, en un libro o en una tienda, presentada por una autoridad reconocida. Debido a que el diseño casi siempre se ha mantenido netamente separado del mundo del arte, la definición "institucional" de arte excluye automáticamente la mayor parte de sus formas.

guardando avanti, consolidando un disegno culturale e una logica professionale basati sulla presenza multipla, sulla proliferazione dei luoghi, sulla reiterazione dei contatti. Tutto è partito da un luogo speciale, nell'entroterra veneto, dove un tempo alloggiavano vecchi dirigibili: degli hangar in muratura, antichi ricoveri di macchine volanti soppiantate dagli aeroplani, il cui fascino iconico rimane fissato nell'immaginario collettivo come metafora di sfida votata all'utopia. Assumendo su di sé la potenza evocativa del genius loci, Hangar Design Group è cresciuto grazie ai fondatori e a coloro che ne hanno condiviso il percorso in questi anni fino a diventare un modello di sviluppo consolidato, fondato dall'origine sulla capacità di attrarre e assorbire molteplici tensioni disciplinari per irradiarle poi in ambiti settoriali affini ma diversi, secondo il principio della trasversalità delle competenze e dei linguaggi creativi. Un modello reticolare, modulare, variegato secondo la natura delle figure professionali che lo abitano, in grado di adattarsi nei rapporti in base alle singole commesse e alle singole persone. Perché se la struttura professionale cresce sulle competenze, sui processi e sulle interazioni tra i singoli, essa si alimenta in primo luogo della passione e della visione degli individui, della loro capacità di abbracciare il progetto e di animare la squadra. Sono loro, al di là di tutte le categorizzazioni, l'anima dell'Hangar.

400

Non siamo inventori. Piuttosto, rielaboriamo, ricostruiamo, riduciamo e miglioriamo l'esistente. E anche se il decorativo non ci intimidisce, siamo convinti che l'eleganza vera debba essere cercata altrove: precisamente, nell'essenza delle cose.

XVII
LINKS
402

Coloro che sanno scoprire qualcosa che gli piace rendono il mondo un luogo più interessante. Il vero viaggio di scoperta non è cercare nuove destinazioni ma guardare il mondo con occhi nuovi. Molte città sono fatte di cemento, ma alcune di esse possono accendere la nostra fantasia collettiva, generando grandi promesse di cambiamento e nuovi stimoli. Alcune città possono catturare la nostra immaginazione senza che le abbiamo mai visitate. Proprio come l'ispirazione, in alcuni luoghi i progetti calano un'ombra esagerata sull'osservatore. Puoi trovare l'ispirazione in ogni cosa. E se non la trovi, guarda ancora.

409

Parole e immagini combinate in modo casuale tradiscono i diversi modi di seguire un'idea, a volte una forma, a volte una funzione, o un colore, o un materiale.
Esse raccontano – e vorremmo sottolineare proprio questo aspetto narrativo – i modi personali e non formali di raccogliere e accogliere le idee e di cercare le soluzioni migliori entrando nel cuore delle cose o rinchiudendole in un layout immediato. Queste immagini raccontano inoltre il lato personale e intimo del nostro impulso di ispirazione, i suoi ostacoli, ma anche i processi creativi, che sono unici e vitali.

411

La nostra società (la cosiddetta società post-moderna) è cresciuta con le citazioni, tratte per la grande maggioranza dalla cultura pop, dai libri alle canzoni, tanto da essere ormai simile a una blogoteca. In un'epoca in cui tutto sembra essere già stato visto e osservato, non resta nient'altro da fare per noi che prendere le cose e rielaborarle.
Uno degli aspetti più seducenti della storia moderna delle idee è la costante instabilità, la metamorfosi infinita. I temi, le immagini e le pulsioni migrano da un campo all'altro, cambiando, in questo passaggio, se stessi e lo scenario in

Es obvio que existe también una teoría del diseño, institucional y bien desarrollada. Se basa en ciertos principios que constituyen un anatema para el mundo del arte: el diseño depende de los comisarios comerciales, se sustenta en la producción de masas y no en creaciones únicas, y carece de contenidos de autor (los diseñadores comunican los mensajes de otros, no los suyos). Pero, como se decía arriba, hoy en día los diseñadores gráficos sobrepasan las rígidas fronteras institucionales del diseño. Desarrollan sus propias obras y las publican en un mundo de "semi-arte" constituido por galerías, blogs y publicaciones que no siguen el modelo de objetos "comisionados por el cliente". Al final, creemos que nuestra relación con el arte es una profunda asociación personal entre nosotros y los objetos o las obras con que nos involucramos. Si pudiéramos liberarnos de las viejas concepciones y los condicionamientos culturales que determinan en gran medida lo que pensamos y hacemos en relación con el arte, nos daríamos cuenta de que, sin salirnos del concepto de arte, es posible encontrar placer estético en cualquier lugar y hacer arte de la forma que se desee.

393

Entendemos la creatividad en un sentido dinámico, debe ser capaz de evolucionar de acuerdo con los nuevos lenguajes, de renovarse, de cambiar. Lo mismo puede decirse de los creativos, que deben ser capaces de una "fertilización cruzada" de diferentes ideas, culturas, sensibilidades y habilidades específicas. La creatividad en nuestro trabajo nunca debe perder de vista la realidad, los cambios y las demandas del mercado, los requisitos del cliente y el hecho de estar en la vanguardia. La creatividad es ante todo un lenguaje indirecto, que debe conjugarse con el rigor del diseño.

394

Hangar Twist. Un alma que sigue siendo joven, incluso después de su larga trayectoria hasta hoy, ya que ha sabido renovarse y aprender nuevos lenguajes, explorar nuevos destinos y transformar el rigor profesional y la sustancia en la ligereza del pensamiento creativo que se eleva libremente en el paisaje aéreo de la imaginación.

397

Treinta años de diseño. No es poco tiempo, para quienes siempre han enfrentado el desafío mirando al futuro, consolidando un diseño cultural y una lógica profesional basada en la presencia y proliferación de múltiples lugares, en la repetición de los contactos. Todo comenzó en un lugar especial en las tierras vénetas que albergaban antaño viejos globos dirigibles. Hangares de mampostería, el antiguo refugio de las máquinas voladoras —que fueron reemplazados por los aviones— cuya icónica fascinación permanece inalterable en la memoria colectiva como la metáfora de un reto consagrado a la utopía. Abrazando el poder evocador del Genius Loci, Hangar Design Group ha evolucionado gracias a sus fundadores y a quienes han compartido su trayectoria en estos años. A quienes la vieron convertirse en un modelo de desarrollo afianzado, basado, desde un principio, en su capacidad de atraer y absorber una multiplicidad de tendencias profesionales y difundirlas hacia otras zonas similares, pero diferentes, de acuerdo con el principio de cruce de las habilidades y lenguajes creativos.
Un modelo reticular, modular, diversificado en relación con la naturaleza de las figuras profesionales que lo habitan, capaz de adaptar su manera de relacionarse a cada uno de los pedidos, a cada una de las personas. Porque si la estructura profesional se desarrolla a partir de las habilidades, los procesos y las interacciones entre los individuos que la componen, esa estructura se alimenta sobre todo por su pasión y visión, su capacidad de abrazar el proyecto y animar al equipo. Son ellos —más allá de cualquier categorización— quienes representan el alma verdadera de Hangar.

cui si collocano.
La chiave di tutto sta nell'andare oltre l'indicazione estetica ricevuta e trovare il modo di comporre tutti gli elementi. Il segreto è molto semplice: assemblare, ma con le idee. Migliorare in modo personale il significato e il messaggio, ad esempio riducendo l'eccesso d'informazione che ci circonda. Il nostro desiderio più grande? Che centinaia di persone vogliano copiarci.

423

Non pensiamo alle nostre amate città come a semplici luoghi geografici, ma come a un'idea: rappresentano uno spazio per la mente. Lo crediamo fermamente. Ci sono persone che hanno le città nella mente – non importa se vivono in Georgia o nel nord-est dell'Italia, o nella campagna di Barcellona. Ciò che conta è avere una mente aperta: un modo di pensare internazionale.

È tutto nel modo di pensare.

400

No somos inventores. Más bien, reelaboramos, reconstruimos, reducimos y mejoramos lo que ya existe. Y, a pesar de no evitar el arte decorativo, estamos convencidos de que hay que buscar la elegancia en otro lugar, es decir, en la esencia de las cosas.

XVII
ENLACES
402

Las personas que encuentran algo que les gusta convierten el mundo en un lugar más interesante. El verdadero viaje de descubrimiento no consiste en buscar nuevos paisajes, sino en mirarlos con nuevos ojos. Muchas ciudades están construidas sólo de hormigón, pero algunas de ellas pueden encender nuestra fantasía colectiva y crear grandes promesas de cambio y de emoción. Pueden llegar a capturar nuestra imaginación antes incluso de haberlas visitado. Al igual que la inspiración, los diseños en algunos lugares proyectan una sombra exageradamente grande sobre el observador.
La inspiración está en cualquier cosa (y si no la encuentras es porque no has mirado bien).

409

Las palabras y las imágenes compiladas a través de la acumulación al azar delatan una manera personal de llevar a cabo una idea, a veces una forma, una función y otras veces un color o un material. Narran —y aquí se hace hincapié en los aspectos narrativos— modos personales, no formales, de captar/acoger las ideas y de la búsqueda de soluciones entrando en las cosas o encerrándolas un diseño de forma inmediata. Estas imágenes también narran el lado personal e íntimo de nuestro impulso de inspiración, sus obstáculos, así como también los procesos creativos únicos y vitales.

411

Nuestra sociedad (la llamada sociedad posmoderna) se basó tanto en las citas —la mayoría procedentes de la cultura pop, de libros, de canciones— que ahora se parece mucho a una blogoteca. En una época en que todo ya ha sido visto y observado, no nos queda nada más que hacer que reunir las cosas y reelaborarlas. Uno de los aspectos más seductores de la historia moderna de las ideas es la inestabilidad perpetua, la incesante metamorfosis. Los temas, las imágenes y las pulsiones migran de un campo a otro, cambiando por el camino y en el escenario en el que se las sitúa.
La clave está en ir más allá de la indicación estética que recibimos y encontrar el modo de alinear todos los elementos. El secreto es muy sencillo: juntar todos los detalles, pero con las ideas. Cultivar de manera personal la solución acerca del significado y del mensaje, con el exceso de información que nos rodea. ¿Nuestro mayor deseo? Que cientos de personas nos copien.

423

Personalmente no pensamos en nuestras queridas ciudades como en lugares geográficos. Pensamos en ellas como en una idea: representan un lugar para la mente. Lo creemos realmente. Hay personas que llevan estas ciudades en sus mentes, no importa si viven en Georgia, en el noreste de Italia, o en los alrededores de Barcelona. Lo que importa es tener un estado mental libre, una manera de pensar internacional.

Todo está en la manera de pensar.

ACKNOWLEDGMENTS

This book would not have been possible without the contribution of many people inside and outside the Hangar Design Group, especially the customers, writers, designers, photographers, archivists and support staff.
We are particularly grateful to Micaela Portinari, Michele Bicego, and Marco Fortini for their determination in ensuring that the concept and texts were created while steadfastly maintaining the distinct style of the Hangar Design Group throughout the book. Special thanks to all those who contributed to the layout and helped to retrieve the creative and photographic material from the archives, especially Cristina Bonaldo, Andrea Piovesan, and Melania Pettenò.

Hangar Design Group Partners

All the pages of the book contain works created or designed by Hangar Design Group.
The texts have been written by the team preparing the book, even partly reworking texts previously written for Hangar Design Group by various authors.

All the images, photos and graphics in the book have been produced by members of the Hangar Design Group creative team during the various trips for supervising works and operational benchmarks or taken from the historical archives of works completed by the various branches of the group.

First published in Italy in 2011 by
Skira Editore S.p.A.
Palazzo Casati Stampa
via Torino 61
20123 Milano
Italy
www.skira.net

Printed and bound in Italy. First edition

ISBN: 978-88-572-0628-8

Distributed in North America by Rizzoli International Publications,
Inc., 300 Park Avenue South, New York, NY 10010, USA.
Distributed elsewhere in the world by Thames and Hudson Ltd.,
181A High Holborn, London WC1V 7QX, United Kingdom.